The New Jersey Municipal Data Book

2006

State & Municipal Profiles Series™

The New Jersey Municipal Data Book

2006

State & Municipal Profiles Series™

[ip] **information publications**

Woodside, California

Also from Information Publications

State & Municipal Profiles Series™

Almanac of the 50 States

California Cities, Towns & Counties	*Connecticut Municipal Profiles*
Florida Municipal Profiles	*Massachusetts Municipal Profiles*
The New Jersey Municipal Data Book	*North Carolina Municipal Profiles*

American Profiles Series™

Asian Americans: A Statistical Sourcebook
Black Americans: A Statistical Sourcebook
Hispanic Americans: A Statistical Sourcebook

ISBN 0-911273-32-8 Paper
ISBN 0-911273-33-6 CD
The New Jersey Municipal Data Book 2006

Information Publications, Inc.
2995 Woodside Rd., Suite 400-182
Woodside, CA 94062-2446

www.informationpublications.com

Toll Free Phone 877.544.INFO (4636)
Toll Free Fax 877.544.4635

Direct Dial Phone 650.851.4250
Direct Dial Fax 650.529.9980

Table of Contents

New Jersey
Municipal Data Book

2006

State & Municipal Profiles Series™

State &
Municipal
Profiles
Series

New Jersey Counties

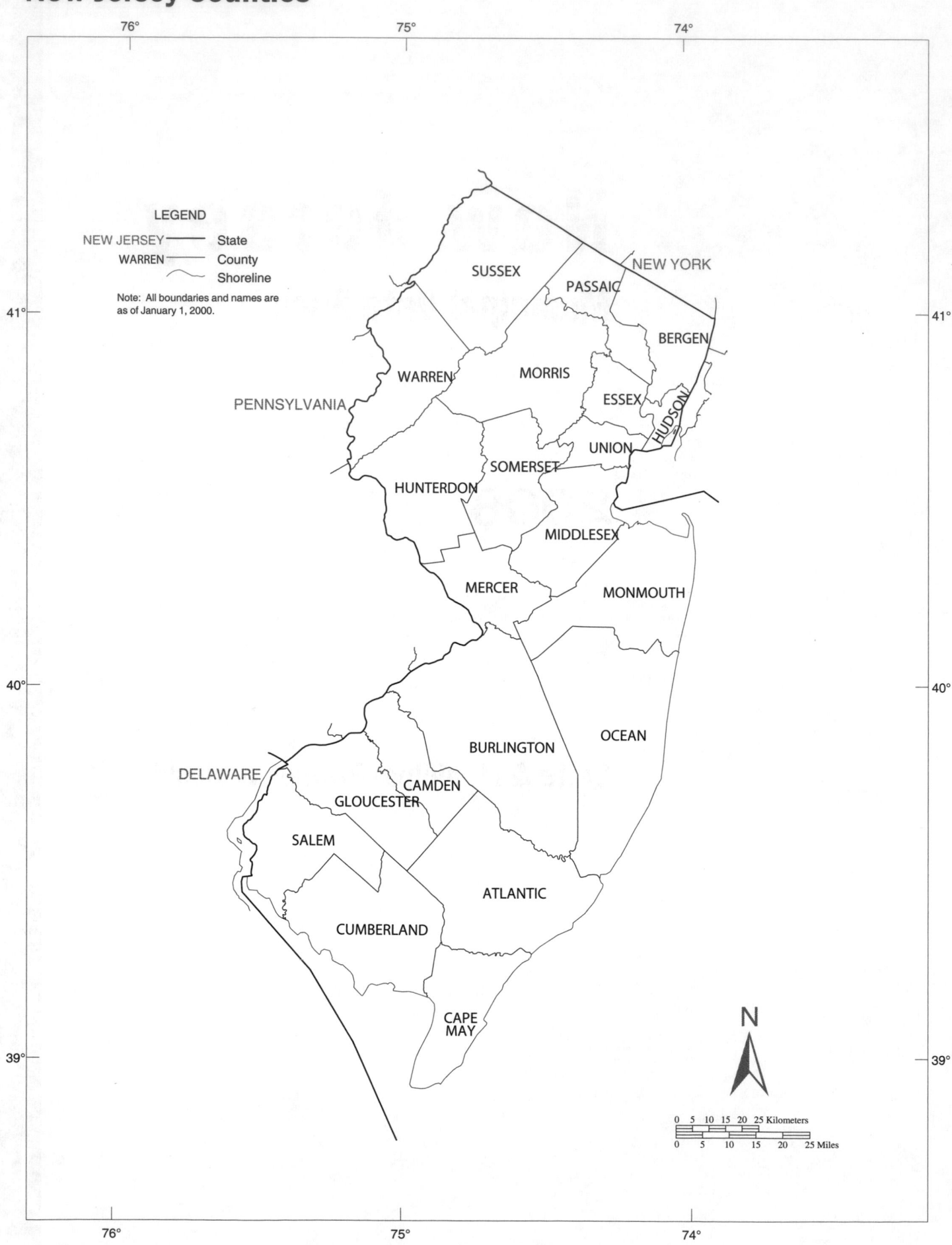

INTRODUCTION

The New Jersey Municipal Data Book is an annual reference publication published by Information Publications, Inc. since 1981. Drawing from a variety of established sources, *New Jersey Municipal Data Book* is designed to provide concise yet comprehensive one page profiles for all 566 municipalities in New Jersey and 21 counties. (The number of municipalities changed from 567 to 566 in 1997, when Pahaquarry Township merged with Hardwick Township.) South Belmar Borough of Monmouth County has changed its named to Lake Como Borough. This name change is reflected in this edition

The book contains one page for every incorporated city and county in the state. These pages are arranged alphabetically by city or county name within the municipal or county profiles sections. Each page has the same format which organizes the data into eight categories, with the result being that information about a specific city or county can be found rapidly and comparisons can be made easily. Following the county profiles section, Appendix A contains the list of municipalities within a county and Appendix B provides additional school data.

INTRODUCTION TO THE DATA

The information in this volume has been obtained from a variety of sources. In order to maximize the usefulness of the volume it is important to disclose where each piece of information came from. This is especially important to researchers who have questions about how the data was gathered and what some of the terms used mean. The best answers to these questions are found in the originators of the data which we will cite in the Explanation of the Categories to follow.

It is also important to cite the year of the data. In all cases this is the latest year for which complete data was available for all local governing bodies as of May 1, 2006. Dates of data are indicated in the headings themselves. Where no date is shown for a given category, one is provided below.

It should be noted that information about a given year is not available for release from the gathering agency until well into the following year or sometimes not until subsequent years. Whenever possible, we will continue to try to provide latest information possible.

Information Publications, Inc. conducts mail and telephone surveys and Internet research between November, 2005 and April, 2006 to obtain most recent names of government officials, police chief, firechief, librarians and school superintendents. Information gathered is used to supplement other sources to provide complete and up-to-date information.

EXPLANATION OF THE CATEGORIES

Demographics & Socio-Economic Characteristics

Information in this category, with a few exceptions, comes from the 2000 U.S. Census. 2000 U.S. Census data as shown here has been revised from the original data published by the Bureau of Census. The exceptions are: The **1980** and **1990** population figures, and the **2004** population estimates, which come from the U.S. Bureau of Census; and the labor force and unemployment rate for **2004**, which are from New Jersey Department of Labor and Workforce Development. **Population density** for **2004** is calculated by Information Publications based on the 2004 population estimates, and Land Area of 2000 U.S. Census

In order to fully appreciate census information, it is important to understand how the Census Bureau collects its data and defines its terms.

Race, as used by the Bureau of the Census is not meant to denote any scientific or biological concept of race. The subgroups displayed here represent the self-categorization of respondents. It should also be noted that **Hispanic origin** is not a racial category. Persons may be of any race, and be of Hispanic origin as well.

Educational Attainment is that of persons who are 25 years or older, and college graduates includes persons with at least a four year degr ee.

Income and Poverty as reported in the 2000 U.S. Census is from the previous calendar year, 1999.

A **household** includes all the persons occupying a housing unit. A **family household** includes a householder and one or more other persons living in the same household who are related to the householder by birth, marriage, or adoption. The number of family households always equals the number of families; however, a family household may also include nonrelatives living with the family. A **nonfamily household** includes a householder living alone or with nonrelatives only. Not all persons live in households. Some, for example, are members of the armed forces, or are inmates of institutions, or live in group quarters. As a result the total number of persons in a city or town can be greater than the number of persons living in all households of that town. The subgroups displayed here under households were selected for potential interest and by no means represent a full breakdown of all types of households. Readers should also note that there is overlapping amongst types of households. For example, the same household may have members both under 18 years of age and over 65.

Total civilian labor force includes all persons who are not members of the armed forces age 16 years old and over who are either employed or unemployed. Self-employed workers are referred to workers in own incorporated businesses.

General Information

The **address** and **telephone number** shown are for the central location of municipal business; i.e., the city hall, city administrative offices, and were obtained from the surveys done by Information Publications. Other information such as **Web site** and **Form of government** was also obtained from the surveys. **Land Area** and **Water Area** are from the 2000 U.S. Census.

It should be noted that land and water area measurement as reported by the 2000 U.S. Census is in square meters. It is converted into square miles in this section. According to the 2000 U.S. Census data dictionary, "land area measurement in square meters. The accuracy of the area measurement is limited by the inaccuracy inherent in the mapping of the various boundary features in the TIGER file. Square miles can be derived by dividing square meters by 2,589,988."

Government

Legislative District comes from the Municipal and County Government section of The Official Web Site of New Jersey. www.state.nj.us. U.S. Congressional District information is also verified against Surveys and U.S. Census 2000.

Names of **Government officials** are from our surveys. Mayors Directory from New Jersey Department of Community Affairs is also used.

Registered Voters data in the county page is compiled from information provided by the Office of the Attorney General, New Jersey Division of Elections. Numbers do not add to total because not all party affiliations are shown, only Democrat, Republican and Unaffiliated.

Housing and Construction

Housing Units, 2000 data comes from the 2000 U.S. Census.

A **housing unit** is a house, apartment, mobile home or trailer, group of rooms, or single room occupied as a separate living quarter or, if vacant, intended as a separate living quarter. Separate living quarters are those in which the occupants live and eat separately from any other persons in the building, and which have direct access from the outside of the building or through a common hall.

For this publication, a **single family unit** is defined as a housing unit which does not share the building with any other housing units, nor is its building attached to any other structure. In Census terminology, it is defined as one (1) unit in structure, detached. **Single family home** as listed

is equivalent to the Census term "specified owner-occupied unit" that is referred to one (1) family houses on less than 10 acres without a business or medical office on the property.

A housing unit is **owner occupied** if the owner or co-owner lives in the unit, even if the unit is mortgaged or not fully paid for. All other housing units are considered renter occupied.

Value is the Census respondent's estimate of how much the house would sell for if it were on the market. **Median value** represents the middle value of the distribution of these estimates. One half the houses have higher values than the median value, and one half have lower value than the median. A similar definition holds true **median rent**.

Total housing units for the county page come from the Population Division, U.S. Census Bureau.

Statistics for **New Privately Owned Housing Units Authorized by Building Permit**, **2004** and **2005** come from annual U.S. Bureau of the Census reports available at http://www.census.gov. Places which issue building permits are asked to report monthly to the Bureau. This data is further compiled by the New Jersey Department of Labor and Workforce Development.

Data for **Real Property Valuation Parcels**, **2005** and **Average Property Value & Tax**, **2005** come from the New Jersey Division of Local Government Services, Department of Community Affairs.

Public Library

The name of the Library Director was obtained by our own annual mail and telephone surveys. Library volumes and expenditures come from New Jersey Public Library Statistics, 2004. Information was downloaded from the web site for New Jersey State Library, under the section for Library Development Bureau.

Public Safety

The names of the **Police** and **Fire Chiefs** (municipal pages) and **Sheriffs** (county pages) come from our surveys. **Number of Officers, Violent crimes, Property crimes** and **Arson** come from "Crime in the United States, 2004" report by Federal Bureau of Investigation. (Violent crime is defined as murder, forcible sex, robbery and aggravated assault).

School System

Only information about locally maintained schools or joint or regional schools with no more than two constituent municipalities are listed in this section. If a governing body does not maintain a school system, the system to which it sends its children is listed. If only an elementary school-system is maintained, this is the information provided. Information about regional school systems has not been included.

Name, address, telephone number and **superintendent**, and **grade plan** of public school districts were obtained from *New Jersey School Directory* published by New Jersey Department of Education. The above information is supplemented with our surveys.

All other school information is for the school year 2004-2005 except where indicated. The information comes from the *New Jersey Report Card 2004-2005*.

Grade plan shows the range of grades available in the schools within the district. K denotes kindergarten; PK denotes pre-kindergarten; 9-12 is a four-year high school. A grade plan of "K-12" means that the school district contains at least one of each of the following types of schools: an elementary school with kindergarten through sixth grade, a junior high with seventh and eighth graders, and a four year high school.

Enrollment includes all regular day school students enrolled for all grades in the district. **Enrollment** and **Grade 12 enrollment** are grouped by school districts. The data shown here is a total enrollment of all schools within the district.

Assessment test results show the sum of percentage of students who are at advanced level and proficient level.

The goals of education are complex and standardized tests are available to measure the degree of attainment of only a few of those goals. Standardized test scores should not be the only criteria used to evaluate a total educational program. The reader must realize that only a small amount of the information that is required for a total evaluation process is provided in district profiles, and for a more in-depth look should talk with the districts directly and do extensive research of all data available from the schools, the districts and the New Jersey Department of Education.

Municipal Finance/County Finance

Information in this section is obtained from the New Jersey Department of Community Affairs, and is the latest available at press time. Information in this section is distilled from a combination of the Property Tax Information, State Aid to Municipalities, and Abstract of Ratables. The majority of municipalities in New Jersey operate on calendar year budgets (January 1-December 31).

Total budget aid reflects the budgeted amount. Total formula aid reflects the projected amount. Expenditure data are not available; hence they are not reported here. For a more detailed explanation, users of this data may find it helpful to call the Department of Community Affairs, Division of Local Government Services, in Trenton, New Jersey.

Taxes

The information shown under this heading was obtained from the New Jersey Department of the Treasury, Division of Taxation's Tables of Equalized Valuations for 2003, 2004 and 2005, and from Abstracts of Ratables from for 2003, 2004 and 2005. The County Equalization Ratio is computed by the State for the purpose of apportioning state school aid. It is computed during the final months of the year, and is used for the following year (ratios appear under the year in which they are used). The County Ratio is used for the purpose of equalizing county taxes. However, there are three counties, Bergen, Middlesex, and Morris which do not make use of the State Ratio.

COUNTY PAGES

All the information on the County Pages is derived from the same source as for those on the Municipal Pages with the following exceptions, notes and additions:

Education

The County Superintendent (a state rather than county official), along with address and phone number of Superintendent's office, was obtained from our own mail and telephone surveys and Web research.

General Information

The number of municipalities and address of the county (county seat) are updated annually by our own mail survey.

Government

The form of government along with number of freeholders has been taken from the 56th Annual Report of the Division of Local Goverment Services, 1993, Trenton, New Jersey. All the names listed in the section come from our own mail survey.

Income Tax

Information in this section is obtained from the New Jersey Annual Report on taxation. Appendix G of the report provides information on Individual Income Tax Returns County Profile. Appendix H provides information on Average Gross Income and Average Income Tax By County.

Taxes

County pages display a State Equalization Ratio which is computed by the State, and unlike the ratios displayed on the municipal pages, appears under the year in which the ratio is struck (one year previous to the year in which it was issued);i. e., ratios appearing under 2002 will be used in 2003.

APPENDICES

The appendices supplement the information that appears on the individual profile pages. Information in the appendices comes from the same source as the corresponding item on the profile page unless otherwise noted below.

Appendix A lists municipalities by county.

Appendix B provides additional school data.

ABBREVIATIONS

"-"	Zero or not applicable / not available
Actg	Acting
Admin/Mgr	Administrator or Manager
Avg	Average
AYP	Adequate Yearly Progress
B	Borough
BCF	Board of Chosen Freeholders
C	Old City Charter
CEP	County Executive Plan
CM'23	Council Manager, 1923
CM'50	County Manager, Optional Municipal Charter, 1950
CMP	County Manager Plan
(County)	Services provided by County
DCA	Department of Community Affairs
Dep	Deputy
DFG	District Factor Group
Dir	Director
ELA	English Language Arts
est.	estimates
FY	Fiscal year ended in June 30
H'holds	Households
Hi-Lo ranking	Ranking from highest to lowest

Int	Interim
MCA	Mayor Council Administrator
Mgr	Manager
N/A or NA	Not available or no information available
NCLB	No Child Left Behind
OCCL'72	Optional County Charter Law, 1972
OMCL	Optional Municipal Charter Law
SC	Special Charter
SM 50	Small Municipality, OMCL, 1950
SAT	Scholastic Achievement/Aptitude Test
T	Town
V	Village
Vol.	Volunteered

DISCLAIMER

New Jersey Municipal Data Book contains thousands of pieces of information. Every reasonable precaution, along with a good deal of care was taken in its preparation. Despite all efforts it is possible that some of the information contained in this book may not be accurate. Some errors may be due to errors in the original source materials, others may have been made by the compilers of this volume. An incorrect spelling may occur, a figure may be inverted and similar mistakes may exist. The compilers, editors, typist, printers, and others are all human, and in a work of this magnitude the possibility of error can never be fully eliminated. If any piece of information is believed to be inaccurate, please contact the publisher. We are eager to eliminate any errors from coming editions and we will be pleased to check a piece of information. The publisher is also aware that some users may apply the data in this book in various remunerative projects. Although we have taken all reasonable, responsible measures to insure total accuracy, we cannot take responsibility for liability or losses suffered by users of the data. The information provided here is believed to be correct at the time of publication. No other guarantees are made or implied. The publisher assumes no liability for losses incurred by users, and warrants only that diligence and due care were used in the production of this volume.

The New Jersey Municipal Data Book

2006

State & Municipal Profiles Series™

County Profiles

State &
Municipal
Profiles
Series

Demographics & Socio-Economic Characteristics
(2000 U.S. Census, except as noted)

Population
1980*	17,235
1990*	17,038
2000	17,454
Male	8,506
Female	8,948
2004 (estimate)*	18,467
Persons per sq. mi. of land	3,335

Race & Hispanic Origin, 2000
Race
White	13,758
Black/African American	2,098
Amer. Indian/Alaska Natv.	24
Asian	962
Natv. Hawaiian/Pac. Islander	1
Other Race	306
Two or more races	305
Hispanic origin, total	1,225
Mexican	90
Puerto Rican	648
Cuban	96
Other Hispanic	391

Age & Nativity, 2000
Under 5 years	1,211
18 years and over	13,185
21 years and over	12,708
65 years and over	1,811
85 years and over	129
Median Age	37
Native born	15,392
Foreign born	1,995

Educational Attainment, 2000
Population 25 years and over	12,263
0-8 yrs of school	3.1%
High School grad or higher	87.9%
Bachelor's degree or higher	34.4%
Graduate degree	11.4%

Income & Poverty, 1999
Per capita income	$28,984
Median household income	$68,125
Median family income	$76,648
Persons in poverty	807
H'holds receiving public assistance	102
H'holds receiving social security	1,432

Households, 2000
Total households	6,421
With persons under 18	2,416
With persons over 65	1,299
Family households	4,774
One-person households	1,300
Persons per household	2.7
Persons per family	3.14

Labor & Employment
Total civilian labor force, 2004**	10,805
Unemployment rate	4.4%
Total civilian labor force, 2000	9,742
Unemployment rate	3.5%

Employed persons 16 years and over by occupation, 2000
Managers & professionals	3,963
Service occupations	1,120
Sales & office occupations	2,712
Farming, fishing & forestry	8
Construction & maintenance	647
Production & transportation	947
Self-employed persons	396

*US Census Bureau
**New Jersey Department of Labor

General Information
Township of Aberdeen
One Aberdeen Square
Aberdeen, NJ 07747
732-583-4200

Web site	www.twp.aberdeen.nj.us
Land area (sq. miles)	5.54
Water area (sq. miles)	2.22
Type of government	Township
Form of government	CM '50

Government

Legislative Districts
US Congressional	6
State Legislative	13

Local Officials, 2006
Mayor	David Sobel
Admin/Manager	Stuart Brown
Clerk	Karen Ventura
Finance Dir/Treas	Angela Morin
Engineer	David Samuel
Attorney	Dan McCarthy
Tax assessor	Ann Barker
Tax collector	Marie Taylor
Building officer	John Quinn
Zoning officer	NA
Public Works	James Lauro

Housing & Construction

Housing Units, 2000*
Total	6,558
Median rent	$817
Median SF home value	$160,800

New Privately Owned Housing Units Authorized by Building Permit
	Units	Value
Total, 2004	45	$3,820,840
Single family	43	$3,670,840
Total, 2005	22	$2,417,400
Single family	22	$2,417,400

Real Property Valuation - parcels, 2005
	Number	Valuation
Total		$843,790,140
Vacant	488	15,059,530
Residential	6,108	707,656,910
Commercial	167	91,048,800
Industrial	4	11,849,700
Apartments	8	17,136,400
Farm land	6	943,200
Farm homestead	14	95,600

Average Property Value & Tax, 2005
Residential value	$115,608
Property tax	$5,503
FAIR rebate	$508

Public Library
Matawan-Aberdeen Public Library†
165 Main St
Matawan, NJ 07747
732-583-9100

Director	Susan Pike

Library statistics, 2004
	Total	per capita
Volumes	89,918	3.41
Expenditure	$636,215	$24.13

†Joint Library with Matawan Borough

Public Safety

Police
Chief	Joseph Kelly
Number of officers, 2004	34

Crime, 2004	Number	Rate
Total	288	15.4
Violent	37	2
Non-violent	251	13.4
Domestic Viol.	243	NA

Emergency/Fire
Director	NA

Public School District
(for school year 2004-2005 except as noted)

Matawan-Aberdeen Regional School District
One Crest Way
Aberdeen, NJ 07747
732-290-2705

Superintendent	Bruce Quinn
Grade plan	K-12
Enrollment	3,839.5
Students per teacher	11.1
Per pupil expenditure	$12,895
Median faculty salary	$50,700
Median administrator salary	$105,944
Grade 12 enrollment	215.0
High school graduation rate	96.5%

Assessment test results
(percent scoring at proficient or advanced level)
	Language	Math
Grade 3	93.4%	88.9%
Grade 8	74.9%	68.7%
High school	86.5%	77.4%

SAT
Percent tested	76%
Average SAT math score	504
Average SAT verbal score	499

No Child Left Behind, 2003-04
Attendence rate (target = 90%)	94.7%
Drop rate	0.5%
Highly-qualified teachers	98.9%
District needs improvement?(AYP)	No

Municipal Finance

Fiscal Year 2005
Total tax levy	$40,224,280
County levy	5,182,338
County taxes	4,892,044
County library	0
County health	0
County open space	290,294
School levy	28,358,113
Local muni. budget	6,683,829
Misc. revenues	6,994,490
Total aid	$2,020,594
CMPTRA	947,908
Muni. block grant	74,552
Energy tax receipts	928,134
Homeland security	70,000

Fiscal Year 2006
Total aid	$2,020,593
CMPTRA	915,423
Muni. block grant	74,552
Energy tax receipts	960,618
Homeland security	70,000

Taxes
	2003	2004	2005
General tax rate per $100	4.27	4.581	4.760
Net valuation taxable	$816,912,147	$831,540,587	$845,098,132
State equalized value	$1,396,908,596	$1,599,223,700	$1,868,446,014
County equalization ratio	67.67	58.48	51.95

Demographics & Socio-Economic Characteristics

(2000 U.S. Census, except as noted)

Population

1980*	6,859
1990*	7,298
2000	7,638
Male	3,660
Female	3,978
2004 (estimate)*	7,905
Persons per sq. mi. of land	1,383

Race & Hispanic Origin, 2000

Race

White	6,363
Black/African American	459
Amer. Indian/Alaska Natv.	13
Asian	570
Natv. Hawaiian/Pac. Islander	0
Other Race	115
Two or more races	118
Hispanic origin, total	288
Mexican	30
Puerto Rican	111
Cuban	19
Other Hispanic	128

Age & Nativity, 2000

Under 5 years	460
18 years and over	5,842
21 years and over	5,672
65 years and over	1,231
85 years and over	165
Median Age	40.3
Native born	6,894
Foreign born	799

Educational Attainment, 2000

Population 25 years and over	5,357
0-8 yrs of school	3.2%
High School grad or higher	86.0%
Bachelor's degree or higher	22.4%
Graduate degree	7.3%

Income & Poverty, 1999

Per capita income	$23,615
Median household income	$55,745
Median family income	$61,563
Persons in poverty	364
H'holds receiving public assistance	30
H'holds receiving social security	836

Households, 2000

Total households	2,773
With persons under 18	996
With persons over 65	777
Family households	2,084
One-person households	532
Persons per household	2.69
Persons per family	3.08

Labor & Employment

Total civilian labor force, 2004**	4,058
Unemployment rate	5.8%
Total civilian labor force, 2000	4,009
Unemployment rate	6.5%

Employed persons 16 years and over by occupation, 2000

Managers & professionals	1,042
Service occupations	1,097
Sales & office occupations	1,087
Farming, fishing & forestry	4
Construction & maintenance	280
Production & transportation	239
Self-employed persons	197

*US Census Bureau
**New Jersey Department of Labor

General Information

City of Absecon
Muni Complex
500 Mill Rd
Absecon, NJ 08201
609-641-0663

Web site	NA
Land area (sq. miles)	5.72
Water area (sq. miles)	1.21
Type of government	City
Form of government	C

Government

Legislative Districts

US Congressional	2
State Legislative	2

Local Officials, 2006

Mayor	Peter C. Elco
Admin/Manager	Terrence Dolan
Clerk	Carie A. Crone
Finance Dir/Treas	Jessica Thompson
Engineer	Edward Walberg
Attorney	Michael Blee
Tax assessor	Brian Conover
Tax collector	Agnes Bambrick
Building officer	Pat Naticchione
Zoning officer	Pat Naticchione
Public Works	Lloyd Jones

Housing & Construction

Housing Units, 2000*

Total	2,902
Median rent	$792
Median SF home value	$123,000

New Privately Owned Housing Units Authorized by Building Permit

	Units	Value
Total, 2004	62	$5,708,215
Single family	38	$4,537,615
Total, 2005	79	$9,966,085
Single family	79	$9,966,085

Real Property Valuation - parcels, 2005

	Number	Valuation
Total		$444,406,700
Vacant	576	12,167,600
Residential	2,990	343,396,700
Commercial	195	88,842,400
Industrial	0	0
Apartments	0	0
Farm land	0	0
Farm homestead	0	0

Average Property Value & Tax, 2005

Residential value	$114,848
Property tax	$4,242
FAIR rebate	$590

Public Library

Absecon Public Library
305 New Jersey Ave
Absecon, NJ 08201
609-646-2228

Director .... Barbara E. Wilson

Library statistics, 2004

	Total	per capita
Volumes	19,686	2.58
Expenditure	$175,283	$22.95

Public Safety

Police

Chief	Charles J. Smith
Number of officers, 2004	26

Crime, 2004	Number	Rate
Total	285	36.4
Violent	37	4.7
Non-violent	248	31.7
Domestic Viol.	90	NA

Emergency/Fire

Director .... Stanley Kolbe

Public School District

(for school year 2004-2005 except as noted)

Absecon City School District
800 Irelan Ave
Absecon, NJ 08201
609-641-5375

Superintendent	James Giaquinto
Grade plan	K-12
Enrollment	910.0
Students per teacher	12.0
Per pupil expenditure	$8,766
Median faculty salary	$52,397
Median administrator salary	$83,782
Grade 12 enrollment	NA
High school graduation rate	NA

Assessment test results

(percent scoring at proficient or advanced level)

	Language	Math
Grade 3	74.4%	91.9%
Grade 8	74.8%	70.5%
High school	NA	NA

SAT

Percent tested	NA
Average SAT math score	NA
Average SAT verbal score	NA

No Child Left Behind, 2003-04

Attendence rate (target = 90%)	95.1%
Drop rate	NA
Highly-qualified teachers	98.8%
District needs improvement?(AYP)	No

Municipal Finance

Fiscal Year 2005

Total tax levy	$16,454,334
County levy	2,288,737
County taxes	2,054,426
County library	0
County health	111,970
County open space	122,342
School levy	8,955,406
Local muni. budget	5,210,191
Misc. revenues	5,521,989
Total aid	$1,103,288
CMPTRA	322,956
Muni. block grant	31,934
Energy tax receipts	695,061
Homeland security	50,000

Fiscal Year 2006

Total aid	$1,103,288
CMPTRA	298,629
Muni. block grant	31,934
Energy tax receipts	719,388
Homeland security	50,000

Taxes

	2003	2004	2005
General tax rate per $100	3.50	3.618	3.694
Net valuation taxable	$422,133,010	$438,292,519	$445,470,853
State equalized value	$507,249,471	$600,778,208	$702,746,258
County equalization ratio	89.79	83.22	72.90

Demographics & Socio-Economic Characteristics

(2000 U.S. Census, except as noted)

Population

1980*	2,798
1990*	3,594
2000	4,698
Male	2,353
Female	2,345
2004 (estimate)*	4,976
Persons per sq. mi. of land	181

Race & Hispanic Origin, 2000

Race
White	4,558
Black/African American	37
Amer. Indian/Alaska Natv.	5
Asian	34
Natv. Hawaiian/Pac. Islander	2
Other Race	21
Two or more races	41
Hispanic origin, total	81
Mexican	17
Puerto Rican	30
Cuban	6
Other Hispanic	28

Age & Nativity, 2000

Under 5 years	331
18 years and over	3,378
21 years and over	3,259
65 years and over	568
85 years and over	124
Median Age	40.2
Native born	4,448
Foreign born	250

Educational Attainment, 2000

Population 25 years and over	3,150
0-8 yrs of school	3.4%
High School grad or higher	93.2%
Bachelor's degree or higher	39.7%
Graduate degree	16.0%

Income & Poverty, 1999

Per capita income	$34,622
Median household income	$92,730
Median family income	$93,619
Persons in poverty	229
H'holds receiving public assistance	8
H'holds receiving social security	319

Households, 2000

Total households	1,535
With persons under 18	679
With persons over 65	289
Family households	1,291
One-person households	207
Persons per household	2.95
Persons per family	3.25

Labor & Employment

Total civilian labor force, 2004**	2,287
Unemployment rate	4.4%
Total civilian labor force, 2000	2,351
Unemployment rate	4.0%

Employed persons 16 years and over by occupation, 2000
Managers & professionals	1,115
Service occupations	187
Sales & office occupations	633
Farming, fishing & forestry	28
Construction & maintenance	153
Production & transportation	142
Self-employed persons	234

*US Census Bureau
**New Jersey Department of Labor

General Information

Township of Alexandria
21 Hog Hollow Rd
Pittstown, NJ 08867
908-996-7071

Web site	www.alexandria-nj.us
Land area (sq. miles)	27.54
Water area (sq. miles)	0.10
Type of government	Township
Form of government	TC

Government

Legislative Districts

US Congressional	7
State Legislative	23

Local Officials, 2006

Mayor	Carol Hoffmann
Admin/Manager	NA
Clerk	Ellen Kluber
Finance Dir/Treas	Dawn Merante
Engineer	Gerald D. Philkill
Attorney	Valerie Bollheimer
Tax assessor	Curtis Schick
Tax collector	Jack Earley
Building officer	James Fania
Zoning officer	NA
Public Works	NA

Housing & Construction

Housing Units, 2000*

Total	1,598
Median rent	$1,021
Median SF home value	$274,100

New Privately Owned Housing Units Authorized by Building Permit

	Units	Value
Total, 2004	27	$7,359,200
Single family	27	$7,359,200
Total, 2005	37	$9,217,984
Single family	37	$9,217,984

Real Property Valuation - parcels, 2005

	Number	Valuation
Total		$739,484,959
Vacant	255	36,947,000
Residential	1,395	580,220,100
Commercial	32	22,067,188
Industrial	3	2,534,800
Apartments	1	418,900
Farm land	232	93,233,700
Farm homestead	372	4,063,271

Average Property Value & Tax, 2005

Residential value	$330,664
Property tax	$6,203
FAIR rebate	$513

Public Library

No public municipal library.

Library statistics, 2004

	Total	per capita
Volumes	NA	NA
Expenditure	NA	NA

Public Safety

Police

Chief	NA
Number of officers, 2004	0

Crime, 2004	Number	Rate
Total	31	6.3
Violent	1	0.2
Non-violent	30	6.1
Domestic Viol.	7	NA

Emergency/Fire

Director	NA

Public School District

(for school year 2004-2005 except as noted)

Alexandria Township School District
557 County Rd 513
Pittstown, NJ 08867
908-996-6811

Superintendent	Wendy Schadt
Grade plan	K-8
Enrollment	656.0
Students per teacher	10.4
Per pupil expenditure	$11,241
Median faculty salary	$51,150
Median administrator salary	$91,600
Grade 12 enrollment	NA
High school graduation rate	NA

Assessment test results

(percent scoring at proficient or advanced level)
	Language	Math
Grade 3	97.2%	94.3%
Grade 8	87.8%	69.6%
High school	NA	NA

SAT

Percent tested	NA
Average SAT math score	NA
Average SAT verbal score	NA

No Child Left Behind, 2003-04

Attendence rate (target = 90%)	95.5%
Drop rate	NA
Highly-qualified teachers	100%
District needs improvement?(AYP)	No

Municipal Finance

Fiscal Year 2005

Total tax levy	$13,907,844
County levy	2,662,900
County taxes	2,260,939
County library	189,184
County health	0
County open space	212,777
School levy	9,835,949
Local muni. budget	1,408,995
Misc. revenues	1,821,477
Total aid	$467,011
CMPTRA	161,085
Muni. block grant	18,421
Energy tax receipts	287,505
Homeland security	0

Fiscal Year 2006

Total aid	$467,010
CMPTRA	151,022
Muni. block grant	18,421
Energy tax receipts	297,567
Homeland security	NA

Taxes

	2003	2004	2005
General tax rate per $100	2.97	1.840	1.880
Net valuation taxable	$405,793,833	$713,815,972	$741,419,296
State equalized value	$574,209,471	$649,506,849	$742,012,906
County equalization ratio	67.66	111.17	105.02

Demographics & Socio-Economic Characteristics
(2000 U.S. Census, except as noted)

Population
1980* 2,560
1990* 3,484
2000 3,877
  Male 1,800
  Female 2,077
2000 (revised) 3,873
2004 (estimate)* 4,007
  Persons per sq. mi. of land 195

Race & Hispanic Origin, 2000
Race
  White 3,702
  Black/African American 36
  Amer. Indian/Alaska Natv. 2
  Asian 72
  Natv. Hawaiian/Pac. Islander 0
  Other Race 27
  Two or more races 38
Hispanic origin, total 104
  Mexican 15
  Puerto Rican 28
  Cuban 9
  Other Hispanic 52

Age & Nativity, 2000
Under 5 years 229
18 years and over 3,142
21 years and over 3,072
65 years and over 637
85 years and over 60
Median Age 44.1
Native born 3,493
Foreign born 384

Educational Attainment, 2000
Population 25 years and over 3,003
0-8 yrs of school 1.0%
High School grad or higher 94.5%
Bachelor's degree or higher 43.8%
Graduate degree 15.2%

Income & Poverty, 1999
Per capita income $43,552
Median household income $70,107
Median family income $89,653
Persons in poverty 71
H'holds receiving public assistance 42
H'holds receiving social security 420

Households, 2000
Total households 1,692
  With persons under 18 423
  With persons over 65 442
  Family households 1,134
  One-person households 482
Persons per household 2.28
Persons per family 2.8

Labor & Employment
Total civilian labor force, 2004** 2,454
  Unemployment rate 4.6%
Total civilian labor force, 2000 2,144
  Unemployment rate 1.7%
Employed persons 16 years and over by occupation, 2000
  Managers & professionals 1,033
  Service occupations 145
  Sales & office occupations 616
  Farming, fishing & forestry 19
  Construction & maintenance 115
  Production & transportation 179
Self-employed persons 138

*US Census Bureau
**New Jersey Department of Labor

General Information
Township of Allamuchy
PO Box A
292 Alphano Rd
Allamuchy, NJ 07820
908-852-5132

Web site .... NA
Land area (sq. miles) 20.54
Water area (sq. miles) 0.23
Type of government .... Township
Form of government .... SM '50

Government

Legislative Districts
US Congressional 5
State Legislative 23

Local Officials, 2006
Mayor .... Robert Resker
Admin/Manager .... Anne Marie Tracy
Clerk .... Anne Marie Tracy
Finance Dir/Treas .. D. Mowrey/J. Kozimor
Engineer .... Paul Sterbenz
Attorney .... Edward Wacks
Tax assessor .... Michael Schmidt
Tax collector .... Betty Drake
Building officer .... Charles Cutler
Zoning officer .... Charles Cutler
Public Works .... NA

Housing & Construction

Housing Units, 2000*
Total 1,774
Median rent $1,075
Median SF home value $192,500

New Privately Owned Housing Units Authorized by Building Permit

	Units	Value
Total, 2004	19	$3,994,510
Single family	19	$3,994,510
Total, 2005	51	$7,146,800
Single family	51	$7,146,800

Real Property Valuation - parcels, 2005

	Number	Valuation
Total		$491,138,970
Vacant	170	13,016,700
Residential	1,718	437,655,500
Commercial	19	18,423,100
Industrial	1	977,300
Apartments	0	0
Farm land	67	19,655,200
Farm homestead	124	1,411,170

Average Property Value & Tax, 2005
Residential value $238,364
Property tax $4,537
FAIR rebate $572

Public Library

No public municipal library.

Library statistics, 2004

	Total	per capita
Volumes	NA	NA
Expenditure	NA	NA

Public Safety

Police
Chief .... (State)
Number of officers, 2004 0

Crime, 2004	Number	Rate
Total	22	5.6
Violent	3	0.8
Non-violent	19	4.8
Domestic Viol.	21	NA

Emergency/Fire
Director .... Daniel Bulka

Public School District
(for school year 2004-2005 except as noted)

Allamuchy Township School District
Allamuchy Township School
Allamuchy, NJ 07820
908-852-1894
Superintendent .... Timothy Frederiks
Grade plan K-12
Enrollment 339.0
Students per teacher 11.0
Per pupil expenditure $13,005
Median faculty salary $38,575
Median administrator salary $46,800
Grade 12 enrollment .... NA
High school graduation rate .... NA

Assessment test results
(percent scoring at proficient or advanced level)

	Language	Math
Grade 3	89.6%	83.3%
Grade 8	93.4%	66.7%
High school	NA	NA

SAT
Percent tested .... NA
Average SAT math score .... NA
Average SAT verbal score .... NA

No Child Left Behind, 2003-04
Attendence rate (target = 90%) 94.9%
Drop rate .... NA
Highly-qualified teachers 99.3%
District needs improvement?(AYP) ..... No

Municipal Finance

Fiscal Year 2005
Total tax levy $9,375,335
  County levy 3,315,314
  County taxes 2,741,188
  County library 264,279
  County health 0
  County open space 309,846
  School levy 5,372,511
  Local muni. budget 687,511
  Misc. revenues 2,186,370
Total aid $510,857
  CMPTRA 145,630
  Muni. block grant 15,245
  Energy tax receipts 349,982
  Homeland security 0

Fiscal Year 2006
Total aid $510,857
  CMPTRA 133,380
  Muni. block grant 15,245
  Energy tax receipts 362,232
  Homeland security .... NA

Taxes

	2003	2004	2005
General tax rate per $100	1.70	1.820	1.910
Net valuation taxable	$478,843,102	$486,949,763	$492,508,822
State equalized value	$455,303,891	$508,653,974	$567,995,412
County equalization ratio	117.97	105.17	95.72

Demographics & Socio-Economic Characteristics
(2000 U.S. Census, except as noted)

Population
1980*	5,901
1990*	5,900
2000	6,699
Male	3,245
Female	3,454
2004 (estimate)*	6,799
Persons per sq. mi. of land	2,176

Race & Hispanic Origin, 2000
Race
White	6,195
Black/African American	26
Amer. Indian/Alaska Natv.	4
Asian	408
Natv. Hawaiian/Pac. Islander	0
Other Race	31
Two or more races	35
Hispanic origin, total	170
Mexican	12
Puerto Rican	41
Cuban	40
Other Hispanic	77

Age & Nativity, 2000
Under 5 years	478
18 years and over	4,663
21 years and over	4,528
65 years and over	945
85 years and over	224
Median Age	39.5
Native born	5,933
Foreign born	766

Educational Attainment, 2000
Population 25 years and over	4,376
0-8 yrs of school	2.7%
High School grad or higher	94.8%
Bachelor's degree or higher	62.5%
Graduate degree	22.6%

Income & Poverty, 1999
Per capita income	$47,772
Median household income	$105,704
Median family income	$113,390
Persons in poverty	117
H'holds receiving public assistance	11
H'holds receiving social security	484

Households, 2000
Total households	2,110
With persons under 18	1,028
With persons over 65	461
Family households	1,796
One-person households	277
Persons per household	3.03
Persons per family	3.33

Labor & Employment
Total civilian labor force, 2004**	3,378
Unemployment rate	3.4%
Total civilian labor force, 2000	3,079
Unemployment rate	2.7%

Employed persons 16 years and over by occupation, 2000
Managers & professionals	1,583
Service occupations	216
Sales & office occupations	913
Farming, fishing & forestry	0
Construction & maintenance	138
Production & transportation	145
Self-employed persons	298

*US Census Bureau
**New Jersey Department of Labor

General Information
Borough of Allendale
500 W Crescent Ave
Allendale, NJ 07401
201-818-4400
Web site	www.allendale.org
Land area (sq. miles)	3.12
Water area (sq. miles)	0.03
Type of government	Borough
Form of government	B

Government

Legislative Districts
US Congressional	5
State Legislative	39

Local Officials, 2006
Mayor	Albert Klomburg
Admin/Manager	Leslie Shenkler
Clerk	Gwen Gabbert
Finance Dir/Treas	Paula Favata
Engineer	John Yakimik
Attorney	David Bole
Tax assessor	Angela Mattiace
Tax collector	Paula Favata
Building officer	John Wittekind
Zoning officer	John Wittekind
Public Works	George Higbie

Housing & Construction

Housing Units, 2000*
Total	2,143
Median rent	$1,778
Median SF home value	$421,800

New Privately Owned Housing Units Authorized by Building Permit
	Units	Value
Total, 2004	2	$3,008,425
Single family	2	$3,008,425
Total, 2005	1	$1,318,950
Single family	1	$1,318,950

Real Property Valuation - parcels, 2005
	Number	Valuation
Total		$1,280,254,200
Vacant	64	9,746,500
Residential	2,107	1,105,020,600
Commercial	50	103,847,100
Industrial	12	60,671,900
Apartments	0	0
Farm land	1	951,900
Farm homestead	5	16,200

Average Property Value & Tax, 2005
Residential value	$523,218
Property tax	$11,404
FAIR rebate	$561

Public Library
Lee Memorial Library
500 W Crescent Ave
Allendale, NJ 07401
201-327-4338
Director	Carol Cannon

Library statistics, 2004
	Total	per capita
Volumes	47,256	7.05
Expenditure	$466,365	$69.62

Public Safety
Police
Chief	Robert Herndon
Number of officers, 2004	14

Crime, 2004	Number	Rate
Total	44	6.5
Violent	0	0
Non-violent	44	6.5
Domestic Viol.	4	NA

Emergency/Fire
Director	John Shute

Public School District
(for school year 2004-2005 except as noted)

Allendale School District
100 Brookside Ave
Allendale, NJ 07401
201-327-2020
Superintendent	Jerilyn Caprio
Grade plan	K-8
Enrollment	1,108.0
Students per teacher	13.2
Per pupil expenditure	$10,483
Median faculty salary	$50,367
Median administrator salary	$125,815
Grade 12 enrollment	NA
High school graduation rate	NA

Assessment test results
(percent scoring at proficient or advanced level)
	Language	Math
Grade 3	95.0%	98.0%
Grade 8	93.9%	90.5%
High school	NA	NA

SAT
Percent tested	NA
Average SAT math score	NA
Average SAT verbal score	NA

No Child Left Behind, 2003-04
Attendence rate (target = 90%)	94.7%
Drop rate	NA
Highly-qualified teachers	100%
District needs improvement?(AYP)	No

Municipal Finance

Fiscal Year 2005
Total tax levy	$27,970,016
County levy	2,895,670
County taxes	2,750,064
County library	0
County health	0
County open space	145,606
School levy	18,234,606
Local muni. budget	6,839,740
Misc. revenues	3,502,688
Total aid	$1,362,001
CMPTRA	159,617
Muni. block grant	26,267
Energy tax receipts	1,126,117
Homeland security	50,000

Fiscal Year 2006
Total aid	$1,362,001
CMPTRA	120,203
Muni. block grant	26,267
Energy tax receipts	1,165,531
Homeland security	50,000

Taxes
	2003	2004	2005
General tax rate per $100	1.91	2.050	2.180
Net valuation taxable	$1,287,122,598	$1,280,372,085	$1,283,268,177
State equalized value	$1,331,460,223	$1,451,197,971	$1,593,923,956
County equalization ratio	107.41	96.67	88.21

Demographics & Socio-Economic Characteristics

(2000 U.S. Census, except as noted)

Population

1980*	912
1990*	759
2000	718
Male	370
Female	348
2004 (estimate)*	714
Persons per sq. mi. of land	2,735

Race & Hispanic Origin, 2000

Race
White	699
Black/African American	6
Amer. Indian/Alaska Natv.	2
Asian	3
Natv. Hawaiian/Pac. Islander	0
Other Race	1
Two or more races	7
Hispanic origin, total	18
Mexican	3
Puerto Rican	3
Cuban	0
Other Hispanic	12

Age & Nativity, 2000

Under 5 years	40
18 years and over	582
21 years and over	569
65 years and over	134
85 years and over	20
Median Age	42.5
Native born	700
Foreign born	23

Educational Attainment, 2000

Population 25 years and over	556
0-8 yrs of school	2.3%
High School grad or higher	96.0%
Bachelor's degree or higher	57.7%
Graduate degree	21.2%

Income & Poverty, 1999

Per capita income	$42,710
Median household income	$85,000
Median family income	$109,180
Persons in poverty	27
H'holds receiving public assistance	2
H'holds receiving social security	96

Households, 2000

Total households	285
With persons under 18	74
With persons over 65	90
Family households	189
One-person households	71
Persons per household	2.52
Persons per family	3.08

Labor & Employment

Total civilian labor force, 2004**	416
Unemployment rate	1.6%
Total civilian labor force, 2000	370
Unemployment rate	3.5%

Employed persons 16 years and over by occupation, 2000
Managers & professionals	181
Service occupations	32
Sales & office occupations	123
Farming, fishing & forestry	0
Construction & maintenance	7
Production & transportation	14
Self-employed persons	41

*US Census Bureau
**New Jersey Department of Labor

General Information

Borough of Allenhurst
125 Corlies Ave
Allenhurst, NJ 07711
732-531-2757

Web site	www.allenhurstnj.org
Land area (sq. miles)	0.26
Water area (sq. miles)	0.02
Type of government	Borough
Form of government	Comm.

Government

Legislative Districts

US Congressional	6
State Legislative	11

Local Officials, 2006

Mayor	Joseph M. Coyne
Admin/Manager	Lori L. Osborn
Clerk	Lori L. Osborn
Finance Dir/Treas	Chris Brown
Engineer	Peter Avakian
Attorney	William O'Hagan
Tax assessor	Peter Barnett
Tax collector	Edward Mazzacco
Building officer	NA
Zoning officer	Thomas Gironda
Public Works	Doug Caron

Housing & Construction

Housing Units, 2000*

Total	370
Median rent	$815
Median SF home value	$359,000

New Privately Owned Housing Units Authorized by Building Permit

	Units	Value
Total, 2004	0	$0
Single family	0	$0
Total, 2005	0	$0
Single family	0	$0

Real Property Valuation - parcels, 2005

	Number	Valuation
Total		$209,814,900
Vacant	9	1,626,300
Residential	295	184,333,700
Commercial	26	18,193,100
Industrial	1	4,294,300
Apartments	4	1,367,500
Farm land	0	0
Farm homestead	0	0

Average Property Value & Tax, 2005

Residential value	$624,860
Property tax	$8,300
FAIR rebate	$533

Public Library

No public municipal library.

Library statistics, 2004

	Total	per capita
Volumes	NA	NA
Expenditure	NA	NA

Public Safety

Police

Chief	Robert Richter
Number of officers, 2004	9

Crime, 2004	Number	Rate
Total	35	49.6
Violent	0	0
Non-violent	35	49.6
Domestic Viol.	6	NA

Emergency/Fire

Director	J.C. Harrington

Public School District

(for school year 2004-2005 except as noted)

Allenhurst School District
125 Corlies Ave
Allenhurst, NJ 07711

Superintendent	NA
Grade plan	NA
Enrollment	NA
Students per teacher	NA
Per pupil expenditure	NA
Median faculty salary	NA
Median administrator salary	NA
Grade 12 enrollment	NA
High school graduation rate	NA

Assessment test results

(percent scoring at proficient or advanced level)
	Language	Math
Grade 3	NA	NA
Grade 8	NA	NA
High school	NA	NA

SAT

Percent tested	NA
Average SAT math score	NA
Average SAT verbal score	NA

No Child Left Behind, 2003-04

Attendence rate (target = 90%)	NA
Drop rate	NA
Highly-qualified teachers	NA
District needs improvement?(AYP)	NA

Municipal Finance

Fiscal Year 2005

Total tax levy	$2,788,496
County levy	995,413
County taxes	893,208
County library	49,201
County health	0
County open space	53,004
School levy	294,532
Local muni. budget	1,498,551
Misc. revenues	1,906,198
Total aid	$233,738
CMPTRA	0
Muni. block grant	3,321
Energy tax receipts	205,417
Homeland security	25,000

Fiscal Year 2006

Total aid	$240,928
CMPTRA	0
Muni. block grant	3,321
Energy tax receipts	212,607
Homeland security	25,000

Taxes

	2003	2004	2005
General tax rate per $100	1.21	1.289	1.329
Net valuation taxable	$207,520,471	$208,165,687	$209,922,567
State equalized value	$256,514,797	$294,548,734	$413,233,400
County equalization ratio	97.66	80.90	70.66

Demographics & Socio-Economic Characteristics
(2000 U.S. Census, except as noted)

Population
1980*	1,962
1990*	1,828
2000	1,882
Male	890
Female	992
2004 (estimate)*	1,875
Persons per sq. mi. of land	3,086

Race & Hispanic Origin, 2000
Race
White	1,706
Black/African American	121
Amer. Indian/Alaska Natv.	11
Asian	12
Natv. Hawaiian/Pac. Islander	0
Other Race	11
Two or more races	21
Hispanic origin, total	36
Mexican	2
Puerto Rican	24
Cuban	3
Other Hispanic	7

Age & Nativity, 2000
Under 5 years	136
18 years and over	1,379
21 years and over	1,327
65 years and over	184
85 years and over	22
Median Age	38.5
Native born	1,827
Foreign born	55

Educational Attainment, 2000
Population 25 years and over	1,269
0-8 yrs of school	1.7%
High School grad or higher	92.5%
Bachelor's degree or higher	41.1%
Graduate degree	15.7%

Income & Poverty, 1999
Per capita income	$29,455
Median household income	$71,193
Median family income	$79,843
Persons in poverty	44
H'holds receiving public assistance	15
H'holds receiving social security	155

Households, 2000
Total households	708
With persons under 18	271
With persons over 65	136
Family households	527
One-person households	151
Persons per household	2.66
Persons per family	3.13

Labor & Employment
Total civilian labor force, 2004**	1,209
Unemployment rate	3.5%
Total civilian labor force, 2000	1,073
Unemployment rate	3.3%

Employed persons 16 years and over by occupation, 2000
Managers & professionals	488
Service occupations	122
Sales & office occupations	276
Farming, fishing & forestry	1
Construction & maintenance	65
Production & transportation	86
Self-employed persons	64

*US Census Bureau
**New Jersey Department of Labor

General Information
Borough of Allentown
PO Box 487
8 N Main St
Allentown, NJ 08501
609-259-3151

Web site	NA
Land area (sq. miles)	0.61
Water area (sq. miles)	0.02
Type of government	Borough
Form of government	Borough

Government

Legislative Districts
US Congressional	4
State Legislative	30

Local Officials, 2006
Mayor	Stuart Fierstein
Admin/Manager	NA
Clerk	Lorene Wright
Finance Dir/Treas	Robert Benick
Engineer	Hatch, Mott MacDonald
Attorney	Donald Driggers
Tax assessor	Victoria Butchon
Tax collector	Barbara Pater
Building officer	Washington Township
Zoning officer	Ron Gafgen
Public Works	NA

Housing & Construction

Housing Units, 2000*
Total	718
Median rent	$792
Median SF home value	$167,100

New Privately Owned Housing Units
Authorized by Building Permit
	Units	Value
Total, 2004	0	$0
Single family	0	$0
Total, 2005	1	$120,000
Single family	1	$120,000

Real Property Valuation - parcels, 2005
	Number	Valuation
Total		$100,751,700
Vacant	30	524,400
Residential	582	88,718,100
Commercial	41	8,744,800
Industrial	0	0
Apartments	2	2,760,100
Farm land	0	0
Farm homestead	2	4,300

Average Property Value & Tax, 2005
Residential value	$151,922
Property tax	$5,838
FAIR rebate	$703

Public Library
Allentown Branch Library†
16 S Main St
Allentown, NJ 08501
609-259-7565

Branch Librarian . . . . Nancy Stein

Library statistics, 2004
	Total	per capita
Volumes	NA	NA
Expenditure	NA	NA

†Branch of County Library

Public Safety

Police
Chief	Harvey Morrell
Number of officers, 2004	6

Crime, 2004	Number	Rate
Total	22	11.8
Violent	1	0.5
Non-violent	21	11.3
Domestic Viol.	2	NA

Emergency/Fire
Director . . . . Jeremy Wyckoff

Public School District
(for school year 2004-2005 except as noted)

Upper Freehold Regional School Dist.
27 High St
Allentown, NJ 08501
609-259-7292

Superintendent	Robert Connelly
Grade plan	K-12
Enrollment	2,109.5
Students per teacher	12.7
Per pupil expenditure	$10,829
Median faculty salary	$48,372
Median administrator salary	$95,000
Grade 12 enrollment	206.5
High school graduation rate	97.7%

Assessment test results
(percent scoring at proficient or advanced level)
	Language	Math
Grade 3	90.5%	85.0%
Grade 8	87.7%	81.5%
High school	88.4%	79.8%

SAT
Percent tested	84%
Average SAT math score	499
Average SAT verbal score	493

No Child Left Behind, 2003-04
Attendence rate (target = 90%)	95.1%
Drop rate	0.9%
Highly-qualified teachers	89.1%
District needs improvement?(AYP)	No

Municipal Finance

Fiscal Year 2005
Total tax levy	$3,919,197
County levy	518,865
County taxes	458,094
County library	25,234
County health	8,354
County open space	27,184
School levy	2,412,633
Local muni. budget	987,699
Misc. revenues	815,554
Total aid	$224,743
CMPTRA	107,086
Muni. block grant	7,999
Energy tax receipts	84,658
Homeland security	25,000

Fiscal Year 2006
Total aid	$224,742
CMPTRA	104,122
Muni. block grant	7,999
Energy tax receipts	87,621
Homeland security	25,000

Taxes
	2003	2004	2005
General tax rate per $100	3.59	3.558	3.843
Net valuation taxable	$101,221,380	$101,620,669	$101,991,312
State equalized value	$133,678,526	$152,070,142	$174,672,567
County equalization ratio	82.06	75.72	66.54

Demographics & Socio-Economic Characteristics
(2000 U.S. Census, except as noted)

Population
1980*	2,680
1990*	2,795
2000	2,774
Male	1,411
Female	1,363
2004 (estimate)*	2,917
Persons per sq. mi. of land	89

Race & Hispanic Origin, 2000
Race
White	2,516
Black/African American	191
Amer. Indian/Alaska Natv.	15
Asian	12
Natv. Hawaiian/Pac. Islander	0
Other Race	11
Two or more races	29
Hispanic origin, total	66
Mexican	3
Puerto Rican	3
Cuban	1
Other Hispanic	59

Age & Nativity, 2000
Under 5 years	181
18 years and over	1,995
21 years and over	1,891
65 years and over	343
85 years and over	37
Median Age	36.7
Native born	2,726
Foreign born	48

Educational Attainment, 2000
Population 25 years and over	1,812
0-8 yrs of school	3.4%
High School grad or higher	87.4%
Bachelor's degree or higher	20.3%
Graduate degree	6.6%

Income & Poverty, 1999
Per capita income	$22,935
Median household income	$56,528
Median family income	$65,132
Persons in poverty	226
H'holds receiving public assistance	16
H'holds receiving social security	235

Households, 2000
Total households	948
With persons under 18	373
With persons over 65	239
Family households	742
One-person households	177
Persons per household	2.8
Persons per family	3.19

Labor & Employment
Total civilian labor force, 2004**	1,371
Unemployment rate	0.8%
Total civilian labor force, 2000	1,465
Unemployment rate	9.4%

Employed persons 16 years and over by occupation, 2000
Managers & professionals	417
Service occupations	159
Sales & office occupations	311
Farming, fishing & forestry	24
Construction & maintenance	218
Production & transportation	199
Self-employed persons	112

*US Census Bureau
**New Jersey Department of Labor

General Information
Township of Alloway
PO Box 425
Alloway, NJ 08001
856-935-4080

Web site	NA
Land area (sq. miles)	32.85
Water area (sq. miles)	0.33
Type of government	Township
Form of government	TC

Government

Legislative Districts
US Congressional	2
State Legislative	3

Local Officials, 2006
Mayor	Joseph G. Fedora
Admin/Manager	NA
Clerk	Mary Lou Rutherford
Finance Dir/Treas	James R. Hackett
Engineer	Carl Gaskill
Attorney	John G. Hoffman
Tax assessor	Lisa Perella
Tax collector	Thomas Freeman
Building officer	Harold Underwood
Zoning officer	Walter Leslie
Public Works	NA

Housing & Construction

Housing Units, 2000*
Total	995
Median rent	$700
Median SF home value	$133,300

New Privately Owned Housing Units Authorized by Building Permit
	Units	Value
Total, 2004	18	$3,170,000
Single family	18	$3,170,000
Total, 2005	34	$5,072,000
Single family	34	$5,072,000

Real Property Valuation - parcels, 2005
	Number	Valuation
Total		$186,897,800
Vacant	414	8,692,100
Residential	1,023	131,452,000
Commercial	29	9,277,900
Industrial	0	0
Apartments	0	0
Farm land	215	32,667,200
Farm homestead	426	4,808,600

Average Property Value & Tax, 2005
Residential value	$94,038
Property tax	$2,733
FAIR rebate	$556

Public Library

No public municipal library.

Library statistics, 2004
	Total	per capita
Volumes	NA	NA
Expenditure	NA	NA

Public Safety

Police
Chief	NA
Number of officers, 2004	0

Crime, 2004	Number	Rate
Total	39	13.7
Violent	4	1.4
Non-violent	35	12.3
Domestic Viol.	9	NA

Emergency/Fire
Director	Jeffery Pompper

Public School District
(for school year 2004-2005 except as noted)

Alloway Township School District
43 Cedar St
Alloway, NJ 08001
856-935-1622

Superintendent	Robert J. Bazzel
Grade plan	K-12
Enrollment	490.0
Students per teacher	13.4
Per pupil expenditure	$9,230
Median faculty salary	$47,255
Median administrator salary	$55,860
Grade 12 enrollment	NA
High school graduation rate	NA

Assessment test results
(percent scoring at proficient or advanced level)
	Language	Math
Grade 3	86.5%	84.6%
Grade 8	82.3%	76.4%
High school	NA	NA

SAT
Percent tested	NA
Average SAT math score	NA
Average SAT verbal score	NA

No Child Left Behind, 2003-04
Attendence rate (target = 90%)	95.9%
Drop rate	NA
Highly-qualified teachers	92.4%
District needs improvement?(AYP)	No

Municipal Finance

Fiscal Year 2005
Total tax levy	$5,451,080
County levy	2,119,482
County taxes	2,077,434
County library	0
County health	0
County open space	42,048
School levy	3,059,640
Local muni. budget	271,958
Misc. revenues	1,372,149
Total aid	$469,744
CMPTRA	115,895
Muni. block grant	12,230
Energy tax receipts	341,431
Homeland security	0

Fiscal Year 2006
Total aid	$469,745
CMPTRA	103,945
Muni. block grant	12,230
Energy tax receipts	353,382
Homeland security	NA

Taxes
	2003	2004	2005
General tax rate per $100	2.64	2.713	2.906
Net valuation taxable	$175,864,991	$179,927,367	$187,580,464
State equalized value	$192,897,873	$200,530,124	$241,633,987
County equalization ratio	96.49	91.17	89.69

Demographics & Socio-Economic Characteristics
(2000 U.S. Census, except as noted)

Population
1980*	2,644
1990*	2,530
2000	2,482
Male	1,208
Female	1,274
2004 (estimate)*	2,480
Persons per sq. mi. of land	1,461

Race & Hispanic Origin, 2000
Race
White	2,409
Black/African American	7
Amer. Indian/Alaska Natv.	1
Asian	30
Natv. Hawaiian/Pac. Islander	0
Other Race	16
Two or more races	19
Hispanic origin, total	47
Mexican	15
Puerto Rican	12
Cuban	1
Other Hispanic	19

Age & Nativity, 2000
Under 5 years	144
18 years and over	1,876
21 years and over	1,812
65 years and over	434
85 years and over	45
Median Age	37.7
Native born	2,433
Foreign born	49

Educational Attainment, 2000
Population 25 years and over	1,729
0-8 yrs of school	6.2%
High School grad or higher	80.6%
Bachelor's degree or higher	11.9%
Graduate degree	4.4%

Income & Poverty, 1999
Per capita income	$20,104
Median household income	$42,209
Median family income	$45,435
Persons in poverty	187
H'holds receiving public assistance	26
H'holds receiving social security	375

Households, 2000
Total households	989
With persons under 18	336
With persons over 65	317
Family households	688
One person households	266
Persons per household	2.5
Persons per family	3.05

Labor & Employment
Total civilian labor force, 2004**	1,538
Unemployment rate	4.5%
Total civilian labor force, 2000	1,268
Unemployment rate	5.7%

Employed persons 16 years and over by occupation, 2000
Managers & professionals	255
Service occupations	212
Sales & office occupations	397
Farming, fishing & forestry	0
Construction & maintenance	144
Production & transportation	188
Self-employed persons	66

*US Census Bureau
**New Jersey Department of Labor

General Information
Borough of Alpha
1001 East Blvd
Alpha, NJ 08865
908-454-0088
Web site	NA
Land area (sq. miles)	1.70
Water area (sq. miles)	0.04
Type of government	Borough
Form of government	B

Government

Legislative Districts
US Congressional	5
State Legislative	23

Local Officials, 2006
Mayor	Harry Zikas Jr.
Admin/Manager	NA
Clerk	Laurie Courter
Finance Dir/Treas	Lorraine Russetti
Engineer	Stanley Schrek
Attorney	Christopher Troxell
Tax assessor	Kathy Degan
Tax collector	NA
Building officer	Kevin Duddy
Zoning officer	NA
Public Works	NA

Housing & Construction

Housing Units, 2000*
Total	1,034
Median rent	$710
Median SF home value	$117,200

New Privately Owned Housing Units
Authorized by Building Permit
	Units	Value
Total, 2004	1	$130,000
Single family	1	$130,000
Total, 2005	1	$170,000
Single family	1	$170,000

Real Property Valuation - parcels, 2005
	Number	Valuation
Total		$194,674,321
Vacant	45	3,429,600
Residential	797	143,242,700
Commercial	49	19,176,600
Industrial	15	21,063,000
Apartments	9	6,491,100
Farm land	3	1,009,300
Farm homestead	16	262,021

Average Property Value & Tax, 2005
Residential value	$176,513
Property tax	$4,469
FAIR rebate	$640

Public Library
W H Walters Free Library
1001 E Boulevard
Alpha, NJ 08865
908-454-1445
Director	Myrna Minardi

Library statistics, 2004
	Total	per capita
Volumes	NA	NA
Expenditure	NA	NA

Public Safety

Police
Chief	NA
Number of officers, 2004	1

Crime, 2004	Number	Rate
Total	20	8
Violent	4	1.6
Non-violent	16	6.4
Domestic Viol.	7	NA

Emergency/Fire
Director	Carl Gercie Jr.

Public School District
(for school year 2004-2005 except as noted)

Alpha School District
817 North Blvd
Alpha, NJ 08865
908-454-5000
Administrator	Mary A. Kildow
Grade plan	K-12
Enrollment	271.0
Students per teacher	8.9
Per pupil expenditure	$11,220
Median faculty salary	$48,100
Median administrator salary	$71,500
Grade 12 enrollment	NA
High school graduation rate	NA

Assessment test results
(percent scoring at proficient or advanced level)
	Language	Math
Grade 3	92.6%	92.6%
Grade 8	83.9%	83.9%
High school	NA	NA

SAT
Percent tested	NA
Average SAT math score	NA
Average SAT verbal score	NA

No Child Left Behind, 2003-04
Attendence rate (target = 90%)	95.4%
Drop rate	NA
Highly-qualified teachers	88.5%
District needs improvement?(AYP)	No

Municipal Finance

Fiscal Year 2005
Total tax levy	$4,938,437
County levy	1,082,504
County taxes	972,186
County library	0
County health	0
County open space	110,318
School levy	2,416,979
Local muni. budget	1,438,953
Misc. revenues	869,122
Total aid	$347,098
CMPTRA	165,458
Muni. block grant	11,070
Energy tax receipts	145,570
Homeland security	25,000

Fiscal Year 2006
Total aid	$347,097
CMPTRA	160,363
Muni. block grant	11,070
Energy tax receipts	150,664
Homeland security	25,000

Taxes
	2003	2004	2005
General tax rate per $100	3.66	2.340	2.540
Net valuation taxable	$122,994,321	$195,717,578	$195,072,549
State equalized value	$156,342,088	$183,399,521	$200,960,697
County equalization ratio	87.24	125.02	106.73

Demographics & Socio-Economic Characteristics
(2000 U.S. Census, except as noted)

Population
1980*	1,549
1990*	1,716
2000	2,183
Male	1,104
Female	1,079
2004 (estimate)*	2,340
Persons per sq. mi. of land	368

Race & Hispanic Origin, 2000
Race
White	1,689
Black/African American	33
Amer. Indian/Alaska Natv.	5
Asian	417
Natv. Hawaiian/Pac. Islander	1
Other Race	7
Two or more races	31
Hispanic origin, total	55
Mexican	1
Puerto Rican	16
Cuban	1
Other Hispanic	37

Age & Nativity, 2000
Under 5 years	104
18 years and over	1,644
21 years and over	1,594
65 years and over	322
85 years and over	26
Median Age	44.2
Native born	1,589
Foreign born	594

Educational Attainment, 2000
Population 25 years and over	1,530
0-8 yrs of school	2.2%
High School grad or higher	93.6%
Bachelor's degree or higher	62.8%
Graduate degree	28.0%

Income & Poverty, 1999
Per capita income	$76,995
Median household income	$130,740
Median family income	$134,068
Persons in poverty	135
H'holds receiving public assistance	0
H'holds receiving social security	165

Households, 2000
Total households	708
With persons under 18	274
With persons over 65	210
Family households	623
One-person households	70
Persons per household	3.08
Persons per family	3.24

Labor & Employment
Total civilian labor force, 2004**	932
Unemployment rate	1.2%
Total civilian labor force, 2000	1,037
Unemployment rate	2.6%

Employed persons 16 years and over by occupation, 2000
Managers & professionals	591
Service occupations	62
Sales & office occupations	278
Farming, fishing & forestry	0
Construction & maintenance	40
Production & transportation	39
Self-employed persons	93

*US Census Bureau
**New Jersey Department of Labor

General Information
Borough of Alpine
100 Church St
Alpine, NJ 07620
201-784-2900

Web site	NA
Land area (sq. miles)	6.36
Water area (sq. miles)	2.82
Type of government	Borough
Form of government	B

Government

Legislative Districts
US Congressional	5
State Legislative	39

Local Officials, 2006
Mayor	Paul Tomasko
Admin/Manager	NA
Clerk	Gail Warming-Tanno
Finance Dir/Treas	Irene Kateris
Engineer	Azzolina & Feury
Attorney	Terry Paul Bottinelli
Tax assessor	Stuart Stolarz
Tax collector	NA
Building officer	James Taormina
Zoning officer	Alden Blackwell
Public Works	Ralph Wehmann

Housing & Construction

Housing Units, 2000*
Total	730
Median rent	$1,844
Median SF home value	$1,000,001

New Privately Owned Housing Units Authorized by Building Permit
	Units	Value
Total, 2004	14	$15,115,000
Single family	14	$15,115,000
Total, 2005	26	$16,910,029
Single family	18	$14,520,029

Real Property Valuation - parcels, 2005
	Number	Valuation
Total		$1,767,454,900
Vacant	81	116,836,800
Residential	640	1,555,206,300
Commercial	20	95,411,800
Industrial	0	0
Apartments	0	0
Farm land	0	0
Farm homestead	0	0

Average Property Value & Tax, 2005
Residential value	$2,430,010
Property tax	$13,335
FAIR rebate	$648

Public Library
No public municipal library.

Library statistics, 2004
	Total	per capita
Volumes	NA	NA
Expenditure	NA	NA

Public Safety

Police
Chief	Thomas Blake
Number of officers, 2004	13

Crime, 2004	Number	Rate
Total	19	8.3
Violent	4	1.7
Non-violent	15	6.5
Domestic Viol.	4	NA

Emergency/Fire
Director	John Veras

Public School District
(for school year 2004-2005 except as noted)

Alpine School District
500 Hillside Ave
Alpine, NJ 07620
201-768-6804

Superintendent	Kathleen Semergieff
Grade plan	K-12
Enrollment	124.0
Students per teacher	6.2
Per pupil expenditure	$21,031
Median faculty salary	$44,575
Median administrator salary	$80,000
Grade 12 enrollment	NA
High school graduation rate	NA

Assessment test results
(percent scoring at proficient or advanced level)
	Language	Math
Grade 3	100%	100%
Grade 8	80.0%	80.0%
High school	NA	NA

SAT
Percent tested	NA
Average SAT math score	NA
Average SAT verbal score	NA

No Child Left Behind, 2003-04
Attendence rate (target = 90%)	96.0%
Drop rate	NA
Highly-qualified teachers	97.5%
District needs improvement?(AYP)	No

Municipal Finance

Fiscal Year 2005
Total tax levy	$9,701,204
County levy	2,586,315
County taxes	2,456,996
County library	0
County health	0
County open space	129,319
School levy	4,511,379
Local muni. budget	2,603,510
Misc. revenues	1,850,102
Total aid	$470,796
CMPTRA	11,160
Muni. block grant	8,560
Energy tax receipts	426,076
Homeland security	25,000

Fiscal Year 2006
Total aid	$474,549
CMPTRA	0
Muni. block grant	8,560
Energy tax receipts	440,989
Homeland security	25,000

Taxes
	2003	2004	2005
General tax rate per $100	1.13	1.180	0.550
Net valuation taxable	$773,659,493	$782,022,065	$1,767,890,565
State equalized value	$1,238,251,429	$1,268,010,105	$1,536,761,618
County equalization ratio	70.31	62.48	136.87

Demographics & Socio-Economic Characteristics

(2000 U.S. Census, except as noted)

Population

1980*	892
1990*	700
2000	658
Male	335
Female	323
2004 (estimate)*	660
Persons per sq. mi. of land	453

Race & Hispanic Origin, 2000

Race

White	610
Black/African American	15
Amer. Indian/Alaska Natv.	5
Asian	15
Natv. Hawaiian/Pac. Islander	1
Other Race	8
Two or more races	4
Hispanic origin, total	17
Mexican	4
Puerto Rican	2
Cuban	0
Other Hispanic	11

Age & Nativity, 2000

Under 5 years	30
18 years and over	515
21 years and over	492
65 years and over	65
85 years and over	5
Median Age	38.3
Native born	622
Foreign born	36

Educational Attainment, 2000

Population 25 years and over	480
0-8 yrs of school	5.4%
High School grad or higher	84.2%
Bachelor's degree or higher	20.0%
Graduate degree	6.5%

Income & Poverty, 1999

Per capita income	$25,914
Median household income	$60,000
Median family income	$69,688
Persons in poverty	18
H'holds receiving public assistance	1
H'holds receiving social security	55

Households, 2000

Total households	261
With persons under 18	85
With persons over 65	50
Family households	181
One-person households	65
Persons per household	2.52
Persons per family	2.98

Labor & Employment

Total civilian labor force, 2004**	531
Unemployment rate	4.3%
Total civilian labor force, 2000	442
Unemployment rate	4.3%

Employed persons 16 years and over by occupation, 2000

Managers & professionals	117
Service occupations	44
Sales & office occupations	127
Farming, fishing & forestry	10
Construction & maintenance	61
Production & transportation	64
Self-employed persons	14

*US Census Bureau
**New Jersey Department of Labor

General Information

Borough of Andover
137 Main St
Andover, NJ 07821
973-786-6688

Web site	NA
Land area (sq. miles)	1.46
Water area (sq. miles)	0.01
Type of government	Borough
Form of government	B

Government

Legislative Districts

US Congressional	5
State Legislative	24

Local Officials, 2006

Mayor	Shirlee Bollard
Admin/Manager	NA
Clerk	Doris Lewis
Finance Dir/Treas	Jessica M. Caruso
Engineer	Harold Pellow
Attorney	Stephen Roseman
Tax assessor	Joseph Ferraris
Tax collector	NA
Building officer	Brendon O'Connor
Zoning officer	Bill Paterson
Public Works	NA

Housing & Construction

Housing Units, 2000*

Total	273
Median rent	$804
Median SF home value	$154,800

New Privately Owned Housing Units
Authorized by Building Permit

	Units	Value
Total, 2004	2	$617,000
Single family	2	$617,000
Total, 2005	0	$0
Single family	0	$0

Real Property Valuation - parcels, 2005

	Number	Valuation
Total		$45,039,200
Vacant	49	1,602,600
Residential	191	28,766,000
Commercial	47	12,687,200
Industrial	1	150,200
Apartments	2	968,100
Farm land	5	751,700
Farm homestead	11	113,400

Average Property Value & Tax, 2005

Residential value	$142,967
Property tax	$4,306
FAIR rebate	$540

Public Library

No public municipal library.

Library statistics, 2004

	Total	per capita
Volumes	NA	NA
Expenditure	NA	NA

Public Safety

Police

Chief	NA
Number of officers, 2004	0

Crime, 2004	Number	Rate
Total	11	16.6
Violent	1	1.5
Non-violent	10	15.1
Domestic Viol.	11	NA

Emergency/Fire

Director................. Dennis Walker

Public School District

(for school year 2004-2005 except as noted)

Andover Regional School District
707 Limecrest Rd
Newton, NJ 07860
973-383-3746

Administrator	Jerry Clymer
Grade plan	K-12
Enrollment	750.0
Students per teacher	10.9
Per pupil expenditure	$10,872
Median faculty salary	$52,695
Median administrator salary	$94,000
Grade 12 enrollment	NA
High school graduation rate	NA

Assessment test results

(percent scoring at proficient or advanced level)

	Language	Math
Grade 3	97.4%	90.6%
Grade 8	84.9%	82.8%
High school	NA	NA

SAT

Percent tested	NA
Average SAT math score	NA
Average SAT verbal score	NA

No Child Left Behind, 2003-04

Attendence rate (target = 90%)	95.3%
Drop rate	NA
Highly-qualified teachers	88.4%
District needs improvement?(AYP)	No

Municipal Finance

Fiscal Year 2005

Total tax levy	$1,367,987
County levy	318,499
County taxes	270,317
County library	23,306
County health	10,971
County open space	13,905
School levy	917,758
Local muni. budget	131,729
Misc. revenues	525,043
Total aid	$171,013
CMPTRA	40,936
Muni. block grant	3,115
Energy tax receipts	126,962
Homeland security	0

Fiscal Year 2006

Total aid	$171,013
CMPTRA	36,492
Muni. block grant	3,115
Energy tax receipts	131,406
Homeland security	NA

Taxes

	2003	2004	2005
General tax rate per $100	2.87	2.890	3.020
Net valuation taxable	$45,865,688	$45,433,644	$45,423,685
State equalized value	$60,628,801	$68,715,363	$75,756,646
County equalization ratio	93.28	75.65	65.89

Demographics & Socio-Economic Characteristics
(2000 U.S. Census, except as noted)

Population
1980*	4,506
1990*	5,438
2000	6,033
Male	2,889
Female	3,144
2004 (estimate)*	6,486
Persons per sq. mi. of land	321

Race & Hispanic Origin, 2000
Race
White	5,698
Black/African American	112
Amer. Indian/Alaska Natv.	5
Asian	139
Natv. Hawaiian/Pac. Islander	2
Other Race	36
Two or more races	41
Hispanic origin, total	136
Mexican	17
Puerto Rican	57
Cuban	12
Other Hispanic	50

Age & Nativity, 2000
Under 5 years	389
18 years and over	4,522
21 years and over	4,392
65 years and over	950
85 years and over	241
Median Age	40.2
Native born	5,587
Foreign born	446

Educational Attainment, 2000
Population 25 years and over	4,298
0-8 yrs of school	8.7%
High School grad or higher	84.2%
Bachelor's degree or higher	28.6%
Graduate degree	8.8%

Income & Poverty, 1999
Per capita income	$29,180
Median household income	$75,748
Median family income	$78,439
Persons in poverty	186
H'holds receiving public assistance	33
H'holds receiving social security	375

Households, 2000
Total households	1,889
With persons under 18	787
With persons over 65	331
Family households	1,500
One-person households	304
Persons per household	2.8
Persons per family	3.16

Labor & Employment
Total civilian labor force, 2004**	3,233
Unemployment rate	3.5%
Total civilian labor force, 2000	2,879
Unemployment rate	2.2%

Employed persons 16 years and over by occupation, 2000
Managers & professionals	1,288
Service occupations	271
Sales & office occupations	804
Farming, fishing & forestry	0
Construction & maintenance	200
Production & transportation	254
Self-employed persons	176

*US Census Bureau
**New Jersey Department of Labor

General Information
Township of Andover
134 Newton-Sparta Rd
Newton, NJ 07860
973-383-4280

Web site	NA
Land area (sq. miles)	20.18
Water area (sq. miles)	0.57
Type of government	Township
Form of government	TC

Government

Legislative Districts
US Congressional	5
State Legislative	24

Local Officials, 2006
Mayor	Tom Walsh
Admin/Manager	Richard Stewart
Clerk	Vita Thompson
Finance Dir/Treas	Jess Theriault
Engineer	Joseph Golden
Attorney	Fred Semrau
Tax assessor	Michael Perugini
Tax collector	NA
Building officer	James Cutler
Zoning officer	NA
Public Works	NA

Housing & Construction

Housing Units, 2000*
Total	1,968
Median rent	$1,033
Median SF home value	$164,600

New Privately Owned Housing Units
Authorized by Building Permit
	Units	Value
Total, 2004	22	$4,698,301
Single family	22	$4,698,301
Total, 2005	31	$5,509,469
Single family	31	$5,509,469

Real Property Valuation - parcels, 2005
	Number	Valuation
Total		$591,144,170
Vacant	278	20,822,300
Residential	1,948	456,099,400
Commercial	122	84,388,200
Industrial	11	5,999,000
Apartments	1	1,700,000
Farm land	54	20,911,900
Farm homestead	155	1,223,370

Average Property Value & Tax, 2005
Residential value	$217,462
Property tax	$5,789
FAIR rebate	$492

Public Library

No public municipal library.

Library statistics, 2004
	Total	per capita
Volumes	NA	NA
Expenditure	NA	NA

Public Safety

Police
Chief	Phillip Coleman
Number of officers, 2004	11

Crime, 2004	Number	Rate
Total	38	5.9
Violent	7	1.1
Non-violent	31	4.8
Domestic Viol.	34	NA

Emergency/Fire
Director	Dan Crater

Public School District
(for school year 2004-2005 except as noted)

Andover Regional School District
707 Limecrest Rd
Newton, NJ 07860
973-383-3746

Administrator	Jerry Clymer
Grade plan	K-12
Enrollment	750.0
Students per teacher	10.9
Per pupil expenditure	$10,872
Median faculty salary	$52,695
Median administrator salary	$94,000
Grade 12 enrollment	NA
High school graduation rate	NA

Assessment test results
(percent scoring at proficient or advanced level)
	Language	Math
Grade 3	97.4%	90.6%
Grade 8	84.9%	82.8%
High school	NA	NA

SAT
Percent tested	NA
Average SAT math score	NA
Average SAT verbal score	NA

No Child Left Behind, 2003-04
Attendence rate (target = 90%)	95.3%
Drop rate	NA
Highly-qualified teachers	88.4%
District needs improvement?(AYP)	No

Municipal Finance

Fiscal Year 2005
Total tax levy	$15,780,752
County levy	3,087,042
County taxes	2,620,033
County library	225,815
County health	106,154
County open space	135,041
School levy	8,863,798
Local muni. budget	3,829,911
Misc. revenues	2,375,461
Total aid	$690,559
CMPTRA	291,582
Muni. block grant	23,734
Energy tax receipts	325,243
Homeland security	50,000

Fiscal Year 2006
Total aid	$690,559
CMPTRA	280,198
Muni. block grant	23,734
Energy tax receipts	336,627
Homeland security	50,000

Taxes
	2003	2004	2005
General tax rate per $100	2.48	2.580	2.670
Net valuation taxable	$574,510,532	$579,110,317	$592,774,536
State equalized value	$581,370,706	$662,481,723	$754,934,457
County equalization ratio	81.17	98.82	87.38

Demographics & Socio-Economic Characteristics
(2000 U.S. Census, except as noted)

Population
1980*	17,015
1990*	16,799
2000	16,930
Male	7,943
Female	8,987
2004 (estimate)*	16,819
Persons per sq. mi. of land	11,764

Race & Hispanic Origin, 2000
Race
White	4,194
Black/African American	10,515
Amer. Indian/Alaska Natv.	55
Asian	119
Natv. Hawaiian/Pac. Islander	12
Other Race	1,098
Two or more races	937
Hispanic origin, total	2,637
Mexican	956
Puerto Rican	1,021
Cuban	35
Other Hispanic	625

Age & Nativity, 2000
Under 5 years	1,539
18 years and over	11,841
21 years and over	11,132
65 years and over	1,891
85 years and over	305
Median Age	30.6
Native born	13,761
Foreign born	3,169

Educational Attainment, 2000
Population 25 years and over	9,936
0-8 yrs of school	9.9%
High School grad or higher	67.6%
Bachelor's degree or higher	11.2%
Graduate degree	3.5%

Income & Poverty, 1999
Per capita income	$13,516
Median household income	$23,081
Median family income	$26,370
Persons in poverty	5,006
H'holds receiving public assistance	707
H'holds receiving social security	1,675

Households, 2000
Total households	6,754
With persons under 18	2,490
With persons over 65	1,622
Family households	3,587
One-person households	2,658
Persons per household	2.46
Persons per family	3.36

Labor & Employment
Total civilian labor force, 2004**	9,251
Unemployment rate	10.2%
Total civilian labor force, 2000	7,094
Unemployment rate	11.6%

Employed persons 16 years and over by occupation, 2000
Managers & professionals	1,324
Service occupations	1,554
Sales & office occupations	1,806
Farming, fishing & forestry	20
Construction & maintenance	590
Production & transportation	978
Self-employed persons	318

*US Census Bureau
**New Jersey Department of Labor

General Information
City of Asbury Park
One Municipal Plaza
Asbury Park, NJ 07712
732-775-2100
Web site	www.cityofasburypark.com
Land area (sq. miles)	1.43
Water area (sq. miles)	0.17
Type of government	City
Form of government	CM '23

Government
Legislative Districts
US Congressional	6
State Legislative	11

Local Officials, 2006
Mayor	Kevin G. Sanders
Admin/Manager	Terence J. Reidy
Clerk	Stephen M. Kay
Finance Dir/Treas	Richard Krawczun
Engineer	Brian Grant
Attorney	Frederick C. Raffetto
Tax assessor	Mary Lou Hartman
Tax collector	Dorothy Ruth (Actg)
Building officer	William Gray
Zoning officer	Andre Willis
Public Works	NA

Housing & Construction
Housing Units, 2000*
Total	7,744
Median rent	$615
Median SF home value	$92,800

New Privately Owned Housing Units Authorized by Building Permit
	Units	Value
Total, 2004	11	$657,000
Single family	6	$490,000
Total, 2005	33	$3,906,300
Single family	30	$3,781,300

Real Property Valuation - parcels, 2005
	Number	Valuation
Total		$412,404,100
Vacant	336	10,616,000
Residential	2,651	236,395,500
Commercial	392	99,240,400
Industrial	3	694,100
Apartments	155	65,458,100
Farm land	0	0
Farm homestead	0	0

Average Property Value & Tax, 2005
Residential value	$89,172
Property tax	$3,697
FAIR rebate	$541

Public Library
Asbury Park Public Library
500 1st Ave
Asbury Park, NJ 07712
732-774-4221
Director	Robert W. Stewart

Library statistics, 2004
	Total	per capita
Volumes	114,267	6.75
Expenditure	$532,478	$31.45

Public Safety
Police
Chief	Gilbert Reed
Number of officers, 2004	82

Crime, 2004	Number	Rate
Total	1,429	85.6
Violent	360	21.6
Non-violent	1,069	64
Domestic Viol.	497	NA

Emergency/Fire
Director	John Murphy

Public School District
(for school year 2004-2005 except as noted)

Asbury Park School District
407 Lake Ave
Asbury Park, NJ 07712
732-776-2606
Superintendent	Antonio Lewis
Grade plan	K-12
Enrollment	2,797.0
Students per teacher	7.2
Per pupil expenditure	$15,730
Median faculty salary	$49,280
Median administrator salary	$89,337
Grade 12 enrollment	105.5
High school graduation rate	66.9%

Assessment test results
(percent scoring at proficient or advanced level)
	Language	Math
Grade 3	51.9%	62.1%
Grade 8	20.3%	14.7%
High school	33.3%	23.1%

SAT
Percent tested	65%
Average SAT math score	344
Average SAT verbal score	351

No Child Left Behind, 2003-04
Attendence rate (target = 90%)	90.0%
Drop rate	8.4%
Highly-qualified teachers	98.7%
District needs improvement?(AYP)	Yes

Municipal Finance
Fiscal Year 2005
Total tax levy	$17,212,367
County levy	2,723,662
County taxes	2,527,565
County library	0
County health	46,094
County open space	150,003
School levy	5,056,381
Local muni. budget	9,432,324
Misc. revenues	20,248,389
Total aid	$9,099,065
CMPTRA	7,811,781
Muni. block grant	73,507
Energy tax receipts	1,143,777
Homeland security	70,000

Fiscal Year 2006
Total aid	$9,099,066
CMPTRA	7,771,749
Muni. block grant	73,507
Energy tax receipts	1,183,810
Homeland security	70,000

Taxes
	2003	2004	2005
General tax rate per $100	3.94	4.069	4.146
Net valuation taxable	$395,997,461	$403,699,568	$415,169,666
State equalized value	$615,093,913	$801,299,658	$1,028,411,360
County equalization ratio	80.97	64.38	50.16

Demographics & Socio-Economic Characteristics
(2000 U.S. Census, except as noted)

Population
1980*	40,199
1990*	37,986
2000	40,517
Male	19,852
Female	20,665
2004 (estimate)*	40,580
Persons per sq. mi. of land	3,575

Race & Hispanic Origin, 2000
Race
White	10,809
Black/African American	17,892
Amer. Indian/Alaska Natv.	193
Asian	4,213
Natv. Hawaiian/Pac. Islander	24
Other Race	5,575
Two or more races	1,811
Hispanic origin, total	10,107
Mexican	2,199
Puerto Rican	3,635
Cuban	238
Other Hispanic	4,035

Age & Nativity, 2000
Under 5 years	3,041
18 years and over	30,090
21 years and over	28,568
65 years and over	5,734
85 years and over	744
Median Age	34.7
Native born	30,508
Foreign born	10,009

Educational Attainment, 2000
Population 25 years and over	26,521
0-8 yrs of school	11.9%
High School grad or higher	61.8%
Bachelor's degree or higher	10.4%
Graduate degree	3.2%

Income & Poverty, 1999
Per capita income	$15,402
Median household income	$26,969
Median family income	$31,997
Persons in poverty	9,427
H'holds receiving public assistance	1,208
H'holds receiving social security	4,821

Households, 2000
Total households	15,848
With persons under 18	5,260
With persons over 65	4,445
Family households	8,708
One-person households	5,902
Persons per household	2.46
Persons per family	3.26

Labor & Employment
Total civilian labor force, 2004**	19,110
Unemployment rate	10.5%
Total civilian labor force, 2000	17,683
Unemployment rate	12.9%

Employed persons 16 years and over by occupation, 2000
Managers & professionals	2,114
Service occupations	7,477
Sales & office occupations	3,430
Farming, fishing & forestry	30
Construction & maintenance	758
Production & transportation	1,599
Self-employed persons	492

*US Census Bureau
**New Jersey Department of Labor

General Information
City of Atlantic
1301 Bacharach Blvd
Atlantic, NJ 08401
609-347-5300

Web site	NA
Land area (sq. miles)	11.35
Water area (sq. miles)	6.00
Type of government	City
Form of government	MC '50

Government

Legislative Districts
US Congressional	2
State Legislative	2

Local Officials, 2006
Mayor	Robert W. Levy Sr.
Admin/Manager	Domenic Cappella
Clerk	Rosemary Adams
Finance Dir/Treas	JoAnne Shepherd
Engineer	William Rafferty
Attorney	Kimberly Baldwin
Tax assessor	Novalette Hopkins
Tax collector	Patricia Gallo
Building officer	Elmer Stocks
Zoning officer	Jack Potts
Public Works	David Callaway

Housing & Construction

Housing Units, 2000*
Total	20,219
Median rent	$561
Median SF home value	$87,500

New Privately Owned Housing Units Authorized by Building Permit
	Units	Value
Total, 2004	85	$9,573,421
Single family	81	$8,868,206
Total, 2005	95	$11,608,648
Single family	64	$8,893,940

Real Property Valuation - parcels, 2005
	Number	Valuation
Total		$7,913,033,200
Vacant	2,160	452,146,600
Residential	10,614	790,629,600
Commercial	1,585	6,573,094,000
Industrial	12	4,315,900
Apartments	193	92,847,100
Farm land	0	0
Farm homestead	0	0

Average Property Value & Tax, 2005
Residential value	$74,489
Property tax	$2,608
FAIR rebate	$644

Public Library
Atlantic City Public Library
1 N Tennesee Ave
Atlantic City, NJ 08401
609-345-2269

Director | Maureen Frank

Library statistics, 2004
	Total	per capita
Volumes	131,794	3.25
Expenditure	$2,272,730	$56.09

Public Safety

Police
Chief	Arthur Snellbaker
Number of officers, 2004	393

Crime, 2004	Number	Rate
Total	5,786	143.3
Violent	707	17.5
Non-violent	5,079	125.8
Domestic Viol.	1,708	NA

Emergency/Fire
Director | John Bereheiko

Public School District
(for school year 2004-2005 except as noted)

Atlantic City School District
1300 Atlantic Ave
Atlantic City, NJ 08401
609-343-7200

Superintendent	Frederick Nickles
Grade plan	K-12
Enrollment	7,080.0
Students per teacher	10.9
Per pupil expenditure	$13,362
Median faculty salary	$57,575
Median administrator salary	$92,880
Grade 12 enrollment	493.0
High school graduation rate	68.9%

Assessment test results
(percent scoring at proficient or advanced level)
	Language	Math
Grade 3	63.1%	57.1%
Grade 8	34.5%	21.1%
High school	61.9%	51.1%

SAT
Percent tested	52%
Average SAT math score	477
Average SAT verbal score	455

No Child Left Behind, 2003-04
Attendence rate (target = 90%)	92.3%
Drop rate	8.7%
Highly-qualified teachers	96.9%
District needs improvement?(AYP)	Yes

Municipal Finance

Fiscal Year 2005
Total tax levy	$273,807,972
County levy	37,624,649
County taxes	35,476,986
County library	0
County health	0
County open space	2,147,663
School levy	96,995,803
Local muni. budget	139,187,520
Misc. revenues	54,079,724
Total aid	$7,889,182
CMPTRA	977,725
Muni. block grant	166,214
Energy tax receipts	6,605,243
Homeland security	140,000

Fiscal Year 2006
Total aid	$7,889,182
CMPTRA	746,542
Muni. block grant	166,214
Energy tax receipts	6,836,426
Homeland security	140,000

Taxes
	2003	2004	2005
General tax rate per $100	3.37	3.421	3.502
Net valuation taxable	$7,378,211,814	$7,793,105,791	$7,820,776,556
State equalized value	$8,869,109,044	$10,642,732,583	$12,067,237,395
County equalization ratio	80.62	86.90	73.20

Demographics & Socio-Economic Characteristics

(2000 U.S. Census, except as noted)

Population

1980*	4,950
1990*	4,629
2000	4,705
Male	2,274
Female	2,431
2004 (estimate)*	4,685
Persons per sq. mi. of land	3,789

Race & Hispanic Origin, 2000

Race

White	4,440
Black/African American	108
Amer. Indian/Alaska Natv.	3
Asian	58
Natv. Hawaiian/Pac. Islander	0
Other Race	48
Two or more races	48
Hispanic origin, total	165
Mexican	32
Puerto Rican	45
Cuban	13
Other Hispanic	75

Age & Nativity, 2000

Under 5 years	285
18 years and over	3,700
21 years and over	3,585
65 years and over	665
85 years and over	69
Median Age	40.2
Native born	4,410
Foreign born	295

Educational Attainment, 2000

Population 25 years and over	3,366
0-8 yrs of school	4.0%
High School grad or higher	91.5%
Bachelor's degree or higher	36.7%
Graduate degree	11.6%

Income & Poverty, 1999

Per capita income	$34,798
Median household income	$64,955
Median family income	$79,044
Persons in poverty	231
H'holds receiving public assistance	10
H'holds receiving social security	518

Households, 2000

Total households	1,969
With persons under 18	567
With persons over 65	508
Family households	1,259
One-person households	585
Persons per household	2.39
Persons per family	3

Labor & Employment

Total civilian labor force, 2004**	2,748
Unemployment rate	3.1%
Total civilian labor force, 2000	2,583
Unemployment rate	5.9%

Employed persons 16 years and over by occupation, 2000

Managers & professionals	1,131
Service occupations	367
Sales & office occupations	663
Farming, fishing & forestry	0
Construction & maintenance	157
Production & transportation	112
Self-employed persons	180

*US Census Bureau
**New Jersey Department of Labor

General Information

Borough of Atlantic Highlands
100 First Ave
Atlantic Highlands, NJ 07716
732-291-1444

Web site	www.ahnj.com
Land area (sq. miles)	1.24
Water area (sq. miles)	3.27
Type of government	Borough
Form of government	B

Government

Legislative Districts

US Congressional	6
State Legislative	11

Local Officials, 2006

Mayor	Peter R. Donoghue
Admin/Manager	Adam Hubeny
Clerk	Dwayne Harris
Finance Dir/Treas	Dawn Babcock
Engineer	Katherine Elliott
Attorney	Janice Miller
Tax assessor	Eldo Magnani
Tax collector	NA
Building officer	Bernard Frotten
Zoning officer	NA
Public Works	Robert Dougherty

Housing & Construction

Housing Units, 2000*

Total	2,056
Median rent	$812
Median SF home value	$187,700

New Privately Owned Housing Units
Authorized by Building Permit

	Units	Value
Total, 2004	5	$1,340,000
Single family	5	$1,340,000
Total, 2005	9	$1,381,521
Single family	9	$1,381,521

Real Property Valuation - parcels, 2005

	Number	Valuation
Total		$610,889,600
Vacant	102	9,710,500
Residential	1,520	527,275,400
Commercial	90	54,145,700
Industrial	4	3,077,000
Apartments	9	16,681,000
Farm land	0	0
Farm homestead	0	0

Average Property Value & Tax, 2005

Residential value	$346,892
Property tax	$7,379
FAIR rebate	$621

Public Library

Atlantic Highlands Public Library
100 1st Ave
Atlantic Highlands, NJ 07716
732-291-1956

Director.............. Marilyn Scherfen

Library statistics, 2004

	Total	per capita
Volumes	20,515	4.36
Expenditure	$74,490	$15.83

Public Safety

Police

Chief	Jerry Vasto
Number of officers, 2004	15

Crime, 2004	Number	Rate
Total	64	13.8
Violent	2	0.4
Non-violent	62	13.4
Domestic Viol.	48	NA

Emergency/Fire

Director.................... Joseph Mess

Public School District

(for school year 2004-2005 except as noted)

Atlantic Highlands School District
140 First Ave
Atlantic Highlands, NJ 07716
732-291-2020

Superintendent	Martha Wallauer
Grade plan	K-6
Enrollment	286.0
Students per teacher	9.7
Per pupil expenditure	$11,056
Median faculty salary	$45,290
Median administrator salary	$73,758
Grade 12 enrollment	NA
High school graduation rate	NA

Assessment test results

(percent scoring at proficient or advanced level)

	Language	Math
Grade 3	73.8%	66.7%
Grade 8	NA	NA
High school	NA	NA

SAT

Percent tested	NA
Average SAT math score	NA
Average SAT verbal score	NA

No Child Left Behind, 2003-04

Attendence rate (target = 90%)	95.0%
Drop rate	NA
Highly-qualified teachers	100%
District needs improvement?(AYP)	No

Municipal Finance

Fiscal Year 2005

Total tax levy	$13,038,666
County levy	2,172,375
County taxes	1,917,982
County library	105,656
County health	34,948
County open space	113,789
School levy	7,328,705
Local muni. budget	3,537,587
Misc. revenues	1,909,376
Total aid	$496,655
CMPTRA	184,680
Muni. block grant	20,255
Energy tax receipts	266,720
Homeland security	25,000

Fiscal Year 2006

Total aid	$496,655
CMPTRA	175,345
Muni. block grant	20,255
Energy tax receipts	276,055
Homeland security	25,000

Taxes

	2003	2004	2005
General tax rate per $100	3.78	2.022	2.128
Net valuation taxable	$300,873,360	$616,469,979	$612,995,415
State equalized value	$537,273,857	$646,492,921	$738,726,699
County equalization ratio	64.89	114.16	95.34

Demographics & Socio-Economic Characteristics
(2000 U.S. Census, except as noted)

Population
1980*	9,533
1990*	9,205
2000	9,182
Male	4,391
Female	4,791
2004 (estimate)*	9,070
Persons per sq. mi. of land	6,087

Race & Hispanic Origin, 2000
Race
White	8,938
Black/African American	48
Amer. Indian/Alaska Natv.	10
Asian	82
Natv. Hawaiian/Pac. Islander	1
Other Race	44
Two or more races	59
Hispanic origin, total	139
Mexican	21
Puerto Rican	68
Cuban	9
Other Hispanic	41

Age & Nativity, 2000
Under 5 years	507
18 years and over	6,907
21 years and over	6,613
65 years and over	1,456
85 years and over	192
Median Age	38.1
Native born	8,935
Foreign born	247

Educational Attainment, 2000
Population 25 years and over	6,289
0-8 yrs of school	4.0%
High School grad or higher	87.4%
Bachelor's degree or higher	25.1%
Graduate degree	6.3%

Income & Poverty, 1999
Per capita income	$24,942
Median household income	$49,250
Median family income	$59,115
Persons in poverty	502
H'holds receiving public assistance	50
H'holds receiving social security	1,159

Households, 2000
Total households	3,673
With persons under 18	1,207
With persons over 65	1,096
Family households	2,388
One-person households	1,113
Persons per household	2.5
Persons per family	3.16

Labor & Employment
Total civilian labor force, 2004**	5,115
Unemployment rate	4.0%
Total civilian labor force, 2000	4,752
Unemployment rate	1.7%

Employed persons 16 years and over by occupation, 2000
Managers & professionals	1,640
Service occupations	675
Sales & office occupations	1,364
Farming, fishing & forestry	6
Construction & maintenance	494
Production & transportation	493
Self-employed persons	211

*US Census Bureau
**New Jersey Department of Labor

General Information
Borough of Audubon
606 W Nicholson Rd
Audubon, NJ 08106
856-547-0711
Web site	NA
Land area (sq. miles)	1.49
Water area (sq. miles)	0.02
Type of government	Borough
Form of government	Comm.

Government
Legislative Districts
US Congressional	1
State Legislative	5

Local Officials, 2006
Mayor	Anthony Pugliese
Admin/Manager	David Taraschi
Clerk	Nancy Doman
Finance Dir/Treas	Jack Bruno
Engineer	Remington & Vernick
Attorney	Kathie Renner
Tax assessor	Douglas Kolton
Tax collector	NA
Building officer	Jack Hargraves
Zoning officer	NA
Public Works	NA

Housing & Construction
Housing Units, 2000*
Total	3,813
Median rent	$598
Median SF home value	$107,200

New Privately Owned Housing Units Authorized by Building Permit
	Units	Value
Total, 2004	6	$310,186
Single family	3	$309,336
Total, 2005	6	$310,186
Single family	3	$309,336

Real Property Valuation - parcels, 2005
	Number	Valuation
Total		$345,014,550
Vacant	49	1,167,700
Residential	2,998	293,193,950
Commercial	154	41,527,600
Industrial	1	140,000
Apartments	16	8,985,300
Farm land	0	0
Farm homestead	0	0

Average Property Value & Tax, 2005
Residential value	$97,797
Property tax	$4,495
FAIR rebate	$589

Public Library
Audubon Public Library
239 Oakland Ave
Audubon, NJ 08106
856-547-8686
Admin. Coord . . . . Kathleen Ostberg

Library statistics, 2004
	Total	per capita
Volumes	36,061	3.93
Expenditure	$115,098	$12.54

Public Safety
Police
Chief	Thomas Tassi
Number of officers, 2004	22

Crime, 2004	Number	Rate
Total	226	24.8
Violent	17	1.9
Non-violent	209	22.9
Domestic Viol.	42	NA

Emergency/Fire
Director . . . . John Carpenter

Public School District
(for school year 2004-2005 except as noted)

Audubon School District
350 Edgewood Ave
Audubon, NJ 08106
856-547-1325
Superintendent	Mary Anne Rende
Grade plan	K-12
Enrollment	1,674.0
Students per teacher	11.7
Per pupil expenditure	$10,075
Median faculty salary	$49,400
Median administrator salary	$92,710
Grade 12 enrollment	175.0
High school graduation rate	91.8%

Assessment test results
(percent scoring at proficient or advanced level)
	Language	Math
Grade 3	85.0%	86.0%
Grade 8	72.9%	76.2%
High school	88.0%	81.3%

SAT
Percent tested	69%
Average SAT math score	507
Average SAT verbal score	475

No Child Left Behind, 2003-04
Attendance rate (target = 90%)	94.7%
Drop rate	2.3%
Highly-qualified teachers	96.5%
District needs improvement?(AYP)	No

Municipal Finance
Fiscal Year 2005
Total tax levy	$15,880,500
County levy	3,846,167
County taxes	3,796,398
County library	0
County health	0
County open space	49,769
School levy	8,744,333
Local muni. budget	3,290,000
Misc. revenues	4,100,000
Total aid	$1,260,896
CMPTRA	537,529
Muni. block grant	40,278
Energy tax receipts	633,089
Homeland security	50,000

Fiscal Year 2006
Total aid	$1,260,896
CMPTRA	515,371
Muni. block grant	40,278
Energy tax receipts	655,247
Homeland security	50,000

Taxes
	2003	2004	2005
General tax rate per $100	4.25	4.334	4.597
Net valuation taxable	$343,783,028	$345,354,318	$345,523,565
State equalized value	$436,771,729	$492,122,370	$565,782,815
County equalization ratio	84.33	78.71	70.14

Demographics & Socio-Economic Characteristics
(2000 U.S. Census, except as noted)

Population
1980*	1,274
1990*	1,150
2000	1,102
Male	492
Female	610
2004 (estimate)*	1,085
Persons per sq. mi. of land	7,445

Race & Hispanic Origin, 2000
Race
White	1,090
Black/African American	4
Amer. Indian/Alaska Natv.	1
Asian	2
Natv. Hawaiian/Pac. Islander	0
Other Race	1
Two or more races	4
Hispanic origin, total	7
Mexican	2
Puerto Rican	0
Cuban	0
Other Hispanic	5

Age & Nativity, 2000
Under 5 years	45
18 years and over	868
21 years and over	843
65 years and over	202
85 years and over	18
Median Age	41.9
Native born	1,092
Foreign born	10

Educational Attainment, 2000
Population 25 years and over	809
0-8 yrs of school	5.4%
High School grad or higher	71.8%
Bachelor's degree or higher	3.2%
Graduate degree	0.4%

Income & Poverty, 1999
Per capita income	$16,926
Median household income	$34,643
Median family income	$41,029
Persons in poverty	97
H'holds receiving public assistance	25
H'holds receiving social security	170

Households, 2000
Total households	496
With persons under 18	128
With persons over 65	165
Family households	302
One-person households	175
Persons per household	2.22
Persons per family	2.88

Labor & Employment
Total civilian labor force, 2004**	568
Unemployment rate	5.5%
Total civilian labor force, 2000	518
Unemployment rate	3.7%

Employed persons 16 years and over by occupation, 2000
Managers & professionals	79
Service occupations	88
Sales & office occupations	178
Farming, fishing & forestry	0
Construction & maintenance	43
Production & transportation	111
Self-employed persons	15

*US Census Bureau
**New Jersey Department of Labor

General Information
Borough of Audubon Park
20 Rd C
Audubon Park, NJ 08106
856-547-5236

Web site	NA
Land area (sq. miles)	0.15
Water area (sq. miles)	0.02
Type of government	Borough
Form of government	B

Government

Legislative Districts
US Congressional	1
State Legislative	6

Local Officials, 2006
Mayor	Donald Pennock
Admin/Manager	NA
Clerk	Patricia McCreery
Finance Dir/Treas	Dawn Pennock
Engineer	Remington & Vernick
Attorney	John Kearney
Tax assessor	Stephen Kessler
Tax collector	NA
Building officer	DCA
Zoning officer	NA
Public Works	NA

Housing & Construction

Housing Units, 2000*
Total	499
Median rent	$474
Median SF home value	$47,400

New Privately Owned Housing Units Authorized by Building Permit
	Units	Value
Total, 2004	0	$0
Single family	0	$0
Total, 2005	0	$0
Single family	0	$0

Real Property Valuation - parcels, 2005
	Number	Valuation
Total		$9,267,500
Vacant	0	0
Residential	0	0
Commercial	0	0
Industrial	0	0
Apartments	1	9,267,500
Farm land	0	0
Farm homestead	0	0

Average Property Value & Tax, 2005
Residential value	NA
Property tax	$0
FAIR rebate	$641

Public Library
Audubon Park Library
20 Road C
Audubon Park, NJ 08106
856-547-9583

Librarian.................. Dorathea Zeoli

Library statistics, 2004
	Total	per capita
Volumes	NA	NA
Expenditure	NA	NA

Public Safety
Police
Chief	NA
Number of officers, 2004	0

Crime, 2004	Number	Rate
Total	25	22.8
Violent	2	1.8
Non-violent	23	20.9
Domestic Viol.	3	NA

Emergency/Fire
Director.................... David Iosrd

Public School District
(for school year 2004-2005 except as noted)

Audubon Park School District†
20 Road C
Audubon Park, NJ 08106

†No schools in district - sends children to Audubon Borough schools.

Grade plan	NA
Enrollment	NA
Students per teacher	NA
Per pupil expenditure	NA
Median faculty salary	NA

Assessment test results
(percent scoring at proficient or advanced level)
	Language	Math
Grade 3	NA	NA
Grade 8	NA	NA
High school	NA	NA

SAT
Percent tested	NA
Average SAT math score	NA
Average SAT verbal score	NA

No Child Left Behind, 2003-04
Attendence rate (target = 90%)	NA
Drop rate	NA
Highly-qualified teachers	NA
District needs improvement?(AYP)	NA

Municipal Finance

Fiscal Year 2005
Total tax levy	$567,368
County levy	78,529
County taxes	72,377
County library	5,203
County health	0
County open space	949
School levy	65,033
Local muni. budget	423,806
Misc. revenues	331,946
Total aid	$159,912
CMPTRA	133,813
Muni. block grant	5,032
Energy tax receipts	21,067
Homeland security	0

Fiscal Year 2006
Total aid	$159,911
CMPTRA	133,075
Muni. block grant	5,032
Energy tax receipts	21,804
Homeland security	NA

Taxes
	2003	2004	2005
General tax rate per $100	4.92	5.241	6.100
Net valuation taxable	$9,303,469	$9,301,246	$9,301,243
State equalized value	$9,303,469	$9,301,246	$9,301,243
County equalization ratio	100	100.00	100.00

Demographics & Socio-Economic Characteristics
(2000 U.S. Census, except as noted)

Population
1980*	2,162
1990*	1,809
2000	2,143
Male	1,043
Female	1,100
2004 (estimate)*	2,164
Persons per sq. mi. of land	513

Race & Hispanic Origin, 2000
Race
White	2,115
Black/African American	3
Amer. Indian/Alaska Natv.	0
Asian	12
Natv. Hawaiian/Pac. Islander	1
Other Race	1
Two or more races	11
Hispanic origin, total	12
Mexican	5
Puerto Rican	3
Cuban	0
Other Hispanic	4

Age & Nativity, 2000
Under 5 years	61
18 years and over	1,841
21 years and over	1,816
65 years and over	701
85 years and over	52
Median Age	56
Native born	2,106
Foreign born	37

Educational Attainment, 2000
Population 25 years and over	1,780
0-8 yrs of school	0.3%
High School grad or higher	93.1%
Bachelor's degree or higher	37.9%
Graduate degree	11.0%

Income & Poverty, 1999
Per capita income	$50,016
Median household income	$59,196
Median family income	$72,750
Persons in poverty	93
H'holds receiving public assistance	0
H'holds receiving social security	475

Households, 2000
Total households	1,045
With persons under 18	147
With persons over 65	479
Family households	669
One-person households	349
Persons per household	2.05
Persons per family	2.56

Labor & Employment
Total civilian labor force, 2004**	1,120
Unemployment rate	5.5%
Total civilian labor force, 2000	884
Unemployment rate	3.3%

Employed persons 16 years and over by occupation, 2000
Managers & professionals	355
Service occupations	109
Sales & office occupations	257
Farming, fishing & forestry	5
Construction & maintenance	73
Production & transportation	56
Self-employed persons	95

*US Census Bureau
**New Jersey Department of Labor

General Information
Borough of Avalon
3100 Dune Dr
Avalon, NJ 08202
609-967-8200

Web site	www.avalonboro.org
Land area (sq. miles)	4.21
Water area (sq. miles)	0.67
Type of government	Borough
Form of government	MC '50

Government

Legislative Districts
US Congressional	2
State Legislative	1

Local Officials, 2006
Mayor	Martin Pagliughi
Admin/Manager	Andrew Bednarek
Clerk	Amy Kleuskens
Finance Dir/Treas	James Craft
Engineer	Thomas Thorton
Attorney	James Waldron
Tax assessor	Jeffrey Hesley
Tax collector	Connie DiCola
Building officer	Salvatore DeSimone
Zoning officer	NA
Public Works	Harry deButts

Housing & Construction

Housing Units, 2000*
Total	5,281
Median rent	$719
Median SF home value	$443,300

New Privately Owned Housing Units Authorized by Building Permit
	Units	Value
Total, 2004	110	$41,248,897
Single family	98	$39,864,297
Total, 2005	196	$67,720,843
Single family	107	$48,725,991

Real Property Valuation - parcels, 2005
	Number	Valuation
Total		$5,462,258,100
Vacant	319	222,676,100
Residential	5,025	5,109,256,600
Commercial	138	130,325,400
Industrial	0	0
Apartments	0	0
Farm land	0	0
Farm homestead	0	0

Average Property Value & Tax, 2005
Residential value	$1,016,767
Property tax	$4,620
FAIR rebate	$886

Public Library
Avalon Branch Library†
26 25th St
Avalon, NJ 08202
609-967-4010

Branch Librarian	NA

Library statistics, 2004
	Total	per capita
Volumes	NA	NA
Expenditure	NA	NA

†Branch of County Library

Public Safety

Police
Chief	Stephen Sykes
Number of officers, 2004	20

Crime, 2004	Number	Rate
Total	195	90.5
Violent	7	3.2
Non-violent	188	87.2
Domestic Viol.	1	NA

Emergency/Fire
Director	Ed Dean

Public School District
(for school year 2004-2005 except as noted)

Avalon School District
32nd & Ocean Drive
Avalon, NJ 08202
609-967-7544

Administrator	David Rauenzahn
Grade plan	K-12
Enrollment	76.0
Students per teacher	4.5
Per pupil expenditure	$24,168
Median faculty salary	$57,266
Median administrator salary	$115,954
Grade 12 enrollment	NA
High school graduation rate	NA

Assessment test results
(percent scoring at proficient or advanced level)
	Language	Math
Grade 3	NA	NA
Grade 8	NA	NA
High school	NA	NA

SAT
Percent tested	NA
Average SAT math score	NA
Average SAT verbal score	NA

No Child Left Behind, 2003-04
Attendence rate (target = 90%)	94.4%
Drop rate	NA
Highly-qualified teachers	100%
District needs improvement?(AYP)	No

Municipal Finance

Fiscal Year 2005
Total tax levy	$24,824,245
County levy	11,592,909
County taxes	11,055,951
County library	0
County health	0
County open space	536,958
School levy	2,411,023
Local muni. budget	10,820,314
Misc. revenues	5,607,368
Total aid	$475,518
CMPTRA	0
Muni. block grant	8,403
Energy tax receipts	472,299
Homeland security	25,000

Fiscal Year 2006
Total aid	$492,049
CMPTRA	0
Muni. block grant	8,403
Energy tax receipts	458,646
Homeland security	25,000

Taxes
	2003	2004	2005
General tax rate per $100	0.86	0.450	0.460
Net valuation taxable	$2,718,430,315	$5,391,047,210	$5,463,821,704
State equalized value	$4,227,072,485	$5,292,115,267	$6,685,209,475
County equalization ratio	71.97	125.63	101.87

Demographics & Socio-Economic Characteristics

(2000 U.S. Census, except as noted)

Population

1980*	2,337
1990*	2,165
2000	2,244
Male	1,084
Female	1,160
2004 (estimate)*	2,231
Persons per sq. mi. of land	5,232

Race & Hispanic Origin, 2000

Race

White	2,180
Black/African American	12
Amer. Indian/Alaska Natv.	10
Asian	20
Natv. Hawaiian/Pac. Islander	0
Other Race	14
Two or more races	8
Hispanic origin, total	54
Mexican	46
Puerto Rican	2
Cuban	0
Other Hispanic	6

Age & Nativity, 2000

Under 5 years	112
18 years and over	1,831
21 years and over	1,784
65 years and over	501
85 years and over	68
Median Age	43.9
Native born	2,161
Foreign born	76

Educational Attainment, 2000

Population 25 years and over	1,746
0-8 yrs of school	0.8%
High School grad or higher	92.6%
Bachelor's degree or higher	48.0%
Graduate degree	21.2%

Income & Poverty, 1999

Per capita income	$41,238
Median household income	$60,192
Median family income	$80,605
Persons in poverty	61
H'holds receiving public assistance	9
H'holds receiving social security	389

Households, 2000

Total households	1,043
With persons under 18	210
With persons over 65	376
Family households	535
One-person households	429
Persons per household	2.15
Persons per family	3.04

Labor & Employment

Total civilian labor force, 2004**	1,224
Unemployment rate	3.3%
Total civilian labor force, 2000	1,198
Unemployment rate	3.7%

Employed persons 16 years and over by occupation, 2000

Managers & professionals	584
Service occupations	132
Sales & office occupations	306
Farming, fishing & forestry	4
Construction & maintenance	72
Production & transportation	56
Self-employed persons	112

*US Census Bureau
**New Jersey Department of Labor

General Information

Borough of Avon-by-the-Sea
301 Main St
Avon-by-the-Sea, NJ 07717
732-502-4510

Web site	www.avon-by-the-sea.com
Land area (sq. miles)	0.43
Water area (sq. miles)	0.12
Type of government	Borough
Form of government	Comm.

Government

Legislative Districts

US Congressional	6
State Legislative	11

Local Officials, 2006

Mayor	Danel J. Gibney
Admin/Manager	Timothy Gallagher
Clerk	Timothy Gallagher
Finance Dir/Treas	John Antonides
Engineer	Charles Rooney
Attorney	Barry Cooke
Tax assessor	Tim Anfuso
Tax collector	Kerry McGrath
Building officer	Patrick McMahon
Zoning officer	NA
Public Works	NA

Housing & Construction

Housing Units, 2000*

Total	1,387
Median rent	$789
Median SF home value	$370,100

New Privately Owned Housing Units
Authorized by Building Permit

	Units	Value
Total, 2004	NA	NA
Single family	NA	NA
Total, 2005	15	$5,339,300
Single family	15	$5,339,300

Real Property Valuation - parcels, 2005

	Number	Valuation
Total		$305,283,600
Vacant	13	2,186,500
Residential	943	278,163,600
Commercial	52	19,143,500
Industrial	2	843,400
Apartments	8	4,946,600
Farm land	0	0
Farm homestead	0	0

Average Property Value & Tax, 2005

Residential value	$294,977
Property tax	$6,925
FAIR rebate	$569

Public Library

Avon Free Public Library
Garfield and Fifth Ave
Avon By The Sea, NJ 07717
732-502-4525

Director ... Sheila Watson

Library statistics, 2004

	Total	per capita
Volumes	22,848	10.18
Expenditure	$154,667	$68.92

Public Safety

Police

Chief	Terry Mahon
Number of officers, 2004	12

Crime, 2004	Number	Rate
Total	96	43
Violent	1	0.4
Non-violent	95	42.5
Domestic Viol.	0	NA

Emergency/Fire

Director ... Harry Cuttrell

Public School District

(for school year 2004-2005 except as noted)

Avon Borough School District
Lincoln and 5th Aves
Avon, NJ 07717
732-775-4328

Superintendent	Helen Payne
Grade plan	K-12
Enrollment	121.0
Students per teacher	8.2
Per pupil expenditure	$16,391
Median faculty salary	$44,083
Median administrator salary	$85,289
Grade 12 enrollment	NA
High school graduation rate	NA

Assessment test results
(percent scoring at proficient or advanced level)

	Language	Math
Grade 3	100%	81.8%
Grade 8	90.9%	90.9%
High school	NA	NA

SAT

Percent tested	NA
Average SAT math score	NA
Average SAT verbal score	NA

No Child Left Behind, 2003-04

Attendence rate (target = 90%)	94.4%
Drop rate	NA
Highly-qualified teachers	89.2%
District needs improvement?(AYP)	No

Municipal Finance

Fiscal Year 2005

Total tax levy	$7,168,550
County levy	2,091,079
County taxes	1,940,539
County library	0
County health	35,386
County open space	115,153
School levy	2,529,458
Local muni. budget	2,548,013
Misc. revenues	4,136,999
Total aid	$233,228
CMPTRA	50,778
Muni. block grant	9,473
Energy tax receipts	147,977
Homeland security	25,000

Fiscal Year 2006

Total aid	$233,228
CMPTRA	45,599
Muni. block grant	9,473
Energy tax receipts	153,156
Homeland security	25,000

Taxes

	2003	2004	2005
General tax rate per $100	2.14	2.211	2.348
Net valuation taxable	$302,052,319	$303,556,954	$305,369,343
State equalized value	$571,635,729	$642,741,443	$732,476,237
County equalization ratio	63.15	52.84	47.22

Demographics & Socio-Economic Characteristics
(2000 U.S. Census, except as noted)

Population
1980*	619
1990*	675
2000	764
Male	389
Female	375
2004 (estimate)*	815
Persons per sq. mi. of land	1,127

Race & Hispanic Origin, 2000
Race
White	751
Black/African American	4
Amer. Indian/Alaska Natv.	0
Asian	2
Natv. Hawaiian/Pac. Islander	2
Other Race	3
Two or more races	2
Hispanic origin, total	6
Mexican	3
Puerto Rican	1
Cuban	0
Other Hispanic	2

Age & Nativity, 2000
Under 5 years	25
18 years and over	654
21 years and over	641
65 years and over	262
85 years and over	23
Median Age	54.9
Native born	747
Foreign born	25

Educational Attainment, 2000
Population 25 years and over	610
0-8 yrs of school	2.0%
High School grad or higher	92.1%
Bachelor's degree or higher	38.9%
Graduate degree	17.4%

Income & Poverty, 1999
Per capita income	$34,599
Median household income	$52,361
Median family income	$66,406
Persons in poverty	36
H'holds receiving public assistance	3
H'holds receiving social security	202

Households, 2000
Total households	371
With persons under 18	61
With persons over 65	182
Family households	230
One-person households	129
Persons per household	2.05
Persons per family	2.6

Labor & Employment
Total civilian labor force, 2004**	400
Unemployment rate	0.8%
Total civilian labor force, 2000	300
Unemployment rate	2.7%

Employed persons 16 years and over by occupation, 2000
Managers & professionals	119
Service occupations	38
Sales & office occupations	68
Farming, fishing & forestry	19
Construction & maintenance	33
Production & transportation	15
Self-employed persons	55

*US Census Bureau
**New Jersey Department of Labor

General Information
Borough of Barnegat Light
Municipal Building
10 W 10th St
Barnegat Light, NJ 08006
609-494-9196
Web site	www.barnlight.com
Land area (sq. miles)	0.72
Water area (sq. miles)	0.14
Type of government	Borough
Form of government	B

Government

Legislative Districts
US Congressional	3
State Legislative	9

Local Officials, 2006
Mayor	Kirk Larson
Admin/Manager	Gail Wetmore
Clerk	Gail Wetmore
Finance Dir/Treas	Elizabeth Jones
Engineer	Frank Little
Attorney	Terry Brady
Tax assessor	Bernard Haney
Tax collector	NA
Building officer	Frank Zappavigna
Zoning officer	Alex Oros
Public Works	NA

Housing & Construction

Housing Units, 2000*
Total	1,207
Median rent	$772
Median SF home value	$299,400

New Privately Owned Housing Units Authorized by Building Permit
	Units	Value
Total, 2004	17	$5,421,000
Single family	17	$5,421,000
Total, 2005	22	$7,845,656
Single family	22	$7,845,656

Real Property Valuation - parcels, 2005
	Number	Valuation
Total		$881,612,200
Vacant	88	34,328,800
Residential	1,143	804,603,300
Commercial	47	39,181,100
Industrial	0	0
Apartments	4	3,499,000
Farm land	0	0
Farm homestead	0	0

Average Property Value & Tax, 2005
Residential value	$703,940
Property tax	$5,693
FAIR rebate	$670

Public Library

No public municipal library.

Library statistics, 2004
	Total	per capita
Volumes	NA	NA
Expenditure	NA	NA

Public Safety

Police
Chief	Michael Bradley
Number of officers, 2004	0

Crime, 2004	Number	Rate
Total	26	32.5
Violent	2	2.5
Non-violent	24	30
Domestic Viol.	2	NA

Emergency/Fire
Director	Keith Anderson

Public School District
(for school year 2004-2005 except as noted)

Sends children to Long Beach Island school district (see Appendix A).
Grade plan	NA
Enrollment	NA
Students per teacher	NA
Per pupil expenditure	NA
Median faculty salary	NA
Median administrator salary	NA
Grade 12 enrollment	NA
High school graduation rate	NA

Assessment test results
(percent scoring at proficient or advanced level)
	Language	Math
Grade 3	NA	NA
Grade 8	NA	NA
High school	NA	NA

SAT
Percent tested	NA
Average SAT math score	NA
Average SAT verbal score	NA

No Child Left Behind, 2003-04
Attendence rate (target = 90%)	NA
Drop rate	NA
Highly-qualified teachers	NA
District needs improvement?(AYP)	NA

Municipal Finance

Fiscal Year 2005
Total tax levy	$7,132,428
County levy	3,177,187
County taxes	2,781,209
County library	292,189
County health	0
County open space	103,789
School levy	2,656,766
Local muni. budget	1,298,475
Misc. revenues	1,198,613
Total aid	$127,333
CMPTRA	9,410
Muni. block grant	2,996
Energy tax receipts	89,927
Homeland security	25,000

Fiscal Year 2006
Total aid	$127,334
CMPTRA	6,263
Muni. block grant	2,996
Energy tax receipts	93,075
Homeland security	25,000

Taxes
	2003	2004	2005
General tax rate per $100	1.93	0.819	0.809
Net valuation taxable	$330,688,655	$879,271,795	$881,983,000
State equalized value	$721,712,473	$861,027,513	$1,014,239,880
County equalization ratio	55.41	120.30	102.12

Demographics & Socio-Economic Characteristics

(2000 U.S. Census, except as noted)

Population

1980*	8,702
1990*	12,235
2000	15,270
Male	7,358
Female	7,912
2004 (estimate)*	19,177
Persons per sq. mi. of land	553

Race & Hispanic Origin, 2000

Race

White	14,468
Black/African American	338
Amer. Indian/Alaska Natv.	14
Asian	152
Natv. Hawaiian/Pac. Islander	0
Other Race	107
Two or more races	191
Hispanic origin, total	590
Mexican	39
Puerto Rican	281
Cuban	68
Other Hispanic	202

Age & Nativity, 2000

Under 5 years	947
18 years and over	11,137
21 years and over	10,637
65 years and over	2,739
85 years and over	223
Median Age	39
Native born	14,656
Foreign born	629

Educational Attainment, 2000

Population 25 years and over	10,068
0-8 yrs of school	3.1%
High School grad or higher	84.8%
Bachelor's degree or higher	15.8%
Graduate degree	4.3%

Income & Poverty, 1999

Per capita income	$19,307
Median household income	$48,572
Median family income	$56,093
Persons in poverty	944
H'holds receiving public assistance	122
H'holds receiving social security	2,164

Households, 2000

Total households	5,493
With persons under 18	2,090
With persons over 65	1,879
Family households	4,192
One-person households	1,110
Persons per household	2.76
Persons per family	3.19

Labor & Employment

Total civilian labor force, 2004**	6,969
Unemployment rate	4.6%
Total civilian labor force, 2000	6,589
Unemployment rate	4.4%

Employed persons 16 years and over by occupation, 2000

Managers & professionals	1,692
Service occupations	1,150
Sales & office occupations	1,864
Farming, fishing & forestry	0
Construction & maintenance	755
Production & transportation	841
Self-employed persons	355

*US Census Bureau
**New Jersey Department of Labor

General Information

Township of Barnegat
900 West Bay Ave
Barnegat, NJ 08005
609-698-0080

Web site	www.ci.barnegat.nj.us
Land area (sq. miles)	34.67
Water area (sq. miles)	6.16
Type of government	Township
Form of government	TC

Government

Legislative Districts

US Congressional	3
State Legislative	9

Local Officials, 2006

Mayor	Thomas E. Hartman Jr.
Admin/Manager	David Breeden
Clerk	Veronica Jasina
Finance Dir/Treas	Kathleen Janeski
Engineer	Birdsall Engineering
Attorney	Jerry J. Dasti
Tax assessor	Ellen Kelleher
Tax collector	NA
Building officer	Carl DiLeo
Zoning officer	John Durasky
Public Works	NA

Housing & Construction

Housing Units, 2000*

Total	6,066
Median rent	$898
Median SF home value	$119,200

New Privately Owned Housing Units Authorized by Building Permit

	Units	Value
Total, 2004	507	$79,976,959
Single family	507	$79,976,959
Total, 2005	386	$43,342,231
Single family	386	$43,342,231

Real Property Valuation - parcels, 2005

	Number	Valuation
Total		$911,494,500
Vacant	4,462	46,802,000
Residential	6,697	787,203,800
Commercial	167	49,163,500
Industrial	15	1,500,400
Apartments	2	25,534,900
Farm land	12	1,204,400
Farm homestead	18	85,500

Average Property Value & Tax, 2005

Residential value	$117,243
Property tax	$4,277
FAIR rebate	$621

Public Library

Barnegat Branch Library†
112 Burr St
Barnegat, NJ 08005
609-698-3331

Branch Librarian	Lydia Lloyd

Library statistics, 2004

	Total	per capita
Volumes	NA	NA
Expenditure	NA	NA

†Branch of County Library

Public Safety

Police

Chief	Joseph Manger
Number of officers, 2004	33

Crime, 2004	Number	Rate
Total	214	12.1
Violent	29	1.6
Non-violent	185	10.5
Domestic Viol.	176	NA

Emergency/Fire

Director	Kevin Kadlubowski

Public School District

(for school year 2004-2005 except as noted)

Barnegat Township School District
550 Barnegat Blvd N
Barnegat, NJ 08005
609-698-5800

Superintendent	Thomas McMahon
Grade plan	K-12
Enrollment	2,513.0
Students per teacher	11.3
Per pupil expenditure	$11,103
Median faculty salary	$46,759
Median administrator salary	$95,748
Grade 12 enrollment	NA
High school graduation rate	NA

Assessment test results

(percent scoring at proficient or advanced level)

	Language	Math
Grade 3	84.6%	91.4%
Grade 8	82.2%	69.3%
High school	NA	NA

SAT

Percent tested	NA
Average SAT math score	NA
Average SAT verbal score	NA

No Child Left Behind, 2003-04

Attendence rate (target = 90%)	94.1%
Drop rate	NA
Highly-qualified teachers	98%
District needs improvement?(AYP)	No

Municipal Finance

Fiscal Year 2005

Total tax levy	$33,365,292
County levy	6,159,245
County taxes	5,189,335
County library	545,185
County health	231,078
County open space	193,647
School levy	19,190,360
Local muni. budget	8,015,687
Misc. revenues	6,222,317
Total aid	$1,469,632
CMPTRA	512,722
Muni. block grant	59,874
Energy tax receipts	812,600
Homeland security	70,000

Fiscal Year 2006

Total aid	$1,469,632
CMPTRA	484,281
Muni. block grant	59,874
Energy tax receipts	841,041
Homeland security	70,000

Taxes

	2003	2004	2005
General tax rate per $100	3.56	3.624	3.649
Net valuation taxable	$727,471,149	$808,269,127	$914,600,898
State equalized value	$1,110,642,976	$1,423,644,356	$2,638,018,166
County equalization ratio	75.68	65.50	56.67

Demographics & Socio-Economic Characteristics
(2000 U.S. Census, except as noted)

Population
1980*	7,418
1990*	6,774
2000	7,084
Male	3,376
Female	3,708
2004 (estimate)*	7,036
Persons per sq. mi. of land	4,382

Race & Hispanic Origin, 2000
Race
White	6,490
Black/African American	295
Amer. Indian/Alaska Natv.	17
Asian	102
Natv. Hawaiian/Pac. Islander	3
Other Race	76
Two or more races	101
Hispanic origin, total	201
Mexican	25
Puerto Rican	122
Cuban	10
Other Hispanic	44

Age & Nativity, 2000
Under 5 years	410
18 years and over	5,588
21 years and over	5,366
65 years and over	1,250
85 years and over	133
Median Age	38.2
Native born	6,825
Foreign born	227

Educational Attainment, 2000
Population 25 years and over	5,030
0-8 yrs of school	4.7%
High School grad or higher	86.2%
Bachelor's degree or higher	25.8%
Graduate degree	5.9%

Income & Poverty, 1999
Per capita income	$24,434
Median household income	$45,148
Median family income	$59,706
Persons in poverty	134
H'holds receiving public assistance	43
H'holds receiving social security	1,001

Households, 2000
Total households	3,028
With persons under 18	842
With persons over 65	968
Family households	1,832
One-person households	1,016
Persons per household	2.34
Persons per family	3.04

Labor & Employment
Total civilian labor force, 2004**	3,780
Unemployment rate	3.8%
Total civilian labor force, 2000	3,733
Unemployment rate	3.0%

Employed persons 16 years and over by occupation, 2000
Managers & professionals	1,432
Service occupations	450
Sales & office occupations	1,187
Farming, fishing & forestry	6
Construction & maintenance	291
Production & transportation	256
Self-employed persons	248

*US Census Bureau
**New Jersey Department of Labor

General Information
Borough of Barrington
229 Trenton Ave
Barrington, NJ 08007
856-547-0706

Web site	www.barringtonboro.com
Land area (sq. miles)	1.61
Water area (sq. miles)	0
Type of government	Borough
Form of government	B

Government

Legislative Districts
US Congressional	1
State Legislative	5

Local Officials, 2006
Mayor	John Rink
Admin/Manager	NA
Clerk	Terry Shannon
Finance Dir/Treas	Denise Moules
Engineer	Kei Assoc.
Attorney	Timothy Higgins
Tax assessor	Steven Kessler
Tax collector	Kristy Emmett
Building officer	John Szczerbinski
Zoning officer	George Jones
Public Works	Mike Ciocco

Housing & Construction

Housing Units, 2000*
Total	3,164
Median rent	$607
Median SF home value	$111,200

New Privately Owned Housing Units Authorized by Building Permit
	Units	Value
Total, 2004	17	$2,431,300
Single family	17	$2,431,300
Total, 2005	9	$1,061,300
Single family	9	$1,061,300

Real Property Valuation - parcels, 2005
	Number	Valuation
Total		$268,904,500
Vacant	74	2,244,800
Residential	2,000	212,639,200
Commercial	79	20,701,700
Industrial	10	16,268,600
Apartments	6	16,746,200
Farm land	1	304,000
Farm homestead	0	0

Average Property Value & Tax, 2005
Residential value	$106,320
Property tax	$5,299
FAIR rebate	$613

Public Library

No public municipal library.

Library statistics, 2004
	Total	per capita
Volumes	NA	NA
Expenditure	NA	NA

Public Safety

Police
Chief	George Preen
Number of officers, 2004	15

Crime, 2004	Number	Rate
Total	87	12.3
Violent	8	1.1
Non-violent	79	11.2
Domestic Viol.	71	NA

Emergency/Fire
Director	Jay Houck

Public School District
(for school year 2004-2005 except as noted)

Barrington Borough School District
311 Reading Ave
Barrington, NJ 08007
856-547-8467

Superintendent	Loyola Garcia
Grade plan	K-12
Enrollment	602.0
Students per teacher	10.3
Per pupil expenditure	$12,270
Median faculty salary	$43,514
Median administrator salary	$86,388
Grade 12 enrollment	NA
High school graduation rate	NA

Assessment test results
(percent scoring at proficient or advanced level)
	Language	Math
Grade 3	79.2%	86.1%
Grade 8	64.6%	61.5%
High school	NA	NA

SAT
Percent tested	NA
Average SAT math score	NA
Average SAT verbal score	NA

No Child Left Behind, 2003-04
Attendence rate (target = 90%)	94.6%
Drop rate	NA
Highly-qualified teachers	99.4%
District needs improvement?(AYP)	No

Municipal Finance

Fiscal Year 2005
Total tax levy	$13,424,266
County levy	3,070,551
County taxes	2,829,661
County library	203,737
County health	0
County open space	37,152
School levy	7,811,636
Local muni. budget	2,542,080
Misc. revenues	2,386,575
Total aid	$1,102,224
CMPTRA	575,787
Muni. block grant	29,720
Energy tax receipts	446,717
Homeland security	50,000

Fiscal Year 2006
Total aid	$1,102,224
CMPTRA	560,152
Muni. block grant	29,720
Energy tax receipts	462,352
Homeland security	50,000

Taxes
	2003	2004	2005
General tax rate per $100	4.29	4.673	4.984
Net valuation taxable	$269,531,617	$269,879,043	$269,369,449
State equalized value	$329,138,621	$365,200,255	$435,661,409
County equalization ratio	88.72	81.89	73.86

Demographics & Socio-Economic Characteristics
(2000 U.S. Census, except as noted)

Population
1980*	1,334
1990*	1,580
2000	1,510
Male	768
Female	742
2004 (estimate)*	1,564
Persons per sq. mi. of land	21

Race & Hispanic Origin, 2000
Race
White	1,493
Black/African American	1
Amer. Indian/Alaska Natv.	1
Asian	2
Natv. Hawaiian/Pac. Islander	0
Other Race	2
Two or more races	11
Hispanic origin, total	33
Mexican	0
Puerto Rican	17
Cuban	10
Other Hispanic	6

Age & Nativity, 2000
Under 5 years	66
18 years and over	1,105
21 years and over	1,048
65 years and over	161
85 years and over	9
Median Age	38.1
Native born	1,504
Foreign born	48

Educational Attainment, 2000
Population 25 years and over	1,011
0-8 yrs of school	4.5%
High School grad or higher	80.5%
Bachelor's degree or higher	17.9%
Graduate degree	4.8%

Income & Poverty, 1999
Per capita income	$20,382
Median household income	$47,469
Median family income	$51,167
Persons in poverty	81
H'holds receiving public assistance	13
H'holds receiving social security	161

Households, 2000
Total households	548
With persons under 18	215
With persons over 65	122
Family households	410
One-person households	106
Persons per household	2.76
Persons per family	3.15

Labor & Employment
Total civilian labor force, 2004**	846
Unemployment rate	4.8%
Total civilian labor force, 2000	804
Unemployment rate	3.9%

Employed persons 16 years and over by occupation, 2000
Managers & professionals	178
Service occupations	122
Sales & office occupations	215
Farming, fishing & forestry	5
Construction & maintenance	171
Production & transportation	82
Self-employed persons	75

*US Census Bureau
**New Jersey Department of Labor

General Information
Township of Bass River
PO Box 307
New Gretna, NJ 08224
609-296-3337

Web site	NA
Land area (sq. miles)	75.88
Water area (sq. miles)	2.37
Type of government	Township
Form of government	Comm

Government

Legislative Districts
US Congressional	3
State Legislative	9

Local Officials, 2006
Mayor	T. Richard Bethea
Admin/Manager	NA
Clerk	Amanda Somes
Finance Dir/Treas	Kathleen Phelan
Engineer	Kris Kluk
Attorney	Peter Nelson
Tax assessor	Jay Renwick
Tax collector	NA
Building officer	John Ewert
Zoning officer	NA
Public Works	NA

Housing & Construction

Housing Units, 2000*
Total	602
Median rent	$650
Median SF home value	$98,800

New Privately Owned Housing Units Authorized by Building Permit
	Units	Value
Total, 2004	3	$435,300
Single family	3	$435,300
Total, 2005	5	$881,823
Single family	5	$881,823

Real Property Valuation - parcels, 2005
	Number	Valuation
Total		$71,291,200
Vacant	481	5,432,600
Residential	524	53,476,600
Commercial	48	10,151,200
Industrial	0	0
Apartments	0	0
Farm land	14	1,799,200
Farm homestead	41	431,600

Average Property Value & Tax, 2005
Residential value	$95,413
Property tax	$3,109
FAIR rebate	$575

Public Library
Bass River Library†
N Maple Ave
North Gretna, NJ 08224
609-296-6942

Branch Librarian .... Sheila Daugherty

Library statistics, 2004
	Total	per capita
Volumes	NA	NA
Expenditure	NA	NA

†Branch of County Library

Public Safety

Police
Chief	NA
Number of officers, 2004	0

Crime, 2004	Number	Rate
Total	41	26.2
Violent	2	1.3
Non-violent	39	25
Domestic Viol.	13	NA

Emergency/Fire
Director .... Kemp Wetmore

Public School District
(for school year 2004-2005 except as noted)

Bass River Township School District
11 N Maple Ave
New Gretna, NJ 08224
609-296-4230

Superintendent	Larry Mathis
Grade plan	K-6
Enrollment	129.0
Students per teacher	9.8
Per pupil expenditure	$15,521
Median faculty salary	$43,224
Median administrator salary	$72,800
Grade 12 enrollment	NA
High school graduation rate	NA

Assessment test results
(percent scoring at proficient or advanced level)
	Language	Math
Grade 3	50.1%	68.8%
Grade 8	NA	NA
High school	NA	NA

SAT
Percent tested	NA
Average SAT math score	NA
Average SAT verbal score	NA

No Child Left Behind, 2003-04
Attendence rate (target = 90%)	94.3%
Drop rate	NA
Highly-qualified teachers	100%
District needs improvement?(AYP)	No

Municipal Finance

Fiscal Year 2005
Total tax levy	$2,350,726
County levy	504,918
County taxes	423,573
County library	37,088
County health	0
County open space	44,257
School levy	1,845,808
Local muni. budget	0
Misc. revenues	1,250,000
Total aid	$317,021
CMPTRA	88,465
Muni. block grant	6,914
Energy tax receipts	122,885
Homeland security	0

Fiscal Year 2006
Total aid	$317,021
CMPTRA	84,164
Muni. block grant	6,914
Energy tax receipts	127,186
Homeland security	NA

Taxes
	2003	2004	2005
General tax rate per $100	3.19	3.179	3.260
Net valuation taxable	$70,947,790	$71,044,087	$72,146,105
State equalized value	$91,333,406	$107,877,101	$129,526,221
County equalization ratio	90.89	77.68	65.51

Demographics & Socio-Economic Characteristics
(2000 U.S. Census, except as noted)

Population
1980*	1,340
1990*	1,226
2000	1,238
Male	587
Female	651
2004 (estimate)*	1,264
Persons per sq. mi. of land	2,138

Race & Hispanic Origin, 2000
Race
White	1,213
Black/African American	2
Amer. Indian/Alaska Natv.	1
Asian	7
Natv. Hawaiian/Pac. Islander	0
Other Race	6
Two or more races	9
Hispanic origin, total	16
Mexican	0
Puerto Rican	0
Cuban	1
Other Hispanic	15

Age & Nativity, 2000
Under 5 years	39
18 years and over	1,047
21 years and over	1,024
65 years and over	312
85 years and over	32
Median Age	51.5
Native born	1,269
Foreign born	23

Educational Attainment, 2000
Population 25 years and over	1,029
0-8 yrs of school	1.3%
High School grad or higher	97.2%
Bachelor's degree or higher	52.8%
Graduate degree	19.9%

Income & Poverty, 1999
Per capita income	$49,639
Median household income	$77,790
Median family income	$93,055
Persons in poverty	39
H'holds receiving public assistance	4
H'holds receiving social security	243

Households, 2000
Total households	584
With persons under 18	103
With persons over 65	223
Family households	350
One-person households	207
Persons per household	2.12
Persons per family	2.73

Labor & Employment
Total civilian labor force, 2004**	872
Unemployment rate	3.1%
Total civilian labor force, 2000	630
Unemployment rate	4.8%

Employed persons 16 years and over by occupation, 2000
Managers & professionals	285
Service occupations	52
Sales & office occupations	168
Farming, fishing & forestry	0
Construction & maintenance	73
Production & transportation	22
Self-employed persons	97

*US Census Bureau
**New Jersey Department of Labor

General Information
Borough of Bay Head
PO Box 248
Bay Head, NJ 08742
732-892-0636

Web site	NA
Land area (sq. miles)	0.59
Water area (sq. miles)	0.11
Type of government	Borough
Form of government	B

Government

Legislative Districts
US Congressional	4
State Legislative	10

Local Officials, 2006
Mayor	Arthur Petracco
Admin/Manager	NA
Clerk	Patricia Applegate
Finance Dir/Treas	Patricia Wojcik
Engineer	William England
Attorney	Kenneth Fitzsimmons
Tax assessor	Mary Anne Clear
Tax collector	NA
Building officer	Douglas Applegate
Zoning officer	NA
Public Works	NA

Housing & Construction

Housing Units, 2000*
Total	1,053
Median rent	$817
Median SF home value	$450,700

New Privately Owned Housing Units
Authorized by Building Permit
	Units	Value
Total, 2004	2	$1,000,003
Single family	2	$1,000,003
Total, 2005	5	$2,223,001
Single family	5	$2,223,001

Real Property Valuation - parcels, 2005
	Number	Valuation
Total		$932,566,100
Vacant	45	14,169,800
Residential	952	868,342,800
Commercial	49	49,500,200
Industrial	0	0
Apartments	1	553,300
Farm land	0	0
Farm homestead	0	0

Average Property Value & Tax, 2005
Residential value	$912,125
Property tax	$8,188
FAIR rebate	$827

Public Library
Bay Head Reading Center†
136 Meadow Ave
Bay Head, NJ 08742
732-892-0662
Director.............Virginia Berkman

Library statistics, 2004
	Total	per capita
Volumes	NA	NA
Expenditure	NA	NA

†Branch of County Library

Public Safety

Police
Chief	Charles B. Grace Jr.
Number of officers, 2004	8

Crime, 2004	Number	Rate
Total	59	46.9
Violent	0	0
Non-violent	59	46.9
Domestic Viol.	1	NA

Emergency/Fire
Director.............William VanDernoot

Public School District
(for school year 2004-2005 except as noted)

Bay Head School District
145 Grove St
Bay Head, NJ 08742
732-892-0668
Superintendent	Cheri Ellen Crowl
Grade plan	K-12
Enrollment	105.0
Students per teacher	8.2
Per pupil expenditure	$15,799
Median faculty salary	$35,934
Median administrator salary	$61,765
Grade 12 enrollment	NA
High school graduation rate	NA

Assessment test results
(percent scoring at proficient or advanced level)
	Language	Math
Grade 3	NA	NA
Grade 8	100%	84.6%
High school	NA	NA

SAT
Percent tested	NA
Average SAT math score	NA
Average SAT verbal score	NA

No Child Left Behind, 2003-04
Attendence rate (target = 90%)	96.2%
Drop rate	NA
Highly-qualified teachers	100%
District needs improvement?(AYP)	No

Municipal Finance

Fiscal Year 2005
Total tax levy	$8,374,995
County levy	4,529,625
County taxes	3,816,334
County library	400,945
County health	169,941
County open space	142,406
School levy	1,796,560
Local muni. budget	2,048,810
Misc. revenues	1,455,299
Total aid	$252,984
CMPTRA	42,697
Muni. block grant	5,365
Energy tax receipts	179,922
Homeland security	25,000

Fiscal Year 2006
Total aid	$252,984
CMPTRA	36,399
Muni. block grant	5,365
Energy tax receipts	186,220
Homeland security	25,000

Taxes
	2003	2004	2005
General tax rate per $100	0.87	0.900	0.898
Net valuation taxable	$921,628,330	$930,174,831	$932,904,536
State equalized value	$1,065,589,467	$1,180,471,325	$1,356,163,012
County equalization ratio	99.35	86.49	78.79

Demographics & Socio-Economic Characteristics
(2000 U.S. Census, except as noted)

Population
1980*	65,047
1990*	61,444
2000	61,842
Male	29,269
Female	32,573
2004 (estimate)*	60,748
Persons per sq. mi. of land	10,798

Race & Hispanic Origin, 2000
Race
White	48,631
Black/African American	3,416
Amer. Indian/Alaska Natv.	106
Asian	2,562
Natv. Hawaiian/Pac. Islander	30
Other Race	4,611
Two or more races	2,486
Hispanic origin, total	11,015
Mexican	631
Puerto Rican	4,244
Cuban	454
Other Hispanic	5,686

Age & Nativity, 2000
Under 5 years	3,603
18 years and over	48,170
21 years and over	46,048
65 years and over	10,237
85 years and over	1,141
Median Age	38.1
Native born	49,372
Foreign born	12,470

Educational Attainment, 2000
Population 25 years and over	43,359
0-8 yrs of school	7.8%
High School grad or higher	78.8%
Bachelor's degree or higher	20.9%
Graduate degree	6.7%

Income & Poverty, 1999
Per capita income	$21,553
Median household income	$41,566
Median family income	$52,413
Persons in poverty	6,262
H'holds receiving public assistance	855
H'holds receiving social security	8,406

Households, 2000
Total households	25,545
With persons under 18	7,795
With persons over 65	8,001
Family households	16,022
One-person households	8,390
Persons per household	2.42
Persons per family	3.1

Labor & Employment
Total civilian labor force, 2004**	32,007
Unemployment rate	3.9%
Total civilian labor force, 2000	29,496
Unemployment rate	6.5%

Employed persons 16 years and over by occupation, 2000
Managers & professionals	8,811
Service occupations	3,896
Sales & office occupations	8,835
Farming, fishing & forestry	18
Construction & maintenance	2,144
Production & transportation	3,861
Self-employed persons	849

*US Census Bureau
**New Jersey Department of Labor

General Information
City of Bayonne
Municipal Building
630 Ave C
Bayonne, NJ 07002
201-858-6000
Web site	www.bayonnenj.org
Land area (sq. miles)	5.63
Water area (sq. miles)	5.63
Type of government	City
Form of government	MC '50

Government

Legislative Districts
US Congressional	10, 13
State Legislative	31

Local Officials, 2006
Mayor	Joseph Doria Jr.
Admin/Manager	Terrence Malloy
Clerk	Robert Sloan
Finance Dir/Treas	Janet Convery
Engineer	Eugene Bryzinski
Attorney	John Coffey
Tax assessor	Joseph Nichols
Tax collector	Joanne Sisk
Building officer	Michael Feurer
Zoning officer	John Zgola
Public Works	Frank Carine

Housing & Construction

Housing Units, 2000*
Total	26,826
Median rent	$681
Median SF home value	$155,600

New Privately Owned Housing Units Authorized by Building Permit
	Units	Value
Total, 2004	201	$17,790,864
Single family	124	$9,814,902
Total, 2005	69	$6,844,018
Single family	23	$2,084,361

Real Property Valuation - parcels, 2005
	Number	Valuation
Total		$2,362,246,200
Vacant	514	89,125,800
Residential	10,867	1,456,827,300
Commercial	1,193	348,639,300
Industrial	142	364,120,400
Apartments	342	103,533,400
Farm land	0	0
Farm homestead	0	0

Average Property Value & Tax, 2005
Residential value	$134,060
Property tax	$6,952
FAIR rebate	$691

Public Library
Bayonne Free Public Library
697 Ave C
Bayonne, NJ 07002
201-858-6972
Director	Sneh Bains

Library statistics, 2004
	Total	per capita
Volumes	261,073	4.22
Expenditure	$1,941,394	$31.39

Public Safety

Police
Chief	Robert Kubert
Number of officers, 2004	230

Crime, 2004	Number	Rate
Total	1,029	16.9
Violent	183	3
Non-violent	846	13.9
Domestic Viol.	392	NA

Emergency/Fire
Director	Thomas Lynch

Public School District
(for school year 2004-2005 except as noted)

Bayonne School District
669 Ave A
Bayonne, NJ 07002
201-858-5817
Superintendent	Patricia McGeehan
Grade plan	K-12
Enrollment	9,240.0
Students per teacher	12.8
Per pupil expenditure	$10,010
Median faculty salary	$54,762
Median administrator salary	$103,807
Grade 12 enrollment	491.0
High school graduation rate	94.0%

Assessment test results
(percent scoring at proficient or advanced level)
	Language	Math
Grade 3	82.8%	82.9%
Grade 8	70.9%	58.1%
High school	81.7%	65.9%

SAT
Percent tested	65%
Average SAT math score	460
Average SAT verbal score	449

No Child Left Behind, 2003-04
Attendence rate (target = 90%)	94.2%
Drop rate	1.2%
Highly-qualified teachers	98.9%
District needs improvement?(AYP)	No

Municipal Finance

Fiscal Year 2005
Total tax levy	$122,664,865
County levy	22,772,519
County taxes	22,341,480
County library	0
County health	0
County open space	431,039
School levy	53,662,094
Local muni. budget	46,230,253
Misc. revenues	42,830,060
Total aid	$11,429,458
CMPTRA	7,519,922
Muni. block grant	268,947
Energy tax receipts	3,500,589
Homeland security	140,000

Fiscal Year 2006
Total aid	$11,429,457
CMPTRA	7,397,401
Muni. block grant	268,947
Energy tax receipts	3,623,109
Homeland security	140,000

Taxes
	2003	2004	2005
General tax rate per $100	4.59	4.852	5.186
Net valuation taxable	$2,327,024,046	$2,347,189,377	$2,365,566,270
State equalized value	$3,527,932,150	$4,188,993,571	$4,854,435,194
County equalization ratio	74.14	65.96	55.99

Demographics & Socio-Economic Characteristics
(2000 U.S. Census, except as noted)

Population
1980*	1,714
1990*	1,475
2000	1,278
Male	595
Female	683
2004 (estimate)*	1,325
Persons per sq. mi. of land	1,350

Race & Hispanic Origin, 2000
Race
White	1,263
Black/African American	1
Amer. Indian/Alaska Natv.	0
Asian	7
Natv. Hawaiian/Pac. Islander	0
Other Race	1
Two or more races	6
Hispanic origin, total	60
Mexican	52
Puerto Rican	2
Cuban	1
Other Hispanic	5

Age & Nativity, 2000
Under 5 years	62
18 years and over	1,059
21 years and over	1,032
65 years and over	354
85 years and over	43
Median Age	48.6
Native born	1,226
Foreign born	54

Educational Attainment, 2000
Population 25 years and over	942
0-8 yrs of school	2.8%
High School grad or higher	90.2%
Bachelor's degree or higher	35.6%
Graduate degree	14.1%

Income & Poverty, 1999
Per capita income	$30,267
Median household income	$48,355
Median family income	$68,036
Persons in poverty	47
H'holds receiving public assistance	12
H'holds receiving social security	264

Households, 2000
Total households	586
With persons under 18	119
With persons over 65	261
Family households	347
One-person households	205
Persons per household	2.17
Persons per family	2.8

Labor & Employment
Total civilian labor force, 2004**	919
Unemployment rate	5.5%
Total civilian labor force, 2000	557
Unemployment rate	7.0%

Employed persons 16 years and over by occupation, 2000
Managers & professionals	208
Service occupations	79
Sales & office occupations	130
Farming, fishing & forestry	0
Construction & maintenance	64
Production & transportation	37
Self-employed persons	52

*US Census Bureau
**New Jersey Department of Labor

General Information
Borough of Beach Haven
300 Engleside Ave
Beach Haven, NJ 08008
609-492-0111
Web site	www.beachhavenborough.com
Land area (sq. miles)	0.98
Water area (sq. miles)	1.34
Type of government	Borough
Form of government	Comm.

Government

Legislative Districts
US Congressional	3
State Legislative	9

Local Officials, 2006
Mayor	Deborah Whitcraft
Admin/Manager	Richard Crane
Clerk	Judith Howard
Finance Dir/Treas	Diane Marshall
Engineer	Frank Little
Attorney	Steven Zabarsky
Tax assessor	Tracy Hafner
Tax collector	Anne White
Building officer	Frank Zappavigna
Zoning officer	Christine Cathcart
Public Works	Kim England

Housing & Construction

Housing Units, 2000*
Total	2,555
Median rent	$697
Median SF home value	$286,300

New Privately Owned Housing Units Authorized by Building Permit
	Units	Value
Total, 2004	68	$12,830,064
Single family	68	$12,830,064
Total, 2005	38	$9,102,354
Single family	38	$9,102,354

Real Property Valuation - parcels, 2005
	Number	Valuation
Total		$1,568,012,392
Vacant	374	65,902,900
Residential	2,126	1,376,696,200
Commercial	116	110,883,492
Industrial	0	0
Apartments	13	14,529,800
Farm land	0	0
Farm homestead	0	0

Average Property Value & Tax, 2005
Residential value	$647,552
Property tax	$6,118
FAIR rebate	$755

Public Library
Beach Haven Public Library
3rd and Beach Ave
Beach Haven, NJ 08008
609-492-7081
Director . . . . Virgina Donnelly

Library statistics, 2004
	Total	per capita
Volumes	29,828	23.34
Expenditure	$130,464	$102.08

Public Safety

Police
Chief	Stanley Markoski
Number of officers, 2004	11

Crime, 2004	Number	Rate
Total	114	87
Violent	2	1.5
Non-violent	112	85.5
Domestic Viol.	5	NA

Emergency/Fire
Director	Thomas Medel

Public School District
(for school year 2004-2005 except as noted)

Beach Haven Borough School District
Beach Ave at Eighth St
Beach Haven, NJ 08008
609-492-7411
Superintendent	Patricia Daggy
Grade plan	K-6
Enrollment	86.0
Students per teacher	7.2
Per pupil expenditure	$13,526
Median faculty salary	$36,994
Median administrator salary	$100,000
Grade 12 enrollment	NA
High school graduation rate	NA

Assessment test results
(percent scoring at proficient or advanced level)
	Language	Math
Grade 3	100%	100%
Grade 8	NA	NA
High school	NA	NA

SAT
Percent tested	NA
Average SAT math score	NA
Average SAT verbal score	NA

No Child Left Behind, 2003-04
Attendence rate (target = 90%)	94.6%
Drop rate	NA
Highly-qualified teachers	100%
District needs improvement?(AYP)	No

Municipal Finance

Fiscal Year 2005
Total tax levy	$14,826,684
County levy	5,102,211
County taxes	4,918,578
County library	0
County health	0
County open space	183,633
School levy	4,875,843
Local muni. budget	4,848,631
Misc. revenues	2,733,712
Total aid	$255,733
CMPTRA	0
Muni. block grant	6,454
Energy tax receipts	238,650
Homeland security	25,000

Fiscal Year 2006
Total aid	$264,086
CMPTRA	0
Muni. block grant	6,454
Energy tax receipts	232,632
Homeland security	25,000

Taxes
	2003	2004	2005
General tax rate per $100	2.28	0.883	0.945
Net valuation taxable	$546,329,624	$1,566,970,564	$1,569,221,700
State equalized value	$1,249,896,189	$1,527,738,343	$1,806,818,307
County equalization ratio	54.23	124.71	102.57

Demographics & Socio-Economic Characteristics
(2000 U.S. Census, except as noted)

Population
1980*	7,687
1990*	9,324
2000	10,375
Male	5,111
Female	5,264
2004 (estimate)*	10,740
Persons per sq. mi. of land	3,889

Race & Hispanic Origin, 2000
Race
White	9,925
Black/African American	101
Amer. Indian/Alaska Natv.	13
Asian	117
Natv. Hawaiian/Pac. Islander	6
Other Race	115
Two or more races	98
Hispanic origin, total	438
Mexican	106
Puerto Rican	196
Cuban	53
Other Hispanic	83

Age & Nativity, 2000
Under 5 years	720
18 years and over	7,415
21 years and over	7,038
65 years and over	896
85 years and over	69
Median Age	35.2
Native born	9,928
Foreign born	388

Educational Attainment, 2000
Population 25 years and over	6,636
0-8 yrs of school	1.6%
High School grad or higher	87.4%
Bachelor's degree or higher	13.2%
Graduate degree	3.4%

Income & Poverty, 1999
Per capita income	$21,247
Median household income	$59,022
Median family income	$64,190
Persons in poverty	462
H'holds receiving public assistance	9
H'holds receiving social security	714

Households, 2000
Total households	3,475
With persons under 18	1,584
With persons over 65	678
Family households	2,817
One-person households	521
Persons per household	2.98
Persons per family	3.31

Labor & Employment
Total civilian labor force, 2004**	6,266
Unemployment rate	5.6%
Total civilian labor force, 2000	5,538
Unemployment rate	4.7%

Employed persons 16 years and over by occupation, 2000
Managers & professionals	1,354
Service occupations	978
Sales & office occupations	1,518
Farming, fishing & forestry	0
Construction & maintenance	769
Production & transportation	656
Self-employed persons	245

*US Census Bureau
**New Jersey Department of Labor

General Information
Borough of Beachwood
1600 Pinewald Rd
Beachwood, NJ 08722
732-286-6000
Web site	www.beachwoodusa.com
Land area (sq. miles)	2.76
Water area (sq. miles)	0
Type of government	Borough
Form of government	B

Government

Legislative Districts
US Congressional	3
State Legislative	9

Local Officials, 2006
Mayor	Harold R. Morris
Admin/Manager	James F. Lacey
Clerk	Elizabeth Mastropasqua
Finance Dir/Treas	John Adams
Engineer	Schoor De Palma
Attorney	William Hiering Jr.
Tax assessor	Denise Siegal
Tax collector	NA
Building officer	County
Zoning officer	NA
Public Works	NA

Housing & Construction

Housing Units, 2000*
Total	3,623
Median rent	$926
Median SF home value	$114,400

New Privately Owned Housing Units Authorized by Building Permit
	Units	Value
Total, 2004	18	$1,704,068
Single family	18	$1,704,068
Total, 2005	15	$1,334,709
Single family	15	$1,334,709

Real Property Valuation - parcels, 2005
	Number	Valuation
Total		$407,110,900
Vacant	409	5,087,100
Residential	3,656	385,903,400
Commercial	74	15,351,700
Industrial	1	125,300
Apartments	4	643,400
Farm land	0	0
Farm homestead	0	0

Average Property Value & Tax, 2005
Residential value	$105,553
Property tax	$3,279
FAIR rebate	$817

Public Library
Beachwood Branch Library†
126 Beachwood Blvd
Beachwood, NJ 08722
732-244-4573
Branch Librarian	Emily Holman

Library statistics, 2004
	Total	per capita
Volumes	NA	NA
Expenditure	NA	NA

†Branch of County Library

Public Safety

Police
Chief	John Wagner
Number of officers, 2004	18

Crime, 2004	Number	Rate
Total	177	16.5
Violent	11	1
Non-violent	166	15.5
Domestic Viol.	139	NA

Emergency/Fire
Director	Roger Hull

Public School District
(for school year 2004-2005 except as noted)

Sends children to Toms River Regional school district (see South Toms River Borough).
Grade plan	NA
Enrollment	NA
Students per teacher	NA
Per pupil expenditure	NA
Median faculty salary	NA
Median administrator salary	NA
Grade 12 enrollment	NA
High school graduation rate	NA

Assessment test results
(percent scoring at proficient or advanced level)
	Language	Math
Grade 3	NA	NA
Grade 8	NA	NA
High school	NA	NA

SAT
Percent tested	NA
Average SAT math score	NA
Average SAT verbal score	NA

No Child Left Behind, 2003-04
Attendence rate (target = 90%)	NA
Drop rate	NA
Highly-qualified teachers	NA
District needs improvement?(AYP)	NA

Municipal Finance

Fiscal Year 2005
Total tax levy	$12,661,509
County levy	2,725,009
County taxes	2,295,895
County library	241,207
County health	102,236
County open space	85,671
School levy	5,742,674
Local muni. budget	4,193,826
Misc. revenues	2,674,352
Total aid	$976,091
CMPTRA	408,559
Muni. block grant	40,799
Energy tax receipts	455,927
Homeland security	70,000

Fiscal Year 2006
Total aid	$976,091
CMPTRA	392,602
Muni. block grant	40,799
Energy tax receipts	471,884
Homeland security	70,000

Taxes
	2003	2004	2005
General tax rate per $100	2.85	2.957	3.107
Net valuation taxable	$399,173,837	$402,943,469	$407,618,972
State equalized value	$591,631,595	$704,132,816	$839,413,040
County equalization ratio	79.03	67.47	57.19

Demographics & Socio-Economic Characteristics
(2000 U.S. Census, except as noted)

Population
1980*	2,469
1990*	7,086
2000	8,302
Male	3,836
Female	4,466
2004 (estimate)*	8,392
Persons per sq. mi. of land	317

Race & Hispanic Origin, 2000
Race
White	7,476
Black/African American	145
Amer. Indian/Alaska Natv.	9
Asian	532
Natv. Hawaiian/Pac. Islander	2
Other Race	69
Two or more races	69
Hispanic origin, total	319
Mexican	32
Puerto Rican	53
Cuban	22
Other Hispanic	212

Age & Nativity, 2000
Under 5 years	482
18 years and over	6,822
21 years and over	6,710
65 years and over	890
85 years and over	64
Median Age	39.3
Native born	7,079
Foreign born	1,223

Educational Attainment, 2000
Population 25 years and over	6,508
0-8 yrs of school	1.5%
High School grad or higher	96.2%
Bachelor's degree or higher	60.4%
Graduate degree	22.6%

Income & Poverty, 1999
Per capita income	$53,549
Median household income	$71,550
Median family income	$96,890
Persons in poverty	254
H'holds receiving public assistance	15
H'holds receiving social security	733

Households, 2000
Total households	4,235
With persons under 18	902
With persons over 65	667
Family households	2,100
One-person households	1,862
Persons per household	1.96
Persons per family	2.76

Labor & Employment
Total civilian labor force, 2004**	5,919
Unemployment rate	3.0%
Total civilian labor force, 2000	5,117
Unemployment rate	2.4%

Employed persons 16 years and over by occupation, 2000
Managers & professionals	2,924
Service occupations	345
Sales & office occupations	1,369
Farming, fishing & forestry	19
Construction & maintenance	115
Production & transportation	223
Self-employed persons	320

*US Census Bureau
**New Jersey Department of Labor

General Information
Township of Bedminster
One Miller Lane
Bedminster, NJ 07921
908-212-7000

Web site	www.bedminster.us
Land area (sq. miles)	26.47
Water area (sq. miles)	0
Type of government	Township
Form of government	TC

Government

Legislative Districts
US Congressional	7
State Legislative	16

Local Officials, 2006
Mayor	Robert Holtaway
Admin/Manager	Susan Stanbury
Clerk	Dorothy Wilkie
Finance Dir/Treas	June Enos
Engineer	Paul Ferriero
Attorney	Jeffery Lehrer
Tax assessor	Edward Kerwin Jr.
Tax collector	NA
Building officer	Joseph Alicino
Zoning officer	NA
Public Works	NA

Housing & Construction

Housing Units, 2000*
Total	4,467
Median rent	$1,430
Median SF home value	$228,000

New Privately Owned Housing Units Authorized by Building Permit
	Units	Value
Total, 2004	5	$11,320,628
Single family	5	$11,320,628
Total, 2005	2	$2,700,000
Single family	2	$2,700,000

Real Property Valuation - parcels, 2005
	Number	Valuation
Total		$2,211,839,045
Vacant	90	17,757,400
Residential	4,054	1,334,556,800
Commercial	122	471,686,700
Industrial	0	0
Apartments	0	0
Farm land	207	384,356,690
Farm homestead	311	3,481,455

Average Property Value & Tax, 2005
Residential value	$306,538
Property tax	$3,660
FAIR rebate	$493

Public Library
Clarence Dillon Public Library
2336 Lamington Rd
Bedminster, NJ 07921
908-234-2325

Director................. Eileen Burnash

Library statistics, 2004
	Total	per capita
Volumes	101,622	11.09
Expenditure	$807,777	$88.18

Public Safety

Police
Chief	William Stephens
Number of officers, 2004	17

Crime, 2004	Number	Rate
Total	52	6.2
Violent	1	0.1
Non-violent	51	6.1
Domestic Viol.	54	NA

Emergency/Fire
Director................. Kevin Sullivan

Public School District
(for school year 2004-2005 except as noted)

Bedminster Township School District
234 Somerville Rd
Bedminster, NJ 07921
908-234-0768

Superintendent	Andrew Rinko
Grade plan	K-12
Enrollment	610.0
Students per teacher	9.3
Per pupil expenditure	$14,592
Median faculty salary	$47,188
Median administrator salary	$102,933
Grade 12 enrollment	NA
High school graduation rate	NA

Assessment test results
(percent scoring at proficient or advanced level)
	Language	Math
Grade 3	93.7%	83.1%
Grade 8	97.3%	82.0%
High school	NA	NA

SAT
Percent tested	NA
Average SAT math score	NA
Average SAT verbal score	NA

No Child Left Behind, 2003-04
Attendance rate (target = 90%)	96.0%
Drop rate	NA
Highly-qualified teachers	98.9%
District needs improvement?(AYP)	No

Municipal Finance

Fiscal Year 2005
Total tax levy	$26,506,247
County levy	7,846,916
County taxes	7,158,427
County library	0
County health	0
County open space	688,489
School levy	12,887,632
Local muni. budget	5,771,699
Misc. revenues	4,011,943
Total aid	$1,168,958
CMPTRA	165,336
Muni. block grant	32,552
Energy tax receipts	921,070
Homeland security	50,000

Fiscal Year 2006
Total aid	$1,168,959
CMPTRA	133,099
Muni. block grant	32,552
Energy tax receipts	953,308
Homeland security	50,000

Taxes
	2003	2004	2005
General tax rate per $100	1.20	1.300	1.200
Net valuation taxable	$2,024,851,749	$2,040,721,079	$2,219,874,678
State equalized value	$2,111,199,822	$2,296,387,030	$2,471,195,233
County equalization ratio	104.22	95.91	95.90

Demographics & Socio-Economic Characteristics
(2000 U.S. Census, except as noted)

Population
1980*	35,367
1990*	34,213
2000	35,928
Male	17,330
Female	18,598
2004 (estimate)*	35,399
Persons per sq. mi. of land	10,586

Race & Hispanic Origin, 2000
Race
White	24,950
Black/African American	1,926
Amer. Indian/Alaska Natv.	60
Asian	4,062
Natv. Hawaiian/Pac. Islander	26
Other Race	3,532
Two or more races	1,372
Hispanic origin, total	8,507
Mexican	158
Puerto Rican	3,430
Cuban	454
Other Hispanic	4,465

Age & Nativity, 2000
Under 5 years	2,133
18 years and over	28,082
21 years and over	26,925
65 years and over	4,806
85 years and over	612
Median Age	36.2
Native born	26,290
Foreign born	9,638

Educational Attainment, 2000
Population 25 years and over	25,114
0-8 yrs of school	8.5%
High School grad or higher	78.2%
Bachelor's degree or higher	21.7%
Graduate degree	5.9%

Income & Poverty, 1999
Per capita income	$22,093
Median household income	$48,576
Median family income	$55,212
Persons in poverty	2,939
H'holds receiving public assistance	321
H'holds receiving social security	3,351

Households, 2000
Total households	13,731
With persons under 18	4,469
With persons over 65	3,543
Family households	9,091
One-person households	3,828
Persons per household	2.6
Persons per family	3.23

Labor & Employment
Total civilian labor force, 2004**	17,791
Unemployment rate	3.4%
Total civilian labor force, 2000	18,387
Unemployment rate	6.6%

Employed persons 16 years and over by occupation, 2000
Managers & professionals	5,282
Service occupations	2,578
Sales & office occupations	5,453
Farming, fishing & forestry	0
Construction & maintenance	1,398
Production & transportation	2,467
Self-employed persons	619

*US Census Bureau
**New Jersey Department of Labor

General Information
Township of Belleville
152 Washington Ave
Belleville, NJ 07109
973-450-3302

Web site	www.bellevillenj.org
Land area (sq. miles)	3.34
Water area (sq. miles)	0.07
Type of government	Township
Form of government	CM '50

Government

Legislative Districts
US Congressional	8
State Legislative	28

Local Officials, 2006
Mayor	Gerald Digori
Admin/Manager	Mayro McTuccl
Clerk	Kelly Nash
Finance Dir/Treas	Arthur Minsky
Engineer	Tom Herits
Attorney	Rodert Gaccione
Tax assessor	William Merdinger
Tax collector	NA
Building officer	Frank DeLorenzo
Zoning officer	NA
Public Works	NA

Housing & Construction

Housing Units, 2000*
Total	14,144
Median rent	$752
Median SF home value	$147,500

New Privately Owned Housing Units Authorized by Building Permit
	Units	Value
Total, 2004	12	$1,267,000
Single family	8	$1,040,000
Total, 2005	54	$1,580,315
Single family	20	$1,055,315

Real Property Valuation - parcels, 2005
	Number	Valuation
Total		$431,775,150
Vacant	295	4,837,400
Residential	8,116	323,434,650
Commercial	534	48,766,700
Industrial	128	24,425,100
Apartments	128	30,311,300
Farm land	0	0
Farm homestead	0	0

Average Property Value & Tax, 2005
Residential value	$39,851
Property tax	$6,002
FAIR rebate	$620

Public Library
Belleville Public Public Library
221 Washington Ave
Belleville, NJ 07109
973-450-3434

Director	Joan Taub

Library statistics, 2004
	Total	per capita
Volumes	102,001	2.84
Expenditure	$982,721	$27.35

Public Safety

Police
Chief	Joseph Rotonda
Number of officers, 2004	110

Crime, 2004	Number	Rate
Total	954	26.8
Violent	104	2.9
Non-violent	850	23.9
Domestic Viol.	79	NA

Emergency/Fire
Director	Robert Caruso

Public School District
(for school year 2004-2005 except as noted)

Belleville School District
102 Passaic Ave
Belleville, NJ 07109
973-450-3500

Superintendent	Edward Kliszus
Grade plan	K-12
Enrollment	4,541.0
Students per teacher	12.0
Per pupil expenditure	$10,059
Median faculty salary	$65,742
Median administrator salary	$105,770
Grade 12 enrollment	354.5
High school graduation rate	86.8%

Assessment test results
(percent scoring at proficient or advanced level)
	Language	Math
Grade 3	75.8%	73.3%
Grade 8	63.8%	51.0%
High school	77.6%	67.7%

SAT
Percent tested	54%
Average SAT math score	491
Average SAT verbal score	476

No Child Left Behind, 2003-04
Attendence rate (target = 90%)	94.4%
Drop rate	4.7%
Highly-qualified teachers	98.1%
District needs improvement?(AYP)	No

Municipal Finance

Fiscal Year 2005
Total tax levy	$65,158,841
County levy	10,894,704
County taxes	10,662,657
County library	0
County health	0
County open space	232,047
School levy	28,792,217
Local muni. budget	25,471,920
Misc. revenues	18,388,667
Total aid	$8,329,997
CMPTRA	5,896,395
Muni. block grant	149,705
Energy tax receipts	2,143,897
Homeland security	140,000

Fiscal Year 2006
Total aid	$8,329,997
CMPTRA	5,821,359
Muni. block grant	149,705
Energy tax receipts	2,218,933
Homeland security	140,000

Taxes
	2003	2004	2005
General tax rate per $100	14.09	14.520	15.070
Net valuation taxable	$429,265,095	$431,050,202	$432,613,316
State equalized value	$2,031,543,280	$2,330,875,884	$2,831,238,979
County equalization ratio	24.23	24.23	18.46

Demographics & Socio-Economic Characteristics
(2000 U.S. Census, except as noted)

Population
1980*	13,721
1990*	12,603
2000	11,262
Male	5,531
Female	5,731
2004 (estimate)*	11,184
Persons per sq. mi. of land	3,690

Race & Hispanic Origin, 2000
Race
White	10,450
Black/African American	133
Amer. Indian/Alaska Natv.	7
Asian	344
Natv. Hawaiian/Pac. Islander	2
Other Race	173
Two or more races	153
Hispanic origin, total	394
Mexican	115
Puerto Rican	202
Cuban	1
Other Hispanic	76

Age & Nativity, 2000
Under 5 years	571
18 years and over	8,922
21 years and over	8,522
65 years and over	1,969
85 years and over	127
Median Age	40.1
Native born	10,415
Foreign born	847

Educational Attainment, 2000
Population 25 years and over	7,925
0-8 yrs of school	6.0%
High School grad or higher	74.5%
Bachelor's degree or higher	10.4%
Graduate degree	2.8%

Income & Poverty, 1999
Per capita income	$19,863
Median household income	$44,653
Median family income	$53,839
Persons in poverty	446
H'holds receiving public assistance	50
H'holds receiving social security	1,690

Households, 2000
Total households	4,446
With persons under 18	1,356
With persons over 65	1,441
Family households	3,136
One-person households	1,124
Persons per household	2.53
Persons per family	3.02

Labor & Employment
Total civilian labor force, 2004**	7,071
Unemployment rate	4.9%
Total civilian labor force, 2000	5,899
Unemployment rate	4.2%

Employed persons 16 years and over by occupation, 2000
Managers & professionals	1,322
Service occupations	761
Sales & office occupations	1,864
Farming, fishing & forestry	4
Construction & maintenance	672
Production & transportation	1,029
Self-employed persons	234

*US Census Bureau
**New Jersey Department of Labor

General Information
Borough of Bellmawr
PO Box 368
Bellmawr, NJ 08099
856-933-1313
Web site	www.bellmawr.com
Land area (sq. miles)	3.03
Water area (sq. miles)	0.10
Type of government	Borough
Form of government	B

Government

Legislative Districts
US Congressional	1
State Legislative	5

Local Officials, 2006
Mayor	Frank Filipek
Admin/Manager	NA
Clerk	Charles Sauter
Finance Dir/Treas	Jasper Garagozzo
Engineer	Gregory Fusco
Attorney	Robert L. Messick
Tax assessor	Anthony Leone
Tax collector	Margaret Sandrock
Building officer	John Warburton
Zoning officer	NA
Public Works	Joseph Ciano Jr.

Housing & Construction

Housing Units, 2000*
Total	4,561
Median rent	$523
Median SF home value	$95,800

New Privately Owned Housing Units Authorized by Building Permit
	Units	Value
Total, 2004	6	$519,000
Single family	6	$519,000
Total, 2005	58	$631,352
Single family	7	$592,750

Real Property Valuation - parcels, 2005
	Number	Valuation
Total		$425,385,400
Vacant	86	3,893,600
Residential	3,385	295,053,800
Commercial	111	39,445,400
Industrial	55	58,431,100
Apartments	9	28,561,500
Farm land	0	0
Farm homestead	0	0

Average Property Value & Tax, 2005
Residential value	$87,165
Property tax	$4,054
FAIR rebate	$659

Public Library
Bellmawr Branch Library†
35 E Browning Rd
Bellmawr, NJ 08031
856-931-1400
Branch librarian	Deborah Stefano

Library statistics, 2004
	Total	per capita
Volumes	NA	NA
Expenditure	NA	NA

†Branch of County Library

Public Safety

Police
Chief	William Walsh
Number of officers, 2004	23

Crime, 2004	Number	Rate
Total	264	23.4
Violent	17	1.5
Non-violent	247	21.9
Domestic Viol.	51	NA

Emergency/Fire
Director	NA

Public School District
(for school year 2004-2005 except as noted)

Bellmawr Borough School District
256 Anderson Ave
Bellmawr, NJ 08031
856-931-3620
Superintendent	Deborah L. Monahan
Grade plan	K-8
Enrollment	1,057.0
Students per teacher	12.7
Per pupil expenditure	$9,517
Median faculty salary	$57,967
Median administrator salary	$83,283
Grade 12 enrollment	NA
High school graduation rate	NA

Assessment test results
(percent scoring at proficient or advanced level)
	Language	Math
Grade 3	82.4%	77.4%
Grade 8	78.3%	67.5%
High school	NA	NA

SAT
Percent tested	NA
Average SAT math score	NA
Average SAT verbal score	NA

No Child Left Behind, 2003-04
Attendence rate (target = 90%)	94.1%
Drop rate	NA
Highly-qualified teachers	83.6%
District needs improvement?(AYP)	No

Municipal Finance

Fiscal Year 2005
Total tax levy	$19,832,245
County levy	4,699,120
County taxes	4,330,576
County library	311,705
County health	0
County open space	56,840
School levy	9,882,853
Local muni. budget	5,250,271
Misc. revenues	4,834,172
Total aid	$1,589,508
CMPTRA	635,955
Muni. block grant	55,147
Energy tax receipts	828,406
Homeland security	70,000

Fiscal Year 2006
Total aid	$1,589,508
CMPTRA	606,961
Muni. block grant	55,147
Energy tax receipts	857,400
Homeland security	70,000

Taxes
	2003	2004	2005
General tax rate per $100	4.27	4.425	4.651
Net valuation taxable	$426,312,890	$426,776,510	$426,409,790
State equalized value	$500,015,118	$565,052,255	$669,823,735
County equalization ratio	87.86	85.26	75.48

Demographics & Socio-Economic Characteristics
(2000 U.S. Census, except as noted)

Population
1980*	6,771
1990*	5,877
2000	6,045
Male	3,020
Female	3,025
2004 (estimate)*	6,033
Persons per sq. mi. of land	5,910

Race & Hispanic Origin, 2000
Race
White	5,533
Black/African American	209
Amer. Indian/Alaska Natv.	11
Asian	62
Natv. Hawaiian/Pac. Islander	0
Other Race	120
Two or more races	110
Hispanic origin, total	414
Mexican	198
Puerto Rican	86
Cuban	6
Other Hispanic	124

Age & Nativity, 2000
Under 5 years	293
18 years and over	5,007
21 years and over	4,850
65 years and over	952
85 years and over	113
Median Age	38.5
Native born	5,524
Foreign born	521

Educational Attainment, 2000
Population 25 years and over	4,553
0-8 yrs of school	4.7%
High School grad or higher	89.3%
Bachelor's degree or higher	34.0%
Graduate degree	11.9%

Income & Poverty, 1999
Per capita income	$29,456
Median household income	$44,896
Median family income	$61,250
Persons in poverty	520
H'holds receiving public assistance	76
H'holds receiving social security	763

Households, 2000
Total households	2,946
With persons under 18	564
With persons over 65	726
Family households	1,318
One-person households	1,305
Persons per household	2.05
Persons per family	2.92

Labor & Employment
Total civilian labor force, 2004**	3,494
Unemployment rate	4.4%
Total civilian labor force, 2000	3,492
Unemployment rate	4.8%

Employed persons 16 years and over by occupation, 2000
Managers & professionals	1,333
Service occupations	461
Sales & office occupations	924
Farming, fishing & forestry	0
Construction & maintenance	314
Production & transportation	292
Self-employed persons	234

*US Census Bureau
**New Jersey Department of Labor

General Information
Borough of Belmar
PO Box A
Belmar, NJ 07719
732-681-1176

Web site	NA
Land area (sq. miles)	1.02
Water area (sq. miles)	0.67
Type of government	Borough
Form of government	SM '50

Government
Legislative Districts
US Congressional	6
State Legislative	11

Local Officials, 2006
Mayor	Kenneth Pringle
Admin/Manager	Robbin D. Kirk
Clerk	Margaret Plummer
Finance Dir/Treas	Robbin Kirk
Engineer	Tom Rospos
Attorney	Karl Kemm
Tax assessor	Edward Mullane
Tax collector	NA
Building officer	Patrick McMahon
Zoning officer	NA
Public Works	NA

Housing & Construction
Housing Units, 2000*
Total	3,996
Median rent	$779
Median SF home value	$186,700

New Privately Owned Housing Units Authorized by Building Permit
	Units	Value
Total, 2004	19	$4,871,144
Single family	9	$4,861,736
Total, 2005	27	$4,887,916
Single family	20	$4,881,352

Real Property Valuation - parcels, 2005
	Number	Valuation
Total		$992,118,400
Vacant	63	14,956,800
Residential	2,504	832,791,500
Commercial	173	108,677,600
Industrial	0	0
Apartments	36	35,692,500
Farm land	0	0
Farm homestead	0	0

Average Property Value & Tax, 2005
Residential value	$332,584
Property tax	$5,282
FAIR rebate	$775

Public Library
Belmar Public Library
517 Tenth Ave
Belmar, NJ 07719
732-681-0775
Director....................Lois Gallagher

Library statistics, 2004
	Total	per capita
Volumes	31,642	5.23
Expenditure	$173,908	$28.77

Public Safety
Police
Chief	Jack Hill
Number of officers, 2004	21

Crime, 2004	Number	Rate
Total	385	64.4
Violent	18	3
Non-violent	367	61.4
Domestic Viol.	114	NA

Emergency/Fire
Director...................John Rizzitello

Public School District
(for school year 2004-2005 except as noted)

Belmar School District
1101 Main St
Belmar, NJ 07719
732-280-9218

Superintendent	Lester Richens
Grade plan	K-12
Enrollment	554.0
Students per teacher	10.9
Per pupil expenditure	$11,551
Median faculty salary	$45,000
Median administrator salary	$112,462
Grade 12 enrollment	NA
High school graduation rate	NA

Assessment test results
(percent scoring at proficient or advanced level)
	Language	Math
Grade 3	75.4%	76.2%
Grade 8	78.0%	80.3%
High school	NA	NA

SAT
Percent tested	NA
Average SAT math score	NA
Average SAT verbal score	NA

No Child Left Behind, 2003-04
Attendence rate (target = 90%)	95.1%
Drop rate	NA
Highly-qualified teachers	95.4%
District needs improvement?(AYP)	No

Municipal Finance
Fiscal Year 2005
Total tax levy	$15,761,559
County levy	3,740,621
County taxes	3,471,338
County library	0
County health	63,300
County open space	205,983
School levy	6,359,465
Local muni. budget	5,661,473
Misc. revenues	5,885,216
Total aid	$671,439
CMPTRA	217,659
Muni. block grant	25,716
Energy tax receipts	378,064
Homeland security	50,000

Fiscal Year 2006
Total aid	$671,440
CMPTRA	204,427
Muni. block grant	25,716
Energy tax receipts	391,297
Homeland security	50,000

Taxes
	2003	2004	2005
General tax rate per $100	1.36	1.460	1.589
Net valuation taxable	$979,601,796	$982,889,788	$992,515,029
State equalized value	$936,432,268	$1,144,675,333	$1,377,345,308
County equalization ratio	57.24	104.60	85.86

Demographics & Socio-Economic Characteristics
(2000 U.S. Census, except as noted)

Population
1980*	2,475
1990*	2,669
2000	2,771
Male	1,328
Female	1,443
2004 (estimate)*	2,761
Persons per sq. mi. of land	2,084

Race & Hispanic Origin, 2000
Race
White	2,716
Black/African American	14
Amer. Indian/Alaska Natv.	1
Asian	14
Natv. Hawaiian/Pac. Islander	0
Other Race	7
Two or more races	19
Hispanic origin, total	64
Mexican	1
Puerto Rican	28
Cuban	12
Other Hispanic	23

Age & Nativity, 2000
Under 5 years	201
18 years and over	1,991
21 years and over	1,903
65 years and over	356
85 years and over	57
Median Age	36.4
Native born	2,703
Foreign born	68

Educational Attainment, 2000
Population 25 years and over	1,823
0-8 yrs of school	2.7%
High School grad or higher	84.0%
Bachelor's degree or higher	26.2%
Graduate degree	7.7%

Income & Poverty, 1999
Per capita income	$23,231
Median household income	$52,792
Median family income	$62,212
Persons in poverty	93
H'holds receiving public assistance	27
H'holds receiving social security	304

Households, 2000
Total households	1,088
With persons under 18	416
With persons over 65	266
Family households	717
One-person households	310
Persons per household	2.54
Persons per family	3.17

Labor & Employment
Total civilian labor force, 2004**	1,589
Unemployment rate	4.1%
Total civilian labor force, 2000	1,454
Unemployment rate	4.6%

Employed persons 16 years and over by occupation, 2000
Managers & professionals	490
Service occupations	192
Sales & office occupations	369
Farming, fishing & forestry	1
Construction & maintenance	116
Production & transportation	219
Self-employed persons	107

*US Census Bureau
**New Jersey Department of Labor

General Information
Town of Belvidere
691 Water St
Belvidere, NJ 07823
908-475-5331

Web site	NA
Land area (sq. miles)	1.32
Water area (sq. miles)	0.02
Type of government	Town
Form of government	T

Government

Legislative Districts
US Congressional	5
State Legislative	23

Local Officials, 2006
Mayor	Charles J. Liegel Sr.
Admin/Manager	Teaesa A. DeMatt
Clerk	Teresa A. DeMont
Finance Dir/Treas	Cathy Gangaware
Engineer	Maser Consulting, Inc.
Attorney	Brian Smith
Tax assessor	David Gill
Tax collector	NA
Building officer	Charles O'Connor
Zoning officer	Charles Hoff
Public Works	NA

Housing & Construction

Housing Units, 2000*
Total	1,165
Median rent	$575
Median SF home value	$124,200

New Privately Owned Housing Units Authorized by Building Permit
	Units	Value
Total, 2004	1	$330,000
Single family	1	$330,000
Total, 2005	2	$382,600
Single family	2	$382,600

Real Property Valuation - parcels, 2005
	Number	Valuation
Total		$143,780,600
Vacant	80	2,786,700
Residential	831	99,081,200
Commercial	92	14,620,500
Industrial	12	24,150,800
Apartments	8	2,487,600
Farm land	3	613,900
Farm homestead	8	39,900

Average Property Value & Tax, 2005
Residential value	$118,142
Property tax	$4,620
FAIR rebate	$550

Public Library
Belvidere Public Library
301 2nd St
Belvidere, NJ 07823
908-475-3941

Director | Teresa Aicher

Library statistics, 2004
	Total	per capita
Volumes	20,867	7.53
Expenditure	$115,088	$41.53

Public Safety

Police
Chief	Kent Sweigert
Number of officers, 2004	6

Crime, 2004	Number	Rate
Total	8	2.9
Violent	3	1.1
Non-violent	5	1.8
Domestic Viol.	33	NA

Emergency/Fire
Director | Keith Wolfinger

Public School District
(for school year 2004-2005 except as noted)

Belvidere School District
809 Oxford St
Belvidere, NJ 07823
908-475-6600

Superintendent	Jean Atkin Gool
Grade plan	K-12
Enrollment	990.0
Students per teacher	11.9
Per pupil expenditure	$9,812
Median faculty salary	$44,150
Median administrator salary	$87,750
Grade 12 enrollment	118.0
High school graduation rate	90.4%

Assessment test results
(percent scoring at proficient or advanced level)
	Language	Math
Grade 3	88.6%	84.1%
Grade 8	63.0%	50.0%
High school	90.4%	79.6%

SAT
Percent tested	59%
Average SAT math score	497
Average SAT verbal score	500

No Child Left Behind, 2003-04
Attendance rate (target = 90%)	97.0%
Drop rate	1.9%
Highly-qualified teachers	83.7%
District needs improvement?(AYP)	No

Municipal Finance

Fiscal Year 2005
Total tax levy	$5,673,649
County levy	1,221,916
County taxes	1,098,120
County library	0
County health	0
County open space	123,796
School levy	3,070,000
Local muni. budget	1,381,732
Misc. revenues	1,385,635
Total aid	$679,443
CMPTRA	204,879
Muni. block grant	11,679
Energy tax receipts	437,885
Homeland security	25,000

Fiscal Year 2006
Total aid	$679,443
CMPTRA	189,553
Muni. block grant	11,679
Energy tax receipts	453,211
Homeland security	25,000

Taxes
	2003	2004	2005
General tax rate per $100	3.56	3.660	3.920
Net valuation taxable	$142,841,323	$145,216,202	$145,090,423
State equalized value	$177,266,472	$203,159,134	$226,562,185
County equalization ratio	86.53	80.58	71.27

Demographics & Socio-Economic Characteristics
(2000 U.S. Census, except as noted)

Population
1980*	25,568
1990*	24,458
2000	26,247
Male	12,534
Female	13,713
2004 (estimate)*	26,210
Persons per sq. mi. of land	9,053

Race & Hispanic Origin, 2000
Race
White	16,510
Black/African American	1,812
Amer. Indian/Alaska Natv.	63
Asian	5,357
Natv. Hawaiian/Pac. Islander	4
Other Race	1,698
Two or more races	803
Hispanic origin, total	4,474
Mexican	220
Puerto Rican	926
Cuban	247
Other Hispanic	3,081

Age & Nativity, 2000
Under 5 years	1,779
18 years and over	19,726
21 years and over	18,881
65 years and over	3,556
85 years and over	387
Median Age	37.6
Native born	17,810
Foreign born	8,437

Educational Attainment, 2000
Population 25 years and over	17,831
0-8 yrs of school	4.9%
High School grad or higher	86.6%
Bachelor's degree or higher	32.3%
Graduate degree	9.9%

Income & Poverty, 1999
Per capita income	$24,706
Median household income	$62,172
Median family income	$71,187
Persons in poverty	919
H'holds receiving public assistance	105
H'holds receiving social security	2,593

Households, 2000
Total households	8,981
With persons under 18	3,542
With persons over 65	2,656
Family households	6,750
One-person households	1,868
Persons per household	2.92
Persons per family	3.41

Labor & Employment
Total civilian labor force, 2004**	14,651
Unemployment rate	4.6%
Total civilian labor force, 2000	13,731
Unemployment rate	3.6%

Employed persons 16 years and over by occupation, 2000
Managers & professionals	5,040
Service occupations	1,898
Sales & office occupations	3,875
Farming, fishing & forestry	0
Construction & maintenance	933
Production & transportation	1,495
Self-employed persons	606

*US Census Bureau
**New Jersey Department of Labor

General Information
Borough of Bergenfield
198 N Washington Ave
Bergenfield, NJ 07621
201-387-4055

Web site	www.bergenfield.com
Land area (sq. miles)	2.90
Water area (sq. miles)	0
Type of government	Borough
Form of government	B

Government

Legislative Districts
US Congressional	5
State Legislative	37

Local Officials, 2006
Mayor	Richard J. Bohan Sr.
Admin/Manager	C. Navarro-Steinel
Clerk	Catherine Navarro-Steinel
Finance Dir/Treas	C. Navarro-Steinel
Engineer	James Feury, AFR Eng. Group
Attorney	Dennis Oury
Tax assessor	James Anzevino
Tax collector	Barbara Kozay
Building officer	Tom Hill
Zoning officer	Robert Byrnes
Public Works	Robert Bartley

Housing & Construction

Housing Units, 2000*
Total	9,147
Median rent	$855
Median SF home value	$184,400

New Privately Owned Housing Units
Authorized by Building Permit
	Units	Value
Total, 2004	9	$1,559,500
Single family	7	$1,232,500
Total, 2005	120	$14,912,100
Single family	16	$3,483,100

Real Property Valuation - parcels, 2005
	Number	Valuation
Total		$2,420,900,400
Vacant	58	9,428,200
Residential	6,874	2,096,005,900
Commercial	257	202,507,300
Industrial	50	34,071,400
Apartments	48	78,887,600
Farm land	0	0
Farm homestead	0	0

Average Property Value & Tax, 2005
Residential value	$304,918
Property tax	$7,829
FAIR rebate	$579

Public Library
Bergenfield Public Library
50 West Clinton Ave
Bergenfield, NJ 07621
201-387-4040

Director	Mary Riskind

Library statistics, 2004
	Total	per capita
Volumes	134,867	5.14
Expenditure	$1,584,090	$60.35

Public Safety

Police
Chief	Thomas Lucas
Number of officers, 2004	45

Crime, 2004	Number	Rate
Total	286	10.9
Violent	25	1
Non-violent	261	10
Domestic Viol.	155	NA

Emergency/Fire
Director	Charles Hartung

Public School District
(for school year 2004-2005 except as noted)

Bergenfield School District
100 S Prospect Ave
Bergenfield, NJ 07621
201-385-8202

Superintendent	Michael Kuchar
Grade plan	K-12
Enrollment	3,754.0
Students per teacher	12.0
Per pupil expenditure	$11,714
Median faculty salary	$54,020
Median administrator salary	$121,005
Grade 12 enrollment	264.0
High school graduation rate	94.9%

Assessment test results
(percent scoring at proficient or advanced level)
	Language	Math
Grade 3	90.4%	90.4%
Grade 8	76.1%	70.1%
High school	87.0%	81.5%

SAT
Percent tested	78%
Average SAT math score	501
Average SAT verbal score	481

No Child Left Behind, 2003-04
Attendence rate (target = 90%)	95.9%
Drop rate	2%
Highly-qualified teachers	97.1%
District needs improvement?(AYP)	No

Municipal Finance

Fiscal Year 2005
Total tax levy	$62,196,752
County levy	4,703,878
County taxes	4,467,236
County library	0
County health	0
County open space	236,643
School levy	36,326,331
Local muni. budget	21,166,543
Misc. revenues	6,393,097
Total aid	$2,657,160
CMPTRA	1,220,221
Muni. block grant	107,020
Energy tax receipts	1,239,919
Homeland security	90,000

Fiscal Year 2006
Total aid	$2,657,160
CMPTRA	1,176,824
Muni. block grant	107,020
Energy tax receipts	1,283,316
Homeland security	90,000

Taxes
	2003	2004	2005
General tax rate per $100	4.41	4.560	2.570
Net valuation taxable	$1,252,413,383	$1,251,432,633	$2,422,312,290
State equalized value	$2,108,440,039	$2,347,138,086	$2,706,796,614
County equalization ratio	67.37	59.40	102.68

Demographics & Socio-Economic Characteristics
(2000 U.S. Census, except as noted)

Population
1980*	12,549
1990*	11,980
2000	13,407
Male	6,389
Female	7,018
2004 (estimate)*	13,619
Persons per sq. mi. of land	2,174

Race & Hispanic Origin, 2000
Race
White	12,019
Black/African American	149
Amer. Indian/Alaska Natv.	11
Asian	1,055
Natv. Hawaiian/Pac. Islander	0
Other Race	82
Two or more races	91
Hispanic origin, total	494
Mexican	37
Puerto Rican	93
Cuban	45
Other Hispanic	319

Age & Nativity, 2000
Under 5 years	1,070
18 years and over	9,812
21 years and over	9,560
65 years and over	2,200
85 years and over	354
Median Age	39.7
Native born	11,552
Foreign born	1,855

Educational Attainment, 2000
Population 25 years and over	9,267
0-8 yrs of school	3.5%
High School grad or higher	92.5%
Bachelor's degree or higher	52.3%
Graduate degree	23.2%

Income & Poverty, 1999
Per capita income	$43,981
Median household income	$107,716
Median family income	$118,862
Persons in poverty	278
H'holds receiving public assistance	12
H'holds receiving social security	1,282

Households, 2000
Total households	4,479
With persons under 18	1,910
With persons over 65	1,249
Family households	3,719
One-person households	661
Persons per household	2.89
Persons per family	3.21

Labor & Employment
Total civilian labor force, 2004**	6,337
Unemployment rate	2.2%
Total civilian labor force, 2000	6,312
Unemployment rate	2.2%

Employed persons 16 years and over by occupation, 2000
Managers & professionals	3,494
Service occupations	541
Sales & office occupations	1,649
Farming, fishing & forestry	0
Construction & maintenance	297
Production & transportation	193
Self-employed persons	464

*US Census Bureau
**New Jersey Department of Labor

General Information
Township of Berkeley Heights
29 Park Ave
Berkeley Heights, NJ 07922
908-464-2700
Web site	www.berkeleyheightstwp.com
Land area (sq. miles)	6.26
Water area (sq. miles)	0.01
Type of government	Township
Form of government	TC

Government
Legislative Districts
US Congressional	7
State Legislative	21

Local Officials, 2006
Mayor	David A. Cohen
Admin/Manager	Angela Devanney
Clerk	Patricia Rapach
Finance Dir/Treas	Tracy Tedesco
Engineer	Jack D'Agostaro
Attorney	Edward J. Kologi
Tax assessor	Stan Belenky
Tax collector	Rachele Sanfilippo
Building officer	Robin Greenwald
Zoning officer	Raymond Sullivan
Public Works	Joseph A. Graziano

Housing & Construction
Housing Units, 2000*
Total	4,562
Median rent	$1,248
Median SF home value	$324,900

New Privately Owned Housing Units Authorized by Building Permit
	Units	Value
Total, 2004	18	$3,258,330
Single family	14	$2,158,330
Total, 2005	25	$3,635,353
Single family	23	$3,468,238

Real Property Valuation - parcels, 2005
	Number	Valuation
Total		$1,836,475,420
Vacant	152	27,152,700
Residential	4,356	1,303,249,400
Commercial	108	294,684,300
Industrial	37	205,031,200
Apartments	3	6,357,400
Farm land	0	0
Farm homestead	1	420

Average Property Value & Tax, 2005
Residential value	$299,116
Property tax	$8,126
FAIR rebate	$592

Public Library
Berkeley Heights Public Library
290 Plainfield Ave
Berkeley Heights, NJ 07922
908-464-9333
Director	Stephanie Bakos

Library statistics, 2004
	Total	per capita
Volumes	73,506	5.48
Expenditure	$894,160	$66.69

Public Safety
Police
Chief	David Zager
Number of officers, 2004	26

Crime, 2004	Number	Rate
Total	97	7.1
Violent	10	0.7
Non-violent	87	6.4
Domestic Viol.	61	NA

Emergency/Fire
Director	Richard Boss

Public School District
(for school year 2004-2005 except as noted)

Berkeley Heights School District
345 Plainfield Ave
Berkeley Heights, NJ 07922
908-464-1718
Superintendent	Judith Rattner
Grade plan	K-12
Enrollment	2,821.0
Students per teacher	10.8
Per pupil expenditure	$12,091
Median faculty salary	$55,450
Median administrator salary	$105,671
Grade 12 enrollment	227.5
High school graduation rate	99.1%

Assessment test results
(percent scoring at proficient or advanced level)
	Language	Math
Grade 3	96.6%	94.6%
Grade 8	92.5%	85.1%
High school	95.4%	91.3%

SAT
Percent tested	102%
Average SAT math score	587
Average SAT verbal score	558

No Child Left Behind, 2003-04
Attendance rate (target = 90%)	96.1%
Drop rate	0%
Highly-qualified teachers	96.8%
District needs improvement?(AYP)	No

Municipal Finance
Fiscal Year 2005
Total tax levy	$49,929,853
County levy	10,521,440
County taxes	10,106,098
County library	0
County health	0
County open space	415,341
School levy	30,464,431
Local muni. budget	8,943,982
Misc. revenues	5,792,752
Total aid	$2,239,704
CMPTRA	1,082,958
Muni. block grant	52,569
Energy tax receipts	1,034,177
Homeland security	70,000

Fiscal Year 2006
Total aid	$2,239,704
CMPTRA	1,046,762
Muni. block grant	52,569
Energy tax receipts	1,070,373
Homeland security	70,000

Taxes
	2003	2004	2005
General tax rate per $100	2.44	2.538	2.717
Net valuation taxable	$1,857,647,055	$1,864,568,931	$1,837,988,047
State equalized value	$2,565,456,505	$2,737,566,320	$2,944,549,899
County equalization ratio	74.33	72.96	67.34

Demographics & Socio-Economic Characteristics
(2000 U.S. Census, except as noted)

Population
1980*	23,151
1990*	37,319
2000	39,991
Male	17,765
Female	22,226
2004 (estimate)*	42,527
Persons per sq. mi. of land	991

Race & Hispanic Origin, 2000
Race
White	38,833
Black/African American	519
Amer. Indian/Alaska Natv.	16
Asian	181
Natv. Hawaiian/Pac. Islander	4
Other Race	173
Two or more races	265
Hispanic origin, total	932
Mexican	228
Puerto Rican	354
Cuban	78
Other Hispanic	272

Age & Nativity, 2000
Under 5 years	1,089
18 years and over	35,433
21 years and over	34,738
65 years and over	20,806
85 years and over	2,376
Median Age	66.3
Native born	37,308
Foreign born	2,680

Educational Attainment, 2000
Population 25 years and over	34,037
0-8 yrs of school	7.4%
High School grad or higher	72.4%
Bachelor's degree or higher	10.3%
Graduate degree	2.8%

Income & Poverty, 1999
Per capita income	$22,198
Median household income	$32,134
Median family income	$40,208
Persons in poverty	2,157
H'holds receiving public assistance	296
H'holds receiving social security	14,125

Households, 2000
Total households	19,828
With persons under 18	2,450
With persons over 65	13,931
Family households	12,175
One-person households	7,110
Persons per household	1.99
Persons per family	2.52

Labor & Employment
Total civilian labor force, 2004**	13,062
Unemployment rate	6.2%
Total civilian labor force, 2000	11,892
Unemployment rate	9.6%

Employed persons 16 years and over by occupation, 2000
Managers & professionals	2,945
Service occupations	1,557
Sales & office occupations	3,571
Farming, fishing & forestry	0
Construction & maintenance	1,381
Production & transportation	1,302
Self-employed persons	607

*US Census Bureau
**New Jersey Department of Labor

General Information
Township of Berkeley
PO Box B
627 Pinewald Keswick Rd
Bayville, NJ 08721
732-244-7400

Web site	NA
Land area (sq. miles)	42.90
Water area (sq. miles)	12.90
Type of government	Township
Form of government	MC '50

Government

Legislative Districts
US Congressional	3
State Legislative	9

Local Officials, 2006
Mayor	Jason Varano
Admin/Manager	Leonard Roeber
Clerk	Beverly Carle
Finance Dir/Treas	John Hannan
Engineer	Chris Theodos
Attorney	Patrick Sheehan
Tax assessor	Eric Zanetti
Tax collector	Gerry Dorso
Building officer	Bill Schultz
Zoning officer	NA
Public Works	Steve Seiler

Housing & Construction

Housing Units, 2000*
Total	22,288
Median rent	$774
Median SF home value	$102,100

New Privately Owned Housing Units
Authorized by Building Permit
	Units	Value
Total, 2004	128	$15,131,070
Single family	128	$15,131,070
Total, 2005	111	$12,142,522
Single family	108	$12,090,022

Real Property Valuation - parcels, 2005
	Number	Valuation
Total		$2,601,551,240
Vacant	3,703	50,153,250
Residential	22,503	2,396,731,790
Commercial	199	118,269,500
Industrial	20	11,358,700
Apartments	9	24,746,400
Farm land	2	270,800
Farm homestead	3	20,800

Average Property Value & Tax, 2005
Residential value	$106,494
Property tax	$3,013
FAIR rebate	$520

Public Library
Berkeley Branch Library†
30 Station Rd
Bayville, NJ 08721
732-269-2144

Branch Librarian	Heather Andolsen

Library statistics, 2004
	Total	per capita
Volumes	NA	NA
Expenditure	NA	NA

†Branch of County Library

Public Safety

Police
Chief	John Weinlein
Number of officers, 2004	71

Crime, 2004	Number	Rate
Total	715	16.9
Violent	34	0.8
Non-violent	681	16.1
Domestic Viol.	461	NA

Emergency/Fire
Director	NA

Public School District
(for school year 2004-2005 except as noted)

Berkeley Township School District
53 Central Parkway
Bayville, NJ 08721
732-269-2233

Superintendent	Joseph H. Vicari
Grade plan	K-6
Enrollment	1,907.0
Students per teacher	10.5
Per pupil expenditure	$11,687
Median faculty salary	$46,141
Median administrator salary	$91,200
Grade 12 enrollment	NA
High school graduation rate	NA

Assessment test results
(percent scoring at proficient or advanced level)
	Language	Math
Grade 3	79.3%	83.7%
Grade 8	NA	NA
High school	NA	NA

SAT
Percent tested	NA
Average SAT math score	NA
Average SAT verbal score	NA

No Child Left Behind, 2003-04
Attendence rate (target = 90%)	95.3%
Drop rate	NA
Highly-qualified teachers	100%
District needs improvement?(AYP)	No

Municipal Finance

Fiscal Year 2005
Total tax levy	$73,750,327
County levy	17,018,925
County taxes	14,338,909
County library	1,506,441
County health	638,508
County open space	535,067
School levy	39,106,420
Local muni. budget	17,624,982
Misc. revenues	14,790,952
Total aid	$5,809,207
CMPTRA	1,041,809
Muni. block grant	163,296
Energy tax receipts	4,395,197
Homeland security	140,000

Fiscal Year 2006
Total aid	$5,809,208
CMPTRA	887,978
Muni. block grant	163,296
Energy tax receipts	4,549,029
Homeland security	140,000

Taxes
	2003	2004	2005
General tax rate per $100	2.52	2.694	2.830
Net valuation taxable	$2,544,685,309	$2,565,591,068	$2,606,388,907
State equalized value	$3,793,508,213	$4,377,889,518	$5,090,603,334
County equalization ratio	77.36	67.08	58.55

Demographics & Socio-Economic Characteristics
(2000 U.S. Census, except as noted)

Population
1980*	5,786
1990*	5,672
2000	6,149
Male	3,045
Female	3,104
2004 (estimate)*	7,595
Persons per sq. mi. of land	2,123

Race & Hispanic Origin, 2000
Race
White	5,784
Black/African American	134
Amer. Indian/Alaska Natv.	13
Asian	104
Natv. Hawaiian/Pac. Islander	4
Other Race	30
Two or more races	80
Hispanic origin, total	130
Mexican	8
Puerto Rican	50
Cuban	21
Other Hispanic	51

Age & Nativity, 2000
Under 5 years	335
18 years and over	4,636
21 years and over	4,438
65 years and over	837
85 years and over	91
Median Age	38.2
Native born	5,896
Foreign born	253

Educational Attainment, 2000
Population 25 years and over	4,222
0-8 yrs of school	5.4%
High School grad or higher	84.2%
Bachelor's degree or higher	24.4%
Graduate degree	6.3%

Income & Poverty, 1999
Per capita income	$24,675
Median household income	$60,286
Median family income	$68,704
Persons in poverty	212
H'holds receiving public assistance	29
H'holds receiving social security	654

Households, 2000
Total households	2,205
With persons under 18	817
With persons over 65	581
Family households	1,660
One-person households	432
Persons per household	2.76
Persons per family	3.19

Labor & Employment
Total civilian labor force, 2004**	2,991
Unemployment rate	4.4%
Total civilian labor force, 2000	3,471
Unemployment rate	4.6%

Employed persons 16 years and over by occupation, 2000
Managers & professionals	1,212
Service occupations	466
Sales & office occupations	971
Farming, fishing & forestry	0
Construction & maintenance	318
Production & transportation	343
Self-employed persons	130

*US Census Bureau
**New Jersey Department of Labor

General Information
Borough of Berlin
59 S White Horse Pike
Berlin, NJ 08009
856-767-7777
Web site	www.berlinnj.org
Land area (sq. miles)	3.58
Water area (sq. miles)	0
Type of government	Borough
Form of government	B

Government

Legislative Districts
US Congressional	1
State Legislative	6

Local Officials, 2006
Mayor	Joseph Keskes
Admin/Manager	Barbara Gilbert
Clerk	Charleen Santora
Finance Dir/Treas	Karen Wingert (Treas)
Engineer	Environmental Resolution
Attorney	George Botcheos
Tax assessor	Blackwell Albertson
Tax collector	L. Eggert/S. Van Dyke
Building officer	Anthony Saccomanno
Zoning officer	NA
Public Works	Matt Siedlecki

Housing & Construction

Housing Units, 2000*
Total	2,275
Median rent	$642
Median SF home value	$135,800

New Privately Owned Housing Units Authorized by Building Permit
	Units	Value
Total, 2004	104	$7,314,326
Single family	64	$5,796,886
Total, 2005	52	$3,828,260
Single family	52	$3,828,260

Real Property Valuation - parcels, 2005
	Number	Valuation
Total		$384,570,740
Vacant	343	13,797,000
Residential	2,346	301,592,600
Commercial	133	57,918,500
Industrial	10	7,239,940
Apartments	15	3,464,300
Farm land	4	476,400
Farm homestead	8	82,000

Average Property Value & Tax, 2005
Residential value	$128,154
Property tax	$5,028
FAIR rebate	$576

Public Library
M Fleche Memorial Library
49 S White Horse Pke
Berlin, NJ 08009
856-767-2448
Director	Mary Rencic

Library statistics, 2004
	Total	per capita
Volumes	28,615	4.65
Expenditure	$104,423	$16.98

Public Safety

Police
Chief	Lawrence Winters
Number of officers, 2004	18

Crime, 2004	Number	Rate
Total	184	27
Violent	7	1
Non-violent	177	26
Domestic Viol.	34	NA

Emergency/Fire
Director	Paul Miller

Public School District
(for school year 2004-2005 except as noted)

Berlin Borough School District
215 S Franklin Ave
Berlin, NJ 08009
856-767-6785
Superintendent	Leonard Binowski
Grade plan	K-8
Enrollment	786.0
Students per teacher	12.5
Per pupil expenditure	$10,011
Median faculty salary	$43,999
Median administrator salary	$85,974
Grade 12 enrollment	NA
High school graduation rate	NA

Assessment test results
(percent scoring at proficient or advanced level)
	Language	Math
Grade 3	92.0%	93.1%
Grade 8	85.5%	68.7%
High school	NA	NA

SAT
Percent tested	NA
Average SAT math score	NA
Average SAT verbal score	NA

No Child Left Behind, 2003-04
Attendence rate (target = 90%)	95.5%
Drop rate	NA
Highly-qualified teachers	99.4%
District needs improvement?(AYP)	No

Municipal Finance

Fiscal Year 2005
Total tax levy	$15,247,593
County levy	4,461,300
County taxes	4,110,957
County library	296,311
County health	0
County open space	54,033
School levy	8,431,842
Local muni. budget	2,354,451
Misc. revenues	3,316,119
Total aid	$1,052,568
CMPTRA	433,112
Muni. block grant	24,818
Energy tax receipts	544,638
Homeland security	50,000

Fiscal Year 2006
Total aid	$1,052,568
CMPTRA	414,050
Muni. block grant	24,818
Energy tax receipts	563,700
Homeland security	50,000

Taxes
	2003	2004	2005
General tax rate per $100	3.63	3.668	3.924
Net valuation taxable	$371,215,010	$380,396,706	$388,627,543
State equalized value	$460,507,394	$525,689,561	$606,946,030
County equalization ratio	88.58	80.61	72.12

Demographics & Socio-Economic Characteristics
(2000 U.S. Census, except as noted)

Population
1980*	5,348
1990*	5,466
2000	5,290
Male	2,632
Female	2,658
2004 (estimate)*	5,372
Persons per sq. mi. of land	1,654

Race & Hispanic Origin, 2000
Race
White	4,362
Black/African American	628
Amer. Indian/Alaska Natv.	9
Asian	143
Natv. Hawaiian/Pac. Islander	4
Other Race	64
Two or more races	80
Hispanic origin, total	254
Mexican	146
Puerto Rican	72
Cuban	6
Other Hispanic	30

Age & Nativity, 2000
Under 5 years	352
18 years and over	3,926
21 years and over	3,722
65 years and over	663
85 years and over	69
Median Age	35.9
Native born	5,015
Foreign born	275

Educational Attainment, 2000
Population 25 years and over	3,495
0-8 yrs of school	5.6%
High School grad or higher	76.7%
Bachelor's degree or higher	15.1%
Graduate degree	4.3%

Income & Poverty, 1999
Per capita income	$22,178
Median household income	$54,448
Median family income	$61,042
Persons in poverty	312
H'holds receiving public assistance	37
H'holds receiving social security	565

Households, 2000
Total households	1,893
With persons under 18	736
With persons over 65	510
Family households	1,368
One-person households	427
Persons per household	2.78
Persons per family	3.28

Labor & Employment
Total civilian labor force, 2004**	2,869
Unemployment rate	4.0%
Total civilian labor force, 2000	2,774
Unemployment rate	3.6%

Employed persons 16 years and over by occupation, 2000
Managers & professionals	728
Service occupations	518
Sales & office occupations	695
Farming, fishing & forestry	0
Construction & maintenance	422
Production & transportation	310
Self-employed persons	75

*US Census Bureau
**New Jersey Department of Labor

General Information
Township of Berlin
170 Bate Ave
West Berlin, NJ 08091
856-767-1854
Web site	www.berlintwp.com
Land area (sq. miles)	3.25
Water area (sq. miles)	0
Type of government	Township
Form of government	SM '50

Government
Legislative Districts
US Congressional	1
State Legislative	6

Local Officials, 2006
Mayor	Phyllis Jeffries-Magazzu
Admin/Manager	NA
Clerk	Jamey Eggers
Finance Dir/Treas	Lori Campisano
Engineer	Charles Riebel Jr.
Attorney	Donafaye Zoll
Tax assessor	Gilbert Goble
Tax collector	NA
Building officer	Mike DePalma
Zoning officer	NA
Public Works	NA

Housing & Construction
Housing Units, 2000*
Total	2,009
Median rent	$590
Median SF home value	$109,600

New Privately Owned Housing Units
Authorized by Building Permit
	Units	Value
Total, 2004	17	$1,115,769
Single family	17	$1,115,769
Total, 2005	21	$1,462,210
Single family	21	$1,462,210

Real Property Valuation - parcels, 2005
	Number	Valuation
Total		$328,191,400
Vacant	297	8,456,900
Residential	1,667	170,025,100
Commercial	312	113,729,700
Industrial	49	31,803,200
Apartments	3	3,955,600
Farm land	2	164,900
Farm homestead	19	56,000

Average Property Value & Tax, 2005
Residential value	$100,878
Property tax	$4,147
FAIR rebate	$608

Public Library
Berlin Township Library
201 Veteran's Ave
West Berlin, NJ 08901
856-767-0439
Director	Mary Holt

Library statistics, 2004
	Total	per capita
Volumes	NA	NA
Expenditure	NA	NA

Public Safety
Police
Chief	Michael Hayden
Number of officers, 2004	18

Crime, 2004	Number	Rate
Total	278	51.9
Violent	21	3.9
Non-violent	257	47.9
Domestic Viol.	52	NA

Emergency/Fire
Director	Joseph Jackson

Public School District
(for school year 2004-2005 except as noted)

Berlin Township School District
225 Grove Ave
West Berlin, NJ 08091
856-767-9480
Superintendent	Brian Betze
Grade plan	K-12
Enrollment	671.0
Students per teacher	9.9
Per pupil expenditure	$11,623
Median faculty salary	$42,641
Median administrator salary	$86,936
Grade 12 enrollment	NA
High school graduation rate	NA

Assessment test results
(percent scoring at proficient or advanced level)
	Language	Math
Grade 3	80.0%	81.8%
Grade 8	78.1%	69.9%
High school	NA	NA

SAT
Percent tested	NA
Average SAT math score	NA
Average SAT verbal score	NA

No Child Left Behind, 2003-04
Attendence rate (target = 90%)	93.7%
Drop rate	NA
Highly-qualified teachers	NA
District needs improvement?(AYP)	No

Municipal Finance
Fiscal Year 2005
Total tax levy	$13,523,055
County levy	3,321,850
County taxes	3,061,556
County library	220,149
County health	0
County open space	40,145
School levy	7,062,475
Local muni. budget	3,138,731
Misc. revenues	3,478,256
Total aid	$1,628,358
CMPTRA	203,058
Muni. block grant	23,917
Energy tax receipts	1,351,063
Homeland security	50,000

Fiscal Year 2006
Total aid	$1,628,358
CMPTRA	155,771
Muni. block grant	23,917
Energy tax receipts	1,398,350
Homeland security	50,000

Taxes
	2003	2004	2005
General tax rate per $100	3.65	3.986	4.111
Net valuation taxable	$322,148,482	$325,486,423	$328,956,262
State equalized value	$362,779,822	$396,066,060	$449,025,747
County equalization ratio	97.23	88.80	82.14

Demographics & Socio-Economic Characteristics
(2000 U.S. Census, except as noted)

Population
1980*	12,920
1990*	17,199
2000	24,575
Male	11,945
Female	12,630
2004 (estimate)*	26,904
Persons per sq. mi. of land	1,121

Race & Hispanic Origin, 2000
Race
White	21,921
Black/African American	354
Amer. Indian/Alaska Natv.	13
Asian	1,928
Natv. Hawaiian/Pac. Islander	3
Other Race	98
Two or more races	258
Hispanic origin, total	646
Mexican	60
Puerto Rican	105
Cuban	82
Other Hispanic	399

Age & Nativity, 2000
Under 5 years	1,962
18 years and over	17,770
21 years and over	17,403
65 years and over	3,063
85 years and over	383
Median Age	39.2
Native born	21,499
Foreign born	3,076

Educational Attainment, 2000
Population 25 years and over	16,950
0-8 yrs of school	1.8%
High School grad or higher	95.8%
Bachelor's degree or higher	67.4%
Graduate degree	30.6%

Income & Poverty, 1999
Per capita income	$56,521
Median household income	$107,204
Median family income	$135,806
Persons in poverty	319
H'holds receiving public assistance	55
H'holds receiving social security	1,927

Households, 2000
Total households	9,242
With persons under 18	3,549
With persons over 65	2,004
Family households	6,484
One-person households	2,442
Persons per household	2.58
Persons per family	3.17

Labor & Employment
Total civilian labor force, 2004**	11,608
Unemployment rate	3.1%
Total civilian labor force, 2000	12,279
Unemployment rate	2.7%

Employed persons 16 years and over by occupation, 2000
Managers & professionals	7,651
Service occupations	629
Sales & office occupations	2,835
Farming, fishing & forestry	0
Construction & maintenance	379
Production & transportation	452
Self-employed persons	713

*US Census Bureau
**New Jersey Department of Labor

General Information
Township of Bernards
1 Collyer Lane
Basking Ridge, NJ 07920
908-766-2510

Web site	www.bernards.org
Land area (sq. miles)	24.00
Water area (sq. miles)	0.01
Type of government	Township
Form of government	TC

Government

Legislative Districts
US Congressional	11
State Legislative	16

Local Officials, 2006
Mayor	John Malay
Admin/Manager	Karen Waldron
Clerk	Denise Szabo
Finance Dir/Treas	J. Bolcato/ B. McArthur
Engineer	Peter Messina
Attorney	John Belardo
Tax assessor	Marcia Sudano
Tax collector	NA
Building officer	Dennis Bettler
Zoning officer	Hosea Harvey
Public Works	NA

Housing & Construction

Housing Units, 2000*
Total	9,485
Median rent	$1,494
Median SF home value	$380,500

New Privately Owned Housing Units
Authorized by Building Permit

	Units	Value
Total, 2004	30	$10,048,567
Single family	28	$9,448,567
Total, 2005	23	$9,721,100
Single family	23	$9,721,100

Real Property Valuation - parcels, 2005
	Number	Valuation
Total		$6,399,159,210
Vacant	306	34,921,300
Residential	9,471	5,625,239,400
Commercial	160	700,421,000
Industrial	7	7,425,000
Apartments	2	7,858,900
Farm land	30	22,896,000
Farm homestead	59	397,610

Average Property Value & Tax, 2005
Residential value	$590,308
Property tax	$9,124
FAIR rebate	$534

Public Library
Bernards Twp Library
32 S Maple Ave
Basking Ridge, NJ 07920
908-204-3031
Director........... Anne Meany

Library statistics, 2004
	Total	per capita
Volumes	122,915	5.00
Expenditure	$1,732,612	$70.50

Public Safety

Police
Chief	Robert Kumph
Number of officers, 2004	39

Crime, 2004	Number	Rate
Total	171	6.5
Violent	3	0.1
Non-violent	168	6.4
Domestic Viol.	89	NA

Emergency/Fire
Director....... E. McMahon/M. Friedman

Public School District
(for school year 2004-2005 except as noted)

Bernards Township School District
101 Peachtree Rd
Basking Ridge, NJ 07920
908-204-2600

Superintendent	Valerie Goger
Grade plan	K-12
Enrollment	5,207.0
Students per teacher	11.3
Per pupil expenditure	$11,328
Median faculty salary	$49,939
Median administrator salary	$105,423
Grade 12 enrollment	311.5
High school graduation rate	99.7%

Assessment test results
(percent scoring at proficient or advanced level)
	Language	Math
Grade 3	94.6%	96.3%
Grade 8	94.4%	91.5%
High school	96.2%	94.8%

SAT
Percent tested	101%
Average SAT math score	609
Average SAT verbal score	583

No Child Left Behind, 2003-04
Attendence rate (target = 90%)	96.1%
Drop rate	0.2%
Highly-qualified teachers	96.9%
District needs improvement?(AYP)	No

Municipal Finance

Fiscal Year 2005
Total tax levy	$99,018,297
County levy	20,191,257
County taxes	18,420,076
County library	0
County health	0
County open space	1,771,181
School levy	59,541,418
Local muni. budget	19,285,622
Misc. revenues	18,783,342
Total aid	$2,598,854
CMPTRA	479,004
Muni. block grant	96,359
Energy tax receipts	1,933,491
Homeland security	90,000

Fiscal Year 2006
Total aid	$2,598,854
CMPTRA	411,332
Muni. block grant	96,359
Energy tax receipts	2,001,163
Homeland security	90,000

Taxes
	2003	2004	2005
General tax rate per $100	1.70	1.760	1.550
Net valuation taxable	$5,250,906,008	$5,309,898,347	$6,406,611,095
State equalized value	$5,384,992,317	$5,846,486,764	$6,423,955,776
County equalization ratio	102.78	97.51	108.69

Demographics & Socio-Economic Characteristics
(2000 U.S. Census, except as noted)

Population
1980*	6,715
1990*	6,597
2000	7,345
Male	3,599
Female	3,746
2004 (estimate)*	7,597
Persons per sq. mi. of land	588

Race & Hispanic Origin, 2000
Race
White	6,900
Black/African American	18
Amer. Indian/Alaska Natv.	11
Asian	194
Natv. Hawaiian/Pac. Islander	0
Other Race	114
Two or more races	108
Hispanic origin, total	439
Mexican	28
Puerto Rican	21
Cuban	10
Other Hispanic	380

Age & Nativity, 2000
Under 5 years	557
18 years and over	5,430
21 years and over	5,280
65 years and over	933
85 years and over	76
Median Age	40
Native born	6,428
Foreign born	917

Educational Attainment, 2000
Population 25 years and over	5,129
0-8 yrs of school	2.3%
High School grad or higher	92.3%
Bachelor's degree or higher	59.6%
Graduate degree	24.3%

Income & Poverty, 1999
Per capita income	$69,854
Median household income	$104,162
Median family income	$126,601
Persons in poverty	202
H'holds receiving public assistance	21
H'holds receiving social security	732

Households, 2000
Total households	2,723
With persons under 18	1,010
With persons over 65	669
Family households	2,050
One-person households	573
Persons per household	2.69
Persons per family	3.12

Labor & Employment
Total civilian labor force, 2004**	4,307
Unemployment rate	3.1%
Total civilian labor force, 2000	3,831
Unemployment rate	1.4%

Employed persons 16 years and over by occupation, 2000
Managers & professionals	1,999
Service occupations	477
Sales & office occupations	905
Farming, fishing & forestry	0
Construction & maintenance	190
Production & transportation	208
Self-employed persons	382

*US Census Bureau
**New Jersey Department of Labor

General Information
Borough of Bernardsville
PO Box 158
Bernardsville, NJ 07924
908-766-3000
Web site	www.bernardsvilleboro.org
Land area (sq. miles)	12.93
Water area (sq. miles)	0.01
Type of government	Borough
Form of government	B

Government
Legislative Districts
US Congressional	7
State Legislative	16

Local Officials, 2006
Mayor	Jay Parsons
Admin/Manager	Ralph Maresca Jr.
Clerk	Sandra Jones
Finance Dir/Treas	Jenny Lin
Engineer	Paul Ferriero
Attorney	John Pidgeon
Tax assessor	Marcia Sudano
Tax collector	Antonietta Marino
Building officer	Joseph Alicino
Zoning officer	Michael Mondok
Public Works	John Macdowell

Housing & Construction
Housing Units, 2000*
Total	2,807
Median rent	$1,039
Median SF home value	$409,700

New Privately Owned Housing Units
Authorized by Building Permit
	Units	Value
Total, 2004	8	$7,206,013
Single family	8	$7,206,013
Total, 2005	10	$8,085,504
Single family	10	$8,085,504

Real Property Valuation - parcels, 2005
	Number	Valuation
Total		$2,336,191,500
Vacant	149	34,828,200
Residential	2,497	2,010,946,100
Commercial	164	156,809,400
Industrial	26	15,759,400
Apartments	12	7,609,100
Farm land	57	107,904,700
Farm homestead	99	2,334,600

Average Property Value & Tax, 2005
Residential value	$775,532
Property tax	$10,919
FAIR rebate	$606

Public Library
Bernardsville Public Library
1 Anderson Hill Rd
Bernardsville, NJ 07924
908-766-0118
Director	Karen Yannetta

Library statistics, 2004
	Total	per capita
Volumes	79,024	10.76
Expenditure	$707,884	$96.38

Public Safety
Police
Chief	Kevin Valentine
Number of officers, 2004	19

Crime, 2004	Number	Rate
Total	85	11.2
Violent	2	0.3
Non-violent	83	11
Domestic Viol.	44	NA

Emergency/Fire
Director	Chuck Feriante

Public School District
(for school year 2004-2005 except as noted)

Somerset Hills Regional School District
25 Olcott Ave
Bernardsville, NJ 07924
908-630-3010
Superintendent	Pete Miller
Grade plan	K-12
Enrollment	1,944.0
Students per teacher	11.8
Per pupil expenditure	$13,957
Median faculty salary	$59,292
Median administrator salary	$122,500
Grade 12 enrollment	136.0
High school graduation rate	97.8%

Assessment test results
(percent scoring at proficient or advanced level)
	Language	Math
Grade 3	94.3%	95.1%
Grade 8	95.1%	86.5%
High school	96.0%	93.0%

SAT
Percent tested	91%
Average SAT math score	561
Average SAT verbal score	557

No Child Left Behind, 2003-04
Attendance rate (target = 90%)	95.5%
Drop rate	0.3%
Highly-qualified teachers	97.5%
District needs improvement?(AYP)	No

Municipal Finance
Fiscal Year 2005
Total tax levy	$32,982,914
County levy	7,229,630
County taxes	6,595,430
County library	0
County health	0
County open space	634,199
School levy	18,684,354
Local muni. budget	7,068,931
Misc. revenues	4,333,056
Total aid	$999,596
CMPTRA	219,406
Muni. block grant	28,866
Energy tax receipts	701,324
Homeland security	50,000

Fiscal Year 2006
Total aid	$999,597
CMPTRA	194,860
Muni. block grant	28,866
Energy tax receipts	725,871
Homeland security	50,000

Taxes
	2003	2004	2005
General tax rate per $100	1.41	1.590	1.410
Net valuation taxable	$1,913,359,634	$1,932,373,601	$2,342,570,600
State equalized value	$1,919,887,251	$2,076,669,826	$2,376,555,341
County equalization ratio	108.29	99.66	111.04

Demographics & Socio-Economic Characteristics
(2000 U.S. Census, except as noted)

Population
1980*	3,045
1990*	3,104
2000	3,820
Male	1,921
Female	1,899
2004 (estimate)*	4,003
Persons per sq. mi. of land	192

Race & Hispanic Origin, 2000
Race
White	3,725
Black/African American	33
Amer. Indian/Alaska Natv.	4
Asian	39
Natv. Hawaiian/Pac. Islander	2
Other Race	1
Two or more races	16
Hispanic origin, total	62
Mexican	5
Puerto Rican	25
Cuban	8
Other Hispanic	24

Age & Nativity, 2000
Under 5 years	283
18 years and over	2,693
21 years and over	2,598
65 years and over	249
85 years and over	27
Median Age	38.8
Native born	3,634
Foreign born	186

Educational Attainment, 2000
Population 25 years and over	2,499
0-8 yrs of school	3.6%
High School grad or higher	92.3%
Bachelor's degree or higher	45.3%
Graduate degree	18.6%

Income & Poverty, 1999
Per capita income	$35,298
Median household income	$88,048
Median family income	$92,768
Persons in poverty	40
H'holds receiving public assistance	7
H'holds receiving social security	221

Households, 2000
Total households	1,266
With persons under 18	575
With persons over 65	188
Family households	1,093
One-person households	131
Persons per household	3.02
Persons per family	3.26

Labor & Employment
Total civilian labor force, 2004**	2,033
Unemployment rate	2.6%
Total civilian labor force, 2000	2,028
Unemployment rate	1.4%

Employed persons 16 years and over by occupation, 2000
Managers & professionals	958
Service occupations	172
Sales & office occupations	538
Farming, fishing & forestry	15
Construction & maintenance	236
Production & transportation	80
Self-employed persons	124

*US Census Bureau
**New Jersey Department of Labor

General Information
Township of Bethlehem
405 Mine Rd
Asbury, NJ 08802
908-735-4107

Web site	www.bethlehem-twp.org
Land area (sq. miles)	20.84
Water area (sq. miles)	0
Type of government	Township
Form of government	TC

Government

Legislative Districts
US Congressional	7
State Legislative	23

Local Officials, 2006
Mayor	Steve Kucinski
Admin/Manager	Diane Pflugfelder
Clerk	Diane Pflugfelder
Finance Dir/Treas	Mary Dobes
Engineer	James Coe
Attorney	Robert Kenny
Tax assessor	Eloise Hagaman
Tax collector	Steve Davis
Building officer	NA
Zoning officer	NA
Public Works	Steve Douglas

Housing & Construction

Housing Units, 2000*
Total	1,303
Median rent	$750
Median SF home value	$278,400

New Privately Owned Housing Units Authorized by Building Permit
	Units	Value
Total, 2004	7	$1,185,707
Single family	7	$1,185,707
Total, 2005	15	$2,967,715
Single family	15	$2,967,715

Real Property Valuation - parcels, 2005
	Number	Valuation
Total		$521,719,158
Vacant	163	8,894,100
Residential	1,265	442,105,800
Commercial	24	21,078,800
Industrial	7	8,333,000
Apartments	0	0
Farm land	126	39,296,200
Farm homestead	218	2,011,258

Average Property Value & Tax, 2005
Residential value	$299,472
Property tax	$7,917
FAIR rebate	$478

Public Library

No public municipal library.

Library statistics, 2004
	Total	per capita
Volumes	NA	NA
Expenditure	NA	NA

Public Safety

Police
Chief	(State)
Number of officers, 2004	0

Crime, 2004	Number	Rate
Total	11	2.8
Violent	1	0.3
Non-violent	10	2.5
Domestic Viol.	5	NA

Emergency/Fire
Director	NA

Public School District
(for school year 2004-2005 except as noted)

Bethlehem Township School District
940 Iron Bridge Rd
Asbury, NJ 08802
908-537-4044

Superintendent	Mario Barbiere
Grade plan	K-8
Enrollment	686.0
Students per teacher	11.9
Per pupil expenditure	$11,768
Median faculty salary	$45,397
Median administrator salary	$92,000
Grade 12 enrollment	NA
High school graduation rate	NA

Assessment test results
(percent scoring at proficient or advanced level)
	Language	Math
Grade 3	90.7%	83.3%
Grade 8	83.3%	78.8%
High school	NA	NA

SAT
Percent tested	NA
Average SAT math score	NA
Average SAT verbal score	NA

No Child Left Behind, 2003-04
Attendence rate (target = 90%)	93.8%
Drop rate	NA
Highly-qualified teachers	81.1%
District needs improvement?(AYP)	No

Municipal Finance

Fiscal Year 2005
Total tax levy	$13,818,106
County levy	2,369,036
County taxes	2,011,458
County library	168,304
County health	0
County open space	189,274
School levy	9,802,823
Local muni. budget	1,646,247
Misc. revenues	1,574,429
Total aid	$369,580
CMPTRA	122,656
Muni. block grant	14,978
Energy tax receipts	231,946
Homeland security	0

Fiscal Year 2006
Total aid	$369,580
CMPTRA	114,538
Muni. block grant	14,978
Energy tax receipts	240,064
Homeland security	NA

Taxes
	2003	2004	2005
General tax rate per $100	2.44	2.580	2.650
Net valuation taxable	$514,354,653	$518,535,781	$522,659,062
State equalized value	$512,713,968	$561,344,180	$610,654,354
County equalization ratio	99.11	93.81	83.14

Demographics & Socio-Economic Characteristics
(2000 U.S. Census, except as noted)

Population
1980*	2,919
1990*	2,973
2000	2,661
Male	1,251
Female	1,410
2004 (estimate)*	2,689
Persons per sq. mi. of land	4,657

Race & Hispanic Origin, 2000
Race
White	1,721
Black/African American	765
Amer. Indian/Alaska Natv.	3
Asian	24
Natv. Hawaiian/Pac. Islander	0
Other Race	38
Two or more races	110
Hispanic origin, total	122
Mexican	6
Puerto Rican	88
Cuban	3
Other Hispanic	25

Age & Nativity, 2000
Under 5 years	172
18 years and over	1,907
21 years and over	1,784
65 years and over	314
85 years and over	33
Median Age	35
Native born	2,596
Foreign born	65

Educational Attainment, 2000
Population 25 years and over	1,689
0-8 yrs of school	4.5%
High School grad or higher	77.0%
Bachelor's degree or higher	11.2%
Graduate degree	4.6%

Income & Poverty, 1999
Per capita income	$17,760
Median household income	$45,054
Median family income	$49,519
Persons in poverty	302
H'holds receiving public assistance	25
H'holds receiving social security	256

Households, 2000
Total households	960
With persons under 18	381
With persons over 65	244
Family households	694
One-person households	207
Persons per household	2.77
Persons per family	3.23

Labor & Employment
Total civilian labor force, 2004**	1,634
Unemployment rate	7.6%
Total civilian labor force, 2000	1,368
Unemployment rate	8.4%

Employed persons 16 years and over by occupation, 2000
Managers & professionals	276
Service occupations	288
Sales & office occupations	311
Farming, fishing & forestry	0
Construction & maintenance	126
Production & transportation	252
Self-employed persons	62

*US Census Bureau
**New Jersey Department of Labor

General Information
City of Beverly
446 Broad St
Beverly, NJ 08010
609-387-1881

Web site	NA
Land area (sq. miles)	0.58
Water area (sq. miles)	0.20
Type of government	City
Form of government	C

Government

Legislative Districts
US Congressional	3
State Legislative	7

Local Officials, 2006
Mayor	Jean C. Wetherill
Admin/Manager	Barbara A. Sheipe
Clerk	Barbara A. Sheipe
Finance Dir/Treas	Beverly Morgan
Engineer	Willian Kirchner
Attorney	Kearns, Vassalo et al
Tax assessor	Joseph Robinson
Tax collector	Victoria Boras
Building officer	Daniel McGonigle
Zoning officer	NA
Public Works	Daniel Schoen

Housing & Construction

Housing Units, 2000*
Total	1,042
Median rent	$645
Median SF home value	$94,300

New Privately Owned Housing Units Authorized by Building Permit
	Units	Value
Total, 2004	0	$0
Single family	0	$0
Total, 2005	3	$186,565
Single family	3	$186,565

Real Property Valuation - parcels, 2005
	Number	Valuation
Total		$82,964,700
Vacant	57	621,500
Residential	866	75,056,900
Commercial	44	4,534,800
Industrial	13	1,954,100
Apartments	5	797,400
Farm land	0	0
Farm homestead	0	0

Average Property Value & Tax, 2005
Residential value	$86,671
Property tax	$4,036
FAIR rebate	$610

Public Library
Beverly Public Library
441 Cooper St
Beverly, NJ 08010
609-387-1259

Director	Margaret Lowden

Library statistics, 2004
	Total	per capita
Volumes	NA	NA
Expenditure	NA	NA

Public Safety
Police
Chief	NA
Number of officers, 2004	7

Crime, 2004	Number	Rate
Total	89	33.2
Violent	15	5.6
Non-violent	74	27.6
Domestic Viol.	87	NA

Emergency/Fire
Director	Sean Richards

Public School District
(for school year 2004-2005 except as noted)

Beverly City School District
601 Bentley Ave
Beverly, NJ 08010
609-387-2200

Superintendent	Glenn Gray
Grade plan	K-12
Enrollment	275.0
Students per teacher	8.2
Per pupil expenditure	$11,980
Median faculty salary	$39,775
Median administrator salary	$104,086
Grade 12 enrollment	NA
High school graduation rate	NA

Assessment test results
(percent scoring at proficient or advanced level)
	Language	Math
Grade 3	70.0%	71.4%
Grade 8	35.1%	36.1%
High school	NA	NA

SAT
Percent tested	NA
Average SAT math score	NA
Average SAT verbal score	NA

No Child Left Behind, 2003-04
Attendance rate (target = 90%)	93.0%
Drop rate	NA
Highly-qualified teachers	100%
District needs improvement?(AYP)	No

Municipal Finance
Fiscal Year 2005
Total tax levy	$3,869,280
County levy	481,765
County taxes	404,150
County library	35,387
County health	0
County open space	42,228
School levy	2,205,718
Local muni. budget	1,181,797
Misc. revenues	1,389,634
Total aid	$429,829
CMPTRA	217,279
Muni. block grant	13,009
Energy tax receipts	174,541
Homeland security	25,000

Fiscal Year 2006
Total aid	$429,829
CMPTRA	211,170
Muni. block grant	13,009
Energy tax receipts	180,650
Homeland security	25,000

Taxes
	2003	2004	2005
General tax rate per $100	4.03	4.357	4.658
Net valuation taxable	$83,531,809	$83,860,255	$83,097,206
State equalized value	$95,421,303	$105,846,617	$119,101,628
County equalization ratio	91.85	87.54	79.20

Demographics & Socio-Economic Characteristics
(2000 U.S. Census, except as noted)

Population
1980*	4,360
1990*	5,331
2000	5,747
Male	2,866
Female	2,881
2004 (estimate)*	6,000
Persons per sq. mi. of land	193

Race & Hispanic Origin, 2000
Race
White	5,642
Black/African American	15
Amer. Indian/Alaska Natv.	8
Asian	32
Natv. Hawaiian/Pac. Islander	1
Other Race	16
Two or more races	33
Hispanic origin, total	114
Mexican	6
Puerto Rican	35
Cuban	15
Other Hispanic	58

Age & Nativity, 2000
Under 5 years	335
18 years and over	4,278
21 years and over	4,110
65 years and over	713
85 years and over	79
Median Age	40.4
Native born	5,450
Foreign born	298

Educational Attainment, 2000
Population 25 years and over	3,957
0-8 yrs of school	5.1%
High School grad or higher	86.7%
Bachelor's degree or higher	29.8%
Graduate degree	12.7%

Income & Poverty, 1999
Per capita income	$27,775
Median household income	$64,809
Median family income	$71,214
Persons in poverty	261
H'holds receiving public assistance	27
H'holds receiving social security	582

Households, 2000
Total households	2,040
With persons under 18	773
With persons over 65	519
Family households	1,638
One-person households	312
Persons per household	2.81
Persons per family	3.14

Labor & Employment
Total civilian labor force, 2004**	3,144
Unemployment rate	2.7%
Total civilian labor force, 2000	2,994
Unemployment rate	3.9%

Employed persons 16 years and over by occupation, 2000
Managers & professionals	1,274
Service occupations	208
Sales & office occupations	641
Farming, fishing & forestry	17
Construction & maintenance	387
Production & transportation	350
Self-employed persons	221

*US Census Bureau
**New Jersey Department of Labor

General Information
Township of Blairstown
PO Box 370
12 Mohican Rd
Blairstown, NJ 07825
908-362-6663

Web site	www.blairstown-nj.org
Land area (sq. miles)	31.02
Water area (sq. miles)	0.75
Type of government	Township
Form of government	TC

Government

Legislative Districts
US Congressional	5
State Legislative	23

Local Officials, 2006
Mayor	Stephen Lance
Admin/Manager	NA
Clerk	Theresa Tamburro
Finance Dir/Treas	Barbara J. Emery (CFO)
Engineer	Norton Rodman
Attorney	Robert Benbrook
Tax assessor	Lydia Zdrodowski
Tax collector	Rita Kelley
Building officer	Ralph Price
Zoning officer	David Diehl
Public Works	Robert DePuy

Housing & Construction

Housing Units, 2000*
Total	2,136
Median rent	$882
Median SF home value	$207,600

New Privately Owned Housing Units Authorized by Building Permit
	Units	Value
Total, 2004	13	$3,512,036
Single family	13	$3,512,036
Total, 2005	18	$5,211,564
Single family	18	$5,211,564

Real Property Valuation - parcels, 2005
	Number	Valuation
Total		$460,335,264
Vacant	216	8,851,850
Residential	1,830	357,848,500
Commercial	118	38,780,125
Industrial	8	6,845,900
Apartments	0	0
Farm land	201	45,794,100
Farm homestead	357	2,214,789

Average Property Value & Tax, 2005
Residential value	$164,638
Property tax	$4,717
FAIR rebate	$569

Public Library
C D Hofman Library†
4 Lambert Rd
Blairstown, NJ 07825
908-362-8335

Branch Librarian	Marilyn Grandin

Library statistics, 2004
	Total	per capita
Volumes	NA	NA
Expenditure	NA	NA

†Branch of County Library

Public Safety

Police
Chief	Tom Krisak
Number of officers, 2004	6

Crime, 2004	Number	Rate
Total	32	5.3
Violent	1	0.2
Non-violent	31	5.2
Domestic Viol.	13	NA

Emergency/Fire
Director	William Weinbrecht

Public School District
(for school year 2004-2005 except as noted)

Blairstown Township School District
1 Sunset Hill Rd
Blairstown, NJ 07825
908-362-6111

Administrator	W. Michael Feeney
Grade plan	K-6
Enrollment	751.0
Students per teacher	12.6
Per pupil expenditure	$9,223
Median faculty salary	$62,953
Median administrator salary	$85,198
Grade 12 enrollment	NA
High school graduation rate	NA

Assessment test results
(percent scoring at proficient or advanced level)
	Language	Math
Grade 3	91.3%	87.5%
Grade 8	NA	NA
High school	NA	NA

SAT
Percent tested	NA
Average SAT math score	NA
Average SAT verbal score	NA

No Child Left Behind, 2003-04
Attendence rate (target = 90%)	95.7%
Drop rate	NA
Highly-qualified teachers	98.5%
District needs improvement?(AYP)	No

Municipal Finance

Fiscal Year 2005
Total tax levy	$13,237,043
County levy	4,498,313
County taxes	3,719,360
County library	358,565
County health	0
County open space	420,388
School levy	8,553,926
Local muni. budget	184,804
Misc. revenues	5,064,342
Total aid	$3,190,936
CMPTRA	116,392
Muni. block grant	23,327
Energy tax receipts	3,051,217
Homeland security	50,000

Fiscal Year 2006
Total aid	$3,190,936
CMPTRA	9,599
Muni. block grant	23,327
Energy tax receipts	3,158,010
Homeland security	NA

Taxes
	2003	2004	2005
General tax rate per $100	2.44	2.660	2.870
Net valuation taxable	$447,680,961	$455,313,508	$462,054,641
State equalized value	$605,792,911	$688,868,748	$782,215,407
County equalization ratio	82.62	73.90	66.00

Demographics & Socio-Economic Characteristics
(2000 U.S. Census, except as noted)

Population
1980*	47,792
1990*	45,061
2000	47,683
Male	22,695
Female	24,988
2004 (estimate)*	46,793
Persons per sq. mi. of land	8,794

Race & Hispanic Origin, 2000
Race
White	33,421
Black/African American	5,573
Amer. Indian/Alaska Natv.	91
Asian	3,998
Natv. Hawaiian/Pac. Islander	31
Other Race	3,061
Two or more races	1,508
Hispanic origin, total	6,901
Mexican	160
Puerto Rican	2,724
Cuban	377
Other Hispanic	3,640

Age & Nativity, 2000
Under 5 years	2,820
18 years and over	37,644
21 years and over	36,087
65 years and over	6,827
85 years and over	871
Median Age	37.1
Native born	36,791
Foreign born	10,892

Educational Attainment, 2000
Population 25 years and over	33,673
0-8 yrs of school	6.1%
High School grad or higher	83.5%
Bachelor's degree or higher	31.8%
Graduate degree	9.9%

Income & Poverty, 1999
Per capita income	$26,049
Median household income	$53,289
Median family income	$64,945
Persons in poverty	2,772
H'holds receiving public assistance	339
H'holds receiving social security	5,146

Households, 2000
Total households	19,017
With persons under 18	5,796
With persons over 65	5,034
Family households	12,069
One-person households	5,789
Persons per household	2.49
Persons per family	3.16

Labor & Employment
Total civilian labor force, 2004**	23,745
Unemployment rate	3.7%
Total civilian labor force, 2000	26,092
Unemployment rate	5.1%

Employed persons 16 years and over by occupation, 2000
Managers & professionals	9,624
Service occupations	2,968
Sales & office occupations	7,522
Farming, fishing & forestry	15
Construction & maintenance	1,635
Production & transportation	3,006
Self-employed persons	840

*US Census Bureau
**New Jersey Department of Labor

General Information
Township of Bloomfield
Municipal Plaza
Bloomfield, NJ 07003
973-680-4000
Web site	www.bloomfieldtwpnj.com
Land area (sq. miles)	5.32
Water area (sq. miles)	0.01
Type of government	Township
Form of government	SC

Government

Legislative Districts
US Congressional	8
State Legislative	28

Local Officials, 2006
Mayor	Raymond J. McCarthy
Admin/Manager	Louise M. Palagano
Clerk	Louise M. Palagano
Finance Dir/Treas	Wayne Hartmann
Engineer	Paul Lasek
Attorney	Vincent A. Pirone
Tax assessor	Joseph Pisauro
Tax collector	Cindy Prochilo
Building officer	Carl Graziano
Zoning officer	NA
Public Works	NA

Housing & Construction

Housing Units, 2000*
Total	19,508
Median rent	$768
Median SF home value	$164,800

New Privately Owned Housing Units Authorized by Building Permit
	Units	Value
Total, 2004	24	$2,406,000
Single family	8	$1,010,000
Total, 2005	1	$153,600
Single family	1	$153,600

Real Property Valuation - parcels, 2005
	Number	Valuation
Total		$2,097,683,400
Vacant	132	8,101,600
Residential	11,644	1,631,317,800
Commercial	671	305,583,000
Industrial	54	42,867,200
Apartments	88	109,813,800
Farm land	0	0
Farm homestead	0	0

Average Property Value & Tax, 2005
Residential value	$140,099
Property tax	$6,706
FAIR rebate	$594

Public Library
Bloomfield Public Library
90 Broad St
Bloomfield, NJ 07003
973-566-6200
Director	Gian Hasija

Library statistics, 2004
	Total	per capita
Volumes	150,444	3.16
Expenditure	$1,280,929	$26.86

Public Safety
Police
Chief	Michael A.Sisco
Number of officers, 2004	125

Crime, 2004	Number	Rate
Total	2,128	45.1
Violent	192	4.1
Non-violent	1,936	41
Domestic Viol.	110	NA

Emergency/Fire
Director	Joseph Intile

Public School District
(for school year 2004-2005 except as noted)
Bloomfield Township School District
155 Broad St
Bloomfield, NJ 07003
973-680-8501
Superintendent	Thomas Dowd
Grade plan	K-12
Enrollment	6,035.0
Students per teacher	11.9
Per pupil expenditure	$9,891
Median faculty salary	$48,331
Median administrator salary	$99,710
Grade 12 enrollment	412.0
High school graduation rate	88.1%

Assessment test results
(percent scoring at proficient or advanced level)
	Language	Math
Grade 3	86.7%	85.8%
Grade 8	59.9%	48.4%
High school	77.2%	65.4%

SAT
Percent tested	77%
Average SAT math score	486
Average SAT verbal score	476

No Child Left Behind, 2003-04
Attendence rate (target = 90%)	94.0%
Drop rate	2.9%
Highly-qualified teachers	95.1%
District needs improvement?(AYP)	No

Municipal Finance

Fiscal Year 2005
Total tax levy	$100,593,744
County levy	17,783,981
County taxes	17,411,727
County library	0
County health	0
County open space	372,254
School levy	48,148,077
Local muni. budget	34,661,686
Misc. revenues	19,518,128
Total aid	$8,296,692
CMPTRA	5,524,959
Muni. block grant	197,172
Energy tax receipts	2,434,561
Homeland security	140,000

Fiscal Year 2006
Total aid	$8,296,692
CMPTRA	5,439,749
Muni. block grant	197,172
Energy tax receipts	2,519,771
Homeland security	140,000

Taxes
	2003	2004	2005
General tax rate per $100	4.23	4.580	4.790
Net valuation taxable	$2,094,444,200	$2,100,582,200	$2,101,703,005
State equalized value	$3,236,662,340	$3,670,752,925	$4,277,840,434
County equalization ratio	75.66	75.66	57.17

Demographics & Socio-Economic Characteristics
(2000 U.S. Census, except as noted)

Population
1980*	7,867
1990*	7,530
2000	7,610
Male	3,763
Female	3,847
2004 (estimate)*	7,699
Persons per sq. mi. of land	875

Race & Hispanic Origin, 2000
Race
White	7,271
Black/African American	32
Amer. Indian/Alaska Natv.	9
Asian	167
Natv. Hawaiian/Pac. Islander	0
Other Race	51
Two or more races	80
Hispanic origin, total	332
Mexican	93
Puerto Rican	100
Cuban	21
Other Hispanic	118

Age & Nativity, 2000
Under 5 years	509
18 years and over	5,914
21 years and over	5,698
65 years and over	903
85 years and over	117
Median Age	37.9
Native born	6,839
Foreign born	771

Educational Attainment, 2000
Population 25 years and over	5,442
0-8 yrs of school	3.4%
High School grad or higher	87.6%
Bachelor's degree or higher	25.7%
Graduate degree	7.7%

Income & Poverty, 1999
Per capita income	$27,736
Median household income	$67,885
Median family income	$75,433
Persons in poverty	251
H'holds receiving public assistance	46
H'holds receiving social security	604

Households, 2000
Total households	2,847
With persons under 18	974
With persons over 65	583
Family households	2,077
One-person households	623
Persons per household	2.63
Persons per family	3.09

Labor & Employment
Total civilian labor force, 2004**	4,644
Unemployment rate	3.3%
Total civilian labor force, 2000	4,546
Unemployment rate	3.1%

Employed persons 16 years and over by occupation, 2000
Managers & professionals	1,649
Service occupations	589
Sales & office occupations	1,243
Farming, fishing & forestry	0
Construction & maintenance	325
Production & transportation	599
Self-employed persons	206

*US Census Bureau
**New Jersey Department of Labor

General Information
Borough of Bloomingdale
101 Hamburg Turnpike
Bloomingdale, NJ 07403
973-838-0778
Web site	www.bloomingdalenj.org
Land area (sq. miles)	8.80
Water area (sq. miles)	0.41
Type of government	Borough
Form of government	B

Government

Legislative Districts
US Congressional	5, 11
State Legislative	26

Local Officials, 2006
Mayor	Craig Ollenschleger
Admin/Manager	Ted Ehrenburg
Clerk	Jane McCarthy
Finance Dir/Treas	Beverly Allen-Miller
Engineer	James Floystrop
Attorney	Joseph MacMahon
Tax assessor	Brian Townsend
Tax collector	Dale Mathews
Building officer	Daniel Hagberg
Zoning officer	Daniel Hagberg
Public Works	Joseph Luke

Housing & Construction

Housing Units, 2000*
Total	2,940
Median rent	$899
Median SF home value	$177,000

New Privately Owned Housing Units
Authorized by Building Permit
	Units	Value
Total, 2004	2	$220,000
Single family	2	$220,000
Total, 2005	2	$566,920
Single family	2	$566,920

Real Property Valuation - parcels, 2005
	Number	Valuation
Total		$421,039,799
Vacant	136	13,450,200
Residential	2,468	361,954,500
Commercial	100	33,637,500
Industrial	1	6,000
Apartments	8	11,573,000
Farm land	2	348,200
Farm homestead	15	70,399

Average Property Value & Tax, 2005
Residential value	$145,801
Property tax	$6,672
FAIR rebate	$560

Public Library
Bloomingdale Public Library
101 Hamburg Tpke
Bloomingdale, NJ 07403
973-838-0077
Director	Theresa Rubin

Library statistics, 2004
	Total	per capita
Volumes	24,543	3.23
Expenditure	$282,226	$37.09

Public Safety

Police
Chief	William Alexander
Number of officers, 2004	16

Crime, 2004	Number	Rate
Total	94	12.2
Violent	3	0.4
Non-violent	91	11.8
Domestic Viol.	75	NA

Emergency/Fire
Director	Barry Marciano

Public School District
(for school year 2004-2005 except as noted)

Bloomingdale School District
Captolene Ave
Bloomingdale, NJ 07403
973-838-3282
Administrator	Thomas W. Comiciotto
Grade plan	K-12
Enrollment	675.0
Students per teacher	10.2
Per pupil expenditure	$13,345
Median faculty salary	$48,315
Median administrator salary	$105,000
Grade 12 enrollment	NA
High school graduation rate	NA

Assessment test results
(percent scoring at proficient or advanced level)
	Language	Math
Grade 3	86.2%	86.2%
Grade 8	76.2%	70.4%
High school	NA	NA

SAT
Percent tested	NA
Average SAT math score	NA
Average SAT verbal score	NA

No Child Left Behind, 2003-04
Attendence rate (target = 90%)	94.8%
Drop rate	NA
Highly-qualified teachers	100%
District needs improvement?(AYP)	No

Municipal Finance

Fiscal Year 2005
Total tax levy	$19,285,687
County levy	4,047,205
County taxes	3,970,247
County library	0
County health	0
County open space	76,958
School levy	10,501,688
Local muni. budget	4,736,794
Misc. revenues	2,782,872
Total aid	$863,579
CMPTRA	392,485
Muni. block grant	32,949
Energy tax receipts	388,145
Homeland security	50,000

Fiscal Year 2006
Total aid	$863,579
CMPTRA	378,900
Muni. block grant	32,949
Energy tax receipts	401,730
Homeland security	50,000

Taxes
	2003	2004	2005
General tax rate per $100	4.22	4.390	4.580
Net valuation taxable	$420,341,205	$420,289,781	$421,434,459
State equalized value	$670,507,585	$765,037,442	$861,124,763
County equalization ratio	69.56	62.69	54.91

Demographics & Socio-Economic Characteristics
(2000 U.S. Census, except as noted)

Population
1980*	864
1990*	890
2000	886
Male	427
Female	459
2004 (estimate)*	894
Persons per sq. mi. of land	984

Race & Hispanic Origin, 2000
Race
White	870
Black/African American	3
Amer. Indian/Alaska Natv.	2
Asian	3
Natv. Hawaiian/Pac. Islander	0
Other Race	1
Two or more races	7
Hispanic origin, total	13
Mexican	1
Puerto Rican	2
Cuban	2
Other Hispanic	8

Age & Nativity, 2000
Under 5 years	102
18 years and over	622
21 years and over	605
65 years and over	89
85 years and over	7
Median Age	35.5
Native born	861
Foreign born	25

Educational Attainment, 2000
Population 25 years and over	581
0-8 yrs of school	0.9%
High School grad or higher	93.6%
Bachelor's degree or higher	33.0%
Graduate degree	11.7%

Income & Poverty, 1999
Per capita income	$26,392
Median household income	$64,375
Median family income	$67,500
Persons in poverty	34
H'holds receiving public assistance	4
H'holds receiving social security	64

Households, 2000
Total households	322
With persons under 18	151
With persons over 65	62
Family households	252
One-person households	51
Persons per household	2.74
Persons per family	3.11

Labor & Employment
Total civilian labor force, 2004**	536
Unemployment rate	5.1%
Total civilian labor force, 2000	472
Unemployment rate	3.2%

Employed persons 16 years and over by occupation, 2000
Managers & professionals	185
Service occupations	66
Sales & office occupations	116
Farming, fishing & forestry	0
Construction & maintenance	56
Production & transportation	34
Self-employed persons	31

*US Census Bureau
**New Jersey Department of Labor

General Information
Borough of Bloomsbury
91 Brunswick Ave
Bloomsbury, NJ 08804
908-479-4200

Web site	NA
Land area (sq. miles)	0.91
Water area (sq. miles)	0
Type of government	Borough
Form of government	B

Government

Legislative Districts
US Congressional	7
State Legislative	23

Local Officials, 2006
Mayor	Mark R. Peck
Admin/Manager	NA
Clerk	Lisa A. Burd
Finance Dir/Treas	Kim Francisco
Engineer	Robert Zederbaum
Attorney	William Edleston
Tax assessor	Eloise Hagaman
Tax collector	NA
Building officer	NA
Zoning officer	Bob Shortell
Public Works	NA

Housing & Construction

Housing Units, 2000*
Total	342
Median rent	$875
Median SF home value	$172,800

New Privately Owned Housing Units Authorized by Building Permit
	Units	Value
Total, 2004	0	$0
Single family	0	$0
Total, 2005	1	$168,000
Single family	1	$168,000

Real Property Valuation - parcels, 2005
	Number	Valuation
Total		$59,168,000
Vacant	39	386,100
Residential	316	46,506,100
Commercial	15	8,559,300
Industrial	5	2,450,100
Apartments	3	724,300
Farm land	2	426,400
Farm homestead	7	115,700

Average Property Value & Tax, 2005
Residential value	$144,340
Property tax	$4,862
FAIR rebate	$525

Public Library
No public municipal library.

Library statistics, 2004
	Total	per capita
Volumes	NA	NA
Expenditure	NA	NA

Public Safety

Police
Chief	NA
Number of officers, 2004	0

Crime, 2004	Number	Rate
Total	33	36.7
Violent	7	7.8
Non-violent	26	28.9
Domestic Viol.	4	NA

Emergency/Fire
Director	Jim Wyant

Public School District
(for school year 2004-2005 except as noted)

Bloomsbury School District
20 Main St
Bloomsbury, NJ 08804
908-479-4414

Administrator	Michael Slattery
Grade plan	K-12
Enrollment	154.0
Students per teacher	9.5
Per pupil expenditure	$10,785
Median faculty salary	$39,573
Median administrator salary	$72,500
Grade 12 enrollment	NA
High school graduation rate	NA

Assessment test results
(percent scoring at proficient or advanced level)
	Language	Math
Grade 3	90.5%	85.8%
Grade 8	78.5%	78.6%
High school	NA	NA

SAT
Percent tested	NA
Average SAT math score	NA
Average SAT verbal score	NA

No Child Left Behind, 2003-04
Attendence rate (target = 90%)	95.4%
Drop rate	NA
Highly-qualified teachers	100%
District needs improvement?(AYP)	No

Municipal Finance

Fiscal Year 2005
Total tax levy	$1,997,662
County levy	374,552
County taxes	318,018
County library	26,609
County health	0
County open space	29,925
School levy	1,371,065
Local muni. budget	252,045
Misc. revenues	402,155
Total aid	$87,213
CMPTRA	43,651
Muni. block grant	3,894
Energy tax receipts	39,668
Homeland security	0

Fiscal Year 2006
Total aid	$87,214
CMPTRA	42,263
Muni. block grant	3,894
Energy tax receipts	41,057
Homeland security	NA

Taxes
	2003	2004	2005
General tax rate per $100	3.16	3.280	3.370
Net valuation taxable	$58,639,883	$59,087,094	$59,307,022
State equalized value	$78,301,353	$88,853,208	$100,299,378
County equalization ratio	75.81	71.73	59.87

Demographics & Socio-Economic Characteristics
(2000 U.S. Census, except as noted)

Population
1980*	8,344
1990*	7,824
2000	8,249
Male	3,917
Female	4,332
2004 (estimate)*	8,208
Persons per sq. mi. of land	10,787

Race & Hispanic Origin, 2000
Race
White	6,246
Black/African American	473
Amer. Indian/Alaska Natv.	12
Asian	639
Natv. Hawaiian/Pac. Islander	5
Other Race	558
Two or more races	316
Hispanic origin, total	1,759
Mexican	83
Puerto Rican	422
Cuban	220
Other Hispanic	1,034

Age & Nativity, 2000
Under 5 years	538
18 years and over	6,161
21 years and over	5,891
65 years and over	915
85 years and over	93
Median Age	36.5
Native born	6,437
Foreign born	1,812

Educational Attainment, 2000
Population 25 years and over	5,542
0-8 yrs of school	5.0%
High School grad or higher	84.4%
Bachelor's degree or higher	28.4%
Graduate degree	9.2%

Income & Poverty, 1999
Per capita income	$25,505
Median household income	$59,813
Median family income	$69,841
Persons in poverty	331
H'holds receiving public assistance	68
H'holds receiving social security	647

Households, 2000
Total households	2,874
With persons under 18	1,129
With persons over 65	694
Family households	2,126
One-person households	628
Persons per household	2.85
Persons per family	3.38

Labor & Employment
Total civilian labor force, 2004**	4,722
Unemployment rate	5.4%
Total civilian labor force, 2000	4,585
Unemployment rate	6.7%

Employed persons 16 years and over by occupation, 2000
Managers & professionals	1,471
Service occupations	637
Sales & office occupations	1,377
Farming, fishing & forestry	0
Construction & maintenance	372
Production & transportation	422
Self-employed persons	132

*US Census Bureau
**New Jersey Department of Labor

General Information
Borough of Bogota
375 Larch Ave
Bogota, NJ 07603
201-342-1736

Web site	www.bogota.nj.us
Land area (sq. miles)	0.76
Water area (sq. miles)	0.06
Type of government	Borough
Form of government	B

Government
Legislative Districts
US Congressional	9
State Legislative	37

Local Officials, 2006
Mayor	Steve Lonegan
Admin/Manager	Patrick O'Brien
Clerk	Fran Garlicki
Finance Dir/Treas	Helen Hegel (Treas)
Engineer	Kenneth Job
Attorney	Andrew Fede
Tax assessor	Dick Mohr
Tax collector	Betty Wiemer
Building officer	Daniel Howell
Zoning officer	NA
Public Works	Don Viviani

Housing & Construction
Housing Units, 2000*
Total	2,915
Median rent	$819
Median SF home value	$166,700

New Privately Owned Housing Units Authorized by Building Permit
	Units	Value
Total, 2004	0	$0
Single family	0	$0
Total, 2005	5	$765,700
Single family	5	$765,700

Real Property Valuation - parcels, 2005
	Number	Valuation
Total		$472,083,780
Vacant	53	2,908,400
Residential	2,018	393,657,680
Commercial	90	35,919,100
Industrial	13	14,862,100
Apartments	25	24,736,500
Farm land	0	0
Farm homestead	0	0

Average Property Value & Tax, 2005
Residential value	$195,073
Property tax	$6,418
FAIR rebate	$566

Public Library
Bogota Public Library
375 Larch Ave
Bogota, NJ 07603
201-488-7185

Director	Jonna Davis

Library statistics, 2004
	Total	per capita
Volumes	34,777	4.22
Expenditure	$172,600	$20.92

Public Safety
Police
Chief	Frank Gurnari
Number of officers, 2004	14

Crime, 2004	Number	Rate
Total	126	15.4
Violent	16	2
Non-violent	110	13.4
Domestic Viol.	49	NA

Emergency/Fire
Director	Anthony Culmone

Public School District
(for school year 2004-2005 except as noted)

Bogota School District
1 Henry C. Luthin Place
Bogota, NJ 07603
201-441-4800

Superintendent	José R. Negrón
Grade plan	K-12
Enrollment	1,115.0
Students per teacher	11.2
Per pupil expenditure	$12,492
Median faculty salary	$48,577
Median administrator salary	$95,000
Grade 12 enrollment	60.0
High school graduation rate	98.3%

Assessment test results
(percent scoring at proficient or advanced level)
	Language	Math
Grade 3	85.7%	87.0%
Grade 8	74.7%	64.5%
High school	87.5%	82.5%

SAT
Percent tested	72%
Average SAT math score	466
Average SAT verbal score	475

No Child Left Behind, 2003-04
Attendence rate (target = 90%)	95.9%
Drop rate	0%
Highly-qualified teachers	95.7%
District needs improvement?(AYP)	No

Municipal Finance
Fiscal Year 2005
Total tax levy	$15,548,654
County levy	1,352,401
County taxes	1,284,712
County library	0
County health	0
County open space	67,689
School levy	9,883,924
Local muni. budget	4,312,329
Misc. revenues	2,260,278
Total aid	$1,088,166
CMPTRA	610,568
Muni. block grant	34,235
Energy tax receipts	393,363
Homeland security	50,000

Fiscal Year 2006
Total aid	$1,088,166
CMPTRA	596,800
Muni. block grant	34,235
Energy tax receipts	407,131
Homeland security	50,000

Taxes
	2003	2004	2005
General tax rate per $100	3.09	3.290	3.290
Net valuation taxable	$469,650,157	$471,549,984	$472,605,507
State equalized value	$580,173,140	$665,909,297	$749,334,877
County equalization ratio	91.9	80.95	70.79

Demographics & Socio-Economic Characteristics
(2000 U.S. Census, except as noted)

Population
1980*	8,620
1990*	8,343
2000	8,496
Male	4,214
Female	4,282
2004 (estimate)*	8,468
Persons per sq. mi. of land	3,608

Race & Hispanic Origin, 2000
Race
White	7,052
Black/African American	337
Amer. Indian/Alaska Natv.	18
Asian	660
Natv. Hawaiian/Pac. Islander	1
Other Race	187
Two or more races	241
Hispanic origin, total	582
Mexican	46
Puerto Rican	140
Cuban	19
Other Hispanic	377

Age & Nativity, 2000
Under 5 years	621
18 years and over	6,633
21 years and over	6,418
65 years and over	1,147
85 years and over	158
Median Age	36.9
Native born	7,112
Foreign born	1,384

Educational Attainment, 2000
Population 25 years and over	6,081
0-8 yrs of school	6.4%
High School grad or higher	86.1%
Bachelor's degree or higher	32.9%
Graduate degree	9.4%

Income & Poverty, 1999
Per capita income	$29,919
Median household income	$65,322
Median family income	$75,147
Persons in poverty	559
H'holds receiving public assistance	94
H'holds receiving social security	865

Households, 2000
Total households	3,272
With persons under 18	1,000
With persons over 65	813
Family households	2,159
One-person households	861
Persons per household	2.55
Persons per family	3.11

Labor & Employment
Total civilian labor force, 2004**	5,246
Unemployment rate	4.3%
Total civilian labor force, 2000	4,792
Unemployment rate	6.0%

Employed persons 16 years and over by occupation, 2000
Managers & professionals	1,845
Service occupations	515
Sales & office occupations	1,265
Farming, fishing & forestry	0
Construction & maintenance	327
Production & transportation	552
Self-employed persons	181

*US Census Bureau
**New Jersey Department of Labor

General Information
Town of Boonton
100 Washington St
Boonton, NJ 07005
973-402-9410

Web site	www.boonton.org
Land area (sq. miles)	2.35
Water area (sq. miles)	0.12
Type of government	Town
Form of government	T

Government

Legislative Districts
US Congressional	11
State Legislative	25

Local Officials, 2006
Mayor	Cyril Wekilsky
Admin/Manager	John Arntz
Clerk	Cynthia Oravits
Finance Dir/Treas	Jeffery Theriault
Engineer	John Miller
Attorney	John Dorsey
Tax assessor	Paul Parsons
Tax collector	NA
Building officer	Russell Heiney
Zoning officer	NA
Public Works	NA

Housing & Construction

Housing Units, 2000*
Total	3,352
Median rent	$897
Median SF home value	$212,000

New Privately Owned Housing Units Authorized by Building Permit
	Units	Value
Total, 2004	NA	NA
Single family	NA	NA
Total, 2005	31	$3,041,612
Single family	31	$3,041,612

Real Property Valuation - parcels, 2005
	Number	Valuation
Total		$560,399,400
Vacant	113	4,983,300
Residential	2,321	428,864,100
Commercial	196	80,196,900
Industrial	39	35,995,800
Apartments	15	10,138,900
Farm land	1	218,700
Farm homestead	1	1,700

Average Property Value & Tax, 2005
Residential value	$184,697
Property tax	$6,111
FAIR rebate	$597

Public Library
Boonton-Holmes Library
621 Main St
Boonton, NJ 07005
973-334-2980

Director.............Joy Ellen Kauffman

Library statistics, 2004
	Total	per capita
Volumes	40,940	4.82
Expenditure	$298,140	$35.09

Public Safety

Police
Chief	Michael Beltran
Number of officers, 2004	22

Crime, 2004	Number	Rate
Total	91	10.8
Violent	16	1.9
Non-violent	75	8.9
Domestic Viol.	78	NA

Emergency/Fire
Director....................James Wendt

Public School District
(for school year 2004-2005 except as noted)

Boonton Town School District
434 Lathrop Ave
Boonton, NJ 07005
973-335-3994

Superintendent	Mario Cardinale
Grade plan	K-12
Enrollment	1,295.5
Students per teacher	8.9
Per pupil expenditure	$12,257
Median faculty salary	$47,750
Median administrator salary	$108,915
Grade 12 enrollment	144.5
High school graduation rate	97.0%

Assessment test results
(percent scoring at proficient or advanced level)
	Language	Math
Grade 3	89.9%	92.6%
Grade 8	77.0%	58.1%
High school	79.5%	74.7%

SAT
Percent tested	82%
Average SAT math score	507
Average SAT verbal score	488

No Child Left Behind, 2003-04
Attendence rate (target = 90%)	95.2%
Drop rate	0.8%
Highly-qualified teachers	96.8%
District needs improvement?(AYP)	No

Municipal Finance

Fiscal Year 2005
Total tax levy	$18,704,753
County levy	2,635,386
County taxes	2,158,739
County library	0
County health	0
County open space	476,648
School levy	11,211,617
Local muni. budget	4,857,750
Misc. revenues	4,345,114
Total aid	$1,437,514
CMPTRA	820,256
Muni. block grant	36,506
Energy tax receipts	524,219
Homeland security	50,000

Fiscal Year 2006
Total aid	$1,437,514
CMPTRA	801,908
Muni. block grant	36,506
Energy tax receipts	542,567
Homeland security	50,000

Taxes
	2003	2004	2005
General tax rate per $100	2.88	3.100	3.310
Net valuation taxable	$553,615,492	$561,004,927	$565,312,920
State equalized value	$853,554,567	$966,956,735	$1,132,437,740
County equalization ratio	76	64.86	57.79

Demographics & Socio-Economic Characteristics
(2000 U.S. Census, except as noted)

Population
1980*	3,273
1990*	3,566
2000	4,287
Male	2,128
Female	2,159
2004 (estimate)*	4,359
Persons per sq. mi. of land	517

Race & Hispanic Origin, 2000
Race
White	3,987
Black/African American	51
Amer. Indian/Alaska Natv.	2
Asian	175
Natv. Hawaiian/Pac. Islander	0
Other Race	27
Two or more races	45
Hispanic origin, total	92
Mexican	11
Puerto Rican	34
Cuban	7
Other Hispanic	40

Age & Nativity, 2000
Under 5 years	247
18 years and over	3,221
21 years and over	3,124
65 years and over	638
85 years and over	99
Median Age	41.6
Native born	3,932
Foreign born	355

Educational Attainment, 2000
Population 25 years and over	3,047
0-8 yrs of school	1.6%
High School grad or higher	93.1%
Bachelor's degree or higher	45.9%
Graduate degree	17.0%

Income & Poverty, 1999
Per capita income	$45,014
Median household income	$91,753
Median family income	$102,944
Persons in poverty	55
H'holds receiving public assistance	11
H'holds receiving social security	340

Households, 2000
Total households	1,476
With persons under 18	567
With persons over 65	383
Family households	1,157
One-person households	258
Persons per household	2.78
Persons per family	3.18

Labor & Employment
Total civilian labor force, 2004**	2,069
Unemployment rate	2.9%
Total civilian labor force, 2000	2,198
Unemployment rate	3.0%

Employed persons 16 years and over by occupation, 2000
Managers & professionals	1,163
Service occupations	133
Sales & office occupations	615
Farming, fishing & forestry	0
Construction & maintenance	133
Production & transportation	88
Self-employed persons	204

*US Census Bureau
**New Jersey Department of Labor

General Information
Township of Boonton
155 Powerville Rd
Boonton, NJ 07005
973-402-4002
Web site	www.boontontownship.com
Land area (sq. miles)	8.42
Water area (sq. miles)	0.16
Type of government	Township
Form of government	TC

Government

Legislative Districts
US Congressional	11
State Legislative	25

Local Officials, 2006
Mayor	Douglas Spender
Admin/Manager	Barbara Shepard
Clerk	Barbara Shepard
Finance Dir/Treas	Norman Eckstein
Engineer	Lincoln H. Edwards
Attorney	John P. Jansen
Tax assessor	Anthony Scozzafava
Tax collector	Norman Eckstein
Building officer	Edward Bucceri
Zoning officer	Edward Bucceri
Public Works	NA

Housing & Construction

Housing Units, 2000*
Total	1,510
Median rent	$1,077
Median SF home value	$322,600

New Privately Owned Housing Units
Authorized by Building Permit
	Units	Value
Total, 2004	12	$4,415,613
Single family	12	$4,415,613
Total, 2005	16	$5,498,376
Single family	16	$5,498,376

Real Property Valuation - parcels, 2005
	Number	Valuation
Total		$514,553,321
Vacant	149	12,281,800
Residential	1,484	471,876,321
Commercial	10	8,049,800
Industrial	7	9,487,200
Apartments	1	183,800
Farm land	31	12,336,700
Farm homestead	46	337,700

Average Property Value & Tax, 2005
Residential value	$308,637
Property tax	$8,616
FAIR rebate	$563

Public Library
No public municipal library.

Library statistics, 2004
	Total	per capita
Volumes	NA	NA
Expenditure	NA	NA

Public Safety

Police
Chief	John Speirs
Number of officers, 2004	12

Crime, 2004	Number	Rate
Total	29	6.7
Violent	1	0.2
Non-violent	28	6.5
Domestic Viol.	27	NA

Emergency/Fire
Director	Scott Para

Public School District
(for school year 2004-2005 except as noted)

Boonton Township School District
11 Valley Rd
Boonton Township, NJ 07005
973-334-4162
Superintendent	Roseann Humphrey
Grade plan	K-12
Enrollment	506.0
Students per teacher	11.2
Per pupil expenditure	$12,448
Median faculty salary	$61,346
Median administrator salary	$100,800
Grade 12 enrollment	NA
High school graduation rate	NA

Assessment test results
(percent scoring at proficient or advanced level)
	Language	Math
Grade 3	93.1%	96.6%
Grade 8	85.7%	77.8%
High school	NA	NA

SAT
Percent tested	NA
Average SAT math score	NA
Average SAT verbal score	NA

No Child Left Behind, 2003-04
Attendence rate (target = 90%)	96.4%
Drop rate	NA
Highly-qualified teachers	90.1%
District needs improvement?(AYP)	No

Municipal Finance

Fiscal Year 2005
Total tax levy	$14,380,859
County levy	2,222,822
County taxes	1,820,806
County library	0
County health	0
County open space	402,016
School levy	9,618,722
Local muni. budget	2,539,315
Misc. revenues	1,756,719
Total aid	$396,049
CMPTRA	148,961
Muni. block grant	16,809
Energy tax receipts	205,279
Homeland security	25,000

Fiscal Year 2006
Total aid	$396,049
CMPTRA	141,776
Muni. block grant	16,809
Energy tax receipts	212,464
Homeland security	25,000

Taxes
	2003	2004	2005
General tax rate per $100	2.46	2.660	2.800
Net valuation taxable	$496,881,975	$504,831,127	$515,119,321
State equalized value	$731,246,468	$816,205,159	$924,478,322
County equalization ratio	74.86	67.95	61.82

Demographics & Socio-Economic Characteristics
(2000 U.S. Census, except as noted)

Population
1980*	4,441
1990*	4,341
2000	3,969
Male	1,881
Female	2,088
2004 (estimate)*	4,010
Persons per sq. mi. of land	4,348

Race & Hispanic Origin, 2000
Race
White	3,225
Black/African American	519
Amer. Indian/Alaska Natv.	2
Asian	76
Natv. Hawaiian/Pac. Islander	1
Other Race	32
Two or more races	114
Hispanic origin, total	112
Mexican	6
Puerto Rican	67
Cuban	5
Other Hispanic	34

Age & Nativity, 2000
Under 5 years	204
18 years and over	3,139
21 years and over	3,019
65 years and over	556
85 years and over	71
Median Age	37.9
Native born	3,896
Foreign born	73

Educational Attainment, 2000
Population 25 years and over	2,837
0-8 yrs of school	3.2%
High School grad or higher	85.7%
Bachelor's degree or higher	26.7%
Graduate degree	7.8%

Income & Poverty, 1999
Per capita income	$25,882
Median household income	$47,279
Median family income	$59,872
Persons in poverty	266
H'holds receiving public assistance	32
H'holds receiving social security	413

Households, 2000
Total households	1,757
With persons under 18	482
With persons over 65	420
Family households	990
One-person households	627
Persons per household	2.23
Persons per family	2.93

Labor & Employment
Total civilian labor force, 2004**	2,856
Unemployment rate	2.4%
Total civilian labor force, 2000	2,352
Unemployment rate	3.8%

Employed persons 16 years and over by occupation, 2000
Managers & professionals	763
Service occupations	412
Sales & office occupations	677
Farming, fishing & forestry	0
Construction & maintenance	192
Production & transportation	219
Self-employed persons	169

*US Census Bureau
**New Jersey Department of Labor

General Information
City of Bordentown
324 Farnsworth Ave
Bordentown, NJ 08505
609-298-0604

Web site	NA
Land area (sq. miles)	0.92
Water area (sq. miles)	0.05
Type of government	City
Form of government	Comm.

Government

Legislative Districts
US Congressional	4
State Legislative	30

Local Officials, 2006
Mayor	John W. Collom
Admin/Manager	NA
Clerk	Patricia Ryan
Finance Dir/Treas	Patricia Ryan
Engineer	BCM Engineers
Attorney	Richard Hunt
Tax assessor	William Tantum
Tax collector	NA
Building officer	Dept. Comm. Affairs
Zoning officer	NA
Public Works	NA

Housing & Construction

Housing Units, 2000*
Total	1,884
Median rent	$736
Median SF home value	$110,200

New Privately Owned Housing Units
Authorized by Building Permit
	Units	Value
Total, 2004	4	$440,000
Single family	4	$440,000
Total, 2005	0	$0
Single family	0	$0

Real Property Valuation - parcels, 2005
	Number	Valuation
Total		$187,894,060
Vacant	78	2,812,200
Residential	1,189	126,472,260
Commercial	111	26,148,700
Industrial	7	18,479,700
Apartments	21	13,981,200
Farm land	0	0
Farm homestead	0	0

Average Property Value & Tax, 2005
Residential value	$106,369
Property tax	$4,574
FAIR rebate	$570

Public Library
Bordentown Branch Library†
18 E Union St
Bordentown, NJ 08505
609-298-0622

Branch Librarian	Isabelle Addis

Library statistics, 2004
	Total	per capita
Volumes	NA	NA
Expenditure	NA	NA

†Branch of County Library

Public Safety

Police
Chief	Matthew J. Simmons III
Number of officers, 2004	10

Crime, 2004	Number	Rate
Total	67	16.7
Violent	7	1.7
Non-violent	60	15
Domestic Viol.	19	NA

Emergency/Fire
Director	Brian Ferguson

Public School District
(for school year 2004-2005 except as noted)

Bordentown Regional School District
48 Dunns Mill Rd
Bordentown, NJ 08505
609-298-0025
Superintendent	John Polomano
Grade plan	K-12
Enrollment	2,042.5
Students per teacher	10.8
Per pupil expenditure	$11,701
Median faculty salary	$50,290
Median administrator salary	$82,774
Grade 12 enrollment	140.0
High school graduation rate	96.3%

Assessment test results
(percent scoring at proficient or advanced level)
	Language	Math
Grade 3	87.5%	87.5%
Grade 8	76.4%	68.5%
High school	84.4%	74.9%

SAT
Percent tested	80%
Average SAT math score	515
Average SAT verbal score	495

No Child Left Behind, 2003-04
Attendence rate (target = 90%)	95.6%
Drop rate	1%
Highly-qualified teachers	98.7%
District needs improvement?(AYP)	No

Municipal Finance

Fiscal Year 2005
Total tax levy	$8,088,710
County levy	1,305,978
County taxes	1,095,577
County library	95,928
County health	0
County open space	114,473
School levy	4,512,598
Local muni. budget	2,270,134
Misc. revenues	2,639,671
Total aid	$579,951
CMPTRA	269,469
Muni. block grant	18,955
Energy tax receipts	266,527
Homeland security	25,000

Fiscal Year 2006
Total aid	$579,950
CMPTRA	260,140
Muni. block grant	18,955
Energy tax receipts	275,855
Homeland security	25,000

Taxes
	2003	2004	2005
General tax rate per $100	3.90	4.083	4.302
Net valuation taxable	$185,193,813	$187,618,093	$188,104,625
State equalized value	$237,915,998	$282,924,743	$303,052,401
County equalization ratio	85.38	77.84	66.28

Demographics & Socio-Economic Characteristics
(2000 U.S. Census, except as noted)

Population
1980*	7,170
1990*	7,683
2000	8,380
Male	4,081
Female	4,299
2004 (estimate)*	9,973
Persons per sq. mi. of land	1,172

Race & Hispanic Origin, 2000
Race
White	7,486
Black/African American	421
Amer. Indian/Alaska Natv.	17
Asian	278
Natv. Hawaiian/Pac. Islander	0
Other Race	57
Two or more races	121
Hispanic origin, total	254
Mexican	15
Puerto Rican	121
Cuban	9
Other Hispanic	109

Age & Nativity, 2000
Under 5 years	556
18 years and over	6,394
21 years and over	6,166
65 years and over	980
85 years and over	73
Median Age	37.6
Native born	7,768
Foreign born	612

Educational Attainment, 2000
Population 25 years and over	5,863
0-8 yrs of school	3.7%
High School grad or higher	87.0%
Bachelor's degree or higher	23.9%
Graduate degree	7.5%

Income & Poverty, 1999
Per capita income	$26,934
Median household income	$60,131
Median family income	$71,627
Persons in poverty	234
H'holds receiving public assistance	18
H'holds receiving social security	808

Households, 2000
Total households	3,293
With persons under 18	1,138
With persons over 65	714
Family households	2,305
One-person households	775
Persons per household	2.53
Persons per family	3.03

Labor & Employment
Total civilian labor force, 2004**	5,185
Unemployment rate	4.7%
Total civilian labor force, 2000	4,833
Unemployment rate	3.4%

Employed persons 16 years and over by occupation, 2000
Managers & professionals	1,622
Service occupations	650
Sales & office occupations	1,567
Farming, fishing & forestry	10
Construction & maintenance	405
Production & transportation	416
Self-employed persons	123

*US Census Bureau
**New Jersey Department of Labor

General Information
Township of Bordentown
Municipal Dr
Bordentown, NJ 08505
609-298-2800
Web site . . . www.bordentowntownship.com	
Land area (sq. miles)	8.51
Water area (sq. miles)	0.77
Type of government	Township
Form of government	TC

Government

Legislative Districts
US Congressional	4
State Legislative	30

Local Officials, 2006
Mayor	Mark Roselli
Admin/Manager	Leonard M. Klepner
Clerk	Colleen Eckert
Finance Dir/Treas	David Kocian
Engineer	Fred Turek
Attorney	Gregory Sullivan
Tax assessor	William Tantum
Tax collector	Mary Picariello
Building officer	Dan McGonigle
Zoning officer	Werner Nitschmann
Public Works	Victor Pangia

Housing & Construction

Housing Units, 2000*
Total	3,436
Median rent	$698
Median SF home value	$136,000

New Privately Owned Housing Units Authorized by Building Permit
	Units	Value
Total, 2004	168	$24,039,131
Single family	168	$24,039,131
Total, 2005	113	$18,428,418
Single family	113	$18,428,418

Real Property Valuation - parcels, 2005
	Number	Valuation
Total		$640,848,140
Vacant	422	51,055,800
Residential	3,188	438,747,050
Commercial	185	114,630,960
Industrial	18	16,937,830
Apartments	6	17,901,800
Farm land	10	1,262,600
Farm homestead	27	312,100

Average Property Value & Tax, 2005
Residential value	$136,566
Property tax	$4,767
FAIR rebate	$542

Public Library

No public municipal library.

Library statistics, 2004
	Total	per capita
Volumes	NA	NA
Expenditure	NA	NA

Public Safety

Police
Chief	Frank Nucera
Number of officers, 2004	23

Crime, 2004	Number	Rate
Total	249	25.8
Violent	13	1.3
Non-violent	236	24.4
Domestic Viol.	53	NA

Emergency/Fire
Director	NA

Public School District
(for school year 2004-2005 except as noted)

Bordentown Regional School District
48 Dunns Mill Rd
Bordentown, NJ 08505
609-298-0025
Superintendent	John Polomano
Grade plan	K-12
Enrollment	2,042.5
Students per teacher	10.8
Per pupil expenditure	$11,701
Median faculty salary	$50,290
Median administrator salary	$82,774
Grade 12 enrollment	140.0
High school graduation rate	96.3%

Assessment test results
(percent scoring at proficient or advanced level)
	Language	Math
Grade 3	87.5%	87.5%
Grade 8	76.4%	68.5%
High school	84.4%	74.9%

SAT
Percent tested	80%
Average SAT math score	515
Average SAT verbal score	495

No Child Left Behind, 2003-04
Attendence rate (target = 90%)	95.6%
Drop rate	1%
Highly-qualified teachers	98.7%
District needs improvement?(AYP)	No

Municipal Finance

Fiscal Year 2005
Total tax levy	$22,469,035
County levy	4,538,951
County taxes	3,807,719
County library	333,383
County health	0
County open space	397,848
School levy	14,874,485
Local muni. budget	3,055,599
Misc. revenues	4,822,558
Total aid	$1,240,364
CMPTRA	495,429
Muni. block grant	33,658
Energy tax receipts	661,277
Homeland security	50,000

Fiscal Year 2006
Total aid	$1,240,363
CMPTRA	472,284
Muni. block grant	33,658
Energy tax receipts	684,421
Homeland security	50,000

Taxes
	2003	2004	2005
General tax rate per $100	3.35	3.543	3.492
Net valuation taxable	$564,263,106	$593,341,036	$643,689,731
State equalized value	$808,052,565	$908,708,009	$1,093,594,514
County equalization ratio	81.25	69.83	65.18

Demographics & Socio-Economic Characteristics
(2000 U.S. Census, except as noted)

Population
1980* 9,710
1990* 9,487
2000 10,155
   Male 5,251
   Female 4,904
2004 (estimate)* 10,174
   Persons per sq. mi. of land 5,965

Race & Hispanic Origin, 2000
Race
   White 8,385
   Black/African American 256
   Amer. Indian/Alaska Natv. 31
   Asian 292
   Natv. Hawaiian/Pac. Islander 7
   Other Race 880
   Two or more races 304
Hispanic origin, total 3,541
   Mexican 706
   Puerto Rican 246
   Cuban 43
   Other Hispanic 2,546

Age & Nativity, 2000
Under 5 years 699
18 years and over 7,950
21 years and over 7,569
65 years and over 1,268
85 years and over 120
Median Age 34.2
Native born 6,535
Foreign born 3,656

Educational Attainment, 2000
Population 25 years and over 7,006
0-8 yrs of school 13.5%
High School grad or higher 75.9%
Bachelor's degree or higher . . . 23.9%
Graduate degree 7.5%

Income & Poverty, 1999
Per capita income $22,395
Median household income $46,858
Median family income $51,346
Persons in poverty 1,109
H'holds receiving public assistance 55
H'holds receiving social security 994

Households, 2000
Total households 3,615
   With persons under 18 1,257
   With persons over 65 931
   Family households 2,461
   One-person households 834
Persons per household 2.81
Persons per family 3.21

Labor & Employment
Total civilian labor force, 2004** 6,872
   Unemployment rate 4.4%
Total civilian labor force, 2000 5,723
   Unemployment rate 4.7%
Employed persons 16 years and over by occupation, 2000
   Managers & professionals 1,406
   Service occupations 1,028
   Sales & office occupations 1,367
   Farming, fishing & forestry 25
   Construction & maintenance 479
   Production & transportation 1,151
Self-employed persons 241

*US Census Bureau
**New Jersey Department of Labor

General Information
Borough of Bound Brook
230 Hamilton St
Bound Brook, NJ 08805
732-356-0833

Web site . . . . NA
Land area (sq. miles) 1.71
Water area (sq. miles) 0
Type of government . . . . Borough
Form of government . . . . .B

Government
Legislative Districts
US Congressional 7
State Legislative 16

Local Officials, 2006
Mayor . . . . Frank Ryan
Admin/Manager . . . . John J.Kennedy
Clerk . . . . Donna Marie Godleski
Finance Dir/Treas . . . . (Vacant)
Engineer . . . . T&M Associates
Attorney . . . . .James O'Donahue
Tax assessor . . . . .Gary Toth
Tax collector . . . . .NA
Building officer . . . . John Kapp
Zoning officer .NA
Public Works .NA

Housing & Construction
Housing Units, 2000*
Total 3,802
Median rent $853
Median SF home value $157,600

New Privately Owned Housing Units Authorized by Building Permit
	Units	Value
Total, 2004	4	$353,500
Single family	4	$353,500
Total, 2005	3	$265,125
Single family	3	$265,125

Real Property Valuation - parcels, 2005
	Number	Valuation
Total		$421,220,900
Vacant	43	2,141,600
Residential	2,302	337,951,400
Commercial	225	59,077,400
Industrial	1	763,300
Apartments	30	21,287,200
Farm land	0	0
Farm homestead	0	0

Average Property Value & Tax, 2005
Residential value $146,808
Property tax $6,607
FAIR rebate $657

Public Library
Bound Brook Memorial Library
402 East High St
Bound Brook, NJ 08805
732-356-0043
Director . . . . Hannah Kerwin

Library statistics, 2004
	Total	per capita
Volumes	67,004	6.60
Expenditure	$579,856	$57.10

Public Safety
Police
Chief . . . . .NA
Number of officers, 2004 22

Crime, 2004	Number	Rate
Total	229	22.6
Violent	13	1.3
Non-violent	216	21.3
Domestic Viol.	261	NA

Emergency/Fire
Director . . . . .James Suk

Public School District
(for school year 2004-2005 except as noted)
Bound Brook Borough School District
West 2nd St
Bound Brook, NJ 08805
732-652-7920
Superintendent . . . . Edward Hoffman
Grade plan K-12
Enrollment .1,569.0
Students per teacher 11.0
Per pupil expenditure $11,049
Median faculty salary $50,190
Median administrator salary $93,197
Grade 12 enrollment 111.0
High school graduation rate 95.5%

Assessment test results
(percent scoring at proficient or advanced level)
	Language	Math
Grade 3	82.6%	66.0%
Grade 8	41.4%	40.8%
High school	72.3%	56.9%

SAT
Percent tested 61%
Average SAT math score 468
Average SAT verbal score 468

No Child Left Behind, 2003-04
Attendence rate (target = 90%) 94.5%
Drop rate 2%
Highly-qualified teachers 88%
District needs improvement?(AYP) . . . . . No

Municipal Finance
Fiscal Year 2005
Total tax levy $19,176,388
   County levy 2,303,410
   County taxes 2,101,352
   County library 0
   County health 0
   County open space 202,059
   School levy 11,363,838
   Local muni. budget 5,509,140
   Misc. revenues 5,042,504
Total aid $1,571,634
   CMPTRA 868,859
   Muni. block grant 41,513
   Energy tax receipts 591,262
   Homeland security 70,000

Fiscal Year 2006
Total aid $1,571,634
   CMPTRA 848,165
   Muni. block grant 41,513
   Energy tax receipts 611,956
   Homeland security 70,000

Taxes
	2003	2004	2005
General tax rate per $100	3.50	4.270	4.510
Net valuation taxable	$422,707,031	$425,074,122	$426,121,949
State equalized value	$600,350,846	$668,447,849	$764,893,105
County equalization ratio	81.53	70.41	63.29

Demographics & Socio-Economic Characteristics
(2000 U.S. Census, except as noted)

Population
1980*	4,772
1990*	4,475
2000	4,793
Male	2,385
Female	2,408
2004 (estimate)*	4,804
Persons per sq. mi. of land	8,116

Race & Hispanic Origin, 2000
Race
White	4,225
Black/African American	185
Amer. Indian/Alaska Natv.	8
Asian	70
Natv. Hawaiian/Pac. Islander	1
Other Race	192
Two or more races	112
Hispanic origin, total	615
Mexican	248
Puerto Rican	213
Cuban	19
Other Hispanic	135

Age & Nativity, 2000
Under 5 years	265
18 years and over	3,931
21 years and over	3,792
65 years and over	590
85 years and over	83
Median Age	36.9
Native born	4,258
Foreign born	535

Educational Attainment, 2000
Population 25 years and over	3,544
0-8 yrs of school	4.8%
High School grad or higher	81.8%
Bachelor's degree or higher	25.2%
Graduate degree	10.0%

Income & Poverty, 1999
Per capita income	$25,438
Median household income	$40,878
Median family income	$49,688
Persons in poverty	439
H'holds receiving public assistance	11
H'holds receiving social security	511

Households, 2000
Total households	2,297
With persons under 18	478
With persons over 65	450
Family households	1,086
One-person households	977
Persons per household	2.09
Persons per family	2.91

Labor & Employment
Total civilian labor force, 2004**	2,614
Unemployment rate	6.3%
Total civilian labor force, 2000	2,714
Unemployment rate	6.5%

Employed persons 16 years and over by occupation, 2000
Managers & professionals	825
Service occupations	431
Sales & office occupations	759
Farming, fishing & forestry	0
Construction & maintenance	247
Production & transportation	275
Self-employed persons	153

*US Census Bureau
**New Jersey Department of Labor

General Information
Borough of Bradley Beach
701 Main St
Bradley Beach, NJ 07720
732-776-2999
Web site	www.bradleybeachonline.com
Land area (sq. miles)	0.59
Water area (sq. miles)	0.02
Type of government	Borough
Form of government	MC

Government

Legislative Districts
US Congressional	6
State Legislative	11

Local Officials, 2006
Mayor	Stephen Schueler
Admin/Manager	Phyllis Quixley
Clerk	Mary Ann Solinski
Finance Dir/Treas	Joyce Wilkins
Engineer	Philip R. Kavanuagh
Attorney	Michael DuPont
Tax assessor	Ed Mullane
Tax collector	Joyce Wilkins
Building officer	Patrick McMahon
Zoning officer	William Gray
Public Works	Richard Bianchi

Housing & Construction

Housing Units, 2000*
Total	3,132
Median rent	$729
Median SF home value	$161,200

New Privately Owned Housing Units Authorized by Building Permit
	Units	Value
Total, 2004	44	$3,644,390
Single family	23	$2,271,390
Total, 2005	45	$4,105,097
Single family	20	$2,470,572

Real Property Valuation - parcels, 2005
	Number	Valuation
Total		$444,922,400
Vacant	79	5,694,500
Residential	1,826	376,549,600
Commercial	103	32,419,500
Industrial	4	868,600
Apartments	39	29,390,200
Farm land	0	0
Farm homestead	0	0

Average Property Value & Tax, 2005
Residential value	$206,216
Property tax	$5,120
FAIR rebate	$632

Public Library
Bradley Beach Public Library
511 4th Ave
Bradley Beach, NJ 07720
732-776-2995
Director — Karen Klapperstuck

Library statistics, 2004
	Total	per capita
Volumes	37,674	7.86
Expenditure	$140,495	$29.31

Public Safety

Police
Chief	Robert DeNardo
Number of officers, 2004	17

Crime, 2004	Number	Rate
Total	241	50.5
Violent	16	3.4
Non-violent	225	47.2
Domestic Viol.	123	NA

Emergency/Fire
Director — Jason Afanador

Public School District
(for school year 2004-2005 except as noted)

Bradley Beach School District
515 Brinley Ave
Bradley Beach, NJ 07720
732-775-4413
Superintendent	Wayne W. Tuner
Grade plan	K-12
Enrollment	322.0
Students per teacher	8.6
Per pupil expenditure	$15,189
Median faculty salary	$54,060
Median administrator salary	$73,500
Grade 12 enrollment	NA
High school graduation rate	NA

Assessment test results
(percent scoring at proficient or advanced level)
	Language	Math
Grade 3	78.9%	75.7%
Grade 8	67.6%	43.2%
High school	NA	NA

SAT
Percent tested	NA
Average SAT math score	NA
Average SAT verbal score	NA

No Child Left Behind, 2003-04
Attendence rate (target = 90%)	94.8%
Drop rate	NA
Highly-qualified teachers	92.8%
District needs improvement?(AYP)	No

Municipal Finance

Fiscal Year 2005
Total tax levy	$11,052,983
County levy	2,274,788
County taxes	2,147,361
County library	0
County health	0
County open space	127,427
School levy	4,729,953
Local muni. budget	4,048,243
Misc. revenues	2,131,243
Total aid	$547,208
CMPTRA	192,806
Muni. block grant	19,582
Energy tax receipts	309,820
Homeland security	25,000

Fiscal Year 2006
Total aid	$547,208
CMPTRA	181,962
Muni. block grant	19,582
Energy tax receipts	320,664
Homeland security	25,000

Taxes
	2003	2004	2005
General tax rate per $100	2.35	2.330	2.483
Net valuation taxable	$438,316,003	$440,707,448	$445,169,128
State equalized value	$576,125,135	$707,659,271	$880,999,660
County equalization ratio	93.56	76.08	62.26

Demographics & Socio-Economic Characteristics
(2000 U.S. Census, except as noted)

Population
1980*	7,846
1990*	10,888
2000	14,566
Male	7,148
Female	7,418
2004 (estimate)*	14,943
Persons per sq. mi. of land	738

Race & Hispanic Origin, 2000
Race
White	13,174
Black/African American	284
Amer. Indian/Alaska Natv.	15
Asian	898
Natv. Hawaiian/Pac. Islander	4
Other Race	57
Two or more races	134
Hispanic origin, total	392
Mexican	20
Puerto Rican	137
Cuban	51
Other Hispanic	184

Age & Nativity, 2000
Under 5 years	1,269
18 years and over	10,583
21 years and over	10,303
65 years and over	1,206
85 years and over	98
Median Age	37.5
Native born	12,997
Foreign born	1,565

Educational Attainment, 2000
Population 25 years and over	9,954
0-8 yrs of school	1.8%
High School grad or higher	94.8%
Bachelor's degree or higher	53.7%
Graduate degree	23.0%

Income & Poverty, 1999
Per capita income	$41,241
Median household income	$96,864
Median family income	$110,268
Persons in poverty	282
H'holds receiving public assistance	63
H'holds receiving social security	942

Households, 2000
Total households	5,272
With persons under 18	2,148
With persons over 65	898
Family households	4,065
One-person households	990
Persons per household	2.76
Persons per family	3.19

Labor & Employment
Total civilian labor force, 2004**	8,006
Unemployment rate	4.2%
Total civilian labor force, 2000	8,018
Unemployment rate	2.1%

Employed persons 16 years and over by occupation, 2000
Managers & professionals	4,376
Service occupations	453
Sales & office occupations	1,984
Farming, fishing & forestry	0
Construction & maintenance	521
Production & transportation	516
Self-employed persons	392

*US Census Bureau
**New Jersey Department of Labor

General Information
Township of Branchburg
1077 US Hwy 202 North
Branchburg, NJ 08876
908-526-1300
Web site	www.branchburg.nj.us
Land area (sq. miles)	20.26
Water area (sq. miles)	0
Type of government	Township
Form of government	TC

Government
Legislative Districts
US Congressional	7
State Legislative	16

Local Officials, 2006
Mayor	M. Kate Sarles
Admin/Manager	Gregory Bonin
Clerk	Sharon Brienza
Finance Dir/Treas	Diane Schubach
Engineer	Douglas Ball
Attorney	M. S. Anderson
Tax assessor	Frances Kuczynski
Tax collector	Diane Wynn
Building officer	John Tamburini
Zoning officer	Thomas Leach
Public Works	Bruce Kosensky

Housing & Construction
Housing Units, 2000*
Total	5,405
Median rent	$1,036
Median SF home value	$278,000

New Privately Owned Housing Units Authorized by Building Permit
	Units	Value
Total, 2004	9	$2,296,650
Single family	9	$2,296,650
Total, 2005	15	$3,996,442
Single family	15	$3,996,442

Real Property Valuation - parcels, 2005
	Number	Valuation
Total		$2,633,727,700
Vacant	169	22,543,100
Residential	4,773	1,978,098,600
Commercial	130	153,500,600
Industrial	152	425,248,400
Apartments	1	20,350,000
Farm land	60	32,591,500
Farm homestead	116	1,395,500

Average Property Value & Tax, 2005
Residential value	$404,887
Property tax	$7,818
FAIR rebate	$485

Public Library
No public municipal library.

Library statistics, 2004
	Total	per capita
Volumes	NA	NA
Expenditure	NA	NA

Public Safety
Police
Chief	Brian Fitzgerald
Number of officers, 2004	26

Crime, 2004	Number	Rate
Total	124	8.4
Violent	2	0.1
Non-violent	122	8.2
Domestic Viol.	103	NA

Emergency/Fire
Director	James McAleer

Public School District
(for school year 2004-2005 except as noted)

Branchburg Township School District
240 Baird Rd
Branchburg, NJ 08876
908-722-3265
Superintendent	Walter Oberwanowicz (Actg)
Grade plan	K-12
Enrollment	1,998.0
Students per teacher	9.9
Per pupil expenditure	$13,005
Median faculty salary	$47,620
Median administrator salary	$109,009
Grade 12 enrollment	NA
High school graduation rate	NA

Assessment test results
(percent scoring at proficient or advanced level)
	Language	Math
Grade 3	93.4%	91.3%
Grade 8	90.5%	92.2%
High school	NA	NA

SAT
Percent tested	NA
Average SAT math score	NA
Average SAT verbal score	NA

No Child Left Behind, 2003-04
Attendence rate (target = 90%)	97.2%
Drop rate	NA
Highly-qualified teachers	86.8%
District needs improvement?(AYP)	No

Municipal Finance
Fiscal Year 2005
Total tax levy	$50,945,957
County levy	9,331,187
County taxes	7,730,854
County library	856,952
County health	0
County open space	743,382
School levy	34,679,634
Local muni. budget	6,935,136
Misc. revenues	7,820,919
Total aid	$3,603,755
CMPTRA	310,031
Muni. block grant	57,114
Energy tax receipts	3,166,610
Homeland security	70,000

Fiscal Year 2006
Total aid	$3,603,756
CMPTRA	199,200
Muni. block grant	57,114
Energy tax receipts	3,277,442
Homeland security	70,000

Taxes
	2003	2004	2005
General tax rate per $100	2.12	2.260	1.940
Net valuation taxable	$2,011,270,853	$2,069,989,725	$2,638,596,002
State equalized value	$2,163,122,019	$2,379,158,538	$2,776,592,657
County equalization ratio	99.57	92.98	106.66

Demographics & Socio-Economic Characteristics
(2000 U.S. Census, except as noted)

Population
1980*	870
1990*	851
2000	845
Male	394
Female	451
2004 (estimate)*	848
Persons per sq. mi. of land	1,427

Race & Hispanic Origin, 2000
Race
White	832
Black/African American	1
Amer. Indian/Alaska Natv.	3
Asian	3
Natv. Hawaiian/Pac. Islander	0
Other Race	1
Two or more races	5
Hispanic origin, total	11
Mexican	7
Puerto Rican	1
Cuban	0
Other Hispanic	3

Age & Nativity, 2000
Under 5 years	29
18 years and over	642
21 years and over	615
65 years and over	153
85 years and over	15
Median Age	41.7
Native born	829
Foreign born	18

Educational Attainment, 2000
Population 25 years and over	613
0-8 yrs of school	3.8%
High School grad or higher	85.2%
Bachelor's degree or higher	18.3%
Graduate degree	6.9%

Income & Poverty, 1999
Per capita income	$22,748
Median household income	$45,855
Median family income	$60,909
Persons in poverty	37
H'holds receiving public assistance	8
H'holds receiving social security	134

Households, 2000
Total households	354
With persons under 18	107
With persons over 65	119
Family households	225
One-person households	114
Persons per household	2.37
Persons per family	3.03

Labor & Employment
Total civilian labor force, 2004**	542
Unemployment rate	4.8%
Total civilian labor force, 2000	435
Unemployment rate	4.4%

Employed persons 16 years and over by occupation, 2000
Managers & professionals	122
Service occupations	54
Sales & office occupations	122
Farming, fishing & forestry	2
Construction & maintenance	57
Production & transportation	59
Self-employed persons	27

*US Census Bureau
**New Jersey Department of Labor

General Information
Borough of Branchville
PO Box 840
Branchville, NJ 07826
973-948-4626

Web site	NA
Land area (sq. miles)	0.59
Water area (sq. miles)	0
Type of government	Borough
Form of government	B

Government

Legislative Districts
US Congressional	5
State Legislative	24

Local Officials, 2006
Mayor	Gerald Van Gorden
Admin/Manager	NA
Clerk	Beverly Bathgate
Finance Dir/Treas	E. Jerome Orr
Engineer	Harold Pellow
Attorney	Thomas Bain
Tax assessor	Katherine Kieb
Tax collector	Beverly Bathgate
Building officer	Wesley Powers
Zoning officer	George Boesze
Public Works	NA

Housing & Construction

Housing Units, 2000*
Total	377
Median rent	$671
Median SF home value	$149,600

New Privately Owned Housing Units
Authorized by Building Permit
	Units	Value
Total, 2004	0	$0
Single family	0	$0
Total, 2005	2	$555,000
Single family	2	$555,000

Real Property Valuation - parcels, 2005
	Number	Valuation
Total		$100,629,100
Vacant	43	1,302,100
Residential	276	37,582,700
Commercial	53	60,854,300
Industrial	0	0
Apartments	4	821,200
Farm land	1	63,600
Farm homestead	2	5,200

Average Property Value & Tax, 2005
Residential value	$135,208
Property tax	$3,091
FAIR rebate	$650

Public Library
No public municipal library.

Library statistics, 2004
	Total	per capita
Volumes	NA	NA
Expenditure	NA	NA

Public Safety

Police
Chief	NA
Number of officers, 2004	0

Crime, 2004	Number	Rate
Total	14	16.4
Violent	0	0
Non-violent	14	16.4
Domestic Viol.	8	NA

Emergency/Fire
Director	Brian Geimer

Public School District
(for school year 2004-2005 except as noted)

Branchville Borough School District
RR 4
Stroudsburg PA, NJ 18360
Superintendent	NA
Grade plan	NA
Enrollment	NA
Students per teacher	NA
Per pupil expenditure	NA
Median faculty salary	NA
Median administrator salary	NA
Grade 12 enrollment	NA
High school graduation rate	NA

Assessment test results
(percent scoring at proficient or advanced level)
	Language	Math
Grade 3	NA	NA
Grade 8	NA	NA
High school	NA	NA

SAT
Percent tested	NA
Average SAT math score	NA
Average SAT verbal score	NA

No Child Left Behind, 2003-04
Attendence rate (target = 90%)	NA
Drop rate	NA
Highly-qualified teachers	NA
District needs improvement?(AYP)	NA

Municipal Finance

Fiscal Year 2005
Total tax levy	$2,303,876
County levy	650,205
County taxes	548,915
County library	48,994
County health	23,064
County open space	29,232
School levy	1,653,671
Local muni. budget	0
Misc. revenues	1,257,500
Total aid	$900,506
CMPTRA	865,279
Muni. block grant	3,724
Energy tax receipts	31,503
Homeland security	0

Fiscal Year 2006
Total aid	$900,506
CMPTRA	864,177
Muni. block grant	3,724
Energy tax receipts	32,605
Homeland security	NA

Taxes
	2003	2004	2005
General tax rate per $100	2.20	2.270	2.290
Net valuation taxable	$100,195,752	$100,568,401	$100,787,356
State equalized value	$120,528,993	$143,690,731	$160,642,901
County equalization ratio	101.17	83.13	69.95

Demographics & Socio-Economic Characteristics

(2000 U.S. Census, except as noted)

Population

1980*	53,629
1990*	66,473
2000	76,119
Male	36,155
Female	39,964
2004 (estimate)*	78,474
Persons per sq. mi. of land	2,991

Race & Hispanic Origin, 2000

Race

White	72,932
Black/African American	751
Amer. Indian/Alaska Natv.	76
Asian	904
Natv. Hawaiian/Pac. Islander	12
Other Race	650
Two or more races	794
Hispanic origin, total	2,930
Mexican	491
Puerto Rican	1,229
Cuban	200
Other Hispanic	1,010

Age & Nativity, 2000

Under 5 years	4,721
18 years and over	57,965
21 years and over	55,790
65 years and over	12,963
85 years and over	1,671
Median Age	39.4
Native born	71,816
Foreign born	4,303

Educational Attainment, 2000

Population 25 years and over	52,965
0-8 yrs of school	3.3%
High School grad or higher	86.6%
Bachelor's degree or higher	19.4%
Graduate degree	5.6%

Income & Poverty, 1999

Per capita income	$24,462
Median household income	$52,092
Median family income	$61,446
Persons in poverty	3,411
H'holds receiving public assistance	420
H'holds receiving social security	10,004

Households, 2000

Total households	29,511
With persons under 18	9,995
With persons over 65	9,081
Family households	20,788
One-person households	7,367
Persons per household	2.56
Persons per family	3.07

Labor & Employment

Total civilian labor force, 2004**	42,386
Unemployment rate	4.7%
Total civilian labor force, 2000	37,840
Unemployment rate	4.1%

Employed persons 16 years and over by occupation, 2000

Managers & professionals	11,269
Service occupations	5,427
Sales & office occupations	11,236
Farming, fishing & forestry	80
Construction & maintenance	4,211
Production & transportation	4,049
Self-employed persons	1,820

*US Census Bureau
**New Jersey Department of Labor

General Information

Township of Brick
401 Chambers Bridge Rd
Brick, NJ 08723
732-262-1000

Web site	www.twp.brick.nj.us
Land area (sq. miles)	26.23
Water area (sq. miles)	6.03
Type of government	Township
Form of government	MC '50

Government

Legislative Districts

US Congressional	4
State Legislative	10

Local Officials, 2006

Mayor	Joseph Scarpelli
Admin/Manager	Scott MacFadden
Clerk	Virginia A. Lampman
Finance Dir/Treas	Scott Pezarras
Engineer	Thomas Rospos
Attorney	Charles Starkey
Tax assessor	Fred Millman
Tax collector	JoAnne Lambusta
Building officer	Daniel Newman Jr.
Zoning officer	Sean Kinnevy
Public Works	Robert Russo

Housing & Construction

Housing Units, 2000*

Total	32,689
Median rent	$820
Median SF home value	$136,800

New Privately Owned Housing Units Authorized by Building Permit

	Units	Value
Total, 2004	76	$11,387,519
Single family	76	$11,387,519
Total, 2005	129	$18,338,409
Single family	117	$15,690,607

Real Property Valuation - parcels, 2005

	Number	Valuation
Total		$4,622,482,800
Vacant	1,519	79,692,200
Residential	30,339	4,007,550,400
Commercial	709	471,112,000
Industrial	22	8,978,700
Apartments	14	55,053,600
Farm land	1	95,900
Farm homestead	0	0

Average Property Value & Tax, 2005

Residential value	$132,092
Property tax	$4,270
FAIR rebate	$944

Public Library

Brick Branch Library†
301 Chambers Bridge Rd
Brick, NJ 08723
732-477-4513

Branch Librarian	Eleanor Clark

Library statistics, 2004

	Total	per capita
Volumes	NA	NA
Expenditure	NA	NA

†Branch of County Library

Public Safety

Police

Chief	Ronald Dougard
Number of officers, 2004	123

Crime, 2004	Number	Rate
Total	1,430	18.2
Violent	100	1.3
Non-violent	1,330	17
Domestic Viol.	813	NA

Emergency/Fire

Director	NA

Public School District

(for school year 2004-2005 except as noted)

Brick Township School District
101 Hendrickson Ave
Brick, NJ 08724
732-785-3000

Superintendent	Thomas Seidenberger
Grade plan	K-12
Enrollment	11,210.0
Students per teacher	12.4
Per pupil expenditure	$9,881
Median faculty salary	$43,355
Median administrator salary	$101,828
Grade 12 enrollment	779.5
High school graduation rate	NA

Assessment test results

(percent scoring at proficient or advanced level)

	Language	Math
Grade 3	85.0%	86.2%
Grade 8	80.6%	64.7%
High school	89.6%	79.3%

SAT

Percent tested	NA
Average SAT math score	NA
Average SAT verbal score	NA

No Child Left Behind, 2003-04

Attendence rate (target = 90%)	94.6%
Drop rate	1.1%
Highly-qualified teachers	96.9%
District needs improvement?(AYP)	No

Municipal Finance

Fiscal Year 2005

Total tax levy	$149,708,320
County levy	34,178,873
County taxes	28,796,638
County library	3,025,372
County health	1,282,308
County open space	1,074,555
School levy	78,104,225
Local muni. budget	37,425,222
Misc. revenues	27,047,473
Total aid	$7,430,534
CMPTRA	2,798,833
Muni. block grant	298,464
Energy tax receipts	4,193,237
Homeland security	140,000

Fiscal Year 2006

Total aid	$7,430,533
CMPTRA	2,652,069
Muni. block grant	298,464
Energy tax receipts	4,340,000
Homeland security	140,000

Taxes

	2003	2004	2005
General tax rate per $100	2.90	3.010	3.233
Net valuation taxable	$4,576,570,768	$4,604,539,942	$4,630,699,335
State equalized value	$7,478,056,810	$8,879,865,054	$10,434,203,098
County equalization ratio	71.12	61.20	51.80

Demographics & Socio-Economic Characteristics
(2000 U.S. Census, except as noted)

Population
1980*	18,795
1990*	18,942
2000	22,771
Male	12,899
Female	9,872
2004 (estimate)*	22,727
Persons per sq. mi. of land	3,653

Race & Hispanic Origin, 2000
Race
White	8,854
Black/African American	9,528
Amer. Indian/Alaska Natv.	271
Asian	159
Natv. Hawaiian/Pac. Islander	20
Other Race	3,112
Two or more races	827
Hispanic origin, total	5,576
Mexican	3,264
Puerto Rican	1,558
Cuban	62
Other Hispanic	692

Age & Nativity, 2000
Under 5 years	1,658
18 years and over	16,843
21 years and over	15,857
65 years and over	2,485
85 years and over	342
Median Age	31.5
Native born	19,942
Foreign born	2,829

Educational Attainment, 2000
Population 25 years and over	14,198
0-8 yrs of school	14.6%
High School grad or higher	57.6%
Bachelor's degree or higher	7.3%
Graduate degree	2.6%

Income & Poverty, 1999
Per capita income	$10,917
Median household income	$26,923
Median family income	$30,502
Persons in poverty	4,880
H'holds receiving public assistance	515
H'holds receiving social security	1,840

Households, 2000
Total households	6,182
With persons under 18	2,665
With persons over 65	1,735
Family households	4,181
One-person households	1,691
Persons per household	2.96
Persons per family	3.49

Labor & Employment
Total civilian labor force, 2004**	8,421
Unemployment rate	9.0%
Total civilian labor force, 2000	7,850
Unemployment rate	13.5%

Employed persons 16 years and over by occupation, 2000
Managers & professionals	1,301
Service occupations	1,607
Sales & office occupations	1,468
Farming, fishing & forestry	340
Construction & maintenance	436
Production & transportation	1,642
Self-employed persons	175

*US Census Bureau
**New Jersey Department of Labor

General Information
City of Bridgeton
181 E Commerce St
Bridgeton, NJ 08302
856-455-3230
Web site	www.cityofbridgeton.com
Land area (sq. miles)	6.22
Water area (sq. miles)	0.23
Type of government	City
Form of government	MC '50

Government

Legislative Districts
US Congressional	2
State Legislative	3

Local Officials, 2006
Mayor	Michael Pirolli
Admin/Manager	Charles Kolakowski
Clerk	Darlene Richmond
Finance Dir/Treas	Terry Delp
Engineer	J. Michael Fralinger
Attorney	Theodore Baker
Tax assessor	Kevin Maloney
Tax collector	Mary Pierce
Building officer	Robert Mixner
Zoning officer	Robert Mixner
Public Works	Wilbert Turpin

Housing & Construction

Housing Units, 2000*
Total	6,795
Median rent	$602
Median SF home value	$71,500

New Privately Owned Housing Units Authorized by Building Permit
	Units	Value
Total, 2004	213	$13,807,512
Single family	213	$13,807,512
Total, 2005	167	$10,837,228
Single family	167	$10,837,228

Real Property Valuation - parcels, 2005
	Number	Valuation
Total		$357,526,500
Vacant	660	3,937,500
Residential	4,432	238,654,700
Commercial	486	71,756,000
Industrial	59	27,428,100
Apartments	53	15,540,300
Farm land	3	178,800
Farm homestead	8	31,100

Average Property Value & Tax, 2005
Residential value	$53,758
Property tax	$2,193
FAIR rebate	$673

Public Library
Bridgeton Public Library
150 E Commerce St
Bridgeton, NJ 08302
856-451-2620
Director	Gail Robinson

Library statistics, 2004
	Total	per capita
Volumes	59,265	2.60
Expenditure	$330,759	$14.53

Public Safety
Police
Chief	Jeffery Wentz
Number of officers, 2004	71

Crime, 2004	Number	Rate
Total	1,490	65.4
Violent	405	17.8
Non-violent	1,085	47.6
Domestic Viol.	636	NA

Emergency/Fire
Director	Dave Schoch

Public School District
(for school year 2004-2005 except as noted)

Bridgeton School District
PO Box 657
Bridgeton, NJ 08302
856-455-8030
Superintendent	H. Victor Gilson
Grade plan	K-12
Enrollment	4,391.0
Students per teacher	8.7
Per pupil expenditure	$13,869
Median faculty salary	$44,250
Median administrator salary	$82,300
Grade 12 enrollment	187.5
High school graduation rate	82.6%

Assessment test results
(percent scoring at proficient or advanced level)
	Language	Math
Grade 3	49.3%	55.0%
Grade 8	32.3%	22.5%
High school	58.9%	37.1%

SAT
Percent tested	37%
Average SAT math score	436
Average SAT verbal score	450

No Child Left Behind, 2003-04
Attendence rate (target = 90%)	92.8%
Drop rate	6.6%
Highly-qualified teachers	96.3%
District needs improvement?(AYP)	No

Municipal Finance

Fiscal Year 2005
Total tax levy	$14,776,693
County levy	4,201,131
County taxes	3,988,594
County library	0
County health	171,702
County open space	40,834
School levy	3,333,454
Local muni. budget	7,242,108
Misc. revenues	10,915,447
Total aid	$5,444,028
CMPTRA	4,331,052
Muni. block grant	89,286
Energy tax receipts	933,690
Homeland security	90,000

Fiscal Year 2006
Total aid	$5,444,028
CMPTRA	4,298,373
Muni. block grant	89,286
Energy tax receipts	966,369
Homeland security	90,000

Taxes
	2003	2004	2005
General tax rate per $100	3.30	3.771	4.082
Net valuation taxable	$358,864,845	$359,901,052	$362,228,210
State equalized value	$392,760,036	$388,081,571	$442,551,265
County equalization ratio	91.16	91.37	92.65

Demographics & Socio-Economic Characteristics
(2000 U.S. Census, except as noted)

Population
1980*	29,175
1990*	32,509
2000	42,940
Male	20,636
Female	22,304
2004 (estimate)*	44,370
Persons per sq. mi. of land	1,368

Race & Hispanic Origin, 2000
Race
White	36,527
Black/African American	931
Amer. Indian/Alaska Natv.	33
Asian	4,525
Natv. Hawaiian/Pac. Islander	5
Other Race	381
Two or more races	538
Hispanic origin, total	2,056
Mexican	194
Puerto Rican	352
Cuban	143
Other Hispanic	1,367

Age & Nativity, 2000
Under 5 years	3,295
18 years and over	31,922
21 years and over	30,977
65 years and over	5,443
85 years and over	778
Median Age	38.2
Native born	36,128
Foreign born	6,754

Educational Attainment, 2000
Population 25 years and over	29,686
0-8 yrs of school	3.2%
High School grad or higher	92.0%
Bachelor's degree or higher	49.9%
Graduate degree	22.0%

Income & Poverty, 1999
Per capita income	$39,555
Median household income	$88,308
Median family income	$99,832
Persons in poverty	885
H'holds receiving public assistance	138
H'holds receiving social security	3,435

Households, 2000
Total households	15,561
With persons under 18	6,121
With persons over 65	3,523
Family households	11,890
One-person households	3,083
Persons per household	2.71
Persons per family	3.14

Labor & Employment
Total civilian labor force, 2004**	23,784
Unemployment rate	2.9%
Total civilian labor force, 2000	23,028
Unemployment rate	2.8%

Employed persons 16 years and over by occupation, 2000
Managers & professionals	12,020
Service occupations	1,705
Sales & office occupations	5,808
Farming, fishing & forestry	18
Construction & maintenance	1,514
Production & transportation	1,323
Self-employed persons	1,045

*US Census Bureau
**New Jersey Department of Labor

General Information
Township of Bridgewater
700 Garretson Rd
Bridgewater, NJ 08807
908-725-6300
Web site	www.bridgewaternj.gov
Land area (sq. miles)	32.45
Water area (sq. miles)	0.09
Type of government	Township
Form of government	Faulkner

Government

Legislative Districts
US Congressional	7, 11
State Legislative	16

Local Officials, 2006
Mayor	Patricia Flannery
Admin/Manager	James Naples
Clerk	Linda Doyle
Finance Dir/Treas	Natasha Turchan
Engineer	Robert Bogart
Attorney	William Savo
Tax assessor	Anthony DiRado
Tax collector	NA
Building officer	William Strohmeyer
Zoning officer	George Jones
Public Works	NA

Housing & Construction

Housing Units, 2000*
Total	15,879
Median rent	$1,096
Median SF home value	$268,100

New Privately Owned Housing Units Authorized by Building Permit
	Units	Value
Total, 2004	38	$9,494,194
Single family	38	$9,319,194
Total, 2005	50	$12,545,008
Single family	44	$11,431,008

Real Property Valuation - parcels, 2005
	Number	Valuation
Total		$8,440,177,100
Vacant	639	120,570,400
Residential	14,638	6,256,325,400
Commercial	378	1,647,929,200
Industrial	48	365,279,800
Apartments	13	44,081,300
Farm land	11	5,860,400
Farm homestead	38	130,600

Average Property Value & Tax, 2005
Residential value	$426,305
Property tax	$7,164
FAIR rebate	$538

Public Library
Somerset County Library
1 Vogt Dr
Bridgewater, NJ 08807
908-526-4016
Branch Director	Kathleen J. Harris

Library statistics, 2004
	Total	per capita
Volumes	NA	NA
Expenditure	NA	NA

Public Safety

Police
Chief	Steve Obal
Number of officers, 2004	79

Crime, 2004	Number	Rate
Total	650	14.8
Violent	15	0.3
Non-violent	635	14.4
Domestic Viol.	123	NA

Emergency/Fire
Director	NA

Public School District
(for school year 2004-2005 except as noted)

Bridgewater-Raritan Regional School Dist.
836 Newmans Lane
Bridgewater, NJ 08807
908-685-2777
Superintendent	Walter Mahler
Grade plan	K-12
Enrollment	8,777.0
Students per teacher	10.9
Per pupil expenditure	$11,750
Median faculty salary	$48,530
Median administrator salary	$109,956
Grade 12 enrollment	520.5
High school graduation rate	98.3%

Assessment test results
(percent scoring at proficient or advanced level)
	Language	Math
Grade 3	92.8%	92.1%
Grade 8	87.3%	77.8%
High school	92.1%	87.7%

SAT
Percent tested	93%
Average SAT math score	578
Average SAT verbal score	543

No Child Left Behind, 2003-04
Attendence rate (target = 90%)	95.5%
Drop rate	0.5%
Highly-qualified teachers	96.9%
District needs improvement?(AYP)	No

Municipal Finance

Fiscal Year 2005
Total tax levy	$142,001,304
County levy	34,037,821
County taxes	28,199,968
County library	3,125,659
County health	0
County open space	2,712,195
School levy	88,160,574
Local muni. budget	19,802,909
Misc. revenues	16,219,637
Total aid	$8,535,828
CMPTRA	3,077,732
Muni. block grant	168,369
Energy tax receipts	5,149,727
Homeland security	140,000

Fiscal Year 2006
Total aid	$8,535,827
CMPTRA	2,897,491
Muni. block grant	168,369
Energy tax receipts	5,329,967
Homeland security	140,000

Taxes
	2003	2004	2005
General tax rate per $100	1.91	2.060	1.690
Net valuation taxable	$6,307,360,331	$6,331,904,915	$8,450,016,633
State equalized value	$7,527,581,252	$8,927,195,960	$9,234,990,856
County equalization ratio	92.42	83.79	94.21

Demographics & Socio-Economic Characteristics

(2000 U.S. Census, except as noted)

Population

1980*	4,068
1990*	4,406
2000	4,893
Male	2,336
Female	2,557
2004 (estimate)*	4,913
Persons per sq. mi. of land	2,766

Race & Hispanic Origin, 2000

Race

White	4,553
Black/African American	172
Amer. Indian/Alaska Natv.	3
Asian	33
Natv. Hawaiian/Pac. Islander	0
Other Race	79
Two or more races	53
Hispanic origin, total	162
Mexican	88
Puerto Rican	31
Cuban	11
Other Hispanic	32

Age & Nativity, 2000

Under 5 years	348
18 years and over	3,733
21 years and over	3,631
65 years and over	868
85 years and over	77
Median Age	42.9
Native born	4,734
Foreign born	159

Educational Attainment, 2000

Population 25 years and over	3,533
0-8 yrs of school	1.8%
High School grad or higher	94.8%
Bachelor's degree or higher	44.7%
Graduate degree	14.7%

Income & Poverty, 1999

Per capita income	$35,785
Median household income	$68,368
Median family income	$82,867
Persons in poverty	193
H'holds receiving public assistance	24
H'holds receiving social security	693

Households, 2000

Total households	1,938
With persons under 18	640
With persons over 65	633
Family households	1,414
One-person households	456
Persons per household	2.52
Persons per family	3

Labor & Employment

Total civilian labor force, 2004**	2,561
Unemployment rate	5.9%
Total civilian labor force, 2000	2,297
Unemployment rate	3.5%

Employed persons 16 years and over by occupation, 2000

Managers & professionals	1,241
Service occupations	225
Sales & office occupations	484
Farming, fishing & forestry	16
Construction & maintenance	107
Production & transportation	144
Self-employed persons	229

*US Census Bureau
**New Jersey Department of Labor

General Information

Borough of Brielle
601 Union Lane
Brielle, NJ 08730
732-528-6600

Web site	www.briellenj.com
Land area (sq. miles)	1.78
Water area (sq. miles)	0.59
Type of government	Borough
Form of government	B

Government

Legislative Districts

US Congressional	4
State Legislative	11

Local Officials, 2006

Mayor	Thomas Nicol
Admin/Manager	Thomas Nolan
Clerk	Thomas Nolan
Finance Dir/Treas	Karen Brisben
Engineer	Alan Hilla Jr.
Attorney	Nicholas Montenegro
Tax assessor	Mary Lou Hartman
Tax collector	Karen Brisben
Building officer	Albert Ratz Jr.
Zoning officer	Albert Ratz Jr.
Public Works	William Burkhardt Jr

Housing & Construction

Housing Units, 2000*

Total	2,123
Median rent	$1,090
Median SF home value	$285,000

New Privately Owned Housing Units
Authorized by Building Permit

	Units	Value
Total, 2004	26	$6,795,612
Single family	26	$6,795,612
Total, 2005	22	$8,014,547
Single family	22	$8,014,547

Real Property Valuation - parcels, 2005

	Number	Valuation
Total		$606,341,300
Vacant	111	16,022,900
Residential	1,874	527,962,400
Commercial	85	54,176,300
Industrial	0	0
Apartments	2	8,179,700
Farm land	0	0
Farm homestead	0	0

Average Property Value & Tax, 2005

Residential value	$281,730
Property tax	$7,971
FAIR rebate	$617

Public Library

Brielle Public Library
610 South St
Brielle, NJ 08730
732-528-9381

Director .... Richard Bidnick

Library statistics, 2004

	Total	per capita
Volumes	32,791	6.70
Expenditure	$232,044	$47.42

Public Safety

Police

Chief	Michael Palmer
Number of officers, 2004	15

Crime, 2004	Number	Rate
Total	41	8.2
Violent	4	0.8
Non-violent	37	7.4
Domestic Viol.	19	NA

Emergency/Fire

Director .... Timothy A. Shaak

Public School District

(for school year 2004-2005 except as noted)

Brielle Borough School District
605 Union Lane
Brielle, NJ 08730
732-528-6400

Superintendent	Joseph Torrone
Grade plan	K-12
Enrollment	661.0
Students per teacher	11.7
Per pupil expenditure	$9,691
Median faculty salary	$43,525
Median administrator salary	$86,500
Grade 12 enrollment	NA
High school graduation rate	NA

Assessment test results
(percent scoring at proficient or advanced level)

	Language	Math
Grade 3	97.8%	86.7%
Grade 8	98.0%	92.2%
High school	NA	NA

SAT

Percent tested	NA
Average SAT math score	NA
Average SAT verbal score	NA

No Child Left Behind, 2003-04

Attendence rate (target = 90%)	95.7%
Drop rate	NA
Highly-qualified teachers	97.6%
District needs improvement?(AYP)	No

Municipal Finance

Fiscal Year 2005

Total tax levy	$17,163,863
County levy	3,798,243
County taxes	3,408,291
County library	187,779
County health	0
County open space	202,172
School levy	9,269,620
Local muni. budget	4,096,000
Misc. revenues	2,554,740
Total aid	$463,402
CMPTRA	125,006
Muni. block grant	19,279
Energy tax receipts	294,117
Homeland security	25,000

Fiscal Year 2006

Total aid	$463,403
CMPTRA	114,712
Muni. block grant	19,279
Energy tax receipts	304,412
Homeland security	25,000

Taxes

	2003	2004	2005
General tax rate per $100	2.66	2.744	2.830
Net valuation taxable	$587,024,170	$595,327,971	$606,638,971
State equalized value	$983,125,389	$1,122,338,988	$1,280,909,989
County equalization ratio	68.78	59.71	53.03

Demographics & Socio-Economic Characteristics

(2000 U.S. Census, except as noted)

Population

1980*	8,318
1990*	11,354
2000	12,594
Male	6,138
Female	6,456
2004 (estimate)*	12,769
Persons per sq. mi. of land	1,986

Race & Hispanic Origin, 2000

Race

White	10,472
Black/African American	496
Amer. Indian/Alaska Natv.	23
Asian	720
Natv. Hawaiian/Pac. Islander	6
Other Race	588
Two or more races	289
Hispanic origin, total	1,185
Mexican	171
Puerto Rican	526
Cuban	29
Other Hispanic	459

Age & Nativity, 2000

Under 5 years	701
18 years and over	9,973
21 years and over	9,689
65 years and over	2,090
85 years and over	161
Median Age	40.7
Native born	11,045
Foreign born	1,549

Educational Attainment, 2000

Population 25 years and over	9,314
0-8 yrs of school	3.0%
High School grad or higher	84.5%
Bachelor's degree or higher	23.8%
Graduate degree	8.5%

Income & Poverty, 1999

Per capita income	$23,950
Median household income	$44,639
Median family income	$51,679
Persons in poverty	1,185
H'holds receiving public assistance	113
H'holds receiving social security	1,711

Households, 2000

Total households	5,473
With persons under 18	1,449
With persons over 65	1,536
Family households	3,338
One-person households	1,678
Persons per household	2.3
Persons per family	2.89

Labor & Employment

Total civilian labor force, 2004**	7,052
Unemployment rate	4.8%
Total civilian labor force, 2000	6,713
Unemployment rate	4.6%

Employed persons 16 years and over by occupation, 2000

Managers & professionals	1,844
Service occupations	2,159
Sales & office occupations	1,652
Farming, fishing & forestry	29
Construction & maintenance	373
Production & transportation	350
Self-employed persons	295

*US Census Bureau
**New Jersey Department of Labor

General Information

City of Brigantine
1417 W Brigantine Ave
Brigantine, NJ 08203
609-266-7600

Web site	www.brigantinebeachnj.com
Land area (sq. miles)	6.43
Water area (sq. miles)	3.36
Type of government	City
Form of government	CM 50

Government

Legislative Districts

US Congressional	2
State Legislative	2

Local Officials, 2006

Mayor	Philip Guenther
Admin/Manager	James Barber
Clerk	Lynn Sweeney
Finance Dir/Treas	Christian Johansen
Engineer	Edward Stinson
Attorney	Timothy Maguire
Tax assessor	Barbara Saccoccia
Tax collector	Dana Wineland
Building officer	Rich Stevens
Zoning officer	Matthew Doran
Public Works	Ernie Purdy

Housing & Construction

Housing Units, 2000*

Total	9,304
Median rent	$792
Median SF home value	$144,400

New Privately Owned Housing Units Authorized by Building Permit

	Units	Value
Total, 2004	155	$15,619,041
Single family	145	$14,880,701
Total, 2005	164	$25,263,626
Single family	158	$24,034,966

Real Property Valuation - parcels, 2005

	Number	Valuation
Total		$1,179,758,700
Vacant	234	12,962,900
Residential	8,358	1,118,543,700
Commercial	123	45,937,700
Industrial	0	0
Apartments	9	2,314,400
Farm land	0	0
Farm homestead	0	0

Average Property Value & Tax, 2005

Residential value	$133,829
Property tax	$4,502
FAIR rebate	$685

Public Library

Brigantine Branch Library†
201 15th St
Brigantine, NJ 08203
609-266-0110

Branch Librarian	Sue Wick

Library statistics, 2004

	Total	per capita
Volumes	NA	NA
Expenditure	NA	NA

†Branch of County Library

Public Safety

Police

Chief	Arthur L. Gordy
Number of officers, 2004	38

Crime, 2004	Number	Rate
Total	242	19.2
Violent	10	0.8
Non-violent	232	18.4
Domestic Viol.	225	NA

Emergency/Fire

Director	Stanley Cwiklinski

Public School District

(for school year 2004-2005 except as noted)

Brigantine City School District
301 E Evans Blvd
Brigantine, NJ 08203
609-266-7671

Superintendent	Robert Previti
Grade plan	K-12
Enrollment	1,140.0
Students per teacher	11.3
Per pupil expenditure	$11,276
Median faculty salary	$50,690
Median administrator salary	$103,466
Grade 12 enrollment	NA
High school graduation rate	NA

Assessment test results

(percent scoring at proficient or advanced level)

	Language	Math
Grade 3	80.4%	94.8%
Grade 8	74.0%	68.9%
High school	NA	NA

SAT

Percent tested	NA
Average SAT math score	NA
Average SAT verbal score	NA

No Child Left Behind, 2003-04

Attendence rate (target = 90%)	93.9%
Drop rate	NA
Highly-qualified teachers	100%
District needs improvement?(AYP)	No

Municipal Finance

Fiscal Year 2005

Total tax levy	$39,717,862
County levy	11,280,028
County taxes	9,209,525
County library	1,020,042
County health	501,981
County open space	548,480
School levy	15,102,001
Local muni. budget	13,335,833
Misc. revenues	5,888,715
Total aid	$991,928
CMPTRA	215,902
Muni. block grant	49,682
Energy tax receipts	656,344
Homeland security	70,000

Fiscal Year 2006

Total aid	$991,928
CMPTRA	192,930
Muni. block grant	49,682
Energy tax receipts	679,316
Homeland security	70,000

Taxes

	2003	2004	2005
General tax rate per $100	2.85	3.074	3.365
Net valuation taxable	$1,150,359,513	$1,159,080,077	$1,180,618,094
State equalized value	$2,166,810,158	$2,690,306,696	$3,311,691,708
County equalization ratio	68.9	53.09	43.06

Demographics & Socio-Economic Characteristics

(2000 U.S. Census, except as noted)

Population

1980*	2,133
1990*	1,805
2000	2,354
Male	1,109
Female	1,245
2004 (estimate)*	2,325
Persons per sq. mi. of land	4,942

Race & Hispanic Origin, 2000

Race

White	2,125
Black/African American	101
Amer. Indian/Alaska Natv.	2
Asian	25
Natv. Hawaiian/Pac. Islander	0
Other Race	56
Two or more races	45
Hispanic origin, total	111
Mexican	7
Puerto Rican	73
Cuban	0
Other Hispanic	31

Age & Nativity, 2000

Under 5 years	165
18 years and over	1,746
21 years and over	1,670
65 years and over	310
85 years and over	40
Median Age	35.2
Native born	2,283
Foreign born	71

Educational Attainment, 2000

Population 25 years and over	1,525
0-8 yrs of school	4.5%
High School grad or higher	80.1%
Bachelor's degree or higher	7.9%
Graduate degree	3.5%

Income & Poverty, 1999

Per capita income	$18,295
Median household income	$39,600
Median family income	$47,891
Persons in poverty	170
H'holds receiving public assistance	12
H'holds receiving social security	249

Households, 2000

Total households	961
With persons under 18	345
With persons over 65	246
Family households	601
One-person households	297
Persons per household	2.45
Persons per family	3.09

Labor & Employment

Total civilian labor force, 2004**	961
Unemployment rate	5.2%
Total civilian labor force, 2000	1,263
Unemployment rate	3.2%

Employed persons 16 years and over by occupation, 2000

Managers & professionals	239
Service occupations	259
Sales & office occupations	352
Farming, fishing & forestry	5
Construction & maintenance	155
Production & transportation	212
Self-employed persons	48

*US Census Bureau
**New Jersey Department of Labor

General Information

Borough of Brooklawn
301 Christiana St
Brooklawn, NJ 08030
856-456-0750

Web site	www.brooklawn.us
Land area (sq. miles)	0.47
Water area (sq. miles)	0.05
Type of government	Borough
Form of government	B

Government

Legislative Districts

US Congressional	1
State Legislative	5

Local Officials, 2006

Mayor	John Soubasis
Admin/Manager	NA
Clerk	Barbara Lewis
Finance Dir/Treas	Barbara Lewis
Engineer	KEI Engr, Chuck Reibel
Attorney	Timothy Higgins
Tax assessor	Anthony Leone
Tax collector	Maureen Mitchell
Building officer	Christopher Mecca
Zoning officer	Christopher Mecca
Public Works	Donna Domico

Housing & Construction

Housing Units, 2000*

Total	1,025
Median rent	$622
Median SF home value	$79,300

New Privately Owned Housing Units Authorized by Building Permit

	Units	Value
Total, 2004	0	$0
Single family	0	$0
Total, 2005	1	$100,000
Single family	1	$100,000

Real Property Valuation - parcels, 2005

	Number	Valuation
Total		$77,783,800
Vacant	41	775,500
Residential	687	52,260,900
Commercial	59	22,897,000
Industrial	3	819,700
Apartments	4	1,030,700
Farm land	0	0
Farm homestead	0	0

Average Property Value & Tax, 2005

Residential value	$76,071
Property tax	$2,885
FAIR rebate	$623

Public Library

No public municipal library.

Library statistics, 2004

	Total	per capita
Volumes	NA	NA
Expenditure	NA	NA

Public Safety

Police

Chief	Francis McKinney
Number of officers, 2004	7

Crime, 2004	Number	Rate
Total	191	81.8
Violent	23	9.8
Non-violent	168	71.9
Domestic Viol.	23	NA

Emergency/Fire

Director	Robert Wentzell

Public School District

(for school year 2004-2005 except as noted)

Brooklawn School District
Haakon Rd
Brooklawn, NJ 08030
856-456-4039

Superintendent	John Kellmayer
Grade plan	K-12
Enrollment	298.0
Students per teacher	11.5
Per pupil expenditure	$10,494
Median faculty salary	$42,050
Median administrator salary	$85,410
Grade 12 enrollment	NA
High school graduation rate	NA

Assessment test results

(percent scoring at proficient or advanced level)

	Language	Math
Grade 3	92.6%	95.1%
Grade 8	89.3%	85.7%
High school	NA	NA

SAT

Percent tested	NA
Average SAT math score	NA
Average SAT verbal score	NA

No Child Left Behind, 2003-04

Attendence rate (target = 90%)	95.4%
Drop rate	NA
Highly-qualified teachers	100%
District needs improvement?(AYP)	No

Municipal Finance

Fiscal Year 2005

Total tax levy	$2,959,662
County levy	745,016
County taxes	686,650
County library	49,364
County health	0
County open space	9,002
School levy	1,181,183
Local muni. budget	1,033,462
Misc. revenues	1,453,196
Total aid	$292,762
CMPTRA	110,929
Muni. block grant	9,230
Energy tax receipts	147,603
Homeland security	25,000

Fiscal Year 2006

Total aid	$292,762
CMPTRA	105,763
Muni. block grant	9,230
Energy tax receipts	152,769
Homeland security	25,000

Taxes

	2003	2004	2005
General tax rate per $100	3.58	3.760	3.793
Net valuation taxable	$77,818,220	$77,743,168	$78,043,592
State equalized value	$85,084,430	$88,674,955	$99,405,925
County equalization ratio	96.59	91.46	87.63

Demographics & Socio-Economic Characteristics
(2000 U.S. Census, except as noted)

Population
1980*	3,642
1990*	4,441
2000	3,873
Male	1,887
Female	1,986
2004 (estimate)*	3,862
Persons per sq. mi. of land	508

Race & Hispanic Origin, 2000
Race
White	2,993
Black/African American	296
Amer. Indian/Alaska Natv.	20
Asian	17
Natv. Hawaiian/Pac. Islander	1
Other Race	408
Two or more races	138
Hispanic origin, total	916
Mexican	175
Puerto Rican	660
Cuban	8
Other Hispanic	73

Age & Nativity, 2000
Under 5 years	245
18 years and over	2,876
21 years and over	2,715
65 years and over	613
85 years and over	59
Median Age	36.2
Native born	3,626
Foreign born	247

Educational Attainment, 2000
Population 25 years and over	2,552
0-8 yrs of school	17.4%
High School grad or higher	62.3%
Bachelor's degree or higher	8.8%
Graduate degree	2.5%

Income & Poverty, 1999
Per capita income	$16,717
Median household income	$35,679
Median family income	$44,352
Persons in poverty	725
H'holds receiving public assistance	28
H'holds receiving social security	513

Households, 2000
Total households	1,454
With persons under 18	525
With persons over 65	475
Family households	978
One person households	407
Persons per household	2.64
Persons per family	3.23

Labor & Employment
Total civilian labor force, 2004**	2,230
Unemployment rate	11.5%
Total civilian labor force, 2000	1,779
Unemployment rate	8.3%

Employed persons 16 years and over by occupation, 2000
Managers & professionals	353
Service occupations	296
Sales & office occupations	401
Farming, fishing & forestry	103
Construction & maintenance	190
Production & transportation	288
Self-employed persons	80

*US Census Bureau
**New Jersey Department of Labor

General Information
Borough of Buena
616 Central Ave
Minotola, NJ 08341
856-697-9393

Web site	buenaboro.org
Land area (sq. miles)	7.61
Water area (sq. miles)	0
Type of government	Borough
Form of government	B

Government

Legislative Districts
US Congressional	2
State Legislative	1

Local Officials, 2006
Mayor	Joseph Baruffi
Admin/Manager	NA
Clerk	Maryann Coraluzzo
Finance Dir/Treas	Nancy Brunini
Engineer	Remington & Vernick
Attorney	Robert DeSanto
Tax assessor	Dennis Deklerk
Tax collector	Mary Ann Coraluzzo
Building officer	Anthony Casadia
Zoning officer	John Keenan
Public Works	William Nimohay

Housing & Construction

Housing Units, 2000*
Total	1,553
Median rent	$639
Median SF home value	$98,100

New Privately Owned Housing Units Authorized by Building Permit
	Units	Value
Total, 2004	9	$1,078,800
Single family	9	$1,078,800
Total, 2005	6	$794,992
Single family	6	$794,992

Real Property Valuation - parcels, 2005
	Number	Valuation
Total		$145,310,200
Vacant	212	3,307,600
Residential	1,205	104,157,000
Commercial	105	17,422,200
Industrial	3	5,075,000
Apartments	8	4,300,400
Farm land	100	9,550,400
Farm homestead	160	1,497,600

Average Property Value & Tax, 2005
Residential value	$77,403
Property tax	$2,920
FAIR rebate	$636

Public Library

No public municipal library.

Library statistics, 2004
	Total	per capita
Volumes	NA	NA
Expenditure	NA	NA

Public Safety

Police
Chief	Douglas Adams
Number of officers, 2004	10

Crime, 2004	Number	Rate
Total	120	31.3
Violent	22	5.7
Non-violent	98	25.6
Domestic Viol.	50	NA

Emergency/Fire
Director	NA

Public School District
(for school year 2004-2005 except as noted)

Buena Regional School District
Harding Highway
Buena, NJ 08310
856-697-0800

Superintendent	Diane DeGiacomo
Grade plan	K-12
Enrollment	2,606.5
Students per teacher	11.9
Per pupil expenditure	$11,076
Median faculty salary	$53,958
Median administrator salary	$92,850
Grade 12 enrollment	220.0
High school graduation rate	88.5%

Assessment test results
(percent scoring at proficient or advanced level)
	Language	Math
Grade 3	85.1%	85.1%
Grade 8	71.8%	59.7%
High school	76.3%	67.2%

SAT
Percent tested	58%
Average SAT math score	489
Average SAT verbal score	483

No Child Left Behind, 2003-04
Attendance rate (target = 90%)	93.6%
Drop rate	3.2%
Highly-qualified teachers	93.1%
District needs improvement?(AYP)	Yes

Municipal Finance

Fiscal Year 2005
Total tax levy	$5,537,497
County levy	805,682
County taxes	657,737
County library	72,886
County health	35,868
County open space	39,191
School levy	3,292,539
Local muni. budget	1,439,277
Misc. revenues	1,435,827
Total aid	$648,738
CMPTRA	317,554
Muni. block grant	19,432
Energy tax receipts	286,752
Homeland security	25,000

Fiscal Year 2006
Total aid	$648,738
CMPTRA	307,518
Muni. block grant	19,432
Energy tax receipts	296,788
Homeland security	25,000

Taxes
	2003	2004	2005
General tax rate per $100	3.25	3.425	3.773
Net valuation taxable	$144,579,001	$145,362,009	$146,766,272
State equalized value	$179,467,479	$192,395,779	$222,812,012
County equalization ratio	87.01	80.56	75.35

Demographics & Socio-Economic Characteristics
(2000 U.S. Census, except as noted)

Population
1980*	6,959
1990*	7,655
2000	7,436
Male	3,622
Female	3,814
2004 (estimate)*	7,563
Persons per sq. mi. of land	183

Race & Hispanic Origin, 2000
Race
White	5,751
Black/African American	1,167
Amer. Indian/Alaska Natv.	16
Asian	17
Natv. Hawaiian/Pac. Islander	1
Other Race	303
Two or more races	181
Hispanic origin, total	689
Mexican	63
Puerto Rican	513
Cuban	7
Other Hispanic	106

Age & Nativity, 2000
Under 5 years	409
18 years and over	5,598
21 years and over	5,317
65 years and over	1,138
85 years and over	120
Median Age	39
Native born	7,174
Foreign born	262

Educational Attainment, 2000
Population 25 years and over	5,007
0-8 yrs of school	9.7%
High School grad or higher	70.3%
Bachelor's degree or higher	12.2%
Graduate degree	3.8%

Income & Poverty, 1999
Per capita income	$18,382
Median household income	$43,770
Median family income	$50,403
Persons in poverty	890
H'holds receiving public assistance	47
H'holds receiving social security	861

Households, 2000
Total households	2,648
With persons under 18	935
With persons over 65	818
Family households	1,973
One-person households	555
Persons per household	2.77
Persons per family	3.2

Labor & Employment
Total civilian labor force, 2004**	3,711
Unemployment rate	7.4%
Total civilian labor force, 2000	3,719
Unemployment rate	6.7%

Employed persons 16 years and over by occupation, 2000
Managers & professionals	683
Service occupations	599
Sales & office occupations	938
Farming, fishing & forestry	40
Construction & maintenance	550
Production & transportation	658
Self-employed persons	195

*US Census Bureau
**New Jersey Department of Labor

General Information
Township of Buena Vista
PO Box 605
890 Harding Hwy
Buena, NJ 08310
856-697-2100
Web site	www.buenavistatownship.org
Land area (sq. miles)	41.36
Water area (sq. miles)	0.16
Type of government	Township
Form of government	TC

Government

Legislative Districts
US Congressional	2
State Legislative	1

Local Officials, 2006
Mayor	Chuck Chiarello
Admin/Manager	Ronald Trebing
Clerk	LaVerne Gunter
Finance Dir/Treas	Ronald Trebing
Engineer	David Scheidegg
Attorney	Joseph Gindhart
Tax assessor	Bernadette Leonardi
Tax collector	Peter Micheletti Sr.
Building officer	NJDCA
Zoning officer	Albert Pellegrini
Public Works	Richard Calareso

Housing & Construction

Housing Units, 2000*
Total	2,827
Median rent	$740
Median SF home value	$96,100

New Privately Owned Housing Units Authorized by Building Permit
	Units	Value
Total, 2004	16	$1,638,450
Single family	16	$1,638,450
Total, 2005	23	$2,575,869
Single family	23	$2,575,869

Real Property Valuation - parcels, 2005
	Number	Valuation
Total		$261,551,000
Vacant	3,275	17,808,100
Residential	2,330	202,693,900
Commercial	76	21,267,400
Industrial	15	6,281,100
Apartments	0	0
Farm land	117	11,207,900
Farm homestead	276	2,292,600

Average Property Value & Tax, 2005
Residential value	$78,659
Property tax	$2,852
FAIR rebate	$575

Public Library

No public municipal library.

Library statistics, 2004
	Total	per capita
Volumes	NA	NA
Expenditure	NA	NA

Public Safety

Police
Chief	(State)
Number of officers, 2004	0

Crime, 2004	Number	Rate
Total	180	23.8
Violent	25	3.3
Non-violent	155	20.5
Domestic Viol.	77	NA

Emergency/Fire
Director	NA

Public School District
(for school year 2004-2005 except as noted)

Buena Regional School District
Harding Highway
Buena, NJ 08310
856-697-0800
Superintendent	Diane DeGiacomo
Grade plan	K-12
Enrollment	2,606.5
Students per teacher	11.9
Per pupil expenditure	$11,076
Median faculty salary	$53,958
Median administrator salary	$92,850
Grade 12 enrollment	220.0
High school graduation rate	88.5%

Assessment test results
(percent scoring at proficient or advanced level)
	Language	Math
Grade 3	85.1%	85.1%
Grade 8	71.8%	59.7%
High school	76.3%	67.2%

SAT
Percent tested	58%
Average SAT math score	489
Average SAT verbal score	483

No Child Left Behind, 2003-04
Attendence rate (target = 90%)	93.6%
Drop rate	3.2%
Highly-qualified teachers	93.1%
District needs improvement?(AYP)	Yes

Municipal Finance

Fiscal Year 2005
Total tax levy	$9,519,352
County levy	1,634,881
County taxes	1,334,332
County library	148,066
County health	72,866
County open space	79,616
School levy	6,579,249
Local muni. budget	1,305,223
Misc. revenues	2,785,786
Total aid	$976,132
CMPTRA	287,721
Muni. block grant	33,496
Energy tax receipts	654,915
Homeland security	0

Fiscal Year 2006
Total aid	$976,132
CMPTRA	264,799
Muni. block grant	33,496
Energy tax receipts	677,837
Homeland security	NA

Taxes
	2003	2004	2005
General tax rate per $100	2.94	3.238	3.626
Net valuation taxable	$253,699,448	$257,753,183	$262,577,992
State equalized value	$353,292,644	$388,776,636	$453,973,015
County equalization ratio	81.51	71.81	66.20

Demographics & Socio-Economic Characteristics
(2000 U.S. Census, except as noted)

Population
1980*	10,246
1990*	9,835
2000	9,736
Male	4,618
Female	5,118
2004 (estimate)*	9,833
Persons per sq. mi. of land	3,277

Race & Hispanic Origin, 2000
Race
White	6,638
Black/African American	2,592
Amer. Indian/Alaska Natv.	26
Asian	125
Natv. Hawaiian/Pac. Islander	1
Other Race	126
Two or more races	228
Hispanic origin, total	332
Mexican	32
Puerto Rican	193
Cuban	7
Other Hispanic	100

Age & Nativity, 2000
Under 5 years	618
18 years and over	7,408
21 years and over	7,072
65 years and over	1,636
85 years and over	189
Median Age	38.1
Native born	9,129
Foreign born	607

Educational Attainment, 2000
Population 25 years and over	6,646
0-8 yrs of school	6.7%
High School grad or higher	77.6%
Bachelor's degree or higher	12.1%
Graduate degree	3.7%

Income & Poverty, 1999
Per capita income	$20,208
Median household income	$43,115
Median family income	$47,969
Persons in poverty	776
H'holds receiving public assistance	156
H'holds receiving social security	1,357

Households, 2000
Total households	3,898
With persons under 18	1,270
With persons over 65	1,254
Family households	2,521
One-person households	1,167
Persons per household	2.48
Persons per family	3.09

Labor & Employment
Total civilian labor force, 2004**	5,819
Unemployment rate	6.3%
Total civilian labor force, 2000	5,004
Unemployment rate	5.6%

Employed persons 16 years and over by occupation, 2000
Managers & professionals	1,161
Service occupations	794
Sales & office occupations	1,414
Farming, fishing & forestry	7
Construction & maintenance	459
Production & transportation	888
Self-employed persons	153

*US Census Bureau
**New Jersey Department of Labor

General Information
City of Burlington
525 High St
Burlington, NJ 08016
609-386-0200
Web site	www.burlingtonnj.us
Land area (sq. miles)	3.00
Water area (sq. miles)	0.72
Type of government	City
Form of government	MC '50

Government

Legislative Districts
US Congressional	4
State Legislative	7

Local Officials, 2006
Mayor	Darlene Scocca
Admin/Manager	Robin Snodgrass
Clerk	Cindy Crivaro
Finance Dir/Treas	Kenneth MacMillan
Engineer	Jeffrey Taylor
Attorney	Anthony Valenti
Tax assessor	Dennis Bianchini
Tax collector	Lynette Miller
Building officer	Robert Wiley
Zoning officer	NA
Public Works	NA

Housing & Construction

Housing Units, 2000*
Total	4,181
Median rent	$620
Median SF home value	$97,600

New Privately Owned Housing Units Authorized by Building Permit
	Units	Value
Total, 2004	12	$971,492
Single family	12	$971,492
Total, 2005	12	$907,442
Single family	12	$907,442

Real Property Valuation - parcels, 2005
	Number	Valuation
Total		$434,697,300
Vacant	263	8,283,500
Residential	3,228	305,062,600
Commercial	331	85,990,100
Industrial	11	26,049,800
Apartments	15	9,311,300
Farm land	0	0
Farm homestead	0	0

Average Property Value & Tax, 2005
Residential value	$94,505
Property tax	$3,078
FAIR rebate	$660

Public Library
Library Co. of Burlington
23 W Union St
Burlington, NJ 08016
609-386-1273
Director ... Michele Stricker

Library statistics, 2004
	Total	per capita
Volumes	22,151	2.28
Expenditure	$143,501	$14.74

Public Safety

Police
Chief	John Lazzarotti
Number of officers, 2004	30

Crime, 2004	Number	Rate
Total	229	23.3
Violent	63	6.4
Non-violent	166	16.9
Domestic Viol.	180	NA

Emergency/Fire
Director ... David Ekelburg

Public School District
(for school year 2004-2005 except as noted)

Burlington City School District
518 Locust Ave
Burlington, NJ 08016
609-387-5874
Superintendent	Edward Gola Jr.
Grade plan	K-12
Enrollment	1,856.0
Students per teacher	8.9
Per pupil expenditure	$14,052
Median faculty salary	$46,302
Median administrator salary	$95,297
Grade 12 enrollment	133.0
High school graduation rate	86.5%

Assessment test results
(percent scoring at proficient or advanced level)
	Language	Math
Grade 3	83.2%	87.2%
Grade 8	64.3%	52.2%
High school	76.8%	66.1%

SAT
Percent tested	64%
Average SAT math score	455
Average SAT verbal score	451

No Child Left Behind, 2003-04
Attendence rate (target = 90%)	93.9%
Drop rate	3.7%
Highly-qualified teachers	100%
District needs improvement?(AYP)	No

Municipal Finance

Fiscal Year 2005
Total tax levy	$14,258,987
County levy	2,451,769
County taxes	2,056,743
County library	180,103
County health	0
County open space	214,922
School levy	7,788,361
Local muni. budget	4,018,857
Misc. revenues	9,172,893
Total aid	$6,064,042
CMPTRA	334,949
Muni. block grant	43,035
Energy tax receipts	5,636,058
Homeland security	50,000

Fiscal Year 2006
Total aid	$6,064,042
CMPTRA	137,687
Muni. block grant	43,035
Energy tax receipts	5,833,320
Homeland security	50,000

Taxes
	2003	2004	2005
General tax rate per $100	3.04	3.159	3.257
Net valuation taxable	$436,805,066	$436,784,940	$437,853,174
State equalized value	$481,009,873	$532,350,607	$630,095,228
County equalization ratio	98.78	90.81	81.92

Demographics & Socio-Economic Characteristics
(2000 U.S. Census, except as noted)

Population
1980*	11,527
1990*	12,454
2000	20,294
Male	9,620
Female	10,674
2004 (estimate)*	21,994
Persons per sq. mi. of land	1,632

Race & Hispanic Origin, 2000
Race
White	13,742
Black/African American	4,971
Amer. Indian/Alaska Natv.	33
Asian	757
Natv. Hawaiian/Pac. Islander	6
Other Race	296
Two or more races	489
Hispanic origin, total	814
Mexican	84
Puerto Rican	401
Cuban	28
Other Hispanic	301

Age & Nativity, 2000
Under 5 years	1,819
18 years and over	14,775
21 years and over	14,289
65 years and over	2,558
85 years and over	536
Median Age	35.6
Native born	18,695
Foreign born	1,599

Educational Attainment, 2000
Population 25 years and over	13,724
0-8 yrs of school	5.0%
High School grad or higher	85.1%
Bachelor's degree or higher	26.0%
Graduate degree	7.2%

Income & Poverty, 1999
Per capita income	$24,754
Median household income	$61,663
Median family income	$70,958
Persons in poverty	969
H'holds receiving public assistance	163
H'holds receiving social security	1,550

Households, 2000
Total households	7,112
With persons under 18	3,081
With persons over 65	1,313
Family households	5,280
One-person households	1,521
Persons per household	2.72
Persons per family	3.18

Labor & Employment
Total civilian labor force, 2004**	7,911
Unemployment rate	4.5%
Total civilian labor force, 2000	10,552
Unemployment rate	3.9%

Employed persons 16 years and over by occupation, 2000
Managers & professionals	3,796
Service occupations	1,429
Sales & office occupations	2,857
Farming, fishing & forestry	43
Construction & maintenance	684
Production & transportation	1,336
Self-employed persons	314

*US Census Bureau
**New Jersey Department of Labor

General Information
Burlington Township
PO Box 340
Burlington, NJ 08016
609-386-4444
Web site	www.twp.burlington.nj.us
Land area (sq. miles)	13.47
Water area (sq. miles)	0.50
Type of government	Township
Form of government	MC '50

Government
Legislative Districts
US Congressional	4
State Legislative	7

Local Officials, 2006
Mayor	Stephen M. George
Admin/Manager	Kevin J.McLernon
Clerk	Anthony J. Carnivale J
Finance Dir/Treas	Dawn M. Hubbard
Engineer	Robert L. Schreibel
Attorney	Kenneth S. Domzalski
Tax assessor	Harry Renwick Jr.
Tax collector	Dolores Coolidge
Building officer	Henry Freck
Zoning officer	Edward M. Stetz Jr.
Public Works	NA

Housing & Construction
Housing Units, 2000*
Total	7,348
Median rent	$621
Median SF home value	$151,600

New Privately Owned Housing Units Authorized by Building Permit
	Units	Value
Total, 2004	15	$1,320,541
Single family	15	$1,320,541
Total, 2005	17	$1,756,479
Single family	17	$1,756,479

Real Property Valuation - parcels, 2005
	Number	Valuation
Total		$2,336,682,510
Vacant	301	62,368,200
Residential	6,563	1,636,150,960
Commercial	184	369,438,400
Industrial	41	203,500,900
Apartments	7	57,190,000
Farm land	11	6,244,000
Farm homestead	63	1,790,050

Average Property Value & Tax, 2005
Residential value	$247,199
Property tax	$4,615
FAIR rebate	$486

Public Library
No public municipal library.

Library statistics, 2004
	Total	per capita
Volumes	NA	NA
Expenditure	NA	NA

Public Safety
Police
Chief	NA
Number of officers, 2004	43

Crime, 2004	Number	Rate
Total	523	24
Violent	29	1.3
Non-violent	494	22.7
Domestic Viol.	158	NA

Emergency/Fire
Director	William Diamond

Public School District
(for school year 2004-2005 except as noted)

Burlington Township School District
PO Box 428
Burlington, NJ 08016
609-387-3955
Superintendent	Christopher Manno
Grade plan	K-12
Enrollment	4,120.0
Students per teacher	12.7
Per pupil expenditure	$9,453
Median faculty salary	$44,351
Median administrator salary	$90,001
Grade 12 enrollment	245.0
High school graduation rate	97.9%

Assessment test results
(percent scoring at proficient or advanced level)
	Language	Math
Grade 3	86.0%	80.2%
Grade 8	76.0%	63.9%
High school	85.1%	80.4%

SAT
Percent tested	82%
Average SAT math score	485
Average SAT verbal score	485

No Child Left Behind, 2003-04
Attendence rate (target = 90%)	95.4%
Drop rate	1%
Highly-qualified teachers	100%
District needs improvement?(AYP)	No

Municipal Finance
Fiscal Year 2005
Total tax levy	$43,712,049
County levy	9,344,409
County taxes	7,838,391
County library	686,639
County health	0
County open space	819,378
School levy	29,222,659
Local muni. budget	5,144,981
Misc. revenues	17,663,902
Total aid	$5,639,724
CMPTRA	661,857
Muni. block grant	79,573
Energy tax receipts	4,808,294
Homeland security	90,000

Fiscal Year 2006
Total aid	$5,639,724
CMPTRA	493,567
Muni. block grant	79,573
Energy tax receipts	4,976,584
Homeland security	90,000

Taxes
	2003	2004	2005
General tax rate per $100	2.84	2.979	1.867
Net valuation taxable	$1,289,327,856	$1,319,352,405	$2,341,425,856
State equalized value	$1,787,505,692	$1,987,961,523	$2,422,081,159
County equalization ratio	84.81	72.13	114.58

Demographics & Socio-Economic Characteristics

(2000 U.S. Census, except as noted)

Population

1980*	7,616
1990*	7,392
2000	7,420
Male	3,655
Female	3,765
2004 (estimate)*	8,118
Persons per sq. mi. of land	3,905

Race & Hispanic Origin, 2000

Race

White	7,041
Black/African American	46
Amer. Indian/Alaska Natv.	15
Asian	137
Natv. Hawaiian/Pac. Islander	1
Other Race	110
Two or more races	70
Hispanic origin, total	379
Mexican	109
Puerto Rican	89
Cuban	38
Other Hispanic	143

Age & Nativity, 2000

Under 5 years	467
18 years and over	5,813
21 years and over	5,609
65 years and over	983
85 years and over	96
Median Age	37.5
Native born	6,690
Foreign born	730

Educational Attainment, 2000

Population 25 years and over	5,293
0-8 yrs of school	4.9%
High School grad or higher	85.8%
Bachelor's degree or higher	24.1%
Graduate degree	7.4%

Income & Poverty, 1999

Per capita income	$27,113
Median household income	$57,455
Median family income	$66,199
Persons in poverty	372
H'holds receiving public assistance	33
H'holds receiving social security	703

Households, 2000

Total households	2,868
With persons under 18	934
With persons over 65	725
Family households	2,025
One-person households	691
Persons per household	2.58
Persons per family	3.09

Labor & Employment

Total civilian labor force, 2004**	4,687
Unemployment rate	4.0%
Total civilian labor force, 2000	4,156
Unemployment rate	3.0%

Employed persons 16 years and over by occupation, 2000

Managers & professionals	1,419
Service occupations	518
Sales & office occupations	1,233
Farming, fishing & forestry	4
Construction & maintenance	378
Production & transportation	481
Self-employed persons	179

*US Census Bureau
**New Jersey Department of Labor

General Information

Borough of Butler
One Ace Rd
Butler, NJ 07405
973-838-7200

Web site	NA
Land area (sq. miles)	2.08
Water area (sq. miles)	0.02
Type of government	Borough
Form of government	B

Government

Legislative Districts

US Congressional	11
State Legislative	26

Local Officials, 2006

Mayor	Joseph Heywang
Admin/Manager	James Lampmann
Clerk	Carol Ashley
Finance Dir/Treas	James Kozimor
Engineer	Paul Darmolfaski
Attorney	Martin Murphy
Tax assessor	Shawn Hopkins
Tax collector	Cora Wright
Building officer	Joseph Montemarano
Zoning officer	Bill Budesheim
Public Works	Ed Becker

Housing & Construction

Housing Units, 2000*

Total	2,923
Median rent	$796
Median SF home value	$187,500

New Privately Owned Housing Units Authorized by Building Permit

	Units	Value
Total, 2004	0	$0
Single family	0	$0
Total, 2005	0	$0
Single family	0	$0

Real Property Valuation - parcels, 2005

	Number	Valuation
Total		$707,156,500
Vacant	109	13,642,100
Residential	2,286	576,221,200
Commercial	130	76,451,000
Industrial	17	21,464,600
Apartments	12	19,376,900
Farm land	0	0
Farm homestead	1	700

Average Property Value & Tax, 2005

Residential value	$251,955
Property tax	$5,906
FAIR rebate	$556

Public Library

Butler Public Library
1 Ace Rd
Butler, NJ 07405
973-838-3262

Director	Debbie Maynard

Library statistics, 2004

	Total	per capita
Volumes	42,558	5.74
Expenditure	$212,818	$28.68

Public Safety

Police

Chief	Dennis Passenti
Number of officers, 2004	17

Crime, 2004	Number	Rate
Total	135	16.7
Violent	12	1.5
Non-violent	123	15.2
Domestic Viol.	73	NA

Emergency/Fire

Director	Earl Dean

Public School District

(for school year 2004-2005 except as noted)

Butler School District
Bartholdi Ave
Butler, NJ 07405
973-492-2032

Superintendent	Rene Rovtar
Grade plan	K-12
Enrollment	1,161.5
Students per teacher	9.6
Per pupil expenditure	$13,611
Median faculty salary	$56,806
Median administrator salary	$103,302
Grade 12 enrollment	133.5
High school graduation rate	90.8%

Assessment test results

(percent scoring at proficient or advanced level)

	Language	Math
Grade 3	86.4%	91.5%
Grade 8	70.2%	63.8%
High school	85.9%	71.0%

SAT

Percent tested	78%
Average SAT math score	523
Average SAT verbal score	510

No Child Left Behind, 2003-04

Attendance rate (target = 90%)	95.2%
Drop rate	2.5%
Highly-qualified teachers	100%
District needs improvement?(AYP)	No

Municipal Finance

Fiscal Year 2005

Total tax levy	$16,593,381
County levy	2,114,313
County taxes	1,731,816
County library	0
County health	0
County open space	382,496
School levy	10,048,230
Local muni. budget	4,430,838
Misc. revenues	4,408,309
Total aid	$1,381,908
CMPTRA	413,240
Muni. block grant	32,345
Energy tax receipts	886,323
Homeland security	50,000

Fiscal Year 2006

Total aid	$1,381,909
CMPTRA	382,219
Muni. block grant	32,345
Energy tax receipts	917,345
Homeland security	50,000

Taxes

	2003	2004	2005
General tax rate per $100	2.13	2.240	2.350
Net valuation taxable	$704,423,345	$705,520,864	$707,936,070
State equalized value	$716,241,327	$788,094,661	$897,371,112
County equalization ratio	108.44	98.35	89.51

Demographics & Socio-Economic Characteristics
(2000 U.S. Census, except as noted)

Population
1980*	7,502
1990*	8,048
2000	8,254
Male	4,098
Female	4,156
2000 (revised)	8,321
2004 (estimate)*	8,662
Persons per sq. mi. of land	411

Race & Hispanic Origin, 2000
Race
White	7,905
Black/African American	80
Amer. Indian/Alaska Natv.	5
Asian	116
Natv. Hawaiian/Pac. Islander	5
Other Race	53
Two or more races	90
Hispanic origin, total	243
Mexican	20
Puerto Rican	75
Cuban	29
Other Hispanic	119

Age & Nativity, 2000
Under 5 years	644
18 years and over	5,874
21 years and over	5,633
65 years and over	501
85 years and over	40
Median Age	36.3
Native born	7,730
Foreign born	505

Educational Attainment, 2000
Population 25 years and over	5,364
0-8 yrs of school	1.2%
High School grad or higher	94.1%
Bachelor's degree or higher	32.2%
Graduate degree	9.4%

Income & Poverty, 1999
Per capita income	$30,710
Median household income	$81,532
Median family income	$89,500
Persons in poverty	143
H'holds receiving public assistance	31
H'holds receiving social security	411

Households, 2000
Total households	2,833
With persons under 18	1,302
With persons over 65	383
Family households	2,317
One-person households	395
Persons per household	2.91
Persons per family	3.24

Labor & Employment
Total civilian labor force, 2004**	5,201
Unemployment rate	2.4%
Total civilian labor force, 2000	4,632
Unemployment rate	3.3%

Employed persons 16 years and over by occupation, 2000
Managers & professionals	1,994
Service occupations	455
Sales & office occupations	1,271
Farming, fishing & forestry	5
Construction & maintenance	408
Production & transportation	345
Self-employed persons	184

*US Census Bureau
**New Jersey Department of Labor

General Information
Township of Byram
10 Mansfield Dr
Stanhope, NJ 07874
973-347-2500

Web site	NA
Land area (sq. miles)	21.07
Water area (sq. miles)	1.11
Type of government	Township
Form of government	CM '50

Government

Legislative Districts
US Congressional	11
State Legislative	24

Local Officials, 2006
Mayor	Eskil Danielson
Admin/Manager	Greg Poff
Clerk	Doris Flynn
Finance Dir/Treas	Lisa Spring
Engineer	Harold Pellow & Asso.
Attorney	Megan Ward
Tax assessor	Penny Holenstein
Tax collector	Lisa Spring
Building officer	Richard O'Connor
Zoning officer	John Gutwerk
Public Works	Adolf Steyh

Housing & Construction

Housing Units, 2000*
Total	3,078
Median rent	$953
Median SF home value	$175,300

New Privately Owned Housing Units
Authorized by Building Permit
	Units	Value
Total, 2004	22	$4,283,452
Single family	22	$4,283,452
Total, 2005	18	$3,119,874
Single family	18	$3,119,874

Real Property Valuation - parcels, 2005
	Number	Valuation
Total		$518,450,630
Vacant	587	11,967,300
Residential	3,152	457,682,600
Commercial	102	40,165,500
Industrial	9	1,877,900
Apartments	3	643,600
Farm land	31	5,842,100
Farm homestead	125	271,630

Average Property Value & Tax, 2005
Residential value	$139,748
Property tax	$6,053
FAIR rebate	$474

Public Library
E. Louise Child Branch Library†
21 Sparta Rd
Stanhope, NJ 07874
973-770-1000
Branch Librarian — Victoria Larson

Library statistics, 2004
	Total	per capita
Volumes	NA	NA
Expenditure	NA	NA

†Branch of County Library

Public Safety

Police
Chief	Raymond Rafferty
Number of officers, 2004	16

Crime, 2004	Number	Rate
Total	80	9.4
Violent	8	0.9
Non-violent	72	8.4
Domestic Viol.	50	NA

Emergency/Fire
Director — Meg Sesselberg

Public School District
(for school year 2004-2005 except as noted)

Byram Township School District
12 Mansfield Drive
Stanhope, NJ 07874
973-347-6663

Superintendent	Joseph Pezak
Grade plan	K-8
Enrollment	1,228.0
Students per teacher	15.0
Per pupil expenditure	$9,320
Median faculty salary	$57,626
Median administrator salary	$113,372
Grade 12 enrollment	NA
High school graduation rate	NA

Assessment test results
(percent scoring at proficient or advanced level)
	Language	Math
Grade 3	92.7%	90.5%
Grade 8	90.7%	72.5%
High school	NA	NA

SAT
Percent tested	NA
Average SAT math score	NA
Average SAT verbal score	NA

No Child Left Behind, 2003-04
Attendence rate (target = 90%)	96.0%
Drop rate	NA
Highly-qualified teachers	79.1%
District needs improvement?(AYP)	No

Municipal Finance

Fiscal Year 2005
Total tax levy	$22,496,461
County levy	4,268,372
County taxes	3,622,650
County library	312,335
County health	147,030
County open space	186,356
School levy	12,924,002
Local muni. budget	5,304,087
Misc. revenues	2,906,120
Total aid	$910,121
CMPTRA	418,660
Muni. block grant	35,482
Energy tax receipts	405,979
Homeland security	50,000

Fiscal Year 2006
Total aid	$910,122
CMPTRA	404,451
Muni. block grant	35,482
Energy tax receipts	420,189
Homeland security	50,000

Taxes
	2003	2004	2005
General tax rate per $100	3.92	4.140	4.340
Net valuation taxable	$510,712,659	$514,626,091	$519,353,941
State equalized value	$788,623,624	$919,282,559	$1,027,203,206
County equalization ratio	78.77	64.76	55.93

Demographics & Socio-Economic Characteristics

(2000 U.S. Census, except as noted)

Population

1980*	7,624
1990*	7,549
2000	7,584
Male	3,423
Female	4,161
2004 (estimate)*	7,594
Persons per sq. mi. of land	6,405

Race & Hispanic Origin, 2000

Race

White	6,918
Black/African American	172
Amer. Indian/Alaska Natv.	8
Asian	308
Natv. Hawaiian/Pac. Islander	5
Other Race	91
Two or more races	82
Hispanic origin, total	352
Mexican	29
Puerto Rican	103
Cuban	26
Other Hispanic	194

Age & Nativity, 2000

Under 5 years	379
18 years and over	6,215
21 years and over	5,885
65 years and over	1,350
85 years and over	226
Median Age	39.1
Native born	6,656
Foreign born	928

Educational Attainment, 2000

Population 25 years and over	5,547
0-8 yrs of school	2.8%
High School grad or higher	91.2%
Bachelor's degree or higher	44.0%
Graduate degree	18.2%

Income & Poverty, 1999

Per capita income	$34,630
Median household income	$61,250
Median family income	$81,989
Persons in poverty	347
H'holds receiving public assistance	64
H'holds receiving social security	1,043

Households, 2000

Total households	3,311
With persons under 18	796
With persons over 65	998
Family households	1,814
One-person households	1,257
Persons per household	2.17
Persons per family	2.93

Labor & Employment

Total civilian labor force, 2004**	4,271
Unemployment rate	1.8%
Total civilian labor force, 2000	4,430
Unemployment rate	2.8%

Employed persons 16 years and over by occupation, 2000

Managers & professionals	2,257
Service occupations	368
Sales & office occupations	1,284
Farming, fishing & forestry	0
Construction & maintenance	201
Production & transportation	197
Self-employed persons	218

*US Census Bureau
**New Jersey Department of Labor

General Information

Borough of Caldwell
1 Provost Square
Caldwell, NJ 07006
973-226-6100

Web site	www.caldwell-nj.com
Land area (sq. miles)	1.19
Water area (sq. miles)	0
Type of government	Borough
Form of government	B

Government

Legislative Districts

US Congressional	11
State Legislative	27

Local Officials, 2006

Mayor	Paul Jemas
Admin/Manager	Maureen Ruane
Clerk	Maureen Ruane
Finance Dir/Treas	Maureen Ruane
Engineer	Anthony Marucci
Attorney	Stuart Koenig
Tax assessor	Jack Kelly
Tax collector	NA
Building officer	Phil Cheff
Zoning officer	Michael Rubin
Public Works	Mario Bifalco

Housing & Construction

Housing Units, 2000*

Total	3,396
Median rent	$905
Median SF home value	$228,800

New Privately Owned Housing Units Authorized by Building Permit

	Units	Value
Total, 2004	0	$15,000
Single family	0	$0
Total, 2005	0	$0
Single family	0	$0

Real Property Valuation - parcels, 2005

	Number	Valuation
Total		$1,029,259,400
Vacant	24	7,176,200
Residential	1,886	815,067,800
Commercial	191	124,774,600
Industrial	0	0
Apartments	30	82,240,800
Farm land	0	0
Farm homestead	0	0

Average Property Value & Tax, 2005

Residential value	$432,167
Property tax	$8,112
FAIR rebate	$602

Public Library

Caldwell Public Library
268 Bloomfield Ave
Caldwell, NJ 07006
973-403-4649

Director	Karen Kleppe-Lembo

Library statistics, 2004

	Total	per capita
Volumes	39,519	5.21
Expenditure	$336,217	$44.33

Public Safety

Police

Chief	John Tofanelli
Number of officers, 2004	21

Crime, 2004	Number	Rate
Total	81	10.6
Violent	10	1.3
Non-violent	71	9.3
Domestic Viol.	34	NA

Emergency/Fire

Director	Anthony Grenci

Public School District

(for school year 2004-2005 except as noted)

Caldwell-West Caldwell School District
Harrison Bldg Gray St
West Caldwell, NJ 07006
973-228-6979

Superintendent	Daniel Gerardi
Grade plan	K-12
Enrollment	2,617.0
Students per teacher	12.0
Per pupil expenditure	$11,912
Median faculty salary	$51,875
Median administrator salary	$103,339
Grade 12 enrollment	207.0
High school graduation rate	97.6%

Assessment test results

(percent scoring at proficient or advanced level)

	Language	Math
Grade 3	95.8%	88.5%
Grade 8	85.0%	78.1%
High school	95.4%	91.6%

SAT

Percent tested	96%
Average SAT math score	551
Average SAT verbal score	542

No Child Left Behind, 2003-04

Attendence rate (target = 90%)	96.7%
Drop rate	0.6%
Highly-qualified teachers	95.7%
District needs improvement?(AYP)	No

Municipal Finance

Fiscal Year 2005

Total tax levy	$19,414,190
County levy	4,270,177
County taxes	4,180,774
County library	0
County health	0
County open space	89,403
School levy	9,749,933
Local muni. budget	5,394,080
Misc. revenues	4,867,338
Total aid	$1,037,150
CMPTRA	391,866
Muni. block grant	33,001
Energy tax receipts	562,283
Homeland security	50,000

Fiscal Year 2006

Total aid	$1,037,150
CMPTRA	372,186
Muni. block grant	33,001
Energy tax receipts	581,963
Homeland security	50,000

Taxes

	2003	2004	2005
General tax rate per $100	15.27	16.140	1.880
Net valuation taxable	$105,041,936	$105,695,147	$1,034,280,810
State equalized value	$748,695,196	$869,278,935	$1,022,825,168
County equalization ratio	15.9	15.90	117.23

Demographics & Socio-Economic Characteristics
(2000 U.S. Census, except as noted)

Population
1980*	1,023
1990*	1,073
2000	1,055
Male	504
Female	551
2004 (estimate)*	1,056
Persons per sq. mi. of land	1,094

Race & Hispanic Origin, 2000
Race
White	1,041
Black/African American	0
Amer. Indian/Alaska Natv.	0
Asian	8
Natv. Hawaiian/Pac. Islander	0
Other Race	0
Two or more races	6
Hispanic origin, total	5
Mexican	3
Puerto Rican	1
Cuban	1
Other Hispanic	0

Age & Nativity, 2000
Under 5 years	67
18 years and over	772
21 years and over	746
65 years and over	112
85 years and over	8
Median Age	39.1
Native born	1,015
Foreign born	40

Educational Attainment, 2000
Population 25 years and over	735
0-8 yrs of school	3.3%
High School grad or higher	93.2%
Bachelor's degree or higher	42.4%
Graduate degree	14.8%

Income & Poverty, 1999
Per capita income	$31,064
Median household income	$76,657
Median family income	$85,963
Persons in poverty	45
H'holds receiving public assistance	2
H'holds receiving social security	75

Households, 2000
Total households	401
With persons under 18	151
With persons over 65	85
Family households	302
One-person households	85
Persons per household	2.63
Persons per family	3.11

Labor & Employment
Total civilian labor force, 2004**	728
Unemployment rate	2.6%
Total civilian labor force, 2000	549
Unemployment rate	0.9%

Employed persons 16 years and over by occupation, 2000
Managers & professionals	264
Service occupations	44
Sales & office occupations	133
Farming, fishing & forestry	0
Construction & maintenance	60
Production & transportation	43
Self-employed persons	43

*US Census Bureau
**New Jersey Department of Labor

General Information
Borough of Califon
PO Box 368
39 Academy St
Califon, NJ 07830
908-832-7850
Web site	www.califonborough-nj.org
Land area (sq. miles)	0.97
Water area (sq. miles)	0.01
Type of government	Borough
Form of government	B

Government

Legislative Districts
US Congressional	7
State Legislative	24

Local Officials, 2006
Mayor	R. Merwin Grimes
Admin/Manager	Laura Eidsvaag
Clerk	Laura Eidsvaag
Finance Dir/Treas	Bonnie Holborow
Engineer	Donald Scott
Attorney	J. Peter Jost
Tax assessor	Eloise Hagaman
Tax collector	Bonnie Holbrow
Building officer	NA
Zoning officer	NA
Public Works	NA

Housing & Construction

Housing Units, 2000*
Total	410
Median rent	$883
Median SF home value	$220,900

New Privately Owned Housing Units Authorized by Building Permit
	Units	Value
Total, 2004	3	$303,900
Single family	3	$303,900
Total, 2005	2	$333,500
Single family	2	$333,500

Real Property Valuation - parcels, 2005
	Number	Valuation
Total		$88,769,349
Vacant	67	1,476,500
Residential	385	76,610,500
Commercial	28	8,919,644
Industrial	0	0
Apartments	2	294,400
Farm land	7	1,439,500
Farm homestead	21	28,805

Average Property Value & Tax, 2005
Residential value	$188,767
Property tax	$7,734
FAIR rebate	$516

Public Library
Bunnvale Library†
23 Bunnvale Rd
Califon, NJ 07830
908-638-8884
Branch Librarian	Marie Taluba

Library statistics, 2004
	Total	per capita
Volumes	NA	NA
Expenditure	NA	NA

†Branch of County Library

Public Safety
Police
Chief	NA
Number of officers, 2004	2

Crime, 2004	Number	Rate
Total	6	5.7
Violent	0	0
Non-violent	6	5.7
Domestic Viol.	0	NA

Emergency/Fire
Director	Michael Mitelski

Public School District
(for school year 2004-2005 except as noted)

Califon School District
6 School St
Califon, NJ 07830
908-832-2828
Administrator	Kathleen Prystash
Grade plan	K-8
Enrollment	140.0
Students per teacher	7.5
Per pupil expenditure	$12,126
Median faculty salary	$38,900
Median administrator salary	$83,750
Grade 12 enrollment	NA
High school graduation rate	NA

Assessment test results
(percent scoring at proficient or advanced level)
	Language	Math
Grade 3	100%	92.3%
Grade 8	100%	84.7%
High school	NA	NA

SAT
Percent tested	NA
Average SAT math score	NA
Average SAT verbal score	NA

No Child Left Behind, 2003-04
Attendence rate (target = 90%)	97.4%
Drop rate	NA
Highly-qualified teachers	100%
District needs improvement?(AYP)	No

Municipal Finance

Fiscal Year 2005
Total tax levy	$3,664,442
County levy	534,637
County taxes	453,937
County library	37,983
County health	0
County open space	42,717
School levy	2,544,612
Local muni. budget	585,193
Misc. revenues	327,800
Total aid	$167,000
CMPTRA	73,655
Muni. block grant	4,696
Energy tax receipts	88,649
Homeland security	0

Fiscal Year 2006
Total aid	$167,000
CMPTRA	70,552
Muni. block grant	4,696
Energy tax receipts	91,752
Homeland security	NA

Taxes
	2003	2004	2005
General tax rate per $100	3.73	3.890	4.100
Net valuation taxable	$89,045,072	$88,700,555	$89,443,444
State equalized value	$118,395,256	$136,160,182	$147,014,208
County equalization ratio	72.48	68.70	62.96

Demographics & Socio-Economic Characteristics
(2000 U.S. Census, except as noted)

Population
1980*	84,910
1990*	87,492
2000	79,904
Male	38,784
Female	41,120
2004 (estimate)*	79,948
Persons per sq. mi. of land	9,062

Race & Hispanic Origin, 2000
Race
White	13,454
Black/African American	42,628
Amer. Indian/Alaska Natv.	435
Asian	1,958
Natv. Hawaiian/Pac. Islander	59
Other Race	18,239
Two or more races	3,131
Hispanic origin, total	31,019
Mexican	1,908
Puerto Rican	23,051
Cuban	206
Other Hispanic	5,854

Age & Nativity, 2000
Under 5 years	7,302
18 years and over	52,230
21 years and over	47,879
65 years and over	6,090
85 years and over	577
Median Age	27.2
Native born	72,804
Foreign born	7,100

Educational Attainment, 2000
Population 25 years and over	42,746
0-8 yrs of school	17.7%
High School grad or higher	51.0%
Bachelor's degree or higher	5.4%
Graduate degree	1.9%

Income & Poverty, 1999
Per capita income	$9,815
Median household income	$23,421
Median family income	$24,612
Persons in poverty	26,786
H'holds receiving public assistance	3,948
H'holds receiving social security	5,714

Households, 2000
Total households	24,177
With persons under 18	12,530
With persons over 65	4,818
Family households	17,434
One-person households	5,439
Persons per household	3.12
Persons per family	3.62

Labor & Employment
Total civilian labor force, 2004**	33,346
Unemployment rate	15.2%
Total civilian labor force, 2000	27,304
Unemployment rate	15.9%

Employed persons 16 years and over by occupation, 2000
Managers & professionals	3,850
Service occupations	5,858
Sales & office occupations	5,763
Farming, fishing & forestry	68
Construction & maintenance	1,528
Production & transportation	5,906
Self-employed persons	637

*US Census Bureau
**New Jersey Department of Labor

General Information
City of Camden
PO Box 95120
Camden, NJ 08101
856-757-7000

Web site	www.ci.camden.nj.us
Land area (sq. miles)	8.82
Water area (sq. miles)	1.56
Type of government	City
Form of government	MC '50

Government

Legislative Districts
US Congressional	1
State Legislative	5

Local Officials, 2006
Mayor	Gwendolyn A. Faison
Admin/Manager	Christine Jones-Tucker
Clerk	Luis Pastoriza
Finance Dir/Treas	Richard Wright
Engineer	Uzo Ahiarakwe
Attorney	Lewis Wilson
Tax assessor	Frank Librizzi
Tax collector	Sherry Garton
Building officer	Roberto Scouler
Zoning officer	NA
Public Works	Roberto Feliz

Housing & Construction

Housing Units, 2000*
Total	29,769
Median rent	$522
Median SF home value	$40,700

New Privately Owned Housing Units Authorized by Building Permit
	Units	Value
Total, 2004	141	$12,978,681
Single family	24	$3,915,214
Total, 2005	17	$1,795,650
Single family	1	$45,000

Real Property Valuation - parcels, 2005
	Number	Valuation
Total		$769,578,907
Vacant	4,407	18,737,352
Residential	20,417	522,547,450
Commercial	1,439	132,275,951
Industrial	97	61,685,500
Apartments	189	34,332,654
Farm land	0	0
Farm homestead	0	0

Average Property Value & Tax, 2005
Residential value	$25,594
Property tax	$1,145
FAIR rebate	$529

Public Library
Camden Free Public Library
418 Federal St
Camden, NJ 08101
856-757-7650

Director .... Theresa Gorman

Library statistics, 2004
	Total	per capita
Volumes	160,125	2.00
Expenditure	$1,239,982	$15.52

Public Safety

Police
Chief	NA
Number of officers, 2004	428

Crime, 2004	Number	Rate
Total	7,156	89.4
Violent	1,829	22.8
Non-violent	5,327	66.5
Domestic Viol.	2,482	NA

Emergency/Fire
Director	Joseph Marini

Public School District
(for school year 2004-2005 except as noted)

Camden City School District
201 N Front St
Camden, NJ 08102
856-966-2040

Superintendent	Annette Knox
Grade plan	K-12
Enrollment	16,385.0
Students per teacher	9.1
Per pupil expenditure	$15,399
Median faculty salary	$54,164
Median administrator salary	$99,912
Grade 12 enrollment	431.0
High school graduation rate	NA

Assessment test results
(percent scoring at proficient or advanced level)
	Language	Math
Grade 3	57.6%	64.3%
Grade 8	28.5%	13.7%
High school	44.7%	30.1%

SAT
Percent tested	NA
Average SAT math score	NA
Average SAT verbal score	NA

No Child Left Behind, 2003-04
Attendence rate (target = 90%)	90.1%
Drop rate	7.6%
Highly-qualified teachers	63.7%
District needs improvement?(AYP)	Yes

Municipal Finance

Fiscal Year 2005
Total tax levy	$35,836,396
County levy	7,993,912
County taxes	7,887,773
County library	0
County health	0
County open space	106,139
School levy	7,396,722
Local muni. budget	20,445,761
Misc. revenues	145,460,898
Total aid	$55,756,082
CMPTRA	49,141,119
Muni. block grant	382,835
Energy tax receipts	6,092,128
Homeland security	140,000

Fiscal Year 2006
Total aid	$55,756,081
CMPTRA	48,927,894
Muni. block grant	382,835
Energy tax receipts	6,305,352
Homeland security	140,000

Taxes
	2003	2004	2005
General tax rate per $100	4.58	4.608	4.473
Net valuation taxable	$807,206,258	$800,144,059	$801,235,072
State equalized value	$1,040,482,416	$973,340,007	$1,074,617,854
County equalization ratio	85.55	77.58	81.66

Demographics & Socio-Economic Characteristics
(2000 U.S. Census, except as noted)

Population
1980*	4,853
1990*	4,668
2000	4,034
Male	1,987
Female	2,047
2004 (estimate)*	3,856
Persons per sq. mi. of land	1,552

Race & Hispanic Origin, 2000
Race
White	3,684
Black/African American	212
Amer. Indian/Alaska Natv.	8
Asian	16
Natv. Hawaiian/Pac. Islander	2
Other Race	51
Two or more races	61
Hispanic origin, total	153
Mexican	49
Puerto Rican	61
Cuban	11
Other Hispanic	32

Age & Nativity, 2000
Under 5 years	167
18 years and over	3,375
21 years and over	3,133
65 years and over	1,148
85 years and over	143
Median Age	47.4
Native born	3,787
Foreign born	247

Educational Attainment, 2000
Population 25 years and over	2,942
0-8 yrs of school	2.6%
High School grad or higher	87.6%
Bachelor's degree or higher	30.8%
Graduate degree	11.8%

Income & Poverty, 1999
Per capita income	$29,902
Median household income	$33,462
Median family income	$46,250
Persons in poverty	336
H'holds receiving public assistance	53
H'holds receiving social security	904

Households, 2000
Total households	1,821
With persons under 18	348
With persons over 65	863
Family households	1,035
One-person households	717
Persons per household	2.02
Persons per family	2.69

Labor & Employment
Total civilian labor force, 2004**	2,265
Unemployment rate	5.7%
Total civilian labor force, 2000	1,494
Unemployment rate	8.8%

Employed persons 16 years and over by occupation, 2000
Managers & professionals	459
Service occupations	286
Sales & office occupations	454
Farming, fishing & forestry	12
Construction & maintenance	81
Production & transportation	71
Self-employed persons	205

*US Census Bureau
**New Jersey Department of Labor

General Information
City of Cape May
643 Washington St
Cape May, NJ 08204
609-884-9530

Web site	NA
Land area (sq. miles)	2.48
Water area (sq. miles)	0.32
Type of government	City
Form of government	CM '23

Government

Legislative Districts
US Congressional	2
State Legislative	1

Local Officials, 2006
Mayor	Jerome Inderwies
Admin/Manager	Luciano Corea
Clerk	Diane Hollingshead
Finance Dir/Treas	Bruce MacLeod
Engineer	Remington & Vernick
Attorney	Anthony Monzo
Tax assessor	Michael Jones
Tax collector	NA
Building officer	William Callahan
Zoning officer	Mary Rothwell
Public Works	Robert Smith

Housing & Construction

Housing Units, 2000*
Total	4,064
Median rent	$564
Median SF home value	$212,900

New Privately Owned Housing Units Authorized by Building Permit
	Units	Value
Total, 2004	28	$11,013,076
Single family	22	$9,100,676
Total, 2005	17	$7,191,327
Single family	13	$6,604,827

Real Property Valuation - parcels, 2005
	Number	Valuation
Total		$2,110,813,500
Vacant	182	52,899,800
Residential	3,185	1,567,400,100
Commercial	277	352,860,500
Industrial	0	0
Apartments	131	137,653,100
Farm land	0	0
Farm homestead	0	0

Average Property Value & Tax, 2005
Residential value	$492,119
Property tax	$3,702
FAIR rebate	$864

Public Library
Cape May Branch Library†
110 Ocean St
Cape May, NJ 08204
609-884-9568

Branch Librarian | Linda Smith

Library statistics, 2004
	Total	per capita
Volumes	NA	NA
Expenditure	NA	NA

†Branch of County Library

Public Safety

Police
Chief	Diane Sorantino
Number of officers, 2004	22

Crime, 2004	Number	Rate
Total	218	55.6
Violent	8	2
Non-violent	210	53.5
Domestic Viol.	60	NA

Emergency/Fire
Director | Jerome Inderwies Jr.

Public School District
(for school year 2004-2005 except as noted)

Cape May City School District
921 Lafayette St
Cape May, NJ 08204
609-884-8485

Administrator	Victoria Zelenak
Grade plan	K-6
Enrollment	193.0
Students per teacher	8.0
Per pupil expenditure	$14,209
Median faculty salary	$46,687
Median administrator salary	$81,000
Grade 12 enrollment	NA
High school graduation rate	NA

Assessment test results
(percent scoring at proficient or advanced level)
	Language	Math
Grade 3	75.0%	80.0%
Grade 8	NA	NA
High school	NA	NA

SAT
Percent tested	NA
Average SAT math score	NA
Average SAT verbal score	NA

No Child Left Behind, 2003-04
Attendence rate (target = 90%)	94.2%
Drop rate	NA
Highly-qualified teachers	NA
District needs improvement?(AYP)	No

Municipal Finance

Fiscal Year 2005
Total tax levy	$15,885,261
County levy	4,750,230
County taxes	3,993,567
County library	562,722
County health	0
County open space	193,941
School levy	6,205,522
Local muni. budget	4,929,509
Misc. revenues	7,387,262
Total aid	$500,471
CMPTRA	102,320
Muni. block grant	20,425
Energy tax receipts	352,726
Homeland security	25,000

Fiscal Year 2006
Total aid	$500,470
CMPTRA	89,974
Muni. block grant	20,425
Energy tax receipts	365,071
Homeland security	25,000

Taxes
	2003	2004	2005
General tax rate per $100	1.84	0.760	0.760
Net valuation taxable	$827,501,963	$2,075,693,395	$2,111,729,697
State equalized value	$1,630,224,513	$1,898,293,361	$2,164,322,740
County equalization ratio	60.31	125.66	109.35

Demographics & Socio-Economic Characteristics

(2000 U.S. Census, except as noted)

Population

1980*	255
1990*	248
2000	241
Male	118
Female	123
2004 (estimate)*	239
Persons per sq. mi. of land	813

Race & Hispanic Origin, 2000

Race
White	229
Black/African American	5
Amer. Indian/Alaska Natv.	0
Asian	1
Natv. Hawaiian/Pac. Islander	0
Other Race	0
Two or more races	6
Hispanic origin, total	4
Mexican	3
Puerto Rican	0
Cuban	0
Other Hispanic	1

Age & Nativity, 2000

Under 5 years	5
18 years and over	225
21 years and over	224
65 years and over	115
85 years and over	18
Median Age	64.2
Native born	226
Foreign born	12

Educational Attainment, 2000

Population 25 years and over	215
0-8 yrs of school	1.9%
High School grad or higher	91.6%
Bachelor's degree or higher	54.9%
Graduate degree	17.7%

Income & Poverty, 1999

Per capita income	$52,689
Median household income	$55,313
Median family income	$69,750
Persons in poverty	4
H'holds receiving public assistance	0
H'holds receiving social security	89

Households, 2000

Total households	133
With persons under 18	11
With persons over 65	81
Family households	78
One-person households	47
Persons per household	1.81
Persons per family	2.27

Labor & Employment

Total civilian labor force, 2004**	107
Unemployment rate	5.6%
Total civilian labor force, 2000	55
Unemployment rate	5.5%

Employed persons 16 years and over by occupation, 2000
Managers & professionals	23
Service occupations	4
Sales & office occupations	25
Farming, fishing & forestry	0
Construction & maintenance	0
Production & transportation	0
Self-employed persons	4

*US Census Bureau
**New Jersey Department of Labor

General Information

Borough of Cape May Point
PO Drawer 490
Cape May Point, NJ 08212
609-884-8468

Web site	www.cmpnj.com
Land area (sq. miles)	0.29
Water area (sq. miles)	0.02
Type of government	Borough
Form of government	Comm.

Government

Legislative Districts

US Congressional	2
State Legislative	1

Local Officials, 2006

Mayor	Malcolm Fraser
Admin/Manager	NA
Clerk	Connie Mahon
Finance Dir/Treas	Francine Springer
Engineer	Bruce Graham
Attorney	George Neidig
Tax assessor	Maryann Mason
Tax collector	Susan Browning
Building officer	John McGraw
Zoning officer	John McGraw
Public Works	NA

Housing & Construction

Housing Units, 2000*

Total	501
Median rent	$850
Median SF home value	$301,400

New Privately Owned Housing Units Authorized by Building Permit

	Units	Value
Total, 2004	10	$2,177,800
Single family	10	$2,177,800
Total, 2005	7	$1,313,700
Single family	7	$1,313,700

Real Property Valuation - parcels, 2005

	Number	Valuation
Total		$280,899,900
Vacant	78	22,025,600
Residential	590	258,464,200
Commercial	1	410,100
Industrial	0	0
Apartments	0	0
Farm land	0	0
Farm homestead	0	0

Average Property Value & Tax, 2005

Residential value	$438,075
Property tax	$3,245
FAIR rebate	$965

Public Library

No public municipal library.

Library statistics, 2004

	Total	per capita
Volumes	NA	NA
Expenditure	NA	NA

Public Safety

Police

Chief	Diane Sorantino
Number of officers, 2004	0

Crime, 2004	Number	Rate
Total	6	24.8
Violent	0	0
Non-violent	6	24.8
Domestic Viol.	0	NA

Emergency/Fire

Director	Robert Shepanski

Public School District

(for school year 2004-2005 except as noted)

Cape May Point School District[†]
921 Lafayette St
Cape May, NJ 08204

[†]No schools in district - sends children to Cape May City schools.

Grade plan	NA
Enrollment	NA
Students per teacher	NA
Per pupil expenditure	NA
Median faculty salary	NA

Assessment test results

(percent scoring at proficient or advanced level)
	Language	Math
Grade 3	NA	NA
Grade 8	NA	NA
High school	NA	NA

SAT

Percent tested	NA
Average SAT math score	NA
Average SAT verbal score	NA

No Child Left Behind, 2003-04

Attendence rate (target = 90%)	NA
Drop rate	NA
Highly-qualified teachers	NA
District needs improvement?(AYP)	NA

Municipal Finance

Fiscal Year 2005

Total tax levy	$2,081,127
County levy	962,976
County taxes	809,628
County library	114,037
County health	0
County open space	39,311
School levy	111,948
Local muni. budget	1,006,203
Misc. revenues	326,256
Total aid	$34,231
CMPTRA	5,239
Muni. block grant	1,085
Energy tax receipts	27,907
Homeland security	0

Fiscal Year 2006

Total aid	$34,231
CMPTRA	4,262
Muni. block grant	1,085
Energy tax receipts	28,884
Homeland security	NA

Taxes

	2003	2004	2005
General tax rate per $100	0.69	0.700	0.750
Net valuation taxable	$278,049,291	$278,113,004	$280,937,095
State equalized value	$318,352,749	$388,769,761	$463,745,617
County equalization ratio	97.97	87.34	71.53

Demographics & Socio-Economic Characteristics
(2000 U.S. Census, except as noted)

Population
1980*	6,166
1990*	5,510
2000	5,917
Male	2,869
Female	3,048
2004 (estimate)*	6,019
Persons per sq. mi. of land	1,522

Race & Hispanic Origin, 2000
Race
White	5,260
Black/African American	81
Amer. Indian/Alaska Natv.	5
Asian	366
Natv. Hawaiian/Pac. Islander	1
Other Race	126
Two or more races	78
Hispanic origin, total	473
Mexican	27
Puerto Rican	97
Cuban	64
Other Hispanic	285

Age & Nativity, 2000
Under 5 years	303
18 years and over	4,790
21 years and over	4,621
65 years and over	904
85 years and over	86
Median Age	38.9
Native born	4,704
Foreign born	1,213

Educational Attainment, 2000
Population 25 years and over	4,306
0-8 yrs of school	7.8%
High School grad or higher	80.0%
Bachelor's degree or higher	21.0%
Graduate degree	5.7%

Income & Poverty, 1999
Per capita income	$28,713
Median household income	$55,058
Median family income	$62,040
Persons in poverty	357
H'holds receiving public assistance	60
H'holds receiving social security	688

Households, 2000
Total households	2,393
With persons under 18	670
With persons over 65	672
Family households	1,593
One-person households	631
Persons per household	2.47
Persons per family	3.04

Labor & Employment
Total civilian labor force, 2004**	3,304
Unemployment rate	3.0%
Total civilian labor force, 2000	3,332
Unemployment rate	3.3%

Employed persons 16 years and over by occupation, 2000
Managers & professionals	1,175
Service occupations	400
Sales & office occupations	1,034
Farming, fishing & forestry	0
Construction & maintenance	259
Production & transportation	355
Self-employed persons	155

*US Census Bureau
**New Jersey Department of Labor

General Information
Borough of Carlstadt
500 Madison St
Carlstadt, NJ 07072
201-939-2850

Web site	NA
Land area (sq. miles)	3.95
Water area (sq. miles)	0.28
Type of government	Borough
Form of government	B

Government
Legislative Districts
US Congressional	9
State Legislative	36

Local Officials, 2006
Mayor	William Jay Roseman
Admin/Manager	Jane Fontana
Clerk	Claire Foy
Finance Dir/Treas	Domenick Giancaspro
Engineer	Paul Sarlo
Attorney	Jay Fahy
Tax assessor	Joyce Ranone
Tax collector	NA
Building officer	Mark Sadomis (Actg.)
Zoning officer	NA
Public Works	NA

Housing & Construction
Housing Units, 2000*
Total	2,473
Median rent	$839
Median SF home value	$201,900

New Privately Owned Housing Units
Authorized by Building Permit
	Units	Value
Total, 2004	17	$1,193,273
Single family	3	$388,600
Total, 2005	27	$2,690,109
Single family	7	$1,189,533

Real Property Valuation - parcels, 2005
	Number	Valuation
Total		$1,052,918,997
Vacant	116	84,942,340
Residential	1,536	237,712,207
Commercial	147	201,179,070
Industrial	292	523,393,480
Apartments	15	5,691,900
Farm land	0	0
Farm homestead	0	0

Average Property Value & Tax, 2005
Residential value	$154,761
Property tax	$4,298
FAIR rebate	$657

Public Library
Dermody Public Library
420 Hackensack St
Carlstadt, NJ 07072
201-438-8866

Director	Mary Disanza

Library statistics, 2004
	Total	per capita
Volumes	31,609	5.34
Expenditure	$536,673	$90.70

Public Safety
Police
Chief	Thomas Nielsen
Number of officers, 2004	31

Crime, 2004	Number	Rate
Total	273	45.5
Violent	12	2
Non-violent	261	43.5
Domestic Viol.	88	NA

Emergency/Fire
Director	Jack Roughgarden

Public School District
(for school year 2004-2005 except as noted)

Carlstadt School District
550 Washington St
Carlstadt, NJ 07072
201-939-6502

Superintendent	Frank Legato
Grade plan	K-8
Enrollment	406.0
Students per teacher	10.8
Per pupil expenditure	$13,957
Median faculty salary	$72,400
Median administrator salary	$117,988
Grade 12 enrollment	NA
High school graduation rate	NA

Assessment test results
(percent scoring at proficient or advanced level)
	Language	Math
Grade 3	91.1%	91.1%
Grade 8	66.6%	62.5%
High school	NA	NA

SAT
Percent tested	NA
Average SAT math score	NA
Average SAT verbal score	NA

No Child Left Behind, 2003-04
Attendence rate (target = 90%)	94.7%
Drop rate	NA
Highly-qualified teachers	94.8%
District needs improvement?(AYP)	No

Municipal Finance
Fiscal Year 2005
Total tax levy	$29,302,004
County levy	3,602,951
County taxes	3,420,837
County library	0
County health	0
County open space	182,114
School levy	13,367,358
Local muni. budget	12,331,695
Misc. revenues	3,702,662
Total aid	$1,486,094
CMPTRA	391,557
Muni. block grant	24,110
Energy tax receipts	1,020,427
Homeland security	50,000

Fiscal Year 2006
Total aid	$1,486,094
CMPTRA	355,842
Muni. block grant	24,110
Energy tax receipts	1,056,142
Homeland security	50,000

Taxes
	2003	2004	2005
General tax rate per $100	2.37	2.550	2.780
Net valuation taxable	$1,045,752,126	$1,049,130,454	$1,055,036,099
State equalized value	$1,598,520,523	$1,791,124,899	$1,948,358,447
County equalization ratio	68.06	65.42	58.53

Demographics & Socio-Economic Characteristics
(2000 U.S. Census, except as noted)

Population
1980*	8,396
1990*	8,443
2000	7,684
Male	3,667
Female	4,017
2004 (estimate)*	7,812
Persons per sq. mi. of land	446

Race & Hispanic Origin, 2000
Race
White	6,034
Black/African American	1,250
Amer. Indian/Alaska Natv.	21
Asian	70
Natv. Hawaiian/Pac. Islander	3
Other Race	161
Two or more races	145
Hispanic origin, total	306
Mexican	42
Puerto Rican	182
Cuban	6
Other Hispanic	76

Age & Nativity, 2000
Under 5 years	467
18 years and over	5,927
21 years and over	5,621
65 years and over	1,243
85 years and over	152
Median Age	38.7
Native born	7,385
Foreign born	299

Educational Attainment, 2000
Population 25 years and over	5,240
0-8 yrs of school	7.6%
High School grad or higher	77.6%
Bachelor's degree or higher	14.1%
Graduate degree	3.8%

Income & Poverty, 1999
Per capita income	$19,978
Median household income	$41,007
Median family income	$52,213
Persons in poverty	808
H'holds receiving public assistance	116
H'holds receiving social security	931

Households, 2000
Total households	3,121
With persons under 18	1,003
With persons over 65	847
Family households	2,052
One-person households	916
Persons per household	2.42
Persons per family	2.99

Labor & Employment
Total civilian labor force, 2004**	3,928
Unemployment rate	6.4%
Total civilian labor force, 2000	3,669
Unemployment rate	8.3%

Employed persons 16 years and over by occupation, 2000
Managers & professionals	849
Service occupations	472
Sales & office occupations	902
Farming, fishing & forestry	13
Construction & maintenance	354
Production & transportation	773
Self-employed persons	130

*US Census Bureau
**New Jersey Department of Labor

General Information
Township of Carneys Point
303 Harding Highway
Carneys Point, NJ 08069
856-299-0070

Web site	NA
Land area (sq. miles)	17.50
Water area (sq. miles)	0.25
Type of government	Township
Form of government	TC

Government

Legislative Districts
US Congressional	2
State Legislative	3

Local Officials, 2006
Mayor	John Lake III
Admin/Manager	Marie Stout
Clerk	Janina Patrus
Finance Dir/Treas	Marie Stout
Engineer	Skinner, Compton & Fralinger
Attorney	John Jordan
Tax assessor	Kevin Maloney
Tax collector	Thomas Freeman
Building officer	Louis Palena
Zoning officer	John Franceschini
Public Works	Eugene Gilbert

Housing & Construction

Housing Units, 2000*
Total	3,330
Median rent	$607
Median SF home value	$89,700

New Privately Owned Housing Units Authorized by Building Permit
	Units	Value
Total, 2004	53	$4,262,463
Single family	27	$3,001,857
Total, 2005	43	$3,534,714
Single family	33	$3,049,866

Real Property Valuation - parcels, 2005
	Number	Valuation
Total		$336,298,705
Vacant	473	10,420,300
Residential	2,388	191,470,625
Commercial	159	65,452,510
Industrial	12	43,856,800
Apartments	8	15,198,000
Farm land	81	7,939,150
Farm homestead	156	1,961,320

Average Property Value & Tax, 2005
Residential value	$76,035
Property tax	$2,846
FAIR rebate	$669

Public Library
Penns Grove-Carneys Point Library†
222 S Broad St
Penns Grove, NJ 08069
856-299-4255
Director......Barbara Hunt

Library statistics, 2004
	Total	per capita
Volumes	NA	NA
Expenditure	NA	NA

†Joint Library with Penns Grove

Public Safety

Police
Chief	Cosmo Mangiocco Jr.
Number of officers, 2004	20

Crime, 2004	Number	Rate
Total	183	24.1
Violent	15	2
Non-violent	168	22.1
Domestic Viol.	55	NA

Emergency/Fire
Director	Tom Heinbaugh

Public School District
(for school year 2004-2005 except as noted)

Penns Grove-Carneys Pt. Reg. School Dist.
100 Iona Ave
Penns Grove, NJ 08069
856-299-4250
Superintendent	Joseph A. Massare
Grade plan	K-12
Enrollment	2,302.5
Students per teacher	10.9
Per pupil expenditure	$11,135
Median faculty salary	$49,835
Median administrator salary	$85,223
Grade 12 enrollment	116.0
High school graduation rate	85.4%

Assessment test results
(percent scoring at proficient or advanced level)
	Language	Math
Grade 3	70.0%	75.0%
Grade 8	48.0%	35.2%
High school	77.9%	64.1%

SAT
Percent tested	63%
Average SAT math score	469
Average SAT verbal score	469

No Child Left Behind, 2003-04
Attendence rate (target = 90%)	92.9%
Drop rate	2.7%
Highly-qualified teachers	96.2%
District needs improvement?(AYP)	No

Municipal Finance

Fiscal Year 2005
Total tax levy	$12,623,857
County levy	4,366,191
County taxes	4,279,562
County library	0
County health	0
County open space	86,628
School levy	6,485,851
Local muni. budget	1,771,815
Misc. revenues	7,965,185
Total aid	$1,254,341
CMPTRA	624,787
Muni. block grant	36,944
Energy tax receipts	542,610
Homeland security	50,000

Fiscal Year 2006
Total aid	$1,254,341
CMPTRA	605,796
Muni. block grant	36,944
Energy tax receipts	561,601
Homeland security	50,000

Taxes
	2003	2004	2005
General tax rate per $100	3.40	3.537	3.743
Net valuation taxable	$324,385,541	$331,026,409	$337,316,561
State equalized value	$366,164,963	$416,343,435	$475,294,577
County equalization ratio	84.16	88.59	79.45

Demographics & Socio-Economic Characteristics
(2000 U.S. Census, except as noted)

Population
1980*	20,598
1990*	19,025
2000	20,709
Male	10,050
Female	10,659
2000 (revised)	20,705
2004 (estimate)*	21,523
Persons per sq. mi. of land	4,934

Race & Hispanic Origin, 2000
Race
White	14,239
Black/African American	1,975
Amer. Indian/Alaska Natv.	49
Asian	1,722
Natv. Hawaiian/Pac. Islander	7
Other Race	1,918
Two or more races	799
Hispanic origin, total	4,839
Mexican	184
Puerto Rican	2,216
Cuban	244
Other Hispanic	2,195

Age & Nativity, 2000
Under 5 years	1,276
18 years and over	15,481
21 years and over	14,723
65 years and over	3,099
85 years and over	332
Median Age	37
Native born	15,866
Foreign born	4,843

Educational Attainment, 2000
Population 25 years and over	13,745
0-8 yrs of school	9.3%
High School grad or higher	74.9%
Bachelor's degree or higher	12.8%
Graduate degree	3.7%

Income & Poverty, 1999
Per capita income	$18,967
Median household income	$47,148
Median family income	$54,609
Persons in poverty	2,253
H'holds receiving public assistance	248
H'holds receiving social security	2,356

Households, 2000
Total households	7,039
With persons under 18	2,807
With persons over 65	2,213
Family households	5,212
One-person households	1,544
Persons per household	2.88
Persons per family	3.38

Labor & Employment
Total civilian labor force, 2004**	10,723
Unemployment rate	5.9%
Total civilian labor force, 2000	9,972
Unemployment rate	9.4%

Employed persons 16 years and over by occupation, 2000
Managers & professionals	1,953
Service occupations	1,348
Sales & office occupations	3,016
Farming, fishing & forestry	8
Construction & maintenance	808
Production & transportation	1,903
Self-employed persons	264

*US Census Bureau
**New Jersey Department of Labor

General Information
Borough of Carteret
61 Cooke Ave
Carteret, NJ 07008
732-541-3800
Web site	www.ci.carteret.nj.us
Land area (sq. miles)	4.36
Water area (sq. miles)	0.63
Type of government	Borough
Form of government	B

Government

Legislative Districts
US Congressional	13
State Legislative	19

Local Officials, 2006
Mayor	Daniel J. Reiman
Admin/Manager	NA
Clerk	Kathleen Barney
Finance Dir/Treas	Patrick DeBlasio
Engineer	John P. Dupont
Attorney	Robert Bergen
Tax assessor	Charles Heck
Tax collector	NA
Building officer	Anthony Neibert
Zoning officer	Anthony Neibert
Public Works	NA

Housing & Construction

Housing Units, 2000*
Total	7,320
Median rent	$741
Median SF home value	$135,500

New Privately Owned Housing Units
Authorized by Building Permit
	Units	Value
Total, 2004	0	$0
Single family	0	$0
Total, 2005	404	$13,354,851
Single family	23	$2,272,251

Real Property Valuation - parcels, 2005
	Number	Valuation
Total		$975,396,300
Vacant	254	21,955,400
Residential	5,052	603,317,100
Commercial	187	114,400,500
Industrial	105	220,093,000
Apartments	9	15,630,300
Farm land	0	0
Farm homestead	0	0

Average Property Value & Tax, 2005
Residential value	$119,421
Property tax	$5,271
FAIR rebate	$639

Public Library
Carteret Public Library
100 Cooke Ave
Carteret, NJ 07008
732-541-3830
Director	Veronica Chan

Library statistics, 2004
	Total	per capita
Volumes	70,635	3.41
Expenditure	$562,468	$27.16

Public Safety

Police
Chief	John Pieczyski
Number of officers, 2004	58

Crime, 2004	Number	Rate
Total	474	21.9
Violent	56	2.6
Non-violent	418	19.3
Domestic Viol.	336	NA

Emergency/Fire
Director	Brian O'Connor

Public School District
(for school year 2004-2005 except as noted)

Carteret Borough School District
599 Roosevelt Ave
Carteret, NJ 07008
732-541-8960
Superintendent	Kevin Ahearn
Grade plan	K-12
Enrollment	3,919.5
Students per teacher	12.4
Per pupil expenditure	$10,353
Median faculty salary	$47,460
Median administrator salary	$96,446
Grade 12 enrollment	210.5
High school graduation rate	89.7%

Assessment test results
(percent scoring at proficient or advanced level)
	Language	Math
Grade 3	75.1%	83.2%
Grade 8	57.8%	49.6%
High school	76.3%	75.1%

SAT
Percent tested	73%
Average SAT math score	484
Average SAT verbal score	454

No Child Left Behind, 2003-04
Attendence rate (target = 90%)	93.0%
Drop rate	2.7%
Highly-qualified teachers	58.9%
District needs improvement?(AYP)	No

Municipal Finance

Fiscal Year 2005
Total tax levy	$43,142,330
County levy	5,339,583
County taxes	4,836,917
County library	0
County health	0
County open space	502,666
School levy	21,989,435
Local muni. budget	15,813,312
Misc. revenues	16,612,491
Total aid	$3,508,327
CMPTRA	1,910,507
Muni. block grant	83,247
Energy tax receipts	1,424,573
Homeland security	90,000

Fiscal Year 2006
Total aid	$3,508,327
CMPTRA	1,860,647
Muni. block grant	83,247
Energy tax receipts	1,474,433
Homeland security	90,000

Taxes
	2003	2004	2005
General tax rate per $100	3.97	4.100	4.420
Net valuation taxable	$964,018,523	$973,184,094	$977,494,346
State equalized value	$1,485,619,545	$1,650,056,786	$2,020,033,780
County equalization ratio	75.52	64.89	58.92

Demographics & Socio-Economic Characteristics
(2000 U.S. Census, except as noted)

Population
1980*	12,600
1990*	12,053
2000	12,300
Male	5,722
Female	6,578
2004 (estimate)*	12,565
Persons per sq. mi. of land	2,976

Race & Hispanic Origin, 2000
Race
White	11,076
Black/African American	368
Amer. Indian/Alaska Natv.	6
Asian	667
Natv. Hawaiian/Pac. Islander	3
Other Race	57
Two or more races	123
Hispanic origin, total	393
Mexican	23
Puerto Rican	112
Cuban	55
Other Hispanic	203

Age & Nativity, 2000
Under 5 years	666
18 years and over	9,934
21 years and over	9,667
65 years and over	2,766
85 years and over	539
Median Age	44
Native born	10,951
Foreign born	1,349

Educational Attainment, 2000
Population 25 years and over	9,264
0-8 yrs of school	3.7%
High School grad or higher	88.4%
Bachelor's degree or higher	41.3%
Graduate degree	14.0%

Income & Poverty, 1999
Per capita income	$36,558
Median household income	$78,863
Median family income	$94,475
Persons in poverty	230
H'holds receiving public assistance	22
H'holds receiving social security	1,529

Households, 2000
Total households	4,403
With persons under 18	1,321
With persons over 65	1,521
Family households	3,240
One-person households	1,017
Persons per household	2.57
Persons per family	3.05

Labor & Employment
Total civilian labor force, 2004**	5,859
Unemployment rate	2.1%
Total civilian labor force, 2000	5,938
Unemployment rate	1.1%

Employed persons 16 years and over by occupation, 2000
Managers & professionals	3,036
Service occupations	530
Sales & office occupations	1,751
Farming, fishing & forestry	0
Construction & maintenance	218
Production & transportation	338
Self-employed persons	348

*US Census Bureau
**New Jersey Department of Labor

General Information
Township of Cedar Grove
525 Pompton Ave
Cedar Grove, NJ 07009
973-239-1410
Web site	www.cedargrovenj.org
Land area (sq. miles)	4.22
Water area (sq. miles)	0.13
Type of government	Township
Form of government	CM '50

Government
Legislative Districts
US Congressional	8
State Legislative	40

Local Officials, 2006
Mayor	Robert O'Toole
Admin/Manager	Thomas Tucci
Clerk	Kathleen Stutz
Finance Dir/Treas	William Homa
Engineer	Stan Omland
Attorney	Thomas Scrivo
Tax assessor	Richard Hamilton
Tax collector	NA
Building officer	John D'Ascensio
Zoning officer	NA
Public Works	NA

Housing & Construction
Housing Units, 2000*
Total	4,470
Median rent	$973
Median SF home value	$237,600

New Privately Owned Housing Units Authorized by Building Permit
	Units	Value
Total, 2004	124	$16,534,963
Single family	46	$7,244,433
Total, 2005	143	$18,785,356
Single family	45	$7,112,637

Real Property Valuation - parcels, 2005
	Number	Valuation
Total		$316,315,000
Vacant	314	10,203,700
Residential	3,716	253,448,100
Commercial	152	29,148,800
Industrial	44	15,921,500
Apartments	6	7,288,500
Farm land	1	302,000
Farm homestead	1	2,400

Average Property Value & Tax, 2005
Residential value	$68,187
Property tax	$7,155
FAIR rebate	$611

Public Library
Cedar Grove Public Library
1 Municipal Plaza
Cedar Grove, NJ 07009
973-239-1447
Director	Catherine Ruf

Library statistics, 2004
	Total	per capita
Volumes	42,846	3.48
Expenditure	$574,570	$46.71

Public Safety
Police
Chief	Jeffrey Rowe
Number of officers, 2004	32

Crime, 2004	Number	Rate
Total	200	16.3
Violent	12	1
Non-violent	188	15.3
Domestic Viol.	46	NA

Emergency/Fire
Director	Tom Wilson

Public School District
(for school year 2004-2005 except as noted)

Cedar Grove Township School District
520 Pompton Ave
Cedar Grove, NJ 07009
973-239-1550
Superintendent	Gene Polles
Grade plan	K-12
Enrollment	1,544.0
Students per teacher	11.2
Per pupil expenditure	$12,696
Median faculty salary	$53,610
Median administrator salary	$112,150
Grade 12 enrollment	118.0
High school graduation rate	99.1%

Assessment test results
(percent scoring at proficient or advanced level)
	Language	Math
Grade 3	90.7%	91.4%
Grade 8	69.3%	57.7%
High school	94.4%	88.6%

SAT
Percent tested	92%
Average SAT math score	518
Average SAT verbal score	501

No Child Left Behind, 2003-04
Attendence rate (target = 90%)	96.1%
Drop rate	0.8%
Highly-qualified teachers	95.3%
District needs improvement?(AYP)	No

Municipal Finance
Fiscal Year 2005
Total tax levy	$33,217,341
County levy	8,732,737
County taxes	8,549,901
County library	0
County health	0
County open space	182,836
School levy	18,918,288
Local muni. budget	5,566,316
Misc. revenues	5,228,854
Total aid	$1,479,858
CMPTRA	462,378
Muni. block grant	52,740
Energy tax receipts	889,053
Homeland security	70,000

Fiscal Year 2006
Total aid	$1,479,859
CMPTRA	431,262
Muni. block grant	52,740
Energy tax receipts	920,170
Homeland security	70,000

Taxes
	2003	2004	2005
General tax rate per $100	9.99	10.430	10.500
Net valuation taxable	$305,334,200	$309,915,700	$316,579,600
State equalized value	$1,603,646,008	$1,770,564,897	$2,092,396,563
County equalization ratio	21.44	21.44	17.49

Demographics & Socio-Economic Characteristics

(2000 U.S. Census, except as noted)

Population

1980*	8,537
1990*	8,007
2000	8,460
Male	4,037
Female	4,423
2004 (estimate)*	8,428
Persons per sq. mi. of land	3,493

Race & Hispanic Origin, 2000

Race

White	8,104
Black/African American	12
Amer. Indian/Alaska Natv.	5
Asian	238
Natv. Hawaiian/Pac. Islander	1
Other Race	42
Two or more races	58
Hispanic origin, total	223
Mexican	22
Puerto Rican	29
Cuban	17
Other Hispanic	155

Age & Nativity, 2000

Under 5 years	871
18 years and over	6,068
21 years and over	5,924
65 years and over	1,098
85 years and over	148
Median Age	36.9
Native born	7,629
Foreign born	831

Educational Attainment, 2000

Population 25 years and over	5,723
0-8 yrs of school	1.5%
High School grad or higher	96.6%
Bachelor's degree or higher	66.7%
Graduate degree	28.3%

Income & Poverty, 1999

Per capita income	$53,027
Median household income	$101,991
Median family income	$119,635
Persons in poverty	188
H'holds receiving public assistance	7
H'holds receiving social security	747

Households, 2000

Total households	3,159
With persons under 18	1,271
With persons over 65	766
Family households	2,384
One-person households	673
Persons per household	2.67
Persons per family	3.14

Labor & Employment

Total civilian labor force, 2004**	4,487
Unemployment rate	2.2%
Total civilian labor force, 2000	4,197
Unemployment rate	2.1%

Employed persons 16 years and over by occupation, 2000

Managers & professionals	2,567
Service occupations	298
Sales & office occupations	986
Farming, fishing & forestry	0
Construction & maintenance	102
Production & transportation	155
Self-employed persons	244

*US Census Bureau
**New Jersey Department of Labor

General Information

Chatham Borough
54 Fairmount Ave
Chatham, NJ 07928
973-635-0674

Web site	www.chathamborough.org
Land area (sq. miles)	2.41
Water area (sq. miles)	0
Type of government	Borough
Form of government	B

Government

Legislative Districts

US Congressional	11
State Legislative	26

Local Officials, 2006

Mayor	Richard Plambeck
Admin/Manager	Robert J. Falzarano
Clerk	Susan Caljean
Finance Dir/Treas	Dorothy Klein
Engineer	Vincent DeNave
Attorney	David Lloyd
Tax assessor	Pat Aceto
Tax collector	Madeline Polidor-LeBoeuf
Building officer	William Jankowski
Zoning officer	Leonard Taylor
Public Works	Robert Venezia

Housing & Construction

Housing Units, 2000*

Total	3,232
Median rent	$1,082
Median SF home value	$376,900

New Privately Owned Housing Units Authorized by Building Permit

	Units	Value
Total, 2004	18	$4,402,763
Single family	10	$2,818,688
Total, 2005	9	$1,655,172
Single family	9	$1,655,172

Real Property Valuation - parcels, 2005

	Number	Valuation
Total		$2,029,387,500
Vacant	59	12,685,100
Residential	2,687	1,739,443,300
Commercial	193	220,482,100
Industrial	28	15,418,000
Apartments	15	41,358,800
Farm land	0	0
Farm homestead	1	200

Average Property Value & Tax, 2005

Residential value	$647,114
Property tax	$8,938
FAIR rebate	$588

Public Library

Library Of The Chathams†
214 Main St
Chatham, NJ 07928
973-635-0603

Director ... Diane O'Brien

Library statistics, 2004

	Total	per capita
Volumes	86,183	4.65
Expenditure	$1,293,697	$69.76

†Joint Library with Chatham Twp

Public Safety

Police

Chief	John Drake
Number of officers, 2004	24

Crime, 2004	Number	Rate
Total	94	11.1
Violent	7	0.8
Non-violent	87	10.3
Domestic Viol.	22	NA

Emergency/Fire

Director ... Peter Gloglolich

Public School District

(for school year 2004-2005 except as noted)

School District of the Chathams
54 Fairmount Ave
Chatham, NJ 07928
973-635-5656

Superintendent	James O'Neill
Grade plan	K-12
Enrollment	3,255.5
Students per teacher	11.5
Per pupil expenditure	$12,233
Median faculty salary	$57,447
Median administrator salary	$123,503
Grade 12 enrollment	204.0
High school graduation rate	98.5%

Assessment test results

(percent scoring at proficient or advanced level)

	Language	Math
Grade 3	98.4%	97.6%
Grade 8	94.5%	90.4%
High school	98.0%	95.6%

SAT

Percent tested	96%
Average SAT math score	602
Average SAT verbal score	591

No Child Left Behind, 2003-04

Attendence rate (target = 90%)	96.3%
Drop rate	0%
Highly-qualified teachers	97.6%
District needs improvement?(AYP)	No

Municipal Finance

Fiscal Year 2005

Total tax levy	$28,055,822
County levy	4,898,824
County taxes	4,012,804
County library	0
County health	0
County open space	886,019
School levy	17,081,123
Local muni. budget	6,075,875
Misc. revenues	6,181,930
Total aid	$915,500
CMPTRA	317,228
Muni. block grant	35,036
Energy tax receipts	510,933
Homeland security	50,000

Fiscal Year 2006

Total aid	$915,500
CMPTRA	299,345
Muni. block grant	35,036
Energy tax receipts	528,816
Homeland security	50,000

Taxes

	2003	2004	2005
General tax rate per $100	3.10	3.310	1.390
Net valuation taxable	$786,691,019	$790,982,131	$2,031,217,435
State equalized value	$1,692,172,551	$1,827,062,134	$2,036,308,206
County equalization ratio	52.46	46.49	110.74

Demographics & Socio-Economic Characteristics
(2000 U.S. Census, except as noted)

Population
1980*	8,883
1990*	9,361
2000	10,086
Male	4,803
Female	5,283
2004 (estimate)*	10,162
Persons per sq. mi. of land	1,089

Race & Hispanic Origin, 2000
Race
White	9,452
Black/African American	45
Amer. Indian/Alaska Natv.	6
Asian	485
Natv. Hawaiian/Pac. Islander	1
Other Race	15
Two or more races	82
Hispanic origin, total	197
Mexican	27
Puerto Rican	26
Cuban	22
Other Hispanic	122

Age & Nativity, 2000
Under 5 years	768
18 years and over	7,392
21 years and over	7,209
65 years and over	1,366
85 years and over	185
Median Age	40.1
Native born	8,874
Foreign born	1,212

Educational Attainment, 2000
Population 25 years and over	7,013
0-8 yrs of school	1.0%
High School grad or higher	96.6%
Bachelor's degree or higher	65.7%
Graduate degree	31.7%

Income & Poverty, 1999
Per capita income	$65,497
Median household income	$106,208
Median family income	$131,609
Persons in poverty	271
H'holds receiving public assistance	13
H'holds receiving social security	911

Households, 2000
Total households	3,920
With persons under 18	1,380
With persons over 65	922
Family households	2,772
One-person households	1,030
Persons per household	2.54
Persons per family	3.11

Labor & Employment
Total civilian labor force, 2004**	5,431
Unemployment rate	2.8%
Total civilian labor force, 2000	4,995
Unemployment rate	1.3%

Employed persons 16 years and over by occupation, 2000
Managers & professionals	3,132
Service occupations	255
Sales & office occupations	1,296
Farming, fishing & forestry	0
Construction & maintenance	134
Production & transportation	111
Self-employed persons	361

*US Census Bureau
**New Jersey Department of Labor

General Information
Township of Chatham
58 Meyersville Rd
Chatham, NJ 07928
973-635-4600
Web site	www.chathamtownship.org
Land area (sq. miles)	9.33
Water area (sq. miles)	0.02
Type of government	Township
Form of government	TC

Government

Legislative Districts
US Congressional	11
State Legislative	21

Local Officials, 2006
Mayor	William P. O'Conner
Admin/Manager	Thomas Ciccarone
Clerk	Joy Wiley
Finance Dir/Treas	Thomas Ciccarone
Engineer	John Ruschke
Attorney	Carl Woodward
Tax assessor	E. Delguercio/E. Hladky
Tax collector	Mary Ellen Babyack
Building officer	Greg Impink
Zoning officer	Donald Schmidt
Public Works	Joseph Smith

Housing & Construction

Housing Units, 2000*
Total	4,019
Median rent	$1,371
Median SF home value	$449,000

New Privately Owned Housing Units Authorized by Building Permit
	Units	Value
Total, 2004	28	$12,832,108
Single family	26	$12,191,106
Total, 2005	43	$20,324,191
Single family	43	$17,778,831

Real Property Valuation - parcels, 2005
	Number	Valuation
Total		$2,733,271,100
Vacant	196	32,899,900
Residential	3,640	2,487,098,300
Commercial	31	127,975,400
Industrial	4	13,725,100
Apartments	3	60,260,000
Farm land	12	10,798,600
Farm homestead	23	513,800

Average Property Value & Tax, 2005
Residential value	$679,119
Property tax	$8,901
FAIR rebate	$595

Public Library
Library Of The Chathams†
214 Main St
Chatham, NJ 07928
973-635-0603
Director	Diane O'Brien

Library statistics, 2004
	Total	per capita
Volumes	86,183	4.65
Expenditure	$1,293,697	$69.76

†Joint Library with Chatham Boro

Public Safety

Police
Chief	Elizabeth Goeckel
Number of officers, 2004	24

Crime, 2004	Number	Rate
Total	50	5
Violent	1	0.1
Non-violent	49	4.9
Domestic Viol.	42	NA

Emergency/Fire
Director	J. Burke/M. Sciaretta

Public School District
(for school year 2004-2005 except as noted)

School District of the Chathams
54 Fairmount Ave
Chatham, NJ 07928
973-635-5656
Superintendent	James O'Neill
Grade plan	K-12
Enrollment	3,255.5
Students per teacher	11.5
Per pupil expenditure	$12,233
Median faculty salary	$57,447
Median administrator salary	$123,503
Grade 12 enrollment	204.0
High school graduation rate	98.5%

Assessment test results
(percent scoring at proficient or advanced level)
	Language	Math
Grade 3	98.4%	97.6%
Grade 8	94.5%	90.4%
High school	98.0%	95.6%

SAT
Percent tested	96%
Average SAT math score	602
Average SAT verbal score	591

No Child Left Behind, 2003-04
Attendence rate (target = 90%)	96.3%
Drop rate	0%
Highly-qualified teachers	97.6%
District needs improvement?(AYP)	No

Municipal Finance

Fiscal Year 2005
Total tax levy	$35,841,193
County levy	6,391,109
County taxes	5,235,408
County library	0
County health	0
County open space	1,155,700
School levy	22,143,135
Local muni. budget	7,306,950
Misc. revenues	3,397,621
Total aid	$1,234,418
CMPTRA	226,986
Muni. block grant	40,961
Energy tax receipts	896,471
Homeland security	70,000

Fiscal Year 2006
Total aid	$1,234,418
CMPTRA	195,610
Muni. block grant	40,961
Energy tax receipts	927,847
Homeland security	70,000

Taxes
	2003	2004	2005
General tax rate per $100	2.44	2.580	1.320
Net valuation taxable	$1,286,893,289	$1,291,888,451	$2,734,636,563
State equalized value	$2,193,069,681	$2,368,393,424	$2,707,292,905
County equalization ratio	64.54	58.68	114.30

Demographics & Socio-Economic Characteristics
(2000 U.S. Census, except as noted)

Population
1980*	68,785
1990*	69,348
2000	69,965
Male	33,450
Female	36,515
2000 (revised)	69,945
2004 (estimate)*	71,929
Persons per sq. mi. of land	2,966

Race & Hispanic Origin, 2000
Race
White	59,240
Black/African American	3,121
Amer. Indian/Alaska Natv.	71
Asian	6,205
Natv. Hawaiian/Pac. Islander	24
Other Race	491
Two or more races	813
Hispanic origin, total	1,778
Mexican	252
Puerto Rican	823
Cuban	96
Other Hispanic	607

Age & Nativity, 2000
Under 5 years	3,928
18 years and over	53,495
21 years and over	51,739
65 years and over	12,570
85 years and over	1,814
Median Age	41.8
Native born	61,245
Foreign born	8,720

Educational Attainment, 2000
Population 25 years and over	49,401
0-8 yrs of school	2.8%
High School grad or higher	91.0%
Bachelor's degree or higher	46.2%
Graduate degree	19.1%

Income & Poverty, 1999
Per capita income	$32,658
Median household income	$69,421
Median family income	$80,766
Persons in poverty	2,725
H'holds receiving public assistance	452
H'holds receiving social security	8,124

Households, 2000
Total households	26,227
With persons under 18	8,930
With persons over 65	8,218
Family households	19,399
One-person households	5,900
Persons per household	2.61
Persons per family	3.08

Labor & Employment
Total civilian labor force, 2004**	38,202
Unemployment rate	2.9%
Total civilian labor force, 2000	35,499
Unemployment rate	3.7%

Employed persons 16 years and over by occupation, 2000
Managers & professionals	18,091
Service occupations	3,249
Sales & office occupations	9,710
Farming, fishing & forestry	23
Construction & maintenance	1,259
Production & transportation	1,865
Self-employed persons	2,383

*US Census Bureau
**New Jersey Department of Labor

General Information
Township of Cherry Hill
PO Box 5002
820 Mercer St
Cherry Hill, NJ 08002
856-665-6500
Web site	www.cherryhill-nj.com
Land area (sq. miles)	24.25
Water area (sq. miles)	0.11
Type of government	Township
Form of government	MC '50

Government

Legislative Districts
US Congressional	3
State Legislative	6

Local Officials, 2006
Mayor	Bernie Platt
Admin/Manager	Maris Kukainis
Clerk	Nancy L. Saffos
Finance Dir/Treas	Peggy Bustard
Engineer	Edward Vernick
Attorney	Lisa Kmiec
Tax assessor	Thomas Glock
Tax collector	Carol Redmond
Building officer	Anthony Saccamanno
Zoning officer	NA
Public Works	NA

Housing & Construction

Housing Units, 2000*
Total	27,074
Median rent	$793
Median SF home value	$154,900

New Privately Owned Housing Units
Authorized by Building Permit
	Units	Value
Total, 2004	40	$7,230,744
Single family	40	$7,230,744
Total, 2005	155	$11,844,863
Single family	31	$8,439,863

Real Property Valuation - parcels, 2005
	Number	Valuation
Total		$4,576,754,700
Vacant	726	74,187,200
Residential	23,625	3,287,141,000
Commercial	911	1,004,921,300
Industrial	222	116,305,100
Apartments	16	90,470,600
Farm land	6	3,550,500
Farm homestead	8	179,000

Average Property Value & Tax, 2005
Residential value	$139,099
Property tax	$6,230
FAIR rebate	$593

Public Library
Cherry Hill Public Library
1100 Kings Hwy North
Cherry Hill, NJ 08034
856-667-0300
Director . . . . Manuel Paredes (Actg)

Library statistics, 2004
	Total	per capita
Volumes	119,052	1.70
Expenditure	$2,062,092	$29.47

Public Safety

Police
Chief	Clarence Jones
Number of officers, 2004	130

Crime, 2004	Number	Rate
Total	2,327	32.7
Violent	104	1.5
Non-violent	2,223	31.3
Domestic Viol.	420	NA

Emergency/Fire
Director . . . . Robert Giorgio

Public School District
(for school year 2004-2005 except as noted)

Cherry Hill Township School District
45 Ranoldo Terrace
Cherry Hill, NJ 08034
856-429-5600
Superintendent	Timothy Brennan (Int)
Grade plan	K-12
Enrollment	11,527.0
Students per teacher	11.8
Per pupil expenditure	$11,821
Median faculty salary	$50,143
Median administrator salary	$105,450
Grade 12 enrollment	904.0
High school graduation rate	NA

Assessment test results
(percent scoring at proficient or advanced level)
	Language	Math
Grade 3	94.5%	94.1%
Grade 8	87.0%	81.9%
High school	94.3%	90.3%

SAT
Percent tested	NA
Average SAT math score	NA
Average SAT verbal score	NA

No Child Left Behind, 2003-04
Attendence rate (target = 90%)	94.6%
Drop rate	0.4%
Highly-qualified teachers	100%
District needs improvement?(AYP)	No

Municipal Finance

Fiscal Year 2005
Total tax levy	$205,525,294
County levy	53,693,081
County taxes	52,998,182
County library	0
County health	0
County open space	694,899
School levy	124,630,828
Local muni. budget	27,201,385
Misc. revenues	24,623,328
Total aid	$11,864,526
CMPTRA	5,644,998
Muni. block grant	303,443
Energy tax receipts	5,776,085
Homeland security	140,000

Fiscal Year 2006
Total aid	$11,864,526
CMPTRA	5,442,835
Muni. block grant	303,443
Energy tax receipts	5,978,248
Homeland security	140,000

Taxes
	2003	2004	2005
General tax rate per $100	3.81	4.093	4.479
Net valuation taxable	$4,566,106,673	$4,577,073,436	$4,588,818,942
State equalized value	$6,015,158,310	$6,878,700,158	$8,438,431,302
County equalization ratio	84.44	75.91	66.47

Demographics & Socio-Economic Characteristics
(2000 U.S. Census, except as noted)

Population
1980*	1,590
1990*	1,526
2000	1,520
Male	760
Female	760
2004 (estimate)*	1,811
Persons per sq. mi. of land	1,055

Race & Hispanic Origin, 2000
Race
White	568
Black/African American	851
Amer. Indian/Alaska Natv.	3
Asian	5
Natv. Hawaiian/Pac. Islander	0
Other Race	44
Two or more races	49
Hispanic origin, total	62
Mexican	6
Puerto Rican	45
Cuban	2
Other Hispanic	9

Age & Nativity, 2000
Under 5 years	66
18 years and over	1,172
21 years and over	1,120
65 years and over	229
85 years and over	21
Median Age	42.1
Native born	1,486
Foreign born	34

Educational Attainment, 2000
Population 25 years and over	1,060
0-8 yrs of school	9.3%
High School grad or higher	65.7%
Bachelor's degree or higher	9.5%
Graduate degree	4.1%

Income & Poverty, 1999
Per capita income	$15,252
Median household income	$41,786
Median family income	$50,263
Persons in poverty	214
H'holds receiving public assistance	20
H'holds receiving social security	196

Households, 2000
Total households	493
With persons under 18	171
With persons over 65	165
Family households	345
One-person households	124
Persons per household	2.81
Persons per family	3.32

Labor & Employment
Total civilian labor force, 2004**	675
Unemployment rate	7.3%
Total civilian labor force, 2000	651
Unemployment rate	8.6%

Employed persons 16 years and over by occupation, 2000
Managers & professionals	150
Service occupations	115
Sales & office occupations	152
Farming, fishing & forestry	4
Construction & maintenance	73
Production & transportation	101
Self-employed persons	26

*US Census Bureau
**New Jersey Department of Labor

General Information
Borough of Chesilhurst
201 Grant Ave
Chesilhurst, NJ 08089
856-767-4153
Web site	www.chesilhurstgov.org
Land area (sq. miles)	1.72
Water area (sq. miles)	0
Type of government	Borough
Form of government	B

Government

Legislative Districts
US Congressional	1
State Legislative	6

Local Officials, 2006
Mayor	Arland Poindexter Jr.
Admin/Manager	NA
Clerk	Sylvia VanNockay
Finance Dir/Treas	Charlene Ganges
Engineer	Steven Back
Attorney	Harvey Johnson
Tax assessor	Theresa Stalgiano
Tax collector	NA
Building officer	NA
Zoning officer	William Morris Sr.
Public Works	NA

Housing & Construction

Housing Units, 2000*
Total	535
Median rent	$817
Median SF home value	$93,300

New Privately Owned Housing Units Authorized by Building Permit
	Units	Value
Total, 2004	23	$1,312,757
Single family	18	$1,043,518
Total, 2005	12	$664,396
Single family	7	$395,157

Real Property Valuation - parcels, 2005
	Number	Valuation
Total		$44,549,736
Vacant	342	3,971,400
Residential	432	37,422,836
Commercial	18	2,337,800
Industrial	3	596,800
Apartments	2	220,900
Farm land	0	0
Farm homestead	0	0

Average Property Value & Tax, 2005
Residential value	$86,627
Property tax	$3,000
FAIR rebate	$638

Public Library

No public municipal library.

Library statistics, 2004
	Total	per capita
Volumes	NA	NA
Expenditure	NA	NA

Public Safety

Police
Chief	Sheldon Fortune
Number of officers, 2004	10

Crime, 2004	Number	Rate
Total	39	22.2
Violent	8	4.6
Non-violent	31	17.7
Domestic Viol.	14	NA

Emergency/Fire
Director	Robert Barney

Public School District
(for school year 2004-2005 except as noted)

Chesilhurst Borough School District
511 Edwards Ave
Chesilhurst, NJ 08089
856-767-5451
Administrator	Abdi Gass
Grade plan	K-12
Enrollment	150.0
Students per teacher	11.0
Per pupil expenditure	$12,327
Median faculty salary	$51,349
Median administrator salary	$87,550
Grade 12 enrollment	NA
High school graduation rate	NA

Assessment test results
(percent scoring at proficient or advanced level)
	Language	Math
Grade 3	31.3%	43.8%
Grade 8	NA	NA
High school	NA	NA

SAT
Percent tested	NA
Average SAT math score	NA
Average SAT verbal score	NA

No Child Left Behind, 2003-04
Attendence rate (target = 90%)	93.8%
Drop rate	NA
Highly-qualified teachers	91.7%
District needs improvement?(AYP)	No

Municipal Finance

Fiscal Year 2005
Total tax levy	$1,551,601
County levy	441,313
County taxes	406,740
County library	29,241
County health	0
County open space	5,332
School levy	773,547
Local muni. budget	336,742
Misc. revenues	1,651,409
Total aid	$889,403
CMPTRA	768,768
Muni. block grant	6,677
Energy tax receipts	88,775
Homeland security	25,000

Fiscal Year 2006
Total aid	$889,403
CMPTRA	765,661
Muni. block grant	6,677
Energy tax receipts	91,882
Homeland security	25,000

Taxes
	2003	2004	2005
General tax rate per $100	3.20	3.225	3.463
Net valuation taxable	$44,192,570	$44,448,735	$44,806,765
State equalized value	$48,745,389	$52,596,738	$57,972,267
County equalization ratio	94.36	90.66	84.42

Demographics & Socio-Economic Characteristics
(2000 U.S. Census, except as noted)

Population
1980*	1433
1990*	1,214
2000	1,635
Male	819
Female	816
2004 (estimate)*	1,655
Persons per sq. mi. of land	1,076

Race & Hispanic Origin, 2000
Race
White	1,548
Black/African American	13
Amer. Indian/Alaska Natv.	0
Asian	28
Natv. Hawaiian/Pac. Islander	0
Other Race	33
Two or more races	13
Hispanic origin, total	112
Mexican	59
Puerto Rican	1
Cuban	4
Other Hispanic	48

Age & Nativity, 2000
Under 5 years	120
18 years and over	1,229
21 years and over	1,192
65 years and over	223
85 years and over	34
Median Age	39.1
Native born	1,434
Foreign born	201

Educational Attainment, 2000
Population 25 years and over	1,138
0-8 yrs of school	3.5%
High School grad or higher	90.2%
Bachelor's degree or higher	48.3%
Graduate degree	19.9%

Income & Poverty, 1999
Per capita income	$42,564
Median household income	$80,398
Median family income	$106,260
Persons in poverty	84
H'holds receiving public assistance	4
H'holds receiving social security	172

Households, 2000
Total households	609
With persons under 18	218
With persons over 65	172
Family households	427
One-person households	145
Persons per household	2.66
Persons per family	3.15

Labor & Employment
Total civilian labor force, 2004**	736
Unemployment rate	2.8%
Total civilian labor force, 2000	836
Unemployment rate	5.0%

Employed persons 16 years and over by occupation, 2000
Managers & professionals	394
Service occupations	108
Sales & office occupations	187
Farming, fishing & forestry	0
Construction & maintenance	51
Production & transportation	54
Self-employed persons	44

*US Census Bureau
**New Jersey Department of Labor

General Information
Borough of Chester
300 Main St
Chester, NJ 07930
908-879-5361
Web site	www.chesterborough.org
Land area (sq. miles)	1.54
Water area (sq. miles)	0
Type of government	Borough
Form of government	B

Government

Legislative Districts
US Congressional	11
State Legislative	24

Local Officials, 2006
Mayor	Dennis Verbaro
Admin/Manager	Ricky Prill
Clerk	Valerie Egan
Finance Dir/Treas	Vidya Nayak
Engineer	Ferriero Engineering
Attorney	Brian Mason
Tax assessor	Edward Kerwin
Tax collector	John Gregory
Building officer	Steven Freedman
Zoning officer	Jack Mendelsohn
Public Works	Paul Kapral

Housing & Construction

Housing Units, 2000*
Total	627
Median rent	$802
Median SF home value	$313,600

New Privately Owned Housing Units Authorized by Building Permit
	Units	Value
Total, 2004	1	$63,752
Single family	1	$63,752
Total, 2005	1	$17,201
Single family	1	$17,201

Real Property Valuation - parcels, 2005
	Number	Valuation
Total		$369,040,600
Vacant	17	5,229,200
Residential	463	217,617,700
Commercial	137	140,571,400
Industrial	0	0
Apartments	3	2,010,000
Farm land	8	3,545,100
Farm homestead	10	67,200

Average Property Value & Tax, 2005
Residential value	$460,222
Property tax	$8,821
FAIR rebate	$576

Public Library
Chester Library†
250 W Main St
Chester, NJ 07930
908-879-7612
Director	Susan Persak

Library statistics, 2004
	Total	per capita
Volumes	46,615	5.23
Expenditure	$487,685	$54.69

†Joint Library with Chester Twp

Public Safety

Police
Chief	Neil Logan
Number of officers, 2004	8

Crime, 2004	Number	Rate
Total	32	19.3
Violent	4	2.4
Non-violent	28	16.9
Domestic Viol.	3	NA

Emergency/Fire
Director	Angelo Bolio

Public School District
(for school year 2004-2005 except as noted)

Chester Township School District
415 Route 24
Chester, NJ 07930
908-879-7383
Superintendent	Michael Roth
Grade plan	K-8
Enrollment	1,332.0
Students per teacher	11.0
Per pupil expenditure	$12,073
Median faculty salary	$53,945
Median administrator salary	$101,975
Grade 12 enrollment	NA
High school graduation rate	NA

Assessment test results
(percent scoring at proficient or advanced level)
	Language	Math
Grade 3	97.7%	95.3%
Grade 8	94.0%	87.9%
High school	NA	NA

SAT
Percent tested	NA
Average SAT math score	NA
Average SAT verbal score	NA

No Child Left Behind, 2003-04
Attendence rate (target = 90%)	95.7%
Drop rate	NA
Highly-qualified teachers	86.5%
District needs improvement?(AYP)	No

Municipal Finance

Fiscal Year 2005
Total tax levy	$7,106,806
County levy	833,956
County taxes	683,141
County library	0
County health	0
County open space	150,815
School levy	3,801,887
Local muni. budget	2,470,963
Misc. revenues	1,134,354
Total aid	$240,208
CMPTRA	68,763
Muni. block grant	6,411
Energy tax receipts	140,034
Homeland security	25,000

Fiscal Year 2006
Total aid	$240,208
CMPTRA	63,862
Muni. block grant	6,411
Energy tax receipts	144,935
Homeland security	25,000

Taxes
	2003	2004	2005
General tax rate per $100	2.11	2.240	1.920
Net valuation taxable	$302,393,233	$304,200,284	$370,787,766
State equalized value	$292,082,713	$308,649,905	$376,587,209
County equalization ratio	108.64	103.53	119.17

Demographics & Socio-Economic Characteristics
(2000 U.S. Census, except as noted)

Population
1980*	5,198
1990*	5,958
2000	7,282
Male	3,586
Female	3,696
2004 (estimate)*	7,765
Persons per sq. mi. of land	265

Race & Hispanic Origin, 2000
Race
White	6,927
Black/African American	84
Amer. Indian/Alaska Natv.	1
Asian	174
Natv. Hawaiian/Pac. Islander	4
Other Race	19
Two or more races	73
Hispanic origin, total	188
Mexican	12
Puerto Rican	49
Cuban	21
Other Hispanic	106

Age & Nativity, 2000
Under 5 years	532
18 years and over	5,064
21 years and over	4,919
65 years and over	664
85 years and over	77
Median Age	39.6
Native born	6,616
Foreign born	666

Educational Attainment, 2000
Population 25 years and over	4,789
0-8 yrs of school	1.4%
High School grad or higher	96.3%
Bachelor's degree or higher	63.7%
Graduate degree	30.7%

Income & Poverty, 1999
Per capita income	$55,353
Median household income	$117,298
Median family income	$133,586
Persons in poverty	163
H'holds receiving public assistance	0
H'holds receiving social security	396

Households, 2000
Total households	2,323
With persons under 18	1,111
With persons over 65	399
Family households	2,013
One-person households	240
Persons per household	3.05
Persons per family	3.29

Labor & Employment
Total civilian labor force, 2004**	3,594
Unemployment rate	2.8%
Total civilian labor force, 2000	3,500
Unemployment rate	2.1%

Employed persons 16 years and over by occupation, 2000
Managers & professionals	2,113
Service occupations	197
Sales & office occupations	816
Farming, fishing & forestry	8
Construction & maintenance	207
Production & transportation	86
Self-employed persons	323

*US Census Bureau
**New Jersey Department of Labor

General Information
Township of Chester
1 Parker Rd
Chester, NJ 07930
908-879-5100
Web site	www.chestertownship.org
Land area (sq. miles)	29.33
Water area (sq. miles)	0.01
Type of government	Township
Form of government	SM '50

Government

Legislative Districts
US Congressional	11
State Legislative	24

Local Officials, 2006
Mayor	Benjamin Spinelli
Admin/Manager	Carol Isemann
Clerk	Carol Isemann
Finance Dir/Treas	E. Naomi Caruso
Engineer	Peter Turek
Attorney	John Suminski
Tax assessor	Maureen Kaman
Tax collector	NA
Building officer	Jim Fania
Zoning officer	Sarah Jane Noll
Public Works	NA

Housing & Construction

Housing Units, 2000*
Total	2,377
Median rent	$1,315
Median SF home value	$407,900

New Privately Owned Housing Units Authorized by Building Permit
	Units	Value
Total, 2004	32	$9,946,516
Single family	32	$9,946,516
Total, 2005	18	$5,637,450
Single family	18	$5,637,450

Real Property Valuation - parcels, 2005
	Number	Valuation
Total		$981,376,242
Vacant	209	16,402,700
Residential	2,468	892,335,662
Commercial	80	29,388,100
Industrial	9	1,930,000
Apartments	1	353,400
Farm land	97	39,767,500
Farm homestead	133	1,198,880

Average Property Value & Tax, 2005
Residential value	$343,535
Property tax	$10,673
FAIR rebate	SM $565

Public Library
Chester Library†
250 W Main St
Chester, NJ 07930
908-879-7612
Director	Susan Persak

Library statistics, 2004
	Total	per capita
Volumes	46,615	5.23
Expenditure	$487,685	$54.69

†Joint Library with Chester Boro

Public Safety
Police
Chief	Adam Schuler
Number of officers, 2004	16

Crime, 2004	Number	Rate
Total	54	7
Violent	3	0.4
Non-violent	51	6.7
Domestic Viol.	22	NA

Emergency/Fire
Director	Dan Taquinto

Public School District
(for school year 2004-2005 except as noted)

Chester Township School District
415 Route 24
Chester, NJ 07930
908-879-7383
Superintendent	Michael Roth
Grade plan	K-8
Enrollment	1,332.0
Students per teacher	11.0
Per pupil expenditure	$12,073
Median faculty salary	$53,945
Median administrator salary	$101,975
Grade 12 enrollment	NA
High school graduation rate	NA

Assessment test results
(percent scoring at proficient or advanced level)
	Language	Math
Grade 3	97.7%	95.3%
Grade 8	94.0%	87.9%
High school	NA	NA

SAT
Percent tested	NA
Average SAT math score	NA
Average SAT verbal score	NA

No Child Left Behind, 2003-04
Attendance rate (target = 90%)	95.7%
Drop rate	NA
Highly-qualified teachers	86.5%
District needs improvement?(AYP)	No

Municipal Finance

Fiscal Year 2005
Total tax levy	$30,532,164
County levy	4,488,188
County taxes	3,676,435
County library	0
County health	0
County open space	811,753
School levy	21,585,901
Local muni. budget	4,458,075
Misc. revenues	12,688,093
Total aid	$1,205,851
CMPTRA	196,919
Muni. block grant	28,553
Energy tax receipts	930,379
Homeland security	50,000

Fiscal Year 2006
Total aid	$1,205,852
CMPTRA	164,356
Muni. block grant	28,553
Energy tax receipts	962,943
Homeland security	50,000

Taxes
	2003	2004	2005
General tax rate per $100	2.76	2.890	3.110
Net valuation taxable	$943,800,188	$971,424,626	$982,730,899
State equalized value	$1,512,500,301	$1,666,061,713	$1,868,309,694
County equalization ratio	67.77	62.40	58.27

Demographics & Socio-Economic Characteristics
(2000 U.S. Census, except as noted)

Population
1980*	3,867
1990*	5,152
2000	5,955
Male	4,619
Female	1,336
2004 (estimate)*	6,110
Persons per sq. mi. of land	285

Race & Hispanic Origin, 2000
Race
White	2,960
Black/African American	2,225
Amer. Indian/Alaska Natv.	40
Asian	38
Natv. Hawaiian/Pac. Islander	5
Other Race	503
Two or more races	184
Hispanic origin, total	735
Mexican	43
Puerto Rican	478
Cuban	27
Other Hispanic	187

Age & Nativity, 2000
Under 5 years	183
18 years and over	5,250
21 years and over	4,581
65 years and over	299
85 years and over	25
Median Age	24.6
Native born	5,752
Foreign born	203

Educational Attainment, 2000
Population 25 years and over	2,790
0-8 yrs of school	2.6%
High School grad or higher	78.5%
Bachelor's degree or higher	26.6%
Graduate degree	7.5%

Income & Poverty, 1999
Per capita income	$17,193
Median household income	$85,428
Median family income	$91,267
Persons in poverty	46
H'holds receiving public assistance	11
H'holds receiving social security	233

Households, 2000
Total households	899
With persons under 18	374
With persons over 65	209
Family households	744
One-person households	115
Persons per household	2.91
Persons per family	3.19

Labor & Employment
Total civilian labor force, 2004**	1,780
Unemployment rate	1.6%
Total civilian labor force, 2000	1,396
Unemployment rate	3.5%

Employed persons 16 years and over by occupation, 2000
Managers & professionals	663
Service occupations	154
Sales & office occupations	296
Farming, fishing & forestry	17
Construction & maintenance	111
Production & transportation	106
Self-employed persons	104

*US Census Bureau
**New Jersey Department of Labor

General Information
Township of Chesterfield
300 Brdntn-Chstrfld Rd
Trenton, NJ 08620
609-298-2311
Web site	www.chesterfieldtwp.com
Land area (sq. miles)	21.41
Water area (sq. miles)	0.09
Type of government	Township
Form of government	TC

Government
Legislative Districts
US Congressional	4
State Legislative	30

Local Officials, 2006
Mayor	Michael Hlubik
Admin/Manager	NA
Clerk	Bonnie Haines
Finance Dir/Treas	Janice Jones
Engineer	Nancy Jamanow
Attorney	John Gillespie
Tax assessor	William Tantum
Tax collector	Janice Jones
Building officer	Raymond Verner
Zoning officer	NA
Public Works	G. Lebak/R. Bartell/W. Idell

Housing & Construction
Housing Units, 2000*
Total	924
Median rent	$940
Median SF home value	$197,500

New Privately Owned Housing Units
Authorized by Building Permit
	Units	Value
Total, 2004	33	$4,894,251
Single family	33	$4,894,251
Total, 2005	105	$11,591,341
Single family	87	$11,495,066

Real Property Valuation - parcels, 2005
	Number	Valuation
Total		$263,696,500
Vacant	363	19,989,000
Residential	883	192,059,500
Commercial	46	19,985,700
Industrial	0	0
Apartments	1	161,700
Farm land	110	25,595,000
Farm homestead	236	5,905,600

Average Property Value & Tax, 2005
Residential value	$176,913
Property tax	$5,490
FAIR rebate	$529

Public Library
Crosswicks Public Library
483 Main St
Crosswicks, NJ 08515
609-298-6271
Director	Alice Bumbera

Library statistics, 2004
	Total	per capita
Volumes	20,249	3.40
Expenditure	$24,703	$4.15

Public Safety
Police
Chief	Kyle Wilson
Number of officers, 2004	9

Crime, 2004	Number	Rate
Total	11	1.8
Violent	0	0
Non-violent	11	1.8
Domestic Viol.	4	NA

Emergency/Fire
Director	B. Wilson

Public School District
(for school year 2004-2005 except as noted)

Chesterfield Township School District
295 Bordentown-Chesterfield Rd
Trenton, NJ 08620
609-298-6900
Administrator	Constance Bauer
Grade plan	K-6
Enrollment	278.0
Students per teacher	10.1
Per pupil expenditure	$11,235
Median faculty salary	$45,819
Median administrator salary	$93,413
Grade 12 enrollment	NA
High school graduation rate	NA

Assessment test results
(percent scoring at proficient or advanced level)
	Language	Math
Grade 3	89.3%	89.4%
Grade 8	NA	NA
High school	NA	NA

SAT
Percent tested	NA
Average SAT math score	NA
Average SAT verbal score	NA

No Child Left Behind, 2003-04
Attendence rate (target = 90%)	95.3%
Drop rate	NA
Highly-qualified teachers	100%
District needs improvement?(AYP)	No

Municipal Finance
Fiscal Year 2005
Total tax levy	$8,201,068
County levy	1,833,546
County taxes	1,538,196
County library	134,660
County health	0
County open space	160,691
School levy	6,132,011
Local muni. budget	235,511
Misc. revenues	2,448,703
Total aid	$794,542
CMPTRA	199,514
Muni. block grant	23,350
Energy tax receipts	521,678
Homeland security	50,000

Fiscal Year 2006
Total aid	$794,542
CMPTRA	181,256
Muni. block grant	23,350
Energy tax receipts	539,936
Homeland security	50,000

Taxes
	2003	2004	2005
General tax rate per $100	3.09	3.134	3.104
Net valuation taxable	$238,400,007	$248,615,304	$264,289,512
State equalized value	$330,468,543	$374,755,017	$432,552,393
County equalization ratio	82.74	72.14	66.28

Demographics & Socio-Economic Characteristics

(2000 U.S. Census, except as noted)

Population

1980*	16,072
1990*	14,583
2000	14,595
Male	7,121
Female	7,474
2004 (estimate)*	15,129
Persons per sq. mi. of land	1,991

Race & Hispanic Origin, 2000

Race

White	13,334
Black/African American	742
Amer. Indian/Alaska Natv.	24
Asian	274
Natv. Hawaiian/Pac. Islander	1
Other Race	72
Two or more races	148
Hispanic origin, total	224
Mexican	24
Puerto Rican	126
Cuban	19
Other Hispanic	55

Age & Nativity, 2000

Under 5 years	701
18 years and over	11,012
21 years and over	10,576
65 years and over	2,794
85 years and over	219
Median Age	42
Native born	13,935
Foreign born	660

Educational Attainment, 2000

Population 25 years and over	10,127
0-8 yrs of school	2.7%
High School grad or higher	89.7%
Bachelor's degree or higher	28.8%
Graduate degree	9.3%

Income & Poverty, 1999

Per capita income	$27,790
Median household income	$68,474
Median family income	$75,920
Persons in poverty	353
H'holds receiving public assistance	67
H'holds receiving social security	1,825

Households, 2000

Total households	5,057
With persons under 18	1,834
With persons over 65	1,838
Family households	4,143
One-person households	786
Persons per household	2.85
Persons per family	3.18

Labor & Employment

Total civilian labor force, 2004**	8,835
Unemployment rate	4.0%
Total civilian labor force, 2000	7,431
Unemployment rate	4.1%

Employed persons 16 years and over by occupation, 2000

Managers & professionals	2,791
Service occupations	652
Sales & office occupations	2,426
Farming, fishing & forestry	4
Construction & maintenance	521
Production & transportation	736
Self-employed persons	462

*US Census Bureau
**New Jersey Department of Labor

General Information

Township of Cinnaminson
PO Box 2100
Cinnaminson, NJ 08077
856-829-6000

Web site	NA
Land area (sq. miles)	7.60
Water area (sq. miles)	0.46
Type of government	Township
Form of government	TC

Government

Legislative Districts

US Congressional	3
State Legislative	7

Local Officials, 2006

Mayor	Sandra Iaquinto
Admin/Manager	John Ostrowski
Clerk	Grace Campbell
Finance Dir/Treas	John Ostrowski
Engineer	Remington & Vernick
Attorney	John Gillespie
Tax assessor	James Mancini
Tax collector	NA
Building officer	Edward Schaefer
Zoning officer	NA
Public Works	NA

Housing & Construction

Housing Units, 2000*

Total	5,147
Median rent	$916
Median SF home value	$158,900

New Privately Owned Housing Units Authorized by Building Permit

	Units	Value
Total, 2004	41	$7,821,708
Single family	41	$4,137,708
Total, 2005	157	$10,487,228
Single family	127	$7,956,448

Real Property Valuation - parcels, 2005

	Number	Valuation
Total		$923,791,100
Vacant	342	12,343,000
Residential	5,273	742,948,850
Commercial	169	98,271,200
Industrial	102	69,599,500
Apartments	1	95,200
Farm land	5	482,300
Farm homestead	7	51,050

Average Property Value & Tax, 2005

Residential value	$140,720
Property tax	$5,283
FAIR rebate	$642

Public Library

Cinnaminson Branch Library†
1619 Riverton Rd
Cinnaminson, NJ 08077
856-829-9340

Branch Librarian .... Isabella Addis

Library statistics, 2004

	Total	per capita
Volumes	NA	NA
Expenditure	NA	NA

†Branch of County Library

Public Safety

Police

Chief	Michael Wallace
Number of officers, 2004	30

Crime, 2004	Number	Rate
Total	397	26.4
Violent	27	1.8
Non-violent	370	24.6
Domestic Viol.	60	NA

Emergency/Fire

Director .... Robert Yearly

Public School District

(for school year 2004-2005 except as noted)

Cinnaminson Township School District
2195 Riverton Rd
Cinnaminson, NJ 08077
856-829-7600

Superintendent	Salvatore Illuzzi
Grade plan	K-12
Enrollment	2,559.5
Students per teacher	11.1
Per pupil expenditure	$11,831
Median faculty salary	$50,626
Median administrator salary	$94,303
Grade 12 enrollment	227.0
High school graduation rate	97.4%

Assessment test results

(percent scoring at proficient or advanced level)

	Language	Math
Grade 3	87.7%	84.5%
Grade 8	86.4%	71.6%
High school	96.7%	82.9%

SAT

Percent tested	84%
Average SAT math score	531
Average SAT verbal score	513

No Child Left Behind, 2003-04

Attendence rate (target = 90%)	95.2%
Drop rate	0.7%
Highly-qualified teachers	97.9%
District needs improvement?(AYP)	No

Municipal Finance

Fiscal Year 2005

Total tax levy	$34,795,121
County levy	6,435,417
County taxes	5,398,636
County library	472,701
County health	0
County open space	564,081
School levy	23,180,464
Local muni. budget	5,179,240
Misc. revenues	5,878,796
Total aid	$2,611,998
CMPTRA	719,176
Muni. block grant	63,810
Energy tax receipts	1,759,012
Homeland security	70,000

Fiscal Year 2006

Total aid	$2,611,999
CMPTRA	657,611
Muni. block grant	63,810
Energy tax receipts	1,820,578
Homeland security	70,000

Taxes

	2003	2004	2005
General tax rate per $100	3.50	3.603	3.756
Net valuation taxable	$895,108,980	$916,218,342	$926,809,520
State equalized value	$1,196,829,763	$1,382,644,485	$1,548,553,918
County equalization ratio	79.37	74.79	66.18

Demographics & Socio-Economic Characteristics
(2000 U.S. Census, except as noted)

Population
1980*	16,699
1990*	14,629
2000	14,597
Male	6,934
Female	7,663
2004 (estimate)*	14,709
Persons per sq. mi. of land	3,385

Race & Hispanic Origin, 2000
Race
White	13,956
Black/African American	44
Amer. Indian/Alaska Natv.	2
Asian	402
Natv. Hawaiian/Pac. Islander	0
Other Race	92
Two or more races	101
Hispanic origin, total	535
Mexican	21
Puerto Rican	99
Cuban	97
Other Hispanic	318

Age & Nativity, 2000
Under 5 years	759
18 years and over	11,562
21 years and over	11,209
65 years and over	3,163
85 years and over	381
Median Age	42.7
Native born	12,976
Foreign born	1,621

Educational Attainment, 2000
Population 25 years and over	10,839
0-8 yrs of school	5.3%
High School grad or higher	88.1%
Bachelor's degree or higher	28.2%
Graduate degree	8.6%

Income & Poverty, 1999
Per capita income	$29,883
Median household income	$65,019
Median family income	$77,291
Persons in poverty	248
H'holds receiving public assistance	28
H'holds receiving social security	2,069

Households, 2000
Total households	5,637
With persons under 18	1,681
With persons over 65	2,150
Family households	4,124
One-person households	1,361
Persons per household	2.56
Persons per family	3.07

Labor & Employment
Total civilian labor force, 2004**	7,833
Unemployment rate	3.4%
Total civilian labor force, 2000	7,098
Unemployment rate	2.0%

Employed persons 16 years and over by occupation, 2000
Managers & professionals	2,572
Service occupations	749
Sales & office occupations	2,402
Farming, fishing & forestry	0
Construction & maintenance	596
Production & transportation	636
Self-employed persons	370

*US Census Bureau
**New Jersey Department of Labor

General Information
Township of Clark
430 Westfield Ave
Clark, NJ 07066
732-388-3600
Web site	www.ourclark.com
Land area (sq. miles)	4.34
Water area (sq. miles)	0.14
Type of government	Township
Form of government	MC '50

Government

Legislative Districts
US Congressional	7
State Legislative	22

Local Officials, 2006
Mayor	Salvatore F. Bonaccorso
Admin/Manager	John Laezza
Clerk	Kathleen Leonard
Finance Dir/Treas	Robert Stanley
Engineer	Richard O'Connor
Attorney	Joseph Triarsi
Tax assessor	Michael Ross
Tax collector	Tom Grady
Building officer	Michael Khoda
Zoning officer	Michael Khoda
Public Works	NA

Housing & Construction

Housing Units, 2000*
Total	5,709
Median rent	$941
Median SF home value	$217,500

New Privately Owned Housing Units
Authorized by Building Permit

	Units	Value
Total, 2004	15	$2,550,460
Single family	15	$2,550,460
Total, 2005	46	$6,589,181
Single family	46	$6,589,181

Real Property Valuation - parcels, 2005
	Number	Valuation
Total		$712,322,000
Vacant	88	7,509,900
Residential	4,813	561,410,500
Commercial	203	90,024,200
Industrial	23	34,650,200
Apartments	6	18,727,200
Farm land	0	0
Farm homestead	0	0

Average Property Value & Tax, 2005
Residential value	$116,645
Property tax	$7,556
FAIR rebate	$649

Public Library
Clark Public Library
303 Westfield Ave
Clark, NJ 07066
732-388-5999
Director............Maureen Wilkinson

Library statistics, 2004
	Total	per capita
Volumes	57,966	3.97
Expenditure	$505,880	$34.66

Public Safety

Police
Chief	Anton Danco
Number of officers, 2004	40

Crime, 2004	Number	Rate
Total	188	12.8
Violent	5	0.3
Non-violent	183	12.4
Domestic Viol.	48	NA

Emergency/Fire
Director............Chris Matthews

Public School District
(for school year 2004-2005 except as noted)

Clark Township School District
365 Westfield Ave
Clark, NJ 07066
732-574-9600
Superintendent	Brian Zychowski
Grade plan	K-12
Enrollment	2,334.0
Students per teacher	11.6
Per pupil expenditure	$10,796
Median faculty salary	$47,700
Median administrator salary	$105,858
Grade 12 enrollment	237.0
High school graduation rate	99.2%

Assessment test results
(percent scoring at proficient or advanced level)
	Language	Math
Grade 3	90.1%	90.7%
Grade 8	86.7%	75.5%
High school	92.4%	88.8%

SAT
Percent tested	86%
Average SAT math score	523
Average SAT verbal score	510

No Child Left Behind, 2003-04
Attendence rate (target = 90%)	96.0%
Drop rate	0.2%
Highly-qualified teachers	86.3%
District needs improvement?(AYP)	No

Municipal Finance

Fiscal Year 2005
Total tax levy	$46,177,385
County levy	8,010,537
County taxes	7,694,106
County library	0
County health	0
County open space	316,431
School levy	26,448,315
Local muni. budget	11,718,533
Misc. revenues	6,286,872
Total aid	$2,461,433
CMPTRA	1,143,100
Muni. block grant	64,011
Energy tax receipts	1,184,322
Homeland security	70,000

Fiscal Year 2006
Total aid	$2,461,433
CMPTRA	1,101,649
Muni. block grant	64,011
Energy tax receipts	1,225,773
Homeland security	70,000

Taxes
	2003	2004	2005
General tax rate per $100	5.69	5.975	6.478
Net valuation taxable	$711,526,855	$712,243,986	$712,884,989
State equalized value	$1,811,422,747	$1,955,597,952	$2,187,434,762
County equalization ratio	42.14	36.69	34.19

Demographics & Socio-Economic Characteristics
(2000 U.S. Census, except as noted)

Population
1980*	6,013
1990*	6,155
2000	7,139
Male	3,415
Female	3,724
2004 (estimate)*	7,424
Persons per sq. mi. of land	1,034

Race & Hispanic Origin, 2000
Race
White	5,656
Black/African American	1,146
Amer. Indian/Alaska Natv.	30
Asian	47
Natv. Hawaiian/Pac. Islander	2
Other Race	68
Two or more races	190
Hispanic origin, total	234
Mexican	25
Puerto Rican	147
Cuban	5
Other Hispanic	57

Age & Nativity, 2000
Under 5 years	551
18 years and over	5,061
21 years and over	4,779
65 years and over	688
85 years and over	50
Median Age	33.6
Native born	6,840
Foreign born	299

Educational Attainment, 2000
Population 25 years and over	4,430
0-8 yrs of school	3.7%
High School grad or higher	83.7%
Bachelor's degree or higher	18.8%
Graduate degree	3.6%

Income & Poverty, 1999
Per capita income	$20,006
Median household income	$53,219
Median family income	$63,097
Persons in poverty	209
H'holds receiving public assistance	25
H'holds receiving social security	592

Households, 2000
Total households	2,464
With persons under 18	1,073
With persons over 65	538
Family households	1,886
One-person households	485
Persons per household	2.89
Persons per family	3.31

Labor & Employment
Total civilian labor force, 2004**	3,623
Unemployment rate	6.3%
Total civilian labor force, 2000	3,800
Unemployment rate	4.6%

Employed persons 16 years and over by occupation, 2000
Managers & professionals	955
Service occupations	460
Sales & office occupations	1,065
Farming, fishing & forestry	8
Construction & maintenance	468
Production & transportation	671
Self-employed persons	112

*US Census Bureau
**New Jersey Department of Labor

General Information
Borough of Clayton
125 N Delsea Dr
Clayton, NJ 08312
856-881-2882

Web site	claytonnj.com
Land area (sq. miles)	7.18
Water area (sq. miles)	0.17
Type of government	Borough
Form of government	B

Government

Legislative Districts
US Congressional	2
State Legislative	3

Local Officials, 2006
Mayor	Patricia Gannon
Admin/Manager	Ted Taylor
Clerk	Christine Newcomb
Finance Dir/Treas	Donna Nestore
Engineer	Sickel & Associates
Attorney	Timothy Scaffidi
Tax assessor	Craig Black
Tax collector	Donna Nestore
Building officer	Jerry Myers
Zoning officer	Joseph Kenney
Public Works	NA

Housing & Construction

Housing Units, 2000*
Total	2,680
Median rent	$544
Median SF home value	$96,300

New Privately Owned Housing Units
Authorized by Building Permit
	Units	Value
Total, 2004	13	$1,926,100
Single family	13	$1,926,100
Total, 2005	23	$2,449,557
Single family	23	$2,449,557

Real Property Valuation - parcels, 2005
	Number	Valuation
Total		$264,856,577
Vacant	303	6,571,302
Residential	2,399	224,030,300
Commercial	76	13,587,800
Industrial	14	11,762,375
Apartments	9	6,222,700
Farm land	19	2,190,400
Farm homestead	35	491,700

Average Property Value & Tax, 2005
Residential value	$92,244
Property tax	$3,878
FAIR rebate	$550

Public Library
Glassboro Public Library†
2 Center St
Glassboro, NJ 08028
856-881-0001

Director	Carol Wolf

Library statistics, 2004
	Total	per capita
Volumes	NA	NA
Expenditure	NA	NA

†Branch of County Library

Public Safety

Police
Chief	N. Frank Winters
Number of officers, 2004	18

Crime, 2004	Number	Rate
Total	260	36.3
Violent	14	2
Non-violent	246	34.4
Domestic Viol.	109	NA

Emergency/Fire
Director	Harry Simpson

Public School District
(for school year 2004-2005 except as noted)

Clayton School District
300 W Chestnut St
Clayton, NJ 08312
856-881-8700

Superintendent	Catherine Hills
Grade plan	K-12
Enrollment	1,262.5
Students per teacher	11.8
Per pupil expenditure	$10,394
Median faculty salary	$40,161
Median administrator salary	$71,500
Grade 12 enrollment	50.5
High school graduation rate	84.6%

Assessment test results
(percent scoring at proficient or advanced level)
	Language	Math
Grade 3	75.0%	76.3%
Grade 8	60.4%	44.7%
High school	83.4%	75.6%

SAT
Percent tested	63%
Average SAT math score	483
Average SAT verbal score	464

No Child Left Behind, 2003-04
Attendence rate (target = 90%)	94.7%
Drop rate	5%
Highly-qualified teachers	98.2%
District needs improvement?(AYP)	No

Municipal Finance

Fiscal Year 2005
Total tax levy	$11,170,131
County levy	2,379,283
County taxes	2,086,835
County library	154,222
County health	0
County open space	138,226
School levy	5,703,848
Local muni. budget	3,087,000
Misc. revenues	4,825,009
Total aid	$844,288
CMPTRA	361,734
Muni. block grant	27,992
Energy tax receipts	404,562
Homeland security	50,000

Fiscal Year 2006
Total aid	$844,287
CMPTRA	347,574
Muni. block grant	27,992
Energy tax receipts	418,721
Homeland security	50,000

Taxes
	2003	2004	2005
General tax rate per $100	3.93	3.865	4.205
Net valuation taxable	$252,220,206	$260,158,758	$265,695,237
State equalized value	$304,834,670	$335,696,807	$385,736,407
County equalization ratio	89.65	82.74	77.43

Demographics & Socio-Economic Characteristics
(2000 U.S. Census, except as noted)

Population
1980*	5,764
1990*	5,601
2000	4,986
Male	2,407
Female	2,579
2004 (estimate)*	4,952
Persons per sq. mi. of land	2,618

Race & Hispanic Origin, 2000
Race
White	4,100
Black/African American	577
Amer. Indian/Alaska Natv.	11
Asian	46
Natv. Hawaiian/Pac. Islander	9
Other Race	117
Two or more races	126
Hispanic origin, total	206
Mexican	31
Puerto Rican	90
Cuban	3
Other Hispanic	82

Age & Nativity, 2000
Under 5 years	361
18 years and over	3,752
21 years and over	3,563
65 years and over	554
85 years and over	60
Median Age	35.3
Native born	4,817
Foreign born	169

Educational Attainment, 2000
Population 25 years and over	3,358
0-8 yrs of school	3.4%
High School grad or higher	77.4%
Bachelor's degree or higher	11.0%
Graduate degree	2.6%

Income & Poverty, 1999
Per capita income	$18,510
Median household income	$42,207
Median family income	$50,963
Persons in poverty	570
H'holds receiving public assistance	72
H'holds receiving social security	473

Households, 2000
Total households	1,978
With persons under 18	660
With persons over 65	438
Family households	1,246
One-person households	583
Persons per household	2.52
Persons per family	3.13

Labor & Employment
Total civilian labor force, 2004**	3,095
Unemployment rate	5.7%
Total civilian labor force, 2000	2,700
Unemployment rate	8.3%

Employed persons 16 years and over by occupation, 2000
Managers & professionals	643
Service occupations	436
Sales & office occupations	737
Farming, fishing & forestry	0
Construction & maintenance	299
Production & transportation	362
Self-employed persons	126

*US Census Bureau
**New Jersey Department of Labor

General Information
Borough of Clementon
101 Gibbsboro Rd
Clementon, NJ 08021
856-783-0284

Web site	NA
Land area (sq. miles)	1.89
Water area (sq. miles)	0.06
Type of government	Borough
Form of government	B

Government
Legislative Districts
US Congressional	1
State Legislative	4

Local Officials, 2006
Mayor	Mark E. Armbruster
Admin/Manager	NA
Clerk	Jenai Johnson
Finance Dir/Treas	Debra Campbell
Engineer	Churchill Consulting
Attorney	George Botcheos
Tax assessor	Charles E. Warrington
Tax collector	NA
Building officer	Albert O. Hallworth
Zoning officer	NA
Public Works	NA

Housing & Construction
Housing Units, 2000*
Total	2,206
Median rent	$604
Median SF home value	$85,300

New Privately Owned Housing Units
Authorized by Building Permit
	Units	Value
Total, 2004	4	$388,000
Single family	4	$388,000
Total, 2005	11	$1,355,223
Single family	11	$1,355,223

Real Property Valuation - parcels, 2005
	Number	Valuation
Total		$170,473,330
Vacant	171	3,431,000
Residential	1,623	132,989,630
Commercial	88	26,409,900
Industrial	0	0
Apartments	6	7,536,100
Farm land	1	103,100
Farm homestead	1	3,600

Average Property Value & Tax, 2005
Residential value	$81,892
Property tax	$3,481
FAIR rebate	$570

Public Library
Clementon Memorial Library
195 Gibbsboro Rd
Clementon, NJ 08021
856-783-3233
Director................. Dale Swanson

Library statistics, 2004
	Total	per capita
Volumes	NA	NA
Expenditure	NA	NA

Public Safety
Police
Chief	David Kunkel
Number of officers, 2004	14

Crime, 2004	Number	Rate
Total	257	51.7
Violent	35	7
Non-violent	222	44.6
Domestic Viol.	142	NA

Emergency/Fire
Director	Randall Freiling

Public School District
(for school year 2004-2005 except as noted)

Clementon Borough School District
Audubon Ave
Clementon, NJ 08021
856-783-2300

Superintendent	Michael Kozak
Grade plan	K-12
Enrollment	630.0
Students per teacher	12.5
Per pupil expenditure	$10,723
Median faculty salary	$48,490
Median administrator salary	$69,200
Grade 12 enrollment	NA
High school graduation rate	NA

Assessment test results
(percent scoring at proficient or advanced level)
	Language	Math
Grade 3	60.3%	76.2%
Grade 8	42.3%	40.4%
High school	NA	NA

SAT
Percent tested	NA
Average SAT math score	NA
Average SAT verbal score	NA

No Child Left Behind, 2003-04
Attendence rate (target = 90%)	93.4%
Drop rate	NA
Highly-qualified teachers	95.6%
District needs improvement?(AYP)	No

Municipal Finance
Fiscal Year 2005
Total tax levy	$7,270,202
County levy	1,614,954
County taxes	1,488,403
County library	107,034
County health	0
County open space	19,518
School levy	3,493,318
Local muni. budget	2,161,930
Misc. revenues	2,097,570
Total aid	$631,204
CMPTRA	324,382
Muni. block grant	24,508
Energy tax receipts	257,314
Homeland security	25,000

Fiscal Year 2006
Total aid	$631,204
CMPTRA	315,376
Muni. block grant	24,508
Energy tax receipts	266,320
Homeland security	25,000

Taxes
	2003	2004	2005
General tax rate per $100	3.91	4.075	4.251
Net valuation taxable	$172,371,897	$172,705,906	$171,035,857
State equalized value	$187,564,632	$195,704,897	$218,855,863
County equalization ratio	95.61	91.90	88.21

Demographics & Socio-Economic Characteristics
(2000 U.S. Census, except as noted)

Population
1980*	21,464
1990*	20,393
2000	23,007
Male	11,091
Female	11,916
2004 (estimate)*	23,012
Persons per sq. mi. of land	23,853

Race & Hispanic Origin, 2000
Race
White	17,911
Black/African American	422
Amer. Indian/Alaska Natv.	58
Asian	2,772
Natv. Hawaiian/Pac. Islander	5
Other Race	1,144
Two or more races	695
Hispanic origin, total	4,177
Mexican	89
Puerto Rican	578
Cuban	565
Other Hispanic	2,945

Age & Nativity, 2000
Under 5 years	1,129
18 years and over	19,126
21 years and over	18,527
65 years and over	4,229
85 years and over	498
Median Age	39.8
Native born	13,054
Foreign born	9,953

Educational Attainment, 2000
Population 25 years and over	17,382
0-8 yrs of school	11.1%
High School grad or higher	78.7%
Bachelor's degree or higher	32.7%
Graduate degree	13.1%

Income & Poverty, 1999
Per capita income	$28,516
Median household income	$46,288
Median family income	$54,915
Persons in poverty	2,462
H'holds receiving public assistance	162
H'holds receiving social security	2,916

Households, 2000
Total households	10,027
With persons under 18	2,393
With persons over 65	3,185
Family households	6,041
One-person households	3,390
Persons per household	2.29
Persons per family	2.95

Labor & Employment
Total civilian labor force, 2004**	11,848
Unemployment rate	5.3%
Total civilian labor force, 2000	11,674
Unemployment rate	4.5%

Employed persons 16 years and over by occupation, 2000
Managers & professionals	3,919
Service occupations	1,604
Sales & office occupations	3,323
Farming, fishing & forestry	5
Construction & maintenance	943
Production & transportation	1,354
Self-employed persons	893

*US Census Bureau
**New Jersey Department of Labor

General Information
Borough of Cliffside Park
525 Palisade Ave
Cliffside Park, NJ 07010
201-945-3456

Web site	NA
Land area (sq. miles)	0.96
Water area (sq. miles)	0
Type of government	Borough
Form of government	B

Government

Legislative Districts
US Congressional	9
State Legislative	38

Local Officials, 2006
Mayor	Gerald A. Calabrese
Admin/Manager	Brian McGuirt
Clerk	Brian McGuirt
Finance Dir/Treas	Frank Berado
Engineer	Stephen Boswell
Attorney	Chris Diktas
Tax assessor	Frank Bucino
Tax collector	NA
Building officer	John Candelmo
Zoning officer	NA
Public Works	NA

Housing & Construction

Housing Units, 2000*
Total	10,375
Median rent	$864
Median SF home value	$227,500

New Privately Owned Housing Units Authorized by Building Permit
	Units	Value
Total, 2004	76	$9,622,750
Single family	15	$3,376,450
Total, 2005	59	$7,862,080
Single family	29	$4,920,940

Real Property Valuation - parcels, 2005
	Number	Valuation
Total		$2,411,263,400
Vacant	124	15,412,600
Residential	6,216	2,034,533,200
Commercial	251	143,532,900
Industrial	12	9,905,100
Apartments	162	207,879,600
Farm land	0	0
Farm homestead	0	0

Average Property Value & Tax, 2005
Residential value	$327,306
Property tax	$6,087
FAIR rebate	$702

Public Library
Cliffside Park Public Library
505 Palisade Ave
Cliffside Park, NJ 07010
201-945-2867

Director	Ana Chelariu

Library statistics, 2004
	Total	per capita
Volumes	65,705	2.86
Expenditure	$668,485	$29.06

Public Safety

Police
Chief	Donald Keane
Number of officers, 2004	45

Crime, 2004	Number	Rate
Total	234	10.2
Violent	25	1.1
Non-violent	209	9.1
Domestic Viol.	85	NA

Emergency/Fire
Director	Al Deleone

Public School District
(for school year 2004-2005 except as noted)

Cliffside Park School District
525 Palisade Ave
Cliffside Park, NJ 07010
201-313-2310

Superintendent	Robert Paladino
Grade plan	K-12
Enrollment	2,600.0
Students per teacher	12.1
Per pupil expenditure	$9,293
Median faculty salary	$60,410
Median administrator salary	$119,114
Grade 12 enrollment	215.0
High school graduation rate	94.5%

Assessment test results
(percent scoring at proficient or advanced level)
	Language	Math
Grade 3	81.8%	80.9%
Grade 8	75.6%	48.6%
High school	80.2%	73.9%

SAT
Percent tested	69%
Average SAT math score	477
Average SAT verbal score	457

No Child Left Behind, 2003-04
Attendence rate (target = 90%)	94.3%
Drop rate	1.3%
Highly-qualified teachers	98%
District needs improvement?(AYP)	No

Municipal Finance

Fiscal Year 2005
Total tax levy	$44,942,807
County levy	4,990,658
County taxes	4,740,997
County library	0
County health	0
County open space	249,661
School levy	22,144,447
Local muni. budget	17,807,703
Misc. revenues	7,267,175
Total aid	$1,646,639
CMPTRA	711,141
Muni. block grant	90,211
Energy tax receipts	755,287
Homeland security	90,000

Fiscal Year 2006
Total aid	$1,646,639
CMPTRA	684,706
Muni. block grant	90,211
Energy tax receipts	781,722
Homeland security	90,000

Taxes
	2003	2004	2005
General tax rate per $100	2.89	1.740	1.860
Net valuation taxable	$1,275,540,807	$2,404,769,448	$2,416,716,438
State equalized value	$2,133,011,383	$2,470,080,316	$2,832,200,209
County equalization ratio	67.02	111.64	97.35

Demographics & Socio-Economic Characteristics
(2000 U.S. Census, except as noted)

Population
1980*	74,388
1990*	71,742
2000	78,672
Male	37,560
Female	41,112
2000 (revised)	79,062
2004 (estimate)*	79,944
Persons per sq. mi. of land	7,078

Race & Hispanic Origin, 2000
Race
White	59,960
Black/African American	2,277
Amer. Indian/Alaska Natv.	192
Asian	5,066
Natv. Hawaiian/Pac. Islander	27
Other Race	7,553
Two or more races	3,597
Hispanic origin, total	15,608
Mexican	1,591
Puerto Rican	3,923
Cuban	510
Other Hispanic	9,584

Age & Nativity, 2000
Under 5 years	4,700
18 years and over	61,700
21 years and over	59,327
65 years and over	13,829
85 years and over	2,037
Median Age	38.8
Native born	55,680
Foreign born	22,992

Educational Attainment, 2000
Population 25 years and over	55,730
0-8 yrs of school	8.8%
High School grad or higher	78.6%
Bachelor's degree or higher	23.6%
Graduate degree	7.6%

Income & Poverty, 1999
Per capita income	$23,638
Median household income	$50,619
Median family income	$60,688
Persons in poverty	4,932
H'holds receiving public assistance	593
H'holds receiving social security	10,239

Households, 2000
Total households	30,244
With persons under 18	9,459
With persons over 65	10,261
Family households	20,352
One-person households	8,448
Persons per household	2.59
Persons per family	3.2

Labor & Employment
Total civilian labor force, 2004**	39,599
Unemployment rate	3.9%
Total civilian labor force, 2000	39,232
Unemployment rate	4.9%

Employed persons 16 years and over by occupation, 2000
Managers & professionals	12,055
Service occupations	4,374
Sales & office occupations	11,520
Farming, fishing & forestry	11
Construction & maintenance	3,146
Production & transportation	6,211
Self-employed persons	1,623

*US Census Bureau
**New Jersey Department of Labor

General Information
City of Clifton
900 Clifton Ave
Clifton, NJ 07013
973-470-5800
Web site	www.cliftonnj.org
Land area (sq. miles)	11.30
Water area (sq. miles)	0.10
Type of government	City
Form of government	CM '23

Government

Legislative Districts
US Congressional	8
State Legislative	34

Local Officials, 2006
Mayor	James Anzaldi
Admin/Manager	Albert Greco
Clerk	Richard C. Moran
Finance Dir/Treas	William Nadolny
Engineer	James Yellen
Attorney	Matthew Priore
Tax assessor	Jon Whiting
Tax collector	NA
Building officer	Joseph Lotorto
Zoning officer	Daniel Howell
Public Works	Vincent Cahill

Housing & Construction

Housing Units, 2000*
Total	31,060
Median rent	$784
Median SF home value	$181,600

New Privately Owned Housing Units Authorized by Building Permit
	Units	Value
Total, 2004	218	$15,935,240
Single family	22	$2,938,676
Total, 2005	145	$12,376,953
Single family	27	$4,552,491

Real Property Valuation - parcels, 2005
	Number	Valuation
Total		$5,263,763,000
Vacant	547	56,024,100
Residential	20,938	3,658,481,800
Commercial	1,088	759,652,800
Industrial	424	653,947,700
Apartments	116	135,033,700
Farm land	2	607,500
Farm homestead	2	15,400

Average Property Value & Tax, 2005
Residential value	$174,713
Property tax	$6,525
FAIR rebate	$644

Public Library
Clifton Public Library
292 Piaget Ave
Clifton, NJ 07011
973-772-5500
Director . . . . Christine Zembicki

Library statistics, 2004
	Total	per capita
Volumes	186,582	2.37
Expenditure	$2,497,277	$31.74

Public Safety
Police
Chief	Robert Ferreri
Number of officers, 2004	156

Crime, 2004	Number	Rate
Total	2,379	29.8
Violent	233	2.9
Non-violent	2,146	26.9
Domestic Viol.	530	NA

Emergency/Fire
Director . . . . John Dubravsky

Public School District
(for school year 2004-2005 except as noted)

Clifton School District
745 Clifton Ave
Clifton, NJ 07015
973-470-2260
Superintendent	Michael Rice
Grade plan	K-12
Enrollment	10,350.0
Students per teacher	11.4
Per pupil expenditure	$10,542
Median faculty salary	$50,010
Median administrator salary	$97,989
Grade 12 enrollment	700.0
High school graduation rate	86.4%

Assessment test results
(percent scoring at proficient or advanced level)
	Language	Math
Grade 3	77.0%	75.8%
Grade 8	61.9%	53.8%
High school	78.4%	74.2%

SAT
Percent tested	68%
Average SAT math score	510
Average SAT verbal score	481

No Child Left Behind, 2003-04
Attendence rate (target = 90%)	95.1%
Drop rate	3.6%
Highly-qualified teachers	97.5%
District needs improvement?(AYP)	No

Municipal Finance

Fiscal Year 2005
Total tax levy	$196,914,693
County levy	43,095,273
County taxes	42,274,864
County library	0
County health	0
County open space	820,409
School levy	103,545,393
Local muni. budget	50,274,026
Misc. revenues	31,381,387
Total aid	$13,554,996
CMPTRA	7,069,881
Muni. block grant	314,977
Energy tax receipts	6,030,138
Homeland security	140,000

Fiscal Year 2006
Total aid	$13,554,996
CMPTRA	6,858,826
Muni. block grant	314,977
Energy tax receipts	6,241,193
Homeland security	140,000

Taxes
	2003	2004	2005
General tax rate per $100	3.26	3.480	3.740
Net valuation taxable	$5,193,187,123	$5,250,461,607	$5,272,195,890
State equalized value	$6,997,961,357	$8,047,526,125	$9,054,088,769
County equalization ratio	83.12	74.21	65.20

Demographics & Socio-Economic Characteristics
(2000 U.S. Census, except as noted)

Population
1980*	1,910
1990*	2,054
2000	2,632
Male	1,284
Female	1,348
2004 (estimate)*	2,639
Persons per sq. mi. of land	1,921

Race & Hispanic Origin, 2000
Race
White	2,423
Black/African American	35
Amer. Indian/Alaska Natv.	12
Asian	98
Natv. Hawaiian/Pac. Islander	0
Other Race	36
Two or more races	28
Hispanic origin, total	108
Mexican	15
Puerto Rican	18
Cuban	6
Other Hispanic	69

Age & Nativity, 2000
Under 5 years	200
18 years and over	1,938
21 years and over	1,892
65 years and over	248
85 years and over	18
Median Age	36.7
Native born	2,349
Foreign born	283

Educational Attainment, 2000
Population 25 years and over	1,852
0-8 yrs of school	2.9%
High School grad or higher	93.6%
Bachelor's degree or higher	49.1%
Graduate degree	20.6%

Income & Poverty, 1999
Per capita income	$37,463
Median household income	$78,121
Median family income	$88,671
Persons in poverty	74
H'holds receiving public assistance	4
H'holds receiving social security	206

Households, 2000
Total households	1,068
With persons under 18	388
With persons over 65	196
Family households	724
One-person households	281
Persons per household	2.46
Persons per family	3

Labor & Employment
Total civilian labor force, 2004**	1,472
Unemployment rate	3.0%
Total civilian labor force, 2000	1,526
Unemployment rate	1.8%

Employed persons 16 years and over by occupation, 2000
Managers & professionals	873
Service occupations	171
Sales & office occupations	329
Farming, fishing & forestry	4
Construction & maintenance	57
Production & transportation	65
Self-employed persons	130

*US Census Bureau
**New Jersey Department of Labor

General Information
Town of Clinton
PO Box 5194
Clinton, NJ 08809
908-735-8616

Web site	NA
Land area (sq. miles)	1.37
Water area (sq. miles)	0.04
Type of government	Town
Form of government	T

Government

Legislative Districts
US Congressional	7
State Legislative	23

Local Officials, 2006
Mayor	Christine Schaumburg
Admin/Manager	Robert Cutter
Clerk	Cecilia Covino
Finance Dir/Treas	Nancy Smith
Engineer	Van Cleef Eng.
Attorney	Richard Cushing
Tax assessor	Marcia Sudano-Kerwin
Tax collector	NA
Building officer	John Leonard
Zoning officer	NA
Public Works	NA

Housing & Construction

Housing Units, 2000*
Total	1,095
Median rent	$862
Median SF home value	$222,100

New Privately Owned Housing Units Authorized by Building Permit
	Units	Value
Total, 2004	0	$0
Single family	0	$0
Total, 2005	0	$0
Single family	0	$0

Real Property Valuation - parcels, 2005
	Number	Valuation
Total		$358,023,100
Vacant	39	3,893,900
Residential	854	275,107,400
Commercial	123	71,988,300
Industrial	0	0
Apartments	8	6,758,200
Farm land	1	201,500
Farm homestead	4	73,800

Average Property Value & Tax, 2005
Residential value	$320,724
Property tax	$7,821
FAIR rebate	$500

Public Library
North County Branch Library†
65 Halstead St
Clinton, NJ 08809
908-730-6262
Branch Librarian	Barbara Riesenfeld

Library statistics, 2004
	Total	per capita
Volumes	NA	NA
Expenditure	NA	NA

†Branch of County Library

Public Safety

Police
Chief	Richard Brett Matheis
Number of officers, 2004	10

Crime, 2004	Number	Rate
Total	15	5.7
Violent	2	0.8
Non-violent	13	4.9
Domestic Viol.	6	NA

Emergency/Fire
Director	Tim Langston

Public School District
(for school year 2004-2005 except as noted)

Clinton Town School District
10 School St
Clinton, NJ 08809
908-735-8512
Superintendent	J. Michael Schilder
Grade plan	K-8
Enrollment	566.0
Students per teacher	10.5
Per pupil expenditure	$10,697
Median faculty salary	$49,750
Median administrator salary	$102,811
Grade 12 enrollment	NA
High school graduation rate	NA

Assessment test results
(percent scoring at proficient or advanced level)
	Language	Math
Grade 3	93.0%	84.2%
Grade 8	83.8%	82.9%
High school	NA	NA

SAT
Percent tested	NA
Average SAT math score	NA
Average SAT verbal score	NA

No Child Left Behind, 2003-04
Attendance rate (target = 90%)	95.6%
Drop rate	NA
Highly-qualified teachers	100%
District needs improvement?(AYP)	No

Municipal Finance

Fiscal Year 2005
Total tax levy	$8,758,845
County levy	1,371,985
County taxes	1,164,899
County library	97,470
County health	0
County open space	109,616
School levy	5,639,060
Local muni. budget	1,747,800
Misc. revenues	1,611,710
Total aid	$263,127
CMPTRA	107,777
Muni. block grant	10,320
Energy tax receipts	120,030
Homeland security	25,000

Fiscal Year 2006
Total aid	$263,127
CMPTRA	103,576
Muni. block grant	10,320
Energy tax receipts	124,231
Homeland security	25,000

Taxes
	2003	2004	2005
General tax rate per $100	2.57	2.690	2.440
Net valuation taxable	$316,545,530	$311,288,892	$359,205,736
State equalized value	$314,501,272	$339,836,368	$382,296,441
County equalization ratio	94.24	92.28	98.92

Demographics & Socio-Economic Characteristics
(2000 U.S. Census, except as noted)

Population
1980*	7,345
1990*	10,816
2000	12,957
Male	7,023
Female	5,934
2004 (estimate)*	13,862
Persons per sq. mi. of land	462

Race & Hispanic Origin, 2000
Race
White	11,365
Black/African American	902
Amer. Indian/Alaska Natv.	26
Asian	304
Natv. Hawaiian/Pac. Islander	9
Other Race	206
Two or more races	145
Hispanic origin, total	507
Mexican	36
Puerto Rican	253
Cuban	46
Other Hispanic	172

Age & Nativity, 2000
Under 5 years	852
18 years and over	9,559
21 years and over	9,081
65 years and over	951
85 years and over	120
Median Age	36.4
Native born	12,039
Foreign born	918

Educational Attainment, 2000
Population 25 years and over	8,100
0-8 yrs of school	1.8%
High School grad or higher	93.0%
Bachelor's degree or higher	50.5%
Graduate degree	22.1%

Income & Poverty, 1999
Per capita income	$37,264
Median household income	$96,570
Median family income	$106,448
Persons in poverty	105
H'holds receiving public assistance	10
H'holds receiving social security	658

Households, 2000
Total households	4,129
With persons under 18	1,782
With persons over 65	655
Family households	3,255
One-person households	717
Persons per household	2.82
Persons per family	3.23

Labor & Employment
Total civilian labor force, 2004**	6,465
Unemployment rate	3.1%
Total civilian labor force, 2000	6,170
Unemployment rate	3.4%

Employed persons 16 years and over by occupation, 2000
Managers & professionals	3,542
Service occupations	411
Sales & office occupations	1,339
Farming, fishing & forestry	0
Construction & maintenance	296
Production & transportation	370
Self-employed persons	423

*US Census Bureau
**New Jersey Department of Labor

General Information
Township of Clinton
1370 Route 31 North
Annandale, NJ 08801
908-735-8800

Web site	www.township.clinton.nj.us
Land area (sq. miles)	30.00
Water area (sq. miles)	3.93
Type of government	Township
Form of government	SM '50

Government

Legislative Districts
US Congressional	7
State Legislative	23

Local Officials, 2006
Mayor	Nick Corcodilos
Admin/Manager	Gail McKane
Clerk	Gail McKane
Finance Dir/Treas	Al Steinberg
Engineer	Cathleen F. Marcelli
Attorney	Kristina P. Hadinger
Tax assessor	Marianne Busher
Tax collector	Margaret Saharic
Building officer	Michael Wright
Zoning officer	NA
Public Works	NA

Housing & Construction

Housing Units, 2000*
Total	4,234
Median rent	$1,062
Median SF home value	$283,900

New Privately Owned Housing Units Authorized by Building Permit
	Units	Value
Total, 2004	79	$16,606,272
Single family	79	$16,606,272
Total, 2005	54	$11,897,316
Single family	54	$11,897,316

Real Property Valuation - parcels, 2005
	Number	Valuation
Total		$1,987,699,144
Vacant	244	25,178,000
Residential	4,277	1,548,702,100
Commercial	246	189,682,244
Industrial	9	149,292,000
Apartments	5	18,623,800
Farm land	133	53,599,400
Farm homestead	231	2,621,600

Average Property Value & Tax, 2005
Residential value	$344,127
Property tax	$8,063
FAIR rebate	$510

Public Library
No public municipal library.

Library statistics, 2004
	Total	per capita
Volumes	NA	NA
Expenditure	NA	NA

Public Safety

Police
Chief	Steven Clancy
Number of officers, 2004	22

Crime, 2004	Number	Rate
Total	81	5.9
Violent	4	0.3
Non-violent	77	5.6
Domestic Viol.	47	NA

Emergency/Fire
Director	Marc Strauss

Public School District
(for school year 2004-2005 except as noted)

Clinton Township School District
PO Box 362
Lebanon, NJ 08833
908-735-8320

Superintendent	Elizabeth Nastus
Grade plan	K-8
Enrollment	1,760.5
Students per teacher	11.0
Per pupil expenditure	$10,339
Median faculty salary	$42,255
Median administrator salary	$107,624
Grade 12 enrollment	NA
High school graduation rate	NA

Assessment test results
(percent scoring at proficient or advanced level)
	Language	Math
Grade 3	93.5%	88.8%
Grade 8	90.0%	86.1%
High school	NA	NA

SAT
Percent tested	NA
Average SAT math score	NA
Average SAT verbal score	NA

No Child Left Behind, 2003-04
Attendence rate (target = 90%)	95.6%
Drop rate	NA
Highly-qualified teachers	100%
District needs improvement?(AYP)	No

Municipal Finance

Fiscal Year 2005
Total tax levy	$46,782,772
County levy	8,824,060
County taxes	7,492,160
County library	626,894
County health	0
County open space	705,007
School levy	32,940,155
Local muni. budget	5,018,557
Misc. revenues	6,387,389
Total aid	$1,462,370
CMPTRA	440,975
Muni. block grant	50,805
Energy tax receipts	900,590
Homeland security	70,000

Fiscal Year 2006
Total aid	$1,462,369
CMPTRA	409,454
Muni. block grant	50,805
Energy tax receipts	932,110
Homeland security	70,000

Taxes
	2003	2004	2005
General tax rate per $100	2.13	2.240	2.350
Net valuation taxable	$1,936,010,344	$1,949,774,990	$1,996,746,013
State equalized value	$1,948,088,493	$2,105,732,875	$2,323,148,357
County equalization ratio	93.03	92.22	85.24

Demographics & Socio-Economic Characteristics
(2000 U.S. Census, except as noted)

Population
1980*	8,164
1990*	8,094
2000	8,383
Male	4,130
Female	4,253
2004 (estimate)*	8,623
Persons per sq. mi. of land	2,720

Race & Hispanic Origin, 2000
Race
White	6,314
Black/African American	78
Amer. Indian/Alaska Natv.	8
Asian	1,807
Natv. Hawaiian/Pac. Islander	0
Other Race	68
Two or more races	108
Hispanic origin, total	343
Mexican	24
Puerto Rican	69
Cuban	55
Other Hispanic	195

Age & Nativity, 2000
Under 5 years	546
18 years and over	6,038
21 years and over	5,839
65 years and over	1,102
85 years and over	108
Median Age	39.6
Native born	6,264
Foreign born	2,119

Educational Attainment, 2000
Population 25 years and over	5,687
0-8 yrs of school	2.9%
High School grad or higher	93.1%
Bachelor's degree or higher	49.9%
Graduate degree	19.6%

Income & Poverty, 1999
Per capita income	$37,065
Median household income	$83,918
Median family income	$94,543
Persons in poverty	229
H'holds receiving public assistance	0
H'holds receiving social security	759

Households, 2000
Total households	2,789
With persons under 18	1,254
With persons over 65	763
Family households	2,321
One-person households	391
Persons per household	2.98
Persons per family	3.3

Labor & Employment
Total civilian labor force, 2004**	4,606
Unemployment rate	3.2%
Total civilian labor force, 2000	3,918
Unemployment rate	1.8%

Employed persons 16 years and over by occupation, 2000
Managers & professionals	1,972
Service occupations	274
Sales & office occupations	1,216
Farming, fishing & forestry	0
Construction & maintenance	198
Production & transportation	186
Self-employed persons	323

*US Census Bureau
**New Jersey Department of Labor

©2006 Information Publications, Inc.
All rights reserved. Photocopying prohibited.
For additional copies, contact the publisher at
www.informationpublications.com or (877)544-INFO (4636)

General Information
Borough of Closter
295 Closter Dock Rd
Closter, NJ 07624
201-784-0600
Web site	www.closterboro.com
Land area (sq. miles)	3.17
Water area (sq. miles)	0.12
Type of government	Borough
Form of government	B

Government
Legislative Districts
US Congressional	5
State Legislative	39

Local Officials, 2006
Mayor	Fred Pitofsky
Admin/Manager	Erik Lenander
Clerk	Loretta Castano
Finance Dir/Treas	E. Lenander /J. Luppino
Engineer	Steven Boswell
Attorney	Edward T. Rogan
Tax assessor	Angela Mattiace
Tax collector	Norma Ketler
Building officer	Keith Sager
Zoning officer	Leonard Sinowitz
Public Works	Robert Stauffer (Dep Supt)

Housing & Construction
Housing Units, 2000*
Total	2,865
Median rent	$1,184
Median SF home value	$346,000

New Privately Owned Housing Units
Authorized by Building Permit

	Units	Value
Total, 2004	35	$13,164,000
Single family	35	$13,164,000
Total, 2005	43	$15,984,602
Single family	43	$15,984,602

Real Property Valuation - parcels, 2005
	Number	Valuation
Total		$1,168,891,100
Vacant	82	15,035,600
Residential	2,698	1,000,581,600
Commercial	153	135,618,900
Industrial	7	14,267,500
Apartments	1	539,200
Farm land	4	2,819,800
Farm homestead	5	28,500

Average Property Value & Tax, 2005
Residential value	$370,185
Property tax	$10,308
FAIR rebate	$605

Public Library
Closter Public Library
280 High St
Closter, NJ 07624
201-768-4197
Director	Ruth Rando

Library statistics, 2004
	Total	per capita
Volumes	60,129	7.17
Expenditure	$701,218	$83.65

Public Safety
Police
Chief	David Berrian
Number of officers, 2004	22

Crime, 2004	Number	Rate
Total	67	7.8
Violent	4	0.5
Non-violent	63	7.4
Domestic Viol.	22	NA

Emergency/Fire
Director	Tom Reinecke

Public School District
(for school year 2004-2005 except as noted)

Closter School District
340 Homans Ave
Closter, NJ 07624
201-768-3001
Superintendent	Jeffrey Feifer
Grade plan	K-8
Enrollment	1,226.0
Students per teacher	13.5
Per pupil expenditure	$10,447
Median faculty salary	$66,869
Median administrator salary	$110,650
Grade 12 enrollment	NA
High school graduation rate	NA

Assessment test results
(percent scoring at proficient or advanced level)
	Language	Math
Grade 3	94.1%	84.1%
Grade 8	95.8%	89.7%
High school	NA	NA

SAT
Percent tested	NA
Average SAT math score	NA
Average SAT verbal score	NA

No Child Left Behind, 2003-04
Attendance rate (target = 90%)	96.5%
Drop rate	NA
Highly-qualified teachers	95.2%
District needs improvement?(AYP)	No

Municipal Finance
Fiscal Year 2005
Total tax levy	$32,653,149
County levy	3,525,184
County taxes	3,348,783
County library	0
County health	0
County open space	176,400
School levy	21,817,405
Local muni. budget	7,310,560
Misc. revenues	4,717,428
Total aid	$1,931,656
CMPTRA	261,779
Muni. block grant	35,417
Energy tax receipts	1,570,971
Homeland security	50,000

Fiscal Year 2006
Total aid	$1,931,656
CMPTRA	206,795
Muni. block grant	35,417
Energy tax receipts	1,625,955
Homeland security	50,000

Taxes
	2003	2004	2005
General tax rate per $100	2.55	2.660	2.790
Net valuation taxable	$1,143,691,651	$1,155,899,463	$1,172,622,035
State equalized value	$1,513,219,967	$1,734,963,848	$1,958,613,721
County equalization ratio	83.54	75.58	66.55

Demographics & Socio-Economic Characteristics

(2000 U.S. Census, except as noted)

Population

1980*	15,838
1990*	15,289
2000	14,326
Male	6,732
Female	7,594
2004 (estimate)*	14,138
Persons per sq. mi. of land	7,732

Race & Hispanic Origin, 2000

Race

White	12,388
Black/African American	955
Amer. Indian/Alaska Natv.	48
Asian	395
Natv. Hawaiian/Pac. Islander	3
Other Race	346
Two or more races	191
Hispanic origin, total	812
Mexican	112
Puerto Rican	450
Cuban	9
Other Hispanic	241

Age & Nativity, 2000

Under 5 years	785
18 years and over	11,209
21 years and over	10,708
65 years and over	2,066
85 years and over	357
Median Age	37.1
Native born	13,511
Foreign born	826

Educational Attainment, 2000

Population 25 years and over	10,095
0-8 yrs of school	3.0%
High School grad or higher	87.5%
Bachelor's degree or higher	30.3%
Graduate degree	10.2%

Income & Poverty, 1999

Per capita income	$24,358
Median household income	$43,175
Median family income	$57,987
Persons in poverty	866
H'holds receiving public assistance	126
H'holds receiving social security	1,710

Households, 2000

Total households	6,263
With persons under 18	1,733
With persons over 65	1,641
Family households	3,461
One-person households	2,291
Persons per household	2.27
Persons per family	3.05

Labor & Employment

Total civilian labor force, 2004**	8,650
Unemployment rate	3.4%
Total civilian labor force, 2000	7,926
Unemployment rate	4.6%

Employed persons 16 years and over by occupation, 2000

Managers & professionals	3,207
Service occupations	803
Sales & office occupations	2,379
Farming, fishing & forestry	0
Construction & maintenance	606
Production & transportation	563
Self-employed persons	347

*US Census Bureau
**New Jersey Department of Labor

General Information

Borough of Collingswood
678 Haddon Ave
Collingswood, NJ 08108
856-854-0720

Web site	www.collingswood.com
Land area (sq. miles)	1.83
Water area (sq. miles)	0.09
Type of government	Borough
Form of government	Comm.

Government

Legislative Districts

US Congressional	1
State Legislative	6

Local Officials, 2006

Mayor	M. James Maley Jr.
Admin/Manager	Bradford Stokes
Clerk	Alice Marks
Finance Dir/Treas	Sandra Powell
Engineer	Remington & Vernick
Attorney	Joseph Nardi III
Tax assessor	John Dymond
Tax collector	Margaret Howard
Building officer	William Joseph
Zoning officer	Mary Ellen Ries
Public Works	Carl Jubb Jr.

Housing & Construction

Housing Units, 2000*

Total	6,866
Median rent	$688
Median SF home value	$101,200

New Privately Owned Housing Units
Authorized by Building Permit

	Units	Value
Total, 2004	1	$180,000
Single family	1	$180,000
Total, 2005	0	$0
Single family	0	$0

Real Property Valuation - parcels, 2005

	Number	Valuation
Total		$479,027,200
Vacant	58	1,112,600
Residential	3,920	401,955,400
Commercial	307	57,440,300
Industrial	0	0
Apartments	40	18,518,900
Farm land	0	0
Farm homestead	0	0

Average Property Value & Tax, 2005

Residential value	$102,540
Property tax	$4,631
FAIR rebate	$561

Public Library

Collingswood Public Library
771 Haddon Ave
Collingswood, NJ 08108
856-858-0649

Director	Bradley Green

Library statistics, 2004

	Total	per capita
Volumes	64,297	4.49
Expenditure	$487,549	$34.03

Public Safety

Police

Chief	Thomas Garrity
Number of officers, 2004	31

Crime, 2004	Number	Rate
Total	421	29.6
Violent	46	3.2
Non-violent	375	26.4
Domestic Viol.	145	NA

Emergency/Fire

Director	John Amet

Public School District

(for school year 2004-2005 except as noted)

Collingswood Borough School District
200 Lees Ave
Collingswood, NJ 08108
856-962-5732

Superintendent	James Bathurst
Grade plan	K-12
Enrollment	1,980.0
Students per teacher	10.3
Per pupil expenditure	$12,369
Median faculty salary	$50,100
Median administrator salary	$88,759
Grade 12 enrollment	186.0
High school graduation rate	83.3%

Assessment test results

(percent scoring at proficient or advanced level)

	Language	Math
Grade 3	87.8%	83.0%
Grade 8	75.7%	60.2%
High school	84.9%	79.0%

SAT

Percent tested	62%
Average SAT math score	497
Average SAT verbal score	503

No Child Left Behind, 2003-04

Attendence rate (target = 90%)	94.2%
Drop rate	3.5%
Highly-qualified teachers	95.1%
District needs improvement?(AYP)	No

Municipal Finance

Fiscal Year 2005

Total tax levy	$21,772,374
County levy	5,211,281
County taxes	5,143,829
County library	0
County health	0
County open space	67,452
School levy	10,862,593
Local muni. budget	5,698,500
Misc. revenues	5,288,104
Total aid	$1,694,828
CMPTRA	846,379
Muni. block grant	66,900
Energy tax receipts	711,549
Homeland security	70,000

Fiscal Year 2006

Total aid	$1,694,827
CMPTRA	821,474
Muni. block grant	66,900
Energy tax receipts	736,453
Homeland security	70,000

Taxes

	2003	2004	2005
General tax rate per $100	3.95	4.158	4.516
Net valuation taxable	$481,395,332	$482,047,931	$482,118,388
State equalized value	$556,462,065	$669,704,798	$809,602,667
County equalization ratio	96.52	86.51	71.82

Demographics & Socio-Economic Characteristics
(2000 U.S. Census, except as noted)

Population
1980*	7,888
1990*	8,559
2000	12,331
Male	6,448
Female	5,883
2000 (revised)	11,179
2004 (estimate)*	11,701
Persons per sq. mi. of land	372

Race & Hispanic Origin, 2000
Race
White	10,544
Black/African American	973
Amer. Indian/Alaska Natv.	28
Asian	447
Natv. Hawaiian/Pac. Islander	1
Other Race	179
Two or more races	159
Hispanic origin, total	520
Mexican	113
Puerto Rican	186
Cuban	15
Other Hispanic	206

Age & Nativity, 2000
Under 5 years	1,019
18 years and over	8,731
21 years and over	8,116
65 years and over	1,003
85 years and over	88
Median Age	33.2
Native born	11,271
Foreign born	1,060

Educational Attainment, 2000
Population 25 years and over	7,254
0-8 yrs of school	2.2%
High School grad or higher	95.0%
Bachelor's degree or higher	47.5%
Graduate degree	19.3%

Income & Poverty, 1999
Per capita income	$46,795
Median household income	$109,190
Median family income	$117,980
Persons in poverty	308
H'holds receiving public assistance	21
H'holds receiving social security	747

Households, 2000
Total households	3,513
With persons under 18	1,813
With persons over 65	697
Family households	3,195
One-person households	262
Persons per household	3.17
Persons per family	3.33

Labor & Employment
Total civilian labor force, 2004**	4,571
Unemployment rate	2.4%
Total civilian labor force, 2000	4,692
Unemployment rate	3.6%

Employed persons 16 years and over by occupation, 2000
Managers & professionals	2,373
Service occupations	442
Sales & office occupations	1,183
Farming, fishing & forestry	8
Construction & maintenance	259
Production & transportation	259
Self-employed persons	375

*US Census Bureau
**New Jersey Department of Labor

General Information
Township of Colts Neck
124 Cedar Dr
Colts Neck, NJ 07722
732-462-5470

Web site	www.colts-neck.nj.us
Land area (sq. miles)	31.43
Water area (sq. miles)	0.68
Type of government	Township
Form of government	TC

Government

Legislative Districts
US Congressional	12
State Legislative	12

Local Officials, 2006
Mayor	Kenneth Florek
Admin/Manager	Robert Bowden
Clerk	Robert Bowden
Finance Dir/Treas	John Antonides
Engineer	Schoor DePalma
Attorney	John Bennett
Tax assessor	Eldo Magnani
Tax collector	John Antonides
Building officer	Henry Salerno
Zoning officer	Timothy Anfuso
Public Works	Edward Thompson

Housing & Construction

Housing Units, 2000*
Total	3,614
Median rent	$974
Median SF home value	$425,500

New Privately Owned Housing Units
Authorized by Building Permit
	Units	Value
Total, 2004	32	$16,795,650
Single family	30	$16,789,650
Total, 2005	19	$9,183,000
Single family	19	$9,183,000

Real Property Valuation - parcels, 2005
	Number	Valuation
Total		$1,364,195,300
Vacant	174	22,918,500
Residential	2,996	1,150,175,800
Commercial	72	72,887,300
Industrial	0	0
Apartments	0	0
Farm land	220	114,367,600
Farm homestead	310	3,846,100

Average Property Value & Tax, 2005
Residential value	$349,069
Property tax	$10,530
FAIR rebate	$631

Public Library
Colts Neck Branch Library†
1 Winthrop Rd
Colts Neck, NJ 07722
732-431-5656
Branch Librarian	Beth Miller

Library statistics, 2004
	Total	per capita
Volumes	NA	NA
Expenditure	NA	NA

†Branch of County Library

Public Safety
Police
Chief	Kevin Sauter
Number of officers, 2004	22

Crime, 2004	Number	Rate
Total	140	11.7
Violent	9	0.8
Non-violent	131	11
Domestic Viol.	32	NA

Emergency/Fire
Director	Richard Galinski

Public School District
(for school year 2004-2005 except as noted)

Colts Neck Township School District
70 Conover Rd
Colts Neck, NJ 07722
732-946-0055
Superintendent	Richard M. Fitzpatrick
Grade plan	K-8
Enrollment	1,508.0
Students per teacher	10.4
Per pupil expenditure	$11,464
Median faculty salary	$45,830
Median administrator salary	$96,685
Grade 12 enrollment	NA
High school graduation rate	NA

Assessment test results
(percent scoring at proficient or advanced level)
	Language	Math
Grade 3	90.6%	87.7%
Grade 8	93.8%	87.7%
High school	NA	NA

SAT
Percent tested	NA
Average SAT math score	NA
Average SAT verbal score	NA

No Child Left Behind, 2003-04
Attendence rate (target = 90%)	95.9%
Drop rate	NA
Highly-qualified teachers	85.5%
District needs improvement?(AYP)	No

Municipal Finance

Fiscal Year 2005
Total tax levy	$41,202,145
County levy	8,905,705
County taxes	7,991,309
County library	440,197
County health	0
County open space	474,198
School levy	28,241,674
Local muni. budget	4,054,766
Misc. revenues	5,462,157
Total aid	$2,401,539
CMPTRA	197,400
Muni. block grant	48,350
Energy tax receipts	2,057,401
Homeland security	70,000

Fiscal Year 2006
Total aid	$2,401,539
CMPTRA	125,391
Muni. block grant	48,350
Energy tax receipts	2,129,410
Homeland security	70,000

Taxes
	2003	2004	2005
General tax rate per $100	2.82	2.915	3.017
Net valuation taxable	$1,317,533,682	$1,335,980,549	$1,365,818,868
State equalized value	$2,319,601,553	$2,607,555,477	$2,931,570,869
County equalization ratio	62.59	56.80	51.20

Demographics & Socio-Economic Characteristics
(2000 U.S. Census, except as noted)

Population
1980*	4,674
1990*	5,026
2000	5,259
Male	2,590
Female	2,669
2004 (estimate)*	5,388
Persons per sq. mi. of land	166

Race & Hispanic Origin, 2000
Race
White	4,364
Black/African American	706
Amer. Indian/Alaska Natv.	22
Asian	12
Natv. Hawaiian/Pac. Islander	1
Other Race	53
Two or more races	101
Hispanic origin, total	203
Mexican	29
Puerto Rican	126
Cuban	1
Other Hispanic	47

Age & Nativity, 2000
Under 5 years	373
18 years and over	3,773
21 years and over	3,534
65 years and over	648
85 years and over	58
Median Age	34
Native born	5,200
Foreign born	59

Educational Attainment, 2000
Population 25 years and over	3,281
0-8 yrs of school	10.3%
High School grad or higher	63.2%
Bachelor's degree or higher	6.3%
Graduate degree	1.3%

Income & Poverty, 1999
Per capita income	$14,663
Median household income	$34,960
Median family income	$37,500
Persons in poverty	827
H'holds receiving public assistance	107
H'holds receiving social security	565

Households, 2000
Total households	1,873
With persons under 18	791
With persons over 65	490
Family households	1,368
One-person households	400
Persons per household	2.8
Persons per family	3.22

Labor & Employment
Total civilian labor force, 2004**	2,344
Unemployment rate	4.4%
Total civilian labor force, 2000	2,362
Unemployment rate	9.1%

Employed persons 16 years and over by occupation, 2000
Managers & professionals	367
Service occupations	420
Sales & office occupations	421
Farming, fishing & forestry	58
Construction & maintenance	289
Production & transportation	593
Self-employed persons	137

*US Census Bureau
**New Jersey Department of Labor

General Information
Township of Commercial
Township Hall
1768 Main St
Port Norris, NJ 08349
856-785-3100

Web site	NA
Land area (sq. miles)	32.46
Water area (sq. miles)	2.04
Type of government	Township
Form of government	TC

Government

Legislative Districts
US Congressional	2
State Legislative	3

Local Officials, 2006
Mayor	Ronald L. Sutton Sr.
Admin/Manager	Judson Moore
Clerk	Hannah E. Nichols
Finance Dir/Treas	Judson Moore
Engineer	Edward Vernick
Attorney	Edward Duffy
Tax assessor	David Brown
Tax collector	Grace Robinson
Building officer	David Dean
Zoning officer	David Dean
Public Works	Orville Harris

Housing & Construction

Housing Units, 2000*
Total	2,171
Median rent	$689
Median SF home value	$66,100

New Privately Owned Housing Units
Authorized by Building Permit
	Units	Value
Total, 2004	9	$618,278
Single family	9	$618,278
Total, 2005	8	$726,588
Single family	8	$726,588

Real Property Valuation - parcels, 2005
	Number	Valuation
Total		$114,661,125
Vacant	1,797	10,367,975
Residential	2,096	92,296,000
Commercial	61	4,146,650
Industrial	19	6,495,100
Apartments	1	62,400
Farm land	23	823,800
Farm homestead	53	469,200

Average Property Value & Tax, 2005
Residential value	$43,167
Property tax	$1,529
FAIR rebate	$595

Public Library
Commercial Township Free Public Library
1628 Main St
Port Norris, NJ 08349
856-785-1900

Librarian	NA

Library statistics, 2004
	Total	per capita
Volumes	NA	NA
Expenditure	NA	NA

Public Safety

Police
Chief	NA
Number of officers, 2004	0

Crime, 2004	Number	Rate
Total	152	28.2
Violent	20	3.7
Non-violent	132	24.5
Domestic Viol.	102	NA

Emergency/Fire
Director	NA

Public School District
(for school year 2004-2005 except as noted)

Commercial Township School District
PO Box 650
Port Norris, NJ 08349
856-785-0840

Superintendent	Barry Ballard
Grade plan	K-12
Enrollment	713.0
Students per teacher	10.1
Per pupil expenditure	$11,118
Median faculty salary	$42,000
Median administrator salary	$82,000
Grade 12 enrollment	NA
High school graduation rate	NA

Assessment test results
(percent scoring at proficient or advanced level)
	Language	Math
Grade 3	71.2%	50.0%
Grade 8	62.8%	40.8%
High school	NA	NA

SAT
Percent tested	NA
Average SAT math score	NA
Average SAT verbal score	NA

No Child Left Behind, 2003-04
Attendence rate (target = 90%)	92.9%
Drop rate	NA
Highly-qualified teachers	88.8%
District needs improvement?(AYP)	No

Municipal Finance

Fiscal Year 2005
Total tax levy	$4,120,889
County levy	1,658,657
County taxes	1,575,603
County library	0
County health	67,097
County open space	15,957
School levy	1,589,835
Local muni. budget	872,397
Misc. revenues	2,361,056
Total aid	$651,905
CMPTRA	318,231
Muni. block grant	21,992
Energy tax receipts	311,682
Homeland security	0

Fiscal Year 2006
Total aid	$651,905
CMPTRA	307,322
Muni. block grant	21,992
Energy tax receipts	322,591
Homeland security	NA

Taxes
	2003	2004	2005
General tax rate per $100	2.90	3.080	3.545
Net valuation taxable	$116,001,917	$115,976,825	$116,304,201
State equalized value	$147,341,442	$157,448,916	$183,300,553
County equalization ratio	84.72	78.73	73.36

Demographics & Socio-Economic Characteristics
(2000 U.S. Census, except as noted)

Population
1980*	254
1990*	412
2000	468
Male	232
Female	236
2004 (estimate)*	525
Persons per sq. mi. of land	67

Race & Hispanic Origin, 2000
Race
White	440
Black/African American	13
Amer. Indian/Alaska Natv.	4
Asian	6
Natv. Hawaiian/Pac. Islander	0
Other Race	3
Two or more races	2
Hispanic origin, total	14
Mexican	3
Puerto Rican	3
Cuban	5
Other Hispanic	3

Age & Nativity, 2000
Under 5 years	38
18 years and over	328
21 years and over	317
65 years and over	49
85 years and over	1
Median Age	36.5
Native born	453
Foreign born	15

Educational Attainment, 2000
Population 25 years and over	325
0-8 yrs of school	4.0%
High School grad or higher	84.6%
Bachelor's degree or higher	20.6%
Graduate degree	4.9%

Income & Poverty, 1999
Per capita income	$21,321
Median household income	$47,083
Median family income	$56,000
Persons in poverty	23
H'holds receiving public assistance	4
H'holds receiving social security	32

Households, 2000
Total households	172
With persons under 18	71
With persons over 65	37
Family households	121
One-person households	39
Persons per household	2.72
Persons per family	3.21

Labor & Employment
Total civilian labor force, 2004**	205
Unemployment rate	4.4%
Total civilian labor force, 2000	231
Unemployment rate	3.5%

Employed persons 16 years and over by occupation, 2000
Managers & professionals	76
Service occupations	60
Sales & office occupations	31
Farming, fishing & forestry	0
Construction & maintenance	28
Production & transportation	28
Self-employed persons	20

*US Census Bureau
**New Jersey Department of Labor

General Information
City of Corbin
316 Route 50
Corbin, NJ 08270
609-628-2673
Email	corbincity@plexi.net
Land area (sq. miles)	7.89
Water area (sq. miles)	1.10
Type of government	City
Form of government	C

Government

Legislative Districts
US Congressional	2
State Legislative	2

Local Officials, 2006
Mayor	Carol Foster
Admin/Manager	NA
Clerk	Joanne Siedlecki
Finance Dir/Treas	James Nicola
Engineer	David Scheidegg
Attorney	Richard Russell
Tax assessor	Bernadette Leonardi
Tax collector	NA
Building officer	NA
Zoning officer	Carl Saunders
Public Works	NA

Housing & Construction

Housing Units, 2000*
Total	204
Median rent	$792
Median SF home value	$150,000

New Privately Owned Housing Units Authorized by Building Permit
	Units	Value
Total, 2004	NA	NA
Single family	NA	NA
Total, 2005	3	$198,580
Single family	3	$198,580

Real Property Valuation - parcels, 2005
	Number	Valuation
Total		$29,155,400
Vacant	81	1,905,800
Residential	207	24,190,000
Commercial	14	2,661,700
Industrial	0	0
Apartments	0	0
Farm land	4	304,000
Farm homestead	12	93,900

Average Property Value & Tax, 2005
Residential value	$110,885
Property tax	$3,765
FAIR rebate	$545

Public Library

No public municipal library.

Library statistics, 2004
	Total	per capita
Volumes	NA	NA
Expenditure	NA	NA

Public Safety
Police
Chief	NA
Number of officers, 2004	0

Crime, 2004	Number	Rate
Total	8	15.4
Violent	2	3.9
Non-violent	6	11.6
Domestic Viol.	1	NA

Emergency/Fire
Director	NA

Public School District
(for school year 2004-2005 except as noted)

Corbin City School District†
501 Atlantic Ave
Ocean City, NJ 08226
609-628-2701

†No schools in district - sends children to Upper Township and Ocean City schools.
Grade plan	NA
Enrollment	NA
Students per teacher	NA
Per pupil expenditure	NA
Median faculty salary	NA

Assessment test results
(percent scoring at proficient or advanced level)
	Language	Math
Grade 3	NA	NA
Grade 8	NA	NA
High school	NA	NA

SAT
Percent tested	NA
Average SAT math score	NA
Average SAT verbal score	NA

No Child Left Behind, 2003-04
Attendence rate (target = 90%)	NA
Drop rate	NA
Highly-qualified teachers	NA
District needs improvement?(AYP)	NA

Municipal Finance

Fiscal Year 2005
Total tax levy	$994,098
County levy	120,038
County taxes	97,968
County library	10,873
County health	5,351
County open space	5,846
School levy	794,617
Local muni. budget	79,444
Misc. revenues	456,224
Total aid	$78,012
CMPTRA	17,797
Muni. block grant	1,835
Energy tax receipts	58,380
Homeland security	0

Fiscal Year 2006
Total aid	$78,013
CMPTRA	15,754
Muni. block grant	1,835
Energy tax receipts	60,424
Homeland security	NA

Taxes
	2003	2004	2005
General tax rate per $100	2.37	3.317	3.396
Net valuation taxable	$27,171,748	$28,499,412	$29,278,025
State equalized value	$28,604,851	$28,391,986	$28,130,308
County equalization ratio	106.71	94.99	100.38

Demographics & Socio-Economic Characteristics
(2000 U.S. Census, except as noted)

Population
1980*	1,927
1990*	2,500
2000	3,227
Male	1,558
Female	1,669
2004 (estimate)*	3,722
Persons per sq. mi. of land	278

Race & Hispanic Origin, 2000
Race
White	2,865
Black/African American	73
Amer. Indian/Alaska Natv.	0
Asian	239
Natv. Hawaiian/Pac. Islander	0
Other Race	7
Two or more races	43
Hispanic origin, total	55
Mexican	4
Puerto Rican	8
Cuban	6
Other Hispanic	37

Age & Nativity, 2000
Under 5 years	214
18 years and over	2,245
21 years and over	2,191
65 years and over	363
85 years and over	64
Median Age	39.6
Native born	2,857
Foreign born	370

Educational Attainment, 2000
Population 25 years and over	2,142
0-8 yrs of school	3.4%
High School grad or higher	93.5%
Bachelor's degree or higher	62.7%
Graduate degree	27.5%

Income & Poverty, 1999
Per capita income	$50,698
Median household income	$111,680
Median family income	$128,410
Persons in poverty	51
H'holds receiving public assistance	2
H'holds receiving social security	261

Households, 2000
Total households	1,091
With persons under 18	517
With persons over 65	236
Family households	877
One-person households	178
Persons per household	2.92
Persons per family	3.31

Labor & Employment
Total civilian labor force, 2004**	1,443
Unemployment rate	1.9%
Total civilian labor force, 2000	1,551
Unemployment rate	1.8%

Employed persons 16 years and over by occupation, 2000
Managers & professionals	920
Service occupations	122
Sales & office occupations	360
Farming, fishing & forestry	0
Construction & maintenance	32
Production & transportation	89
Self-employed persons	114

*US Census Bureau
**New Jersey Department of Labor

General Information
Township of Cranbury
23A N Main St
Cranbury, NJ 08512
609-395-0900

Web site	www.cranburytownship.org
Land area (sq. miles)	13.41
Water area (sq. miles)	0.04
Type of government	Township
Form of government	TC

Government

Legislative Districts
US Congressional	12
State Legislative	14

Local Officials, 2006
Mayor	Thomas Panconi Jr.
Admin/Manager	Thomas C. Witt
Clerk	Kathleen Cunningham
Finance Dir/Treas	Denise Marabello
Engineer	Cathleen Marcell
Attorney	Trishka Waterbury
Tax assessor	Steve Benner
Tax collector	NA
Building officer	Greg Farrington
Zoning officer	NA
Public Works	Thomas C. Witt

Housing & Construction

Housing Units, 2000*
Total	1,121
Median rent	$756
Median SF home value	$361,000

New Privately Owned Housing Units
Authorized by Building Permit
	Units	Value
Total, 2004	81	$13,666,843
Single family	81	$13,666,843
Total, 2005	2	$457,803
Single family	2	$457,803

Real Property Valuation - parcels, 2005
	Number	Valuation
Total		$587,018,965
Vacant	158	18,638,415
Residential	1,086	237,932,250
Commercial	79	106,000,500
Industrial	31	212,048,800
Apartments	1	400,000
Farm land	48	10,060,500
Farm homestead	100	1,938,500

Average Property Value & Tax, 2005
Residential value	$202,252
Property tax	$7,270
FAIR rebate	$556

Public Library
Cranbury Public Library
23 N Main St
Cranbury, NJ 08512
609-655-0555

Director................. Howard Zogott

Library statistics, 2004
	Total	per capita
Volumes	23,036	7.14
Expenditure	$255,195	$79.08

Public Safety

Police
Chief	Jay Hansen
Number of officers, 2004	17

Crime, 2004	Number	Rate
Total	88	25.6
Violent	0	0
Non-violent	88	25.6
Domestic Viol.	3	NA

Emergency/Fire
Director................. Sam Distasio

Public School District
(for school year 2004-2005 except as noted)

Cranbury Township School District
23 N Main St
Cranbury, NJ 08512
609-395-1700

Superintendent	Carol Malouf
Grade plan	K-12
Enrollment	599.0
Students per teacher	9.8
Per pupil expenditure	$14,741
Median faculty salary	$54,560
Median administrator salary	$100,800
Grade 12 enrollment	NA
High school graduation rate	NA

Assessment test results
(percent scoring at proficient or advanced level)
	Language	Math
Grade 3	97.1%	94.3%
Grade 8	97.2%	95.9%
High school	NA	NA

SAT
Percent tested	NA
Average SAT math score	NA
Average SAT verbal score	NA

No Child Left Behind, 2003-04
Attendence rate (target = 90%)	96.4%
Drop rate	NA
Highly-qualified teachers	95.9%
District needs improvement?(AYP)	No

Municipal Finance

Fiscal Year 2005
Total tax levy	$21,143,333
County levy	3,627,530
County taxes	3,284,772
County library	0
County health	0
County open space	342,758
School levy	12,837,978
Local muni. budget	4,677,825
Misc. revenues	7,055,789
Total aid	$693,130
CMPTRA	182,597
Muni. block grant	12,653
Energy tax receipts	472,880
Homeland security	25,000

Fiscal Year 2006
Total aid	$693,129
CMPTRA	166,046
Muni. block grant	12,653
Energy tax receipts	489,430
Homeland security	25,000

Taxes
	2003	2004	2005
General tax rate per $100	3.53	3.660	3.600
Net valuation taxable	$490,779,329	$545,329,430	$588,192,697
State equalized value	$979,599,459	$1,096,003,674	$1,390,197,818
County equalization ratio	57.49	50.10	49.70

Demographics & Socio-Economic Characteristics
(2000 U.S. Census, except as noted)

Population
1980*	24,573
1990*	22,633
2000	22,578
Male	10,724
Female	11,854
2004 (estimate)*	22,617
Persons per sq. mi. of land	4,692

Race & Hispanic Origin, 2000
Race
White	21,156
Black/African American	583
Amer. Indian/Alaska Natv.	9
Asian	485
Natv. Hawaiian/Pac. Islander	5
Other Race	151
Two or more races	189
Hispanic origin, total	879
Mexican	47
Puerto Rican	241
Cuban	198
Other Hispanic	393

Age & Nativity, 2000
Under 5 years	1,465
18 years and over	17,316
21 years and over	16,793
65 years and over	4,048
85 years and over	615
Median Age	40.4
Native born	20,613
Foreign born	1,965

Educational Attainment, 2000
Population 25 years and over	16,204
0-8 yrs of school	2.9%
High School grad or higher	91.5%
Bachelor's degree or higher	43.0%
Graduate degree	16.0%

Income & Poverty, 1999
Per capita income	$33,283
Median household income	$76,338
Median family income	$86,624
Persons in poverty	553
H'holds receiving public assistance	54
H'holds receiving social security	2,438

Households, 2000
Total households	8,397
With persons under 18	2,902
With persons over 65	2,509
Family households	6,225
One-person households	1,842
Persons per household	2.62
Persons per family	3.09

Labor & Employment
Total civilian labor force, 2004**	12,757
Unemployment rate	2.1%
Total civilian labor force, 2000	12,149
Unemployment rate	4.1%

Employed persons 16 years and over by occupation, 2000
Managers & professionals	5,895
Service occupations	1,065
Sales & office occupations	3,161
Farming, fishing & forestry	0
Construction & maintenance	798
Production & transportation	727
Self-employed persons	584

*US Census Bureau
**New Jersey Department of Labor

General Information
Township of Cranford
8 Springfield Ave
Cranford, NJ 07016
908-709-7200

Web site	www.cranford.com/township
Land area (sq. miles)	4.82
Water area (sq. miles)	0.02
Type of government	Township
Form of government	TC

Government

Legislative Districts
US Congressional	7
State Legislative	21

Local Officials, 2006
Mayor	Daniel J. Aschenbach
Admin/Manager	Marlena Schmid
Clerk	Rosalie Hellenbrecht
Finance Dir/Treas	Thomas Grady
Engineer	Richard Marsden
Attorney	Robert Renaud
Tax assessor	Peter Barnett
Tax collector	Thomas Grady
Building officer	Richard Belluscio
Zoning officer	(Vacant)
Public Works	Wayne Rozman

Housing & Construction

Housing Units, 2000*
Total	8,560
Median rent	$867
Median SF home value	$233,600

New Privately Owned Housing Units Authorized by Building Permit
	Units	Value
Total, 2004	17	$2,021,164
Single family	15	$1,875,164
Total, 2005	21	$3,161,442
Single family	19	$2,969,942

Real Property Valuation - parcels, 2005
	Number	Valuation
Total		$1,670,597,900
Vacant	72	6,819,500
Residential	7,467	1,333,744,900
Commercial	290	273,396,600
Industrial	44	50,021,300
Apartments	9	6,510,400
Farm land	0	0
Farm homestead	1	105,200

Average Property Value & Tax, 2005
Residential value	$178,609
Property tax	$7,006
FAIR rebate	$604

Public Library
Cranford Public Library
224 Walnut Ave
Cranford, NJ 07016
908-709-7272

Director......................John Malar

Library statistics, 2004
	Total	per capita
Volumes	105,163	4.66
Expenditure	$1,035,844	$45.88

Public Safety
Police
Chief	Eric G. Mason
Number of officers, 2004	52

Crime, 2004	Number	Rate
Total	270	11.9
Violent	10	0.4
Non-violent	260	11.5
Domestic Viol.	68	NA

Emergency/Fire
Director	Leonard Dolan III

Public School District
(for school year 2004-2005 except as noted)

Cranford Township School District
132 Thomas St
Cranford, NJ 07016
908-709-6202

Superintendent	Lawrence Feinsod
Grade plan	K-12
Enrollment	3,651.0
Students per teacher	11.4
Per pupil expenditure	$11,710
Median faculty salary	$53,276
Median administrator salary	$102,110
Grade 12 enrollment	227.0
High school graduation rate	97.4%

Assessment test results
(percent scoring at proficient or advanced level)
	Language	Math
Grade 3	95.6%	92.6%
Grade 8	93.8%	82.4%
High school	91.9%	86.5%

SAT
Percent tested	96%
Average SAT math score	563
Average SAT verbal score	561

No Child Left Behind, 2003-04
Attendance rate (target = 90%)	95.8%
Drop rate	0.5%
Highly-qualified teachers	96.9%
District needs improvement?(AYP)	No

Municipal Finance

Fiscal Year 2005
Total tax levy	$65,667,305
County levy	13,282,306
County taxes	12,759,169
County library	0
County health	0
County open space	523,137
School levy	36,878,298
Local muni. budget	15,506,701
Misc. revenues	8,527,585
Total aid	$3,944,116
CMPTRA	1,157,202
Muni. block grant	99,034
Energy tax receipts	2,597,880
Homeland security	90,000

Fiscal Year 2006
Total aid	$3,944,115
CMPTRA	1,066,276
Muni. block grant	99,034
Energy tax receipts	2,688,805
Homeland security	90,000

Taxes
	2003	2004	2005
General tax rate per $100	3.53	3.722	3.923
Net valuation taxable	$1,665,985,038	$1,671,466,265	$1,674,054,231
State equalized value	$2,929,461,998	$3,251,776,158	$3,617,230,404
County equalization ratio	60.21	53.21	48.22

Demographics & Socio-Economic Characteristics
(2000 U.S. Census, except as noted)

Population
1980*	7,609
1990*	7,558
2000	7,746
Male	3,726
Female	4,020
2004 (estimate)*	8,212
Persons per sq. mi. of land	3,844

Race & Hispanic Origin, 2000
Race
White	6,046
Black/African American	71
Amer. Indian/Alaska Natv.	3
Asian	1,444
Natv. Hawaiian/Pac. Islander	0
Other Race	50
Two or more races	132
Hispanic origin, total	309
Mexican	7
Puerto Rican	71
Cuban	79
Other Hispanic	152

Age & Nativity, 2000
Under 5 years	530
18 years and over	5,710
21 years and over	5,563
65 years and over	1,308
85 years and over	177
Median Age	40.9
Native born	5,848
Foreign born	1,898

Educational Attainment, 2000
Population 25 years and over	5,408
0-8 yrs of school	2.6%
High School grad or higher	92.3%
Bachelor's degree or higher	50.1%
Graduate degree	17.6%

Income & Poverty, 1999
Per capita income	$41,573
Median household income	$84,692
Median family income	$96,245
Persons in poverty	232
H'holds receiving public assistance	36
H'holds receiving social security	807

Households, 2000
Total households	2,630
With persons under 18	1,113
With persons over 65	873
Family households	2,163
One-person households	418
Persons per household	2.91
Persons per family	3.26

Labor & Employment
Total civilian labor force, 2004**	3,975
Unemployment rate	3.0%
Total civilian labor force, 2000	3,731
Unemployment rate	2.3%

Employed persons 16 years and over by occupation, 2000
Managers & professionals	1,955
Service occupations	284
Sales & office occupations	982
Farming, fishing & forestry	0
Construction & maintenance	291
Production & transportation	132
Self-employed persons	274

*US Census Bureau
**New Jersey Department of Labor

General Information
Borough of Cresskill
67 Union Ave
Cresskill, NJ 07626
201-569-5400
Web site	www.cresskillboro.com
Land area (sq. miles)	2.14
Water area (sq. miles)	0
Type of government	Borough
Form of government	B

Government

Legislative Districts
US Congressional	5
State Legislative	39

Local Officials, 2006
Mayor	Benedict Romeo
Admin/Manager	NA
Clerk	Barbara Nasuto
Finance Dir/Treas	Robert Camasto
Engineer	Azzolina,Feury,Raimondo
Attorney	Robert Quinn
Tax assessor	James Anzevino
Tax collector	NA
Building officer	Edward Rossi
Zoning officer	NA
Public Works	NA

Housing & Construction

Housing Units, 2000*
Total	2,702
Median rent	$1,571
Median SF home value	$281,100

New Privately Owned Housing Units Authorized by Building Permit
	Units	Value
Total, 2004	104	$24,991,052
Single family	25	$11,514,052
Total, 2005	17	$11,027,125
Single family	17	$11,027,125

Real Property Valuation - parcels, 2005
	Number	Valuation
Total		$1,705,614,000
Vacant	110	45,143,800
Residential	2,629	1,538,106,200
Commercial	81	102,017,800
Industrial	4	15,005,400
Apartments	5	5,340,800
Farm land	0	0
Farm homestead	0	0

Average Property Value & Tax, 2005
Residential value	$585,054
Property tax	$10,421
FAIR rebate	$640

Public Library
Cresskill Public Library
53 Union Ave
Cresskill, NJ 07626
201-567-3521
Director	Alice Chi

Library statistics, 2004
	Total	per capita
Volumes	50,897	6.57
Expenditure	$505,682	$65.28

Public Safety

Police
Chief	Frank Tino Jr.
Number of officers, 2004	25

Crime, 2004
	Number	Rate
Total	103	13
Violent	4	0.5
Non-violent	99	12.5
Domestic Viol.	1	NA

Emergency/Fire
Director	John Birnie

Public School District
(for school year 2004-2005 except as noted)

Cresskill School District
1 Lincoln Drive
Cresskill, NJ 07626
201-567-5919
Superintendent	Charles Khoury
Grade plan	K-12
Enrollment	1,614.0
Students per teacher	12.5
Per pupil expenditure	$11,694
Median faculty salary	$65,667
Median administrator salary	$112,658
Grade 12 enrollment	114.0
High school graduation rate	98.4%

Assessment test results
(percent scoring at proficient or advanced level)
	Language	Math
Grade 3	96.7%	87.4%
Grade 8	83.8%	77.4%
High school	90.8%	89.8%

SAT
Percent tested	102%
Average SAT math score	597
Average SAT verbal score	555

No Child Left Behind, 2003-04
Attendence rate (target = 90%)	96.3%
Drop rate	0%
Highly-qualified teachers	99.2%
District needs improvement?(AYP)	No

Municipal Finance

Fiscal Year 2005
Total tax levy	$30,397,111
County levy	3,342,435
County taxes	3,172,400
County library	0
County health	0
County open space	170,035
School levy	18,760,894
Local muni. budget	8,293,782
Misc. revenues	3,549,312
Total aid	$1,182,008
CMPTRA	227,335
Muni. block grant	33,072
Energy tax receipts	871,601
Homeland security	50,000

Fiscal Year 2006
Total aid	$1,182,008
CMPTRA	196,829
Muni. block grant	33,072
Energy tax receipts	902,107
Homeland security	50,000

Taxes
	2003	2004	2005
General tax rate per $100	3.18	1.650	1.790
Net valuation taxable	$832,134,268	$1,706,022,079	$1,706,514,983
State equalized value	$1,488,878,633	$1,697,032,643	$1,948,076,465
County equalization ratio	63.2	114.02	100.53

Demographics & Socio-Economic Characteristics
(2000 U.S. Census, except as noted)

Population
1980*	1,952
1990*	1,179
2000	1,070
Male	535
Female	535
2004 (estimate)*	1,055
Persons per sq. mi. of land	868

Race & Hispanic Origin, 2000
Race
White	1,010
Black/African American	13
Amer. Indian/Alaska Natv.	1
Asian	3
Natv. Hawaiian/Pac. Islander	0
Other Race	29
Two or more races	14
Hispanic origin, total	54
Mexican	10
Puerto Rican	7
Cuban	2
Other Hispanic	35

Age & Nativity, 2000
Under 5 years	53
18 years and over	851
21 years and over	818
65 years and over	286
85 years and over	25
Median Age	44.6
Native born	935
Foreign born	135

Educational Attainment, 2000
Population 25 years and over	756
0-8 yrs of school	2.2%
High School grad or higher	88.6%
Bachelor's degree or higher	26.9%
Graduate degree	8.2%

Income & Poverty, 1999
Per capita income	$38,510
Median household income	$58,472
Median family income	$65,313
Persons in poverty	120
H'holds receiving public assistance	3
H'holds receiving social security	191

Households, 2000
Total households	434
With persons under 18	96
With persons over 65	194
Family households	290
One-person households	126
Persons per household	2.46
Persons per family	3.02

Labor & Employment
Total civilian labor force, 2004**	629
Unemployment rate	2.9%
Total civilian labor force, 2000	359
Unemployment rate	3.1%

Employed persons 16 years and over by occupation, 2000
Managers & professionals	131
Service occupations	51
Sales & office occupations	139
Farming, fishing & forestry	0
Construction & maintenance	15
Production & transportation	12
Self-employed persons	35

*US Census Bureau
**New Jersey Department of Labor

General Information
Borough of Deal
PO Box 56
Deal, NJ 07723
732-531-1454

Web site	dealborough.com
Land area (sq. miles)	1.22
Water area (sq. miles)	0.08
Type of government	Borough
Form of government	Comm.

Government

Legislative Districts
US Congressional	6
State Legislative	11

Local Officials, 2006
Mayor	Harry Franco
Admin/Manager	James Rogers
Clerk	James Rogers
Finance Dir/Treas	Theresa Davis
Engineer	Leon Avakian
Attorney	Martin Barger
Tax assessor	Peter Barnett
Tax collector	Theresa Davis
Building officer	William Doolittle
Zoning officer	NA
Public Works	Brendan Kelly

Housing & Construction

Housing Units, 2000*
Total	953
Median rent	$950
Median SF home value	$553,800

New Privately Owned Housing Units Authorized by Building Permit
	Units	Value
Total, 2004	6	$1,128,000
Single family	6	$1,128,000
Total, 2005	8	$5,075,000
Single family	8	$5,075,000

Real Property Valuation - parcels, 2005
	Number	Valuation
Total		$1,091,885,400
Vacant	57	42,010,000
Residential	856	1,034,099,500
Commercial	16	13,305,400
Industrial	0	0
Apartments	4	2,470,500
Farm land	0	0
Farm homestead	0	0

Average Property Value & Tax, 2005
Residential value	$1,208,060
Property tax	$9,911
FAIR rebate	$572

Public Library
No public municipal library.

Library statistics, 2004
	Total	per capita
Volumes	NA	NA
Expenditure	NA	NA

Public Safety

Police
Chief	Michael Sylvester
Number of officers, 2004	15

Crime, 2004	Number	Rate
Total	87	81.2
Violent	2	1.9
Non-violent	85	79.4
Domestic Viol.	14	NA

Emergency/Fire
Director	Robert Simmen III

Public School District
(for school year 2004-2005 except as noted)

Deal Borough School District
Roseld Ave
Deal, NJ 07723
732-531-0480

Superintendent	Anthony Moro Jr.
Grade plan	K-12
Enrollment	124.0
Students per teacher	9.5
Per pupil expenditure	$14,570
Median faculty salary	$39,218
Median administrator salary	$119,870
Grade 12 enrollment	NA
High school graduation rate	NA

Assessment test results
(percent scoring at proficient or advanced level)
	Language	Math
Grade 3	90.9%	100%
Grade 8	85.7%	85.7%
High school	NA	NA

SAT
Percent tested	NA
Average SAT math score	NA
Average SAT verbal score	NA

No Child Left Behind, 2003-04
Attendence rate (target = 90%)	94.6%
Drop rate	NA
Highly-qualified teachers	100%
District needs improvement?(AYP)	No

Municipal Finance

Fiscal Year 2005
Total tax levy	$8,967,459
County levy	4,193,321
County taxes	3,762,761
County library	207,273
County health	0
County open space	223,287
School levy	1,599,402
Local muni. budget	3,174,736
Misc. revenues	2,889,151
Total aid	$492,983
CMPTRA	0
Muni. block grant	5,159
Energy tax receipts	475,209
Homeland security	25,000

Fiscal Year 2006
Total aid	$509,615
CMPTRA	0
Muni. block grant	5,159
Energy tax receipts	479,456
Homeland security	25,000

Taxes
	2003	2004	2005
General tax rate per $100	0.76	0.769	0.821
Net valuation taxable	$1,075,384,059	$1,083,745,500	$1,093,026,348
State equalized value	$1,117,166,070	$1,245,229,826	$1,878,052,144
County equalization ratio	109.77	96.26	87.02

Demographics & Socio-Economic Characteristics
(2000 U.S. Census, except as noted)

Population
1980*	2,523
1990*	2,933
2000	2,927
Male	1,425
Female	1,502
2004 (estimate)*	3,147
Persons per sq. mi. of land	187

Race & Hispanic Origin, 2000
Race
White	2,289
Black/African American	382
Amer. Indian/Alaska Natv.	45
Asian	30
Natv. Hawaiian/Pac. Islander	0
Other Race	89
Two or more races	92
Hispanic origin, total	174
Mexican	27
Puerto Rican	104
Cuban	1
Other Hispanic	42

Age & Nativity, 2000
Under 5 years	160
18 years and over	2,154
21 years and over	2,037
65 years and over	412
85 years and over	39
Median Age	38.8
Native born	2,841
Foreign born	86

Educational Attainment, 2000
Population 25 years and over	1,912
0-8 yrs of school	12.2%
High School grad or higher	73.4%
Bachelor's degree or higher	10.6%
Graduate degree	2.6%

Income & Poverty, 1999
Per capita income	$18,468
Median household income	$45,365
Median family income	$47,225
Persons in poverty	268
H'holds receiving public assistance	12
H'holds receiving social security	334

Households, 2000
Total households	1,013
With persons under 18	412
With persons over 65	304
Family households	785
One-person households	178
Persons per household	2.86
Persons per family	3.22

Labor & Employment
Total civilian labor force, 2004**	1,581
Unemployment rate	6.7%
Total civilian labor force, 2000	1,402
Unemployment rate	6.1%

Employed persons 16 years and over by occupation, 2000
Managers & professionals	275
Service occupations	224
Sales & office occupations	357
Farming, fishing & forestry	11
Construction & maintenance	146
Production & transportation	303
Self-employed persons	60

*US Census Bureau
**New Jersey Department of Labor

General Information
Township of Deerfield
PO Box 350
Rosenhayn, NJ 08352
856-455-3200
Web site	www.deerfieldtownship.org
Land area (sq. miles)	16.84
Water area (sq. miles)	0
Type of government	Township
Form of government	TC

Government

Legislative Districts
US Congressional	2
State Legislative	3

Local Officials, 2006
Mayor	Charlotte Brago
Admin/Manager	Karen Seifrit
Clerk	Karen Seifrit
Finance Dir/Treas	Ruth Moynihan
Engineer	Michael Fralinger
Attorney	Michael Testa
Tax assessor	Donald Seifrit
Tax collector	Ruth Moynihan
Building officer	Kevin Kirchner
Zoning officer	Anthony Lamanteer
Public Works	NA

Housing & Construction

Housing Units, 2000*
Total	1,065
Median rent	$646
Median SF home value	$99,500

New Privately Owned Housing Units Authorized by Building Permit
	Units	Value
Total, 2004	21	$2,291,978
Single family	21	$2,291,978
Total, 2005	15	$2,011,189
Single family	15	$2,011,189

Real Property Valuation - parcels, 2005
	Number	Valuation
Total		$170,301,500
Vacant	285	7,052,600
Residential	924	118,485,100
Commercial	69	15,534,400
Industrial	2	8,193,600
Apartments	0	0
Farm land	154	18,295,400
Farm homestead	259	2,740,400

Average Property Value & Tax, 2005
Residential value	$102,473
Property tax	$2,933
FAIR rebate	$625

Public Library
No public municipal library.

Library statistics, 2004
	Total	per capita
Volumes	NA	NA
Expenditure	NA	NA

Public Safety

Police
Chief	NA
Number of officers, 2004	0

Crime, 2004	Number	Rate
Total	64	20.9
Violent	9	2.9
Non-violent	55	17.9
Domestic Viol.	45	NA

Emergency/Fire
Director	NA

Public School District
(for school year 2004-2005 except as noted)

Deerfield Township School District
PO Box 375
Rosenhayn, NJ 08352
856-451-6610
Administrator	Edythe Austermuhl
Grade plan	K-8
Enrollment	327.0
Students per teacher	9.5
Per pupil expenditure	$11,514
Median faculty salary	$56,925
Median administrator salary	$83,575
Grade 12 enrollment	NA
High school graduation rate	NA

Assessment test results
(percent scoring at proficient or advanced level)
	Language	Math
Grade 3	95.0%	80.0%
Grade 8	61.3%	54.6%
High school	NA	NA

SAT
Percent tested	NA
Average SAT math score	NA
Average SAT verbal score	NA

No Child Left Behind, 2003-04
Attendence rate (target = 90%)	94.9%
Drop rate	NA
Highly-qualified teachers	100%
District needs improvement?(AYP)	No

Municipal Finance

Fiscal Year 2005
Total tax levy	$4,905,544
County levy	1,703,696
County taxes	1,617,774
County library	0
County health	69,414
County open space	16,508
School levy	3,182,220
Local muni. budget	19,629
Misc. revenues	1,708,371
Total aid	$434,220
CMPTRA	150,149
Muni. block grant	12,834
Energy tax receipts	271,237
Homeland security	0

Fiscal Year 2006
Total aid	$434,220
CMPTRA	140,656
Muni. block grant	12,834
Energy tax receipts	280,730
Homeland security	NA

Taxes
	2003	2004	2005
General tax rate per $100	3.92	2.636	2.866
Net valuation taxable	$104,410,023	$171,956,001	$171,360,347
State equalized value	$148,774,612	$164,115,807	$169,932,911
County equalization ratio	76.04	114.27	104.81

Demographics & Socio-Economic Characteristics

(2000 U.S. Census, except as noted)

Population

1980*	3,730
1990*	3,316
2000	3,237
Male	1,568
Female	1,669
2004 (estimate)*	3,701
Persons per sq. mi. of land	1,488

Race & Hispanic Origin, 2000

Race

White	3,104
Black/African American	62
Amer. Indian/Alaska Natv.	8
Asian	13
Natv. Hawaiian/Pac. Islander	0
Other Race	13
Two or more races	37
Hispanic origin, total	63
Mexican	13
Puerto Rican	42
Cuban	2
Other Hispanic	6

Age & Nativity, 2000

Under 5 years	184
18 years and over	2,430
21 years and over	2,326
65 years and over	430
85 years and over	36
Median Age	37
Native born	3,076
Foreign born	161

Educational Attainment, 2000

Population 25 years and over	2,213
0-8 yrs of school	4.7%
High School grad or higher	85.2%
Bachelor's degree or higher	14.8%
Graduate degree	4.7%

Income & Poverty, 1999

Per capita income	$21,096
Median household income	$50,106
Median family income	$56,985
Persons in poverty	305
H'holds receiving public assistance	36
H'holds receiving social security	268

Households, 2000

Total households	1,227
With persons under 18	444
With persons over 65	325
Family households	892
One-person households	280
Persons per household	2.64
Persons per family	3.09

Labor & Employment

Total civilian labor force, 2004**	2,060
Unemployment rate	3.1%
Total civilian labor force, 2000	1,731
Unemployment rate	6.0%

Employed persons 16 years and over by occupation, 2000

Managers & professionals	426
Service occupations	223
Sales & office occupations	528
Farming, fishing & forestry	3
Construction & maintenance	178
Production & transportation	269
Self-employed persons	80

*US Census Bureau
**New Jersey Department of Labor

General Information

Township of Delanco
770 Coopertown Rd
Delanco, NJ 08075
856-461-0561

Web site	www.delancotownship.com
Land area (sq. miles)	2.49
Water area (sq. miles)	0.90
Type of government	Township
Form of government	TC

Government

Legislative Districts

US Congressional	3
State Legislative	7

Local Officials, 2006

Mayor	Kate Fitzpatrick
Admin/Manager	Steven Corcoran
Clerk	Janice Lohr
Finance Dir/Treas	Robert Hudnell
Engineer	William Birdsall
Attorney	Douglas Heinold
Tax assessor	Marie Procacci
Tax collector	Lynn Davis
Building officer	Edward Schaefer
Zoning officer	Phil Goffredo
Public Works	John Fenimore

Housing & Construction

Housing Units, 2000*

Total	1,285
Median rent	$615
Median SF home value	$111,600

New Privately Owned Housing Units Authorized by Building Permit

	Units	Value
Total, 2004	117	$9,998,240
Single family	113	$9,650,240
Total, 2005	121	$10,037,842
Single family	117	$9,675,342

Real Property Valuation - parcels, 2005

	Number	Valuation
Total		$202,841,400
Vacant	435	11,245,300
Residential	1,364	157,747,600
Commercial	40	19,703,600
Industrial	11	12,290,000
Apartments	6	1,146,400
Farm land	5	670,900
Farm homestead	7	37,600

Average Property Value & Tax, 2005

Residential value	$115,088
Property tax	$4,137
FAIR rebate	$615

Public Library

Delanco Public Library
1303 Burlington Ave
Delanco, NJ 08075
856-461-6850

Director	Patricia Krull

Library statistics, 2004

	Total	per capita
Volumes	51,836	16.01
Expenditure	$62,216	$19.22

Public Safety

Police

Chief	Edmund Parsons
Number of officers, 2004	9

Crime, 2004	Number	Rate
Total	56	16.2
Violent	6	1.7
Non-violent	50	14.4
Domestic Viol.	21	NA

Emergency/Fire

Director	Keith Mohrmann

Public School District

(for school year 2004-2005 except as noted)

Delanco Township School District
411 Walnut St
Delanco, NJ 08075
856-461-0859

Superintendent	Michael Livengood
Grade plan	K-12
Enrollment	357.0
Students per teacher	10.2
Per pupil expenditure	$11,858
Median faculty salary	$51,582
Median administrator salary	$74,163
Grade 12 enrollment	NA
High school graduation rate	NA

Assessment test results

(percent scoring at proficient or advanced level)

	Language	Math
Grade 3	81.1%	78.9%
Grade 8	56.6%	54.7%
High school	NA	NA

SAT

Percent tested	NA
Average SAT math score	NA
Average SAT verbal score	NA

No Child Left Behind, 2003-04

Attendence rate (target = 90%)	95.7%
Drop rate	NA
Highly-qualified teachers	99%
District needs improvement?(AYP)	No

Municipal Finance

Fiscal Year 2005

Total tax levy	$7,302,323
County levy	1,289,526
County taxes	1,081,765
County library	94,724
County health	0
County open space	113,038
School levy	4,316,537
Local muni. budget	1,696,260
Misc. revenues	2,596,036
Total aid	$621,600
CMPTRA	306,042
Muni. block grant	14,510
Energy tax receipts	276,048
Homeland security	25,000

Fiscal Year 2006

Total aid	$621,600
CMPTRA	296,380
Muni. block grant	14,510
Energy tax receipts	285,710
Homeland security	25,000

Taxes

	2003	2004	2005
General tax rate per $100	3.47	3.466	3.596
Net valuation taxable	$166,046,527	$183,454,279	$203,136,315
State equalized value	$210,212,086	$250,290,226	$315,527,050
County equalization ratio	86.07	78.99	73.26

Demographics & Socio-Economic Characteristics

(2000 U.S. Census, except as noted)

Population

1980*	3,816
1990*	4,512
2000	4,478
Male	2,226
Female	2,252
2004 (estimate)*	4,701
Persons per sq. mi. of land	128

Race & Hispanic Origin, 2000

Race

White	4,375
Black/African American	18
Amer. Indian/Alaska Natv.	2
Asian	46
Natv. Hawaiian/Pac. Islander	1
Other Race	11
Two or more races	25
Hispanic origin, total	51
Mexican	3
Puerto Rican	15
Cuban	12
Other Hispanic	21

Age & Nativity, 2000

Under 5 years	220
18 years and over	3,429
21 years and over	3,301
65 years and over	530
85 years and over	43
Median Age	42.4
Native born	4,279
Foreign born	202

Educational Attainment, 2000

Population 25 years and over	3,163
0-8 yrs of school	1.9%
High School grad or higher	91.1%
Bachelor's degree or higher	39.1%
Graduate degree	17.8%

Income & Poverty, 1999

Per capita income	$38,285
Median household income	$80,756
Median family income	$90,842
Persons in poverty	154
H'holds receiving public assistance	13
H'holds receiving social security	374

Households, 2000

Total households	1,643
With persons under 18	573
With persons over 65	367
Family households	1,303
One-person households	243
Persons per household	2.72
Persons per family	3.06

Labor & Employment

Total civilian labor force, 2004**	3,025
Unemployment rate	3.1%
Total civilian labor force, 2000	2,482
Unemployment rate	1.8%

Employed persons 16 years and over by occupation, 2000

Managers & professionals	1,124
Service occupations	302
Sales & office occupations	587
Farming, fishing & forestry	5
Construction & maintenance	235
Production & transportation	184
Self-employed persons	291

*US Census Bureau
**New Jersey Department of Labor

General Information

Township of Delaware
PO Box 500
Sergeantsville, NJ 08557
609-397-3240

Web site	NA
Land area (sq. miles)	36.74
Water area (sq. miles)	0.28
Type of government	Township
Form of government	TC

Government

Legislative Districts

US Congressional	12
State Legislative	23

Local Officials, 2006

Mayor	Richard W. Madden
Admin/Manager	NA
Clerk	Judith Allen
Finance Dir/Treas	Linda Zengel
Engineer	Peter Turek
Attorney	Kristina Hadinger
Tax assessor	Michelle Tivigno
Tax collector	NA
Building officer	Edward Noval
Zoning officer	NA
Public Works	NA

Housing & Construction

Housing Units, 2000*

Total	1,701
Median rent	$1,130
Median SF home value	$275,900

New Privately Owned Housing Units
Authorized by Building Permit

	Units	Value
Total, 2004	22	$7,937,572
Single family	22	$7,937,572
Total, 2005	15	$5,374,566
Single family	15	$5,374,566

Real Property Valuation - parcels, 2005

	Number	Valuation
Total		$875,203,420
Vacant	133	12,665,020
Residential	1,282	571,992,300
Commercial	33	17,992,600
Industrial	9	8,602,300
Apartments	2	1,065,700
Farm land	468	256,267,800
Farm homestead	701	6,617,700

Average Property Value & Tax, 2005

Residential value	$291,785
Property tax	$5,249
FAIR rebate	$573

Public Library

No public municipal library.

Library statistics, 2004

	Total	per capita
Volumes	NA	NA
Expenditure	NA	NA

Public Safety

Police

Chief	Bruce Must
Number of officers, 2004	7

Crime, 2004	Number	Rate
Total	37	7.9
Violent	2	0.4
Non-violent	35	7.5
Domestic Viol.	12	NA

Emergency/Fire

Director	Sean Conway

Public School District

(for school year 2004-2005 except as noted)

Delaware Township School District
501 Rosemont-Ringoes Rd
Sergeantsville, NJ 08557
609-397-3179

Superintendent	Richard Wiener
Grade plan	K-8
Enrollment	523.0
Students per teacher	10.5
Per pupil expenditure	$12,051
Median faculty salary	$54,260
Median administrator salary	$97,457
Grade 12 enrollment	NA
High school graduation rate	NA

Assessment test results

(percent scoring at proficient or advanced level)

	Language	Math
Grade 3	98.2%	86.2%
Grade 8	84.7%	82.2%
High school	NA	NA

SAT

Percent tested	NA
Average SAT math score	NA
Average SAT verbal score	NA

No Child Left Behind, 2003-04

Attendence rate (target = 90%)	96.2%
Drop rate	NA
Highly-qualified teachers	100%
District needs improvement?(AYP)	No

Municipal Finance

Fiscal Year 2005

Total tax levy	$15,777,079
County levy	3,190,004
County taxes	2,708,455
County library	226,648
County health	0
County open space	254,900
School levy	10,709,307
Local muni. budget	1,877,768
Misc. revenues	1,649,667
Total aid	$548,026
CMPTRA	210,477
Muni. block grant	19,743
Energy tax receipts	292,806
Homeland security	25,000

Fiscal Year 2006

Total aid	$548,026
CMPTRA	200,229
Muni. block grant	19,743
Energy tax receipts	303,054
Homeland security	25,000

Taxes

	2003	2004	2005
General tax rate per $100	1.90	2.000	1.800
Net valuation taxable	$722,512,441	$732,200,010	$876,960,532
State equalized value	$732,325,604	$781,561,278	$871,383,676
County equalization ratio	105.29	99.40	103.74

Demographics & Socio-Economic Characteristics
(2000 U.S. Census, except as noted)

Population
1980*	14,811
1990*	13,178
2000	15,536
Male	7,646
Female	7,890
2004 (estimate)*	17,309
Persons per sq. mi. of land	2,607

Race & Hispanic Origin, 2000
Race
White	12,875
Black/African American	1,464
Amer. Indian/Alaska Natv.	27
Asian	435
Natv. Hawaiian/Pac. Islander	25
Other Race	253
Two or more races	457
Hispanic origin, total	505
Mexican	51
Puerto Rican	253
Cuban	7
Other Hispanic	194

Age & Nativity, 2000
Under 5 years	970
18 years and over	11,722
21 years and over	11,197
65 years and over	1,672
85 years and over	132
Median Age	36.7
Native born	13,931
Foreign born	1,605

Educational Attainment, 2000
Population 25 years and over	10,463
0-8 yrs of school	3.9%
High School grad or higher	88.2%
Bachelor's degree or higher	27.3%
Graduate degree	8.1%

Income & Poverty, 1999
Per capita income	$25,312
Median household income	$58,526
Median family income	$67,895
Persons in poverty	637
H'holds receiving public assistance	140
H'holds receiving social security	1,249

Households, 2000
Total households	5,816
With persons under 18	2,175
With persons over 65	1,233
Family households	4,330
One-person households	1,222
Persons per household	2.67
Persons per family	3.11

Labor & Employment
Total civilian labor force, 2004**	8,361
Unemployment rate	4.3%
Total civilian labor force, 2000	8,665
Unemployment rate	3.0%

Employed persons 16 years and over by occupation, 2000
Managers & professionals	3,206
Service occupations	858
Sales & office occupations	2,442
Farming, fishing & forestry	7
Construction & maintenance	738
Production & transportation	1,152
Self-employed persons	267

*US Census Bureau
**New Jersey Department of Labor

General Information
Township of Delran
900 Chester Ave
Delran, NJ 08075
856-461-7734

Web site	NA
Land area (sq. miles)	6.64
Water area (sq. miles)	0.61
Type of government	Township
Form of government	MC '50

Government
Legislative Districts
US Congressional	3
State Legislative	7

Local Officials, 2006
Mayor	Joseph Stellwag
Admin/Manager	Jeffrey Hatcher
Clerk	Bernadette McPhee
Finance Dir/Treas	Teresa Leisse (Treas)
Engineer	Pennoni Assoc.
Attorney	Brian Guest
Tax assessor	Tom Davis
Tax collector	Donna Ibbetson
Building officer	Hugh McCurley
Zoning officer	NA
Public Works	NA

Housing & Construction
Housing Units, 2000*
Total	5,936
Median rent	$698
Median SF home value	$145,600

New Privately Owned Housing Units
Authorized by Building Permit
	Units	Value
Total, 2004	80	$5,617,600
Single family	80	$5,617,600
Total, 2005	6	$1,108,000
Single family	6	$1,108,000

Real Property Valuation - parcels, 2005
	Number	Valuation
Total		$1,511,167,900
Vacant	208	15,137,600
Residential	5,058	1,179,037,100
Commercial	157	248,448,500
Industrial	5	2,869,100
Apartments	2	62,667,200
Farm land	11	2,823,700
Farm homestead	18	184,700

Average Property Value & Tax, 2005
Residential value	$232,313
Property tax	$5,222
FAIR rebate	$552

Public Library
No public municipal library.

Library statistics, 2004
	Total	per capita
Volumes	NA	NA
Expenditure	NA	NA

Public Safety
Police
Chief	Al Parente
Number of officers, 2004	30

Crime, 2004	Number	Rate
Total	287	17.3
Violent	21	1.3
Non-violent	266	16.1
Domestic Viol.	135	NA

Emergency/Fire
Director	Joseph Bennett Sr.

Public School District
(for school year 2004-2005 except as noted)

Delran Township School District
52 Hartford Rd
Delran, NJ 08075
856-461-6800

Superintendent	George Sharp
Grade plan	K-12
Enrollment	2,762.5
Students per teacher	12.5
Per pupil expenditure	$10,580
Median faculty salary	$51,150
Median administrator salary	$96,355
Grade 12 enrollment	166.0
High school graduation rate	96.1%

Assessment test results
(percent scoring at proficient or advanced level)
	Language	Math
Grade 3	87.8%	80.0%
Grade 8	75.3%	67.9%
High school	90.2%	82.6%

SAT
Percent tested	87%
Average SAT math score	526
Average SAT verbal score	503

No Child Left Behind, 2003-04
Attendence rate (target = 90%)	94.9%
Drop rate	0.7%
Highly-qualified teachers	96.9%
District needs improvement?(AYP)	No

Municipal Finance
Fiscal Year 2005
Total tax levy	$34,022,651
County levy	6,025,674
County taxes	5,054,886
County library	442,612
County health	0
County open space	528,176
School levy	21,536,977
Local muni. budget	6,460,000
Misc. revenues	6,391,500
Total aid	$1,792,016
CMPTRA	696,760
Muni. block grant	60,917
Energy tax receipts	964,339
Homeland security	70,000

Fiscal Year 2006
Total aid	$1,792,016
CMPTRA	663,009
Muni. block grant	60,917
Energy tax receipts	998,090
Homeland security	70,000

Taxes
	2003	2004	2005
General tax rate per $100	3.33	3.611	2.249
Net valuation taxable	$827,315,417	$849,311,054	$1,513,499,343
State equalized value	$1,022,134,194	$1,238,600,736	$1,529,714,315
County equalization ratio	87.87	80.94	115.24

Demographics & Socio-Economic Characteristics
(2000 U.S. Census, except as noted)

Population
1980*	4,963
1990*	4,800
2000	4,845
Male	2,376
Female	2,469
2004 (estimate)*	4,938
Persons per sq. mi. of land	2,389

Race & Hispanic Origin, 2000
Race
White	3,744
Black/African American	24
Amer. Indian/Alaska Natv.	1
Asian	981
Natv. Hawaiian/Pac. Islander	1
Other Race	23
Two or more races	71
Hispanic origin, total	167
Mexican	14
Puerto Rican	27
Cuban	48
Other Hispanic	78

Age & Nativity, 2000
Under 5 years	297
18 years and over	3,444
21 years and over	3,320
65 years and over	698
85 years and over	67
Median Age	41.1
Native born	3,661
Foreign born	1,184

Educational Attainment, 2000
Population 25 years and over	3,251
0-8 yrs of school	2.9%
High School grad or higher	94.4%
Bachelor's degree or higher	58.9%
Graduate degree	24.1%

Income & Poverty, 1999
Per capita income	$51,939
Median household income	$103,286
Median family income	$113,144
Persons in poverty	79
H'holds receiving public assistance	14
H'holds receiving social security	448

Households, 2000
Total households	1,601
With persons under 18	752
With persons over 65	487
Family households	1,387
One-person households	186
Persons per household	3.02
Persons per family	3.27

Labor & Employment
Total civilian labor force, 2004**	2,657
Unemployment rate	2.5%
Total civilian labor force, 2000	2,267
Unemployment rate	3.9%

Employed persons 16 years and over by occupation, 2000
Managers & professionals	1,344
Service occupations	186
Sales & office occupations	502
Farming, fishing & forestry	0
Construction & maintenance	75
Production & transportation	72
Self-employed persons	208

*US Census Bureau
**New Jersey Department of Labor

General Information
Borough of Demarest
118 Serpentine Rd
Demarest, NJ 07627
201-768-0167
Web site	www.demarestnj.net
Land area (sq. miles)	2.07
Water area (sq. miles)	0
Type of government	Borough
Form of government	B

Government

Legislative Districts
US Congressional	5
State Legislative	39

Local Officials, 2006
Mayor	Jim Carroll
Admin/Manager	NA
Clerk	Carol Kroepke
Finance Dir/Treas	Maureen Neville
Engineer	AFR Group
Attorney	Gregg Paster
Tax assessor	George Reggo
Tax collector	Maureen Neville
Building officer	Edward Rossi
Zoning officer	Edward Rossi
Public Works	John Crosman

Housing & Construction

Housing Units, 2000*
Total	1,634
Median rent	$2,001
Median SF home value	$360,300

New Privately Owned Housing Units Authorized by Building Permit
	Units	Value
Total, 2004	34	$15,028,830
Single family	34	$15,028,830
Total, 2005	47	$21,562,084
Single family	47	$21,562,084

Real Property Valuation - parcels, 2005
	Number	Valuation
Total		$1,112,624,700
Vacant	36	23,938,600
Residential	1,602	1,050,060,500
Commercial	8	37,275,600
Industrial	0	0
Apartments	1	1,350,000
Farm land	0	0
Farm homestead	0	0

Average Property Value & Tax, 2005
Residential value	$655,468
Property tax	$12,812
FAIR rebate	$628

Public Library
Demarest Public Library
90 Hardenburgh Ave
Demarest, NJ 07627
201-768-8714
Director	Edna Ortega

Library statistics, 2004
	Total	per capita
Volumes	24,049	4.96
Expenditure	$215,986	$44.58

Public Safety

Police
Chief	James Brower
Number of officers, 2004	13

Crime, 2004	Number	Rate
Total	38	7.7
Violent	3	0.6
Non-violent	35	7.1
Domestic Viol.	9	NA

Emergency/Fire
Director	Richard Motta

Public School District
(for school year 2004-2005 except as noted)

Demarest School District
568 Piermont Rd
Demarest, NJ 07627
201-768-6060
Superintendent	Lawrence Hughes
Grade plan	K-8
Enrollment	723.0
Students per teacher	10.8
Per pupil expenditure	$12,352
Median faculty salary	$54,154
Median administrator salary	$110,804
Grade 12 enrollment	NA
High school graduation rate	NA

Assessment test results
(percent scoring at proficient or advanced level)
	Language	Math
Grade 3	95.8%	97.2%
Grade 8	92.7%	89.2%
High school	NA	NA

SAT
Percent tested	NA
Average SAT math score	NA
Average SAT verbal score	NA

No Child Left Behind, 2003-04
Attendence rate (target = 90%)	96.8%
Drop rate	NA
Highly-qualified teachers	100%
District needs improvement?(AYP)	No

Municipal Finance

Fiscal Year 2005
Total tax levy	$21,755,738
County levy	2,179,506
County taxes	2,070,282
County library	0
County health	0
County open space	109,224
School levy	14,809,014
Local muni. budget	4,767,218
Misc. revenues	2,012,844
Total aid	$609,387
CMPTRA	131,164
Muni. block grant	21,003
Energy tax receipts	432,220
Homeland security	25,000

Fiscal Year 2006
Total aid	$609,387
CMPTRA	116,037
Muni. block grant	21,003
Energy tax receipts	447,347
Homeland security	25,000

Taxes
	2003	2004	2005
General tax rate per $100	1.72	1.870	1.960
Net valuation taxable	$1,109,706,712	$1,097,243,887	$1,113,022,663
State equalized value	$983,259,536	$1,076,581,503	$1,186,844,384
County equalization ratio	127.75	112.86	101.92

Demographics & Socio-Economic Characteristics

(2000 U.S. Census, except as noted)

Population

1980*	3,989
1990*	5,574
2000	6,492
Male	3,188
Female	3,304
2004 (estimate)*	6,225
Persons per sq. mi. of land	102

Race & Hispanic Origin, 2000

Race

White	6,325
Black/African American	62
Amer. Indian/Alaska Natv.	6
Asian	28
Natv. Hawaiian/Pac. Islander	1
Other Race	40
Two or more races	30
Hispanic origin, total	98
Mexican	45
Puerto Rican	34
Cuban	6
Other Hispanic	13

Age & Nativity, 2000

Under 5 years	429
18 years and over	4,656
21 years and over	4,442
65 years and over	798
85 years and over	162
Median Age	37.4
Native born	6,351
Foreign born	152

Educational Attainment, 2000

Population 25 years and over	4,275
0-8 yrs of school	5.2%
High School grad or higher	83.2%
Bachelor's degree or higher	20.5%
Graduate degree	5.1%

Income & Poverty, 1999

Per capita income	$21,455
Median household income	$56,595
Median family income	$61,445
Persons in poverty	346
H'holds receiving public assistance	38
H'holds receiving social security	533

Households, 2000

Total households	2,159
With persons under 18	970
With persons over 65	460
Family households	1,738
One-person households	333
Persons per household	2.91
Persons per family	3.24

Labor & Employment

Total civilian labor force, 2004**	3,764
Unemployment rate	4.7%
Total civilian labor force, 2000	3,362
Unemployment rate	4.8%

Employed persons 16 years and over by occupation, 2000

Managers & professionals	968
Service occupations	557
Sales & office occupations	769
Farming, fishing & forestry	6
Construction & maintenance	574
Production & transportation	328
Self-employed persons	249

*US Census Bureau
**New Jersey Department of Labor

General Information

Township of Dennis
571 Petersburg Rd
Dennisville, NJ 08214
609-861-9700

Web site	www.dennistwp.org
Land area (sq. miles)	61.35
Water area (sq. miles)	2.94
Type of government	Township
Form of government	TC

Government

Legislative Districts

US Congressional	2
State Legislative	1

Local Officials, 2006

Mayor	Ruth J. Blessing
Admin/Manager	NA
Clerk	Jacqueline B. Justice
Finance Dir/Treas	Glenn Clarke
Engineer	Andrew Previti
Attorney	Jeffrey April
Tax assessor	Patricia Sutton
Tax collector	Darlene Muller
Building officer	Ralph James
Zoning officer	Eileen McFillin
Public Works	Clarence Ryan

Housing & Construction

Housing Units, 2000*

Total	2,327
Median rent	$981
Median SF home value	$135,500

New Privately Owned Housing Units Authorized by Building Permit

	Units	Value
Total, 2004	23	$2,911,560
Single family	23	$2,911,560
Total, 2005	18	$2,427,164
Single family	18	$2,427,164

Real Property Valuation - parcels, 2005

	Number	Valuation
Total		$391,820,600
Vacant	1,450	31,973,300
Residential	2,508	291,257,600
Commercial	132	59,711,000
Industrial	0	0
Apartments	0	0
Farm land	61	7,314,300
Farm homestead	205	1,564,400

Average Property Value & Tax, 2005

Residential value	$107,933
Property tax	$2,440
FAIR rebate	$539

Public Library

No public municipal library.

Library statistics, 2004

	Total	per capita
Volumes	NA	NA
Expenditure	NA	NA

Public Safety

Police

Chief	NA
Number of officers, 2004	0

Crime, 2004	Number	Rate
Total	124	19.6
Violent	15	2.4
Non-violent	109	17.2
Domestic Viol.	37	NA

Emergency/Fire

Director	NA

Public School District

(for school year 2004-2005 except as noted)

Dennis Township School District
601 Hagen Rd
Cape May Court House, NJ 08210
609-861-0549

Superintendent	George Papp
Grade plan	K-12
Enrollment	723.0
Students per teacher	9.6
Per pupil expenditure	$11,644
Median faculty salary	$56,572
Median administrator salary	$81,348
Grade 12 enrollment	NA
High school graduation rate	NA

Assessment test results

(percent scoring at proficient or advanced level)

	Language	Math
Grade 3	84.6%	92.3%
Grade 8	94.0%	85.0%
High school	NA	NA

SAT

Percent tested	NA
Average SAT math score	NA
Average SAT verbal score	NA

No Child Left Behind, 2003-04

Attendence rate (target = 90%)	95.3%
Drop rate	NA
Highly-qualified teachers	88%
District needs improvement?(AYP)	No

Municipal Finance

Fiscal Year 2005

Total tax levy	$8,895,714
County levy	1,570,431
County taxes	1,320,338
County library	185,983
County health	0
County open space	64,110
School levy	6,773,941
Local muni. budget	551,342
Misc. revenues	3,787,360
Total aid	$1,769,295
CMPTRA	143,566
Muni. block grant	25,455
Energy tax receipts	1,586,496
Homeland security	0

Fiscal Year 2006

Total aid	$1,769,296
CMPTRA	88,039
Muni. block grant	25,455
Energy tax receipts	1,642,024
Homeland security	NA

Taxes

	2003	2004	2005
General tax rate per $100	2.08	2.260	2.270
Net valuation taxable	$375,423,997	$384,663,419	$393,439,189
State equalized value	$536,933,634	$625,274,633	$751,268,262
County equalization ratio	77.98	69.92	61.40

Demographics & Socio-Economic Characteristics
(2000 U.S. Census, except as noted)

Population
1980*	14,380
1990*	13,812
2000	15,824
Male	7,617
Female	8,207
2004 (estimate)*	16,188
Persons per sq. mi. of land	1,337

Race & Hispanic Origin, 2000
Race
White	14,659
Black/African American	181
Amer. Indian/Alaska Natv.	12
Asian	734
Natv. Hawaiian/Pac. Islander	5
Other Race	70
Two or more races	163
Hispanic origin, total	418
Mexican	30
Puerto Rican	115
Cuban	55
Other Hispanic	218

Age & Nativity, 2000
Under 5 years	1,147
18 years and over	12,047
21 years and over	11,689
65 years and over	2,376
85 years and over	487
Median Age	39.7
Native born	14,151
Foreign born	1,673

Educational Attainment, 2000
Population 25 years and over	11,319
0-8 yrs of school	2.0%
High School grad or higher	92.3%
Bachelor's degree or higher	44.0%
Graduate degree	17.0%

Income & Poverty, 1999
Per capita income	$38,607
Median household income	$76,778
Median family income	$90,651
Persons in poverty	436
H'holds receiving public assistance	49
H'holds receiving social security	1,656

Households, 2000
Total households	5,990
With persons under 18	2,074
With persons over 65	1,624
Family households	4,315
One-person households	1,416
Persons per household	2.59
Persons per family	3.11

Labor & Employment
Total civilian labor force, 2004**	8,676
Unemployment rate	2.8%
Total civilian labor force, 2000	8,054
Unemployment rate	2.8%

Employed persons 16 years and over by occupation, 2000
Managers & professionals	3,821
Service occupations	559
Sales & office occupations	2,297
Farming, fishing & forestry	6
Construction & maintenance	599
Production & transportation	548
Self-employed persons	507

*US Census Bureau
**New Jersey Department of Labor

General Information
Township of Denville
1 St Mary's Place
Denville, NJ 07834
973-625-8300

Web site	www.denvillenj.org
Land area (sq. miles)	12.11
Water area (sq. miles)	0.52
Type of government	Township
Form of government	MC '50

Government

Legislative Districts
US Congressional	11
State Legislative	25

Local Officials, 2006
Mayor	Gene Feyl
Admin/Manager	Ellen M. Sandman
Clerk	Donna Costello
Finance Dir/Treas	Marie Goble
Engineer	Nick Rosania
Attorney	John Jansen
Tax assessor	Ginny Klein
Tax collector	Annemarie Hopler
Building officer	Walter Stefanacci
Zoning officer	NA
Public Works	Joe Lowell

Housing & Construction

Housing Units, 2000*
Total	6,178
Median rent	$1,129
Median SF home value	$228,300

New Privately Owned Housing Units Authorized by Building Permit
	Units	Value
Total, 2004	141	$20,583,490
Single family	30	$5,484,390
Total, 2005	57	$11,020,790
Single family	43	$8,422,790

Real Property Valuation - parcels, 2005
	Number	Valuation
Total		$2,141,620,400
Vacant	857	63,044,100
Residential	5,682	1,692,079,500
Commercial	354	298,571,500
Industrial	39	73,457,400
Apartments	3	8,173,600
Farm land	18	6,156,100
Farm homestead	31	138,200

Average Property Value & Tax, 2005
Residential value	$296,205
Property tax	$6,632
FAIR rebate	$569

Public Library
Denville Public Library
121 Diamond Spring Rd
Denville, NJ 07834
973-627-6555
Director................Betsy Kanouse

Library statistics, 2004
	Total	per capita
Volumes	61,762	3.9
Expenditure	$721,013	$45.56

Public Safety

Police
Chief	Anthony P. Strungis III
Number of officers, 2004	33

Crime, 2004	Number	Rate
Total	204	12.8
Violent	14	0.9
Non-violent	190	11.9
Domestic Viol.	79	NA

Emergency/Fire
Director....................John Egbert

Public School District
(for school year 2004-2005 except as noted)

Denville Township School District
501 Openaki Rd
Denville, NJ 07834
973-366-1001

Superintendent	John Sakala
Grade plan	K-8
Enrollment	1,927.0
Students per teacher	13.3
Per pupil expenditure	$10,127
Median faculty salary	$44,928
Median administrator salary	$99,560
Grade 12 enrollment	NA
High school graduation rate	NA

Assessment test results
(percent scoring at proficient or advanced level)
	Language	Math
Grade 3	91.3%	85.3%
Grade 8	86.9%	85.1%
High school	NA	NA

SAT
Percent tested	NA
Average SAT math score	NA
Average SAT verbal score	NA

No Child Left Behind, 2003-04
Attendence rate (target = 90%)	96.5%
Drop rate	NA
Highly-qualified teachers	92.5%
District needs improvement?(AYP)	No

Municipal Finance

Fiscal Year 2005
Total tax levy	$48,068,026
County levy	6,892,159
County taxes	5,645,465
County library	0
County health	0
County open space	1,246,695
School levy	32,630,082
Local muni. budget	8,545,785
Misc. revenues	8,247,112
Total aid	$2,463,593
CMPTRA	529,485
Muni. block grant	62,046
Energy tax receipts	1,802,062
Homeland security	70,000

Fiscal Year 2006
Total aid	$2,463,594
CMPTRA	466,413
Muni. block grant	62,046
Energy tax receipts	1,865,135
Homeland security	70,000

Taxes
	2003	2004	2005
General tax rate per $100	1.97	2.150	2.240
Net valuation taxable	$2,076,259,078	$2,110,367,320	$2,146,959,541
State equalized value	$2,270,128,010	$2,538,945,584	$2,888,027,362
County equalization ratio	100.04	91.46	83.08

Demographics & Socio-Economic Characteristics
(2000 U.S. Census, except as noted)

Population
1980*	23,473
1990*	24,137
2000	26,763
Male	12,911
Female	13,852
2004 (estimate)*	28,943
Persons per sq. mi. of land	1,654

Race & Hispanic Origin, 2000
Race
White	22,330
Black/African American	3,314
Amer. Indian/Alaska Natv.	56
Asian	410
Natv. Hawaiian/Pac. Islander	9
Other Race	266
Two or more races	378
Hispanic origin, total	766
Mexican	114
Puerto Rican	421
Cuban	25
Other Hispanic	206

Age & Nativity, 2000
Under 5 years	1,668
18 years and over	20,383
21 years and over	19,533
65 years and over	4,012
85 years and over	421
Median Age	37.3
Native born	25,646
Foreign born	1,117

Educational Attainment, 2000
Population 25 years and over	18,448
0-8 yrs of school	4.5%
High School grad or higher	80.0%
Bachelor's degree or higher	15.2%
Graduate degree	4.2%

Income & Poverty, 1999
Per capita income	$21,477
Median household income	$50,147
Median family income	$56,642
Persons in poverty	1,535
H'holds receiving public assistance	140
H'holds receiving social security	2,935

Households, 2000
Total households	10,013
With persons under 18	3,572
With persons over 65	2,648
Family households	7,083
One-person households	2,435
Persons per household	2.62
Persons per family	3.12

Labor & Employment
Total civilian labor force, 2004**	15,585
Unemployment rate	5.0%
Total civilian labor force, 2000	13,829
Unemployment rate	5.5%

Employed persons 16 years and over by occupation, 2000
Managers & professionals	3,508
Service occupations	1,752
Sales & office occupations	3,886
Farming, fishing & forestry	5
Construction & maintenance	1,612
Production & transportation	2,305
Self-employed persons	446

*US Census Bureau
**New Jersey Department of Labor

General Information
Township of Deptford
1011 Cooper St
Deptford, NJ 08096
856-845-5300

Web site	NA
Land area (sq. miles)	17.50
Water area (sq. miles)	0.08
Type of government	Township
Form of government	CM '50

Government

Legislative Districts
US Congressional	1
State Legislative	5

Local Officials, 2006
Mayor	Paul Medany
Admin/Manager	William Saunders
Clerk	Dina Zawadski
Finance Dir/Treas	Joanne Strange
Engineer	Alaimo Group
Attorney	Harvey C. Johnson
Tax assessor	Joseph Harasta
Tax collector	NA
Building officer	William Coughlin
Zoning officer	NA
Public Works	NA

Housing & Construction

Housing Units, 2000*
Total	10,647
Median rent	$664
Median SF home value	$106,000

New Privately Owned Housing Units
Authorized by Building Permit
	Units	Value
Total, 2004	382	$18,581,167
Single family	233	$18,171,911
Total, 2005	276	$20,110,055
Single family	257	$20,057,868

Real Property Valuation - parcels, 2005
	Number	Valuation
Total		$1,602,396,300
Vacant	2,080	46,464,600
Residential	9,374	1,016,827,400
Commercial	335	473,928,000
Industrial	6	10,371,000
Apartments	13	47,880,800
Farm land	67	6,459,800
Farm homestead	154	464,700

Average Property Value & Tax, 2005
Residential value	$106,769
Property tax	$3,500
FAIR rebate	$611

Public Library
Johnson Memorial Library
670 Ward Dr
Deptford, NJ 08096
856-848-9149

Director	Arn Winter

Library statistics, 2004
	Total	per capita
Volumes	66,133	2.47
Expenditure	$597,707	$22.33

Public Safety

Police
Chief	John Marolt
Number of officers, 2004	68

Crime, 2004	Number	Rate
Total	1,656	59
Violent	133	4.7
Non-violent	1,523	54.3
Domestic Viol.	432	NA

Emergency/Fire
Director	Steve Hubbs (Actg)

Public School District
(for school year 2004-2005 except as noted)

Deptford Township School District
2022 Good Intent Rd
Deptford, NJ 08096
856-232-2700

Superintendent	Marie R. Louis
Grade plan	K-12
Enrollment	4,233.0
Students per teacher	12.5
Per pupil expenditure	$10,730
Median faculty salary	$47,000
Median administrator salary	$95,355
Grade 12 enrollment	220.5
High school graduation rate	92.3%

Assessment test results
(percent scoring at proficient or advanced level)
	Language	Math
Grade 3	77.0%	85.0%
Grade 8	75.2%	47.5%
High school	84.3%	73.0%

SAT
Percent tested	65%
Average SAT math score	493
Average SAT verbal score	485

No Child Left Behind, 2003-04
Attendence rate (target = 90%)	94.6%
Drop rate	1%
Highly-qualified teachers	95.8%
District needs improvement?(AYP)	No

Municipal Finance

Fiscal Year 2005
Total tax levy	$52,656,686
County levy	12,775,426
County taxes	11,979,027
County library	0
County health	0
County open space	796,400
School levy	28,199,593
Local muni. budget	11,681,666
Misc. revenues	10,326,560
Total aid	$3,076,522
CMPTRA	1,198,194
Muni. block grant	105,616
Energy tax receipts	1,682,712
Homeland security	90,000

Fiscal Year 2006
Total aid	$3,076,522
CMPTRA	1,139,299
Muni. block grant	105,616
Energy tax receipts	1,741,607
Homeland security	90,000

Taxes
	2003	2004	2005
General tax rate per $100	3.00	3.104	3.279
Net valuation taxable	$1,505,471,533	$1,544,710,038	$1,606,111,389
State equalized value	$1,723,296,169	$1,908,905,685	$2,361,928,513
County equalization ratio	98.24	87.36	80.88

Demographics & Socio-Economic Characteristics
(2000 U.S. Census, except as noted)

Population
1980*	14,681
1990*	15,115
2000	18,188
Male	9,377
Female	8,811
2004 (estimate)*	18,463
Persons per sq. mi. of land	6,891

Race & Hispanic Origin, 2000
Race
White	12,631
Black/African American	1,242
Amer. Indian/Alaska Natv.	62
Asian	450
Natv. Hawaiian/Pac. Islander	5
Other Race	2,909
Two or more races	889
Hispanic origin, total	10,539
Mexican	1,557
Puerto Rican	2,413
Cuban	98
Other Hispanic	6,471

Age & Nativity, 2000
Under 5 years	1,278
18 years and over	13,976
21 years and over	13,203
65 years and over	1,922
85 years and over	310
Median Age	33.7
Native born	10,400
Foreign born	7,788

Educational Attainment, 2000
Population 25 years and over	12,011
0-8 yrs of school	16.8%
High School grad or higher	66.9%
Bachelor's degree or higher	12.5%
Graduate degree	4.4%

Income & Poverty, 1999
Per capita income	$18,056
Median household income	$53,423
Median family income	$57,141
Persons in poverty	2,381
H'holds receiving public assistance	183
H'holds receiving social security	1,446

Households, 2000
Total households	5,436
With persons under 18	2,242
With persons over 65	1,277
Family households	3,918
One-person households	1,156
Persons per household	3.29
Persons per family	3.55

Labor & Employment
Total civilian labor force, 2004**	9,707
Unemployment rate	7.3%
Total civilian labor force, 2000	9,523
Unemployment rate	7.4%

Employed persons 16 years and over by occupation, 2000
Managers & professionals	1,713
Service occupations	1,845
Sales & office occupations	2,262
Farming, fishing & forestry	0
Construction & maintenance	789
Production & transportation	2,207
Self-employed persons	296

*US Census Bureau
**New Jersey Department of Labor

General Information
Town of Dover
PO Box 798
Dover, NJ 07802
973-366-2200

Web site	www.dover.nj.us
Land area (sq. miles)	2.68
Water area (sq. miles)	0.03
Type of government	Town
Form of government	T

Government

Legislative Districts
US Congressional	11
State Legislative	25

Local Officials, 2006
Mayor	James Dodd
Admin/Manager	Bibi Stewart Garvin
Clerk	Paul McDougall
Finance Dir/Treas	Kelly Toohey
Engineer	Mike Hantson
Attorney	David Pennella
Tax assessor	Robert Sweeney
Tax collector	Ana Hopler
Building officer	Robert Young
Zoning officer	Mike Hantson
Public Works	Luis Acevedo

Housing & Construction

Housing Units, 2000*
Total	5,568
Median rent	$870
Median SF home value	$150,500

New Privately Owned Housing Units
Authorized by Building Permit
	Units	Value
Total, 2004	11	$1,236,185
Single family	11	$1,236,185
Total, 2005	10	$1,142,600
Single family	10	$1,142,600

Real Property Valuation - parcels, 2005
	Number	Valuation
Total		$682,852,800
Vacant	149	6,796,500
Residential	3,593	475,811,600
Commercial	329	115,146,300
Industrial	53	61,978,300
Apartments	28	23,120,100
Farm land	0	0
Farm homestead	0	0

Average Property Value & Tax, 2005
Residential value	$132,427
Property tax	$4,819
FAIR rebate	$593

Public Library
Dover Free Public Library
32 E Clinton St
Dover, NJ 07801
973-366-0172
Director	Robert Tambini

Library statistics, 2004
	Total	per capita
Volumes	52,336	2.88
Expenditure	$413,906	$22.76

Public Safety

Police
Chief	Harold Valentine
Number of officers, 2004	36

Crime, 2004	Number	Rate
Total	480	26.1
Violent	54	2.9
Non-violent	426	23.2
Domestic Viol.	112	NA

Emergency/Fire
Director	William Gilbert

Public School District
(for school year 2004-2005 except as noted)

Dover Town School District
100 Grace St
Dover, NJ 07801
973-989-2000
Superintendent	Robert Becker
Grade plan	K-12
Enrollment	3,042.0
Students per teacher	12.3
Per pupil expenditure	$10,768
Median faculty salary	$44,722
Median administrator salary	$85,906
Grade 12 enrollment	191.5
High school graduation rate	93.2%

Assessment test results
(percent scoring at proficient or advanced level)
	Language	Math
Grade 3	79.4%	86.4%
Grade 8	63.4%	41.6%
High school	71.9%	66.7%

SAT
Percent tested	35%
Average SAT math score	480
Average SAT verbal score	461

No Child Left Behind, 2003-04
Attendence rate (target = 90%)	94.5%
Drop rate	0.9%
Highly-qualified teachers	93.3%
District needs improvement?(AYP)	No

Municipal Finance

Fiscal Year 2005
Total tax levy	$24,980,897
County levy	3,208,431
County taxes	2,628,126
County library	0
County health	0
County open space	580,305
School levy	12,505,087
Local muni. budget	9,267,380
Misc. revenues	7,264,432
Total aid	$1,753,668
CMPTRA	980,483
Muni. block grant	71,316
Energy tax receipts	631,869
Homeland security	70,000

Fiscal Year 2006
Total aid	$1,753,669
CMPTRA	958,368
Muni. block grant	71,316
Energy tax receipts	653,985
Homeland security	70,000

Taxes
	2003	2004	2005
General tax rate per $100	3.25	3.370	3.640
Net valuation taxable	$683,976,791	$685,724,255	$686,483,971
State equalized value	$1,014,501,322	$1,192,184,259	$1,341,575,085
County equalization ratio	77.69	67.42	57.37

Demographics & Socio-Economic Characteristics
(2000 U.S. Census, except as noted)

Population
1980*	64,455
1990*	76,371
2000	89,706
Male	43,160
Female	46,546
2004 (estimate)*	94,320
Persons per sq. mi. of land	2,302

Race & Hispanic Origin, 2000
Race
White	83,939
Black/African American	1,568
Amer. Indian/Alaska Natv.	117
Asian	2,207
Natv. Hawaiian/Pac. Islander	21
Other Race	850
Two or more races	1,004
Hispanic origin, total	4,070
Mexican	720
Puerto Rican	1,764
Cuban	326
Other Hispanic	1,260

Age & Nativity, 2000
Under 5 years	4,956
18 years and over	68,815
21 years and over	65,852
65 years and over	15,464
85 years and over	1,708
Median Age	40.2
Native born	83,513
Foreign born	6,254

Educational Attainment, 2000
Population 25 years and over	62,453
0-8 yrs of school	3.2%
High School grad or higher	86.2%
Bachelor's degree or higher	23.8%
Graduate degree	8.0%

Income & Poverty, 1999
Per capita income	$25,010
Median household income	$54,776
Median family income	$62,561
Persons in poverty	4,988
H'holds receiving public assistance	608
H'holds receiving social security	11,254

Households, 2000
Total households	33,510
With persons under 18	11,247
With persons over 65	10,409
Family households	24,427
One-person households	7,619
Persons per household	2.62
Persons per family	3.09

Labor & Employment
Total civilian labor force, 2004**	48,274
Unemployment rate	4.2%
Total civilian labor force, 2000	43,541
Unemployment rate	4.6%

Employed persons 16 years and over by occupation, 2000
Managers & professionals	14,278
Service occupations	6,463
Sales & office occupations	12,729
Farming, fishing & forestry	39
Construction & maintenance	4,206
Production & transportation	3,831
Self-employed persons	2,373

*US Census Bureau
**New Jersey Department of Labor

General Information
Township of Dover
PO Box 728
Toms River, NJ 08754
732-341-1000

Web site	twp.dover.nj.us
Land area (sq. miles)	40.97
Water area (sq. miles)	11.96
Type of government	Township
Form of government	Township Council

Government

Legislative Districts
US Congressional	3, 4
State Legislative	10

Local Officials, 2006
Mayor	Paul C. Brush
Admin/Manager	Fred Ebenau
Clerk	J. Mark Mutter
Finance Dir/Treas	Christine Manolio
Engineer	Robert Chankalian
Attorney	Mark Troncone
Tax assessor	Glen Seelhorst
Tax collector	NA
Building officer	Pramod Pathak
Zoning officer	NA
Public Works	NA

Housing & Construction

Housing Units, 2000*
Total	41,116
Median rent	$789
Median SF home value	$149,900

New Privately Owned Housing Units Authorized by Building Permit
	Units	Value
Total, 2004	440	$47,100,965
Single family	434	$46,532,965
Total, 2005	252	$30,759,218
Single family	252	$30,759,218

Real Property Valuation - parcels, 2005
	Number	Valuation
Total		$6,270,976,300
Vacant	1,729	129,588,400
Residential	37,694	5,094,418,200
Commercial	1,503	895,754,900
Industrial	47	56,327,800
Apartments	34	91,788,300
Farm land	18	2,989,900
Farm homestead	24	108,800

Average Property Value & Tax, 2005
Residential value	$135,069
Property tax	$4,017
FAIR rebate	$630

Public Library
Toms River Branch Library
101 Washington St
Toms River, NJ 08753
732-349-6300
Branch Librarian .... Diane Tralka

Library statistics, 2004
	Total	per capita
Volumes	NA	NA
Expenditure	NA	NA

Public Safety
Police
Chief	Michael Mastronardy
Number of officers, 2004	153

Crime, 2004	Number	Rate
Total	2,011	21.5
Violent	122	1.3
Non-violent	1,889	20.2
Domestic Viol.	767	NA

Emergency/Fire
Director	John Lightbody

Public School District
(for school year 2004-2005 except as noted)

Sends children to Toms River Regional school district (see South Toms River Borough).
Grade plan	NA
Enrollment	NA
Students per teacher	NA
Per pupil expenditure	NA
Median faculty salary	NA
Median administrator salary	NA
Grade 12 enrollment	NA
High school graduation rate	NA

Assessment test results
(percent scoring at proficient or advanced level)
	Language	Math
Grade 3	NA	NA
Grade 8	NA	NA
High school	NA	NA

SAT
Percent tested	NA
Average SAT math score	NA
Average SAT verbal score	NA

No Child Left Behind, 2003-04
Attendance rate (target = 90%)	NA
Drop rate	NA
Highly-qualified teachers	NA
District needs improvement?(AYP)	NA

Municipal Finance

Fiscal Year 2005
Total tax levy	$187,100,243
County levy	46,815,043
County taxes	39,442,934
County library	4,143,810
County health	1,756,376
County open space	1,471,923
School levy	98,064,149
Local muni. budget	42,221,051
Misc. revenues	37,688,878
Total aid	$11,490,497
CMPTRA	3,547,682
Muni. block grant	351,739
Energy tax receipts	7,451,076
Homeland security	140,000

Fiscal Year 2006
Total aid	$11,490,498
CMPTRA	3,286,895
Muni. block grant	351,739
Energy tax receipts	7,711,864
Homeland security	140,000

Taxes
	2003	2004	2005
General tax rate per $100	2.71	2.754	2.975
Net valuation taxable	$6,106,905,362	$6,195,811,366	$6,291,172,914
State equalized value	$10,135,942,510	$12,024,046,664	$14,223,768,741
County equalization ratio	69.73	60.25	51.43

Demographics & Socio-Economic Characteristics
(2000 U.S. Census, except as noted)

Population
1980*	1,803
1990*	1,702
2000	1,631
Male	846
Female	785
2004 (estimate)*	1,670
Persons per sq. mi. of land	33

Race & Hispanic Origin, 2000
Race
White	1,485
Black/African American	79
Amer. Indian/Alaska Natv.	24
Asian	3
Natv. Hawaiian/Pac. Islander	0
Other Race	16
Two or more races	24
Hispanic origin, total	55
Mexican	4
Puerto Rican	49
Cuban	0
Other Hispanic	2

Age & Nativity, 2000
Under 5 years	91
18 years and over	1,247
21 years and over	1,201
65 years and over	309
85 years and over	13
Median Age	42.3
Native born	1,607
Foreign born	24

Educational Attainment, 2000
Population 25 years and over	1,151
0-8 yrs of school	9.9%
High School grad or higher	71.2%
Bachelor's degree or higher	7.8%
Graduate degree	2.2%

Income & Poverty, 1999
Per capita income	$17,366
Median household income	$34,667
Median family income	$39,375
Persons in poverty	213
H'holds receiving public assistance	23
H'holds receiving social security	255

Households, 2000
Total households	658
With persons under 18	216
With persons over 65	232
Family households	439
One-person households	180
Persons per household	2.48
Persons per family	3.03

Labor & Employment
Total civilian labor force, 2004**	858
Unemployment rate	7.5%
Total civilian labor force, 2000	704
Unemployment rate	6.8%

Employed persons 16 years and over by occupation, 2000
Managers & professionals	110
Service occupations	117
Sales & office occupations	168
Farming, fishing & forestry	13
Construction & maintenance	84
Production & transportation	164
Self-employed persons	42

*US Census Bureau
**New Jersey Department of Labor

General Information
Township of Downe
288 Main St
Newport, NJ 08345
856-447-3100

Web site	www.downetwpnj.org
Land area (sq. miles)	50.76
Water area (sq. miles)	3.47
Type of government	Township
Form of government	TC

Government

Legislative Districts
US Congressional	2
State Legislative	3

Local Officials, 2006
Mayor	Harry Wilson
Admin/Manager	NA
Clerk	Lois R.Buttner (Actg.)
Finance Dir/Treas	Lois Buttner
Engineer	Mike Fralinger
Attorney	Frank Di Domenico
Tax assessor	Doris Sanza (tp)
Tax collector	NA
Building officer	State Construction
Zoning officer	Bob Camphell
Public Works	NA

Housing & Construction

Housing Units, 2000*
Total	1,134
Median rent	$581
Median SF home value	$74,500

New Privately Owned Housing Units Authorized by Building Permit
	Units	Value
Total, 2004	3	$140,250
Single family	3	$140,250
Total, 2005	7	$333,250
Single family	7	$333,250

Real Property Valuation - parcels, 2005
	Number	Valuation
Total		$76,311,700
Vacant	721	8,955,300
Residential	929	56,094,800
Commercial	53	7,159,200
Industrial	3	67,500
Apartments	1	123,500
Farm land	61	3,649,500
Farm homestead	54	261,900

Average Property Value & Tax, 2005
Residential value	$57,331
Property tax	$1,929
FAIR rebate	$666

Public Library

No public municipal library.

Library statistics, 2004
	Total	per capita
Volumes	NA	NA
Expenditure	NA	NA

Public Safety

Police
Chief	NA
Number of officers, 2004	0

Crime, 2004	Number	Rate
Total	27	16.3
Violent	5	3
Non-violent	22	13.3
Domestic Viol.	18	NA

Emergency/Fire
Director	NA

Public School District
(for school year 2004-2005 except as noted)

Downe Township School District
220 Main St
Newport, NJ 08345
856-447-3878

Superintendent	Mary Ann Russell
Grade plan	K-12
Enrollment	245.0
Students per teacher	9.2
Per pupil expenditure	$17,478
Median faculty salary	$54,757
Median administrator salary	$85,856
Grade 12 enrollment	NA
High school graduation rate	NA

Assessment test results
(percent scoring at proficient or advanced level)
	Language	Math
Grade 3	64.3%	78.6%
Grade 8	70.8%	66.7%
High school	NA	NA

SAT
Percent tested	NA
Average SAT math score	NA
Average SAT verbal score	NA

No Child Left Behind, 2003-04
Attendence rate (target = 90%)	94.1%
Drop rate	NA
Highly-qualified teachers	100%
District needs improvement?(AYP)	No

Municipal Finance

Fiscal Year 2005
Total tax levy	$2,581,945
County levy	1,088,483
County taxes	1,033,986
County library	0
County health	44,027
County open space	10,470
School levy	1,493,462
Local muni. budget	0
Misc. revenues	1,454,514
Total aid	$307,911
CMPTRA	107,480
Muni. block grant	7,448
Energy tax receipts	192,983
Homeland security	0

Fiscal Year 2006
Total aid	$307,911
CMPTRA	100,725
Muni. block grant	7,448
Energy tax receipts	199,738
Homeland security	NA

Taxes
	2003	2004	2005
General tax rate per $100	3.16	3.099	3.367
Net valuation taxable	$76,134,166	$76,371,198	$76,737,907
State equalized value	$91,047,795	$102,872,588	$132,398,045
County equalization ratio	86.35	83.62	74.11

Demographics & Socio-Economic Characteristics
(2000 U.S. Census, except as noted)

Population
1980*	18,334
1990*	17,187
2000	17,503
Male	8,416
Female	9,087
2004 (estimate)*	17,571
Persons per sq. mi. of land	8,847

Race & Hispanic Origin, 2000
Race
White	14,663
Black/African American	261
Amer. Indian/Alaska Natv.	17
Asian	1,918
Natv. Hawaiian/Pac. Islander	1
Other Race	339
Two or more races	304
Hispanic origin, total	1,463
Mexican	59
Puerto Rican	419
Cuban	160
Other Hispanic	825

Age & Nativity, 2000
Under 5 years	1,173
18 years and over	13,239
21 years and over	12,787
65 years and over	2,702
85 years and over	309
Median Age	38.4
Native born	14,250
Foreign born	3,253

Educational Attainment, 2000
Population 25 years and over	12,229
0-8 yrs of school	3.6%
High School grad or higher	88.5%
Bachelor's degree or higher	27.4%
Graduate degree	8.2%

Income & Poverty, 1999
Per capita income	$26,489
Median household income	$65,490
Median family income	$73,880
Persons in poverty	459
H'holds receiving public assistance	119
H'holds receiving social security	2,009

Households, 2000
Total households	6,370
With persons under 18	2,345
With persons over 65	2,000
Family households	4,757
One-person households	1,422
Persons per household	2.75
Persons per family	3.24

Labor & Employment
Total civilian labor force, 2004**	9,870
Unemployment rate	3.7%
Total civilian labor force, 2000	9,072
Unemployment rate	2.9%

Employed persons 16 years and over by occupation, 2000
Managers & professionals	3,319
Service occupations	1,154
Sales & office occupations	2,776
Farming, fishing & forestry	10
Construction & maintenance	766
Production & transportation	784
Self-employed persons	356

*US Census Bureau
**New Jersey Department of Labor

General Information
Borough of Dumont
50 Washington Ave
Dumont, NJ 07628
201-387-5022
Web site	www.dumont.us
Land area (sq. miles)	1.99
Water area (sq. miles)	0
Type of government	Borough
Form of government	B

Government

Legislative Districts
US Congressional	5
State Legislative	39

Local Officials, 2006
Mayor	Matthew McHale
Admin/Manager	John Perkins
Clerk	Jack Eckel
Finance Dir/Treas	Denise Randazzo
Engineer	T & M Associates
Attorney	Gregg Paster
Tax assessor	James Anzevino
Tax collector	Barbara Kozay
Building officer	James Taorming (Actg)
Zoning officer	NA
Public Works	John Cook

Housing & Construction

Housing Units, 2000*
Total	6,465
Median rent	$882
Median SF home value	$195,000

New Privately Owned Housing Units Authorized by Building Permit
	Units	Value
Total, 2004	9	$1,658,901
Single family	9	$1,658,901
Total, 2005	8	$1,395,925
Single family	8	$1,395,925

Real Property Valuation - parcels, 2005
	Number	Valuation
Total		$2,079,408,900
Vacant	15	1,181,800
Residential	4,968	1,898,270,100
Commercial	145	103,507,200
Industrial	11	7,064,200
Apartments	25	69,375,100
Farm land	0	0
Farm homestead	1	10,500

Average Property Value & Tax, 2005
Residential value	$382,025
Property tax	$7,396
FAIR rebate	$606

Public Library
Dixon Homestead Library
180 Washington Ave
Dumont, NJ 07628
201-384-2030
Director	Carolyn Blowers

Library statistics, 2004
	Total	per capita
Volumes	38,143	2.18
Expenditure	$648,777	$37.07

Public Safety

Police
Chief	Brian Venezio
Number of officers, 2004	32

Crime, 2004	Number	Rate
Total	186	10.6
Violent	15	0.9
Non-violent	171	9.8
Domestic Viol.	125	NA

Emergency/Fire
Director	Tony Spina

Public School District
(for school year 2004-2005 except as noted)

Dumont School District
25 Depew St
Dumont, NJ 07628
201-387-3082
Superintendent	James Montesano
Grade plan	K-12
Enrollment	2,648.0
Students per teacher	11.9
Per pupil expenditure	$11,516
Median faculty salary	$71,769
Median administrator salary	$115,746
Grade 12 enrollment	176.0
High school graduation rate	98.9%

Assessment test results
(percent scoring at proficient or advanced level)
	Language	Math
Grade 3	91.1%	88.7%
Grade 8	80.5%	75.7%
High school	89.4%	86.0%

SAT
Percent tested	86%
Average SAT math score	504
Average SAT verbal score	482

No Child Left Behind, 2003-04
Attendence rate (target = 90%)	95.4%
Drop rate	0.8%
Highly-qualified teachers	96.6%
District needs improvement?(AYP)	No

Municipal Finance

Fiscal Year 2005
Total tax levy	$40,337,596
County levy	3,354,607
County taxes	3,186,811
County library	0
County health	0
County open space	167,796
School levy	25,514,545
Local muni. budget	11,468,444
Misc. revenues	3,731,046
Total aid	$1,905,979
CMPTRA	765,927
Muni. block grant	75,204
Energy tax receipts	994,848
Homeland security	70,000

Fiscal Year 2006
Total aid	$1,905,978
CMPTRA	731,107
Muni. block grant	75,204
Energy tax receipts	1,029,667
Homeland security	70,000

Taxes
	2003	2004	2005
General tax rate per $100	3.53	3.770	1.940
Net valuation taxable	$964,223,771	$967,351,047	$2,083,517,734
State equalized value	$1,500,036,980	$1,666,625,852	$1,962,250,644
County equalization ratio	73.7	64.28	124.38

Demographics & Socio-Economic Characteristics

(2000 U.S. Census, except as noted)

Population

1980*	6,593
1990*	6,528
2000	6,823
Male	3,428
Female	3,395
2004 (estimate)*	6,995
Persons per sq. mi. of land	6,740

Race & Hispanic Origin, 2000

Race
White	5,736
Black/African American	250
Amer. Indian/Alaska Natv.	17
Asian	243
Natv. Hawaiian/Pac. Islander	1
Other Race	435
Two or more races	141
Hispanic origin, total	1,010
Mexican	71
Puerto Rican	121
Cuban	29
Other Hispanic	789

Age & Nativity, 2000

Under 5 years	503
18 years and over	5,124
21 years and over	4,917
65 years and over	773
85 years and over	91
Median Age	35.8
Native born	5,715
Foreign born	1,108

Educational Attainment, 2000

Population 25 years and over	4,715
0-8 yrs of school	3.0%
High School grad or higher	86.0%
Bachelor's degree or higher	22.2%
Graduate degree	6.2%

Income & Poverty, 1999

Per capita income	$26,529
Median household income	$59,205
Median family income	$67,188
Persons in poverty	224
H'holds receiving public assistance	24
H'holds receiving social security	550

Households, 2000

Total households	2,451
With persons under 18	918
With persons over 65	559
Family households	1,711
One-person households	575
Persons per household	2.75
Persons per family	3.3

Labor & Employment

Total civilian labor force, 2004**	4,121
Unemployment rate	3.7%
Total civilian labor force, 2000	3,779
Unemployment rate	7.8%

Employed persons 16 years and over by occupation, 2000
Managers & professionals	1,233
Service occupations	444
Sales & office occupations	909
Farming, fishing & forestry	11
Construction & maintenance	363
Production & transportation	524
Self-employed persons	220

*US Census Bureau
**New Jersey Department of Labor

General Information

Borough of Dunellen
355 North Ave
Dunellen, NJ 08812
732-968-3033

Web site	NA
Land area (sq. miles)	1.04
Water area (sq. miles)	0
Type of government	Borough
Form of government	B

Government

Legislative Districts

US Congressional	6
State Legislative	22

Local Officials, 2006

Mayor	Robert Seader
Admin/Manager	William Robins
Clerk	William Robins
Finance Dir/Treas	Scott Olsen
Engineer	CME
Attorney	John Bruder
Tax assessor	Thomas Boyle
Tax collector	NA
Building officer	Scott Luthman
Zoning officer	NA
Public Works	NA

Housing & Construction

Housing Units, 2000*

Total	2,520
Median rent	$811
Median SF home value	$155,800

New Privately Owned Housing Units Authorized by Building Permit

	Units	Value
Total, 2004	11	$897,378
Single family	6	$619,600
Total, 2005	20	$1,356,202
Single family	5	$522,868

Real Property Valuation - parcels, 2005

	Number	Valuation
Total		$143,208,975
Vacant	32	534,500
Residential	1,924	123,223,800
Commercial	100	14,420,600
Industrial	6	3,581,575
Apartments	7	1,448,500
Farm land	0	0
Farm homestead	0	0

Average Property Value & Tax, 2005

Residential value	$64,046
Property tax	$5,406
FAIR rebate	$567

Public Library

Dunellen Free Public Library
New Market Rd
Dunellen, NJ 08812
732-968-4585

Director...................Joan Henry

Library statistics, 2004

	Total	per capita
Volumes	39,171	5.74
Expenditure	$206,843	$30.32

Public Safety

Police

Chief	Robert Moore
Number of officers, 2004	16

Crime, 2004	Number	Rate
Total	172	24.5
Violent	27	3.9
Non-violent	145	20.7
Domestic Viol.	44	NA

Emergency/Fire

Director...................William Scott

Public School District

(for school year 2004-2005 except as noted)

Dunellen School District
High St & Lehigh St
Dunellen, NJ 08812
732-968-3226

Superintendent	Joyce Baynes
Grade plan	K-12
Enrollment	1,136.0
Students per teacher	11.4
Per pupil expenditure	$9,586
Median faculty salary	$47,598
Median administrator salary	$100,051
Grade 12 enrollment	78.0
High school graduation rate	98.7%

Assessment test results

(percent scoring at proficient or advanced level)
	Language	Math
Grade 3	83.4%	88.1%
Grade 8	82.7%	65.5%
High school	84.2%	79.5%

SAT

Percent tested	82%
Average SAT math score	483
Average SAT verbal score	491

No Child Left Behind, 2003-04

Attendance rate (target = 90%)	94.5%
Drop rate	0%
Highly-qualified teachers	95.8%
District needs improvement?(AYP)	No

Municipal Finance

Fiscal Year 2005

Total tax levy	$12,168,699
County levy	1,599,615
County taxes	1,449,027
County library	0
County health	0
County open space	150,588
School levy	7,545,891
Local muni. budget	3,023,193
Misc. revenues	2,674,842
Total aid	$959,849
CMPTRA	500,461
Muni. block grant	28,565
Energy tax receipts	380,823
Homeland security	50,000

Fiscal Year 2006

Total aid	$959,849
CMPTRA	487,132
Muni. block grant	28,565
Energy tax receipts	394,152
Homeland security	50,000

Taxes

	2003	2004	2005
General tax rate per $100	7.54	7.990	8.450
Net valuation taxable	$142,765,014	$142,908,252	$144,169,538
State equalized value	$441,041,131	$493,679,461	$575,527,098
County equalization ratio	37.5	32.37	28.79

Demographics & Socio-Economic Characteristics
(2000 U.S. Census, except as noted)

Population
1980*	1,009
1990*	1,476
2000	1,441
Male	726
Female	715
2004 (estimate)*	1,534
Persons per sq. mi. of land	94

Race & Hispanic Origin, 2000
Race
White	1,426
Black/African American	1
Amer. Indian/Alaska Natv.	4
Asian	3
Natv. Hawaiian/Pac. Islander	0
Other Race	0
Two or more races	7
Hispanic origin, total	16
Mexican	1
Puerto Rican	8
Cuban	4
Other Hispanic	3

Age & Nativity, 2000
Under 5 years	73
18 years and over	1,085
21 years and over	1,038
65 years and over	207
85 years and over	16
Median Age	39.4
Native born	1,413
Foreign born	28

Educational Attainment, 2000
Population 25 years and over	974
0-8 yrs of school	4.4%
High School grad or higher	75.8%
Bachelor's degree or higher	10.1%
Graduate degree	2.4%

Income & Poverty, 1999
Per capita income	$20,617
Median household income	$38,625
Median family income	$49,453
Persons in poverty	51
H'holds receiving public assistance	10
H'holds receiving social security	194

Households, 2000
Total households	546
With persons under 18	190
With persons over 65	156
Family households	395
One-person households	122
Persons per household	2.64
Persons per family	3.11

Labor & Employment
Total civilian labor force, 2004**	985
Unemployment rate	4.7%
Total civilian labor force, 2000	717
Unemployment rate	3.8%

Employed persons 16 years and over by occupation, 2000
Managers & professionals	131
Service occupations	105
Sales & office occupations	186
Farming, fishing & forestry	4
Construction & maintenance	183
Production & transportation	81
Self-employed persons	104

*US Census Bureau
**New Jersey Department of Labor

General Information
Township of Eagleswood
PO Box 409
146 Division St
West Creek, NJ 08092
609-296-3040

Web site	NA
Land area (sq. miles)	16.37
Water area (sq. miles)	2.49
Type of government	Township
Form of government	TC

Government

Legislative Districts
US Congressional	3
State Legislative	9

Local Officials, 2006
Mayor	Wayne Thomas
Admin/Manager	Michael McFadden
Clerk	Michael McFadden
Finance Dir/Treas	Wanda Holman
Engineer	Jack Mallon
Attorney	Tom Monahan
Tax assessor	Fred Millman
Tax collector	Barbara Stover
Building officer	Robert Gaestel
Zoning officer	Karl Sillitoe
Public Works	Richard Lombardo

Housing & Construction

Housing Units, 2000*
Total	693
Median rent	$678
Median SF home value	$115,700

New Privately Owned Housing Units Authorized by Building Permit
	Units	Value
Total, 2004	20	$4,103,242
Single family	20	$4,103,242
Total, 2005	27	$5,997,094
Single family	27	$5,997,094

Real Property Valuation - parcels, 2005
	Number	Valuation
Total		$98,698,700
Vacant	410	14,435,700
Residential	638	68,145,000
Commercial	64	13,207,700
Industrial	6	2,485,900
Apartments	1	205,000
Farm land	1	177,600
Farm homestead	16	41,800

Average Property Value & Tax, 2005
Residential value	$104,261
Property tax	$3,500
FAIR rebate	$619

Public Library

No public municipal library.

Library statistics, 2004
	Total	per capita
Volumes	NA	NA
Expenditure	NA	NA

Public Safety

Police
Chief	(State)
Number of officers, 2004	0

Crime, 2004	Number	Rate
Total	24	15.6
Violent	2	1.3
Non-violent	22	14.3
Domestic Viol.	13	NA

Emergency/Fire
Director	Tony Cahill

Public School District
(for school year 2004-2005 except as noted)

Eagleswood Township School District
y11 Route 9
West Creek, NJ 08092
609-597-3663

Superintendent	Deborah Snyder
Grade plan	K-6
Enrollment	146.0
Students per teacher	8.7
Per pupil expenditure	$10,088
Median faculty salary	$42,274
Median administrator salary	$70,025
Grade 12 enrollment	NA
High school graduation rate	NA

Assessment test results
(percent scoring at proficient or advanced level)
	Language	Math
Grade 3	96.2%	88.4%
Grade 8	NA	NA
High school	NA	NA

SAT
Percent tested	NA
Average SAT math score	NA
Average SAT verbal score	NA

No Child Left Behind, 2003-04
Attendence rate (target = 90%)	95.2%
Drop rate	NA
Highly-qualified teachers	89.6%
District needs improvement?(AYP)	No

Municipal Finance

Fiscal Year 2005
Total tax levy	$3,323,966
County levy	611,512
County taxes	515,212
County library	54,127
County health	22,943
County open space	19,230
School levy	2,188,554
Local muni. budget	523,900
Misc. revenues	1,057,902
Total aid	270,193
CMPTRA	61,029
Muni. block grant	6,459
Energy tax receipts	185,221
Homeland security	0

Fiscal Year 2006
Total aid	$270,194
CMPTRA	54,547
Muni. block grant	6,459
Energy tax receipts	191,704
Homeland security	NA

Taxes
	2003	2004	2005
General tax rate per $100	3.03	3.201	3.358
Net valuation taxable	$93,894,851	$95,708,222	$99,006,855
State equalized value	$126,101,062	$154,621,067	$219,527,395
County equalization ratio	84.28	74.46	61.79

Demographics & Socio-Economic Characteristics
(2000 U.S. Census, except as noted)

Population

1980*	3,468
1990*	4,332
2000	4,455
Male	2,265
Female	2,190
2004 (estimate)*	4,564
Persons per sq. mi. of land	159

Race & Hispanic Origin, 2000
Race

White	4,320
Black/African American	32
Amer. Indian/Alaska Natv.	6
Asian	41
Natv. Hawaiian/Pac. Islander	1
Other Race	21
Two or more races	34
Hispanic origin, total	68
Mexican	15
Puerto Rican	6
Cuban	6
Other Hispanic	41

Age & Nativity, 2000

Under 5 years	269
18 years and over	3,328
21 years and over	3,218
65 years and over	455
85 years and over	52
Median Age	40.8
Native born	4,189
Foreign born	266

Educational Attainment, 2000

Population 25 years and over	3,135
0-8 yrs of school	1.8%
High School grad or higher	92.2%
Bachelor's degree or higher	39.6%
Graduate degree	15.9%

Income & Poverty, 1999

Per capita income	$37,187
Median household income	$85,664
Median family income	$90,000
Persons in poverty	74
H'holds receiving public assistance	45
H'holds receiving social security	382

Households, 2000

Total households	1,581
With persons under 18	606
With persons over 65	336
Family households	1,306
One-person households	210
Persons per household	2.8
Persons per family	3.07

Labor & Employment

Total civilian labor force, 2004**	2,834
Unemployment rate	2.2%
Total civilian labor force, 2000	2,426
Unemployment rate	2.5%

Employed persons 16 years and over by occupation, 2000

Managers & professionals	1,144
Service occupations	137
Sales & office occupations	534
Farming, fishing & forestry	20
Construction & maintenance	262
Production & transportation	269
Self-employed persons	248

*US Census Bureau
**New Jersey Department of Labor

General Information

Township of East Amwell
1070 Route 202
Ringoes, NJ 08551
908-782-8536

Web site	NA
Land area (sq. miles)	28.68
Water area (sq. miles)	0.04
Type of government	Township
Form of government	TC

Government

Legislative Districts

US Congressional	12
State Legislative	23

Local Officials, 2006

Mayor	Kurt Hoffman
Admin/Manager	Karl Posselt
Clerk	Teresa Stahl
Finance Dir/Treas	Jane Luhrs
Engineer	Dennis O'Neal
Attorney	Richard Cushing
Tax assessor	Marianne Busher
Tax collector	NA
Building officer	Stewart Doddy
Zoning officer	(Vacant)
Public Works	NA

Housing & Construction

Housing Units, 2000*

Total	1,624
Median rent	$913
Median SF home value	$252,500

New Privately Owned Housing Units Authorized by Building Permit

	Units	Value
Total, 2004	NA	NA
Single family	NA	NA
Total, 2005	13	$4,151,922
Single family	13	$4,151,922

Real Property Valuation - parcels, 2005

	Number	Valuation
Total		$783,287,061
Vacant	174	16,302,500
Residential	1,211	516,517,300
Commercial	61	105,138,342
Industrial	0	0
Apartments	5	2,258,400
Farm land	250	139,278,000
Farm homestead	432	3,792,519

Average Property Value & Tax, 2005

Residential value	$316,683
Property tax	$5,266
FAIR rebate	$536

Public Library

No public municipal library.

Library statistics, 2004

	Total	per capita
Volumes	NA	NA
Expenditure	NA	NA

Public Safety

Police

Chief	(State)
Number of officers, 2004	0

Crime, 2004	Number	Rate
Total	30	6.6
Violent	2	0.4
Non-violent	28	6.1
Domestic Viol.	10	NA

Emergency/Fire

Director	Robert Jason

Public School District
(for school year 2004-2005 except as noted)

East Amwell Township School District
43 Wertsville Rd
Ringoes, NJ 08551
908-782-6464

Superintendent	Edward Stoloski
Grade plan	K-8
Enrollment	478.0
Students per teacher	9.8
Per pupil expenditure	$12,093
Median faculty salary	$49,405
Median administrator salary	$88,530
Grade 12 enrollment	NA
High school graduation rate	NA

Assessment test results
(percent scoring at proficient or advanced level)

	Language	Math
Grade 3	91.5%	91.5%
Grade 8	85.2%	87.1%
High school	NA	NA

SAT

Percent tested	NA
Average SAT math score	NA
Average SAT verbal score	NA

No Child Left Behind, 2003-04

Attendence rate (target = 90%)	96.7%
Drop rate	NA
Highly-qualified teachers	100%
District needs improvement?(AYP)	No

Municipal Finance

Fiscal Year 2005

Total tax levy	$13,046,268
County levy	2,655,079
County taxes	2,253,905
County library	188,558
County health	0
County open space	212,616
School levy	9,018,969
Local muni. budget	1,372,220
Misc. revenues	1,820,367
Total aid	$465,875
CMPTRA	195,876
Muni. block grant	18,955
Energy tax receipts	251,044
Homeland security	0

Fiscal Year 2006

Total aid	$465,874
CMPTRA	187,089
Muni. block grant	18,955
Energy tax receipts	259,830
Homeland security	NA

Taxes

	2003	2004	2005
General tax rate per $100	2.87	3.090	1.670
Net valuation taxable	$395,405,187	$398,750,297	$784,572,366
State equalized value	$583,451,656	$636,868,442	$752,154,507
County equalization ratio	69.69	64.93	111.31

Demographics & Socio-Economic Characteristics
(2000 U.S. Census, except as noted)

Population
1980*	37,711
1990*	43,548
2000	46,756
Male	22,692
Female	24,064
2004 (estimate)*	48,317
Persons per sq. mi. of land	2,201

Race & Hispanic Origin, 2000
Race
White	36,265
Black/African American	1,321
Amer. Indian/Alaska Natv.	42
Asian	7,607
Natv. Hawaiian/Pac. Islander	5
Other Race	526
Two or more races	990
Hispanic origin, total	1,957
Mexican	160
Puerto Rican	718
Cuban	189
Other Hispanic	890

Age & Nativity, 2000
Under 5 years	2,768
18 years and over	34,588
21 years and over	33,305
65 years and over	5,429
85 years and over	480
Median Age	39.1
Native born	35,774
Foreign born	10,982

Educational Attainment, 2000
Population 25 years and over	31,652
0-8 yrs of school	3.2%
High School grad or higher	92.1%
Bachelor's degree or higher	47.1%
Graduate degree	19.5%

Income & Poverty, 1999
Per capita income	$33,286
Median household income	$75,956
Median family income	$86,863
Persons in poverty	1,321
H'holds receiving public assistance	186
H'holds receiving social security	3,764

Households, 2000
Total households	16,372
With persons under 18	6,916
With persons over 65	3,836
Family households	13,074
One-person households	2,815
Persons per household	2.84
Persons per family	3.23

Labor & Employment
Total civilian labor force, 2004**	27,193
Unemployment rate	3.4%
Total civilian labor force, 2000	25,008
Unemployment rate	3.5%

Employed persons 16 years and over by occupation, 2000
Managers & professionals	11,965
Service occupations	1,840
Sales & office occupations	7,210
Farming, fishing & forestry	0
Construction & maintenance	1,364
Production & transportation	1,757
Self-employed persons	1,276

*US Census Bureau
**New Jersey Department of Labor

General Information
Township of East Brunswick
PO Box 1081
East Brunswick, NJ 08816
732-390-6810
Web site	www.eastbrunswick.org
Land area (sq. miles)	21.95
Water area (sq. miles)	0.43
Type of government	Township
Form of government	Faulkner Plan E

Government

Legislative Districts
US Congressional	12
State Legislative	18

Local Officials, 2006
Mayor	William Neary
Admin/Manager	James White
Clerk	Elizabeth Kiss
Finance Dir/Treas	L. Mason Neely
Engineer	Schoor DePalma
Attorney	Michael Baker
Tax assessor	Frank Colon
Tax collector	Michelle O'Hara
Building officer	Edward Grobelny
Zoning officer	NA
Public Works	Thomas Williams

Housing & Construction

Housing Units, 2000*
Total	16,640
Median rent	$877
Median SF home value	$212,800

New Privately Owned Housing Units Authorized by Building Permit
	Units	Value
Total, 2004	19	$8,462,810
Single family	19	$8,462,810
Total, 2005	15	$5,287,543
Single family	15	$5,287,543

Real Property Valuation - parcels, 2005
	Number	Valuation
Total		$2,020,124,300
Vacant	850	17,435,400
Residential	15,243	1,498,193,000
Commercial	617	364,725,700
Industrial	109	103,127,500
Apartments	13	33,814,700
Farm land	22	2,538,700
Farm homestead	70	289,300

Average Property Value & Tax, 2005
Residential value	$97,857
Property tax	$6,804
FAIR rebate	$539

Public Library
E. Brunswick Public Library
2 Jean Walling Civic Ctr
E Brunswick, NJ 08816
732-390-6761
Director . . . . Carol Nersinger (Actg)

Library statistics, 2004
	Total	per capita
Volumes	188,409	4.03
Expenditure	$3,964,352	$84.79

Public Safety
Police
Chief	Barry Roberson (Dir)
Number of officers, 2004	93

Crime, 2004	Number	Rate
Total	887	18.4
Violent	38	0.8
Non-violent	849	17.6
Domestic Viol.	221	NA

Emergency/Fire
Director	NA

Public School District
(for school year 2004-2005 except as noted)

East Brunswick Township School District
760 Route #18
East Brunswick, NJ 08816
732-613-6705
Superintendent	Jo Ann Magistro
Grade plan	K-12
Enrollment	9,047.0
Students per teacher	12.7
Per pupil expenditure	$12,021
Median faculty salary	$68,365
Median administrator salary	$108,390
Grade 12 enrollment	641.5
High school graduation rate	98.2%

Assessment test results
(percent scoring at proficient or advanced level)
	Language	Math
Grade 3	92.5%	91.4%
Grade 8	84.1%	80.8%
High school	96.6%	92.2%

SAT
Percent tested	95%
Average SAT math score	583
Average SAT verbal score	543

No Child Left Behind, 2003-04
Attendence rate (target = 90%)	96.1%
Drop rate	0.5%
Highly-qualified teachers	100%
District needs improvement?(AYP)	No

Municipal Finance

Fiscal Year 2005
Total tax levy	$140,791,440
County levy	20,225,368
County taxes	18,320,855
County library	0
County health	0
County open space	1,904,514
School levy	96,063,754
Local muni. budget	24,502,318
Misc. revenues	35,296,326
Total aid	$5,745,132
CMPTRA	2,130,475
Muni. block grant	190,552
Energy tax receipts	3,276,538
Homeland security	NA

Fiscal Year 2006
Total aid	$5,745,132
CMPTRA	2,015,796
Muni. block grant	190,552
Energy tax receipts	3,391,217
Homeland security	140,000

Taxes
	2003	2004	2005
General tax rate per $100	6.22	6.510	6.960
Net valuation taxable	$2,008,626,584	$2,038,785,147	$2,024,791,877
State equalized value	$5,443,432,477	$6,436,660,850	$7,127,039,342
County equalization ratio	41.5	36.90	31.62

Demographics & Socio-Economic Characteristics
(2000 U.S. Census, except as noted)

Population
1980*	4,144
1990*	5,258
2000	5,430
Male	2,591
Female	2,839
2004 (estimate)*	6,114
Persons per sq. mi. of land	414

Race & Hispanic Origin, 2000
Race
White	5,141
Black/African American	177
Amer. Indian/Alaska Natv.	7
Asian	35
Natv. Hawaiian/Pac. Islander	0
Other Race	13
Two or more races	57
Hispanic origin, total	76
Mexican	15
Puerto Rican	40
Cuban	7
Other Hispanic	14

Age & Nativity, 2000
Under 5 years	311
18 years and over	4,070
21 years and over	3,891
65 years and over	811
85 years and over	120
Median Age	40.7
Native born	5,241
Foreign born	189

Educational Attainment, 2000
Population 25 years and over	3,661
0-8 yrs of school	3.6%
High School grad or higher	88.1%
Bachelor's degree or higher	23.9%
Graduate degree	7.0%

Income & Poverty, 1999
Per capita income	$25,345
Median household income	$65,701
Median family income	$74,455
Persons in poverty	203
H'holds receiving public assistance	11
H'holds receiving social security	558

Households, 2000
Total households	1,901
With persons under 18	732
With persons over 65	507
Family households	1,516
One-person households	330
Persons per household	2.77
Persons per family	3.12

Labor & Employment
Total civilian labor force, 2004**	3,015
Unemployment rate	5.0%
Total civilian labor force, 2000	2,672
Unemployment rate	3.0%

Employed persons 16 years and over by occupation, 2000
Managers & professionals	1,051
Service occupations	237
Sales & office occupations	683
Farming, fishing & forestry	9
Construction & maintenance	260
Production & transportation	351
Self-employed persons	103

*US Census Bureau
**New Jersey Department of Labor

General Information
Township of East Greenwich
159 Democrat Rd
Mickleton, NJ 08056
856-423-0654

Web site	NA
Land area (sq. miles)	14.75
Water area (sq. miles)	0.22
Type of government	Township
Form of government	TC

Government

Legislative Districts
US Congressional	1
State Legislative	3

Local Officials, 2006
Mayor	John DeGeorge
Admin/Manager	NA
Clerk	Susan Costill
Finance Dir/Treas	Susan Costill
Engineer	Remington & Vernick
Attorney	Thomas North
Tax assessor	Nicholas Monahan
Tax collector	NA
Building officer	James Sabetta
Zoning officer	NA
Public Works	NA

Housing & Construction

Housing Units, 2000*
Total	1,971
Median rent	$706
Median SF home value	$155,000

New Privately Owned Housing Units Authorized by Building Permit
	Units	Value
Total, 2004	107	$13,450,201
Single family	107	$13,450,201
Total, 2005	169	$22,076,404
Single family	169	$22,076,404

Real Property Valuation - parcels, 2005
	Number	Valuation
Total		$418,960,200
Vacant	526	17,566,200
Residential	2,288	341,938,500
Commercial	64	26,999,500
Industrial	20	11,818,300
Apartments	7	1,799,600
Farm land	105	15,788,300
Farm homestead	242	3,049,800

Average Property Value & Tax, 2005
Residential value	$136,359
Property tax	$5,114
FAIR rebate	$555

Public Library
E. Greenwich Public Library
535 Kings Highway
Mickleton, NJ 08056
856-423-1149

Director................Carol Baughman

Library statistics, 2004
	Total	per capita
Volumes	16,628	3.06
Expenditure	$46,956	$8.65

Public Safety

Police
Chief	William Giordano
Number of officers, 2004	17

Crime, 2004	Number	Rate
Total	84	14.3
Violent	7	1.2
Non-violent	77	13.1
Domestic Viol.	36	NA

Emergency/Fire
Director	NA

Public School District
(for school year 2004-2005 except as noted)

East Greenwich Township School District
535 Kings Highway
Mickleton, NJ 08056
856-423-0412

Superintendent	Joseph Conroy
Grade plan	K-6
Enrollment	655.0
Students per teacher	12.0
Per pupil expenditure	$11,072
Median faculty salary	$53,978
Median administrator salary	$76,531
Grade 12 enrollment	NA
High school graduation rate	NA

Assessment test results
(percent scoring at proficient or advanced level)
	Language	Math
Grade 3	90.5%	94.3%
Grade 8	NA	NA
High school	NA	NA

SAT
Percent tested	NA
Average SAT math score	NA
Average SAT verbal score	NA

No Child Left Behind, 2003-04
Attendence rate (target = 90%)	96.2%
Drop rate	NA
Highly-qualified teachers	100%
District needs improvement?(AYP)	No

Municipal Finance

Fiscal Year 2005
Total tax levy	$15,750,878
County levy	4,088,842
County taxes	3,585,466
County library	264,979
County health	0
County open space	238,396
School levy	10,871,831
Local muni. budget	790,205
Misc. revenues	4,491,640
Total aid	$2,141,331
CMPTRA	149,084
Muni. block grant	23,007
Energy tax receipts	1,919,240
Homeland security	50,000

Fiscal Year 2006
Total aid	$2,141,331
CMPTRA	81,910
Muni. block grant	23,007
Energy tax receipts	1,986,414
Homeland security	50,000

Taxes
	2003	2004	2005
General tax rate per $100	3.15	3.464	3.751
Net valuation taxable	$380,062,814	$392,743,335	$419,994,197
State equalized value	$484,403,281	$556,188,372	$668,780,568
County equalization ratio	83.93	78.46	70.55

Demographics & Socio-Economic Characteristics

(2000 U.S. Census, except as noted)

Population

1980*	9,319
1990*	9,926
2000	11,393
Male	5,520
Female	5,873
2004 (estimate)*	11,535
Persons per sq. mi. of land	1,414

Race & Hispanic Origin, 2000

Race

White	9,921
Black/African American	66
Amer. Indian/Alaska Natv.	3
Asian	1,269
Natv. Hawaiian/Pac. Islander	0
Other Race	27
Two or more races	107
Hispanic origin, total	312
Mexican	22
Puerto Rican	71
Cuban	53
Other Hispanic	166

Age & Nativity, 2000

Under 5 years	713
18 years and over	8,828
21 years and over	8,511
65 years and over	1,662
85 years and over	138
Median Age	40.7
Native born	9,274
Foreign born	2,119

Educational Attainment, 2000

Population 25 years and over	8,147
0-8 yrs of school	4.9%
High School grad or higher	88.1%
Bachelor's degree or higher	33.4%
Graduate degree	13.4%

Income & Poverty, 1999

Per capita income	$32,129
Median household income	$82,133
Median family income	$88,348
Persons in poverty	192
H'holds receiving public assistance	23
H'holds receiving social security	1,214

Households, 2000

Total households	3,843
With persons under 18	1,407
With persons over 65	1,163
Family households	3,214
One-person households	521
Persons per household	2.96
Persons per family	3.26

Labor & Employment

Total civilian labor force, 2004**	6,306
Unemployment rate	3.0%
Total civilian labor force, 2000	5,952
Unemployment rate	3.1%

Employed persons 16 years and over by occupation, 2000

Managers & professionals	2,553
Service occupations	748
Sales & office occupations	1,528
Farming, fishing & forestry	0
Construction & maintenance	474
Production & transportation	462
Self-employed persons	317

*US Census Bureau
**New Jersey Department of Labor

General Information

Township of East Hanover
411 Ridgedale Ave
East Hanover, NJ 07936
973-428-3000

Web site	NA
Land area (sq. miles)	8.16
Water area (sq. miles)	0
Type of government	Township
Form of government	SM '50

Government

Legislative Districts

US Congressional	11
State Legislative	26

Local Officials, 2006

Mayor	William Agnellino
Admin/Manager	C. Richard Paduch
Clerk	Marilyn J. Snow
Finance Dir/Treas	Smruti Amin
Engineer	Lawrence Palmer
Attorney	Joseph Bell
Tax assessor	Stan Belenky
Tax collector	Carole Reardon
Building officer	Thomas Pershouse
Zoning officer	Thomas Pershouse
Public Works	Marc Macaluso

Housing & Construction

Housing Units, 2000*

Total	3,895
Median rent	$1,504
Median SF home value	$322,800

New Privately Owned Housing Units Authorized by Building Permit

	Units	Value
Total, 2004	30	$4,197,255
Single family	28	$4,097,255
Total, 2005	24	$4,429,623
Single family	24	$4,429,623

Real Property Valuation - parcels, 2005

	Number	Valuation
Total		$2,457,281,200
Vacant	228	30,941,400
Residential	3,890	1,373,868,900
Commercial	176	891,080,700
Industrial	91	161,390,200
Apartments	0	0
Farm land	0	0
Farm homestead	0	0

Average Property Value & Tax, 2005

Residential value	$353,180
Property tax	$5,881
FAIR rebate	$629

Public Library

E. Hanover Township Library
415 Ridgedale Ave
East Hanover, NJ 07936
973-428-3075

Director .... Gayle Carlson

Library statistics, 2004

	Total	per capita
Volumes	70,151	6.16
Expenditure	$741,276	$65.06

Public Safety

Police

Chief	Stanley Hansen
Number of officers, 2004	34

Crime, 2004	Number	Rate
Total	212	18.5
Violent	8	0.7
Non-violent	204	17.8
Domestic Viol.	79	NA

Emergency/Fire

Director .... Raymond Serra

Public School District

(for school year 2004-2005 except as noted)

East Hanover Township School District
20 School Ave
East Hanover, NJ 07936
973-887-2112

Superintendent	Larry Santos
Grade plan	K-8
Enrollment	1,134.0
Students per teacher	9.8
Per pupil expenditure	$12,944
Median faculty salary	$50,863
Median administrator salary	$99,916
Grade 12 enrollment	NA
High school graduation rate	NA

Assessment test results

(percent scoring at proficient or advanced level)

	Language	Math
Grade 3	84.4%	88.5%
Grade 8	89.7%	70.1%
High school	NA	NA

SAT

Percent tested	NA
Average SAT math score	NA
Average SAT verbal score	NA

No Child Left Behind, 2003-04

Attendence rate (target = 90%)	95.8%
Drop rate	NA
Highly-qualified teachers	92.1%
District needs improvement?(AYP)	No

Municipal Finance

Fiscal Year 2005

Total tax levy	$40,957,400
County levy	7,848,437
County taxes	6,425,851
County library	0
County health	0
County open space	1,422,586
School levy	21,503,086
Local muni. budget	11,605,878
Misc. revenues	6,276,445
Total aid	$3,492,922
CMPTRA	425,587
Muni. block grant	44,672
Energy tax receipts	2,952,663
Homeland security	70,000

Fiscal Year 2006

Total aid	$3,492,921
CMPTRA	322,243
Muni. block grant	44,672
Energy tax receipts	3,056,006
Homeland security	70,000

Taxes

	2003	2004	2005
General tax rate per $100	1.46	1.510	1.670
Net valuation taxable	$2,471,585,657	$2,476,663,255	$2,459,779,889
State equalized value	$2,570,819,281	$3,013,408,987	$3,267,941,928
County equalization ratio	100.6	96.14	82.17

Demographics & Socio-Economic Characteristics

(2000 U.S. Census, except as noted)

Population

1980*	1,923
1990*	2,157
2000	2,377
Male	1,211
Female	1,166
2004 (estimate)*	2,307
Persons per sq. mi. of land	22,643

Race & Hispanic Origin, 2000

Race

White	1,593
Black/African American	40
Amer. Indian/Alaska Natv.	12
Asian	60
Natv. Hawaiian/Pac. Islander	1
Other Race	499
Two or more races	172
Hispanic origin, total	1,130
Mexican	48
Puerto Rican	124
Cuban	59
Other Hispanic	899

Age & Nativity, 2000

Under 5 years	161
18 years and over	1,761
21 years and over	1,657
65 years and over	181
85 years and over	23
Median Age	32.3
Native born	1,104
Foreign born	1,273

Educational Attainment, 2000

Population 25 years and over	1,495
0-8 yrs of school	22.9%
High School grad or higher	60.9%
Bachelor's degree or higher	13.2%
Graduate degree	5.0%

Income & Poverty, 1999

Per capita income	$16,415
Median household income	$44,352
Median family income	$46,375
Persons in poverty	298
H'holds receiving public assistance	18
H'holds receiving social security	152

Households, 2000

Total households	767
With persons under 18	351
With persons over 65	137
Family households	605
One-person households	123
Persons per household	3.1
Persons per family	3.4

Labor & Employment

Total civilian labor force, 2004**	1,249
Unemployment rate	3.8%
Total civilian labor force, 2000	1,122
Unemployment rate	6.4%

Employed persons 16 years and over by occupation, 2000

Managers & professionals	163
Service occupations	184
Sales & office occupations	278
Farming, fishing & forestry	4
Construction & maintenance	150
Production & transportation	271
Self-employed persons	29

*US Census Bureau
**New Jersey Department of Labor

General Information

Borough of East Newark
34 Sherman Ave
East Newark, NJ 07029
973-481-2902

Web site	NA
Land area (sq. miles)	0.10
Water area (sq. miles)	0.02
Type of government	Borough
Form of government	B

Government

Legislative Districts

US Congressional	13
State Legislative	32

Local Officials, 2006

Mayor	Joseph R. Smith
Admin/Manager	NA
Clerk	Robert Knapp (Actg.)
Finance Dir/Treas	James Mangin
Engineer	Boswell Engineering
Attorney	Neil Marotta
Tax assessor	Denis McGuire
Tax collector	Anthony Blasi
Building officer	Mark Sadonis
Zoning officer	NA
Public Works	NA

Housing & Construction

Housing Units, 2000*

Total	799
Median rent	$725
Median SF home value	$126,300

New Privately Owned Housing Units Authorized by Building Permit

	Units	Value
Total, 2004	0	$0
Single family	0	$0
Total, 2005	0	$0
Single family	0	$0

Real Property Valuation - parcels, 2005

	Number	Valuation
Total		$38,937,400
Vacant	14	516,700
Residential	327	24,063,400
Commercial	26	3,212,500
Industrial	6	9,650,500
Apartments	12	1,494,300
Farm land	0	0
Farm homestead	0	0

Average Property Value & Tax, 2005

Residential value	$73,588
Property tax	$5,134
FAIR rebate	$633

Public Library

No public municipal library.

Library statistics, 2004

	Total	per capita
Volumes	NA	NA
Expenditure	NA	NA

Public Safety

Police

Chief	Kenneth Sheehan
Number of officers, 2004	7

Crime, 2004	Number	Rate
Total	43	18.4
Violent	10	4.3
Non-violent	33	14.1
Domestic Viol.	11	NA

Emergency/Fire

Director	Lawrence Handlin

Public School District

(for school year 2004-2005 except as noted)

East Newark School District
501 -11 N Third St
East Newark, NJ 07029
973-481-6803

Administrator	Robert Van Zanten
Grade plan	K-12
Enrollment	246.0
Students per teacher	13.3
Per pupil expenditure	$9,968
Median faculty salary	$37,915
Median administrator salary	$43,665
Grade 12 enrollment	NA
High school graduation rate	NA

Assessment test results

(percent scoring at proficient or advanced level)

	Language	Math
Grade 3	68.1%	86.4%
Grade 8	21.4%	22.3%
High school	NA	NA

SAT

Percent tested	NA
Average SAT math score	NA
Average SAT verbal score	NA

No Child Left Behind, 2003-04

Attendence rate (target = 90%)	97.6%
Drop rate	NA
Highly-qualified teachers	100%
District needs improvement?(AYP)	No

Municipal Finance

Fiscal Year 2005

Total tax levy	$2,718,449
County levy	710,914
County taxes	697,477
County library	0
County health	0
County open space	13,437
School levy	946,435
Local muni. budget	1,061,100
Misc. revenues	1,977,988
Total aid	$791,321
CMPTRA	654,339
Muni. block grant	9,438
Energy tax receipts	102,544
Homeland security	25,000

Fiscal Year 2006

Total aid	$791,321
CMPTRA	650,750
Muni. block grant	9,438
Energy tax receipts	106,133
Homeland security	25,000

Taxes

	2003	2004	2005
General tax rate per $100	6.57	6.880	6.978
Net valuation taxable	$38,909,548	$39,045,694	$38,962,213
State equalized value	$113,438,915	$125,163,837	$137,481,344
County equalization ratio	42.32	34.30	31.18

Demographics & Socio-Economic Characteristics

(2000 U.S. Census, except as noted)

Population

1980*	77,025
1990*	73,552
2000	69,824
Male	31,429
Female	38,395
2004 (estimate)*	68,930
Persons per sq. mi. of land	17,549

Race & Hispanic Origin, 2000

Race

White	2,683
Black/African American	62,462
Amer. Indian/Alaska Natv.	177
Asian	302
Natv. Hawaiian/Pac. Islander	51
Other Race	1,496
Two or more races	2,653
Hispanic origin, total	3,284
Mexican	196
Puerto Rican	1,248
Cuban	138
Other Hispanic	1,702

Age & Nativity, 2000

Under 5 years	5,535
18 years and over	50,188
21 years and over	47,327
65 years and over	7,845
85 years and over	879
Median Age	33
Native born	57,145
Foreign born	12,759

Educational Attainment, 2000

Population 25 years and over	43,509
0-8 yrs of school	7.5%
High School grad or higher	72.4%
Bachelor's degree or higher	15.0%
Graduate degree	4.5%

Income & Poverty, 1999

Per capita income	$16,488
Median household income	$32,346
Median family income	$38,562
Persons in poverty	13,159
H'holds receiving public assistance	2,415
H'holds receiving social security	6,691

Households, 2000

Total households	26,024
With persons under 18	10,289
With persons over 65	6,072
Family households	16,079
One-person households	8,584
Persons per household	2.63
Persons per family	3.37

Labor & Employment

Total civilian labor force, 2004**	14,396
Unemployment rate	6.6%
Total civilian labor force, 2000	31,605
Unemployment rate	13.3%

Employed persons 16 years and over by occupation, 2000

Managers & professionals	6,740
Service occupations	6,079
Sales & office occupations	8,823
Farming, fishing & forestry	9
Construction & maintenance	1,612
Production & transportation	4,136
Self-employed persons	821

*US Census Bureau
**New Jersey Department of Labor

General Information

City of East Orange
44 City Hall Plaza
East Orange, NJ 07019
973-266-5100

Web site	www.eastorange-nj.org
Land area (sq. miles)	3.93
Water area (sq. miles)	0
Type of government	City
Form of government	C

Government

Legislative Districts

US Congressional	10
State Legislative	34

Local Officials, 2006

Mayor	Robert L. Bowser
Admin/Manager	Joseph W. Jenkins
Clerk	Cynthia Brown
Finance Dir/Treas	Soe Myint
Engineer	Michael Johnson
Attorney	Jason Holt
Tax assessor	Barbara Williams
Tax collector	Annmarie Corbitt
Building officer	Lloyd Abdul Raheem
Zoning officer	Lloyd Abdul Raheem
Public Works	Calvin Gibson

Housing & Construction

Housing Units, 2000*

Total	28,485
Median rent	$650
Median SF home value	$122,000

New Privately Owned Housing Units Authorized by Building Permit

	Units	Value
Total, 2004	114	$15,721,070
Single family	22	$2,352,952
Total, 2005	68	$4,777,652
Single family	15	$1,491,800

Real Property Valuation - parcels, 2005

	Number	Valuation
Total		$302,791,900
Vacant	469	4,367,900
Residential	8,379	177,398,800
Commercial	615	51,514,500
Industrial	32	3,788,500
Apartments	327	65,722,200
Farm land	0	0
Farm homestead	0	0

Average Property Value & Tax, 2005

Residential value	$21,172
Property tax	$5,733
FAIR rebate	$656

Public Library

East Orange Public Library
21 S Arlington Ave
East Orange, NJ 07018
973-266-5600

Director................Carolyn Ryan Reed

Library statistics, 2004

	Total	per capita
Volumes	366,200	5.24
Expenditure	$4,074,655	$58.36

Public Safety

Police

Chief	Michael Cleary (Actg)
Number of officers, 2004	270

Crime, 2004	Number	Rate
Total	5,369	77.6
Violent	1,121	16.2
Non-violent	4,248	61.4
Domestic Viol.	70	NA

Emergency/Fire

Director..............Carl Manns (Actg)

Public School District

(for school year 2004-2005 except as noted)

East Orange School District
715 Park Ave
East Orange, NJ 07017
973-266-5760

Superintendent	Laval S. Wilson
Grade plan	K-12
Enrollment	11,250.0
Students per teacher	11.1
Per pupil expenditure	$14,615
Median faculty salary	$68,800
Median administrator salary	$116,185
Grade 12 enrollment	462.0
High school graduation rate	NA

Assessment test results

(percent scoring at proficient or advanced level)

	Language	Math
Grade 3	65.3%	68.1%
Grade 8	38.0%	22.0%
High school	54.5%	36.8%

SAT

Percent tested	NA
Average SAT math score	NA
Average SAT verbal score	NA

No Child Left Behind, 2003-04

Attendance rate (target = 90%)	93.9%
Drop rate	7.1%
Highly-qualified teachers	99.8%
District needs improvement?(AYP)	Yes

Municipal Finance

Fiscal Year 2005

Total tax levy	$82,351,948
County levy	9,394,432
County taxes	9,197,639
County library	0
County health	0
County open space	196,793
School levy	18,931,200
Local muni. budget	54,026,316
Misc. revenues	621,783
Total aid	$26,774,033
CMPTRA	23,004,997
Muni. block grant	321,839
Energy tax receipts	3,307,197
Homeland security	140,000

Fiscal Year 2006

Total aid	$26,774,033
CMPTRA	22,889,245
Muni. block grant	321,839
Energy tax receipts	3,422,949
Homeland security	140,000

Taxes

	2003	2004	2005
General tax rate per $100	27.12	27.050	27.090
Net valuation taxable	$300,137,900	$301,068,230	$304,103,330
State equalized value	$1,649,109,341	$1,917,909,432	$2,298,589,040
County equalization ratio	19.85	19.85	15.63

Demographics & Socio-Economic Characteristics
(2000 U.S. Census, except as noted)

Population
1980*	7,849
1990*	7,902
2000	8,716
Male	4,241
Female	4,475
2004 (estimate)*	8,754
Persons per sq. mi. of land	2,299

Race & Hispanic Origin, 2000
Race
White	6,945
Black/African American	324
Amer. Indian/Alaska Natv.	10
Asian	932
Natv. Hawaiian/Pac. Islander	4
Other Race	280
Two or more races	221
Hispanic origin, total	928
Mexican	42
Puerto Rican	221
Cuban	91
Other Hispanic	574

Age & Nativity, 2000
Under 5 years	475
18 years and over	7,027
21 years and over	6,803
65 years and over	1,250
85 years and over	168
Median Age	37.9
Native born	6,202
Foreign born	2,514

Educational Attainment, 2000
Population 25 years and over	6,434
0-8 yrs of school	9.0%
High School grad or higher	78.5%
Bachelor's degree or higher	25.5%
Graduate degree	10.0%

Income & Poverty, 1999
Per capita income	$28,072
Median household income	$50,163
Median family income	$59,583
Persons in poverty	832
H'holds receiving public assistance	55
H'holds receiving social security	980

Households, 2000
Total households	3,644
With persons under 18	1,004
With persons over 65	952
Family households	2,156
One-person households	1,216
Persons per household	2.35
Persons per family	3.05

Labor & Employment
Total civilian labor force, 2004**	4,683
Unemployment rate	4.5%
Total civilian labor force, 2000	4,809
Unemployment rate	5.5%

Employed persons 16 years and over by occupation, 2000
Managers & professionals	1,557
Service occupations	647
Sales & office occupations	1,402
Farming, fishing & forestry	12
Construction & maintenance	285
Production & transportation	643
Self-employed persons	188

*US Census Bureau
**New Jersey Department of Labor

General Information
Borough of East Rutherford
One Everett Place
East Rutherford, NJ 07073
201-933-3444

Web site	NA
Land area (sq. miles)	3.81
Water area (sq. miles)	0.34
Type of government	Borough
Form of government	B

Government

Legislative Districts
US Congressional	9
State Legislative	36

Local Officials, 2006
Mayor	James Cassella
Admin/Manager	NA
Clerk	Danielle Micci
Finance Dir/Treas	Anthony Bianchi
Engineer	Glenn Beckmeyer
Attorney	Peter Melchionne
Tax assessor	Maurice Nafash
Tax collector	Linda Ramsaier
Building officer	Charles Flenner
Zoning officer	NA
Public Works	NA

Housing & Construction

Housing Units, 2000*
Total	3,771
Median rent	$817
Median SF home value	$196,200

New Privately Owned Housing Units Authorized by Building Permit
	Units	Value
Total, 2004	117	$11,560,800
Single family	2	$97,200
Total, 2005	15	$2,162,800
Single family	3	$577,600

Real Property Valuation - parcels, 2005
	Number	Valuation
Total		$880,117,231
Vacant	76	47,465,600
Residential	1,905	272,871,460
Commercial	171	228,767,671
Industrial	96	296,208,000
Apartments	34	34,804,500
Farm land	0	0
Farm homestead	0	0

Average Property Value & Tax, 2005
Residential value	$143,240
Property tax	$3,579
FAIR rebate	$633

Public Library
East Rutherford Mem Library
143 Boiling Springs Ave
East Rutherford, NJ 07073
201-939-3930
Director . . . . Karen DiNardo

Library statistics, 2004
	Total	per capita
Volumes	29,175	3.35
Expenditure	$311,289	$35.71

Public Safety
Police
Chief	John LaGreca
Number of officers, 2004	32

Crime, 2004	Number	Rate
Total	389	44.7
Violent	11	1.3
Non-violent	378	43.5
Domestic Viol.	45	NA

Emergency/Fire
Director . . . . Jerome Winston

Public School District
(for school year 2004-2005 except as noted)

East Rutherford School District
Uhland and Grove Sts
East Rutherford, NJ 07073
201-804-3100
Superintendent	Gayle Strauss
Grade plan	K-8
Enrollment	777.0
Students per teacher	9.9
Per pupil expenditure	$13,423
Median faculty salary	$68,728
Median administrator salary	$114,250
Grade 12 enrollment	NA
High school graduation rate	NA

Assessment test results
(percent scoring at proficient or advanced level)
	Language	Math
Grade 3	88.6%	84.8%
Grade 8	75.8%	65.3%
High school	NA	NA

SAT
Percent tested	NA
Average SAT math score	NA
Average SAT verbal score	NA

No Child Left Behind, 2003-04
Attendence rate (target = 90%)	95.4%
Drop rate	NA
Highly-qualified teachers	94%
District needs improvement?(AYP)	No

Municipal Finance

Fiscal Year 2005
Total tax levy	$22,050,865
County levy	2,739,250
County taxes	2,602,249
County library	0
County health	0
County open space	137,001
School levy	14,582,073
Local muni. budget	4,729,542
Misc. revenues	11,774,471
Total aid	$2,056,628
CMPTRA	500,239
Muni. block grant	34,576
Energy tax receipts	1,471,813
Homeland security	50,000

Fiscal Year 2006
Total aid	$2,056,627
CMPTRA	448,725
Muni. block grant	34,576
Energy tax receipts	1,523,326
Homeland security	50,000

Taxes
	2003	2004	2005
General tax rate per $100	2.24	2.390	2.500
Net valuation taxable	$843,074,398	$868,410,644	$882,647,583
State equalized value	$1,239,450,747	$1,323,856,358	$1,518,141,698
County equalization ratio	81.24	68.02	65.53

Demographics & Socio-Economic Characteristics
(2000 U.S. Census, except as noted)

Population
1980*	21,041
1990*	22,353
2000	24,919
Male	12,153
Female	12,766
2004 (estimate)*	26,872
Persons per sq. mi. of land	1,718

Race & Hispanic Origin, 2000
Race
White	18,545
Black/African American	2,217
Amer. Indian/Alaska Natv.	49
Asian	2,380
Natv. Hawaiian/Pac. Islander	31
Other Race	1,148
Two or more races	549
Hispanic origin, total	3,559
Mexican	282
Puerto Rican	515
Cuban	96
Other Hispanic	2,666

Age & Nativity, 2000
Under 5 years	1,915
18 years and over	18,935
21 years and over	18,221
65 years and over	2,062
85 years and over	402
Median Age	35.6
Native born	19,155
Foreign born	5,764

Educational Attainment, 2000
Population 25 years and over	17,196
0-8 yrs of school	4.0%
High School grad or higher	88.6%
Bachelor's degree or higher	42.0%
Graduate degree	15.5%

Income & Poverty, 1999
Per capita income	$28,695
Median household income	$63,616
Median family income	$73,461
Persons in poverty	1,312
H'holds receiving public assistance	67
H'holds receiving social security	1,451

Households, 2000
Total households	9,448
With persons under 18	3,451
With persons over 65	1,485
Family households	6,557
One-person households	2,320
Persons per household	2.61
Persons per family	3.12

Labor & Employment
Total civilian labor force, 2004**	14,340
Unemployment rate	2.7%
Total civilian labor force, 2000	14,352
Unemployment rate	3.1%

Employed persons 16 years and over by occupation, 2000
Managers & professionals	6,312
Service occupations	1,332
Sales & office occupations	4,026
Farming, fishing & forestry	19
Construction & maintenance	498
Production & transportation	1,721
Self-employed persons	476

*US Census Bureau
**New Jersey Department of Labor

General Information
Township of East Windsor
16 Lanning Blvd
East Windsor, NJ 08520
609-443-4000
Web site	www.east-windsor.nj.us
Land area (sq. miles)	15.65
Water area (sq. miles)	0.05
Type of government	Township
Form of government	CM '50

Government
Legislative Districts
US Congressional	4
State Legislative	12

Local Officials, 2006
Mayor	Janice Mironov
Admin/Manager	Alan M. Fishher
Clerk	Cindy A. Dye
Finance Dir/Treas	Kathleen Kovach
Engineer	Raymond Jordan
Attorney	David Orron
Tax assessor	H. Rick Kline
Tax collector	Lois A. Burns
Building officer	Stanley Rodefeld
Zoning officer	Marvin Lesser
Public Works	William Askenstedt

Housing & Construction
Housing Units, 2000*
Total	9,880
Median rent	$791
Median SF home value	$152,600

New Privately Owned Housing Units Authorized by Building Permit
	Units	Value
Total, 2004	99	$10,986,800
Single family	99	$10,986,800
Total, 2005	93	$10,655,800
Single family	93	$10,655,800

Real Property Valuation - parcels, 2005
	Number	Valuation
Total		$1,361,256,080
Vacant	590	36,165,800
Residential	7,395	966,184,800
Commercial	144	218,563,900
Industrial	12	55,773,500
Apartments	19	76,560,000
Farm land	35	6,482,800
Farm homestead	118	1,525,280

Average Property Value & Tax, 2005
Residential value	$128,805
Property tax	$5,818
FAIR rebate	$464

Public Library
Hickory Corner Branch Library†
138 Hickory Corner Rd
East Windsor, NJ 08520
609-448-1330
Branch Librarian	Marilyn Fischer

Library statistics, 2004
	Total	per capita
Volumes	NA	NA
Expenditure	NA	NA

†Branch of County Library

Public Safety
Police
Chief	William Spain
Number of officers, 2004	48

Crime, 2004	Number	Rate
Total	428	16
Violent	23	0.9
Non-violent	405	15.2
Domestic Viol.	166	NA

Emergency/Fire
Director	NA

Public School District
(for school year 2004-2005 except as noted)

East Windsor Regional School District
384 Stockton St
Hightstown, NJ 08520
609-443-7704
Superintendent	Ronald Bolandi
Grade plan	K-12
Enrollment	4,884.0
Students per teacher	11.7
Per pupil expenditure	$12,424
Median faculty salary	$64,685
Median administrator salary	$99,282
Grade 12 enrollment	270.5
High school graduation rate	90.5%

Assessment test results
(percent scoring at proficient or advanced level)
	Language	Math
Grade 3	89.5%	87.8%
Grade 8	80.4%	71.0%
High school	81.1%	74.5%

SAT
Percent tested	81%
Average SAT math score	535
Average SAT verbal score	525

No Child Left Behind, 2003-04
Attendence rate (target = 90%)	95.2%
Drop rate	1.7%
Highly-qualified teachers	96.9%
District needs improvement?(AYP)	No

Municipal Finance
Fiscal Year 2005
Total tax levy	$61,588,052
County levy	13,980,680
County taxes	12,211,977
County library	1,082,787
County health	0
County open space	685,916
School levy	41,523,056
Local muni. budget	6,084,317
Misc. revenues	12,075,914
Total aid	$4,733,438
CMPTRA	1,127,878
Muni. block grant	97,810
Energy tax receipts	3,417,750
Homeland security	90,000

Fiscal Year 2006
Total aid	$4,733,438
CMPTRA	1,008,257
Muni. block grant	97,810
Energy tax receipts	3,537,371
Homeland security	90,000

Taxes
	2003	2004	2005
General tax rate per $100	3.90	4.140	4.520
Net valuation taxable	$1,284,438,653	$1,336,155,372	$1,363,476,665
State equalized value	$1,871,541,094	$2,230,658,450	$2,648,041,688
County equalization ratio	76.18	68.63	59.85

Demographics & Socio-Economic Characteristics
(2000 U.S. Census, except as noted)

Population
1980*	3,814
1990*	4,962
2000	6,202
Male	3,085
Female	3,117
2004 (estimate)*	6,745
Persons per sq. mi. of land	1,172

Race & Hispanic Origin, 2000
Race
White	4,853
Black/African American	730
Amer. Indian/Alaska Natv.	14
Asian	336
Natv. Hawaiian/Pac. Islander	0
Other Race	89
Two or more races	180
Hispanic origin, total	293
Mexican	28
Puerto Rican	149
Cuban	17
Other Hispanic	99

Age & Nativity, 2000
Under 5 years	443
18 years and over	4,371
21 years and over	4,185
65 years and over	444
85 years and over	26
Median Age	34.9
Native born	5,705
Foreign born	497

Educational Attainment, 2000
Population 25 years and over	3,945
0-8 yrs of school	2.7%
High School grad or higher	90.1%
Bachelor's degree or higher	29.6%
Graduate degree	8.6%

Income & Poverty, 1999
Per capita income	$24,534
Median household income	$66,406
Median family income	$71,765
Persons in poverty	179
H'holds receiving public assistance	28
H'holds receiving social security	321

Households, 2000
Total households	2,226
With persons under 18	995
With persons over 65	338
Family households	1,639
One-person households	478
Persons per household	2.78
Persons per family	3.29

Labor & Employment
Total civilian labor force, 2004**	3,155
Unemployment rate	4.4%
Total civilian labor force, 2000	3,453
Unemployment rate	2.5%

Employed persons 16 years and over by occupation, 2000
Managers & professionals	1,200
Service occupations	442
Sales & office occupations	1,021
Farming, fishing & forestry	8
Construction & maintenance	251
Production & transportation	446
Self-employed persons	141

*US Census Bureau
**New Jersey Department of Labor

General Information
Township of Eastampton
12 Manor House Ct
Eastampton, NJ 08060
609-267-5723

Web site	www.eastampton.com
Land area (sq. miles)	5.75
Water area (sq. miles)	0.08
Type of government	Township
Form of government	CM '50

Government

Legislative Districts
US Congressional	4
State Legislative	8

Local Officials, 2006
Mayor	Donald G. Hartman
Admin/Manager	Scott Carew
Clerk	Linda M. Peryer
Finance Dir/Treas	D. Lavacca/G. Mingin
Engineer	Nancy Jamanow
Attorney	Eileen Fahey
Tax assessor	Harry Renwick
Tax collector	Doris LaVacca
Building officer	Stephen Murray
Zoning officer	NA
Public Works	Richard Parks

Housing & Construction

Housing Units, 2000*
Total	2,312
Median rent	$722
Median SF home value	$143,100

New Privately Owned Housing Units Authorized by Building Permit
	Units	Value
Total, 2004	8	$669,580
Single family	6	$569,580
Total, 2005	6	$685,413
Single family	4	$379,720

Real Property Valuation - parcels, 2005
	Number	Valuation
Total		$249,700,212
Vacant	92	4,162,629
Residential	1,610	211,389,792
Commercial	32	12,873,907
Industrial	3	615,000
Apartments	5	16,415,700
Farm land	21	3,772,120
Farm homestead	40	471,064

Average Property Value & Tax, 2005
Residential value	$128,401
Property tax	$5,367
FAIR rebate	$470

Public Library
No public municipal library.

Library statistics, 2004
	Total	per capita
Volumes	NA	NA
Expenditure	NA	NA

Public Safety

Police
Chief	Gerald Mingin
Number of officers, 2004	18

Crime, 2004	Number	Rate
Total	108	16.2
Violent	12	1.8
Non-violent	96	14.4
Domestic Viol.	53	NA

Emergency/Fire
Director	Phillip Polios

Public School District
(for school year 2004-2005 except as noted)

Eastampton Township School District
1380 Woodlane Rd
Eastampton, NJ 08060
609-518-7402

Superintendent	Susan Mintz
Grade plan	K-8
Enrollment	811.0
Students per teacher	11.3
Per pupil expenditure	$9,354
Median faculty salary	$43,500
Median administrator salary	$79,923
Grade 12 enrollment	NA
High school graduation rate	NA

Assessment test results
(percent scoring at proficient or advanced level)
	Language	Math
Grade 3	89.4%	90.9%
Grade 8	78.7%	72.2%
High school	NA	NA

SAT
Percent tested	NA
Average SAT math score	NA
Average SAT verbal score	NA

No Child Left Behind, 2003-04
Attendence rate (target = 90%)	96.5%
Drop rate	NA
Highly-qualified teachers	95.9%
District needs improvement?(AYP)	No

Municipal Finance

Fiscal Year 2005
Total tax levy	$10,456,812
County levy	1,725,486
County taxes	1,447,490
County library	126,746
County health	0
County open space	151,250
School levy	6,058,257
Local muni. budget	2,673,069
Misc. revenues	1,673,887
Total aid	$660,522
CMPTRA	218,964
Muni. block grant	24,318
Energy tax receipts	367,240
Homeland security	50,000

Fiscal Year 2006
Total aid	$660,522
CMPTRA	206,111
Muni. block grant	24,318
Energy tax receipts	380,093
Homeland security	50,000

Taxes
	2003	2004	2005
General tax rate per $100	3.54	3.745	4.187
Net valuation taxable	$249,556,948	$249,770,425	$250,161,950
State equalized value	$330,189,135	$377,122,516	$426,897,526
County equalization ratio	85.03	75.58	66.18

Demographics & Socio-Economic Characteristics
(2000 U.S. Census, except as noted)

Population
1980*	12,703
1990*	13,800
2000	14,008
Male	6,813
Female	7,195
2004 (estimate)*	14,139
Persons per sq. mi. of land	2,389

Race & Hispanic Origin, 2000
Race
White	10,267
Black/African American	1,626
Amer. Indian/Alaska Natv.	48
Asian	1,305
Natv. Hawaiian/Pac. Islander	5
Other Race	323
Two or more races	434
Hispanic origin, total	928
Mexican	158
Puerto Rican	378
Cuban	35
Other Hispanic	357

Age & Nativity, 2000
Under 5 years	958
18 years and over	10,796
21 years and over	10,441
65 years and over	1,867
85 years and over	288
Median Age	36.6
Native born	11,691
Foreign born	2,307

Educational Attainment, 2000
Population 25 years and over	9,877
0-8 yrs of school	3.7%
High School grad or higher	89.1%
Bachelor's degree or higher	33.5%
Graduate degree	13.4%

Income & Poverty, 1999
Per capita income	$26,965
Median household income	$53,833
Median family income	$69,397
Persons in poverty	777
H'holds receiving public assistance	110
H'holds receiving social security	1,206

Households, 2000
Total households	5,780
With persons under 18	1,783
With persons over 65	1,232
Family households	3,447
One-person households	1,951
Persons per household	2.35
Persons per family	3.08

Labor & Employment
Total civilian labor force, 2004**	7,885
Unemployment rate	4.1%
Total civilian labor force, 2000	7,511
Unemployment rate	4.4%

Employed persons 16 years and over by occupation, 2000
Managers & professionals	3,215
Service occupations	958
Sales & office occupations	2,046
Farming, fishing & forestry	0
Construction & maintenance	384
Production & transportation	579
Self-employed persons	288

*US Census Bureau
**New Jersey Department of Labor

General Information
Borough of Eatontown
47 Broad St
Eatontown, NJ 07724
732-389-7621

Web site	NA
Land area (sq. miles)	5.92
Water area (sq. miles)	0.01
Type of government	Borough
Form of government	B

Government

Legislative Districts
US Congressional	12
State Legislative	11

Local Officials, 2006
Mayor	Gerald Tarantolo
Admin/Manager	Michael Trotta
Clerk	Karen Siano
Finance Dir/Treas	Lesley Connolly
Engineer	Edward Broberg
Attorney	Gene Anthony
Tax assessor	Thomas Lenahan
Tax collector	Patricia DePonti
Building officer	Wallace Englehart
Zoning officer	NA
Public Works	Nate Albert

Housing & Construction

Housing Units, 2000*
Total	6,341
Median rent	$766
Median SF home value	$178,200

New Privately Owned Housing Units Authorized by Building Permit
	Units	Value
Total, 2004	58	$9,156,395
Single family	58	$9,156,395
Total, 2005	27	$4,079,375
Single family	27	$4,079,375

Real Property Valuation - parcels, 2005
	Number	Valuation
Total		$1,064,791,600
Vacant	221	28,217,800
Residential	2,727	408,337,700
Commercial	187	433,482,900
Industrial	43	110,972,100
Apartments	23	83,336,400
Farm land	4	429,700
Farm homestead	8	15,000

Average Property Value & Tax, 2005
Residential value	$149,306
Property tax	$4,959
FAIR rebate	$884

Public Library
Eatontown Public Library
33 Broad St
Eatontown, NJ 07724
732-389-2665

Director . . . . Amy Garibay

Library statistics, 2004
	Total	per capita
Volumes	NA	NA
Expenditure	NA	NA

Public Safety

Police
Chief	George Jackson
Number of officers, 2004	36

Crime, 2004	Number	Rate
Total	610	43.2
Violent	35	2.5
Non-violent	575	40.7
Domestic Viol.	83	NA

Emergency/Fire
Director . . . . Brian Denegar

Public School District
(for school year 2004-2005 except as noted)

Eatontown School District
215 Broad St
Eatontown, NJ 07724
732-542-1310

Superintendent	Jean Hoover
Grade plan	K-8
Enrollment	1,244.0
Students per teacher	9.9
Per pupil expenditure	$12,794
Median faculty salary	$63,882
Median administrator salary	$110,900
Grade 12 enrollment	NA
High school graduation rate	NA

Assessment test results
(percent scoring at proficient or advanced level)
	Language	Math
Grade 3	87.0%	83.4%
Grade 8	77.9%	72.0%
High school	NA	NA

SAT
Percent tested	NA
Average SAT math score	NA
Average SAT verbal score	NA

No Child Left Behind, 2003-04
Attendence rate (target = 90%)	96.0%
Drop rate	NA
Highly-qualified teachers	98.4%
District needs improvement?(AYP)	No

Municipal Finance

Fiscal Year 2005
Total tax levy	$35,530,205
County levy	5,663,094
County taxes	5,081,600
County library	279,969
County health	0
County open space	301,525
School levy	19,746,577
Local muni. budget	10,120,534
Misc. revenues	8,146,155
Total aid	$2,031,642
CMPTRA	770,929
Muni. block grant	60,384
Energy tax receipts	1,130,329
Homeland security	70,000

Fiscal Year 2006
Total aid	$2,031,642
CMPTRA	731,368
Muni. block grant	60,384
Energy tax receipts	1,169,890
Homeland security	70,000

Taxes
	2003	2004	2005
General tax rate per $100	2.98	3.286	3.322
Net valuation taxable	$1,061,272,075	$1,063,608,445	$1,069,828,539
State equalized value	$1,560,464,748	$1,695,488,755	$2,066,502,876
County equalization ratio	86.59	68.01	62.61

Demographics & Socio-Economic Characteristics
(2000 U.S. Census, except as noted)

Population
1980*	4,628
1990*	5,001
2000	7,677
Male	3,739
Female	3,938
2000 (revised)	7,734
2004 (estimate)*	9,358
Persons per sq. mi. of land	11,044

Race & Hispanic Origin, 2000
Race
White	5,153
Black/African American	270
Amer. Indian/Alaska Natv.	16
Asian	1,775
Natv. Hawaiian/Pac. Islander	3
Other Race	226
Two or more races	234
Hispanic origin, total	802
Mexican	71
Puerto Rican	169
Cuban	102
Other Hispanic	460

Age & Nativity, 2000
Under 5 years	430
18 years and over	6,494
21 years and over	6,362
65 years and over	687
85 years and over	67
Median Age	36.3
Native born	4,954
Foreign born	2,723

Educational Attainment, 2000
Population 25 years and over	6,124
0-8 yrs of school	2.8%
High School grad or higher	90.8%
Bachelor's degree or higher	51.4%
Graduate degree	18.6%

Income & Poverty, 1999
Per capita income	$42,650
Median household income	$63,455
Median family income	$72,692
Persons in poverty	662
H'holds receiving public assistance	51
H'holds receiving social security	551

Households, 2000
Total households	3,836
With persons under 18	800
With persons over 65	551
Family households	1,973
One-person households	1,499
Persons per household	2.0
Persons per family	2.7

Labor & Employment
Total civilian labor force, 2004**	3,487
Unemployment rate	3.0%
Total civilian labor force, 2000	4,817
Unemployment rate	4.0%

Employed persons 16 years and over by occupation, 2000
Managers & professionals	2,494
Service occupations	342
Sales & office occupations	1,203
Farming, fishing & forestry	0
Construction & maintenance	202
Production & transportation	385
Self-employed persons	174

*US Census Bureau
**New Jersey Department of Labor

General Information
Borough of Edgewater
916 River Rd
Edgewater, NJ 07020
201-943-1700
Web site	www.edgewaternj.org
Land area (sq. miles)	0.85
Water area (sq. miles)	1.57
Type of government	Borough
Form of government	B

Government
Legislative Districts
US Congressional	9
State Legislative	38

Local Officials, 2006
Mayor	Nancy Merse
Admin/Manager	Harvey Weber Jr.
Clerk	Barbara Rae
Finance Dir/Treas	Joseph Iannaconi Jr.
Engineer	Schoor DePalma
Attorney	Robert Regan
Tax assessor	Harvey Weber Jr.
Tax collector	NA
Building officer	John Candelmo
Zoning officer	John Candelmo
Public Works	NA

Housing & Construction
Housing Units, 2000*
Total	4,277
Median rent	$1,209
Median SF home value	$283,900

New Privately Owned Housing Units
Authorized by Building Permit
	Units	Value
Total, 2004	193	$3,494,201
Single family	0	$179,001
Total, 2005	24	$1,834,000
Single family	0	$0

Real Property Valuation - parcels, 2005
	Number	Valuation
Total		$1,062,226,300
Vacant	195	33,282,500
Residential	2,701	556,259,300
Commercial	107	207,103,000
Industrial	14	40,935,900
Apartments	50	224,645,600
Farm land	0	0
Farm homestead	0	0

Average Property Value & Tax, 2005
Residential value	$205,946
Property tax	$5,601
FAIR rebate	$494

Public Library
Edgewater Free Public Library
49 Hudson Ave
Edgewater, NJ 07020
201-224-6144

Director.............Donna Bachowski

Library statistics, 2004
	Total	per capita
Volumes	20,334	2.65
Expenditure	$363,619	$47.36

Public Safety
Police
Chief	Donald Martin
Number of officers, 2004	30

Crime, 2004	Number	Rate
Total	171	18.4
Violent	14	1.5
Non-violent	157	16.9
Domestic Viol.	13	NA

Emergency/Fire
Director................Steven Stewart

Public School District
(for school year 2004-2005 except as noted)

Edgewater School District
251 Undercliff Ave
Edgewater, NJ 07020
201-945-4106
Superintendent	Ted Blumstein
Grade plan	K-12
Enrollment	394.0
Students per teacher	10.4
Per pupil expenditure	$14,559
Median faculty salary	$46,023
Median administrator salary	$86,855
Grade 12 enrollment	NA
High school graduation rate	NA

Assessment test results
(percent scoring at proficient or advanced level)
	Language	Math
Grade 3	92.8%	92.9%
Grade 8	NA	NA
High school	NA	NA

SAT
Percent tested	NA
Average SAT math score	NA
Average SAT verbal score	NA

No Child Left Behind, 2003-04
Attendence rate (target = 90%)	95.8%
Drop rate	NA
Highly-qualified teachers	96.7%
District needs improvement?(AYP)	No

Municipal Finance
Fiscal Year 2005
Total tax levy	$28,906,400
County levy	3,894,183
County taxes	3,698,110
County library	0
County health	0
County open space	196,073
School levy	10,569,051
Local muni. budget	14,443,167
Misc. revenues	6,951,494
Total aid	$1,280,001
CMPTRA	834,349
Muni. block grant	30,102
Energy tax receipts	365,550
Homeland security	50,000

Fiscal Year 2006
Total aid	$1,280,001
CMPTRA	821,555
Muni. block grant	30,102
Energy tax receipts	378,344
Homeland security	50,000

Taxes
	2003	2004	2005
General tax rate per $100	2.52	2.610	2.720
Net valuation taxable	$1,008,926,008	$1,037,677,148	$1,062,824,270
State equalized value	$1,573,987,532	$1,846,828,810	$1,916,725,464
County equalization ratio	66.63	64.10	56.17

Demographics & Socio-Economic Characteristics

(2000 U.S. Census, except as noted)

Population

1980*	9,273
1990*	8,388
2000	7,864
Male	3,789
Female	4,075
2004 (estimate)*	8,069
Persons per sq. mi. of land	2,772

Race & Hispanic Origin, 2000

Race

White	5,353
Black/African American	1,683
Amer. Indian/Alaska Natv.	13
Asian	256
Natv. Hawaiian/Pac. Islander	1
Other Race	252
Two or more races	306
Hispanic origin, total	519
Mexican	70
Puerto Rican	211
Cuban	4
Other Hispanic	234

Age & Nativity, 2000

Under 5 years	462
18 years and over	6,053
21 years and over	5,773
65 years and over	1,025
85 years and over	58
Median Age	37.9
Native born	7,188
Foreign born	676

Educational Attainment, 2000

Population 25 years and over	5,527
0-8 yrs of school	3.5%
High School grad or higher	85.8%
Bachelor's degree or higher	19.6%
Graduate degree	4.1%

Income & Poverty, 1999

Per capita income	$22,920
Median household income	$48,936
Median family income	$52,016
Persons in poverty	677
H'holds receiving public assistance	95
H'holds receiving social security	973

Households, 2000

Total households	3,152
With persons under 18	1,044
With persons over 65	782
Family households	2,099
One-person households	868
Persons per household	2.49
Persons per family	3.03

Labor & Employment

Total civilian labor force, 2004**	5,644
Unemployment rate	3.1%
Total civilian labor force, 2000	4,322
Unemployment rate	4.8%

Employed persons 16 years and over by occupation, 2000

Managers & professionals	1,384
Service occupations	578
Sales & office occupations	1,105
Farming, fishing & forestry	0
Construction & maintenance	389
Production & transportation	658
Self-employed persons	192

*US Census Bureau
**New Jersey Department of Labor

General Information

Township of Edgewater Park
400 Delanco Rd
Edgewater Park, NJ 08010
609-877-2050

Web site	www.edgewaterpark-nj.com
Land area (sq. miles)	2.91
Water area (sq. miles)	0.13
Type of government	Township
Form of government	TC

Government

Legislative Districts

US Congressional	3
State Legislative	7

Local Officials, 2006

Mayor	Judy Hall
Admin/Manager	Linda Dougherty
Clerk	Linda Dougherty
Finance Dir/Treas	Frank VanGelder
Engineer	Remington and Vernick
Attorney	William Kearns
Tax assessor	Leo Midure
Tax collector	Tanyika Johns
Building officer	Jim Scott
Zoning officer	Charles Fisher
Public Works	Aubrey Painter

Housing & Construction

Housing Units, 2000*

Total	3,301
Median rent	$661
Median SF home value	$119,800

New Privately Owned Housing Units Authorized by Building Permit

	Units	Value
Total, 2004	0	$161,000
Single family	0	$161,000
Total, 2005	8	$1,101,708
Single family	3	$1,011,708

Real Property Valuation - parcels, 2005

	Number	Valuation
Total		$310,496,800
Vacant	72	4,151,800
Residential	2,384	236,336,300
Commercial	56	33,648,200
Industrial	9	4,442,100
Apartments	9	31,181,500
Farm land	4	602,200
Farm homestead	10	134,700

Average Property Value & Tax, 2005

Residential value	$98,777
Property tax	$3,427
FAIR rebate	$640

Public Library

Beverly Public Library
441 Cooper St
Beverly, NJ 08010
609-387-1259

Director	Margaret Lowden

Library statistics, 2004

	Total	per capita
Volumes	NA	NA
Expenditure	NA	NA

Public Safety

Police

Chief	Robert Brian (PS Dir)
Number of officers, 2004	14

Crime, 2004	Number	Rate
Total	265	33
Violent	29	3.6
Non-violent	236	29.4
Domestic Viol.	191	NA

Emergency/Fire

Director	Beverly Fire Dept.

Public School District

(for school year 2004-2005 except as noted)

Edgewater Park Township School District
25 Washington Ave
Edgewater Park, NJ 08010
609-877-2124

Superintendent	Scott Streckenbein
Grade plan	K-12
Enrollment	930.0
Students per teacher	11.0
Per pupil expenditure	$11,105
Median faculty salary	$50,564
Median administrator salary	$90,002
Grade 12 enrollment	NA
High school graduation rate	NA

Assessment test results

(percent scoring at proficient or advanced level)

	Language	Math
Grade 3	74.2%	75.2%
Grade 8	66.3%	59.4%
High school	NA	NA

SAT

Percent tested	NA
Average SAT math score	NA
Average SAT verbal score	NA

No Child Left Behind, 2003-04

Attendence rate (target = 90%)	94.4%
Drop rate	NA
Highly-qualified teachers	100%
District needs improvement?(AYP)	No

Municipal Finance

Fiscal Year 2005

Total tax levy	$10,789,644
County levy	2,110,823
County taxes	1,770,746
County library	155,053
County health	0
County open space	185,024
School levy	6,227,866
Local muni. budget	2,450,956
Misc. revenues	2,595,250
Total aid	$1,044,967
CMPTRA	454,295
Muni. block grant	36,703
Energy tax receipts	503,969
Homeland security	50,000

Fiscal Year 2006

Total aid	$1,044,967
CMPTRA	436,656
Muni. block grant	36,703
Energy tax receipts	521,608
Homeland security	50,000

Taxes

	2003	2004	2005
General tax rate per $100	3.09	3.158	3.470
Net valuation taxable	$297,095,888	$311,115,510	$311,021,411
State equalized value	$388,919,869	$458,866,111	$495,099,349
County equalization ratio	85.89	76.39	67.76

Demographics & Socio-Economic Characteristics
(2000 U.S. Census, except as noted)

Population
1980*	70,193
1990*	88,680
2000	97,687
Male	47,926
Female	49,761
2000 (revised)	97,597
2004 (estimate)*	100,142
Persons per sq. mi. of land	3,324

Race & Hispanic Origin, 2000
Race
White	58,116
Black/African American	6,728
Amer. Indian/Alaska Natv.	132
Asian	28,597
Natv. Hawaiian/Pac. Islander	37
Other Race	1,973
Two or more races	2,104
Hispanic origin, total	6,226
Mexican	546
Puerto Rican	2,095
Cuban	590
Other Hispanic	2,995

Age & Nativity, 2000
Under 5 years	6,299
18 years and over	75,365
21 years and over	72,264
65 years and over	11,668
85 years and over	1,247
Median Age	36.3
Native born	65,336
Foreign born	32,351

Educational Attainment, 2000
Population 25 years and over	67,649
0-8 yrs of school	4.4%
High School grad or higher	87.6%
Bachelor's degree or higher	42.3%
Graduate degree	17.2%

Income & Poverty, 1999
Per capita income	$30,148
Median household income	$69,746
Median family income	$77,976
Persons in poverty	4,606
H'holds receiving public assistance	455
H'holds receiving social security	7,681

Households, 2000
Total households	35,136
With persons under 18	12,887
With persons over 65	7,991
Family households	25,881
One-person households	7,419
Persons per household	2.72
Persons per family	3.19

Labor & Employment
Total civilian labor force, 2004**	56,333
Unemployment rate	4.0%
Total civilian labor force, 2000	52,409
Unemployment rate	4.1%

Employed persons 16 years and over by occupation, 2000
Managers & professionals	23,944
Service occupations	4,449
Sales & office occupations	14,077
Farming, fishing & forestry	13
Construction & maintenance	2,626
Production & transportation	5,144
Self-employed persons	1,684

*US Census Bureau
**New Jersey Department of Labor

General Information
Township of Edison
100 Municipal Blvd
Edison, NJ 08817
732-248-7200

Web site	www.edisonnj.org
Land area (sq. miles)	30.12
Water area (sq. miles)	0.57
Type of government	Township
Form of government	MC '50

Government

Legislative Districts
US Congressional	6
State Legislative	18

Local Officials, 2006
Mayor	Jun H. Choi
Admin/Manager	Howard Dill (Actg)
Clerk	Reina Murphy
Finance Dir/Treas	Ross Bobal
Engineer	Rick Brown
Attorney	Jeffrey Lehrer
Tax assessor	Victoria Riddle
Tax collector	Gary Farinich
Building officer	Victoria Riddle
Zoning officer	Steve Lombardi
Public Works	Howard Dill (Actg)

Housing & Construction

Housing Units, 2000*
Total	36,018
Median rent	$913
Median SF home value	$186,900

New Privately Owned Housing Units Authorized by Building Permit
	Units	Value
Total, 2004	226	$25,766,801
Single family	81	$18,837,126
Total, 2005	137	$20,784,475
Single family	95	$19,734,475

Real Property Valuation - parcels, 2005
	Number	Valuation
Total		$7,262,295,200
Vacant	1,202	170,124,500
Residential	24,339	4,212,307,800
Commercial	839	1,133,600,900
Industrial	313	1,279,202,000
Apartments	73	467,037,800
Farm land	0	0
Farm homestead	6	22,200

Average Property Value & Tax, 2005
Residential value	$173,026
Property tax	$5,795
FAIR rebate	$560

Public Library
Edison Public Library
340 Plainfield Ave
Edison, NJ 08817
732-548-3045

Director	Susan M. Krieger

Library statistics, 2004
	Total	per capita
Volumes	254,447	2.60
Expenditure	$4,990,611	$51.09

Public Safety

Police
Chief	George Mieczkowski
Number of officers, 2004	208

Crime, 2004	Number	Rate
Total	2,678	26.7
Violent	216	2.2
Non-violent	2,462	24.6
Domestic Viol.	376	NA

Emergency/Fire
Director	G. Robert Campbell

Public School District
(for school year 2004-2005 except as noted)

Edison Township School District
312 Pierson Ave
Edison, NJ 08837
732-452-4900

Superintendent	Carol Toth
Grade plan	K-12
Enrollment	13,563.0
Students per teacher	11.3
Per pupil expenditure	$11,964
Median faculty salary	$55,035
Median administrator salary	$105,897
Grade 12 enrollment	1,021.5
High school graduation rate	NA

Assessment test results
(percent scoring at proficient or advanced level)
	Language	Math
Grade 3	89.5%	88.0%
Grade 8	84.0%	76.8%
High school	89.6%	88.4%

SAT
Percent tested	NA
Average SAT math score	NA
Average SAT verbal score	NA

No Child Left Behind, 2003-04
Attendence rate (target = 90%)	96.3%
Drop rate	0.5%
Highly-qualified teachers	79.4%
District needs improvement?(AYP)	No

Municipal Finance

Fiscal Year 2005
Total tax levy	$243,702,979
County levy	35,300,844
County taxes	31,976,887
County library	0
County health	0
County open space	3,323,957
School levy	151,317,673
Local muni. budget	57,084,462
Misc. revenues	42,739,208
Total aid	$20,498,476
CMPTRA	3,073,105
Muni. block grant	388,033
Energy tax receipts	16,897,338
Homeland security	140,000

Fiscal Year 2006
Total aid	$20,498,476
CMPTRA	2,481,698
Muni. block grant	388,033
Energy tax receipts	17,488,745
Homeland security	140,000

Taxes
	2003	2004	2005
General tax rate per $100	3.11	3.250	3.350
Net valuation taxable	$7,214,867,544	$7,243,388,197	$7,276,174,542
State equalized value	$10,071,004,389	$11,091,280,835	$12,534,323,070
County equalization ratio	77.87	71.64	65.26

Demographics & Socio-Economic Characteristics
(2000 U.S. Census, except as noted)

Population
1980*	4,618
1990*	4,583
2000	4,545
Male	2,197
Female	2,348
2004 (estimate)*	4,500
Persons per sq. mi. of land	405

Race & Hispanic Origin, 2000
Race
White	3,036
Black/African American	645
Amer. Indian/Alaska Natv.	17
Asian	57
Natv. Hawaiian/Pac. Islander	4
Other Race	613
Two or more races	173
Hispanic origin, total	1,116
Mexican	77
Puerto Rican	880
Cuban	10
Other Hispanic	149

Age & Nativity, 2000
Under 5 years	305
18 years and over	3,261
21 years and over	3,070
65 years and over	633
85 years and over	57
Median Age	34.9
Native born	4,286
Foreign born	259

Educational Attainment, 2000
Population 25 years and over	2,928
0-8 yrs of school	8.5%
High School grad or higher	70.0%
Bachelor's degree or higher	10.2%
Graduate degree	2.5%

Income & Poverty, 1999
Per capita income	$15,151
Median household income	$32,956
Median family income	$40,040
Persons in poverty	588
H'holds receiving public assistance	33
H'holds receiving social security	534

Households, 2000
Total households	1,658
With persons under 18	645
With persons over 65	459
Family households	1,150
One-person households	413
Persons per household	2.7
Persons per family	3.2

Labor & Employment
Total civilian labor force, 2004**	2,227
Unemployment rate	8.4%
Total civilian labor force, 2000	2,170
Unemployment rate	9.7%

Employed persons 16 years and over by occupation, 2000
Managers & professionals	297
Service occupations	455
Sales & office occupations	579
Farming, fishing & forestry	0
Construction & maintenance	242
Production & transportation	387
Self-employed persons	49

*US Census Bureau
**New Jersey Department of Labor

General Information
City of Egg Harbor
500 London Ave
Egg Harbor, NJ 08215
609-965-0081

Web site	NA
Land area (sq. miles)	11.11
Water area (sq. miles)	0.43
Type of government	City
Form of government	SC

Government

Legislative Districts
US Congressional	2
State Legislative	2

Local Officials, 2006
Mayor	Joseph A. Kuehner Jr.
Admin/Manager	Thomas Henshaw
Clerk	Lillian DeBow
Finance Dir/Treas	Betty Wenzel
Engineer	Edward Walberg
Attorney	James Carroll
Tax assessor	Gregory Busa
Tax collector	Beverly Totten
Building officer	Robert Lemon
Zoning officer	Frank DeClementi
Public Works	NA

Housing & Construction

Housing Units, 2000*
Total	1,770
Median rent	$615
Median SF home value	$86,800

New Privately Owned Housing Units
Authorized by Building Permit
	Units	Value
Total, 2004	17	$1,364,212
Single family	17	$1,364,212
Total, 2005	11	$1,016,764
Single family	11	$1,016,764

Real Property Valuation - parcels, 2005
	Number	Valuation
Total		$123,834,900
Vacant	1,106	3,005,500
Residential	1,217	87,561,200
Commercial	149	23,661,900
Industrial	12	5,038,200
Apartments	11	4,568,100
Farm land	0	0
Farm homestead	0	0

Average Property Value & Tax, 2005
Residential value	$71,948
Property tax	$3,729
FAIR rebate	$607

Public Library

No public municipal library.

Library statistics, 2004
	Total	per capita
Volumes	NA	NA
Expenditure	NA	NA

Public Safety

Police
Chief	Mark Emmer
Number of officers, 2004	15

Crime, 2004	Number	Rate
Total	110	24.5
Violent	16	3.6
Non-violent	94	21
Domestic Viol.	78	NA

Emergency/Fire
Director	Russell Fenton

Public School District
(for school year 2004-2005 except as noted)

Egg Harbor City School District
527 Philadelphia Ave
Egg Harbor City, NJ 08215
609-965-1034

Superintendent	John Gilly III
Grade plan	K-8
Enrollment	518.0
Students per teacher	8.0
Per pupil expenditure	$13,661
Median faculty salary	$40,537
Median administrator salary	$76,219
Grade 12 enrollment	NA
High school graduation rate	NA

Assessment test results
(percent scoring at proficient or advanced level)
	Language	Math
Grade 3	55.8%	61.3%
Grade 8	38.6%	46.6%
High school	NA	NA

SAT
Percent tested	NA
Average SAT math score	NA
Average SAT verbal score	NA

No Child Left Behind, 2003-04
Attendance rate (target = 90%)	93.5%
Drop rate	NA
Highly-qualified teachers	97.4%
District needs improvement?(AYP)	No

Municipal Finance

Fiscal Year 2005
Total tax levy	$6,501,440
County levy	797,091
County taxes	650,792
County library	72,075
County health	35,469
County open space	38,755
School levy	2,983,233
Local muni. budget	2,721,115
Misc. revenues	2,591,138
Total aid	$666,972
CMPTRA	336,680
Muni. block grant	20,054
Energy tax receipts	285,238
Homeland security	25,000

Fiscal Year 2006
Total aid	$666,971
CMPTRA	326,696
Muni. block grant	20,054
Energy tax receipts	295,221
Homeland security	25,000

Taxes
	2003	2004	2005
General tax rate per $100	4.73	4.751	5.183
Net valuation taxable	$123,555,899	$123,634,391	$125,448,242
State equalized value	$167,374,558	$186,947,843	$224,535,962
County equalization ratio	79.61	73.82	65.80

Demographics & Socio-Economic Characteristics
(2000 U.S. Census, except as noted)

Population
1980*	19,381
1990*	24,544
2000	30,726
Male	14,934
Female	15,792
2004 (estimate)*	36,877
Persons per sq. mi. of land	548

Race & Hispanic Origin, 2000
Race
White	24,404
Black/African American	3,185
Amer. Indian/Alaska Natv.	66
Asian	1,552
Natv. Hawaiian/Pac. Islander	15
Other Race	868
Two or more races	636
Hispanic origin, total	2,076
Mexican	213
Puerto Rican	1,098
Cuban	44
Other Hispanic	721

Age & Nativity, 2000
Under 5 years	2,278
18 years and over	22,142
21 years and over	21,198
65 years and over	2,815
85 years and over	274
Median Age	36
Native born	28,047
Foreign born	2,572

Educational Attainment, 2000
Population 25 years and over	20,071
0-8 yrs of school	5.4%
High School grad or higher	82.8%
Bachelor's degree or higher	19.0%
Graduate degree	5.5%

Income & Poverty, 1999
Per capita income	$22,328
Median household income	$52,550
Median family income	$60,032
Persons in poverty	1,637
H'holds receiving public assistance	245
H'holds receiving social security	2,411

Households, 2000
Total households	11,199
With persons under 18	4,617
With persons over 65	2,167
Family households	8,106
One-person households	2,467
Persons per household	2.74
Persons per family	3.23

Labor & Employment
Total civilian labor force, 2004**	14,354
Unemployment rate	5.0%
Total civilian labor force, 2000	16,367
Unemployment rate	4.2%

Employed persons 16 years and over by occupation, 2000
Managers & professionals	4,188
Service occupations	4,276
Sales & office occupations	4,058
Farming, fishing & forestry	16
Construction & maintenance	1,708
Production & transportation	1,437
Self-employed persons	803

*US Census Bureau
**New Jersey Department of Labor

General Information
Egg Harbor Township
3515 Bargaintown Rd
Egg Harbor Township, NJ 08234
609-926-4000

Web site	www.ehtgov.org
Land area (sq. miles)	67.35
Water area (sq. miles)	7.61
Type of government	Township
Form of government	TC

Government

Legislative Districts
US Congressional	2
State Legislative	2

Local Officials, 2006
Mayor	James McCollough
Admin/Manager	Peter J. Miller
Clerk	Patricia Indrieri
Finance Dir/Treas	Charlene Canale
Engineer	James Mott
Attorney	Marc Friedman
Tax assessor	Maryanne Lavner
Tax collector	Sharon Miller
Building officer	Thomas Leonardis
Zoning officer	Patty Chatigny
Public Works	Al Simerson

Housing & Construction

Housing Units, 2000*
Total	12,067
Median rent	$700
Median SF home value	$131,300

New Privately Owned Housing Units Authorized by Building Permit
	Units	Value
Total, 2004	619	$63,378,108
Single family	619	$63,378,108
Total, 2005	519	$53,683,246
Single family	519	$53,683,246

Real Property Valuation - parcels, 2005
	Number	Valuation
Total		$2,165,297,525
Vacant	5,876	174,390,925
Residential	12,069	1,550,498,400
Commercial	868	427,746,000
Industrial	0	0
Apartments	21	8,452,000
Farm land	22	3,732,900
Farm homestead	64	477,300

Average Property Value & Tax, 2005
Residential value	$127,831
Property tax	$4,148
FAIR rebate	$481

Public Library
Egg Harbor Twp. Branch Library†
1 Swift Ave
Egg Harbor Twp., NJ 08234
609-927-8664
Branch Librarian | Jean MacPherson

Library statistics, 2004
	Total	per capita
Volumes	NA	NA
Expenditure	NA	NA

†Branch of County Library

Public Safety

Police
Chief	John Coyle
Number of officers, 2004	95

Crime, 2004	Number	Rate
Total	1,061	30.3
Violent	96	2.7
Non-violent	965	27.5
Domestic Viol.	435	NA

Emergency/Fire
Director	Wallace Shields

Public School District
(for school year 2004-2005 except as noted)

Egg Harbor Township School District
202 Naples Ave
West Atlantic City, NJ 08232
609-646-7911

Superintendent	Philip Heery
Grade plan	K-12
Enrollment	6,953.0
Students per teacher	11.8
Per pupil expenditure	$10,060
Median faculty salary	$43,680
Median administrator salary	$83,262
Grade 12 enrollment	405.0
High school graduation rate	95.8%

Assessment test results
(percent scoring at proficient or advanced level)
	Language	Math
Grade 3	76.8%	78.8%
Grade 8	63.3%	57.5%
High school	80.1%	67.5%

SAT
Percent tested	56%
Average SAT math score	510
Average SAT verbal score	507

No Child Left Behind, 2003-04
Attendance rate (target = 90%)	95.2%
Drop rate	0.7%
Highly-qualified teachers	94.7%
District needs improvement?(AYP)	No

Municipal Finance

Fiscal Year 2005
Total tax levy	$70,546,639
County levy	13,150,499
County taxes	10,731,470
County library	1,191,745
County health	586,480
County open space	640,805
School levy	49,496,124
Local muni. budget	7,900,015
Misc. revenues	19,608,068
Total aid	$7,210,298
CMPTRA	618,027
Muni. block grant	120,477
Energy tax receipts	6,315,015
Homeland security	140,000

Fiscal Year 2006
Total aid	$7,210,298
CMPTRA	397,001
Muni. block grant	120,477
Energy tax receipts	6,536,041
Homeland security	140,000

Taxes
	2003	2004	2005
General tax rate per $100	2.96	3.184	3.245
Net valuation taxable	$1,876,692,869	$2,011,909,673	$2,174,128,643
State equalized value	$2,475,848,112	$2,944,078,910	$3,794,953,121
County equalization ratio	84.76	75.80	68.23

Demographics & Socio-Economic Characteristics
(2000 U.S. Census, except as noted)

Population
1980*	106,201
1990*	110,002
2000	120,568
Male	59,674
Female	60,894
2004 (estimate)*	124,724
Persons per sq. mi. of land	10,206

Race & Hispanic Origin, 2000
Race
White	67,250
Black/African American	24,090
Amer. Indian/Alaska Natv.	580
Asian	2,830
Natv. Hawaiian/Pac. Islander	55
Other Race	18,702
Two or more races	7,061
Hispanic origin, total	59,627
Mexican	1,612
Puerto Rican	12,989
Cuban	7,069
Other Hispanic	37,957

Age & Nativity, 2000
Under 5 years	9,266
18 years and over	88,888
21 years and over	83,630
65 years and over	12,041
85 years and over	1,556
Median Age	32.6
Native born	67,593
Foreign born	52,975

Educational Attainment, 2000
Population 25 years and over	75,912
0-8 yrs of school	18.1%
High School grad or higher	61.7%
Bachelor's degree or higher	12.1%
Graduate degree	4.2%

Income & Poverty, 1999
Per capita income	$15,114
Median household income	$35,175
Median family income	$38,370
Persons in poverty	20,963
H'holds receiving public assistance	2,532
H'holds receiving social security	8,924

Households, 2000
Total households	40,482
With persons under 18	16,813
With persons over 65	9,034
Family households	28,170
One-person households	9,944
Persons per household	2.91
Persons per family	3.45

Labor & Employment
Total civilian labor force, 2004**	55,643
Unemployment rate	8.3%
Total civilian labor force, 2000	52,403
Unemployment rate	9.0%

Employed persons 16 years and over by occupation, 2000
Managers & professionals	8,698
Service occupations	8,488
Sales & office occupations	12,356
Farming, fishing & forestry	44
Construction & maintenance	4,539
Production & transportation	13,546
Self-employed persons	1,774

*US Census Bureau
**New Jersey Department of Labor

General Information
City of Elizabeth
50 Winfield Scott Plaza
Elizabeth, NJ 07201
908-820-4000

Web site	www.elizabethnj.org
Land area (sq. miles)	12.22
Water area (sq. miles)	1.43
Type of government	City
Form of government	MC '50

Government

Legislative Districts
US Congressional	10, 13
State Legislative	20

Local Officials, 2006
Mayor	J. Christian Bollwage
Admin/Manager	Bridget S. Zellner
Clerk	Yolanda M. Roberts (Actg)
Finance Dir/Treas	Robert Mack
Engineer	Ernesto Marticorena
Attorney	William Holzapfel
Tax assessor	Enrico Emma
Tax collector	Robert A. Mack
Building officer	Michael Mazza
Zoning officer	NA
Public Works	John F. Papetti Jr.

Housing & Construction

Housing Units, 2000*
Total	42,838
Median rent	$681
Median SF home value	$143,000

New Privately Owned Housing Units Authorized by Building Permit
	Units	Value
Total, 2004	761	$42,553,551
Single family	8	$902,500
Total, 2005	446	$32,124,799
Single family	2	$156,800

Real Property Valuation - parcels, 2005
	Number	Valuation
Total		$906,731,580
Vacant	872	43,000,300
Residential	14,374	472,332,580
Commercial	1,927	191,062,600
Industrial	191	98,873,100
Apartments	592	101,463,000
Farm land	0	0
Farm homestead	0	0

Average Property Value & Tax, 2005
Residential value	$32,860
Property tax	$5,127
FAIR rebate	$644

Public Library
Elizabeth Free Public Library
11 South Broad St
Elizabeth, NJ 07202
908-354-6060

Director .... Dorothy Key

Library statistics, 2004
	Total	per capita
Volumes	326,962	2.71
Expenditure	$3,455,702	$28.66

Public Safety

Police
Chief	Ronald Simon
Number of officers, 2004	341

Crime, 2004	Number	Rate
Total	6,373	51.7
Violent	700	5.7
Non-violent	5,673	46
Domestic Viol.	856	NA

Emergency/Fire
Director .... Edward Sisk

Public School District
(for school year 2004-2005 except as noted)

Elizabeth School District
500 N Broad St
Elizabeth, NJ 07207
908-436-5010

Superintendent	Pablo Muñoz
Grade plan	K-12
Enrollment	21,124.0
Students per teacher	9.1
Per pupil expenditure	$14,260
Median faculty salary	$47,291
Median administrator salary	$94,778
Grade 12 enrollment	1,019.0
High school graduation rate	77.6%

Assessment test results
(percent scoring at proficient or advanced level)
	Language	Math
Grade 3	69.5%	72.9%
Grade 8	44.8%	29.4%
High school	58.0%	46.9%

SAT
Percent tested	45%
Average SAT math score	411
Average SAT verbal score	399

No Child Left Behind, 2003-04
Attendance rate (target = 90%)	92.8%
Drop rate	5.2%
Highly-qualified teachers	96%
District needs improvement?(AYP)	Yes

Municipal Finance

Fiscal Year 2005
Total tax levy	$141,887,335
County levy	24,335,561
County taxes	23,363,270
County library	0
County health	0
County open space	972,291
School levy	37,165,104
Local muni. budget	80,386,670
Misc. revenues	86,181,388
Total aid	$35,199,186
CMPTRA	21,846,476
Muni. block grant	481,332
Energy tax receipts	12,731,378
Homeland security	140,000

Fiscal Year 2006
Total aid	$35,199,187
CMPTRA	21,400,878
Muni. block grant	401,332
Energy tax receipts	13,176,977
Homeland security	140,000

Taxes
	2003	2004	2005
General tax rate per $100	14.22	14.810	15.604
Net valuation taxable	$909,772,698	$912,079,216	$909,344,204
State equalized value	$5,034,713,326	$5,839,922,006	$6,883,756,276
County equalization ratio	20.11	17.11	14.29

Demographics & Socio-Economic Characteristics
(2000 U.S. Census, except as noted)

Population
1980*	3,187
1990*	3,806
2000	3,514
Male	1,722
Female	1,792
2004 (estimate)*	3,679
Persons per sq. mi. of land	187

Race & Hispanic Origin, 2000
Race
White	2,884
Black/African American	501
Amer. Indian/Alaska Natv.	20
Asian	15
Natv. Hawaiian/Pac. Islander	0
Other Race	48
Two or more races	46
Hispanic origin, total	103
Mexican	34
Puerto Rican	57
Cuban	2
Other Hispanic	10

Age & Nativity, 2000
Under 5 years	213
18 years and over	2,558
21 years and over	2,432
65 years and over	443
85 years and over	44
Median Age	38.2
Native born	3,444
Foreign born	70

Educational Attainment, 2000
Population 25 years and over	2,349
0-8 yrs of school	6.0%
High School grad or higher	78.6%
Bachelor's degree or higher	13.8%
Graduate degree	5.2%

Income & Poverty, 1999
Per capita income	$18,621
Median household income	$51,047
Median family income	$55,472
Persons in poverty	297
H'holds receiving public assistance	8
H'holds receiving social security	393

Households, 2000
Total households	1,263
With persons under 18	489
With persons over 65	326
Family households	959
One-person households	248
Persons per household	2.74
Persons per family	3.16

Labor & Employment
Total civilian labor force, 2004**	2,252
Unemployment rate	4.6%
Total civilian labor force, 2000	1,641
Unemployment rate	4.7%

Employed persons 16 years and over by occupation, 2000
Managers & professionals	479
Service occupations	273
Sales & office occupations	367
Farming, fishing & forestry	11
Construction & maintenance	223
Production & transportation	211
Self-employed persons	130

*US Census Bureau
**New Jersey Department of Labor

General Information
Township of Elk
667 Whig Lane Rd
Monroeville, NJ 08343
856-881-6525

Web site	www.elktwp.org
Land area (sq. miles)	19.63
Water area (sq. miles)	0.08
Type of government	Township
Form of government	TC

Government

Legislative Districts
US Congressional	2
State Legislative	3

Local Officials, 2006
Mayor	William Rainey
Admin/Manager	NA
Clerk	Debbie Pine
Finance Dir/Treas	Steve Considine
Engineer	James Sickels
Attorney	Bob Becker
Tax assessor	Darlene Campbell
Tax collector	Susan DeFrancesco
Building officer	Anthony Dariano Sr.
Zoning officer	Dave Mc Creery
Public Works	Steven Alexander

Housing & Construction

Housing Units, 2000*
Total	1,347
Median rent	$715
Median SF home value	$127,900

New Privately Owned Housing Units Authorized by Building Permit
	Units	Value
Total, 2004	51	$5,056,658
Single family	51	$5,056,658
Total, 2005	38	$5,511,247
Single family	38	$5,511,247

Real Property Valuation - parcels, 2005
	Number	Valuation
Total		$183,214,800
Vacant	475	10,854,400
Residential	1,247	139,700,900
Commercial	63	16,383,900
Industrial	1	813,500
Apartments	0	0
Farm land	99	11,109,300
Farm homestead	301	4,352,800

Average Property Value & Tax, 2005
Residential value	$93,058
Property tax	$3,216
FAIR rebate	$575

Public Library
Glassboro Public Library
2 Center St
Glassboro, NJ 08028
856-881-0001

Director	Carol Wolf

Library statistics, 2004
	Total	per capita
Volumes	NA	NA
Expenditure	NA	NA

Public Safety
Police
Chief	Steve Brogan
Number of officers, 2004	11

Crime, 2004	Number	Rate
Total	89	24.6
Violent	3	0.8
Non-violent	86	23.7
Domestic Viol.	44	NA

Emergency/Fire
Director	NA

Public School District
(for school year 2004-2005 except as noted)

Elk Township School District
98 Unionville Rd
Glassboro, NJ 08028
856-881-4551

Superintendent	Robert Campbell
Grade plan	K-6
Enrollment	383.0
Students per teacher	11.3
Per pupil expenditure	$10,301
Median faculty salary	$42,911
Median administrator salary	$64,318
Grade 12 enrollment	NA
High school graduation rate	NA

Assessment test results
(percent scoring at proficient or advanced level)
	Language	Math
Grade 3	85.8%	85.7%
Grade 8	NA	NA
High school	NA	NA

SAT
Percent tested	NA
Average SAT math score	NA
Average SAT verbal score	NA

No Child Left Behind, 2003-04
Attendence rate (target = 90%)	94.7%
Drop rate	NA
Highly-qualified teachers	100%
District needs improvement?(AYP)	No

Municipal Finance

Fiscal Year 2005
Total tax levy	$6,576,836
County levy	1,609,839
County taxes	1,411,358
County library	104,298
County health	0
County open space	94,182
School levy	3,636,782
Local muni. budget	1,330,215
Misc. revenues	2,671,981
Total aid	$544,166
CMPTRA	203,889
Muni. block grant	16,654
Energy tax receipts	298,623
Homeland security	25,000

Fiscal Year 2006
Total aid	$544,165
CMPTRA	193,437
Muni. block grant	16,654
Energy tax receipts	309,074
Homeland security	25,000

Taxes
	2003	2004	2005
General tax rate per $100	3.35	3.451	3.572
Net valuation taxable	$167,931,559	$174,412,278	$184,143,896
State equalized value	$199,419,973	$223,229,263	$259,540,375
County equalization ratio	86.04	84.21	78.03

Demographics & Socio-Economic Characteristics
(2000 U.S. Census, except as noted)

Population
1980*	1,569
1990*	1,571
2000	1,384
Male	671
Female	713
2004 (estimate)*	1,371
Persons per sq. mi. of land	1,584

Race & Hispanic Origin, 2000
Race
White	1,346
Black/African American	9
Amer. Indian/Alaska Natv.	0
Asian	7
Natv. Hawaiian/Pac. Islander	0
Other Race	10
Two or more races	12
Hispanic origin, total	21
Mexican	0
Puerto Rican	15
Cuban	0
Other Hispanic	6

Age & Nativity, 2000
Under 5 years	75
18 years and over	1,046
21 years and over	982
65 years and over	214
85 years and over	24
Median Age	36.7
Native born	1,368
Foreign born	16

Educational Attainment, 2000
Population 25 years and over	920
0-8 yrs of school	3.7%
High School grad or higher	85.2%
Bachelor's degree or higher	14.8%
Graduate degree	3.8%

Income & Poverty, 1999
Per capita income	$21,356
Median household income	$46,172
Median family income	$58,438
Persons in poverty	73
H'holds receiving public assistance	12
H'holds receiving social security	150

Households, 2000
Total households	524
With persons under 18	194
With persons over 65	146
Family households	385
One-person households	117
Persons per household	2.61
Persons per family	3.06

Labor & Employment
Total civilian labor force, 2004**	703
Unemployment rate	3.0%
Total civilian labor force, 2000	757
Unemployment rate	5.8%

Employed persons 16 years and over by occupation, 2000
Managers & professionals	181
Service occupations	91
Sales & office occupations	209
Farming, fishing & forestry	2
Construction & maintenance	80
Production & transportation	150
Self-employed persons	39

*US Census Bureau
**New Jersey Department of Labor

General Information
Borough of Elmer
PO Box 882
120 South Main St
Elmer, NJ 08318
856-358-4010
Web site	www.elmerboroughnj.com
Land area (sq. miles)	0.87
Water area (sq. miles)	0.01
Type of government	Borough
Form of government	B

Government

Legislative Districts
US Congressional	2
State Legislative	3

Local Officials, 2006
Mayor	Herbert Stiles Jr
Admin/Manager	NA
Clerk	Beverly Richards
Finance Dir/Treas	Darla Timberman
Engineer	John Schweppenheiser
Attorney	Charles J. Girard
Tax assessor	James Milliken
Tax collector	NA
Building officer	Pittsgrove Township
Zoning officer	NA
Public Works	NA

Housing & Construction

Housing Units, 2000*
Total	557
Median rent	$643
Median SF home value	$103,900

New Privately Owned Housing Units
Authorized by Building Permit
	Units	Value
Total, 2004	2	$285,450
Single family	2	$285,450
Total, 2005	1	$20,000
Single family	1	$20,000

Real Property Valuation - parcels, 2005
	Number	Valuation
Total		$56,935,425
Vacant	69	753,525
Residential	477	42,164,200
Commercial	59	13,591,700
Industrial	0	0
Apartments	0	0
Farm land	5	369,100
Farm homestead	19	56,900

Average Property Value & Tax, 2005
Residential value	$85,123
Property tax	$3,348
FAIR rebate	$630

Public Library
Elmer Public Library
120 S Main St
Elmer, NJ 08318
856-358-2449
Director	Linda Fritz

Library statistics, 2004
	Total	per capita
Volumes	10,450	7.55
Expenditure	$25,545	$18.46

Public Safety

Police
Chief	Patrick Bryan (Capt)
Number of officers, 2004	1

Crime, 2004	Number	Rate
Total	16	11.7
Violent	1	0.7
Non-violent	15	10.9
Domestic Viol.	1	NA

Emergency/Fire
Director	Benjamin Hitzelberger Jr.

Public School District
(for school year 2004-2005 except as noted)

Elmer Borough School District
PO Box 596
Elmer, NJ 08318
856-358-6761
Administrator	Stephen Berkowitz
Grade plan	K-12
Enrollment	76.0
Students per teacher	10.9
Per pupil expenditure	$11,881
Median faculty salary	$44,068
Median administrator salary	$90,293
Grade 12 enrollment	NA
High school graduation rate	NA

Assessment test results
(percent scoring at proficient or advanced level)
	Language	Math
Grade 3	77.8%	100%
Grade 8	NA	NA
High school	NA	NA

SAT
Percent tested	NA
Average SAT math score	NA
Average SAT verbal score	NA

No Child Left Behind, 2003-04
Attendance rate (target = 90%)	96.9%
Drop rate	NA
Highly-qualified teachers	100%
District needs improvement?(AYP)	No

Municipal Finance

Fiscal Year 2005
Total tax levy	$2,281,566
County levy	782,339
County taxes	766,819
County library	0
County health	0
County open space	15,520
School levy	1,182,783
Local muni. budget	316,444
Misc. revenues	753,993
Total aid	$196,321
CMPTRA	121,058
Muni. block grant	6,875
Energy tax receipts	68,388
Homeland security	0

Fiscal Year 2006
Total aid	$196,322
CMPTRA	118,665
Muni. block grant	6,875
Energy tax receipts	70,782
Homeland security	NA

Taxes
	2003	2004	2005
General tax rate per $100	3.91	3.882	3.934
Net valuation taxable	$57,321,054	$57,913,996	$58,002,872
State equalized value	$72,918,272	$76,893,897	$87,091,399
County equalization ratio	82.2	78.61	74.96

Demographics & Socio-Economic Characteristics

(2000 U.S. Census, except as noted)

Population

1980*	18,377
1990*	17,623
2000	18,925
Male	9,042
Female	9,883
2004 (estimate)*	19,005
Persons per sq. mi. of land	7,160

Race & Hispanic Origin, 2000

Race

White	15,619
Black/African American	409
Amer. Indian/Alaska Natv.	21
Asian	1,477
Natv. Hawaiian/Pac. Islander	1
Other Race	841
Two or more races	557
Hispanic origin, total	2,535
Mexican	43
Puerto Rican	535
Cuban	237
Other Hispanic	1,720

Age & Nativity, 2000

Under 5 years	1,084
18 years and over	14,971
21 years and over	14,380
65 years and over	3,115
85 years and over	386
Median Age	38.5
Native born	13,217
Foreign born	5,708

Educational Attainment, 2000

Population 25 years and over	13,537
0-8 yrs of school	7.7%
High School grad or higher	80.0%
Bachelor's degree or higher	20.6%
Graduate degree	6.0%

Income & Poverty, 1999

Per capita income	$22,588
Median household income	$52,319
Median family income	$59,131
Persons in poverty	1,212
H'holds receiving public assistance	140
H'holds receiving social security	2,336

Households, 2000

Total households	7,089
With persons under 18	2,275
With persons over 65	2,311
Family households	5,077
One-person households	1,645
Persons per household	2.66
Persons per family	3.17

Labor & Employment

Total civilian labor force, 2004**	9,991
Unemployment rate	4.6%
Total civilian labor force, 2000	9,945
Unemployment rate	4.9%

Employed persons 16 years and over by occupation, 2000

Managers & professionals	2,680
Service occupations	1,145
Sales & office occupations	3,345
Farming, fishing & forestry	0
Construction & maintenance	871
Production & transportation	1,421
Self-employed persons	496

*US Census Bureau
**New Jersey Department of Labor

General Information

Borough of Elmwood Park
182 Market St
Elmwood Park, NJ 07407
201-796-1457

Web site	NA
Land area (sq. miles)	2.65
Water area (sq. miles)	0.11
Type of government	Borough
Form of government	B

Government

Legislative Districts

US Congressional	9
State Legislative	38

Local Officials, 2006

Mayor	Richard A. Mola
Admin/Manager	NA
Clerk	Dolores Camlet
Finance Dir/Treas	Roy Riggitano
Engineer	Vincent J. DeNave T & N A
Attorney	Louis Mangano
Tax assessor	Pasquale Aceto
Tax collector	Frank Santora
Building officer	John Buonanno
Zoning officer	John Buonanno
Public Works	Joseph Mulligan

Housing & Construction

Housing Units, 2000*

Total	7,242
Median rent	$897
Median SF home value	$184,100

New Privately Owned Housing Units

Authorized by Building Permit

	Units	Value
Total, 2004	10	$941,484
Single family	0	$0
Total, 2005	6	$564,891
Single family	0	$0

Real Property Valuation - parcels, 2005

	Number	Valuation
Total		$2,042,858,000
Vacant	59	29,615,900
Residential	4,623	1,524,319,000
Commercial	223	294,413,900
Industrial	58	124,847,100
Apartments	19	67,596,700
Farm land	1	2,065,400
Farm homestead	0	0

Average Property Value & Tax, 2005

Residential value	$329,725
Property tax	$5,978
FAIR rebate	$657

Public Library

Elmwood Park Public Library
210 Lee St
Elmwood Park, NJ 07407
201-796-8888

Director................Ethan Gavin (Int.)

Library statistics, 2004

	Total	per capita
Volumes	66,847	3.53
Expenditure	$682,795	$36.08

Public Safety

Police

Chief	Donald Ingrasselino
Number of officers, 2004	37

Crime, 2004	Number	Rate
Total	523	27.6
Violent	31	1.6
Non-violent	492	25.9
Domestic Viol.	236	NA

Emergency/Fire

Director..................Philip Cheski

Public School District

(for school year 2004-2005 except as noted)

Elmwood Park School District
465 Blvd
Elmwood Park, NJ 07407
201-794-2979

Superintendent	Joseph Casapulla
Grade plan	K-12
Enrollment	2,108.0
Students per teacher	13.8
Per pupil expenditure	$11,377
Median faculty salary	$45,845
Median administrator salary	$97,000
Grade 12 enrollment	156.0
High school graduation rate	91.5%

Assessment test results

(percent scoring at proficient or advanced level)

	Language	Math
Grade 3	89.6%	86.9%
Grade 8	72.3%	52.5%
High school	78.2%	71.7%

SAT

Percent tested	66%
Average SAT math score	482
Average SAT verbal score	447

No Child Left Behind, 2003-04

Attendence rate (target = 90%)	94.7%
Drop rate	2.5%
Highly-qualified teachers	94.1%
District needs improvement?(AYP)	No

Municipal Finance

Fiscal Year 2005

Total tax levy	$38,055,272
County levy	3,895,815
County taxes	3,701,033
County library	0
County health	0
County open space	194,782
School levy	22,492,616
Local muni. budget	11,666,841
Misc. revenues	8,185,536
Total aid	$2,049,633
CMPTRA	939,105
Muni. block grant	77,113
Energy tax receipts	963,415
Homeland security	70,000

Fiscal Year 2006

Total aid	$2,049,634
CMPTRA	905,386
Muni. block grant	77,113
Energy tax receipts	997,135
Homeland security	70,000

Taxes

	2003	2004	2005
General tax rate per $100	2.90	3.090	1.870
Net valuation taxable	$1,135,821,962	$1,144,386,769	$2,044,940,201
State equalized value	$1,689,205,773	$1,923,361,033	$2,265,610,681
County equalization ratio	75.67	67.24	106.05

Demographics & Socio-Economic Characteristics

(2000 U.S. Census, except as noted)

Population

1980*	1,290
1990*	1,170
2000	1,092
Male	518
Female	574
2004 (estimate)*	1,077
Persons per sq. mi. of land	88

Race & Hispanic Origin, 2000

Race

White	1,038
Black/African American	39
Amer. Indian/Alaska Natv.	2
Asian	0
Natv. Hawaiian/Pac. Islander	0
Other Race	3
Two or more races	10
Hispanic origin, total	7
Mexican	0
Puerto Rican	5
Cuban	0
Other Hispanic	2

Age & Nativity, 2000

Under 5 years	52
18 years and over	861
21 years and over	847
65 years and over	216
85 years and over	17
Median Age	43.6
Native born	1,085
Foreign born	7

Educational Attainment, 2000

Population 25 years and over	814
0-8 yrs of school	4.8%
High School grad or higher	83.9%
Bachelor's degree or higher	16.5%
Graduate degree	6.9%

Income & Poverty, 1999

Per capita income	$25,415
Median household income	$50,972
Median family income	$59,688
Persons in poverty	19
H'holds receiving public assistance	5
H'holds receiving social security	170

Households, 2000

Total households	468
With persons under 18	129
With persons over 65	158
Family households	325
One-person households	123
Persons per household	2.33
Persons per family	2.8

Labor & Employment

Total civilian labor force, 2004**	566
Unemployment rate	3.0%
Total civilian labor force, 2000	559
Unemployment rate	2.9%

Employed persons 16 years and over by occupation, 2000

Managers & professionals	162
Service occupations	77
Sales & office occupations	142
Farming, fishing & forestry	5
Construction & maintenance	67
Production & transportation	90
Self-employed persons	36

*US Census Bureau
**New Jersey Department of Labor

General Information

Township of Elsinboro
619 Salem-Ft Elfsborg Rd
Salem, NJ 08079
856-935-4031 or 935

Web site	NA
Land area (sq. miles)	12.27
Water area (sq. miles)	1.06
Type of government	Township
Form of government	TC

Government

Legislative Districts

US Congressional	2
State Legislative	3

Local Officials, 2006

Mayor	John Elk
Admin/Manager	NA
Clerk	Betty Jean Eby
Finance Dir/Treas	John Willadsen
Engineer	Albert Fralinger
Attorney	Mr. Hoffman
Tax assessor	R. Shidner
Tax collector	NA
Building officer	Robert DeAngelo
Zoning officer	Robert DeAngelo
Public Works	NA

Housing & Construction

Housing Units, 2000*

Total	530
Median rent	$639
Median SF home value	$110,100

New Privately Owned Housing Units Authorized by Building Permit

	Units	Value
Total, 2004	0	$0
Single family	0	$0
Total, 2005	1	$150,232
Single family	1	$150,232

Real Property Valuation - parcels, 2005

	Number	Valuation
Total		$56,864,800
Vacant	158	1,518,900
Residential	538	46,421,700
Commercial	10	2,713,500
Industrial	0	0
Apartments	0	0
Farm land	43	5,191,400
Farm homestead	96	1,019,300

Average Property Value & Tax, 2005

Residential value	$74,828
Property tax	$2,792
FAIR rebate	$647

Public Library

No public municipal library.

Library statistics, 2004

	Total	per capita
Volumes	NA	NA
Expenditure	NA	NA

Public Safety

Police

Chief	Carlton Bowers
Number of officers, 2004	0

Crime, 2004	Number	Rate
Total	14	13
Violent	1	0.9
Non-violent	13	12
Domestic Viol.	3	NA

Emergency/Fire

Director	Steve Hannah

Public School District

(for school year 2004-2005 except as noted)

Elsinboro Township School District
631 Salem-Fort Elfsborg Rd
Salem, NJ 08079
856-935-3817

Administrator	Frank Vogel
Grade plan	K-12
Enrollment	116.0
Students per teacher	10.4
Per pupil expenditure	$12,306
Median faculty salary	$39,415
Median administrator salary	$84,871
Grade 12 enrollment	NA
High school graduation rate	NA

Assessment test results

(percent scoring at proficient or advanced level)

	Language	Math
Grade 3	42.9%	50.0%
Grade 8	69.2%	69.3%
High school	NA	NA

SAT

Percent tested	NA
Average SAT math score	NA
Average SAT verbal score	NA

No Child Left Behind, 2003-04

Attendance rate (target = 90%)	95.9%
Drop rate	NA
Highly-qualified teachers	66.7%
District needs improvement?(AYP)	No

Municipal Finance

Fiscal Year 2005

Total tax levy	$2,129,337
County levy	776,864
County taxes	761,427
County library	0
County health	0
County open space	15,438
School levy	1,152,731
Local muni. budget	199,741
Misc. revenues	444,029
Total aid	$171,537
CMPTRA	61,811
Muni. block grant	5,120
Energy tax receipts	104,606
Homeland security	0

Fiscal Year 2006

Total aid	$171,537
CMPTRA	58,150
Muni. block grant	5,120
Energy tax receipts	108,267
Homeland security	NA

Taxes

	2003	2004	2005
General tax rate per $100	3.48	3.588	3.732
Net valuation taxable	$56,502,969	$56,795,975	$57,069,015
State equalized value	$71,153,468	$76,496,397	$81,318,061
County equalization ratio	87.25	79.41	74.16

Demographics & Socio-Economic Characteristics
(2000 U.S. Census, except as noted)

Population
1980*	7,793
1990*	6,930
2000	7,197
Male	3,432
Female	3,765
2004 (estimate)*	7,339
Persons per sq. mi. of land	3,280

Race & Hispanic Origin, 2000
Race
White	6,450
Black/African American	61
Amer. Indian/Alaska Natv.	4
Asian	568
Natv. Hawaiian/Pac. Islander	0
Other Race	63
Two or more races	51
Hispanic origin, total	332
Mexican	22
Puerto Rican	65
Cuban	62
Other Hispanic	183

Age & Nativity, 2000
Under 5 years	500
18 years and over	5,527
21 years and over	5,357
65 years and over	1,351
85 years and over	262
Median Age	41.1
Native born	6,072
Foreign born	1,125

Educational Attainment, 2000
Population 25 years and over	5,166
0-8 yrs of school	4.3%
High School grad or higher	89.0%
Bachelor's degree or higher	40.3%
Graduate degree	12.3%

Income & Poverty, 1999
Per capita income	$31,506
Median household income	$74,556
Median family income	$80,468
Persons in poverty	166
H'holds receiving public assistance	0
H'holds receiving social security	759

Households, 2000
Total households	2,373
With persons under 18	907
With persons over 65	770
Family households	1,964
One-person households	344
Persons per household	2.91
Persons per family	3.23

Labor & Employment
Total civilian labor force, 2004**	3,850
Unemployment rate	3.9%
Total civilian labor force, 2000	3,413
Unemployment rate	1.8%

Employed persons 16 years and over by occupation, 2000
Managers & professionals	1,598
Service occupations	395
Sales & office occupations	1,031
Farming, fishing & forestry	0
Construction & maintenance	174
Production & transportation	152
Self-employed persons	286

*US Census Bureau
**New Jersey Department of Labor

General Information
Borough of Emerson
Municipal Place
Emerson, NJ 07630
201-262-6086

Web site	www.emersonnj.org
Land area (sq. miles)	2.24
Water area (sq. miles)	0.18
Type of government	Borough
Form of government	B

Government
Legislative Districts
US Congressional	5
State Legislative	39

Local Officials, 2006
Mayor	Steve Setteducati
Admin/Manager	Joseph Scarpa
Clerk	Carol Dray
Finance Dir/Treas	Nancy Burns
Engineer	Job & Job
Attorney	William Smith
Tax assessor	Claire Psoto
Tax collector	Barbara Kozay
Building officer	Michael Sartori
Zoning officer	Michael Sartori
Public Works	Joseph Solimando

Housing & Construction
Housing Units, 2000*
Total	2,398
Median rent	$1,096
Median SF home value	$260,600

New Privately Owned Housing Units Authorized by Building Permit
	Units	Value
Total, 2004	14	$1,349,985
Single family	14	$1,349,985
Total, 2005	12	$1,599,886
Single family	12	$1,599,886

Real Property Valuation - parcels, 2005
	Number	Valuation
Total		$646,696,550
Vacant	80	10,093,200
Residential	2,275	545,996,850
Commercial	123	87,879,700
Industrial	9	2,392,200
Apartments	0	0
Farm land	1	329,500
Farm homestead	1	5,100

Average Property Value & Tax, 2005
Residential value	$239,895
Property tax	$8,201
FAIR rebate	$616

Public Library
Emerson Public Library
20 Palisade Ave
Emerson, NJ 07630
201-261-5569
Director | Jodi L. Fulgione

Library statistics, 2004
	Total	per capita
Volumes	29,949	4.16
Expenditure	$302,313	$42.01

Public Safety
Police
Chief	Michael Saudino
Number of officers, 2004	18

Crime, 2004	Number	Rate
Total	48	6.6
Violent	4	0.5
Non-violent	44	6
Domestic Viol.	18	NA

Emergency/Fire
Director | Thomas Carlos

Public School District
(for school year 2004-2005 except as noted)

Emerson School District
Administration Building
Emerson, NJ 07630
201-262-2828
Superintendent	Vincent Taffaro
Grade plan	K-12
Enrollment	1,148.5
Students per teacher	13.5
Per pupil expenditure	$12,121
Median faculty salary	$51,860
Median administrator salary	$109,970
Grade 12 enrollment	74.5
High school graduation rate	98.7%

Assessment test results
(percent scoring at proficient or advanced level)
	Language	Math
Grade 3	93.7%	86.0%
Grade 8	93.8%	90.0%
High school	90.1%	87.3%

SAT
Percent tested	97%
Average SAT math score	519
Average SAT verbal score	507

No Child Left Behind, 2003-04
Attendence rate (target = 90%)	95.6%
Drop rate	0.4%
Highly-qualified teachers	100%
District needs improvement?(AYP)	No

Municipal Finance
Fiscal Year 2005
Total tax levy	$22,130,040
County levy	2,069,123
County taxes	1,965,659
County library	0
County health	0
County open space	103,464
School levy	13,729,349
Local muni. budget	6,331,568
Misc. revenues	2,687,215
Total aid	$953,977
CMPTRA	333,413
Muni. block grant	30,324
Energy tax receipts	522,051
Homeland security	50,000

Fiscal Year 2006
Total aid	$953,977
CMPTRA	315,141
Muni. block grant	30,324
Energy tax receipts	540,323
Homeland security	50,000

Taxes
	2003	2004	2005
General tax rate per $100	3.12	3.240	3.420
Net valuation taxable	$642,112,465	$645,111,834	$647,381,792
State equalized value	$919,668,383	$1,028,191,659	$1,156,245,387
County equalization ratio	78.03	69.82	62.71

Demographics & Socio-Economic Characteristics

(2000 U.S. Census, except as noted)

Population

1980*	23,701
1990*	24,850
2000	26,203
Male	12,318
Female	13,885
2004 (estimate)*	26,353
Persons per sq. mi. of land	5,352

Race & Hispanic Origin, 2000

Race

White	11,134
Black/African American	10,215
Amer. Indian/Alaska Natv.	71
Asian	1,366
Natv. Hawaiian/Pac. Islander	12
Other Race	2,226
Two or more races	1,179
Hispanic origin, total	5,703
Mexican	251
Puerto Rican	666
Cuban	257
Other Hispanic	4,529

Age & Nativity, 2000

Under 5 years	1,814
18 years and over	19,947
21 years and over	19,112
65 years and over	3,491
85 years and over	439
Median Age	37.4
Native born	18,124
Foreign born	8,079

Educational Attainment, 2000

Population 25 years and over	18,010
0-8 yrs of school	6.8%
High School grad or higher	82.7%
Bachelor's degree or higher	36.7%
Graduate degree	16.5%

Income & Poverty, 1999

Per capita income	$35,275
Median household income	$58,379
Median family income	$67,194
Persons in poverty	2,295
H'holds receiving public assistance	289
H'holds receiving social security	2,478

Households, 2000

Total households	9,273
With persons under 18	3,342
With persons over 65	2,559
Family households	6,486
One-person households	2,299
Persons per household	2.79
Persons per family	3.29

Labor & Employment

Total civilian labor force, 2004**	14,588
Unemployment rate	4.8%
Total civilian labor force, 2000	13,298
Unemployment rate	6.0%

Employed persons 16 years and over by occupation, 2000

Managers & professionals	4,826
Service occupations	2,005
Sales & office occupations	3,403
Farming, fishing & forestry	18
Construction & maintenance	698
Production & transportation	1,545
Self-employed persons	721

*US Census Bureau
**New Jersey Department of Labor

General Information

City of Englewood
PO Box 228
Englewood, NJ 07631
201-871-6637

Web site	www.cityofenglewood.org
Land area (sq. miles)	4.92
Water area (sq. miles)	0.01
Type of government	City
Form of government	SC

Government

Legislative Districts

US Congressional	9
State Legislative	37

Local Officials, 2006

Mayor	Michael Wildes
Admin/Manager	Cheryl G. Fuller
Clerk	Lenore Schiavelli
Finance Dir/Treas	D. Patino/C. Fuller
Engineer	Kenneth Albert
Attorney	William F. Rupp
Tax assessor	Raymond D. Picciano
Tax collector	NA
Building officer	Piero Abballe
Zoning officer	Don Porrino
Public Works	NA

Housing & Construction

Housing Units, 2000*

Total	9,614
Median rent	$825
Median SF home value	$212,400

New Privately Owned Housing Units Authorized by Building Permit

	Units	Value
Total, 2004	11	$2,991,400
Single family	11	$2,991,400
Total, 2005	685	$78,378,173
Single family	22	$10,771,890

Real Property Valuation - parcels, 2005

	Number	Valuation
Total		$2,038,385,900
Vacant	112	10,366,200
Residential	6,477	1,540,883,600
Commercial	522	298,024,500
Industrial	133	134,260,300
Apartments	53	54,851,300
Farm land	0	0
Farm homestead	0	0

Average Property Value & Tax, 2005

Residential value	$237,901
Property tax	$9,371
FAIR rebate	$613

Public Library

Englewood Public Library
31 Engle St
Englewood, NJ 07631
201-568-2215

Director	Donald Jacobsen

Library statistics, 2004

	Total	per capita
Volumes	126,149	4.81
Expenditure	$2,052,709	$78.34

Public Safety

Police

Chief	David Bowman
Number of officers, 2004	82

Crime, 2004	Number	Rate
Total	580	22.2
Violent	56	2.1
Non-violent	524	20.1
Domestic Viol.	311	NA

Emergency/Fire

Director	Robert Moran

Public School District

(for school year 2004-2005 except as noted)

Englewood City School District
12 Tenafly Rd
Englewood, NJ 07631
201-862-6241

Superintendent	Carol Lisa
Grade plan	K-12
Enrollment	2,689.0
Students per teacher	9.8
Per pupil expenditure	$16,618
Median faculty salary	$57,580
Median administrator salary	$106,217
Grade 12 enrollment	119.0
High school graduation rate	85.2%

Assessment test results

(percent scoring at proficient or advanced level)

	Language	Math
Grade 3	76.3%	70.9%
Grade 8	49.5%	30.5%
High school	76.2%	62.8%

SAT

Percent tested	82%
Average SAT math score	408
Average SAT verbal score	387

No Child Left Behind, 2003-04

Attendence rate (target = 90%)	94.2%
Drop rate	2.4%
Highly-qualified teachers	98%
District needs improvement?(AYP)	No

Municipal Finance

Fiscal Year 2005

Total tax levy	$82,038,476
County levy	7,566,727
County taxes	7,187,755
County library	0
County health	0
County open space	378,972
School levy	40,263,536
Local muni. budget	34,208,213
Misc. revenues	14,091,950
Total aid	$3,698,447
CMPTRA	1,311,970
Muni. block grant	108,735
Energy tax receipts	2,187,742
Homeland security	90,000

Fiscal Year 2006

Total aid	$3,698,447
CMPTRA	1,235,399
Muni. block grant	108,735
Energy tax receipts	2,264,313
Homeland security	90,000

Taxes

	2003	2004	2005
General tax rate per $100	3.46	3.810	4.020
Net valuation taxable	$2,026,213,856	$2,032,445,033	$2,044,264,194
State equalized value	$3,357,994,458	$3,740,758,045	$4,199,392,346
County equalization ratio	67.47	60.34	54.25

Demographics & Socio-Economic Characteristics

(2000 U.S. Census, except as noted)

Population

1980*	5,698
1990*	5,634
2000	5,322
Male	2,508
Female	2,814
2004 (estimate)*	5,655
Persons per sq. mi. of land	2,704

Race & Hispanic Origin, 2000

Race
White	3,557
Black/African American	73
Amer. Indian/Alaska Natv.	2
Asian	1,580
Natv. Hawaiian/Pac. Islander	0
Other Race	38
Two or more races	72
Hispanic origin, total	260
Mexican	10
Puerto Rican	24
Cuban	96
Other Hispanic	130

Age & Nativity, 2000

Under 5 years	304
18 years and over	4,221
21 years and over	4,098
65 years and over	1,171
85 years and over	106
Median Age	44.8
Native born	3,261
Foreign born	2,061

Educational Attainment, 2000

Population 25 years and over	3,921
0-8 yrs of school	4.6%
High School grad or higher	92.7%
Bachelor's degree or higher	52.5%
Graduate degree	23.7%

Income & Poverty, 1999

Per capita income	$57,399
Median household income	$106,478
Median family income	$113,187
Persons in poverty	136
H'holds receiving public assistance	20
H'holds receiving social security	660

Households, 2000

Total households	1,818
With persons under 18	599
With persons over 65	775
Family households	1,560
One-person households	228
Persons per household	2.9
Persons per family	3.16

Labor & Employment

Total civilian labor force, 2004**	3,001
Unemployment rate	2.2%
Total civilian labor force, 2000	2,577
Unemployment rate	3.4%

Employed persons 16 years and over by occupation, 2000
Managers & professionals	1,421
Service occupations	135
Sales & office occupations	760
Farming, fishing & forestry	0
Construction & maintenance	79
Production & transportation	94
Self-employed persons	269

*US Census Bureau
**New Jersey Department of Labor

General Information

Borough of Englewood Cliffs
10 Kahn Terrace
Englewood Cliffs, NJ 07632
201-569-5252

Web site	NA
Land area (sq. miles)	2.09
Water area (sq. miles)	1.29
Type of government	Borough
Form of government	B

Government

Legislative Districts

US Congressional	9
State Legislative	37

Local Officials, 2006

Mayor	Joseph Parisi
Admin/Manager	Joseph Favaro
Clerk	Joseph Favaro
Finance Dir/Treas	Joseph Iannaconi
Engineer	Stephen Boswell
Attorney	Michael Kates
Tax assessor	George Reggo
Tax collector	Joseph Iannaconi
Building officer	Alan Marcus
Zoning officer	NA
Public Works	Rodney Bialko

Housing & Construction

Housing Units, 2000*

Total	1,889
Median rent	$2,001
Median SF home value	$507,100

New Privately Owned Housing Units Authorized by Building Permit

	Units	Value
Total, 2004	42	$17,513,740
Single family	42	$17,513,740
Total, 2005	34	$18,385,186
Single family	34	$18,385,186

Real Property Valuation - parcels, 2005

	Number	Valuation
Total		$2,019,660,100
Vacant	87	38,990,500
Residential	1,905	1,297,156,300
Commercial	113	681,157,200
Industrial	1	1,383,600
Apartments	1	972,500
Farm land	0	0
Farm homestead	0	0

Average Property Value & Tax, 2005

Residential value	$680,922
Property tax	$6,918
FAIR rebate	$710

Public Library

No public municipal library.

Library statistics, 2004

	Total	per capita
Volumes	NA	NA
Expenditure	NA	NA

Public Safety

Police

Chief	Lawrence Whiting
Number of officers, 2004	27

Crime, 2004	Number	Rate
Total	125	22.5
Violent	10	1.8
Non-violent	115	20.7
Domestic Viol.	19	NA

Emergency/Fire

Director | George Drimones

Public School District

(for school year 2004-2005 except as noted)

Englewood Cliffs School District
143 Charlotte Place
Englewood Cliffs, NJ 07632
201-567-7292

Superintendent	Philomena Pezzano
Grade plan	K-12
Enrollment	437.0
Students per teacher	7.8
Per pupil expenditure	$19,555
Median faculty salary	$47,691
Median administrator salary	$118,437
Grade 12 enrollment	NA
High school graduation rate	NA

Assessment test results

(percent scoring at proficient or advanced level)
	Language	Math
Grade 3	97.0%	98.5%
Grade 8	89.2%	84.2%
High school	NA	NA

SAT

Percent tested	NA
Average SAT math score	NA
Average SAT verbal score	NA

No Child Left Behind, 2003-04

Attendence rate (target = 90%)	95.9%
Drop rate	NA
Highly-qualified teachers	93.3%
District needs improvement?(AYP)	No

Municipal Finance

Fiscal Year 2005

Total tax levy	$20,532,330
County levy	4,448,145
County taxes	4,220,337
County library	0
County health	0
County open space	227,808
School levy	8,088,766
Local muni. budget	7,995,419
Misc. revenues	3,199,550
Total aid	$1,069,801
CMPTRA	349,664
Muni. block grant	24,652
Energy tax receipts	645,485
Homeland security	50,000

Fiscal Year 2006

Total aid	$1,069,801
CMPTRA	327,072
Muni. block grant	24,652
Energy tax receipts	668,077
Homeland security	50,000

Taxes

	2003	2004	2005
General tax rate per $100	0.94	0.950	1.020
Net valuation taxable	$1,948,052,675	$1,994,134,724	$2,021,066,288
State equalized value	$1,962,575,735	$2,217,698,577	$2,557,987,961
County equalization ratio	102.21	99.26	89.91

Demographics & Socio-Economic Characteristics
(2000 U.S. Census, except as noted)

Population
1980*	976
1990*	1,268
2000	1,764
Male	843
Female	921
2004 (estimate)*	1,814
Persons per sq. mi. of land	3,190

Race & Hispanic Origin, 2000
Race
White	1,559
Black/African American	73
Amer. Indian/Alaska Natv.	2
Asian	79
Natv. Hawaiian/Pac. Islander	0
Other Race	29
Two or more races	22
Hispanic origin, total	110
Mexican	14
Puerto Rican	49
Cuban	16
Other Hispanic	31

Age & Nativity, 2000
Under 5 years	161
18 years and over	1,251
21 years and over	1,204
65 years and over	194
85 years and over	52
Median Age	34.9
Native born	1,556
Foreign born	208

Educational Attainment, 2000
Population 25 years and over	1,162
0-8 yrs of school	7.2%
High School grad or higher	81.6%
Bachelor's degree or higher	18.8%
Graduate degree	5.9%

Income & Poverty, 1999
Per capita income	$23,438
Median household income	$57,557
Median family income	$73,750
Persons in poverty	126
H'holds receiving public assistance	13
H'holds receiving social security	177

Households, 2000
Total households	643
With persons under 18	269
With persons over 65	161
Family households	416
One-person households	183
Persons per household	2.74
Persons per family	3.51

Labor & Employment
Total civilian labor force, 2004**	752
Unemployment rate	4.8%
Total civilian labor force, 2000	881
Unemployment rate	3.5%

Employed persons 16 years and over by occupation, 2000
Managers & professionals	266
Service occupations	133
Sales & office occupations	230
Farming, fishing & forestry	1
Construction & maintenance	113
Production & transportation	107
Self-employed persons	47

*US Census Bureau
**New Jersey Department of Labor

General Information
Borough of Englishtown
15 Main St
Englishtown, NJ 07726
732-446-9235

Web site	www.englishtownnj.com
Land area (sq. miles)	0.57
Water area (sq. miles)	0.01
Type of government	Borough
Form of government	B

Government

Legislative Districts
US Congressional	12
State Legislative	12

Local Officials, 2006
Mayor	Thomas E. Reynolds
Admin/Manager	Laurie Finger
Clerk	Julie Martin
Finance Dir/Treas	Laurie Finger
Engineer	Thomas Herits
Attorney	Stuart Moskovitz
Tax assessor	Sharon Hartman
Tax collector	Janice Garcia
Building officer	Richard Hogan
Zoning officer	NA
Public Works	NA

Housing & Construction

Housing Units, 2000*
Total	680
Median rent	$772
Median SF home value	$150,600

New Privately Owned Housing Units
Authorized by Building Permit
	Units	Value
Total, 2004	8	$848,945
Single family	8	$848,945
Total, 2005	46	$4,493,405
Single family	46	$4,493,405

Real Property Valuation - parcels, 2005
	Number	Valuation
Total		$93,512,500
Vacant	33	1,576,400
Residential	562	74,384,600
Commercial	30	13,476,100
Industrial	5	3,275,900
Apartments	2	633,000
Farm land	1	164,000
Farm homestead	1	2,500

Average Property Value & Tax, 2005
Residential value	$132,126
Property tax	$4,876
FAIR rebate	$572

Public Library

No public municipal library.

Library statistics, 2004
	Total	per capita
Volumes	NA	NA
Expenditure	NA	NA

Public Safety

Police
Chief	John Niziolek
Number of officers, 2004	8

Crime, 2004	Number	Rate
Total	17	9.5
Violent	5	2.8
Non-violent	12	6.7
Domestic Viol.	2	NA

Emergency/Fire
Director	Ralph Kirkland

Public School District
(for school year 2004-2005 except as noted)

Manalapan-Englishtown Reg. School Dist.
54 Main St
Englishtown, NJ 07726
732-786-2500

Superintendent	Maureen Lally
Grade plan	K-8
Enrollment	5,486.0
Students per teacher	12.3
Per pupil expenditure	$9,756
Median faculty salary	$49,200
Median administrator salary	$90,160
Grade 12 enrollment	NA
High school graduation rate	NA

Assessment test results
(percent scoring at proficient or advanced level)
	Language	Math
Grade 3	93.9%	88.5%
Grade 8	92.5%	82.7%
High school	NA	NA

SAT
Percent tested	NA
Average SAT math score	NA
Average SAT verbal score	NA

No Child Left Behind, 2003-04
Attendance rate (target = 90%)	95.5%
Drop rate	NA
Highly-qualified teachers	97.8%
District needs improvement?(AYP)	No

Municipal Finance

Fiscal Year 2005
Total tax levy	$3,514,469
County levy	583,647
County taxes	515,289
County library	28,384
County health	9,396
County open space	30,578
School levy	2,240,731
Local muni. budget	690,091
Misc. revenues	1,246,216
Total aid	$238,303
CMPTRA	112,793
Muni. block grant	6,917
Energy tax receipts	93,593
Homeland security	25,000

Fiscal Year 2006
Total aid	$238,304
CMPTRA	109,518
Muni. block grant	6,917
Energy tax receipts	96,869
Homeland security	25,000

Taxes
	2003	2004	2005
General tax rate per $100	3.36	3.604	3.691
Net valuation taxable	$96,066,387	$94,551,582	$95,237,609
State equalized value	$153,362,687	$169,651,537	$191,125,043
County equalization ratio	73.14	62.64	55.21

Demographics & Socio-Economic Characteristics

(2000 U.S. Census, except as noted)

Population

1980*	2,363
1990*	2,139
2000	2,162
Male	1,064
Female	1,098
2004 (estimate)*	2,130
Persons per sq. mi. of land	1,511

Race & Hispanic Origin, 2000

Race

White	2,096
Black/African American	10
Amer. Indian/Alaska Natv.	4
Asian	22
Natv. Hawaiian/Pac. Islander	0
Other Race	3
Two or more races	27
Hispanic origin, total	26
Mexican	1
Puerto Rican	3
Cuban	4
Other Hispanic	18

Age & Nativity, 2000

Under 5 years	198
18 years and over	1,520
21 years and over	1,484
65 years and over	318
85 years and over	27
Median Age	40.3
Native born	2,004
Foreign born	158

Educational Attainment, 2000

Population 25 years and over	1,438
0-8 yrs of school	1.2%
High School grad or higher	97.1%
Bachelor's degree or higher	72.4%
Graduate degree	32.0%

Income & Poverty, 1999

Per capita income	$77,434
Median household income	$148,173
Median family income	$175,000
Persons in poverty	23
H'holds receiving public assistance	3
H'holds receiving social security	219

Households, 2000

Total households	737
With persons under 18	304
With persons over 65	222
Family households	605
One-person households	111
Persons per household	2.93
Persons per family	3.28

Labor & Employment

Total civilian labor force, 2004**	34,761
Unemployment rate	8.0%
Total civilian labor force, 2000	954
Unemployment rate	1.2%

Employed persons 16 years and over by occupation, 2000

Managers & professionals	617
Service occupations	43
Sales & office occupations	247
Farming, fishing & forestry	0
Construction & maintenance	23
Production & transportation	13
Self-employed persons	110

*US Census Bureau
**New Jersey Department of Labor

General Information

Borough of Essex Fells
255 Roseland Ave
Essex Fells, NJ 07021
973-226-3400

Web site	www.essexfellsboro.com
Land area (sq. miles)	1.41
Water area (sq. miles)	0
Type of government	Borough
Form of government	B

Government

Legislative Districts

US Congressional	11
State Legislative	27

Local Officials, 2006

Mayor	Edward P. Abbot
Admin/Manager	Frank Bastone
Clerk	Francine T. Paserchia
Finance Dir/Treas	Kerry Geisler
Engineer	Frank Ziccelli
Attorney	Martin Murphy
Tax assessor	Jack Kelly
Tax collector	Kerry Geisler
Building officer	Robert Young
Zoning officer	Robert Young
Public Works	Roger Kerr

Housing & Construction

Housing Units, 2000*

Total	761
Median rent	$1,656
Median SF home value	$584,100

New Privately Owned Housing Units Authorized by Building Permit

	Units	Value
Total, 2004	2	$2,553,700
Single family	2	$2,553,700
Total, 2005	1	$1,436,600
Single family	1	$1,436,600

Real Property Valuation - parcels, 2005

	Number	Valuation
Total		$808,820,000
Vacant	34	7,903,700
Residential	748	778,885,700
Commercial	6	22,030,600
Industrial	0	0
Apartments	0	0
Farm land	0	0
Farm homestead	0	0

Average Property Value & Tax, 2005

Residential value	$1,041,291
Property tax	$14,503
FAIR rebate	$631

Public Library

No public municipal library.

Library statistics, 2004

	Total	per capita
Volumes	NA	NA
Expenditure	NA	NA

Public Safety

Police

Chief	Kelly J. Reilly
Number of officers, 2004	13

Crime, 2004	Number	Rate
Total	15	7
Violent	1	0.5
Non-violent	14	6.5
Domestic Viol.	5	NA

Emergency/Fire

Director	James Egan

Public School District

(for school year 2004-2005 except as noted)

Essex Fells School District
102 Hawthorne Rd
Essex Fells, NJ 07021
973-226-0505

Superintendent	Raymond Hyman
Grade plan	K-6
Enrollment	273.0
Students per teacher	10.7
Per pupil expenditure	$10,182
Median faculty salary	$46,634
Median administrator salary	$82,729
Grade 12 enrollment	NA
High school graduation rate	NA

Assessment test results

(percent scoring at proficient or advanced level)

	Language	Math
Grade 3	100.0%	100%
Grade 8	NA	NA
High school	NA	NA

SAT

Percent tested	NA
Average SAT math score	NA
Average SAT verbal score	NA

No Child Left Behind, 2003-04

Attendence rate (target = 90%)	95.9%
Drop rate	NA
Highly-qualified teachers	100%
District needs improvement?(AYP)	No

Municipal Finance

Fiscal Year 2005

Total tax levy	$11,269,383
County levy	3,319,803
County taxes	3,250,334
County library	0
County health	0
County open space	69,468
School levy	5,569,874
Local muni. budget	2,379,707
Misc. revenues	2,334,607
Total aid	$278,205
CMPTRA	29,022
Muni. block grant	9,359
Energy tax receipts	214,824
Homeland security	25,000

Fiscal Year 2006

Total aid	$278,205
CMPTRA	21,503
Muni. block grant	9,359
Energy tax receipts	222,343
Homeland security	25,000

Taxes

	2003	2004	2005
General tax rate per $100	14.04	1.300	1.400
Net valuation taxable	$70,645,013	$814,258,058	$809,115,363
State equalized value	$597,168,326	$697,024,801	$807,903,508
County equalization ratio	12.88	12.88	116.82

Demographics & Socio-Economic Characteristics

(2000 U.S. Census, except as noted)

Population

1980*	848
1990*	1,404
2000	1,585
Male	800
Female	785
2004 (estimate)*	1,707
Persons per sq. mi. of land	32

Race & Hispanic Origin, 2000

Race

White	1,493
Black/African American	57
Amer. Indian/Alaska Natv.	7
Asian	5
Natv. Hawaiian/Pac. Islander	0
Other Race	2
Two or more races	21
Hispanic origin, total	15
Mexican	1
Puerto Rican	10
Cuban	0
Other Hispanic	4

Age & Nativity, 2000

Under 5 years	111
18 years and over	1,107
21 years and over	1,053
65 years and over	153
85 years and over	13
Median Age	36.6
Native born	1,522
Foreign born	70

Educational Attainment, 2000

Population 25 years and over	1,008
0-8 yrs of school	4.1%
High School grad or higher	84.8%
Bachelor's degree or higher	17.0%
Graduate degree	4.9%

Income & Poverty, 1999

Per capita income	$19,469
Median household income	$54,653
Median family income	$56,548
Persons in poverty	77
H'holds receiving public assistance	10
H'holds receiving social security	133

Households, 2000

Total households	528
With persons under 18	234
With persons over 65	116
Family households	433
One-person households	73
Persons per household	2.95
Persons per family	3.27

Labor & Employment

Total civilian labor force, 2004**	756
Unemployment rate	3.0%
Total civilian labor force, 2000	729
Unemployment rate	5.8%

Employed persons 16 years and over by occupation, 2000

Managers & professionals	238
Service occupations	111
Sales & office occupations	155
Farming, fishing & forestry	2
Construction & maintenance	105
Production & transportation	76
Self-employed persons	46

*US Census Bureau
**New Jersey Department of Labor

General Information

City of Estell Manor
PO Box 102
Estell Manor, NJ 08319
609-476-2692

Web site	NA
Land area (sq. miles)	53.57
Water area (sq. miles)	1.34
Type of government	City
Form of government	SM '50

Government

Legislative Districts

US Congressional	2
State Legislative	2

Local Officials, 2006

Mayor	Joseph Venezia
Admin/Manager	NA
Clerk	Catherine Cornew
Finance Dir/Treas	Dawn Gorman
Engineer	J. Michael Fralinger
Attorney	Daniel Gallagher
Tax assessor	James Mancini
Tax collector	NA
Building officer	Charles Kane
Zoning officer	NA
Public Works	NA

Housing & Construction

Housing Units, 2000*

Total	546
Median rent	$838
Median SF home value	$123,500

New Privately Owned Housing Units Authorized by Building Permit

	Units	Value
Total, 2004	11	$1,285,026
Single family	11	$1,285,026
Total, 2005	8	$642,590
Single family	8	$642,590

Real Property Valuation - parcels, 2005

	Number	Valuation
Total		$113,515,000
Vacant	824	13,238,900
Residential	706	90,412,400
Commercial	6	3,372,200
Industrial	5	1,573,300
Apartments	1	700,000
Farm land	17	2,568,500
Farm homestead	48	1,649,700

Average Property Value & Tax, 2005

Residential value	$122,098
Property tax	$2,939
FAIR rebate	$537

Public Library

No public municipal library.

Library statistics, 2004

	Total	per capita
Volumes	NA	NA
Expenditure	NA	NA

Public Safety

Police

Chief	NA
Number of officers, 2004	0

Crime, 2004	Number	Rate
Total	24	14.5
Violent	0	0
Non-violent	24	14.5
Domestic Viol.	11	NA

Emergency/Fire

Director	John Wagner

Public School District

(for school year 2004-2005 except as noted)

Estell Manor City School District
128 Cape May Ave
Estell Manor, NJ 08319
609-476-2267

Superintendent	John Cressey
Grade plan	K-12
Enrollment	220.0
Students per teacher	9.2
Per pupil expenditure	$11,255
Median faculty salary	$47,400
Median administrator salary	$82,800
Grade 12 enrollment	NA
High school graduation rate	NA

Assessment test results

(percent scoring at proficient or advanced level)

	Language	Math
Grade 3	82.8%	86.2%
Grade 8	81.8%	59.0%
High school	NA	NA

SAT

Percent tested	NA
Average SAT math score	NA
Average SAT verbal score	NA

No Child Left Behind, 2003-04

Attendence rate (target = 90%)	95.6%
Drop rate	NA
Highly-qualified teachers	100%
District needs improvement?(AYP)	No

Municipal Finance

Fiscal Year 2005

Total tax levy	$2,745,358
County levy	569,523
County taxes	464,978
County library	51,505
County health	25,346
County open space	27,694
School levy	1,981,804
Local muni. budget	194,031
Misc. revenues	1,168,709
Total aid	$259,363
CMPTRA	49,301
Muni. block grant	6,215
Energy tax receipts	203,847
Homeland security	0

Fiscal Year 2006

Total aid	$259,363
CMPTRA	42,167
Muni. block grant	6,215
Energy tax receipts	210,981
Homeland security	NA

Taxes

	2003	2004	2005
General tax rate per $100	2.08	2.276	2.408
Net valuation taxable	$109,762,031	$111,034,227	$114,052,299
State equalized value	$121,498,817	$134,427,644	$164,625,143
County equalization ratio	102.5	90.34	82.52

Demographics & Socio-Economic Characteristics
(2000 U.S. Census, except as noted)

Population
1980*	21,659
1990*	35,309
2000	42,275
Male	20,498
Female	21,777
2004 (estimate)*	46,858
Persons per sq. mi. of land	1,586

Race & Hispanic Origin, 2000
Race
White	38,579
Black/African American	1,313
Amer. Indian/Alaska Natv.	31
Asian	1,721
Natv. Hawaiian/Pac. Islander	8
Other Race	203
Two or more races	420
Hispanic origin, total	829
Mexican	136
Puerto Rican	330
Cuban	81
Other Hispanic	282

Age & Nativity, 2000
Under 5 years	3,090
18 years and over	30,790
21 years and over	29,702
65 years and over	3,750
85 years and over	368
Median Age	36
Native born	39,688
Foreign born	2,740

Educational Attainment, 2000
Population 25 years and over	28,565
0-8 yrs of school	1.5%
High School grad or higher	93.3%
Bachelor's degree or higher	39.7%
Graduate degree	12.3%

Income & Poverty, 1999
Per capita income	$29,494
Median household income	$67,010
Median family income	$77,245
Persons in poverty	1,174
H'holds receiving public assistance	123
H'holds receiving social security	3,011

Households, 2000
Total households	15,712
With persons under 18	6,297
With persons over 65	2,733
Family households	11,346
One-person households	3,584
Persons per household	2.68
Persons per family	3.21

Labor & Employment
Total civilian labor force, 2004**	23,646
Unemployment rate	2.4%
Total civilian labor force, 2000	23,374
Unemployment rate	2.6%

Employed persons 16 years and over by occupation, 2000
Managers & professionals	10,930
Service occupations	2,200
Sales & office occupations	7,092
Farming, fishing & forestry	8
Construction & maintenance	1,158
Production & transportation	1,382
Self-employed persons	1,228

*US Census Bureau
**New Jersey Department of Labor

General Information
Township of Evesham
984 Tuckerton Rd
Marlton, NJ 08053
856-983-2900

Web site	www.evesham-nj.gov
Land area (sq. miles)	29.54
Water area (sq. miles)	0.17
Type of government	Township
Form of government	CM '50

Government
Legislative Districts
US Congressional	3
State Legislative	8

Local Officials, 2006
Mayor	Augustus Tamburro
Admin/Manager	Edward Sasdelli
Clerk	Carmela Bonfrisco
Finance Dir/Treas	Eileen Zaharchak
Engineer	James Ruddiman
Attorney	John Gillespie
Tax assessor	Blackwell Albertson
Tax collector	Kathie Sanders
Building officer	Carlos Martinez
Zoning officer	F. Robert Perry
Public Works	Paul Tomasetti

Housing & Construction
Housing Units, 2000*
Total	16,324
Median rent	$886
Median SF home value	$157,000

New Privately Owned Housing Units
Authorized by Building Permit
	Units	Value
Total, 2004	135	$17,041,545
Single family	135	$17,041,545
Total, 2005	46	$9,476,682
Single family	46	$9,476,682

Real Property Valuation - parcels, 2005
	Number	Valuation
Total		$2,760,016,100
Vacant	865	26,635,200
Residential	14,973	2,191,515,000
Commercial	477	408,684,000
Industrial	18	20,048,300
Apartments	22	106,365,100
Farm land	45	6,052,800
Farm homestead	96	715,700

Average Property Value & Tax, 2005
Residential value	$145,480
Property tax	$5,651
FAIR rebate	$492

Public Library
Evesham Branch Library†
984 Tuckerton Rd
Marlton, NJ 08053
856-983-1444

Branch Librarian	Susan Szymanik

Library statistics, 2004
	Total	per capita
Volumes	NA	NA
Expenditure	NA	NA

†Branch of County Library

Public Safety
Police
Chief	Joseph Cornely
Number of officers, 2004	73

Crime, 2004	Number	Rate
Total	756	16.4
Violent	49	1.1
Non-violent	707	15.3
Domestic Viol.	303	NA

Emergency/Fire
Director	Ted Lowden

Public School District
(for school year 2004-2005 except as noted)

Evesham Township School District
25 S Maple Ave
Marlton, NJ 08053
856-983-1800

Superintendent	Patricia Lucas
Grade plan	K-8
Enrollment	5,277.0
Students per teacher	11.2
Per pupil expenditure	$11,398
Median faculty salary	$46,500
Median administrator salary	$93,650
Grade 12 enrollment	NA
High school graduation rate	NA

Assessment test results
(percent scoring at proficient or advanced level)
	Language	Math
Grade 3	89.1%	87.1%
Grade 8	86.6%	77.5%
High school	NA	NA

SAT
Percent tested	NA
Average SAT math score	NA
Average SAT verbal score	NA

No Child Left Behind, 2003-04
Attendence rate (target = 90%)	96.3%
Drop rate	NA
Highly-qualified teachers	99.2%
District needs improvement?(AYP)	No

Municipal Finance
Fiscal Year 2005
Total tax levy	$107,617,134
County levy	19,394,936
County taxes	16,270,247
County library	1,424,641
County health	0
County open space	1,700,048
School levy	74,064,249
Local muni. budget	14,157,949
Misc. revenues	14,433,239
Total aid	$4,476,334
CMPTRA	1,532,311
Muni. block grant	165,761
Energy tax receipts	2,572,110
Homeland security	140,000

Fiscal Year 2006
Total aid	$4,476,333
CMPTRA	1,442,287
Muni. block grant	165,761
Energy tax receipts	2,662,133
Homeland security	140,000

Taxes
	2003	2004	2005
General tax rate per $100	3.44	3.725	3.885
Net valuation taxable	$2,641,630,956	$2,724,297,149	$2,770,634,123
State equalized value	$3,763,007,060	$4,172,251,226	$4,675,386,640
County equalization ratio	81.53	70.20	65.20

Demographics & Socio-Economic Characteristics

(2000 U.S. Census, except as noted)

Population

1980*	34,842
1990*	34,185
2000	35,707
Male	17,203
Female	18,504
2004 (estimate)*	37,057
Persons per sq. mi. of land	2,417

Race & Hispanic Origin, 2000

Race

White	24,645
Black/African American	8,863
Amer. Indian/Alaska Natv.	55
Asian	811
Natv. Hawaiian/Pac. Islander	22
Other Race	653
Two or more races	658
Hispanic origin, total	1,586
Mexican	97
Puerto Rican	900
Cuban	72
Other Hispanic	517

Age & Nativity, 2000

Under 5 years	1,623
18 years and over	29,263
21 years and over	25,573
65 years and over	5,631
85 years and over	761
Median Age	37
Native born	32,778
Foreign born	2,929

Educational Attainment, 2000

Population 25 years and over	23,114
0-8 yrs of school	4.7%
High School grad or higher	84.1%
Bachelor's degree or higher	29.1%
Graduate degree	12.0%

Income & Poverty, 1999

Per capita income	$24,268
Median household income	$57,274
Median family income	$67,618
Persons in poverty	1,964
H'holds receiving public assistance	155
H'holds receiving social security	4,007

Households, 2000

Total households	12,551
With persons under 18	3,645
With persons over 65	3,978
Family households	8,211
One-person households	3,480
Persons per household	2.45
Persons per family	3

Labor & Employment

Total civilian labor force, 2004**	20,381
Unemployment rate	3.1%
Total civilian labor force, 2000	18,364
Unemployment rate	4.6%

Employed persons 16 years and over by occupation, 2000

Managers & professionals	6,765
Service occupations	2,785
Sales & office occupations	5,269
Farming, fishing & forestry	26
Construction & maintenance	1,013
Production & transportation	1,664
Self-employed persons	686

*US Census Bureau
**New Jersey Department of Labor

General Information

Township of Ewing
2 Jake Garzio Dr
Ewing, NJ 08628
609-883-2900

Web site	www.ewingtwp.net
Land area (sq. miles)	15.33
Water area (sq. miles)	0.27
Type of government	Township
Form of government	TC

Government

Legislative Districts

US Congressional	12
State Legislative	15

Local Officials, 2006

Mayor	Wendell Pribila
Admin/Manager	Jim McManimon
Clerk	Charles Green (Actg)
Finance Dir/Treas	Shannon Keyes
Engineer	Schoor DePalma
Attorney	Maeve Cannon
Tax assessor	Jeff Burd
Tax collector	Thomas Hespe
Building officer	William Erney
Zoning officer	William Erney
Public Works	Jim McManimon

Housing & Construction

Housing Units, 2000*

Total	12,924
Median rent	$720
Median SF home value	$133,100

New Privately Owned Housing Units Authorized by Building Permit

	Units	Value
Total, 2004	212	$25,267,535
Single family	20	$2,442,535
Total, 2005	51	$5,983,689
Single family	25	$2,892,804

Real Property Valuation - parcels, 2005

	Number	Valuation
Total		$1,772,191,250
Vacant	697	21,225,300
Residential	10,323	1,259,468,500
Commercial	581	404,333,450
Industrial	20	17,769,300
Apartments	19	68,868,500
Farm land	1	461,700
Farm homestead	3	64,500

Average Property Value & Tax, 2005

Residential value	$121,977
Property tax	$4,804
FAIR rebate	$621

Public Library

Ewing Branch Library†
61 Scotch Rd
W. Trenton, NJ 08628
609-882-3130

Branch Librarian	Jacquelyn Huff

Library statistics, 2004

	Total	per capita
Volumes	NA	NA
Expenditure	NA	NA

†Branch of County Library

Public Safety

Police

Chief	Robert Coulton
Number of officers, 2004	78

Crime, 2004	Number	Rate
Total	1,039	28.4
Violent	92	2.5
Non-violent	947	25.9
Domestic Viol.	222	NA

Emergency/Fire

Director	NA

Public School District

(for school year 2004-2005 except as noted)

Ewing Township School District
1331 Lower Ferry Rd
Ewing, NJ 08618
609-538-9800

Superintendent	Raymond Broach
Grade plan	K-12
Enrollment	4,247.0
Students per teacher	11.7
Per pupil expenditure	$11,861
Median faculty salary	$49,400
Median administrator salary	$112,309
Grade 12 enrollment	248.5
High school graduation rate	91.4%

Assessment test results

(percent scoring at proficient or advanced level)

	Language	Math
Grade 3	85.0%	76.5%
Grade 8	72.4%	50.6%
High school	82.6%	66.7%

SAT

Percent tested	68%
Average SAT math score	488
Average SAT verbal score	481

No Child Left Behind, 2003-04

Attendence rate (target = 90%)	95.6%
Drop rate	1.2%
Highly-qualified teachers	98.7%
District needs improvement?(AYP)	No

Municipal Finance

Fiscal Year 2005

Total tax levy	$70,215,706
County levy	16,145,376
County taxes	14,102,816
County library	1,250,381
County health	0
County open space	792,180
School levy	44,719,712
Local muni. budget	9,350,618
Misc. revenues	28,869,455
Total aid	$13,114,268
CMPTRA	10,349,993
Muni. block grant	149,582
Energy tax receipts	2,474,693
Homeland security	140,000

Fiscal Year 2006

Total aid	$13,114,267
CMPTRA	10,263,378
Muni. block grant	149,582
Energy tax receipts	2,561,307
Homeland security	140,000

Taxes

	2003	2004	2005
General tax rate per $100	3.73	3.780	3.940
Net valuation taxable	$1,747,085,150	$1,758,782,989	$1,782,975,217
State equalized value	$2,416,438,658	$2,558,808,553	$2,931,560,699
County equalization ratio	80.83	72.30	68.60

Demographics & Socio-Economic Characteristics

(2000 U.S. Census, except as noted)

Population

1980*	5,679
1990*	5,270
2000	5,937
Male	2,877
Female	3,060
2004 (estimate)*	5,961
Persons per sq. mi. of land	3,574

Race & Hispanic Origin, 2000

Race
White	5,573
Black/African American	243
Amer. Indian/Alaska Natv.	2
Asian	58
Natv. Hawaiian/Pac. Islander	0
Other Race	13
Two or more races	48
Hispanic origin, total	79
Mexican	10
Puerto Rican	8
Cuban	14
Other Hispanic	47

Age & Nativity, 2000

Under 5 years	537
18 years and over	3,976
21 years and over	3,858
65 years and over	614
85 years and over	65
Median Age	37.4
Native born	5,655
Foreign born	282

Educational Attainment, 2000

Population 25 years and over	3,747
0-8 yrs of school	1.4%
High School grad or higher	97.1%
Bachelor's degree or higher	61.8%
Graduate degree	26.4%

Income & Poverty, 1999

Per capita income	$44,018
Median household income	$97,220
Median family income	$109,760
Persons in poverty	139
H'holds receiving public assistance	7
H'holds receiving social security	424

Households, 2000

Total households	1,998
With persons under 18	980
With persons over 65	438
Family households	1,658
One-person households	304
Persons per household	2.97
Persons per family	3.33

Labor & Employment

Total civilian labor force, 2004**	2,989
Unemployment rate	4.7%
Total civilian labor force, 2000	2,728
Unemployment rate	2.9%

Employed persons 16 years and over by occupation, 2000
Managers & professionals	1,474
Service occupations	183
Sales & office occupations	717
Farming, fishing & forestry	5
Construction & maintenance	164
Production & transportation	107
Self-employed persons	298

*US Census Bureau
**New Jersey Department of Labor

General Information

Borough of Fair Haven
748 River Rd
Fair Haven, NJ 07704
732-747-0241

Web site	www.fairhavennj.net
Land area (sq. miles)	1.67
Water area (sq. miles)	0.01
Type of government	Borough
Form of government	B

Government

Legislative Districts

US Congressional	12
State Legislative	12

Local Officials, 2006

Mayor	Joseph Szostak
Admin/Manager	Julie Horner-Keizer
Clerk	Julie Horner-Keizer
Finance Dir/Treas	Mike Martin
Engineer	Richard Moralle
Attorney	Salvatore Alfieri
Tax assessor	Stephen Walters
Tax collector	Dale Connor
Building officer	Paul Reinhold
Zoning officer	Paul Reinhold
Public Works	Tom Curcio

Housing & Construction

Housing Units, 2000*

Total	2,037
Median rent	$1,219
Median SF home value	$305,900

New Privately Owned Housing Units Authorized by Building Permit

	Units	Value
Total, 2004	18	$3,977,138
Single family	18	$3,977,138
Total, 2005	13	$2,479,664
Single family	13	$2,479,664

Real Property Valuation - parcels, 2005

	Number	Valuation
Total		$1,104,561,500
Vacant	42	7,457,300
Residential	2,016	1,060,201,400
Commercial	63	36,902,800
Industrial	0	0
Apartments	0	0
Farm land	0	0
Farm homestead	0	0

Average Property Value & Tax, 2005

Residential value	$525,894
Property tax	$10,589
FAIR rebate	$432

Public Library

Fair Haven Public Library
748 River Rd
Fair Haven, NJ 07704
732-747-5031

Director.............Donna Powers

Library statistics, 2004

	Total	per capita
Volumes	NA	NA
Expenditure	NA	NA

Public Safety

Police

Chief	Darryl Breckenridge
Number of officers, 2004	13

Crime, 2004	Number	Rate
Total	51	8.6
Violent	4	0.7
Non-violent	47	7.9
Domestic Viol.	2	NA

Emergency/Fire

Director.................Paul Lenskold

Public School District

(for school year 2004-2005 except as noted)

Fair Haven Borough School District
224 Hance Rd
Fair Haven, NJ 07704
732-747-2294

Superintendent	William Presutti
Grade plan	K-8
Enrollment	973.0
Students per teacher	11.7
Per pupil expenditure	$8,713
Median faculty salary	$44,775
Median administrator salary	$104,165
Grade 12 enrollment	NA
High school graduation rate	NA

Assessment test results

(percent scoring at proficient or advanced level)
	Language	Math
Grade 3	97.2%	89.8%
Grade 8	89.8%	83.3%
High school	NA	NA

SAT

Percent tested	NA
Average SAT math score	NA
Average SAT verbal score	NA

No Child Left Behind, 2003-04

Attendence rate (target = 90%)	95.8%
Drop rate	NA
Highly-qualified teachers	99.6%
District needs improvement?(AYP)	No

Municipal Finance

Fiscal Year 2005

Total tax levy	$22,248,272
County levy	3,938,219
County taxes	3,533,865
County library	194,664
County health	0
County open space	209,690
School levy	13,453,461
Local muni. budget	4,856,591
Misc. revenues	1,904,840
Total aid	$724,579
CMPTRA	219,423
Muni. block grant	23,279
Energy tax receipts	431,877
Homeland security	50,000

Fiscal Year 2006

Total aid	$724,579
CMPTRA	204,307
Muni. block grant	23,279
Energy tax receipts	446,993
Homeland security	50,000

Taxes

	2003	2004	2005
General tax rate per $100	1.77	1.848	2.014
Net valuation taxable	$1,098,367,430	$1,099,256,983	$1,104,975,059
State equalized value	$1,041,995,475	$1,173,385,577	$1,315,289,917
County equalization ratio	60.18	105.41	96.68

Demographics & Socio-Economic Characteristics
(2000 U.S. Census, except as noted)

Population
1980*	32,229
1990*	30,548
2000	31,637
Male	15,039
Female	16,598
2004 (estimate)*	31,613
Persons per sq. mi. of land	6,116

Race & Hispanic Origin, 2000
Race
White	28,960
Black/African American	234
Amer. Indian/Alaska Natv.	13
Asian	1,558
Natv. Hawaiian/Pac. Islander	1
Other Race	434
Two or more races	437
Hispanic origin, total	1,744
Mexican	55
Puerto Rican	456
Cuban	171
Other Hispanic	1,062

Age & Nativity, 2000
Under 5 years	1,673
18 years and over	24,423
21 years and over	23,584
65 years and over	5,919
85 years and over	711
Median Age	41.8
Native born	23,161
Foreign born	8,476

Educational Attainment, 2000
Population 25 years and over	22,452
0-8 yrs of school	3.3%
High School grad or higher	89.9%
Bachelor's degree or higher	44.8%
Graduate degree	17.6%

Income & Poverty, 1999
Per capita income	$32,273
Median household income	$72,127
Median family income	$81,220
Persons in poverty	1,161
H'holds receiving public assistance	86
H'holds receiving social security	3,823

Households, 2000
Total households	11,806
With persons under 18	4,135
With persons over 65	4,163
Family households	8,906
One-person households	2,516
Persons per household	2.67
Persons per family	3.12

Labor & Employment
Total civilian labor force, 2004**	16,870
Unemployment rate	3.4%
Total civilian labor force, 2000	16,156
Unemployment rate	2.7%

Employed persons 16 years and over by occupation, 2000
Managers & professionals	7,563
Service occupations	1,428
Sales & office occupations	4,602
Farming, fishing & forestry	0
Construction & maintenance	912
Production & transportation	1,222
Self-employed persons	1,046

*US Census Bureau
**New Jersey Department of Labor

General Information
Borough of Fair Lawn
8-01 Fair Lawn Ave
Fair Lawn, NJ 07410
201-796-1700

Web site	www.fairlawn.org
Land area (sq. miles)	5.17
Water area (sq. miles)	0.05
Type of government	Borough
Form of government	CM '50

Government

Legislative Districts
US Congressional	5, 9
State Legislative	38

Local Officials, 2006
Mayor	Martin Etler
Admin/Manager	Thomas Metzler
Clerk	Joanne Kwasniewski
Finance Dir/Treas	Barry Eccleston
Engineer	Kenneth Garrison
Attorney	Michael Kates
Tax assessor	Timothy Henderson
Tax collector	Alice Lee
Building officer	Dennis Kolano
Zoning officer	NA
Public Works	NA

Housing & Construction

Housing Units, 2000*
Total	12,006
Median rent	$923
Median SF home value	$218,000

New Privately Owned Housing Units Authorized by Building Permit
	Units	Value
Total, 2004	4	$787,424
Single family	4	$787,424
Total, 2005	27	$4,022,793
Single family	13	$2,377,793

Real Property Valuation - parcels, 2005
	Number	Valuation
Total		$2,291,728,000
Vacant	128	7,158,600
Residential	10,205	1,870,791,800
Commercial	405	230,735,000
Industrial	68	125,153,800
Apartments	13	57,888,800
Farm land	0	0
Farm homestead	0	0

Average Property Value & Tax, 2005
Residential value	$183,321
Property tax	$7,127
FAIR rebate	$616

Public Library
Maurice M Pine Library
10-01 Fair Lawn Ave
Fair Lawn, NJ 07410
201-796-3400

Director	Timothy Murphy

Library statistics, 2004
	Total	per capita
Volumes	166,053	5.25
Expenditure	$2,020,064	$63.85

Public Safety

Police
Chief	Erik Rose
Number of officers, 2004	55

Crime, 2004	Number	Rate
Total	550	17.4
Violent	56	1.8
Non-violent	494	15.6
Domestic Viol.	163	NA

Emergency/Fire
Director	Scott Osback

Public School District
(for school year 2004-2005 except as noted)

Fair Lawn School District
37-01 Fair Lawn Ave
Fair Lawn, NJ 07410
201-794-5510

Superintendent	Bruce Watson
Grade plan	K-12
Enrollment	4,700.0
Students per teacher	11.3
Per pupil expenditure	$12,892
Median faculty salary	$60,022
Median administrator salary	$116,925
Grade 12 enrollment	381.5
High school graduation rate	97.2%

Assessment test results
(percent scoring at proficient or advanced level)
	Language	Math
Grade 3	90.7%	86.1%
Grade 8	88.8%	78.6%
High school	94.5%	89.3%

SAT
Percent tested	92%
Average SAT math score	553
Average SAT verbal score	524

No Child Left Behind, 2003-04
Attendence rate (target = 90%)	95.5%
Drop rate	0.8%
Highly-qualified teachers	99.9%
District needs improvement?(AYP)	No

Municipal Finance

Fiscal Year 2005
Total tax levy	$89,312,009
County levy	8,071,021
County taxes	7,666,450
County library	0
County health	0
County open space	404,571
School levy	56,845,238
Local muni. budget	24,395,751
Misc. revenues	11,010,940
Total aid	$5,121,039
CMPTRA	1,491,368
Muni. block grant	133,668
Energy tax receipts	3,356,003
Homeland security	140,000

Fiscal Year 2006
Total aid	$5,121,039
CMPTRA	1,373,908
Muni. block grant	133,668
Energy tax receipts	3,473,463
Homeland security	140,000

Taxes
	2003	2004	2005
General tax rate per $100	3.37	3.670	3.890
Net valuation taxable	$2,286,241,910	$2,289,302,164	$2,297,274,817
State equalized value	$3,616,899,082	$4,000,382,728	$4,533,796,757
County equalization ratio	71.1	63.21	57.16

Demographics & Socio-Economic Characteristics
(2000 U.S. Census, except as noted)

Population
1980*	5,693
1990*	5,699
2000	6,283
Male	3,736
Female	2,547
2004 (estimate)*	6,688
Persons per sq. mi. of land	158

Race & Hispanic Origin, 2000
Race
White	2,602
Black/African American	2,980
Amer. Indian/Alaska Natv.	319
Asian	35
Natv. Hawaiian/Pac. Islander	2
Other Race	150
Two or more races	195
Hispanic origin, total	557
Mexican	123
Puerto Rican	149
Cuban	0
Other Hispanic	285

Age & Nativity, 2000
Under 5 years	279
18 years and over	5,037
21 years and over	4,823
65 years and over	670
85 years and over	53
Median Age	36.8
Native born	6,165
Foreign born	118

Educational Attainment, 2000
Population 25 years and over	4,491
0-8 yrs of school	8.2%
High School grad or higher	63.3%
Bachelor's degree or higher	5.1%
Graduate degree	1.5%

Income & Poverty, 1999
Per capita income	$17,547
Median household income	$37,891
Median family income	$41,326
Persons in poverty	551
H'holds receiving public assistance	67
H'holds receiving social security	591

Households, 2000
Total households	1,751
With persons under 18	660
With persons over 65	484
Family households	1,322
One-person households	358
Persons per household	2.78
Persons per family	3.19

Labor & Employment
Total civilian labor force, 2004**	3,008
Unemployment rate	11.8%
Total civilian labor force, 2000	2,288
Unemployment rate	12.3%

Employed persons 16 years and over by occupation, 2000
Managers & professionals	398
Service occupations	460
Sales & office occupations	433
Farming, fishing & forestry	7
Construction & maintenance	176
Production & transportation	532
Self-employed persons	101

*US Census Bureau
**New Jersey Department of Labor

General Information
Township of Fairfield
PO Box 240
Fairton, NJ 08320
856-451-9284

Web site	NA
Land area (sq. miles)	42.29
Water area (sq. miles)	1.51
Type of government	Township
Form of government	TC

Government

Legislative Districts
US Congressional	2
State Legislative	3

Local Officials, 2006
Mayor	A. Craig Thomas
Admin/Manager	R. J. DeVillasanta
Clerk	R. J. DeVillasanta
Finance Dir/Treas	R.J. DeVillasanta
Engineer	Uzo Ahiarakwe
Attorney	Phillip George
Tax assessor	Michelle Sharp
Tax collector	Heddi Sutherland
Building officer	Milt Truxton
Zoning officer	Mario Santiago
Public Works	NA

Housing & Construction

Housing Units, 2000*
Total	1,915
Median rent	$596
Median SF home value	$84,100

New Privately Owned Housing Units
Authorized by Building Permit
	Units	Value
Total, 2004	10	$1,498,950
Single family	10	$1,498,950
Total, 2005	11	$1,408,969
Single family	11	$1,408,969

Real Property Valuation - parcels, 2005
	Number	Valuation
Total		$157,865,900
Vacant	735	9,493,000
Residential	1,561	124,562,600
Commercial	66	12,893,200
Industrial	0	0
Apartments	0	0
Farm land	63	7,934,600
Farm homestead	184	2,982,500

Average Property Value & Tax, 2005
Residential value	$73,092
Property tax	$1,954
FAIR rebate	$643

Public Library

No public municipal library.

Library statistics, 2004
	Total	per capita
Volumes	NA	NA
Expenditure	NA	NA

Public Safety

Police
Chief	NA
Number of officers, 2004	0

Crime, 2004	Number	Rate
Total	156	23.6
Violent	22	3.3
Non-violent	134	20.3
Domestic Viol.	99	NA

Emergency/Fire
Director	NA

Public School District
(for school year 2004-2005 except as noted)

Fairfield Township School District
13 Ramah Rd
Bridgeton, NJ 08302
856-451-1128

Superintendent	Thomas Smith
Grade plan	K-8
Enrollment	534.0
Students per teacher	9.8
Per pupil expenditure	$12,876
Median faculty salary	$47,925
Median administrator salary	$71,414
Grade 12 enrollment	NA
High school graduation rate	NA

Assessment test results
(percent scoring at proficient or advanced level)
	Language	Math
Grade 3	70.7%	63.5%
Grade 8	45.7%	22.9%
High school	NA	NA

SAT
Percent tested	NA
Average SAT math score	NA
Average SAT verbal score	NA

No Child Left Behind, 2003-04
Attendence rate (target = 90%)	96.0%
Drop rate	NA
Highly-qualified teachers	100%
District needs improvement?(AYP)	No

Municipal Finance

Fiscal Year 2005
Total tax levy	$4,253,528
County levy	1,815,896
County taxes	1,724,943
County library	0
County health	73,478
County open space	17,475
School levy	2,086,566
Local muni. budget	351,066
Misc. revenues	1,925,224
Total aid	$628,418
CMPTRA	263,235
Muni. block grant	24,937
Energy tax receipts	340,246
Homeland security	0

Fiscal Year 2006
Total aid	$628,419
CMPTRA	251,327
Muni. block grant	24,937
Energy tax receipts	352,155
Homeland security	NA

Taxes
	2003	2004	2005
General tax rate per $100	2.23	2.510	2.676
Net valuation taxable	$157,780,656	$157,904,546	$159,109,561
State equalized value	$168,102,127	$172,546,288	$203,699,348
County equalization ratio	97.47	93.86	91.45

Demographics & Socio-Economic Characteristics
(2000 U.S. Census, except as noted)

Population
1980*	7,987
1990*	7,615
2000	7,063
Male	3,454
Female	3,609
2004 (estimate)*	7,827
Persons per sq. mi. of land	749

Race & Hispanic Origin, 2000
Race
White	6,754
Black/African American	37
Amer. Indian/Alaska Natv.	7
Asian	199
Natv. Hawaiian/Pac. Islander	0
Other Race	28
Two or more races	38
Hispanic origin, total	244
Mexican	33
Puerto Rican	68
Cuban	32
Other Hispanic	111

Age & Nativity, 2000
Under 5 years	390
18 years and over	5,506
21 years and over	5,300
65 years and over	1,065
85 years and over	118
Median Age	40.7
Native born	6,174
Foreign born	889

Educational Attainment, 2000
Population 25 years and over	5,028
0-8 yrs of school	4.9%
High School grad or higher	86.9%
Bachelor's degree or higher	34.8%
Graduate degree	11.6%

Income & Poverty, 1999
Per capita income	$32,099
Median household income	$83,120
Median family income	$90,998
Persons in poverty	195
H'holds receiving public assistance	8
H'holds receiving social security	776

Households, 2000
Total households	2,296
With persons under 18	837
With persons over 65	703
Family households	1,982
One-person households	251
Persons per household	3.04
Persons per family	3.29

Labor & Employment
Total civilian labor force, 2004**	950
Unemployment rate	1.4%
Total civilian labor force, 2000	3,652
Unemployment rate	2.7%

Employed persons 16 years and over by occupation, 2000
Managers & professionals	1,500
Service occupations	341
Sales & office occupations	1,136
Farming, fishing & forestry	0
Construction & maintenance	307
Production & transportation	270
Self-employed persons	255

*US Census Bureau
**New Jersey Department of Labor

General Information
Township of Fairfield
230 Fairfield Rd
Fairfield, NJ 07004
973-882-2700

Web site	NA
Land area (sq. miles)	10.45
Water area (sq. miles)	0
Type of government	Township
Form of government	SM '50

Government

Legislative Districts
US Congressional	11
State Legislative	27

Local Officials, 2006
Mayor	Rocco Palmieri
Admin/Manager	Joseph Catenaro
Clerk	Patricia Fahy
Finance Dir/Treas	Gordon Stelter
Engineer	Laurence Gonnello
Attorney	David Paris
Tax assessor	E. Romeo Longo
Tax collector	Marita Shatzel
Building officer	Phil Cheff
Zoning officer	Glenn Plumstead
Public Works	Michael deMontaigne

Housing & Construction

Housing Units, 2000*
Total	2,326
Median rent	$988
Median SF home value	$274,800

New Privately Owned Housing Units Authorized by Building Permit
	Units	Value
Total, 2004	14	$3,082,200
Single family	14	$3,082,200
Total, 2005	26	$8,391,170
Single family	26	$8,391,170

Real Property Valuation - parcels, 2005
	Number	Valuation
Total		$1,538,296,800
Vacant	281	25,041,300
Residential	2,435	628,088,400
Commercial	399	414,582,700
Industrial	276	470,085,300
Apartments	0	0
Farm land	2	434,600
Farm homestead	9	64,500

Average Property Value & Tax, 2005
Residential value	$257,018
Property tax	$6,255
FAIR rebate	$611

Public Library
A. P. Costa Memorial Library
261 Hollywood Ave
Fairfield, NJ 07004
973-227-3575

Director	John Helle

Library statistics, 2004
	Total	per capita
Volumes	64,926	9.19
Expenditure	$577,559	$81.77

Public Safety
Police
Chief	C. Centonze
Number of officers, 2004	40

Crime, 2004	Number	Rate
Total	348	46.8
Violent	21	2.8
Non-violent	327	43.9
Domestic Viol.	46	NA

Emergency/Fire
Director	Christopher Barrella

Public School District
(for school year 2004-2005 except as noted)

Fairfield Township School District
233 Fairfield Rd
Fairfield, NJ 07004
973-227-5586

Superintendent	Lois Capobianco
Grade plan	K-6
Enrollment	742.0
Students per teacher	11.8
Per pupil expenditure	$10,726
Median faculty salary	$43,467
Median administrator salary	$100,500
Grade 12 enrollment	NA
High school graduation rate	NA

Assessment test results
(percent scoring at proficient or advanced level)
	Language	Math
Grade 3	93.1%	86.9%
Grade 8	NA	NA
High school	NA	NA

SAT
Percent tested	NA
Average SAT math score	NA
Average SAT verbal score	NA

No Child Left Behind, 2003-04
Attendence rate (target = 90%)	94.8%
Drop rate	NA
Highly-qualified teachers	94.4%
District needs improvement?(AYP)	No

Municipal Finance

Fiscal Year 2005
Total tax levy	$37,597,534
County levy	10,731,035
County taxes	10,506,276
County library	0
County health	0
County open space	224,758
School levy	18,319,252
Local muni. budget	8,547,248
Misc. revenues	6,741,843
Total aid	$1,762,667
CMPTRA	699,778
Muni. block grant	33,180
Energy tax receipts	979,709
Homeland security	50,000

Fiscal Year 2006
Total aid	$1,762,667
CMPTRA	665,488
Muni. block grant	33,180
Energy tax receipts	1,013,999
Homeland security	50,000

Taxes
	2003	2004	2005
General tax rate per $100	2.32	2.370	2.440
Net valuation taxable	$1,505,920,800	$1,522,760,100	$1,544,958,000
State equalized value	$2,044,421,396	$2,179,517,487	$2,539,378,698
County equalization ratio	80.26	80.26	69.77

Demographics & Socio-Economic Characteristics
(2000 U.S. Census, except as noted)

Population
1980*	10,519
1990*	10,733
2000	13,255
Male	6,844
Female	6,411
2004 (estimate)*	13,561
Persons per sq. mi. of land	15,945

Race & Hispanic Origin, 2000
Race
White	9,605
Black/African American	226
Amer. Indian/Alaska Natv.	51
Asian	659
Natv. Hawaiian/Pac. Islander	4
Other Race	1,712
Two or more races	998
Hispanic origin, total	4,911
Mexican	149
Puerto Rican	452
Cuban	562
Other Hispanic	3,748

Age & Nativity, 2000
Under 5 years	852
18 years and over	10,456
21 years and over	9,843
65 years and over	1,824
85 years and over	191
Median Age	34.5
Native born	6,841
Foreign born	6,414

Educational Attainment, 2000
Population 25 years and over	8,859
0-8 yrs of school	19.6%
High School grad or higher	65.4%
Bachelor's degree or higher	16.5%
Graduate degree	4.0%

Income & Poverty, 1999
Per capita income	$18,835
Median household income	$40,393
Median family income	$46,365
Persons in poverty	1,557
H'holds receiving public assistance	221
H'holds receiving social security	1,364

Households, 2000
Total households	4,861
With persons under 18	1,600
With persons over 65	1,395
Family households	3,178
One-person households	1,362
Persons per household	2.73
Persons per family	3.31

Labor & Employment
Total civilian labor force, 2004**	6,194
Unemployment rate	7.0%
Total civilian labor force, 2000	6,053
Unemployment rate	7.0%

Employed persons 16 years and over by occupation, 2000
Managers & professionals	1,345
Service occupations	894
Sales & office occupations	1,770
Farming, fishing & forestry	0
Construction & maintenance	656
Production & transportation	964
Self-employed persons	269

*US Census Bureau
**New Jersey Department of Labor

General Information
Borough of Fairview
59 Anderson Ave
Fairview, NJ 07022
201-943-3300
Web site	NA
Land area (sq. miles)	0.85
Water area (sq. miles)	0
Type of government	Borough
Form of government	B

Government
Legislative Districts
US Congressional	9
State Legislative	32

Local Officials, 2006
Mayor	Vincent Bellucci Jr.
Admin/Manager	Diane Testa
Clerk	Diane Testa
Finance Dir/Treas	Joseph Rutch
Engineer	Boswell Engineering
Attorney	John Schettino
Tax assessor	George Reggo
Tax collector	Eugene Pedoto
Building officer	Gary Ippolito
Zoning officer	NA
Public Works	NA

Housing & Construction
Housing Units, 2000*
Total	4,988
Median rent	$846
Median SF home value	$179,900

New Privately Owned Housing Units Authorized by Building Permit
	Units	Value
Total, 2004	35	$4,095,182
Single family	2	$209,250
Total, 2005	57	$6,958,033
Single family	9	$1,119,200

Real Property Valuation - parcels, 2005
	Number	Valuation
Total		$611,651,200
Vacant	69	7,040,600
Residential	2,033	376,778,600
Commercial	203	113,726,000
Industrial	115	46,166,300
Apartments	123	67,939,700
Farm land	0	0
Farm homestead	0	0

Average Property Value & Tax, 2005
Residential value	$185,331
Property tax	$6,356
FAIR rebate	$707

Public Library
Fairview Free Public Library
213 Anderson Ave
Fairview, NJ 07022
201-943-6244
Director	Roger Verdi

Library statistics, 2004
	Total	per capita
Volumes	18,981	1.43
Expenditure	$304,882	$23.00

Public Safety
Police
Chief	John Pinzone
Number of officers, 2004	32

Crime, 2004	Number	Rate
Total	261	19.5
Violent	58	4.3
Non-violent	203	15.2
Domestic Viol.	171	NA

Emergency/Fire
Director	Michael Mesisca

Public School District
(for school year 2004-2005 except as noted)

Fairview School District
130 Hamilton Ave
Fairview, NJ 07022
201-943-1699
Superintendent	Louis DeLisio
Grade plan	K-12
Enrollment	1,015.0
Students per teacher	12.2
Per pupil expenditure	$10,128
Median faculty salary	$41,600
Median administrator salary	$89,778
Grade 12 enrollment	NA
High school graduation rate	NA

Assessment test results
(percent scoring at proficient or advanced level)
	Language	Math
Grade 3	77.5%	69.6%
Grade 8	50.8%	50.8%
High school	NA	NA

SAT
Percent tested	NA
Average SAT math score	NA
Average SAT verbal score	NA

No Child Left Behind, 2003-04
Attendence rate (target = 90%)	94.6%
Drop rate	NA
Highly-qualified teachers	99.6%
District needs improvement?(AYP)	No

Municipal Finance
Fiscal Year 2005
Total tax levy	$20,991,401
County levy	1,934,698
County taxes	1,837,720
County library	0
County health	0
County open space	96,978
School levy	10,351,107
Local muni. budget	8,705,597
Misc. revenues	3,845,642
Total aid	$1,415,427
CMPTRA	686,664
Muni. block grant	51,973
Energy tax receipts	606,790
Homeland security	70,000

Fiscal Year 2006
Total aid	$1,415,427
CMPTRA	665,426
Muni. block grant	51,973
Energy tax receipts	628,028
Homeland security	70,000

Taxes
	2003	2004	2005
General tax rate per $100	3.14	3.290	3.430
Net valuation taxable	$607,350,709	$609,616,295	$612,105,473
State equalized value	$830,621,867	$955,557,729	$1,089,155,646
County equalization ratio	84.93	73.12	63.78

Demographics & Socio-Economic Characteristics
(2000 U.S. Census, except as noted)

Population
1980*	7,767
1990*	7,115
2000	7,174
Male	3,422
Female	3,752
2004 (estimate)*	7,255
Persons per sq. mi. of land	5,424

Race & Hispanic Origin, 2000
Race
White	6,335
Black/African American	369
Amer. Indian/Alaska Natv.	7
Asian	315
Natv. Hawaiian/Pac. Islander	2
Other Race	57
Two or more races	89
Hispanic origin, total	268
Mexican	13
Puerto Rican	105
Cuban	26
Other Hispanic	124

Age & Nativity, 2000
Under 5 years	608
18 years and over	5,323
21 years and over	5,183
65 years and over	1,055
85 years and over	136
Median Age	38.6
Native born	6,316
Foreign born	858

Educational Attainment, 2000
Population 25 years and over	4,999
0-8 yrs of school	1.9%
High School grad or higher	95.0%
Bachelor's degree or higher	51.0%
Graduate degree	18.3%

Income & Poverty, 1999
Per capita income	$34,804
Median household income	$85,233
Median family income	$99,232
Persons in poverty	243
H'holds receiving public assistance	44
H'holds receiving social security	709

Households, 2000
Total households	2,574
With persons under 18	1,042
With persons over 65	727
Family households	2,053
One-person households	463
Persons per household	2.76
Persons per family	3.13

Labor & Employment
Total civilian labor force, 2004**	4,018
Unemployment rate	2.4%
Total civilian labor force, 2000	3,756
Unemployment rate	4.7%

Employed persons 16 years and over by occupation, 2000
Managers & professionals	1,984
Service occupations	214
Sales & office occupations	1,004
Farming, fishing & forestry	0
Construction & maintenance	181
Production & transportation	195
Self-employed persons	179

*US Census Bureau
**New Jersey Department of Labor

General Information
Borough of Fanwood
75 North Martine Ave
Fanwood, NJ 07023
908-322-8236

Web site	NA
Land area (sq. miles)	1.34
Water area (sq. miles)	0
Type of government	Borough
Form of government	B

Government
Legislative Districts
US Congressional	7
State Legislative	22

Local Officials, 2006
Mayor	Colleen Mahr
Admin/Manager	Eleanor McGovern
Clerk	Eleanor McGovern
Finance Dir/Treas	Fred Tomkins
Engineer	Joseph Pryor
Attorney	Dennis Estis
Tax assessor	Michael Ross
Tax collector	NA
Building officer	Bruce Helmstetter
Zoning officer	NA
Public Works	NA

Housing & Construction
Housing Units, 2000*
Total	2,615
Median rent	$1,077
Median SF home value	$224,300

New Privately Owned Housing Units
Authorized by Building Permit
	Units	Value
Total, 2004	12	$1,794,315
Single family	12	$1,794,315
Total, 2005	13	$2,339,334
Single family	13	$2,339,334

Real Property Valuation - parcels, 2005
	Number	Valuation
Total		$223,642,200
Vacant	45	1,394,400
Residential	2,474	206,646,200
Commercial	75	13,015,600
Industrial	16	2,586,000
Apartments	0	0
Farm land	0	0
Farm homestead	0	0

Average Property Value & Tax, 2005
Residential value	$83,527
Property tax	$7,833
FAIR rebate	$561

Public Library
Fanwood Memorial Library
N Ave and Tillotson Rd
Fanwood, NJ 07023
908-322-6400

Director...................... Daniel Weiss

Library statistics, 2004
	Total	per capita
Volumes	47,809	6.66
Expenditure	$426,933	$59.51

Public Safety
Police
Chief	Donald Domanoski
Number of officers, 2004	21

Crime, 2004	Number	Rate
Total	99	13.6
Violent	6	0.8
Non-violent	93	12.8
Domestic Viol.	17	NA

Emergency/Fire
Director.................... David Ziegler

Public School District
(for school year 2004-2005 except as noted)

Scotch Plains-Fanwood School District
Evergreen Ave & Cedar St
Scotch Plains, NJ 07076
908-232-6161

Superintendent	Carol Choye
Grade plan	K-12
Enrollment	5,048.0
Students per teacher	12.3
Per pupil expenditure	$11,962
Median faculty salary	$52,325
Median administrator salary	$113,500
Grade 12 enrollment	346.0
High school graduation rate	100.0%

Assessment test results
(percent scoring at proficient or advanced level)
	Language	Math
Grade 3	93.5%	91.9%
Grade 8	83.3%	83.5%
High school	91.6%	88.7%

SAT
Percent tested	93%
Average SAT math score	548
Average SAT verbal score	526

No Child Left Behind, 2003-04
Attendence rate (target = 90%)	96.3%
Drop rate	0.1%
Highly-qualified teachers	97.7%
District needs improvement?(AYP)	No

Municipal Finance
Fiscal Year 2005
Total tax levy	$20,983,605
County levy	3,542,933
County taxes	3,403,060
County library	0
County health	0
County open space	139,873
School levy	13,406,729
Local muni. budget	4,033,943
Misc. revenues	3,242,277
Total aid	$1,095,387
CMPTRA	305,857
Muni. block grant	31,133
Energy tax receipts	708,397
Homeland security	50,000

Fiscal Year 2006
Total aid	$1,095,387
CMPTRA	281,063
Muni. block grant	31,133
Energy tax receipts	733,191
Homeland security	50,000

Taxes
	2003	2004	2005
General tax rate per $100	8.52	8.868	9.378
Net valuation taxable	$220,755,629	$221,411,427	$223,765,836
State equalized value	$790,106,045	$890,129,620	$1,006,593,954
County equalization ratio	29.94	26.86	24.03

Demographics & Socio-Economic Characteristics
(2000 U.S. Census, except as noted)

Population
1980*	.677
1990*	.657
2000	.859
Male	.404
Female	.455
2004 (estimate)*	.919
Persons per sq. mi. of land	.189

Race & Hispanic Origin, 2000
Race
White	.825
Black/African American	.7
Amer. Indian/Alaska Natv.	.1
Asian	.18
Natv. Hawaiian/Pac. Islander	.0
Other Race	.0
Two or more races	.8
Hispanic origin, total	.31
Mexican	.6
Puerto Rican	.0
Cuban	.0
Other Hispanic	.25

Age & Nativity, 2000
Under 5 years	.52
18 years and over	.701
21 years and over	.688
65 years and over	.142
85 years and over	.12
Median Age	.44.6
Native born	.756
Foreign born	.100

Educational Attainment, 2000
Population 25 years and over	.669
0-8 yrs of school	.2.1%
High School grad or higher	.94.8%
Bachelor's degree or higher	.58.1%
Graduate degree	.23.5%

Income & Poverty, 1999
Per capita income	.$81,535
Median household income	.$112,817
Median family income	.$149,095
Persons in poverty	.21
H'holds receiving public assistance	.0
H'holds receiving social security	.104

Households, 2000
Total households	.368
With persons under 18	.91
With persons over 65	.97
Family households	.253
One-person households	.94
Persons per household	.2.33
Persons per family	.2.76

Labor & Employment
Total civilian labor force, 2004**	.447
Unemployment rate	.4.7%
Total civilian labor force, 2000	.444
Unemployment rate	.2.5%

Employed persons 16 years and over by occupation, 2000
Managers & professionals	.240
Service occupations	.57
Sales & office occupations	.91
Farming, fishing & forestry	.4
Construction & maintenance	.30
Production & transportation	.11
Self-employed persons	.49

*US Census Bureau
**New Jersey Department of Labor

General Information
Borough of Far Hills
PO Box 249
Far Hills, NJ 07931
908-234-0611

Web site	.NA
Land area (sq. miles)	.4.86
Water area (sq. miles)	.0.06
Type of government	.Borough
Form of government	.B

Government

Legislative Districts
US Congressional	.7
State Legislative	.16

Local Officials, 2006
Mayor	.Carl Torsilieri
Admin/Manager	.NA
Clerk	.Robin Collins (Actg)
Finance Dir/Treas	.Deborah Stern
Engineer	.Paul Ferriero
Attorney	.Mary Ann Nergaard
Tax assessor	.Edward Kerwin
Tax collector	.Deborah Giordano
Building officer	.Joseph Alicino
Zoning officer	.Leonard Taylor
Public Works	.NA

Housing & Construction

Housing Units, 2000*
Total	.386
Median rent	.$1,208
Median SF home value	.$393,300

New Privately Owned Housing Units Authorized by Building Permit
	Units	Value
Total, 2004	2	$5,100,000
Single family	2	$5,100,000
Total, 2005	1	$2,000,000
Single family	1	$2,000,000

Real Property Valuation - parcels, 2005
	Number	Valuation
Total		$434,362,416
Vacant	20	13,530,800
Residential	313	306,851,800
Commercial	27	29,355,900
Industrial	0	0
Apartments	1	390,000
Farm land	39	83,853,100
Farm homestead	50	380,816

Average Property Value & Tax, 2005
Residential value	.$846,371
Property tax	.$8,083
FAIR rebate	.$593

Public Library
Clarence Dillon Public Library
2336 Lamington Rd
Bedminster, NJ 07921
908-234-2325

Director	.Eileen Burnash

Library statistics, 2004
	Total	per capita
Volumes	101,622	11.09
Expenditure	$807,777	$88.18

Public Safety

Police
Chief	.Kenneth Hartman
Number of officers, 2004	.6

Crime, 2004	Number	Rate
Total	3	3.3
Violent	0	0
Non-violent	3	3.3
Domestic Viol.	7	NA

Emergency/Fire
Director	.Brian Wilde

Public School District
(for school year 2004-2005 except as noted)

Sends children to Somerset Hills Regional school district (see Bernardsville Borough).
Grade plan	.NA
Enrollment	.NA
Students per teacher	.NA
Per pupil expenditure	.NA
Median faculty salary	.NA
Median administrator salary	.NA
Grade 12 enrollment	.NA
High school graduation rate	.NA

Assessment test results
(percent scoring at proficient or advanced level)
	Language	Math
Grade 3	NA	NA
Grade 8	NA	NA
High school	NA	NA

SAT
Percent tested	.NA
Average SAT math score	.NA
Average SAT verbal score	.NA

No Child Left Behind, 2003-04
Attendence rate (target = 90%)	.NA
Drop rate	.NA
Highly-qualified teachers	.NA
District needs improvement?(AYP)	.NA

Municipal Finance

Fiscal Year 2005
Total tax levy	.$4,151,645
County levy	.1,428,648
County taxes	.1,303,326
County library	.0
County health	.0
County open space	.125,322
School levy	.1,403,618
Local muni. budget	.1,319,378
Misc. revenues	.767,689
Total aid	.$117,981
CMPTRA	.19,821
Muni. block grant	.3,368
Energy tax receipts	.69,792
Homeland security	.25,000

Fiscal Year 2006
Total aid	.$117,981
CMPTRA	.17,378
Muni. block grant	.3,368
Energy tax receipts	.72,235
Homeland security	.25,000

Taxes
	2003	2004	2005
General tax rate per $100	1.05	1.120	0.960
Net valuation taxable	$351,372,209	$356,989,599	$434,723,333
State equalized value	$373,363,308	$413,940,062	$438,759,924
County equalization ratio	105.75	94.11	104.32

Demographics & Socio-Economic Characteristics
(2000 U.S. Census, except as noted)

Population
1980*	1,348
1990*	1,462
2000	1,587
Male	802
Female	785
2004 (estimate)*	1,586
Persons per sq. mi. of land	2,970

Race & Hispanic Origin, 2000
Race
White	1,486
Black/African American	18
Amer. Indian/Alaska Natv.	0
Asian	37
Natv. Hawaiian/Pac. Islander	0
Other Race	33
Two or more races	13
Hispanic origin, total	61
Mexican	12
Puerto Rican	27
Cuban	0
Other Hispanic	22

Age & Nativity, 2000
Under 5 years	102
18 years and over	1,159
21 years and over	1,117
65 years and over	143
85 years and over	7
Median Age	34.7
Native born	1,496
Foreign born	91

Educational Attainment, 2000
Population 25 years and over	1,041
0-8 yrs of school	2.2%
High School grad or higher	88.5%
Bachelor's degree or higher	19.0%
Graduate degree	6.3%

Income & Poverty, 1999
Per capita income	$21,667
Median household income	$48,889
Median family income	$59,625
Persons in poverty	90
H'holds receiving public assistance	20
H'holds receiving social security	120

Households, 2000
Total households	625
With persons under 18	244
With persons over 65	105
Family households	406
One-person households	181
Persons per household	2.54
Persons per family	3.21

Labor & Employment
Total civilian labor force, 2004**	911
Unemployment rate	3.9%
Total civilian labor force, 2000	860
Unemployment rate	3.1%

Employed persons 16 years and over by occupation, 2000
Managers & professionals	274
Service occupations	121
Sales & office occupations	230
Farming, fishing & forestry	0
Construction & maintenance	114
Production & transportation	94
Self-employed persons	40

*US Census Bureau
**New Jersey Department of Labor

General Information
Borough of Farmingdale
PO Box 58
11 Asbury Ave
Farmingdale, NJ 07727
732-938-4077
Email	farmingdale.borough@verizon.net
Land area (sq. miles)	0.53
Water area (sq. miles)	0
Type of government	Borough
Form of government	B

Government

Legislative Districts
US Congressional	4
State Legislative	30

Local Officials, 2006
Mayor	John P. Morgan
Admin/Manager	NA
Clerk	Bryan Marks
Finance Dir/Treas	Robbin Kirk
Engineer	Matt Shafai
Attorney	John O. Bennett III
Tax assessor	Thomas Glock
Tax collector	Robbin Kirk
Building officer	Robert Corby
Zoning officer	NA
Public Works	NA

Housing & Construction

Housing Units, 2000*
Total	638
Median rent	$780
Median SF home value	$154,100

New Privately Owned Housing Units
Authorized by Building Permit
	Units	Value
Total, 2004	0	$0
Single family	0	$0
Total, 2005	2	$59,000
Single family	2	$59,000

Real Property Valuation - parcels, 2005
	Number	Valuation
Total		$148,273,800
Vacant	26	2,312,300
Residential	350	109,362,000
Commercial	35	19,613,700
Industrial	3	2,742,800
Apartments	3	13,507,100
Farm land	1	721,700
Farm homestead	1	14,200

Average Property Value & Tax, 2005
Residential value	$311,613
Property tax	$5,372
FAIR rebate	$548

Public Library
No public municipal library.

Library statistics, 2004
	Total	per capita
Volumes	NA	NA
Expenditure	NA	NA

Public Safety

Police
Chief	NA
Number of officers, 2004	0

Crime, 2004	Number	Rate
Total	11	7
Violent	0	0
Non-violent	11	7
Domestic Viol.	7	NA

Emergency/Fire
Director	Robert D. Bradley Jr.

Public School District
(for school year 2004-2005 except as noted)

Farmingdale Borough School District
Academy St
Farmingdale, NJ 07727
732-938-9611
Superintendent	Janet Munger
Grade plan	K-8
Enrollment	150.0
Students per teacher	8.8
Per pupil expenditure	$14,007
Median faculty salary	$63,025
Median administrator salary	$61,591
Grade 12 enrollment	NA
High school graduation rate	NA

Assessment test results
(percent scoring at proficient or advanced level)
	Language	Math
Grade 3	81.3%	93.8%
Grade 8	90.5%	81.8%
High school	NA	NA

SAT
Percent tested	NA
Average SAT math score	NA
Average SAT verbal score	NA

No Child Left Behind, 2003-04
Attendence rate (target = 90%)	95.0%
Drop rate	NA
Highly-qualified teachers	89.3%
District needs improvement?(AYP)	No

Municipal Finance

Fiscal Year 2005
Total tax levy	$2,596,260
County levy	497,269
County taxes	439,027
County library	24,183
County health	8,006
County open space	26,052
School levy	1,934,950
Local muni. budget	164,042
Misc. revenues	593,222
Total aid	$223,304
CMPTRA	138,982
Muni. block grant	6,397
Energy tax receipts	77,925
Homeland security	0

Fiscal Year 2006
Total aid	$223,305
CMPTRA	136,255
Muni. block grant	6,397
Energy tax receipts	80,653
Homeland security	NA

Taxes
	2003	2004	2005
General tax rate per $100	3.46	3.659	1.725
Net valuation taxable	$66,170,318	$65,952,242	$150,594,944
State equalized value	$117,677,962	$143,425,224	$150,159,482
County equalization ratio	69.39	56.23	103.57

Demographics & Socio-Economic Characteristics
(2000 U.S. Census, except as noted)

Population
1980*	597
1990*	579
2000	522
Male	245
Female	277
2004 (estimate)*	586
Persons per sq. mi. of land	2,156

Race & Hispanic Origin, 2000
Race
White	426
Black/African American	83
Amer. Indian/Alaska Natv.	1
Asian	0
Natv. Hawaiian/Pac. Islander	0
Other Race	2
Two or more races	10
Hispanic origin, total	13
Mexican	0
Puerto Rican	5
Cuban	1
Other Hispanic	7

Age & Nativity, 2000
Under 5 years	39
18 years and over	390
21 years and over	378
65 years and over	65
85 years and over	3
Median Age	35.4
Native born	508
Foreign born	20

Educational Attainment, 2000
Population 25 years and over	351
0-8 yrs of school	1.7%
High School grad or higher	88.6%
Bachelor's degree or higher	27.6%
Graduate degree	5.4%

Income & Poverty, 1999
Per capita income	$23,908
Median household income	$58,958
Median family income	$66,607
Persons in poverty	10
H'holds receiving public assistance	0
H'holds receiving social security	34

Households, 2000
Total households	189
With persons under 18	76
With persons over 65	45
Family households	139
One-person households	33
Persons per household	2.76
Persons per family	3.17

Labor & Employment
Total civilian labor force, 2004**	327
Unemployment rate	8.1%
Total civilian labor force, 2000	303
Unemployment rate	4.0%

Employed persons 16 years and over by occupation, 2000
Managers & professionals	84
Service occupations	39
Sales & office occupations	99
Farming, fishing & forestry	0
Construction & maintenance	18
Production & transportation	51
Self-employed persons	8

*US Census Bureau
**New Jersey Department of Labor

General Information
Borough of Fieldsboro
18 Washington St
Fieldsboro, NJ 08505
609-298-6344

Web site	www.fieldsboro.us
Land area (sq. miles)	0.27
Water area (sq. miles)	0
Type of government	Borough
Form of government	B

Government

Legislative Districts
US Congressional	4
State Legislative	30

Local Officials, 2006
Mayor	Edward Tyler Sr.
Admin/Manager	NA
Clerk	Patrice Hansell
Finance Dir/Treas	Peter Federico
Engineer	Birdsall Engineering
Attorney	George Kotch
Tax assessor	Walter Kosul
Tax collector	Lan Chen Shen
Building officer	DCA
Zoning officer	NA
Public Works	NA

Housing & Construction

Housing Units, 2000*
Total	204
Median rent	$1,050
Median SF home value	$103,900

New Privately Owned Housing Units
Authorized by Building Permit
	Units	Value
Total, 2004	0	$0
Single family	0	$0
Total, 2005	1	$52,510
Single family	1	$52,510

Real Property Valuation - parcels, 2005
	Number	Valuation
Total		$28,557,200
Vacant	34	830,500
Residential	200	18,576,300
Commercial	7	1,284,500
Industrial	1	7,865,900
Apartments	0	0
Farm land	0	0
Farm homestead	0	0

Average Property Value & Tax, 2005
Residential value	$92,882
Property tax	$3,378
FAIR rebate	$583

Public Library
No public municipal library.

Library statistics, 2004
	Total	per capita
Volumes	NA	NA
Expenditure	NA	NA

Public Safety
Police
Chief	Edward Tyler Sr.
Number of officers, 2004	0

Crime, 2004	Number	Rate
Total	7	12.3
Violent	2	3.5
Non-violent	5	8.8
Domestic Viol.	2	NA

Emergency/Fire
Director	NA

Public School District
(for school year 2004-2005 except as noted)

Sends children to Bordentown Regional school district (see Bordentown City or Bordentown Township).
Grade plan	NA
Enrollment	NA
Students per teacher	NA
Per pupil expenditure	NA
Median faculty salary	NA
Median administrator salary	NA
Grade 12 enrollment	NA
High school graduation rate	NA

Assessment test results
(percent scoring at proficient or advanced level)
	Language	Math
Grade 3	NA	NA
Grade 8	NA	NA
High school	NA	NA

SAT
Percent tested	NA
Average SAT math score	NA
Average SAT verbal score	NA

No Child Left Behind, 2003-04
Attendence rate (target = 90%)	NA
Drop rate	NA
Highly-qualified teachers	NA
District needs improvement?(AYP)	NA

Municipal Finance

Fiscal Year 2005
Total tax levy	$1,040,046
County levy	186,273
County taxes	156,273
County library	13,671
County health	0
County open space	16,328
School levy	640,055
Local muni. budget	213,718
Misc. revenues	374,365
Total aid	$138,780
CMPTRA	97,247
Muni. block grant	2,534
Energy tax receipts	38,999
Homeland security	0

Fiscal Year 2006
Total aid	$138,780
CMPTRA	95,882
Muni. block grant	2,534
Energy tax receipts	40,364
Homeland security	NA

Taxes
	2003	2004	2005
General tax rate per $100	3.45	3.539	3.637
Net valuation taxable	$28,520,794	$28,594,554	$28,596,674
State equalized value	$35,302,381	$38,489,872	$49,690,137
County equalization ratio	88.38	80.79	74.25

Demographics & Socio-Economic Characteristics
(2000 U.S. Census, except as noted)

Population
1980*	4,132
1990*	4,047
2000	4,200
Male	2,038
Female	2,162
2004 (estimate)*	4,206
Persons per sq. mi. of land	3,933

Race & Hispanic Origin, 2000
Race
White	3,684
Black/African American	134
Amer. Indian/Alaska Natv.	13
Asian	131
Natv. Hawaiian/Pac. Islander	7
Other Race	132
Two or more races	99
Hispanic origin, total	461
Mexican	143
Puerto Rican	40
Cuban	3
Other Hispanic	275

Age & Nativity, 2000
Under 5 years	296
18 years and over	3,267
21 years and over	3,134
65 years and over	510
85 years and over	87
Median Age	34.9
Native born	3,618
Foreign born	582

Educational Attainment, 2000
Population 25 years and over	2,942
0-8 yrs of school	5.6%
High School grad or higher	82.6%
Bachelor's degree or higher	27.4%
Graduate degree	11.2%

Income & Poverty, 1999
Per capita income	$23,769
Median household income	$39,886
Median family income	$51,582
Persons in poverty	281
H'holds receiving public assistance	72
H'holds receiving social security	496

Households, 2000
Total households	1,804
With persons under 18	518
With persons over 65	406
Family households	998
One-person households	680
Persons per household	2.26
Persons per family	3

Labor & Employment
Total civilian labor force, 2004**	2,701
Unemployment rate	4.9%
Total civilian labor force, 2000	2,259
Unemployment rate	2.9%

Employed persons 16 years and over by occupation, 2000
Managers & professionals	694
Service occupations	439
Sales & office occupations	640
Farming, fishing & forestry	37
Construction & maintenance	165
Production & transportation	219
Self-employed persons	130

*US Census Bureau
**New Jersey Department of Labor

General Information
Borough of Flemington
38 Park Ave
Flemington, NJ 08822
908-782-8840

Web site	www.historicflemington.com
Land area (sq. miles)	1.07
Water area (sq. miles)	0
Type of government	Borough
Form of government	B

Government

Legislative Districts
US Congressional	7
State Legislative	23

Local Officials, 2006
Mayor	William Martin Jr.
Admin/Manager	NA
Clerk	Diane Schottman
Finance Dir/Treas	William Hance
Engineer	Robert Clerico
Attorney	Barry Goodman
Tax assessor	Edward Kerwin
Tax collector	NA
Building officer	Jeffrey Klein
Zoning officer	Jeffrey Klein
Public Works	NA

Housing & Construction

Housing Units, 2000*
Total	1,876
Median rent	$828
Median SF home value	$163,300

New Privately Owned Housing Units Authorized by Building Permit
	Units	Value
Total, 2004	0	$0
Single family	0	$0
Total, 2005	60	$3,085,000
Single family	0	$0

Real Property Valuation - parcels, 2005
	Number	Valuation
Total		$435,915,700
Vacant	39	3,529,400
Residential	845	208,390,600
Commercial	223	184,883,700
Industrial	2	2,859,000
Apartments	10	36,253,000
Farm land	0	0
Farm homestead	0	0

Average Property Value & Tax, 2005
Residential value	$246,616
Property tax	$5,887
FAIR rebate	$560

Public Library
Flemington Free Public Library
118 Main St
Flemington, NJ 08822
908-782-5733
Director...............Shaun Armington

Library statistics, 2004
	Total	per capita
Volumes	47,575	11.33
Expenditure	$219,065	$52.16

Public Safety

Police
Chief	George Becker
Number of officers, 2004	14

Crime, 2004	Number	Rate
Total	100	23.6
Violent	0	0
Non-violent	100	23.6
Domestic Viol.	0	NA

Emergency/Fire
Director	Robert Bogart

Public School District
(for school year 2004-2005 except as noted)

Flemington-Raritan Regional School Dist.
50 Court St
Flemington, NJ 08822
908-284-7561

Superintendent	Jack Farr
Grade plan	K-8
Enrollment	3,555.0
Students per teacher	11.4
Per pupil expenditure	$11,042
Median faculty salary	$47,520
Median administrator salary	$100,477
Grade 12 enrollment	NA
High school graduation rate	NA

Assessment test results
(percent scoring at proficient or advanced level)
	Language	Math
Grade 3	92.2%	91.6%
Grade 8	88.3%	78.1%
High school	NA	NA

SAT
Percent tested	NA
Average SAT math score	NA
Average SAT verbal score	NA

No Child Left Behind, 2003-04
Attendance rate (target = 90%)	96.2%
Drop rate	NA
Highly-qualified teachers	100%
District needs improvement?(AYP)	No

Municipal Finance

Fiscal Year 2005
Total tax levy	$10,521,875
County levy	1,576,422
County taxes	1,440,842
County library	0
County health	0
County open space	135,580
School levy	6,699,458
Local muni. budget	2,245,995
Misc. revenues	2,059,652
Total aid	$572,992
CMPTRA	278,396
Muni. block grant	17,708
Energy tax receipts	251,888
Homeland security	25,000

Fiscal Year 2006
Total aid	$572,992
CMPTRA	269,580
Muni. block grant	17,708
Energy tax receipts	260,704
Homeland security	25,000

Taxes
	2003	2004	2005
General tax rate per $100	2.71	2.780	2.390
Net valuation taxable	$364,698,898	$365,527,467	$440,812,963
State equalized value	$389,469,135	$421,034,721	$510,969,008
County equalization ratio	95.11	93.11	98.62

Demographics & Socio-Economic Characteristics
(2000 U.S. Census, except as noted)

Population
1980*	9,084
1990*	10,266
2000	10,746
Male	5,140
Female	5,606
2004 (estimate)*	11,262
Persons per sq. mi. of land	1,160

Race & Hispanic Origin, 2000
Race
White	9,190
Black/African American	1,047
Amer. Indian/Alaska Natv.	19
Asian	253
Natv. Hawaiian/Pac. Islander	1
Other Race	70
Two or more races	166
Hispanic origin, total	253
Mexican	23
Puerto Rican	126
Cuban	11
Other Hispanic	93

Age & Nativity, 2000
Under 5 years	660
18 years and over	8,039
21 years and over	7,680
65 years and over	1,277
85 years and over	123
Median Age	36.9
Native born	10,059
Foreign born	687

Educational Attainment, 2000
Population 25 years and over	7,210
0-8 yrs of school	5.1%
High School grad or higher	85.5%
Bachelor's degree or higher	19.9%
Graduate degree	6.8%

Income & Poverty, 1999
Per capita income	$23,529
Median household income	$56,843
Median family income	$67,412
Persons in poverty	654
H'holds receiving public assistance	86
H'holds receiving social security	1,082

Households, 2000
Total households	4,149
With persons under 18	1,501
With persons over 65	949
Family households	2,892
One-person households	1,037
Persons per household	2.58
Persons per family	3.1

Labor & Employment
Total civilian labor force, 2004**	6,299
Unemployment rate	4.3%
Total civilian labor force, 2000	5,661
Unemployment rate	4.9%

Employed persons 16 years and over by occupation, 2000
Managers & professionals	1,770
Service occupations	684
Sales & office occupations	1,544
Farming, fishing & forestry	6
Construction & maintenance	482
Production & transportation	895
Self-employed persons	174

*US Census Bureau
**New Jersey Department of Labor

General Information
Township of Florence
Municipal Complex
711 Broad St
Florence, NJ 08518
609-499-2525

Web site	www.florence-nj.com
Land area (sq. miles)	9.71
Water area (sq. miles)	0.42
Type of government	Township
Form of government	MC '50

Government

Legislative Districts
US Congressional	4
State Legislative	7

Local Officials, 2006
Mayor	Michael J. Muchowski
Admin/Manager	Richard A. Brook
Clerk	Joy M. Weiler
Finance Dir/Treas	Sandra A. Blacker
Engineer	Dante Guzzi
Attorney	William J. Kearns Jr.
Tax assessor	Dennis Bianchini
Tax collector	Ann Schubert
Building officer	Thomas Layou
Zoning officer	Thomas Sahol
Public Works	Richard Pendle

Housing & Construction

Housing Units, 2000*
Total	4,391
Median rent	$680
Median SF home value	$115,900

New Privately Owned Housing Units Authorized by Building Permit
	Units	Value
Total, 2004	103	$10,293,310
Single family	101	$10,291,810
Total, 2005	127	$12,571,053
Single family	127	$12,571,053

Real Property Valuation - parcels, 2005
	Number	Valuation
Total		$538,709,350
Vacant	362	17,652,800
Residential	4,061	454,006,650
Commercial	136	24,286,500
Industrial	20	28,909,500
Apartments	9	6,277,300
Farm land	31	4,879,500
Farm homestead	66	2,697,100

Average Property Value & Tax, 2005
Residential value	$110,662
Property tax	$3,935
FAIR rebate	$548

Public Library
Florence Twp. Public Library
1350 Hornberger Ave
Roebling, NJ 08554
609-499-0143

Director	Dorothy Revay

Library statistics, 2004
	Total	per capita
Volumes	25,008	2.33
Expenditure	$97,176	$9.04

Public Safety
Police
Chief	Gordon Dawson
Number of officers, 2004	24

Crime, 2004	Number	Rate
Total	168	14.9
Violent	25	2.2
Non-violent	143	12.7
Domestic Viol.	117	NA

Emergency/Fire
Director	Edward Kensler

Public School District
(for school year 2004-2005 except as noted)

Florence Township School District
201 Cedar St
Florence, NJ 08518
609-499-4600

Superintendent	Louis Talarico
Grade plan	K-12
Enrollment	1,509.0
Students per teacher	10.2
Per pupil expenditure	$10,849
Median faculty salary	$47,132
Median administrator salary	$97,380
Grade 12 enrollment	102.0
High school graduation rate	92.5%

Assessment test results
(percent scoring at proficient or advanced level)
	Language	Math
Grade 3	84.3%	75.5%
Grade 8	70.2%	58.2%
High school	80.2%	74.7%

SAT
Percent tested	74%
Average SAT math score	475
Average SAT verbal score	483

No Child Left Behind, 2003-04
Attendance rate (target = 90%)	93.8%
Drop rate	0.7%
Highly-qualified teachers	93.9%
District needs improvement?(AYP)	No

Municipal Finance

Fiscal Year 2005
Total tax levy	$19,227,122
County levy	3,510,044
County taxes	2,944,559
County library	257,822
County health	0
County open space	307,663
School levy	12,434,136
Local muni. budget	3,282,942
Misc. revenues	5,509,458
Total aid	$1,874,059
CMPTRA	884,959
Muni. block grant	44,921
Energy tax receipts	874,179
Homeland security	70,000

Fiscal Year 2006
Total aid	$1,874,059
CMPTRA	854,363
Muni. block grant	44,921
Energy tax receipts	904,775
Homeland security	70,000

Taxes
	2003	2004	2005
General tax rate per $100	3.06	3.280	3.557
Net valuation taxable	$522,894,749	$529,199,350	$540,769,035
State equalized value	$637,365,613	$736,905,994	$863,158,875
County equalization ratio	89.07	82.04	71.72

Demographics & Socio-Economic Characteristics
(2000 U.S. Census, except as noted)

Population
1980*	9,359
1990*	8,521
2000	8,857
Male	4,095
Female	4,762
2000 (revised)	10,296
2004 (estimate)*	12,556
Persons per sq. mi. of land	1,689

Race & Hispanic Origin, 2000
Race
White	8,326
Black/African American	88
Amer. Indian/Alaska Natv.	1
Asian	343
Natv. Hawaiian/Pac. Islander	5
Other Race	34
Two or more races	60
Hispanic origin, total	190
Mexican	14
Puerto Rican	30
Cuban	28
Other Hispanic	118

Age & Nativity, 2000
Under 5 years	542
18 years and over	6,935
21 years and over	6,756
65 years and over	1,806
85 years and over	261
Median Age	43.8
Native born	7,927
Foreign born	930

Educational Attainment, 2000
Population 25 years and over	6,484
0-8 yrs of school	2.9%
High School grad or higher	92.2%
Bachelor's degree or higher	57.7%
Graduate degree	24.4%

Income & Poverty, 1999
Per capita income	$42,133
Median household income	$88,706
Median family income	$102,047
Persons in poverty	507
H'holds receiving public assistance	52
H'holds receiving social security	1,044

Households, 2000
Total households	3,239
With persons under 18	1,040
With persons over 65	1,067
Family households	2,474
One-person households	671
Persons per household	2.62
Persons per family	3.05

Labor & Employment
Total civilian labor force, 2004**	5,378
Unemployment rate	3.6%
Total civilian labor force, 2000	4,399
Unemployment rate	3.3%

Employed persons 16 years and over by occupation, 2000
Managers & professionals	2,346
Service occupations	451
Sales & office occupations	1,074
Farming, fishing & forestry	0
Construction & maintenance	213
Production & transportation	172
Self-employed persons	246

*US Census Bureau
**New Jersey Department of Labor

General Information
Borough of Florham Park
111 Ridgedale Ave
Florham Park, NJ 07932
973-410-5300

Web site	www.florhamparkboro.net
Land area (sq. miles)	7.43
Water area (sq. miles)	0.02
Type of government	Borough
Form of government	B

Government

Legislative Districts
US Congressional	11
State Legislative	26

Local Officials, 2006
Mayor	Frank D. Tinari
Admin/Manager	John R. Massarano
Clerk	Judith Beecher
Finance Dir/Treas	Sheila A. Williams
Engineer	Robert Kirkpatrick
Attorney	Joseph Bell
Tax assessor	Lisa Baratto
Tax collector	NA
Building officer	Stephen Jones
Zoning officer	James Campbell
Public Works	NA

Housing & Construction

Housing Units, 2000*
Total	3,342
Median rent	$917
Median SF home value	$322,400

New Privately Owned Housing Units
Authorized by Building Permit
	Units	Value
Total, 2004	23	$6,454,765
Single family	23	$6,454,765
Total, 2005	15	$5,132,076
Single family	15	$5,132,076

Real Property Valuation - parcels, 2005
	Number	Valuation
Total		$1,586,480,000
Vacant	104	37,898,500
Residential	3,047	804,072,800
Commercial	198	517,707,600
Industrial	19	139,829,100
Apartments	4	86,852,200
Farm land	0	0
Farm homestead	1	119,800

Average Property Value & Tax, 2005
Residential value	$263,843
Property tax	$5,917
FAIR rebate	$641

Public Library
Florham Park Public Library
107 Ridgedale Ave
Florham Park, NJ 07932
973-377-2694

Director	Barbara McConville

Library statistics, 2004
	Total	per capita
Volumes	38,541	4.35
Expenditure	$594,017	$67.07

Public Safety

Police
Chief	Kim Chapman
Number of officers, 2004	31

Crime, 2004	Number	Rate
Total	120	9.6
Violent	4	0.3
Non-violent	116	9.3
Domestic Viol.	33	NA

Emergency/Fire
Director	Alban Kellogg

Public School District
(for school year 2004-2005 except as noted)

Florham Park School District
PO Box 39
Florham Park, NJ 07932
973-822-3880

Superintendent	William Ronzitti
Grade plan	K-8
Enrollment	982.0
Students per teacher	10.5
Per pupil expenditure	$13,092
Median faculty salary	$41,160
Median administrator salary	$93,950
Grade 12 enrollment	NA
High school graduation rate	NA

Assessment test results
(percent scoring at proficient or advanced level)
	Language	Math
Grade 3	92.9%	94.6%
Grade 8	89.2%	83.3%
High school	NA	NA

SAT
Percent tested	NA
Average SAT math score	NA
Average SAT verbal score	NA

No Child Left Behind, 2003-04
Attendence rate (target = 90%)	96.1%
Drop rate	NA
Highly-qualified teachers	89.5%
District needs improvement?(AYP)	No

Municipal Finance

Fiscal Year 2005
Total tax levy	$35,641,480
County levy	7,459,305
County taxes	6,107,975
County library	0
County health	0
County open space	1,351,330
School levy	18,882,374
Local muni. budget	9,299,801
Misc. revenues	4,437,664
Total aid	$1,510,944
CMPTRA	393,737
Muni. block grant	37,285
Energy tax receipts	1,009,922
Homeland security	70,000

Fiscal Year 2006
Total aid	$1,510,944
CMPTRA	358,390
Muni. block grant	37,285
Energy tax receipts	1,045,269
Homeland security	70,000

Taxes
	2003	2004	2005
General tax rate per $100	1.96	2.100	2.250
Net valuation taxable	$1,591,994,757	$1,592,303,999	$1,589,186,314
State equalized value	$2,617,981,840	$2,830,262,335	$2,948,397,614
County equalization ratio	67.2	60.81	56.21

Demographics & Socio-Economic Characteristics
(2000 U.S. Census, except as noted)

Population
1980*	1,892
1990*	2,181
2000	1,972
Male	967
Female	1,005
2004 (estimate)*	1,979
Persons per sq. mi. of land	239

Race & Hispanic Origin, 2000
Race
White	1,809
Black/African American	87
Amer. Indian/Alaska Natv.	3
Asian	17
Natv. Hawaiian/Pac. Islander	3
Other Race	31
Two or more races	22
Hispanic origin, total	68
Mexican	9
Puerto Rican	50
Cuban	5
Other Hispanic	4

Age & Nativity, 2000
Under 5 years	102
18 years and over	1,481
21 years and over	1,399
65 years and over	193
85 years and over	20
Median Age	37.5
Native born	1,919
Foreign born	53

Educational Attainment, 2000
Population 25 years and over	1,301
0-8 yrs of school	4.3%
High School grad or higher	83.0%
Bachelor's degree or higher	16.4%
Graduate degree	4.5%

Income & Poverty, 1999
Per capita income	$20,617
Median household income	$56,406
Median family income	$59,231
Persons in poverty	111
H'holds receiving public assistance	26
H'holds receiving social security	151

Households, 2000
Total households	671
With persons under 18	286
With persons over 65	133
Family households	552
One-person households	92
Persons per household	2.93
Persons per family	3.18

Labor & Employment
Total civilian labor force, 2004**	1,171
Unemployment rate	4.3%
Total civilian labor force, 2000	1,084
Unemployment rate	3.3%

Employed persons 16 years and over by occupation, 2000
Managers & professionals	251
Service occupations	153
Sales & office occupations	327
Farming, fishing & forestry	2
Construction & maintenance	147
Production & transportation	168
Self-employed persons	36

*US Census Bureau
**New Jersey Department of Labor

General Information
Borough of Folsom
Route 54
1700 12th St
Folsom, NJ 08037
609-561-3178

Web site	NA
Land area (sq. miles)	8.27
Water area (sq. miles)	0.19
Type of government	Borough
Form of government	B

Government

Legislative Districts
US Congressional	2
State Legislative	9

Local Officials, 2006
Mayor	Thomas Ballistreri
Admin/Manager	NA
Clerk	Gail Macera
Finance Dir/Treas	Dawn Stollenwerk
Engineer	Pollistina & Assoc.
Attorney	Michael Fitzgerald
Tax assessor	Joseph Ingemi
Tax collector	NA
Building officer	John Aloisio
Zoning officer	Lou DeStefano
Public Works	NA

Housing & Construction

Housing Units, 2000*
Total	702
Median rent	$883
Median SF home value	$104,700

New Privately Owned Housing Units Authorized by Building Permit
	Units	Value
Total, 2004	4	$648,087
Single family	4	$648,087
Total, 2005	2	$65,442
Single family	2	$65,442

Real Property Valuation - parcels, 2005
	Number	Valuation
Total		$101,250,475
Vacant	488	4,469,000
Residential	651	74,876,050
Commercial	46	9,488,120
Industrial	12	11,139,255
Apartments	0	0
Farm land	10	1,071,100
Farm homestead	58	206,950

Average Property Value & Tax, 2005
Residential value	$105,900
Property tax	$2,527
FAIR rebate	$552

Public Library
Hammonton Branch Library
451 Egg Harbor Rd
Hammonton, NJ 08037
609-561-2264

Branch Manager .... David Munn

Library statistics, 2004
	Total	per capita
Volumes	NA	NA
Expenditure	NA	NA

Public Safety

Police
Chief	NA
Number of officers, 2004	0

Crime, 2004	Number	Rate
Total	42	21.2
Violent	6	3
Non-violent	36	18.2
Domestic Viol.	19	NA

Emergency/Fire
Director .... Larry Smith

Public School District
(for school year 2004-2005 except as noted)

Folsom School District
1357 Mays Landing Rd
Folsom, NJ 08037
609-561-8666

Administrator	Robert Garguilo
Grade plan	K-12
Enrollment	381.0
Students per teacher	11.6
Per pupil expenditure	$9,573
Median faculty salary	$44,845
Median administrator salary	$62,265
Grade 12 enrollment	NA
High school graduation rate	NA

Assessment test results
(percent scoring at proficient or advanced level)
	Language	Math
Grade 3	78.3%	71.8%
Grade 8	81.1%	83.7%
High school	NA	NA

SAT
Percent tested	NA
Average SAT math score	NA
Average SAT verbal score	NA

No Child Left Behind, 2003-04
Attendence rate (target = 90%)	95.0%
Drop rate	NA
Highly-qualified teachers	100%
District needs improvement?(AYP)	No

Municipal Finance

Fiscal Year 2005
Total tax levy	$2,427,654
County levy	573,043
County taxes	467,866
County library	51,816
County health	25,500
County open space	27,862
School levy	1,463,990
Local muni. budget	390,621
Misc. revenues	928,678
Total aid	$272,227
CMPTRA	121,173
Muni. block grant	9,544
Energy tax receipts	141,510
Homeland security	0

Fiscal Year 2006
Total aid	$272,228
CMPTRA	116,221
Muni. block grant	9,544
Energy tax receipts	146,463
Homeland security	NA

Taxes
	2003	2004	2005
General tax rate per $100	2.20	2.330	2.387
Net valuation taxable	$100,716,780	$101,123,135	$101,736,617
State equalized value	$114,269,095	$137,348,669	$146,320,462
County equalization ratio	91.35	88.14	73.51

Demographics & Socio-Economic Characteristics
(2000 U.S. Census, except as noted)

Population

1980*	32,449
1990*	31,997
2000	35,461
Male	16,569
Female	18,892
2000 (revised)	35,404
2004 (estimate)*	37,310
Persons per sq. mi. of land	14,732

Race & Hispanic Origin, 2000
Race

White	22,253
Black/African American	615
Amer. Indian/Alaska Natv.	25
Asian	11,146
Natv. Hawaiian/Pac. Islander	20
Other Race	600
Two or more races	802
Hispanic origin, total	2,791
Mexican	78
Puerto Rican	562
Cuban	425
Other Hispanic	1,726

Age & Nativity, 2000

Under 5 years	1,870
18 years and over	29,261
21 years and over	28,499
65 years and over	7,151
85 years and over	901
Median Age	41.6
Native born	19,597
Foreign born	15,864

Educational Attainment, 2000

Population 25 years and over	27,490
0-8 yrs of school	4.7%
High School grad or higher	89.5%
Bachelor's degree or higher	48.2%
Graduate degree	18.5%

Income & Poverty, 1999

Per capita income	$37,899
Median household income	$58,161
Median family income	$72,140
Persons in poverty	2,807
H'holds receiving public assistance	188
H'holds receiving social security	4,843

Households, 2000

Total households	16,544
With persons under 18	3,909
With persons over 65	5,452
Family households	9,402
One-person households	6,448
Persons per household	2.14
Persons per family	2.88

Labor & Employment

Total civilian labor force, 2004**	18,257
Unemployment rate	4.3%
Total civilian labor force, 2000	17,802
Unemployment rate	3.4%

Employed persons 16 years and over by occupation, 2000

Managers & professionals	8,870
Service occupations	1,430
Sales & office occupations	5,324
Farming, fishing & forestry	0
Construction & maintenance	561
Production & transportation	1,020
Self-employed persons	1,160

*US Census Bureau
**New Jersey Department of Labor

General Information
Borough of Fort Lee
309 Main St
Fort Lee, NJ 07024
201-592-3546 x 1505

Web site	www.fortleenj.org
Land area (sq. miles)	2.53
Water area (sq. miles)	0.35
Type of government	Borough
Form of government	B

Government

Legislative Districts

US Congressional	9
State Legislative	38

Local Officials, 2006

Mayor	Jack Alter
Admin/Manager	Peggy Thomas
Clerk	Neil Grant
Finance Dir/Treas	Joseph Iannaconi
Engineer	Steven Boswell
Attorney	J. Sheldon Cohen
Tax assessor	Tim Leodori
Tax collector	Joseph Iannaconi
Building officer	Eric Swanson
Zoning officer	Barbara Klein
Public Works	Anthony Lione

Housing & Construction

Housing Units, 2000*

Total	17,446
Median rent	$1,101
Median SF home value	$287,000

New Privately Owned Housing Units
Authorized by Building Permit

	Units	Value
Total, 2004	42	$8,722,399
Single family	18	$5,209,049
Total, 2005	37	$9,116,661
Single family	29	$7,900,961

Real Property Valuation - parcels, 2005

	Number	Valuation
Total		$5,799,513,620
Vacant	109	42,856,900
Residential	7,935	3,167,290,200
Commercial	394	978,031,400
Industrial	9	10,568,600
Apartments	72	1,600,766,520
Farm land	0	0
Farm homestead	0	0

Average Property Value & Tax, 2005

Residential value	$399,154
Property tax	$6,342
FAIR rebate	$652

Public Library
Fort Lee Public Library
320 Main St
Fort Lee, NJ 07024
201-592-3628

Director	Rita Altomara

Library statistics, 2004

	Total	per capita
Volumes	126,498	3.57
Expenditure	$1,414,992	$39.90

Public Safety

Police

Chief	Tom Ripoli
Number of officers, 2004	102

Crime, 2004	Number	Rate
Total	513	13.8
Violent	35	0.9
Non-violent	478	12.9
Domestic Viol.	80	NA

Emergency/Fire

Director	Stephan Ferraro (Capt)

Public School District
(for school year 2004-2005 except as noted)

Fort Lee School District
255 Whiteman St
Fort Lee, NJ 07024
201-585-4610

Superintendent	Joanne Calabro
Grade plan	K-12
Enrollment	3,443.0
Students per teacher	12.3
Per pupil expenditure	$12,491
Median faculty salary	$65,490
Median administrator salary	$107,929
Grade 12 enrollment	253.0
High school graduation rate	97.0%

Assessment test results
(percent scoring at proficient or advanced level)

	Language	Math
Grade 3	91.8%	87.7%
Grade 8	75.7%	83.1%
High school	88.2%	91.5%

SAT

Percent tested	79%
Average SAT math score	571
Average SAT verbal score	515

No Child Left Behind, 2003-04

Attendance rate (target = 90%)	95.8%
Drop rate	0.8%
Highly-qualified teachers	97.9%
District needs improvement?(AYP)	No

Municipal Finance

Fiscal Year 2005

Total tax levy	$92,304,731
County levy	10,698,498
County taxes	10,158,232
County library	0
County health	0
County open space	540,266
School levy	38,592,292
Local muni. budget	43,013,942
Misc. revenues	10,190,093
Total aid	$2,511,469
CMPTRA	823,675
Muni. block grant	140,009
Energy tax receipts	1,407,785
Homeland security	140,000

Fiscal Year 2006

Total aid	$2,511,469
CMPTRA	774,402
Muni. block grant	140,009
Energy tax receipts	1,457,058
Homeland security	140,000

Taxes

	2003	2004	2005
General tax rate per $100	2.65	1.500	1.590
Net valuation taxable	$3,082,319,704	$5,861,219,604	$5,809,064,016
State equalized value	$4,501,050,970	$5,442,875,330	$5,684,015,671
County equalization ratio	79.74	129.91	107.70

Demographics & Socio-Economic Characteristics
(2000 U.S. Census, except as noted)

Population
1980*	4,654
1990*	5,114
2000	5,420
Male	2,664
Female	2,756
2004 (estimate)*	5,660
Persons per sq. mi. of land	166

Race & Hispanic Origin, 2000
Race
White	5,320
Black/African American	21
Amer. Indian/Alaska Natv.	3
Asian	21
Natv. Hawaiian/Pac. Islander	0
Other Race	27
Two or more races	28
Hispanic origin, total	96
Mexican	13
Puerto Rican	41
Cuban	17
Other Hispanic	25

Age & Nativity, 2000
Under 5 years	267
18 years and over	4,067
21 years and over	3,885
65 years and over	703
85 years and over	149
Median Age	40.8
Native born	5,254
Foreign born	165

Educational Attainment, 2000
Population 25 years and over	3,731
0-8 yrs of school	3.9%
High School grad or higher	88.8%
Bachelor's degree or higher	25.2%
Graduate degree	7.8%

Income & Poverty, 1999
Per capita income	$25,051
Median household income	$64,444
Median family income	$69,449
Persons in poverty	269
H'holds receiving public assistance	46
H'holds receiving social security	498

Households, 2000
Total households	1,839
With persons under 18	727
With persons over 65	390
Family households	1,473
One-person households	303
Persons per household	2.81
Persons per family	3.17

Labor & Employment
Total civilian labor force, 2004**	3,142
Unemployment rate	3.8%
Total civilian labor force, 2000	2,779
Unemployment rate	3.2%

Employed persons 16 years and over by occupation, 2000
Managers & professionals	1,000
Service occupations	449
Sales & office occupations	639
Farming, fishing & forestry	10
Construction & maintenance	302
Production & transportation	291
Self-employed persons	262

*US Census Bureau
**New Jersey Department of Labor

General Information
Township of Frankford
151 State Hwy 206
Augusta, NJ 07822
973-948-5566
Web site	www.frankfordtownship.com
Land area (sq. miles)	34.11
Water area (sq. miles)	1.31
Type of government	Township
Form of government	TC

Government

Legislative Districts
US Congressional	5
State Legislative	24

Local Officials, 2006
Mayor	William Hahn
Admin/Manager	NA
Clerk	Louanne Cular
Finance Dir/Treas	Gail Magura
Engineer	Harold Pellow
Attorney	Peter Laemers
Tax assessor	John Dyksen
Tax collector	NA
Building officer	Jeff Fette
Zoning officer	NA
Public Works	NA

Housing & Construction

Housing Units, 2000*
Total	2,295
Median rent	$675
Median SF home value	$179,100

New Privately Owned Housing Units Authorized by Building Permit
	Units	Value
Total, 2004	22	$4,035,246
Single family	22	$4,035,246
Total, 2005	19	$3,830,619
Single family	19	$3,830,619

Real Property Valuation - parcels, 2005
	Number	Valuation
Total		$422,687,380
Vacant	472	14,626,050
Residential	2,126	324,594,785
Commercial	99	35,181,300
Industrial	10	2,989,600
Apartments	2	485,500
Farm land	221	41,616,645
Farm homestead	377	3,193,500

Average Property Value & Tax, 2005
Residential value	$130,958
Property tax	$4,292
FAIR rebate	$539

Public Library
Sussex County Library
125 Morris Turnpike
Newton, NJ 07860
973-948-3660
Director	Stan Pollakoff

Library statistics, 2004
	Total	per capita
Volumes	NA	NA
Expenditure	NA	NA

Public Safety

Police
Chief	NA
Number of officers, 2004	0

Crime, 2004	Number	Rate
Total	80	14.2
Violent	3	0.5
Non-violent	77	13.7
Domestic Viol.	44	NA

Emergency/Fire
Director	Tom Jocquin

Public School District
(for school year 2004-2005 except as noted)

Frankford Township School District
4 Pines Rd
Branchville, NJ 07826
973-948-3727
Superintendent	Harry Tachovsky
Grade plan	K-8
Enrollment	760.0
Students per teacher	10.6
Per pupil expenditure	$11,581
Median faculty salary	$66,047
Median administrator salary	$95,000
Grade 12 enrollment	NA
High school graduation rate	NA

Assessment test results
(percent scoring at proficient or advanced level)
	Language	Math
Grade 3	92.0%	85.3%
Grade 8	84.3%	78.4%
High school	NA	NA

SAT
Percent tested	NA
Average SAT math score	NA
Average SAT verbal score	NA

No Child Left Behind, 2003-04
Attendence rate (target = 90%)	95.3%
Drop rate	NA
Highly-qualified teachers	99.5%
District needs improvement?(AYP)	No

Municipal Finance

Fiscal Year 2005
Total tax levy	$13,912,296
County levy	2,922,009
County taxes	2,479,964
County library	213,814
County health	100,651
County open space	127,580
School levy	9,673,040
Local muni. budget	1,317,247
Misc. revenues	2,115,785
Total aid	$702,771
CMPTRA	274,849
Muni. block grant	22,377
Energy tax receipts	392,479
Homeland security	0

Fiscal Year 2006
Total aid	$702,771
CMPTRA	261,112
Muni. block grant	22,377
Energy tax receipts	406,216
Homeland security	NA

Taxes
	2003	2004	2005
General tax rate per $100	3.07	3.150	3.280
Net valuation taxable	$417,134,332	$423,539,160	$424,539,664
State equalized value	$542,860,921	$631,998,101	$723,729,397
County equalization ratio	89.92	76.84	66.90

Demographics & Socio-Economic Characteristics
(2000 U.S. Census, except as noted)

Population
1980*	4,486
1990*	4,977
2000	5,160
Male	2,444
Female	2,716
2004 (estimate)*	5,233
Persons per sq. mi. of land	1,166

Race & Hispanic Origin, 2000
Race
White	4,907
Black/African American	32
Amer. Indian/Alaska Natv.	18
Asian	76
Natv. Hawaiian/Pac. Islander	0
Other Race	63
Two or more races	64
Hispanic origin, total	228
Mexican	16
Puerto Rican	96
Cuban	12
Other Hispanic	104

Age & Nativity, 2000
Under 5 years	357
18 years and over	3,741
21 years and over	3,579
65 years and over	603
85 years and over	85
Median Age	36.7
Native born	4,805
Foreign born	382

Educational Attainment, 2000
Population 25 years and over	3,325
0-8 yrs of school	3.6%
High School grad or higher	86.8%
Bachelor's degree or higher	15.3%
Graduate degree	4.7%

Income & Poverty, 1999
Per capita income	$19,386
Median household income	$44,985
Median family income	$52,682
Persons in poverty	360
H'holds receiving public assistance	35
H'holds receiving social security	581

Households, 2000
Total households	1,898
With persons under 18	751
With persons over 65	472
Family households	1,325
One-person households	457
Persons per household	2.69
Persons per family	3.22

Labor & Employment
Total civilian labor force, 2004**	3,000
Unemployment rate	3.9%
Total civilian labor force, 2000	2,547
Unemployment rate	3.6%

Employed persons 16 years and over by occupation, 2000
Managers & professionals	626
Service occupations	369
Sales & office occupations	703
Farming, fishing & forestry	0
Construction & maintenance	302
Production & transportation	456
Self-employed persons	156

*US Census Bureau
**New Jersey Department of Labor

General Information
Borough of Franklin
46 Main St
Franklin, NJ 07416
973-827-9280

Web site	www.franklinboro.com
Land area (sq. miles)	4.49
Water area (sq. miles)	0.06
Type of government	Borough
Form of government	B

Government

Legislative Districts
US Congressional	5
State Legislative	24

Local Officials, 2006
Mayor	Douglas C. Kistle
Admin/Manager	Richard R. Wolak
Clerk	Patricia Leasure
Finance Dir/Treas	Grant Rome
Engineer	Thomas Grau
Attorney	Richard Clark
Tax assessor	Scott Holzhauer
Tax collector	Terry Beshada
Building officer	Anthony Piechowski
Zoning officer	Patricia Fischer
Public Works	Mike Gunderman

Housing & Construction

Housing Units, 2000*
Total	1,997
Median rent	$771
Median SF home value	$123,000

New Privately Owned Housing Units Authorized by Building Permit
	Units	Value
Total, 2004	9	$1,117,627
Single family	9	$1,117,627
Total, 2005	9	$1,229,615
Single family	9	$1,229,615

Real Property Valuation - parcels, 2005
	Number	Valuation
Total		$240,998,800
Vacant	118	5,889,700
Residential	1,420	162,777,200
Commercial	115	58,002,400
Industrial	10	6,966,000
Apartments	20	4,994,300
Farm land	13	2,225,900
Farm homestead	17	143,300

Average Property Value & Tax, 2005
Residential value	$113,375
Property tax	$4,511
FAIR rebate	$557

Public Library
Franklin Branch Library†
103 Main St
Franklin, NJ 07416
973-827-6555

Branch Librarian . . . . Carol Crowley

Library statistics, 2004
	Total	per capita
Volumes	NA	NA
Expenditure	NA	NA

†Branch of County Library

Public Safety

Police
Chief	Joseph Kistle
Number of officers, 2004	14

Crime, 2004	Number	Rate
Total	136	25.9
Violent	5	1
Non-violent	131	25
Domestic Viol.	77	NA

Emergency/Fire
Director	Jason Doyle

Public School District
(for school year 2004-2005 except as noted)

Franklin Borough School District
50 Washington Ave
Franklin, NJ 07416
973-827-9775

Administrator	Thomas Turner
Grade plan	K-8
Enrollment	547.0
Students per teacher	9.0
Per pupil expenditure	$12,585
Median faculty salary	$44,000
Median administrator salary	$94,369
Grade 12 enrollment	NA
High school graduation rate	NA

Assessment test results
(percent scoring at proficient or advanced level)
	Language	Math
Grade 3	67.2%	82.8%
Grade 8	70.0%	57.1%
High school	NA	NA

SAT
Percent tested	NA
Average SAT math score	NA
Average SAT verbal score	NA

No Child Left Behind, 2003-04
Attendence rate (target = 90%)	95.5%
Drop rate	NA
Highly-qualified teachers	83.5%
District needs improvement?(AYP)	No

Municipal Finance

Fiscal Year 2005
Total tax levy	$9,680,715
County levy	1,672,516
County taxes	1,469,973
County library	126,649
County health	0
County open space	75,894
School levy	5,537,500
Local muni. budget	2,470,699
Misc. revenues	2,811,844
Total aid	$901,395
CMPTRA	280,100
Muni. block grant	21,778
Energy tax receipts	545,428
Homeland security	50,000

Fiscal Year 2006
Total aid	$901,395
CMPTRA	261,010
Muni. block grant	21,778
Energy tax receipts	564,518
Homeland security	50,000

Taxes
	2003	2004	2005
General tax rate per $100	4.08	4.090	3.980
Net valuation taxable	$230,548,897	$231,030,927	$243,330,078
State equalized value	$321,681,173	$364,613,184	$442,418,324
County equalization ratio	86.69	71.67	63.09

Demographics & Socio-Economic Characteristics
(2000 U.S. Census, except as noted)

Population
1980*	8,769
1990*	9,873
2000	10,422
Male	5,146
Female	5,276
2004 (estimate)*	11,260
Persons per sq. mi. of land	1,191

Race & Hispanic Origin, 2000
Race
White	9,521
Black/African American	96
Amer. Indian/Alaska Natv.	11
Asian	660
Natv. Hawaiian/Pac. Islander	1
Other Race	43
Two or more races	90
Hispanic origin, total	286
Mexican	11
Puerto Rican	62
Cuban	60
Other Hispanic	153

Age & Nativity, 2000
Under 5 years	703
18 years and over	7,433
21 years and over	7,209
65 years and over	1,164
85 years and over	104
Median Age	40.7
Native born	9,191
Foreign born	1,231

Educational Attainment, 2000
Population 25 years and over	6,885
0-8 yrs of school	1.7%
High School grad or higher	94.7%
Bachelor's degree or higher	52.9%
Graduate degree	21.5%

Income & Poverty, 1999
Per capita income	$59,763
Median household income	$132,373
Median family income	$142,930
Persons in poverty	331
H'holds receiving public assistance	17
H'holds receiving social security	798

Households, 2000
Total households	3,322
With persons under 18	1,508
With persons over 65	803
Family households	2,960
One-person households	287
Persons per household	3.13
Persons per family	3.34

Labor & Employment
Total civilian labor force, 2004**	5,449
Unemployment rate	3.0%
Total civilian labor force, 2000	4,900
Unemployment rate	2.3%

Employed persons 16 years and over by occupation, 2000
Managers & professionals	2,601
Service occupations	286
Sales & office occupations	1,442
Farming, fishing & forestry	0
Construction & maintenance	221
Production & transportation	235
Self-employed persons	483

*US Census Bureau
**New Jersey Department of Labor

General Information
Borough of Franklin Lakes
De Korte Dr
Franklin Lakes, NJ 07417
201-891-0048
Web site	www.franklinlakes.org
Land area (sq. miles)	9.45
Water area (sq. miles)	0.38
Type of government	Borough
Form of government	B

Government

Legislative Districts
US Congressional	5
State Legislative	40

Local Officials, 2006
Mayor	G. Thomas Donch
Admin/Manager	Robert Hoffmann
Clerk	Sally Bleeker
Finance Dir/Treas	Harold Laufeld III
Engineer	Boswell Engineering
Attorney	William Smith
Tax assessor	Claire Psota
Tax collector	Harold Laufeld III
Building officer	Michael Balala
Zoning officer	Joseph McDonnell
Public Works	Brian Peterson

Housing & Construction

Housing Units, 2000*
Total	3,395
Median rent	$1,313
Median SF home value	$609,400

New Privately Owned Housing Units Authorized by Building Permit
	Units	Value
Total, 2004	35	$21,795,750
Single family	35	$21,795,750
Total, 2005	36	$22,372,010
Single family	36	$22,372,010

Real Property Valuation - parcels, 2005
	Number	Valuation
Total		$2,193,072,532
Vacant	230	46,127,800
Residential	3,383	1,845,092,402
Commercial	53	274,931,030
Industrial	15	13,438,000
Apartments	1	9,783,000
Farm land	8	3,681,300
Farm homestead	10	19,000

Average Property Value & Tax, 2005
Residential value	$543,799
Property tax	$12,349
FAIR rebate	$590

Public Library
Franklin Lakes Public Library
470 DeKorte Dr
Franklin Lakes, NJ 07417
201-891-2224
Director . . . . Gerry McMahon (Actg.)

Library statistics, 2004
	Total	per capita
Volumes	70,048	6.72
Expenditure	$924,612	$88.72

Public Safety
Police
Chief	Irving Conklin
Number of officers, 2004	22

Crime, 2004	Number	Rate
Total	117	10.5
Violent	3	0.3
Non-violent	114	10.2
Domestic Viol.	43	NA

Emergency/Fire
Director . . . . Christopher Donch

Public School District
(for school year 2004-2005 except as noted)

Franklin Lakes School District
490 Pulis Ave
Franklin Lakes, NJ 07417
201-891-1856
Superintendent	Roger Bayersdorfer
Grade plan	K-8
Enrollment	1,547.0
Students per teacher	9.3
Per pupil expenditure	$13,481
Median faculty salary	$49,125
Median administrator salary	$101,978
Grade 12 enrollment	NA
High school graduation rate	NA

Assessment test results
(percent scoring at proficient or advanced level)
	Language	Math
Grade 3	96.4%	94.7%
Grade 8	87.5%	83.9%
High school	NA	NA

SAT
Percent tested	NA
Average SAT math score	NA
Average SAT verbal score	NA

No Child Left Behind, 2003-04
Attendance rate (target = 90%)	96.4%
Drop rate	NA
Highly-qualified teachers	100%
District needs improvement?(AYP)	No

Municipal Finance

Fiscal Year 2005
Total tax levy	$49,833,505
County levy	7,349,176
County taxes	6,981,696
County library	0
County health	0
County open space	367,480
School levy	34,871,034
Local muni. budget	7,613,295
Misc. revenues	6,098,015
Total aid	$2,156,244
CMPTRA	166,560
Muni. block grant	43,201
Energy tax receipts	1,870,514
Homeland security	70,000

Fiscal Year 2006
Total aid	$2,156,244
CMPTRA	101,092
Muni. block grant	43,201
Energy tax receipts	1,935,982
Homeland security	70,000

Taxes
	2003	2004	2005
General tax rate per $100	2.04	2.150	2.280
Net valuation taxable	$2,143,339,816	$2,170,458,118	$2,194,474,587
State equalized value	$3,286,322,932	$3,630,832,348	$4,008,172,762
County equalization ratio	71.63	65.22	59.76

Demographics & Socio-Economic Characteristics
(2000 U.S. Census, except as noted)

Population
1980*	12,396
1990*	14,482
2000	15,466
Male	7,723
Female	7,743
2004 (estimate)*	16,378
Persons per sq. mi. of land	292

Race & Hispanic Origin, 2000
Race
White	13,954
Black/African American	1,030
Amer. Indian/Alaska Natv.	48
Asian	63
Natv. Hawaiian/Pac. Islander	2
Other Race	193
Two or more races	176
Hispanic origin, total	543
Mexican	86
Puerto Rican	365
Cuban	13
Other Hispanic	79

Age & Nativity, 2000
Under 5 years	956
18 years and over	11,185
21 years and over	10,543
65 years and over	1,480
85 years and over	110
Median Age	36.4
Native born	15,111
Foreign born	355

Educational Attainment, 2000
Population 25 years and over	9,811
0-8 yrs of school	4.8%
High School grad or higher	81.8%
Bachelor's degree or higher	14.9%
Graduate degree	3.4%

Income & Poverty, 1999
Per capita income	$20,277
Median household income	$55,169
Median family income	$60,518
Persons in poverty	778
H'holds receiving public assistance	103
H'holds receiving social security	1,412

Households, 2000
Total households	5,225
With persons under 18	2,333
With persons over 65	1,085
Family households	4,190
One-person households	831
Persons per household	2.94
Persons per family	3.29

Labor & Employment
Total civilian labor force, 2004**	8,777
Unemployment rate	5.5%
Total civilian labor force, 2000	7,856
Unemployment rate	6.1%

Employed persons 16 years and over by occupation, 2000
Managers & professionals	1,949
Service occupations	1,105
Sales & office occupations	1,884
Farming, fishing & forestry	41
Construction & maintenance	1,291
Production & transportation	1,105
Self-employed persons	481

*US Census Bureau
**New Jersey Department of Labor

General Information
Township of Franklin
1571 Delsea Dr
Franklinville, NJ 08322
856-694-1234
Web site	www.franklintownship.com
Land area (sq. miles)	56.01
Water area (sq. miles)	0.42
Type of government	Township
Form of government	TC

Government

Legislative Districts
US Congressional	2
State Legislative	4

Local Officials, 2006
Mayor	David Ferrucci
Admin/Manager	NA
Clerk	Carol Coulbourn
Finance Dir/Treas	Frances Carder
Engineer	J. Michael Fralinger
Attorney	William Ziegler
Tax assessor	Timothy Mead
Tax collector	Lawrence Nightlinger Jr.
Building officer	Steven Rickerschauser
Zoning officer	Robert Errera
Public Works	William Nese

Housing & Construction

Housing Units, 2000*
Total	5,461
Median rent	$710
Median SF home value	$111,700

New Privately Owned Housing Units
Authorized by Building Permit
	Units	Value
Total, 2004	126	$17,400,753
Single family	123	$17,389,753
Total, 2005	101	$18,620,396
Single family	101	$18,620,396

Real Property Valuation - parcels, 2005
	Number	Valuation
Total		$702,628,000
Vacant	1,295	30,250,800
Residential	5,151	573,994,100
Commercial	264	59,033,600
Industrial	0	0
Apartments	8	1,981,200
Farm land	297	31,929,600
Farm homestead	720	5,438,700

Average Property Value & Tax, 2005
Residential value	$98,694
Property tax	$3,351
FAIR rebate	$546

Public Library
Franklin Twp. Free Pub Library
1584 Coles Mill Rd
Franklinville, NJ 08322
856-694-2833
Director	Denise Saia

Library statistics, 2004
	Total	per capita
Volumes	39,087	2.53
Expenditure	$330,756	$21.39

Public Safety

Police
Chief	Michael DiGiorgio
Number of officers, 2004	27

Crime, 2004	Number	Rate
Total	369	23
Violent	30	1.9
Non-violent	339	21.2
Domestic Viol.	171	NA

Emergency/Fire
Director	NA

Public School District
(for school year 2004-2005 except as noted)

Franklin Township School District
3228 Coles Mill Rd
Franklinville, NJ 08322
856-629-9500
Superintendent	John Scavelli Jr.
Grade plan	K-6
Enrollment	1,431.0
Students per teacher	12.3
Per pupil expenditure	$9,683
Median faculty salary	$52,670
Median administrator salary	$82,950
Grade 12 enrollment	NA
High school graduation rate	NA

Assessment test results
(percent scoring at proficient or advanced level)
	Language	Math
Grade 3	88.7%	83.2%
Grade 8	NA	NA
High school	NA	NA

SAT
Percent tested	NA
Average SAT math score	NA
Average SAT verbal score	NA

No Child Left Behind, 2003-04
Attendance rate (target = 90%)	95.1%
Drop rate	NA
Highly-qualified teachers	100%
District needs improvement?(AYP)	No

Municipal Finance

Fiscal Year 2005
Total tax levy	$23,979,857
County levy	6,013,656
County taxes	5,638,787
County library	0
County health	0
County open space	374,869
School levy	12,981,534
Local muni. budget	4,984,667
Misc. revenues	4,689,842
Total aid	$2,007,769
CMPTRA	658,378
Muni. block grant	63,369
Energy tax receipts	1,216,022
Homeland security	70,000

Fiscal Year 2006
Total aid	$2,007,769
CMPTRA	615,817
Muni. block grant	63,369
Energy tax receipts	1,258,583
Homeland security	70,000

Taxes
	2003	2004	2005
General tax rate per $100	3.14	3.218	3.396
Net valuation taxable	$663,239,078	$680,829,095	$706,202,585
State equalized value	$788,350,265	$900,718,752	$1,070,490,503
County equalization ratio	90.86	84.13	75.47

Demographics & Socio-Economic Characteristics
(2000 U.S. Census, except as noted)

Population
1980*	2,294
1990*	2,851
2000	2,990
Male	1,482
Female	1,508
2004 (estimate)*	3,133
Persons per sq. mi. of land	137

Race & Hispanic Origin, 2000
Race
White	2,916
Black/African American	12
Amer. Indian/Alaska Natv.	7
Asian	23
Natv. Hawaiian/Pac. Islander	0
Other Race	10
Two or more races	22
Hispanic origin, total	67
Mexican	13
Puerto Rican	20
Cuban	7
Other Hispanic	27

Age & Nativity, 2000
Under 5 years	174
18 years and over	2,244
21 years and over	2,183
65 years and over	361
85 years and over	33
Median Age	41.6
Native born	2,785
Foreign born	205

Educational Attainment, 2000
Population 25 years and over	2,112
0-8 yrs of school	2.2%
High School grad or higher	93.5%
Bachelor's degree or higher	44.5%
Graduate degree	16.2%

Income & Poverty, 1999
Per capita income	$39,668
Median household income	$91,364
Median family income	$96,320
Persons in poverty	49
H'holds receiving public assistance	5
H'holds receiving social security	258

Households, 2000
Total households	1,091
With persons under 18	403
With persons over 65	260
Family households	890
One-person households	155
Persons per household	2.74
Persons per family	3.04

Labor & Employment
Total civilian labor force, 2004**	1,878
Unemployment rate	3.6%
Total civilian labor force, 2000	1,668
Unemployment rate	3.0%

Employed persons 16 years and over by occupation, 2000
Managers & professionals	831
Service occupations	118
Sales & office occupations	374
Farming, fishing & forestry	4
Construction & maintenance	148
Production & transportation	143
Self-employed persons	194

*US Census Bureau
**New Jersey Department of Labor

General Information
Township of Franklin
202 Sidney Rd
Pittstown, NJ 08867
908-735-5215

Web site	NA
Land area (sq. miles)	22.88
Water area (sq. miles)	0.04
Type of government	Township
Form of government	TC

Government

Legislative Districts
US Congressional	12
State Legislative	23

Local Officials, 2006
Mayor	Lawrence Remaly
Admin/Manager	NA
Clerk	Ursula Stryker
Finance Dir/Treas	Ronald Mathews
Engineer	Robert C. Bogart
Attorney	William J. Caldwell
Tax assessor	Mary Mastro
Tax collector	NA
Building officer	George Reichert
Zoning officer	NA
Public Works	NA

Housing & Construction

Housing Units, 2000*
Total	1,125
Median rent	$892
Median SF home value	$283,500

New Privately Owned Housing Units Authorized by Building Permit
	Units	Value
Total, 2004	18	$5,501,800
Single family	18	$5,501,800
Total, 2005	8	$1,666,081
Single family	8	$1,666,081

Real Property Valuation - parcels, 2005
	Number	Valuation
Total		$527,084,987
Vacant	81	8,714,400
Residential	860	359,765,100
Commercial	23	39,024,100
Industrial	6	3,712,400
Apartments	3	1,246,700
Farm land	248	110,437,600
Farm homestead	391	4,184,687

Average Property Value & Tax, 2005
Residential value	$290,927
Property tax	$5,980
FAIR rebate	$549

Public Library

No public municipal library.

Library statistics, 2004
	Total	per capita
Volumes	NA	NA
Expenditure	NA	NA

Public Safety

Police
Chief	Edward Mangini
Number of officers, 2004	6

Crime, 2004	Number	Rate
Total	40	12.8
Violent	1	0.3
Non-violent	39	12.4
Domestic Viol.	9	NA

Emergency/Fire
Director	Christopher Vallat

Public School District
(for school year 2004-2005 except as noted)

Franklin Township School District
226 Quakertown Rd
Quakertown, NJ 08868
908-735-7929

Administrator	Karen Lewis
Grade plan	K-8
Enrollment	400.0
Students per teacher	10.7
Per pupil expenditure	$11,906
Median faculty salary	$49,665
Median administrator salary	$81,120
Grade 12 enrollment	NA
High school graduation rate	NA

Assessment test results
(percent scoring at proficient or advanced level)
	Language	Math
Grade 3	90.7%	95.4%
Grade 8	88.5%	86.7%
High school	NA	NA

SAT
Percent tested	NA
Average SAT math score	NA
Average SAT verbal score	NA

No Child Left Behind, 2003-04
Attendence rate (target = 90%)	96.0%
Drop rate	NA
Highly-qualified teachers	100%
District needs improvement?(AYP)	No

Municipal Finance

Fiscal Year 2005
Total tax levy	$10,858,463
County levy	1,956,072
County taxes	1,659,150
County library	139,310
County health	0
County open space	157,612
School levy	7,261,797
Local muni. budget	1,640,594
Misc. revenues	1,525,962
Total aid	$421,004
CMPTRA	142,944
Muni. block grant	12,475
Energy tax receipts	240,585
Homeland security	25,000

Fiscal Year 2006
Total aid	$421,003
CMPTRA	134,523
Muni. block grant	12,475
Energy tax receipts	249,005
Homeland security	25,000

Taxes
	2003	2004	2005
General tax rate per $100	3.06	2.010	2.060
Net valuation taxable	$327,123,362	$521,592,762	$528,248,963
State equalized value	$469,397,850	$530,377,300	$571,203,463
County equalization ratio	66.6	100.58	95.95

Demographics & Socio-Economic Characteristics
(2000 U.S. Census, except as noted)

Population
1980*	31,358
1990*	42,780
2000	50,903
Male	24,353
Female	26,550
2004 (estimate)*	56,863
Persons per sq. mi. of land	1,216

Race & Hispanic Origin, 2000
Race
White	28,052
Black/African American	13,223
Amer. Indian/Alaska Natv.	93
Asian	6,486
Natv. Hawaiian/Pac. Islander	21
Other Race	1,811
Two or more races	1,217
Hispanic origin, total	4,127
Mexican	522
Puerto Rican	1,372
Cuban	206
Other Hispanic	2,027

Age & Nativity, 2000
Under 5 years	3,733
18 years and over	39,361
21 years and over	38,095
65 years and over	5,805
85 years and over	943
Median Age	36.1
Native born	39,092
Foreign born	11,811

Educational Attainment, 2000
Population 25 years and over	36,111
0-8 yrs of school	4.6%
High School grad or higher	88.2%
Bachelor's degree or higher	43.3%
Graduate degree	16.0%

Income & Poverty, 1999
Per capita income	$31,209
Median household income	$67,923
Median family income	$78,177
Persons in poverty	2,535
H'holds receiving public assistance	350
H'holds receiving social security	3,694

Households, 2000
Total households	19,355
With persons under 18	6,560
With persons over 65	3,699
Family households	12,989
One-person households	4,975
Persons per household	2.58
Persons per family	3.14

Labor & Employment
Total civilian labor force, 2004**	31,591
Unemployment rate	3.3%
Total civilian labor force, 2000	27,856
Unemployment rate	3.5%

Employed persons 16 years and over by occupation, 2000
Managers & professionals	13,889
Service occupations	2,450
Sales & office occupations	6,833
Farming, fishing & forestry	18
Construction & maintenance	1,384
Production & transportation	2,312
Self-employed persons	913

*US Census Bureau
**New Jersey Department of Labor

General Information
Township of Franklin
475 De Mott Lane
Somerset, NJ 08873
732-873-2500
Web site	www.franklintwpnj.org
Land area (sq. miles)	46.77
Water area (sq. miles)	0.07
Type of government	Township
Form of government	CM '50

Government

Legislative Districts
US Congressional	6, 12
State Legislative	17

Local Officials, 2006
Mayor	Brian D. Levine
Admin/Manager	Kenneth Daly
Clerk	Ann Marie McCarthy
Finance Dir/Treas	Marc D. Dashield
Engineer	Thomas Zilinek
Attorney	Louis Rainone
Tax assessor	Burnham Hobbs
Tax collector	Carol Langone
Building officer	Vincent Lupo
Zoning officer	Vincent Dominach
Public Works	Thomas Zilinek

Housing & Construction

Housing Units, 2000*
Total	19,789
Median rent	$897
Median SF home value	$169,700

New Privately Owned Housing Units Authorized by Building Permit
	Units	Value
Total, 2004	1,075	$134,141,112
Single family	522	$59,305,869
Total, 2005	475	$56,429,466
Single family	412	$52,825,753

Real Property Valuation - parcels, 2005
	Number	Valuation
Total		$7,439,956,470
Vacant	1,689	146,613,750
Residential	17,808	5,533,243,600
Commercial	467	879,781,300
Industrial	162	611,447,300
Apartments	26	209,567,220
Farm land	125	56,405,400
Farm homestead	234	2,897,900

Average Property Value & Tax, 2005
Residential value	$306,847
Property tax	$5,892
FAIR rebate	$520

Public Library
Franklin Township Library
485 De Mott Lane
Somerset, NJ 08873
732-873-8700
Director	January Adams

Library statistics, 2004
	Total	per capita
Volumes	117,998	2.32
Expenditure	$1,588,142	$31.20

Public Safety

Police
Chief	Craig Novick
Number of officers, 2004	100

Crime, 2004	Number	Rate
Total	874	15.9
Violent	112	2
Non-violent	762	13.9
Domestic Viol.	494	NA

Emergency/Fire
Director	John Hauss

Public School District
(for school year 2004-2005 except as noted)

Franklin Township School District
1755 Amwell Rd
Somerset, NJ 08873
732-873-2400
Superintendent	William Westfield
Grade plan	K-12
Enrollment	6,724.0
Students per teacher	11.0
Per pupil expenditure	$13,353
Median faculty salary	$53,400
Median administrator salary	$107,862
Grade 12 enrollment	323.5
High school graduation rate	93.1%

Assessment test results
(percent scoring at proficient or advanced level)
	Language	Math
Grade 3	75.8%	80.0%
Grade 8	65.7%	56.2%
High school	83.0%	73.5%

SAT
Percent tested	79%
Average SAT math score	507
Average SAT verbal score	489

No Child Left Behind, 2003-04
Attendence rate (target = 90%)	94.4%
Drop rate	0.4%
Highly-qualified teachers	93.5%
District needs improvement?(AYP)	Yes

Municipal Finance

Fiscal Year 2005
Total tax levy	$143,112,133
County levy	23,294,601
County taxes	21,250,937
County library	0
County health	0
County open space	2,043,664
School levy	90,270,019
Local muni. budget	29,547,513
Misc. revenues	20,226,707
Total aid	$6,287,545
CMPTRA	2,264,467
Muni. block grant	199,592
Energy tax receipts	3,683,486
Homeland security	140,000

Fiscal Year 2006
Total aid	$6,287,545
CMPTRA	2,135,545
Muni. block grant	199,592
Energy tax receipts	3,812,408
Homeland security	140,000

Taxes
	2003	2004	2005
General tax rate per $100	2.19	2.060	1.930
Net valuation taxable	$5,761,931,443	$6,327,503,738	$7,453,186,258
State equalized value	$5,847,895,507	$6,598,121,626	$7,694,803,075
County equalization ratio	111.08	106.41	109.36

Demographics & Socio-Economic Characteristics
(2000 U.S. Census, except as noted)

Population
1980*	2,341
1990*	2,404
2000	2,768
Male	1,403
Female	1,365
2004 (estimate)*	3,199
Persons per sq. mi. of land	133

Race & Hispanic Origin, 2000
Race
White	2,686
Black/African American	23
Amer. Indian/Alaska Natv.	2
Asian	24
Natv. Hawaiian/Pac. Islander	0
Other Race	3
Two or more races	30
Hispanic origin, total	55
Mexican	8
Puerto Rican	18
Cuban	3
Other Hispanic	26

Age & Nativity, 2000
Under 5 years	195
18 years and over	1,970
21 years and over	1,903
65 years and over	281
85 years and over	20
Median Age	38.2
Native born	2,666
Foreign born	102

Educational Attainment, 2000
Population 25 years and over	1,818
0-8 yrs of school	3.7%
High School grad or higher	87.0%
Bachelor's degree or higher	21.5%
Graduate degree	6.7%

Income & Poverty, 1999
Per capita income	$27,224
Median household income	$69,115
Median family income	$72,763
Persons in poverty	86
H'holds receiving public assistance	25
H'holds receiving social security	189

Households, 2000
Total households	972
With persons under 18	415
With persons over 65	211
Family households	750
One-person households	181
Persons per household	2.84
Persons per family	3.28

Labor & Employment
Total civilian labor force, 2004**	1,605
Unemployment rate	5.2%
Total civilian labor force, 2000	1,463
Unemployment rate	2.7%

Employed persons 16 years and over by occupation, 2000
Managers & professionals	408
Service occupations	191
Sales & office occupations	385
Farming, fishing & forestry	17
Construction & maintenance	224
Production & transportation	198
Self-employed persons	82

*US Census Bureau
**New Jersey Department of Labor

General Information
Township of Franklin
PO Box 547
2093 Rt 57
Broadway, NJ 08808
908-689-3994
Web site	www.franklintwpwarren.org
Land area (sq. miles)	23.99
Water area (sq. miles)	0.04
Type of government	Township
Form of government	TC

Government
Legislative Districts
US Congressional	5
State Legislative	23

Local Officials, 2006
Mayor	Larry Adams
Admin/Manager	NA
Clerk	Denise L.Cicerelle
Finance Dir/Treas	Dawn Merante
Engineer	Michael Finelli
Attorney	James Broscious
Tax assessor	Eloise Hagaman
Tax collector	Karin Kneafsey
Building officer	Walter Van Lieu
Zoning officer	Jim Onembo
Public Works	NA

Housing & Construction
Housing Units, 2000*
Total	1,019
Median rent	$725
Median SF home value	$176,200

New Privately Owned Housing Units
Authorized by Building Permit
	Units	Value
Total, 2004	9	$2,038,950
Single family	9	$2,038,950
Total, 2005	8	$2,028,975
Single family	8	$2,028,975

Real Property Valuation - parcels, 2005
	Number	Valuation
Total		$398,475,105
Vacant	120	6,415,300
Residential	937	282,125,400
Commercial	46	32,808,300
Industrial	15	26,257,900
Apartments	1	306,300
Farm land	142	45,366,500
Farm homestead	395	5,195,405

Average Property Value & Tax, 2005
Residential value	$215,706
Property tax	$4,798
FAIR rebate	$512

Public Library
Franklin Branch Library†
1502 Rte 57 West
Washington, NJ 07882
908-689-7922
Branch Librarian	Chris Reedell

Library statistics, 2004
	Total	per capita
Volumes	NA	NA
Expenditure	NA	NA

†Branch of County Library

Public Safety
Police
Chief	(State)
Number of officers, 2004	0

Crime, 2004	Number	Rate
Total	27	8.5
Violent	2	0.6
Non-violent	25	7.8
Domestic Viol.	13	NA

Emergency/Fire
Director	Raymond Read

Public School District
(for school year 2004-2005 except as noted)

Franklin Township School District
52 Asbury Broadway Rd
Washington, NJ 07882
908-689-2958
Superintendent	Roger Jinks
Grade plan	K-6
Enrollment	382.0
Students per teacher	10.7
Per pupil expenditure	$9,760
Median faculty salary	$42,500
Median administrator salary	$83,387
Grade 12 enrollment	NA
High school graduation rate	NA

Assessment test results
(percent scoring at proficient or advanced level)
	Language	Math
Grade 3	82.7%	71.2%
Grade 8	NA	NA
High school	NA	NA

SAT
Percent tested	NA
Average SAT math score	NA
Average SAT verbal score	NA

No Child Left Behind, 2003-04
Attendence rate (target = 90%)	95.7%
Drop rate	NA
Highly-qualified teachers	100%
District needs improvement?(AYP)	No

Municipal Finance
Fiscal Year 2005
Total tax levy	$8,888,312
County levy	2,411,828
County taxes	1,993,639
County library	192,499
County health	0
County open space	225,690
School levy	5,789,199
Local muni. budget	687,285
Misc. revenues	1,344,945
Total aid	$382,894
CMPTRA	144,288
Muni. block grant	10,853
Energy tax receipts	227,753
Homeland security	0

Fiscal Year 2006
Total aid	$382,894
CMPTRA	136,317
Muni. block grant	10,853
Energy tax receipts	235,724
Homeland security	NA

Taxes
	2003	2004	2005
General tax rate per $100	3.04	2.100	2.230
Net valuation taxable	$244,098,181	$399,181,582	$399,556,586
State equalized value	$319,877,055	$373,108,781	$406,218,571
County equalization ratio	84.54	115.25	107.01

Demographics & Socio-Economic Characteristics
(2000 U.S. Census, except as noted)

Population
1980*	2,281
1990*	2,763
2000	2,860
Male	1,399
Female	1,461
2004 (estimate)*	3,253
Persons per sq. mi. of land	183

Race & Hispanic Origin, 2000
Race
White	2,779
Black/African American	15
Amer. Indian/Alaska Natv.	7
Asian	24
Natv. Hawaiian/Pac. Islander	0
Other Race	16
Two or more races	19
Hispanic origin, total	62
Mexican	9
Puerto Rican	16
Cuban	12
Other Hispanic	25

Age & Nativity, 2000
Under 5 years	197
18 years and over	2,099
21 years and over	2,017
65 years and over	266
85 years and over	27
Median Age	39.3
Native born	2,721
Foreign born	139

Educational Attainment, 2000
Population 25 years and over	1,946
0-8 yrs of school	2.8%
High School grad or higher	92.9%
Bachelor's degree or higher	34.0%
Graduate degree	10.9%

Income & Poverty, 1999
Per capita income	$31,430
Median household income	$75,710
Median family income	$84,038
Persons in poverty	62
H'holds receiving public assistance	6
H'holds receiving social security	210

Households, 2000
Total households	982
With persons under 18	401
With persons over 65	194
Family households	818
One-person households	131
Persons per household	2.89
Persons per family	3.18

Labor & Employment
Total civilian labor force, 2004**	1,677
Unemployment rate	2.4%
Total civilian labor force, 2000	1,645
Unemployment rate	1.1%

Employed persons 16 years and over by occupation, 2000
Managers & professionals	678
Service occupations	234
Sales & office occupations	434
Farming, fishing & forestry	5
Construction & maintenance	144
Production & transportation	132
Self-employed persons	171

*US Census Bureau
**New Jersey Department of Labor

General Information
Township of Fredon
443 Rt 94
Newton, NJ 07860
973-383-7025
Web site	www.twp.fredon.nj.us
Land area (sq. miles)	17.76
Water area (sq. miles)	0.19
Type of government	Township
Form of government	TC

Government

Legislative Districts
US Congressional	5
State Legislative	24

Local Officials, 2006
Mayor	John Richardson Sr.
Admin/Manager	NA
Clerk	Joanne Charner
Finance Dir/Treas	William Liverance
Engineer	Harold E. Pellow
Attorney	William Hinkes
Tax assessor	Donald DeKorte
Tax collector	Gisela Boltzer
Building officer	John de Jager
Zoning officer	Arlene Fisher
Public Works	Donald Nelson

Housing & Construction

Housing Units, 2000*
Total	1,019
Median rent	$708
Median SF home value	$199,700

New Privately Owned Housing Units Authorized by Building Permit
	Units	Value
Total, 2004	29	$5,279,352
Single family	29	$5,279,352
Total, 2005	25	$5,460,820
Single family	25	$5,460,820

Real Property Valuation - parcels, 2005
	Number	Valuation
Total		$262,866,200
Vacant	154	7,003,300
Residential	1,029	212,702,400
Commercial	31	12,114,600
Industrial	5	3,912,700
Apartments	0	0
Farm land	106	25,193,400
Farm homestead	188	1,939,800

Average Property Value & Tax, 2005
Residential value	$176,370
Property tax	$5,428
FAIR rebate	$491

Public Library
No public municipal library.

Library statistics, 2004
	Total	per capita
Volumes	NA	NA
Expenditure	NA	NA

Public Safety

Police
Chief	NA
Number of officers, 2004	0

Crime, 2004	Number	Rate
Total	11	3.5
Violent	1	0.3
Non-violent	10	3.2
Domestic Viol.	11	NA

Emergency/Fire
Director	Robert Lewis

Public School District
(for school year 2004-2005 except as noted)

Fredon Township School District
459 Route 94
Newton, NJ 07860
973-383-4151
Superintendent	Randy Pratt
Grade plan	K-6
Enrollment	327.0
Students per teacher	12.4
Per pupil expenditure	$10,036
Median faculty salary	$38,899
Median administrator salary	$81,900
Grade 12 enrollment	NA
High school graduation rate	NA

Assessment test results
(percent scoring at proficient or advanced level)
	Language	Math
Grade 3	90.0%	90.0%
Grade 8	NA	NA
High school	NA	NA

SAT
Percent tested	NA
Average SAT math score	NA
Average SAT verbal score	NA

No Child Left Behind, 2003-04
Attendence rate (target = 90%)	95.4%
Drop rate	NA
Highly-qualified teachers	100%
District needs improvement?(AYP)	No

Municipal Finance

Fiscal Year 2005
Total tax levy	$8,113,178
County levy	1,848,926
County taxes	1,569,219
County library	135,293
County health	63,688
County open space	80,725
School levy	5,101,928
Local muni. budget	1,162,323
Misc. revenues	1,431,200
Total aid	$377,516
CMPTRA	156,060
Muni. block grant	12,090
Energy tax receipts	209,366
Homeland security	0

Fiscal Year 2006
Total aid	$377,516
CMPTRA	148,732
Muni. block grant	12,090
Energy tax receipts	216,694
Homeland security	NA

Taxes
	2003	2004	2005
General tax rate per $100	3.01	3.070	3.080
Net valuation taxable	$239,397,337	$250,259,567	$263,630,328
State equalized value	$333,608,329	$380,475,836	$455,713,618
County equalization ratio	88.16	71.76	65.70

Demographics & Socio-Economic Characteristics
(2000 U.S. Census, except as noted)

Population
1980*	10,020
1990*	10,742
2000	10,976
Male	5,656
Female	5,320
2004 (estimate)*	11,527
Persons per sq. mi. of land	5,777

Race & Hispanic Origin, 2000
Race
White	7,795
Black/African American	1,738
Amer. Indian/Alaska Natv.	60
Asian	269
Natv. Hawaiian/Pac. Islander	2
Other Race	729
Two or more races	383
Hispanic origin, total	3,081
Mexican	1,903
Puerto Rican	627
Cuban	31
Other Hispanic	520

Age & Nativity, 2000
Under 5 years	858
18 years and over	8,258
21 years and over	7,788
65 years and over	1,171
85 years and over	169
Median Age	33
Native born	8,720
Foreign born	2,256

Educational Attainment, 2000
Population 25 years and over	7,148
0-8 yrs of school	10.7%
High School grad or higher	76.0%
Bachelor's degree or higher	19.7%
Graduate degree	4.6%

Income & Poverty, 1999
Per capita income	$19,910
Median household income	$48,654
Median family income	$53,374
Persons in poverty	1,314
H'holds receiving public assistance	108
H'holds receiving social security	931

Households, 2000
Total households	3,695
With persons under 18	1,436
With persons over 65	898
Family households	2,570
One-person households	898
Persons per household	2.96
Persons per family	3.39

Labor & Employment
Total civilian labor force, 2004**	6,436
Unemployment rate	5.6%
Total civilian labor force, 2000	5,833
Unemployment rate	7.0%

Employed persons 16 years and over by occupation, 2000
Managers & professionals	1,410
Service occupations	1,374
Sales & office occupations	1,378
Farming, fishing & forestry	36
Construction & maintenance	542
Production & transportation	683
Self-employed persons	228

*US Census Bureau
**New Jersey Department of Labor

General Information
Freehold Borough
51 W Main St
Freehold, NJ 07728
732-462-1410

Web site	NA
Land area (sq. miles)	2.00
Water area (sq. miles)	0
Type of government	Borough
Form of government	B

Government
Legislative Districts
US Congressional	12
State Legislative	12

Local Officials, 2006
Mayor	Michael Wilson
Admin/Manager	Joseph Bellina
Clerk	Linda Cottrell
Finance Dir/Treas	Nancy Forman
Engineer	Jim Kovacs
Attorney	Kerry Higgins
Tax assessor	Mitchell Elias
Tax collector	Edward Lewis
Building officer	Henry Stryker
Zoning officer	Henry Stryker
Public Works	Bobby Holmes

Housing & Construction
Housing Units, 2000*
Total	3,821
Median rent	$821
Median SF home value	$137,500

New Privately Owned Housing Units Authorized by Building Permit
	Units	Value
Total, 2004	29	$2,555,145
Single family	27	$2,386,646
Total, 2005	21	$1,865,935
Single family	21	$1,865,935

Real Property Valuation - parcels, 2005
	Number	Valuation
Total		$1,075,070,000
Vacant	95	16,243,200
Residential	2,935	756,435,500
Commercial	251	243,404,500
Industrial	4	35,266,400
Apartments	12	23,720,400
Farm land	0	0
Farm homestead	0	0

Average Property Value & Tax, 2005
Residential value	$257,729
Property tax	$4,676
FAIR rebate	$539

Public Library
Freehold Public Library
28 1/2 E Main St
Freehold, NJ 07728
732-462-5135
Director.............Barbara Greenberg

Library statistics, 2004
	Total	per capita
Volumes	26,194	2.39
Expenditure	$274,590	$25.02

Public Safety
Police
Chief	Michael Beierschmitt
Number of officers, 2004	35

Crime, 2004	Number	Rate
Total	369	32.2
Violent	55	4.8
Non-violent	314	27.4
Domestic Viol.	159	NA

Emergency/Fire
Director.................Charles Megill

Public School District
(for school year 2004-2005 except as noted)

Freehold Borough School District
280 Park Ave
Freehold, NJ 07728
732-761-2102

Superintendent	Phil Meara
Grade plan	K-8
Enrollment	1,347.0
Students per teacher	12.3
Per pupil expenditure	$9,344
Median faculty salary	$50,850
Median administrator salary	$99,015
Grade 12 enrollment	NA
High school graduation rate	NA

Assessment test results
(percent scoring at proficient or advanced level)
	Language	Math
Grade 3	66.0%	57.9%
Grade 8	56.1%	45.6%
High school	NA	NA

SAT
Percent tested	NA
Average SAT math score	NA
Average SAT verbal score	NA

No Child Left Behind, 2003-04
Attendence rate (target = 90%)	95.6%
Drop rate	NA
Highly-qualified teachers	87.1%
District needs improvement?(AYP)	No

Municipal Finance
Fiscal Year 2005
Total tax levy	$19,693,556
County levy	2,923,773
County taxes	2,759,996
County library	0
County health	0
County open space	163,777
School levy	10,279,306
Local muni. budget	6,490,478
Misc. revenues	5,155,898
Total aid	$1,748,854
CMPTRA	942,395
Muni. block grant	47,003
Energy tax receipts	689,456
Homeland security	70,000

Fiscal Year 2006
Total aid	$1,748,854
CMPTRA	918,264
Muni. block grant	47,003
Energy tax receipts	713,587
Homeland security	70,000

Taxes
	2003	2004	2005
General tax rate per $100	3.38	3.552	1.815
Net valuation taxable	$484,548,775	$487,574,695	$1,085,562,930
State equalized value	$734,832,840	$904,115,361	$1,074,921,210
County equalization ratio	76.16	65.94	119.00

Demographics & Socio-Economic Characteristics
(2000 U.S. Census, except as noted)

Population

1980*	19,202
1990*	24,710
2000	31,537
Male	15,588
Female	15,949
2004 (estimate)*	33,853
Persons per sq. mi. of land	880

Race & Hispanic Origin, 2000

Race

White	27,466
Black/African American	1,616
Amer. Indian/Alaska Natv.	44
Asian	1,623
Natv. Hawaiian/Pac. Islander	5
Other Race	374
Two or more races	409
Hispanic origin, total	1,637
Mexican	328
Puerto Rican	607
Cuban	133
Other Hispanic	569

Age & Nativity, 2000

Under 5 years	2,137
18 years and over	23,564
21 years and over	22,722
65 years and over	3,781
85 years and over	613
Median Age	38.3
Native born	28,008
Foreign born	3,529

Educational Attainment, 2000

Population 25 years and over	21,808
0-8 yrs of school	3.6%
High School grad or higher	88.8%
Bachelor's degree or higher	37.5%
Graduate degree	13.1%

Income & Poverty, 1999

Per capita income	$31,505
Median household income	$77,185
Median family income	$89,845
Persons in poverty	1,155
H'holds receiving public assistance	113
H'holds receiving social security	2,726

Households, 2000

Total households	10,814
With persons under 18	4,266
With persons over 65	2,468
Family households	8,279
One-person households	2,163
Persons per household	2.76
Persons per family	3.21

Labor & Employment

Total civilian labor force, 2004**	15,172
Unemployment rate	2.8%
Total civilian labor force, 2000	15,970
Unemployment rate	2.8%

Employed persons 16 years and over by occupation, 2000

Managers & professionals	7,117
Service occupations	1,422
Sales & office occupations	5,002
Farming, fishing & forestry	24
Construction & maintenance	1,031
Production & transportation	934
Self-employed persons	787

*US Census Bureau
**New Jersey Department of Labor

General Information

Freehold Township
1 Municipal Plaza
Freehold, NJ 07728
732-294-2000

Web site	www.twp.freehold.nj.us
Land area (sq. miles)	38.45
Water area (sq. miles)	0.08
Type of government	Township
Form of government	TC

Government

Legislative Districts

US Congressional	12
State Legislative	12

Local Officials, 2006

Mayor	Anthony Ammiano
Admin/Manager	Thomas Antus
Clerk	Romeo Cascaes
Finance Dir/Treas	D. Defeo
Engineer	Joseph Mavuro
Attorney	Duane O. Davison
Tax assessor	Helen Ward
Tax collector	NA
Building officer	Tom Luongo
Zoning officer	NA
Public Works	NA

Housing & Construction

Housing Units, 2000*

Total	11,032
Median rent	$904
Median SF home value	$227,500

New Privately Owned Housing Units Authorized by Building Permit

	Units	Value
Total, 2004	103	$17,212,209
Single family	103	$17,212,209
Total, 2005	331	$16,250,668
Single family	26	$11,154,096

Real Property Valuation - parcels, 2005

	Number	Valuation
Total		$2,927,214,300
Vacant	790	66,615,000
Residential	10,905	2,096,875,500
Commercial	356	636,922,000
Industrial	24	78,428,200
Apartments	2	30,958,400
Farm land	87	15,635,600
Farm homestead	165	1,779,600

Average Property Value & Tax, 2005

Residential value	$189,580
Property tax	$5,991
FAIR rebate	$573

Public Library

No public municipal library.

Library statistics, 2004

	Total	per capita
Volumes	NA	NA
Expenditure	NA	NA

Public Safety

Police

Chief	Ernest Schriefer
Number of officers, 2004	68

Crime, 2004	Number	Rate
Total	1,019	30.3
Violent	44	1.3
Non-violent	975	29
Domestic Viol.	277	NA

Emergency/Fire

Director	Tom Luongo

Public School District
(for school year 2004-2005 except as noted)

Freehold Township School District
384 W Main St
Freehold, NJ 07728
732-462-8400

Superintendent	Catherine M. Snyder
Grade plan	K-8
Enrollment	4,603.0
Students per teacher	12.4
Per pupil expenditure	$10,696
Median faculty salary	$46,070
Median administrator salary	$104,225
Grade 12 enrollment	NA
High school graduation rate	NA

Assessment test results
(percent scoring at proficient or advanced level)

	Language	Math
Grade 3	93.7%	92.3%
Grade 8	91.6%	78.3%
High school	NA	NA

SAT

Percent tested	NA
Average SAT math score	NA
Average SAT verbal score	NA

No Child Left Behind, 2003-04

Attendence rate (target = 90%)	95.8%
Drop rate	NA
Highly-qualified teachers	97.7%
District needs improvement?(AYP)	No

Municipal Finance

Fiscal Year 2005

Total tax levy	$94,024,018
County levy	16,086,690
County taxes	14,434,971
County library	795,149
County health	0
County open space	856,570
School levy	66,368,358
Local muni. budget	11,568,971
Misc. revenues	23,330,637
Total aid	$10,341,096
CMPTRA	2,957,884
Muni. block grant	123,657
Energy tax receipts	7,119,555
Homeland security	140,000

Fiscal Year 2006

Total aid	$10,341,097
CMPTRA	2,708,700
Muni. block grant	123,657
Energy tax receipts	7,368,740
Homeland security	140,000

Taxes

	2003	2004	2005
General tax rate per $100	2.87	3.019	3.161
Net valuation taxable	$2,845,300,247	$2,889,763,510	$2,975,359,174
State equalized value	$4,207,156,953	$4,663,434,469	$5,431,469,832
County equalization ratio	74.17	67.63	61.49

Demographics & Socio-Economic Characteristics
(2000 U.S. Census, except as noted)

Population
1980*	1,435
1990*	1,779
2000	2,083
Male	1,028
Female	1,055
2004 (estimate)*	2,181
Persons per sq. mi. of land	93

Race & Hispanic Origin, 2000
Race
White	2,037
Black/African American	7
Amer. Indian/Alaska Natv.	1
Asian	8
Natv. Hawaiian/Pac. Islander	4
Other Race	10
Two or more races	16
Hispanic origin, total	55
Mexican	1
Puerto Rican	17
Cuban	16
Other Hispanic	21

Age & Nativity, 2000
Under 5 years	132
18 years and over	1,540
21 years and over	1,487
65 years and over	230
85 years and over	43
Median Age	40.3
Native born	1,986
Foreign born	97

Educational Attainment, 2000
Population 25 years and over	1,438
0-8 yrs of school	4.0%
High School grad or higher	89.6%
Bachelor's degree or higher	33.4%
Graduate degree	12.7%

Income & Poverty, 1999
Per capita income	$28,792
Median household income	$72,434
Median family income	$78,464
Persons in poverty	46
H'holds receiving public assistance	11
H'holds receiving social security	146

Households, 2000
Total households	722
With persons under 18	287
With persons over 65	133
Family households	578
One-person households	105
Persons per household	2.81
Persons per family	3.13

Labor & Employment
Total civilian labor force, 2004**	1,106
Unemployment rate	3.1%
Total civilian labor force, 2000	1,082
Unemployment rate	3.3%

Employed persons 16 years and over by occupation, 2000
Managers & professionals	450
Service occupations	135
Sales & office occupations	252
Farming, fishing & forestry	4
Construction & maintenance	126
Production & transportation	79
Self-employed persons	90

*US Census Bureau
**New Jersey Department of Labor

General Information
Township of Frelinghuysen
PO Box 417
Johnsonburg, NJ 07846
908-852-4121

Web site	NA
Land area (sq. miles)	23.43
Water area (sq. miles)	0.12
Type of government	Township
Form of government	TC

Government

Legislative Districts
US Congressional	5
State Legislative	23

Local Officials, 2006
Mayor	Thomas K. Charles
Admin/Manager	NA
Clerk	Brenda Kleber
Finance Dir/Treas	Arthur Merrill
Engineer	Maser Consulting
Attorney	Edward Wacks
Tax assessor	David Gill
Tax collector	NA
Building officer	Richard O'Connor
Zoning officer	NA
Public Works	NA

Housing & Construction

Housing Units, 2000*
Total	755
Median rent	$817
Median SF home value	$211,000

New Privately Owned Housing Units Authorized by Building Permit
	Units	Value
Total, 2004	12	$2,653,667
Single family	12	$2,653,667
Total, 2005	12	$2,649,216
Single family	12	$2,649,216

Real Property Valuation - parcels, 2005
	Number	Valuation
Total		$264,275,178
Vacant	111	7,422,700
Residential	588	180,493,500
Commercial	25	8,159,478
Industrial	0	0
Apartments	0	0
Farm land	187	65,710,900
Farm homestead	395	2,488,600

Average Property Value & Tax, 2005
Residential value	$186,147
Property tax	$3,814
FAIR rebate	$505

Public Library

No public municipal library.

Library statistics, 2004
	Total	per capita
Volumes	NA	NA
Expenditure	NA	NA

Public Safety
Police
Chief	NA
Number of officers, 2004	0

Crime, 2004	Number	Rate
Total	13	6
Violent	3	1.4
Non-violent	10	4.6
Domestic Viol.	13	NA

Emergency/Fire
Director	NA

Public School District
(for school year 2004-2005 except as noted)

Frelinghuysen Township School District
780 Route 94
Johnsonburg, NJ 07846
908-362-6319

Administrator	Dwight Klett
Grade plan	K-6
Enrollment	205.0
Students per teacher	10.1
Per pupil expenditure	$11,415
Median faculty salary	$42,660
Median administrator salary	$80,500
Grade 12 enrollment	NA
High school graduation rate	NA

Assessment test results
(percent scoring at proficient or advanced level)
	Language	Math
Grade 3	97.0%	94.1%
Grade 8	NA	NA
High school	NA	NA

SAT
Percent tested	NA
Average SAT math score	NA
Average SAT verbal score	NA

No Child Left Behind, 2003-04
Attendence rate (target = 90%)	95.5%
Drop rate	NA
Highly-qualified teachers	80.8%
District needs improvement?(AYP)	No

Municipal Finance

Fiscal Year 2005
Total tax levy	$5,430,644
County levy	1,611,783
County taxes	1,331,052
County library	129,225
County health	0
County open space	151,506
School levy	3,447,218
Local muni. budget	371,642
Misc. revenues	753,978
Total aid	$278,498
CMPTRA	108,774
Muni. block grant	8,167
Energy tax receipts	161,557
Homeland security	0

Fiscal Year 2006
Total aid	$278,497
CMPTRA	103,119
Muni. block grant	8,167
Energy tax receipts	167,211
Homeland security	NA

Taxes
	2003	2004	2005
General tax rate per $100	2.85	1.960	2.050
Net valuation taxable	$162,765,522	$262,401,569	$265,076,647
State equalized value	$216,962,839	$248,648,474	$273,331,251
County equalization ratio	83.44	118.32	105.55

Demographics & Socio-Economic Characteristics
(2000 U.S. Census, except as noted)

Population
1980*	1,573
1990*	1,528
2000	1,488
Male	721
Female	767
2004 (estimate)*	1,512
Persons per sq. mi. of land	1,179

Race & Hispanic Origin, 2000
Race
White	1,428
Black/African American	6
Amer. Indian/Alaska Natv.	3
Asian	18
Natv. Hawaiian/Pac. Islander	0
Other Race	20
Two or more races	13
Hispanic origin, total	39
Mexican	2
Puerto Rican	5
Cuban	0
Other Hispanic	32

Age & Nativity, 2000
Under 5 years	94
18 years and over	1,153
21 years and over	1,102
65 years and over	146
85 years and over	12
Median Age	38
Native born	1,385
Foreign born	103

Educational Attainment, 2000
Population 25 years and over	1,051
0-8 yrs of school	3.0%
High School grad or higher	85.6%
Bachelor's degree or higher	32.4%
Graduate degree	13.1%

Income & Poverty, 1999
Per capita income	$27,765
Median household income	$52,109
Median family income	$62,132
Persons in poverty	49
H'holds receiving public assistance	9
H'holds receiving social security	120

Households, 2000
Total households	613
With persons under 18	199
With persons over 65	107
Family households	376
One-person households	177
Persons per household	2.38
Persons per family	2.99

Labor & Employment
Total civilian labor force, 2004**	943
Unemployment rate	3.6%
Total civilian labor force, 2000	862
Unemployment rate	3.2%

Employed persons 16 years and over by occupation, 2000
Managers & professionals	356
Service occupations	78
Sales & office occupations	199
Farming, fishing & forestry	0
Construction & maintenance	104
Production & transportation	97
Self-employed persons	99

*US Census Bureau
**New Jersey Department of Labor

General Information
Borough of Frenchtown
Borough Hall
29 Second St
Frenchtown, NJ 08825
908-996-4524
Web site	NA
Land area (sq. miles)	1.28
Water area (sq. miles)	0.06
Type of government	Borough
Form of government	B

Government

Legislative Districts
US Congressional	12
State Legislative	23

Local Officials, 2006
Mayor	Ronald Sworen
Admin/Manager	NA
Clerk	Brenda Shepherd
Finance Dir/Treas	Diane Laudenbach
Engineer	Robert Clerico
Attorney	Douglas Cole
Tax assessor	Curtis Schick
Tax collector	Diane Laudenbach
Building officer	DCA
Zoning officer	Richard DeCroce
Public Works	NA

Housing & Construction

Housing Units, 2000*
Total	630
Median rent	$755
Median SF home value	$165,900

New Privately Owned Housing Units Authorized by Building Permit
	Units	Value
Total, 2004	2	$254,390
Single family	2	$254,390
Total, 2005	0	$0
Single family	0	$0

Real Property Valuation - parcels, 2005
	Number	Valuation
Total		$149,031,155
Vacant	47	2,704,600
Residential	414	108,135,800
Commercial	61	26,621,400
Industrial	6	3,726,350
Apartments	10	6,867,600
Farm land	2	898,600
Farm homestead	8	76,805

Average Property Value & Tax, 2005
Residential value	$256,428
Property tax	$5,760
FAIR rebate	$566

Public Library
Frenchtown Public Library
29 Second St
Frenchtown, NJ 08825
908-996-4788
Director	Sara Heil

Library statistics, 2004
	Total	per capita
Volumes	NA	NA
Expenditure	NA	NA

Public Safety
Police
Chief	Allan Kurylka
Number of officers, 2004	2

Crime, 2004	Number	Rate
Total	31	20.4
Violent	1	0.7
Non-violent	30	19.7
Domestic Viol.	11	NA

Emergency/Fire
Director	Gerald Hoffman

Public School District
(for school year 2004-2005 except as noted)

Frenchtown Borough School District
902 Harrison St
Frenchtown, NJ 08825
908-996-2751
Administrator	Joyce Brennan
Grade plan	K-8
Enrollment	132.0
Students per teacher	6.5
Per pupil expenditure	$15,756
Median faculty salary	$44,801
Median administrator salary	$98,722
Grade 12 enrollment	NA
High school graduation rate	NA

Assessment test results
(percent scoring at proficient or advanced level)
	Language	Math
Grade 3	100%	92.9%
Grade 8	72.2%	77.8%
High school	NA	NA

SAT
Percent tested	NA
Average SAT math score	NA
Average SAT verbal score	NA

No Child Left Behind, 2003-04
Attendence rate (target = 90%)	95.5%
Drop rate	NA
Highly-qualified teachers	100%
District needs improvement?(AYP)	No

Municipal Finance

Fiscal Year 2005
Total tax levy	$3,367,673
County levy	540,811
County taxes	459,177
County library	38,422
County health	0
County open space	43,212
School levy	2,167,910
Local muni. budget	658,951
Misc. revenues	654,049
Total aid	$180,092
CMPTRA	109,177
Muni. block grant	6,686
Energy tax receipts	64,229
Homeland security	0

Fiscal Year 2006
Total aid	$180,092
CMPTRA	106,929
Muni. block grant	6,686
Energy tax receipts	66,477
Homeland security	NA

Taxes
	2003	2004	2005
General tax rate per $100	3.54	2.130	2.250
Net valuation taxable	$83,522,960	$151,214,466	$149,912,746
State equalized value	$122,395,897	$144,111,230	$156,714,140
County equalization ratio	66.76	116.76	105.49

Demographics & Socio-Economic Characteristics
(2000 U.S. Census, except as noted)

Population
1980*	12,176
1990*	23,330
2000	31,209
Male	14,984
Female	16,225
2004 (estimate)*	35,058
Persons per sq. mi. of land	387

Race & Hispanic Origin, 2000
Race
White	24,081
Black/African American	3,058
Amer. Indian/Alaska Natv.	75
Asian	2,498
Natv. Hawaiian/Pac. Islander	15
Other Race	807
Two or more races	675
Hispanic origin, total	1,924
Mexican	126
Puerto Rican	1,048
Cuban	69
Other Hispanic	681

Age & Nativity, 2000
Under 5 years	2,030
18 years and over	23,147
21 years and over	20,991
65 years and over	2,830
85 years and over	237
Median Age	34
Native born	27,665
Foreign born	3,494

Educational Attainment, 2000
Population 25 years and over	18,733
0-8 yrs of school	3.0%
High School grad or higher	87.3%
Bachelor's degree or higher	22.8%
Graduate degree	7.3%

Income & Poverty, 1999
Per capita income	$21,048
Median household income	$51,592
Median family income	$57,156
Persons in poverty	1,907
H'holds receiving public assistance	206
H'holds receiving social security	2,344

Households, 2000
Total households	10,772
With persons under 18	4,451
With persons over 65	2,106
Family households	7,681
One-person households	2,317
Persons per household	2.7
Persons per family	3.18

Labor & Employment
Total civilian labor force, 2004**	13,691
Unemployment rate	4.5%
Total civilian labor force, 2000	16,928
Unemployment rate	10.1%

Employed persons 16 years and over by occupation, 2000
Managers & professionals	4,380
Service occupations	4,332
Sales & office occupations	4,193
Farming, fishing & forestry	0
Construction & maintenance	1,244
Production & transportation	1,067
Self-employed persons	661

*US Census Bureau
**New Jersey Department of Labor

General Information
Township of Galloway
300 E Jimmie Leeds Rd
Galloway, NJ 08205
609-652-3700

Web site	NA
Land area (sq. miles)	90.49
Water area (sq. miles)	24.31
Type of government	Township
Form of government	CM '50

Government

Legislative Districts
US Congressional	2
State Legislative	2

Local Officials, 2006
Mayor	Tom Bassford
Admin/Manager	Jill A. Gougher
Clerk	Karen Bacon
Finance Dir/Treas	Jill Gougher
Engineer	Kevin Dixon
Attorney	Michael Blee
Tax assessor	David Jackson
Tax collector	Albert Stanley
Building officer	Richard Roesch
Zoning officer	Jody Loen
Public Works	Stephen Bonanni

Housing & Construction

Housing Units, 2000*
Total	11,406
Median rent	$811
Median SF home value	$130,000

New Privately Owned Housing Units
Authorized by Building Permit
	Units	Value
Total, 2004	423	$66,880,627
Single family	423	$66,880,627
Total, 2005	346	$36,258,119
Single family	346	$36,258,119

Real Property Valuation - parcels, 2005
	Number	Valuation
Total		$1,760,042,300
Vacant	4,451	70,489,500
Residential	12,334	1,436,646,800
Commercial	398	188,482,200
Industrial	2	11,426,300
Apartments	17	40,396,300
Farm land	93	11,066,300
Farm homestead	264	1,534,900

Average Property Value & Tax, 2005
Residential value	$114,160
Property tax	$3,697
FAIR rebate	$538

Public Library
Galloway Twp. Branch Library†
306 E Jimmie Leeds Rd
Absecon, NJ 08201
609-652-2352
Branch Librarian ... Katherine Ostrum

Library statistics, 2004
	Total	per capita
Volumes	NA	NA
Expenditure	NA	NA

†Branch of County Library

Public Safety

Police
Chief	Keith Spencer
Number of officers, 2004	61

Crime, 2004	Number	Rate
Total	742	21.7
Violent	79	2.3
Non-violent	663	19.4
Domestic Viol.	697	NA

Emergency/Fire
Director	Brian Berchtold

Public School District
(for school year 2004-2005 except as noted)

Galloway Township School District
101 S Reeds Rd
Galloway, NJ 08205
609-748-1250

Superintendent	Douglas Groff
Grade plan	K-8
Enrollment	3,667.0
Students per teacher	10.3
Per pupil expenditure	$9,630
Median faculty salary	$42,213
Median administrator salary	$85,171
Grade 12 enrollment	NA
High school graduation rate	NA

Assessment test results
(percent scoring at proficient or advanced level)
	Language	Math
Grade 3	73.5%	77.2%
Grade 8	70.0%	65.1%
High school	NA	NA

SAT
Percent tested	NA
Average SAT math score	NA
Average SAT verbal score	NA

No Child Left Behind, 2003-04
Attendence rate (target = 90%)	95.1%
Drop rate	NA
Highly-qualified teachers	94.8%
District needs improvement?(AYP)	No

Municipal Finance

Fiscal Year 2005
Total tax levy	$57,235,743
County levy	10,447,416
County taxes	8,527,229
County library	945,988
County health	465,538
County open space	508,661
School levy	36,868,779
Local muni. budget	9,919,549
Misc. revenues	9,779,293
Total aid	$3,728,235
CMPTRA	1,061,544
Muni. block grant	122,371
Energy tax receipts	2,261,747
Homeland security	140,000

Fiscal Year 2006
Total aid	$3,728,235
CMPTRA	982,383
Muni. block grant	122,371
Energy tax receipts	2,340,908
Homeland security	140,000

Taxes
	2003	2004	2005
General tax rate per $100	2.98	3.086	3.239
Net valuation taxable	$1,628,097,412	$1,706,482,575	$1,767,441,446
State equalized value	$2,002,579,843	$2,450,343,753	$2,891,756,293
County equalization ratio	91.02	81.30	69.53

Demographics & Socio-Economic Characteristics
(2000 U.S. Census, except as noted)

Population
1980*	26,803
1990*	26,727
2000	29,786
Male	14,514
Female	15,272
2004 (estimate)*	29,833
Persons per sq. mi. of land	13,998

Race & Hispanic Origin, 2000
Race
White	24,456
Black/African American	887
Amer. Indian/Alaska Natv.	99
Asian	800
Natv. Hawaiian/Pac. Islander	2
Other Race	2,414
Two or more races	1,128
Hispanic origin, total	5,989
Mexican	469
Puerto Rican	1,348
Cuban	130
Other Hispanic	4,042

Age & Nativity, 2000
Under 5 years	1,809
18 years and over	23,124
21 years and over	22,039
65 years and over	4,185
85 years and over	479
Median Age	35.6
Native born	18,150
Foreign born	11,636

Educational Attainment, 2000
Population 25 years and over	20,271
0-8 yrs of school	13.5%
High School grad or higher	70.3%
Bachelor's degree or higher	14.0%
Graduate degree	3.8%

Income & Poverty, 1999
Per capita income	$19,530
Median household income	$42,748
Median family income	$51,654
Persons in poverty	2,305
H'holds receiving public assistance	253
H'holds receiving social security	3,264

Households, 2000
Total households	11,250
With persons under 18	3,748
With persons over 65	3,242
Family households	7,426
One-person households	3,077
Persons per household	2.64
Persons per family	3.26

Labor & Employment
Total civilian labor force, 2004**	15,164
Unemployment rate	5.8%
Total civilian labor force, 2000	15,594
Unemployment rate	7.6%

Employed persons 16 years and over by occupation, 2000
Managers & professionals	2,954
Service occupations	2,237
Sales & office occupations	4,059
Farming, fishing & forestry	69
Construction & maintenance	2,107
Production & transportation	2,986
Self-employed persons	543

*US Census Bureau
**New Jersey Department of Labor

General Information
City of Garfield
111 Outwater Lane
Garfield, NJ 07026
973-340-2001

Web site	www.garfieldnj.org
Land area (sq. miles)	2.13
Water area (sq. miles)	0.06
Type of government	City
Form of government	CM '23

Government

Legislative Districts
US Congressional	9
State Legislative	36

Local Officials, 2006
Mayor	Frank Calandriello
Admin/Manager	Thomas J. Duch
Clerk	Andrew J. Pavlica
Finance Dir/Treas	Roy Riggitano
Engineer	Kevin Boswell
Attorney	Joseph Rotolo
Tax assessor	Kurt Hielle
Tax collector	Rosemarie Cokinos
Building officer	James Mazzer
Zoning officer	NA
Public Works	Sam Garofalo

Housing & Construction

Housing Units, 2000*
Total	11,698
Median rent	$777
Median SF home value	$161,500

New Privately Owned Housing Units Authorized by Building Permit
	Units	Value
Total, 2004	57	$5,095,439
Single family	1	$141,500
Total, 2005	38	$3,240,795
Single family	0	$0

Real Property Valuation - parcels, 2005
	Number	Valuation
Total		$1,182,272,900
Vacant	153	12,280,400
Residential	5,431	877,558,700
Commercial	460	153,271,100
Industrial	82	87,474,000
Apartments	121	51,688,700
Farm land	0	0
Farm homestead	0	0

Average Property Value & Tax, 2005
Residential value	$161,583
Property tax	$5,363
FAIR rebate	$686

Public Library
Garfield Public Library
500 Midland Ave
Garfield, NJ 07026
973-478-3800
Director — I. MacArthur Nickles

Library statistics, 2004
	Total	per capita
Volumes	82,885	2.78
Expenditure	$855,449	$28.72

Public Safety

Police
Chief	Robert Andrezzi
Number of officers, 2004	58

Crime, 2004	Number	Rate
Total	609	20.5
Violent	73	2.5
Non-violent	536	18
Domestic Viol.	221	NA

Emergency/Fire
Director	Glann Zalarick

Public School District
(for school year 2004-2005 except as noted)

Garfield School District
125 Outwater Lane
Garfield, NJ 07026
973-340-5000

Superintendent	Nicholas Perrapato
Grade plan	K-12
Enrollment	4,480.0
Students per teacher	11.1
Per pupil expenditure	$12,483
Median faculty salary	$46,380
Median administrator salary	$118,675
Grade 12 enrollment	248.5
High school graduation rate	83.4%

Assessment test results
(percent scoring at proficient or advanced level)
	Language	Math
Grade 3	82.6%	91.7%
Grade 8	63.7%	53.6%
High school	67.5%	63.4%

SAT
Percent tested	52%
Average SAT math score	459
Average SAT verbal score	428

No Child Left Behind, 2003-04
Attendence rate (target = 90%)	94.3%
Drop rate	3.6%
Highly-qualified teachers	100%
District needs improvement?(AYP)	No

Municipal Finance

Fiscal Year 2005
Total tax levy	$39,273,466
County levy	3,843,959
County taxes	3,651,616
County library	0
County health	0
County open space	192,342
School levy	19,860,353
Local muni. budget	15,569,155
Misc. revenues	8,739,373
Total aid	$3,517,458
CMPTRA	2,189,124
Muni. block grant	116,948
Energy tax receipts	1,121,386
Homeland security	90,000

Fiscal Year 2006
Total aid	$3,517,458
CMPTRA	2,149,876
Muni. block grant	116,948
Energy tax receipts	1,160,634
Homeland security	90,000

Taxes
	2003	2004	2005
General tax rate per $100	2.95	3.110	3.320
Net valuation taxable	$1,178,460,586	$1,182,318,059	$1,183,265,460
State equalized value	$1,690,518,700	$1,900,122,618	$2,217,929,634
County equalization ratio	80.93	69.71	62.20

Demographics & Socio-Economic Characteristics
(2000 U.S. Census, except as noted)

Population
1980*	4,752
1990*	4,227
2000	4,153
Male	2,005
Female	2,148
2004 (estimate)*	4,166
Persons per sq. mi. of land	6,313

Race & Hispanic Origin, 2000
Race
White	3,983
Black/African American	15
Amer. Indian/Alaska Natv.	0
Asian	55
Natv. Hawaiian/Pac. Islander	0
Other Race	64
Two or more races	36
Hispanic origin, total	207
Mexican	30
Puerto Rican	15
Cuban	30
Other Hispanic	132

Age & Nativity, 2000
Under 5 years	231
18 years and over	3,322
21 years and over	3,215
65 years and over	716
85 years and over	75
Median Age	38.3
Native born	3,718
Foreign born	435

Educational Attainment, 2000
Population 25 years and over	3,090
0-8 yrs of school	4.1%
High School grad or higher	86.5%
Bachelor's degree or higher	27.6%
Graduate degree	11.2%

Income & Poverty, 1999
Per capita income	$26,944
Median household income	$52,571
Median family income	$64,053
Persons in poverty	210
H'holds receiving public assistance	11
H'holds receiving social security	572

Households, 2000
Total households	1,731
With persons under 18	487
With persons over 65	527
Family households	1,125
One-person households	496
Persons per household	2.4
Persons per family	2.96

Labor & Employment
Total civilian labor force, 2004**	2,377
Unemployment rate	4.7%
Total civilian labor force, 2000	2,382
Unemployment rate	2.6%

Employed persons 16 years and over by occupation, 2000
Managers & professionals	893
Service occupations	243
Sales & office occupations	743
Farming, fishing & forestry	0
Construction & maintenance	245
Production & transportation	196
Self-employed persons	118

*US Census Bureau
**New Jersey Department of Labor

General Information
Borough of Garwood
403 South Ave
Garwood, NJ 07027
908-789-0710

Web site	www.garwood.org
Land area (sq. miles)	0.66
Water area (sq. miles)	0
Type of government	Borough
Form of government	B

Government

Legislative Districts
US Congressional	7
State Legislative	21

Local Officials, 2006
Mayor	Dennis McCarthy
Admin/Manager	Christina M. Ariemma
Clerk	Christina M. Ariemma
Finance Dir/Treas	Sue Wright
Engineer	Donald Guarriello
Attorney	Robert Renaud
Tax assessor	Annmarie Switzer
Tax collector	Loretta J. Glogorski
Building officer	Richard Belluscio
Zoning officer	Ron Meeks
Public Works	Fred Corbitt

Housing & Construction

Housing Units, 2000*
Total	1,782
Median rent	$913
Median SF home value	$181,500

New Privately Owned Housing Units Authorized by Building Permit
	Units	Value
Total, 2004	6	$735,850
Single family	6	$735,850
Total, 2005	52	$1,789,242
Single family	8	$789,242

Real Property Valuation - parcels, 2005
	Number	Valuation
Total		$179,575,000
Vacant	44	859,000
Residential	1,258	126,173,300
Commercial	119	41,703,600
Industrial	25	8,589,100
Apartments	8	2,250,000
Farm land	0	0
Farm homestead	0	0

Average Property Value & Tax, 2005
Residential value	$100,297
Property tax	$6,551
FAIR rebate	$669

Public Library
Garwood Public Library
411 Third Ave
Garwood, NJ 07027
908-789-1670

Director................Carol Lombardo

Library statistics, 2004
	Total	per capita
Volumes	35,755	8.61
Expenditure	$129,422	$31.16

Public Safety

Police
Chief	William Legg
Number of officers, 2004	16

Crime, 2004	Number	Rate
Total	65	15.6
Violent	3	0.7
Non-violent	62	14.9
Domestic Viol.	14	NA

Emergency/Fire
Director...............Richard Bonfanti

Public School District
(for school year 2004-2005 except as noted)

Garwood School District
500 East St
Garwood, NJ 07027
908-789-0165

Superintendent	William Murphy
Grade plan	K-12
Enrollment	398.0
Students per teacher	11.2
Per pupil expenditure	$10,498
Median faculty salary	$49,015
Median administrator salary	$83,600
Grade 12 enrollment	NA
High school graduation rate	NA

Assessment test results
(percent scoring at proficient or advanced level)
	Language	Math
Grade 3	92.5%	85.4%
Grade 8	94.1%	68.6%
High school	NA	NA

SAT
Percent tested	NA
Average SAT math score	NA
Average SAT verbal score	NA

No Child Left Behind, 2003-04
Attendence rate (target = 90%)	95.3%
Drop rate	NA
Highly-qualified teachers	100%
District needs improvement?(AYP)	No

Municipal Finance

Fiscal Year 2005
Total tax levy	$11,737,265
County levy	2,064,687
County taxes	1,983,106
County library	0
County health	0
County open space	81,581
School levy	5,773,133
Local muni. budget	3,899,445
Misc. revenues	2,025,211
Total aid	$752,929
CMPTRA	403,612
Muni. block grant	18,496
Energy tax receipts	305,821
Homeland security	25,000

Fiscal Year 2006
Total aid	$752,929
CMPTRA	392,908
Muni. block grant	18,496
Energy tax receipts	316,525
Homeland security	25,000

Taxes
	2003	2004	2005
General tax rate per $100	5.87	6.272	6.533
Net valuation taxable	$177,438,923	$179,545,971	$179,687,144
State equalized value	$423,481,916	$480,183,881	$525,862,289
County equalization ratio	44.72	38.53	33.62

Demographics & Socio-Economic Characteristics
(2000 U.S. Census, except as noted)

Population
1980*	2,510
1990*	2,383
2000	2,435
Male	1,211
Female	1,224
2004 (estimate)*	2,473
Persons per sq. mi. of land	1,127

Race & Hispanic Origin, 2000
Race
White	2,289
Black/African American	68
Amer. Indian/Alaska Natv.	10
Asian	26
Natv. Hawaiian/Pac. Islander	0
Other Race	18
Two or more races	24
Hispanic origin, total	58
Mexican	17
Puerto Rican	16
Cuban	0
Other Hispanic	25

Age & Nativity, 2000
Under 5 years	140
18 years and over	1,819
21 years and over	1,732
65 years and over	330
85 years and over	20
Median Age	38.6
Native born	2,334
Foreign born	101

Educational Attainment, 2000
Population 25 years and over	1,650
0-8 yrs of school	2.7%
High School grad or higher	84.7%
Bachelor's degree or higher	23.3%
Graduate degree	6.6%

Income & Poverty, 1999
Per capita income	$26,035
Median household income	$57,326
Median family income	$63,864
Persons in poverty	101
H'holds receiving public assistance	10
H'holds receiving social security	272

Households, 2000
Total households	829
With persons under 18	333
With persons over 65	222
Family households	665
One-person households	138
Persons per household	2.91
Persons per family	3.28

Labor & Employment
Total civilian labor force, 2004**	1,435
Unemployment rate	4.6%
Total civilian labor force, 2000	1,319
Unemployment rate	3.9%

Employed persons 16 years and over by occupation, 2000
Managers & professionals	515
Service occupations	98
Sales & office occupations	388
Farming, fishing & forestry	0
Construction & maintenance	145
Production & transportation	121
Self-employed persons	58

*US Census Bureau
**New Jersey Department of Labor

General Information
Borough of Gibbsboro
49 Kirkwood Rd
Gibbsboro, NJ 08026
856-783-6655
Web site	www.gibbsborotownhall.com
Land area (sq. miles)	2.20
Water area (sq. miles)	0.04
Type of government	Borough
Form of government	B

Government
Legislative Districts
US Congressional	1
State Legislative	6

Local Officials, 2006
Mayor	Edward Campbell III
Admin/Manager	NA
Clerk	Anne Levy
Finance Dir/Treas	Jennifer Hernandez
Engineer	Greg Fusco
Attorney	John Jehl
Tax assessor	Lawrence O. Vituscka
Tax collector	NA
Building officer	John White
Zoning officer	John White
Public Works	NA

Housing & Construction
Housing Units, 2000*
Total	847
Median rent	$782
Median SF home value	$117,500

New Privately Owned Housing Units
Authorized by Building Permit
	Units	Value
Total, 2004	1	$184,200
Single family	1	$184,200
Total, 2005	2	$320,630
Single family	2	$320,630

Real Property Valuation - parcels, 2005
	Number	Valuation
Total		$183,211,800
Vacant	123	8,746,700
Residential	800	127,466,900
Commercial	100	29,526,200
Industrial	11	17,052,900
Apartments	1	225,000
Farm land	1	169,400
Farm homestead	2	24,700

Average Property Value & Tax, 2005
Residential value	$158,967
Property tax	$5,317
FAIR rebate	$616

Public Library
Gibbsboro Public Library
49 Kirkwood Rd
Gibbsboro, NJ 08026
856-435-3656
Director	Jodie Favat

Library statistics, 2004
	Total	per capita
Volumes	15,505	6.37
Expenditure	$16,125	$6.62

Public Safety
Police
Chief	Patrick Gleason
Number of officers, 2004	3

Crime, 2004	Number	Rate
Total	69	27.8
Violent	4	1.6
Non-violent	65	26.2
Domestic Viol.	21	NA

Emergency/Fire
Director	Chas Thawley

Public School District
(for school year 2004-2005 except as noted)

Gibbsboro School District
37 Kirkwood Rd
Gibbsboro, NJ 08026
856-783-1140
Superintendent	Dennis Vespe
Grade plan	K-8
Enrollment	271.0
Students per teacher	8.1
Per pupil expenditure	$12,543
Median faculty salary	$47,761
Median administrator salary	$89,150
Grade 12 enrollment	NA
High school graduation rate	NA

Assessment test results
(percent scoring at proficient or advanced level)
	Language	Math
Grade 3	90.3%	87.1%
Grade 8	70.0%	70.0%
High school	NA	NA

SAT
Percent tested	NA
Average SAT math score	NA
Average SAT verbal score	NA

No Child Left Behind, 2003-04
Attendance rate (target = 90%)	95.7%
Drop rate	NA
Highly-qualified teachers	98.1%
District needs improvement?(AYP)	No

Municipal Finance
Fiscal Year 2005
Total tax levy	$6,149,094
County levy	1,727,839
County taxes	1,592,311
County library	114,625
County health	0
County open space	20,902
School levy	3,501,091
Local muni. budget	920,165
Misc. revenues	1,415,551
Total aid	$428,751
CMPTRA	163,179
Muni. block grant	10,427
Energy tax receipts	230,145
Homeland security	25,000

Fiscal Year 2006
Total aid	$428,751
CMPTRA	155,124
Muni. block grant	10,427
Energy tax receipts	238,200
Homeland security	25,000

Taxes
	2003	2004	2005
General tax rate per $100	2.81	3.073	3.345
Net valuation taxable	$182,077,230	$182,316,641	$183,861,193
State equalized value	$181,877,165	$204,986,462	$235,719,478
County equalization ratio	118.43	100.11	88.90

Demographics & Socio-Economic Characteristics
(2000 U.S. Census, except as noted)

Population
1980*	14,574
1990*	15,614
2000	19,068
Male	9,126
Female	9,942
2004 (estimate)*	19,177
Persons per sq. mi. of land	2,083

Race & Hispanic Origin, 2000
Race
White	14,212
Black/African American	3,712
Amer. Indian/Alaska Natv.	32
Asian	441
Natv. Hawaiian/Pac. Islander	17
Other Race	282
Two or more races	372
Hispanic origin, total	728
Mexican	62
Puerto Rican	468
Cuban	28
Other Hispanic	170

Age & Nativity, 2000
Under 5 years	1,216
18 years and over	14,859
21 years and over	12,445
65 years and over	1,866
85 years and over	176
Median Age	27.1
Native born	18,310
Foreign born	758

Educational Attainment, 2000
Population 25 years and over	9,943
0-8 yrs of school	5.9%
High School grad or higher	82.1%
Bachelor's degree or higher	24.0%
Graduate degree	7.8%

Income & Poverty, 1999
Per capita income	$18,113
Median household income	$44,992
Median family income	$55,246
Persons in poverty	2,525
H'holds receiving public assistance	153
H'holds receiving social security	1,508

Households, 2000
Total households	6,225
With persons under 18	2,225
With persons over 65	1,386
Family households	4,049
One-person households	1,472
Persons per household	2.66
Persons per family	3.17

Labor & Employment
Total civilian labor force, 2004**	9,712
Unemployment rate	8.0%
Total civilian labor force, 2000	10,552
Unemployment rate	19.2%

Employed persons 16 years and over by occupation, 2000
Managers & professionals	2,903
Service occupations	1,479
Sales & office occupations	2,348
Farming, fishing & forestry	6
Construction & maintenance	675
Production & transportation	1,114
Self-employed persons	236

*US Census Bureau
**New Jersey Department of Labor

General Information
Borough of Glassboro
1 S Main St
Glassboro, NJ 08028
856-881-9230

Web site	www.glassboroonline.com
Land area (sq. miles)	9.21
Water area (sq. miles)	0.01
Type of government	Borough
Form of government	B

Government
Legislative Districts
US Congressional	2
State Legislative	4

Local Officials, 2006
Mayor	Leo McCabe
Admin/Manager	Joseph Brigandi Jr.
Clerk	Patricia A. Frontino
Finance Dir/Treas	Josephine Myers
Engineer	Sickels & Associates
Attorney	Timothy Scaffidi
Tax assessor	Rosemary A. Turner
Tax collector	NA
Building officer	R. Angelo Martilini
Zoning officer	William Kirsch
Public Works	Russell Clark

Housing & Construction
Housing Units, 2000*
Total	6,555
Median rent	$567
Median SF home value	$114,100

New Privately Owned Housing Units
Authorized by Building Permit
	Units	Value
Total, 2004	53	$4,047,570
Single family	53	$4,047,570
Total, 2005	56	$5,787,522
Single family	56	$5,787,522

Real Property Valuation - parcels, 2005
	Number	Valuation
Total		$637,067,000
Vacant	667	19,858,200
Residential	4,587	477,275,100
Commercial	254	102,392,100
Industrial	8	8,116,200
Apartments	34	27,107,600
Farm land	15	2,131,200
Farm homestead	40	186,600

Average Property Value & Tax, 2005
Residential value	$103,190
Property tax	$4,512
FAIR rebate	$568

Public Library
Glassboro Public Library†
2 Center St
Glassboro, NJ 08028
856-881-0001

Branch Librarian	Carol Wolf

Library statistics, 2004
	Total	per capita
Volumes	NA	NA
Expenditure	NA	NA

†Branch of County Library

Public Safety
Police
Chief	Alex Fanfarillo
Number of officers, 2004	47

Crime, 2004	Number	Rate
Total	890	46.6
Violent	78	4.1
Non-violent	812	42.5
Domestic Viol.	280	NA

Emergency/Fire
Director	Ralph Johnson

Public School District
(for school year 2004-2005 except as noted)

Glassboro School District
George Beach Adm Bldg
Glassboro, NJ 08028
856-881-0123

Superintendent	Michael Gorman
Grade plan	K-12
Enrollment	2,411.0
Students per teacher	10.9
Per pupil expenditure	$11,592
Median faculty salary	$51,057
Median administrator salary	$102,906
Grade 12 enrollment	153.5
High school graduation rate	87.7%

Assessment test results
(percent scoring at proficient or advanced level)
	Language	Math
Grade 3	71.2%	71.5%
Grade 8	60.8%	49.8%
High school	85.0%	76.6%

SAT
Percent tested	76%
Average SAT math score	484
Average SAT verbal score	450

No Child Left Behind, 2003-04
Attendence rate (target = 90%)	94.5%
Drop rate	3.6%
Highly-qualified teachers	99.6%
District needs improvement?(AYP)	No

Municipal Finance
Fiscal Year 2005
Total tax levy	$28,091,196
County levy	5,396,096
County taxes	4,731,772
County library	349,694
County health	0
County open space	314,630
School levy	14,394,900
Local muni. budget	8,300,200
Misc. revenues	8,401,034
Total aid	$3,210,025
CMPTRA	1,609,875
Muni. block grant	74,766
Energy tax receipts	1,455,384
Homeland security	70,000

Fiscal Year 2006
Total aid	$3,210,025
CMPTRA	1,558,937
Muni. block grant	74,766
Energy tax receipts	1,506,322
Homeland security	70,000

Taxes
	2003	2004	2005
General tax rate per $100	3.89	4.119	4.373
Net valuation taxable	$626,532,189	$629,132,577	$642,433,197
State equalized value	$698,241,601	$762,930,444	$890,166,547
County equalization ratio	94.72	89.73	82.32

Demographics & Socio-Economic Characteristics
(2000 U.S. Census, except as noted)

Population
1980*	834
1990*	1,665
2000	1,902
Male	929
Female	973
2004 (estimate)*	1,998
Persons per sq. mi. of land	1,279

Race & Hispanic Origin, 2000
Race
White	1,820
Black/African American	17
Amer. Indian/Alaska Natv.	2
Asian	28
Natv. Hawaiian/Pac. Islander	2
Other Race	11
Two or more races	22
Hispanic origin, total	65
Mexican	9
Puerto Rican	23
Cuban	7
Other Hispanic	26

Age & Nativity, 2000
Under 5 years	135
18 years and over	1,421
21 years and over	1,374
65 years and over	145
85 years and over	17
Median Age	35.4
Native born	1,810
Foreign born	92

Educational Attainment, 2000
Population 25 years and over	1,304
0-8 yrs of school	3.0%
High School grad or higher	91.0%
Bachelor's degree or higher	35.3%
Graduate degree	11.5%

Income & Poverty, 1999
Per capita income	$28,647
Median household income	$59,917
Median family income	$75,369
Persons in poverty	84
H'holds receiving public assistance	11
H'holds receiving social security	148

Households, 2000
Total households	805
With persons under 18	275
With persons over 65	123
Family households	474
One-person households	275
Persons per household	2.33
Persons per family	3.07

Labor & Employment
Total civilian labor force, 2004**	1,222
Unemployment rate	4.7%
Total civilian labor force, 2000	1,079
Unemployment rate	2.0%

Employed persons 16 years and over by occupation, 2000
Managers & professionals	486
Service occupations	134
Sales & office occupations	269
Farming, fishing & forestry	5
Construction & maintenance	112
Production & transportation	51
Self-employed persons	47

*US Census Bureau
**New Jersey Department of Labor

General Information
Borough of Glen Gardner
PO Box 307
Glen Gardner, NJ 08826
908-537-4748

Web site	www.glengardnernj.org
Land area (sq. miles)	1.56
Water area (sq. miles)	0
Type of government	Borough
Form of government	B

Government

Legislative Districts
US Congressional	7
State Legislative	23

Local Officials, 2006
Mayor	Stanley Kovach
Admin/Manager	NA
Clerk	Marilyn Hodgson
Finance Dir/Treas	Nancy Smith
Engineer	Robert Clerico
Attorney	J. Peter Jost
Tax assessor	Robert McN. Vance
Tax collector	Diane Laudenbach
Building officer	Charles Herring
Zoning officer	Judy Bass
Public Works	Richard Meyer

Housing & Construction

Housing Units, 2000*
Total	829
Median rent	$866
Median SF home value	$170,700

New Privately Owned Housing Units
Authorized by Building Permit
	Units	Value
Total, 2004	7	$737,151
Single family	7	$737,151
Total, 2005	3	$315,921
Single family	3	$315,921

Real Property Valuation - parcels, 2005
	Number	Valuation
Total		$139,078,390
Vacant	44	1,338,903
Residential	711	129,505,200
Commercial	16	4,827,800
Industrial	1	568,600
Apartments	3	880,000
Farm land	7	1,908,200
Farm homestead	14	49,687

Average Property Value & Tax, 2005
Residential value	$178,696
Property tax	$4,400
FAIR rebate	$444

Public Library

No public municipal library.

Library statistics, 2004
	Total	per capita
Volumes	NA	NA
Expenditure	NA	NA

Public Safety

Police
Chief	NA
Number of officers, 2004	0

Crime, 2004	Number	Rate
Total	13	6.5
Violent	1	0.5
Non-violent	12	6
Domestic Viol.	10	NA

Emergency/Fire
Director	William Clawson

Public School District
(for school year 2004-2005 except as noted)

Glen Gardner Borough School District
PO Box 158
Glen Gardner, NJ 08826

Superintendent	NA
Grade plan	NA
Enrollment	NA
Students per teacher	NA
Per pupil expenditure	NA
Median faculty salary	NA
Median administrator salary	NA
Grade 12 enrollment	NA
High school graduation rate	NA

Assessment test results
(percent scoring at proficient or advanced level)
	Language	Math
Grade 3	NA	NA
Grade 8	NA	NA
High school	NA	NA

SAT
Percent tested	NA
Average SAT math score	NA
Average SAT verbal score	NA

No Child Left Behind, 2003-04
Attendence rate (target = 90%)	NA
Drop rate	NA
Highly-qualified teachers	NA
District needs improvement?(AYP)	NA

Municipal Finance

Fiscal Year 2005
Total tax levy	$3,436,527
County levy	626,138
County taxes	531,631
County library	44,483
County health	0
County open space	50,025
School levy	2,223,896
Local muni. budget	586,493
Misc. revenues	673,268
Total aid	$176,889
CMPTRA	79,868
Muni. block grant	7,458
Energy tax receipts	89,563
Homeland security	0

Fiscal Year 2006
Total aid	$176,890
CMPTRA	76,734
Muni. block grant	7,458
Energy tax receipts	92,698
Homeland security	NA

Taxes
	2003	2004	2005
General tax rate per $100	2.41	2.430	2.470
Net valuation taxable	$140,053,867	$139,864,345	$139,551,793
State equalized value	$138,584,867	$152,775,765	$170,392,910
County equalization ratio	96.87	90.67	83.96

Demographics & Socio-Economic Characteristics
(2000 U.S. Census, except as noted)

Population
1980*	7,855
1990*	7,076
2000	7,271
Male	3,540
Female	3,731
2004 (estimate)*	7,123
Persons per sq. mi. of land	5,579

Race & Hispanic Origin, 2000
Race
White	6,484
Black/African American	362
Amer. Indian/Alaska Natv.	11
Asian	243
Natv. Hawaiian/Pac. Islander	0
Other Race	72
Two or more races	99
Hispanic origin, total	251
Mexican	22
Puerto Rican	63
Cuban	36
Other Hispanic	130

Age & Nativity, 2000
Under 5 years	679
18 years and over	5,039
21 years and over	4,885
65 years and over	757
85 years and over	102
Median Age	37.8
Native born	6,617
Foreign born	654

Educational Attainment, 2000
Population 25 years and over	4,727
0-8 yrs of school	2.2%
High School grad or higher	96.2%
Bachelor's degree or higher	65.8%
Graduate degree	31.0%

Income & Poverty, 1999
Per capita income	$48,456
Median household income	$105,638
Median family income	$120,650
Persons in poverty	219
H'holds receiving public assistance	36
H'holds receiving social security	520

Households, 2000
Total households	2,458
With persons under 18	1,170
With persons over 65	555
Family households	1,978
One-person households	410
Persons per household	2.95
Persons per family	3.33

Labor & Employment
Total civilian labor force, 2004**	4,195
Unemployment rate	2.2%
Total civilian labor force, 2000	3,551
Unemployment rate	2.8%

Employed persons 16 years and over by occupation, 2000
Managers & professionals	2,125
Service occupations	205
Sales & office occupations	924
Farming, fishing & forestry	0
Construction & maintenance	117
Production & transportation	82
Self-employed persons	224

*US Census Bureau
**New Jersey Department of Labor

General Information
Borough of Glen Ridge
825 Bloomfield Ave
Glen Ridge, NJ 07028
973-748-8400

Web site	www.glenridgenj.org
Land area (sq. miles)	1.28
Water area (sq. miles)	0
Type of government	Borough
Form of government	B

Government
Legislative Districts
US Congressional	8
State Legislative	34

Local Officials, 2006
Mayor	Carl Bergmanson
Admin/Manager	Michael Rohal
Clerk	Michael Rohal
Finance Dir/Treas	Cindy Goldberg
Engineer	Michael Rohal
Attorney	John Malyska
Tax assessor	William Merdinger
Tax collector	Donna Altschuler
Building officer	Ronald Young
Zoning officer	Ronal Young
Public Works	NA

Housing & Construction
Housing Units, 2000*
Total	2,490
Median rent	$1,058
Median SF home value	$264,700

New Privately Owned Housing Units Authorized by Building Permit
	Units	Value
Total, 2004	0	$0
Single family	0	$0
Total, 2005	0	$0
Single family	0	$0

Real Property Valuation - parcels, 2005
	Number	Valuation
Total		$233,114,800
Vacant	10	130,000
Residential	2,232	219,328,400
Commercial	20	9,056,400
Industrial	0	0
Apartments	2	4,600,000
Farm land	0	0
Farm homestead	0	0

Average Property Value & Tax, 2005
Residential value	$98,265
Property tax	$14,018
FAIR rebate	$548

Public Library
Glen Ridge Public Library
240 Ridgewood Ave
Glen Ridge, NJ 07028
973-748-5482

Director	John Sitnik

Library statistics, 2004
	Total	per capita
Volumes	42,753	5.88
Expenditure	$612,662	$84.26

Public Safety
Police
Chief	John Magnier
Number of officers, 2004	26

Crime, 2004	Number	Rate
Total	282	39.4
Violent	21	2.9
Non-violent	261	36.4
Domestic Viol.	22	NA

Emergency/Fire
Director	NA

Public School District
(for school year 2004-2005 except as noted)

Glen Ridge School District
12 High St
Glen Ridge, NJ 07028
973-429-8302

Superintendent	Daniel Fishbein
Grade plan	K-12
Enrollment	1,778.5
Students per teacher	12.0
Per pupil expenditure	$10,703
Median faculty salary	$54,608
Median administrator salary	$107,459
Grade 12 enrollment	92.5
High school graduation rate	100.0%

Assessment test results
(percent scoring at proficient or advanced level)
	Language	Math
Grade 3	95.9%	93.1%
Grade 8	96.7%	90.1%
High school	96.6%	91.6%

SAT
Percent tested	91%
Average SAT math score	575
Average SAT verbal score	584

No Child Left Behind, 2003-04
Attendence rate (target = 90%)	96.0%
Drop rate	0%
Highly-qualified teachers	90.5%
District needs improvement?(AYP)	No

Municipal Finance
Fiscal Year 2005
Total tax levy	$33,268,723
County levy	5,607,343
County taxes	5,489,906
County library	0
County health	0
County open space	117,437
School levy	20,489,845
Local muni. budget	7,171,535
Misc. revenues	3,101,450
Total aid	$673,172
CMPTRA	278,011
Muni. block grant	30,962
Energy tax receipts	314,199
Homeland security	50,000

Fiscal Year 2006
Total aid	$673,172
CMPTRA	267,014
Muni. block grant	30,962
Energy tax receipts	325,196
Homeland security	50,000

Taxes
	2003	2004	2005
General tax rate per $100	12.76	13.340	14.270
Net valuation taxable	$232,465,002	$233,507,481	$233,220,100
State equalized value	$1,054,263,048	$1,173,470,050	$1,288,508,840
County equalization ratio	25.61	25.61	19.89

Demographics & Socio-Economic Characteristics
(2000 U.S. Census, except as noted)

Population

1980*	11,497
1990*	10,883
2000	11,546
Male	5,622
Female	5,924
2004 (estimate)*	11,525
Persons per sq. mi. of land	4,238

Race & Hispanic Origin, 2000
Race

White	10,399
Black/African American	209
Amer. Indian/Alaska Natv.	18
Asian	748
Natv. Hawaiian/Pac. Islander	2
Other Race	71
Two or more races	99
Hispanic origin, total	314
Mexican	37
Puerto Rican	99
Cuban	57
Other Hispanic	121

Age & Nativity, 2000

Under 5 years	962
18 years and over	8,151
21 years and over	7,945
65 years and over	1,579
85 years and over	193
Median Age	39.5
Native born	10,270
Foreign born	1,276

Educational Attainment, 2000

Population 25 years and over	7,714
0-8 yrs of school	1.3%
High School grad or higher	96.0%
Bachelor's degree or higher	61.1%
Graduate degree	24.3%

Income & Poverty, 1999

Per capita income	$45,091
Median household income	$104,192
Median family income	$111,280
Persons in poverty	278
H'holds receiving public assistance	7
H'holds receiving social security	1,135

Households, 2000

Total households	3,977
With persons under 18	1,785
With persons over 65	1,121
Family households	3,322
One-person households	586
Persons per household	2.89
Persons per family	3.22

Labor & Employment

Total civilian labor force, 2004**	5,914
Unemployment rate	2.0%
Total civilian labor force, 2000	5,757
Unemployment rate	3.0%

Employed persons 16 years and over by occupation, 2000

Managers & professionals	3,501
Service occupations	289
Sales & office occupations	1,426
Farming, fishing & forestry	0
Construction & maintenance	159
Production & transportation	208
Self-employed persons	374

*US Census Bureau
**New Jersey Department of Labor

General Information
Borough of Glen Rock
Municipal Building
Harding Plaza
Glen Rock, NJ 07452
201-670-3956

Web site	NA
Land area (sq. miles)	2.72
Water area (sq. miles)	0.01
Type of government	Borough
Form of government	B

Government

Legislative Districts

US Congressional	5
State Legislative	35

Local Officials, 2006

Mayor	John VanKeuren
Admin/Manager	Lenora Benjamin
Clerk	Jacqueline Scalia
Finance Dir/Treas	Lenora Benjamin
Engineer	Vollmer Assoc.
Attorney	Robert Garibaldi Jr.
Tax assessor	Steven Rubenstein
Tax collector	Patricia McCormick
Building officer	Brian Frugis
Zoning officer	NA
Public Works	NA

Housing & Construction

Housing Units, 2000*

Total	4,024
Median rent	$1,188
Median SF home value	$316,900

New Privately Owned Housing Units
Authorized by Building Permit

	Units	Value
Total, 2004	4	$1,457,550
Single family	4	$1,457,550
Total, 2005	4	$1,621,319
Single family	4	$1,621,319

Real Property Valuation - parcels, 2005

	Number	Valuation
Total		$1,821,145,700
Vacant	56	8,401,700
Residential	3,846	1,661,491,200
Commercial	99	127,787,000
Industrial	7	23,465,800
Apartments	0	0
Farm land	0	0
Farm homestead	0	0

Average Property Value & Tax, 2005

Residential value	$432,005
Property tax	$10,957
FAIR rebate	$586

Public Library
Glen Rock Public Library
315 Rock Rd
Glen Rock, NJ 07452
201-670-3970

Director	Roz Pelcyger

Library statistics, 2004

	Total	per capita
Volumes	86,016	7.45
Expenditure	$827,237	$71.65

Public Safety

Police

Chief	Steven Cherry
Number of officers, 2004	21

Crime, 2004	Number	Rate
Total	100	8.7
Violent	2	0.2
Non-violent	98	8.5
Domestic Viol.	7	NA

Emergency/Fire

Director	Art Zanotti

Public School District
(for school year 2004-2005 except as noted)

Glen Rock School District
620 Harristown Rd
Glen Rock, NJ 07452
201-445-7700

Superintendent	Patrick Fletcher
Grade plan	K-12
Enrollment	2,416.0
Students per teacher	10.8
Per pupil expenditure	$13,258
Median faculty salary	$54,963
Median administrator salary	$105,186
Grade 12 enrollment	144.0
High school graduation rate	100.0%

Assessment test results
(percent scoring at proficient or advanced level)

	Language	Math
Grade 3	93.7%	95.3%
Grade 8	87.5%	84.5%
High school	97.7%	93.8%

SAT

Percent tested	103%
Average SAT math score	585
Average SAT verbal score	558

No Child Left Behind, 2003-04

Attendance rate (target = 90%)	96.6%
Drop rate	0%
Highly-qualified teachers	98.5%
District needs improvement?(AYP)	No

Municipal Finance

Fiscal Year 2005

Total tax levy	$46,216,086
County levy	4,023,803
County taxes	3,822,425
County library	0
County health	0
County open space	201,378
School levy	32,130,618
Local muni. budget	10,061,665
Misc. revenues	4,396,979
Total aid	$1,470,979
CMPTRA	498,259
Muni. block grant	47,620
Energy tax receipts	855,100
Homeland security	70,000

Fiscal Year 2006

Total aid	$1,470,980
CMPTRA	468,331
Muni. block grant	47,620
Energy tax receipts	885,029
Homeland security	70,000

Taxes

	2003	2004	2005
General tax rate per $100	2.21	2.410	2.540
Net valuation taxable	$1,801,185,953	$1,807,161,207	$1,822,099,032
State equalized value	$1,794,009,913	$1,991,030,803	$2,215,587,344
County equalization ratio	111.22	100.40	90.76

Demographics & Socio-Economic Characteristics
(2000 U.S. Census, except as noted)

Population

1980*	13,121
1990*	12,649
2000	11,484
Male	5,594
Female	5,890
2004 (estimate)*	11,608
Persons per sq. mi. of land	5,270

Race & Hispanic Origin, 2000
Race

White	11,155
Black/African American	79
Amer. Indian/Alaska Natv.	21
Asian	78
Natv. Hawaiian/Pac. Islander	4
Other Race	74
Two or more races	73
Hispanic origin, total	216
Mexican	15
Puerto Rican	142
Cuban	10
Other Hispanic	49

Age & Nativity, 2000

Under 5 years	736
18 years and over	8,435
21 years and over	7,953
65 years and over	1,582
85 years and over	136
Median Age	36.4
Native born	11,366
Foreign born	109

Educational Attainment, 2000

Population 25 years and over	7,438
0-8 yrs of school	6.7%
High School grad or higher	72.4%
Bachelor's degree or higher	8.2%
Graduate degree	1.7%

Income & Poverty, 1999

Per capita income	$16,912
Median household income	$36,855
Median family income	$46,038
Persons in poverty	1,155
H'holds receiving public assistance	148
H'holds receiving social security	1,458

Households, 2000

Total households	4,213
With persons under 18	1,556
With persons over 65	1,248
Family households	2,840
One-person households	1,145
Persons per household	2.72
Persons per family	3.32

Labor & Employment

Total civilian labor force, 2004**	6,344
Unemployment rate	5.5%
Total civilian labor force, 2000	5,482
Unemployment rate	8.5%

Employed persons 16 years and over by occupation, 2000

Managers & professionals	1,010
Service occupations	769
Sales & office occupations	1,500
Farming, fishing & forestry	0
Construction & maintenance	550
Production & transportation	1,188
Self-employed persons	203

*US Census Bureau
**New Jersey Department of Labor

General Information

City of Gloucester
512 Monmouth St
Gloucester, NJ 08030
856-456-0205

Web site	NA
Land area (sq. miles)	2.20
Water area (sq. miles)	0.63
Type of government	City
Form of government	SC

Government

Legislative Districts

US Congressional	1
State Legislative	5

Local Officials, 2006

Mayor	Thomas Kilcourse
Admin/Manager	NA
Clerk	Paul Kain
Finance Dir/Treas	Frank Robertson
Engineer	Edward Vernick
Attorney	M. James Maley Jr.
Tax assessor	John Dymond
Tax collector	Joanne Monroe
Building officer	John Hargraves
Zoning officer	NA
Public Works	NA

Housing & Construction

Housing Units, 2000*

Total	4,604
Median rent	$625
Median SF home value	$79,500

New Privately Owned Housing Units Authorized by Building Permit

	Units	Value
Total, 2004	8	$941,774
Single family	8	$941,774
Total, 2005	5	$573,966
Single family	5	$573,966

Real Property Valuation - parcels, 2005

	Number	Valuation
Total		$354,475,100
Vacant	233	6,503,300
Residential	3,637	255,242,100
Commercial	278	75,066,000
Industrial	32	13,005,500
Apartments	19	4,658,200
Farm land	0	0
Farm homestead	0	0

Average Property Value & Tax, 2005

Residential value	$70,179
Property tax	$2,548
FAIR rebate	$634

Public Library

Gloucester City Library
Hudson & Monmonth Sts
Gloucester City, NJ 08030
856-456-4181

Director | Elizabeth Egan

Library statistics, 2004

	Total	per capita
Volumes	53,119	4.63
Expenditure	$468,800	$40.82

Public Safety

Police

Chief	William Crothers
Number of officers, 2004	29

Crime, 2004	Number	Rate
Total	310	27.1
Violent	32	2.8
Non-violent	278	24.3
Domestic Viol.	206	NA

Emergency/Fire

Director | William Glassman

Public School District
(for school year 2004-2005 except as noted)

Gloucester City School District
520 Cumberland St
Gloucester City, NJ 08030
856-456-9394

Superintendent	Mary Stansky
Grade plan	K-12
Enrollment	2,094.0
Students per teacher	7.8
Per pupil expenditure	$16,239
Median faculty salary	$41,898
Median administrator salary	$90,082
Grade 12 enrollment	112.0
High school graduation rate	94.7%

Assessment test results
(percent scoring at proficient or advanced level)

	Language	Math
Grade 3	84.0%	77.7%
Grade 8	55.1%	43.9%
High school	78.1%	62.9%

SAT

Percent tested	46%
Average SAT math score	488
Average SAT verbal score	475

No Child Left Behind, 2003-04

Attendance rate (target = 90%)	94.5%
Drop rate	1.5%
Highly-qualified teachers	100%
District needs improvement?(AYP)	No

Municipal Finance

Fiscal Year 2005

Total tax levy	$13,043,093
County levy	3,185,005
County taxes	3,143,724
County library	0
County health	0
County open space	41,281
School levy	3,386,088
Local muni. budget	6,472,000
Misc. revenues	7,823,850
Total aid	$3,339,674
CMPTRA	1,504,135
Muni. block grant	55,348
Energy tax receipts	1,710,191
Homeland security	70,000

Fiscal Year 2006

Total aid	$3,339,673
CMPTRA	1,444,278
Muni. block grant	55,348
Energy tax receipts	1,770,047
Homeland security	70,000

Taxes

	2003	2004	2005
General tax rate per $100	3.35	3.498	3.632
Net valuation taxable	$362,039,313	$360,420,598	$359,186,253
State equalized value	$397,889,123	$401,049,455	$457,795,377
County equalization ratio	100.09	90.99	89.74

Demographics & Socio-Economic Characteristics
(2000 U.S. Census, except as noted)

Population
1980*	45,156
1990*	53,797
2000	64,350
Male	31,309
Female	33,041
2004 (estimate)*	66,286
Persons per sq. mi. of land	2,855

Race & Hispanic Origin, 2000
Race
White	53,484
Black/African American	7,432
Amer. Indian/Alaska Natv.	100
Asian	1,688
Natv. Hawaiian/Pac. Islander	16
Other Race	715
Two or more races	915
Hispanic origin, total	1,962
Mexican	248
Puerto Rican	1,160
Cuban	81
Other Hispanic	473

Age & Nativity, 2000
Under 5 years	4,405
18 years and over	47,057
21 years and over	44,616
65 years and over	6,052
85 years and over	536
Median Age	34.6
Native born	61,187
Foreign born	3,128

Educational Attainment, 2000
Population 25 years and over	41,473
0-8 yrs of school	2.8%
High School grad or higher	85.8%
Bachelor's degree or higher	22.0%
Graduate degree	6.1%

Income & Poverty, 1999
Per capita income	$22,604
Median household income	$54,280
Median family income	$62,992
Persons in poverty	3,934
H'holds receiving public assistance	523
H'holds receiving social security	4,983

Households, 2000
Total households	23,150
With persons under 18	9,456
With persons over 65	4,351
Family households	16,878
One-person households	4,948
Persons per household	2.75
Persons per family	3.24

Labor & Employment
Total civilian labor force, 2004**	30,048
Unemployment rate	4.8%
Total civilian labor force, 2000	34,739
Unemployment rate	4.9%

Employed persons 16 years and over by occupation, 2000
Managers & professionals	11,214
Service occupations	4,410
Sales & office occupations	10,334
Farming, fishing & forestry	0
Construction & maintenance	3,332
Production & transportation	3,753
Self-employed persons	1,485

*US Census Bureau
**New Jersey Department of Labor

General Information
Gloucester Township
PO Box 8
Blackwood, NJ 08012
856-228-4000
Web site	www.glotwp.com
Land area (sq. miles)	23.22
Water area (sq. miles)	0.10
Type of government	Township
Form of government	MC '50

Government

Legislative Districts
US Congressional	1
State Legislative	4

Local Officials, 2006
Mayor	Sandra Love
Admin/Manager	Thomas Cardis
Clerk	Rosemary Di Josie
Finance Dir/Treas	Candace Prince
Engineer	Remington & Vernick
Attorney	David Carlamere
Tax assessor	Charles G. Palumbo Jr.
Tax collector	Sandra Ferguson
Building officer	Bernie Shepherd
Zoning officer	Edward Sayers
Public Works	Gabe Busa

Housing & Construction

Housing Units, 2000*
Total	24,257
Median rent	$706
Median SF home value	$116,100

New Privately Owned Housing Units Authorized by Building Permit
	Units	Value
Total, 2004	165	$15,647,809
Single family	157	$15,041,009
Total, 2005	221	$20,565,617
Single family	171	$15,172,426

Real Property Valuation - parcels, 2005
	Number	Valuation
Total		$2,368,026,800
Vacant	1,556	30,229,100
Residential	19,305	2,070,257,700
Commercial	463	145,046,600
Industrial	33	34,200,800
Apartments	26	83,623,300
Farm land	32	4,125,100
Farm homestead	70	544,200

Average Property Value & Tax, 2005
Residential value	$106,880
Property tax	$4,978
FAIR rebate	$514

Public Library
Gloucester Twp. Branch Library†
15 S Black Horse Pike
Blackwood, NJ 08012
856-228-0022
Branch Librarian	Ann Ackroyd

Library statistics, 2004
	Total	per capita
Volumes	NA	NA
Expenditure	NA	NA

†Branch of County Library

Public Safety

Police
Chief	John Stollsteimer
Number of officers, 2004	109

Crime, 2004	Number	Rate
Total	1,833	27.8
Violent	209	3.2
Non-violent	1,624	24.6
Domestic Viol.	626	NA

Emergency/Fire
Director	NA

Public School District
(for school year 2004-2005 except as noted)

Gloucester Township School District
17 Erial Rd
Blackwood, NJ 08012
856-227-1400
Superintendent	Thomas D. Seddon
Grade plan	K-8
Enrollment	7,879.0
Students per teacher	12.4
Per pupil expenditure	$9,749
Median faculty salary	$53,015
Median administrator salary	$91,350
Grade 12 enrollment	NA
High school graduation rate	NA

Assessment test results
(percent scoring at proficient or advanced level)
	Language	Math
Grade 3	87.3%	87.9%
Grade 8	77.4%	57.0%
High school	NA	NA

SAT
Percent tested	NA
Average SAT math score	NA
Average SAT verbal score	NA

No Child Left Behind, 2003-04
Attendance rate (target = 90%)	95.3%
Drop rate	NA
Highly-qualified teachers	99.3%
District needs improvement?(AYP)	No

Municipal Finance

Fiscal Year 2005
Total tax levy	$110,676,253
County levy	27,048,709
County taxes	24,926,548
County library	1,794,864
County health	0
County open space	327,297
School levy	59,650,018
Local muni. budget	23,977,526
Misc. revenues	13,453,006
Total aid	$6,880,140
CMPTRA	3,151,736
Muni. block grant	252,318
Energy tax receipts	3,336,086
Homeland security	140,000

Fiscal Year 2006
Total aid	$6,880,140
CMPTRA	3,034,973
Muni. block grant	252,318
Energy tax receipts	3,452,849
Homeland security	140,000

Taxes
	2003	2004	2005
General tax rate per $100	3.84	4.255	4.658
Net valuation taxable	$2,310,548,316	$2,335,593,392	$2,376,365,270
State equalized value	$2,816,368,011	$3,201,605,703	$3,905,925,822
County equalization ratio	89.11	82.04	72.87

Demographics & Socio-Economic Characteristics
(2000 U.S. Census, except as noted)

Population
1980*	4,640
1990*	4,460
2000	5,654
Male	2,704
Female	2,950
2004 (estimate)*	6,673
Persons per sq. mi. of land	1,457

Race & Hispanic Origin, 2000
Race
White	5,000
Black/African American	95
Amer. Indian/Alaska Natv.	4
Asian	452
Natv. Hawaiian/Pac. Islander	2
Other Race	40
Two or more races	61
Hispanic origin, total	231
Mexican	7
Puerto Rican	65
Cuban	48
Other Hispanic	111

Age & Nativity, 2000
Under 5 years	371
18 years and over	4,278
21 years and over	4,160
65 years and over	884
85 years and over	157
Median Age	39.9
Native born	4,912
Foreign born	742

Educational Attainment, 2000
Population 25 years and over	3,984
0-8 yrs of school	6.9%
High School grad or higher	88.3%
Bachelor's degree or higher	39.7%
Graduate degree	14.9%

Income & Poverty, 1999
Per capita income	$37,290
Median household income	$80,644
Median family income	$87,744
Persons in poverty	130
H'holds receiving public assistance	14
H'holds receiving social security	490

Households, 2000
Total households	1,893
With persons under 18	735
With persons over 65	449
Family households	1,508
One-person households	301
Persons per household	2.84
Persons per family	3.2

Labor & Employment
Total civilian labor force, 2004**	2,813
Unemployment rate	2.9%
Total civilian labor force, 2000	2,939
Unemployment rate	3.0%

Employed persons 16 years and over by occupation, 2000
Managers & professionals	1,326
Service occupations	220
Sales & office occupations	802
Farming, fishing & forestry	0
Construction & maintenance	242
Production & transportation	261
Self-employed persons	187

*US Census Bureau
**New Jersey Department of Labor

General Information
Township of Green Brook
111 Greenbrook Rd
Green Brook, NJ 08812
732-968-1023
Web site	www.greenbrooktwp,org
Land area (sq. miles)	4.58
Water area (sq. miles)	0
Type of government	Township
Form of government	TC

Government
Legislative Districts
US Congressional	7
State Legislative	22

Local Officials, 2006
Mayor	Patricia L Walsh
Admin/Manager	Kathryn Kitchener
Clerk	Kathryn Kitchener
Finance Dir/Treas	Raymond S. Murray
Engineer	C. Richard Roseberry
Attorney	Robert Rusignola
Tax assessor	Rosalie Lauerman
Tax collector	Raymond S. Murray
Building officer	Thomas Carisone
Zoning officer	C. Richard Roseberry
Public Works	C. Richard Roseberry

Housing & Construction
Housing Units, 2000*
Total	1,916
Median rent	$1,148
Median SF home value	$242,500

New Privately Owned Housing Units
Authorized by Building Permit
	Units	Value
Total, 2004	17	$5,319,641
Single family	17	$5,319,641
Total, 2005	39	$11,287,255
Single family	39	$11,287,255

Real Property Valuation - parcels, 2005
	Number	Valuation
Total		$1,429,227,100
Vacant	206	31,763,300
Residential	2,301	1,160,862,600
Commercial	178	216,466,500
Industrial	9	13,768,400
Apartments	8	6,365,200
Farm land	0	0
Farm homestead	1	1,100

Average Property Value & Tax, 2005
Residential value	$504,285
Property tax	$8,225
FAIR rebate	$526

Public Library
No public municipal library.

Library statistics, 2004
	Total	per capita
Volumes	NA	NA
Expenditure	NA	NA

Public Safety
Police
Chief	Martin Rasmussen
Number of officers, 2004	21

Crime, 2004	Number	Rate
Total	133	20.2
Violent	7	1.1
Non-violent	126	19.1
Domestic Viol.	74	NA

Emergency/Fire
Director	Geno Panella

Public School District
(for school year 2004-2005 except as noted)

Green Brook Township School District
132 Jefferson Ave
Green Brook, NJ 08812
732-968-7734
Superintendent	Stephanie Bilenker
Grade plan	K-12
Enrollment	906.0
Students per teacher	10.9
Per pupil expenditure	$11,734
Median faculty salary	$43,875
Median administrator salary	$100,008
Grade 12 enrollment	NA
High school graduation rate	NA

Assessment test results
(percent scoring at proficient or advanced level)
	Language	Math
Grade 3	97.6%	98.8%
Grade 8	94.8%	73.7%
High school	NA	NA

SAT
Percent tested	NA
Average SAT math score	NA
Average SAT verbal score	NA

No Child Left Behind, 2003-04
Attendence rate (target = 90%)	96.2%
Drop rate	NA
Highly-qualified teachers	97%
District needs improvement?(AYP)	No

Municipal Finance
Fiscal Year 2005
Total tax levy	$23,326,489
County levy	4,444,648
County taxes	3,682,375
County library	408,183
County health	0
County open space	354,090
School levy	14,727,830
Local muni. budget	4,154,012
Misc. revenues	2,377,399
Total aid	$805,418
CMPTRA	57,223
Muni. block grant	22,169
Energy tax receipts	676,026
Homeland security	50,000

Fiscal Year 2006
Total aid	$805,418
CMPTRA	33,562
Muni. block grant	22,169
Energy tax receipts	699,687
Homeland security	50,000

Taxes
	2003	2004	2005
General tax rate per $100	2.96	3.230	1.640
Net valuation taxable	$678,202,251	$688,093,657	$1,430,231,789
State equalized value	$1,057,542,883	$1,163,817,872	$1,328,224,173
County equalization ratio	70.73	64.13	121.51

Demographics & Socio-Economic Characteristics
(2000 U.S. Census, except as noted)

Population
1980*	2,450
1990*	2,709
2000	3,220
Male	1,647
Female	1,573
2000 (revised)	3,224
2004 (estimate)*	3,506
Persons per sq. mi. of land	217

Race & Hispanic Origin, 2000
Race
White	3,107
Black/African American	30
Amer. Indian/Alaska Natv.	1
Asian	31
Natv. Hawaiian/Pac. Islander	0
Other Race	9
Two or more races	42
Hispanic origin, total	103
Mexican	6
Puerto Rican	40
Cuban	12
Other Hispanic	45

Age & Nativity, 2000
Under 5 years	254
18 years and over	2,227
21 years and over	2,137
65 years and over	193
85 years and over	19
Median Age	36.3
Native born	2,948
Foreign born	264

Educational Attainment, 2000
Population 25 years and over	2,079
0-8 yrs of school	2.2%
High School grad or higher	93.9%
Bachelor's degree or higher	34.2%
Graduate degree	10.7%

Income & Poverty, 1999
Per capita income	$34,127
Median household income	$84,847
Median family income	$89,788
Persons in poverty	52
H'holds receiving public assistance	0
H'holds receiving social security	150

Households, 2000
Total households	1,046
With persons under 18	499
With persons over 65	144
Family households	890
One-person households	115
Persons per household	3.07
Persons per family	3.34

Labor & Employment
Total civilian labor force, 2004**	1,733
Unemployment rate	2.5%
Total civilian labor force, 2000	1,729
Unemployment rate	2.8%

Employed persons 16 years and over by occupation, 2000
Managers & professionals	788
Service occupations	117
Sales & office occupations	480
Farming, fishing & forestry	4
Construction & maintenance	158
Production & transportation	134
Self-employed persons	57

*US Census Bureau
**New Jersey Department of Labor

General Information
Township of Green
PO Box 65
150 Kennedy Rd
Tranquility, NJ 07879
908-852-9333

Web site	www.greentwp.com
Land area (sq. miles)	16.18
Water area (sq. miles)	0.13
Type of government	Township
Form of government	TC

Government

Legislative Districts
US Congressional	5
State Legislative	24

Local Officials, 2006
Mayor	Roger Michaud
Admin/Manager	A. Denise Stagnari
Clerk	A. Denise Stagnari
Finance Dir/Treas	Linda Padula
Engineer	John Miller
Attorney	William Hinkes
Tax assessor	Penny Holenstein
Tax collector	Victoria Trogani
Building officer	Edward Vanderberg
Zoning officer	NA
Public Works	Watson Perigo Jr.

Housing & Construction

Housing Units, 2000*
Total	1,069
Median rent	$968
Median SF home value	$182,500

New Privately Owned Housing Units Authorized by Building Permit
	Units	Value
Total, 2004	NA	NA
Single family	NA	NA
Total, 2005	16	$3,100,298
Single family	16	$3,100,298

Real Property Valuation - parcels, 2005
	Number	Valuation
Total		$521,399,100
Vacant	110	15,418,200
Residential	1,090	440,573,500
Commercial	25	17,278,100
Industrial	1	6,142,000
Apartments	0	0
Farm land	92	40,358,600
Farm homestead	185	1,628,700

Average Property Value & Tax, 2005
Residential value	$346,825
Property tax	$6,402
FAIR rebate	$464

Public Library

No public municipal library.

Library statistics, 2004
	Total	per capita
Volumes	NA	NA
Expenditure	NA	NA

Public Safety

Police
Chief	NA
Number of officers, 2004	0

Crime, 2004	Number	Rate
Total	21	6.1
Violent	2	0.6
Non-violent	19	5.5
Domestic Viol.	25	NA

Emergency/Fire
Director	Michael Carlin

Public School District
(for school year 2004-2005 except as noted)

Green Township School District
PO Box 14
Greendell, NJ 07839
973-383-6666

Superintendent	William Caldwell (Int)
Grade plan	K-12
Enrollment	487.0
Students per teacher	11.4
Per pupil expenditure	$10,439
Median faculty salary	$53,632
Median administrator salary	$86,000
Grade 12 enrollment	NA
High school graduation rate	NA

Assessment test results
(percent scoring at proficient or advanced level)
	Language	Math
Grade 3	93.6%	91.5%
Grade 8	86.9%	76.1%
High school	NA	NA

SAT
Percent tested	NA
Average SAT math score	NA
Average SAT verbal score	NA

No Child Left Behind, 2003-04
Attendence rate (target = 90%)	95.4%
Drop rate	NA
Highly-qualified teachers	100%
District needs improvement?(AYP)	No

Municipal Finance

Fiscal Year 2005
Total tax levy	$9,640,857
County levy	1,960,357
County taxes	1,663,794
County library	143,447
County health	67,526
County open space	85,590
School levy	5,967,938
Local muni. budget	1,712,562
Misc. revenues	1,408,536
Total aid	$304,367
CMPTRA	147,258
Muni. block grant	12,626
Energy tax receipts	144,483
Homeland security	0

Fiscal Year 2006
Total aid	$304,367
CMPTRA	142,201
Muni. block grant	12,626
Energy tax receipts	149,540
Homeland security	NA

Taxes
	2003	2004	2005
General tax rate per $100	3.36	3.540	1.850
Net valuation taxable	$250,055,464	$254,478,502	$522,299,256
State equalized value	$364,671,816	$411,946,743	$482,850,380
County equalization ratio	84.4	68.57	122.74

Demographics & Socio-Economic Characteristics
(2000 U.S. Census, except as noted)

Population
1980*	973
1990*	911
2000	847
Male	420
Female	427
2004 (estimate)*	872
Persons per sq. mi. of land	48

Race & Hispanic Origin, 2000
Race
White	762
Black/African American	43
Amer. Indian/Alaska Natv.	22
Asian	2
Natv. Hawaiian/Pac. Islander	0
Other Race	1
Two or more races	17
Hispanic origin, total	13
Mexican	4
Puerto Rican	1
Cuban	0
Other Hispanic	8

Age & Nativity, 2000
Under 5 years	47
18 years and over	661
21 years and over	629
65 years and over	126
85 years and over	13
Median Age	43.4
Native born	838
Foreign born	4

Educational Attainment, 2000
Population 25 years and over	627
0-8 yrs of school	3.8%
High School grad or higher	86.3%
Bachelor's degree or higher	22.0%
Graduate degree	7.2%

Income & Poverty, 1999
Per capita income	$22,233
Median household income	$52,188
Median family income	$56,111
Persons in poverty	67
H'holds receiving public assistance	6
H'holds receiving social security	94

Households, 2000
Total households	326
With persons under 18	104
With persons over 65	92
Family households	245
One-person households	71
Persons per household	2.6
Persons per family	3.05

Labor & Employment
Total civilian labor force, 2004**	453
Unemployment rate	5.8%
Total civilian labor force, 2000	460
Unemployment rate	4.3%

Employed persons 16 years and over by occupation, 2000
Managers & professionals	185
Service occupations	52
Sales & office occupations	98
Farming, fishing & forestry	5
Construction & maintenance	39
Production & transportation	61
Self-employed persons	61

*US Census Bureau
**New Jersey Department of Labor

General Information
Township of Greenwich
Box 64
Greenwich, NJ 08323
856-455-4677

Web site	NA
Land area (sq. miles)	18.16
Water area (sq. miles)	0.72
Type of government	Township
Form of government	TC

Government

Legislative Districts
US Congressional	2
State Legislative	3

Local Officials, 2006
Mayor	Theodore Kiefer
Admin/Manager	NA
Clerk	Elaine Hancock
Finance Dir/Treas	Barbara Schofield
Engineer	Alexander Churchill
Attorney	Thomas Seeley
Tax assessor	Lois Mazza
Tax collector	NA
Building officer	Gordon Gross
Zoning officer	NA
Public Works	NA

Housing & Construction

Housing Units, 2000*
Total	361
Median rent	$742
Median SF home value	$112,000

New Privately Owned Housing Units Authorized by Building Permit
	Units	Value
Total, 2004	2	$266,688
Single family	2	$266,688
Total, 2005	8	$864,470
Single family	8	$864,470

Real Property Valuation - parcels, 2005
	Number	Valuation
Total		$61,475,100
Vacant	121	3,767,800
Residential	295	40,632,800
Commercial	11	2,928,300
Industrial	0	0
Apartments	0	0
Farm land	63	10,835,700
Farm homestead	159	3,310,500

Average Property Value & Tax, 2005
Residential value	$96,791
Property tax	$2,717
FAIR rebate	$624

Public Library
No public municipal library.

Library statistics, 2004
	Total	per capita
Volumes	NA	NA
Expenditure	NA	NA

Public Safety

Police
Chief	NA
Number of officers, 2004	0

Crime, 2004	Number	Rate
Total	4	4.7
Violent	1	1.2
Non-violent	3	3.5
Domestic Viol.	12	NA

Emergency/Fire
Director	Wade McFarland

Public School District
(for school year 2004-2005 except as noted)

Greenwich Township School District
839 Ye Greate St
Greenwich, NJ 08323
856-451-5513

Superintendent	Nancy Nosta
Grade plan	K-8
Enrollment	88.0
Students per teacher	7.7
Per pupil expenditure	$12,248
Median faculty salary	$46,000
Median administrator salary	$47,123
Grade 12 enrollment	NA
High school graduation rate	NA

Assessment test results
(percent scoring at proficient or advanced level)
	Language	Math
Grade 3	NA	NA
Grade 8	NA	NA
High school	NA	NA

SAT
Percent tested	NA
Average SAT math score	NA
Average SAT verbal score	NA

No Child Left Behind, 2003-04
Attendence rate (target = 90%)	95.9%
Drop rate	NA
Highly-qualified teachers	100%
District needs improvement?(AYP)	No

Municipal Finance

Fiscal Year 2005
Total tax levy	$1,732,651
County levy	544,465
County taxes	517,174
County library	0
County health	22,048
County open space	5,243
School levy	1,011,911
Local muni. budget	176,275
Misc. revenues	433,608
Total aid	$123,911
CMPTRA	61,903
Muni. block grant	3,986
Energy tax receipts	58,022
Homeland security	0

Fiscal Year 2006
Total aid	$123,911
CMPTRA	59,872
Muni. block grant	3,986
Energy tax receipts	60,053
Homeland security	NA

Taxes
	2003	2004	2005
General tax rate per $100	4.36	2.635	2.809
Net valuation taxable	$36,451,520	$62,079,954	$61,732,103
State equalized value	$52,140,638	$52,093,370	$57,715,130
County equalization ratio	74.85	119.26	119.27

Demographics & Socio-Economic Characteristics
(2000 U.S. Census, except as noted)

Population
1980*	5,404
1990*	5,102
2000	4,879
Male	2,382
Female	2,497
2004 (estimate)*	4,994
Persons per sq. mi. of land	536

Race & Hispanic Origin, 2000
Race
White	4,613
Black/African American	162
Amer. Indian/Alaska Natv.	5
Asian	33
Natv. Hawaiian/Pac. Islander	1
Other Race	13
Two or more races	52
Hispanic origin, total	75
Mexican	19
Puerto Rican	21
Cuban	3
Other Hispanic	32

Age & Nativity, 2000
Under 5 years	281
18 years and over	3,767
21 years and over	3,594
65 years and over	884
85 years and over	92
Median Age	40.1
Native born	4,702
Foreign born	177

Educational Attainment, 2000
Population 25 years and over	3,394
0-8 yrs of school	5.2%
High School grad or higher	86.9%
Bachelor's degree or higher	17.4%
Graduate degree	2.9%

Income & Poverty, 1999
Per capita income	$24,791
Median household income	$53,651
Median family income	$60,565
Persons in poverty	174
H'holds receiving public assistance	21
H'holds receiving social security	700

Households, 2000
Total households	1,866
With persons under 18	640
With persons over 65	642
Family households	1,393
One-person households	413
Persons per household	2.61
Persons per family	3.05

Labor & Employment
Total civilian labor force, 2004**	3,023
Unemployment rate	2.6%
Total civilian labor force, 2000	2,424
Unemployment rate	3.1%

Employed persons 16 years and over by occupation, 2000
Managers & professionals	666
Service occupations	264
Sales & office occupations	652
Farming, fishing & forestry	10
Construction & maintenance	312
Production & transportation	446
Self-employed persons	82

*US Census Bureau
**New Jersey Department of Labor

General Information
Township of Greenwich
420 Washington St
Gibbstown, NJ 08027
856-423-1038
Web site	www.greenwichtwp.com
Land area (sq. miles)	9.32
Water area (sq. miles)	2.74
Type of government	Township
Form of government	SM '50

Government
Legislative Districts
US Congressional	1
State Legislative	3

Local Officials, 2006
Mayor	George Shivery Jr.
Admin/Manager	Horace Spoto
Clerk	Lori Biermann (Actg)
Finance Dir/Treas	Merrie Schmidt
Engineer	Annia Hogan
Attorney	Kenneth DiMuzio
Tax assessor	Brian Schneider
Tax collector	Barbara Hoffman
Building officer	Phillip Zimm
Zoning officer	NA
Public Works	Richard Middleton

Housing & Construction
Housing Units, 2000*
Total	1,944
Median rent	$778
Median SF home value	$114,400

New Privately Owned Housing Units
Authorized by Building Permit
	Units	Value
Total, 2004	4	$542,000
Single family	4	$542,000
Total, 2005	6	$720,000
Single family	6	$720,000

Real Property Valuation - parcels, 2005
	Number	Valuation
Total		$541,747,251
Vacant	191	6,519,200
Residential	1,808	183,134,900
Commercial	65	27,092,900
Industrial	17	323,144,851
Apartments	3	410,300
Farm land	10	941,600
Farm homestead	49	503,500

Average Property Value & Tax, 2005
Residential value	$98,890
Property tax	$3,288
FAIR rebate	$657

Public Library
Greenwich Branch Library†
415 Swedesboro Rd
Gibbstown, NJ 08027
856-423-0684
Branch Librarian	Pat Woodruff

Library statistics, 2004
	Total	per capita
Volumes	NA	NA
Expenditure	NA	NA

†Branch of County library

Public Safety
Police
Chief	Carmel Morina
Number of officers, 2004	16

Crime, 2004	Number	Rate
Total	124	24.8
Violent	9	1.8
Non-violent	115	23
Domestic Viol.	88	NA

Emergency/Fire
Director	James Schmidt

Public School District
(for school year 2004-2005 except as noted)

Greenwich Township School District
415 Swedesboro Rd
Gibbstown, NJ 08027
856-224-4920
Superintendent	Francine Marteski
Grade plan	K-12
Enrollment	532.0
Students per teacher	9.4
Per pupil expenditure	$13,795
Median faculty salary	$60,407
Median administrator salary	$83,345
Grade 12 enrollment	NA
High school graduation rate	NA

Assessment test results
(percent scoring at proficient or advanced level)
	Language	Math
Grade 3	71.4%	78.6%
Grade 8	88.9%	64.5%
High school	NA	NA

SAT
Percent tested	NA
Average SAT math score	NA
Average SAT verbal score	NA

No Child Left Behind, 2003-04
Attendence rate (target = 90%)	95.4%
Drop rate	NA
Highly-qualified teachers	93.5%
District needs improvement?(AYP)	No

Municipal Finance
Fiscal Year 2005
Total tax levy	$19,563,763
County levy	5,234,735
County taxes	4,590,059
County library	339,378
County health	0
County open space	305,299
School levy	8,080,418
Local muni. budget	6,248,610
Misc. revenues	4,130,943
Total aid	$1,119,204
CMPTRA	594,347
Muni. block grant	22,325
Energy tax receipts	477,532
Homeland security	25,000

Fiscal Year 2006
Total aid	$1,144,203
CMPTRA	577,633
Muni. block grant	22,325
Energy tax receipts	494,245
Homeland security	50,000

Taxes
	2003	2004	2005
General tax rate per $100	2.87	3.032	3.326
Net valuation taxable	$622,504,474	$593,340,061	$588,372,774
State equalized value	$761,659,701	$751,149,566	$840,772,755
County equalization ratio	88.44	81.73	77.30

Demographics & Socio-Economic Characteristics
(2000 U.S. Census, except as noted)

Population
1980*	1,738
1990*	1,899
2000	4,365
Male	2,154
Female	2,211
2004 (estimate)*	5,223
Persons per sq. mi. of land	495

Race & Hispanic Origin, 2000
Race
White	4,071
Black/African American	108
Amer. Indian/Alaska Natv.	12
Asian	97
Natv. Hawaiian/Pac. Islander	3
Other Race	25
Two or more races	49
Hispanic origin, total	166
Mexican	10
Puerto Rican	64
Cuban	4
Other Hispanic	88

Age & Nativity, 2000
Under 5 years	527
18 years and over	2,897
21 years and over	2,823
65 years and over	270
85 years and over	27
Median Age	33.9
Native born	4,111
Foreign born	254

Educational Attainment, 2000
Population 25 years and over	2,763
0-8 yrs of school	2.6%
High School grad or higher	91.6%
Bachelor's degree or higher	39.0%
Graduate degree	11.1%

Income & Poverty, 1999
Per capita income	$32,886
Median household income	$87,613
Median family income	$92,579
Persons in poverty	106
H'holds receiving public assistance	20
H'holds receiving social security	226

Households, 2000
Total households	1,421
With persons under 18	752
With persons over 65	197
Family households	1,224
One-person households	162
Persons per household	3.07
Persons per family	3.34

Labor & Employment
Total civilian labor force, 2004**	1,206
Unemployment rate	3.9%
Total civilian labor force, 2000	2,132
Unemployment rate	2.3%

Employed persons 16 years and over by occupation, 2000
Managers & professionals	1,012
Service occupations	192
Sales & office occupations	570
Farming, fishing & forestry	0
Construction & maintenance	148
Production & transportation	161
Self-employed persons	84

*US Census Bureau
**New Jersey Department of Labor

General Information
Township of Greenwich
321 Greenwich St
Stewartsville, NJ 08886
908-859-0909

Web site	NA
Land area (sq. miles)	10.55
Water area (sq. miles)	0
Type of government	Township
Form of government	TC

Government

Legislative Districts
US Congressional	5
State Legislative	23

Local Officials, 2006
Mayor	William Kanyuck
Admin/Manager	NA
Clerk	Kim Viscomi
Finance Dir/Treas	Greg Della Pia
Engineer	Michael Finelli
Attorney	Michael DiMarco
Tax assessor	Eloise Hagman
Tax collector	NA
Building officer	DCA
Zoning officer	NA
Public Works	NA

Housing & Construction

Housing Units, 2000*
Total	1,477
Median rent	$871
Median SF home value	$233,300

New Privately Owned Housing Units
Authorized by Building Permit
	Units	Value
Total, 2004	19	$3,599,179
Single family	19	$3,599,179
Total, 2005	12	$2,861,134
Single family	10	$2,407,134

Real Property Valuation - parcels, 2005
	Number	Valuation
Total		$572,568,490
Vacant	83	3,244,500
Residential	1,751	464,024,890
Commercial	44	76,932,100
Industrial	5	14,698,000
Apartments	0	0
Farm land	49	11,269,300
Farm homestead	113	2,399,700

Average Property Value & Tax, 2005
Residential value	$250,228
Property tax	$5,845
FAIR rebate	$442

Public Library

No public municipal library.

Library statistics, 2004
	Total	per capita
Volumes	NA	NA
Expenditure	NA	NA

Public Safety

Police
Chief	Richard Guzzo
Number of officers, 2004	9

Crime, 2004	Number	Rate
Total	111	21.4
Violent	3	0.6
Non-violent	108	20.8
Domestic Viol.	38	NA

Emergency/Fire
Director	Joseph Mecsey III

Public School District
(for school year 2004-2005 except as noted)

Greenwich Township School District
642 S Main St
Stewartsville, NJ 08886
908-859-2022

Superintendent	Kevin Brennan
Grade plan	K-12
Enrollment	947.0
Students per teacher	11.4
Per pupil expenditure	$9,325
Median faculty salary	$39,110
Median administrator salary	$87,633
Grade 12 enrollment	NA
High school graduation rate	NA

Assessment test results
(percent scoring at proficient or advanced level)
	Language	Math
Grade 3	91.7%	91.7%
Grade 8	70.1%	72.2%
High school	NA	NA

SAT
Percent tested	NA
Average SAT math score	NA
Average SAT verbal score	NA

No Child Left Behind, 2003-04
Attendence rate (target = 90%)	96.1%
Drop rate	NA
Highly-qualified teachers	95.7%
District needs improvement?(AYP)	No

Municipal Finance

Fiscal Year 2005
Total tax levy	$13,422,588
County levy	4,216,512
County taxes	3,486,322
County library	336,118
County health	0
County open space	394,071
School levy	7,009,616
Local muni. budget	2,196,460
Misc. revenues	1,281,047
Total aid	$484,445
CMPTRA	105,319
Muni. block grant	17,115
Energy tax receipts	312,011
Homeland security	50,000

Fiscal Year 2006
Total aid	$484,446
CMPTRA	94,399
Muni. block grant	17,115
Energy tax receipts	322,932
Homeland security	50,000

Taxes
	2003	2004	2005
General tax rate per $100	2.10	2.140	2.340
Net valuation taxable	$555,879,148	$572,354,751	$574,611,201
State equalized value	$575,206,072	$652,900,666	$757,862,307
County equalization ratio	101.46	96.64	87.62

Demographics & Socio-Economic Characteristics
(2000 U.S. Census, except as noted)

Population
1980*	7,340
1990*	8,268
2000	10,807
Male	5,205
Female	5,602
2004 (estimate)*	11,011
Persons per sq. mi. of land	57,069

Race & Hispanic Origin, 2000
Race
White	7,022
Black/African American	412
Amer. Indian/Alaska Natv.	41
Asian	789
Natv. Hawaiian/Pac. Islander	1
Other Race	1,775
Two or more races	767
Hispanic origin, total	5,871
Mexican	233
Puerto Rican	608
Cuban	1,203
Other Hispanic	3,827

Age & Nativity, 2000
Under 5 years	695
18 years and over	8,520
21 years and over	8,175
65 years and over	1,273
85 years and over	170
Median Age	35.5
Native born	5,434
Foreign born	5,259

Educational Attainment, 2000
Population 25 years and over	7,566
0-8 yrs of school	11.9%
High School grad or higher	75.0%
Bachelor's degree or higher	29.8%
Graduate degree	13.4%

Income & Poverty, 1999
Per capita income	$27,931
Median household income	$44,515
Median family income	$47,440
Persons in poverty	1,377
H'holds receiving public assistance	128
H'holds receiving social security	969

Households, 2000
Total households	4,493
With persons under 18	1,344
With persons over 65	964
Family households	2,620
One-person households	1,576
Persons per household	2.38
Persons per family	3.13

Labor & Employment
Total civilian labor force, 2004**	4,945
Unemployment rate	3.1%
Total civilian labor force, 2000	5,596
Unemployment rate	6.7%

Employed persons 16 years and over by occupation, 2000
Managers & professionals	1,798
Service occupations	714
Sales & office occupations	1,548
Farming, fishing & forestry	0
Construction & maintenance	331
Production & transportation	828
Self-employed persons	276

*US Census Bureau
**New Jersey Department of Labor

General Information
Town of Guttenberg
6808 Park Ave
Guttenberg, NJ 07093
201-868-2315

Web site	www.guttenbergnj.org
Land area (sq. miles)	0.19
Water area (sq. miles)	0.04
Type of government	Town
Form of government	M&C

Government
Legislative Districts
US Congressional	13
State Legislative	33

Local Officials, 2006
Mayor	David Delle Donna
Admin/Manager	Linda Martin
Clerk	Linda Martin
Finance Dir/Treas	Nicholas Goldsack
Engineer	Wendell Bibbs
Attorney	Charles Daglian
Tax assessor	Gerald Pontrelli
Tax collector	Nicholas Goldsack
Building officer	Brian Ribarro
Zoning officer	Brian Ribarro
Public Works	Michael Ronchi

Housing & Construction
Housing Units, 2000*
Total	4,650
Median rent	$794
Median SF home value	$150,200

New Privately Owned Housing Units Authorized by Building Permit
	Units	Value
Total, 2004	36	$2,619,098
Single family	9	$736,400
Total, 2005	29	$2,161,863
Single family	7	$572,754

Real Property Valuation - parcels, 2005
	Number	Valuation
Total		$405,065,200
Vacant	26	1,703,600
Residential	2,289	316,786,500
Commercial	130	36,983,200
Industrial	70	15,033,500
Apartments	73	34,558,400
Farm land	0	0
Farm homestead	0	0

Average Property Value & Tax, 2005
Residential value	$138,395
Property tax	$6,168
FAIR rebate	$586

Public Library
No public municipal library.

Library statistics, 2004
	Total	per capita
Volumes	NA	NA
Expenditure	NA	NA

Public Safety
Police
Chief	Nicholas Lordo (PS Dir)
Number of officers, 2004	22

Crime, 2004	Number	Rate
Total	226	20.5
Violent	42	3.8
Non-violent	184	16.7
Domestic Viol.	67	NA

Emergency/Fire
Director	(Police Dept)

Public School District
(for school year 2004-2005 except as noted)

Guttenberg School District
301 69th St
Guttenberg, NJ 07093
201-861-3100

Superintendent	Robert Penna
Grade plan	K-12
Enrollment	948.0
Students per teacher	14.2
Per pupil expenditure	$8,698
Median faculty salary	$44,921
Median administrator salary	$109,277
Grade 12 enrollment	NA
High school graduation rate	NA

Assessment test results
(percent scoring at proficient or advanced level)
	Language	Math
Grade 3	80.7%	79.3%
Grade 8	69.0%	69.2%
High school	NA	NA

SAT
Percent tested	NA
Average SAT math score	NA
Average SAT verbal score	NA

No Child Left Behind, 2003-04
Attendence rate (target = 90%)	94.9%
Drop rate	NA
Highly-qualified teachers	94.5%
District needs improvement?(AYP)	No

Municipal Finance
Fiscal Year 2005
Total tax levy	$19,062,661
County levy	4,096,054
County taxes	4,018,628
County library	0
County health	0
County open space	77,426
School levy	7,166,288
Local muni. budget	7,800,319
Misc. revenues	4,202,052
Total aid	$1,060,847
CMPTRA	697,401
Muni. block grant	42,375
Energy tax receipts	251,071
Homeland security	70,000

Fiscal Year 2006
Total aid	$1,060,847
CMPTRA	688,614
Muni. block grant	42,375
Energy tax receipts	259,858
Homeland security	70,000

Taxes
	2003	2004	2005
General tax rate per $100	4.27	4.534	4.704
Net valuation taxable	$402,265,850	$403,813,503	$405,269,784
State equalized value	$716,412,912	$767,351,552	$869,491,062
County equalization ratio	61.9	56.15	52.61

Demographics & Socio-Economic Characteristics
(2000 U.S. Census, except as noted)

Population
1980*	36,039
1990*	37,049
2000	42,677
Male	21,199
Female	21,478
2004 (estimate)*	43,681
Persons per sq. mi. of land	10,602

Race & Hispanic Origin, 2000
Race
White	22,451
Black/African American	10,518
Amer. Indian/Alaska Natv.	191
Asian	3,181
Natv. Hawaiian/Pac. Islander	23
Other Race	4,144
Two or more races	2,169
Hispanic origin, total	11,061
Mexican	340
Puerto Rican	1,371
Cuban	298
Other Hispanic	9,052

Age & Nativity, 2000
Under 5 years	2,465
18 years and over	34,906
21 years and over	33,607
65 years and over	5,329
85 years and over	768
Median Age	36.2
Native born	28,231
Foreign born	14,446

Educational Attainment, 2000
Population 25 years and over	31,518
0-8 yrs of school	8.5%
High School grad or higher	79.7%
Bachelor's degree or higher	29.1%
Graduate degree	10.7%

Income & Poverty, 1999
Per capita income	$26,856
Median household income	$49,316
Median family income	$56,953
Persons in poverty	3,867
H'holds receiving public assistance	417
H'holds receiving social security	4,019

Households, 2000
Total households	18,113
With persons under 18	4,503
With persons over 65	3,924
Family households	9,549
One-person households	7,206
Persons per household	2.26
Persons per family	3.08

Labor & Employment
Total civilian labor force, 2004**	23,460
Unemployment rate	5.3%
Total civilian labor force, 2000	23,543
Unemployment rate	6.8%

Employed persons 16 years and over by occupation, 2000
Managers & professionals	7,817
Service occupations	3,262
Sales & office occupations	6,534
Farming, fishing & forestry	4
Construction & maintenance	1,344
Production & transportation	2,992
Self-employed persons	926

*US Census Bureau
**New Jersey Department of Labor

General Information
City of Hackensack
65 Central Ave
Hackensack, NJ 07602
201-646-3980
Web site	www.hackensack.org
Land area (sq. miles)	4.12
Water area (sq. miles)	0.19
Type of government	City
Form of government	CM '23

Government
Legislative Districts
US Congressional	9
State Legislative	37

Local Officials, 2006
Mayor	Marlin G. Townes Jr.
Admin/Manager	Stephen Lo Iacono
Clerk	Debra Heck
Finance Dir/Treas	Louis Garbaccio
Engineer	Vincent DeNave
Attorney	Joseph C. Zisa
Tax assessor	Arthur Carlson
Tax collector	NA
Building officer	John Greenwood
Zoning officer	NA
Public Works	Jesse D'Amore

Housing & Construction
Housing Units, 2000*
Total	18,945
Median rent	$848
Median SF home value	$187,300

New Privately Owned Housing Units
Authorized by Building Permit
	Units	Value
Total, 2004	147	$10,485,850
Single family	6	$1,090,200
Total, 2005	104	$11,706,000
Single family	3	$256,000

Real Property Valuation - parcels, 2005
	Number	Valuation
Total		$2,262,748,000
Vacant	287	24,754,500
Residential	7,932	928,798,000
Commercial	1,004	773,001,000
Industrial	241	150,088,200
Apartments	212	386,106,300
Farm land	0	0
Farm homestead	0	0

Average Property Value & Tax, 2005
Residential value	$117,095
Property tax	$5,492
FAIR rebate	$601

Public Library
Johnson Free Pub Library
274 Moore St
Hackensack, NJ 07601
201-343-4169
Director	Maureen Taffe

Library statistics, 2004
	Total	per capita
Volumes	159,624	3.74
Expenditure	$1,974,769	$46.27

Public Safety
Police
Chief	Charles Zisa
Number of officers, 2004	110

Crime, 2004	Number	Rate
Total	1,306	30
Violent	139	3.2
Non-violent	1,167	26.8
Domestic Viol.	404	NA

Emergency/Fire
Director	Joel Thornton

Public School District
(for school year 2004-2005 except as noted)

Hackensack School District
355 State St
Hackensack, NJ 07601
201-646-7830
Superintendent	Joseph Montesano
Grade plan	K-12
Enrollment	5,416.0
Students per teacher	12.0
Per pupil expenditure	$13,055
Median faculty salary	$69,308
Median administrator salary	$118,223
Grade 12 enrollment	403.5
High school graduation rate	85.5%

Assessment test results
(percent scoring at proficient or advanced level)
	Language	Math
Grade 3	75.3%	76.7%
Grade 8	63.6%	46.7%
High school	73.5%	72.1%

SAT
Percent tested	61%
Average SAT math score	492
Average SAT verbal score	463

No Child Left Behind, 2003-04
Attendence rate (target = 90%)	94.6%
Drop rate	1.8%
Highly-qualified teachers	96.7%
District needs improvement?(AYP)	No

Municipal Finance
Fiscal Year 2005
Total tax levy	$106,766,279
County levy	8,931,910
County taxes	8,484,418
County library	0
County health	0
County open space	447,491
School levy	51,499,840
Local muni. budget	46,334,530
Misc. revenues	19,675,646
Total aid	$5,640,845
CMPTRA	2,627,422
Muni. block grant	167,338
Energy tax receipts	2,706,085
Homeland security	140,000

Fiscal Year 2006
Total aid	$5,640,845
CMPTRA	2,532,709
Muni. block grant	167,338
Energy tax receipts	2,800,798
Homeland security	140,000

Taxes
	2003	2004	2005
General tax rate per $100	4.30	4.480	4.690
Net valuation taxable	$2,270,426,898	$2,277,263,377	$2,276,491,440
State equalized value	$3,733,026,797	$4,425,547,412	$4,981,381,707
County equalization ratio	69.57	60.82	51.29

Demographics & Socio-Economic Characteristics
(2000 U.S. Census, except as noted)

Population
1980*	8,850
1990*	8,120
2000	10,403
Male	5,006
Female	5,397
2000 (revised)	8,984
2004 (estimate)*	9,339
Persons per sq. mi. of land	2,522

Race & Hispanic Origin, 2000
Race
White	9,389
Black/African American	227
Amer. Indian/Alaska Natv.	13
Asian	303
Natv. Hawaiian/Pac. Islander	6
Other Race	208
Two or more races	257
Hispanic origin, total	833
Mexican	79
Puerto Rican	188
Cuban	48
Other Hispanic	518

Age & Nativity, 2000
Under 5 years	658
18 years and over	8,043
21 years and over	7,536
65 years and over	1,270
85 years and over	208
Median Age	35.4
Native born	9,100
Foreign born	1,303

Educational Attainment, 2000
Population 25 years and over	6,994
0-8 yrs of school	3.6%
High School grad or higher	87.1%
Bachelor's degree or higher	24.5%
Graduate degree	6.8%

Income & Poverty, 1999
Per capita income	$24,742
Median household income	$51,955
Median family income	$64,383
Persons in poverty	475
H'holds receiving public assistance	86
H'holds receiving social security	1,013

Households, 2000
Total households	4,134
With persons under 18	1,327
With persons over 65	918
Family households	2,532
One-person households	1,311
Persons per household	2.41
Persons per family	3.1

Labor & Employment
Total civilian labor force, 2004**	5,463
Unemployment rate	4.9%
Total civilian labor force, 2000	5,820
Unemployment rate	4.7%

Employed persons 16 years and over by occupation, 2000
Managers & professionals	1,855
Service occupations	813
Sales & office occupations	1,584
Farming, fishing & forestry	11
Construction & maintenance	620
Production & transportation	665
Self-employed persons	160

*US Census Bureau
**New Jersey Department of Labor

General Information
Town of Hackettstown
215 Stiger St
Hackettstown, NJ 07840
908-852-3130

Web site	www.hackettstown.net
Land area (sq. miles)	3.70
Water area (sq. miles)	0
Type of government	Town
Form of government	SC

Government

Legislative Districts
US Congressional	5
State Legislative	23

Local Officials, 2006
Mayor	Michael B. Lavery
Admin/Manager	William Kuster Jr.
Clerk	William Kuster Jr.
Finance Dir/Treas	Danette Dyer
Engineer	Paul Sterbenz
Attorney	Thomas Thorp
Tax assessor	Bernard Murdoch
Tax collector	Regina McKenna
Building officer	Richard O'Connor
Zoning officer	David Diehl
Public Works	NA

Housing & Construction

Housing Units, 2000*
Total	4,347
Median rent	$719
Median SF home value	$154,000

New Privately Owned Housing Units
Authorized by Building Permit
	Units	Value
Total, 2004	56	$1,870,675
Single family	9	$1,126,444
Total, 2005	74	$6,110,192
Single family	8	$972,811

Real Property Valuation - parcels, 2005
	Number	Valuation
Total		$582,376,872
Vacant	80	12,180,100
Residential	2,255	378,924,822
Commercial	282	106,024,300
Industrial	29	52,897,850
Apartments	33	32,349,800
Farm land	0	0
Farm homestead	0	0

Average Property Value & Tax, 2005
Residential value	$168,038
Property tax	$6,181
FAIR rebate	$543

Public Library
Hackettstown Free Public Library
110 Church St
Hackettstown, NJ 07840
908-852-4936
Director ... J. Rona Mosler

Library statistics, 2004
	Total	per capita
Volumes	34,389	3.31
Expenditure	$318,227	$30.59

Public Safety
Police
Chief	Leonard Kunz
Number of officers, 2004	21

Crime, 2004	Number	Rate
Total	156	16.7
Violent	14	1.5
Non-violent	142	15.2
Domestic Viol.	97	NA

Emergency/Fire
Director ... Christopher Biamonte

Public School District
(for school year 2004-2005 except as noted)

Hackettstown School District
315 Washington Ave
Hackettstown, NJ 07840
908-850-6500
Superintendent	Robert Gratz
Grade plan	K-12
Enrollment	1,947.5
Students per teacher	11.1
Per pupil expenditure	$11,646
Median faculty salary	$54,435
Median administrator salary	$101,450
Grade 12 enrollment	220.5
High school graduation rate	94.8%

Assessment test results
(percent scoring at proficient or advanced level)
	Language	Math
Grade 3	81.9%	85.7%
Grade 8	74.3%	65.5%
High school	89.3%	84.2%

SAT
Percent tested	77%
Average SAT math score	493
Average SAT verbal score	497

No Child Left Behind, 2003-04
Attendence rate (target = 90%)	94.8%
Drop rate	2.2%
Highly-qualified teachers	100%
District needs improvement?(AYP)	No

Municipal Finance

Fiscal Year 2005
Total tax levy	$21,569,598
County levy	4,562,802
County taxes	4,099,180
County library	0
County health	0
County open space	463,622
School levy	12,879,110
Local muni. budget	4,127,686
Misc. revenues	3,236,655
Total aid	$1,153,342
CMPTRA	559,923
Muni. block grant	40,790
Energy tax receipts	482,629
Homeland security	70,000

Fiscal Year 2006
Total aid	$1,153,342
CMPTRA	543,031
Muni. block grant	40,790
Energy tax receipts	499,521
Homeland security	70,000

Taxes
	2003	2004	2005
General tax rate per $100	3.31	3.550	3.680
Net valuation taxable	$574,400,289	$573,763,640	$586,384,815
State equalized value	$691,965,172	$746,614,971	$846,520,593
County equalization ratio	92.5	83.01	76.71

Demographics & Socio-Economic Characteristics
(2000 U.S. Census, except as noted)

Population
1980*	8,361
1990*	7,860
2000	7,547
Male	3,554
Female	3,993
2004 (estimate)*	7,453
Persons per sq. mi. of land	4,795

Race & Hispanic Origin, 2000
Race
White	7,394
Black/African American	30
Amer. Indian/Alaska Natv.	8
Asian	49
Natv. Hawaiian/Pac. Islander	3
Other Race	20
Two or more races	43
Hispanic origin, total	79
Mexican	17
Puerto Rican	27
Cuban	3
Other Hispanic	32

Age & Nativity, 2000
Under 5 years	464
18 years and over	5,731
21 years and over	5,541
65 years and over	1,373
85 years and over	154
Median Age	40.6
Native born	7,325
Foreign born	222

Educational Attainment, 2000
Population 25 years and over	5,366
0-8 yrs of school	2.6%
High School grad or higher	90.7%
Bachelor's degree or higher	38.1%
Graduate degree	13.4%

Income & Poverty, 1999
Per capita income	$28,198
Median household income	$58,424
Median family income	$73,460
Persons in poverty	211
H'holds receiving public assistance	7
H'holds receiving social security	1,041

Households, 2000
Total households	3,039
With persons under 18	989
With persons over 65	1,012
Family households	2,039
One-person households	867
Persons per household	2.48
Persons per family	3.09

Labor & Employment
Total civilian labor force, 2004**	4,102
Unemployment rate	2.1%
Total civilian labor force, 2000	3,863
Unemployment rate	3.3%

Employed persons 16 years and over by occupation, 2000
Managers & professionals	1,830
Service occupations	432
Sales & office occupations	1,022
Farming, fishing & forestry	0
Construction & maintenance	242
Production & transportation	211
Self-employed persons	232

*US Census Bureau
**New Jersey Department of Labor

General Information
Borough of Haddon Heights
625 Station Ave
Haddon Heights, NJ 08035
856-547-7164

Web site	www.haddonhts.com
Land area (sq. miles)	1.55
Water area (sq. miles)	0
Type of government	Borough
Form of government	B

Government

Legislative Districts
US Congressional	1
State Legislative	5

Local Officials, 2006
Mayor	Susan Griffith
Admin/Manager	Joan Moreland
Clerk	Joan Moreland
Finance Dir/Treas	Ernest Merlino
Engineer	Remington & Vernick
Attorney	John Kearney
Tax assessor	Thomas Glock
Tax collector	Audrea Penny
Building officer	Mengste Thomas El
Zoning officer	Mengste Thomas El
Public Works	NA

Housing & Construction

Housing Units, 2000*
Total	3,136
Median rent	$586
Median SF home value	$139,800

New Privately Owned Housing Units
Authorized by Building Permit
	Units	Value
Total, 2004	2	$229,200
Single family	2	$229,200
Total, 2005	1	$114,600
Single family	1	$114,600

Real Property Valuation - parcels, 2005
	Number	Valuation
Total		$399,581,700
Vacant	31	810,700
Residential	2,514	347,159,800
Commercial	159	45,563,800
Industrial	2	295,700
Apartments	17	5,751,700
Farm land	0	0
Farm homestead	0	0

Average Property Value & Tax, 2005
Residential value	$138,091
Property tax	$6,316
FAIR rebate	$601

Public Library
Haddon Heights Public Library
608 Station Ave
Haddon Heights, NJ 08035
856-547-7132

Director | Robert Hunter

Library statistics, 2004
	Total	per capita
Volumes	49,061	6.50
Expenditure	$268,873	$35.63

Public Safety

Police
Chief	Ronald Shute
Number of officers, 2004	18

Crime, 2004	Number	Rate
Total	163	21.7
Violent	8	1.1
Non-violent	155	20.7
Domestic Viol.	17	NA

Emergency/Fire
Director | Steve Kinky (Chief)

Public School District
(for school year 2004-2005 except as noted)

Haddon Heights School District
300 Second Ave
Haddon Heights, NJ 08035
856-547-1412

Superintendent	Nancy Hacker
Grade plan	K-12
Enrollment	1,294.0
Students per teacher	10.6
Per pupil expenditure	$12,192
Median faculty salary	$49,772
Median administrator salary	$77,289
Grade 12 enrollment	176.0
High school graduation rate	98.3%

Assessment test results
(percent scoring at proficient or advanced level)
	Language	Math
Grade 3	94.9%	98.3%
Grade 8	81.5%	59.3%
High school	90.5%	80.9%

SAT
Percent tested	74%
Average SAT math score	503
Average SAT verbal score	504

No Child Left Behind, 2003-04
Attendence rate (target = 90%)	94.7%
Drop rate	0%
Highly-qualified teachers	100%
District needs improvement?(AYP)	No

Municipal Finance

Fiscal Year 2005
Total tax levy	$18,298,972
County levy	4,447,238
County taxes	4,389,637
County library	0
County health	0
County open space	57,601
School levy	9,947,782
Local muni. budget	3,903,952
Misc. revenues	2,415,548
Total aid	$1,122,999
CMPTRA	397,785
Muni. block grant	34,393
Energy tax receipts	640,821
Homeland security	50,000

Fiscal Year 2006
Total aid	$1,122,999
CMPTRA	375,356
Muni. block grant	34,393
Energy tax receipts	663,250
Homeland security	50,000

Taxes
	2003	2004	2005
General tax rate per $100	4.23	4.322	4.574
Net valuation taxable	$398,463,180	$399,551,205	$400,081,674
State equalized value	$506,177,820	$572,823,076	$666,691,675
County equalization ratio	85.72	78.72	69.72

Demographics & Socio-Economic Characteristics

(2000 U.S. Census, except as noted)

Population

1980*	15,875
1990*	14,837
2000	14,651
Male	6,876
Female	7,775
2004 (estimate)*	14,592
Persons per sq. mi. of land	5,422

Race & Hispanic Origin, 2000

Race

White	13,980
Black/African American	173
Amer. Indian/Alaska Natv.	8
Asian	294
Natv. Hawaiian/Pac. Islander	6
Other Race	82
Two or more races	108
Hispanic origin, total	226
Mexican	39
Puerto Rican	114
Cuban	19
Other Hispanic	54

Age & Nativity, 2000

Under 5 years	801
18 years and over	11,340
21 years and over	10,972
65 years and over	2,929
85 years and over	386
Median Age	40.7
Native born	14,084
Foreign born	576

Educational Attainment, 2000

Population 25 years and over	10,348
0-8 yrs of school	2.9%
High School grad or higher	89.5%
Bachelor's degree or higher	30.6%
Graduate degree	9.7%

Income & Poverty, 1999

Per capita income	$25,610
Median household income	$51,076
Median family income	$65,269
Persons in poverty	607
H'holds receiving public assistance	81
H'holds receiving social security	2,214

Households, 2000

Total households	6,207
With persons under 18	1,804
With persons over 65	2,224
Family households	3,889
One-person households	2,048
Persons per household	2.36
Persons per family	3.05

Labor & Employment

Total civilian labor force, 2004**	7,925
Unemployment rate	2.1%
Total civilian labor force, 2000	7,474
Unemployment rate	3.5%

Employed persons 16 years and over by occupation, 2000

Managers & professionals	3,000
Service occupations	883
Sales & office occupations	2,112
Farming, fishing & forestry	0
Construction & maintenance	633
Production & transportation	586
Self-employed persons	373

*US Census Bureau
**New Jersey Department of Labor

General Information

Township of Haddon
135 Haddon Ave
Westmont, NJ 08108
856-854-1176

Web site	www.haddontwp.com
Land area (sq. miles)	2.69
Water area (sq. miles)	0.11
Type of government	Township
Form of government	Comm.

Government

Legislative Districts

US Congressional	1, 3
State Legislative	6

Local Officials, 2006

Mayor	William J. Park Jr.
Admin/Manager	NA
Clerk	Denise P. Adams
Finance Dir/Treas	Denise P.Adams
Engineer	Schoor DePalma Inc.
Attorney	Timothy Higgins
Tax assessor	Martin Blaskey
Tax collector	NA
Building officer	Lawrence Orcutt
Zoning officer	NA
Public Works	NA

Housing & Construction

Housing Units, 2000*

Total	6,423
Median rent	$690
Median SF home value	$122,200

New Privately Owned Housing Units
Authorized by Building Permit

	Units	Value
Total, 2004	19	$953,619
Single family	4	$287,619
Total, 2005	24	$1,445,643
Single family	4	$557,643

Real Property Valuation - parcels, 2005

	Number	Valuation
Total		$679,429,900
Vacant	131	2,884,900
Residential	4,722	558,785,100
Commercial	272	80,631,200
Industrial	23	4,967,800
Apartments	17	32,160,900
Farm land	0	0
Farm homestead	0	0

Average Property Value & Tax, 2005

Residential value	$118,337
Property tax	$5,175
FAIR rebate	$603

Public Library

Haddon Township Branch Library†
15 MacArthur Blvd
Westmont, NJ 08108
856-854-2752

Branch Librarian | Nan Rosenthal

Library statistics, 2004

	Total	per capita
Volumes	NA	NA
Expenditure	NA	NA

†Branch of county library

Public Safety

Police

Chief	Joseph Gallagher Jr.
Number of officers, 2004	30

Crime, 2004	Number	Rate
Total	381	25.9
Violent	26	1.8
Non-violent	355	24.2
Domestic Viol.	112	NA

Emergency/Fire

Director	NA

Public School District

(for school year 2004-2005 except as noted)

Haddon Township School District
500 Rhoads Ave
Westmont, NJ 08108
856-869-7700

Superintendent	Mark Raivetz
Grade plan	K-12
Enrollment	2,258.0
Students per teacher	12.7
Per pupil expenditure	$10,870
Median faculty salary	$54,050
Median administrator salary	$93,610
Grade 12 enrollment	155.0
High school graduation rate	96.4%

Assessment test results

(percent scoring at proficient or advanced level)

	Language	Math
Grade 3	87.5%	86.7%
Grade 8	78.7%	79.2%
High school	90.0%	85.4%

SAT

Percent tested	88%
Average SAT math score	512
Average SAT verbal score	517

No Child Left Behind, 2003-04

Attendence rate (target = 90%)	95.1%
Drop rate	2.3%
Highly-qualified teachers	98.7%
District needs improvement?(AYP)	No

Municipal Finance

Fiscal Year 2005

Total tax levy	$29,737,584
County levy	7,944,139
County taxes	7,321,642
County library	526,490
County health	0
County open space	96,007
School levy	16,518,062
Local muni. budget	5,275,383
Misc. revenues	4,759,617
Total aid	$1,776,294
CMPTRA	765,656
Muni. block grant	64,921
Energy tax receipts	875,717
Homeland security	70,000

Fiscal Year 2006

Total aid	$1,776,294
CMPTRA	735,006
Muni. block grant	64,921
Energy tax receipts	906,367
Homeland security	70,000

Taxes

	2003	2004	2005
General tax rate per $100	3.84	4.073	4.373
Net valuation taxable	$675,724,452	$677,431,896	$680,072,447
State equalized value	$847,197,156	$951,151,667	$1,090,034,376
County equalization ratio	89.4	79.76	71.20

Demographics & Socio-Economic Characteristics
(2000 U.S. Census, except as noted)

Population
1980*	12,337
1990*	11,628
2000	11,659
Male	5,536
Female	6,123
2004 (estimate)*	11,596
Persons per sq. mi. of land	4,102

Race & Hispanic Origin, 2000
Race
White	11,247
Black/African American	148
Amer. Indian/Alaska Natv.	15
Asian	131
Natv. Hawaiian/Pac. Islander	3
Other Race	37
Two or more races	78
Hispanic origin, total	170
Mexican	22
Puerto Rican	54
Cuban	24
Other Hispanic	70

Age & Nativity, 2000
Under 5 years	743
18 years and over	8,488
21 years and over	8,250
65 years and over	1,850
85 years and over	222
Median Age	41.3
Native born	11,290
Foreign born	370

Educational Attainment, 2000
Population 25 years and over	8,091
0-8 yrs of school	1.0%
High School grad or higher	95.1%
Bachelor's degree or higher	64.8%
Graduate degree	28.9%

Income & Poverty, 1999
Per capita income	$43,170
Median household income	$86,872
Median family income	$103,597
Persons in poverty	250
H'holds receiving public assistance	33
H'holds receiving social security	1,338

Households, 2000
Total households	4,496
With persons under 18	1,620
With persons over 65	1,297
Family households	3,253
One-person households	1,085
Persons per household	2.57
Persons per family	3.09

Labor & Employment
Total civilian labor force, 2004**	6,099
Unemployment rate	1.6%
Total civilian labor force, 2000	5,872
Unemployment rate	2.8%

Employed persons 16 years and over by occupation, 2000
Managers & professionals	3,855
Service occupations	355
Sales & office occupations	1,169
Farming, fishing & forestry	5
Construction & maintenance	76
Production & transportation	245
Self-employed persons	545

*US Census Bureau
**New Jersey Department of Labor

General Information
Borough of Haddonfield
PO Box 3005
242 Kings Highway E
Haddonfield, NJ 08033
856-429-4700
Web site	haddonfield-nj.org
Land area (sq. miles)	2.83
Water area (sq. miles)	0.03
Type of government	Borough
Form of government	Comm.

Government

Legislative Districts
US Congressional	1, 3
State Legislative	6

Local Officials, 2006
Mayor	Letitia Colombi
Admin/Manager	Richard Schwab
Clerk	Deanna Speck
Finance Dir/Treas	Terry Henry
Engineer	Edward Vernick
Attorney	Mario Iavicoli
Tax assessor	Thomas Colavecchio
Tax collector	NA
Building officer	Steven Walko
Zoning officer	NA
Public Works	Howard Frazier

Housing & Construction

Housing Units, 2000*
Total	4,620
Median rent	$732
Median SF home value	$225,300

New Privately Owned Housing Units Authorized by Building Permit
	Units	Value
Total, 2004	15	$3,762,300
Single family	15	$3,762,300
Total, 2005	16	$3,336,000
Single family	16	$3,336,000

Real Property Valuation - parcels, 2005
	Number	Valuation
Total		$1,014,759,600
Vacant	55	2,709,900
Residential	4,074	900,204,200
Commercial	274	105,631,300
Industrial	0	0
Apartments	11	6,214,200
Farm land	0	0
Farm homestead	0	0

Average Property Value & Tax, 2005
Residential value	$220,963
Property tax	$9,831
FAIR rebate	$609

Public Library
Haddonfield Public Library
60 N Haddon Ave
Haddonfield, NJ 08033
856-429-1304
Director | Douglas Rauschenberger

Library statistics, 2004
	Total	per capita
Volumes	79,340	6.81
Expenditure	$875,278	$75.07

Public Safety

Police
Chief	Richard Tsonis
Number of officers, 2004	25

Crime, 2004	Number	Rate
Total	162	13.9
Violent	9	0.8
Non-violent	153	13.2
Domestic Viol.	27	NA

Emergency/Fire
Director | Joseph Riggs Jr.

Public School District
(for school year 2004-2005 except as noted)

Haddonfield Borough School District
One Lincoln Ave
Haddonfield, NJ 08033
856-429-4130
Superintendent	Joseph O'Brien
Grade plan	K-12
Enrollment	2,490.0
Students per teacher	12.8
Per pupil expenditure	$11,206
Median faculty salary	$57,763
Median administrator salary	$104,991
Grade 12 enrollment	187.0
High school graduation rate	100.0%

Assessment test results
(percent scoring at proficient or advanced level)
	Language	Math
Grade 3	98.2%	95.1%
Grade 8	93.9%	94.5%
High school	96.0%	93.1%

SAT
Percent tested	101%
Average SAT math score	578
Average SAT verbal score	575

No Child Left Behind, 2003-04
Attendence rate (target = 90%)	94.9%
Drop rate	0%
Highly-qualified teachers	94.8%
District needs improvement?(AYP)	No

Municipal Finance

Fiscal Year 2005
Total tax levy	$45,330,539
County levy	12,161,368
County taxes	12,003,980
County library	0
County health	0
County open space	157,389
School levy	26,649,142
Local muni. budget	6,520,029
Misc. revenues	5,194,424
Total aid	$1,428,767
CMPTRA	524,444
Muni. block grant	50,903
Energy tax receipts	783,420
Homeland security	70,000

Fiscal Year 2006
Total aid	$1,428,768
CMPTRA	497,025
Muni. block grant	50,903
Energy tax receipts	810,840
Homeland security	70,000

Taxes
	2003	2004	2005
General tax rate per $100	4.00	4.202	4.450
Net valuation taxable	$1,008,013,448	$1,011,118,379	$1,018,820,904
State equalized value	$1,403,332,101	$1,555,236,374	$1,752,056,585
County equalization ratio	78.08	71.83	64.91

Demographics & Socio-Economic Characteristics
(2000 U.S. Census, except as noted)

Population
1980*	3,236
1990*	3,249
2000	4,126
Male	2,018
Female	2,108
2004 (estimate)*	6,106
Persons per sq. mi. of land	936

Race & Hispanic Origin, 2000
Race
White	3,882
Black/African American	110
Amer. Indian/Alaska Natv.	4
Asian	70
Natv. Hawaiian/Pac. Islander	0
Other Race	21
Two or more races	39
Hispanic origin, total	88
Mexican	9
Puerto Rican	63
Cuban	6
Other Hispanic	10

Age & Nativity, 2000
Under 5 years	321
18 years and over	3,042
21 years and over	2,936
65 years and over	485
85 years and over	41
Median Age	38.4
Native born	4,007
Foreign born	119

Educational Attainment, 2000
Population 25 years and over	2,784
0-8 yrs of school	0.9%
High School grad or higher	88.6%
Bachelor's degree or higher	24.7%
Graduate degree	7.7%

Income & Poverty, 1999
Per capita income	$28,091
Median household income	$66,417
Median family income	$72,005
Persons in poverty	121
H'holds receiving public assistance	9
H'holds receiving social security	385

Households, 2000
Total households	1,477
With persons under 18	569
With persons over 65	355
Family households	1,150
One-person households	259
Persons per household	2.78
Persons per family	3.16

Labor & Employment
Total civilian labor force, 2004**	1,839
Unemployment rate	2.9%
Total civilian labor force, 2000	2,307
Unemployment rate	2.7%

Employed persons 16 years and over by occupation, 2000
Managers & professionals	843
Service occupations	278
Sales & office occupations	662
Farming, fishing & forestry	4
Construction & maintenance	191
Production & transportation	266
Self-employed persons	84

*US Census Bureau
**New Jersey Department of Labor

General Information
Township of Hainesport
PO Box 477
One Hainesport Centre
Hainesport, NJ 08036
609-267-2730

Web site	www.hainesporttownship.com
Land area (sq. miles)	6.52
Water area (sq. miles)	0.20
Type of government	Township
Form of government	TC

Government

Legislative Districts
US Congressional	3
State Legislative	8

Local Officials, 2006
Mayor	Bruce MacLachlan
Admin/Manager	Paul Tuliano Jr.
Clerk	Paul Tuliano Jr.
Finance Dir/Treas	Dawn Robertson
Engineer	Richard Alaimo
Attorney	Ted Costa
Tax assessor	Edward Burek
Tax collector	Sharon Deviney
Building officer	M. Gene Blair
Zoning officer	Kathy Newcomb
Public Works	Jay Jones Jr.

Housing & Construction

Housing Units, 2000*
Total	1,555
Median rent	$744
Median SF home value	$144,400

New Privately Owned Housing Units
Authorized by Building Permit
	Units	Value
Total, 2004	19	$2,123,971
Single family	19	$2,123,971
Total, 2005	38	$5,328,427
Single family	38	$5,328,427

Real Property Valuation - parcels, 2005
	Number	Valuation
Total		$413,026,300
Vacant	295	11,632,100
Residential	2,119	330,499,200
Commercial	84	38,929,900
Industrial	29	26,315,800
Apartments	2	247,500
Farm land	24	5,174,600
Farm homestead	40	227,200

Average Property Value & Tax, 2005
Residential value	$153,185
Property tax	$4,751
FAIR rebate	$557

Public Library
No public municipal library.

Library statistics, 2004
	Total	per capita
Volumes	NA	NA
Expenditure	NA	NA

Public Safety
Police
Chief	(State)
Number of officers, 2004	0

Crime, 2004	Number	Rate
Total	141	24.8
Violent	11	1.9
Non-violent	130	22.9
Domestic Viol.	20	NA

Emergency/Fire
Director	William Wiley

Public School District
(for school year 2004-2005 except as noted)

Hainesport Township School District
PO Box 538
Hainesport, NJ 08036
609-265-8050

Superintendent	Mark Silverstein
Grade plan	K-8
Enrollment	633.0
Students per teacher	11.3
Per pupil expenditure	$10,432
Median faculty salary	$43,370
Median administrator salary	$77,984
Grade 12 enrollment	NA
High school graduation rate	NA

Assessment test results
(percent scoring at proficient or advanced level)
	Language	Math
Grade 3	84.6%	83.1%
Grade 8	74.3%	70.7%
High school	NA	NA

SAT
Percent tested	NA
Average SAT math score	NA
Average SAT verbal score	NA

No Child Left Behind, 2003-04
Attendence rate (target = 90%)	94.9%
Drop rate	NA
Highly-qualified teachers	100%
District needs improvement?(AYP)	No

Municipal Finance

Fiscal Year 2005
Total tax levy	$12,842,973
County levy	2,822,926
County taxes	2,368,163
County library	207,340
County health	0
County open space	247,423
School levy	8,316,784
Local muni. budget	1,703,264
Misc. revenues	2,375,391
Total aid	$562,842
CMPTRA	192,463
Muni. block grant	16,178
Energy tax receipts	354,201
Homeland security	0

Fiscal Year 2006
Total aid	$562,842
CMPTRA	180,066
Muni. block grant	16,178
Energy tax receipts	366,598
Homeland security	NA

Taxes
	2003	2004	2005
General tax rate per $100	2.76	2.946	3.103
Net valuation taxable	$344,365,635	$385,600,428	$414,129,405
State equalized value	$456,113,424	$571,907,783	$682,368,438
County equalization ratio	85.61	75.50	67.34

Demographics & Socio-Economic Characteristics
(2000 U.S. Census, except as noted)

Population
1980*	6,607
1990*	6,951
2000	8,252
Male	3,894
Female	4,358
2004 (estimate)*	8,440
Persons per sq. mi. of land	7,273

Race & Hispanic Origin, 2000
Race
White	6,073
Black/African American	585
Amer. Indian/Alaska Natv.	14
Asian	377
Natv. Hawaiian/Pac. Islander	2
Other Race	833
Two or more races	368
Hispanic origin, total	1,865
Mexican	66
Puerto Rican	729
Cuban	48
Other Hispanic	1,022

Age & Nativity, 2000
Under 5 years	576
18 years and over	6,144
21 years and over	5,847
65 years and over	1,163
85 years and over	191
Median Age	34.6
Native born	6,097
Foreign born	2,155

Educational Attainment, 2000
Population 25 years and over	5,393
0-8 yrs of school	12.2%
High School grad or higher	77.1%
Bachelor's degree or higher	18.5%
Graduate degree	6.1%

Income & Poverty, 1999
Per capita income	$19,099
Median household income	$45,599
Median family income	$49,014
Persons in poverty	872
H'holds receiving public assistance	78
H'holds receiving social security	725

Households, 2000
Total households	2,820
With persons under 18	1,090
With persons over 65	744
Family households	1,975
One-person households	660
Persons per household	2.83
Persons per family	3.41

Labor & Employment
Total civilian labor force, 2004**	3,499
Unemployment rate	3.5%
Total civilian labor force, 2000	4,168
Unemployment rate	7.2%

Employed persons 16 years and over by occupation, 2000
Managers & professionals	1,083
Service occupations	567
Sales & office occupations	1,200
Farming, fishing & forestry	0
Construction & maintenance	371
Production & transportation	645
Self-employed persons	198

*US Census Bureau
**New Jersey Department of Labor

General Information
Borough of Haledon
510 Belmont Ave
Haledon, NJ 07508
973-595-7766

Web site	NA
Land area (sq. miles)	1.16
Water area (sq. miles)	0
Type of government	Borough
Form of government	B

Government
Legislative Districts
US Congressional	8
State Legislative	35

Local Officials, 2006
Mayor	Kenneth Pengitore
Admin/Manager	William Close
Clerk	Allan Susen
Finance Dir/Treas	William Close
Engineer	Stephen Boswell
Attorney	Andrew Oddo
Tax assessor	Brian Townsend
Tax collector	NA
Building officer	John Pallotta
Zoning officer	NA
Public Works	NA

Housing & Construction
Housing Units, 2000*
Total	2,906
Median rent	$826
Median SF home value	$164,100

New Privately Owned Housing Units
Authorized by Building Permit
	Units	Value
Total, 2004	6	$568,760
Single family	2	$268,760
Total, 2005	9	$1,087,700
Single family	5	$802,000

Real Property Valuation - parcels, 2005
	Number	Valuation
Total		$321,664,800
Vacant	64	3,939,500
Residential	1,623	259,105,400
Commercial	128	36,769,600
Industrial	27	13,331,300
Apartments	8	8,519,000
Farm land	0	0
Farm homestead	0	0

Average Property Value & Tax, 2005
Residential value	$159,646
Property tax	$6,974
FAIR rebate	$604

Public Library
Haledon Free Public Library
404 Morrissee Ave
Haledon, NJ 07508
973-790-3808

Director ... Judie Erk

Library statistics, 2004
	Total	per capita
Volumes	15,554	1.88
Expenditure	$177,798	$21.55

Public Safety
Police
Chief	Louis Mercuro
Number of officers, 2004	14

Crime, 2004	Number	Rate
Total	122	14.5
Violent	9	1.1
Non-violent	113	13.4
Domestic Viol.	39	NA

Emergency/Fire
Director ... Robert DeVirgilio

Public School District
(for school year 2004-2005 except as noted)

Haledon School District
70 Church St
Haledon, NJ 07508
973-956-2582

Administrator	Raymond Kwak
Grade plan	K-8
Enrollment	961.0
Students per teacher	10.3
Per pupil expenditure	$10,550
Median faculty salary	$42,240
Median administrator salary	$83,928
Grade 12 enrollment	NA
High school graduation rate	NA

Assessment test results
(percent scoring at proficient or advanced level)
	Language	Math
Grade 3	76.5%	77.9%
Grade 8	60.0%	60.0%
High school	NA	NA

SAT
Percent tested	NA
Average SAT math score	NA
Average SAT verbal score	NA

No Child Left Behind, 2003-04
Attendence rate (target = 90%)	95.7%
Drop rate	NA
Highly-qualified teachers	74.6%
District needs improvement?(AYP)	No

Municipal Finance
Fiscal Year 2005
Total tax levy	$14,187,613
County levy	2,685,370
County taxes	2,634,256
County library	0
County health	0
County open space	51,114
School levy	7,775,295
Local muni. budget	3,726,948
Misc. revenues	3,159,003
Total aid	$1,044,782
CMPTRA	509,342
Muni. block grant	32,356
Energy tax receipts	453,084
Homeland security	50,000

Fiscal Year 2006
Total aid	$1,044,781
CMPTRA	493,484
Muni. block grant	32,356
Energy tax receipts	468,941
Homeland security	50,000

Taxes
	2003	2004	2005
General tax rate per $100	3.78	4.110	4.370
Net valuation taxable	$324,057,146	$324,693,859	$324,795,464
State equalized value	$447,716,422	$508,090,694	$580,717,797
County equalization ratio	83.16	72.38	63.64

Demographics & Socio-Economic Characteristics

(2000 U.S. Census, except as noted)

Population

1980*	1,832
1990*	2,566
2000	3,105
Male	1,489
Female	1,616
2004 (estimate)*	3,528
Persons per sq. mi. of land	3,053

Race & Hispanic Origin, 2000

Race
White	2,892
Black/African American	23
Amer. Indian/Alaska Natv.	9
Asian	71
Natv. Hawaiian/Pac. Islander	0
Other Race	52
Two or more races	58
Hispanic origin, total	131
Mexican	7
Puerto Rican	70
Cuban	6
Other Hispanic	48

Age & Nativity, 2000

Under 5 years	229
18 years and over	2,274
21 years and over	2,194
65 years and over	252
85 years and over	14
Median Age	35
Native born	2,925
Foreign born	180

Educational Attainment, 2000

Population 25 years and over	2,060
0-8 yrs of school	3.3%
High School grad or higher	88.8%
Bachelor's degree or higher	19.8%
Graduate degree	6.1%

Income & Poverty, 1999

Per capita income	$24,651
Median household income	$58,246
Median family income	$64,773
Persons in poverty	142
H'holds receiving public assistance	7
H'holds receiving social security	199

Households, 2000

Total households	1,173
With persons under 18	466
With persons over 65	188
Family households	844
One-person households	273
Persons per household	2.65
Persons per family	3.14

Labor & Employment

Total civilian labor force, 2004**	1,772
Unemployment rate	6.0%
Total civilian labor force, 2000	1,726
Unemployment rate	3.9%

Employed persons 16 years and over by occupation, 2000
Managers & professionals	594
Service occupations	215
Sales & office occupations	443
Farming, fishing & forestry	4
Construction & maintenance	170
Production & transportation	233
Self-employed persons	76

*US Census Bureau
**New Jersey Department of Labor

General Information

Borough of Hamburg
16 Wallkill Ave
Hamburg, NJ 07419
973-827-9230

Web site	www.hamburgnj.org
Land area (sq. miles)	1.16
Water area (sq. miles)	0.01
Type of government	Borough
Form of government	B

Government

Legislative Districts

US Congressional	5
State Legislative	24

Local Officials, 2006

Mayor	Paul Marino
Admin/Manager	NA
Clerk	Doreen Schott
Finance Dir/Treas	Charles Wood
Engineer	John Ruschke
Attorney	Richard Clemack
Tax assessor	John Dyksen
Tax collector	NA
Building officer	Anthony Piechowski
Zoning officer	NA
Public Works	NA

Housing & Construction

Housing Units, 2000*

Total	1,233
Median rent	$864
Median SF home value	$124,500

New Privately Owned Housing Units
Authorized by Building Permit

	Units	Value
Total, 2004	21	$1,431,116
Single family	21	$1,431,116
Total, 2005	8	$545,188
Single family	8	$545,188

Real Property Valuation - parcels, 2005

	Number	Valuation
Total		$204,679,850
Vacant	180	6,566,750
Residential	1,299	174,416,900
Commercial	58	19,814,900
Industrial	3	3,375,700
Apartments	1	331,500
Farm land	1	169,000
Farm homestead	2	5,100

Average Property Value & Tax, 2005

Residential value	$134,068
Property tax	$4,230
FAIR rebate	$526

Public Library

No public municipal library.

Library statistics, 2004

	Total	per capita
Volumes	NA	NA
Expenditure	NA	NA

Public Safety

Police

Chief	E. Gregory Kresge
Number of officers, 2004	9

Crime, 2004	Number	Rate
Total	34	9.7
Violent	3	0.9
Non-violent	31	8.9
Domestic Viol.	56	NA

Emergency/Fire

Director	Daniel Shane

Public School District

(for school year 2004-2005 except as noted)

Hamburg Borough School District
30 Linwood Ave
Hamburg, NJ 07419
973-827-7440

Administrator	Robert McCann
Grade plan	K-8
Enrollment	331.0
Students per teacher	9.4
Per pupil expenditure	$12,175
Median faculty salary	$46,545
Median administrator salary	$90,443
Grade 12 enrollment	NA
High school graduation rate	NA

Assessment test results

(percent scoring at proficient or advanced level)
	Language	Math
Grade 3	83.9%	67.8%
Grade 8	88.0%	74.0%
High school	NA	NA

SAT

Percent tested	NA
Average SAT math score	NA
Average SAT verbal score	NA

No Child Left Behind, 2003-04

Attendence rate (target = 90%)	95.1%
Drop rate	NA
Highly-qualified teachers	81.9%
District needs improvement?(AYP)	No

Municipal Finance

Fiscal Year 2005

Total tax levy	$6,472,901
County levy	1,190,756
County taxes	1,010,618
County library	87,133
County health	41,017
County open space	51,988
School levy	3,977,322
Local muni. budget	1,304,823
Misc. revenues	1,366,816
Total aid	$360,395
CMPTRA	162,486
Muni. block grant	12,175
Energy tax receipts	160,734
Homeland security	25,000

Fiscal Year 2006

Total aid	$360,395
CMPTRA	156,860
Muni. block grant	12,175
Energy tax receipts	166,360
Homeland security	25,000

Taxes

	2003	2004	2005
General tax rate per $100	2.86	3.010	3.160
Net valuation taxable	$192,190,772	$199,059,549	$205,165,577
State equalized value	$206,701,196	$250,119,635	$301,625,370
County equalization ratio	110.07	92.98	79.54

Demographics & Socio-Economic Characteristics
(2000 U.S. Census, except as noted)

Population
1980*	9,499
1990*	16,012
2000	20,499
Male	10,217
Female	10,282
2004 (estimate)*	23,699
Persons per sq. mi. of land	213

Race & Hispanic Origin, 2000
Race
White	14,646
Black/African American	3,949
Amer. Indian/Alaska Natv.	60
Asian	675
Natv. Hawaiian/Pac. Islander	10
Other Race	682
Two or more races	477
Hispanic origin, total	1,621
Mexican	91
Puerto Rican	960
Cuban	34
Other Hispanic	536

Age & Nativity, 2000
Under 5 years	1,431
18 years and over	14,946
21 years and over	14,202
65 years and over	1,683
85 years and over	182
Median Age	34.5
Native born	19,152
Foreign born	1,347

Educational Attainment, 2000
Population 25 years and over	13,351
0-8 yrs of school	4.7%
High School grad or higher	80.4%
Bachelor's degree or higher	19.3%
Graduate degree	5.0%

Income & Poverty, 1999
Per capita income	$21,309
Median household income	$50,259
Median family income	$54,899
Persons in poverty	1,280
H'holds receiving public assistance	130
H'holds receiving social security	1,318

Households, 2000
Total households	7,148
With persons under 18	2,976
With persons over 65	1,241
Family households	5,039
One-person households	1,586
Persons per household	2.72
Persons per family	3.21

Labor & Employment
Total civilian labor force, 2004**	9,230
Unemployment rate	4.3%
Total civilian labor force, 2000	10,275
Unemployment rate	5.2%

Employed persons 16 years and over by occupation, 2000
Managers & professionals	2,918
Service occupations	2,553
Sales & office occupations	2,507
Farming, fishing & forestry	31
Construction & maintenance	904
Production & transportation	828
Self-employed persons	341

*US Census Bureau
**New Jersey Department of Labor

General Information
Township of Hamilton
6101 Thirteenth St
Mays Landing, NJ 08330
609-625-1511
Web site	www.townshipofhamilton.com
Land area (sq. miles)	111.28
Water area (sq. miles)	1.71
Type of government	Township
Form of government	TC

Government
Legislative Districts
US Congressional	2
State Legislative	2

Local Officials, 2006
Mayor	Thomas Palmentieri
Admin/Manager	Edward Perugini
Clerk	Joan Anderson
Finance Dir/Treas	Richard Tuthill
Engineer	Robert Smith
Attorney	Norman Zlotnick
Tax assessor	Gerard Mead
Tax collector	Renee DeSalvo
Building officer	Glen Franzoi
Zoning officer	N. Rainbow/S. Maimon
Public Works	Oliver Thies

Housing & Construction
Housing Units, 2000*
Total	7,567
Median rent	$806
Median SF home value	$105,700

New Privately Owned Housing Units Authorized by Building Permit
	Units	Value
Total, 2004	164	$16,043,101
Single family	152	$14,933,801
Total, 2005	331	$23,156,945
Single family	236	$22,633,945

Real Property Valuation - parcels, 2005
	Number	Valuation
Total		$1,189,634,900
Vacant	5,185	62,879,100
Residential	7,650	729,117,100
Commercial	226	333,970,800
Industrial	11	16,516,000
Apartments	14	37,103,100
Farm land	57	8,089,000
Farm homestead	171	1,959,800

Average Property Value & Tax, 2005
Residential value	$93,476
Property tax	$3,135
FAIR rebate	$496

Public Library
No public municipal library.

Library statistics, 2004
	Total	per capita
Volumes	NA	NA
Expenditure	NA	NA

Public Safety
Police
Chief	Jay McKeen
Number of officers, 2004	61

Crime, 2004	Number	Rate
Total	1,151	50.7
Violent	84	3.7
Non-violent	1,067	47
Domestic Viol.	608	NA

Emergency/Fire
Director	(Volunteer)

Public School District
(for school year 2004-2005 except as noted)

Hamilton Township School District
1876 Dr. Dennis Foreman Dr
Mays Landing, NJ 08330
609-476-6300
Superintendent	Frederick Donatucci (Int)
Grade plan	K-8
Enrollment	2,810.0
Students per teacher	10.8
Per pupil expenditure	$9,888
Median faculty salary	$41,778
Median administrator salary	$72,219
Grade 12 enrollment	NA
High school graduation rate	NA

Assessment test results
(percent scoring at proficient or advanced level)
	Language	Math
Grade 3	82.3%	83.3%
Grade 8	75.4%	66.0%
High school	NA	NA

SAT
Percent tested	NA
Average SAT math score	NA
Average SAT verbal score	NA

No Child Left Behind, 2003-04
Attendence rate (target = 90%)	94.6%
Drop rate	NA
Highly-qualified teachers	100%
District needs improvement?(AYP)	No

Municipal Finance
Fiscal Year 2005
Total tax levy	$40,076,101
County levy	7,188,278
County taxes	5,869,022
County library	649,937
County health	319,846
County open space	349,473
School levy	23,349,018
Local muni. budget	9,538,805
Misc. revenues	8,624,195
Total aid	$3,820,391
CMPTRA	704,363
Muni. block grant	80,377
Energy tax receipts	2,850,938
Homeland security	90,000

Fiscal Year 2006
Total aid	$3,820,391
CMPTRA	604,580
Muni. block grant	80,377
Energy tax receipts	2,950,721
Homeland security	90,000

Taxes
	2003	2004	2005
General tax rate per $100	3.08	3.171	3.355
Net valuation taxable	$1,077,799,552	$1,122,503,753	$1,194,829,436
State equalized value	$1,367,765,929	$1,635,437,136	$2,050,153,459
County equalization ratio	85.87	78.80	68.52

Demographics & Socio-Economic Characteristics
(2000 U.S. Census, except as noted)

Population
1980*	82,801
1990*	86,553
2000	87,109
Male	41,530
Female	45,579
2004 (estimate)*	90,058
Persons per sq. mi. of land	2,283

Race & Hispanic Origin, 2000
Race
White	74,173
Black/African American	7,112
Amer. Indian/Alaska Natv.	121
Asian	2,234
Natv. Hawaiian/Pac. Islander	31
Other Race	1,908
Two or more races	1,530
Hispanic origin, total	4,471
Mexican	221
Puerto Rican	2,409
Cuban	113
Other Hispanic	1,728

Age & Nativity, 2000
Under 5 years	5,006
18 years and over	66,909
21 years and over	64,219
65 years and over	13,623
85 years and over	1,520
Median Age	39.1
Native born	78,943
Foreign born	8,311

Educational Attainment, 2000
Population 25 years and over	61,062
0-8 yrs of school	5.1%
High School grad or higher	83.0%
Bachelor's degree or higher	22.5%
Graduate degree	7.2%

Income & Poverty, 1999
Per capita income	$25,441
Median household income	$57,110
Median family income	$66,986
Persons in poverty	3,619
H'holds receiving public assistance	686
H'holds receiving social security	9,939

Households, 2000
Total households	33,523
With persons under 18	11,338
With persons over 65	9,655
Family households	23,681
One-person households	8,222
Persons per household	2.58
Persons per family	3.1

Labor & Employment
Total civilian labor force, 2004**	52,796
Unemployment rate	2.9%
Total civilian labor force, 2000	46,420
Unemployment rate	3.7%

Employed persons 16 years and over by occupation, 2000
Managers & professionals	16,451
Service occupations	6,001
Sales & office occupations	13,647
Farming, fishing & forestry	60
Construction & maintenance	3,744
Production & transportation	4,813
Self-employed persons	1,942

*US Census Bureau
**New Jersey Department of Labor

General Information
Township of Hamilton
2090 Greenwood Ave
Hamilton, NJ 08650
609-890-3500
Web site	www.hamiltonnj.com
Land area (sq. miles)	39.45
Water area (sq. miles)	0.92
Type of government	Township
Form of government	Mayor-Council, Plan E

Government
Legislative Districts
US Congressional	4
State Legislative	14

Local Officials, 2006
Mayor	Glen Gilmore
Admin/Manager	John F Mason
Clerk	Jean Chianese
Finance Dir/Treas	Phil Del Turco
Engineer	Tom Dunn
Attorney	Paul Adezio
Tax assessor	Donald Kosul
Tax collector	Michele Rossi
Building officer	Ray Lumio
Zoning officer	Mike Cosma
Public Works	Richard Balgowan

Housing & Construction
Housing Units, 2000*
Total	34,535
Median rent	$739
Median SF home value	$136,700

New Privately Owned Housing Units
Authorized by Building Permit
	Units	Value
Total, 2004	336	$31,925,519
Single family	330	$31,925,018
Total, 2005	497	$27,021,682
Single family	492	$26,996,182

Real Property Valuation - parcels, 2005
	Number	Valuation
Total		$4,943,307,883
Vacant	1,545	81,689,609
Residential	28,161	3,715,915,750
Commercial	1,473	874,110,250
Industrial	62	97,721,900
Apartments	58	156,379,434
Farm land	69	15,224,000
Farm homestead	133	2,266,940

Average Property Value & Tax, 2005
Residential value	$131,412
Property tax	$4,391
FAIR rebate	$608

Public Library
Hamilton Twp Public Library
1 Municipal Dr
Hamilton, NJ 08619
609-631-4100
Director.................George Cornwell

Library statistics, 2004
	Total	per capita
Volumes	272,701	3.13
Expenditure	$2,494,953	$28.64

Public Safety
Police
Chief	James Collins
Number of officers, 2004	182

Crime, 2004	Number	Rate
Total	1,904	21.2
Violent	162	1.8
Non-violent	1,742	19.4
Domestic Viol.	773	NA

Emergency/Fire
Director.............................NA

Public School District
(for school year 2004-2005 except as noted)

Hamilton Township School District
90 Park Ave
Hamilton Square, NJ 08690
609-631-4100
Superintendent	Neil Bencivengo
Grade plan	K-12
Enrollment	13,309.0
Students per teacher	12.3
Per pupil expenditure	$10,530
Median faculty salary	$52,114
Median administrator salary	$94,825
Grade 12 enrollment	889.0
High school graduation rate	NA

Assessment test results
(percent scoring at proficient or advanced level)
	Language	Math
Grade 3	84.8%	82.3%
Grade 8	70.3%	56.9%
High school	82.8%	73.2%

SAT
Percent tested	NA
Average SAT math score	NA
Average SAT verbal score	NA

No Child Left Behind, 2003-04
Attendance rate (target = 90%)	93.6%
Drop rate	1.4%
Highly-qualified teachers	97.8%
District needs improvement?(AYP)	No

Municipal Finance
Fiscal Year 2005
Total tax levy	$165,877,916
County levy	39,744,120
County taxes	37,630,106
County library	0
County health	0
County open space	2,114,014
School levy	87,972,642
Local muni. budget	38,161,155
Misc. revenues	37,049,934
Total aid	$25,337,749
CMPTRA	7,888,734
Muni. block grant	378,726
Energy tax receipts	16,930,289
Homeland security	140,000

Fiscal Year 2006
Total aid	$25,337,749
CMPTRA	7,296,174
Muni. block grant	378,726
Energy tax receipts	17,522,849
Homeland security	140,000

Taxes
	2003	2004	2005
General tax rate per $100	2.94	3.180	3.350
Net valuation taxable	$4,832,256,559	$4,944,630,277	$4,964,076,086
State equalized value	$5,977,556,357	$6,982,066,703	$7,774,590,581
County equalization ratio	88.6	80.84	70.72

Demographics & Socio-Economic Characteristics
(2000 U.S. Census, except as noted)

Population
1980*	12,298
1990*	12,208
2000	12,604
Male	6,105
Female	6,499
2004 (estimate)*	13,280
Persons per sq. mi. of land	322

Race & Hispanic Origin, 2000
Race
White	11,073
Black/African American	219
Amer. Indian/Alaska Natv.	18
Asian	144
Natv. Hawaiian/Pac. Islander	3
Other Race	987
Two or more races	160
Hispanic origin, total	1,876
Mexican	685
Puerto Rican	994
Cuban	11
Other Hispanic	186

Age & Nativity, 2000
Under 5 years	754
18 years and over	9,730
21 years and over	9,292
65 years and over	2,265
85 years and over	355
Median Age	38.7
Native born	11,581
Foreign born	1,023

Educational Attainment, 2000
Population 25 years and over	8,696
0-8 yrs of school	12.1%
High School grad or higher	72.5%
Bachelor's degree or higher	16.2%
Graduate degree	4.6%

Income & Poverty, 1999
Per capita income	$19,889
Median household income	$43,137
Median family income	$52,205
Persons in poverty	1,119
H'holds receiving public assistance	103
H'holds receiving social security	1,565

Households, 2000
Total households	4,619
With persons under 18	1,564
With persons over 65	1,513
Family households	3,269
One-person households	1,103
Persons per household	2.65
Persons per family	3.14

Labor & Employment
Total civilian labor force, 2004**	6,462
Unemployment rate	5.1%
Total civilian labor force, 2000	6,249
Unemployment rate	8.9%

Employed persons 16 years and over by occupation, 2000
Managers & professionals	1,459
Service occupations	1,069
Sales & office occupations	1,689
Farming, fishing & forestry	97
Construction & maintenance	577
Production & transportation	803
Self-employed persons	327

*US Census Bureau
**New Jersey Department of Labor

General Information
Town of Hammonton
100 Central Ave
Hammonton, NJ 08037
609-567-4300
Web site	www.townofhammonton.org
Land area (sq. miles)	41.26
Water area (sq. miles)	0.21
Type of government	Town
Form of government	SC

Government
Legislative Districts
US Congressional	2
State Legislative	9

Local Officials, 2006
Mayor	John DiDonato
Admin/Manager	Susanne Oddo
Clerk	Susanne Oddo
Finance Dir/Treas	Rosemarie Jacobs
Engineer	Adams, Raymond et al
Attorney	Frank Olivo
Tax assessor	Mary Joan Wyatt
Tax collector	NA
Building officer	John Aloisio
Zoning officer	NA
Public Works	NA

Housing & Construction
Housing Units, 2000*
Total	4,843
Median rent	$689
Median SF home value	$125,200

New Privately Owned Housing Units
Authorized by Building Permit
	Units	Value
Total, 2004	175	$19,149,500
Single family	175	$19,149,500
Total, 2005	79	$10,339,738
Single family	79	$10,339,738

Real Property Valuation - parcels, 2005
	Number	Valuation
Total		$751,201,100
Vacant	946	23,939,500
Residential	4,238	533,381,500
Commercial	393	137,120,600
Industrial	28	21,007,300
Apartments	12	7,708,100
Farm land	173	22,279,600
Farm homestead	425	5,764,500

Average Property Value & Tax, 2005
Residential value	$115,622
Property tax	$3,726
FAIR rebate	$630

Public Library
Hammonton West Branch†
451 S Egg Harbor Rd
Hammonton, NJ 08037
609-561-2264
Branch Librarian	Dave Munn

Library statistics, 2004
	Total	per capita
Volumes	NA	NA
Expenditure	NA	NA

†Branch of County Library

Public Safety
Police
Chief	Frank Ingemi
Number of officers, 2004	31

Crime, 2004	Number	Rate
Total	244	18.8
Violent	28	2.2
Non-violent	216	16.6
Domestic Viol.	275	NA

Emergency/Fire
Director	Frank Domenko

Public School District
(for school year 2004-2005 except as noted)

Hammonton Town School District
566 Old Forks Rd
Hammonton, NJ 08037
609-567-7000
Superintendent	Mary Lou DeFrancisco
Grade plan	K-12
Enrollment	3,314.0
Students per teacher	13.1
Per pupil expenditure	$9,228
Median faculty salary	$46,815
Median administrator salary	$86,596
Grade 12 enrollment	276.0
High school graduation rate	92.9%

Assessment test results
(percent scoring at proficient or advanced level)
	Language	Math
Grade 3	82.8%	85.8%
Grade 8	70.7%	59.5%
High school	78.7%	73.4%

SAT
Percent tested	58%
Average SAT math score	519
Average SAT verbal score	512

No Child Left Behind, 2003-04
Attendence rate (target = 90%)	93.7%
Drop rate	1.7%
Highly-qualified teachers	95.8%
District needs improvement?(AYP)	No

Municipal Finance
Fiscal Year 2005
Total tax levy	$24,380,075
County levy	3,856,013
County taxes	3,147,831
County library	348,889
County health	171,694
County open space	187,599
School levy	14,881,618
Local muni. budget	5,642,444
Misc. revenues	5,370,941
Total aid	$1,740,092
CMPTRA	738,559
Muni. block grant	53,418
Energy tax receipts	871,072
Homeland security	70,000

Fiscal Year 2006
Total aid	$1,740,092
CMPTRA	708,071
Muni. block grant	53,418
Energy tax receipts	901,560
Homeland security	70,000

Taxes
	2003	2004	2005
General tax rate per $100	3.00	3.131	3.223
Net valuation taxable	$702,383,477	$725,377,253	$756,627,824
State equalized value	$782,948,921	$884,760,199	$1,101,190,255
County equalization ratio	94.91	89.71	81.86

Demographics & Socio-Economic Characteristics
(2000 U.S. Census, except as noted)

Population
1980*	1,614
1990*	1,515
2000	1,546
Male	798
Female	748
2004 (estimate)*	1,591
Persons per sq. mi. of land	1,036

Race & Hispanic Origin, 2000
Race
White	1,407
Black/African American	77
Amer. Indian/Alaska Natv.	6
Asian	15
Natv. Hawaiian/Pac. Islander	0
Other Race	12
Two or more races	29
Hispanic origin, total	44
Mexican	3
Puerto Rican	26
Cuban	2
Other Hispanic	13

Age & Nativity, 2000
Under 5 years	126
18 years and over	1,148
21 years and over	1,086
65 years and over	170
85 years and over	15
Median Age	34.7
Native born	1,476
Foreign born	70

Educational Attainment, 2000
Population 25 years and over	972
0-8 yrs of school	2.8%
High School grad or higher	86.9%
Bachelor's degree or higher	22.0%
Graduate degree	6.6%

Income & Poverty, 1999
Per capita income	$22,440
Median household income	$51,111
Median family income	$64,583
Persons in poverty	121
H'holds receiving public assistance	21
H'holds receiving social security	150

Households, 2000
Total households	559
With persons under 18	218
With persons over 65	138
Family households	378
One-person households	155
Persons per household	2.58
Persons per family	3.2

Labor & Employment
Total civilian labor force, 2004**	975
Unemployment rate	4.6%
Total civilian labor force, 2000	779
Unemployment rate	4.4%

Employed persons 16 years and over by occupation, 2000
Managers & professionals	247
Service occupations	130
Sales & office occupations	185
Farming, fishing & forestry	2
Construction & maintenance	95
Production & transportation	86
Self-employed persons	38

*US Census Bureau
**New Jersey Department of Labor

General Information
Borough of Hampton
PO Box 418
Hampton, NJ 08827
908-537-2329

Web site	NA
Land area (sq. miles)	1.54
Water area (sq. miles)	0
Type of government	Borough
Form of government	B

Government

Legislative Districts
US Congressional	7
State Legislative	23

Local Officials, 2006
Mayor	Stephen Dilts
Admin/Manager	NA
Clerk	Cathy Drummond
Finance Dir/Treas	Kathleen Olsen
Engineer	Robert Bogart & Assoc.
Attorney	Richard Cushing
Tax assessor	Robert Vance
Tax collector	Diane Laudenbach
Building officer	NA
Zoning officer	Salvatore Melillo
Public Works	John Spiridigliozzi

Housing & Construction

Housing Units, 2000*
Total	574
Median rent	$543
Median SF home value	$165,200

New Privately Owned Housing Units Authorized by Building Permit
	Units	Value
Total, 2004	12	$1,645,108
Single family	12	$1,645,108
Total, 2005	25	$4,160,364
Single family	25	$4,160,364

Real Property Valuation - parcels, 2005
	Number	Valuation
Total		$67,310,425
Vacant	72	2,824,151
Residential	431	56,733,600
Commercial	18	3,670,600
Industrial	2	562,400
Apartments	3	1,648,000
Farm land	8	1,764,800
Farm homestead	18	106,874

Average Property Value & Tax, 2005
Residential value	$126,593
Property tax	$5,482
FAIR rebate	$500

Public Library

No public municipal library.

Library statistics, 2004
	Total	per capita
Volumes	NA	NA
Expenditure	NA	NA

Public Safety

Police
Chief	NA
Number of officers, 2004	0

Crime, 2004	Number	Rate
Total	27	17
Violent	1	0.6
Non-violent	26	16.3
Domestic Viol.	7	NA

Emergency/Fire
Director	Howard Eick

Public School District
(for school year 2004-2005 except as noted)

Hampton Borough School District
32-41 South St
Hampton, NJ 08827
908-537-4101

Administrator	Frank Albert
Grade plan	K-8
Enrollment	198.0
Students per teacher	8.7
Per pupil expenditure	$13,386
Median faculty salary	$41,515
Median administrator salary	$73,000
Grade 12 enrollment	NA
High school graduation rate	NA

Assessment test results
(percent scoring at proficient or advanced level)
	Language	Math
Grade 3	83.3%	66.7%
Grade 8	62.0%	72.4%
High school	NA	NA

SAT
Percent tested	NA
Average SAT math score	NA
Average SAT verbal score	NA

No Child Left Behind, 2003-04
Attendence rate (target = 90%)	95.0%
Drop rate	NA
Highly-qualified teachers	52.9%
District needs improvement?(AYP)	No

Municipal Finance

Fiscal Year 2005
Total tax levy	$2,941,971
County levy	410,600
County taxes	348,625
County library	29,170
County health	0
County open space	32,805
School levy	2,150,238
Local muni. budget	381,132
Misc. revenues	649,964
Total aid	$151,584
CMPTRA	96,106
Muni. block grant	6,629
Energy tax receipts	48,849
Homeland security	0

Fiscal Year 2006
Total aid	$151,584
CMPTRA	94,396
Muni. block grant	6,629
Energy tax receipts	50,559
Homeland security	NA

Taxes
	2003	2004	2005
General tax rate per $100	4.03	4.440	4.340
Net valuation taxable	$66,400,110	$67,447,377	$67,942,703
State equalized value	$91,535,856	$102,052,184	$113,256,714
County equalization ratio	80.93	72.60	62.18

Demographics & Socio-Economic Characteristics
(2000 U.S. Census, except as noted)

Population
1980*	3,916
1990*	4,438
2000	4,943
Male	2,413
Female	2,530
2000 (revised)	4,928
2004 (estimate)*	5,175
Persons per sq. mi. of land	210

Race & Hispanic Origin, 2000
Race
White	4,809
Black/African American	48
Amer. Indian/Alaska Natv.	1
Asian	33
Natv. Hawaiian/Pac. Islander	1
Other Race	15
Two or more races	36
Hispanic origin, total	94
Mexican	7
Puerto Rican	38
Cuban	13
Other Hispanic	36

Age & Nativity, 2000
Under 5 years	276
18 years and over	3,632
21 years and over	3,503
65 years and over	547
85 years and over	63
Median Age	39.8
Native born	4,766
Foreign born	177

Educational Attainment, 2000
Population 25 years and over	3,373
0-8 yrs of school	2.1%
High School grad or higher	91.4%
Bachelor's degree or higher	27.3%
Graduate degree	7.1%

Income & Poverty, 1999
Per capita income	$25,353
Median household income	$60,698
Median family income	$67,386
Persons in poverty	101
H'holds receiving public assistance	32
H'holds receiving social security	466

Households, 2000
Total households	1,857
With persons under 18	720
With persons over 65	400
Family households	1,413
One-person households	384
Persons per household	2.65
Persons per family	3.1

Labor & Employment
Total civilian labor force, 2004**	2,892
Unemployment rate	3.5%
Total civilian labor force, 2000	2,596
Unemployment rate	2.6%

Employed persons 16 years and over by occupation, 2000
Managers & professionals	941
Service occupations	324
Sales & office occupations	641
Farming, fishing & forestry	13
Construction & maintenance	326
Production & transportation	283
Self-employed persons	183

*US Census Bureau
**New Jersey Department of Labor

General Information
Township of Hampton
1 Municipal Complex Rd
Newton, NJ 07860
973-383-5570
Email	klose@njtown.net
Land area (sq. miles)	24.62
Water area (sq. miles)	0.69
Type of government	Township
Form of government	TC

Government

Legislative Districts
US Congressional	5
State Legislative	24

Local Officials, 2006
Mayor	Philip Yetter
Admin/Manager	Eileen Klose
Clerk	Eileen Klose
Finance Dir/Treas	Jessica Caruso
Engineer	Harold Pellow
Attorney	Stephen Roseman
Tax assessor	John Dyksen
Tax collector	Donna Clouse
Building officer	John deJager
Zoning officer	John deJager
Public Works	Daniel Rumsey

Housing & Construction

Housing Units, 2000*
Total	2,026
Median rent	$953
Median SF home value	$149,500

New Privately Owned Housing Units
Authorized by Building Permit
	Units	Value
Total, 2004	22	$5,224,704
Single family	22	$5,224,704
Total, 2005	20	$4,479,257
Single family	20	$4,479,257

Real Property Valuation - parcels, 2005
	Number	Valuation
Total		$367,702,660
Vacant	501	7,782,400
Residential	1,861	270,649,300
Commercial	70	60,717,900
Industrial	3	610,000
Apartments	0	0
Farm land	119	25,705,600
Farm homestead	237	2,237,460

Average Property Value & Tax, 2005
Residential value	$130,070
Property tax	$4,187
FAIR rebate	$535

Public Library

No public municipal library.

Library statistics, 2004
	Total	per capita
Volumes	NA	NA
Expenditure	NA	NA

Public Safety

Police
Chief	NA
Number of officers, 2004	0

Crime, 2004	Number	Rate
Total	79	15.4
Violent	9	1.8
Non-violent	70	13.7
Domestic Viol.	31	NA

Emergency/Fire
Director	David Gunderman

Public School District
(for school year 2004-2005 except as noted)

Hampton Township School District
One School Rd
Newton, NJ 07860
973-383-5300
Administrator	Everett Burns
Grade plan	K-6
Enrollment	438.0
Students per teacher	9.9
Per pupil expenditure	$12,061
Median faculty salary	$51,197
Median administrator salary	$85,380
Grade 12 enrollment	NA
High school graduation rate	NA

Assessment test results
(percent scoring at proficient or advanced level)
	Language	Math
Grade 3	87.1%	91.4%
Grade 8	NA	NA
High school	NA	NA

SAT
Percent tested	NA
Average SAT math score	NA
Average SAT verbal score	NA

No Child Left Behind, 2003-04
Attendence rate (target = 90%)	95.8%
Drop rate	NA
Highly-qualified teachers	88.6%
District needs improvement?(AYP)	No

Municipal Finance

Fiscal Year 2005
Total tax levy	$11,880,441
County levy	2,558,575
County taxes	2,171,514
County library	187,218
County health	88,130
County open space	111,714
School levy	7,779,331
Local muni. budget	1,542,535
Misc. revenues	1,843,951
Total aid	$592,044
CMPTRA	236,794
Muni. block grant	19,420
Energy tax receipts	335,830
Homeland security	0

Fiscal Year 2006
Total aid	$592,043
CMPTRA	225,039
Muni. block grant	19,420
Energy tax receipts	347,584
Homeland security	NA

Taxes
	2003	2004	2005
General tax rate per $100	3.07	3.150	3.220
Net valuation taxable	$356,691,610	$362,270,294	$369,027,457
State equalized value	$473,819,886	$544,992,198	$642,904,977
County equalization ratio	93.2	75.28	66.38

Demographics & Socio-Economic Characteristics
(2000 U.S. Census, except as noted)

Population
1980*	11,846
1990*	11,538
2000	12,898
Male	6,273
Female	6,625
2004 (estimate)*	13,556
Persons per sq. mi. of land	1,271

Race & Hispanic Origin, 2000
Race
White	11,452
Black/African American	140
Amer. Indian/Alaska Natv.	7
Asian	1,123
Natv. Hawaiian/Pac. Islander	1
Other Race	76
Two or more races	99
Hispanic origin, total	452
Mexican	44
Puerto Rican	63
Cuban	56
Other Hispanic	289

Age & Nativity, 2000
Under 5 years	828
18 years and over	9,956
21 years and over	9,658
65 years and over	1,921
85 years and over	173
Median Age	40.1
Native born	10,868
Foreign born	2,030

Educational Attainment, 2000
Population 25 years and over	9,272
0-8 yrs of school	4.6%
High School grad or higher	89.5%
Bachelor's degree or higher	41.5%
Graduate degree	15.3%

Income & Poverty, 1999
Per capita income	$37,661
Median household income	$84,115
Median family income	$93,937
Persons in poverty	152
H'holds receiving public assistance	23
H'holds receiving social security	1,449

Households, 2000
Total households	4,745
With persons under 18	1,631
With persons over 65	1,363
Family households	3,619
One-person households	930
Persons per household	2.71
Persons per family	3.13

Labor & Employment
Total civilian labor force, 2004**	7,090
Unemployment rate	3.0%
Total civilian labor force, 2000	6,941
Unemployment rate	1.5%

Employed persons 16 years and over by occupation, 2000
Managers & professionals	3,150
Service occupations	638
Sales & office occupations	2,050
Farming, fishing & forestry	0
Construction & maintenance	510
Production & transportation	486
Self-employed persons	308

*US Census Bureau
**New Jersey Department of Labor

General Information
Township of Hanover
PO Box 250
1000 Route 10
Whippany, NJ 07981
973-428-2500

Web site	www.hanovertownship.com
Land area (sq. miles)	10.66
Water area (sq. miles)	0.03
Type of government	Township
Form of government	TC

Government
Legislative Districts
US Congressional	11
State Legislative	26

Local Officials, 2006
Mayor	Ronald Francioli
Admin/Manager	Joseph Giorgio
Clerk	Joseph Giorgio
Finance Dir/Treas	Michael Zambito
Engineer	Samuel Berman
Attorney	John Dorsey
Tax assessor	John Dyksen
Tax collector	Michael Zambito
Building officer	Steven Kaplan
Zoning officer	Stephen Kaplan
Public Works	George Baldwin

Housing & Construction
Housing Units, 2000*
Total	4,818
Median rent	$1,098
Median SF home value	$286,100

New Privately Owned Housing Units
Authorized by Building Permit
	Units	Value
Total, 2004	66	$6,482,230
Single family	23	$4,028,700
Total, 2005	32	$6,048,410
Single family	32	$6,048,410

Real Property Valuation - parcels, 2005
	Number	Valuation
Total		$2,010,539,333
Vacant	223	71,739,900
Residential	4,698	1,107,353,322
Commercial	208	542,556,011
Industrial	148	260,008,400
Apartments	6	28,868,800
Farm land	2	9,100
Farm homestead	1	3,800

Average Property Value & Tax, 2005
Residential value	$235,658
Property tax	$5,126
FAIR rebate	$587

Public Library
Whippanong Library
1000 Rte 10
Whippany, NJ 07981
973-428-2460

Director	Sulekha Das

Library statistics, 2004
	Total	per capita
Volumes	43,475	3.37
Expenditure	$380,861	$29.53

Public Safety
Police
Chief	Stephen Gallaguer
Number of officers, 2004	32

Crime, 2004	Number	Rate
Total	190	14.2
Violent	16	1.2
Non-violent	174	13
Domestic Viol.	91	NA

Emergency/Fire
Director	J. Davidson/J. Cortright

Public School District
(for school year 2004-2005 except as noted)

Hanover Township School District
61 Highland Ave
Whippany, NJ 07981
973-515-2404

Superintendent	Scott Pepper
Grade plan	K-8
Enrollment	1,520.0
Students per teacher	10.6
Per pupil expenditure	$12,445
Median faculty salary	$52,877
Median administrator salary	$114,000
Grade 12 enrollment	NA
High school graduation rate	NA

Assessment test results
(percent scoring at proficient or advanced level)
	Language	Math
Grade 3	96.3%	95.1%
Grade 8	84.8%	82.6%
High school	NA	NA

SAT
Percent tested	NA
Average SAT math score	NA
Average SAT verbal score	NA

No Child Left Behind, 2003-04
Attendance rate (target = 90%)	96.4%
Drop rate	NA
Highly-qualified teachers	100%
District needs improvement?(AYP)	No

Municipal Finance
Fiscal Year 2005
Total tax levy	$44,083,753
County levy	8,180,159
County taxes	6,700,440
County library	0
County health	0
County open space	1,479,718
School levy	25,053,683
Local muni. budget	10,849,911
Misc. revenues	8,375,359
Total aid	$3,183,386
CMPTRA	1,423,327
Muni. block grant	50,573
Energy tax receipts	1,639,486
Homeland security	70,000

Fiscal Year 2006
Total aid	$3,183,386
CMPTRA	1,365,915
Muni. block grant	50,573
Energy tax receipts	1,696,868
Homeland security	70,000

Taxes
	2003	2004	2005
General tax rate per $100	1.96	2.080	2.180
Net valuation taxable	$2,055,518,136	$2,042,548,810	$2,026,835,617
State equalized value	$2,914,388,396	$3,042,119,260	$3,563,353,757
County equalization ratio	74.91	70.53	66.94

Demographics & Socio-Economic Characteristics
(2000 U.S. Census, except as noted)

Population
1980*	3,236
1990*	3,640
2000	3,180
Male	1,540
Female	1,640
2004 (estimate)*	3,292
Persons per sq. mi. of land	161

Race & Hispanic Origin, 2000
Race
White	3,091
Black/African American	13
Amer. Indian/Alaska Natv.	0
Asian	34
Natv. Hawaiian/Pac. Islander	1
Other Race	7
Two or more races	34
Hispanic origin, total	57
Mexican	3
Puerto Rican	2
Cuban	10
Other Hispanic	42

Age & Nativity, 2000
Under 5 years	199
18 years and over	2,379
21 years and over	2,321
65 years and over	521
85 years and over	56
Median Age	44.5
Native born	2,984
Foreign born	196

Educational Attainment, 2000
Population 25 years and over	2,265
0-8 yrs of school	0.7%
High School grad or higher	97.5%
Bachelor's degree or higher	66.0%
Graduate degree	31.9%

Income & Poverty, 1999
Per capita income	$72,689
Median household income	$111,297
Median family income	$128,719
Persons in poverty	36
H'holds receiving public assistance	9
H'holds receiving social security	342

Households, 2000
Total households	1,180
With persons under 18	393
With persons over 65	361
Family households	941
One-person households	208
Persons per household	2.69
Persons per family	3.03

Labor & Employment
Total civilian labor force, 2004**	2,114
Unemployment rate	2.1%
Total civilian labor force, 2000	1,369
Unemployment rate	2.3%

Employed persons 16 years and over by occupation, 2000
Managers & professionals	821
Service occupations	109
Sales & office occupations	313
Farming, fishing & forestry	0
Construction & maintenance	72
Production & transportation	23
Self-employed persons	129

*US Census Bureau
**New Jersey Department of Labor

General Information
Township of Harding
PO Box 666
New Vernon, NJ 07976
973-267-8000
Web site	NA
Land area (sq. miles)	20.44
Water area (sq. miles)	0.04
Type of government	Township
Form of government	TC

Government
Legislative Districts
US Congressional	11
State Legislative	21

Local Officials, 2006
Mayor	John Murray
Admin/Manager	Lyn A. Evers
Clerk	Linda Peralta
Finance Dir/Treas	Lyn A. Evers
Engineer	Paul Fox
Attorney	Maryann Hergaard
Tax assessor	Pat Aceto
Tax collector	NA
Building officer	Mary Ellen Balady
Zoning officer	Russ Heiney
Public Works	Tracy Toribio

Housing & Construction
Housing Units, 2000*
Total	1,243
Median rent	$1,125
Median SF home value	$665,400

New Privately Owned Housing Units Authorized by Building Permit
	Units	Value
Total, 2004	12	$8,177,300
Single family	12	$8,177,300
Total, 2005	9	$7,568,924
Single family	9	$7,568,924

Real Property Valuation - parcels, 2005
	Number	Valuation
Total		$1,951,482,871
Vacant	193	63,611,900
Residential	1,411	1,650,120,163
Commercial	43	76,648,200
Industrial	3	9,641,900
Apartments	0	0
Farm land	86	149,679,800
Farm homestead	141	1,780,908

Average Property Value & Tax, 2005
Residential value	$1,064,369
Property tax	$9,803
FAIR rebate	$688

Public Library
Harding Township Library
Blue Mill Rd
New Vernon, NJ 07976
973-267-8001
Director	Anne Thomas

Library statistics, 2004
	Total	per capita
Volumes	6,452	2.03
Expenditure	$63,719	$20.04

Public Safety
Police
Chief	Kevin Gaffney
Number of officers, 2004	15

Crime, 2004	Number	Rate
Total	10	3.1
Violent	1	0.3
Non-violent	9	2.8
Domestic Viol.	9	NA

Emergency/Fire
Director	Kenneth Noetzli

Public School District
(for school year 2004-2005 except as noted)

Harding Township School District
PO Box 248
New Vernon, NJ 07976
973-267-6398
Superintendent	Dennis Pallozzi
Grade plan	K-12
Enrollment	334.0
Students per teacher	9.2
Per pupil expenditure	$16,000
Median faculty salary	$43,079
Median administrator salary	$89,860
Grade 12 enrollment	NA
High school graduation rate	NA

Assessment test results
(percent scoring at proficient or advanced level)
	Language	Math
Grade 3	100%	100%
Grade 8	87.5%	84.4%
High school	NA	NA

SAT
Percent tested	NA
Average SAT math score	NA
Average SAT verbal score	NA

No Child Left Behind, 2003-04
Attendance rate (target = 90%)	96.0%
Drop rate	NA
Highly-qualified teachers	94.3%
District needs improvement?(AYP)	No

Municipal Finance
Fiscal Year 2005
Total tax levy	$17,985,821
County levy	5,477,906
County taxes	4,486,969
County library	0
County health	0
County open space	990,937
School levy	7,447,449
Local muni. budget	5,060,466
Misc. revenues	3,323,926
Total aid	$558,380
CMPTRA	42,539
Muni. block grant	15,927
Energy tax receipts	474,914
Homeland security	25,000

Fiscal Year 2006
Total aid	$558,380
CMPTRA	25,917
Muni. block grant	15,927
Energy tax receipts	491,536
Homeland security	25,000

Taxes
	2003	2004	2005
General tax rate per $100	0.84	0.880	0.930
Net valuation taxable	$1,932,977,780	$1,941,875,430	$1,952,896,363
State equalized value	$1,894,704,744	$2,050,041,157	$2,243,419,142
County equalization ratio	111.16	102.02	94.72

Demographics & Socio-Economic Characteristics
(2000 U.S. Census, except as noted)

Population
1980*	947
1990*	1,235
2000	1,464
Male	731
Female	733
2004 (estimate)*	1,612
Persons per sq. mi. of land	44

Race & Hispanic Origin, 2000
Race
White	1,421
Black/African American	9
Amer. Indian/Alaska Natv.	1
Asian	6
Natv. Hawaiian/Pac. Islander	0
Other Race	13
Two or more races	14
Hispanic origin, total	34
Mexican	2
Puerto Rican	11
Cuban	1
Other Hispanic	20

Age & Nativity, 2000
Under 5 years	92
18 years and over	1,075
21 years and over	1,035
65 years and over	141
85 years and over	13
Median Age	39.4
Native born	1,398
Foreign born	65

Educational Attainment, 2000
Population 25 years and over	994
0-8 yrs of school	2.0%
High School grad or higher	92.1%
Bachelor's degree or higher	29.8%
Graduate degree	9.6%

Income & Poverty, 1999
Per capita income	$30,038
Median household income	$72,167
Median family income	$76,111
Persons in poverty	38
H'holds receiving public assistance	4
H'holds receiving social security	102

Households, 2000
Total households	502
With persons under 18	206
With persons over 65	98
Family households	410
One-person households	70
Persons per household	2.85
Persons per family	3.15

Labor & Employment
Total civilian labor force, 2004**	762
Unemployment rate	3.3%
Total civilian labor force, 2000	784
Unemployment rate	3.1%

Employed persons 16 years and over by occupation, 2000
Managers & professionals	328
Service occupations	89
Sales & office occupations	200
Farming, fishing & forestry	8
Construction & maintenance	80
Production & transportation	55
Self-employed persons	68

*US Census Bureau
**New Jersey Department of Labor

General Information
Township of Hardwick
40 Spring Valley Rd
Hardwick, NJ 07825
908-362-6528

Web site	NA
Land area (sq. miles)	36.48
Water area (sq. miles)	1.44
Type of government	Township
Form of government	TC

Government

Legislative Districts
US Congressional	5
State Legislative	23

Local Officials, 2006
Mayor	Kevin Duffy
Admin/Manager	NA
Clerk	Judith Fisher
Finance Dir/Treas	Gregory Della Pia
Engineer	Ted Rodman
Attorney	Michael Lavery
Tax assessor	David Gill
Tax collector	Donna Clouse
Building officer	Al Ivany
Zoning officer	Arlene Fisher
Public Works	NA

Housing & Construction

Housing Units, 2000*
Total	530
Median rent	$775
Median SF home value	$196,700

New Privately Owned Housing Units Authorized by Building Permit
	Units	Value
Total, 2004	7	$1,153,000
Single family	7	$1,153,000
Total, 2005	10	$1,982,570
Single family	10	$1,982,570

Real Property Valuation - parcels, 2005
	Number	Valuation
Total		$148,901,300
Vacant	97	7,246,100
Residential	447	107,392,600
Commercial	3	1,506,200
Industrial	1	627,000
Apartments	0	0
Farm land	123	31,035,800
Farm homestead	246	1,093,600

Average Property Value & Tax, 2005
Residential value	$156,546
Property tax	$4,395
FAIR rebate	$546

Public Library

No public municipal library.

Library statistics, 2004
	Total	per capita
Volumes	NA	NA
Expenditure	NA	NA

Public Safety
Police
Chief	(State)
Number of officers, 2004	0

Crime, 2004	Number	Rate
Total	10	6.3
Violent	0	0
Non-violent	10	6.3
Domestic Viol.	7	NA

Emergency/Fire
Director	NA

Public School District
(for school year 2004-2005 except as noted)

Hardwick Township School District†
2551 Belvidere Rd
Phillipsburg, NJ 08865

†No schools in district - sends children to Blairstown schools.

Grade plan	NA
Enrollment	NA
Students per teacher	NA
Per pupil expenditure	NA
Median faculty salary	NA

Assessment test results
(percent scoring at proficient or advanced level)
	Language	Math
Grade 3	NA	NA
Grade 8	NA	NA
High school	NA	NA

SAT
Percent tested	NA
Average SAT math score	NA
Average SAT verbal score	NA

No Child Left Behind, 2003-04
Attendence rate (target = 90%)	NA
Drop rate	NA
Highly-qualified teachers	NA
District needs improvement?(AYP)	NA

Municipal Finance
Fiscal Year 2005
Total tax levy	$4,192,688
County levy	1,252,042
County taxes	1,035,235
County library	99,800
County health	0
County open space	117,007
School levy	2,668,487
Local muni. budget	272,159
Misc. revenues	681,450
Total aid	$175,929
CMPTRA	47,238
Muni. block grant	5,740
Energy tax receipts	122,951
Homeland security	0

Fiscal Year 2006
Total aid	$175,930
CMPTRA	42,935
Muni. block grant	5,740
Energy tax receipts	127,255
Homeland security	NA

Taxes
	2003	2004	2005
General tax rate per $100	2.35	2.480	2.810
Net valuation taxable	$143,359,816	$146,149,367	$149,347,090
State equalized value	$165,753,054	$190,436,504	$210,823,108
County equalization ratio	96.45	86.49	76.68

Demographics & Socio-Economic Characteristics

(2000 U.S. Census, except as noted)

Population

1980*	4,553
1990*	5,275
2000	6,171
Male	3,038
Female	3,133
2004 (estimate)*	7,591
Persons per sq. mi. of land	236

Race & Hispanic Origin, 2000

Race

White	5,897
Black/African American	52
Amer. Indian/Alaska Natv.	10
Asian	97
Natv. Hawaiian/Pac. Islander	0
Other Race	30
Two or more races	85
Hispanic origin, total	199
Mexican	10
Puerto Rican	105
Cuban	10
Other Hispanic	74

Age & Nativity, 2000

Under 5 years	424
18 years and over	4,588
21 years and over	4,436
65 years and over	630
85 years and over	54
Median Age	38.4
Native born	5,848
Foreign born	296

Educational Attainment, 2000

Population 25 years and over	4,267
0-8 yrs of school	2.8%
High School grad or higher	90.4%
Bachelor's degree or higher	26.7%
Graduate degree	10.4%

Income & Poverty, 1999

Per capita income	$28,457
Median household income	$65,511
Median family income	$72,199
Persons in poverty	285
H'holds receiving public assistance	35
H'holds receiving social security	503

Households, 2000

Total households	2,319
With persons under 18	869
With persons over 65	465
Family households	1,715
One-person households	500
Persons per household	2.66
Persons per family	3.12

Labor & Employment

Total civilian labor force, 2004**	3,494
Unemployment rate	3.3%
Total civilian labor force, 2000	3,340
Unemployment rate	3.8%

Employed persons 16 years and over by occupation, 2000

Managers & professionals	1,160
Service occupations	409
Sales & office occupations	851
Farming, fishing & forestry	11
Construction & maintenance	404
Production & transportation	378
Self-employed persons	178

*US Census Bureau
**New Jersey Department of Labor

General Information

Township of Hardyston
149 Wheatsworth Rd
Hardyston, NJ 07419
973-823-7020

Web site	www.hardyston.com
Land area (sq. miles)	32.09
Water area (sq. miles)	0.55
Type of government	Township
Form of government	SC

Government

Legislative Districts

US Congressional	5
State Legislative	24

Local Officials, 2006

Mayor	Leslie G. Hamilton
Admin/Manager	Marianne Smith
Clerk	Jane Bakalarczyk
Finance Dir/Treas	Grant Rome
Engineer	Robert Guerin
Attorney	Kevin Kelly
Tax assessor	Scott Holzhauer
Tax collector	Terry Beshada
Building officer	Keith Utter
Zoning officer	Arden P. Svedman
Public Works	Robert F. Schultz

Housing & Construction

Housing Units, 2000*

Total	2,690
Median rent	$740
Median SF home value	$152,300

New Privately Owned Housing Units
Authorized by Building Permit

	Units	Value
Total, 2004	155	$15,369,353
Single family	131	$13,465,353
Total, 2005	195	$22,205,304
Single family	195	$22,205,304

Real Property Valuation - parcels, 2005

	Number	Valuation
Total		$569,162,200
Vacant	907	32,552,400
Residential	2,985	450,695,200
Commercial	120	55,522,700
Industrial	21	10,586,800
Apartments	4	9,688,000
Farm land	47	8,984,900
Farm homestead	116	1,132,200

Average Property Value & Tax, 2005

Residential value	$145,704
Property tax	$4,785
FAIR rebate	$530

Public Library

No public municipal library.

Library statistics, 2004

	Total	per capita
Volumes	NA	NA
Expenditure	NA	NA

Public Safety

Police

Chief	Keith Armstrong
Number of officers, 2004	17

Crime, 2004	Number	Rate
Total	106	14.3
Violent	1	0.1
Non-violent	105	14.2
Domestic Viol.	75	NA

Emergency/Fire

Director	William Hickerson

Public School District

(for school year 2004-2005 except as noted)

Hardyston Township School District
50 Route 23
Franklin, NJ 07416
973-823-7000

Administrator	Dennis Tobin
Grade plan	K-8
Enrollment	764.0
Students per teacher	11.5
Per pupil expenditure	$9,838
Median faculty salary	$53,406
Median administrator salary	$81,096
Grade 12 enrollment	NA
High school graduation rate	NA

Assessment test results

(percent scoring at proficient or advanced level)

	Language	Math
Grade 3	85.2%	86.7%
Grade 8	76.4%	65.3%
High school	NA	NA

SAT

Percent tested	NA
Average SAT math score	NA
Average SAT verbal score	NA

No Child Left Behind, 2003-04

Attendence rate (target = 90%)	94.6%
Drop rate	NA
Highly-qualified teachers	100%
District needs improvement?(AYP)	No

Municipal Finance

Fiscal Year 2005

Total tax levy	$18,746,379
County levy	3,981,789
County taxes	3,499,983
County library	301,759
County health	0
County open space	180,046
School levy	10,969,381
Local muni. budget	3,795,209
Misc. revenues	3,510,337
Total aid	$956,900
CMPTRA	259,934
Muni. block grant	24,197
Energy tax receipts	428,048
Homeland security	50,000

Fiscal Year 2006

Total aid	$956,900
CMPTRA	244,952
Muni. block grant	24,197
Energy tax receipts	443,030
Homeland security	50,000

Taxes

	2003	2004	2005
General tax rate per $100	3.20	3.280	3.290
Net valuation taxable	$513,790,913	$539,082,988	$570,828,703
State equalized value	$715,685,908	$845,755,198	$1,012,646,271
County equalization ratio	88.65	71.79	63.66

Demographics & Socio-Economic Characteristics
(2000 U.S. Census, except as noted)

Population
1980*	2,592
1990*	2,653
2000	2,729
Male	1,349
Female	1,380
2004 (estimate)*	2,812
Persons per sq. mi. of land	118

Race & Hispanic Origin, 2000
Race
White	2,672
Black/African American	19
Amer. Indian/Alaska Natv.	2
Asian	11
Natv. Hawaiian/Pac. Islander	0
Other Race	5
Two or more races	20
Hispanic origin, total	35
Mexican	1
Puerto Rican	22
Cuban	2
Other Hispanic	10

Age & Nativity, 2000
Under 5 years	163
18 years and over	2,071
21 years and over	2,005
65 years and over	379
85 years and over	51
Median Age	40.1
Native born	2,690
Foreign born	39

Educational Attainment, 2000
Population 25 years and over	1,936
0-8 yrs of school	4.0%
High School grad or higher	84.5%
Bachelor's degree or higher	16.0%
Graduate degree	5.3%

Income & Poverty, 1999
Per capita income	$25,776
Median household income	$60,977
Median family income	$64,196
Persons in poverty	122
H'holds receiving public assistance	18
H'holds receiving social security	280

Households, 2000
Total households	1,010
With persons under 18	370
With persons over 65	263
Family households	787
One-person households	180
Persons per household	2.68
Persons per family	3.05

Labor & Employment
Total civilian labor force, 2004**	1,696
Unemployment rate	3.5%
Total civilian labor force, 2000	1,457
Unemployment rate	2.3%

Employed persons 16 years and over by occupation, 2000
Managers & professionals	414
Service occupations	184
Sales & office occupations	419
Farming, fishing & forestry	4
Construction & maintenance	202
Production & transportation	200
Self-employed persons	102

*US Census Bureau
**New Jersey Department of Labor

General Information
Township of Harmony
3003 Belvidere Rd
Phillipsburg, NJ 08865
908-213-1600
Web site	www.harmonytwp-nj.gov
Land area (sq. miles)	23.81
Water area (sq. miles)	0.33
Type of government	Township
Form of government	TC

Government

Legislative Districts
US Congressional	5
State Legislative	23

Local Officials, 2006
Mayor	Abigail Postma
Admin/Manager	NA
Clerk	Kelley D. Smith
Finance Dir/Treas	Mary Dobes
Engineer	Nevitt S. Duveneck
Attorney	Sieglinde K Rath
Tax assessor	Richard Motyka
Tax collector	NA
Building officer	DCA
Zoning officer	John Fritts
Public Works	NA

Housing & Construction

Housing Units, 2000*
Total	1,076
Median rent	$745
Median SF home value	$156,000

New Privately Owned Housing Units Authorized by Building Permit
	Units	Value
Total, 2004	12	$1,614,674
Single family	12	$1,614,674
Total, 2005	27	$2,194,403
Single family	17	$2,028,403

Real Property Valuation - parcels, 2005
	Number	Valuation
Total		$521,372,000
Vacant	264	13,092,600
Residential	965	188,724,800
Commercial	38	20,036,800
Industrial	7	269,837,600
Apartments	1	180,900
Farm land	109	25,605,800
Farm homestead	276	3,893,500

Average Property Value & Tax, 2005
Residential value	$155,212
Property tax	$2,863
FAIR rebate	$576

Public Library

No public municipal library.

Library statistics, 2004
	Total	per capita
Volumes	NA	NA
Expenditure	NA	NA

Public Safety

Police
Chief	NA
Number of officers, 2004	0

Crime, 2004	Number	Rate
Total	19	6.8
Violent	2	0.7
Non-violent	17	6.1
Domestic Viol.	8	NA

Emergency/Fire
Director	Wesley Garrison

Public School District
(for school year 2004-2005 except as noted)

Harmony Township School District
2551 Belvidere Rd
Phillipsburg, NJ 08865
908-859-1001
Administrator	Vicki Pede
Grade plan	K-12
Enrollment	309.0
Students per teacher	9.0
Per pupil expenditure	$13,067
Median faculty salary	$50,289
Median administrator salary	$67,820
Grade 12 enrollment	NA
High school graduation rate	NA

Assessment test results
(percent scoring at proficient or advanced level)
	Language	Math
Grade 3	100%	90.0%
Grade 8	80.7%	73.0%
High school	NA	NA

SAT
Percent tested	NA
Average SAT math score	NA
Average SAT verbal score	NA

No Child Left Behind, 2003-04
Attendence rate (target = 90%)	95.7%
Drop rate	NA
Highly-qualified teachers	100%
District needs improvement?(AYP)	No

Municipal Finance

Fiscal Year 2005
Total tax levy	$9,634,331
County levy	3,652,287
County taxes	3,019,609
County library	291,232
County health	0
County open space	341,446
School levy	4,995,010
Local muni. budget	987,034
Misc. revenues	1,926,523
Total aid	$385,846
CMPTRA	175,916
Muni. block grant	11,609
Energy tax receipts	198,321
Homeland security	0

Fiscal Year 2006
Total aid	$385,845
CMPTRA	168,974
Muni. block grant	11,609
Energy tax receipts	205,262
Homeland security	NA

Taxes
	2003	2004	2005
General tax rate per $100	1.70	1.800	1.850
Net valuation taxable	$519,183,628	$520,229,019	$522,265,386
State equalized value	$518,457,787	$563,670,132	$719,968,825
County equalization ratio	110.24	100.14	92.28

Demographics & Socio-Economic Characteristics
(2000 U.S. Census, except as noted)

Population
1980*	4,532
1990*	4,623
2000	4,740
Male	2,305
Female	2,435
2004 (estimate)*	4,895
Persons per sq. mi. of land	2,638

Race & Hispanic Origin, 2000
Race
White	3,959
Black/African American	32
Amer. Indian/Alaska Natv.	2
Asian	695
Natv. Hawaiian/Pac. Islander	0
Other Race	30
Two or more races	22
Hispanic origin, total	122
Mexican	6
Puerto Rican	46
Cuban	13
Other Hispanic	57

Age & Nativity, 2000
Under 5 years	344
18 years and over	3,384
21 years and over	3,279
65 years and over	606
85 years and over	41
Median Age	40.2
Native born	3,959
Foreign born	781

Educational Attainment, 2000
Population 25 years and over	3,114
0-8 yrs of school	1.3%
High School grad or higher	96.1%
Bachelor's degree or higher	58.4%
Graduate degree	21.9%

Income & Poverty, 1999
Per capita income	$39,017
Median household income	$100,302
Median family income	$105,223
Persons in poverty	138
H'holds receiving public assistance	5
H'holds receiving social security	421

Households, 2000
Total households	1,563
With persons under 18	716
With persons over 65	430
Family households	1,344
One-person households	191
Persons per household	3.03
Persons per family	3.31

Labor & Employment
Total civilian labor force, 2004**	2,721
Unemployment rate	2.0%
Total civilian labor force, 2000	2,299
Unemployment rate	2.9%

Employed persons 16 years and over by occupation, 2000
Managers & professionals	1,217
Service occupations	112
Sales & office occupations	676
Farming, fishing & forestry	0
Construction & maintenance	100
Production & transportation	127
Self-employed persons	153

*US Census Bureau
**New Jersey Department of Labor

General Information
Borough of Harrington Park
PO Box 174
85 Harriot Ave
Harrington Park, NJ 07640
201-768-1700

Web site	www.hpboro.net
Land area (sq. miles)	1.86
Water area (sq. miles)	0.21
Type of government	Borough
Form of government	B

Government

Legislative Districts
US Congressional	5
State Legislative	39

Local Officials, 2006
Mayor	Paul Hoelscher
Admin/Manager	NA
Clerk	Lou Anne Horsey (Actg.)
Finance Dir/Treas	Anne Murphy
Engineer	Neglia Engineering
Attorney	John Dineen
Tax assessor	Raymond Damiano
Tax collector	Anne Murphy
Building officer	Robert Waldron
Zoning officer	Robert Waldron
Public Works	Mark Kiernan

Housing & Construction

Housing Units, 2000*
Total	1,583
Median rent	$1,281
Median SF home value	$349,700

New Privately Owned Housing Units Authorized by Building Permit
	Units	Value
Total, 2004	14	$4,277,258
Single family	14	$4,277,258
Total, 2005	15	$4,817,890
Single family	15	$4,817,890

Real Property Valuation - parcels, 2005
	Number	Valuation
Total		$514,736,000
Vacant	73	8,330,700
Residential	1,570	487,020,700
Commercial	27	19,384,600
Industrial	0	0
Apartments	0	0
Farm land	0	0
Farm homestead	0	0

Average Property Value & Tax, 2005
Residential value	$310,204
Property tax	$10,115
FAIR rebate	$591

Public Library
Harrington Park Public Library
10 Herring St
Harrington Park, NJ 07640
201-768-5675
Director ... Judith Heldman

Library statistics, 2004
	Total	per capita
Volumes	32,054	6.76
Expenditure	$250,717	$52.89

Public Safety

Police
Chief	David Moppert
Number of officers, 2004	10

Crime, 2004	Number	Rate
Total	21	4.3
Violent	0	0
Non-violent	21	4.3
Domestic Viol.	17	NA

Emergency/Fire
Director	Chris Oakes

Public School District
(for school year 2004-2005 except as noted)

Harrington Park School District
191 Harriot Ave
Harrington Park, NJ 07640
201-768-5700

Superintendent	Richard Weisenfeld
Grade plan	K-8
Enrollment	673.0
Students per teacher	12.6
Per pupil expenditure	$11,093
Median faculty salary	$48,033
Median administrator salary	$101,558
Grade 12 enrollment	NA
High school graduation rate	NA

Assessment test results
(percent scoring at proficient or advanced level)
	Language	Math
Grade 3	100%	96.1%
Grade 8	93.2%	88.5%
High school	NA	NA

SAT
Percent tested	NA
Average SAT math score	NA
Average SAT verbal score	NA

No Child Left Behind, 2003-04
Attendence rate (target = 90%)	96.4%
Drop rate	NA
Highly-qualified teachers	95.9%
District needs improvement?(AYP)	No

Municipal Finance

Fiscal Year 2005
Total tax levy	$16,793,837
County levy	1,657,411
County taxes	1,574,473
County library	0
County health	0
County open space	82,937
School levy	11,752,966
Local muni. budget	3,383,461
Misc. revenues	2,076,268
Total aid	$670,343
CMPTRA	178,939
Muni. block grant	20,228
Energy tax receipts	425,919
Homeland security	25,000

Fiscal Year 2006
Total aid	$670,342
CMPTRA	164,031
Muni. block grant	20,228
Energy tax receipts	440,826
Homeland security	25,000

Taxes
	2003	2004	2005
General tax rate per $100	3.01	3.050	3.270
Net valuation taxable	$499,278,144	$503,958,783	$515,032,901
State equalized value	$748,542,945	$811,321,009	$953,235,056
County equalization ratio	76.08	66.70	62.10

Demographics & Socio-Economic Characteristics
(2000 U.S. Census, except as noted)

Population
1980*	12,242
1990*	13,425
2000	14,424
Male	7,352
Female	7,072
2004 (estimate)*	14,164
Persons per sq. mi. of land	11,598

Race & Hispanic Origin, 2000
Race
White	9,534
Black/African American	142
Amer. Indian/Alaska Natv.	57
Asian	1,715
Natv. Hawaiian/Pac. Islander	4
Other Race	2,302
Two or more races	670
Hispanic origin, total	5,333
Mexican	139
Puerto Rican	605
Cuban	438
Other Hispanic	4,151

Age & Nativity, 2000
Under 5 years	931
18 years and over	11,320
21 years and over	10,725
65 years and over	1,481
85 years and over	132
Median Age	34.1
Native born	6,346
Foreign born	8,078

Educational Attainment, 2000
Population 25 years and over	9,737
0-8 yrs of school	17.0%
High School grad or higher	69.3%
Bachelor's degree or higher	20.9%
Graduate degree	10.1%

Income & Poverty, 1999
Per capita income	$18,490
Median household income	$41,350
Median family income	$48,489
Persons in poverty	1,791
H'holds receiving public assistance	164
H'holds receiving social security	1,148

Households, 2000
Total households	5,136
With persons under 18	1,883
With persons over 65	1,165
Family households	3,638
One-person households	1,154
Persons per household	2.81
Persons per family	3.27

Labor & Employment
Total civilian labor force, 2004**	7,388
Unemployment rate	5.0%
Total civilian labor force, 2000	7,287
Unemployment rate	7.7%

Employed persons 16 years and over by occupation, 2000
Managers & professionals	1,578
Service occupations	1,434
Sales & office occupations	1,637
Farming, fishing & forestry	3
Construction & maintenance	680
Production & transportation	1,394
Self-employed persons	487

*US Census Bureau
**New Jersey Department of Labor

General Information
Town of Harrison
318 Harrison Ave
Harrison, NJ 07029
973-268-2425

Web site	NA
Land area (sq. miles)	1.22
Water area (sq. miles)	0.09
Type of government	Town
Form of government	T

Government

Legislative Districts
US Congressional	13
State Legislative	32

Local Officials, 2006
Mayor	Raymond McDonough
Admin/Manager	NA
Clerk	Paul Zarbetski
Finance Dir/Treas	Elizabeth Higgins
Engineer	Rocco Rossomano
Attorney	Paul Zarbetski
Tax assessor	Albert Cifelli
Tax collector	NA
Building officer	Rocco Russomano
Zoning officer	NA
Public Works	NA

Housing & Construction

Housing Units, 2000*
Total	5,254
Median rent	$723
Median SF home value	$135,000

New Privately Owned Housing Units Authorized by Building Permit
	Units	Value
Total, 2004	66	$1,613,488
Single family	0	$45,499
Total, 2005	71	$5,217,184
Single family	2	$129,219

Real Property Valuation - parcels, 2005
	Number	Valuation
Total		$479,844,265
Vacant	84	6,005,990
Residential	1,934	266,541,465
Commercial	269	63,896,480
Industrial	75	125,767,530
Apartments	74	17,632,800
Farm land	0	0
Farm homestead	0	0

Average Property Value & Tax, 2005
Residential value	$137,819
Property tax	$6,096
FAIR rebate	$673

Public Library
Harrison Public Library
415 Harrison Ave
Harrison, NJ 07029
973-483-2366

Director	Ellen Lucas

Library statistics, 2004
	Total	per capita
Volumes	NA	NA
Expenditure	NA	NA

Public Safety

Police
Chief	Derek Kearns
Number of officers, 2004	51

Crime, 2004	Number	Rate
Total	400	28
Violent	44	3.1
Non-violent	356	25
Domestic Viol.	106	NA

Emergency/Fire
Director	Thomas Dolaghan

Public School District
(for school year 2004-2005 except as noted)

Harrison School District
430 William St
Harrison, NJ 07029
973-483-4627

Superintendent	Anthony Comprelli
Grade plan	K-12
Enrollment	1,905.0
Students per teacher	11.6
Per pupil expenditure	$16,988
Median faculty salary	$55,973
Median administrator salary	$100,582
Grade 12 enrollment	183.0
High school graduation rate	99.4%

Assessment test results
(percent scoring at proficient or advanced level)
	Language	Math
Grade 3	87.6%	87.6%
Grade 8	59.2%	41.1%
High school	65.9%	60.8%

SAT
Percent tested	59%
Average SAT math score	463
Average SAT verbal score	434

No Child Left Behind, 2003-04
Attendence rate (target = 90%)	93.7%
Drop rate	0.3%
Highly-qualified teachers	96.7%
District needs improvement?(AYP)	No

Municipal Finance

Fiscal Year 2005
Total tax levy	$21,258,053
County levy	5,098,459
County taxes	5,002,031
County library	0
County health	0
County open space	96,428
School levy	8,093,476
Local muni. budget	8,066,118
Misc. revenues	22,576,993
Total aid	$10,001,404
CMPTRA	3,096,700
Muni. block grant	58,744
Energy tax receipts	6,775,960
Homeland security	70,000

Fiscal Year 2006
Total aid	$10,001,404
CMPTRA	2,859,541
Muni. block grant	58,744
Energy tax receipts	7,013,119
Homeland security	70,000

Taxes
	2003	2004	2005
General tax rate per $100	4.14	4.253	4.424
Net valuation taxable	$474,671,340	$479,620,270	$480,599,440
State equalized value	$763,628,282	$920,411,589	$1,035,551,476
County equalization ratio	65.22	62.16	52.07

Demographics & Socio-Economic Characteristics
(2000 U.S. Census, except as noted)

Population

1980*	3,585
1990*	4,715
2000	8,788
Male	4,360
Female	4,428
2004 (estimate)*	10,903
Persons per sq. mi. of land	570

Race & Hispanic Origin, 2000

Race

White	8,363
Black/African American	260
Amer. Indian/Alaska Natv.	11
Asian	64
Natv. Hawaiian/Pac. Islander	0
Other Race	36
Two or more races	54
Hispanic origin, total	156
Mexican	18
Puerto Rican	79
Cuban	12
Other Hispanic	47

Age & Nativity, 2000

Under 5 years	757
18 years and over	5,866
21 years and over	5,620
65 years and over	582
85 years and over	61
Median Age	35.1
Native born	8,609
Foreign born	179

Educational Attainment, 2000

Population 25 years and over	5,469
0-8 yrs of school	1.9%
High School grad or higher	91.1%
Bachelor's degree or higher	38.5%
Graduate degree	10.8%

Income & Poverty, 1999

Per capita income	$28,645
Median household income	$77,143
Median family income	$84,379
Persons in poverty	278
H'holds receiving public assistance	23
H'holds receiving social security	516

Households, 2000

Total households	2,848
With persons under 18	1,466
With persons over 65	433
Family households	2,324
One-person households	435
Persons per household	3.06
Persons per family	3.44

Labor & Employment

Total civilian labor force, 2004**	3,009
Unemployment rate	3.5%
Total civilian labor force, 2000	4,374
Unemployment rate	3.5%

Employed persons 16 years and over by occupation, 2000

Managers & professionals	1,951
Service occupations	289
Sales & office occupations	1,206
Farming, fishing & forestry	48
Construction & maintenance	454
Production & transportation	271
Self-employed persons	193

*US Census Bureau
**New Jersey Department of Labor

General Information

Township of Harrison
114 Bridgeton Pike
Mullica Hill, NJ 08062
856-478-4111

Web site	www.harrisontwp.us
Land area (sq. miles)	19.13
Water area (sq. miles)	0.05
Type of government	Township
Form of government	TC

Government

Legislative Districts

US Congressional	2
State Legislative	3

Local Officials, 2006

Mayor	Phillip S. Rhudy
Admin/Manager	Carole Rieck
Clerk	Jennifer Kilborn (Actg)
Finance Dir/Treas	Yvonne Bullock
Engineer	Michael Fralengr
Attorney	Herbert Butler Jr.
Tax assessor	Timothy Mead
Tax collector	Michelle Mitchell
Building officer	Jeffrey Kier
Zoning officer	Sue Champion
Public Works	Mike Micklasavage

Housing & Construction

Housing Units, 2000*

Total	2,939
Median rent	$590
Median SF home value	$181,900

New Privately Owned Housing Units Authorized by Building Permit

	Units	Value
Total, 2004	151	$19,094,382
Single family	151	$19,094,382
Total, 2005	208	$31,540,153
Single family	208	$31,540,153

Real Property Valuation - parcels, 2005

	Number	Valuation
Total		$644,102,400
Vacant	586	26,494,200
Residential	3,089	561,065,400
Commercial	94	29,169,500
Industrial	0	0
Apartments	3	4,532,900
Farm land	116	19,440,600
Farm homestead	264	3,399,800

Average Property Value & Tax, 2005

Residential value	$168,346
Property tax	$6,273
FAIR rebate	$466

Public Library

No public municipal library.

Library statistics, 2004

	Total	per capita
Volumes	NA	NA
Expenditure	NA	NA

Public Safety

Police

Chief	Frank Rodgers
Number of officers, 2004	16

Crime, 2004	Number	Rate
Total	196	19
Violent	8	0.8
Non-violent	188	18.3
Domestic Viol.	93	NA

Emergency/Fire

Director	NA

Public School District
(for school year 2004-2005 except as noted)

Harrison Township School District
120 N Main St
Mullica Hill, NJ 08062
856-478-2016

Superintendent	Patricia Hoey
Grade plan	K-6
Enrollment	1,430.0
Students per teacher	12.7
Per pupil expenditure	$8,760
Median faculty salary	$41,280
Median administrator salary	$83,769
Grade 12 enrollment	NA
High school graduation rate	NA

Assessment test results
(percent scoring at proficient or advanced level)

	Language	Math
Grade 3	91.3%	86.3%
Grade 8	NA	NA
High school	NA	NA

SAT

Percent tested	NA
Average SAT math score	NA
Average SAT verbal score	NA

No Child Left Behind, 2003-04

Attendence rate (target = 90%)	96.0%
Drop rate	NA
Highly-qualified teachers	93%
District needs improvement?(AYP)	No

Municipal Finance

Fiscal Year 2005

Total tax levy	$24,113,157
County levy	6,373,841
County taxes	5,589,201
County library	413,063
County health	0
County open space	371,577
School levy	15,622,213
Local muni. budget	2,117,102
Misc. revenues	3,971,330
Total aid	$825,511
CMPTRA	218,319
Muni. block grant	34,458
Energy tax receipts	522,734
Homeland security	50,000

Fiscal Year 2006

Total aid	$845,511
CMPTRA	200,023
Muni. block grant	34,458
Energy tax receipts	541,030
Homeland security	70,000

Taxes

	2003	2004	2005
General tax rate per $100	3.38	3.494	3.727
Net valuation taxable	$557,270,771	$608,778,837	$647,137,264
State equalized value	$735,088,736	$872,351,326	$1,036,580,593
County equalization ratio	82.18	75.81	69.67

Demographics & Socio-Economic Characteristics

(2000 U.S. Census, except as noted)

Population

1980*	363
1990*	362
2000	359
Male	182
Female	177
2004 (estimate)*	380
Persons per sq. mi. of land	696

Race & Hispanic Origin, 2000

Race
White	348
Black/African American	2
Amer. Indian/Alaska Natv.	1
Asian	1
Natv. Hawaiian/Pac. Islander	0
Other Race	7
Two or more races	0
Hispanic origin, total	13
Mexican	12
Puerto Rican	0
Cuban	0
Other Hispanic	1

Age & Nativity, 2000

Under 5 years	11
18 years and over	307
21 years and over	299
65 years and over	109
85 years and over	4
Median Age	53.7
Native born	339
Foreign born	14

Educational Attainment, 2000

Population 25 years and over	308
0-8 yrs of school	1.9%
High School grad or higher	95.1%
Bachelor's degree or higher	46.1%
Graduate degree	14.3%

Income & Poverty, 1999

Per capita income	$36,757
Median household income	$61,875
Median family income	$69,722
Persons in poverty	18
H'holds receiving public assistance	6
H'holds receiving social security	102

Households, 2000

Total households	167
With persons under 18	31
With persons over 65	76
Family households	112
One-person households	49
Persons per household	2.15
Persons per family	2.61

Labor & Employment

Total civilian labor force, 2004**	215
Unemployment rate	6.4%
Total civilian labor force, 2000	134
Unemployment rate	0.0%

Employed persons 16 years and over by occupation, 2000
Managers & professionals	56
Service occupations	20
Sales & office occupations	36
Farming, fishing & forestry	0
Construction & maintenance	18
Production & transportation	4
Self-employed persons	24

*US Census Bureau
**New Jersey Department of Labor

General Information

Borough of Harvey Cedars
PO Box 3185
Harvey Cedars, NJ 08008
609-361-6000

Web site	www.harveycedars.org
Land area (sq. miles)	0.55
Water area (sq. miles)	0.65
Type of government	Borough
Form of government	Comm.

Government

Legislative Districts

US Congressional	3
State Legislative	9

Local Officials, 2006

Mayor	Jonathan Oldham
Admin/Manager	NA
Clerk	Daina Dale
Finance Dir/Treas	Sharon Sulecki
Engineer	Frank Little
Attorney	John Cerefice
Tax assessor	Bernard Haney
Tax collector	NA
Building officer	Frank Zappavigna
Zoning officer	John Gerkens
Public Works	Lloyd Vosseller

Housing & Construction

Housing Units, 2000*

Total	1,205
Median rent	$870
Median SF home value	$456,500

New Privately Owned Housing Units Authorized by Building Permit

	Units	Value
Total, 2004	25	$8,208,419
Single family	25	$8,208,419
Total, 2005	17	$5,993,935
Single family	17	$5,993,935

Real Property Valuation - parcels, 2005

	Number	Valuation
Total		$1,048,257,500
Vacant	33	12,677,300
Residential	1,194	1,022,884,100
Commercial	26	12,696,100
Industrial	0	0
Apartments	0	0
Farm land	0	0
Farm homestead	0	0

Average Property Value & Tax, 2005

Residential value	$856,687
Property tax	$7,108
FAIR rebate	$569

Public Library

No public municipal library.

Library statistics, 2004

	Total	per capita
Volumes	NA	NA
Expenditure	NA	NA

Public Safety

Police

Chief	Jerry Falkowski
Number of officers, 2004	8

Crime, 2004	Number	Rate
Total	16	42.9
Violent	0	0
Non-violent	16	42.9
Domestic Viol.	3	NA

Emergency/Fire

Director	Sean Marti

Public School District

(for school year 2004-2005 except as noted)

Sends children to Long Beach Island school district (see Appendix A).

Grade plan	NA
Enrollment	NA
Students per teacher	NA
Per pupil expenditure	NA
Median faculty salary	NA
Median administrator salary	NA
Grade 12 enrollment	NA
High school graduation rate	NA

Assessment test results

(percent scoring at proficient or advanced level)
	Language	Math
Grade 3	NA	NA
Grade 8	NA	NA
High school	NA	NA

SAT

Percent tested	NA
Average SAT math score	NA
Average SAT verbal score	NA

No Child Left Behind, 2003-04

Attendence rate (target = 90%)	NA
Drop rate	NA
Highly-qualified teachers	NA
District needs improvement?(AYP)	NA

Municipal Finance

Fiscal Year 2005

Total tax levy	$8,700,738
County levy	3,746,036
County taxes	3,279,157
County library	344,494
County health	0
County open space	122,386
School levy	2,881,248
Local muni. budget	2,073,455
Misc. revenues	1,150,819
Total aid	$135,273
CMPTRA	0
Muni. block grant	1,584
Energy tax receipts	110,532
Homeland security	25,000

Fiscal Year 2006

Total aid	$139,141
CMPTRA	0
Muni. block grant	1,584
Energy tax receipts	112,557
Homeland security	25,000

Taxes

	2003	2004	2005
General tax rate per $100	2.14	0.832	0.830
Net valuation taxable	$380,678,259	$1,050,317,761	$1,048,636,368
State equalized value	$850,487,621	$1,021,423,167	$1,231,950,620
County equalization ratio	52.22	121.79	102.83

Demographics & Socio-Economic Characteristics
(2000 U.S. Census, except as noted)

Population
1980*	12,166
1990*	11,488
2000	11,662
Male	5,605
Female	6,057
2004 (estimate)*	11,679
Persons per sq. mi. of land	7,746

Race & Hispanic Origin, 2000
Race
White	10,247
Black/African American	200
Amer. Indian/Alaska Natv.	5
Asian	776
Natv. Hawaiian/Pac. Islander	1
Other Race	255
Two or more races	178
Hispanic origin, total	964
Mexican	28
Puerto Rican	241
Cuban	184
Other Hispanic	511

Age & Nativity, 2000
Under 5 years	671
18 years and over	9,076
21 years and over	8,752
65 years and over	1,986
85 years and over	235
Median Age	40.1
Native born	9,685
Foreign born	1,977

Educational Attainment, 2000
Population 25 years and over	8,311
0-8 yrs of school	5.4%
High School grad or higher	86.9%
Bachelor's degree or higher	29.9%
Graduate degree	8.1%

Income & Poverty, 1999
Per capita income	$29,626
Median household income	$64,529
Median family income	$75,032
Persons in poverty	492
H'holds receiving public assistance	45
H'holds receiving social security	1,438

Households, 2000
Total households	4,521
With persons under 18	1,475
With persons over 65	1,469
Family households	3,144
One-person households	1,185
Persons per household	2.58
Persons per family	3.16

Labor & Employment
Total civilian labor force, 2004**	6,647
Unemployment rate	4.2%
Total civilian labor force, 2000	5,916
Unemployment rate	3.9%

Employed persons 16 years and over by occupation, 2000
Managers & professionals	2,456
Service occupations	595
Sales & office occupations	1,805
Farming, fishing & forestry	6
Construction & maintenance	351
Production & transportation	473
Self-employed persons	195

*US Census Bureau
**New Jersey Department of Labor

General Information
Borough of Hasbrouck Heights
320 Boulevard
Hasbrouck Heights, NJ 07604
201-288-0195
Web site	www.hasbrouck-heights.nj.us
Land area (sq. miles)	1.51
Water area (sq. miles)	0
Type of government	Borough
Form of government	B

Government

Legislative Districts
US Congressional	9
State Legislative	38

Local Officials, 2006
Mayor	Ronald R. Jones
Admin/Manager	Michael Kronyak
Clerk	Rose Marie Sees
Finance Dir/Treas	Michael Kronyak
Engineer	Kenneth G. B. Job
Attorney	Ralph W. Chandless Jr.
Tax assessor	George Reggo
Tax collector	NA
Building officer	Nicholas Melfi
Zoning officer	NA
Public Works	NA

Housing & Construction

Housing Units, 2000*
Total	4,617
Median rent	$874
Median SF home value	$215,300

New Privately Owned Housing Units Authorized by Building Permit
	Units	Value
Total, 2004	18	$4,368,426
Single family	18	$4,368,426
Total, 2005	26	$7,976,164
Single family	26	$7,976,164

Real Property Valuation - parcels, 2005
	Number	Valuation
Total		$874,976,600
Vacant	114	5,860,500
Residential	3,298	658,500,400
Commercial	177	164,497,200
Industrial	12	12,015,600
Apartments	24	34,102,900
Farm land	0	0
Farm homestead	0	0

Average Property Value & Tax, 2005
Residential value	$199,667
Property tax	$7,008
FAIR rebate	$616

Public Library
Hasbrouck Heights Public Library
301 Division Ave
Hasbrouck Heights, NJ 07604
201-288-0488
Director................. Michele Reutty

Library statistics, 2004
	Total	per capita
Volumes	47,436	4.07
Expenditure	$588,013	$50.42

Public Safety

Police
Chief	Michael Colaneri
Number of officers, 2004	32

Crime, 2004	Number	Rate
Total	157	13.5
Violent	4	0.3
Non-violent	153	13.1
Domestic Viol.	88	NA

Emergency/Fire
Director.................Joseph Taylor

Public School District
(for school year 2004-2005 except as noted)

Hasbrouck Heights School District
379 Blvd
Hasbrouck Heights, NJ 07604
201-393-8145
Superintendent	Joseph Luongo
Grade plan	K-12
Enrollment	1,566.5
Students per teacher	11.6
Per pupil expenditure	$11,939
Median faculty salary	$51,978
Median administrator salary	$97,074
Grade 12 enrollment	113.5
High school graduation rate	98.3%

Assessment test results
(percent scoring at proficient or advanced level)
	Language	Math
Grade 3	94.0%	97.0%
Grade 8	78.1%	74.2%
High school	94.5%	91.8%

SAT
Percent tested	76%
Average SAT math score	537
Average SAT verbal score	503

No Child Left Behind, 2003-04
Attendence rate (target = 90%)	95.9%
Drop rate	0.7%
Highly-qualified teachers	94.3%
District needs improvement?(AYP)	No

Municipal Finance

Fiscal Year 2005
Total tax levy	$30,738,141
County levy	2,893,897
County taxes	2,749,152
County library	0
County health	0
County open space	144,745
School levy	17,517,933
Local muni. budget	10,326,312
Misc. revenues	4,253,835
Total aid	$1,524,451
CMPTRA	503,319
Muni. block grant	50,268
Energy tax receipts	900,864
Homeland security	70,000

Fiscal Year 2006
Total aid	$1,524,451
CMPTRA	471,788
Muni. block grant	50,268
Energy tax receipts	932,395
Homeland security	70,000

Taxes
	2003	2004	2005
General tax rate per $100	3.10	3.360	3.520
Net valuation taxable	$872,992,173	$871,267,476	$875,710,063
State equalized value	$1,272,027,063	$1,436,228,480	$1,617,491,805
County equalization ratio	78.81	68.63	60.64

Demographics & Socio-Economic Characteristics
(2000 U.S. Census, except as noted)

Population
1980*	3,509
1990*	3,384
2000	3,390
Male	1,661
Female	1,729
2004 (estimate)*	3,419
Persons per sq. mi. of land	1,747

Race & Hispanic Origin, 2000
Race
White	2,981
Black/African American	41
Amer. Indian/Alaska Natv.	0
Asian	312
Natv. Hawaiian/Pac. Islander	0
Other Race	25
Two or more races	31
Hispanic origin, total	92
Mexican	1
Puerto Rican	12
Cuban	28
Other Hispanic	51

Age & Nativity, 2000
Under 5 years	232
18 years and over	2,411
21 years and over	2,349
65 years and over	474
85 years and over	51
Median Age	41.1
Native born	2,857
Foreign born	533

Educational Attainment, 2000
Population 25 years and over	2,259
0-8 yrs of school	1.6%
High School grad or higher	93.9%
Bachelor's degree or higher	57.0%
Graduate degree	23.9%

Income & Poverty, 1999
Per capita income	$45,615
Median household income	$101,836
Median family income	$112,500
Persons in poverty	68
H'holds receiving public assistance	13
H'holds receiving social security	304

Households, 2000
Total households	1,134
With persons under 18	519
With persons over 65	336
Family households	971
One-person households	145
Persons per household	2.98
Persons per family	3.25

Labor & Employment
Total civilian labor force, 2004**	1,822
Unemployment rate	3.0%
Total civilian labor force, 2000	1,628
Unemployment rate	3.6%

Employed persons 16 years and over by occupation, 2000
Managers & professionals	928
Service occupations	84
Sales & office occupations	443
Farming, fishing & forestry	0
Construction & maintenance	67
Production & transportation	47
Self-employed persons	141

*US Census Bureau
**New Jersey Department of Labor

General Information
Borough of Haworth
300 Haworth Ave
Haworth, NJ 07641
201-384-4785
Web site	www.haworthnj.org
Land area (sq. miles)	1.96
Water area (sq. miles)	0.40
Type of government	Borough
Form of government	B

Government
Legislative Districts
US Congressional	5
State Legislative	39

Local Officials, 2006
Mayor	John DeRienzo
Admin/Manager	Ann Fay
Clerk	Ann Fay
Finance Dir/Treas	Rebecca Overgaard
Engineer	Schwanewede/Hals
Attorney	Peter Scandariato
Tax assessor	Neil Rubenstein
Tax collector	Rebecca Overgaard
Building officer	Harry Kraus
Zoning officer	NA
Public Works	Martin Mahon

Housing & Construction
Housing Units, 2000*
Total	1,146
Median rent	$1,625
Median SF home value	$378,400

New Privately Owned Housing Units Authorized by Building Permit
	Units	Value
Total, 2004	6	$2,188,750
Single family	6	$2,188,750
Total, 2005	15	$6,456,042
Single family	15	$6,456,042

Real Property Valuation - parcels, 2005
	Number	Valuation
Total		$732,739,300
Vacant	49	15,935,000
Residential	1,124	640,147,700
Commercial	44	76,656,600
Industrial	0	0
Apartments	0	0
Farm land	0	0
Farm homestead	0	0

Average Property Value & Tax, 2005
Residential value	$569,526
Property tax	$11,932
FAIR rebate	$595

Public Library
Haworth Municipal Library
300 Haworth Ave
Haworth, NJ 07641
201-384-1020
Director. . . . . .Elizabeth Rosenberg

Library statistics, 2004
	Total	per capita
Volumes	28,268	8.34
Expenditure	$246,215	$72.63

Public Safety
Police
Chief	Patrick O'Dea
Number of officers, 2004	12

Crime, 2004	Number	Rate
Total	5	1.5
Violent	0	0
Non-violent	5	1.5
Domestic Viol.	3	NA

Emergency/Fire
Director. . . . . .Matthew Carey

Public School District
(for school year 2004-2005 except as noted)

Haworth School District
205 Valley Rd
Haworth, NJ 07641
201-501-7077
Superintendent	Joanne Newberry
Grade plan	K-8
Enrollment	522.0
Students per teacher	11.8
Per pupil expenditure	$12,312
Median faculty salary	$55,772
Median administrator salary	$133,056
Grade 12 enrollment	NA
High school graduation rate	NA

Assessment test results
(percent scoring at proficient or advanced level)
	Language	Math
Grade 3	98.3%	95.0%
Grade 8	90.0%	90.0%
High school	NA	NA

SAT
Percent tested	NA
Average SAT math score	NA
Average SAT verbal score	NA

No Child Left Behind, 2003-04
Attendance rate (target = 90%)	95.5%
Drop rate	NA
Highly-qualified teachers	100%
District needs improvement?(AYP)	No

Municipal Finance
Fiscal Year 2005
Total tax levy	$15,358,867
County levy	1,469,673
County taxes	1,396,171
County library	0
County health	0
County open space	73,502
School levy	9,830,553
Local muni. budget	4,058,641
Misc. revenues	1,532,145
Total aid	$786,822
CMPTRA	77,451
Muni. block grant	14,807
Energy tax receipts	650,294
Homeland security	25,000

Fiscal Year 2006
Total aid	$786,821
CMPTRA	54,690
Muni. block grant	14,807
Energy tax receipts	673,054
Homeland security	25,000

Taxes
	2003	2004	2005
General tax rate per $100	3.33	1.990	2.100
Net valuation taxable	$410,270,542	$729,754,445	$733,076,067
State equalized value	$641,649,268	$731,142,938	$830,116,710
County equalization ratio	69.87	112.59	99.81

Demographics & Socio-Economic Characteristics
(2000 U.S. Census, except as noted)

Population
1980*	18,200
1990*	17,084
2000	18,218
Male	8,686
Female	9,532
2004 (estimate)*	18,378
Persons per sq. mi. of land	5,412

Race & Hispanic Origin, 2000
Race
White	17,080
Black/African American	137
Amer. Indian/Alaska Natv.	25
Asian	344
Natv. Hawaiian/Pac. Islander	3
Other Race	287
Two or more races	342
Hispanic origin, total	1,354
Mexican	55
Puerto Rican	345
Cuban	99
Other Hispanic	855

Age & Nativity, 2000
Under 5 years	1,155
18 years and over	14,252
21 years and over	13,797
65 years and over	2,817
85 years and over	347
Median Age	38.2
Native born	15,684
Foreign born	2,534

Educational Attainment, 2000
Population 25 years and over	13,122
0-8 yrs of school	6.4%
High School grad or higher	84.3%
Bachelor's degree or higher	25.6%
Graduate degree	7.9%

Income & Poverty, 1999
Per capita income	$26,551
Median household income	$55,340
Median family income	$65,451
Persons in poverty	619
H'holds receiving public assistance	59
H'holds receiving social security	2,140

Households, 2000
Total households	7,260
With persons under 18	2,216
With persons over 65	2,095
Family households	4,933
One-person households	1,922
Persons per household	2.5
Persons per family	3.07

Labor & Employment
Total civilian labor force, 2004**	9,538
Unemployment rate	3.3%
Total civilian labor force, 2000	9,925
Unemployment rate	2.9%

Employed persons 16 years and over by occupation, 2000
Managers & professionals	3,462
Service occupations	1,387
Sales & office occupations	3,090
Farming, fishing & forestry	13
Construction & maintenance	826
Production & transportation	858
Self-employed persons	574

*US Census Bureau
**New Jersey Department of Labor

General Information
Borough of Hawthorne
445 Lafayette Ave
Hawthorne, NJ 07506
973-427-5555

Web site	www.hawthornenj.org
Land area (sq. miles)	3.40
Water area (sq. miles)	0.02
Type of government	Borough
Form of government	Mayor-Council

Government

Legislative Districts
US Congressional	9
State Legislative	35

Local Officials, 2006
Mayor	Patrick J. Botbyl
Admin/Manager	Eric Maurer
Clerk	Jean Mele
Finance Dir/Treas	Mary Jeanne Hewitt
Engineer	Boswell Engineering
Attorney	Michael Pasquale
Tax assessor	Tim Henderson
Tax collector	NA
Building officer	John Pallotta
Zoning officer	John Pallotta
Public Works	NA

Housing & Construction

Housing Units, 2000*
Total	7,419
Median rent	$949
Median SF home value	$198,600

New Privately Owned Housing Units
Authorized by Building Permit
	Units	Value
Total, 2004	9	$778,250
Single family	5	$605,750
Total, 2005	17	$388,690
Single family	1	$221,000

Real Property Valuation - parcels, 2005
	Number	Valuation
Total		$1,216,448,750
Vacant	118	8,010,600
Residential	5,346	975,174,150
Commercial	275	121,777,900
Industrial	111	89,296,600
Apartments	18	22,189,500
Farm land	0	0
Farm homestead	0	0

Average Property Value & Tax, 2005
Residential value	$182,412
Property tax	$7,058
FAIR rebate	$609

Public Library
Louis Bay 2nd Library
345 Lafayette Ave
Hawthorne, NJ 07506
973-427-5745

Director............. Jeanne Marie Ryan

Library statistics, 2004
	Total	per capita
Volumes	83,155	4.56
Expenditure	$988,707	$54.27

Public Safety

Police
Chief	Martin Boyd
Number of officers, 2004	33

Crime, 2004	Number	Rate
Total	267	14.5
Violent	11	0.6
Non-violent	256	13.9
Domestic Viol.	133	NA

Emergency/Fire
Director................. Joseph Speranza

Public School District
(for school year 2004-2005 except as noted)

Hawthorne School District
445 Lafayette Ave
Hawthorne, NJ 07506
973-423-6401

Administrator	Richard Spirito
Grade plan	K-12
Enrollment	2,320.0
Students per teacher	11.0
Per pupil expenditure	$11,859
Median faculty salary	$51,840
Median administrator salary	$101,446
Grade 12 enrollment	159.0
High school graduation rate	98.1%

Assessment test results
(percent scoring at proficient or advanced level)
	Language	Math
Grade 3	88.3%	85.7%
Grade 8	83.6%	65.5%
High school	86.8%	79.6%

SAT
Percent tested	72%
Average SAT math score	523
Average SAT verbal score	514

No Child Left Behind, 2003-04
Attendance rate (target = 90%)	95.8%
Drop rate	0.5%
Highly-qualified teachers	100%
District needs improvement?(AYP)	No

Municipal Finance

Fiscal Year 2005
Total tax levy	$47,108,529
County levy	10,950,348
County taxes	10,741,811
County library	0
County health	0
County open space	208,537
School levy	26,146,955
Local muni. budget	10,011,226
Misc. revenues	5,694,333
Total aid	$2,050,391
CMPTRA	759,445
Muni. block grant	74,754
Energy tax receipts	1,146,192
Homeland security	70,000

Fiscal Year 2006
Total aid	$2,050,391
CMPTRA	719,328
Muni. block grant	74,754
Energy tax receipts	1,186,309
Homeland security	70,000

Taxes
	2003	2004	2005
General tax rate per $100	3.57	3.730	3.870
Net valuation taxable	$1,209,940,730	$1,216,871,463	$1,217,455,045
State equalized value	$1,839,654,447	$2,072,904,726	$2,308,409,262
County equalization ratio	73.57	65.77	58.68

Demographics & Socio-Economic Characteristics
(2000 U.S. Census, except as noted)

Population
1980*	23,013
1990*	21,976
2000	21,378
Male	10,217
Female	11,161
2004 (estimate)*	21,226
Persons per sq. mi. of land	3,775

Race & Hispanic Origin, 2000
Race
White	19,918
Black/African American	235
Amer. Indian/Alaska Natv.	12
Asian	725
Natv. Hawaiian/Pac. Islander	1
Other Race	242
Two or more races	245
Hispanic origin, total	1,254
Mexican	137
Puerto Rican	564
Cuban	107
Other Hispanic	446

Age & Nativity, 2000
Under 5 years	1,400
18 years and over	15,932
21 years and over	15,259
65 years and over	2,879
85 years and over	294
Median Age	38.5
Native born	19,719
Foreign born	1,659

Educational Attainment, 2000
Population 25 years and over	14,567
0-8 yrs of school	3.7%
High School grad or higher	83.8%
Bachelor's degree or higher	19.2%
Graduate degree	6.0%

Income & Poverty, 1999
Per capita income	$25,262
Median household income	$65,697
Median family income	$71,361
Persons in poverty	727
H'holds receiving public assistance	108
H'holds receiving social security	2,274

Households, 2000
Total households	7,244
With persons under 18	2,925
With persons over 65	2,054
Family households	5,799
One-person households	1,253
Persons per household	2.92
Persons per family	3.32

Labor & Employment
Total civilian labor force, 2004**	13,583
Unemployment rate	4.4%
Total civilian labor force, 2000	10,746
Unemployment rate	4.6%

Employed persons 16 years and over by occupation, 2000
Managers & professionals	3,424
Service occupations	1,320
Sales & office occupations	3,265
Farming, fishing & forestry	25
Construction & maintenance	1,082
Production & transportation	1,138
Self-employed persons	373

*US Census Bureau
**New Jersey Department of Labor

General Information
Township of Hazlet
PO Box 371
1776 Union Av
Hazlet, NJ 07730
732-264-1700
Web site	www.hazlettwp.org
Land area (sq. miles)	5.62
Water area (sq. miles)	0.04
Type of government	Township
Form of government	TC

Government

Legislative Districts
US Congressional	6
State Legislative	13

Local Officials, 2006
Mayor	Michael C. Sachs
Admin/Manager	Margaret Margiotta
Clerk	Mary L. Lynch
Finance Dir/Treas	Adeline Schmidt
Engineer	Robert Bucco
Attorney	James Gorman
Tax assessor	Evelyn Cranwell
Tax collector	Patricia A. McCarthy
Building officer	Dennis Pino
Zoning officer	Sharon Keegan
Public Works	David Rooke

Housing & Construction

Housing Units, 2000*
Total	7,406
Median rent	$510
Median SF home value	$173,700

New Privately Owned Housing Units
Authorized by Building Permit
	Units	Value
Total, 2004	NA	NA
Single family	NA	NA
Total, 2005	25	$3,166,405
Single family	25	$3,166,405

Real Property Valuation - parcels, 2005
	Number	Valuation
Total		$1,056,443,500
Vacant	190	10,406,400
Residential	6,201	832,054,500
Commercial	362	196,283,700
Industrial	7	17,690,400
Apartments	0	0
Farm land	0	0
Farm homestead	2	8,500

Average Property Value & Tax, 2005
Residential value	$134,139
Property tax	$5,506
FAIR rebate	$631

Public Library
Hazlet Township Library†
251 Middle Rd
Hazlet, NJ 07730
732-264-7164
Branch Librarian .... Beth Henderson

Library statistics, 2004
	Total	per capita
Volumes	NA	NA
Expenditure	NA	NA

†Branch of County Library

Public Safety

Police
Chief	James Broderick
Number of officers, 2004	47

Crime, 2004	Number	Rate
Total	270	12.7
Violent	8	0.4
Non-violent	262	12.3
Domestic Viol.	188	NA

Emergency/Fire
Director	Frank Oliva Jr.

Public School District
(for school year 2004-2005 except as noted)

Hazlet Township School District
421 Middle Rd
Hazlet, NJ 07730
732-264-8402
Superintendent	Renae LaPrete
Grade plan	K-12
Enrollment	3,428.5
Students per teacher	11.3
Per pupil expenditure	$11,755
Median faculty salary	$47,115
Median administrator salary	$102,707
Grade 12 enrollment	245.0
High school graduation rate	99.6%

Assessment test results
(percent scoring at proficient or advanced level)
	Language	Math
Grade 3	92.3%	89.5%
Grade 8	87.9%	73.8%
High school	92.1%	86.5%

SAT
Percent tested	82%
Average SAT math score	514
Average SAT verbal score	501

No Child Left Behind, 2003-04
Attendence rate (target = 90%)	95.2%
Drop rate	0.1%
Highly-qualified teachers	100%
District needs improvement?(AYP)	No

Municipal Finance

Fiscal Year 2005
Total tax levy	$43,402,408
County levy	6,369,128
County taxes	5,715,172
County library	314,814
County health	0
County open space	339,142
School levy	27,812,997
Local muni. budget	9,220,283
Misc. revenues	6,351,125
Total aid	$2,634,950
CMPTRA	1,086,874
Muni. block grant	96,159
Energy tax receipts	1,361,917
Homeland security	90,000

Fiscal Year 2006
Total aid	$2,634,950
CMPTRA	1,039,207
Muni. block grant	96,159
Energy tax receipts	1,409,584
Homeland security	90,000

Taxes
	2003	2004	2005
General tax rate per $100	3.69	3.849	4.105
Net valuation taxable	$1,053,461,423	$1,053,107,871	$1,057,465,395
State equalized value	$1,656,125,488	$1,892,758,411	$2,136,725,389
County equalization ratio	70.7	63.61	55.61

Demographics & Socio-Economic Characteristics
(2000 U.S. Census, except as noted)

Population
1980*	955
1990*	1,211
2000	1,825
Male	905
Female	920
2004 (estimate)*	2,023
Persons per sq. mi. of land	2,387

Race & Hispanic Origin, 2000
Race
White	1,700
Black/African American	44
Amer. Indian/Alaska Natv.	4
Asian	44
Natv. Hawaiian/Pac. Islander	1
Other Race	16
Two or more races	16
Hispanic origin, total	97
Mexican	4
Puerto Rican	43
Cuban	2
Other Hispanic	48

Age & Nativity, 2000
Under 5 years	124
18 years and over	1,422
21 years and over	1,358
65 years and over	113
85 years and over	12
Median Age	35.8
Native born	1,659
Foreign born	166

Educational Attainment, 2000
Population 25 years and over	1,308
0-8 yrs of school	4.2%
High School grad or higher	88.8%
Bachelor's degree or higher	18.4%
Graduate degree	3.2%

Income & Poverty, 1999
Per capita income	$26,668
Median household income	$60,125
Median family income	$64,659
Persons in poverty	61
H'holds receiving public assistance	11
H'holds receiving social security	116

Households, 2000
Total households	746
With persons under 18	256
With persons over 65	89
Family households	495
One-person households	191
Persons per household	2.45
Persons per family	3.01

Labor & Employment
Total civilian labor force, 2004**	792
Unemployment rate	4.9%
Total civilian labor force, 2000	1,141
Unemployment rate	3.9%

Employed persons 16 years and over by occupation, 2000
Managers & professionals	319
Service occupations	168
Sales & office occupations	344
Farming, fishing & forestry	0
Construction & maintenance	110
Production & transportation	156
Self-employed persons	40

*US Census Bureau
**New Jersey Department of Labor

General Information
Borough of Helmetta
PO Box 378
60 Main St
Helmetta, NJ 08828
732-521-4946
Web site	www.helmettaboro.com
Land area (sq. miles)	0.85
Water area (sq. miles)	0.05
Type of government	Borough
Form of government	B

Government
Legislative Districts
US Congressional	12
State Legislative	18

Local Officials, 2006
Mayor	Nancy Martin
Admin/Manager	William Schmeling
Clerk	Sandra Bohinski
Finance Dir/Treas	Denise Biancamano
Engineer	Michael Vena
Attorney	David Clark
Tax assessor	Kenneth Pacera
Tax collector	Denise Jawidzik
Building officer	Robert Simonelli
Zoning officer	NA
Public Works	Darren Doran

Housing & Construction
Housing Units, 2000*
Total	769
Median rent	$1,051
Median SF home value	$148,300

New Privately Owned Housing Units Authorized by Building Permit
	Units	Value
Total, 2004	14	$1,360,053
Single family	14	$1,360,053
Total, 2005	1	$167,000
Single family	1	$167,000

Real Property Valuation - parcels, 2005
	Number	Valuation
Total		$63,681,000
Vacant	57	617,000
Residential	853	60,543,400
Commercial	11	1,978,600
Industrial	5	542,000
Apartments	0	0
Farm land	0	0
Farm homestead	0	0

Average Property Value & Tax, 2005
Residential value	$70,977
Property tax	$4,425
FAIR rebate	$468

Public Library
No public municipal library.

Library statistics, 2004
	Total	per capita
Volumes	NA	NA
Expenditure	NA	NA

Public Safety
Police
Chief	Cully Lewis
Number of officers, 2004	5

Crime, 2004	Number	Rate
Total	17	8.7
Violent	6	3.1
Non-violent	11	5.6
Domestic Viol.	0	NA

Emergency/Fire
Director	Gregory Bennett

Public School District
(for school year 2004-2005 except as noted)

Helmetta School District
PO Box 287
Helmetta, NJ 08828
732-521-0482
Superintendent	NA
Grade plan	NA
Enrollment	NA
Students per teacher	NA
Per pupil expenditure	NA
Median faculty salary	NA
Median administrator salary	NA
Grade 12 enrollment	NA
High school graduation rate	NA

Assessment test results
(percent scoring at proficient or advanced level)
	Language	Math
Grade 3	NA	NA
Grade 8	NA	NA
High school	NA	NA

SAT
Percent tested	NA
Average SAT math score	NA
Average SAT verbal score	NA

No Child Left Behind, 2003-04
Attendence rate (target = 90%)	NA
Drop rate	NA
Highly-qualified teachers	NA
District needs improvement?(AYP)	NA

Municipal Finance
Fiscal Year 2005
Total tax levy	$3,976,772
County levy	579,853
County taxes	525,220
County library	0
County health	0
County open space	54,632
School levy	2,552,396
Local muni. budget	844,523
Misc. revenues	1,059,290
Total aid	$241,680
CMPTRA	123,746
Muni. block grant	7,156
Energy tax receipts	85,778
Homeland security	25,000

Fiscal Year 2006
Total aid	$241,680
CMPTRA	120,744
Muni. block grant	7,156
Energy tax receipts	88,780
Homeland security	25,000

Taxes
	2003	2004	2005
General tax rate per $100	6.57	5.970	6.240
Net valuation taxable	$58,209,654	$61,552,276	$63,787,570
State equalized value	$145,742,749	$175,902,173	$215,062,610
County equalization ratio	45.81	39.94	34.95

Demographics & Socio-Economic Characteristics

(2000 U.S. Census, except as noted)

Population

1980*	3,435
1990*	3,886
2000	3,776
Male	1,830
Female	1,946
2004 (estimate)*	3,793
Persons per sq. mi. of land	1,573

Race & Hispanic Origin, 2000

Race

White	3,634
Black/African American	30
Amer. Indian/Alaska Natv.	13
Asian	54
Natv. Hawaiian/Pac. Islander	1
Other Race	17
Two or more races	27
Hispanic origin, total	80
Mexican	11
Puerto Rican	39
Cuban	4
Other Hispanic	26

Age & Nativity, 2000

Under 5 years	326
18 years and over	2,732
21 years and over	2,636
65 years and over	246
85 years and over	26
Median Age	36.1
Native born	3,531
Foreign born	245

Educational Attainment, 2000

Population 25 years and over	2,530
0-8 yrs of school	1.9%
High School grad or higher	92.4%
Bachelor's degree or higher	39.1%
Graduate degree	12.1%

Income & Poverty, 1999

Per capita income	$29,276
Median household income	$68,719
Median family income	$75,357
Persons in poverty	120
H'holds receiving public assistance	9
H'holds receiving social security	202

Households, 2000

Total households	1,428
With persons under 18	587
With persons over 65	187
Family households	1,051
One-person households	298
Persons per household	2.64
Persons per family	3.1

Labor & Employment

Total civilian labor force, 2004**	2,540
Unemployment rate	2.8%
Total civilian labor force, 2000	2,273
Unemployment rate	2.7%

Employed persons 16 years and over by occupation, 2000

Managers & professionals	892
Service occupations	310
Sales & office occupations	642
Farming, fishing & forestry	0
Construction & maintenance	212
Production & transportation	156
Self-employed persons	142

*US Census Bureau
**New Jersey Department of Labor

General Information

Borough of High Bridge
71 Main St
High Bridge, NJ 08829
908-638-6455

Web site	NA
Land area (sq. miles)	2.41
Water area (sq. miles)	0.02
Type of government	Borough
Form of government	B

Government

Legislative Districts

US Congressional	7
State Legislative	23

Local Officials, 2006

Mayor	Alfred Schweikert
Admin/Manager	W. Barnum Wahl
Clerk	W. Barnum Wahl
Finance Dir/Treas	Bonnie Fleming
Engineer	H. Clay McEldowney
Attorney	Joseph Novak
Tax assessor	Michael Ross
Tax collector	Bonnie Fleming
Building officer	Al Hopping
Zoning officer	John Barczyk
Public Works	Mark Banks

Housing & Construction

Housing Units, 2000*

Total	1,478
Median rent	$788
Median SF home value	$163,300

New Privately Owned Housing Units
Authorized by Building Permit

	Units	Value
Total, 2004	3	$437,500
Single family	3	$437,500
Total, 2005	7	$1,104,099
Single family	7	$1,104,099

Real Property Valuation - parcels, 2005

	Number	Valuation
Total		$380,033,200
Vacant	96	5,474,600
Residential	1,330	347,544,200
Commercial	28	10,888,200
Industrial	9	11,236,700
Apartments	8	3,786,200
Farm land	3	1,084,200
Farm homestead	9	19,100

Average Property Value & Tax, 2005

Residential value	$259,569
Property tax	$6,180
FAIR rebate	$472

Public Library

High Bridge Public Library
71 Main St
High Bridge, NJ 08829
908-638-8231

Director.................... Theresa Steets

Library statistics, 2004

	Total	per capita
Volumes	11,740	3.11
Expenditure	$23,382	$6.19

Public Safety

Police

Chief	Edward Spinks
Number of officers, 2004	6

Crime, 2004	Number	Rate
Total	31	8.1
Violent	1	0.3
Non-violent	30	7.9
Domestic Viol.	36	NA

Emergency/Fire

Director....................... Jeff Smith

Public School District

(for school year 2004-2005 except as noted)

High Bridge Borough School District
50 Thomas St
High Bridge, NJ 08829
908-638-4103

Superintendent	Patricia Ash
Grade plan	K-8
Enrollment	449.0
Students per teacher	9.4
Per pupil expenditure	$11,921
Median faculty salary	$59,216
Median administrator salary	$82,362
Grade 12 enrollment	NA
High school graduation rate	NA

Assessment test results

(percent scoring at proficient or advanced level)

	Language	Math
Grade 3	90.9%	79.6%
Grade 8	92.3%	90.0%
High school	NA	NA

SAT

Percent tested	NA
Average SAT math score	NA
Average SAT verbal score	NA

No Child Left Behind, 2003-04

Attendence rate (target = 90%)	95.8%
Drop rate	NA
Highly-qualified teachers	100%
District needs improvement?(AYP)	No

Municipal Finance

Fiscal Year 2005

Total tax levy	$9,075,113
County levy	1,373,793
County taxes	1,166,431
County library	97,599
County health	0
County open space	109,763
School levy	6,645,643
Local muni. budget	1,055,676
Misc. revenues	1,584,999
Total aid	$481,829
CMPTRA	289,434
Muni. block grant	17,004
Energy tax receipts	150,391
Homeland security	25,000

Fiscal Year 2006

Total aid	$481,829
CMPTRA	284,170
Muni. block grant	17,004
Energy tax receipts	155,655
Homeland security	25,000

Taxes

	2003	2004	2005
General tax rate per $100	3.55	3.790	2.390
Net valuation taxable	$227,782,200	$228,238,700	$381,159,200
State equalized value	$301,219,519	$330,494,390	$381,770,032
County equalization ratio	75.39	71.64	105.25

Demographics & Socio-Economic Characteristics
(2000 U.S. Census, except as noted)

Population
1980*	13,396
1990*	13,279
2000	13,999
Male	6,758
Female	7,241
2004 (estimate)*	14,172
Persons per sq. mi. of land	7,708

Race & Hispanic Origin, 2000
Race
White	10,087
Black/African American	1,111
Amer. Indian/Alaska Natv.	16
Asian	1,908
Natv. Hawaiian/Pac. Islander	12
Other Race	503
Two or more races	362
Hispanic origin, total	1,145
Mexican	247
Puerto Rican	287
Cuban	46
Other Hispanic	565

Age & Nativity, 2000
Under 5 years	836
18 years and over	10,955
21 years and over	10,579
65 years and over	1,672
85 years and over	220
Median Age	34.7
Native born	9,914
Foreign born	4,085

Educational Attainment, 2000
Population 25 years and over	9,801
0-8 yrs of school	2.3%
High School grad or higher	91.1%
Bachelor's degree or higher	59.5%
Graduate degree	35.2%

Income & Poverty, 1999
Per capita income	$28,767
Median household income	$53,250
Median family income	$71,267
Persons in poverty	1,181
H'holds receiving public assistance	141
H'holds receiving social security	1,279

Households, 2000
Total households	5,899
With persons under 18	1,729
With persons over 65	1,266
Family households	3,412
One-person households	1,857
Persons per household	2.37
Persons per family	3.06

Labor & Employment
Total civilian labor force, 2004**	8,792
Unemployment rate	4.7%
Total civilian labor force, 2000	7,846
Unemployment rate	3.8%

Employed persons 16 years and over by occupation, 2000
Managers & professionals	4,646
Service occupations	616
Sales & office occupations	1,502
Farming, fishing & forestry	0
Construction & maintenance	258
Production & transportation	526
Self-employed persons	318

*US Census Bureau
**New Jersey Department of Labor

General Information
Borough of Highland Park
PO Box 1330
221 So 5th Ave
Highland Park, NJ 08904
732-572-3400
Web site	www.hpboro.com
Land area (sq. miles)	1.84
Water area (sq. miles)	0
Type of government	Borough
Form of government	B

Government
Legislative Districts
US Congressional	6
State Legislative	17

Local Officials, 2006
Mayor	Meryl Frank
Admin/Manager	Nick Trasente
Clerk	Joan Hullings
Finance Dir/Treas	Nick Trasente
Engineer	David Samuel
Attorney	Daniel McCarthy
Tax assessor	Thomas Boyle
Tax collector	Jessica Miller
Building officer	Scott Luthman
Zoning officer	NA
Public Works	Donald Rish

Housing & Construction
Housing Units, 2000*
Total	6,071
Median rent	$848
Median SF home value	$183,300

New Privately Owned Housing Units
Authorized by Building Permit
	Units	Value
Total, 2004	67	$9,043,850
Single family	7	$843,850
Total, 2005	54	$7,703,716
Single family	8	$1,417,050

Real Property Valuation - parcels, 2005
	Number	Valuation
Total		$532,061,300
Vacant	77	3,243,500
Residential	2,829	389,950,600
Commercial	194	49,871,800
Industrial	10	5,026,400
Apartments	89	83,969,000
Farm land	0	0
Farm homestead	0	0

Average Property Value & Tax, 2005
Residential value	$137,840
Property tax	$7,428
FAIR rebate	$622

Public Library
Highland Park Public Library
31 N 5th Ave
Highland Park, NJ 08904
732-572-2750
Director	Jane Stanley

Library statistics, 2004
	Total	per capita
Volumes	65,570	4.68
Expenditure	$798,392	$57.03

Public Safety
Police
Chief	Francis Kinney
Number of officers, 2004	29

Crime, 2004	Number	Rate
Total	217	15.3
Violent	12	0.8
Non-violent	205	14.4
Domestic Viol.	56	NA

Emergency/Fire
Director	Jay Littman

Public School District
(for school year 2004-2005 except as noted)

Highland Park School District
435 Mansfield St
Highland Park, NJ 08904
732-572-6990
Superintendent	David Ottaviano
Grade plan	K-12
Enrollment	1,541.0
Students per teacher	10.5
Per pupil expenditure	$12,820
Median faculty salary	$53,306
Median administrator salary	$108,000
Grade 12 enrollment	97.0
High school graduation rate	100.0%

Assessment test results
(percent scoring at proficient or advanced level)
	Language	Math
Grade 3	88.6%	87.7%
Grade 8	74.0%	65.8%
High school	86.9%	81.3%

SAT
Percent tested	94%
Average SAT math score	595
Average SAT verbal score	557

No Child Left Behind, 2003-04
Attendance rate (target = 90%)	95.4%
Drop rate	0.4%
Highly-qualified teachers	100%
District needs improvement?(AYP)	No

Municipal Finance
Fiscal Year 2005
Total tax levy	$28,694,977
County levy	3,611,739
County taxes	3,271,733
County library	0
County health	0
County open space	340,006
School levy	17,774,311
Local muni. budget	7,308,928
Misc. revenues	5,211,044
Total aid	$1,407,270
CMPTRA	693,721
Muni. block grant	58,104
Energy tax receipts	585,445
Homeland security	70,000

Fiscal Year 2006
Total aid	$1,407,269
CMPTRA	673,230
Muni. block grant	58,104
Energy tax receipts	605,935
Homeland security	70,000

Taxes
	2003	2004	2005
General tax rate per $100	4.95	5.160	5.390
Net valuation taxable	$530,108,257	$531,097,561	$532,483,063
State equalized value	$1,070,493,249	$1,135,933,896	$1,274,492,731
County equalization ratio	62.44	53.18	46.73

Demographics & Socio-Economic Characteristics
(2000 U.S. Census, except as noted)

Population
1980*	5,187
1990*	4,849
2000	5,097
Male	2,554
Female	2,543
2000 (revised)	5,318
2004 (estimate)*	5,072
Persons per sq. mi. of land	6,656

Race & Hispanic Origin, 2000
Race
White	4,847
Black/African American	81
Amer. Indian/Alaska Natv.	17
Asian	51
Natv. Hawaiian/Pac. Islander	0
Other Race	30
Two or more races	71
Hispanic origin, total	207
Mexican	22
Puerto Rican	100
Cuban	21
Other Hispanic	64

Age & Nativity, 2000
Under 5 years	259
18 years and over	4,140
21 years and over	3,998
65 years and over	576
85 years and over	70
Median Age	38.6
Native born	4,789
Foreign born	308

Educational Attainment, 2000
Population 25 years and over	3,791
0-8 yrs of school	1.0%
High School grad or higher	87.9%
Bachelor's degree or higher	26.4%
Graduate degree	9.2%

Income & Poverty, 1999
Per capita income	$29,369
Median household income	$45,692
Median family income	$50,985
Persons in poverty	625
H'holds receiving public assistance	44
H'holds receiving social security	646

Households, 2000
Total households	2,450
With persons under 18	542
With persons over 65	450
Family households	1,194
One-person households	1,021
Persons per household	2.08
Persons per family	2.9

Labor & Employment
Total civilian labor force, 2004**	3,112
Unemployment rate	6.7%
Total civilian labor force, 2000	2,905
Unemployment rate	5.7%

Employed persons 16 years and over by occupation, 2000
Managers & professionals	955
Service occupations	454
Sales & office occupations	771
Farming, fishing & forestry	23
Construction & maintenance	293
Production & transportation	242
Self-employed persons	256

*US Census Bureau
**New Jersey Department of Labor

General Information
Borough of Highlands
171 Bay Ave
Highlands, NJ 07732
732-872-1224
Web site	www.highlandsnj.com
Land area (sq. miles)	0.76
Water area (sq. miles)	0.56
Type of government	Borough
Form of government	SM '50

Government

Legislative Districts
US Congressional	6
State Legislative	11

Local Officials, 2006
Mayor	Richard O'Neil
Admin/Manager	David Gilson
Clerk	Nina Light Flannery
Finance Dir/Treas	Stephen Pfeffer
Engineer	Robert Bucco
Attorney	Dominick Manco
Tax assessor	Charles Heck
Tax collector	Patrick DeBlaso
Building officer	Paul Reinhold
Zoning officer	NA
Public Works	NA

Housing & Construction

Housing Units, 2000*
Total	2,820
Median rent	$760
Median SF home value	$139,300

New Privately Owned Housing Units Authorized by Building Permit
	Units	Value
Total, 2004	13	$1,700,673
Single family	13	$1,700,673
Total, 2005	11	$1,634,642
Single family	11	$1,634,642

Real Property Valuation - parcels, 2005
	Number	Valuation
Total		$531,652,100
Vacant	159	6,848,500
Residential	2,239	470,561,400
Commercial	103	49,373,000
Industrial	0	0
Apartments	10	4,869,200
Farm land	0	0
Farm homestead	0	0

Average Property Value & Tax, 2005
Residential value	$210,166
Property tax	$5,006
FAIR rebate	$525

Public Library

No public municipal library.

Library statistics, 2004
	Total	per capita
Volumes	NA	NA
Expenditure	NA	NA

Public Safety

Police
Chief	Joseph Blewett
Number of officers, 2004	13

Crime, 2004	Number	Rate
Total	100	18.6
Violent	12	2.2
Non-violent	88	16.4
Domestic Viol.	111	NA

Emergency/Fire
Director	NA

Public School District
(for school year 2004-2005 except as noted)

Highlands Borough School District
360 Navesink Ave
Highlands, NJ 07732
732-872-1476
Superintendent	Maryann Galassetti
Grade plan	K-6
Enrollment	240.0
Students per teacher	8.3
Per pupil expenditure	$13,071
Median faculty salary	$40,770
Median administrator salary	$98,404
Grade 12 enrollment	NA
High school graduation rate	NA

Assessment test results
(percent scoring at proficient or advanced level)
	Language	Math
Grade 3	82.4%	82.3%
Grade 8	NA	NA
High school	NA	NA

SAT
Percent tested	NA
Average SAT math score	NA
Average SAT verbal score	NA

No Child Left Behind, 2003-04
Attendance rate (target = 90%)	94.0%
Drop rate	NA
Highly-qualified teachers	84.4%
District needs improvement?(AYP)	No

Municipal Finance

Fiscal Year 2005
Total tax levy	$12,673,639
County levy	1,806,809
County taxes	1,621,287
County library	89,328
County health	0
County open space	96,194
School levy	6,275,903
Local muni. budget	4,590,926
Misc. revenues	2,371,017
Total aid	$569,811
CMPTRA	223,997
Muni. block grant	21,218
Energy tax receipts	274,596
Homeland security	50,000

Fiscal Year 2006
Total aid	$569,811
CMPTRA	214,386
Muni. block grant	21,218
Energy tax receipts	284,207
Homeland security	50,000

Taxes
	2003	2004	2005
General tax rate per $100	5.18	2.245	2.382
Net valuation taxable	$230,157,679	$533,295,363	$532,068,848
State equalized value	$448,737,920	$544,669,813	$636,522,129
County equalization ratio	61.73	117.95	97.91

Demographics & Socio-Economic Characteristics
(2000 U.S. Census, except as noted)

Population
1980*	4,581
1990*	5,126
2000	5,216
Male	2,651
Female	2,565
2004 (estimate)*	5,326
Persons per sq. mi. of land	4,342

Race & Hispanic Origin, 2000
Race
White	3,992
Black/African American	444
Amer. Indian/Alaska Natv.	19
Asian	119
Natv. Hawaiian/Pac. Islander	4
Other Race	503
Two or more races	135
Hispanic origin, total	1,046
Mexican	69
Puerto Rican	135
Cuban	12
Other Hispanic	830

Age & Nativity, 2000
Under 5 years	379
18 years and over	4,042
21 years and over	3,873
65 years and over	562
85 years and over	141
Median Age	35.5
Native born	4,115
Foreign born	1,101

Educational Attainment, 2000
Population 25 years and over	3,671
0-8 yrs of school	8.0%
High School grad or higher	82.1%
Bachelor's degree or higher	39.5%
Graduate degree	17.4%

Income & Poverty, 1999
Per capita income	$28,605
Median household income	$64,299
Median family income	$72,092
Persons in poverty	380
H'holds receiving public assistance	25
H'holds receiving social security	426

Households, 2000
Total households	2,001
With persons under 18	658
With persons over 65	423
Family households	1,300
One-person households	559
Persons per household	2.6
Persons per family	3.15

Labor & Employment
Total civilian labor force, 2004**	3,417
Unemployment rate	4.5%
Total civilian labor force, 2000	3,076
Unemployment rate	3.0%

Employed persons 16 years and over by occupation, 2000
Managers & professionals	1,257
Service occupations	405
Sales & office occupations	690
Farming, fishing & forestry	15
Construction & maintenance	207
Production & transportation	411
Self-employed persons	100

*US Census Bureau
**New Jersey Department of Labor

General Information
Borough of Hightstown
148 N Main St
Hightstown, NJ 08520
609-490-5100
Web site	www.hightstownborough.com
Land area (sq. miles)	1.23
Water area (sq. miles)	0.02
Type of government	Borough
Form of government	B

Government

Legislative Districts
US Congressional	4
State Legislative	12

Local Officials, 2006
Mayor	Robert Patten
Admin/Manager	Candace Gallagher
Clerk	Candace Gallagher
Finance Dir/Treas	Arlene O'Rourke
Engineer	Carmela Roberts
Attorney	Fred Raffetto
Tax assessor	Ken Pacera
Tax collector	Nancy Martin
Building officer	Harry Wetterskog
Zoning officer	Harry Wetterskog
Public Works	Larry Blake

Housing & Construction

Housing Units, 2000*
Total	2,081
Median rent	$820
Median SF home value	$141,300

New Privately Owned Housing Units Authorized by Building Permit
	Units	Value
Total, 2004	7	$707,078
Single family	7	$707,078
Total, 2005	10	$1,434,700
Single family	10	$1,434,700

Real Property Valuation - parcels, 2005
	Number	Valuation
Total		$212,848,200
Vacant	68	1,865,600
Residential	1,375	162,761,600
Commercial	98	37,727,100
Industrial	8	2,997,400
Apartments	5	7,492,000
Farm land	0	0
Farm homestead	1	4,500

Average Property Value & Tax, 2005
Residential value	$118,289
Property tax	$6,280
FAIR rebate	$510

Public Library
Hightstown Mem Library†
114 Franklin St
Hightstown, NJ 08520
609-448-1474
Branch Librarian .... Linda Chorewiak

Library statistics, 2004
	Total	per capita
Volumes	NA	NA
Expenditure	NA	NA

†Branch of County Library

Public Safety
Police
Chief	James Eufemia
Number of officers, 2004	13

Crime, 2004	Number	Rate
Total	111	20.9
Violent	16	3
Non-violent	95	17.9
Domestic Viol.	45	NA

Emergency/Fire
Director	John Archer

Public School District
(for school year 2004-2005 except as noted)

East Windsor Regional School District
384 Stockton St
Hightstown, NJ 08520
609-443-7704
Superintendent	Ronald Bolandi
Grade plan	K-12
Enrollment	4,884.0
Students per teacher	11.7
Per pupil expenditure	$12,424
Median faculty salary	$64,685
Median administrator salary	$99,282
Grade 12 enrollment	270.5
High school graduation rate	90.5%

Assessment test results
(percent scoring at proficient or advanced level)
	Language	Math
Grade 3	89.5%	87.8%
Grade 8	80.4%	71.0%
High school	81.1%	74.5%

SAT
Percent tested	81%
Average SAT math score	535
Average SAT verbal score	525

No Child Left Behind, 2003-04
Attendance rate (target = 90%)	95.2%
Drop rate	1.7%
Highly-qualified teachers	96.9%
District needs improvement?(AYP)	No

Municipal Finance

Fiscal Year 2005
Total tax levy	$11,428,845
County levy	2,204,657
County taxes	1,925,745
County library	170,750
County health	0
County open space	108,161
School levy	6,802,260
Local muni. budget	2,421,929
Misc. revenues	2,381,096
Total aid	$815,483
CMPTRA	443,234
Muni. block grant	22,430
Energy tax receipts	299,819
Homeland security	50,000

Fiscal Year 2006
Total aid	$815,484
CMPTRA	432,741
Muni. block grant	22,430
Energy tax receipts	310,313
Homeland security	50,000

Taxes
	2003	2004	2005
General tax rate per $100	4.77	5.030	5.310
Net valuation taxable	$213,731,490	$215,431,591	$215,287,797
State equalized value	$321,739,410	$358,069,242	$421,719,485
County equalization ratio	74.11	66.43	59.87

Demographics & Socio-Economic Characteristics
(2000 U.S. Census, except as noted)

Population
1980*	19,061
1990*	28,808
2000	36,634
Male	18,091
Female	18,543
2004 (estimate)*	37,851
Persons per sq. mi. of land	692

Race & Hispanic Origin, 2000
Race
White	31,491
Black/African American	1,379
Amer. Indian/Alaska Natv.	32
Asian	2,679
Natv. Hawaiian/Pac. Islander	23
Other Race	468
Two or more races	562
Hispanic origin, total	1,740
Mexican	203
Puerto Rican	436
Cuban	133
Other Hispanic	968

Age & Nativity, 2000
Under 5 years	2,898
18 years and over	25,963
21 years and over	24,938
65 years and over	2,508
85 years and over	257
Median Age	35.7
Native born	32,233
Foreign born	4,421

Educational Attainment, 2000
Population 25 years and over	23,743
0-8 yrs of school	2.6%
High School grad or higher	92.7%
Bachelor's degree or higher	46.6%
Graduate degree	16.2%

Income & Poverty, 1999
Per capita income	$33,091
Median household income	$83,290
Median family income	$93,933
Persons in poverty	1,140
H'holds receiving public assistance	87
H'holds receiving social security	1,867

Households, 2000
Total households	12,649
With persons under 18	5,843
With persons over 65	1,740
Family households	9,797
One-person households	2,249
Persons per household	2.88
Persons per family	3.31

Labor & Employment
Total civilian labor force, 2004**	20,936
Unemployment rate	3.7%
Total civilian labor force, 2000	20,181
Unemployment rate	2.0%

Employed persons 16 years and over by occupation, 2000
Managers & professionals	10,534
Service occupations	1,632
Sales & office occupations	5,063
Farming, fishing & forestry	92
Construction & maintenance	1,133
Production & transportation	1,326
Self-employed persons	862

*US Census Bureau
**New Jersey Department of Labor

General Information
Township of Hillsborough
379 South Branch Rd
Hillsborough, NJ 08844
908-369-4313
Web site	www.hillsborough-nj.org
Land area (sq. miles)	54.69
Water area (sq. miles)	0.10
Type of government	Township
Form of government	TC

Government
Legislative Districts
US Congressional	7
State Legislative	16

Local Officials, 2006
Mayor	Carl Suraci
Admin/Manager	Kevin Davis
Clerk	Kevin Davis
Finance Dir/Treas	Ronald Zilinski
Engineer	Maser Consulting
Attorney	Albert Cruz
Tax assessor	Debra Blaney
Tax collector	NA
Building officer	Ron Skobo
Zoning officer	NA
Public Works	Buck Sixt

Housing & Construction
Housing Units, 2000*
Total	12,854
Median rent	$931
Median SF home value	$238,600

New Privately Owned Housing Units
Authorized by Building Permit
	Units	Value
Total, 2004	4	$2,209,685
Single family	4	$2,209,685
Total, 2005	15	$15,067,622
Single family	15	$15,067,622

Real Property Valuation - parcels, 2005
	Number	Valuation
Total		$3,593,264,390
Vacant	719	44,270,900
Residential	11,998	3,031,272,600
Commercial	340	278,193,000
Industrial	118	131,960,700
Apartments	9	42,254,100
Farm land	185	61,748,300
Farm homestead	358	3,564,790

Average Property Value & Tax, 2005
Residential value	$245,616
Property tax	$6,711
FAIR rebate	$463

Public Library
Hillsborough Branch Library†
379 S Branch Rd
Hillsborough, NJ 08844
908-369-2200
Branch Librarian	Edward Hoag

Library statistics, 2004
	Total	per capita
Volumes	NA	NA
Expenditure	NA	NA

†Branch of County Library

Public Safety
Police
Chief	Robert Gazaway
Number of officers, 2004	54

Crime, 2004	Number	Rate
Total	376	10
Violent	19	0.5
Non-violent	357	9.5
Domestic Viol.	396	NA

Emergency/Fire
Director	NA

Public School District
(for school year 2004-2005 except as noted)

Hillsborough Township School District
379 S Branch Rd
Hillsborough, NJ 08844
908-369-0030
Superintendent	Karen Lake
Grade plan	K-12
Enrollment	7,669.0
Students per teacher	10.7
Per pupil expenditure	$10,683
Median faculty salary	$53,000
Median administrator salary	$99,769
Grade 12 enrollment	517.0
High school graduation rate	97.9%

Assessment test results
(percent scoring at proficient or advanced level)
	Language	Math
Grade 3	91.4%	88.9%
Grade 8	88.6%	76.7%
High school	95.5%	89.8%

SAT
Percent tested	85%
Average SAT math score	566
Average SAT verbal score	537

No Child Left Behind, 2003-04
Attendence rate (target = 90%)	96.0%
Drop rate	0.6%
Highly-qualified teachers	99.1%
District needs improvement?(AYP)	No

Municipal Finance
Fiscal Year 2005
Total tax levy	$98,460,466
County levy	17,849,924
County taxes	14,788,617
County library	1,639,279
County health	0
County open space	1,422,027
School levy	66,210,250
Local muni. budget	14,400,293
Misc. revenues	10,570,596
Total aid	$4,494,401
CMPTRA	1,326,030
Muni. block grant	143,643
Energy tax receipts	2,884,728
Homeland security	140,000

Fiscal Year 2006
Total aid	$4,494,401
CMPTRA	1,225,064
Muni. block grant	143,643
Energy tax receipts	2,985,694
Homeland security	140,000

Taxes
	2003	2004	2005
General tax rate per $100	2.47	2.590	2.740
Net valuation taxable	$3,532,030,470	$3,582,026,890	$3,603,640,564
State equalized value	$4,126,685,910	$4,703,296,929	$5,141,447,516
County equalization ratio	93.66	85.59	76.10

Demographics & Socio-Economic Characteristics
(2000 U.S. Census, except as noted)

Population
1980*	10,495
1990*	9,750
2000	10,087
Male	4,915
Female	5,172
2004 (estimate)*	10,138
Persons per sq. mi. of land	3,400

Race & Hispanic Origin, 2000
Race
White	9,321
Black/African American	86
Amer. Indian/Alaska Natv.	7
Asian	512
Natv. Hawaiian/Pac. Islander	4
Other Race	87
Two or more races	70
Hispanic origin, total	429
Mexican	76
Puerto Rican	70
Cuban	55
Other Hispanic	228

Age & Nativity, 2000
Under 5 years	736
18 years and over	7,465
21 years and over	7,235
65 years and over	1,493
85 years and over	146
Median Age	39.5
Native born	8,744
Foreign born	1,343

Educational Attainment, 2000
Population 25 years and over	6,903
0-8 yrs of school	2.4%
High School grad or higher	92.4%
Bachelor's degree or higher	45.8%
Graduate degree	17.0%

Income & Poverty, 1999
Per capita income	$34,651
Median household income	$82,904
Median family income	$90,861
Persons in poverty	334
H'holds receiving public assistance	51
H'holds receiving social security	1,021

Households, 2000
Total households	3,502
With persons under 18	1,405
With persons over 65	1,041
Family households	2,849
One-person households	551
Persons per household	2.87
Persons per family	3.2

Labor & Employment
Total civilian labor force, 2004**	5,523
Unemployment rate	3.7%
Total civilian labor force, 2000	5,207
Unemployment rate	2.8%

Employed persons 16 years and over by occupation, 2000
Managers & professionals	2,326
Service occupations	553
Sales & office occupations	1,612
Farming, fishing & forestry	0
Construction & maintenance	382
Production & transportation	186
Self-employed persons	348

*US Census Bureau
**New Jersey Department of Labor

General Information
Borough of Hillsdale
380 Hillsdale Ave
Hillsdale, NJ 07642
201-666-4800

Web site	www.hillsdalenj.org
Land area (sq. miles)	2.98
Water area (sq. miles)	0
Type of government	Borough
Form of government	B

Government
Legislative Districts
US Congressional	5
State Legislative	39

Local Officials, 2006
Mayor	Dennis S. Deutsch
Admin/Manager	Harold Karns
Clerk	Robert Sandt
Finance Dir/Treas	Colleen Ennis
Engineer	Christopher Statile
Attorney	Harold Ritvo
Tax assessor	Richard Mohr
Tax collector	Colleen Ennis
Building officer	Keith Durie
Zoning officer	NA
Public Works	NA

Housing & Construction
Housing Units, 2000*
Total	3,547
Median rent	$926
Median SF home value	$291,800

New Privately Owned Housing Units
Authorized by Building Permit
	Units	Value
Total, 2004	6	$2,075,031
Single family	6	$2,075,031
Total, 2005	13	$4,668,380
Single family	13	$4,668,380

Real Property Valuation - parcels, 2005
	Number	Valuation
Total		$843,681,900
Vacant	89	7,840,800
Residential	3,285	776,463,400
Commercial	97	50,529,000
Industrial	12	7,490,000
Apartments	2	950,100
Farm land	2	396,200
Farm homestead	2	12,400

Average Property Value & Tax, 2005
Residential value	$236,226
Property tax	$8,297
FAIR rebate	$569

Public Library
Hillsdale Public Library
509 Hillsdale Ave
Hillsdale, NJ 07642
201-358-5072

Director	David Franz

Library statistics, 2004
	Total	per capita
Volumes	50,725	5.03
Expenditure	$515,881	$51.14

Public Safety
Police
Chief	Frank Mikulski
Number of officers, 2004	20

Crime, 2004	Number	Rate
Total	67	6.6
Violent	9	0.9
Non-violent	58	5.7
Domestic Viol.	24	NA

Emergency/Fire
Director	Max Arnowitz

Public School District
(for school year 2004-2005 except as noted)

Hillsdale School District
32 Ruckman Rd
Hillsdale, NJ 07642
201-664-0282

Superintendent	Anthony DeNorchia
Grade plan	K-8
Enrollment	1,379.0
Students per teacher	12.4
Per pupil expenditure	$10,641
Median faculty salary	$49,884
Median administrator salary	$114,506
Grade 12 enrollment	NA
High school graduation rate	NA

Assessment test results
(percent scoring at proficient or advanced level)
	Language	Math
Grade 3	97.8%	91.2%
Grade 8	92.5%	85.9%
High school	NA	NA

SAT
Percent tested	NA
Average SAT math score	NA
Average SAT verbal score	NA

No Child Left Behind, 2003-04
Attendence rate (target = 90%)	96.4%
Drop rate	NA
Highly-qualified teachers	99.5%
District needs improvement?(AYP)	No

Municipal Finance
Fiscal Year 2005
Total tax levy	$29,761,767
County levy	3,070,101
County taxes	2,916,567
County library	0
County health	0
County open space	153,534
School levy	21,285,606
Local muni. budget	5,406,061
Misc. revenues	4,503,629
Total aid	$1,641,273
CMPTRA	423,381
Muni. block grant	42,663
Energy tax receipts	1,102,926
Homeland security	70,000

Fiscal Year 2006
Total aid	$1,641,274
CMPTRA	384,779
Muni. block grant	42,663
Energy tax receipts	1,141,529
Homeland security	70,000

Taxes
	2003	2004	2005
General tax rate per $100	3.02	3.260	3.520
Net valuation taxable	$837,609,166	$844,171,530	$847,398,387
State equalized value	$1,366,409,732	$1,525,692,227	$1,743,618,080
County equalization ratio	67.89	61.30	55.21

Demographics & Socio-Economic Characteristics

(2000 U.S. Census, except as noted)

Population

1980*	21,440
1990*	21,044
2000	21,747
Male	10,199
Female	11,548
2004 (estimate)*	21,891
Persons per sq. mi. of land	7,845

Race & Hispanic Origin, 2000

Race

White	8,705
Black/African American	10,122
Amer. Indian/Alaska Natv.	50
Asian	751
Natv. Hawaiian/Pac. Islander	17
Other Race	1,144
Two or more races	958
Hispanic origin, total	3,153
Mexican	56
Puerto Rican	832
Cuban	402
Other Hispanic	1,863

Age & Nativity, 2000

Under 5 years	1,390
18 years and over	16,185
21 years and over	15,321
65 years and over	2,410
85 years and over	253
Median Age	35.7
Native born	15,788
Foreign born	5,959

Educational Attainment, 2000

Population 25 years and over	14,279
0-8 yrs of school	10.0%
High School grad or higher	76.1%
Bachelor's degree or higher	18.5%
Graduate degree	5.6%

Income & Poverty, 1999

Per capita income	$21,724
Median household income	$59,136
Median family income	$64,635
Persons in poverty	1,147
H'holds receiving public assistance	279
H'holds receiving social security	1,849

Households, 2000

Total households	7,161
With persons under 18	3,081
With persons over 65	1,808
Family households	5,579
One-person households	1,288
Persons per household	3.04
Persons per family	3.45

Labor & Employment

Total civilian labor force, 2004**	12,032
Unemployment rate	5.3%
Total civilian labor force, 2000	11,436
Unemployment rate	7.0%

Employed persons 16 years and over by occupation, 2000

Managers & professionals	2,935
Service occupations	1,567
Sales & office occupations	3,210
Farming, fishing & forestry	9
Construction & maintenance	969
Production & transportation	1,943
Self-employed persons	295

*US Census Bureau
**New Jersey Department of Labor

General Information

Township of Hillside
Liberty & Hillside Aves
Hillside, NJ 07205
973-926-3000

Web site	NA
Land area (sq. miles)	2.79
Water area (sq. miles)	0
Type of government	Township
Form of government	OMCL

Government

Legislative Districts

US Congressional	10
State Legislative	29

Local Officials, 2006

Mayor	Karen McCoy Oliver
Admin/Manager	NA
Clerk	Janet Vlaisavljevic
Finance Dir/Treas	Gene Leporiere
Engineer	Victor Vinegra
Attorney	Dwayne Warren
Tax assessor	Benard Murdoch
Tax collector	Joe Skelly
Building officer	Larry Ditzel
Zoning officer	NA
Public Works	Scott Anderson

Housing & Construction

Housing Units, 2000*

Total	7,388
Median rent	$797
Median SF home value	$135,200

New Privately Owned Housing Units Authorized by Building Permit

	Units	Value
Total, 2004	11	$942,450
Single family	3	$434,100
Total, 2005	40	$3,625,726
Single family	16	$1,931,650

Real Property Valuation - parcels, 2005

	Number	Valuation
Total		$910,517,427
Vacant	181	7,100,600
Residential	5,616	684,988,294
Commercial	267	71,783,900
Industrial	179	135,813,333
Apartments	21	10,831,300
Farm land	0	0
Farm homestead	0	0

Average Property Value & Tax, 2005

Residential value	$121,971
Property tax	$6,297
FAIR rebate	$597

Public Library

Hillside Free Public Library
JFK Plaza & Liberty Ave
Hillside, NJ 07205
973-923-4413

Director ... Joyce Goldberg

Library statistics, 2004

	Total	per capita
Volumes	126,366	5.81
Expenditure	$773,254	$35.56

Public Safety

Police

Chief	Robert Quinlan
Number of officers, 2004	76

Crime, 2004	Number	Rate
Total	921	42.1
Violent	121	5.5
Non-violent	800	36.5
Domestic Viol.	325	NA

Emergency/Fire

Director ... Robert Kreszl

Public School District

(for school year 2004-2005 except as noted)

Hillside Township School District
195 Virginia St
Hillside, NJ 07205
908-352-7664

Superintendent	Raymond Bandlow
Grade plan	K-12
Enrollment	3,427.0
Students per teacher	14.6
Per pupil expenditure	$11,830
Median faculty salary	$56,368
Median administrator salary	$108,247
Grade 12 enrollment	211.5
High school graduation rate	79.3%

Assessment test results

(percent scoring at proficient or advanced level)

	Language	Math
Grade 3	74.4%	71.9%
Grade 8	54.5%	27.2%
High school	71.3%	53.7%

SAT

Percent tested	69%
Average SAT math score	408
Average SAT verbal score	406

No Child Left Behind, 2003-04

Attendence rate (target = 90%)	93.8%
Drop rate	5%
Highly-qualified teachers	98.1%
District needs improvement?(AYP)	No

Municipal Finance

Fiscal Year 2005

Total tax levy	$47,050,077
County levy	6,077,156
County taxes	5,834,811
County library	0
County health	0
County open space	242,345
School levy	22,913,283
Local muni. budget	18,059,638
Misc. revenues	15,679,219
Total aid	$5,568,314
CMPTRA	3,711,478
Muni. block grant	92,082
Energy tax receipts	1,674,754
Homeland security	90,000

Fiscal Year 2006

Total aid	$5,568,314
CMPTRA	3,652,861
Muni. block grant	92,082
Energy tax receipts	1,733,371
Homeland security	90,000

Taxes

	2003	2004	2005
General tax rate per $100	4.66	5.061	5.163
Net valuation taxable	$907,889,854	$911,218,354	$911,322,839
State equalized value	$1,354,655,109	$1,498,602,188	$1,741,492,144
County equalization ratio	73.88	63.14	57.47

Demographics & Socio-Economic Characteristics
(2000 U.S. Census, except as noted)

Population
1980*	1,250
1990*	1,045
2000	1,029
Male	485
Female	544
2004 (estimate)*	1,019
Persons per sq. mi. of land	4,493

Race & Hispanic Origin, 2000
Race
White	731
Black/African American	198
Amer. Indian/Alaska Natv.	0
Asian	32
Natv. Hawaiian/Pac. Islander	0
Other Race	45
Two or more races	23
Hispanic origin, total	71
Mexican	12
Puerto Rican	42
Cuban	5
Other Hispanic	12

Age & Nativity, 2000
Under 5 years	78
18 years and over	772
21 years and over	735
65 years and over	141
85 years and over	11
Median Age	31.8
Native born	965
Foreign born	68

Educational Attainment, 2000
Population 25 years and over	696
0-8 yrs of school	2.4%
High School grad or higher	79.2%
Bachelor's degree or higher	13.8%
Graduate degree	3.9%

Income & Poverty, 1999
Per capita income	$19,285
Median household income	$34,948
Median family income	$38,393
Persons in poverty	126
H'holds receiving public assistance	12
H'holds receiving social security	112

Households, 2000
Total households	472
With persons under 18	142
With persons over 65	105
Family households	260
One-person households	172
Persons per household	2.18
Persons per family	2.83

Labor & Employment
Total civilian labor force, 2004**	605
Unemployment rate	6.3%
Total civilian labor force, 2000	539
Unemployment rate	8.2%

Employed persons 16 years and over by occupation, 2000
Managers & professionals	117
Service occupations	73
Sales & office occupations	190
Farming, fishing & forestry	0
Construction & maintenance	40
Production & transportation	75
Self-employed persons	9

*US Census Bureau
**New Jersey Department of Labor

General Information
Borough of Hi-Nella
100 Wykagyl Rd
Hi-Nella, NJ 08083
856-784-6237

Web site	NA
Land area (sq. miles)	0.23
Water area (sq. miles)	0
Type of government	Borough
Form of government	B

Government

Legislative Districts
US Congressional	1
State Legislative	5

Local Officials, 2006
Mayor	Irene Wolick
Admin/Manager	NA
Clerk	Phyllis Twisler (Actg.)
Finance Dir/Treas	William Hales Jr
Engineer	Churchill Consulting
Attorney	Robert Messick
Tax assessor	Richard Arrowood
Tax collector	Janice Gattone
Building officer	DCA
Zoning officer	NA
Public Works	NA

Housing & Construction

Housing Units, 2000*
Total	495
Median rent	$650
Median SF home value	$96,700

New Privately Owned Housing Units Authorized by Building Permit
	Units	Value
Total, 2004	0	$0
Single family	0	$0
Total, 2005	0	$0
Single family	0	$0

Real Property Valuation - parcels, 2005
	Number	Valuation
Total		$23,087,700
Vacant	3	96,000
Residential	126	11,709,400
Commercial	12	5,025,800
Industrial	0	0
Apartments	2	6,104,900
Farm land	1	140,000
Farm homestead	1	11,600

Average Property Value & Tax, 2005
Residential value	$92,291
Property tax	$5,046
FAIR rebate	$698

Public Library

No public municipal library.

Library statistics, 2004
	Total	per capita
Volumes	NA	NA
Expenditure	NA	NA

Public Safety

Police
Chief	Dominic Palese
Number of officers, 2004	5

Crime, 2004	Number	Rate
Total	46	44.9
Violent	6	5.9
Non-violent	40	39
Domestic Viol.	3	NA

Emergency/Fire
Director	Brian Cunningham

Public School District
(for school year 2004-2005 except as noted)

Hi Nella School District†
501 S Warwick Rd
Somerdale, NJ 08083

†No schools in district - sends children to Oaklyn schools.

Grade plan	NA
Enrollment	NA
Students per teacher	NA
Per pupil expenditure	NA
Median faculty salary	NA

Assessment test results
(percent scoring at proficient or advanced level)
	Language	Math
Grade 3	NA	NA
Grade 8	NA	NA
High school	NA	NA

SAT
Percent tested	NA
Average SAT math score	NA
Average SAT verbal score	NA

No Child Left Behind, 2003-04
Attendence rate (target = 90%)	NA
Drop rate	NA
Highly-qualified teachers	NA
District needs improvement?(AYP)	NA

Municipal Finance

Fiscal Year 2005
Total tax levy	$1,304,343
County levy	260,359
County taxes	239,759
County library	17,423
County health	0
County open space	3,177
School levy	787,488
Local muni. budget	256,496
Misc. revenues	575,926
Total aid	$113,711
CMPTRA	52,872
Muni. block grant	4,573
Energy tax receipts	56,266
Homeland security	0

Fiscal Year 2006
Total aid	$113,710
CMPTRA	50,902
Muni. block grant	4,573
Energy tax receipts	58,235
Homeland security	NA

Taxes
	2003	2004	2005
General tax rate per $100	5.57	5.441	5.636
Net valuation taxable	$23,468,965	$23,195,607	$23,147,047
State equalized value	$28,603,248	$31,674,760	$35,594,413
County equalization ratio	89.48	82.05	73.17

Demographics & Socio-Economic Characteristics
(2000 U.S. Census, except as noted)

Population
1980*	42,460
1990*	33,397
2000	38,577
Male	19,654
Female	18,923
2004 (estimate)*	40,175
Persons per sq. mi. of land	31,492

Race & Hispanic Origin, 2000
Race
White	31,178
Black/African American	1,644
Amer. Indian/Alaska Natv.	60
Asian	1,661
Natv. Hawaiian/Pac. Islander	21
Other Race	2,942
Two or more races	1,071
Hispanic origin, total	7,783
Mexican	359
Puerto Rican	4,660
Cuban	560
Other Hispanic	2,204

Age & Nativity, 2000
Under 5 years	1,232
18 years and over	34,543
21 years and over	33,399
65 years and over	3,483
85 years and over	392
Median Age	30.4
Native born	33,081
Foreign born	5,588

Educational Attainment, 2000
Population 25 years and over	28,637
0-8 yrs of school	8.4%
High School grad or higher	83.3%
Bachelor's degree or higher	59.4%
Graduate degree	18.7%

Income & Poverty, 1999
Per capita income	$43,195
Median household income	$62,550
Median family income	$67,500
Persons in poverty	4,124
H'holds receiving public assistance	472
H'holds receiving social security	3,118

Households, 2000
Total households	19,418
With persons under 18	2,498
With persons over 65	2,819
Family households	6,842
One-person households	8,126
Persons per household	1.92
Persons per family	2.73

Labor & Employment
Total civilian labor force, 2004**	20,967
Unemployment rate	4.1%
Total civilian labor force, 2000	26,850
Unemployment rate	4.4%

Employed persons 16 years and over by occupation, 2000
Managers & professionals	15,655
Service occupations	1,687
Sales & office occupations	6,635
Farming, fishing & forestry	5
Construction & maintenance	495
Production & transportation	1,184
Self-employed persons	852

*US Census Bureau
**New Jersey Department of Labor

General Information
City of Hoboken
94 Washington St
Hoboken, NJ 07030
201-420-2000
Web site	www.hobokennj.org
Land area (sq. miles)	1.28
Water area (sq. miles)	0.70
Type of government	City
Form of government	MC '50

Government

Legislative Districts
US Congressional	13
State Legislative	33

Local Officials, 2006
Mayor	David Roberts
Admin/Manager	Richdrs England
Clerk	James J. Farina
Finance Dir/Treas	Louis Piccardo (Actg)
Engineer	Ralph Tango
Attorney	Joseph Sherman
Tax assessor	Sal Bonaccorsi
Tax collector	NA
Building officer	Alfred N. Arezzo
Zoning officer	NA
Public Works	NA

Housing & Construction

Housing Units, 2000*
Total	19,915
Median rent	$1,002
Median SF home value	$428,900

New Privately Owned Housing Units Authorized by Building Permit
	Units	Value
Total, 2004	272	$26,454,032
Single family	44	$7,138,307
Total, 2005	476	$95,698,487
Single family	21	$3,074,959

Real Property Valuation - parcels, 2005
	Number	Valuation
Total		$2,579,785,200
Vacant	334	53,724,200
Residential	9,713	1,588,634,900
Commercial	963	464,629,900
Industrial	55	52,450,400
Apartments	399	420,345,800
Farm land	0	0
Farm homestead	0	0

Average Property Value & Tax, 2005
Residential value	$163,558
Property tax	$5,375
FAIR rebate	$433

Public Library
Hoboken Public Library
500 Park Ave
Hoboken, NJ 07030
201-420-2281
Director	Lina Podles

Library statistics, 2004
	Total	per capita
Volumes	78,919	2.05
Expenditure	$1,323,063	$34.30

Public Safety

Police
Chief	Carmen LaBruno
Number of officers, 2004	167

Crime, 2004	Number	Rate
Total	1,640	41.5
Violent	153	3.9
Non-violent	1,487	37.7
Domestic Viol.	130	NA

Emergency/Fire
Director	John Cassesa

Public School District
(for school year 2004-2005 except as noted)

Hoboken School District
1115 Clinton St
Hoboken, NJ 07030
201-356-3601
Superintendent	Patrick Gagliardi
Grade plan	K-12
Enrollment	2,014.0
Students per teacher	8.7
Per pupil expenditure	$14,498
Median faculty salary	$77,320
Median administrator salary	$116,996
Grade 12 enrollment	151.0
High school graduation rate	88.6%

Assessment test results
(percent scoring at proficient or advanced level)
	Language	Math
Grade 3	67.1%	54.8%
Grade 8	84.7%	71.2%
High school	76.7%	73.3%

SAT
Percent tested	39%
Average SAT math score	454
Average SAT verbal score	427

No Child Left Behind, 2003-04
Attendance rate (target = 90%)	90.8%
Drop rate	2.7%
Highly-qualified teachers	97.7%
District needs improvement?(AYP)	No

Municipal Finance

Fiscal Year 2005
Total tax levy	$84,838,995
County levy	32,103,595
County taxes	31,493,369
County library	0
County health	0
County open space	610,226
School levy	31,235,400
Local muni. budget	21,500,000
Misc. revenues	51,893,713
Total aid	$15,721,335
CMPTRA	13,423,836
Muni. block grant	151,261
Energy tax receipts	2,006,238
Homeland security	140,000

Fiscal Year 2006
Total aid	$15,721,336
CMPTRA	13,353,618
Muni. block grant	151,261
Energy tax receipts	2,076,457
Homeland security	140,000

Taxes
	2003	2004	2005
General tax rate per $100	3.24	3.216	3.287
Net valuation taxable	$2,341,208,216	$2,427,704,862	$2,581,437,395
State equalized value	$4,730,669,258	$5,622,446,580	$6,791,469,074
County equalization ratio	53.33	49.49	43.16

Demographics & Socio-Economic Characteristics
(2000 U.S. Census, except as noted)

Population
1980*	4,129
1990*	3,935
2000	4,060
Male	1,944
Female	2,116
2004 (estimate)*	4,095
Persons per sq. mi. of land	2,351

Race & Hispanic Origin, 2000
Race
White	3,762
Black/African American	24
Amer. Indian/Alaska Natv.	4
Asian	212
Natv. Hawaiian/Pac. Islander	8
Other Race	15
Two or more races	35
Hispanic origin, total	80
Mexican	5
Puerto Rican	16
Cuban	21
Other Hispanic	38

Age & Nativity, 2000
Under 5 years	343
18 years and over	2,942
21 years and over	2,877
65 years and over	618
85 years and over	58
Median Age	41.1
Native born	3,700
Foreign born	360

Educational Attainment, 2000
Population 25 years and over	2,776
0-8 yrs of school	1.3%
High School grad or higher	97.7%
Bachelor's degree or higher	68.3%
Graduate degree	22.6%

Income & Poverty, 1999
Per capita income	$63,594
Median household income	$129,900
Median family income	$144,588
Persons in poverty	83
H'holds receiving public assistance	0
H'holds receiving social security	381

Households, 2000
Total households	1,433
With persons under 18	574
With persons over 65	416
Family households	1,199
One-person households	209
Persons per household	2.82
Persons per family	3.11

Labor & Employment
Total civilian labor force, 2004**	2,180
Unemployment rate	1.9%
Total civilian labor force, 2000	1,915
Unemployment rate	0.3%

Employed persons 16 years and over by occupation, 2000
Managers & professionals	1,175
Service occupations	81
Sales & office occupations	524
Farming, fishing & forestry	0
Construction & maintenance	62
Production & transportation	67
Self-employed persons	151

*US Census Bureau
**New Jersey Department of Labor

General Information
Borough of Ho-Ho-Kus
333 Warren Ave
Ho-Ho-Kus, NJ 07423
201-652-4400
Web site	www.ho-ho-kusboro.com
Land area (sq. miles)	1.74
Water area (sq. miles)	0.01
Type of government	Borough
Form of government	B

Government

Legislative Districts
US Congressional	5
State Legislative	39

Local Officials, 2006
Mayor	Thomas W. Randall
Admin/Manager	Catherine Henderson
Clerk	Laura Berchens (Actg.)
Finance Dir/Treas	Catherine Henderson
Engineer	Schwanewede/Hals Eng.
Attorney	David Bole
Tax assessor	Marie Merolla
Tax collector	NA
Building officer	Lawrence Scorzelli
Zoning officer	John Hanlen
Public Works	Michael Frank

Housing & Construction

Housing Units, 2000*
Total	1,465
Median rent	$1,479
Median SF home value	$456,600

New Privately Owned Housing Units
Authorized by Building Permit
	Units	Value
Total, 2004	8	$4,018,224
Single family	8	$4,018,224
Total, 2005	13	$5,205,541
Single family	13	$5,205,541

Real Property Valuation - parcels, 2005
	Number	Valuation
Total		$666,801,600
Vacant	52	6,103,000
Residential	1,434	622,940,600
Commercial	41	37,758,000
Industrial	0	0
Apartments	0	0
Farm land	0	0
Farm homestead	0	0

Average Property Value & Tax, 2005
Residential value	$434,408
Property tax	$10,715
FAIR rebate	$621

Public Library
Worth-Pinkham Memorial Library
91 Warren Ave
Ho-Ho-Kus, NJ 07423
201-445-8078
Director . . . . Mildred Thurklsen

Library statistics, 2004
	Total	per capita
Volumes	22,612	5.57
Expenditure	$546,444	$134.59

Public Safety
Police
Chief	Gregory Kallenberg
Number of officers, 2004	16

Crime, 2004	Number	Rate
Total	20	4.9
Violent	0	0
Non-violent	20	4.9
Domestic Viol.	10	NA

Emergency/Fire
Director . . . . Christopher Jey Sr.

Public School District
(for school year 2004-2005 except as noted)

Ho-Ho-Kus School District
70 Lloyd Rd
Ho-Ho-Kus, NJ 07423
201-652-4555
Superintendent	Loretta Bellina
Grade plan	K-12
Enrollment	619.0
Students per teacher	11.3
Per pupil expenditure	$11,238
Median faculty salary	$56,810
Median administrator salary	$115,500
Grade 12 enrollment	NA
High school graduation rate	NA

Assessment test results
(percent scoring at proficient or advanced level)
	Language	Math
Grade 3	96.0%	93.2%
Grade 8	98.6%	91.4%
High school	NA	NA

SAT
Percent tested	NA
Average SAT math score	NA
Average SAT verbal score	NA

No Child Left Behind, 2003-04
Attendence rate (target = 90%)	96.2%
Drop rate	NA
Highly-qualified teachers	99.7%
District needs improvement?(AYP)	No

Municipal Finance

Fiscal Year 2005
Total tax levy	$16,455,586
County levy	2,152,617
County taxes	2,044,996
County library	0
County health	0
County open space	107,621
School levy	9,432,972
Local muni. budget	4,869,997
Misc. revenues	1,649,385
Total aid	$444,540
CMPTRA	83,180
Muni. block grant	17,218
Energy tax receipts	319,142
Homeland security	25,000

Fiscal Year 2006
Total aid	$444,540
CMPTRA	72,010
Muni. block grant	17,218
Energy tax receipts	330,312
Homeland security	25,000

Taxes
	2003	2004	2005
General tax rate per $100	2.23	2.410	2.470
Net valuation taxable	$658,673,836	$663,065,596	$667,161,897
State equalized value	$980,023,562	$1,068,006,325	$1,167,387,396
County equalization ratio	73.44	67.21	62.07

Demographics & Socio-Economic Characteristics
(2000 U.S. Census, except as noted)

Population

1980*	4,593
1990*	4,892
2000	5,124
Male	2,532
Female	2,592
2004 (estimate)*	5,308
Persons per sq. mi. of land	224

Race & Hispanic Origin, 2000
Race

White	5,026
Black/African American	22
Amer. Indian/Alaska Natv.	2
Asian	22
Natv. Hawaiian/Pac. Islander	0
Other Race	20
Two or more races	32
Hispanic origin, total	87
Mexican	21
Puerto Rican	21
Cuban	10
Other Hispanic	35

Age & Nativity, 2000

Under 5 years	290
18 years and over	3,856
21 years and over	3,715
65 years and over	741
85 years and over	74
Median Age	41.2
Native born	4,990
Foreign born	134

Educational Attainment, 2000

Population 25 years and over	3,557
0-8 yrs of school	3.1%
High School grad or higher	90.9%
Bachelor's degree or higher	24.3%
Graduate degree	8.3%

Income & Poverty, 1999

Per capita income	$28,581
Median household income	$68,083
Median family income	$71,925
Persons in poverty	111
H'holds receiving public assistance	47
H'holds receiving social security	549

Households, 2000

Total households	1,881
With persons under 18	665
With persons over 65	501
Family households	1,523
One-person households	291
Persons per household	2.72
Persons per family	3.06

Labor & Employment

Total civilian labor force, 2004**	3,013
Unemployment rate	3.2%
Total civilian labor force, 2000	2,677
Unemployment rate	2.9%

Employed persons 16 years and over by occupation, 2000

Managers & professionals	958
Service occupations	302
Sales & office occupations	729
Farming, fishing & forestry	9
Construction & maintenance	327
Production & transportation	274
Self-employed persons	198

*US Census Bureau
**New Jersey Department of Labor

General Information

Township of Holland
61 Church Rd
Milford, NJ 08848
908-995-4847

Web site	NA
Land area (sq. miles)	23.70
Water area (sq. miles)	0.39
Type of government	Township
Form of government	TC

Government

Legislative Districts

US Congressional	7
State Legislative	23

Local Officials, 2006

Mayor	Bernard O'Brien
Admin/Manager	NA
Clerk	Catherine M. Miller
Finance Dir/Treas	Michael Balogh
Engineer	Gerald Philkill
Attorney	Richard Dieterly
Tax assessor	Michelle Trivigno
Tax collector	NA
Building officer	DCA
Zoning officer	NA
Public Works	NA

Housing & Construction

Housing Units, 2000*

Total	1,942
Median rent	$905
Median SF home value	$199,000

New Privately Owned Housing Units
Authorized by Building Permit

	Units	Value
Total, 2004	18	$3,020,874
Single family	18	$3,020,874
Total, 2005	14	$2,551,762
Single family	14	$2,551,762

Real Property Valuation - parcels, 2005

	Number	Valuation
Total		$760,609,600
Vacant	183	19,866,700
Residential	1,837	631,566,600
Commercial	22	16,210,700
Industrial	8	26,004,800
Apartments	1	409,900
Farm land	161	64,036,700
Farm homestead	245	2,514,200

Average Property Value & Tax, 2005

Residential value	$304,554
Property tax	$5,096
FAIR rebate	$581

Public Library

Holland Township Library
129 Spring Mill Rd
Milford, NJ 08848
908-995-4767

Director	Donna Longcor

Library statistics, 2004

	Total	per capita
Volumes	26,460	2.69
Expenditure	$59,996	$6.11

Public Safety

Police

Chief	Stephen Verish
Number of officers, 2004	6

Crime, 2004	Number	Rate
Total	34	6.4
Violent	0	0
Non-violent	34	6.4
Domestic Viol.	7	NA

Emergency/Fire

Director	Skip LaVigna

Public School District
(for school year 2004-2005 except as noted)

Holland Township School District
714 Milford-Warren Glen Rd
Milford, NJ 08848
908-995-2401

Superintendent	Eugene Costa
Grade plan	K-8
Enrollment	720.0
Students per teacher	10.4
Per pupil expenditure	$11,193
Median faculty salary	$45,195
Median administrator salary	$82,548
Grade 12 enrollment	NA
High school graduation rate	NA

Assessment test results
(percent scoring at proficient or advanced level)

	Language	Math
Grade 3	91.9%	92.0%
Grade 8	86.3%	78.0%
High school	NA	NA

SAT

Percent tested	NA
Average SAT math score	NA
Average SAT verbal score	NA

No Child Left Behind, 2003-04

Attendence rate (target = 90%)	96.2%
Drop rate	NA
Highly-qualified teachers	100%
District needs improvement?(AYP)	No

Municipal Finance

Fiscal Year 2005

Total tax levy	$12,763,587
County levy	2,868,808
County taxes	2,435,785
County library	203,814
County health	0
County open space	229,210
School levy	9,894,779
Local muni. budget	0
Misc. revenues	5,452,335
Total aid	$2,907,225
CMPTRA	85,584
Muni. block grant	21,406
Energy tax receipts	2,800,235
Homeland security	50,000

Fiscal Year 2006

Total aid	$2,919,649
CMPTRA	0
Muni. block grant	21,406
Energy tax receipts	2,898,243
Homeland security	NA

Taxes

	2003	2004	2005
General tax rate per $100	1.74	1.930	1.680
Net valuation taxable	$609,008,242	$620,287,282	$762,806,228
State equalized value	$617,279,791	$677,408,927	$770,122,391
County equalization ratio	99.37	94.41	100.38

Demographics & Socio-Economic Characteristics
(2000 U.S. Census, except as noted)

Population
1980*	8,447
1990*	11,532
2000	15,781
Male	7,557
Female	8,224
2004 (estimate)*	16,956
Persons per sq. mi. of land	944

Race & Hispanic Origin, 2000
Race
White	12,657
Black/African American	102
Amer. Indian/Alaska Natv.	4
Asian	2,753
Natv. Hawaiian/Pac. Islander	1
Other Race	82
Two or more races	182
Hispanic origin, total	387
Mexican	30
Puerto Rican	105
Cuban	78
Other Hispanic	174

Age & Nativity, 2000
Under 5 years	917
18 years and over	11,279
21 years and over	10,871
65 years and over	1,926
85 years and over	378
Median Age	40.8
Native born	12,811
Foreign born	2,970

Educational Attainment, 2000
Population 25 years and over	10,400
0-8 yrs of school	3.6%
High School grad or higher	91.1%
Bachelor's degree or higher	54.8%
Graduate degree	28.1%

Income & Poverty, 1999
Per capita income	$47,898
Median household income	$112,879
Median family income	$122,785
Persons in poverty	518
H'holds receiving public assistance	42
H'holds receiving social security	972

Households, 2000
Total households	4,947
With persons under 18	2,393
With persons over 65	1,043
Family households	4,330
One-person households	549
Persons per household	3.09
Persons per family	3.35

Labor & Employment
Total civilian labor force, 2004**	6,358
Unemployment rate	2.3%
Total civilian labor force, 2000	7,210
Unemployment rate	2.6%

Employed persons 16 years and over by occupation, 2000
Managers & professionals	4,506
Service occupations	394
Sales & office occupations	1,582
Farming, fishing & forestry	0
Construction & maintenance	279
Production & transportation	262
Self-employed persons	379

*US Census Bureau
**New Jersey Department of Labor

General Information
Township of Holmdel
PO Box 410
Holmdel, NJ 07733
732-946-2820
Web site	www.holmdeltownship-nj.com
Land area (sq. miles)	17.97
Water area (sq. miles)	0.12
Type of government	Township
Form of government	TC

Government

Legislative Districts
US Congressional	12
State Legislative	13

Local Officials, 2006
Mayor	Serena DiMaso
Admin/Manager	Christopher Schultz
Clerk	Maureen Doloughty
Finance Dir/Treas	Joseph Annecharico
Engineer	Edward Broberg
Attorney	Duane Davison
Tax assessor	Eldo Magnani
Tax collector	NA
Building officer	Django Wiegers
Zoning officer	Alice Karlquist
Public Works	NA

Housing & Construction

Housing Units, 2000*
Total	5,137
Median rent	$1,512
Median SF home value	$404,200

New Privately Owned Housing Units Authorized by Building Permit
	Units	Value
Total, 2004	53	$12,411,507
Single family	53	$12,411,507
Total, 2005	24	$6,765,730
Single family	24	$6,765,730

Real Property Valuation - parcels, 2005
	Number	Valuation
Total		$2,027,750,834
Vacant	185	19,113,800
Residential	5,417	1,690,716,364
Commercial	164	186,775,455
Industrial	7	116,598,000
Apartments	3	4,497,600
Farm land	35	9,191,200
Farm homestead	65	858,415

Average Property Value & Tax, 2005
Residential value	$308,569
Property tax	$9,990
FAIR rebate	$543

Public Library
Holmdel Public Library†
4 Crawford's Corner Rd
Holmdel, NJ 07733
732-946-4118
Branch Librarian	Karen Nealis

Library statistics, 2004
	Total	per capita
Volumes	NA	NA
Expenditure	NA	NA

†Branch of County Library

Public Safety

Police
Chief	Raymond Wilson
Number of officers, 2004	41

Crime, 2004	Number	Rate
Total	260	15.5
Violent	17	1
Non-violent	243	14.5
Domestic Viol.	118	NA

Emergency/Fire
Director	Ron Pontrelli

Public School District
(for school year 2004-2005 except as noted)

Holmdel Township School District
4 Crawford's Corner Rd
Holmdel, NJ 07733
732-946-1800
Superintendent	Mark Franceschini (Int)
Grade plan	K-12
Enrollment	3,561.0
Students per teacher	12.8
Per pupil expenditure	$11,435
Median faculty salary	$60,830
Median administrator salary	$104,965
Grade 12 enrollment	275.0
High school graduation rate	98.6%

Assessment test results
(percent scoring at proficient or advanced level)
	Language	Math
Grade 3	95.5%	91.4%
Grade 8	89.5%	86.7%
High school	96.0%	94.4%

SAT
Percent tested	99%
Average SAT math score	614
Average SAT verbal score	580

No Child Left Behind, 2003-04
Attendence rate (target = 90%)	96.2%
Drop rate	0.4%
Highly-qualified teachers	92.2%
District needs improvement?(AYP)	No

Municipal Finance

Fiscal Year 2005
Total tax levy	$65,818,314
County levy	12,382,986
County taxes	11,111,554
County library	612,079
County health	0
County open space	659,353
School levy	44,064,483
Local muni. budget	9,370,845
Misc. revenues	8,455,588
Total aid	$2,846,784
CMPTRA	681,587
Muni. block grant	61,878
Energy tax receipts	2,028,243
Homeland security	70,000

Fiscal Year 2006
Total aid	$2,846,783
CMPTRA	610,598
Muni. block grant	61,878
Energy tax receipts	2,099,231
Homeland security	70,000

Taxes
	2003	2004	2005
General tax rate per $100	2.96	3.152	3.238
Net valuation taxable	$1,979,072,912	$2,014,427,810	$2,033,008,578
State equalized value	$3,382,452,422	$3,656,149,573	$4,005,928,233
County equalization ratio	65.09	58.51	55.03

Demographics & Socio-Economic Characteristics
(2000 U.S. Census, except as noted)

Population
1980*	15,531
1990*	15,586
2000	15,888
Male	8,022
Female	7,866
2004 (estimate)*	16,035
Persons per sq. mi. of land	1,463

Race & Hispanic Origin, 2000
Race
White	14,792
Black/African American	310
Amer. Indian/Alaska Natv.	18
Asian	286
Natv. Hawaiian/Pac. Islander	0
Other Race	226
Two or more races	256
Hispanic origin, total	952
Mexican	45
Puerto Rican	352
Cuban	72
Other Hispanic	483

Age & Nativity, 2000
Under 5 years	1,148
18 years and over	11,687
21 years and over	11,159
65 years and over	1,073
85 years and over	102
Median Age	35.7
Native born	14,915
Foreign born	1,036

Educational Attainment, 2000
Population 25 years and over	10,653
0-8 yrs of school	2.1%
High School grad or higher	89.3%
Bachelor's degree or higher	19.4%
Graduate degree	4.5%

Income & Poverty, 1999
Per capita income	$26,698
Median household income	$65,799
Median family income	$73,277
Persons in poverty	480
H'holds receiving public assistance	123
H'holds receiving social security	972

Households, 2000
Total households	5,656
With persons under 18	2,325
With persons over 65	826
Family households	4,239
One-person households	1,054
Persons per household	2.81
Persons per family	3.24

Labor & Employment
Total civilian labor force, 2004**	10,648
Unemployment rate	4.4%
Total civilian labor force, 2000	9,207
Unemployment rate	4.3%

Employed persons 16 years and over by occupation, 2000
Managers & professionals	2,862
Service occupations	903
Sales & office occupations	2,962
Farming, fishing & forestry	0
Construction & maintenance	972
Production & transportation	1,114
Self-employed persons	337

*US Census Bureau
**New Jersey Department of Labor

General Information
Borough of Hopatcong
111 River Styx Rd
Hopatcong, NJ 07843
973-770-1200
Web site	www.hopatcong.org
Land area (sq. miles)	10.96
Water area (sq. miles)	1.38
Type of government	Borough
Form of government	B

Government
Legislative Districts
US Congressional	5, 11
State Legislative	24

Local Officials, 2006
Mayor	Richard Hodson
Admin/Manager	Steven Ward
Clerk	Lorraine Stark
Finance Dir/Treas	Kelleyanne McGann
Engineer	John Rushke
Attorney	Richard Stein
Tax assessor	Therese Auriemma
Tax collector	Regina Thomas
Building officer	William O'Connor
Zoning officer	William Donegan
Public Works	Daniel Wills

Housing & Construction
Housing Units, 2000*
Total	6,190
Median rent	$915
Median SF home value	$141,300

New Privately Owned Housing Units Authorized by Building Permit
	Units	Value
Total, 2004	14	$1,899,288
Single family	14	$1,899,288
Total, 2005	14	$1,760,930
Single family	14	$1,760,930

Real Property Valuation - parcels, 2005
	Number	Valuation
Total		$873,938,900
Vacant	1,134	18,572,600
Residential	6,026	821,842,500
Commercial	73	30,555,800
Industrial	1	195,700
Apartments	0	0
Farm land	7	2,573,600
Farm homestead	18	198,700

Average Property Value & Tax, 2005
Residential value	$136,009
Property tax	$4,947
FAIR rebate	$486

Public Library
E. Louise Childs Branch Library†
21 Sparta Rd
Stanhope, NJ 07874
973-770-1000
Branch Librarian	Victoria Larson

Library statistics, 2004
	Total	per capita
Volumes	NA	NA
Expenditure	NA	NA

†Branch of County Library

Public Safety
Police
Chief	John Swanson
Number of officers, 2004	29

Crime, 2004	Number	Rate
Total	154	9.6
Violent	14	0.9
Non-violent	140	8.7
Domestic Viol.	224	NA

Emergency/Fire
Director	James Byron

Public School District
(for school year 2004-2005 except as noted)

Hopatcong Borough School District
PO Box 1029
Hopatcong, NJ 07843
973-398-8801
Administrator	Wayne Threlkeld
Grade plan	K-12
Enrollment	2,636.0
Students per teacher	11.8
Per pupil expenditure	$11,075
Median faculty salary	$61,650
Median administrator salary	$112,659
Grade 12 enrollment	185.5
High school graduation rate	94.8%

Assessment test results
(percent scoring at proficient or advanced level)
	Language	Math
Grade 3	85.6%	82.1%
Grade 8	75.5%	64.6%
High school	86.2%	79.4%

SAT
Percent tested	64%
Average SAT math score	495
Average SAT verbal score	491

No Child Left Behind, 2003-04
Attendance rate (target = 90%)	93.6%
Drop rate	1.5%
Highly-qualified teachers	99%
District needs improvement?(AYP)	No

Municipal Finance
Fiscal Year 2005
Total tax levy	$31,820,345
County levy	5,845,026
County taxes	5,137,766
County library	442,965
County health	0
County open space	264,295
School levy	18,041,378
Local muni. budget	7,933,941
Misc. revenues	5,441,609
Total aid	$1,381,705
CMPTRA	716,059
Muni. block grant	68,199
Energy tax receipts	527,447
Homeland security	70,000

Fiscal Year 2006
Total aid	$1,381,705
CMPTRA	697,598
Muni. block grant	68,199
Energy tax receipts	545,908
Homeland security	70,000

Taxes
	2003	2004	2005
General tax rate per $100	3.37	3.450	3.640
Net valuation taxable	$871,305,492	$872,588,943	$874,871,569
State equalized value	$1,158,805,017	$1,313,167,188	$1,509,179,867
County equalization ratio	92.59	75.19	66.42

Demographics & Socio-Economic Characteristics
(2000 U.S. Census, except as noted)

Population
1980*	1,468
1990*	1,719
2000	1,891
Male	947
Female	944
2004 (estimate)*	1,963
Persons per sq. mi. of land	106

Race & Hispanic Origin, 2000
Race
White	1,858
Black/African American	8
Amer. Indian/Alaska Natv.	0
Asian	8
Natv. Hawaiian/Pac. Islander	0
Other Race	1
Two or more races	16
Hispanic origin, total	28
Mexican	2
Puerto Rican	6
Cuban	0
Other Hispanic	20

Age & Nativity, 2000
Under 5 years	122
18 years and over	1,391
21 years and over	1,342
65 years and over	208
85 years and over	20
Median Age	39.5
Native born	1,813
Foreign born	78

Educational Attainment, 2000
Population 25 years and over	1,312
0-8 yrs of school	2.2%
High School grad or higher	90.9%
Bachelor's degree or higher	26.9%
Graduate degree	8.1%

Income & Poverty, 1999
Per capita income	$27,902
Median household income	$61,319
Median family income	$68,750
Persons in poverty	36
H'holds receiving public assistance	10
H'holds receiving social security	171

Households, 2000
Total households	697
With persons under 18	267
With persons over 65	155
Family households	539
One-person households	137
Persons per household	2.71
Persons per family	3.12

Labor & Employment
Total civilian labor force, 2004**	1,176
Unemployment rate	4.4%
Total civilian labor force, 2000	989
Unemployment rate	4.2%

Employed persons 16 years and over by occupation, 2000
Managers & professionals	342
Service occupations	113
Sales & office occupations	275
Farming, fishing & forestry	5
Construction & maintenance	108
Production & transportation	104
Self-employed persons	60

*US Census Bureau
**New Jersey Department of Labor

General Information
Township of Hope
Box 284
Hope, NJ 07844
908-459-5011
Email	clerk@hopetwp-nj.us
Land area (sq. miles)	18.50
Water area (sq. miles)	0.18
Type of government	Township
Form of government	TC

Government

Legislative Districts
US Congressional	5
State Legislative	23

Local Officials, 2006
Mayor	Timothy McDonough
Admin/Manager	NA
Clerk	Mary Pat Quinn
Finance Dir/Treas	Peter Kowalick Jr.
Engineer	Ted Rodman
Attorney	Kevin Benbrook
Tax assessor	Richard Motyka
Tax collector	Stephen Lance
Building officer	Ralph Price
Zoning officer	David Diehl
Public Works	Donald Whitmore

Housing & Construction

Housing Units, 2000*
Total	747
Median rent	$711
Median SF home value	$179,500

New Privately Owned Housing Units Authorized by Building Permit
	Units	Value
Total, 2004	11	$1,801,900
Single family	11	$1,801,900
Total, 2005	7	$1,632,310
Single family	7	$1,632,310

Real Property Valuation - parcels, 2005
	Number	Valuation
Total		$138,690,000
Vacant	154	4,923,400
Residential	635	103,246,200
Commercial	29	7,994,900
Industrial	1	209,300
Apartments	1	264,200
Farm land	108	20,209,800
Farm homestead	214	1,842,200

Average Property Value & Tax, 2005
Residential value	$123,779
Property tax	$4,005
FAIR rebate	$532

Public Library
No public municipal library.

Library statistics, 2004
	Total	per capita
Volumes	NA	NA
Expenditure	NA	NA

Public Safety

Police
Chief	NA
Number of officers, 2004	0

Crime, 2004	Number	Rate
Total	18	9.2
Violent	1	0.5
Non-violent	17	8.7
Domestic Viol.	15	NA

Emergency/Fire
Director	Chad Koonz

Public School District
(for school year 2004-2005 except as noted)

Hope Township School District
Hope Township School
Hope, NJ 07844
908-459-4242
Superintendent	Alfred Annunziata
Grade plan	K-12
Enrollment	225.0
Students per teacher	10.7
Per pupil expenditure	$10,754
Median faculty salary	$41,850
Median administrator salary	$86,438
Grade 12 enrollment	NA
High school graduation rate	NA

Assessment test results
(percent scoring at proficient or advanced level)
	Language	Math
Grade 3	94.7%	100%
Grade 8	70.0%	90.0%
High school	NA	NA

SAT
Percent tested	NA
Average SAT math score	NA
Average SAT verbal score	NA

No Child Left Behind, 2003-04
Attendence rate (target = 90%)	95.6%
Drop rate	NA
Highly-qualified teachers	97%
District needs improvement?(AYP)	No

Municipal Finance

Fiscal Year 2005
Total tax levy	$4,518,315
County levy	1,416,197
County taxes	1,170,964
County library	112,884
County health	0
County open space	132,348
School levy	2,769,308
Local muni. budget	332,810
Misc. revenues	967,842
Total aid	$271,558
CMPTRA	88,508
Muni. block grant	7,521
Energy tax receipts	175,529
Homeland security	0

Fiscal Year 2006
Total aid	$271,559
CMPTRA	82,365
Muni. block grant	7,521
Energy tax receipts	181,673
Homeland security	NA

Taxes
	2003	2004	2005
General tax rate per $100	2.80	2.970	3.240
Net valuation taxable	$136,953,866	$138,185,766	$139,629,354
State equalized value	$189,529,291	$217,195,929	$245,912,917
County equalization ratio	83.09	72.26	63.40

Demographics & Socio-Economic Characteristics

(2000 U.S. Census, except as noted)

Population

1980*	2,001
1990*	1,968
2000	2,035
Male	986
Female	1,049
2004 (estimate)*	2,051
Persons per sq. mi. of land	2,987

Race & Hispanic Origin, 2000

Race

White	1,942
Black/African American	22
Amer. Indian/Alaska Natv.	10
Asian	20
Natv. Hawaiian/Pac. Islander	0
Other Race	25
Two or more races	16
Hispanic origin, total	47
Mexican	6
Puerto Rican	3
Cuban	0
Other Hispanic	38

Age & Nativity, 2000

Under 5 years	118
18 years and over	1,503
21 years and over	1,457
65 years and over	215
85 years and over	33
Median Age	39.7
Native born	1,878
Foreign born	157

Educational Attainment, 2000

Population 25 years and over	1,417
0-8 yrs of school	3.4%
High School grad or higher	89.6%
Bachelor's degree or higher	53.9%
Graduate degree	28.8%

Income & Poverty, 1999

Per capita income	$38,413
Median household income	$77,270
Median family income	$91,205
Persons in poverty	43
H'holds receiving public assistance	0
H'holds receiving social security	174

Households, 2000

Total households	813
With persons under 18	305
With persons over 65	167
Family households	562
One-person households	204
Persons per household	2.5
Persons per family	3.01

Labor & Employment

Total civilian labor force, 2004**	1,276
Unemployment rate	1.5%
Total civilian labor force, 2000	1,228
Unemployment rate	1.0%

Employed persons 16 years and over by occupation, 2000

Managers & professionals	672
Service occupations	122
Sales & office occupations	243
Farming, fishing & forestry	0
Construction & maintenance	112
Production & transportation	67
Self-employed persons	95

*US Census Bureau
**New Jersey Department of Labor

General Information

Borough of Hopewell
PO Box 128
4 Columbia Ave
Hopewell, NJ 08525
609-466-2636

Web site	www.hopewell-nj.us
Land area (sq. miles)	0.69
Water area (sq. miles)	0
Type of government	Borough
Form of government	B

Government

Legislative Districts

US Congressional	12
State Legislative	15

Local Officials, 2006

Mayor	David R. Nettles
Admin/Manager	Michele Hovan
Clerk	Michele Hovan
Finance Dir/Treas	Judie McGrorey
Engineer	Dennis O'Neal
Attorney	Edmond Konin
Tax assessor	Christopher Fuges
Tax collector	Donna Griffiths
Building officer	Robert Ward
Zoning officer	Harry Agin
Public Works	Herbert Ruehle

Housing & Construction

Housing Units, 2000*

Total	836
Median rent	$843
Median SF home value	$221,900

New Privately Owned Housing Units Authorized by Building Permit

	Units	Value
Total, 2004	2	$230,000
Single family	2	$230,000
Total, 2005	1	$172,000
Single family	1	$172,000

Real Property Valuation - parcels, 2005

	Number	Valuation
Total		$154,966,600
Vacant	28	1,562,100
Residential	662	129,566,200
Commercial	70	19,776,800
Industrial	3	1,654,700
Apartments	5	1,478,600
Farm land	3	907,800
Farm homestead	3	20,400

Average Property Value & Tax, 2005

Residential value	$194,867
Property tax	$7,367
FAIR rebate	$544

Public Library

Hopewell Public Library
13 E Broad St
Hopewell, NJ 08525
609-466-1625

Director ... Jennifer Spencer

Library statistics, 2004

	Total	per capita
Volumes	14,874	7.31
Expenditure	$92,306	$45.36

Public Safety

Police

Chief	Michael Chipowski
Number of officers, 2004	0

Crime, 2004	Number	Rate
Total	22	10.8
Violent	2	1
Non-violent	20	9.8
Domestic Viol.	9	NA

Emergency/Fire

Director ... Edwart Van Dorew

Public School District

(for school year 2004-2005 except as noted)

Sends children to Hopewell Valley Regional school district (see Appendix A).

Grade plan	NA
Enrollment	NA
Students per teacher	NA
Per pupil expenditure	NA
Median faculty salary	NA
Median administrator salary	NA
Grade 12 enrollment	NA
High school graduation rate	NA

Assessment test results

(percent scoring at proficient or advanced level)

	Language	Math
Grade 3	NA	NA
Grade 8	NA	NA
High school	NA	NA

SAT

Percent tested	NA
Average SAT math score	NA
Average SAT verbal score	NA

No Child Left Behind, 2003-04

Attendence rate (target = 90%)	NA
Drop rate	NA
Highly-qualified teachers	NA
District needs improvement?(AYP)	NA

Municipal Finance

Fiscal Year 2005

Total tax levy	$5,896,779
County levy	1,491,063
County taxes	1,411,772
County library	0
County health	0
County open space	79,291
School levy	3,531,538
Local muni. budget	874,177
Misc. revenues	1,420,623
Total aid	$276,118
CMPTRA	118,368
Muni. block grant	8,611
Energy tax receipts	124,139
Homeland security	25,000

Fiscal Year 2006

Total aid	$276,118
CMPTRA	114,023
Muni. block grant	8,611
Energy tax receipts	128,484
Homeland security	25,000

Taxes

	2003	2004	2005
General tax rate per $100	3.33	3.460	3.790
Net valuation taxable	$154,977,997	$155,140,492	$155,969,562
State equalized value	$242,494,128	$261,388,386	$306,483,714
County equalization ratio	74.05	63.91	59.19

Demographics & Socio-Economic Characteristics
(2000 U.S. Census, except as noted)

Population
1980*	4,365
1990*	4,215
2000	4,434
Male	2,103
Female	2,331
2004 (estimate)*	4,687
Persons per sq. mi. of land	157

Race & Hispanic Origin, 2000
Race
White	3,862
Black/African American	306
Amer. Indian/Alaska Natv.	103
Asian	25
Natv. Hawaiian/Pac. Islander	1
Other Race	64
Two or more races	73
Hispanic origin, total	159
Mexican	55
Puerto Rican	86
Cuban	0
Other Hispanic	18

Age & Nativity, 2000
Under 5 years	210
18 years and over	3,430
21 years and over	3,290
65 years and over	906
85 years and over	129
Median Age	42.4
Native born	4,321
Foreign born	111

Educational Attainment, 2000
Population 25 years and over	3,177
0-8 yrs of school	7.1%
High School grad or higher	83.2%
Bachelor's degree or higher	18.8%
Graduate degree	7.6%

Income & Poverty, 1999
Per capita income	$22,783
Median household income	$49,767
Median family income	$59,675
Persons in poverty	279
H'holds receiving public assistance	16
H'holds receiving social security	577

Households, 2000
Total households	1,628
With persons under 18	549
With persons over 65	539
Family households	1,206
One-person households	372
Persons per household	2.58
Persons per family	3.03

Labor & Employment
Total civilian labor force, 2004**	2,302
Unemployment rate	4.6%
Total civilian labor force, 2000	2,284
Unemployment rate	3.9%

Employed persons 16 years and over by occupation, 2000
Managers & professionals	713
Service occupations	408
Sales & office occupations	484
Farming, fishing & forestry	29
Construction & maintenance	169
Production & transportation	391
Self-employed persons	161

*US Census Bureau
**New Jersey Department of Labor

General Information
Township of Hopewell
590 Shiloh Pike
Bridgeton, NJ 08302
856-455-1230

Web site	hopewelltwp-nj.com
Land area (sq. miles)	29.90
Water area (sq. miles)	0.88
Type of government	Township
Form of government	TC

Government

Legislative Districts
US Congressional	2
State Legislative	3

Local Officials, 2006
Mayor	Harold Bickings Jr.
Admin/Manager	Ted Ritter
Clerk	Ted Ritter
Finance Dir/Treas	Barb Spatola
Engineer	J. Michael Fralinger
Attorney	T. Henry Ritter
Tax assessor	Lois Mazza
Tax collector	Liz Wallender
Building officer	Gordon Gross
Zoning officer	William Cassidy
Public Works	Ken Hildreth

Housing & Construction

Housing Units, 2000*
Total	1,683
Median rent	$495
Median SF home value	$97,000

New Privately Owned Housing Units Authorized by Building Permit
	Units	Value
Total, 2004	17	$2,100,232
Single family	17	$2,100,232
Total, 2005	18	$2,228,547
Single family	18	$2,228,547

Real Property Valuation - parcels, 2005
	Number	Valuation
Total		$223,973,100
Vacant	247	4,670,400
Residential	1,414	167,507,400
Commercial	55	14,749,000
Industrial	0	0
Apartments	2	415,400
Farm land	196	29,779,400
Farm homestead	463	6,851,500

Average Property Value & Tax, 2005
Residential value	$92,892
Property tax	$2,998
FAIR rebate	$637

Public Library

No public municipal library.

Library statistics, 2004
	Total	per capita
Volumes	NA	NA
Expenditure	NA	NA

Public Safety

Police
Chief	(State)
Number of officers, 2004	0

Crime, 2004	Number	Rate
Total	66	14.4
Violent	7	1.5
Non-violent	59	12.8
Domestic Viol.	42	NA

Emergency/Fire
Director	Maxwell Dilks

Public School District
(for school year 2004-2005 except as noted)

Hopewell Township School District
122 Sewall Rd
Bridgeton, NJ 08302
856-451-9203

Administrator	Terry Van Zoren
Grade plan	K-8
Enrollment	540.0
Students per teacher	11.9
Per pupil expenditure	$10,246
Median faculty salary	$59,910
Median administrator salary	$86,425
Grade 12 enrollment	NA
High school graduation rate	NA

Assessment test results
(percent scoring at proficient or advanced level)
	Language	Math
Grade 3	88.7%	85.2%
Grade 8	71.3%	68.8%
High school	NA	NA

SAT
Percent tested	NA
Average SAT math score	NA
Average SAT verbal score	NA

No Child Left Behind, 2003-04
Attendence rate (target = 90%)	95.7%
Drop rate	NA
Highly-qualified teachers	100%
District needs improvement?(AYP)	No

Municipal Finance

Fiscal Year 2005
Total tax levy	$7,260,357
County levy	2,555,737
County taxes	2,427,732
County library	0
County health	103,411
County open space	24,593
School levy	4,538,332
Local muni. budget	166,288
Misc. revenues	2,365,676
Total aid	$460,971
CMPTRA	223,400
Muni. block grant	18,444
Energy tax receipts	219,127
Homeland security	0

Fiscal Year 2006
Total aid	$460,972
CMPTRA	215,731
Muni. block grant	18,444
Energy tax receipts	226,797
Homeland security	NA

Taxes
	2003	2004	2005
General tax rate per $100	2.74	2.889	3.230
Net valuation taxable	$220,152,490	$222,645,464	$224,987,536
State equalized value	$223,119,986	$241,858,775	$272,217,224
County equalization ratio	103.16	98.67	92.02

Demographics & Socio-Economic Characteristics
(2000 U.S. Census, except as noted)

Population
1980*	10,893
1990*	11,590
2000	16,105
Male	8,208
Female	7,897
2004 (estimate)*	17,582
Persons per sq. mi. of land	303

Race & Hispanic Origin, 2000
Race
White	14,220
Black/African American	939
Amer. Indian/Alaska Natv.	20
Asian	639
Natv. Hawaiian/Pac. Islander	4
Other Race	107
Two or more races	176
Hispanic origin, total	395
Mexican	36
Puerto Rican	152
Cuban	50
Other Hispanic	157

Age & Nativity, 2000
Under 5 years	1,076
18 years and over	11,833
21 years and over	11,413
65 years and over	1,845
85 years and over	130
Median Age	39.1
Native born	14,862
Foreign born	1,243

Educational Attainment, 2000
Population 25 years and over	10,956
0-8 yrs of school	1.2%
High School grad or higher	93.0%
Bachelor's degree or higher	55.8%
Graduate degree	27.7%

Income & Poverty, 1999
Per capita income	$43,947
Median household income	$93,640
Median family income	$101,579
Persons in poverty	173
H'holds receiving public assistance	15
H'holds receiving social security	1,334

Households, 2000
Total households	5,498
With persons under 18	2,310
With persons over 65	1,279
Family households	4,429
One-person households	878
Persons per household	2.77
Persons per family	3.11

Labor & Employment
Total civilian labor force, 2004**	6,799
Unemployment rate	1.7%
Total civilian labor force, 2000	7,738
Unemployment rate	2.1%

Employed persons 16 years and over by occupation, 2000
Managers & professionals	4,625
Service occupations	638
Sales & office occupations	1,534
Farming, fishing & forestry	23
Construction & maintenance	422
Production & transportation	334
Self-employed persons	540

*US Census Bureau
**New Jersey Department of Labor

General Information
Township of Hopewell
201 Wash. Crossing-Penn Rd
Titusville, NJ 08560
609-737-0605
Web site	www.hopewelltwp.org
Land area (sq. miles)	58.11
Water area (sq. miles)	0.54
Type of government	Township
Form of government	TC

Government

Legislative Districts
US Congressional	12
State Legislative	15

Local Officials, 2006
Mayor	Vanessa Sandom
Admin/Manager	Bruce Hilling
Clerk	Annette Bielawski
Finance Dir/Treas	Elaine Borges
Engineer	Paul Pogorzelski
Attorney	Steven Goodell
Tax assessor	Antoinette Sost
Tax collector	Kathleen Cantwell
Building officer	William White
Zoning officer	Robert Miller
Public Works	NA

Housing & Construction

Housing Units, 2000*
Total	5,629
Median rent	$925
Median SF home value	$252,600

New Privately Owned Housing Units Authorized by Building Permit
	Units	Value
Total, 2004	120	$17,106,558
Single family	112	$16,222,558
Total, 2005	129	$21,526,928
Single family	129	$21,526,928

Real Property Valuation - parcels, 2005
	Number	Valuation
Total		$2,365,832,000
Vacant	595	59,764,100
Residential	5,683	1,548,527,400
Commercial	154	382,824,000
Industrial	28	235,967,600
Apartments	9	4,063,500
Farm land	319	128,654,100
Farm homestead	520	6,031,300

Average Property Value & Tax, 2005
Residential value	$250,614
Property tax	$8,298
FAIR rebate	$566

Public Library
Hopewell Twp. Branch Library†
245 Pennington/Titusville Rd
Pennington, NJ 08534
609-737-2610
Branch Librarian	Andrea Merrick

Library statistics, 2004
	Total	per capita
Volumes	NA	NA
Expenditure	NA	NA

†Branch of County Library

Public Safety

Police
Chief	George Meyer
Number of officers, 2004	36

Crime, 2004	Number	Rate
Total	116	6.9
Violent	18	1.1
Non-violent	98	5.8
Domestic Viol.	46	NA

Emergency/Fire
Director	NA

Public School District
(for school year 2004-2005 except as noted)

Sends children to Hopewell Valley Regional school district (see Appendix A).
Grade plan	NA
Enrollment	NA
Students per teacher	NA
Per pupil expenditure	NA
Median faculty salary	NA
Median administrator salary	NA
Grade 12 enrollment	NA
High school graduation rate	NA

Assessment test results
(percent scoring at proficient or advanced level)
	Language	Math
Grade 3	NA	NA
Grade 8	NA	NA
High school	NA	NA

SAT
Percent tested	NA
Average SAT math score	NA
Average SAT verbal score	NA

No Child Left Behind, 2003-04
Attendence rate (target = 90%)	NA
Drop rate	NA
Highly-qualified teachers	NA
District needs improvement?(AYP)	NA

Municipal Finance

Fiscal Year 2005
Total tax levy	$78,445,342
County levy	21,536,507
County taxes	18,811,892
County library	1,667,912
County health	0
County open space	1,056,703
School levy	46,248,165
Local muni. budget	10,660,670
Misc. revenues	7,053,708
Total aid	$2,318,200
CMPTRA	562,585
Muni. block grant	63,148
Energy tax receipts	1,622,467
Homeland security	70,000

Fiscal Year 2006
Total aid	$2,318,200
CMPTRA	505,798
Muni. block grant	63,148
Energy tax receipts	1,679,254
Homeland security	70,000

Taxes
	2003	2004	2005
General tax rate per $100	2.96	3.130	3.320
Net valuation taxable	$2,251,214,397	$2,315,218,983	$2,369,199,280
State equalized value	$3,160,930,072	$3,430,734,700	$4,016,272,724
County equalization ratio	74.17	71.22	67.45

Demographics & Socio-Economic Characteristics
(2000 U.S. Census, except as noted)

Population
1980*	25,065
1990*	38,987
2000	48,903
Male	23,864
Female	25,039
2004 (estimate)*	50,320
Persons per sq. mi. of land	826

Race & Hispanic Origin, 2000
Race
White	44,008
Black/African American	1,739
Amer. Indian/Alaska Natv.	58
Asian	1,749
Natv. Hawaiian/Pac. Islander	5
Other Race	633
Two or more races	711
Hispanic origin, total	2,610
Mexican	229
Puerto Rican	1,252
Cuban	202
Other Hispanic	927

Age & Nativity, 2000
Under 5 years	3,910
18 years and over	33,815
21 years and over	32,333
65 years and over	4,295
85 years and over	451
Median Age	35.7
Native born	44,543
Foreign born	4,360

Educational Attainment, 2000
Population 25 years and over	30,878
0-8 yrs of school	3.3%
High School grad or higher	88.2%
Bachelor's degree or higher	29.0%
Graduate degree	8.7%

Income & Poverty, 1999
Per capita income	$26,143
Median household income	$68,069
Median family income	$74,623
Persons in poverty	2,049
H'holds receiving public assistance	196
H'holds receiving social security	3,473

Households, 2000
Total households	16,063
With persons under 18	7,962
With persons over 65	3,249
Family households	13,006
One-person households	2,466
Persons per household	3.04
Persons per family	3.42

Labor & Employment
Total civilian labor force, 2004**	22,504
Unemployment rate	4.6%
Total civilian labor force, 2000	24,937
Unemployment rate	4.2%

Employed persons 16 years and over by occupation, 2000
Managers & professionals	9,175
Service occupations	3,020
Sales & office occupations	7,350
Farming, fishing & forestry	67
Construction & maintenance	2,016
Production & transportation	2,258
Self-employed persons	1,221

*US Census Bureau
**New Jersey Department of Labor

General Information
Township of Howell
PO Box 580
251 Preventorium Rd
Howell, NJ 07731
732-938-4500

Web site	www.twp.howell.nj.us
Land area (sq. miles)	60.91
Water area (sq. miles)	0.09
Type of government	Township
Form of government	TC

Government

Legislative Districts
US Congressional	4
State Legislative	30

Local Officials, 2006
Mayor	Joseph M. Di Bella
Admin/Manager	Thomas Czerniecki
Clerk	Bruce Davis
Finance Dir/Treas	Jeffrey L. Fillatreault
Engineer	William Nunziato
Attorney	Thomas G. Gannon
Tax assessor	Thomas P. Lenahan
Tax collector	NA
Building officer	Chet Philips
Zoning officer	Vito M. Marinaccio
Public Works	NA

Housing & Construction

Housing Units, 2000*
Total	16,572
Median rent	$816
Median SF home value	$172,400

New Privately Owned Housing Units
Authorized by Building Permit
	Units	Value
Total, 2004	254	$31,692,623
Single family	254	$31,692,623
Total, 2005	250	$41,721,459
Single family	250	$41,721,459

Real Property Valuation - parcels, 2005
	Number	Valuation
Total		$2,895,524,640
Vacant	5,824	120,597,750
Residential	15,710	2,375,496,640
Commercial	431	296,105,200
Industrial	64	57,612,450
Apartments	0	0
Farm land	267	43,161,300
Farm homestead	389	2,551,300

Average Property Value & Tax, 2005
Residential value	$147,714
Property tax	$5,580
FAIR rebate	$549

Public Library
Howell Public Library†
318 Old Tavern Rd
Howell, NJ 07731
732-938-2300

Branch Librarian	Beth Miller

Library statistics, 2004
	Total	per capita
Volumes	NA	NA
Expenditure	NA	NA

†Branch of County Library

Public Safety

Police
Chief	Ronald T. Carter
Number of officers, 2004	94

Crime, 2004	Number	Rate
Total	671	13.4
Violent	51	1
Non-violent	620	12.4
Domestic Viol.	295	NA

Emergency/Fire
Director	Robert H. Hotman

Public School District
(for school year 2004-2005 except as noted)

Howell Township School District
200 Squankum-Yellowbrook Rd
Howell, NJ 07731
732-751-2480

Superintendent	Enid Golden
Grade plan	K-8
Enrollment	7,244.0
Students per teacher	11.4
Per pupil expenditure	$11,753
Median faculty salary	$45,225
Median administrator salary	$105,468
Grade 12 enrollment	NA
High school graduation rate	NA

Assessment test results
(percent scoring at proficient or advanced level)
	Language	Math
Grade 3	91.7%	91.7%
Grade 8	83.4%	77.7%
High school	NA	NA

SAT
Percent tested	NA
Average SAT math score	NA
Average SAT verbal score	NA

No Child Left Behind, 2003-04
Attendence rate (target = 90%)	95.2%
Drop rate	NA
Highly-qualified teachers	98.6%
District needs improvement?(AYP)	No

Municipal Finance

Fiscal Year 2005
Total tax levy	$109,590,371
County levy	17,051,975
County taxes	15,054,584
County library	829,406
County health	274,540
County open space	893,445
School levy	78,708,989
Local muni. budget	13,829,407
Misc. revenues	23,605,050
Total aid	$10,318,082
CMPTRA	1,652,118
Muni. block grant	191,750
Energy tax receipts	8,334,214
Homeland security	140,000

Fiscal Year 2006
Total aid	$10,318,082
CMPTRA	1,360,421
Muni. block grant	191,750
Energy tax receipts	8,625,911
Homeland security	140,000

Taxes
	2003	2004	2005
General tax rate per $100	3.39	3.627	3.778
Net valuation taxable	$2,755,414,388	$2,819,043,222	$2,900,931,838
State equalized value	$4,236,491,986	$4,892,925,316	$5,792,595,523
County equalization ratio	74.55	65.04	57.56

Demographics & Socio-Economic Characteristics
(2000 U.S. Census, except as noted)

Population
1980*	2,829
1990*	3,940
2000	5,603
Male	2,710
Female	2,893
2004 (estimate)*	5,796
Persons per sq. mi. of land	292

Race & Hispanic Origin, 2000
Race
White	5,322
Black/African American	65
Amer. Indian/Alaska Natv.	3
Asian	97
Natv. Hawaiian/Pac. Islander	0
Other Race	44
Two or more races	72
Hispanic origin, total	211
Mexican	17
Puerto Rican	54
Cuban	17
Other Hispanic	123

Age & Nativity, 2000
Under 5 years	364
18 years and over	4,104
21 years and over	3,969
65 years and over	451
85 years and over	42
Median Age	36.8
Native born	5,193
Foreign born	410

Educational Attainment, 2000
Population 25 years and over	3,811
0-8 yrs of school	2.3%
High School grad or higher	91.3%
Bachelor's degree or higher	35.7%
Graduate degree	9.9%

Income & Poverty, 1999
Per capita income	$30,555
Median household income	$67,247
Median family income	$79,819
Persons in poverty	158
H'holds receiving public assistance	37
H'holds receiving social security	384

Households, 2000
Total households	2,146
With persons under 18	819
With persons over 65	354
Family households	1,490
One-person households	525
Persons per household	2.61
Persons per family	3.18

Labor & Employment
Total civilian labor force, 2004**	2,668
Unemployment rate	2.3%
Total civilian labor force, 2000	3,191
Unemployment rate	1.2%

Employed persons 16 years and over by occupation, 2000
Managers & professionals	1,258
Service occupations	466
Sales & office occupations	834
Farming, fishing & forestry	0
Construction & maintenance	313
Production & transportation	281
Self-employed persons	150

*US Census Bureau
**New Jersey Department of Labor

General Information
Township of Independence
286-B Route 46
Great Meadows, NJ 07838
908-637-4133
Web site	www.independencenj.com
Land area (sq. miles)	19.84
Water area (sq. miles)	0.05
Type of government	Township
Form of government	TC

Government

Legislative Districts
US Congressional	5
State Legislative	23

Local Officials, 2006
Mayor	Robert M. Giordano
Admin/Manager	NA
Clerk	Deborah Hrebenak
Finance Dir/Treas	Kevin Lifer
Engineer	Michael Finelli
Attorney	William Edleston
Tax assessor	Michael Schmidt
Tax collector	Patricia Noll
Building officer	Richard O'Connor
Zoning officer	Donald Hendershot
Public Works	Alan Shimchook

Housing & Construction

Housing Units, 2000*
Total	2,210
Median rent	$720
Median SF home value	$169,500

New Privately Owned Housing Units Authorized by Building Permit
	Units	Value
Total, 2004	12	$3,319,130
Single family	12	$3,319,130
Total, 2005	14	$3,865,671
Single family	14	$3,865,671

Real Property Valuation - parcels, 2005
	Number	Valuation
Total		$680,408,542
Vacant	145	15,253,200
Residential	1,861	585,789,800
Commercial	55	28,825,700
Industrial	6	3,947,300
Apartments	9	16,364,300
Farm land	92	28,080,800
Farm homestead	196	2,147,442

Average Property Value & Tax, 2005
Residential value	$285,823
Property tax	$4,918
FAIR rebate	$488

Public Library
Northeast Branch Library†
63 US Hwy 46
Hackettstown, NJ 07840
908-813-3858
Branch Librarian	Patricia Optiz

Library statistics, 2004
	Total	per capita
Volumes	NA	NA
Expenditure	NA	NA

†Branch of County Library

Public Safety
Police
Chief	Robert Petersen
Number of officers, 2004	7

Crime, 2004	Number	Rate
Total	51	8.8
Violent	2	0.3
Non-violent	49	8.5
Domestic Viol.	50	NA

Emergency/Fire
Director	Ernest Kinney

Public School District
(for school year 2004-2005 except as noted)

Great Meadows Regional School District
PO BOX 74
Great Meadows, NJ 07838
908-637-6576
Superintendent	Jason Bing
Grade plan	K-12
Enrollment	1,009.0
Students per teacher	11.3
Per pupil expenditure	$10,889
Median faculty salary	$48,259
Median administrator salary	$71,106
Grade 12 enrollment	NA
High school graduation rate	NA

Assessment test results
(percent scoring at proficient or advanced level)
	Language	Math
Grade 3	92.8%	85.6%
Grade 8	85.3%	78.2%
High school	NA	NA

SAT
Percent tested	NA
Average SAT math score	NA
Average SAT verbal score	NA

No Child Left Behind, 2003-04
Attendence rate (target = 90%)	96.0%
Drop rate	NA
Highly-qualified teachers	98.8%
District needs improvement?(AYP)	No

Municipal Finance

Fiscal Year 2005
Total tax levy	$11,736,829
County levy	3,659,324
County taxes	3,021,192
County library	293,742
County health	0
County open space	344,389
School levy	6,741,290
Local muni. budget	1,336,216
Misc. revenues	2,084,618
Total aid	$511,808
CMPTRA	192,315
Muni. block grant	21,969
Energy tax receipts	247,524
Homeland security	50,000

Fiscal Year 2006
Total aid	$511,808
CMPTRA	183,652
Muni. block grant	21,969
Energy tax receipts	256,187
Homeland security	50,000

Taxes
	2003	2004	2005
General tax rate per $100	3.13	3.280	1.730
Net valuation taxable	$330,821,153	$336,157,209	$682,095,974
State equalized value	$498,074,606	$563,897,664	$649,800,871
County equalization ratio	75.19	66.42	119.14

Demographics & Socio-Economic Characteristics
(2000 U.S. Census, except as noted)

Population
1980*	1,037
1990*	910
2000	900
Male	435
Female	465
2004 (estimate)*	895
Persons per sq. mi. of land	2,542

Race & Hispanic Origin, 2000
Race
White	888
Black/African American	0
Amer. Indian/Alaska Natv.	0
Asian	2
Natv. Hawaiian/Pac. Islander	1
Other Race	0
Two or more races	9
Hispanic origin, total	10
Mexican	2
Puerto Rican	5
Cuban	0
Other Hispanic	3

Age & Nativity, 2000
Under 5 years	36
18 years and over	739
21 years and over	724
65 years and over	205
85 years and over	21
Median Age	47.6
Native born	861
Foreign born	39

Educational Attainment, 2000
Population 25 years and over	705
0-8 yrs of school	1.0%
High School grad or higher	97.7%
Bachelor's degree or higher	53.5%
Graduate degree	21.7%

Income & Poverty, 1999
Per capita income	$47,307
Median household income	$82,842
Median family income	$104,618
Persons in poverty	27
H'holds receiving public assistance	0
H'holds receiving social security	144

Households, 2000
Total households	386
With persons under 18	86
With persons over 65	152
Family households	261
One-person households	106
Persons per household	2.33
Persons per family	2.86

Labor & Employment
Total civilian labor force, 2004**	526
Unemployment rate	2.0%
Total civilian labor force, 2000	465
Unemployment rate	3.0%

Employed persons 16 years and over by occupation, 2000
Managers & professionals	246
Service occupations	36
Sales & office occupations	126
Farming, fishing & forestry	0
Construction & maintenance	23
Production & transportation	20
Self-employed persons	58

*US Census Bureau
**New Jersey Department of Labor

General Information
Borough of Interlaken
100 Grassmere Ave
Interlaken, NJ 07712
732-531-7405

Web site	NA
Land area (sq. miles)	0.35
Water area (sq. miles)	0.04
Type of government	Borough
Form of government	B

Government
Legislative Districts
US Congressional	12
State Legislative	11

Local Officials, 2006
Mayor	Robert Wolf
Admin/Manager	Aime Sweeney
Clerk	Aime Sweeney
Finance Dir/Treas	Aime SweeneyAime Sweeney
Engineer	Peter Avakian
Attorney	Dennis Crawford
Tax assessor	Ed Mullane
Tax collector	Eleanor Cottrell
Building officer	Paul Vitale
Zoning officer	Vito Marinachio
Public Works	Norman Cottrell

Housing & Construction
Housing Units, 2000*
Total	397
Median rent	$1,333
Median SF home value	$280,600

New Privately Owned Housing Units Authorized by Building Permit
	Units	Value
Total, 2004	1	$422,000
Single family	1	$422,000
Total, 2005	0	$0
Single family	0	$0

Real Property Valuation - parcels, 2005
	Number	Valuation
Total		$196,827,200
Vacant	11	1,057,900
Residential	396	195,769,300
Commercial	0	0
Industrial	0	0
Apartments	0	0
Farm land	0	0
Farm homestead	0	0

Average Property Value & Tax, 2005
Residential value	$494,367
Property tax	$6,000
FAIR rebate	$544

Public Library
No public municipal library.

Library statistics, 2004
	Total	per capita
Volumes	NA	NA
Expenditure	NA	NA

Public Safety
Police
Chief	James Lanza
Number of officers, 2004	5

Crime, 2004	Number	Rate
Total	13	14.5
Violent	0	0
Non-violent	13	14.5
Domestic Viol.	2	NA

Emergency/Fire
Director	NA

Public School District
(for school year 2004-2005 except as noted)

Interlaken Borough School District†
100 Grassmere Ave
Interlaken, NJ 07712

†No schools in district - sends children to Asbury Park schools.

Grade plan	NA
Enrollment	NA
Students per teacher	NA
Per pupil expenditure	NA
Median faculty salary	NA

Assessment test results
(percent scoring at proficient or advanced level)
	Language	Math
Grade 3	NA	NA
Grade 8	NA	NA
High school	NA	NA

SAT
Percent tested	NA
Average SAT math score	NA
Average SAT verbal score	NA

No Child Left Behind, 2003-04
Attendence rate (target = 90%)	NA
Drop rate	NA
Highly-qualified teachers	NA
District needs improvement?(AYP)	NA

Municipal Finance
Fiscal Year 2005
Total tax levy	$2,390,107
County levy	698,520
County taxes	626,799
County library	34,527
County health	0
County open space	37,195
School levy	271,523
Local muni. budget	1,420,064
Misc. revenues	307,542
Total aid	$152,544
CMPTRA	9,800
Muni. block grant	3,982
Energy tax receipts	113,762
Homeland security	25,000

Fiscal Year 2006
Total aid	$152,545
CMPTRA	5,819
Muni. block grant	3,982
Energy tax receipts	117,744
Homeland security	25,000

Taxes
	2003	2004	2005
General tax rate per $100	1.10	1.161	1.214
Net valuation taxable	$196,796,989	$196,914,937	$196,919,396
State equalized value	$174,620,221	$209,233,474	$249,770,923
County equalization ratio	58.78	112.70	94.11

Demographics & Socio-Economic Characteristics

(2000 U.S. Census, except as noted)

Population

1980*	61,493
1990*	61,018
2000	60,695
Male	28,353
Female	32,342
2004 (estimate)*	59,689
Persons per sq. mi. of land	20,188

Race & Hispanic Origin, 2000

Race

White	5,446
Black/African American	49,566
Amer. Indian/Alaska Natv.	146
Asian	669
Natv. Hawaiian/Pac. Islander	59
Other Race	2,234
Two or more races	2,575
Hispanic origin, total	5,086
Mexican	357
Puerto Rican	2,083
Cuban	105
Other Hispanic	2,541

Age & Nativity, 2000

Under 5 years	4,891
18 years and over	43,691
21 years and over	41,138
65 years and over	4,576
85 years and over	507
Median Age	31.5
Native born	45,937
Foreign born	14,678

Educational Attainment, 2000

Population 25 years and over	37,143
0-8 yrs of school	7.6%
High School grad or higher	72.0%
Bachelor's degree or higher	12.1%
Graduate degree	2.7%

Income & Poverty, 1999

Per capita income	$16,874
Median household income	$36,575
Median family income	$41,098
Persons in poverty	10,420
H'holds receiving public assistance	1,778
H'holds receiving social security	4,020

Households, 2000

Total households	22,032
With persons under 18	9,079
With persons over 65	3,679
Family households	14,403
One-person households	6,453
Persons per household	2.74
Persons per family	3.39

Labor & Employment

Total civilian labor force, 2004**	3,715
Unemployment rate	3.3%
Total civilian labor force, 2000	29,740
Unemployment rate	12.5%

Employed persons 16 years and over by occupation, 2000

Managers & professionals	5,480
Service occupations	5,654
Sales & office occupations	8,445
Farming, fishing & forestry	4
Construction & maintenance	1,547
Production & transportation	4,878
Self-employed persons	698

*US Census Bureau
**New Jersey Department of Labor

General Information

Township of Irvington
Civic Square
Irvington, NJ 07111
973-399-8111

Web site	www.irvinton.net
Land area (sq. miles)	2.96
Water area (sq. miles)	0
Type of government	Township
Form of government	MC '50

Government

Legislative Districts

US Congressional	10
State Legislative	28

Local Officials, 2006

Mayor	Wayne Smith
Admin/Manager	Wayne Bradley
Clerk	Harold Wiener
Finance Dir/Treas	Faheem Ra'Oof
Engineer	John Wiggins
Attorney	Marvin Braker
Tax assessor	James Gibbs
Tax collector	NA
Building officer	Nagy Sileem
Zoning officer	Judith Deinhardt
Public Works	NA

Housing & Construction

Housing Units, 2000*

Total	24,116
Median rent	$678
Median SF home value	$112,200

New Privately Owned Housing Units

Authorized by Building Permit

	Units	Value
Total, 2004	28	$778,635
Single family	1	$100,450
Total, 2005	50	$3,449,335
Single family	5	$409,700

Real Property Valuation - parcels, 2005

	Number	Valuation
Total		$262,197,400
Vacant	345	2,922,100
Residential	7,987	172,677,400
Commercial	635	35,823,000
Industrial	174	14,687,500
Apartments	336	36,087,400
Farm land	0	0
Farm homestead	0	0

Average Property Value & Tax, 2005

Residential value	$21,620
Property tax	$5,148
FAIR rebate	$552

Public Library

Irvington Public Library
Civic Square
Irvington, NJ 07111
973-372-6400

Director..................Joan Whitaker

Library statistics, 2004

	Total	per capita
Volumes	176,853	2.91
Expenditure	$1,592,589	$26.24

Public Safety

Police

Chief	Michael Chase
Number of officers, 2004	185

Crime, 2004	Number	Rate
Total	4,811	80.1
Violent	1,440	24
Non-violent	3,371	56.1
Domestic Viol.	656	NA

Emergency/Fire

Director..................Donald Huber

Public School District

(for school year 2004-2005 except as noted)

Irvington Township School District
1 University Place
Irvington, NJ 07111
973-399-6800

Superintendent	Ethel Davion (Int)
Grade plan	K-12
Enrollment	7,948.0
Students per teacher	12.1
Per pupil expenditure	$14,025
Median faculty salary	$53,827
Median administrator salary	$96,705
Grade 12 enrollment	392.5
High school graduation rate	93.1%

Assessment test results

(percent scoring at proficient or advanced level)

	Language	Math
Grade 3	58.4%	50.4%
Grade 8	37.3%	18.2%
High school	55.0%	24.7%

SAT

Percent tested	43%
Average SAT math score	354
Average SAT verbal score	359

No Child Left Behind, 2003-04

Attendence rate (target = 90%)	83.4%
Drop rate	2.5%
Highly-qualified teachers	76.7%
District needs improvement?(AYP)	Yes

Municipal Finance

Fiscal Year 2005

Total tax levy	$62,822,903
County levy	8,335,586
County taxes	8,160,953
County library	0
County health	0
County open space	174,633
School levy	17,459,529
Local muni. budget	37,027,788
Misc. revenues	43,519,346
Total aid	$14,275,889
CMPTRA	11,527,528
Muni. block grant	266,995
Energy tax receipts	2,341,366
Homeland security	140,000

Fiscal Year 2006

Total aid	$14,275,888
CMPTRA	11,445,580
Muni. block grant	266,995
Energy tax receipts	2,423,313
Homeland security	140,000

Taxes

	2003	2004	2005
General tax rate per $100	23.02	23.030	23.820
Net valuation taxable	$265,852,229	$264,230,308	$263,815,483
State equalized value	$1,547,451,857	$1,726,457,148	$2,075,652,895
County equalization ratio	19.13	19.13	15.23

Demographics & Socio-Economic Characteristics
(2000 U.S. Census, except as noted)

Population

1980*	1,575
1990*	1,470
2000	1,751
Male	843
Female	908
2004 (estimate)*	1,849
Persons per sq. mi. of land	3,072

Race & Hispanic Origin, 2000
Race

White	1,712
Black/African American	2
Amer. Indian/Alaska Natv.	8
Asian	11
Natv. Hawaiian/Pac. Islander	0
Other Race	1
Two or more races	17
Hispanic origin, total	24
Mexican	0
Puerto Rican	16
Cuban	4
Other Hispanic	4

Age & Nativity, 2000

Under 5 years	84
18 years and over	1,359
21 years and over	1,308
65 years and over	303
85 years and over	31
Median Age	43
Native born	1,663
Foreign born	86

Educational Attainment, 2000

Population 25 years and over	1,175
0-8 yrs of school	1.4%
High School grad or higher	90.8%
Bachelor's degree or higher	33.4%
Graduate degree	12.8%

Income & Poverty, 1999

Per capita income	$26,975
Median household income	$61,125
Median family income	$72,596
Persons in poverty	71
H'holds receiving public assistance	8
H'holds receiving social security	235

Households, 2000

Total households	705
With persons under 18	218
With persons over 65	212
Family households	498
One-person households	171
Persons per household	2.48
Persons per family	2.97

Labor & Employment

Total civilian labor force, 2004**	902
Unemployment rate	1.7%
Total civilian labor force, 2000	856
Unemployment rate	4.7%

Employed persons 16 years and over by occupation, 2000

Managers & professionals	351
Service occupations	89
Sales & office occupations	202
Farming, fishing & forestry	0
Construction & maintenance	119
Production & transportation	55
Self-employed persons	79

*US Census Bureau
**New Jersey Department of Labor

General Information
Borough of Island Heights
PO Box AH
Island Heights, NJ 08732
732-270-6415

Web site	NA
Land area (sq. miles)	0.60
Water area (sq. miles)	0.27
Type of government	Borough
Form of government	SM '50

Government

Legislative Districts

US Congressional	3
State Legislative	10

Local Officials, 2006

Mayor	David Siddons
Admin/Manager	Adrian Fanning
Clerk	Eleanor Rogalski
Finance Dir/Treas	Adrian Fanning
Engineer	Michael O'Donnell
Attorney	Robert Grietz
Tax assessor	Victoria Mickiewicz
Tax collector	Wendy Prior
Building officer	Ken Anderson
Zoning officer	NA
Public Works	Jay Price

Housing & Construction

Housing Units, 2000*

Total	807
Median rent	$830
Median SF home value	$167,400

New Privately Owned Housing Units
Authorized by Building Permit

	Units	Value
Total, 2004	11	$850,927
Single family	11	$850,927
Total, 2005	11	$850,927
Single family	11	$850,927

Real Property Valuation - parcels, 2005

	Number	Valuation
Total		$342,831,700
Vacant	52	10,949,600
Residential	806	308,750,600
Commercial	30	22,642,200
Industrial	0	0
Apartments	1	489,300
Farm land	0	0
Farm homestead	0	0

Average Property Value & Tax, 2005

Residential value	$383,065
Property tax	$5,210
FAIR rebate	$790

Public Library
Island Heights Branch Library†
Summit & Central
Island Heights, NJ 08732
732-270-6266

Branch Librarian............Emily Holman

Library statistics, 2004

	Total	per capita
Volumes	NA	NA
Expenditure	NA	NA

†Branch of County Library

Public Safety

Police

Chief	NA
Number of officers, 2004	5

Crime, 2004	Number	Rate
Total	22	12
Violent	4	2.2
Non-violent	18	9.8
Domestic Viol.	9	NA

Emergency/Fire

Director............Robert Wilber Jr.

Public School District
(for school year 2004-2005 except as noted)

Island Heights School District
115 Summit Ave
Island Heights, NJ 08732
732-929-1222

Superintendent	John Lichtenberg
Grade plan	K-6
Enrollment	103.0
Students per teacher	7.9
Per pupil expenditure	$16,281
Median faculty salary	$37,549
Median administrator salary	$113,900
Grade 12 enrollment	NA
High school graduation rate	NA

Assessment test results
(percent scoring at proficient or advanced level)

	Language	Math
Grade 3	84.2%	94.7%
Grade 8	NA	NA
High school	NA	NA

SAT

Percent tested	NA
Average SAT math score	NA
Average SAT verbal score	NA

No Child Left Behind, 2003-04

Attendance rate (target = 90%)	95.6%
Drop rate	NA
Highly-qualified teachers	100%
District needs improvement?(AYP)	No

Municipal Finance

Fiscal Year 2005

Total tax levy	$4,665,882
County levy	966,691
County taxes	814,460
County library	85,566
County health	36,268
County open space	30,397
School levy	2,597,212
Local muni. budget	1,101,979
Misc. revenues	1,160,728
Total aid	$198,016
CMPTRA	63,911
Muni. block grant	6,866
Energy tax receipts	102,239
Homeland security	25,000

Fiscal Year 2006

Total aid	$198,015
CMPTRA	60,332
Muni. block grant	6,866
Energy tax receipts	105,817
Homeland security	25,000

Taxes

	2003	2004	2005
General tax rate per $100	3.43	3.492	1.361
Net valuation taxable	$126,993,439	$129,245,436	$343,054,532
State equalized value	$219,143,122	$249,716,830	$340,080,280
County equalization ratio	66.94	57.95	135.67

Demographics & Socio-Economic Characteristics

(2000 U.S. Census, except as noted)

Population

1980*	25,644
1990*	33,233
2000	42,816
Male	20,911
Female	21,905
2004 (estimate)*	51,607
Persons per sq. mi. of land	516

Race & Hispanic Origin, 2000

Race

White	39,073
Black/African American	1,670
Amer. Indian/Alaska Natv.	57
Asian	882
Natv. Hawaiian/Pac. Islander	3
Other Race	414
Two or more races	717
Hispanic origin, total	2,474
Mexican	201
Puerto Rican	1,316
Cuban	161
Other Hispanic	796

Age & Nativity, 2000

Under 5 years	3,515
18 years and over	30,114
21 years and over	28,764
65 years and over	4,009
85 years and over	456
Median Age	35.2
Native born	40,097
Foreign born	2,713

Educational Attainment, 2000

Population 25 years and over	27,385
0-8 yrs of school	3.6%
High School grad or higher	86.9%
Bachelor's degree or higher	23.1%
Graduate degree	6.0%

Income & Poverty, 1999

Per capita income	$23,981
Median household income	$65,218
Median family income	$71,045
Persons in poverty	1,573
H'holds receiving public assistance	193
H'holds receiving social security	3,181

Households, 2000

Total households	14,176
With persons under 18	6,676
With persons over 65	2,750
Family households	11,264
One-person households	2,267
Persons per household	2.99
Persons per family	3.38

Labor & Employment

Total civilian labor force, 2004**	22,787
Unemployment rate	4.8%
Total civilian labor force, 2000	21,325
Unemployment rate	4.3%

Employed persons 16 years and over by occupation, 2000

Managers & professionals	7,163
Service occupations	2,825
Sales & office occupations	5,568
Farming, fishing & forestry	26
Construction & maintenance	2,508
Production & transportation	2,320
Self-employed persons	915

*US Census Bureau
**New Jersey Department of Labor

General Information

Township of Jackson
95 W Veteran's Hwy
Jackson, NJ 08527
732-928-1200

Web site	www.jacksontwpnj.net
Land area (sq. miles)	100.06
Water area (sq. miles)	0.75
Type of government	Township
Form of government	TC

Government

Legislative Districts

US Congressional	4
State Legislative	30

Local Officials, 2006

Mayor	Sean Giblin
Admin/Manager	Andrew J. Salerno
Clerk	Ann Marie Eden
Finance Dir/Treas	Lily Ann Farley
Engineer	Daniel Burke
Attorney	Kevin Starkey
Tax assessor	Dennis Raftery
Tax collector	Michael Campbell
Building officer	Barry Olejarz
Zoning officer	Richard Megill
Public Works	Sergio Panunzio

Housing & Construction

Housing Units, 2000*

Total	14,640
Median rent	$863
Median SF home value	$156,300

New Privately Owned Housing Units Authorized by Building Permit

	Units	Value
Total, 2004	201	$34,175,252
Single family	194	$33,440,754
Total, 2005	209	$42,840,003
Single family	209	$42,840,003

Real Property Valuation - parcels, 2005

	Number	Valuation
Total		$2,655,746,550
Vacant	3,001	98,997,550
Residential	15,259	2,248,532,000
Commercial	210	247,695,000
Industrial	53	17,296,600
Apartments	10	30,084,100
Farm land	74	12,457,000
Farm homestead	106	684,300

Average Property Value & Tax, 2005

Residential value	$146,386
Property tax	$5,060
FAIR rebate	$620

Public Library

Jackson Branch Library†
2nd Jackson Rd
Jackson, NJ 08527
732-928-4400

Branch Librarian	John Glace

Library statistics, 2004

	Total	per capita
Volumes	NA	NA
Expenditure	NA	NA

†Branch of County Library

Public Safety

Police

Chief	Christopher Dunton (PS Dir)
Number of officers, 2004	85

Crime, 2004	Number	Rate
Total	636	12.8
Violent	63	1.3
Non-violent	573	11.5
Domestic Viol.	389	NA

Emergency/Fire

Director	Barry Olejarz

Public School District

(for school year 2004-2005 except as noted)

Jackson Township School District
151 Don Connor Blvd
Jackson, NJ 08527
732-833-4600

Superintendent	Thomas Gialanella
Grade plan	K-12
Enrollment	9,528.0
Students per teacher	12.5
Per pupil expenditure	$10,401
Median faculty salary	$44,975
Median administrator salary	$117,319
Grade 12 enrollment	598.0
High school graduation rate	96.3%

Assessment test results

(percent scoring at proficient or advanced level)

	Language	Math
Grade 3	91.0%	90.5%
Grade 8	82.0%	72.6%
High school	90.8%	81.3%

SAT

Percent tested	74%
Average SAT math score	498
Average SAT verbal score	486

No Child Left Behind, 2003-04

Attendance rate (target = 90%)	94.4%
Drop rate	0.9%
Highly-qualified teachers	96.4%
District needs improvement?(AYP)	No

Municipal Finance

Fiscal Year 2005

Total tax levy	$91,994,841
County levy	19,567,273
County taxes	16,485,500
County library	1,731,782
County health	734,152
County open space	615,838
School levy	55,680,533
Local muni. budget	16,747,036
Misc. revenues	16,507,077
Total aid	$4,664,905
CMPTRA	1,715,717
Muni. block grant	167,883
Energy tax receipts	2,634,433
Homeland security	140,000

Fiscal Year 2006

Total aid	$4,664,905
CMPTRA	1,623,512
Muni. block grant	167,883
Energy tax receipts	2,726,638
Homeland security	140,000

Taxes

	2003	2004	2005
General tax rate per $100	3.22	3.307	3.457
Net valuation taxable	$2,426,416,852	$2,539,193,051	$2,661,659,878
State equalized value	$3,978,384,738	$4,911,604,535	$5,676,391,295
County equalization ratio	70.9	60.99	51.63

Demographics & Socio-Economic Characteristics
(2000 U.S. Census, except as noted)

Population
1980*	4,114
1990*	5,294
2000	6,025
Male	2,935
Female	3,090
2004 (estimate)*	6,524
Persons per sq. mi. of land	7,740

Race & Hispanic Origin, 2000
Race
White	4,990
Black/African American	532
Amer. Indian/Alaska Natv.	12
Asian	134
Natv. Hawaiian/Pac. Islander	0
Other Race	229
Two or more races	128
Hispanic origin, total	606
Mexican	119
Puerto Rican	180
Cuban	26
Other Hispanic	281

Age & Nativity, 2000
Under 5 years	457
18 years and over	4,541
21 years and over	4,364
65 years and over	646
85 years and over	117
Median Age	35.4
Native born	5,344
Foreign born	681

Educational Attainment, 2000
Population 25 years and over	4,089
0-8 yrs of school	5.5%
High School grad or higher	82.9%
Bachelor's degree or higher	20.2%
Graduate degree	5.0%

Income & Poverty, 1999
Per capita income	$23,325
Median household income	$59,461
Median family income	$67,887
Persons in poverty	206
H'holds receiving public assistance	65
H'holds receiving social security	424

Households, 2000
Total households	2,176
With persons under 18	843
With persons over 65	402
Family households	1,551
One-person households	487
Persons per household	2.7
Persons per family	3.18

Labor & Employment
Total civilian labor force, 2004**	3,257
Unemployment rate	3.2%
Total civilian labor force, 2000	3,327
Unemployment rate	4.3%

Employed persons 16 years and over by occupation, 2000
Managers & professionals	855
Service occupations	429
Sales & office occupations	980
Farming, fishing & forestry	0
Construction & maintenance	324
Production & transportation	595
Self-employed persons	127

*US Census Bureau
**New Jersey Department of Labor

General Information
Borough of Jamesburg
131 Perrineville Rd
Jamesburg, NJ 08831
732-521-2222
Web site	www.jamesburgborough.org
Land area (sq. miles)	0.84
Water area (sq. miles)	0
Type of government	Borough
Form of government	B

Government
Legislative Districts
US Congressional	12
State Legislative	14

Local Officials, 2006
Mayor	Anthony La Mantia
Admin/Manager	Denise Jawidzik
Clerk	Gretchen McCarthy
Finance Dir/Treas	Denise Jawidzik
Engineer	Remington,Vernick et.al
Attorney	Frederick Raffetto
Tax assessor	Edward Heindel
Tax collector	NA
Building officer	NA
Zoning officer	Bernard Long
Public Works	Joseph Intravartola

Housing & Construction
Housing Units, 2000*
Total	2,240
Median rent	$777
Median SF home value	$139,300

New Privately Owned Housing Units
Authorized by Building Permit

	Units	Value
Total, 2004	7	$279,546
Single family	7	$279,546
Total, 2005	0	$0
Single family	0	$0

Real Property Valuation - parcels, 2005
	Number	Valuation
Total		$237,597,300
Vacant	124	3,077,200
Residential	1,565	192,994,600
Commercial	101	32,210,400
Industrial	1	925,000
Apartments	14	8,390,100
Farm land	0	0
Farm homestead	0	0

Average Property Value & Tax, 2005
Residential value	$123,319
Property tax	$5,323
FAIR rebate	$510

Public Library
Jamesburg Public Library
229 Gatzmer Ave
Jamesburg, NJ 08831
732-521-0440
Director	Cynthia Yasher

Library statistics, 2004
	Total	per capita
Volumes	21,518	3.57
Expenditure	$120,747	$20.04

Public Safety
Police
Chief	David Lester
Number of officers, 2004	13

Crime, 2004	Number	Rate
Total	75	11.6
Violent	9	1.4
Non-violent	66	10.2
Domestic Viol.	56	NA

Emergency/Fire
Director	Tom Cooper

Public School District
(for school year 2004-2005 except as noted)

Jamesburg School District
Augusta St
Jamesburg, NJ 08831
732-521-0303
Superintendent	Shirley Ann Bzdewka
Grade plan	K-12
Enrollment	636.0
Students per teacher	12.3
Per pupil expenditure	$11,428
Median faculty salary	$43,725
Median administrator salary	$75,158
Grade 12 enrollment	NA
High school graduation rate	NA

Assessment test results
(percent scoring at proficient or advanced level)
	Language	Math
Grade 3	66.2%	79.8%
Grade 8	60.3%	57.1%
High school	NA	NA

SAT
Percent tested	NA
Average SAT math score	NA
Average SAT verbal score	NA

No Child Left Behind, 2003-04
Attendence rate (target = 90%)	94.2%
Drop rate	NA
Highly-qualified teachers	94%
District needs improvement?(AYP)	No

Municipal Finance
Fiscal Year 2005
Total tax levy	$10,324,575
County levy	1,240,045
County taxes	1,123,290
County library	0
County health	0
County open space	116,755
School levy	6,617,393
Local muni. budget	2,467,137
Misc. revenues	2,360,044
Total aid	$667,780
CMPTRA	304,844
Muni. block grant	23,624
Energy tax receipts	289,312
Homeland security	50,000

Fiscal Year 2006
Total aid	$667,780
CMPTRA	294,718
Muni. block grant	23,624
Energy tax receipts	299,438
Homeland security	50,000

Taxes
	2003	2004	2005
General tax rate per $100	4.03	4.100	4.320
Net valuation taxable	$235,967,641	$238,752,856	$239,196,175
State equalized value	$335,801,396	$391,494,173	$446,095,067
County equalization ratio	81.91	70.27	60.80

Demographics & Socio-Economic Characteristics

(2000 U.S. Census, except as noted)

Population

1980*	16,413
1990*	17,825
2000	19,717
Male	9,775
Female	9,942
2004 (estimate)*	21,280
Persons per sq. mi. of land	524

Race & Hispanic Origin, 2000

Race

White	18,955
Black/African American	163
Amer. Indian/Alaska Natv.	32
Asian	211
Natv. Hawaiian/Pac. Islander	10
Other Race	122
Two or more races	224
Hispanic origin, total	672
Mexican	50
Puerto Rican	244
Cuban	53
Other Hispanic	325

Age & Nativity, 2000

Under 5 years	1,452
18 years and over	14,407
21 years and over	13,861
65 years and over	1,690
85 years and over	158
Median Age	37.2
Native born	18,474
Foreign born	1,243

Educational Attainment, 2000

Population 25 years and over	13,398
0-8 yrs of school	2.6%
High School grad or higher	89.6%
Bachelor's degree or higher	27.8%
Graduate degree	7.1%

Income & Poverty, 1999

Per capita income	$27,950
Median household income	$68,837
Median family income	$76,974
Persons in poverty	468
H'holds receiving public assistance	33
H'holds receiving social security	1,371

Households, 2000

Total households	7,131
With persons under 18	2,907
With persons over 65	1,281
Family households	5,446
One-person households	1,316
Persons per household	2.76
Persons per family	3.17

Labor & Employment

Total civilian labor force, 2004**	11,391
Unemployment rate	3.0%
Total civilian labor force, 2000	11,023
Unemployment rate	3.1%

Employed persons 16 years and over by occupation, 2000

Managers & professionals	4,036
Service occupations	1,132
Sales & office occupations	3,210
Farming, fishing & forestry	9
Construction & maintenance	1,326
Production & transportation	968
Self-employed persons	447

*US Census Bureau
**New Jersey Department of Labor

General Information

Township of Jefferson
1033 Weldon Rd
Lake Hopatcong, NJ 07849
973-697-1500

Web site	www.jeffersontownship.net
Land area (sq. miles)	40.63
Water area (sq. miles)	2.41
Type of government	Township
Form of government	MC '50

Government

Legislative Districts

US Congressional	11
State Legislative	25

Local Officials, 2006

Mayor	Russell Felter
Admin/Manager	James Leach
Clerk	Lydia Magnotti
Finance Dir/Treas	Bill Eagen
Engineer	H. Mott McDonald /J. Co
Attorney	Lawrence Cohen
Tax assessor	Shawn Hopkins
Tax collector	Elizabeth Recksiek
Building officer	Tom Mahoney
Zoning officer	Bruce Decker
Public Works	Jeff Elam

Housing & Construction

Housing Units, 2000*

Total	7,527
Median rent	$847
Median SF home value	$180,400

New Privately Owned Housing Units Authorized by Building Permit

	Units	Value
Total, 2004	149	$12,994,201
Single family	109	$12,985,801
Total, 2005	115	$14,463,649
Single family	115	$14,463,649

Real Property Valuation - parcels, 2005

	Number	Valuation
Total		$1,382,616,300
Vacant	960	49,954,500
Residential	7,710	1,214,815,700
Commercial	204	100,286,700
Industrial	6	2,339,000
Apartments	19	11,709,400
Farm land	15	3,354,100
Farm homestead	35	156,900

Average Property Value & Tax, 2005

Residential value	$156,872
Property tax	$5,452
FAIR rebate	$498

Public Library

Jefferson Twp Municipal Library
1031 Weldon Rd
Oak Ridge, NJ 07438
973-208-6115

Director .... Seth Stephens

Library statistics, 2004

	Total	per capita
Volumes	49,364	2.5
Expenditure	$660,891	$33.52

Public Safety

Police

Chief	John Palko
Number of officers, 2004	39

Crime, 2004	Number	Rate
Total	304	14.8
Violent	10	0.5
Non-violent	294	14.3
Domestic Viol.	104	NA

Emergency/Fire

Director .... V. Corsoro/S. Shatzel

Public School District

(for school year 2004-2005 except as noted)

Jefferson Township School District
28 Bowling Green Parkway
Lake Hopatcong, NJ 07849
973-663-5780

Superintendent	Gary Bowen
Grade plan	K-12
Enrollment	3,602.0
Students per teacher	11.8
Per pupil expenditure	$11,599
Median faculty salary	$48,760
Median administrator salary	$105,700
Grade 12 enrollment	221.5
High school graduation rate	94.1%

Assessment test results

(percent scoring at proficient or advanced level)

	Language	Math
Grade 3	84.5%	82.4%
Grade 8	78.6%	75.8%
High school	92.2%	89.2%

SAT

Percent tested	74%
Average SAT math score	517
Average SAT verbal score	500

No Child Left Behind, 2003-04

Attendance rate (target = 90%)	94.9%
Drop rate	1.8%
Highly-qualified teachers	96.5%
District needs improvement?(AYP)	No

Municipal Finance

Fiscal Year 2005

Total tax levy	$48,147,275
County levy	6,267,249
County taxes	5,133,742
County library	0
County health	0
County open space	1,133,507
School levy	30,849,655
Local muni. budget	11,030,371
Misc. revenues	7,350,405
Total aid	$2,755,021
CMPTRA	549,332
Muni. block grant	77,996
Energy tax receipts	1,864,899
Homeland security	70,000

Fiscal Year 2006

Total aid	$2,775,021
CMPTRA	101,061
Muni. block grant	77,996
Energy tax receipts	1,930,170
Homeland security	90,000

Taxes

	2003	2004	2005
General tax rate per $100	3.09	3.220	3.480
Net valuation taxable	$1,305,600,553	$1,352,533,505	$1,385,310,610
State equalized value	$1,970,420,394	$2,297,255,143	$2,643,722,538
County equalization ratio	74.98	66.26	58.82

Demographics & Socio-Economic Characteristics
(2000 U.S. Census, except as noted)

Population
1980*	223,532
1990*	228,537
2000	240,055
Male	117,144
Female	122,911
2004 (estimate)*	239,079
Persons per sq. mi. of land	16,028

Race & Hispanic Origin, 2000
Race
White	81,637
Black/African American	67,994
Amer. Indian/Alaska Natv.	1,071
Asian	38,881
Natv. Hawaiian/Pac. Islander	181
Other Race	36,280
Two or more races	14,011
Hispanic origin, total	67,952
Mexican	2,495
Puerto Rican	29,777
Cuban	1,860
Other Hispanic	33,820

Age & Nativity, 2000
Under 5 years	16,631
18 years and over	180,652
21 years and over	170,621
65 years and over	23,438
85 years and over	2,805
Median Age	32.4
Native born	158,501
Foreign born	81,554

Educational Attainment, 2000
Population 25 years and over	155,460
0-8 yrs of school	10.6%
High School grad or higher	72.6%
Bachelor's degree or higher	27.5%
Graduate degree	9.3%

Income & Poverty, 1999
Per capita income	$19,410
Median household income	$37,862
Median family income	$41,639
Persons in poverty	44,075
H'holds receiving public assistance	5,977
H'holds receiving social security	17,981

Households, 2000
Total households	88,632
With persons under 18	31,837
With persons over 65	17,802
Family households	55,636
One-person households	25,921
Persons per household	2.67
Persons per family	3.37

Labor & Employment
Total civilian labor force, 2004**	118,229
Unemployment rate	7.3%
Total civilian labor force, 2000	114,909
Unemployment rate	10.0%

Employed persons 16 years and over by occupation, 2000
Managers & professionals	34,111
Service occupations	16,436
Sales & office occupations	31,502
Farming, fishing & forestry	81
Construction & maintenance	5,313
Production & transportation	16,005
Self-employed persons	3,448

*US Census Bureau
**New Jersey Department of Labor

General Information
City of Jersey
280 Grove St
Jersey, NJ 07302
201-547-5000

Web site	www.cityofjerseycity.com
Land area (sq. miles)	14.92
Water area (sq. miles)	6.20
Type of government	City
Form of government	MC '50

Government

Legislative Districts
US Congressional	9, 10
State Legislative	31, 32, 33

Local Officials, 2006
Mayor	Jerramiah T. Healy
Admin/Manager	Brian O'Reilly
Clerk	Robert Byrne
Finance Dir/Treas	Paul Soyka
Engineer	William Goble
Attorney	William Matsikoudis
Tax assessor	Eduardo Toloza
Tax collector	Maureen Cosgrove
Building officer	Raymond Meyer
Zoning officer	Anthony Lambiase
Public Works	John M. Yurchak

Housing & Construction

Housing Units, 2000*
Total	93,648
Median rent	$675
Median SF home value	$125,000

New Privately Owned Housing Units
Authorized by Building Permit
	Units	Value
Total, 2004	2,153	$120,776,083
Single family	84	$2,882,876
Total, 2005	3,194	$283,593,019
Single family	175	$15,524,051

Real Property Valuation - parcels, 2005
	Number	Valuation
Total		$5,440,421,373
Vacant	4,884	347,031,000
Residential	32,383	2,940,771,675
Commercial	3,420	1,236,195,348
Industrial	728	504,392,700
Apartments	1,714	412,030,650
Farm land	0	0
Farm homestead	0	0

Average Property Value & Tax, 2005
Residential value	$90,812
Property tax	$4,181
FAIR rebate	$594

Public Library
Jersey City Public Library
472 Jersey Ave
Jersey City, NJ 07302
201-547-4500

Director. . . . . Priscilla Gardner

Library statistics, 2004
	Total	per capita
Volumes	387,425	1.61
Expenditure	$7,691,811	$32.04

Public Safety

Police
Chief	Robert Troy
Number of officers, 2004	813

Crime, 2004	Number	Rate
Total	11,251	47.1
Violent	2,942	12.3
Non-violent	8,309	34.8
Domestic Viol.	2,091	NA

Emergency/Fire
Director. . . . . Frederick Eggers

Public School District
(for school year 2004-2005 except as noted)

Jersey City School District
346 Claremont Ave
Jersey City, NJ 07305
201-915-6202

Superintendent	Charles Epps Jr.
Grade plan	K-12
Enrollment	30,074.0
Students per teacher	9.2
Per pupil expenditure	$14,218
Median faculty salary	$44,420
Median administrator salary	$102,662
Grade 12 enrollment	1,469.0
High school graduation rate	NA

Assessment test results
(percent scoring at proficient or advanced level)
	Language	Math
Grade 3	73.8%	68.8%
Grade 8	56.0%	42.9%
High school	63.1%	49.6%

SAT
Percent tested	NA
Average SAT math score	NA
Average SAT verbal score	NA

No Child Left Behind, 2003-04
Attendence rate (target = 90%)	93.7%
Drop rate	5.9%
Highly-qualified teachers	74.6%
District needs improvement?(AYP)	Yes

Municipal Finance

Fiscal Year 2005
Total tax levy	$251,889,591
County levy	66,547,027
County taxes	65,277,811
County library	0
County health	0
County open space	1,269,216
School levy	79,742,565
Local muni. budget	105,600,000
Misc. revenues	275,954,268
Total aid	$81,472,468
CMPTRA	48,915,137
Muni. block grant	999,914
Energy tax receipts	31,417,417
Homeland security	140,000

Fiscal Year 2006
Total aid	$81,472,468
CMPTRA	47,815,528
Muni. block grant	999,914
Energy tax receipts	32,517,026
Homeland security	140,000

Taxes
	2003	2004	2005
General tax rate per $100	4.61	4.606	4.605
Net valuation taxable	$5,207,668,677	$5,326,519,066	$5,470,850,530
State equalized value	$10,310,173,583	$12,058,937,186	$15,816,277,913
County equalization ratio	60.33	50.51	44.01

Demographics & Socio-Economic Characteristics
(2000 U.S. Census, except as noted)

Population
1980*	10,613
1990*	11,069
2000	10,732
Male	5,237
Female	5,495
2000 (revised)	10,871
2004 (estimate)*	10,739
Persons per sq. mi. of land	9,961

Race & Hispanic Origin, 2000
Race
White	10,014
Black/African American	229
Amer. Indian/Alaska Natv.	11
Asian	132
Natv. Hawaiian/Pac. Islander	7
Other Race	187
Two or more races	152
Hispanic origin, total	853
Mexican	61
Puerto Rican	473
Cuban	70
Other Hispanic	249

Age & Nativity, 2000
Under 5 years	755
18 years and over	7,814
21 years and over	7,407
65 years and over	1,207
85 years and over	152
Median Age	34.4
Native born	9,950
Foreign born	782

Educational Attainment, 2000
Population 25 years and over	6,854
0-8 yrs of school	6.7%
High School grad or higher	69.8%
Bachelor's degree or higher	9.5%
Graduate degree	2.8%

Income & Poverty, 1999
Per capita income	$17,417
Median household income	$36,383
Median family income	$45,438
Persons in poverty	1,874
H'holds receiving public assistance	138
H'holds receiving social security	1,052

Households, 2000
Total households	3,872
With persons under 18	1,525
With persons over 65	859
Family households	2,563
One-person households	1,059
Persons per household	2.71
Persons per family	3.35

Labor & Employment
Total civilian labor force, 2004**	5,941
Unemployment rate	9.5%
Total civilian labor force, 2000	5,159
Unemployment rate	7.5%

Employed persons 16 years and over by occupation, 2000
Managers & professionals	1,001
Service occupations	808
Sales & office occupations	1,461
Farming, fishing & forestry	15
Construction & maintenance	678
Production & transportation	810
Self-employed persons	217

*US Census Bureau
**New Jersey Department of Labor

General Information
Borough of Keansburg
29 Church St
Keansburg, NJ 07734
732-787-0215
Web site	keansburgboro.com
Land area (sq. miles)	1.08
Water area (sq. miles)	15.75
Type of government	Borough
Form of government	CM '50

Government
Legislative Districts
US Congressional	6
State Legislative	13

Local Officials, 2006
Mayor	Lisa Strydio
Admin/Manager	Terence Wall
Clerk	Thomas Cusick
Finance Dir/Treas	Angela Morin
Engineer	Allan Hila Jr.
Attorney	Michael Hanus
Tax assessor	Michael Frangella
Tax collector	Thomas Cusick
Building officer	NA
Zoning officer	Owen McKenna
Public Works	Dennis O'Keefe

Housing & Construction
Housing Units, 2000*
Total	4,269
Median rent	$718
Median SF home value	$99,000

New Privately Owned Housing Units Authorized by Building Permit
	Units	Value
Total, 2004	4	$391,200
Single family	4	$391,200
Total, 2005	21	$977,950
Single family	7	$877,950

Real Property Valuation - parcels, 2005
	Number	Valuation
Total		$275,839,790
Vacant	129	2,924,200
Residential	3,006	234,885,990
Commercial	123	25,053,600
Industrial	3	1,328,200
Apartments	51	11,647,800
Farm land	0	0
Farm homestead	0	0

Average Property Value & Tax, 2005
Residential value	$78,139
Property tax	$3,587
FAIR rebate	$501

Public Library
Keansburg Public Library
55 Shore Blvd
Keansburg, NJ 07734
732-787-0636
Director	Ellen O'Brien

Library statistics, 2004
	Total	per capita
Volumes	NA	NA
Expenditure	NA	NA

Public Safety
Police
Chief	Raymond O'Hare
Number of officers, 2004	23

Crime, 2004	Number	Rate
Total	356	33.1
Violent	55	5.1
Non-violent	301	28
Domestic Viol.	593	NA

Emergency/Fire
Director	Kevin Rogers

Public School District
(for school year 2004-2005 except as noted)
Keansburg Borough School District
100 Palmer Place
Keansburg, NJ 07734
732-787-2007
Superintendent	Barbara Trzeszkowski
Grade plan	K-12
Enrollment	2,027.0
Students per teacher	7.5
Per pupil expenditure	$18,228
Median faculty salary	$42,810
Median administrator salary	$89,206
Grade 12 enrollment	102.0
High school graduation rate	95.9%

Assessment test results
(percent scoring at proficient or advanced level)
	Language	Math
Grade 3	83.8%	81.9%
Grade 8	50.6%	50.3%
High school	69.5%	58.4%

SAT
Percent tested	55%
Average SAT math score	458
Average SAT verbal score	419

No Child Left Behind, 2003-04
Attendance rate (target = 90%)	92.6%
Drop rate	0.8%
Highly-qualified teachers	97.5%
District needs improvement?(AYP)	No

Municipal Finance
Fiscal Year 2005
Total tax levy	$12,673,497
County levy	1,701,426
County taxes	1,526,732
County library	84,098
County health	0
County open space	90,595
School levy	4,324,721
Local muni. budget	6,647,350
Misc. revenues	4,835,359
Total aid	$2,341,460
CMPTRA	1,781,486
Muni. block grant	48,434
Energy tax receipts	441,540
Homeland security	70,000

Fiscal Year 2006
Total aid	$2,341,459
CMPTRA	1,766,032
Muni. block grant	48,434
Energy tax receipts	456,993
Homeland security	70,000

Taxes
	2003	2004	2005
General tax rate per $100	4.33	4.264	4.591
Net valuation taxable	$270,964,742	$274,127,870	$276,085,830
State equalized value	$424,909,428	$504,233,314	$606,915,432
County equalization ratio	73.3	63.77	54.34

Demographics & Socio-Economic Characteristics
(2000 U.S. Census, except as noted)

Population
1980*	35,735
1990*	34,874
2000	40,513
Male	20,901
Female	19,612
2004 (estimate)*	39,496
Persons per sq. mi. of land	4,322

Race & Hispanic Origin, 2000
Race
White	30,687
Black/African American	1,609
Amer. Indian/Alaska Natv.	148
Asian	2,228
Natv. Hawaiian/Pac. Islander	27
Other Race	4,068
Two or more races	1,746
Hispanic origin, total	11,075
Mexican	375
Puerto Rican	2,237
Cuban	847
Other Hispanic	7,616

Age & Nativity, 2000
Under 5 years	2,328
18 years and over	31,814
21 years and over	30,154
65 years and over	4,407
85 years and over	506
Median Age	34.7
Native born	25,038
Foreign born	15,475

Educational Attainment, 2000
Population 25 years and over	27,690
0-8 yrs of school	12.6%
High School grad or higher	70.9%
Bachelor's degree or higher	17.4%
Graduate degree	6.6%

Income & Poverty, 1999
Per capita income	$20,886
Median household income	$47,757
Median family income	$54,596
Persons in poverty	3,262
H'holds receiving public assistance	400
H'holds receiving social security	3,358

Households, 2000
Total households	13,539
With persons under 18	5,100
With persons over 65	3,276
Family households	9,809
One-person households	2,958
Persons per household	2.81
Persons per family	3.28

Labor & Employment
Total civilian labor force, 2004**	19,697
Unemployment rate	4.2%
Total civilian labor force, 2000	19,045
Unemployment rate	6.8%

Employed persons 16 years and over by occupation, 2000
Managers & professionals	4,747
Service occupations	2,658
Sales & office occupations	5,261
Farming, fishing & forestry	15
Construction & maintenance	2,044
Production & transportation	3,016
Self-employed persons	757

*US Census Bureau
**New Jersey Department of Labor

General Information
Town of Kearny
402 Kearny Ave
Kearny, NJ 07032
201-955-7400
Web site	www.kearnyusa.com
Land area (sq. miles)	9.14
Water area (sq. miles)	1.05
Type of government	Town
Form of government	T

Government

Legislative Districts
US Congressional	9, 13
State Legislative	32

Local Officials, 2006
Mayor	Alberto Santos
Admin/Manager	Joseph D'Arco
Clerk	Doreen Cali
Finance Dir/Treas	Frederick Tomkins
Engineer	Joseph Neglia
Attorney	Gregory Castano
Tax assessor	Gerard Pontrelli
Tax collector	Sharon Curran
Building officer	Michael Martello
Zoning officer	Michael Martello
Public Works	Gerard Kerr

Housing & Construction

Housing Units, 2000*
Total	13,872
Median rent	$769
Median SF home value	$158,200

New Privately Owned Housing Units Authorized by Building Permit
	Units	Value
Total, 2004	3	$216,700
Single family	1	$120,000
Total, 2005	8	$666,500
Single family	0	$0

Real Property Valuation - parcels, 2005
	Number	Valuation
Total		$1,055,719,600
Vacant	192	16,379,100
Residential	7,082	659,958,000
Commercial	494	97,218,200
Industrial	224	246,934,400
Apartments	140	35,229,900
Farm land	0	0
Farm homestead	0	0

Average Property Value & Tax, 2005
Residential value	$93,188
Property tax	$6,829
FAIR rebate	$624

Public Library
Kearny Public Library
318 Kearny Ave
Kearny, NJ 07032
201-998-2666
Director	Julie McCarthy

Library statistics, 2004
	Total	per capita
Volumes	87,434	2.16
Expenditure	$904,547	$22.33

Public Safety

Police
Chief	John Dowie
Number of officers, 2004	118

Crime, 2004	Number	Rate
Total	1,230	30.9
Violent	111	2.8
Non-violent	1,119	28.1
Domestic Viol.	516	NA

Emergency/Fire
Director	Joseph Lapsanski

Public School District
(for school year 2004-2005 except as noted)

Kearny School District
100 Davis Ave
Kearny, NJ 07032
201-955-5021
Superintendent	Robert Mooney
Grade plan	K-12
Enrollment	5,339.0
Students per teacher	11.7
Per pupil expenditure	$11,447
Median faculty salary	$56,402
Median administrator salary	$105,609
Grade 12 enrollment	362.0
High school graduation rate	89.5%

Assessment test results
(percent scoring at proficient or advanced level)
	Language	Math
Grade 3	84.0%	87.1%
Grade 8	73.2%	61.0%
High school	83.8%	75.2%

SAT
Percent tested	60%
Average SAT math score	472
Average SAT verbal score	454

No Child Left Behind, 2003-04
Attendance rate (target = 90%)	94.6%
Drop rate	3.3%
Highly-qualified teachers	91.4%
District needs improvement?(AYP)	No

Municipal Finance

Fiscal Year 2005
Total tax levy	$77,588,723
County levy	14,883,864
County taxes	14,602,604
County library	0
County health	0
County open space	281,260
School levy	40,436,465
Local muni. budget	22,268,394
Misc. revenues	37,326,913
Total aid	$21,977,828
CMPTRA	5,601,582
Muni. block grant	158,852
Energy tax receipts	16,077,394
Homeland security	140,000

Fiscal Year 2006
Total aid	$21,977,828
CMPTRA	5,038,873
Muni. block grant	158,852
Energy tax receipts	16,640,103
Homeland security	140,000

Taxes
	2003	2004	2005
General tax rate per $100	6.61	7.030	7.329
Net valuation taxable	$1,054,290,950	$1,060,034,824	$1,058,747,069
State equalized value	$2,420,318,985	$2,754,411,642	$3,246,694,477
County equalization ratio	47.26	43.56	38.41

Demographics & Socio-Economic Characteristics
(2000 U.S. Census, except as noted)

Population
1980*	8,221
1990*	7,574
2000	7,675
Male	3,723
Female	3,952
2004 (estimate)*	7,764
Persons per sq. mi. of land	3,626

Race & Hispanic Origin, 2000
Race
White	7,007
Black/African American	184
Amer. Indian/Alaska Natv.	19
Asian	221
Natv. Hawaiian/Pac. Islander	0
Other Race	138
Two or more races	106
Hispanic origin, total	663
Mexican	71
Puerto Rican	117
Cuban	93
Other Hispanic	382

Age & Nativity, 2000
Under 5 years	423
18 years and over	6,079
21 years and over	5,864
65 years and over	1,399
85 years and over	144
Median Age	39.7
Native born	6,322
Foreign born	1,353

Educational Attainment, 2000
Population 25 years and over	5,574
0-8 yrs of school	7.8%
High School grad or higher	80.0%
Bachelor's degree or higher	15.5%
Graduate degree	4.1%

Income & Poverty, 1999
Per capita income	$24,343
Median household income	$59,929
Median family income	$66,500
Persons in poverty	157
H'holds receiving public assistance	13
H'holds receiving social security	1,060

Households, 2000
Total households	2,854
With persons under 18	908
With persons over 65	1,009
Family households	2,117
One-person households	611
Persons per household	2.69
Persons per family	3.15

Labor & Employment
Total civilian labor force, 2004**	3,944
Unemployment rate	4.6%
Total civilian labor force, 2000	3,992
Unemployment rate	4.6%

Employed persons 16 years and over by occupation, 2000
Managers & professionals	1,161
Service occupations	619
Sales & office occupations	1,194
Farming, fishing & forestry	8
Construction & maintenance	402
Production & transportation	426
Self-employed persons	198

*US Census Bureau
**New Jersey Department of Labor

General Information
Borough of Kenilworth
567 Boulevard
Kenilworth, NJ 07033
908-276-9090

Web site	NA
Land area (sq. miles)	2.14
Water area (sq. miles)	0
Type of government	Borough
Form of government	B

Government
Legislative Districts
US Congressional	7
State Legislative	20

Local Officials, 2006
Mayor	Gregg David
Admin/Manager	NA
Clerk	Hedy Lipke
Finance Dir/Treas	Nancy Nichols
Engineer	PMK Group
Attorney	Jeffrey Cohen
Tax assessor	Paul Parsons
Tax collector	Nancy Nichols
Building officer	Richard Malanda
Zoning officer	NA
Public Works	NA

Housing & Construction
Housing Units, 2000*
Total	2,926
Median rent	$967
Median SF home value	$175,900

New Privately Owned Housing Units Authorized by Building Permit
	Units	Value
Total, 2004	16	$2,230,708
Single family	14	$2,095,708
Total, 2005	21	$2,881,726
Single family	17	$2,467,226

Real Property Valuation - parcels, 2005
	Number	Valuation
Total		$870,834,200
Vacant	133	8,344,100
Residential	2,502	431,560,600
Commercial	175	84,377,600
Industrial	155	346,551,900
Apartments	0	0
Farm land	0	0
Farm homestead	0	0

Average Property Value & Tax, 2005
Residential value	$172,486
Property tax	$5,224
FAIR rebate	$667

Public Library
Kenilworth Free Public Library
548 Boulevard
Kenilworth, NJ 07033
908-276-2451

Director ... Dale Spindel

Library statistics, 2004
	Total	per capita
Volumes	37,349	4.87
Expenditure	$398,738	$51.95

Public Safety
Police
Chief	William Dowd
Number of officers, 2004	30

Crime, 2004	Number	Rate
Total	151	19.5
Violent	4	0.5
Non-violent	147	19
Domestic Viol.	38	NA

Emergency/Fire
Director ... Lou Giordino

Public School District
(for school year 2004-2005 except as noted)

Kenilworth School District
426 Blvd
Kenilworth, NJ 07033
908-276-1644

Superintendent	Lloyd Leschuk
Grade plan	K-12
Enrollment	1,288.5
Students per teacher	12.0
Per pupil expenditure	$11,134
Median faculty salary	$53,493
Median administrator salary	$101,727
Grade 12 enrollment	86.0
High school graduation rate	100.0%

Assessment test results
(percent scoring at proficient or advanced level)
	Language	Math
Grade 3	86.1%	88.6%
Grade 8	73.7%	75.5%
High school	87.2%	79.3%

SAT
Percent tested	99%
Average SAT math score	476
Average SAT verbal score	476

No Child Left Behind, 2003-04
Attendance rate (target = 90%)	95.5%
Drop rate	0.2%
Highly-qualified teachers	95.5%
District needs improvement?(AYP)	No

Municipal Finance
Fiscal Year 2005
Total tax levy	$26,390,865
County levy	5,665,722
County taxes	5,442,042
County library	0
County health	0
County open space	223,679
School levy	13,702,923
Local muni. budget	7,022,221
Misc. revenues	4,261,870
Total aid	$1,525,442
CMPTRA	658,749
Muni. block grant	33,141
Energy tax receipts	783,552
Homeland security	50,000

Fiscal Year 2006
Total aid	$1,525,442
CMPTRA	631,326
Muni. block grant	33,141
Energy tax receipts	810,976
Homeland security	50,000

Taxes
	2003	2004	2005
General tax rate per $100	2.66	2.824	3.029
Net valuation taxable	$857,338,445	$867,210,689	$871,435,353
State equalized value	$1,124,230,848	$1,270,736,112	$1,538,551,118
County equalization ratio	78.6	67.20	59.37

Demographics & Socio-Economic Characteristics
(2000 U.S. Census, except as noted)

Population
1980*	7,413
1990*	7,586
2000	7,568
Male	3,648
Female	3,920
2004 (estimate)*	7,570
Persons per sq. mi. of land	5,360

Race & Hispanic Origin, 2000
Race
White	6,447
Black/African American	531
Amer. Indian/Alaska Natv.	9
Asian	168
Natv. Hawaiian/Pac. Islander	3
Other Race	224
Two or more races	186
Hispanic origin, total	839
Mexican	151
Puerto Rican	385
Cuban	29
Other Hispanic	274

Age & Nativity, 2000
Under 5 years	443
18 years and over	5,919
21 years and over	5,677
65 years and over	1,219
85 years and over	199
Median Age	38.1
Native born	6,750
Foreign born	818

Educational Attainment, 2000
Population 25 years and over	5,345
0-8 yrs of school	5.9%
High School grad or higher	82.9%
Bachelor's degree or higher	15.9%
Graduate degree	6.6%

Income & Poverty, 1999
Per capita income	$23,288
Median household income	$43,869
Median family income	$58,176
Persons in poverty	587
H'holds receiving public assistance	90
H'holds receiving social security	1,055

Households, 2000
Total households	3,264
With persons under 18	921
With persons over 65	1,013
Family households	1,797
One-person households	1,253
Persons per household	2.31
Persons per family	3.11

Labor & Employment
Total civilian labor force, 2004**	4,416
Unemployment rate	4.2%
Total civilian labor force, 2000	3,986
Unemployment rate	4.8%

Employed persons 16 years and over by occupation, 2000
Managers & professionals	1,233
Service occupations	624
Sales & office occupations	1,176
Farming, fishing & forestry	11
Construction & maintenance	315
Production & transportation	434
Self-employed persons	156

*US Census Bureau
**New Jersey Department of Labor

General Information
Borough of Keyport
70 West Front St
Keyport, NJ 07735
732-739-3900
Web site	www.keyportonline.com
Land area (sq. miles)	1.41
Water area (sq. miles)	0.01
Type of government	Borough
Form of government	B

Government
Legislative Districts
US Congressional	6
State Legislative	13

Local Officials, 2006
Mayor	John Merla
Admin/Manager	Thomas W. Antonucci
Clerk	Judith Poling
Finance Dir/Treas	K. Stencel /T. Fallon
Engineer	Donald Norbut
Attorney	John Wisniewski
Tax assessor	Scott Pezzaras
Tax collector	Keri R. Stencel
Building officer	Robert Burlew
Zoning officer	Anthony Vecchio
Public Works	George Sappah

Housing & Construction
Housing Units, 2000*
Total	3,400
Median rent	$673
Median SF home value	$141,100

New Privately Owned Housing Units
Authorized by Building Permit
	Units	Value
Total, 2004	15	$1,229,802
Single family	15	$1,229,802
Total, 2005	15	$1,245,135
Single family	15	$1,245,135

Real Property Valuation - parcels, 2005
	Number	Valuation
Total		$326,062,000
Vacant	135	4,830,300
Residential	1,929	233,712,200
Commercial	216	66,044,600
Industrial	6	6,218,500
Apartments	19	15,256,400
Farm land	0	0
Farm homestead	0	0

Average Property Value & Tax, 2005
Residential value	$121,157
Property tax	$5,061
FAIR rebate	$695

Public Library
Keyport Public Library
Broad St
Keyport, NJ 07735
732-264-0543
Director............. Jacqueline LaPolla

Library statistics, 2004
	Total	per capita
Volumes	38,767	5.12
Expenditure	$180,907	$23.90

Public Safety
Police
Chief	Theodore Gajewski
Number of officers, 2004	19

Crime, 2004	Number	Rate
Total	135	18
Violent	13	1.7
Non-violent	122	16.3
Domestic Viol.	68	NA

Emergency/Fire
Director................. Timothy Regan

Public School District
(for school year 2004-2005 except as noted)

Keyport School District
335 Broad St
Keyport, NJ 07735
732-264-2840
Superintendent	John Dumford
Grade plan	K-12
Enrollment	1,155.0
Students per teacher	10.6
Per pupil expenditure	$12,015
Median faculty salary	$51,110
Median administrator salary	$84,900
Grade 12 enrollment	86.0
High school graduation rate	97.1%

Assessment test results
(percent scoring at proficient or advanced level)
	Language	Math
Grade 3	91.1%	76.8%
Grade 8	63.6%	53.0%
High school	77.1%	60.0%

SAT
Percent tested	69%
Average SAT math score	466
Average SAT verbal score	448

No Child Left Behind, 2003-04
Attendence rate (target = 90%)	91.9%
Drop rate	0.3%
Highly-qualified teachers	100%
District needs improvement?(AYP)	No

Municipal Finance
Fiscal Year 2005
Total tax levy	$13,730,960
County levy	1,829,017
County taxes	1,726,565
County library	0
County health	0
County open space	102,452
School levy	7,822,007
Local muni. budget	4,079,936
Misc. revenues	3,269,313
Total aid	$1,129,789
CMPTRA	601,309
Muni. block grant	33,194
Energy tax receipts	445,286
Homeland security	50,000

Fiscal Year 2006
Total aid	$1,129,789
CMPTRA	585,724
Muni. block grant	33,194
Energy tax receipts	460,871
Homeland security	50,000

Taxes
	2003	2004	2005
General tax rate per $100	3.62	3.986	4.178
Net valuation taxable	$326,385,163	$328,039,901	$328,694,446
State equalized value	$486,343,560	$571,497,922	$647,418,645
County equalization ratio	76.31	67.11	57.17

Demographics & Socio-Economic Characteristics
(2000 U.S. Census, except as noted)

Population
1980*	2,772
1990*	3,325
2000	3,782
Male	1,910
Female	1,872
2004 (estimate)*	4,011
Persons per sq. mi. of land	114

Race & Hispanic Origin, 2000
Race
White	3,692
Black/African American	23
Amer. Indian/Alaska Natv.	3
Asian	29
Natv. Hawaiian/Pac. Islander	0
Other Race	7
Two or more races	28
Hispanic origin, total	70
Mexican	7
Puerto Rican	22
Cuban	16
Other Hispanic	25

Age & Nativity, 2000
Under 5 years	262
18 years and over	2,750
21 years and over	2,653
65 years and over	399
85 years and over	35
Median Age	38.8
Native born	3,621
Foreign born	161

Educational Attainment, 2000
Population 25 years and over	2,618
0-8 yrs of school	4.3%
High School grad or higher	89.1%
Bachelor's degree or higher	26.5%
Graduate degree	9.5%

Income & Poverty, 1999
Per capita income	$30,219
Median household income	$71,551
Median family income	$81,642
Persons in poverty	108
H'holds receiving public assistance	19
H'holds receiving social security	346

Households, 2000
Total households	1,340
With persons under 18	550
With persons over 65	291
Family households	1,042
One-person households	236
Persons per household	2.82
Persons per family	3.21

Labor & Employment
Total civilian labor force, 2004**	2,169
Unemployment rate	4.7%
Total civilian labor force, 2000	2,115
Unemployment rate	2.8%

Employed persons 16 years and over by occupation, 2000
Managers & professionals	749
Service occupations	383
Sales & office occupations	460
Farming, fishing & forestry	9
Construction & maintenance	326
Production & transportation	128
Self-employed persons	238

*US Census Bureau
**New Jersey Department of Labor

General Information
Township of Kingwood
PO Box 199
Baptistown, NJ 08803
908-996-4276

Web site	www.kingwoodtownship.com
Land area (sq. miles)	35.23
Water area (sq. miles)	0.59
Type of government	Township
Form of government	TC

Government

Legislative Districts
US Congressional	12
State Legislative	23

Local Officials, 2006
Mayor	Stephen A. Zdepski
Admin/Manager	NA
Clerk	Mary MacConnell
Finance Dir/Treas	Diane Laudenbach
Engineer	Robert Lorentz
Attorney	Joseph Novak
Tax assessor	Kathleen Degan
Tax collector	NA
Building officer	Wayne Degan
Zoning officer	Michael DeSapio
Public Works	Jack Search

Housing & Construction

Housing Units, 2000*
Total	1,422
Median rent	$787
Median SF home value	$231,700

New Privately Owned Housing Units
Authorized by Building Permit

	Units	Value
Total, 2004	16	$2,432,383
Single family	16	$2,432,383
Total, 2005	20	$4,359,626
Single family	20	$4,359,626

Real Property Valuation - parcels, 2005
	Number	Valuation
Total		$333,602,142
Vacant	157	9,292,379
Residential	1,136	232,456,100
Commercial	52	16,010,415
Industrial	5	8,325,610
Apartments	4	1,210,500
Farm land	278	62,830,700
Farm homestead	483	3,476,438

Average Property Value & Tax, 2005
Residential value	$145,727
Property tax	$4,486
FAIR rebate	$536

Public Library

No public municipal library.

Library statistics, 2004
	Total	per capita
Volumes	NA	NA
Expenditure	NA	NA

Public Safety
Police
Chief	NA
Number of officers, 2004	0

Crime, 2004	Number	Rate
Total	34	8.5
Violent	6	1.5
Non-violent	28	7
Domestic Viol.	14	NA

Emergency/Fire
Director	Jack Search

Public School District
(for school year 2004-2005 except as noted)

Kingwood Township School District
880 County Rd 519
Frenchtown, NJ 08825
908-996-2941

Administrator	Laura Hartner
Grade plan	K-8
Enrollment	505.0
Students per teacher	10.5
Per pupil expenditure	$11,046
Median faculty salary	$46,124
Median administrator salary	$73,500
Grade 12 enrollment	NA
High school graduation rate	NA

Assessment test results
(percent scoring at proficient or advanced level)
	Language	Math
Grade 3	94.7%	87.7%
Grade 8	82.0%	72.1%
High school	NA	NA

SAT
Percent tested	NA
Average SAT math score	NA
Average SAT verbal score	NA

No Child Left Behind, 2003-04
Attendence rate (target = 90%)	96.0%
Drop rate	NA
Highly-qualified teachers	99.2%
District needs improvement?(AYP)	No

Municipal Finance

Fiscal Year 2005
Total tax levy	$10,299,496
County levy	2,179,339
County taxes	1,850,364
County library	154,839
County health	0
County open space	174,135
School levy	7,070,593
Local muni. budget	1,049,564
Misc. revenues	1,158,875
Total aid	$435,076
CMPTRA	157,881
Muni. block grant	14,829
Energy tax receipts	262,366
Homeland security	0

Fiscal Year 2006
Total aid	$435,076
CMPTRA	148,698
Muni. block grant	14,829
Energy tax receipts	271,549
Homeland security	NA

Taxes

	2003	2004	2005
General tax rate per $100	2.68	2.800	3.080
Net valuation taxable	$320,531,085	$326,172,613	$334,549,335
State equalized value	$458,425,465	$530,744,456	$596,770,130
County equalization ratio	69.02	64.18	57.91

Demographics & Socio-Economic Characteristics
(2000 U.S. Census, except as noted)

Population
1980*	7,770
1990*	8,470
2000	9,365
Male	4,673
Female	4,692
2004 (estimate)*	9,542
Persons per sq. mi. of land	533

Race & Hispanic Origin, 2000
Race
White	8,953
Black/African American	54
Amer. Indian/Alaska Natv.	4
Asian	266
Natv. Hawaiian/Pac. Islander	9
Other Race	22
Two or more races	57
Hispanic origin, total	218
Mexican	10
Puerto Rican	54
Cuban	49
Other Hispanic	105

Age & Nativity, 2000
Under 5 years	702
18 years and over	6,556
21 years and over	6,358
65 years and over	841
85 years and over	66
Median Age	39.6
Native born	8,465
Foreign born	900

Educational Attainment, 2000
Population 25 years and over	6,182
0-8 yrs of school	1.4%
High School grad or higher	96.4%
Bachelor's degree or higher	57.4%
Graduate degree	25.2%

Income & Poverty, 1999
Per capita income	$45,796
Median household income	$105,991
Median family income	$110,593
Persons in poverty	244
H'holds receiving public assistance	28
H'holds receiving social security	572

Households, 2000
Total households	3,062
With persons under 18	1,440
With persons over 65	586
Family households	2,685
One-person households	287
Persons per household	3.06
Persons per family	3.27

Labor & Employment
Total civilian labor force, 2004**	5,136
Unemployment rate	2.4%
Total civilian labor force, 2000	4,664
Unemployment rate	1.8%

Employed persons 16 years and over by occupation, 2000
Managers & professionals	2,701
Service occupations	302
Sales & office occupations	1,169
Farming, fishing & forestry	0
Construction & maintenance	214
Production & transportation	192
Self-employed persons	353

*US Census Bureau
**New Jersey Department of Labor

General Information
Borough of Kinnelon
130 Kinnelon Rd
Kinnelon, NJ 07405
973-838-5401
Web site	www.kinnelonboro.org
Land area (sq. miles)	17.89
Water area (sq. miles)	0.93
Type of government	Borough
Form of government	B

Government

Legislative Districts
US Congressional	11
State Legislative	26

Local Officials, 2006
Mayor	Glenn L. Sisco
Admin/Manager	NA
Clerk	Mary J. Ricker
Finance Dir/Treas	Mary J. Ricker
Engineer	Paul Darmofalski
Attorney	Edward J. Buzak
Tax assessor	Robert Edgar
Tax collector	Irene Kwasnik
Building officer	Russell Heiney
Zoning officer	NA
Public Works	NA

Housing & Construction

Housing Units, 2000*
Total	3,123
Median rent	$1,538
Median SF home value	$354,000

New Privately Owned Housing Units
Authorized by Building Permit
	Units	Value
Total, 2004	39	$11,593,617
Single family	39	$11,593,617
Total, 2005	32	$9,455,999
Single family	32	$9,455,999

Real Property Valuation - parcels, 2005
	Number	Valuation
Total		$1,585,663,000
Vacant	393	54,674,400
Residential	3,338	1,454,945,000
Commercial	92	54,332,000
Industrial	0	0
Apartments	2	18,360,100
Farm land	4	3,156,600
Farm homestead	9	194,900

Average Property Value & Tax, 2005
Residential value	$434,759
Property tax	$10,391
FAIR rebate	$536

Public Library
Kinnelon Public Library
132 Kinnelon Rd
Kinnelon, NJ 07405
973-838-1321
Director | Barbara Owens

Library statistics, 2004
	Total	per capita
Volumes	65,924	7.04
Expenditure	$655,593	$70.00

Public Safety

Police
Chief	John Finkle
Number of officers, 2004	17

Crime, 2004	Number	Rate
Total	91	9.6
Violent	6	0.6
Non-violent	85	9
Domestic Viol.	26	NA

Emergency/Fire
Director | Patrick Avello

Public School District
(for school year 2004-2005 except as noted)

Kinnelon Borough School District
109 Kiel Ave
Kinnelon, NJ 07405
973-838-1418
Superintendent	James Opiekun
Grade plan	K-12
Enrollment	2,112.0
Students per teacher	11.8
Per pupil expenditure	$11,479
Median faculty salary	$54,900
Median administrator salary	$108,500
Grade 12 enrollment	141.0
High school graduation rate	99.3%

Assessment test results
(percent scoring at proficient or advanced level)
	Language	Math
Grade 3	88.7%	91.5%
Grade 8	92.6%	88.9%
High school	98.3%	90.1%

SAT
Percent tested	101%
Average SAT math score	559
Average SAT verbal score	536

No Child Left Behind, 2003-04
Attendence rate (target = 90%)	95.9%
Drop rate	0.6%
Highly-qualified teachers	98.6%
District needs improvement?(AYP)	No

Municipal Finance

Fiscal Year 2005
Total tax levy	$37,938,818
County levy	5,167,081
County taxes	4,232,150
County library	0
County health	0
County open space	934,931
School levy	25,819,801
Local muni. budget	6,951,936
Misc. revenues	3,384,096
Total aid	$927,442
CMPTRA	253,777
Muni. block grant	37,062
Energy tax receipts	541,342
Homeland security	50,000

Fiscal Year 2006
Total aid	$927,442
CMPTRA	234,830
Muni. block grant	37,062
Energy tax receipts	560,289
Homeland security	50,000

Taxes
	2003	2004	2005
General tax rate per $100	2.19	2.280	2.390
Net valuation taxable	$1,552,557,221	$1,568,814,771	$1,587,429,281
State equalized value	$1,775,974,858	$1,933,955,873	$2,131,349,733
County equalization ratio	95.73	87.42	81.10

Demographics & Socio-Economic Characteristics
(2000 U.S. Census, except as noted)

Population
1980*	2,074
1990*	2,543
2000	2,977
Male	1,502
Female	1,475
2004 (estimate)*	3,139
Persons per sq. mi. of land	127

Race & Hispanic Origin, 2000
Race
White	2,901
Black/African American	12
Amer. Indian/Alaska Natv.	2
Asian	19
Natv. Hawaiian/Pac. Islander	0
Other Race	14
Two or more races	29
Hispanic origin, total	55
Mexican	8
Puerto Rican	24
Cuban	7
Other Hispanic	16

Age & Nativity, 2000
Under 5 years	208
18 years and over	2,154
21 years and over	2,069
65 years and over	333
85 years and over	41
Median Age	38
Native born	2,887
Foreign born	129

Educational Attainment, 2000
Population 25 years and over	2,021
0-8 yrs of school	4.0%
High School grad or higher	87.1%
Bachelor's degree or higher	26.8%
Graduate degree	6.5%

Income & Poverty, 1999
Per capita income	$24,631
Median household income	$63,409
Median family income	$72,130
Persons in poverty	103
H'holds receiving public assistance	8
H'holds receiving social security	240

Households, 2000
Total households	1,028
With persons under 18	432
With persons over 65	228
Family households	816
One-person households	154
Persons per household	2.87
Persons per family	3.21

Labor & Employment
Total civilian labor force, 2004**	1,526
Unemployment rate	3.8%
Total civilian labor force, 2000	1,655
Unemployment rate	4.6%

Employed persons 16 years and over by occupation, 2000
Managers & professionals	553
Service occupations	245
Sales & office occupations	346
Farming, fishing & forestry	13
Construction & maintenance	192
Production & transportation	230
Self-employed persons	109

*US Census Bureau
**New Jersey Department of Labor

General Information
Township of Knowlton
628, Rt 94
Columbia, NJ 07832
908-496-4816

Web site	NA
Land area (sq. miles)	24.78
Water area (sq. miles)	0.53
Type of government	Township
Form of government	TC

Government

Legislative Districts
US Congressional	5
State Legislative	23

Local Officials, 2006
Mayor	Frank Van Horn
Admin/Manager	NA
Clerk	Lisa Patton
Finance Dir/Treas	Greg Della Pia
Engineer	Ted Rodman
Attorney	Richard Cushing
Tax assessor	Richard Motyka
Tax collector	Evan Howell
Building officer	Lou Cevetello
Zoning officer	George Rabtzow
Public Works	Ramon Cowell

Housing & Construction

Housing Units, 2000*
Total	1,135
Median rent	$739
Median SF home value	$180,300

New Privately Owned Housing Units Authorized by Building Permit
	Units	Value
Total, 2004	24	$5,214,350
Single family	24	$5,214,350
Total, 2005	14	$3,721,129
Single family	14	$3,721,129

Real Property Valuation - parcels, 2005
	Number	Valuation
Total		$241,485,440
Vacant	199	9,306,100
Residential	903	176,446,500
Commercial	60	20,910,100
Industrial	0	0
Apartments	3	665,700
Farm land	130	31,166,700
Farm homestead	314	2,990,340

Average Property Value & Tax, 2005
Residential value	$147,442
Property tax	$4,105
FAIR rebate	$521

Public Library

No public municipal library.

Library statistics, 2004
	Total	per capita
Volumes	NA	NA
Expenditure	NA	NA

Public Safety
Police
Chief	(State)
Number of officers, 2004	0

Crime, 2004	Number	Rate
Total	55	17.7
Violent	10	3.2
Non-violent	45	14.5
Domestic Viol.	18	NA

Emergency/Fire
Director	Dave Fisher

Public School District
(for school year 2004-2005 except as noted)

Knowlton Township School District
Knowlton Township Elementary
Delaware, NJ 07833
908-475-5118
Superintendent	Sharon Mooney
Grade plan	K-6
Enrollment	383.0
Students per teacher	11.9
Per pupil expenditure	$10,378
Median faculty salary	$49,201
Median administrator salary	$81,970
Grade 12 enrollment	NA
High school graduation rate	NA

Assessment test results
(percent scoring at proficient or advanced level)
	Language	Math
Grade 3	88.4%	97.7%
Grade 8	NA	NA
High school	NA	NA

SAT
Percent tested	NA
Average SAT math score	NA
Average SAT verbal score	NA

No Child Left Behind, 2003-04
Attendence rate (target = 90%)	95.7%
Drop rate	NA
Highly-qualified teachers	100%
District needs improvement?(AYP)	No

Municipal Finance

Fiscal Year 2005
Total tax levy	$6,749,829
County levy	1,971,850
County taxes	1,630,140
County library	157,295
County health	0
County open space	184,415
School levy	4,302,450
Local muni. budget	475,529
Misc. revenues	1,484,441
Total aid	$394,219
CMPTRA	141,121
Muni. block grant	11,673
Energy tax receipts	241,425
Homeland security	0

Fiscal Year 2006
Total aid	$394,219
CMPTRA	132,671
Muni. block grant	11,673
Energy tax receipts	249,875
Homeland security	NA

Taxes
	2003	2004	2005
General tax rate per $100	2.49	2.650	2.790
Net valuation taxable	$234,946,237	$236,666,637	$242,420,098
State equalized value	$265,535,982	$298,577,686	$334,973,191
County equalization ratio	98.74	88.48	79.18

Demographics & Socio-Economic Characteristics
(2000 U.S. Census, except as noted)

Population
1980*	14,161
1990*	22,141
2000	25,346
Male	12,343
Female	13,003
2004 (estimate)*	26,221
Persons per sq. mi. of land	312

Race & Hispanic Origin, 2000
Race
White	24,800
Black/African American	91
Amer. Indian/Alaska Natv.	38
Asian	139
Natv. Hawaiian/Pac. Islander	2
Other Race	103
Two or more races	173
Hispanic origin, total	545
Mexican	78
Puerto Rican	216
Cuban	49
Other Hispanic	202

Age & Nativity, 2000
Under 5 years	1,565
18 years and over	18,863
21 years and over	18,094
65 years and over	3,854
85 years and over	360
Median Age	38.9
Native born	24,671
Foreign born	675

Educational Attainment, 2000
Population 25 years and over	17,180
0-8 yrs of school	3.5%
High School grad or higher	86.1%
Bachelor's degree or higher	19.5%
Graduate degree	6.0%

Income & Poverty, 1999
Per capita income	$23,136
Median household income	$55,938
Median family income	$61,298
Persons in poverty	1,140
H'holds receiving public assistance	107
H'holds receiving social security	2,941

Households, 2000
Total households	9,336
With persons under 18	3,480
With persons over 65	2,719
Family households	7,245
One-person households	1,714
Persons per household	2.71
Persons per family	3.08

Labor & Employment
Total civilian labor force, 2004**	13,501
Unemployment rate	5.1%
Total civilian labor force, 2000	12,542
Unemployment rate	4.3%

Employed persons 16 years and over by occupation, 2000
Managers & professionals	3,584
Service occupations	1,975
Sales & office occupations	3,519
Farming, fishing & forestry	0
Construction & maintenance	1,719
Production & transportation	1,209
Self-employed persons	555

*US Census Bureau
**New Jersey Department of Labor

General Information
Township of Lacey
818 W Lacey Rd
Forked River, NJ 08731
609-693-1100
Web site	www.laceytownship.org
Land area (sq. miles)	84.00
Water area (sq. miles)	14.52
Type of government	Township
Form of government	TC

Government
Legislative Districts
US Congressional	3
State Legislative	9

Local Officials, 2006
Mayor	Mark Dycoff
Admin/Manager	John Adams
Clerk	Veronica Laureigh
Finance Dir/Treas	John Adams
Engineer	James Stanton
Attorney	George Gilmore
Tax assessor	Theresa Poznanski
Tax collector	Joe Regatts
Building officer	Frank Crandall
Zoning officer	John Downing
Public Works	Casey Parker

Housing & Construction
Housing Units, 2000*
Total	10,580
Median rent	$915
Median SF home value	$131,900

New Privately Owned Housing Units Authorized by Building Permit
	Units	Value
Total, 2004	71	$11,856,697
Single family	71	$11,856,697
Total, 2005	63	$10,699,626
Single family	63	$10,699,626

Real Property Valuation - parcels, 2005
	Number	Valuation
Total		$1,686,206,100
Vacant	4,563	46,132,800
Residential	11,101	1,448,942,600
Commercial	247	123,632,100
Industrial	38	64,705,600
Apartments	0	0
Farm land	9	1,943,100
Farm homestead	14	849,900

Average Property Value & Tax, 2005
Residential value	$130,436
Property tax	$3,882
FAIR rebate	$519

Public Library
Lacey Branch Library†
10 E Lacey Rd
Forked River, NJ 08731
609-693-8566
Branch Librarian	Kathlyn Lanzim

Library statistics, 2004
	Total	per capita
Volumes	NA	NA
Expenditure	NA	NA

†Branch of County Library

Public Safety
Police
Chief	William Nally
Number of officers, 2004	40

Crime, 2004	Number	Rate
Total	599	22.8
Violent	29	1.1
Non-violent	570	21.7
Domestic Viol.	255	NA

Emergency/Fire
Director	NA

Public School District
(for school year 2004-2005 except as noted)

Lacey Township School District
200 Western Blvd
Lanoka Harbor, NJ 08734
609-971-2002
Superintendent	Richard Starodub
Grade plan	K-12
Enrollment	5,011.0
Students per teacher	12.7
Per pupil expenditure	$9,951
Median faculty salary	$49,505
Median administrator salary	$105,023
Grade 12 enrollment	320.0
High school graduation rate	96.8%

Assessment test results
(percent scoring at proficient or advanced level)
	Language	Math
Grade 3	92.2%	92.6%
Grade 8	77.5%	69.4%
High school	89.9%	75.8%

SAT
Percent tested	59%
Average SAT math score	530
Average SAT verbal score	498

No Child Left Behind, 2003-04
Attendence rate (target = 90%)	93.0%
Drop rate	0.8%
Highly-qualified teachers	100%
District needs improvement?(AYP)	No

Municipal Finance
Fiscal Year 2005
Total tax levy	$50,303,223
County levy	11,538,284
County taxes	9,721,205
County library	1,021,274
County health	432,900
County open space	362,905
School levy	34,811,383
Local muni. budget	3,953,556
Misc. revenues	18,563,050
Total aid	$11,976,415
CMPTRA	142,070
Muni. block grant	99,382
Energy tax receipts	11,573,145
Homeland security	90,000

Fiscal Year 2006
Total aid	$12,239,405
CMPTRA	0
Muni. block grant	99,382
Energy tax receipts	11,978,205
Homeland security	90,000

Taxes
	2003	2004	2005
General tax rate per $100	2.72	2.868	2.976
Net valuation taxable	$1,641,904,687	$1,664,749,300	$1,690,296,493
State equalized value	$2,533,021,732	$2,978,531,907	$3,559,268,252
County equalization ratio	75.11	64.82	55.82

Demographics & Socio-Economic Characteristics
(2000 U.S. Census, except as noted)

Population
1980*	1,614
1990*	1,902
2000	2,300
Male	1,154
Female	1,146
2000 (revised)	2,315
2004 (estimate)*	2,478
Persons per sq. mi. of land	138

Race & Hispanic Origin, 2000
Race
White	2,232
Black/African American	24
Amer. Indian/Alaska Natv.	2
Asian	18
Natv. Hawaiian/Pac. Islander	0
Other Race	8
Two or more races	16
Hispanic origin, total	54
Mexican	0
Puerto Rican	21
Cuban	11
Other Hispanic	22

Age & Nativity, 2000
Under 5 years	150
18 years and over	1,669
21 years and over	1,611
65 years and over	213
85 years and over	13
Median Age	38.9
Native born	2,177
Foreign born	122

Educational Attainment, 2000
Population 25 years and over	1,509
0-8 yrs of school	2.7%
High School grad or higher	91.8%
Bachelor's degree or higher	33.3%
Graduate degree	11.3%

Income & Poverty, 1999
Per capita income	$30,491
Median household income	$82,805
Median family income	$87,650
Persons in poverty	85
H'holds receiving public assistance	14
H'holds receiving social security	143

Households, 2000
Total households	771
With persons under 18	314
With persons over 65	150
Family households	648
One-person households	93
Persons per household	2.95
Persons per family	3.2

Labor & Employment
Total civilian labor force, 2004**	1,228
Unemployment rate	2.6%
Total civilian labor force, 2000	1,270
Unemployment rate	4.4%

Employed persons 16 years and over by occupation, 2000
Managers & professionals	491
Service occupations	134
Sales & office occupations	302
Farming, fishing & forestry	16
Construction & maintenance	167
Production & transportation	104
Self-employed persons	90

*US Census Bureau
**New Jersey Department of Labor

General Information
Township of Lafayette
33 Morris Faim Rd
Lafayette, NJ 07848
973-383-1817

Web site	NA
Land area (sq. miles)	18.02
Water area (sq. miles)	0.03
Type of government	Township
Form of government	TC

Government

Legislative Districts
US Congressional	5
State Legislative	24

Local Officials, 2006
Mayor	George Sweeney
Admin/Manager	NA
Clerk	Anna Rose Fedish
Finance Dir/Treas	Gail Magura
Engineer	Michael S. Finelli
Attorney	Roy Kurnos
Tax assessor	Maureen Kaman
Tax collector	Linda L. Pettenger
Building officer	Charles O'Connor
Zoning officer	Charles O'Connor
Public Works	W. Macko (Rd Foreman)

Housing & Construction

Housing Units, 2000*
Total	799
Median rent	$815
Median SF home value	$221,100

New Privately Owned Housing Units
Authorized by Building Permit
	Units	Value
Total, 2004	12	$2,830,900
Single family	12	$2,830,900
Total, 2005	15	$5,643,760
Single family	15	$5,643,760

Real Property Valuation - parcels, 2005
	Number	Valuation
Total		$205,545,500
Vacant	84	4,463,400
Residential	698	126,706,900
Commercial	49	22,058,800
Industrial	17	22,057,700
Apartments	0	0
Farm land	154	28,675,100
Farm homestead	334	1,583,600

Average Property Value & Tax, 2005
Residential value	$124,313
Property tax	$4,182
FAIR rebate	$542

Public Library

No public municipal library.

Library statistics, 2004
	Total	per capita
Volumes	NA	NA
Expenditure	NA	NA

Public Safety
Police
Chief	(State)
Number of officers, 2004	0

Crime, 2004	Number	Rate
Total	25	10.2
Violent	3	1.2
Non-violent	22	9
Domestic Viol.	18	NA

Emergency/Fire
Director	Joseph Farischon

Public School District
(for school year 2004-2005 except as noted)

Lafayette Township School District
178 Beaver Run Rd
Lafayette, NJ 07848
973-875-3344

Administrator	Craig Hutcheson
Grade plan	K-8
Enrollment	347.0
Students per teacher	9.9
Per pupil expenditure	$10,715
Median faculty salary	$43,271
Median administrator salary	$77,751
Grade 12 enrollment	NA
High school graduation rate	NA

Assessment test results
(percent scoring at proficient or advanced level)
	Language	Math
Grade 3	94.3%	97.1%
Grade 8	91.5%	70.2%
High school	NA	NA

SAT
Percent tested	NA
Average SAT math score	NA
Average SAT verbal score	NA

No Child Left Behind, 2003-04
Attendence rate (target = 90%)	96.4%
Drop rate	NA
Highly-qualified teachers	99.1%
District needs improvement?(AYP)	No

Municipal Finance

Fiscal Year 2005
Total tax levy	$6,944,599
County levy	1,569,085
County taxes	1,331,706
County library	114,799
County health	54,028
County open space	68,551
School levy	5,124,245
Local muni. budget	251,268
Misc. revenues	1,628,020
Total aid	$282,138
CMPTRA	123,418
Muni. block grant	9,018
Energy tax receipts	149,702
Homeland security	0

Fiscal Year 2006
Total aid	$282,139
CMPTRA	118,179
Muni. block grant	9,018
Energy tax receipts	154,942
Homeland security	NA

Taxes
	2003	2004	2005
General tax rate per $100	3.01	3.210	3.370
Net valuation taxable	$202,445,712	$205,277,691	$206,450,276
State equalized value	$297,977,203	$339,389,235	$378,321,928
County equalization ratio	83.17	67.94	60.37

Demographics & Socio-Economic Characteristics
(2000 U.S. Census, except as noted)

Population
1980*	1,566
1990*	1,482
2000	1,806
Male	913
Female	893
2004 (estimate)*	1,796
Persons per sq. mi. of land	7,282

Race & Hispanic Origin, 2000
Race
White	1,484
Black/African American	140
Amer. Indian/Alaska Natv.	8
Asian	23
Natv. Hawaiian/Pac. Islander	1
Other Race	106
Two or more races	44
Hispanic origin, total	183
Mexican	110
Puerto Rican	37
Cuban	1
Other Hispanic	35

Age & Nativity, 2000
Under 5 years	113
18 years and over	1,413
21 years and over	1,350
65 years and over	234
85 years and over	31
Median Age	35.8
Native born	1,666
Foreign born	140

Educational Attainment, 2000
Population 25 years and over	1,253
0-8 yrs of school	2.1%
High School grad or higher	87.5%
Bachelor's degree or higher	25.2%
Graduate degree	6.6%

Income & Poverty, 1999
Per capita income	$27,111
Median household income	$47,566
Median family income	$56,538
Persons in poverty	134
H'holds receiving public assistance	14
H'holds receiving social security	171

Households, 2000
Total households	824
With persons under 18	215
With persons over 65	191
Family households	391
One-person households	339
Persons per household	2.19
Persons per family	3.1

Labor & Employment
Total civilian labor force, 2004**	886
Unemployment rate	5.4%
Total civilian labor force, 2000	1,051
Unemployment rate	4.2%

Employed persons 16 years and over by occupation, 2000
Managers & professionals	346
Service occupations	166
Sales & office occupations	241
Farming, fishing & forestry	6
Construction & maintenance	110
Production & transportation	138
Self-employed persons	49

*US Census Bureau
**New Jersey Department of Labor

General Information
Borough of Lake Como
PO Box 569
1740 Main St
Lake Como, NJ 07719
732-681-3232
Web site	lakecomonj.org
Land area (sq. miles)	0.25
Water area (sq. miles)	0.01
Type of government	Borough
Form of government	B

Government

Legislative Districts
US Congressional	6
State Legislative	11

Local Officials, 2006
Mayor	Lawrence Chiaravallo
Admin/Manager	Louise Mekosh
Clerk	Louise Mekosh
Finance Dir/Treas	Louise Mekosh
Engineer	William Birdsall
Attorney	William Gallagher Jr.
Tax assessor	Mary Lou Hartman
Tax collector	Esther Kiss
Building officer	William Fisher
Zoning officer	John Rowe
Public Works	Filmore Treadwell

Housing & Construction

Housing Units, 2000*
Total	1,107
Median rent	$811
Median SF home value	$124,300

New Privately Owned Housing Units Authorized by Building Permit
	Units	Value
Total, 2004	5	$867,706
Single family	5	$867,706
Total, 2005	22	$1,837,800
Single family	15	$1,822,800

Real Property Valuation - parcels, 2005
	Number	Valuation
Total		$106,005,750
Vacant	33	1,004,100
Residential	874	92,673,150
Commercial	40	10,959,800
Industrial	2	452,700
Apartments	1	916,000
Farm land	0	0
Farm homestead	0	0

Average Property Value & Tax, 2005
Residential value	$106,033
Property tax	$4,227
FAIR rebate	$801

Public Library

No public municipal library.

Library statistics, 2004
	Total	per capita
Volumes	NA	NA
Expenditure	NA	NA

Public Safety

Police
Chief	Rosman Cash
Number of officers, 2004	9

Crime, 2004	Number	Rate
Total	30	16.7
Violent	7	3.9
Non-violent	23	12.8
Domestic Viol.	8	NA

Emergency/Fire
Director	Ronald Whille

Public School District
(for school year 2004-2005 except as noted)

Lake Como School District†
Borough Hall - F Street
Lake Como, NJ 07719
732-681-6626

†No schools in district - sends children to Belmar Elementary and Manasquan High School.

Grade plan	NA
Enrollment	NA
Students per teacher	NA
Per pupil expenditure	NA
Median faculty salary	NA

Assessment test results
(percent scoring at proficient or advanced level)
	Language	Math
Grade 3	NA	NA
Grade 8	NA	NA
High school	NA	NA

SAT
Percent tested	NA
Average SAT math score	NA
Average SAT verbal score	NA

No Child Left Behind, 2003-04
Attendence rate (target = 90%)	NA
Drop rate	NA
Highly-qualified teachers	NA
District needs improvement?(AYP)	NA

Municipal Finance

Fiscal Year 2005
Total tax levy	$4,229,949
County levy	836,343
County taxes	738,389
County library	40,675
County health	13,464
County open space	43,815
School levy	2,351,521
Local muni. budget	1,042,085
Misc. revenues	1,907,594
Total aid	$563,002
CMPTRA	434,442
Muni. block grant	7,081
Energy tax receipts	96,479
Homeland security	25,000

Fiscal Year 2006
Total aid	$563,002
CMPTRA	431,065
Muni. block grant	7,081
Energy tax receipts	99,856
Homeland security	25,000

Taxes
	2003	2004	2005
General tax rate per $100	3.66	3.680	3.987
Net valuation taxable	$105,663,868	$105,932,178	$106,097,865
State equalized value	$187,347,284	$245,952,867	$293,899,903
County equalization ratio	68.74	56.40	43.04

Demographics & Socio-Economic Characteristics
(2000 U.S. Census, except as noted)

Population
1980*	2,908
1990*	3,078
2000	2,522
Male	1,301
Female	1,221
2000 (revised)	2,650
2004 (estimate)*	2,690
Persons per sq. mi. of land	2,916

Race & Hispanic Origin, 2000
Race
White	2,124
Black/African American	198
Amer. Indian/Alaska Natv.	16
Asian	59
Natv. Hawaiian/Pac. Islander	2
Other Race	69
Two or more races	54
Hispanic origin, total	201
Mexican	50
Puerto Rican	94
Cuban	6
Other Hispanic	51

Age & Nativity, 2000
Under 5 years	207
18 years and over	1,751
21 years and over	1,666
65 years and over	201
85 years and over	15
Median Age	32.3
Native born	2,291
Foreign born	231

Educational Attainment, 2000
Population 25 years and over	1,558
0-8 yrs of school	5.3%
High School grad or higher	73.3%
Bachelor's degree or higher	7.5%
Graduate degree	3.1%

Income & Poverty, 1999
Per capita income	$18,390
Median household income	$43,567
Median family income	$48,833
Persons in poverty	179
H'holds receiving public assistance	35
H'holds receiving social security	192

Households, 2000
Total households	870
With persons under 18	405
With persons over 65	151
Family households	662
One-person households	172
Persons per household	2.9
Persons per family	3.33

Labor & Employment
Total civilian labor force, 2004**	1,767
Unemployment rate	3.9%
Total civilian labor force, 2000	1,173
Unemployment rate	6.1%

Employed persons 16 years and over by occupation, 2000
Managers & professionals	225
Service occupations	298
Sales & office occupations	236
Farming, fishing & forestry	5
Construction & maintenance	195
Production & transportation	142
Self-employed persons	72

*US Census Bureau
**New Jersey Department of Labor

General Information
Borough of Lakehurst
5 Union Ave
Lakehurst, NJ 08733
732-657-4141
Web site	www.lakehurstnj.org
Land area (sq. miles)	0.92
Water area (sq. miles)	0.09
Type of government	Borough
Form of government	B

Government
Legislative Districts
US Congressional	4
State Legislative	9

Local Officials, 2006
Mayor	Stephen Childers
Admin/Manager	Norbert B. MacLean Jr.
Clerk	Bernadette Dugan
Finance Dir/Treas	Christine Thorne
Engineer	Alan Dittenhofer
Attorney	Sean Gertner
Tax assessor	Matcene Hopkins
Tax collector	Marie C. Bell
Building officer	County Service
Zoning officer	NA
Public Works	NA

Housing & Construction
Housing Units, 2000*
Total	961
Median rent	$833
Median SF home value	$89,300

New Privately Owned Housing Units
Authorized by Building Permit
	Units	Value
Total, 2004	3	$226,900
Single family	3	$226,900
Total, 2005	1	$200,000
Single family	1	$200,000

Real Property Valuation - parcels, 2005
	Number	Valuation
Total		$73,888,200
Vacant	46	954,300
Residential	684	55,611,200
Commercial	59	16,937,400
Industrial	0	0
Apartments	3	385,300
Farm land	0	0
Farm homestead	0	0

Average Property Value & Tax, 2005
Residential value	$81,303
Property tax	$3,101
FAIR rebate	$607

Public Library
Manchester Branch Library†
21 Colonial Dr
Lakehurst, NJ 08733
732-657-7600
Branch Librarian .... Louise Innella

Library statistics, 2004
	Total	per capita
Volumes	NA	NA
Expenditure	NA	NA

†Branch of County Library

Public Safety
Police
Chief	Eric Higgins
Number of officers, 2004	10

Crime, 2004	Number	Rate
Total	39	15.1
Violent	4	1.5
Non-violent	35	13.6
Domestic Viol.	41	NA

Emergency/Fire
Director	Gerald Dugan

Public School District
(for school year 2004-2005 except as noted)

Lakehurst School District
301 Union Ave
Lakehurst, NJ 08733
732-657-5741
Superintendent	Kevin Carroll
Grade plan	K-12
Enrollment	484.5
Students per teacher	10.8
Per pupil expenditure	$10,897
Median faculty salary	$42,726
Median administrator salary	$91,350
Grade 12 enrollment	NA
High school graduation rate	NA

Assessment test results
(percent scoring at proficient or advanced level)
	Language	Math
Grade 3	61.2%	64.2%
Grade 8	57.7%	55.8%
High school	NA	NA

SAT
Percent tested	NA
Average SAT math score	NA
Average SAT verbal score	NA

No Child Left Behind, 2003-04
Attendence rate (target = 90%)	94.3%
Drop rate	NA
Highly-qualified teachers	100%
District needs improvement?(AYP)	No

Municipal Finance
Fiscal Year 2005
Total tax levy	$2,861,949
County levy	472,592
County taxes	398,172
County library	41,832
County health	17,731
County open space	14,858
School levy	1,001,499
Local muni. budget	1,387,858
Misc. revenues	2,068,705
Total aid	$446,571
CMPTRA	254,704
Muni. block grant	13,469
Energy tax receipts	153,398
Homeland security	25,000

Fiscal Year 2006
Total aid	$446,571
CMPTRA	249,335
Muni. block grant	13,469
Energy tax receipts	158,767
Homeland security	25,000

Taxes
	2003	2004	2005
General tax rate per $100	3.75	3.787	3.815
Net valuation taxable	$74,454,653	$74,545,307	$75,035,610
State equalized value	$104,762,422	$122,346,705	$150,764,738
County equalization ratio	83.22	71.07	60.50

Demographics & Socio-Economic Characteristics
(2000 U.S. Census, except as noted)

Population
1980*	38,464
1990*	45,048
2000	60,352
Male	28,845
Female	31,507
2004 (estimate)*	66,661
Persons per sq. mi. of land	2,686

Race & Hispanic Origin, 2000
Race
White	47,542
Black/African American	7,270
Amer. Indian/Alaska Natv.	105
Asian	836
Natv. Hawaiian/Pac. Islander	19
Other Race	2,783
Two or more races	1,797
Hispanic origin, total	8,935
Mexican	2,825
Puerto Rican	3,730
Cuban	214
Other Hispanic	2,166

Age & Nativity, 2000
Under 5 years	7,169
18 years and over	41,166
21 years and over	39,014
65 years and over	11,429
85 years and over	2,147
Median Age	30.6
Native born	52,031
Foreign born	8,321

Educational Attainment, 2000
Population 25 years and over	35,168
0-8 yrs of school	8.4%
High School grad or higher	78.6%
Bachelor's degree or higher	21.0%
Graduate degree	8.2%

Income & Poverty, 1999
Per capita income	$16,700
Median household income	$35,634
Median family income	$43,806
Persons in poverty	11,440
H'holds receiving public assistance	969
H'holds receiving social security	8,186

Households, 2000
Total households	19,876
With persons under 18	7,019
With persons over 65	7,763
Family households	13,355
One-person households	5,674
Persons per household	2.92
Persons per family	3.64

Labor & Employment
Total civilian labor force, 2004**	22,418
Unemployment rate	6.2%
Total civilian labor force, 2000	21,234
Unemployment rate	7.5%

Employed persons 16 years and over by occupation, 2000
Managers & professionals	6,553
Service occupations	3,266
Sales & office occupations	5,137
Farming, fishing & forestry	43
Construction & maintenance	1,657
Production & transportation	2,985
Self-employed persons	974

*US Census Bureau
**New Jersey Department of Labor

General Information
Township of Lakewood
231 Third St
Lakewood, NJ 08701
732-364-2500
Web site	www.lakewood.nj.us
Land area (sq. miles)	24.82
Water area (sq. miles)	0.30
Type of government	Township
Form of government	TC

Government

Legislative Districts
US Congressional	4
State Legislative	30

Local Officials, 2006
Mayor	Meir Lichtenstein
Admin/Manager	Frank Edwards
Clerk	Bernadette Standowski
Finance Dir/Treas	William Reiker
Engineer	Glenn Lines
Attorney	Steven Secare
Tax assessor	Linda Solakian
Tax collector	NA
Building officer	Edward Mack
Zoning officer	NA
Public Works	NA

Housing & Construction

Housing Units, 2000*
Total	21,214
Median rent	$849
Median SF home value	$126,400

New Privately Owned Housing Units
Authorized by Building Permit
	Units	Value
Total, 2004	957	$51,451,251
Single family	507	$45,168,591
Total, 2005	344	$30,168,174
Single family	344	$30,168,174

Real Property Valuation - parcels, 2005
	Number	Valuation
Total		$2,867,283,600
Vacant	3,705	142,288,700
Residential	17,713	1,978,934,000
Commercial	521	299,146,300
Industrial	174	299,362,700
Apartments	91	144,374,200
Farm land	14	3,120,800
Farm homestead	24	56,900

Average Property Value & Tax, 2005
Residential value	$111,574
Property tax	$3,845
FAIR rebate	$545

Public Library
Lakewood Branch Library†
301 Lexington Ave
Lakewood, NJ 08701
732-363-1435
Director	Jeff Kesper

Library statistics, 2004
	Total	per capita
Volumes	NA	NA
Expenditure	NA	NA

†Branch of County Library

Public Safety
Police
Chief	Wayne Youst
Number of officers, 2004	107

Crime, 2004	Number	Rate
Total	1,948	29.6
Violent	220	3.3
Non-violent	1,728	26.3
Domestic Viol.	985	NA

Emergency/Fire
Director	Robert Reddington

Public School District
(for school year 2004-2005 except as noted)

Lakewood Township School District
655 Princeton Ave
Lakewood, NJ 08701
732-905-3633
Superintendent	Edward Luick
Grade plan	K-12
Enrollment	5,358.0
Students per teacher	10.3
Per pupil expenditure	$15,560
Median faculty salary	$46,011
Median administrator salary	$102,073
Grade 12 enrollment	277.0
High school graduation rate	76.7%

Assessment test results
(percent scoring at proficient or advanced level)
	Language	Math
Grade 3	70.2%	73.1%
Grade 8	39.8%	42.0%
High school	65.3%	58.6%

SAT
Percent tested	54%
Average SAT math score	465
Average SAT verbal score	448

No Child Left Behind, 2003-04
Attendence rate (target = 90%)	93.0%
Drop rate	4.9%
Highly-qualified teachers	94.9%
District needs improvement?(AYP)	Yes

Municipal Finance

Fiscal Year 2005
Total tax levy	$99,112,678
County levy	19,805,228
County taxes	16,685,287
County library	1,752,926
County health	743,268
County open space	623,747
School levy	55,465,650
Local muni. budget	23,841,800
Misc. revenues	27,377,622
Total aid	$6,926,388
CMPTRA	3,074,726
Muni. block grant	236,642
Energy tax receipts	3,475,020
Homeland security	140,000

Fiscal Year 2006
Total aid	$6,926,388
CMPTRA	2,953,101
Muni. block grant	236,642
Energy tax receipts	3,596,645
Homeland security	140,000

Taxes
	2003	2004	2005
General tax rate per $100	3.15	3.316	3.447
Net valuation taxable	$2,698,682,514	$2,760,747,386	$2,876,116,816
State equalized value	$4,229,247,005	$4,989,292,120	$6,411,317,022
County equalization ratio	72.31	63.81	55.24

Demographics & Socio-Economic Characteristics
(2000 U.S. Census, except as noted)

Population
1980*	4,044
1990*	3,927
2000	3,868
Male	1,882
Female	1,986
2004 (estimate)*	3,872
Persons per sq. mi. of land	3,412

Race & Hispanic Origin, 2000
Race
White	3,661
Black/African American	75
Amer. Indian/Alaska Natv.	13
Asian	41
Natv. Hawaiian/Pac. Islander	2
Other Race	35
Two or more races	41
Hispanic origin, total	120
Mexican	69
Puerto Rican	19
Cuban	5
Other Hispanic	27

Age & Nativity, 2000
Under 5 years	145
18 years and over	3,274
21 years and over	3,156
65 years and over	589
85 years and over	62
Median Age	42.8
Native born	3,671
Foreign born	197

Educational Attainment, 2000
Population 25 years and over	3,082
0-8 yrs of school	4.1%
High School grad or higher	87.9%
Bachelor's degree or higher	37.5%
Graduate degree	18.5%

Income & Poverty, 1999
Per capita income	$36,267
Median household income	$52,647
Median family income	$80,669
Persons in poverty	230
H'holds receiving public assistance	31
H'holds receiving social security	482

Households, 2000
Total households	1,860
With persons under 18	365
With persons over 65	445
Family households	940
One-person households	721
Persons per household	2.06
Persons per family	2.82

Labor & Employment
Total civilian labor force, 2004**	2,730
Unemployment rate	2.9%
Total civilian labor force, 2000	2,509
Unemployment rate	2.4%

Employed persons 16 years and over by occupation, 2000
Managers & professionals	1,099
Service occupations	319
Sales & office occupations	614
Farming, fishing & forestry	13
Construction & maintenance	212
Production & transportation	192
Self-employed persons	251

*US Census Bureau
**New Jersey Department of Labor

General Information
City of Lambertville
18 York St
Lambertville, NJ 08530
609-397-0110
Web site	www.lambertvillenj.org
Land area (sq. miles)	1.13
Water area (sq. miles)	0.12
Type of government	City
Form of government	SM '50

Government

Legislative Districts
US Congressional	12
State Legislative	23

Local Officials, 2006
Mayor	David DelVecchio
Admin/Manager	NA
Clerk	Loretta Buckelew
Finance Dir/Treas	Linda Monteverde
Engineer	Robert Clerico
Attorney	Phillip Faherty III
Tax assessor	Richard Carmosino
Tax collector	Bonnie Eick
Building officer	Allen Rowles
Zoning officer	John Barczky
Public Works	Paul Cronce

Housing & Construction

Housing Units, 2000*
Total	1,961
Median rent	$811
Median SF home value	$170,500

New Privately Owned Housing Units
Authorized by Building Permit
	Units	Value
Total, 2004	1	$168,635
Single family	1	$168,635
Total, 2005	0	$0
Single family	0	$0

Real Property Valuation - parcels, 2005
	Number	Valuation
Total		$565,572,183
Vacant	372	18,672,298
Residential	1,451	419,401,000
Commercial	193	98,120,071
Industrial	11	9,459,550
Apartments	34	18,561,500
Farm land	2	1,229,500
Farm homestead	10	128,264

Average Property Value & Tax, 2005
Residential value	$287,152
Property tax	$4,766
FAIR rebate	$575

Public Library
Lambertville Public Library
6 Lilly St
Lambertville, NJ 08530
609-397-0275
Director	Harold Dunn

Library statistics, 2004
	Total	per capita
Volumes	19,283	4.99
Expenditure	$135,028	$34.91

Public Safety

Police
Chief	Bruce Cocuzza
Number of officers, 2004	11

Crime, 2004	Number	Rate
Total	91	23.5
Violent	8	2.1
Non-violent	83	21.4
Domestic Viol.	24	NA

Emergency/Fire
Director	Matt Hartigan

Public School District
(for school year 2004-2005 except as noted)

Lambertville School District
200 N Main St
Lambertville, NJ 08530
609-397-0183
Administrator	Madeline Gavin
Grade plan	K-6
Enrollment	169.0
Students per teacher	7.9
Per pupil expenditure	$15,835
Median faculty salary	$55,037
Median administrator salary	$88,608
Grade 12 enrollment	NA
High school graduation rate	NA

Assessment test results
(percent scoring at proficient or advanced level)
	Language	Math
Grade 3	77.2%	81.9%
Grade 8	NA	NA
High school	NA	NA

SAT
Percent tested	NA
Average SAT math score	NA
Average SAT verbal score	NA

No Child Left Behind, 2003-04
Attendence rate (target = 90%)	94.9%
Drop rate	NA
Highly-qualified teachers	100%
District needs improvement?(AYP)	No

Municipal Finance

Fiscal Year 2005
Total tax levy	$9,411,896
County levy	2,152,651
County taxes	1,967,502
County library	0
County health	0
County open space	185,149
School levy	6,018,362
Local muni. budget	1,240,884
Misc. revenues	1,178,355
Total aid	$706,089
CMPTRA	448,128
Muni. block grant	17,183
Energy tax receipts	215,778
Homeland security	25,000

Fiscal Year 2006
Total aid	$706,089
CMPTRA	440,576
Muni. block grant	17,183
Energy tax receipts	223,330
Homeland security	25,000

Taxes
	2003	2004	2005
General tax rate per $100	2.08	1.790	1.660
Net valuation taxable	$412,565,436	$504,447,121	$567,008,832
State equalized value	$511,043,523	$572,219,660	$634,948,300
County equalization ratio	87.41	90.63	92.68

Demographics & Socio-Economic Characteristics
(2000 U.S. Census, except as noted)

Population
1980*	2,249
1990*	2,341
2000	1,970
Male	983
Female	987
2004 (estimate)*	1,947
Persons per sq. mi. of land	4,164

Race & Hispanic Origin, 2000
Race
White	1,859
Black/African American	54
Amer. Indian/Alaska Natv.	5
Asian	19
Natv. Hawaiian/Pac. Islander	0
Other Race	14
Two or more races	19
Hispanic origin, total	32
Mexican	4
Puerto Rican	10
Cuban	2
Other Hispanic	16

Age & Nativity, 2000
Under 5 years	106
18 years and over	1,495
21 years and over	1,411
65 years and over	281
85 years and over	22
Median Age	36.9
Native born	1,929
Foreign born	41

Educational Attainment, 2000
Population 25 years and over	1,333
0-8 yrs of school	2.7%
High School grad or higher	87.0%
Bachelor's degree or higher	22.5%
Graduate degree	6.7%

Income & Poverty, 1999
Per capita income	$23,254
Median household income	$52,500
Median family income	$58,854
Persons in poverty	72
H'holds receiving public assistance	10
H'holds receiving social security	242

Households, 2000
Total households	762
With persons under 18	262
With persons over 65	204
Family households	534
One-person households	199
Persons per household	2.59
Persons per family	3.16

Labor & Employment
Total civilian labor force, 2004**	1,198
Unemployment rate	5.5%
Total civilian labor force, 2000	1,059
Unemployment rate	4.0%

Employed persons 16 years and over by occupation, 2000
Managers & professionals	359
Service occupations	150
Sales & office occupations	288
Farming, fishing & forestry	0
Construction & maintenance	95
Production & transportation	125
Self-employed persons	43

*US Census Bureau
**New Jersey Department of Labor

General Information
Borough of Laurel Springs
135 Broadway
Laurel Springs, NJ 08021
856-784-0500
Web site	www.laurelsprings-nj.com
Land area (sq. miles)	0.47
Water area (sq. miles)	0
Type of government	Borough
Form of government	B

Government

Legislative Districts
US Congressional	1
State Legislative	4

Local Officials, 2006
Mayor	David Thatcher
Admin/Manager	NA
Clerk	Barbara M. Hawk
Finance Dir/Treas	M. Mitchel/D. Ciminera
Engineer	Ed Vernick
Attorney	George Botcheos
Tax assessor	Richard Arrowood
Tax collector	Janice M. Gattone
Building officer	Albert Hallworth
Zoning officer	NA
Public Works	Eric P. Warner

Housing & Construction

Housing Units, 2000*
Total	806
Median rent	$605
Median SF home value	$110,200

New Privately Owned Housing Units
Authorized by Building Permit
	Units	Value
Total, 2004	0	$0
Single family	0	$0
Total, 2005	1	$107,500
Single family	1	$107,500

Real Property Valuation - parcels, 2005
	Number	Valuation
Total		$79,758,300
Vacant	13	329,500
Residential	631	67,669,400
Commercial	38	9,919,100
Industrial	0	0
Apartments	3	1,840,300
Farm land	0	0
Farm homestead	0	0

Average Property Value & Tax, 2005
Residential value	$107,242
Property tax	$4,700
FAIR rebate	$577

Public Library

No public municipal library.

Library statistics, 2004
	Total	per capita
Volumes	NA	NA
Expenditure	NA	NA

Public Safety

Police
Chief	Michael Wolcott
Number of officers, 2004	7

Crime, 2004	Number	Rate
Total	59	30.1
Violent	8	4.1
Non-violent	51	26.1
Domestic Viol.	17	NA

Emergency/Fire
Director	Ken Cheeseman

Public School District
(for school year 2004-2005 except as noted)

Laurel Springs School District
y23 Grand Ave
Laurel Springs, NJ 08021
856-783-1086
Superintendent	Albert Brown
Grade plan	K-12.
Enrollment	181.0
Students per teacher	12.9
Per pupil expenditure	$11,498
Median faculty salary	$48,209
Median administrator salary	$28,561
Grade 12 enrollment	NA
High school graduation rate	NA

Assessment test results
(percent scoring at proficient or advanced level)
	Language	Math
Grade 3	78.2%	91.3%
Grade 8	NA	NA
High school	NA	NA

SAT
Percent tested	NA
Average SAT math score	NA
Average SAT verbal score	NA

No Child Left Behind, 2003-04
Attendence rate (target = 90%)	95.4%
Drop rate	NA
Highly-qualified teachers	100%
District needs improvement?(AYP)	No

Municipal Finance

Fiscal Year 2005
Total tax levy	$3,730,185
County levy	902,000
County taxes	831,157
County library	59,917
County health	0
County open space	10,926
School levy	1,875,686
Local muni. budget	952,500
Misc. revenues	1,063,500
Total aid	$488,086
CMPTRA	284,853
Muni. block grant	10,244
Energy tax receipts	167,989
Homeland security	25,000

Fiscal Year 2006
Total aid	$488,086
CMPTRA	278,973
Muni. block grant	10,244
Energy tax receipts	173,869
Homeland security	25,000

Taxes
	2003	2004	2005
General tax rate per $100	3.92	4.129	4.383
Net valuation taxable	$85,853,385	$85,514,805	$85,110,694
State equalized value	$102,560,489	$109,094,507	$127,354,024
County equalization ratio	90.57	83.71	77.14

Demographics & Socio-Economic Characteristics
(2000 U.S. Census, except as noted)

Population
1980*	2,072
1990*	2,299
2000	2,665
Male	1,220
Female	1,445
2004 (estimate)*	2,743
Persons per sq. mi. of land	3,412

Race & Hispanic Origin, 2000
Race
White	2,615
Black/African American	7
Amer. Indian/Alaska Natv.	3
Asian	4
Natv. Hawaiian/Pac. Islander	0
Other Race	17
Two or more races	19
Hispanic origin, total	43
Mexican	19
Puerto Rican	3
Cuban	10
Other Hispanic	11

Age & Nativity, 2000
Under 5 years	89
18 years and over	2,316
21 years and over	2,250
65 years and over	970
85 years and over	162
Median Age	56.4
Native born	2,578
Foreign born	87

Educational Attainment, 2000
Population 25 years and over	2,168
0-8 yrs of school	5.1%
High School grad or higher	85.1%
Bachelor's degree or higher	26.5%
Graduate degree	10.7%

Income & Poverty, 1999
Per capita income	$28,588
Median household income	$43,846
Median family income	$57,778
Persons in poverty	201
H'holds receiving public assistance	34
H'holds receiving social security	613

Households, 2000
Total households	1,208
With persons under 18	197
With persons over 65	588
Family households	742
One-person households	417
Persons per household	2.09
Persons per family	2.66

Labor & Employment
Total civilian labor force, 2004**	1,248
Unemployment rate	4.5%
Total civilian labor force, 2000	1,062
Unemployment rate	2.7%

Employed persons 16 years and over by occupation, 2000
Managers & professionals	417
Service occupations	101
Sales & office occupations	310
Farming, fishing & forestry	0
Construction & maintenance	128
Production & transportation	77
Self-employed persons	81

*US Census Bureau
**New Jersey Department of Labor

General Information
Borough of Lavallette
PO Box 67
1306 Grand Central
Lavallette, NJ 08735
732-793-7477
Web site	lavalletteboro.com
Land area (sq. miles)	0.80
Water area (sq. miles)	0.12
Type of government	Borough
Form of government	B

Government

Legislative Districts
US Congressional	3
State Legislative	10

Local Officials, 2006
Mayor	Thomas Walls
Admin/Manager	Christopher Parlow
Clerk	Christopher Parlow
Finance Dir/Treas	Michele Burk
Engineer	Mike O'Donnell
Attorney	Eric M. Bernstein
Tax assessor	Scott Pezarras
Tax collector	Chrissa Sierfeld
Building officer	Jim Erdman
Zoning officer	Richard Laird
Public Works	Gary Schlosser

Housing & Construction

Housing Units, 2000*
Total	3,210
Median rent	$786
Median SF home value	$323,100

New Privately Owned Housing Units
Authorized by Building Permit
	Units	Value
Total, 2004	23	$3,701,758
Single family	23	$3,701,758
Total, 2005	20	$3,410,564
Single family	20	$3,410,564

Real Property Valuation - parcels, 2005
	Number	Valuation
Total		$1,773,593,960
Vacant	50	26,871,700
Residential	2,498	1,700,885,500
Commercial	69	40,381,360
Industrial	0	0
Apartments	9	5,455,400
Farm land	0	0
Farm homestead	0	0

Average Property Value & Tax, 2005
Residential value	$680,899
Property tax	$5,045
FAIR rebate	$807

Public Library
Upper Shores Branch Library†
112 Jersey City Ave
Lavallette, NJ 08735
732-793-3996
Branch Librarian	Rita Oakes

Library statistics, 2004
	Total	per capita
Volumes	NA	NA
Expenditure	NA	NA

†Branch of County Library

Public Safety
Police
Chief	Colin Grant
Number of officers, 2004	12

Crime, 2004	Number	Rate
Total	50	18.4
Violent	2	0.7
Non-violent	48	17.7
Domestic Viol.	6	NA

Emergency/Fire
Director	Michael Phillips (Chief)

Public School District
(for school year 2004-2005 except as noted)

Lavallette Borough School District
105 Brooklyn Ave
Lavallette, NJ 08735
732-793-7722
Superintendent	Peter Morris
Grade plan	K-12
Enrollment	143.0
Students per teacher	7.9
Per pupil expenditure	$12,665
Median faculty salary	$37,730
Median administrator salary	$100,000
Grade 12 enrollment	NA
High school graduation rate	NA

Assessment test results
(percent scoring at proficient or advanced level)
	Language	Math
Grade 3	92.9%	85.7%
Grade 8	95.2%	95.5%
High school	NA	NA

SAT
Percent tested	NA
Average SAT math score	NA
Average SAT verbal score	NA

No Child Left Behind, 2003-04
Attendance rate (target = 90%)	94.7%
Drop rate	NA
Highly-qualified teachers	98.3%
District needs improvement?(AYP)	No

Municipal Finance

Fiscal Year 2005
Total tax levy	$13,159,809
County levy	6,224,372
County taxes	5,244,193
County library	550,927
County health	233,519
County open space	195,732
School levy	2,862,908
Local muni. budget	4,072,530
Misc. revenues	1,907,415
Total aid	$228,696
CMPTRA	10,908
Muni. block grant	10,450
Energy tax receipts	182,338
Homeland security	25,000

Fiscal Year 2006
Total aid	$228,696
CMPTRA	4,526
Muni. block grant	10,450
Energy tax receipts	188,720
Homeland security	25,000

Taxes
	2003	2004	2005
General tax rate per $100	1.72	0.684	0.741
Net valuation taxable	$673,488,165	$1,772,558,240	$1,776,114,173
State equalized value	$1,326,025,133	$1,627,452,348	$1,895,128,226
County equalization ratio	60.6	132.58	108.93

Demographics & Socio-Economic Characteristics
(2000 U.S. Census, except as noted)

Population
1980*	3,042
1990*	2,841
2000	2,692
Male	1,224
Female	1,468
2004 (estimate)*	2,748
Persons per sq. mi. of land	1,960

Race & Hispanic Origin, 2000
Race
White	47
Black/African American	2,520
Amer. Indian/Alaska Natv.	27
Asian	14
Natv. Hawaiian/Pac. Islander	2
Other Race	13
Two or more races	69
Hispanic origin, total	64
Mexican	8
Puerto Rican	40
Cuban	3
Other Hispanic	13

Age & Nativity, 2000
Under 5 years	108
18 years and over	2,065
21 years and over	1,968
65 years and over	507
85 years and over	59
Median Age	42.4
Native born	2,561
Foreign born	163

Educational Attainment, 2000
Population 25 years and over	1,856
0-8 yrs of school	6.8%
High School grad or higher	79.0%
Bachelor's degree or higher	18.8%
Graduate degree	7.0%

Income & Poverty, 1999
Per capita income	$18,831
Median household income	$45,192
Median family income	$55,197
Persons in poverty	289
H'holds receiving public assistance	48
H'holds receiving social security	419

Households, 2000
Total households	1,026
With persons under 18	331
With persons over 65	396
Family households	701
One-person households	291
Persons per household	2.62
Persons per family	3.23

Labor & Employment
Total civilian labor force, 2004**	1,388
Unemployment rate	8.8%
Total civilian labor force, 2000	1,356
Unemployment rate	7.2%

Employed persons 16 years and over by occupation, 2000
Managers & professionals	392
Service occupations	225
Sales & office occupations	405
Farming, fishing & forestry	0
Construction & maintenance	41
Production & transportation	195
Self-employed persons	26

*US Census Bureau
**New Jersey Department of Labor

General Information
Borough of Lawnside
4 Douglas Ave
Lawnside, NJ 08045
856-573-6200

Web site	www.lawnside.net
Land area (sq. miles)	1.40
Water area (sq. miles)	0
Type of government	Borough
Form of government	B

Government

Legislative Districts
US Congressional	1
State Legislative	5

Local Officials, 2006
Mayor	Mark Bryant
Admin/Manager	Jessie Harris
Clerk	Sylvia VanNockay
Finance Dir/Treas	Jessie Harris
Engineer	Smith Co. Group, Inc.
Attorney	Allen Zeller
Tax assessor	Thomas Colavecchio
Tax collector	Jessie Harris
Building officer	Mengste Thomas El
Zoning officer	Clarence Cannon
Public Works	Alex Barr

Housing & Construction

Housing Units, 2000*
Total	1,110
Median rent	$566
Median SF home value	$99,900

New Privately Owned Housing Units Authorized by Building Permit
	Units	Value
Total, 2004	16	$1,827,276
Single family	16	$1,827,276
Total, 2005	20	$4,970,500
Single family	20	$4,970,500

Real Property Valuation - parcels, 2005
	Number	Valuation
Total		$143,843,200
Vacant	268	3,948,600
Residential	944	86,211,800
Commercial	58	39,191,200
Industrial	1	11,250,000
Apartments	5	3,241,600
Farm land	0	0
Farm homestead	0	0

Average Property Value & Tax, 2005
Residential value	$91,326
Property tax	$3,254
FAIR rebate	$721

Public Library

No public municipal library.

Library statistics, 2004
	Total	per capita
Volumes	NA	NA
Expenditure	NA	NA

Public Safety
Police
Chief	Jessie Harris (Actg)
Number of officers, 2004	9

Crime, 2004	Number	Rate
Total	137	50.2
Violent	24	8.8
Non-violent	113	41.4
Domestic Viol.	6	NA

Emergency/Fire
Director	Samuel Funches Jr.

Public School District
(for school year 2004-2005 except as noted)

Lawnside Borough School District
426 Charleston Ave
Lawnside, NJ 08045
856-546-4850

Superintendent	Cassandra Brown
Grade plan	K-12
Enrollment	283.0
Students per teacher	9.2
Per pupil expenditure	$13,793
Median faculty salary	$49,308
Median administrator salary	$70,821
Grade 12 enrollment	NA
High school graduation rate	NA

Assessment test results
(percent scoring at proficient or advanced level)
	Language	Math
Grade 3	65.0%	90.0%
Grade 8	42.4%	33.3%
High school	NA	NA

SAT
Percent tested	NA
Average SAT math score	NA
Average SAT verbal score	NA

No Child Left Behind, 2003-04
Attendence rate (target = 90%)	94.3%
Drop rate	NA
Highly-qualified teachers	100%
District needs improvement?(AYP)	No

Municipal Finance

Fiscal Year 2005
Total tax levy	$5,134,575
County levy	1,302,793
County taxes	1,200,730
County library	86,322
County health	0
County open space	15,741
School levy	2,881,019
Local muni. budget	950,763
Misc. revenues	2,535,000
Total aid	$734,602
CMPTRA	154,098
Muni. block grant	12,431
Energy tax receipts	543,073
Homeland security	25,000

Fiscal Year 2006
Total aid	$734,602
CMPTRA	135,091
Muni. block grant	12,431
Energy tax receipts	562,080
Homeland security	25,000

Taxes
	2003	2004	2005
General tax rate per $100	3.36	3.386	3.564
Net valuation taxable	$138,814,911	$141,277,390	$144,107,889
State equalized value	$145,768,047	$152,709,668	$187,934,128
County equalization ratio	100.87	95.23	92.50

Demographics & Socio-Economic Characteristics
(2000 U.S. Census, except as noted)

Population
1980*	2,166
1990*	2,433
2000	2,721
Male	1,356
Female	1,365
2004 (estimate)*	2,863
Persons per sq. mi. of land	76

Race & Hispanic Origin, 2000
Race
White	2,228
Black/African American	283
Amer. Indian/Alaska Natv.	29
Asian	7
Natv. Hawaiian/Pac. Islander	5
Other Race	93
Two or more races	76
Hispanic origin, total	191
Mexican	77
Puerto Rican	79
Cuban	2
Other Hispanic	33

Age & Nativity, 2000
Under 5 years	168
18 years and over	1,946
21 years and over	1,854
65 years and over	287
85 years and over	21
Median Age	35.7
Native born	2,613
Foreign born	108

Educational Attainment, 2000
Population 25 years and over	1,801
0-8 yrs of school	7.9%
High School grad or higher	75.2%
Bachelor's degree or higher	11.0%
Graduate degree	2.7%

Income & Poverty, 1999
Per capita income	$17,654
Median household income	$46,083
Median family income	$48,456
Persons in poverty	242
H'holds receiving public assistance	36
H'holds receiving social security	291

Households, 2000
Total households	920
With persons under 18	402
With persons over 65	228
Family households	712
One-person households	164
Persons per household	2.9
Persons per family	3.27

Labor & Employment
Total civilian labor force, 2004**	1,201
Unemployment rate	8.4%
Total civilian labor force, 2000	1,276
Unemployment rate	8.4%

Employed persons 16 years and over by occupation, 2000
Managers & professionals	249
Service occupations	163
Sales & office occupations	246
Farming, fishing & forestry	12
Construction & maintenance	183
Production & transportation	316
Self-employed persons	99

*US Census Bureau
**New Jersey Department of Labor

General Information
Township of Lawrence
357 Main St
Cedarville, NJ 08311
856-447-4554
Email	lawrencemayor@comcast.net
Land area (sq. miles)	37.47
Water area (sq. miles)	0.98
Type of government	Township
Form of government	TC

Government

Legislative Districts
US Congressional	2
State Legislative	3

Local Officials, 2006
Mayor	Elmer Bowman
Admin/Manager	NA
Clerk	Ruth Dawson
Finance Dir/Treas	Teresa Delp
Engineer	Albert Fralinger Jr.
Attorney	Tom Seeley
Tax assessor	Donald Seifrit
Tax collector	Ruth Dawson
Building officer	David Dean
Zoning officer	NA
Public Works	Michael Day

Housing & Construction

Housing Units, 2000*
Total	1,023
Median rent	$680
Median SF home value	$91,500

New Privately Owned Housing Units Authorized by Building Permit
	Units	Value
Total, 2004	9	$1,018,000
Single family	9	$1,018,000
Total, 2005	7	$909,000
Single family	7	$909,000

Real Property Valuation - parcels, 2005
	Number	Valuation
Total		$107,234,700
Vacant	2,019	8,984,500
Residential	1,034	82,799,600
Commercial	32	2,893,900
Industrial	2	2,802,500
Apartments	1	80,000
Farm land	108	8,488,800
Farm homestead	175	1,185,400

Average Property Value & Tax, 2005
Residential value	$69,467
Property tax	$2,358
FAIR rebate	$567

Public Library
No public municipal library.

Library statistics, 2004
	Total	per capita
Volumes	NA	NA
Expenditure	NA	NA

Public Safety
Police
Chief	NA
Number of officers, 2004	0

Crime, 2004	Number	Rate
Total	66	23.6
Violent	6	2.1
Non-violent	60	21.4
Domestic Viol.	30	NA

Emergency/Fire
Director	Bruce Conti

Public School District
(for school year 2004-2005 except as noted)

Lawrence Township School District
225 Main St
Cedarville, NJ 08311
856-447-4237
Administrator	Ralph Scazafabo
Grade plan	K-12
Enrollment	502.0
Students per teacher	12.1
Per pupil expenditure	$10,868
Median faculty salary	$44,449
Median administrator salary	$65,835
Grade 12 enrollment	NA
High school graduation rate	NA

Assessment test results
(percent scoring at proficient or advanced level)
	Language	Math
Grade 3	69.0%	61.0%
Grade 8	57.2%	42.2%
High school	NA	NA

SAT
Percent tested	NA
Average SAT math score	NA
Average SAT verbal score	NA

No Child Left Behind, 2003-04
Attendence rate (target = 90%)	94.9%
Drop rate	NA
Highly-qualified teachers	92.9%
District needs improvement?(AYP)	No

Municipal Finance

Fiscal Year 2005
Total tax levy	$3,678,194
County levy	1,372,906
County taxes	1,304,178
County library	0
County health	55,524
County open space	13,205
School levy	1,709,288
Local muni. budget	596,000
Misc. revenues	1,199,158
Total aid	$328,337
CMPTRA	147,855
Muni. block grant	10,669
Energy tax receipts	169,813
Homeland security	0

Fiscal Year 2006
Total aid	$328,338
CMPTRA	141,912
Muni. block grant	10,669
Energy tax receipts	175,757
Homeland security	NA

Taxes
	2003	2004	2005
General tax rate per $100	2.88	2.941	3.397
Net valuation taxable	$103,537,030	$105,478,982	$108,372,677
State equalized value	$114,684,349	$127,414,885	$146,370,444
County equalization ratio	88.89	90.28	82.61

Demographics & Socio-Economic Characteristics
(2000 U.S. Census, except as noted)

Population
1980*	19,724
1990*	25,787
2000	29,159
Male	13,650
Female	15,509
2004 (estimate)*	31,391
Persons per sq. mi. of land	1,418

Race & Hispanic Origin, 2000
Race
White	23,101
Black/African American	2,707
Amer. Indian/Alaska Natv.	23
Asian	2,306
Natv. Hawaiian/Pac. Islander	31
Other Race	523
Two or more races	468
Hispanic origin, total	1,344
Mexican	180
Puerto Rican	365
Cuban	42
Other Hispanic	757

Age & Nativity, 2000
Under 5 years	1,678
18 years and over	22,836
21 years and over	20,879
65 years and over	3,953
85 years and over	524
Median Age	36.7
Native born	24,062
Foreign born	5,097

Educational Attainment, 2000
Population 25 years and over	19,151
0-8 yrs of school	3.7%
High School grad or higher	89.2%
Bachelor's degree or higher	50.5%
Graduate degree	24.0%

Income & Poverty, 1999
Per capita income	$33,120
Median household income	$67,959
Median family income	$82,704
Persons in poverty	1,311
H'holds receiving public assistance	100
H'holds receiving social security	2,771

Households, 2000
Total households	10,797
With persons under 18	3,595
With persons over 65	2,724
Family households	7,239
One-person households	2,892
Persons per household	2.49
Persons per family	3.05

Labor & Employment
Total civilian labor force, 2004**	15,803
Unemployment rate	2.4%
Total civilian labor force, 2000	16,554
Unemployment rate	10.0%

Employed persons 16 years and over by occupation, 2000
Managers & professionals	8,020
Service occupations	1,571
Sales & office occupations	3,748
Farming, fishing & forestry	0
Construction & maintenance	673
Production & transportation	884
Self-employed persons	826

*US Census Bureau
**New Jersey Department of Labor

General Information
Township of Lawrence
PO Box 6006
2207 Lawrenceville Rd
Lawrenceville, NJ 08648
609-844-7000

Web site	www.lawrencetwp.com
Land area (sq. miles)	22.14
Water area (sq. miles)	0.04
Type of government	Township
Form of government	CM '50

Government

Legislative Districts
US Congressional	12
State Legislative	15

Local Officials, 2006
Mayor	Michael Powers
Admin/Manager	Richard Krawczun
Clerk	Kathleen Norcia
Finance Dir/Treas	Richard Krawczun
Engineer	Christopher Budzinski
Attorney	Kevin Nerwenski
Tax assessor	Geoffrey Acolia
Tax collector	Alice Fish
Building officer	Anthony Cermele
Zoning officer	Christopher Budzinski
Public Works	Greg Whitehead

Housing & Construction

Housing Units, 2000*
Total	11,180
Median rent	$935
Median SF home value	$177,900

New Privately Owned Housing Units Authorized by Building Permit
	Units	Value
Total, 2004	117	$12,492,777
Single family	117	$12,492,777
Total, 2005	130	$17,545,070
Single family	130	$17,545,070

Real Property Valuation - parcels, 2005
	Number	Valuation
Total		$2,656,698,023
Vacant	1,051	59,386,700
Residential	9,514	1,554,582,950
Commercial	403	861,171,173
Industrial	36	44,769,600
Apartments	21	119,651,900
Farm land	46	16,467,900
Farm homestead	88	667,800

Average Property Value & Tax, 2005
Residential value	$161,972
Property tax	$5,761
FAIR rebate	$573

Public Library
Mercer County Library
2751 Brunswick Pike
Lawrenceville, NJ 08648
609-989-6920

Director	Ellen Brown

Library statistics, 2004
	Total	per capita
Volumes	NA	NA
Expenditure	NA	NA

Public Safety

Police
Chief	Daniel Posluszny
Number of officers, 2004	70

Crime, 2004	Number	Rate
Total	1,172	37.8
Violent	52	1.7
Non-violent	1,120	36.2
Domestic Viol.	217	NA

Emergency/Fire
Director	NA

Public School District
(for school year 2004-2005 except as noted)

Lawrence Township School District
2565 Princeton Pike
Lawrenceville, NJ 08648
609-671-5405

Administrator	Philip Meara
Grade plan	K-12
Enrollment	4,244.0
Students per teacher	12.4
Per pupil expenditure	$12,818
Median faculty salary	$51,920
Median administrator salary	$105,807
Grade 12 enrollment	375.0
High school graduation rate	94.4%

Assessment test results
(percent scoring at proficient or advanced level)
	Language	Math
Grade 3	87.3%	83.1%
Grade 8	73.9%	58.8%
High school	86.0%	82.2%

SAT
Percent tested	83%
Average SAT math score	537
Average SAT verbal score	519

No Child Left Behind, 2003-04
Attendence rate (target = 90%)	95.2%
Drop rate	1.4%
Highly-qualified teachers	99.4%
District needs improvement?(AYP)	No

Municipal Finance

Fiscal Year 2005
Total tax levy	$94,638,864
County levy	25,169,699
County taxes	21,983,525
County library	1,946,827
County health	0
County open space	1,239,347
School levy	52,172,850
Local muni. budget	17,296,315
Misc. revenues	18,330,286
Total aid	$5,401,883
CMPTRA	1,565,650
Muni. block grant	114,333
Energy tax receipts	3,581,900
Homeland security	140,000

Fiscal Year 2006
Total aid	$5,401,882
CMPTRA	1,440,283
Muni. block grant	114,333
Energy tax receipts	3,707,266
Homeland security	140,000

Taxes
	2003	2004	2005
General tax rate per $100	2.99	3.240	3.560
Net valuation taxable	$2,612,998,236	$2,636,187,803	$2,660,737,130
State equalized value	$3,471,039,102	$4,094,812,646	$4,385,589,468
County equalization ratio	83.92	75.28	64.33

Demographics & Socio-Economic Characteristics
(2000 U.S. Census, except as noted)

Population
1980* 820
1990* 1,036
2000 1,065
    Male 511
    Female .554
2004 (estimate)* 1,566
    Persons per sq. mi. of land 1,805

Race & Hispanic Origin, 2000
Race
    White 1,016
    Black/African American 7
    Amer. Indian/Alaska Natv. 2
    Asian 33
    Natv. Hawaiian/Pac. Islander 0
    Other Race .4
    Two or more races 3
Hispanic origin, total 22
    Mexican 4
    Puerto Rican 14
    Cuban 1
    Other Hispanic 3

Age & Nativity, 2000
Under 5 years .81
18 years and over 808
21 years and over 786
65 years and over 124
85 years and over 13
Median Age 39.3
Native born .997
Foreign born .68

Educational Attainment, 2000
Population 25 years and over 764
0-8 yrs of school 1.4%
High School grad or higher 93.2%
Bachelor's degree or higher 39.7%
Graduate degree 13.2%

Income & Poverty, 1999
Per capita income $34,066
Median household income $68,542
Median family income $83,436
Persons in poverty 38
H'holds receiving public assistance 4
H'holds receiving social security 90

Households, 2000
Total households 458
    With persons under 18 147
    With persons over 65 96
    Family households 287
    One-person households 151
Persons per household 2.33
Persons per family 2.97

Labor & Employment
Total civilian labor force, 2004** 773
    Unemployment rate 1.2%
Total civilian labor force, 2000 657
    Unemployment rate 3.8%
Employed persons 16 years and over by occupation, 2000
    Managers & professionals 270
    Service occupations 54
    Sales & office occupations 206
    Farming, fishing & forestry 0
    Construction & maintenance 54
    Production & transportation 48
Self-employed persons 42

*US Census Bureau
**New Jersey Department of Labor

General Information
Borough of Lebanon
6 High St
Lebanon, NJ 08833
908-236-2425
Web site . . . . www.lebanonboro.com
Land area (sq. miles) 0.87
Water area (sq. miles) 0
Type of government . . . . Borough
Form of government . . . . .B

Government

Legislative Districts
US Congressional 7
State Legislative 23

Local Officials, 2006
Mayor . . . . Lisa Uchrin
Admin/Manager . . . . .NA
Clerk . . . . .Cecelia Bogart
Finance Dir/Treas . . . . Kay Winzenried
Engineer . . . . Paul Ferriero
Attorney . . . . Joseph Novak
Tax assessor . . . . .Curtis Schick
Tax collector . . . . Kay Winzenried
Building officer . . . . (Clinton Twp)
Zoning officer . . . . Joseph Hauck
Public Works .NA

Housing & Construction

Housing Units, 2000*
Total 477
Median rent $969
Median SF home value $168,100

New Privately Owned Housing Units
Authorized by Building Permit

	Units	Value
Total, 2004	89	$4,014,542
Single family	89	$4,014,542
Total, 2005	49	$1,977,185
Single family	49	$1,977,185

Real Property Valuation - parcels, 2005

	Number	Valuation
Total		$149,157,414
Vacant	34	7,729,514
Residential	457	73,224,100
Commercial	56	58,005,300
Industrial	6	9,741,900
Apartments	0	0
Farm land	1	436,900
Farm homestead	6	19,700

Average Property Value & Tax, 2005
Residential value $158,194
Property tax $4,736
FAIR rebate $590

Public Library

No public municipal library.

Library statistics, 2004

	Total	per capita
Volumes	NA	NA
Expenditure	NA	NA

Public Safety

Police
Chief . . . .(State)
Number of officers, 2004 0

Crime, 2004	Number	Rate
Total	14	12
Violent	1	0.9
Non-violent	13	11.2
Domestic Viol.	3	NA

Emergency/Fire
Director . . . . Kevin Saharic

Public School District
(for school year 2004-2005 except as noted)

Lebanon Borough School District
6 Maple St
Lebanon, NJ 08833
908-735-8320
Superintendent . . . . .Elizabeth Nastas
Grade plan K-8
Enrollment 88.0
Students per teacher 9.3
Per pupil expenditure $15,169
Median faculty salary $50,963
Median administrator salary $53,010
Grade 12 enrollment . . . . .NA
High school graduation rate . . . . .NA

Assessment test results
(percent scoring at proficient or advanced level)

	Language	Math
Grade 3	91.7%	83.3%
Grade 8	NA	NA
High school	NA	NA

SAT
Percent tested .NA
Average SAT math score . . . . .NA
Average SAT verbal score . . . . .NA

No Child Left Behind, 2003-04
Attendence rate (target = 90%) 96.2%
Drop rate . . . . .NA
Highly-qualified teachers 91.7%
District needs improvement?(AYP) . . . . . No

Municipal Finance

Fiscal Year 2005
Total tax levy $4,490,650
  County levy 952,042
  County taxes 808,307
  County library 67,648
  County health .0
  County open space 76,087
  School levy 3,013,582
  Local muni. budget 525,026
  Misc. revenues 885,881
Total aid $134,536
  CMPTRA 38,781
  Muni. block grant 4,534
  Energy tax receipts 91,221
  Homeland security 0

Fiscal Year 2006
Total aid $134,536
  CMPTRA 35,588
  Muni. block grant 4,534
  Energy tax receipts 94,414
  Homeland security . . . . .NA

Taxes

	2003	2004	2005
General tax rate per $100	3.02	2.910	3.000
Net valuation taxable	$136,668,284	$149,806,770	$150,007,459
State equalized value	$182,175,798	$214,634,805	$252,537,810
County equalization ratio	67.2	64.20	59.08

Demographics & Socio-Economic Characteristics

(2000 U.S. Census, except as noted)

Population

1980*	5,459
1990*	5,679
2000	5,816
Male	2,869
Female	2,947
2004 (estimate)*	6,283
Persons per sq. mi. of land	198

Race & Hispanic Origin, 2000

Race

White	5,640
Black/African American	47
Amer. Indian/Alaska Natv.	6
Asian	54
Natv. Hawaiian/Pac. Islander	1
Other Race	22
Two or more races	46
Hispanic origin, total	100
Mexican	18
Puerto Rican	27
Cuban	9
Other Hispanic	46

Age & Nativity, 2000

Under 5 years	352
18 years and over	4,332
21 years and over	4,180
65 years and over	680
85 years and over	100
Median Age	40.3
Native born	5,639
Foreign born	177

Educational Attainment, 2000

Population 25 years and over	4,028
0-8 yrs of school	1.4%
High School grad or higher	94.1%
Bachelor's degree or higher	37.0%
Graduate degree	12.7%

Income & Poverty, 1999

Per capita income	$30,793
Median household income	$77,662
Median family income	$86,145
Persons in poverty	112
H'holds receiving public assistance	22
H'holds receiving social security	400

Households, 2000

Total households	1,963
With persons under 18	791
With persons over 65	354
Family households	1,556
One-person households	305
Persons per household	2.79
Persons per family	3.15

Labor & Employment

Total civilian labor force, 2004**	3,642
Unemployment rate	3.8%
Total civilian labor force, 2000	3,213
Unemployment rate	4.5%

Employed persons 16 years and over by occupation, 2000

Managers & professionals	1,344
Service occupations	305
Sales & office occupations	788
Farming, fishing & forestry	12
Construction & maintenance	323
Production & transportation	296
Self-employed persons	222

*US Census Bureau
**New Jersey Department of Labor

General Information

Lebanon Township
530 W Hill Rd
Glen Gardner, NJ 08826
908-638-8523

Web site	www.lebanontownship.net
Land area (sq. miles)	31.69
Water area (sq. miles)	0.04
Type of government	Township
Form of government	TC

Government

Legislative Districts

US Congressional	7
State Legislative	23

Local Officials, 2006

Mayor	Patricia Schriver
Admin/Manager	NA
Clerk	Karen J. Sandorse
Finance Dir/Treas	Gregory DellaPia
Engineer	Steve Risse
Attorney	Eric Bernstein
Tax assessor	Mary Mastro
Tax collector	Mary Hyland
Building officer	William Skene
Zoning officer	NA
Public Works	Paul R. Jones

Housing & Construction

Housing Units, 2000*

Total	2,020
Median rent	$871
Median SF home value	$233,400

New Privately Owned Housing Units Authorized by Building Permit

	Units	Value
Total, 2004	29	$6,411,033
Single family	29	$6,411,033
Total, 2005	9	$2,134,464
Single family	9	$2,134,464

Real Property Valuation - parcels, 2005

	Number	Valuation
Total		$726,998,507
Vacant	332	17,875,534
Residential	2,009	595,140,100
Commercial	73	33,884,000
Industrial	5	3,410,900
Apartments	4	1,857,800
Farm land	214	72,055,900
Farm homestead	366	2,774,273

Average Property Value & Tax, 2005

Residential value	$251,753
Property tax	$6,364
FAIR rebate	$523

Public Library

Bunnvale Library†
23 Bunnvale Rd
Califon, NJ 07830
908-638-8884

Branch Librarian | Maria Taluba

Library statistics, 2004

	Total	per capita
Volumes	NA	NA
Expenditure	NA	NA

†Branch of County Library

Public Safety

Police

Chief	Pamela Schell
Number of officers, 2004	9

Crime, 2004	Number	Rate
Total	68	10.9
Violent	4	0.6
Non-violent	64	10.3
Domestic Viol.	27	NA

Emergency/Fire

Director | Warren Gadriel

Public School District

(for school year 2004-2005 except as noted)

Lebanon Township School District
70 Bunnvale Rd
Califon, NJ 07830
908-638-4521

Superintendent	Judy Burd
Grade plan	K-8
Enrollment	834.0
Students per teacher	9.4
Per pupil expenditure	$12,892
Median faculty salary	$45,490
Median administrator salary	$101,407
Grade 12 enrollment	NA
High school graduation rate	NA

Assessment test results

(percent scoring at proficient or advanced level)

	Language	Math
Grade 3	83.9%	89.2%
Grade 8	86.7%	80.0%
High school	NA	NA

SAT

Percent tested	NA
Average SAT math score	NA
Average SAT verbal score	NA

No Child Left Behind, 2003-04

Attendence rate (target = 90%)	95.9%
Drop rate	NA
Highly-qualified teachers	92.4%
District needs improvement?(AYP)	No

Municipal Finance

Fiscal Year 2005

Total tax levy	$18,417,444
County levy	3,628,564
County taxes	3,080,876
County library	257,785
County health	0
County open space	289,904
School levy	14,488,880
Local muni. budget	300,000
Misc. revenues	4,228,820
Total aid	$2,914,909
CMPTRA	151,931
Muni. block grant	24,849
Energy tax receipts	2,738,129
Homeland security	50,000

Fiscal Year 2006

Total aid	$2,914,909
CMPTRA	56,096
Muni. block grant	24,849
Energy tax receipts	2,833,964
Homeland security	NA

Taxes

	2003	2004	2005
General tax rate per $100	2.24	2.440	2.530
Net valuation taxable	$702,161,875	$718,012,699	$728,557,848
State equalized value	$779,486,984	$873,015,799	$967,540,303
County equalization ratio	87.96	85.49	75.68

Demographics & Socio-Economic Characteristics
(2000 U.S. Census, except as noted)

Population
1980*	8,027
1990*	8,365
2000	8,914
Male	4,289
Female	4,625
2004 (estimate)*	8,911
Persons per sq. mi. of land	5,919

Race & Hispanic Origin, 2000
Race
White	5,860
Black/African American	202
Amer. Indian/Alaska Natv.	8
Asian	2,323
Natv. Hawaiian/Pac. Islander	1
Other Race	285
Two or more races	235
Hispanic origin, total	1,135
Mexican	44
Puerto Rican	171
Cuban	204
Other Hispanic	716

Age & Nativity, 2000
Under 5 years	513
18 years and over	6,725
21 years and over	6,484
65 years and over	1,223
85 years and over	155
Median Age	39.9
Native born	5,719
Foreign born	3,195

Educational Attainment, 2000
Population 25 years and over	6,221
0-8 yrs of school	2.4%
High School grad or higher	92.7%
Bachelor's degree or higher	49.9%
Graduate degree	20.4%

Income & Poverty, 1999
Per capita income	$35,352
Median household income	$72,440
Median family income	$84,591
Persons in poverty	574
H'holds receiving public assistance	37
H'holds receiving social security	872

Households, 2000
Total households	3,271
With persons under 18	1,257
With persons over 65	915
Family households	2,437
One-person households	722
Persons per household	2.72
Persons per family	3.2

Labor & Employment
Total civilian labor force, 2004**	4,890
Unemployment rate	2.6%
Total civilian labor force, 2000	4,700
Unemployment rate	2.7%

Employed persons 16 years and over by occupation, 2000
Managers & professionals	2,335
Service occupations	499
Sales & office occupations	1,209
Farming, fishing & forestry	18
Construction & maintenance	212
Production & transportation	299
Self-employed persons	413

*US Census Bureau
**New Jersey Department of Labor

General Information
Borough of Leonia
312 Broad Ave
Leonia, NJ 07605
201-592-5741
Web site	www.leonianj.gov
Land area (sq. miles)	1.51
Water area (sq. miles)	0.12
Type of government	Borough
Form of government	B

Government

Legislative Districts
US Congressional	9
State Legislative	37

Local Officials, 2006
Mayor	Laurence Cherchi
Admin/Manager	Victoria Miragliotta
Clerk	Fran Lehmann
Finance Dir/Treas	Myrna Becker
Engineer	Job & Job
Attorney	David Russo
Tax assessor	Tim Henderson
Tax collector	NA
Building officer	Donald Porrino
Zoning officer	Jack Peters
Public Works	Tony Saitta

Housing & Construction

Housing Units, 2000*
Total	3,343
Median rent	$892
Median SF home value	$282,500

New Privately Owned Housing Units Authorized by Building Permit
	Units	Value
Total, 2004	1	$114,400
Single family	1	$114,400
Total, 2005	0	$0
Single family	0	$0

Real Property Valuation - parcels, 2005
	Number	Valuation
Total		$716,404,700
Vacant	47	4,029,500
Residential	2,445	623,749,800
Commercial	58	39,037,500
Industrial	5	14,381,900
Apartments	30	35,206,000
Farm land	0	0
Farm homestead	0	0

Average Property Value & Tax, 2005
Residential value	$255,112
Property tax	$8,827
FAIR rebate	$587

Public Library
Leonia Public Library
227 Fort Lee Rd
Leonia, NJ 07605
201-592-5770
Director ... Deborah Bigelow

Library statistics, 2004
	Total	per capita
Volumes	39,962	4.48
Expenditure	$709,945	$79.64

Public Safety
Police
Chief	Jay Ziegler
Number of officers, 2004	19

Crime, 2004	Number	Rate
Total	105	11.8
Violent	13	1.5
Non-violent	92	10.4
Domestic Viol.	9	NA

Emergency/Fire
Director ... John Dunn (Chief)

Public School District
(for school year 2004-2005 except as noted)
Leonia School District
570 Grand Ave
Leonia, NJ 07605
201-947-5655
Superintendent	Bernard Josefsberg
Grade plan	K-12
Enrollment	1,777.0
Students per teacher	8.9
Per pupil expenditure	$11,698
Median faculty salary	$43,025
Median administrator salary	$95,550
Grade 12 enrollment	131.0
High school graduation rate	98.1%

Assessment test results
(percent scoring at proficient or advanced level)
	Language	Math
Grade 3	83.6%	84.1%
Grade 8	77.8%	71.9%
High school	84.4%	85.6%

SAT
Percent tested	105%
Average SAT math score	550
Average SAT verbal score	518

No Child Left Behind, 2003-04
Attendence rate (target = 90%)	95.9%
Drop rate	0.6%
Highly-qualified teachers	98.6%
District needs improvement?(AYP)	No

Municipal Finance

Fiscal Year 2005
Total tax levy	$24,807,190
County levy	2,319,020
County taxes	2,203,021
County library	0
County health	0
County open space	115,999
School levy	14,835,321
Local muni. budget	7,652,849
Misc. revenues	3,373,446
Total aid	$1,440,559
CMPTRA	315,257
Muni. block grant	36,603
Energy tax receipts	1,038,699
Homeland security	50,000

Fiscal Year 2006
Total aid	$1,440,560
CMPTRA	278,903
Muni. block grant	36,603
Energy tax receipts	1,075,054
Homeland security	50,000

Taxes
	2003	2004	2005
General tax rate per $100	2.99	3.240	3.460
Net valuation taxable	$718,014,193	$716,016,698	$717,001,996
State equalized value	$1,005,481,295	$1,156,670,592	$1,325,327,165
County equalization ratio	79.37	71.41	61.88

Demographics & Socio-Economic Characteristics
(2000 U.S. Census, except as noted)

Population
1980*	1,730
1990*	2,493
2000	2,765
Male	1,373
Female	1,392
2004 (estimate)*	2,931
Persons per sq. mi. of land	248

Race & Hispanic Origin, 2000
Race
White	2,693
Black/African American	10
Amer. Indian/Alaska Natv.	3
Asian	16
Natv. Hawaiian/Pac. Islander	0
Other Race	15
Two or more races	28
Hispanic origin, total	74
Mexican	14
Puerto Rican	15
Cuban	13
Other Hispanic	32

Age & Nativity, 2000
Under 5 years	195
18 years and over	1,981
21 years and over	1,915
65 years and over	234
85 years and over	30
Median Age	37.6
Native born	2,556
Foreign born	170

Educational Attainment, 2000
Population 25 years and over	1,806
0-8 yrs of school	3.4%
High School grad or higher	88.3%
Bachelor's degree or higher	25.7%
Graduate degree	8.7%

Income & Poverty, 1999
Per capita income	$24,743
Median household income	$62,535
Median family income	$68,529
Persons in poverty	95
H'holds receiving public assistance	11
H'holds receiving social security	220

Households, 2000
Total households	980
With persons under 18	413
With persons over 65	171
Family households	751
One-person households	172
Persons per household	2.79
Persons per family	3.23

Labor & Employment
Total civilian labor force, 2004**	1,653
Unemployment rate	3.6%
Total civilian labor force, 2000	1,424
Unemployment rate	4.4%

Employed persons 16 years and over by occupation, 2000
Managers & professionals	472
Service occupations	154
Sales & office occupations	300
Farming, fishing & forestry	20
Construction & maintenance	201
Production & transportation	215
Self-employed persons	78

*US Census Bureau
**New Jersey Department of Labor

General Information
Township of Liberty
349 Mountain Lake Rd
Great Meadows, NJ 07838
908-637-4579
Web site	www.llibertytownship.org
Land area (sq. miles)	11.80
Water area (sq. miles)	0.21
Type of government	Township
Form of government	TC

Government

Legislative Districts
US Congressional	5
State Legislative	23

Local Officials, 2006
Mayor	John Inscho
Admin/Manager	Willa Reilly
Clerk	Willa Reilly
Finance Dir/Treas	Kevin Lifer
Engineer	Median Consulting Eng.
Attorney	Michael Lavery
Tax assessor	Lydia Zdrodowski
Tax collector	Doris Maney
Building officer	Ralph Price
Zoning officer	Eric Snyder
Public Works	Steve Romanowitch

Housing & Construction

Housing Units, 2000*
Total	1,088
Median rent	$686
Median SF home value	$169,600

New Privately Owned Housing Units Authorized by Building Permit
	Units	Value
Total, 2004	22	$3,121,400
Single family	22	$3,121,400
Total, 2005	10	$1,652,028
Single family	10	$1,652,028

Real Property Valuation - parcels, 2005
	Number	Valuation
Total		$259,124,890
Vacant	236	7,579,500
Residential	1,000	220,888,500
Commercial	30	7,898,700
Industrial	0	0
Apartments	1	308,800
Farm land	86	21,503,700
Farm homestead	185	945,690

Average Property Value & Tax, 2005
Residential value	$187,202
Property tax	$4,736
FAIR rebate	$480

Public Library

No public municipal library.

Library statistics, 2004
	Total	per capita
Volumes	NA	NA
Expenditure	NA	NA

Public Safety

Police
Chief	(State)
Number of officers, 2004	0

Crime, 2004	Number	Rate
Total	16	5.5
Violent	1	0.3
Non-violent	15	5.1
Domestic Viol.	19	NA

Emergency/Fire
Director	Ken Lunden

Public School District
(for school year 2004-2005 except as noted)

Great Meadows Regional School District
PO BOX 74
Great Meadows, NJ 07838
908-637-6576
Superintendent	Jason Bing
Grade plan	K-12
Enrollment	1,009.0
Students per teacher	11.3
Per pupil expenditure	$10,889
Median faculty salary	$48,259
Median administrator salary	$71,106
Grade 12 enrollment	NA
High school graduation rate	NA

Assessment test results
(percent scoring at proficient or advanced level)
	Language	Math
Grade 3	92.8%	85.6%
Grade 8	85.3%	78.2%
High school	NA	NA

SAT
Percent tested	NA
Average SAT math score	NA
Average SAT verbal score	NA

No Child Left Behind, 2003-04
Attendence rate (target = 90%)	96.0%
Drop rate	NA
Highly-qualified teachers	98.8%
District needs improvement?(AYP)	No

Municipal Finance

Fiscal Year 2005
Total tax levy	$6,574,928
County levy	1,775,885
County taxes	1,468,202
County library	141,631
County health	0
County open space	166,051
School levy	3,988,929
Local muni. budget	810,114
Misc. revenues	1,332,434
Total aid	$279,604
CMPTRA	118,626
Muni. block grant	10,908
Energy tax receipts	150,070
Homeland security	0

Fiscal Year 2006
Total aid	$279,605
CMPTRA	113,374
Muni. block grant	10,908
Energy tax receipts	155,323
Homeland security	NA

Taxes
	2003	2004	2005
General tax rate per $100	2.25	2.440	2.530
Net valuation taxable	$252,162,536	$255,104,363	$259,912,044
State equalized value	$238,429,024	$271,218,654	$310,639,469
County equalization ratio	120.48	105.76	94.04

Demographics & Socio-Economic Characteristics
(2000 U.S. Census, except as noted)

Population
1980*	8,806
1990*	10,978
2000	10,930
Male	5,239
Female	5,691
2004 (estimate)*	10,894
Persons per sq. mi. of land	1,619

Race & Hispanic Origin, 2000
Race
White	9,845
Black/African American	191
Amer. Indian/Alaska Natv.	13
Asian	578
Natv. Hawaiian/Pac. Islander	1
Other Race	142
Two or more races	160
Hispanic origin, total	633
Mexican	41
Puerto Rican	214
Cuban	75
Other Hispanic	303

Age & Nativity, 2000
Under 5 years	632
18 years and over	8,716
21 years and over	8,466
65 years and over	1,622
85 years and over	266
Median Age	39.6
Native born	9,449
Foreign born	1,481

Educational Attainment, 2000
Population 25 years and over	8,139
0-8 yrs of school	4.5%
High School grad or higher	86.3%
Bachelor's degree or higher	32.9%
Graduate degree	11.0%

Income & Poverty, 1999
Per capita income	$30,389
Median household income	$69,050
Median family income	$77,307
Persons in poverty	286
H'holds receiving public assistance	37
H'holds receiving social security	890

Households, 2000
Total households	4,026
With persons under 18	1,251
With persons over 65	853
Family households	2,707
One-person households	1,072
Persons per household	2.54
Persons per family	3.14

Labor & Employment
Total civilian labor force, 2004**	7,028
Unemployment rate	3.8%
Total civilian labor force, 2000	6,021
Unemployment rate	3.2%

Employed persons 16 years and over by occupation, 2000
Managers & professionals	2,484
Service occupations	482
Sales & office occupations	1,731
Farming, fishing & forestry	11
Construction & maintenance	492
Production & transportation	629
Self-employed persons	340

*US Census Bureau
**New Jersey Department of Labor

General Information
Borough of Lincoln Park
34 Chapel Hill Rd
Lincoln Park, NJ 07035
973-694-6100

Web site	www.linconpark.org
Land area (sq. miles)	6.73
Water area (sq. miles)	0.24
Type of government	Borough
Form of government	Faulkner Plan F

Government

Legislative Districts
US Congressional	11
State Legislative	26

Local Officials, 2006
Mayor	David Baker Jr.
Admin/Manager	Joseph Maiella
Clerk	Annette Maida-Smith
Finance Dir/Treas	Dennis Gerber
Engineer	Joseph Maiella
Attorney	David Dixon
Tax assessor	Tom Lenhardt
Tax collector	Kristen Runfeldt
Building officer	Gary McNabb
Zoning officer	Gary McNabb
Public Works	Tom Piorkowski

Housing & Construction

Housing Units, 2000*
Total	4,110
Median rent	$947
Median SF home value	$194,300

New Privately Owned Housing Units Authorized by Building Permit
	Units	Value
Total, 2004	8	$1,367,630
Single family	6	$1,192,630
Total, 2005	0	$56,000
Single family	0	$56,000

Real Property Valuation - parcels, 2005
	Number	Valuation
Total		$744,487,100
Vacant	135	4,452,100
Residential	3,585	609,327,400
Commercial	77	60,482,400
Industrial	27	44,084,200
Apartments	3	22,954,100
Farm land	14	2,853,400
Farm homestead	20	333,500

Average Property Value & Tax, 2005
Residential value	$169,115
Property tax	$5,917
FAIR rebate	$526

Public Library
Lincoln Park Public Library
12 Boonton Tpke
Lincoln Park, NJ 07035
973-694-8283
Director | Francis Kaiser Jr.

Library statistics, 2004
	Total	per capita
Volumes	66,659	6.1
Expenditure	$346,189	$31.67

Public Safety
Police
Chief	Sean Cannig
Number of officers, 2004	26

Crime, 2004	Number	Rate
Total	99	9.1
Violent	4	0.4
Non-violent	95	8.7
Domestic Viol.	48	NA

Emergency/Fire
Director | George Gilliland

Public School District
(for school year 2004-2005 except as noted)

Lincoln Park Borough School District
92 Ryerson Rd
Lincoln Park, NJ 07035
973-696-5500

Superintendent	Joyce Valenza
Grade plan	K-12
Enrollment	950.0
Students per teacher	10.6
Per pupil expenditure	$12,304
Median faculty salary	$52,727
Median administrator salary	$109,310
Grade 12 enrollment	NA
High school graduation rate	NA

Assessment test results
(percent scoring at proficient or advanced level)
	Language	Math
Grade 3	87.4%	96.4%
Grade 8	87.1%	77.5%
High school	NA	NA

SAT
Percent tested	NA
Average SAT math score	NA
Average SAT verbal score	NA

No Child Left Behind, 2003-04
Attendence rate (target = 90%)	96.1%
Drop rate	NA
Highly-qualified teachers	99.2%
District needs improvement?(AYP)	No

Municipal Finance

Fiscal Year 2005
Total tax levy	$26,078,939
County levy	3,347,320
County taxes	2,741,859
County library	0
County health	0
County open space	605,461
School levy	14,423,857
Local muni. budget	8,307,762
Misc. revenues	5,448,677
Total aid	$1,262,739
CMPTRA	539,658
Muni. block grant	48,037
Energy tax receipts	605,044
Homeland security	70,000

Fiscal Year 2006
Total aid	$1,262,740
CMPTRA	518,482
Muni. block grant	48,037
Energy tax receipts	626,221
Homeland security	70,000

Taxes
	2003	2004	2005
General tax rate per $100	3.24	3.360	3.500
Net valuation taxable	$738,154,113	$742,808,590	$745,330,899
State equalized value	$1,105,683,213	$1,251,935,871	$1,425,924,812
County equalization ratio	75.05	66.76	59.30

Demographics & Socio-Economic Characteristics
(2000 U.S. Census, except as noted)

Population
1980*	37,836
1990*	36,701
2000	39,394
Male	18,703
Female	20,691
2004 (estimate)*	40,004
Persons per sq. mi. of land	3,702

Race & Hispanic Origin, 2000
Race
White	26,031
Black/African American	8,981
Amer. Indian/Alaska Natv.	56
Asian	925
Natv. Hawaiian/Pac. Islander	15
Other Race	1,923
Two or more races	1,463
Hispanic origin, total	5,674
Mexican	153
Puerto Rican	1,512
Cuban	593
Other Hispanic	3,416

Age & Nativity, 2000
Under 5 years	2,345
18 years and over	30,548
21 years and over	29,186
65 years and over	6,426
85 years and over	881
Median Age	38
Native born	29,043
Foreign born	10,351

Educational Attainment, 2000
Population 25 years and over	27,238
0-8 yrs of school	8.7%
High School grad or higher	78.2%
Bachelor's degree or higher	14.1%
Graduate degree	4.5%

Income & Poverty, 1999
Per capita income	$21,314
Median household income	$46,345
Median family income	$54,903
Persons in poverty	2,490
H'holds receiving public assistance	389
H'holds receiving social security	4,896

Households, 2000
Total households	15,052
With persons under 18	4,980
With persons over 65	4,786
Family households	10,087
One-person households	4,207
Persons per household	2.6
Persons per family	3.21

Labor & Employment
Total civilian labor force, 2004**	18,935
Unemployment rate	5.6%
Total civilian labor force, 2000	19,892
Unemployment rate	5.6%

Employed persons 16 years and over by occupation, 2000
Managers & professionals	4,311
Service occupations	2,805
Sales & office occupations	6,071
Farming, fishing & forestry	11
Construction & maintenance	1,723
Production & transportation	3,851
Self-employed persons	654

*US Census Bureau
**New Jersey Department of Labor

General Information
City of Linden
301 N Wood Ave
Linden, NJ 07036
908-474-8452

Web site	NA
Land area (sq. miles)	10.81
Water area (sq. miles)	0.41
Type of government	City
Form of government	C

Government

Legislative Districts
US Congressional	7, 10
State Legislative	22

Local Officials, 2006
Mayor	John Gregorio
Admin/Manager	NA
Clerk	Val D. Imbriaco
Finance Dir/Treas	Alexis Zack
Engineer	John A. Ziemian
Attorney	Edward J. Kologi
Tax assessor	Michael Frangella
Tax collector	Kimberly Allorto
Building officer	Thomas Caverly
Zoning officer	Matthew O'Halloran
Public Works	John Mesler III

Housing & Construction

Housing Units, 2000*
Total	15,567
Median rent	$795
Median SF home value	$148,800

New Privately Owned Housing Units Authorized by Building Permit
	Units	Value
Total, 2004	131	$18,811,718
Single family	43	$3,195,953
Total, 2005	57	$7,730,035
Single family	36	$3,639,116

Real Property Valuation - parcels, 2005
	Number	Valuation
Total		$2,930,808,400
Vacant	491	34,410,200
Residential	9,966	1,389,489,100
Commercial	928	463,569,700
Industrial	230	976,458,400
Apartments	90	66,881,000
Farm land	0	0
Farm homestead	0	0

Average Property Value & Tax, 2005
Residential value	$139,423
Property tax	$5,258
FAIR rebate	$661

Public Library
Linden Free Public Library
31 East Henry St
Linden, NJ 07036
908-298-3830

Director ... Dennis Purves

Library statistics, 2004
	Total	per capita
Volumes	78,448	1.99
Expenditure	$1,537,633	$39.03

Public Safety
Police
Chief	John Miliano
Number of officers, 2004	128

Crime, 2004	Number	Rate
Total	1,665	41.8
Violent	149	3.7
Non-violent	1,516	38
Domestic Viol.	338	NA

Emergency/Fire
Director ... Arthur J. Murray

Public School District
(for school year 2004-2005 except as noted)

Linden School District
2 E Gibbons St
Linden, NJ 07036
908-486-5818

Superintendent	Joseph Martino
Grade plan	K-12
Enrollment	6,163.0
Students per teacher	10.9
Per pupil expenditure	$12,168
Median faculty salary	$48,021
Median administrator salary	$107,302
Grade 12 enrollment	417.0
High school graduation rate	88.4%

Assessment test results
(percent scoring at proficient or advanced level)
	Language	Math
Grade 3	72.6%	72.8%
Grade 8	59.2%	48.3%
High school	74.8%	56.6%

SAT
Percent tested	64%
Average SAT math score	431
Average SAT verbal score	421

No Child Left Behind, 2003-04
Attendence rate (target = 90%)	94.1%
Drop rate	3%
Highly-qualified teachers	83.4%
District needs improvement?(AYP)	No

Municipal Finance

Fiscal Year 2005
Total tax levy	$110,757,224
County levy	18,628,951
County taxes	17,893,609
County library	0
County health	0
County open space	735,342
School levy	59,327,804
Local muni. budget	32,800,469
Misc. revenues	41,824,496
Total aid	$23,730,177
CMPTRA	2,698,906
Muni. block grant	160,592
Energy tax receipts	20,730,679
Homeland security	140,000

Fiscal Year 2006
Total aid	$23,730,178
CMPTRA	1,973,333
Muni. block grant	160,592
Energy tax receipts	21,456,253
Homeland security	140,000

Taxes
	2003	2004	2005
General tax rate per $100	3.36	3.618	3.771
Net valuation taxable	$2,891,306,965	$2,927,122,959	$2,937,112,324
State equalized value	$3,884,598,905	$4,282,452,932	$4,892,740,836
County equalization ratio	79.91	68.70	61.24

Demographics & Socio-Economic Characteristics
(2000 U.S. Census, except as noted)

Population
1980*	18,196
1990*	18,734
2000	17,414
Male	8,312
Female	9,102
2004 (estimate)*	17,297
Persons per sq. mi. of land	4,386

Race & Hispanic Origin, 2000
Race
White	10,695
Black/African American	4,915
Amer. Indian/Alaska Natv.	83
Asian	614
Natv. Hawaiian/Pac. Islander	10
Other Race	564
Two or more races	533
Hispanic origin, total	1,316
Mexican	203
Puerto Rican	587
Cuban	30
Other Hispanic	496

Age & Nativity, 2000
Under 5 years	1,258
18 years and over	13,299
21 years and over	12,619
65 years and over	1,539
85 years and over	132
Median Age	33.3
Native born	16,160
Foreign born	1,254

Educational Attainment, 2000
Population 25 years and over	11,593
0-8 yrs of school	7.0%
High School grad or higher	77.6%
Bachelor's degree or higher	13.3%
Graduate degree	3.7%

Income & Poverty, 1999
Per capita income	$18,659
Median household income	$36,080
Median family income	$40,931
Persons in poverty	2,047
H'holds receiving public assistance	267
H'holds receiving social security	1,565

Households, 2000
Total households	7,465
With persons under 18	2,422
With persons over 65	1,230
Family households	4,301
One-person households	2,558
Persons per household	2.32
Persons per family	3

Labor & Employment
Total civilian labor force, 2004**	11,818
Unemployment rate	5.8%
Total civilian labor force, 2000	9,721
Unemployment rate	8.0%

Employed persons 16 years and over by occupation, 2000
Managers & professionals	2,106
Service occupations	1,783
Sales & office occupations	2,897
Farming, fishing & forestry	10
Construction & maintenance	922
Production & transportation	1,228
Self-employed persons	235

*US Census Bureau
**New Jersey Department of Labor

General Information
Borough of Lindenwold
2001 Egg Harbor Rd
Lindenwold, NJ 08021
856-783-2121

Web site	www.lindenwold.net
Land area (sq. miles)	3.94
Water area (sq. miles)	0.03
Type of government	Borough
Form of government	B

Government

Legislative Districts
US Congressional	1
State Legislative	4

Local Officials, 2006
Mayor	Frank Delucca Jr.
Admin/Manager	Frank Delucca Jr.
Clerk	Jane Barber
Finance Dir/Treas	Dawn Thompson
Engineer	Remington & Vernick
Attorney	John Kearney
Tax assessor	Thomas Glock
Tax collector	Margie Schieber
Building officer	Albert Hallworth
Zoning officer	NA
Public Works	Robert Lodovici

Housing & Construction

Housing Units, 2000*
Total	8,244
Median rent	$615
Median SF home value	$84,000

New Privately Owned Housing Units Authorized by Building Permit
	Units	Value
Total, 2004	7	$544,819
Single family	7	$544,819
Total, 2005	10	$932,293
Single family	10	$932,293

Real Property Valuation - parcels, 2005
	Number	Valuation
Total		$427,519,000
Vacant	338	5,285,800
Residential	4,028	281,456,100
Commercial	143	36,282,300
Industrial	3	1,424,900
Apartments	25	103,069,900
Farm land	0	0
Farm homestead	0	0

Average Property Value & Tax, 2005
Residential value	$69,875
Property tax	$3,542
FAIR rebate	$559

Public Library
Lindenwold Public Library†
310 E Linden Ave
Lindenwold, NJ 08021
856-784-5602

Branch Librarian . . B. Roach/M. Cavanaugh

Library statistics, 2004
	Total	per capita
Volumes	NA	NA
Expenditure	NA	NA

†Branch of County Library

Public Safety

Police
Chief	Francis McHenry
Number of officers, 2004	42

Crime, 2004	Number	Rate
Total	669	38.5
Violent	114	6.6
Non-violent	555	31.9
Domestic Viol.	378	NA

Emergency/Fire
Director . . . . . Delucca/McManus/Majchrz

Public School District
(for school year 2004-2005 except as noted)

Lindenwold Borough School District
1017 E Linden Ave
Lindenwold, NJ 08021
856-784-4071

Superintendent	Geraldine Carroll
Grade plan	K-12
Enrollment	2,491.0
Students per teacher	10.1
Per pupil expenditure	$11,986
Median faculty salary	$44,881
Median administrator salary	$84,210
Grade 12 enrollment	141.0
High school graduation rate	79.9%

Assessment test results
(percent scoring at proficient or advanced level)
	Language	Math
Grade 3	84.0%	85.2%
Grade 8	50.9%	46.2%
High school	67.7%	56.7%

SAT
Percent tested	50%
Average SAT math score	467
Average SAT verbal score	441

No Child Left Behind, 2003-04
Attendence rate (target = 90%)	93.0%
Drop rate	6.9%
Highly-qualified teachers	98.6%
District needs improvement?(AYP)	No

Municipal Finance

Fiscal Year 2005
Total tax levy	$21,733,604
County levy	4,355,102
County taxes	4,013,749
County library	288,707
County health	0
County open space	52,646
School levy	11,746,688
Local muni. budget	5,631,814
Misc. revenues	5,898,365
Total aid	$2,660,543
CMPTRA	1,793,287
Muni. block grant	81,973
Energy tax receipts	715,283
Homeland security	70,000

Fiscal Year 2006
Total aid	$2,660,543
CMPTRA	1,768,252
Muni. block grant	81,973
Energy tax receipts	740,318
Homeland security	70,000

Taxes
	2003	2004	2005
General tax rate per $100	4.53	4.769	5.070
Net valuation taxable	$429,361,012	$429,614,532	$428,699,889
State equalized value	$473,960,715	$525,976,783	$632,860,775
County equalization ratio	97.68	90.59	81.63

Demographics & Socio-Economic Characteristics
(2000 U.S. Census, except as noted)

Population
1980*	6,144
1990*	6,866
2000	7,172
Male	3,343
Female	3,829
2004 (estimate)*	7,415
Persons per sq. mi. of land	1,937

Race & Hispanic Origin, 2000
Race
White	6,828
Black/African American	76
Amer. Indian/Alaska Natv.	8
Asian	173
Natv. Hawaiian/Pac. Islander	0
Other Race	16
Two or more races	71
Hispanic origin, total	130
Mexican	13
Puerto Rican	64
Cuban	2
Other Hispanic	51

Age & Nativity, 2000
Under 5 years	375
18 years and over	5,291
21 years and over	5,163
65 years and over	1,345
85 years and over	231
Median Age	42.8
Native born	6,877
Foreign born	318

Educational Attainment, 2000
Population 25 years and over	5,111
0-8 yrs of school	3.0%
High School grad or higher	90.5%
Bachelor's degree or higher	37.9%
Graduate degree	15.0%

Income & Poverty, 1999
Per capita income	$32,159
Median household income	$60,000
Median family income	$71,415
Persons in poverty	275
H'holds receiving public assistance	28
H'holds receiving social security	905

Households, 2000
Total households	2,647
With persons under 18	976
With persons over 65	878
Family households	1,966
One-person households	590
Persons per household	2.65
Persons per family	3.13

Labor & Employment
Total civilian labor force, 2004**	3,577
Unemployment rate	3.2%
Total civilian labor force, 2000	3,300
Unemployment rate	4.0%

Employed persons 16 years and over by occupation, 2000
Managers & professionals	1,420
Service occupations	536
Sales & office occupations	806
Farming, fishing & forestry	0
Construction & maintenance	274
Production & transportation	133
Self-employed persons	264

*US Census Bureau
**New Jersey Department of Labor

General Information
City of Linwood
400 Poplar Ave
Linwood, NJ 08221
609-926-7953

Web site	www.linwoodcity.org
Land area (sq. miles)	3.83
Water area (sq. miles)	0.31
Type of government	City
Form of government	C

Government

Legislative Districts
US Congressional	2
State Legislative	2

Local Officials, 2006
Mayor	Richard DePamphilis III
Admin/Manager	Kenneth Mosca
Clerk	Leigh Ann Napoli
Finance Dir/Treas	F. Bonnie Tiemann
Engineer	Concord Atlantic/Dixon
Attorney	Joseph Youngblood Jr.
Tax assessor	Arthur Amonette
Tax collector	Carl Wentzell
Building officer	James Galentino
Zoning officer	Lynn Roesch
Public Works	Hank Kolakowski

Housing & Construction

Housing Units, 2000*
Total	2,751
Median rent	$714
Median SF home value	$165,100

New Privately Owned Housing Units
Authorized by Building Permit
	Units	Value
Total, 2004	20	$4,146,096
Single family	20	$4,146,096
Total, 2005	26	$5,085,294
Single family	24	$4,793,294

Real Property Valuation - parcels, 2005
	Number	Valuation
Total		$750,646,000
Vacant	143	15,595,700
Residential	2,694	645,565,600
Commercial	146	88,700,700
Industrial	0	0
Apartments	0	0
Farm land	2	749,400
Farm homestead	2	34,600

Average Property Value & Tax, 2005
Residential value	$239,466
Property tax	$7,255
FAIR rebate	$627

Public Library
Linwood Public Library
301 Davis Ave
Linwood, NJ 08221
609-926-7991

Director	Maria Moss

Library statistics, 2004
	Total	per capita
Volumes	37,686	5.25
Expenditure	$254,836	$35.53

Public Safety

Police
Chief	Charles Desch
Number of officers, 2004	20

Crime, 2004	Number	Rate
Total	102	13.8
Violent	6	0.8
Non-violent	96	13
Domestic Viol.	119	NA

Emergency/Fire
Director	Demetrios Foster

Public School District
(for school year 2004-2005 except as noted)

Linwood City School District
Belhaven Ave School
Linwood, NJ 08221
609-926-6703

Superintendent	Thomas Baruffi
Grade plan	K-8
Enrollment	1,035.0
Students per teacher	12.2
Per pupil expenditure	$10,343
Median faculty salary	$52,115
Median administrator salary	$86,500
Grade 12 enrollment	NA
High school graduation rate	NA

Assessment test results
(percent scoring at proficient or advanced level)
	Language	Math
Grade 3	92.7%	96.3%
Grade 8	89.4%	79.3%
High school	NA	NA

SAT
Percent tested	NA
Average SAT math score	NA
Average SAT verbal score	NA

No Child Left Behind, 2003-04
Attendence rate (target = 90%)	95.0%
Drop rate	NA
Highly-qualified teachers	94.2%
District needs improvement?(AYP)	No

Municipal Finance

Fiscal Year 2005
Total tax levy	$22,768,540
County levy	3,225,925
County taxes	2,894,584
County library	0
County health	158,337
County open space	173,004
School levy	14,036,958
Local muni. budget	5,505,656
Misc. revenues	4,261,765
Total aid	$865,778
CMPTRA	296,403
Muni. block grant	30,044
Energy tax receipts	489,331
Homeland security	50,000

Fiscal Year 2006
Total aid	$865,777
CMPTRA	279,276
Muni. block grant	30,044
Energy tax receipts	506,457
Homeland security	50,000

Taxes
	2003	2004	2005
General tax rate per $100	2.77	2.961	3.030
Net valuation taxable	$745,500,217	$748,510,322	$751,545,247
State equalized value	$759,010,606	$860,102,514	$1,005,008,354
County equalization ratio	112.6	98.22	87.01

Demographics & Socio-Economic Characteristics
(2000 U.S. Census, except as noted)

Population
1980*	8,483
1990*	13,333
2000	15,945
Male	7,655
Female	8,290
2004 (estimate)*	19,334
Persons per sq. mi. of land	394

Race & Hispanic Origin, 2000
Race
White	15,342
Black/African American	126
Amer. Indian/Alaska Natv.	41
Asian	96
Natv. Hawaiian/Pac. Islander	1
Other Race	156
Two or more races	183
Hispanic origin, total	520
Mexican	79
Puerto Rican	253
Cuban	19
Other Hispanic	169

Age & Nativity, 2000
Under 5 years	931
18 years and over	12,091
21 years and over	11,618
65 years and over	2,821
85 years and over	271
Median Age	39.9
Native born	15,525
Foreign born	494

Educational Attainment, 2000
Population 25 years and over	10,971
0-8 yrs of school	3.5%
High School grad or higher	81.0%
Bachelor's degree or higher	15.1%
Graduate degree	4.5%

Income & Poverty, 1999
Per capita income	$20,619
Median household income	$45,628
Median family income	$51,580
Persons in poverty	1,028
H'holds receiving public assistance	107
H'holds receiving social security	2,299

Households, 2000
Total households	6,179
With persons under 18	2,065
With persons over 65	1,916
Family households	4,442
One-person households	1,389
Persons per household	2.55
Persons per family	2.98

Labor & Employment
Total civilian labor force, 2004**	7,734
Unemployment rate	6.6%
Total civilian labor force, 2000	7,505
Unemployment rate	5.2%

Employed persons 16 years and over by occupation, 2000
Managers & professionals	1,875
Service occupations	1,571
Sales & office occupations	1,985
Farming, fishing & forestry	26
Construction & maintenance	943
Production & transportation	711
Self-employed persons	432

*US Census Bureau
**New Jersey Department of Labor

General Information
Township of Little Egg Harbor
665 Radio Rd
Little Egg Harbor, NJ 08087
609-296-7241

Web site	www.leht.com
Land area (sq. miles)	49.11
Water area (sq. miles)	24.07
Type of government	Township
Form of government	TC

Government

Legislative Districts
US Congressional	3
State Legislative	9

Local Officials, 2006
Mayor	Barbara Jo Crea
Admin/Manager	Raymond Urezzio
Clerk	Diana K. Mc Cracken
Finance Dir/Treas	Raymond Urezzio
Engineer	Schoor DePalma
Attorney	G. Gilmore & Monahan
Tax assessor	Joseph Sorrentino
Tax collector	Dayna Cook
Building officer	Jay Haines
Zoning officer	Scotty Esposito
Public Works	Anthony Savino

Housing & Construction

Housing Units, 2000*
Total	7,931
Median rent	$817
Median SF home value	$98,800

New Privately Owned Housing Units Authorized by Building Permit
	Units	Value
Total, 2004	315	$32,666,589
Single family	315	$32,666,589
Total, 2005	266	$37,810,479
Single family	266	$37,810,479

Real Property Valuation - parcels, 2005
	Number	Valuation
Total		$1,138,966,400
Vacant	1,926	67,864,470
Residential	9,215	983,935,214
Commercial	173	82,559,600
Industrial	2	291,800
Apartments	2	2,318,500
Farm land	8	1,966,200
Farm homestead	13	30,616

Average Property Value & Tax, 2005
Residential value	$106,628
Property tax	$3,531
FAIR rebate	$889

Public Library
Little Egg Harbor Branch Library†
290 Mathistown Rd
Little Egg Harbor, NJ 08087
609-294-1197

Branch Librarian .... Kathy Erickson

Library statistics, 2004
	Total	per capita
Volumes	NA	NA
Expenditure	NA	NA

†Branch of County Library

Public Safety

Police
Chief	Mark Siino
Number of officers, 2004	39

Crime, 2004	Number	Rate
Total	394	21.2
Violent	32	1.7
Non-violent	362	19.4
Domestic Viol.	271	NA

Emergency/Fire
Director	NA

Public School District
(for school year 2004-2005 except as noted)

Little Egg Harbor Township School Dist.
307 Frog Pond Rd
Little Egg Harbor, NJ 08087
609-296-1719

Superintendent	Frank Kasyan
Grade plan	K-6
Enrollment	1,630.0
Students per teacher	10.4
Per pupil expenditure	$10,735
Median faculty salary	$47,740
Median administrator salary	$82,080
Grade 12 enrollment	NA
High school graduation rate	NA

Assessment test results
(percent scoring at proficient or advanced level)
	Language	Math
Grade 3	87.0%	79.6%
Grade 8	NA	NA
High school	NA	NA

SAT
Percent tested	NA
Average SAT math score	NA
Average SAT verbal score	NA

No Child Left Behind, 2003-04
Attendence rate (target = 90%)	93.4%
Drop rate	NA
Highly-qualified teachers	100%
District needs improvement?(AYP)	No

Municipal Finance

Fiscal Year 2005
Total tax levy	$37,838,244
County levy	7,192,367
County taxes	6,059,705
County library	636,624
County health	269,848
County open space	226,190
School levy	20,121,069
Local muni. budget	10,524,808
Misc. revenues	5,834,443
Total aid	$1,818,289
CMPTRA	558,730
Muni. block grant	62,521
Energy tax receipts	1,125,221
Homeland security	70,000

Fiscal Year 2006
Total aid	$1,818,289
CMPTRA	519,347
Muni. block grant	62,521
Energy tax receipts	1,164,604
Homeland security	70,000

Taxes
	2003	2004	2005
General tax rate per $100	3.25	3.276	3.312
Net valuation taxable	$978,000,103	$1,067,966,901	$1,142,744,520
State equalized value	$1,386,447,552	$1,759,914,165	$2,215,909,482
County equalization ratio	83.23	70.54	60.58

Demographics & Socio-Economic Characteristics

(2000 U.S. Census, except as noted)

Population

1980*	11,496
1990*	11,294
2000	10,855
Male	5,134
Female	5,721
2000 (revised)	11,793
2004 (estimate)*	11,946
Persons per sq. mi. of land	4,338

Race & Hispanic Origin, 2000

Race

White	10,001
Black/African American	71
Amer. Indian/Alaska Natv.	7
Asian	456
Natv. Hawaiian/Pac. Islander	2
Other Race	144
Two or more races	174
Hispanic origin, total	579
Mexican	56
Puerto Rican	166
Cuban	66
Other Hispanic	291

Age & Nativity, 2000

Under 5 years	556
18 years and over	8,888
21 years and over	8,604
65 years and over	1,938
85 years and over	213
Median Age	40.6
Native born	9,369
Foreign born	1,486

Educational Attainment, 2000

Population 25 years and over	8,178
0-8 yrs of school	6.0%
High School grad or higher	85.3%
Bachelor's degree or higher	34.7%
Graduate degree	12.3%

Income & Poverty, 1999

Per capita income	$33,242
Median household income	$58,857
Median family income	$70,223
Persons in poverty	493
H'holds receiving public assistance	61
H'holds receiving social security	1,491

Households, 2000

Total households	4,687
With persons under 18	1,139
With persons over 65	1,474
Family households	2,871
One-person households	1,552
Persons per household	2.32
Persons per family	2.99

Labor & Employment

Total civilian labor force, 2004**	6,717
Unemployment rate	3.3%
Total civilian labor force, 2000	5,821
Unemployment rate	4.4%

Employed persons 16 years and over by occupation, 2000

Managers & professionals	2,430
Service occupations	531
Sales & office occupations	1,804
Farming, fishing & forestry	0
Construction & maintenance	349
Production & transportation	452
Self-employed persons	291

*US Census Bureau
**New Jersey Department of Labor

General Information

Township of Little Falls
225 Main St
Little Falls, NJ 07424
973-256-0170

Web site	www.lfnj.com
Land area (sq. miles)	2.75
Water area (sq. miles)	0.07
Type of government	Township
Form of government	TC

Government

Legislative Districts

US Congressional	8
State Legislative	40

Local Officials, 2006

Mayor	Eugene Kulick
Admin/Manager	William Wilk
Clerk	William Wilk
Finance Dir/Treas	Kathy Albanese
Engineer	Robert Schilling
Attorney	Joseph Trapanese
Tax assessor	E. Romeo Longo
Tax collector	NA
Building officer	William Cullen
Zoning officer	NA
Public Works	NA

Housing & Construction

Housing Units, 2000*

Total	4,797
Median rent	$909
Median SF home value	$212,300

New Privately Owned Housing Units Authorized by Building Permit

	Units	Value
Total, 2004	12	$1,529,509
Single family	12	$1,529,509
Total, 2005	8	$981,257
Single family	8	$981,257

Real Property Valuation - parcels, 2005

	Number	Valuation
Total		$720,905,300
Vacant	191	17,259,300
Residential	3,670	537,946,300
Commercial	174	95,293,200
Industrial	43	29,779,200
Apartments	9	40,627,300
Farm land	0	0
Farm homestead	0	0

Average Property Value & Tax, 2005

Residential value	$146,579
Property tax	$6,031
FAIR rebate	$635

Public Library

Little Falls Public Library
8 Warren St
Little Falls, NJ 07424
973-256-2784

Director..........Patricia Pelak

Library statistics, 2004

	Total	per capita
Volumes	51,995	4.79
Expenditure	$422,027	$38.88

Public Safety

Police

Chief	Gerald Hunter
Number of officers, 2004	24

Crime, 2004	Number	Rate
Total	384	32.1
Violent	18	1.5
Non-violent	366	30.6
Domestic Viol.	138	NA

Emergency/Fire

Director..........Edmund Pomponio

Public School District

(for school year 2004-2005 except as noted)

Little Falls Township School District
560 Main St
Little Falls, NJ 07424
973-256-1034

Administrator	Bruce DeLyon
Grade plan	K-8
Enrollment	840.0
Students per teacher	10.9
Per pupil expenditure	$11,674
Median faculty salary	$57,044
Median administrator salary	$97,500
Grade 12 enrollment	NA
High school graduation rate	NA

Assessment test results

(percent scoring at proficient or advanced level)

	Language	Math
Grade 3	96.5%	91.6%
Grade 8	88.7%	67.3%
High school	NA	NA

SAT

Percent tested	NA
Average SAT math score	NA
Average SAT verbal score	NA

No Child Left Behind, 2003-04

Attendence rate (target = 90%)	96.0%
Drop rate	NA
Highly-qualified teachers	99.7%
District needs improvement?(AYP)	No

Municipal Finance

Fiscal Year 2005

Total tax levy	$29,801,564
County levy	8,194,168
County taxes	8,038,067
County library	0
County health	0
County open space	156,102
School levy	14,937,326
Local muni. budget	6,670,070
Misc. revenues	4,555,805
Total aid	$1,784,538
CMPTRA	652,770
Muni. block grant	49,419
Energy tax receipts	1,010,892
Homeland security	70,000

Fiscal Year 2006

Total aid	$1,784,538
CMPTRA	617,389
Muni. block grant	49,419
Energy tax receipts	1,046,273
Homeland security	70,000

Taxes

	2003	2004	2005
General tax rate per $100	3.67	3.890	4.120
Net valuation taxable	$722,929,792	$723,963,919	$724,283,752
State equalized value	$1,368,925,946	$1,549,302,516	$1,684,772,626
County equalization ratio	59.27	52.81	46.60

Demographics & Socio-Economic Characteristics
(2000 U.S. Census, except as noted)

Population
1980*	9,399
1990*	9,989
2000	10,800
Male	5,261
Female	5,539
2004 (estimate)*	10,840
Persons per sq. mi. of land	7,101

Race & Hispanic Origin, 2000
Race
White	7,426
Black/African American	509
Amer. Indian/Alaska Natv.	16
Asian	1,847
Natv. Hawaiian/Pac. Islander	6
Other Race	621
Two or more races	375
Hispanic origin, total	1,641
Mexican	43
Puerto Rican	344
Cuban	199
Other Hispanic	1,055

Age & Nativity, 2000
Under 5 years	687
18 years and over	8,616
21 years and over	8,314
65 years and over	1,342
85 years and over	133
Median Age	37.1
Native born	7,443
Foreign born	3,357

Educational Attainment, 2000
Population 25 years and over	7,762
0-8 yrs of school	5.7%
High School grad or higher	81.5%
Bachelor's degree or higher	24.1%
Graduate degree	8.0%

Income & Poverty, 1999
Per capita income	$24,210
Median household income	$49,958
Median family income	$59,176
Persons in poverty	677
H'holds receiving public assistance	65
H'holds receiving social security	1,017

Households, 2000
Total households	4,366
With persons under 18	1,300
With persons over 65	1,002
Family households	2,785
One-person households	1,364
Persons per household	2.47
Persons per family	3.16

Labor & Employment
Total civilian labor force, 2004**	6,460
Unemployment rate	5.6%
Total civilian labor force, 2000	6,021
Unemployment rate	4.6%

Employed persons 16 years and over by occupation, 2000
Managers & professionals	1,979
Service occupations	676
Sales & office occupations	1,920
Farming, fishing & forestry	0
Construction & maintenance	413
Production & transportation	758
Self-employed persons	246

*US Census Bureau
**New Jersey Department of Labor

General Information
Borough of Little Ferry
215-217 Liberty St
Little Ferry, NJ 07643
201-641-9234

Web site	NA
Land area (sq. miles)	1.53
Water area (sq. miles)	0.16
Type of government	Borough
Form of government	B

Government
Legislative Districts
US Congressional	9
State Legislative	38

Local Officials, 2006
Mayor	Thomas Quirico
Admin/Manager	(Vacant)
Clerk	Barbara Maldonado
Finance Dir/Treas	(Vacant)
Engineer	Kenneth Job
Attorney	Joseph Monaghan
Tax assessor	George Reggo
Tax collector	NA
Building officer	Wayne McCotter
Zoning officer	Wayne McCotter
Public Works	NA

Housing & Construction
Housing Units, 2000*
Total	4,449
Median rent	$822
Median SF home value	$192,800

New Privately Owned Housing Units Authorized by Building Permit
	Units	Value
Total, 2004	1	$100,500
Single family	1	$100,500
Total, 2005	1	$200,000
Single family	1	$200,000

Real Property Valuation - parcels, 2005
	Number	Valuation
Total		$1,228,253,700
Vacant	41	11,074,200
Residential	2,240	798,263,100
Commercial	167	154,722,200
Industrial	78	151,511,000
Apartments	25	112,683,200
Farm land	0	0
Farm homestead	0	0

Average Property Value & Tax, 2005
Residential value	$356,367
Property tax	$6,337
FAIR rebate	$623

Public Library
Little Ferry Public Library
239 Liberty St
Little Ferry, NJ 07643
201-641-3721
Director................... Ellen Yamrick

Library statistics, 2004
	Total	per capita
Volumes	28,811	2.67
Expenditure	$274,421	$25.41

Public Safety
Police
Chief	Ralph Verdi
Number of officers, 2004	27

Crime, 2004	Number	Rate
Total	117	10.8
Violent	10	0.9
Non-violent	107	9.9
Domestic Viol.	91	NA

Emergency/Fire
Director................... Steven Turato

Public School District
(for school year 2004-2005 except as noted)

Little Ferry School District
130 Liberty St
Little Ferry, NJ 07643
201-641-6192
Superintendent	Frank Scarafile
Grade plan	K-12
Enrollment	992.0
Students per teacher	13.4
Per pupil expenditure	$10,715
Median faculty salary	$59,945
Median administrator salary	$110,842
Grade 12 enrollment	NA
High school graduation rate	NA

Assessment test results
(percent scoring at proficient or advanced level)
	Language	Math
Grade 3	75.8%	72.2%
Grade 8	80.0%	75.9%
High school	NA	NA

SAT
Percent tested	NA
Average SAT math score	NA
Average SAT verbal score	NA

No Child Left Behind, 2003-04
Attendence rate (target = 90%)	96.1%
Drop rate	NA
Highly-qualified teachers	98.7%
District needs improvement?(AYP)	No

Municipal Finance
Fiscal Year 2005
Total tax levy	$21,973,962
County levy	1,987,106
County taxes	1,887,747
County library	0
County health	0
County open space	99,359
School levy	12,522,663
Local muni. budget	7,464,193
Misc. revenues	4,611,719
Total aid	$1,333,995
CMPTRA	571,538
Muni. block grant	43,709
Energy tax receipts	648,748
Homeland security	70,000

Fiscal Year 2006
Total aid	$1,333,996
CMPTRA	548,832
Muni. block grant	43,709
Energy tax receipts	671,455
Homeland security	70,000

Taxes
	2003	2004	2005
General tax rate per $100	3.47	3.690	1.780
Net valuation taxable	$576,861,395	$578,180,852	$1,235,795,240
State equalized value	$893,665,988	$981,757,127	$1,088,806,379
County equalization ratio	76.54	64.55	125.09

Demographics & Socio-Economic Characteristics
(2000 U.S. Census, except as noted)

Population
1980*	5,548
1990*	5,721
2000	6,170
Male	2,979
Female	3,191
2004 (estimate)*	6,191
Persons per sq. mi. of land	2,234

Race & Hispanic Origin, 2000
Race
White	5,994
Black/African American	19
Amer. Indian/Alaska Natv.	10
Asian	93
Natv. Hawaiian/Pac. Islander	1
Other Race	12
Two or more races	41
Hispanic origin, total	81
Mexican	16
Puerto Rican	14
Cuban	11
Other Hispanic	40

Age & Nativity, 2000
Under 5 years	452
18 years and over	4,479
21 years and over	4,344
65 years and over	967
85 years and over	97
Median Age	41.1
Native born	5,810
Foreign born	360

Educational Attainment, 2000
Population 25 years and over	4,199
0-8 yrs of school	0.5%
High School grad or higher	96.8%
Bachelor's degree or higher	60.5%
Graduate degree	22.0%

Income & Poverty, 1999
Per capita income	$46,798
Median household income	$94,094
Median family income	$104,033
Persons in poverty	48
H'holds receiving public assistance	21
H'holds receiving social security	659

Households, 2000
Total households	2,232
With persons under 18	869
With persons over 65	666
Family households	1,810
One-person households	375
Persons per household	2.76
Persons per family	3.13

Labor & Employment
Total civilian labor force, 2004**	3,198
Unemployment rate	2.7%
Total civilian labor force, 2000	2,934
Unemployment rate	2.7%

Employed persons 16 years and over by occupation, 2000
Managers & professionals	1,694
Service occupations	166
Sales & office occupations	810
Farming, fishing & forestry	5
Construction & maintenance	126
Production & transportation	53
Self-employed persons	288

*US Census Bureau
**New Jersey Department of Labor

General Information
Borough of Little Silver
480 Prospect Ave
Little Silver, NJ 07739
732-842-2400
Web site	www.littlesilver.org
Land area (sq. miles)	2.77
Water area (sq. miles)	0.60
Type of government	Borough
Form of government	B

Government

Legislative Districts
US Congressional	12
State Legislative	12

Local Officials, 2006
Mayor	Suzanne Castleman
Admin/Manager	Michael Biehl
Clerk	Michael Biehl
Finance Dir/Treas	Lynn Marie Gale
Engineer	Gregory Blash
Attorney	John O. Bennett III
Tax assessor	J. Stephen Walters
Tax collector	Lynn Marie Gale
Building officer	Stanley Sickels
Zoning officer	Dianne Ramsey
Public Works	John Clark

Housing & Construction

Housing Units, 2000*
Total	2,288
Median rent	$1,125
Median SF home value	$300,400

New Privately Owned Housing Units Authorized by Building Permit
	Units	Value
Total, 2004	9	$3,623,530
Single family	9	$3,623,530
Total, 2005	22	$5,171,101
Single family	22	$5,171,101

Real Property Valuation - parcels, 2005
	Number	Valuation
Total		$1,224,515,300
Vacant	88	11,932,100
Residential	2,282	1,127,214,700
Commercial	143	81,976,200
Industrial	0	0
Apartments	0	0
Farm land	2	3,376,500
Farm homestead	3	15,800

Average Property Value & Tax, 2005
Residential value	$493,318
Property tax	$9,924
FAIR rebate	$563

Public Library
Little Silver Public Library
484 Prospect Ave
Little Silver, NJ 07739
732-747-9649
Director................. Susan Edwards

Library statistics, 2004
	Total	per capita
Volumes	31,397	5.09
Expenditure	$217,447	$35.24

Public Safety

Police
Chief	Stephen Greenwood III (Actg)
Number of officers, 2004	15

Crime, 2004	Number	Rate
Total	97	15.8
Violent	2	0.3
Non-violent	95	15.5
Domestic Viol.	20	NA

Emergency/Fire
Director............. Pete Gibson (Chief)

Public School District
(for school year 2004-2005 except as noted)

Little Silver Borough School District
124 Willow Drive
Little Silver, NJ 07739
732-741-2188
Superintendent	Marjorie Heller
Grade plan	K-8
Enrollment	821.0
Students per teacher	10.3
Per pupil expenditure	$11,145
Median faculty salary	$41,800
Median administrator salary	$99,500
Grade 12 enrollment	NA
High school graduation rate	NA

Assessment test results
(percent scoring at proficient or advanced level)
	Language	Math
Grade 3	96.5%	93.0%
Grade 8	89.1%	88.1%
High school	NA	NA

SAT
Percent tested	NA
Average SAT math score	NA
Average SAT verbal score	NA

No Child Left Behind, 2003-04
Attendence rate (target = 90%)	96.0%
Drop rate	NA
Highly-qualified teachers	100%
District needs improvement?(AYP)	No

Municipal Finance

Fiscal Year 2005
Total tax levy	$24,655,386
County levy	4,358,336
County taxes	3,910,840
County library	215,425
County health	0
County open space	232,071
School levy	14,785,117
Local muni. budget	5,511,933
Misc. revenues	3,386,170
Total aid	$906,318
CMPTRA	254,694
Muni. block grant	25,034
Energy tax receipts	576,590
Homeland security	50,000

Fiscal Year 2006
Total aid	$906,319
CMPTRA	234,514
Muni. block grant	25,034
Energy tax receipts	596,771
Homeland security	50,000

Taxes
	2003	2004	2005
General tax rate per $100	1.85	1.976	2.012
Net valuation taxable	$1,218,719,540	$1,221,819,447	$1,225,631,503
State equalized value	$1,148,218,900	$1,299,314,885	$1,442,937,960
County equalization ratio	62.2	106.14	94.03

Demographics & Socio-Economic Characteristics
(2000 U.S. Census, except as noted)

Population
1980*	28,040
1990*	26,609
2000	27,391
Male	13,322
Female	14,069
2004 (estimate)*	27,861
Persons per sq. mi. of land	2,007

Race & Hispanic Origin, 2000
Race
White	22,637
Black/African American	328
Amer. Indian/Alaska Natv.	14
Asian	3,982
Natv. Hawaiian/Pac. Islander	3
Other Race	190
Two or more races	237
Hispanic origin, total	695
Mexican	39
Puerto Rican	128
Cuban	88
Other Hispanic	440

Age & Nativity, 2000
Under 5 years	1,917
18 years and over	20,107
21 years and over	19,495
65 years and over	4,221
85 years and over	420
Median Age	40.6
Native born	22,237
Foreign born	5,154

Educational Attainment, 2000
Population 25 years and over	18,769
0-8 yrs of school	2.2%
High School grad or higher	94.0%
Bachelor's degree or higher	57.7%
Graduate degree	26.7%

Income & Poverty, 1999
Per capita income	$47,218
Median household income	$98,869
Median family income	$108,049
Persons in poverty	480
H'holds receiving public assistance	56
H'holds receiving social security	2,779

Households, 2000
Total households	9,300
With persons under 18	4,003
With persons over 65	2,911
Family households	7,936
One-person households	1,207
Persons per household	2.93
Persons per family	3.21

Labor & Employment
Total civilian labor force, 2004**	30,162
Unemployment rate	6.7%
Total civilian labor force, 2000	13,724
Unemployment rate	2.1%

Employed persons 16 years and over by occupation, 2000
Managers & professionals	7,514
Service occupations	988
Sales & office occupations	3,984
Farming, fishing & forestry	0
Construction & maintenance	524
Production & transportation	420
Self-employed persons	927

*US Census Bureau
**New Jersey Department of Labor

General Information
Township of Livingston
357 S Livingston Ave
Livingston, NJ 07039
973-992-5000
Web site	www.livingstonnj.org
Land area (sq. miles)	13.88
Water area (sq. miles)	0.19
Type of government	Township
Form of government	CM '50

Government

Legislative Districts
US Congressional	11
State Legislative	27

Local Officials, 2006
Mayor	Renee Green
Admin/Manager	Michele Mead
Clerk	Glenn Turtletaub
Finance Dir/Treas	Russell Jones Jr.
Engineer	Robert Schaefer
Attorney	Sharon Weiner
Tax assessor	Lidia Dumytsch
Tax collector	Vibha Desai
Building officer	Marty Chiarolanzio
Zoning officer	Edwin Allmann
Public Works	NA

Housing & Construction

Housing Units, 2000*
Total	9,457
Median rent	$1,244
Median SF home value	$290,200

New Privately Owned Housing Units Authorized by Building Permit
	Units	Value
Total, 2004	103	$20,607,476
Single family	55	$19,207,476
Total, 2005	410	$84,165,888
Single family	84	$68,579,387

Real Property Valuation - parcels, 2005
	Number	Valuation
Total		$950,404,800
Vacant	410	18,081,000
Residential	9,612	744,319,000
Commercial	290	171,727,800
Industrial	44	16,140,200
Apartments	0	0
Farm land	2	124,300
Farm homestead	4	12,500

Average Property Value & Tax, 2005
Residential value	$77,406
Property tax	$9,772
FAIR rebate	$590

Public Library
R.L. Rockwood Memorial Library
10 Robert H Harp Dr
Livingston, NJ 07039
973-992-4600
Director......Barbara Jean Sikora

Library statistics, 2004
	Total	per capita
Volumes	219,524	8.01
Expenditure	$2,544,493	$92.90

Public Safety
Police
Chief	Michael Erb
Number of officers, 2004	73

Crime, 2004	Number	Rate
Total	541	19.3
Violent	33	1.2
Non-violent	508	18.2
Domestic Viol.	84	NA

Emergency/Fire
Director......Christopher Mullin

Public School District
(for school year 2004-2005 except as noted)

Livingston Township School District
11 Foxcroft Drive
Livingston, NJ 07039
973-535-8000
Superintendent	Brad Draeger
Grade plan	K-12
Enrollment	5,233.0
Students per teacher	10.4
Per pupil expenditure	$13,800
Median faculty salary	$63,850
Median administrator salary	$103,128
Grade 12 enrollment	360.5
High school graduation rate	99.4%

Assessment test results
(percent scoring at proficient or advanced level)
	Language	Math
Grade 3	94.0%	95.9%
Grade 8	95.9%	87.2%
High school	96.5%	93.7%

SAT
Percent tested	99%
Average SAT math score	611
Average SAT verbal score	574

No Child Left Behind, 2003-04
Attendence rate (target = 90%)	96.4%
Drop rate	0.5%
Highly-qualified teachers	94.5%
District needs improvement?(AYP)	No

Municipal Finance

Fiscal Year 2005
Total tax levy	$120,197,982
County levy	28,107,537
County taxes	27,518,882
County library	0
County health	0
County open space	588,655
School levy	73,587,647
Local muni. budget	18,502,798
Misc. revenues	18,520,299
Total aid	$4,260,090
CMPTRA	1,406,668
Muni. block grant	116,432
Energy tax receipts	2,636,180
Homeland security	90,000

Fiscal Year 2006
Total aid	$4,260,090
CMPTRA	1,314,402
Muni. block grant	116,432
Energy tax receipts	2,728,446
Homeland security	90,000

Taxes
	2003	2004	2005
General tax rate per $100	11.98	12.280	12.630
Net valuation taxable	$935,913,400	$945,477,400	$952,120,200
State equalized value	$5,272,751,549	$5,826,333,911	$6,477,008,163
County equalization ratio	19.71	19.71	16.20

Demographics & Socio-Economic Characteristics
(2000 U.S. Census, except as noted)

Population
1980*	369
1990*	380
2000	280
Male	144
Female	136
2004 (estimate)*	279
Persons per sq. mi. of land	2,884

Race & Hispanic Origin, 2000
Race
White	266
Black/African American	6
Amer. Indian/Alaska Natv.	0
Asian	2
Natv. Hawaiian/Pac. Islander	0
Other Race	1
Two or more races	5
Hispanic origin, total	2
Mexican	0
Puerto Rican	1
Cuban	0
Other Hispanic	1

Age & Nativity, 2000
Under 5 years	18
18 years and over	231
21 years and over	225
65 years and over	44
85 years and over	6
Median Age	43
Native born	273
Foreign born	2

Educational Attainment, 2000
Population 25 years and over	200
0-8 yrs of school	0.0%
High School grad or higher	100.0%
Bachelor's degree or higher	50.0%
Graduate degree	20.0%

Income & Poverty, 1999
Per capita income	$34,037
Median household income	$68,542
Median family income	$74,250
Persons in poverty	13
H'holds receiving public assistance	0
H'holds receiving social security	24

Households, 2000
Total households	120
With persons under 18	28
With persons over 65	30
Family households	77
One-person households	33
Persons per household	2.33
Persons per family	2.88

Labor & Employment
Total civilian labor force, 2004**	253
Unemployment rate	3.7%
Total civilian labor force, 2000	162
Unemployment rate	7.4%

Employed persons 16 years and over by occupation, 2000
Managers & professionals	89
Service occupations	10
Sales & office occupations	34
Farming, fishing & forestry	0
Construction & maintenance	12
Production & transportation	5
Self-employed persons	18

*US Census Bureau
**New Jersey Department of Labor

General Information
Village of Loch Arbour
550 Main St
Loch Arbour, NJ 07711
732-531-4740

Web site	NA
Land area (sq. miles)	0.10
Water area (sq. miles)	0.04
Type of government	Village
Form of government	V

Government
Legislative Districts
US Congressional	6
State Legislative	11

Local Officials, 2006
Mayor	Ed Lee
Admin/Manager	NA
Clerk	Lorraine Carafa
Finance Dir/Treas	L. Carafa
Engineer	Peter Avakian
Attorney	Kenneth Fitzsimmons
Tax assessor	Eldo Magnani
Tax collector	NA
Building officer	Alan Decker
Zoning officer	Vito M. Marinaccio
Public Works	NA

Housing & Construction
Housing Units, 2000*
Total	156
Median rent	$755
Median SF home value	$322,400

New Privately Owned Housing Units
Authorized by Building Permit
	Units	Value
Total, 2004	NA	NA
Single family	NA	NA
Total, 2005	1	$16,000
Single family	1	$16,000

Real Property Valuation - parcels, 2005
	Number	Valuation
Total		$71,842,800
Vacant	5	1,233,400
Residential	135	66,770,000
Commercial	6	3,576,000
Industrial	0	0
Apartments	1	263,400
Farm land	0	0
Farm homestead	0	0

Average Property Value & Tax, 2005
Residential value	$494,593
Property tax	$7,187
FAIR rebate	$544

Public Library
Monmouth County Library
125 Symmes Dr
Manalapan, NJ 07726
732-431-7220

Director .... Kenneth Sheinbaum

Library statistics, 2004
	Total	per capita
Volumes	NA	NA
Expenditure	NA	NA

Public Safety
Police
Chief	Antonio Amodio
Number of officers, 2004	0

Crime, 2004	Number	Rate
Total	9	32.7
Violent	0	0
Non-violent	9	32.7
Domestic Viol.	0	NA

Emergency/Fire
Director .... Thomas Gironda

Public School District
(for school year 2004-2005 except as noted)

Ocean Township School District
163 Monmouth Rd
Oakhurst, NJ 07755
732-531-5600

Superintendent	Thomas Pagano
Grade plan	K-12
Enrollment	4,447.0
Students per teacher	11.6
Per pupil expenditure	$11,976
Median faculty salary	$61,760
Median administrator salary	$105,800
Grade 12 enrollment	328.0
High school graduation rate	98.5%

Assessment test results
(percent scoring at proficient or advanced level)
	Language	Math
Grade 3	91.2%	86.8%
Grade 8	81.2%	75.7%
High school	92.8%	91.1%

SAT
Percent tested	94%
Average SAT math score	543
Average SAT verbal score	522

No Child Left Behind, 2003-04
Attendance rate (target = 90%)	95.8%
Drop rate	0.1%
Highly-qualified teachers	84.5%
District needs improvement?(AYP)	No

Municipal Finance
Fiscal Year 2005
Total tax levy	$1,044,708
County levy	332,808
County taxes	298,636
County library	16,450
County health	0
County open space	17,721
School levy	300,000
Local muni. budget	411,900
Misc. revenues	365,088
Total aid	$54,475
CMPTRA	20,190
Muni. block grant	1,663
Energy tax receipts	32,622
Homeland security	0

Fiscal Year 2006
Total aid	$54,474
CMPTRA	19,048
Muni. block grant	1,663
Energy tax receipts	33,763
Homeland security	NA

Taxes
	2003	2004	2005
General tax rate per $100	1.37	1.410	1.454
Net valuation taxable	$71,753,024	$71,621,815	$71,891,574
State equalized value	$84,734,322	$98,997,671	$137,934,716
County equalization ratio	99.89	84.68	72.33

Demographics & Socio-Economic Characteristics

(2000 U.S. Census, except as noted)

Population

1980*	23,956
1990*	22,355
2000	23,971
Male	11,378
Female	12,593
2004 (estimate)*	24,336
Persons per sq. mi. of land	10,752

Race & Hispanic Origin, 2000

Race

White	18,736
Black/African American	852
Amer. Indian/Alaska Natv.	40
Asian	2,124
Natv. Hawaiian/Pac. Islander	8
Other Race	1,498
Two or more races	713
Hispanic origin, total	4,309
Mexican	212
Puerto Rican	912
Cuban	178
Other Hispanic	3,007

Age & Nativity, 2000

Under 5 years	1,533
18 years and over	18,865
21 years and over	18,157
65 years and over	3,564
85 years and over	425
Median Age	36.4
Native born	16,840
Foreign born	7,131

Educational Attainment, 2000

Population 25 years and over	17,017
0-8 yrs of school	11.7%
High School grad or higher	75.8%
Bachelor's degree or higher	18.7%
Graduate degree	5.1%

Income & Poverty, 1999

Per capita income	$21,667
Median household income	$43,421
Median family income	$51,959
Persons in poverty	1,921
H'holds receiving public assistance	227
H'holds receiving social security	2,742

Households, 2000

Total households	9,528
With persons under 18	3,002
With persons over 65	2,619
Family households	6,100
One-person households	2,871
Persons per household	2.5
Persons per family	3.16

Labor & Employment

Total civilian labor force, 2004**	13,019
Unemployment rate	6.4%
Total civilian labor force, 2000	12,425
Unemployment rate	4.7%

Employed persons 16 years and over by occupation, 2000

Managers & professionals	3,251
Service occupations	1,501
Sales & office occupations	4,050
Farming, fishing & forestry	5
Construction & maintenance	1,083
Production & transportation	1,949
Self-employed persons	435

*US Census Bureau
**New Jersey Department of Labor

General Information

Borough of Lodi
One Memorial Dr
Lodi, NJ 07644
973-365-4005

Web site	www.lodi-nj.org
Land area (sq. miles)	2.26
Water area (sq. miles)	0.01
Type of government	Borough
Form of government	MC '50

Government

Legislative Districts

US Congressional	9
State Legislative	38

Local Officials, 2006

Mayor	Gary Paparozzi
Admin/Manager	Tony Luna
Clerk	Debra Cannizzo
Finance Dir/Treas	Debra Paci
Engineer	Job & Job Eng.
Attorney	John Baldino
Tax assessor	George Reggo
Tax collector	Gary Stramandino
Building officer	Joel Lavin
Zoning officer	George DeNobile
Public Works	Gerald Woods

Housing & Construction

Housing Units, 2000*

Total	9,908
Median rent	$811
Median SF home value	$172,600

New Privately Owned Housing Units
Authorized by Building Permit

	Units	Value
Total, 2004	54	$3,188,235
Single family	24	$978,500
Total, 2005	73	$5,643,110
Single family	3	$469,800

Real Property Valuation - parcels, 2005

	Number	Valuation
Total		$1,928,946,700
Vacant	87	10,692,700
Residential	4,393	1,386,121,300
Commercial	312	265,527,500
Industrial	101	127,407,000
Apartments	91	139,198,200
Farm land	0	0
Farm homestead	0	0

Average Property Value & Tax, 2005

Residential value	$315,530
Property tax	$7,569
FAIR rebate	$689

Public Library

Lodi Memorial Library
1 Memorial Dr
Lodi, NJ 07644
973-365-4044

Director — Anthony Taormina

Library statistics, 2004

	Total	per capita
Volumes	94,129	3.93
Expenditure	$873,370	$36.43

Public Safety

Police

Chief	Vincent Caruso
Number of officers, 2004	42

Crime, 2004	Number	Rate
Total	510	21.1
Violent	44	1.8
Non-violent	466	19.3
Domestic Viol.	263	NA

Emergency/Fire

Director — Michael Panasiuk

Public School District

(for school year 2004-2005 except as noted)

Lodi School District
8 Hunter St
Lodi, NJ 07644
973-778-4620

Superintendent	Frank Quatrone
Grade plan	K-12
Enrollment	3,105.5
Students per teacher	11.8
Per pupil expenditure	$11,795
Median faculty salary	$58,464
Median administrator salary	$111,850
Grade 12 enrollment	185.5
High school graduation rate	90.9%

Assessment test results

(percent scoring at proficient or advanced level)

	Language	Math
Grade 3	84.5%	86.8%
Grade 8	80.3%	56.6%
High school	82.3%	75.7%

SAT

Percent tested	59%
Average SAT math score	503
Average SAT verbal score	463

No Child Left Behind, 2003-04

Attendance rate (target = 90%)	95.0%
Drop rate	1.1%
Highly-qualified teachers	97.5%
District needs improvement?(AYP)	No

Municipal Finance

Fiscal Year 2005

Total tax levy	$46,326,960
County levy	3,548,824
County taxes	3,370,245
County library	0
County health	0
County open space	178,579
School levy	29,241,551
Local muni. budget	13,536,585
Misc. revenues	6,794,120
Total aid	$2,682,484
CMPTRA	1,548,154
Muni. block grant	97,818
Energy tax receipts	946,512
Homeland security	90,000

Fiscal Year 2006

Total aid	$2,682,484
CMPTRA	1,515,020
Muni. block grant	97,818
Energy tax receipts	979,640
Homeland security	90,000

Taxes

	2003	2004	2005
General tax rate per $100	4.11	2.240	2.400
Net valuation taxable	$950,566,331	$1,932,375,203	$1,931,260,753
State equalized value	$1,547,649,513	$1,774,665,152	$2,053,440,460
County equalization ratio	69.67	124.70	108.90

Demographics & Socio-Economic Characteristics
(2000 U.S. Census, except as noted)

Population
1980*	3,078
1990*	5,147
2000	6,032
Male	2,974
Female	3,058
2004 (estimate)*	6,107
Persons per sq. mi. of land	270

Race & Hispanic Origin, 2000
Race
White	4,946
Black/African American	815
Amer. Indian/Alaska Natv.	8
Asian	107
Natv. Hawaiian/Pac. Islander	1
Other Race	73
Two or more races	82
Hispanic origin, total	165
Mexican	34
Puerto Rican	97
Cuban	11
Other Hispanic	23

Age & Nativity, 2000
Under 5 years	514
18 years and over	4,095
21 years and over	3,906
65 years and over	372
85 years and over	40
Median Age	33.6
Native born	5,813
Foreign born	219

Educational Attainment, 2000
Population 25 years and over	3,740
0-8 yrs of school	2.3%
High School grad or higher	89.5%
Bachelor's degree or higher	25.0%
Graduate degree	7.6%

Income & Poverty, 1999
Per capita income	$26,853
Median household income	$67,148
Median family income	$70,771
Persons in poverty	257
H'holds receiving public assistance	16
H'holds receiving social security	372

Households, 2000
Total households	2,001
With persons under 18	1,020
With persons over 65	277
Family households	1,610
One-person households	314
Persons per household	3.0
Persons per family	3.38

Labor & Employment
Total civilian labor force, 2004**	3,164
Unemployment rate	3.8%
Total civilian labor force, 2000	3,138
Unemployment rate	1.9%

Employed persons 16 years and over by occupation, 2000
Managers & professionals	1,157
Service occupations	335
Sales & office occupations	923
Farming, fishing & forestry	20
Construction & maintenance	199
Production & transportation	443
Self-employed persons	116

*US Census Bureau
**New Jersey Department of Labor

General Information
Township of Logan
PO Box 314
125 Main St
Bridgeport, NJ 08014
856-467-3424

Web site	www.logan-twp.org
Land area (sq. miles)	22.62
Water area (sq. miles)	4.21
Type of government	Township
Form of government	SM '50

Government

Legislative Districts
US Congressional	1
State Legislative	3

Local Officials, 2006
Mayor	Frank W. Minor
Admin/Manager	Jan L. Pine
Clerk	Linda L. Oswald
Finance Dir/Treas	Robert Best
Engineer	Michael Myer
Attorney	Robert P. Becker Jr.
Tax assessor	Horace Spoto
Tax collector	NA
Building officer	Phyllis Atkinson
Zoning officer	NA
Public Works	NA

Housing & Construction

Housing Units, 2000*
Total	2,077
Median rent	$764
Median SF home value	$114,200

New Privately Owned Housing Units Authorized by Building Permit
	Units	Value
Total, 2004	43	$6,631,574
Single family	43	$6,631,574
Total, 2005	0	$166,500
Single family	0	$166,500

Real Property Valuation - parcels, 2005
	Number	Valuation
Total		$588,337,290
Vacant	513	12,917,300
Residential	2,001	203,020,500
Commercial	143	329,411,800
Industrial	8	34,662,590
Apartments	1	127,200
Farm land	51	4,896,100
Farm homestead	188	3,301,800

Average Property Value & Tax, 2005
Residential value	$94,254
Property tax	$2,672
FAIR rebate	$457

Public Library
Logan Twp. Branch Library†
101 Beckett Rd
Swedesboro, NJ 08085
856-241-0202
Branch Librarian .... Anne Woonick

Library statistics, 2004
	Total	per capita
Volumes	NA	NA
Expenditure	NA	NA

†Branch of County Library

Public Safety

Police
Chief	Michael Smith
Number of officers, 2004	19

Crime, 2004	Number	Rate
Total	139	23.1
Violent	15	2.5
Non-violent	124	20.6
Domestic Viol.	57	NA

Emergency/Fire
Director .... Patrick Spring

Public School District
(for school year 2004-2005 except as noted)

Logan Township School District
110 School Lane
Logan Township, NJ 08085
856-467-5133
Superintendent	John Herbst
Grade plan	K-12
Enrollment	933.0
Students per teacher	10.6
Per pupil expenditure	$11,077
Median faculty salary	$49,462
Median administrator salary	$92,940
Grade 12 enrollment	NA
High school graduation rate	NA

Assessment test results
(percent scoring at proficient or advanced level)
	Language	Math
Grade 3	87.8%	91.5%
Grade 8	76.4%	67.9%
High school	NA	NA

SAT
Percent tested	NA
Average SAT math score	NA
Average SAT verbal score	NA

No Child Left Behind, 2003-04
Attendence rate (target = 90%)	96.0%
Drop rate	NA
Highly-qualified teachers	98.9%
District needs improvement?(AYP)	No

Municipal Finance

Fiscal Year 2005
Total tax levy	$16,732,265
County levy	4,777,473
County taxes	4,182,438
County library	310,799
County health	0
County open space	284,237
School levy	10,258,503
Local muni. budget	1,696,289
Misc. revenues	6,025,445
Total aid	$773,899
CMPTRA	209,121
Muni. block grant	23,652
Energy tax receipts	491,126
Homeland security	50,000

Fiscal Year 2006
Total aid	$773,899
CMPTRA	191,932
Muni. block grant	23,652
Energy tax receipts	508,315
Homeland security	50,000

Taxes
	2003	2004	2005
General tax rate per $100	2.58	2.704	2.835
Net valuation taxable	$556,217,160	$584,469,719	$590,278,043
State equalized value	$603,665,249	$702,978,208	$782,239,654
County equalization ratio	106.5	92.14	83.08

Demographics & Socio-Economic Characteristics

(2000 U.S. Census, except as noted)

Population

1980*	3,488
1990*	3,407
2000	3,329
Male	1,579
Female	1,750
2004 (estimate)*	3,450
Persons per sq. mi. of land	650

Race & Hispanic Origin, 2000

Race

White	3,280
Black/African American	8
Amer. Indian/Alaska Natv.	1
Asian	12
Natv. Hawaiian/Pac. Islander	0
Other Race	11
Two or more races	17
Hispanic origin, total	70
Mexican	53
Puerto Rican	14
Cuban	0
Other Hispanic	3

Age & Nativity, 2000

Under 5 years	88
18 years and over	2,940
21 years and over	2,884
65 years and over	1,214
85 years and over	111
Median Age	57.3
Native born	3,203
Foreign born	122

Educational Attainment, 2000

Population 25 years and over	2,847
0-8 yrs of school	2.0%
High School grad or higher	92.0%
Bachelor's degree or higher	36.7%
Graduate degree	12.8%

Income & Poverty, 1999

Per capita income	$33,404
Median household income	$48,697
Median family income	$59,833
Persons in poverty	171
H'holds receiving public assistance	41
H'holds receiving social security	842

Households, 2000

Total households	1,664
With persons under 18	224
With persons over 65	857
Family households	1,039
One-person households	562
Persons per household	2.0
Persons per family	2.5

Labor & Employment

Total civilian labor force, 2004**	2,115
Unemployment rate	3.4%
Total civilian labor force, 2000	1,351
Unemployment rate	5.0%

Employed persons 16 years and over by occupation, 2000

Managers & professionals	429
Service occupations	205
Sales & office occupations	413
Farming, fishing & forestry	0
Construction & maintenance	111
Production & transportation	125
Self-employed persons	141

*US Census Bureau
**New Jersey Department of Labor

General Information

Township of Long Beach
6805 Long Beach Blvd
Brant Beach, NJ 08008
609-361-1000

Web site	www.longbeachtownship.com
Land area (sq. miles)	5.31
Water area (sq. miles)	16.69
Type of government	Township
Form of government	Comm.

Government

Legislative Districts

US Congressional	3
State Legislative	9

Local Officials, 2006

Mayor	DiAnne C. Gove
Admin/Manager	Bonnie Leonetti
Clerk	Bonnie Leonetti
Finance Dir/Treas	MaryAnn Mayo
Engineer	Frank Little Jr.
Attorney	Shackleton, Hazeltine
Tax assessor	Tracy A. Hafner
Tax collector	NA
Building officer	Ron Pingaro
Zoning officer	JoAnne Tallon
Public Works	NA

Housing & Construction

Housing Units, 2000*

Total	9,023
Median rent	$766
Median SF home value	$334,400

New Privately Owned Housing Units Authorized by Building Permit

	Units	Value
Total, 2004	93	$35,060,612
Single family	79	$31,698,375
Total, 2005	115	$42,798,709
Single family	97	$39,532,428

Real Property Valuation - parcels, 2005

	Number	Valuation
Total		$7,071,087,600
Vacant	1,092	293,364,400
Residential	7,649	6,609,712,200
Commercial	166	159,866,100
Industrial	0	0
Apartments	10	8,144,900
Farm land	0	0
Farm homestead	0	0

Average Property Value & Tax, 2005

Residential value	$864,128
Property tax	$6,747
FAIR rebate	$666

Public Library

Long Beach Island Branch Library†
217 S Central Ave
Surf City, NJ 08008
609-494-2480

Branch Librarian	Elise Weber

Library statistics, 2004

	Total	per capita
Volumes	NA	NA
Expenditure	NA	NA

†Branch of County Library

Public Safety

Police

Chief	Michael Bradley
Number of officers, 2004	40

Crime, 2004	Number	Rate
Total	197	57.5
Violent	7	2
Non-violent	190	55.4
Domestic Viol.	15	NA

Emergency/Fire

Director	NA

Public School District

(for school year 2004-2005 except as noted)

Sends children to Long Beach Island school district (see Appendix A).

Grade plan	NA
Enrollment	NA
Students per teacher	NA
Per pupil expenditure	NA
Median faculty salary	NA
Median administrator salary	NA
Grade 12 enrollment	NA
High school graduation rate	NA

Assessment test results

(percent scoring at proficient or advanced level)

	Language	Math
Grade 3	NA	NA
Grade 8	NA	NA
High school	NA	NA

SAT

Percent tested	NA
Average SAT math score	NA
Average SAT verbal score	NA

No Child Left Behind, 2003-04

Attendence rate (target = 90%)	NA
Drop rate	NA
Highly-qualified teachers	NA
District needs improvement?(AYP)	NA

Municipal Finance

Fiscal Year 2005

Total tax levy	$55,230,854
County levy	22,973,073
County taxes	20,109,921
County library	2,112,750
County health	0
County open space	750,402
School levy	18,106,034
Local muni. budget	14,151,747
Misc. revenues	3,845,605
Total aid	$739,096
CMPTRA	0
Muni. block grant	14,908
Energy tax receipts	710,354
Homeland security	25,000

Fiscal Year 2006

Total aid	$763,959
CMPTRA	0
Muni. block grant	14,908
Energy tax receipts	724,051
Homeland security	25,000

Taxes

	2003	2004	2005
General tax rate per $100	1.79	1.931	0.781
Net valuation taxable	$2,549,181,942	$2,572,144,178	$7,073,611,662
State equalized value	$5,199,228,925	$6,202,501,219	$7,459,255,153
County equalization ratio	59.06	49.03	113.33

Demographics & Socio-Economic Characteristics
(2000 U.S. Census, except as noted)

Population
1980*	29,819
1990*	28,658
2000	31,340
Male	15,210
Female	16,130
2004 (estimate)*	31,526
Persons per sq. mi. of land	6,044

Race & Hispanic Origin, 2000
Race
White	21,320
Black/African American	5,847
Amer. Indian/Alaska Natv.	113
Asian	513
Natv. Hawaiian/Pac. Islander	15
Other Race	2,220
Two or more races	1,312
Hispanic origin, total	6,477
Mexican	1,448
Puerto Rican	2,778
Cuban	84
Other Hispanic	2,167

Age & Nativity, 2000
Under 5 years	2,183
18 years and over	23,890
21 years and over	22,628
65 years and over	4,036
85 years and over	495
Median Age	34.7
Native born	25,176
Foreign born	6,164

Educational Attainment, 2000
Population 25 years and over	20,774
0-8 yrs of school	8.3%
High School grad or higher	76.3%
Bachelor's degree or higher	20.2%
Graduate degree	7.2%

Income & Poverty, 1999
Per capita income	$20,532
Median household income	$38,651
Median family income	$42,825
Persons in poverty	5,208
H'holds receiving public assistance	551
H'holds receiving social security	3,119

Households, 2000
Total households	12,594
With persons under 18	3,885
With persons over 65	3,027
Family households	7,248
One-person households	4,295
Persons per household	2.47
Persons per family	3.19

Labor & Employment
Total civilian labor force, 2004**	16,693
Unemployment rate	7.4%
Total civilian labor force, 2000	15,398
Unemployment rate	7.4%

Employed persons 16 years and over by occupation, 2000
Managers & professionals	4,077
Service occupations	2,925
Sales & office occupations	4,016
Farming, fishing & forestry	22
Construction & maintenance	1,503
Production & transportation	1,720
Self-employed persons	1,002

*US Census Bureau
**New Jersey Department of Labor

General Information
City of Long Branch
344 Broadway
Long Branch, NJ 07740
732-222-7000
Web site	www.longbranch.org
Land area (sq. miles)	5.22
Water area (sq. miles)	0.97
Type of government	City
Form of government	MC '50

Government

Legislative Districts
US Congressional	6
State Legislative	11

Local Officials, 2006
Mayor	Adam Schneider
Admin/Manager	Howard Woolley Jr.
Clerk	Irene Joline
Finance Dir/Treas	Ronald Mehlhorn Sr.
Engineer	Birdsall Engineering
Attorney	James Aaron
Tax assessor	William Fitzpatrick
Tax collector	Ed Mazzacco
Building officer	Kevin Hayes
Zoning officer	Carl Turner
Public Works	Fred Migliaccio

Housing & Construction

Housing Units, 2000*
Total	13,983
Median rent	$727
Median SF home value	$135,300

New Privately Owned Housing Units Authorized by Building Permit
	Units	Value
Total, 2004	10	$1,443,000
Single family	10	$1,443,000
Total, 2005	94	$18,171,417
Single family	94	$18,171,417

Real Property Valuation - parcels, 2005
	Number	Valuation
Total		$2,380,141,100
Vacant	485	74,494,600
Residential	7,681	1,853,118,800
Commercial	772	278,010,600
Industrial	7	7,670,600
Apartments	161	165,697,400
Farm land	1	1,145,300
Farm homestead	1	3,800

Average Property Value & Tax, 2005
Residential value	$241,229
Property tax	$5,678
FAIR rebate	$602

Public Library
Long Branch Public Library
328 Broadway
Long Branch, NJ 07740
732-222-3900
Director ... Ingrid Bruck

Library statistics, 2004
	Total	per capita
Volumes	68,361	2.18
Expenditure	$946,927	$30.21

Public Safety

Police
Chief	William Richards (PS Dir)
Number of officers, 2004	99

Crime, 2004	Number	Rate
Total	889	28.2
Violent	147	4.7
Non-violent	742	23.5
Domestic Viol.	283	NA

Emergency/Fire
Director ... John Zambrano

Public School District
(for school year 2004-2005 except as noted)

Long Branch School District
540 Broadway
Long Branch, NJ 07740
732-571-2868
Superintendent	Joseph Ferraina
Grade plan	K-12
Enrollment	5,065.0
Students per teacher	9.8
Per pupil expenditure	$13,629
Median faculty salary	$43,805
Median administrator salary	$103,470
Grade 12 enrollment	298.0
High school graduation rate	87.9%

Assessment test results
(percent scoring at proficient or advanced level)
	Language	Math
Grade 3	73.4%	70.2%
Grade 8	51.8%	40.4%
High school	63.8%	59.4%

SAT
Percent tested	44%
Average SAT math score	453
Average SAT verbal score	437

No Child Left Behind, 2003-04
Attendence rate (target = 90%)	92.3%
Drop rate	1.4%
Highly-qualified teachers	92.4%
District needs improvement?(AYP)	Yes

Municipal Finance

Fiscal Year 2005
Total tax levy	$56,162,950
County levy	9,061,184
County taxes	8,553,720
County library	0
County health	0
County open space	507,463
School levy	24,611,452
Local muni. budget	22,490,315
Misc. revenues	15,688,558
Total aid	$5,870,914
CMPTRA	3,639,819
Muni. block grant	125,399
Energy tax receipts	1,965,696
Homeland security	140,000

Fiscal Year 2006
Total aid	$5,870,915
CMPTRA	3,571,020
Muni. block grant	125,399
Energy tax receipts	2,034,496
Homeland security	140,000

Taxes
	2003	2004	2005
General tax rate per $100	2.16	2.302	2.354
Net valuation taxable	$2,341,970,789	$2,350,370,336	$2,386,074,565
State equalized value	$2,353,266,468	$2,812,722,419	$3,567,161,855
County equalization ratio	69.14	99.52	83.52

Demographics & Socio-Economic Characteristics
(2000 U.S. Census, except as noted)

Population
1980*	7,275
1990*	7,826
2000	8,777
Male	4,258
Female	4,519
2004 (estimate)*	8,787
Persons per sq. mi. of land	728

Race & Hispanic Origin, 2000
Race
White	8,141
Black/African American	34
Amer. Indian/Alaska Natv.	15
Asian	420
Natv. Hawaiian/Pac. Islander	3
Other Race	49
Two or more races	115
Hispanic origin, total	303
Mexican	26
Puerto Rican	41
Cuban	32
Other Hispanic	204

Age & Nativity, 2000
Under 5 years	680
18 years and over	6,470
21 years and over	6,292
65 years and over	1,109
85 years and over	98
Median Age	39.2
Native born	7,785
Foreign born	992

Educational Attainment, 2000
Population 25 years and over	5,995
0-8 yrs of school	1.9%
High School grad or higher	93.8%
Bachelor's degree or higher	49.3%
Graduate degree	18.9%

Income & Poverty, 1999
Per capita income	$42,613
Median household income	$84,532
Median family income	$103,037
Persons in poverty	286
H'holds receiving public assistance	14
H'holds receiving social security	801

Households, 2000
Total households	3,139
With persons under 18	1,202
With persons over 65	782
Family households	2,458
One-person households	570
Persons per household	2.79
Persons per family	3.19

Labor & Employment
Total civilian labor force, 2004**	4,999
Unemployment rate	2.1%
Total civilian labor force, 2000	4,559
Unemployment rate	2.8%

Employed persons 16 years and over by occupation, 2000
Managers & professionals	2,143
Service occupations	529
Sales & office occupations	1,222
Farming, fishing & forestry	14
Construction & maintenance	198
Production & transportation	325
Self-employed persons	228

*US Census Bureau
**New Jersey Department of Labor

General Information
Township of Long Hill
915 Valley Rd
Gillette, NJ 07933
908-647-8000

Web site	www.longhillnj.us
Land area (sq. miles)	12.08
Water area (sq. miles)	0
Type of government	Township
Form of government	TC

Government

Legislative Districts
US Congressional	11
State Legislative	21

Local Officials, 2006
Mayor	Gina Genovese
Admin/Manager	Kevin Sluka
Clerk	Kevin Sluka (Actg)
Finance Dir/Treas	R. Tebbs
Engineer	Justin Lizza
Attorney	John Pidgeon
Tax assessor	Ernest Del Guercio
Tax collector	Joan Donat
Building officer	Tom Yotka
Zoning officer	NA
Public Works	Justin Lizza

Housing & Construction

Housing Units, 2000*
Total	3,206
Median rent	$1,024
Median SF home value	$297,000

New Privately Owned Housing Units Authorized by Building Permit
	Units	Value
Total, 2004	13	$4,997,253
Single family	13	$4,997,253
Total, 2005	4	$1,381,000
Single family	4	$1,381,000

Real Property Valuation - parcels, 2005
	Number	Valuation
Total		$1,259,322,530
Vacant	253	23,592,900
Residential	2,885	1,108,267,030
Commercial	112	101,187,800
Industrial	21	16,641,200
Apartments	7	7,408,000
Farm land	6	2,185,600
Farm homestead	18	40,000

Average Property Value & Tax, 2005
Residential value	$381,780
Property tax	$8,778
FAIR rebate	$578

Public Library
Long Hill Twp Public Library
917 Valley Rd
Gillette, NJ 07933
908-647-2088

Director	Peggy Neubig

Library statistics, 2004
	Total	per capita
Volumes	55,749	6.35
Expenditure	$362,490	$41.30

Public Safety

Police
Chief	Michael Peoples
Number of officers, 2004	29

Crime, 2004	Number	Rate
Total	110	12.5
Violent	5	0.6
Non-violent	105	12
Domestic Viol.	24	NA

Emergency/Fire
Director	NA

Public School District
(for school year 2004-2005 except as noted)

Long Hill Township School District
759 Valley Rd
Gillette, NJ 07933
908-647-1200

Superintendent	Arthur DiBenedetto
Grade plan	K-8
Enrollment	1,098.0
Students per teacher	11.5
Per pupil expenditure	$10,561
Median faculty salary	$48,017
Median administrator salary	$95,130
Grade 12 enrollment	NA
High school graduation rate	NA

Assessment test results
(percent scoring at proficient or advanced level)
	Language	Math
Grade 3	92.9%	92.3%
Grade 8	94.1%	85.6%
High school	NA	NA

SAT
Percent tested	NA
Average SAT math score	NA
Average SAT verbal score	NA

No Child Left Behind, 2003-04
Attendence rate (target = 90%)	95.2%
Drop rate	NA
Highly-qualified teachers	97.5%
District needs improvement?(AYP)	No

Municipal Finance

Fiscal Year 2005
Total tax levy	$29,061,386
County levy	3,920,179
County taxes	3,211,149
County library	0
County health	0
County open space	709,030
School levy	16,898,091
Local muni. budget	8,243,115
Misc. revenues	6,030,728
Total aid	$1,789,080
CMPTRA	276,702
Muni. block grant	34,415
Energy tax receipts	1,427,963
Homeland security	50,000

Fiscal Year 2006
Total aid	$1,789,079
CMPTRA	226,723
Muni. block grant	34,415
Energy tax receipts	1,477,941
Homeland security	50,000

Taxes
	2003	2004	2005
General tax rate per $100	1.98	2.150	2.300
Net valuation taxable	$1,257,102,551	$1,259,632,490	$1,264,002,788
State equalized value	$1,344,207,176	$1,464,396,795	$1,641,348,900
County equalization ratio	101.84	93.52	85.97

Demographics & Socio-Economic Characteristics
(2000 U.S. Census, except as noted)

Population
1980*	1,249
1990*	1,224
2000	1,054
Male	489
Female	565
2004 (estimate)*	1,083
Persons per sq. mi. of land	2,841

Race & Hispanic Origin, 2000
Race
White	1,039
Black/African American	1
Amer. Indian/Alaska Natv.	0
Asian	12
Natv. Hawaiian/Pac. Islander	0
Other Race	0
Two or more races	2
Hispanic origin, total	5
Mexican	1
Puerto Rican	3
Cuban	0
Other Hispanic	1

Age & Nativity, 2000
Under 5 years	34
18 years and over	934
21 years and over	927
65 years and over	364
85 years and over	47
Median Age	56.6
Native born	1,022
Foreign born	32

Educational Attainment, 2000
Population 25 years and over	900
0-8 yrs of school	2.8%
High School grad or higher	86.9%
Bachelor's degree or higher	39.0%
Graduate degree	15.8%

Income & Poverty, 1999
Per capita income	$50,884
Median household income	$51,324
Median family income	$68,194
Persons in poverty	39
H'holds receiving public assistance	0
H'holds receiving social security	244

Households, 2000
Total households	544
With persons under 18	65
With persons over 65	261
Family households	317
One-person households	204
Persons per household	1.94
Persons per family	2.53

Labor & Employment
Total civilian labor force, 2004**	569
Unemployment rate	7.3%
Total civilian labor force, 2000	505
Unemployment rate	4.0%

Employed persons 16 years and over by occupation, 2000
Managers & professionals	247
Service occupations	87
Sales & office occupations	113
Farming, fishing & forestry	0
Construction & maintenance	18
Production & transportation	20
Self-employed persons	48

*US Census Bureau
**New Jersey Department of Labor

General Information
Borough of Longport
2305 Atlantic Ave
Longport, NJ 08403
609-823-2731

Web site	NA
Land area (sq. miles)	0.38
Water area (sq. miles)	1.24
Type of government	Borough
Form of government	Comm.

Government

Legislative Districts
US Congressional	2
State Legislative	2

Local Officials, 2006
Mayor	John Stroebele
Admin/Manager	NA
Clerk	Thomas Hiltner
Finance Dir/Treas	Maria Mento
Engineer	Richard Carter
Attorney	Thomas Subranni
Tax assessor	Jeffrey Hesley
Tax collector	NA
Building officer	James Agnesino
Zoning officer	NA
Public Works	NA

Housing & Construction

Housing Units, 2000*
Total	1,574
Median rent	$909
Median SF home value	$267,300

New Privately Owned Housing Units Authorized by Building Permit
	Units	Value
Total, 2004	27	$10,093,043
Single family	27	$10,093,043
Total, 2005	23	$12,786,661
Single family	23	$12,786,661

Real Property Valuation - parcels, 2005
	Number	Valuation
Total		$1,527,926,300
Vacant	64	50,857,900
Residential	1,572	1,471,190,300
Commercial	7	5,878,100
Industrial	0	0
Apartments	0	0
Farm land	0	0
Farm homestead	0	0

Average Property Value & Tax, 2005
Residential value	$935,872
Property tax	$6,266
FAIR rebate	$836

Public Library
Longport Branch Library†
2305 Atlantic Ave
Longport, NJ 08403
609-487-0272

Director ... Kathy Gindin

Library statistics, 2004
	Total	per capita
Volumes	NA	NA
Expenditure	NA	NA

†Branch of County Library

Public Safety

Police
Chief	A. Scott Porter
Number of officers, 2004	15

Crime, 2004	Number	Rate
Total	13	12.3
Violent	0	0
Non-violent	13	12.3
Domestic Viol.	6	NA

Emergency/Fire
Director ... Levon Clayton

Public School District
(for school year 2004-2005 except as noted)

Longport School District
2305 Atlantic Ave
Longport, NJ 08403
609-822-9368

Superintendent	NA
Grade plan	NA
Enrollment	NA
Students per teacher	NA
Per pupil expenditure	NA
Median faculty salary	NA
Median administrator salary	NA
Grade 12 enrollment	NA
High school graduation rate	NA

Assessment test results
(percent scoring at proficient or advanced level)
	Language	Math
Grade 3	NA	NA
Grade 8	NA	NA
High school	NA	NA

SAT
Percent tested	NA
Average SAT math score	NA
Average SAT verbal score	NA

No Child Left Behind, 2003-04
Attendence rate (target = 90%)	NA
Drop rate	NA
Highly-qualified teachers	NA
District needs improvement?(AYP)	NA

Municipal Finance

Fiscal Year 2005
Total tax levy	$10,231,617
County levy	5,032,158
County taxes	4,108,315
County library	455,135
County health	223,980
County open space	244,728
School levy	842,959
Local muni. budget	4,356,500
Misc. revenues	1,340,430
Total aid	$161,004
CMPTRA	0
Muni. block grant	5,356
Energy tax receipts	130,648
Homeland security	25,000

Fiscal Year 2006
Total aid	$165,577
CMPTRA	0
Muni. block grant	5,356
Energy tax receipts	135,221
Homeland security	25,000

Taxes
	2003	2004	2005
General tax rate per $100	1.07	1.136	0.670
Net valuation taxable	$844,022,087	$845,050,774	$1,528,140,594
State equalized value	$1,045,876,192	$1,203,526,093	$1,441,914,129
County equalization ratio	95.04	80.70	124.96

Demographics & Socio-Economic Characteristics
(2000 U.S. Census, except as noted)

Population
1980*	4,998
1990*	5,052
2000	5,765
Male	2,655
Female	3,110
2004 (estimate)*	8,042
Persons per sq. mi. of land	1,136

Race & Hispanic Origin, 2000
Race
White	5,550
Black/African American	65
Amer. Indian/Alaska Natv.	4
Asian	94
Natv. Hawaiian/Pac. Islander	0
Other Race	28
Two or more races	24
Hispanic origin, total	115
Mexican	6
Puerto Rican	50
Cuban	16
Other Hispanic	43

Age & Nativity, 2000
Under 5 years	385
18 years and over	4,351
21 years and over	4,227
65 years and over	1,279
85 years and over	269
Median Age	41.3
Native born	5,502
Foreign born	263

Educational Attainment, 2000
Population 25 years and over	4,137
0-8 yrs of school	7.0%
High School grad or higher	82.5%
Bachelor's degree or higher	22.4%
Graduate degree	7.0%

Income & Poverty, 1999
Per capita income	$24,333
Median household income	$50,918
Median family income	$65,545
Persons in poverty	350
H'holds receiving public assistance	28
H'holds receiving social security	736

Households, 2000
Total households	2,143
With persons under 18	735
With persons over 65	746
Family households	1,524
One-person households	562
Persons per household	2.55
Persons per family	3.09

Labor & Employment
Total civilian labor force, 2004**	2,978
Unemployment rate	3.1%
Total civilian labor force, 2000	2,578
Unemployment rate	1.9%

Employed persons 16 years and over by occupation, 2000
Managers & professionals	1,086
Service occupations	331
Sales & office occupations	621
Farming, fishing & forestry	14
Construction & maintenance	242
Production & transportation	235
Self-employed persons	124

*US Census Bureau
**New Jersey Department of Labor

General Information
Township of Lopatcong
232 S Third St
Phillipsburg, NJ 08865
908-859-3355
Web site	www.lopatcongtwp.com
Land area (sq. miles)	7.08
Water area (sq. miles)	0.06
Type of government	Township
Form of government	SM '50

Government

Legislative Districts
US Congressional	5
State Legislative	23

Local Officials, 2006
Mayor	Douglas Steinhardt
Admin/Manager	M. Beth Dilts
Clerk	M. Beth Dilts
Finance Dir/Treas	Mary Dobes
Engineer	Masur Consulting
Attorney	Michael Lavery
Tax assessor	Kathleen Degan
Tax collector	Mary Dobes
Building officer	John Fritts
Zoning officer	Wayne Degan
Public Works	NA

Housing & Construction

Housing Units, 2000*
Total	2,429
Median rent	$624
Median SF home value	$156,600

New Privately Owned Housing Units
Authorized by Building Permit
	Units	Value
Total, 2004	128	$13,795,013
Single family	128	$13,795,013
Total, 2005	113	$12,462,128
Single family	101	$11,007,128

Real Property Valuation - parcels, 2005
	Number	Valuation
Total		$538,077,136
Vacant	418	15,314,240
Residential	2,528	402,876,756
Commercial	131	90,167,800
Industrial	12	11,611,500
Apartments	2	11,787,600
Farm land	28	5,597,100
Farm homestead	69	722,140

Average Property Value & Tax, 2005
Residential value	$155,410
Property tax	$4,789
FAIR rebate	$547

Public Library

No public municipal library.

Library statistics, 2004
	Total	per capita
Volumes	NA	NA
Expenditure	NA	NA

Public Safety

Police
Chief	Scott Marinelli
Number of officers, 2004	13

Crime, 2004	Number	Rate
Total	83	10.6
Violent	7	0.9
Non-violent	76	9.7
Domestic Viol.	35	NA

Emergency/Fire
Director	Pat Rivoli

Public School District
(for school year 2004-2005 except as noted)

Lopatcong Township School District
263 Route 57
Phillipsburg, NJ 08865
908-859-0800
Superintendent	Michael Rossi
Grade plan	K-12
Enrollment	848.0
Students per teacher	12.8
Per pupil expenditure	$9,596
Median faculty salary	$49,158
Median administrator salary	$82,981
Grade 12 enrollment	NA
High school graduation rate	NA

Assessment test results
(percent scoring at proficient or advanced level)
	Language	Math
Grade 3	94.1%	77.7%
Grade 8	71.2%	55.8%
High school	NA	NA

SAT
Percent tested	NA
Average SAT math score	NA
Average SAT verbal score	NA

No Child Left Behind, 2003-04
Attendence rate (target = 90%)	96.3%
Drop rate	NA
Highly-qualified teachers	96.6%
District needs improvement?(AYP)	No

Municipal Finance

Fiscal Year 2005
Total tax levy	$16,617,626
County levy	4,799,475
County taxes	3,952,699
County library	389,785
County health	0
County open space	456,991
School levy	10,322,053
Local muni. budget	1,496,097
Misc. revenues	4,279,349
Total aid	$1,326,644
CMPTRA	255,499
Muni. block grant	22,605
Energy tax receipts	998,540
Homeland security	50,000

Fiscal Year 2006
Total aid	$1,326,643
CMPTRA	220,550
Muni. block grant	22,605
Energy tax receipts	1,033,488
Homeland security	50,000

Taxes
	2003	2004	2005
General tax rate per $100	2.78	2.990	3.090
Net valuation taxable	$497,140,781	$518,081,639	$539,276,816
State equalized value	$626,279,643	$728,813,943	$858,037,893
County equalization ratio	86.56	79.38	71.03

Demographics & Socio-Economic Characteristics
(2000 U.S. Census, except as noted)

Population
1980*	1,547
1990*	1,858
2000	1,851
Male	894
Female	957
2004 (estimate)*	1,904
Persons per sq. mi. of land	41

Race & Hispanic Origin, 2000
Race
White	1,784
Black/African American	40
Amer. Indian/Alaska Natv.	2
Asian	12
Natv. Hawaiian/Pac. Islander	0
Other Race	3
Two or more races	10
Hispanic origin, total	9
Mexican	1
Puerto Rican	4
Cuban	2
Other Hispanic	2

Age & Nativity, 2000
Under 5 years	121
18 years and over	1,400
21 years and over	1,338
65 years and over	258
85 years and over	30
Median Age	39.5
Native born	1,837
Foreign born	14

Educational Attainment, 2000
Population 25 years and over	1,284
0-8 yrs of school	6.2%
High School grad or higher	82.4%
Bachelor's degree or higher	11.7%
Graduate degree	2.2%

Income & Poverty, 1999
Per capita income	$21,962
Median household income	$55,078
Median family income	$59,653
Persons in poverty	135
H'holds receiving public assistance	6
H'holds receiving social security	208

Households, 2000
Total households	693
With persons under 18	246
With persons over 65	178
Family households	538
One-person households	126
Persons per household	2.67
Persons per family	3.0

Labor & Employment
Total civilian labor force, 2004**	908
Unemployment rate	5.1%
Total civilian labor force, 2000	947
Unemployment rate	3.0%

Employed persons 16 years and over by occupation, 2000
Managers & professionals	244
Service occupations	171
Sales & office occupations	201
Farming, fishing & forestry	8
Construction & maintenance	119
Production & transportation	176
Self-employed persons	44

*US Census Bureau
**New Jersey Department of Labor

General Information
Township of Lower Alloways Creek
PO Box 157
501 Locust Island Rd
Hancock's Bridge, NJ 08038
856-935-1549

Web site	NA
Land area (sq. miles)	46.78
Water area (sq. miles)	25.80
Type of government	Township
Form of government	TC

Government

Legislative Districts
US Congressional	2
State Legislative	3

Local Officials, 2006
Mayor	Wallace Bradway
Admin/Manager	NA
Clerk	Lisa Montagna (Actg)
Finance Dir/Treas	Kevin Clour
Engineer	Richard Alaimo
Attorney	Herb Butler
Tax assessor	Joseph Harasta
Tax collector	D. Michelle Mitchell
Building officer	Wayne Serfass
Zoning officer	Lance Kaufmann
Public Works	Dennis Carlson

Housing & Construction

Housing Units, 2000*
Total	730
Median rent	$640
Median SF home value	$118,000

New Privately Owned Housing Units Authorized by Building Permit
	Units	Value
Total, 2004	7	$1,070,000
Single family	7	$1,070,000
Total, 2005	1	$200,000
Single family	1	$200,000

Real Property Valuation - parcels, 2005
	Number	Valuation
Total		$204,188,310
Vacant	185	2,679,200
Residential	498	58,728,500
Commercial	10	1,527,200
Industrial	1	111,615,200
Apartments	0	0
Farm land	186	25,396,200
Farm homestead	382	4,242,010

Average Property Value & Tax, 2005
Residential value	$71,557
Property tax	$812
FAIR rebate	$646

Public Library

No public municipal library.

Library statistics, 2004
	Total	per capita
Volumes	NA	NA
Expenditure	NA	NA

Public Safety

Police
Chief	Carl Bowers
Number of officers, 2004	12

Crime, 2004	Number	Rate
Total	13	6.9
Violent	0	0
Non-violent	13	6.9
Domestic Viol.	5	NA

Emergency/Fire
Director	Steve Fisher

Public School District
(for school year 2004-2005 except as noted)

Lower Alloways Creek Township Dist.
967 Main St-Canton
Salem, NJ 08079
856-935-2707

Administrator	Fred Pratta
Grade plan	K-12
Enrollment	228.0
Students per teacher	8.8
Per pupil expenditure	$13,490
Median faculty salary	$49,850
Median administrator salary	$89,265
Grade 12 enrollment	NA
High school graduation rate	NA

Assessment test results
(percent scoring at proficient or advanced level)
	Language	Math
Grade 3	80.0%	80.0%
Grade 8	76.9%	88.4%
High school	NA	NA

SAT
Percent tested	NA
Average SAT math score	NA
Average SAT verbal score	NA

No Child Left Behind, 2003-04
Attendence rate (target = 90%)	96.2%
Drop rate	NA
Highly-qualified teachers	49.1%
District needs improvement?(AYP)	No

Municipal Finance

Fiscal Year 2005
Total tax levy	$2,325,378
County levy	2,325,378
County taxes	2,279,252
County library	0
County health	0
County open space	46,126
School levy	0
Local muni. budget	0
Misc. revenues	8,591,772
Total aid	$7,449,377
CMPTRA	0
Muni. block grant	8,130
Energy tax receipts	7,455,055
Homeland security	25,000

Fiscal Year 2006
Total aid	$7,710,304
CMPTRA	0
Muni. block grant	8,130
Energy tax receipts	7,702,174
Homeland security	NA

Taxes
	2003	2004	2005
General tax rate per $100	1.50	1.111	1.136
Net valuation taxable	$140,411,811	$202,783,752	$204,829,688
State equalized value	$224,658,898	$226,838,773	$220,626,549
County equalization ratio	66.77	90.04	89.36

Demographics & Socio-Economic Characteristics
(2000 U.S. Census, except as noted)

Population
1980*	17,105
1990*	20,820
2000	22,945
Male	10,888
Female	12,057
2004 (estimate)*	22,019
Persons per sq. mi. of land	780

Race & Hispanic Origin, 2000
Race
White	22,088
Black/African American	319
Amer. Indian/Alaska Natv.	52
Asian	121
Natv. Hawaiian/Pac. Islander	5
Other Race	150
Two or more races	210
Hispanic origin, total	432
Mexican	74
Puerto Rican	250
Cuban	30
Other Hispanic	78

Age & Nativity, 2000
Under 5 years	1,177
18 years and over	17,504
21 years and over	16,815
65 years and over	4,740
85 years and over	543
Median Age	41.8
Native born	22,293
Foreign born	655

Educational Attainment, 2000
Population 25 years and over	16,099
0-8 yrs of school	4.3%
High School grad or higher	77.0%
Bachelor's degree or higher	13.1%
Graduate degree	3.4%

Income & Poverty, 1999
Per capita income	$19,786
Median household income	$38,977
Median family income	$45,058
Persons in poverty	1,742
H'holds receiving public assistance	219
H'holds receiving social security	3,693

Households, 2000
Total households	9,328
With persons under 18	2,894
With persons over 65	3,361
Family households	6,379
One-person households	2,535
Persons per household	2.43
Persons per family	2.95

Labor & Employment
Total civilian labor force, 2004**	12,205
Unemployment rate	7.2%
Total civilian labor force, 2000	10,530
Unemployment rate	9.9%

Employed persons 16 years and over by occupation, 2000
Managers & professionals	2,269
Service occupations	2,290
Sales & office occupations	2,623
Farming, fishing & forestry	137
Construction & maintenance	1,298
Production & transportation	869
Self-employed persons	669

*US Census Bureau
**New Jersey Department of Labor

General Information
Township of Lower
2600 Bayshore Rd
Villas, NJ 08251
609-886-2005

Web site	townshipoflower.org
Land area (sq. miles)	28.22
Water area (sq. miles)	2.85
Type of government	Township
Form of government	CM '50

Government

Legislative Districts
US Congressional	2
State Legislative	1

Local Officials, 2006
Mayor	Walt Craig
Admin/Manager	Kathleen McPherson
Clerk	Claudia R. Kammer
Finance Dir/Treas	Lauren Read
Engineer	Bill Rafferty
Attorney	Anthony Monzo
Tax assessor	Arthur Amonette
Tax collector	Susan Jackson
Building officer	Jim Cannon
Zoning officer	NA
Public Works	Gary Douglas

Housing & Construction

Housing Units, 2000*
Total	13,924
Median rent	$687
Median SF home value	$95,900

New Privately Owned Housing Units Authorized by Building Permit
	Units	Value
Total, 2004	107	$12,262,397
Single family	99	$11,107,597
Total, 2005	85	$9,751,769
Single family	73	$8,735,519

Real Property Valuation - parcels, 2005
	Number	Valuation
Total		$1,493,797,400
Vacant	932	30,765,500
Residential	13,800	1,320,048,900
Commercial	349	131,287,900
Industrial	5	1,124,800
Apartments	4	6,059,200
Farm land	26	3,564,400
Farm homestead	94	946,700

Average Property Value & Tax, 2005
Residential value	$95,077
Property tax	$2,591
FAIR rebate	$696

Public Library
Lower Cape Branch Library†
2600 Bayshore Rd
Villas, NJ 08251
609-886-8999

Branch Librarian	Edward Carson

Library statistics, 2004
	Total	per capita
Volumes	NA	NA
Expenditure	NA	NA

†Branch of County Library

Public Safety

Police
Chief	Edward Donohue
Number of officers, 2004	46

Crime, 2004	Number	Rate
Total	708	31.4
Violent	44	2
Non-violent	664	29.5
Domestic Viol.	417	NA

Emergency/Fire
Director	NA

Public School District
(for school year 2004-2005 except as noted)

Lower Township School District
834 Seashore Rd
Cape May, NJ 08204
609-884-9400

Superintendent	Joseph Cirrinicione
Grade plan	K-6
Enrollment	1,866.0
Students per teacher	11.8
Per pupil expenditure	$12,301
Median faculty salary	$63,273
Median administrator salary	$95,317
Grade 12 enrollment	NA
High school graduation rate	NA

Assessment test results
(percent scoring at proficient or advanced level)
	Language	Math
Grade 3	81.4%	85.4%
Grade 8	NA	NA
High school	NA	NA

SAT
Percent tested	NA
Average SAT math score	NA
Average SAT verbal score	NA

No Child Left Behind, 2003-04
Attendence rate (target = 90%)	94.4%
Drop rate	NA
Highly-qualified teachers	100%
District needs improvement?(AYP)	No

Municipal Finance

Fiscal Year 2005
Total tax levy	$40,809,414
County levy	7,138,672
County taxes	6,001,813
County library	845,428
County health	0
County open space	291,431
School levy	21,708,763
Local muni. budget	11,961,978
Misc. revenues	7,340,060
Total aid	$2,095,371
CMPTRA	723,589
Muni. block grant	91,102
Energy tax receipts	1,190,680
Homeland security	90,000

Fiscal Year 2006
Total aid	$2,095,371
CMPTRA	681,915
Muni. block grant	91,102
Energy tax receipts	1,232,354
Homeland security	90,000

Taxes
	2003	2004	2005
General tax rate per $100	2.61	2.640	2.730
Net valuation taxable	$1,448,553,091	$1,470,213,914	$1,497,333,183
State equalized value	$2,307,348,026	$2,850,785,908	$3,467,654,430
County equalization ratio	76.22	62.78	51.50

Demographics & Socio-Economic Characteristics
(2000 U.S. Census, except as noted)

Population
1980*	5,236
1990*	6,705
2000	10,461
Male	4,990
Female	5,471
2004 (estimate)*	12,297
Persons per sq. mi. of land	956

Race & Hispanic Origin, 2000
Race
White	8,192
Black/African American	1,438
Amer. Indian/Alaska Natv.	24
Asian	354
Natv. Hawaiian/Pac. Islander	2
Other Race	199
Two or more races	252
Hispanic origin, total	539
Mexican	46
Puerto Rican	337
Cuban	17
Other Hispanic	139

Age & Nativity, 2000
Under 5 years	873
18 years and over	7,524
21 years and over	7,262
65 years and over	1,158
85 years and over	156
Median Age	35.6
Native born	9,665
Foreign born	676

Educational Attainment, 2000
Population 25 years and over	6,790
0-8 yrs of school	4.5%
High School grad or higher	86.2%
Bachelor's degree or higher	30.9%
Graduate degree	9.6%

Income & Poverty, 1999
Per capita income	$25,789
Median household income	$60,571
Median family income	$70,329
Persons in poverty	381
H'holds receiving public assistance	69
H'holds receiving social security	747

Households, 2000
Total households	3,930
With persons under 18	1,630
With persons over 65	784
Family households	2,730
One-person households	988
Persons per household	2.61
Persons per family	3.17

Labor & Employment
Total civilian labor force, 2004**	4,208
Unemployment rate	3.8%
Total civilian labor force, 2000	5,175
Unemployment rate	3.7%

Employed persons 16 years and over by occupation, 2000
Managers & professionals	2,217
Service occupations	526
Sales & office occupations	1,317
Farming, fishing & forestry	0
Construction & maintenance	336
Production & transportation	587
Self-employed persons	217

*US Census Bureau
**New Jersey Department of Labor

General Information
Township of Lumberton
PO Box 1860
Lumberton, NJ 08048
609-267-3217
Web site	www.lumbertontwp.com
Land area (sq. miles)	12.87
Water area (sq. miles)	0.17
Type of government	Township
Form of government	TC

Government

Legislative Districts
US Congressional	3
State Legislative	8

Local Officials, 2006
Mayor	John Pagenkopf
Admin/Manager	Daniel Van Pelt
Clerk	Maureen Horton Gross
Finance Dir/Treas	Paula Matson
Engineer	Alaimo Group
Attorney	Anthony Valenti
Tax assessor	Dennis DeKlerk
Tax collector	Maureen Horton Gross
Building officer	Brad Regn
Zoning officer	Cathy Borstad
Public Works	Steve Moorer

Housing & Construction

Housing Units, 2000*
Total	4,080
Median rent	$702
Median SF home value	$163,300

New Privately Owned Housing Units
Authorized by Building Permit
	Units	Value
Total, 2004	78	$11,150,351
Single family	78	$11,150,351
Total, 2005	7	$1,115,466
Single family	7	$1,115,466

Real Property Valuation - parcels, 2005
	Number	Valuation
Total		$711,511,900
Vacant	304	10,342,300
Residential	3,567	576,900,100
Commercial	149	63,004,800
Industrial	10	29,140,800
Apartments	8	21,610,300
Farm land	47	9,314,100
Farm homestead	118	1,199,500

Average Property Value & Tax, 2005
Residential value	$156,879
Property tax	$5,314
FAIR rebate	$472

Public Library

No public municipal library.

Library statistics, 2004
	Total	per capita
Volumes	NA	NA
Expenditure	NA	NA

Public Safety

Police
Chief	Marc Sano
Number of officers, 2004	31

Crime, 2004	Number	Rate
Total	415	34.5
Violent	33	2.7
Non-violent	382	31.7
Domestic Viol.	164	NA

Emergency/Fire
Director	Tim Pearson

Public School District
(for school year 2004-2005 except as noted)

Lumberton Township School District
33 Municipal Dr
Lumberton, NJ 08048
609-265-7709
Superintendent	Frank Logandro
Grade plan	K-8
Enrollment	1,782.5
Students per teacher	11.2
Per pupil expenditure	$10,071
Median faculty salary	$42,504
Median administrator salary	$93,608
Grade 12 enrollment	NA
High school graduation rate	NA

Assessment test results
(percent scoring at proficient or advanced level)
	Language	Math
Grade 3	91.0%	86.3%
Grade 8	83.1%	70.7%
High school	NA	NA

SAT
Percent tested	NA
Average SAT math score	NA
Average SAT verbal score	NA

No Child Left Behind, 2003-04
Attendence rate (target = 90%)	96.2%
Drop rate	NA
Highly-qualified teachers	92.3%
District needs improvement?(AYP)	No

Municipal Finance

Fiscal Year 2005
Total tax levy	$24,149,612
County levy	4,826,017
County taxes	4,048,491
County library	354,501
County health	0
County open space	423,025
School levy	16,431,687
Local muni. budget	2,891,908
Misc. revenues	6,938,994
Total aid	$1,766,784
CMPTRA	327,955
Muni. block grant	41,018
Energy tax receipts	1,327,811
Homeland security	70,000

Fiscal Year 2006
Total aid	$1,766,784
CMPTRA	281,482
Muni. block grant	41,018
Energy tax receipts	1,374,284
Homeland security	70,000

Taxes
	2003	2004	2005
General tax rate per $100	2.82	3.415	3.388
Net valuation taxable	$663,270,235	$697,086,404	$712,960,292
State equalized value	$866,793,302	$1,031,645,413	$1,220,195,605
County equalization ratio	84.22	76.52	67.52

Demographics & Socio-Economic Characteristics

(2000 U.S. Census, except as noted)

Population

1980*	20,326
1990*	18,262
2000	19,383
Male	9,242
Female	10,141
2004 (estimate)*	19,540
Persons per sq. mi. of land	4,203

Race & Hispanic Origin, 2000

Race
White	17,433
Black/African American	119
Amer. Indian/Alaska Natv.	9
Asian	1,046
Natv. Hawaiian/Pac. Islander	1
Other Race	397
Two or more races	378
Hispanic origin, total	1,744
Mexican	97
Puerto Rican	465
Cuban	273
Other Hispanic	909

Age & Nativity, 2000

Under 5 years	959
18 years and over	15,690
21 years and over	15,142
65 years and over	3,440
85 years and over	382
Median Age	39.5
Native born	15,904
Foreign born	3,479

Educational Attainment, 2000

Population 25 years and over	14,263
0-8 yrs of school	7.8%
High School grad or higher	81.4%
Bachelor's degree or higher	21.9%
Graduate degree	6.2%

Income & Poverty, 1999

Per capita income	$25,940
Median household income	$53,375
Median family income	$63,758
Persons in poverty	890
H'holds receiving public assistance	92
H'holds receiving social security	2,664

Households, 2000

Total households	7,877
With persons under 18	2,200
With persons over 65	2,564
Family households	5,205
One-person households	2,269
Persons per household	2.46
Persons per family	3.06

Labor & Employment

Total civilian labor force, 2004**	10,313
Unemployment rate	4.1%
Total civilian labor force, 2000	10,363
Unemployment rate	5.3%

Employed persons 16 years and over by occupation, 2000
Managers & professionals	2,976
Service occupations	1,280
Sales & office occupations	3,313
Farming, fishing & forestry	0
Construction & maintenance	882
Production & transportation	1,358
Self-employed persons	429

*US Census Bureau
**New Jersey Department of Labor

General Information

Township of Lyndhurst
367 Valley Brook Ave
Lyndhurst, NJ 07071
201-804-2457

Web site	www.lyndhurstnj.org
Land area (sq. miles)	4.65
Water area (sq. miles)	0.26
Type of government	Township
Form of government	Comm.

Government

Legislative Districts

US Congressional	9
State Legislative	36

Local Officials, 2006

Mayor	Richard J. DiLascio
Admin/Manager	NA
Clerk	Helen Polito
Finance Dir/Treas	Deborah Ferrato
Engineer	Michael Neglia
Attorney	Henry J. Amoroso
Tax assessor	Denis McGuire
Tax collector	Deborah Ferrato
Building officer	Mark Sadonis
Zoning officer	NA
Public Works	Matthew T. Ruzzo

Housing & Construction

Housing Units, 2000*

Total	8,103
Median rent	$805
Median SF home value	$182,800

New Privately Owned Housing Units
Authorized by Building Permit

	Units	Value
Total, 2004	14	$2,131,330
Single family	6	$1,109,000
Total, 2005	185	$14,639,590
Single family	7	$2,540,450

Real Property Valuation - parcels, 2005

	Number	Valuation
Total		$1,429,352,900
Vacant	170	53,112,300
Residential	5,063	857,397,800
Commercial	306	214,826,600
Industrial	99	276,304,600
Apartments	50	27,711,600
Farm land	0	0
Farm homestead	0	0

Average Property Value & Tax, 2005

Residential value	$169,346
Property tax	$5,408
FAIR rebate	$675

Public Library

Lyndhurst Public Library
355 Valley Brook Ave
Lyndhurst, NJ 07071
201-804-2486

Director............Donna Vincenzino

Library statistics, 2004

	Total	per capita
Volumes	49,213	2.54
Expenditure	$656,115	$33.85

Public Safety

Police

Chief	James O'Connor
Number of officers, 2004	50

Crime, 2004	Number	Rate
Total	359	18.4
Violent	21	1.1
Non-violent	338	17.4
Domestic Viol.	212	NA

Emergency/Fire

Director..................Keith Carroll

Public School District

(for school year 2004-2005 except as noted)

Lyndhurst Township School District
1050 Wall St W
Lyndhurst, NJ 07071
201-438-5683

Superintendent	Joseph Abate Jr.
Grade plan	K-12
Enrollment	2,183.5
Students per teacher	12.5
Per pupil expenditure	$11,340
Median faculty salary	$61,420
Median administrator salary	$102,609
Grade 12 enrollment	133.5
High school graduation rate	95.5%

Assessment test results

(percent scoring at proficient or advanced level)
	Language	Math
Grade 3	85.4%	82.3%
Grade 8	77.8%	73.3%
High school	90.1%	80.3%

SAT

Percent tested	70%
Average SAT math score	523
Average SAT verbal score	471

No Child Left Behind, 2003-04

Attendence rate (target = 90%)	94.9%
Drop rate	1%
Highly-qualified teachers	99.3%
District needs improvement?(AYP)	No

Municipal Finance

Fiscal Year 2005

Total tax levy	$45,715,490
County levy	4,599,591
County taxes	4,369,270
County library	0
County health	0
County open space	230,321
School levy	24,184,808
Local muni. budget	16,931,092
Misc. revenues	5,620,803
Total aid	$1,985,238
CMPTRA	948,447
Muni. block grant	79,909
Energy tax receipts	886,882
Homeland security	70,000

Fiscal Year 2006

Total aid	$1,985,237
CMPTRA	917,406
Muni. block grant	79,909
Energy tax receipts	917,922
Homeland security	70,000

Taxes

	2003	2004	2005
General tax rate per $100	2.99	3.060	3.200
Net valuation taxable	$1,406,988,333	$1,411,640,653	$1,431,510,850
State equalized value	$2,015,742,597	$2,250,433,432	$2,590,969,864
County equalization ratio	78.42	69.80	62.69

Demographics & Socio-Economic Characteristics
(2000 U.S. Census, except as noted)

Population
1980*	15,357
1990*	15,850
2000	16,530
Male	7,832
Female	8,698
2000 (revised)	15,460
2004 (estimate)*	16,005
Persons per sq. mi. of land	3,811

Race & Hispanic Origin, 2000
Race
White	14,826
Black/African American	496
Amer. Indian/Alaska Natv.	21
Asian	624
Natv. Hawaiian/Pac. Islander	38
Other Race	256
Two or more races	269
Hispanic origin, total	987
Mexican	43
Puerto Rican	70
Cuban	30
Other Hispanic	844

Age & Nativity, 2000
Under 5 years	981
18 years and over	13,126
21 years and over	11,333
65 years and over	2,157
85 years and over	301
Median Age	34.3
Native born	14,323
Foreign born	2,207

Educational Attainment, 2000
Population 25 years and over	10,178
0-8 yrs of school	3.8%
High School grad or higher	90.8%
Bachelor's degree or higher	56.8%
Graduate degree	26.0%

Income & Poverty, 1999
Per capita income	$38,416
Median household income	$82,847
Median family income	$101,798
Persons in poverty	469
H'holds receiving public assistance	59
H'holds receiving social security	1,524

Households, 2000
Total households	5,520
With persons under 18	1,807
With persons over 65	1,501
Family households	3,785
One-person households	1,415
Persons per household	2.53
Persons per family	3.05

Labor & Employment
Total civilian labor force, 2004**	9,485
Unemployment rate	3.6%
Total civilian labor force, 2000	9,199
Unemployment rate	12.5%

Employed persons 16 years and over by occupation, 2000
Managers & professionals	4,256
Service occupations	789
Sales & office occupations	2,219
Farming, fishing & forestry	12
Construction & maintenance	228
Production & transportation	545
Self-employed persons	468

*US Census Bureau
**New Jersey Department of Labor

General Information
Borough of Madison
Hartley Dodge Memorial
50 Kings Rd
Madison, NJ 07940
973-593-3042
Web site	www.rosenet.org/gov
Land area (sq. miles)	4.20
Water area (sq. miles)	0
Type of government	Borough
Form of government	B

Government

Legislative Districts
US Congressional	11
State Legislative	21

Local Officials, 2006
Mayor	Ellwood Kerkeslager
Admin/Manager	James Allison
Clerk	Marilyn Schaefer
Finance Dir/Treas	Robert Kalafut
Engineer	Robert Vogel
Attorney	Joseph Mezzacca Jr.
Tax assessor	Lisa Baratto
Tax collector	Francine DeAngelis
Building officer	Stephen Jones
Zoning officer	Leonard Taylor
Public Works	David Maines

Housing & Construction

Housing Units, 2000*
Total	5,641
Median rent	$1,036
Median SF home value	$362,400

New Privately Owned Housing Units
Authorized by Building Permit
	Units	Value
Total, 2004	18	$3,800,060
Single family	13	$3,595,060
Total, 2005	30	$12,876,860
Single family	30	$12,876,860

Real Property Valuation - parcels, 2005
	Number	Valuation
Total		$2,089,587,600
Vacant	90	19,401,800
Residential	4,168	1,664,970,400
Commercial	229	351,608,500
Industrial	6	3,422,000
Apartments	37	50,184,900
Farm land	0	0
Farm homestead	0	0

Average Property Value & Tax, 2005
Residential value	$399,465
Property tax	$8,221
FAIR rebate	$648

Public Library
Madison Public Library
39 Keep St
Madison, NJ 07940
973-377-0722
Director	Nancy Adamczyk

Library statistics, 2004
	Total	per capita
Volumes	128,873	7.8
Expenditure	$1,415,529	$85.63

Public Safety

Police
Chief	Vincent Chirico
Number of officers, 2004	35

Crime, 2004	Number	Rate
Total	145	9.4
Violent	9	0.6
Non-violent	136	8.9
Domestic Viol.	45	NA

Emergency/Fire
Director	Douglas Atchison

Public School District
(for school year 2004-2005 except as noted)

Madison School District
359 Woodland Rd
Madison, NJ 07940
973-593-3100
Superintendent	Arthur Travlos
Grade plan	K-12
Enrollment	2,213.5
Students per teacher	10.2
Per pupil expenditure	$12,613
Median faculty salary	$52,920
Median administrator salary	$106,895
Grade 12 enrollment	162.5
High school graduation rate	98.8%

Assessment test results
(percent scoring at proficient or advanced level)
	Language	Math
Grade 3	94.7%	93.0%
Grade 8	87.8%	81.3%
High school	97.4%	92.2%

SAT
Percent tested	91%
Average SAT math score	571
Average SAT verbal score	555

No Child Left Behind, 2003-04
Attendence rate (target = 90%)	96.1%
Drop rate	0.1%
Highly-qualified teachers	98.6%
District needs improvement?(AYP)	No

Municipal Finance

Fiscal Year 2005
Total tax levy	$43,265,610
County levy	7,575,992
County taxes	6,205,673
County library	0
County health	0
County open space	1,370,319
School levy	26,122,869
Local muni. budget	9,566,749
Misc. revenues	11,475,845
Total aid	$1,228,115
CMPTRA	522,093
Muni. block grant	69,355
Energy tax receipts	566,667
Homeland security	70,000

Fiscal Year 2006
Total aid	$1,228,114
CMPTRA	502,259
Muni. block grant	69,355
Energy tax receipts	586,500
Homeland security	70,000

Taxes
	2003	2004	2005
General tax rate per $100	1.92	1.990	2.060
Net valuation taxable	$2,164,434,220	$2,166,737,354	$2,102,380,915
State equalized value	$2,775,271,471	$2,929,329,780	$3,191,227,861
County equalization ratio	86.37	77.99	73.85

Demographics & Socio-Economic Characteristics

(2000 U.S. Census, except as noted)

Population

1980*	4,881
1990*	4,861
2000	4,409
Male	2,134
Female	2,275
2004 (estimate)*	4,392
Persons per sq. mi. of land	4,526

Race & Hispanic Origin, 2000

Race

White	3,395
Black/African American	785
Amer. Indian/Alaska Natv.	10
Asian	41
Natv. Hawaiian/Pac. Islander	1
Other Race	68
Two or more races	109
Hispanic origin, total	179
Mexican	21
Puerto Rican	104
Cuban	12
Other Hispanic	42

Age & Nativity, 2000

Under 5 years	298
18 years and over	3,318
21 years and over	3,164
65 years and over	563
85 years and over	39
Median Age	36.1
Native born	4,262
Foreign born	141

Educational Attainment, 2000

Population 25 years and over	2,979
0-8 yrs of school	5.0%
High School grad or higher	80.7%
Bachelor's degree or higher	12.2%
Graduate degree	2.7%

Income & Poverty, 1999

Per capita income	$19,032
Median household income	$43,728
Median family income	$50,791
Persons in poverty	346
H'holds receiving public assistance	30
H'holds receiving social security	444

Households, 2000

Total households	1,710
With persons under 18	599
With persons over 65	421
Family households	1,162
One-person households	439
Persons per household	2.57
Persons per family	3.12

Labor & Employment

Total civilian labor force, 2004**	2,908
Unemployment rate	3.7%
Total civilian labor force, 2000	2,482
Unemployment rate	7.9%

Employed persons 16 years and over by occupation, 2000

Managers & professionals	626
Service occupations	365
Sales & office occupations	678
Farming, fishing & forestry	0
Construction & maintenance	302
Production & transportation	316
Self-employed persons	120

*US Census Bureau
**New Jersey Department of Labor

General Information

Borough of Magnolia
438 W Evesham Ave
Magnolia, NJ 08049
856-783-1520

Web site	magnolia-nj.org
Land area (sq. miles)	0.97
Water area (sq. miles)	0
Type of government	Borough
Form of government	B

Government

Legislative Districts

US Congressional	1
State Legislative	5

Local Officials, 2006

Mayor	BettyAnn Cowling-Carson
Admin/Manager	John D. Keenan Jr.
Clerk	John D. Keenan Jr.
Finance Dir/Treas	Maureen Mitchell
Engineer	Bach Associates
Attorney	Sal Siciliano
Tax assessor	Thomas Davis
Tax collector	Maureen Mitchell
Building officer	Chris Mecca
Zoning officer	NA
Public Works	Steve Pacella

Housing & Construction

Housing Units, 2000*

Total	1,836
Median rent	$599
Median SF home value	$90,900

New Privately Owned Housing Units
Authorized by Building Permit

	Units	Value
Total, 2004	5	$170,924
Single family	2	$169,224
Total, 2005	13	$754,723
Single family	10	$753,023

Real Property Valuation - parcels, 2005

	Number	Valuation
Total		$159,222,000
Vacant	134	2,838,200
Residential	1,415	127,653,600
Commercial	76	16,452,400
Industrial	4	5,331,900
Apartments	5	6,945,900
Farm land	0	0
Farm homestead	0	0

Average Property Value & Tax, 2005

Residential value	$90,215
Property tax	$4,182
FAIR rebate	$620

Public Library

No public municipal library.

Library statistics, 2004

	Total	per capita
Volumes	NA	NA
Expenditure	NA	NA

Public Safety

Police

Chief	Rob Doyle
Number of officers, 2004	12

Crime, 2004	Number	Rate
Total	150	34
Violent	25	5.7
Non-violent	125	28.4
Domestic Viol.	53	NA

Emergency/Fire

Director	Gary Riebel

Public School District

(for school year 2004-2005 except as noted)

Magnolia Borough School District
420 N Warwick Rd
Magnolia, NJ 08049
856-783-6343

Superintendent	Warren Pross
Grade plan	K-8
Enrollment	494.0
Students per teacher	11.9
Per pupil expenditure	$11,533
Median faculty salary	$55,917
Median administrator salary	$62,041
Grade 12 enrollment	NA
High school graduation rate	NA

Assessment test results
(percent scoring at proficient or advanced level)

	Language	Math
Grade 3	78.3%	61.7%
Grade 8	58.3%	40.9%
High school	NA	NA

SAT

Percent tested	NA
Average SAT math score	NA
Average SAT verbal score	NA

No Child Left Behind, 2003-04

Attendence rate (target = 90%)	95.1%
Drop rate	NA
Highly-qualified teachers	100%
District needs improvement?(AYP)	No

Municipal Finance

Fiscal Year 2005

Total tax levy	$7,390,219
County levy	1,562,776
County taxes	1,440,345
County library	103,549
County health	0
County open space	18,882
School levy	4,144,935
Local muni. budget	1,682,508
Misc. revenues	1,548,962
Total aid	$643,526
CMPTRA	274,994
Muni. block grant	21,270
Energy tax receipts	322,262
Homeland security	25,000

Fiscal Year 2006

Total aid	$643,526
CMPTRA	263,715
Muni. block grant	21,270
Energy tax receipts	333,541
Homeland security	25,000

Taxes

	2003	2004	2005
General tax rate per $100	4.36	4.546	4.636
Net valuation taxable	$159,072,143	$159,205,664	$159,430,251
State equalized value	$174,939,121	$187,369,201	$224,739,570
County equalization ratio	97.77	90.93	84.95

Demographics & Socio-Economic Characteristics

(2000 U.S. Census, except as noted)

Population

1980*	12,127
1990*	17,905
2000	24,062
Male	11,435
Female	12,627
2004 (estimate)*	24,682
Persons per sq. mi. of land	952

Race & Hispanic Origin, 2000

Race
White	21,157
Black/African American	519
Amer. Indian/Alaska Natv.	169
Asian	1,518
Natv. Hawaiian/Pac. Islander	7
Other Race	361
Two or more races	331
Hispanic origin, total	1,028
Mexican	136
Puerto Rican	264
Cuban	89
Other Hispanic	539

Age & Nativity, 2000

Under 5 years	1,672
18 years and over	18,717
21 years and over	17,492
65 years and over	2,572
85 years and over	204
Median Age	37.3
Native born	20,868
Foreign born	3,194

Educational Attainment, 2000

Population 25 years and over	16,374
0-8 yrs of school	2.3%
High School grad or higher	93.6%
Bachelor's degree or higher	49.5%
Graduate degree	17.1%

Income & Poverty, 1999

Per capita income	$44,709
Median household income	$79,500
Median family income	$94,484
Persons in poverty	458
H'holds receiving public assistance	71
H'holds receiving social security	1,984

Households, 2000

Total households	9,340
With persons under 18	2,955
With persons over 65	1,923
Family households	6,288
One-person households	2,612
Persons per household	2.43
Persons per family	3.01

Labor & Employment

Total civilian labor force, 2004**	11,599
Unemployment rate	3.6%
Total civilian labor force, 2000	13,481
Unemployment rate	5.6%

Employed persons 16 years and over by occupation, 2000
Managers & professionals	6,323
Service occupations	1,181
Sales & office occupations	3,932
Farming, fishing & forestry	8
Construction & maintenance	533
Production & transportation	754
Self-employed persons	777

*US Census Bureau
**New Jersey Department of Labor

General Information

Township of Mahwah
475 Corporate Dr
Mahwah, NJ 07430
201-529-5757

Web site	www.mahwahtwp.org
Land area (sq. miles)	25.93
Water area (sq. miles)	0.27
Type of government	Township
Form of government	MC '50

Government

Legislative Districts

US Congressional	5
State Legislative	40

Local Officials, 2006

Mayor	Richard Martel
Admin/Manager	Brian Campion
Clerk	Kathrine Coletta
Finance Dir/Treas	Kenneth Sesholtz
Engineer	Kevin Boswell
Attorney	Terry Paul Bottinelli
Tax assessor	Stuart Stolarz
Tax collector	Elizabeth Villano
Building officer	Gary Montroy
Zoning officer	NA
Public Works	Stanley Spiech

Housing & Construction

Housing Units, 2000*

Total	9,577
Median rent	$1,160
Median SF home value	$334,100

New Privately Owned Housing Units Authorized by Building Permit

	Units	Value
Total, 2004	31	$13,316,525
Single family	31	$13,316,525
Total, 2005	25	$10,387,177
Single family	25	$10,387,177

Real Property Valuation - parcels, 2005

	Number	Valuation
Total		$4,083,356,399
Vacant	486	84,574,300
Residential	9,142	3,201,297,499
Commercial	154	513,734,000
Industrial	66	245,746,200
Apartments	8	31,751,800
Farm land	10	5,746,200
Farm homestead	18	506,400

Average Property Value & Tax, 2005

Residential value	$349,542
Property tax	$5,896
FAIR rebate	$553

Public Library

Mahwah Public Library
100 Ridge Rd
Mahwah, NJ 07430
201-529-7323

Director ... Kenneth Giaimo

Library statistics, 2004

	Total	per capita
Volumes	95,616	3.97
Expenditure	$1,482,294	$61.60

Public Safety

Police

Chief	James Batelli
Number of officers, 2004	55

Crime, 2004	Number	Rate
Total	244	10
Violent	13	0.5
Non-violent	231	9.4
Domestic Viol.	158	NA

Emergency/Fire

Director ... Joseph Mantineo

Public School District

(for school year 2004-2005 except as noted)

Mahwah Township School District
60 Ridge Rd
Mahwah, NJ 07430
201-529-6803

Superintendent	Charles Montesano
Grade plan	K-12
Enrollment	3,428.5
Students per teacher	11.5
Per pupil expenditure	$13,328
Median faculty salary	$54,203
Median administrator salary	$110,315
Grade 12 enrollment	172.0
High school graduation rate	91.3%

Assessment test results

(percent scoring at proficient or advanced level)
	Language	Math
Grade 3	94.8%	89.5%
Grade 8	82.8%	75.2%
High school	95.8%	92.0%

SAT

Percent tested	90%
Average SAT math score	565
Average SAT verbal score	538

No Child Left Behind, 2003-04

Attendence rate (target = 90%)	96.5%
Drop rate	2.2%
Highly-qualified teachers	96.6%
District needs improvement?(AYP)	No

Municipal Finance

Fiscal Year 2005

Total tax levy	$68,968,376
County levy	10,340,562
County taxes	9,822,655
County library	0
County health	0
County open space	517,907
School levy	43,693,908
Local muni. budget	14,933,907
Misc. revenues	14,033,466
Total aid	$5,955,617
CMPTRA	618,340
Muni. block grant	94,348
Energy tax receipts	5,152,929
Homeland security	90,000

Fiscal Year 2006

Total aid	$5,955,616
CMPTRA	437,987
Muni. block grant	94,348
Energy tax receipts	5,333,281
Homeland security	90,000

Taxes

	2003	2004	2005
General tax rate per $100	1.41	1.550	1.690
Net valuation taxable	$4,047,413,095	$4,063,097,743	$4,088,426,805
State equalized value	$4,674,226,926	$5,118,221,305	$5,805,775,071
County equalization ratio	95.18	86.59	79.36

Demographics & Socio-Economic Characteristics

(2000 U.S. Census, except as noted)

Population

1980*	18,914
1990*	26,716
2000	33,423
Male	16,029
Female	17,394
2004 (estimate)*	36,988
Persons per sq. mi. of land	1,200

Race & Hispanic Origin, 2000

Race

White	30,687
Black/African American	664
Amer. Indian/Alaska Natv.	9
Asian	1,514
Natv. Hawaiian/Pac. Islander	5
Other Race	177
Two or more races	367
Hispanic origin, total	1,183
Mexican	86
Puerto Rican	579
Cuban	143
Other Hispanic	375

Age & Nativity, 2000

Under 5 years	2,220
18 years and over	23,283
21 years and over	22,349
65 years and over	3,883
85 years and over	589
Median Age	38.2
Native born	29,956
Foreign born	3,467

Educational Attainment, 2000

Population 25 years and over	21,286
0-8 yrs of school	2.4%
High School grad or higher	92.5%
Bachelor's degree or higher	39.3%
Graduate degree	14.5%

Income & Poverty, 1999

Per capita income	$32,142
Median household income	$83,575
Median family income	$94,112
Persons in poverty	1,259
H'holds receiving public assistance	56
H'holds receiving social security	2,982

Households, 2000

Total households	10,781
With persons under 18	5,252
With persons over 65	2,800
Family households	9,001
One-person households	1,607
Persons per household	3.09
Persons per family	3.45

Labor & Employment

Total civilian labor force, 2004**	14,185
Unemployment rate	3.7%
Total civilian labor force, 2000	15,892
Unemployment rate	3.4%

Employed persons 16 years and over by occupation, 2000

Managers & professionals	7,206
Service occupations	1,264
Sales & office occupations	4,897
Farming, fishing & forestry	23
Construction & maintenance	1,047
Production & transportation	922
Self-employed persons	1,041

*US Census Bureau
**New Jersey Department of Labor

General Information

Township of Manalapan
120 Route 522 & Taylors Mills Rd
Manalapan, NJ 07726
732-446-3200

Web site	www.twp.manalapan.nj.us
Land area (sq. miles)	30.82
Water area (sq. miles)	0.05
Type of government	Township
Form of government	TC

Government

Legislative Districts

US Congressional	12
State Legislative	12

Local Officials, 2006

Mayor	Drew Shapiro
Admin/Manager	Alayne M. Shepler
Clerk	Rose Ann Weeden
Finance Dir/Treas	Patricia Addario
Engineer	Greg Valesi
Attorney	James Kinneally
Tax assessor	Sharon Hartman
Tax collector	Hope Lewis
Building officer	Richard Hogan
Zoning officer	Mark Micali
Public Works	John Lewis

Housing & Construction

Housing Units, 2000*

Total	11,066
Median rent	$1,124
Median SF home value	$257,100

New Privately Owned Housing Units Authorized by Building Permit

	Units	Value
Total, 2004	284	$44,055,439
Single family	269	$42,979,816
Total, 2005	202	$35,767,435
Single family	199	$35,583,137

Real Property Valuation - parcels, 2005

	Number	Valuation
Total		$2,445,598,100
Vacant	1,110	79,348,800
Residential	12,217	2,154,592,600
Commercial	300	181,799,700
Industrial	9	11,519,100
Apartments	0	0
Farm land	96	16,211,800
Farm homestead	186	2,126,100

Average Property Value & Tax, 2005

Residential value	$173,887
Property tax	$6,134
FAIR rebate	$606

Public Library

Monmouth County Library
125 Symmes Rd
Manalapan Twp., NJ 07726
732-431-7220

Director ... Ken Sheinbaum

Library statistics, 2004

	Total	per capita
Volumes	NA	NA
Expenditure	NA	NA

Public Safety

Police

Chief	Stuart C. Brown
Number of officers, 2004	65

Crime, 2004	Number	Rate
Total	304	8.5
Violent	20	0.6
Non-violent	284	8
Domestic Viol.	214	NA

Emergency/Fire

Director ... Richard Hogan

Public School District

(for school year 2004-2005 except as noted)

Manalapan-Englishtown Reg. School Dist.
54 Main St
Englishtown, NJ 07726
732-786-2500

Superintendent	Maureen Lally
Grade plan	K-8
Enrollment	5,486.0
Students per teacher	12.3
Per pupil expenditure	$9,756
Median faculty salary	$49,200
Median administrator salary	$90,160
Grade 12 enrollment	NA
High school graduation rate	NA

Assessment test results

(percent scoring at proficient or advanced level)

	Language	Math
Grade 3	93.9%	88.5%
Grade 8	92.5%	82.7%
High school	NA	NA

SAT

Percent tested	NA
Average SAT math score	NA
Average SAT verbal score	NA

No Child Left Behind, 2003-04

Attendence rate (target = 90%)	95.5%
Drop rate	NA
Highly-qualified teachers	97.8%
District needs improvement?(AYP)	No

Municipal Finance

Fiscal Year 2005

Total tax levy	$86,368,512
County levy	15,412,646
County taxes	13,830,144
County library	761,826
County health	0
County open space	820,675
School levy	58,860,866
Local muni. budget	12,095,001
Misc. revenues	16,361,230
Total aid	$5,248,407
CMPTRA	1,121,262
Muni. block grant	131,052
Energy tax receipts	3,856,093
Homeland security	140,000

Fiscal Year 2006

Total aid	$5,248,408
CMPTRA	986,299
Muni. block grant	131,052
Energy tax receipts	3,991,057
Homeland security	140,000

Taxes

	2003	2004	2005
General tax rate per $100	3.46	3.591	3.528
Net valuation taxable	$2,341,783,362	$2,377,859,516	$2,448,575,455
State equalized value	$3,980,593,850	$4,480,195,412	$5,060,085,669
County equalization ratio	65.41	58.83	53.04

Demographics & Socio-Economic Characteristics
(2000 U.S. Census, except as noted)

Population
1980*	5,354
1990*	5,369
2000	6,310
Male	3,106
Female	3,204
2004 (estimate)*	6,286
Persons per sq. mi. of land	4,562

Race & Hispanic Origin, 2000
Race
White	6,177
Black/African American	26
Amer. Indian/Alaska Natv.	7
Asian	28
Natv. Hawaiian/Pac. Islander	0
Other Race	30
Two or more races	42
Hispanic origin, total	283
Mexican	174
Puerto Rican	18
Cuban	11
Other Hispanic	80

Age & Nativity, 2000
Under 5 years	391
18 years and over	4,808
21 years and over	4,623
65 years and over	942
85 years and over	113
Median Age	39
Native born	6,021
Foreign born	289

Educational Attainment, 2000
Population 25 years and over	4,398
0-8 yrs of school	1.8%
High School grad or higher	92.9%
Bachelor's degree or higher	40.4%
Graduate degree	13.2%

Income & Poverty, 1999
Per capita income	$32,898
Median household income	$63,079
Median family income	$73,670
Persons in poverty	195
H'holds receiving public assistance	46
H'holds receiving social security	696

Households, 2000
Total households	2,600
With persons under 18	810
With persons over 65	715
Family households	1,635
One-person households	785
Persons per household	2.43
Persons per family	3.06

Labor & Employment
Total civilian labor force, 2004**	2,985
Unemployment rate	2.3%
Total civilian labor force, 2000	3,328
Unemployment rate	2.4%

Employed persons 16 years and over by occupation, 2000
Managers & professionals	1,289
Service occupations	455
Sales & office occupations	1,007
Farming, fishing & forestry	9
Construction & maintenance	214
Production & transportation	273
Self-employed persons	251

*US Census Bureau
**New Jersey Department of Labor

General Information
Borough of Manasquan
201 East Main St
Manasquan, NJ 08736
732-223-0544
Web site	www.manasquan-nj.com
Land area (sq. miles)	1.38
Water area (sq. miles)	1.15
Type of government	Borough
Form of government	B

Government

Legislative Districts
US Congressional	4
State Legislative	10

Local Officials, 2006
Mayor	Richard Dunne
Admin/Manager	John Trengrove
Clerk	Colleen Scimeca
Finance Dir/Treas	Joanne Madden
Engineer	T & M Associates
Attorney	Kenneth Fitzsimmons
Tax assessor	Holly Reycraft
Tax collector	NA
Building officer	Sandy Ratz
Zoning officer	NA
Public Works	NA

Housing & Construction

Housing Units, 2000*
Total	3,531
Median rent	$808
Median SF home value	$265,300

New Privately Owned Housing Units
Authorized by Building Permit
	Units	Value
Total, 2004	40	$8,286,073
Single family	40	$8,286,073
Total, 2005	91	$19,677,176
Single family	91	$19,677,176

Real Property Valuation - parcels, 2005
	Number	Valuation
Total		$1,527,700,400
Vacant	133	31,962,200
Residential	2,811	1,348,029,700
Commercial	186	129,656,800
Industrial	12	8,353,300
Apartments	9	9,698,400
Farm land	0	0
Farm homestead	0	0

Average Property Value & Tax, 2005
Residential value	$479,555
Property tax	$6,556
FAIR rebate	$627

Public Library
Manasquan Public Library
55 Broad St
Manasquan, NJ 08736
732-223-1503
Director . . . . Margo Petersen

Library statistics, 2004
	Total	per capita
Volumes	34,062	5.40
Expenditure	$144,827	$22.95

Public Safety
Police
Chief	Daniel Scimeca
Number of officers, 2004	18

Crime, 2004	Number	Rate
Total	159	24.8
Violent	15	2.3
Non-violent	144	22.5
Domestic Viol.	22	NA

Emergency/Fire
Director . . . . David Walker

Public School District
(for school year 2004-2005 except as noted)

Manasquan School District
169 Broad St
Manasquan, NJ 08736
732-528-8800
Superintendent	Carole Morris
Grade plan	K-12
Enrollment	1,727.0
Students per teacher	11.8
Per pupil expenditure	$10,187
Median faculty salary	$51,700
Median administrator salary	$109,475
Grade 12 enrollment	231.5
High school graduation rate	96.1%

Assessment test results
(percent scoring at proficient or advanced level)
	Language	Math
Grade 3	96.4%	96.4%
Grade 8	87.3%	82.5%
High school	96.6%	88.9%

SAT
Percent tested	92%
Average SAT math score	519
Average SAT verbal score	516

No Child Left Behind, 2003-04
Attendence rate (target = 90%)	95.1%
Drop rate	1.7%
Highly-qualified teachers	100%
District needs improvement?(AYP)	No

Municipal Finance
Fiscal Year 2005
Total tax levy	$20,894,071
County levy	5,380,976
County taxes	4,750,726
County library	261,704
County health	86,631
County open space	281,915
School levy	10,922,412
Local muni. budget	4,590,683
Misc. revenues	2,643,394
Total aid	$636,301
CMPTRA	154,705
Muni. block grant	24,742
Energy tax receipts	406,854
Homeland security	50,000

Fiscal Year 2006
Total aid	$636,301
CMPTRA	140,465
Muni. block grant	24,742
Energy tax receipts	421,094
Homeland security	50,000

Taxes
	2003	2004	2005
General tax rate per $100	2.94	1.234	1.368
Net valuation taxable	$607,982,236	$1,526,940,760	$1,528,308,179
State equalized value	$1,246,120,590	$1,584,263,971	$1,737,701,170
County equalization ratio	58.02	120.61	96.38

Demographics & Socio-Economic Characteristics
(2000 U.S. Census, except as noted)

Population
1980*	27,987
1990*	35,976
2000	38,928
Male	16,459
Female	22,469
2000 (revised)	38,800
2004 (estimate)*	42,112
Persons per sq. mi. of land	510

Race & Hispanic Origin, 2000
Race
White	36,724
Black/African American	1,190
Amer. Indian/Alaska Natv.	45
Asian	338
Natv. Hawaiian/Pac. Islander	10
Other Race	267
Two or more races	354
Hispanic origin, total	1,024
Mexican	62
Puerto Rican	590
Cuban	48
Other Hispanic	324

Age & Nativity, 2000
Under 5 years	1,019
18 years and over	34,744
21 years and over	34,114
65 years and over	21,210
85 years and over	3,645
Median Age	67.7
Native born	35,971
Foreign born	2,989

Educational Attainment, 2000
Population 25 years and over	33,532
0-8 yrs of school	7.2%
High School grad or higher	75.5%
Bachelor's degree or higher	12.7%
Graduate degree	4.1%

Income & Poverty, 1999
Per capita income	$22,409
Median household income	$29,525
Median family income	$43,363
Persons in poverty	2,102
H'holds receiving public assistance	396
H'holds receiving social security	15,035

Households, 2000
Total households	20,688
With persons under 18	2,242
With persons over 65	15,118
Family households	10,814
One-person households	9,318
Persons per household	1.85
Persons per family	2.53

Labor & Employment
Total civilian labor force, 2004**	10,261
Unemployment rate	6.0%
Total civilian labor force, 2000	10,165
Unemployment rate	6.8%

Employed persons 16 years and over by occupation, 2000
Managers & professionals	2,597
Service occupations	1,683
Sales & office occupations	2,567
Farming, fishing & forestry	8
Construction & maintenance	1,155
Production & transportation	1,467
Self-employed persons	531

*US Census Bureau
**New Jersey Department of Labor

General Information
Township of Manchester
1 Colonial Dr
Manchester, NJ 08759
732-657-8121

Web site	www.manchestertwp.com
Land area (sq. miles)	82.60
Water area (sq. miles)	0.29
Type of government	Township
Form of government	MC'50

Government

Legislative Districts
US Congressional	4
State Legislative	9

Local Officials, 2006
Mayor	Michael Fressola
Admin/Manager	Karen Infanger
Clerk	Marie Pellecchia
Finance Dir/Treas	William Garofalo
Engineer	T & M Assoc.
Attorney	Steve Secare
Tax assessor	Martin Lynch
Tax collector	Andrea Gaskill
Building officer	Michael Martin
Zoning officer	John Tilton
Public Works	Stephen Stanziano

Housing & Construction

Housing Units, 2000*
Total	22,681
Median rent	$940
Median SF home value	$85,000

New Privately Owned Housing Units Authorized by Building Permit
	Units	Value
Total, 2004	17	$1,996,520
Single family	11	$1,824,641
Total, 2005	24	$2,195,472
Single family	11	$2,023,922

Real Property Valuation - parcels, 2005
	Number	Valuation
Total		$1,986,893,581
Vacant	4,360	63,232,600
Residential	14,849	1,510,419,781
Commercial	118	132,491,900
Industrial	10	9,971,600
Apartments	32	269,122,200
Farm land	8	1,151,200
Farm homestead	21	504,300

Average Property Value & Tax, 2005
Residential value	$101,609
Property tax	$2,802
FAIR rebate	$849

Public Library
Manchester Branch Library†
21 Colonial Dr
Manchester, NJ 08759
732-657-7600

Branch Librarian	Susan Scro

Library statistics, 2004
	Total	per capita
Volumes	NA	NA
Expenditure	NA	NA

†Branch of County Library

Public Safety

Police
Chief	William Brase
Number of officers, 2004	66

Crime, 2004	Number	Rate
Total	394	9.3
Violent	25	0.6
Non-violent	369	8.7
Domestic Viol.	254	NA

Emergency/Fire
Director	NA

Public School District
(for school year 2004-2005 except as noted)

Manchester Township School District
121 Route 539
Whiting, NJ 08759
732-350-5900

Superintendent	William DeFeo
Grade plan	K-12
Enrollment	3,225.0
Students per teacher	10.6
Per pupil expenditure	$10,798
Median faculty salary	$48,622
Median administrator salary	$97,620
Grade 12 enrollment	242.0
High school graduation rate	89.2%

Assessment test results
(percent scoring at proficient or advanced level)
	Language	Math
Grade 3	85.8%	87.4%
Grade 8	76.6%	70.5%
High school	81.2%	77.1%

SAT
Percent tested	55%
Average SAT math score	491
Average SAT verbal score	462

No Child Left Behind, 2003-04
Attendence rate (target = 90%)	94.5%
Drop rate	1.4%
Highly-qualified teachers	98.4%
District needs improvement?(AYP)	No

Municipal Finance

Fiscal Year 2005
Total tax levy	$54,920,600
County levy	12,518,496
County taxes	10,547,152
County library	1,108,066
County health	469,664
County open space	393,615
School levy	30,056,570
Local muni. budget	12,345,534
Misc. revenues	13,151,083
Total aid	$4,274,921
CMPTRA	1,480,237
Muni. block grant	157,420
Energy tax receipts	2,486,104
Homeland security	140,000

Fiscal Year 2006
Total aid	$4,274,921
CMPTRA	1,393,223
Muni. block grant	157,420
Energy tax receipts	2,573,118
Homeland security	140,000

Taxes
	2003	2004	2005
General tax rate per $100	2.57	2.653	2.759
Net valuation taxable	$1,848,932,872	$1,923,170,288	$1,991,302,044
State equalized value	$2,525,174,641	$3,163,298,447	$3,649,747,148
County equalization ratio	82.44	73.22	60.73

Demographics & Socio-Economic Characteristics
(2000 U.S. Census, except as noted)

Population
1980*	1,740
1990*	1,693
2000	1,559
Male	763
Female	796
2004 (estimate)*	1,572
Persons per sq. mi. of land	45

Race & Hispanic Origin, 2000
Race
White	1,179
Black/African American	326
Amer. Indian/Alaska Natv.	8
Asian	6
Natv. Hawaiian/Pac. Islander	0
Other Race	27
Two or more races	13
Hispanic origin, total	52
Mexican	12
Puerto Rican	23
Cuban	0
Other Hispanic	17

Age & Nativity, 2000
Under 5 years	86
18 years and over	1,207
21 years and over	1,182
65 years and over	365
85 years and over	78
Median Age	42.7
Native born	1,534
Foreign born	25

Educational Attainment, 2000
Population 25 years and over	1,140
0-8 yrs of school	10.2%
High School grad or higher	76.1%
Bachelor's degree or higher	20.6%
Graduate degree	6.0%

Income & Poverty, 1999
Per capita income	$24,262
Median household income	$52,625
Median family income	$62,500
Persons in poverty	98
H'holds receiving public assistance	17
H'holds receiving social security	185

Households, 2000
Total households	539
With persons under 18	173
With persons over 65	184
Family households	409
One-person households	111
Persons per household	2.63
Persons per family	3.02

Labor & Employment
Total civilian labor force, 2004**	715
Unemployment rate	5.8%
Total civilian labor force, 2000	724
Unemployment rate	4.1%

Employed persons 16 years and over by occupation, 2000
Managers & professionals	269
Service occupations	70
Sales & office occupations	185
Farming, fishing & forestry	14
Construction & maintenance	52
Production & transportation	104
Self-employed persons	42

*US Census Bureau
**New Jersey Department of Labor

General Information
Township of Mannington
491 Route 45
Mannington, NJ 08079
856-935-2359

Web site	NA
Land area (sq. miles)	34.78
Water area (sq. miles)	3.64
Type of government	Township
Form of government	TC

Government

Legislative Districts
US Congressional	2
State Legislative	3

Local Officials, 2006
Mayor	Donald Asay
Admin/Manager	Mary Hancock
Clerk	Mary Hancock
Finance Dir/Treas	Nancy Sutton
Engineer	Fralinger Engineering
Attorney	William C. Horner
Tax assessor	Donna Harris
Tax collector	NA
Building officer	NA
Zoning officer	NA
Public Works	NA

Housing & Construction

Housing Units, 2000*
Total	573
Median rent	$613
Median SF home value	$115,400

New Privately Owned Housing Units Authorized by Building Permit
	Units	Value
Total, 2004	6	$903,452
Single family	6	$903,452
Total, 2005	7	$844,300
Single family	5	$842,000

Real Property Valuation - parcels, 2005
	Number	Valuation
Total		$123,691,700
Vacant	228	1,464,400
Residential	403	36,980,900
Commercial	39	26,732,900
Industrial	4	28,112,200
Apartments	0	0
Farm land	177	25,433,100
Farm homestead	430	4,968,200

Average Property Value & Tax, 2005
Residential value	$50,359
Property tax	$1,479
FAIR rebate	$541

Public Library

No public municipal library.

Library statistics, 2004
	Total	per capita
Volumes	NA	NA
Expenditure	NA	NA

Public Safety

Police
Chief	NA
Number of officers, 2004	0

Crime, 2004	Number	Rate
Total	22	14
Violent	4	2.6
Non-violent	18	11.5
Domestic Viol.	6	NA

Emergency/Fire
Director	S. Lee Butcher

Public School District
(for school year 2004-2005 except as noted)

Mannington Township School District
495 Route 45
Salem, NJ 08079
856-935-1078

Superintendent	Jean Rishel
Grade plan	K-12
Enrollment	188.0
Students per teacher	9.8
Per pupil expenditure	$12,290
Median faculty salary	$46,736
Median administrator salary	$86,944
Grade 12 enrollment	NA
High school graduation rate	NA

Assessment test results
(percent scoring at proficient or advanced level)
	Language	Math
Grade 3	83.4%	77.7%
Grade 8	78.6%	64.3%
High school	NA	NA

SAT
Percent tested	NA
Average SAT math score	NA
Average SAT verbal score	NA

No Child Left Behind, 2003-04
Attendence rate (target = 90%)	96.4%
Drop rate	NA
Highly-qualified teachers	100%
District needs improvement?(AYP)	No

Municipal Finance

Fiscal Year 2005
Total tax levy	$3,831,436
County levy	1,806,258
County taxes	1,770,418
County library	0
County health	0
County open space	35,840
School levy	1,893,711
Local muni. budget	131,467
Misc. revenues	838,804
Total aid	$384,887
CMPTRA	150,726
Muni. block grant	7,408
Energy tax receipts	226,753
Homeland security	0

Fiscal Year 2006
Total aid	$384,888
CMPTRA	142,790
Muni. block grant	7,408
Energy tax receipts	234,690
Homeland security	NA

Taxes
	2003	2004	2005
General tax rate per $100	2.98	2.781	3.082
Net valuation taxable	$122,834,067	$123,593,492	$124,321,529
State equalized value	$149,287,879	$173,992,707	$187,626,817
County equalization ratio	73	82.28	70.91

Demographics & Socio-Economic Characteristics
(2000 U.S. Census, except as noted)

Population
1980*	2,523
1990*	3,874
2000	5,090
Male	2,442
Female	2,648
2004 (estimate)*	7,800
Persons per sq. mi. of land	359

Race & Hispanic Origin, 2000
Race
White	4,857
Black/African American	97
Amer. Indian/Alaska Natv.	9
Asian	76
Natv. Hawaiian/Pac. Islander	2
Other Race	11
Two or more races	38
Hispanic origin, total	93
Mexican	9
Puerto Rican	55
Cuban	4
Other Hispanic	25

Age & Nativity, 2000
Under 5 years	241
18 years and over	4,140
21 years and over	4,019
65 years and over	1,623
85 years and over	87
Median Age	48.8
Native born	4,824
Foreign born	266

Educational Attainment, 2000
Population 25 years and over	3,816
0-8 yrs of school	3.6%
High School grad or higher	85.6%
Bachelor's degree or higher	25.1%
Graduate degree	11.4%

Income & Poverty, 1999
Per capita income	$26,559
Median household income	$50,757
Median family income	$59,040
Persons in poverty	228
H'holds receiving public assistance	4
H'holds receiving social security	1,149

Households, 2000
Total households	2,077
With persons under 18	523
With persons over 65	1,067
Family households	1,561
One-person households	469
Persons per household	2.45
Persons per family	2.86

Labor & Employment
Total civilian labor force, 2004**	1,919
Unemployment rate	2.7%
Total civilian labor force, 2000	2,105
Unemployment rate	4.4%

Employed persons 16 years and over by occupation, 2000
Managers & professionals	674
Service occupations	282
Sales & office occupations	563
Farming, fishing & forestry	14
Construction & maintenance	257
Production & transportation	222
Self-employed persons	112

*US Census Bureau
**New Jersey Department of Labor

General Information
Township of Mansfield
PO Box 249
Columbus, NJ 08022
609-298-0542

Web site	NA
Land area (sq. miles)	21.72
Water area (sq. miles)	0.14
Type of government	Township
Form of government	TC

Government

Legislative Districts
US Congressional	4
State Legislative	8

Local Officials, 2006
Mayor	Arthur R. Puglia
Admin/Manager	Joseph Broski
Clerk	Linda Semus
Finance Dir/Treas	Joseph Monzo
Engineer	Leonard Faiola
Attorney	Michael Magee
Tax assessor	Harry Supple Jr.
Tax collector	NA
Building officer	Jeffrey Jones
Zoning officer	NA
Public Works	NA

Housing & Construction

Housing Units, 2000*
Total	2,122
Median rent	$706
Median SF home value	$153,800

New Privately Owned Housing Units
Authorized by Building Permit
	Units	Value
Total, 2004	69	$9,616,467
Single family	69	$9,616,467
Total, 2005	79	$16,087,902
Single family	79	$16,087,902

Real Property Valuation - parcels, 2005
	Number	Valuation
Total		$630,629,115
Vacant	305	13,961,600
Residential	3,171	541,902,415
Commercial	80	44,453,400
Industrial	2	2,331,200
Apartments	5	918,900
Farm land	123	24,745,000
Farm homestead	231	2,316,600

Average Property Value & Tax, 2005
Residential value	$159,970
Property tax	$5,381
FAIR rebate	$729

Public Library

No public municipal library.

Library statistics, 2004
	Total	per capita
Volumes	NA	NA
Expenditure	NA	NA

Public Safety

Police
Chief	Richard Bendel (Civ. PS Dir)
Number of officers, 2004	12

Crime, 2004	Number	Rate
Total	176	23.8
Violent	4	0.5
Non-violent	172	23.2
Domestic Viol.	13	NA

Emergency/Fire
Director	Sean Gable

Public School District
(for school year 2004-2005 except as noted)

Mansfield Township School District
200 Mansfield Rd E
Columbus, NJ 08022
609-298-2037

Superintendent	Charles McGlone (Int)
Grade plan	K-6
Enrollment	635.0
Students per teacher	10.2
Per pupil expenditure	$9,901
Median faculty salary	$38,880
Median administrator salary	$91,287
Grade 12 enrollment	NA
High school graduation rate	NA

Assessment test results
(percent scoring at proficient or advanced level)
	Language	Math
Grade 3	91.8%	90.7%
Grade 8	NA	NA
High school	NA	NA

SAT
Percent tested	NA
Average SAT math score	NA
Average SAT verbal score	NA

No Child Left Behind, 2003-04
Attendence rate (target = 90%)	95.4%
Drop rate	NA
Highly-qualified teachers	100%
District needs improvement?(AYP)	No

Municipal Finance

Fiscal Year 2005
Total tax levy	$21,264,740
County levy	4,302,464
County taxes	3,609,341
County library	316,020
County health	0
County open space	377,103
School levy	15,003,432
Local muni. budget	1,958,843
Misc. revenues	3,454,820
Total aid	$750,277
CMPTRA	135,210
Muni. block grant	19,958
Energy tax receipts	545,109
Homeland security	50,000

Fiscal Year 2006
Total aid	$750,278
CMPTRA	116,132
Muni. block grant	19,958
Energy tax receipts	564,188
Homeland security	50,000

Taxes
	2003	2004	2005
General tax rate per $100	2.91	3.243	3.365
Net valuation taxable	$555,241,449	$601,702,067	$632,142,896
State equalized value	$753,994,363	$894,169,669	$1,050,944,133
County equalization ratio	80.16	73.64	67.23

Demographics & Socio-Economic Characteristics
(2000 U.S. Census, except as noted)

Population
1980*	5,780
1990*	7,154
2000	6,653
Male	3,237
Female	3,416
2000 (revised)	8,072
2004 (estimate)*	8,322
Persons per sq. mi. of land	278

Race & Hispanic Origin, 2000
Race
White	6,048
Black/African American	300
Amer. Indian/Alaska Natv.	16
Asian	81
Natv. Hawaiian/Pac. Islander	0
Other Race	106
Two or more races	102
Hispanic origin, total	291
Mexican	25
Puerto Rican	63
Cuban	30
Other Hispanic	173

Age & Nativity, 2000
Under 5 years	493
18 years and over	4,857
21 years and over	4,670
65 years and over	776
85 years and over	126
Median Age	37.1
Native born	6,290
Foreign born	363

Educational Attainment, 2000
Population 25 years and over	4,457
0-8 yrs of school	3.5%
High School grad or higher	88.6%
Bachelor's degree or higher	27.5%
Graduate degree	9.3%

Income & Poverty, 1999
Per capita income	$26,277
Median household income	$61,763
Median family income	$76,102
Persons in poverty	251
H'holds receiving public assistance	30
H'holds receiving social security	508

Households, 2000
Total households	2,334
With persons under 18	961
With persons over 65	457
Family households	1,750
One-person households	441
Persons per household	2.76
Persons per family	3.18

Labor & Employment
Total civilian labor force, 2004**	4,991
Unemployment rate	4.4%
Total civilian labor force, 2000	3,536
Unemployment rate	4.0%

Employed persons 16 years and over by occupation, 2000
Managers & professionals	1,259
Service occupations	476
Sales & office occupations	882
Farming, fishing & forestry	9
Construction & maintenance	366
Production & transportation	403
Self-employed persons	363

*US Census Bureau
**New Jersey Department of Labor

General Information
Township of Mansfield
100 Port Murray Rd
Port Murray, NJ 07865
908-689-6151
Web site	www.mansfieldtownship-nj.gov
Land area (sq. miles)	29.92
Water area (sq. miles)	0.02
Type of government	Township
Form of government	TC

Government

Legislative Districts
US Congressional	5
State Legislative	23

Local Officials, 2006
Mayor	Joseph Watters
Admin/Manager	Charles Lee
Clerk	Laurie Courter
Finance Dir/Treas	Andrew Coppola
Engineer	Douglas Mace
Attorney	Charles Lee
Tax assessor	William Merdinger
Tax collector	Carrie Rochelle
Building officer	Charles O'Connor
Zoning officer	Dena Hrebenak
Public Works	Brent Sliker

Housing & Construction

Housing Units, 2000*
Total	2,415
Median rent	$731
Median SF home value	$177,200

New Privately Owned Housing Units Authorized by Building Permit
	Units	Value
Total, 2004	13	$3,526,844
Single family	13	$3,526,844
Total, 2005	21	$2,694,900
Single family	15	$2,336,400

Real Property Valuation - parcels, 2005
	Number	Valuation
Total		$639,707,500
Vacant	577	15,322,700
Residential	1,803	424,186,900
Commercial	53	83,240,900
Industrial	13	16,513,100
Apartments	4	49,489,900
Farm land	168	48,128,800
Farm homestead	305	2,825,200

Average Property Value & Tax, 2005
Residential value	$202,567
Property tax	$5,134
FAIR rebate	$518

Public Library

No public municipal library.

Library statistics, 2004
	Total	per capita
Volumes	NA	NA
Expenditure	NA	NA

Public Safety
Police
Chief	Douglas Ort
Number of officers, 2004	13

Crime, 2004	Number	Rate
Total	117	14.1
Violent	4	0.5
Non-violent	113	13.6
Domestic Viol.	150	NA

Emergency/Fire
Director	Jason Wester

Public School District
(for school year 2004-2005 except as noted)

Mansfield Township School District
50 Port Murray Rd
Port Murray, NJ 07865
908-689-3212
Superintendent	Rita Seipp
Grade plan	K-6
Enrollment	719.0
Students per teacher	10.0
Per pupil expenditure	$9,976
Median faculty salary	$50,110
Median administrator salary	$93,957
Grade 12 enrollment	NA
High school graduation rate	NA

Assessment test results
(percent scoring at proficient or advanced level)
	Language	Math
Grade 3	84.1%	75.0%
Grade 8	NA	NA
High school	NA	NA

SAT
Percent tested	NA
Average SAT math score	NA
Average SAT verbal score	NA

No Child Left Behind, 2003-04
Attendence rate (target = 90%)	95.5%
Drop rate	NA
Highly-qualified teachers	100%
District needs improvement?(AYP)	No

Municipal Finance

Fiscal Year 2005
Total tax levy	$16,259,271
County levy	4,502,600
County taxes	3,712,573
County library	363,662
County health	0
County open space	426,365
School levy	9,614,488
Local muni. budget	2,142,184
Misc. revenues	3,059,925
Total aid	$1,239,207
CMPTRA	337,730
Muni. block grant	31,304
Energy tax receipts	820,173
Homeland security	50,000

Fiscal Year 2006
Total aid	$1,239,207
CMPTRA	309,024
Muni. block grant	31,304
Energy tax receipts	848,879
Homeland security	50,000

Taxes
	2003	2004	2005
General tax rate per $100	2.22	2.420	2.540
Net valuation taxable	$639,615,775	$640,760,585	$641,532,820
State equalized value	$646,468,339	$707,877,812	$804,429,868
County equalization ratio	123.88	98.94	90.49

Demographics & Socio-Economic Characteristics
(2000 U.S. Census, except as noted)

Population

1980*	433
1990*	334
2000	423
Male	208
Female	215
2004 (estimate)*	451
Persons per sq. mi. of land	1,022

Race & Hispanic Origin, 2000
Race

White	413
Black/African American	7
Amer. Indian/Alaska Natv.	0
Asian	2
Natv. Hawaiian/Pac. Islander	0
Other Race	1
Two or more races	0
Hispanic origin, total	3
Mexican	0
Puerto Rican	0
Cuban	0
Other Hispanic	3

Age & Nativity, 2000

Under 5 years	9
18 years and over	380
21 years and over	372
65 years and over	153
85 years and over	12
Median Age	58
Native born	345
Foreign born	24

Educational Attainment, 2000

Population 25 years and over	322
0-8 yrs of school	0.0%
High School grad or higher	99.1%
Bachelor's degree or higher	59.9%
Graduate degree	20.5%

Income & Poverty, 1999

Per capita income	$114,017
Median household income	$105,841
Median family income	$125,000
Persons in poverty	3
H'holds receiving public assistance	0
H'holds receiving social security	104

Households, 2000

Total households	207
With persons under 18	25
With persons over 65	111
Family households	141
One-person households	63
Persons per household	2.02
Persons per family	2.45

Labor & Employment

Total civilian labor force, 2004**	168
Unemployment rate	3.2%
Total civilian labor force, 2000	137
Unemployment rate	0.0%

Employed persons 16 years and over by occupation, 2000

Managers & professionals	89
Service occupations	0
Sales & office occupations	39
Farming, fishing & forestry	0
Construction & maintenance	7
Production & transportation	2
Self-employed persons	25

*US Census Bureau
**New Jersey Department of Labor

General Information
Borough of Mantoloking
PO Box 247
Mantoloking, NJ 08738
732-899-6600

Web site	www.mantoloking.org
Land area (sq. miles)	0.44
Water area (sq. miles)	0.22
Type of government	Borough
Form of government	B

Government

Legislative Districts

US Congressional	4
State Legislative	10

Local Officials, 2006

Mayor	William Dunbar III
Admin/Manager	Irene Ryan
Clerk	Irene Ryan
Finance Dir/Treas	Michelle Swisher
Engineer	Thomas Guldin
Attorney	Edwin O'Malley Jr.
Tax assessor	James Anderson
Tax collector	NA
Building officer	John Wardell
Zoning officer	Thomas Guldin
Public Works	NA

Housing & Construction

Housing Units, 2000*

Total	522
Median rent	$2,001
Median SF home value	$761,000

New Privately Owned Housing Units Authorized by Building Permit

	Units	Value
Total, 2004	2	$2,239,200
Single family	2	$2,239,200
Total, 2005	4	$2,450,425
Single family	4	$2,450,425

Real Property Valuation - parcels, 2005

	Number	Valuation
Total		$958,173,300
Vacant	38	23,808,900
Residential	518	925,256,500
Commercial	5	9,107,900
Industrial	0	0
Apartments	0	0
Farm land	0	0
Farm homestead	0	0

Average Property Value & Tax, 2005

Residential value	$1,786,209
Property tax	$12,729
FAIR rebate	$857

Public Library

No public municipal library.

Library statistics, 2004

	Total	per capita
Volumes	NA	NA
Expenditure	NA	NA

Public Safety

Police

Chief	Richard Ortley
Number of officers, 2004	8

Crime, 2004	Number	Rate
Total	11	24.7
Violent	0	0
Non-violent	11	24.7
Domestic Viol.	0	NA

Emergency/Fire

Director	Douglas Popaca

Public School District
(for school year 2004-2005 except as noted)

Mantoloking School District†
PO Box 881
Mantoloking, NJ 08738

†No schools in district - sends children to Point Pleasant Beach schools.

Grade plan	NA
Enrollment	NA
Students per teacher	NA
Per pupil expenditure	NA
Median faculty salary	NA

Assessment test results
(percent scoring at proficient or advanced level)

	Language	Math
Grade 3	NA	NA
Grade 8	NA	NA
High school	NA	NA

SAT

Percent tested	NA
Average SAT math score	NA
Average SAT verbal score	NA

No Child Left Behind, 2003-04

Attendance rate (target = 90%)	NA
Drop rate	NA
Highly-qualified teachers	NA
District needs improvement?(AYP)	NA

Municipal Finance

Fiscal Year 2005

Total tax levy	$6,829,358
County levy	4,627,941
County taxes	3,899,168
County library	409,647
County health	173,629
County open space	145,497
School levy	107,821
Local muni. budget	2,093,596
Misc. revenues	932,976
Total aid	$177,793
CMPTRA	0
Muni. block grant	1,659
Energy tax receipts	153,873
Homeland security	25,000

Fiscal Year 2006

Total aid	$183,179
CMPTRA	0
Muni. block grant	1,659
Energy tax receipts	156,520
Homeland security	25,000

Taxes

	2003	2004	2005
General tax rate per $100	0.73	0.737	0.713
Net valuation taxable	$922,946,941	$935,843,051	$958,311,859
State equalized value	$1,096,787,809	$1,182,176,695	$1,371,564,132
County equalization ratio	95.51	84.15	79.16

Demographics & Socio-Economic Characteristics

(2000 U.S. Census, except as noted)

Population

1980*	9,193
1990*	10,074
2000	14,217
Male	6,964
Female	7,253
2004 (estimate)*	14,290
Persons per sq. mi. of land	899

Race & Hispanic Origin, 2000

Race

White	13,622
Black/African American	294
Amer. Indian/Alaska Natv.	28
Asian	122
Natv. Hawaiian/Pac. Islander	0
Other Race	40
Two or more races	111
Hispanic origin, total	179
Mexican	19
Puerto Rican	81
Cuban	12
Other Hispanic	67

Age & Nativity, 2000

Under 5 years	1,131
18 years and over	10,423
21 years and over	9,986
65 years and over	1,582
85 years and over	101
Median Age	36.3
Native born	13,784
Foreign born	433

Educational Attainment, 2000

Population 25 years and over	9,517
0-8 yrs of school	3.0%
High School grad or higher	85.7%
Bachelor's degree or higher	23.5%
Graduate degree	6.7%

Income & Poverty, 1999

Per capita income	$24,147
Median household income	$58,256
Median family income	$63,391
Persons in poverty	510
H'holds receiving public assistance	68
H'holds receiving social security	1,326

Households, 2000

Total households	5,265
With persons under 18	2,104
With persons over 65	1,145
Family households	3,947
One-person households	1,111
Persons per household	2.69
Persons per family	3.14

Labor & Employment

Total civilian labor force, 2004**	6,361
Unemployment rate	3.1%
Total civilian labor force, 2000	7,934
Unemployment rate	4.5%

Employed persons 16 years and over by occupation, 2000

Managers & professionals	2,679
Service occupations	954
Sales & office occupations	2,230
Farming, fishing & forestry	15
Construction & maintenance	770
Production & transportation	926
Self-employed persons	362

*US Census Bureau
**New Jersey Department of Labor

General Information

Mantua Township
401 Main St
Mantua, NJ 08051
856-468-1500

Web site	www.mantuatownship.com
Land area (sq. miles)	15.90
Water area (sq. miles)	0.01
Type of government	Township
Form of government	TC

Government

Legislative Districts

US Congressional	1, 2
State Legislative	3

Local Officials, 2006

Mayor	Timothy Chell
Admin/Manager	Richard Subers
Clerk	Shawn Menzies (Actg)
Finance Dir/Treas	Gayle Tschopp
Engineer	Consulting Engineer Svc
Attorney	Michael Angelini
Tax assessor	Sandra Elliot
Tax collector	NA
Building officer	James Gallagher
Zoning officer	Ted Bamford
Public Works	Michael Datz

Housing & Construction

Housing Units, 2000*

Total	5,411
Median rent	$656
Median SF home value	$123,200

New Privately Owned Housing Units Authorized by Building Permit

	Units	Value
Total, 2004	17	$4,916,665
Single family	17	$4,916,665
Total, 2005	29	$4,867,994
Single family	29	$4,867,994

Real Property Valuation - parcels, 2005

	Number	Valuation
Total		$701,964,000
Vacant	302	11,191,800
Residential	5,032	595,248,800
Commercial	152	70,010,400
Industrial	7	7,790,800
Apartments	6	2,088,800
Farm land	94	14,211,800
Farm homestead	178	1,421,600

Average Property Value & Tax, 2005

Residential value	$114,524
Property tax	$4,726
FAIR rebate	$515

Public Library

Gloucester County Library
389 Wolfert Station Rd
Mullica Hill, NJ 08062
856-223-6000

Director	Robert Wetherall

Library statistics, 2004

	Total	per capita
Volumes	NA	NA
Expenditure	NA	NA

Public Safety

Police

Chief	Graham Land
Number of officers, 2004	27

Crime, 2004	Number	Rate
Total	335	23.5
Violent	29	2
Non-violent	306	21.4
Domestic Viol.	189	NA

Emergency/Fire

Director	William Beckett

Public School District

(for school year 2004-2005 except as noted)

Mantua Township School District
684 Main St
Sewell, NJ 08080
856-468-2225

Superintendent	Steven Crispin
Grade plan	K-6
Enrollment	1,652.0
Students per teacher	13.5
Per pupil expenditure	$9,618
Median faculty salary	$48,353
Median administrator salary	$101,936
Grade 12 enrollment	NA
High school graduation rate	NA

Assessment test results

(percent scoring at proficient or advanced level)

	Language	Math
Grade 3	92.5%	85.6%
Grade 8	NA	NA
High school	NA	NA

SAT

Percent tested	NA
Average SAT math score	NA
Average SAT verbal score	NA

No Child Left Behind, 2003-04

Attendence rate (target = 90%)	95.9%
Drop rate	NA
Highly-qualified teachers	100%
District needs improvement?(AYP)	No

Municipal Finance

Fiscal Year 2005

Total tax levy	$29,101,786
County levy	6,898,877
County taxes	6,049,583
County library	447,088
County health	0
County open space	402,206
School levy	17,368,418
Local muni. budget	4,834,492
Misc. revenues	6,500,916
Total aid	$1,701,033
CMPTRA	478,815
Muni. block grant	55,745
Energy tax receipts	1,096,473
Homeland security	70,000

Fiscal Year 2006

Total aid	$1,701,032
CMPTRA	440,438
Muni. block grant	55,745
Energy tax receipts	1,134,849
Homeland security	70,000

Taxes

	2003	2004	2005
General tax rate per $100	3.59	3.851	4.127
Net valuation taxable	$662,996,717	$682,978,110	$705,190,601
State equalized value	$847,171,885	$969,111,785	$1,146,464,967
County equalization ratio	85.88	78.26	70.36

Demographics & Socio-Economic Characteristics

(2000 U.S. Census, except as noted)

Population

1980*	11,278
1990*	10,567
2000	10,343
Male	5,072
Female	5,271
2004 (estimate)*	10,416
Persons per sq. mi. of land	4,197

Race & Hispanic Origin, 2000

Race

White	9,928
Black/African American	47
Amer. Indian/Alaska Natv.	7
Asian	136
Natv. Hawaiian/Pac. Islander	3
Other Race	118
Two or more races	104
Hispanic origin, total	559
Mexican	46
Puerto Rican	121
Cuban	7
Other Hispanic	385

Age & Nativity, 2000

Under 5 years	516
18 years and over	8,203
21 years and over	7,905
65 years and over	1,826
85 years and over	143
Median Age	39.5
Native born	8,917
Foreign born	1,390

Educational Attainment, 2000

Population 25 years and over	7,425
0-8 yrs of school	8.3%
High School grad or higher	78.2%
Bachelor's degree or higher	13.7%
Graduate degree	3.7%

Income & Poverty, 1999

Per capita income	$23,293
Median household income	$51,258
Median family income	$61,151
Persons in poverty	394
H'holds receiving public assistance	88
H'holds receiving social security	1,386

Households, 2000

Total households	4,115
With persons under 18	1,209
With persons over 65	1,375
Family households	2,758
One-person households	1,100
Persons per household	2.51
Persons per family	3.05

Labor & Employment

Total civilian labor force, 2004**	7,152
Unemployment rate	4.5%
Total civilian labor force, 2000	5,509
Unemployment rate	3.2%

Employed persons 16 years and over by occupation, 2000

Managers & professionals	1,369
Service occupations	788
Sales & office occupations	1,639
Farming, fishing & forestry	12
Construction & maintenance	646
Production & transportation	880
Self-employed persons	246

*US Census Bureau
**New Jersey Department of Labor

General Information

Borough of Manville
325 N Main St
Manville, NJ 08835
908-725-9478

Web site	www.manvillenj.org
Land area (sq. miles)	2.48
Water area (sq. miles)	0
Type of government	Borough
Form of government	B

Government

Legislative Districts

US Congressional	7
State Legislative	16

Local Officials, 2006

Mayor	Angelo Corradino
Admin/Manager	Gary Garwacke
Clerk	Philip Petrone
Finance Dir/Treas	Lori Majeski
Engineer	Gary Garwacke
Attorney	C. Douglas Reina
Tax assessor	Catherine Gantner
Tax collector	NA
Building officer	Lou Gara
Zoning officer	Walter Wilczek
Public Works	Philip Petrone

Housing & Construction

Housing Units, 2000*

Total	4,296
Median rent	$789
Median SF home value	$146,200

New Privately Owned Housing Units
Authorized by Building Permit

	Units	Value
Total, 2004	9	$1,008,650
Single family	9	$1,008,650
Total, 2005	5	$560,360
Single family	5	$560,360

Real Property Valuation - parcels, 2005

	Number	Valuation
Total		$531,644,700
Vacant	127	3,587,000
Residential	3,237	440,059,070
Commercial	146	61,837,830
Industrial	31	19,435,700
Apartments	20	6,725,100
Farm land	0	0
Farm homestead	0	0

Average Property Value & Tax, 2005

Residential value	$135,947
Property tax	$4,830
FAIR rebate	$699

Public Library

Manville Public Library
100 S 10th Ave
Manville, NJ 08835
908-722-9722

Director .... Ed Smith

Library statistics, 2004

	Total	per capita
Volumes	48,861	4.72
Expenditure	$344,312	$33.29

Public Safety

Police

Chief	Mark Peltack
Number of officers, 2004	22

Crime, 2004	Number	Rate
Total	245	23.6
Violent	7	0.7
Non-violent	238	22.9
Domestic Viol.	95	NA

Emergency/Fire

Director .... Mark Malinowski

Public School District

(for school year 2004-2005 except as noted)

Manville Borough School District
410 Brooks Blvd
Manville, NJ 08835
908-231-8545

Superintendent	Donald Burkhardt
Grade plan	K-12
Enrollment	1,302.5
Students per teacher	10.7
Per pupil expenditure	$10,992
Median faculty salary	$42,245
Median administrator salary	$97,878
Grade 12 enrollment	106.0
High school graduation rate	86.0%

Assessment test results

(percent scoring at proficient or advanced level)

	Language	Math
Grade 3	80.2%	79.4%
Grade 8	81.8%	74.6%
High school	78.0%	63.9%

SAT

Percent tested	59%
Average SAT math score	480
Average SAT verbal score	459

No Child Left Behind, 2003-04

Attendence rate (target = 90%)	93.2%
Drop rate	3.2%
Highly-qualified teachers	88.3%
District needs improvement?(AYP)	No

Municipal Finance

Fiscal Year 2005

Total tax levy	$18,911,381
County levy	3,015,896
County taxes	2,751,338
County library	0
County health	0
County open space	264,558
School levy	10,647,043
Local muni. budget	5,248,442
Misc. revenues	6,547,951
Total aid	$2,203,408
CMPTRA	1,538,024
Muni. block grant	46,238
Energy tax receipts	549,146
Homeland security	70,000

Fiscal Year 2006

Total aid	$2,203,408
CMPTRA	1,518,804
Muni. block grant	46,238
Energy tax receipts	568,366
Homeland security	70,000

Taxes

	2003	2004	2005
General tax rate per $100	3.14	3.330	3.560
Net valuation taxable	$519,514,716	$519,518,295	$532,272,883
State equalized value	$730,373,564	$835,716,666	$945,422,528
County equalization ratio	80.71	71.13	62.13

Demographics & Socio-Economic Characteristics

(2000 U.S. Census, except as noted)

Population

1980*	20,525
1990*	19,211
2000	19,079
Male	9,339
Female	9,740
2004 (estimate)*	19,330
Persons per sq. mi. of land	5,025

Race & Hispanic Origin, 2000

Race
White	15,868
Black/African American	1,376
Amer. Indian/Alaska Natv.	30
Asian	1,164
Natv. Hawaiian/Pac. Islander	8
Other Race	323
Two or more races	310
Hispanic origin, total	850
Mexican	154
Puerto Rican	446
Cuban	19
Other Hispanic	231

Age & Nativity, 2000

Under 5 years	1,072
18 years and over	15,382
21 years and over	14,835
65 years and over	2,930
85 years and over	315
Median Age	36.5
Native born	17,349
Foreign born	1,730

Educational Attainment, 2000

Population 25 years and over	13,711
0-8 yrs of school	4.6%
High School grad or higher	82.3%
Bachelor's degree or higher	21.4%
Graduate degree	7.1%

Income & Poverty, 1999

Per capita income	$23,812
Median household income	$45,426
Median family income	$53,912
Persons in poverty	1,009
H'holds receiving public assistance	120
H'holds receiving social security	2,125

Households, 2000

Total households	8,462
With persons under 18	2,207
With persons over 65	2,103
Family households	4,718
One-person households	3,047
Persons per household	2.22
Persons per family	2.95

Labor & Employment

Total civilian labor force, 2004**	12,884
Unemployment rate	4.8%
Total civilian labor force, 2000	10,723
Unemployment rate	3.6%

Employed persons 16 years and over by occupation, 2000
Managers & professionals	3,403
Service occupations	1,462
Sales & office occupations	2,965
Farming, fishing & forestry	5
Construction & maintenance	909
Production & transportation	1,598
Self-employed persons	454

*US Census Bureau
**New Jersey Department of Labor

General Information

Township of Maple Shade
200 Stiles Ave
Maple Shade, NJ 08052
856-779-9610

Web site	NA
Land area (sq. miles)	3.85
Water area (sq. miles)	0
Type of government	Township
Form of government	CM '50

Government

Legislative Districts

US Congressional	1
State Legislative	7

Local Officials, 2006

Mayor	John D. Galloway
Admin/Manager	George Haeuber
Clerk	Andrea T. DeGolia
Finance Dir/Treas	Adriane McKendry
Engineer	Doug Traver
Attorney	Eileen Fahey
Tax assessor	Harry Renwick
Tax collector	Denise Lawler
Building officer	Charles Bogardus
Zoning officer	NA
Public Works	John Vanelli

Housing & Construction

Housing Units, 2000*

Total	9,009
Median rent	$767
Median SF home value	$107,900

New Privately Owned Housing Units Authorized by Building Permit

	Units	Value
Total, 2004	141	$7,377,399
Single family	6	$719,214
Total, 2005	101	$5,366,235
Single family	4	$499,738

Real Property Valuation - parcels, 2005

	Number	Valuation
Total		$821,411,300
Vacant	128	8,011,300
Residential	4,666	450,036,100
Commercial	255	210,557,300
Industrial	28	15,602,100
Apartments	23	137,204,500
Farm land	0	0
Farm homestead	0	0

Average Property Value & Tax, 2005

Residential value	$96,450
Property tax	$3,614
FAIR rebate	$636

Public Library

Maple Shade Branch Library
200 Stiles Ave
Maple Shade, NJ 08052
856-779-9767

Director	Jessica Hildreth

Library statistics, 2004

	Total	per capita
Volumes	NA	NA
Expenditure	NA	NA

Public Safety

Police

Chief	Edmund Vernier
Number of officers, 2004	32

Crime, 2004	Number	Rate
Total	504	26.2
Violent	69	3.6
Non-violent	435	22.6
Domestic Viol.	162	NA

Emergency/Fire

Director	Anthony Saporito

Public School District

(for school year 2004-2005 except as noted)

Maple Shade Township School District
Frederick and Clinton Aves
Maple Shade, NJ 08052
856-779-1750

Superintendent	Cheryl Smith
Grade plan	K-12
Enrollment	2,150.0
Students per teacher	11.7
Per pupil expenditure	$11,368
Median faculty salary	$48,924
Median administrator salary	$99,069
Grade 12 enrollment	118.0
High school graduation rate	93.8%

Assessment test results

(percent scoring at proficient or advanced level)
	Language	Math
Grade 3	84.2%	83.3%
Grade 8	72.1%	56.8%
High school	80.9%	66.5%

SAT

Percent tested	59%
Average SAT math score	474
Average SAT verbal score	466

No Child Left Behind, 2003-04

Attendance rate (target = 90%)	93.4%
Drop rate	1.3%
Highly-qualified teachers	97.8%
District needs improvement?(AYP)	No

Municipal Finance

Fiscal Year 2005

Total tax levy	$30,839,379
County levy	5,167,766
County taxes	4,334,937
County library	379,710
County health	0
County open space	453,119
School levy	19,675,351
Local muni. budget	5,996,261
Misc. revenues	4,931,849
Total aid	$2,375,238
CMPTRA	964,736
Muni. block grant	84,061
Energy tax receipts	1,256,441
Homeland security	70,000

Fiscal Year 2006

Total aid	$2,375,238
CMPTRA	920,761
Muni. block grant	84,061
Energy tax receipts	1,300,416
Homeland security	70,000

Taxes

	2003	2004	2005
General tax rate per $100	3.15	3.312	3.748
Net valuation taxable	$811,041,552	$823,800,370	$822,970,817
State equalized value	$992,463,965	$1,134,879,812	$1,289,720,760
County equalization ratio	89.74	81.72	72.55

Demographics & Socio-Economic Characteristics

(2000 U.S. Census, except as noted)

Population

1980*	22,950
1990*	21,652
2000	23,868
Male	11,347
Female	12,521
2004 (estimate)*	23,450
Persons per sq. mi. of land	6,098

Race & Hispanic Origin, 2000

Race

White	14,030
Black/African American	7,788
Amer. Indian/Alaska Natv.	31
Asian	682
Natv. Hawaiian/Pac. Islander	7
Other Race	373
Two or more races	957
Hispanic origin, total	1,248
Mexican	69
Puerto Rican	438
Cuban	97
Other Hispanic	644

Age & Nativity, 2000

Under 5 years	1,882
18 years and over	17,175
21 years and over	16,560
65 years and over	2,890
85 years and over	505
Median Age	37.7
Native born	19,614
Foreign born	4,254

Educational Attainment, 2000

Population 25 years and over	15,987
0-8 yrs of school	2.5%
High School grad or higher	91.9%
Bachelor's degree or higher	50.8%
Graduate degree	22.0%

Income & Poverty, 1999

Per capita income	$36,794
Median household income	$79,637
Median family income	$92,724
Persons in poverty	1,049
H'holds receiving public assistance	77
H'holds receiving social security	1,896

Households, 2000

Total households	8,452
With persons under 18	3,646
With persons over 65	2,136
Family households	6,379
One-person households	1,720
Persons per household	2.81
Persons per family	3.27

Labor & Employment

Total civilian labor force, 2004**	13,921
Unemployment rate	1.7%
Total civilian labor force, 2000	12,848
Unemployment rate	3.9%

Employed persons 16 years and over by occupation, 2000

Managers & professionals	6,478
Service occupations	1,124
Sales & office occupations	3,263
Farming, fishing & forestry	0
Construction & maintenance	604
Production & transportation	883
Self-employed persons	823

*US Census Bureau
**New Jersey Department of Labor

General Information

Township of Maplewood
574 Valley St
Maplewood, NJ 07040
973-762-8120

Web site	www.twp.maplewood.nj.us
Land area (sq. miles)	3.85
Water area (sq. miles)	0
Type of government	Township
Form of government	TC

Government

Legislative Districts

US Congressional	8, 10
State Legislative	27

Local Officials, 2006

Mayor	Fred R. Profeta Jr.
Admin/Manager	Joseph Manning
Clerk	Elizabeth Fritzen
Finance Dir/Treas	Peter Fresulone
Engineer	Richard Calbi Jr.
Attorney	Roger Desiderio
Tax assessor	Edward Galante
Tax collector	Peter Fresulone
Building officer	Robert Mittermaier
Zoning officer	NA
Public Works	Gary Lenci

Housing & Construction

Housing Units, 2000*

Total	8,615
Median rent	$950
Median SF home value	$222,700

New Privately Owned Housing Units
Authorized by Building Permit

	Units	Value
Total, 2004	12	$793,215
Single family	2	$225,415
Total, 2005	12	$1,098,958
Single family	2	$333,058

Real Property Valuation - parcels, 2005

	Number	Valuation
Total		$2,046,184,200
Vacant	41	2,188,600
Residential	6,849	1,830,312,400
Commercial	313	187,813,200
Industrial	34	15,140,600
Apartments	12	10,729,400
Farm land	0	0
Farm homestead	0	0

Average Property Value & Tax, 2005

Residential value	$267,238
Property tax	$10,123
FAIR rebate	$542

Public Library

Maplewood Mem Library
51 Baker St
Maplewood, NJ 07040
973-762-1622

Director.....................Jane Kennedy

Library statistics, 2004

	Total	per capita
Volumes	131,795	5.52
Expenditure	$1,636,522	$68.57

Public Safety

Police

Chief	Robert Cimino
Number of officers, 2004	59

Crime, 2004	Number	Rate
Total	732	31
Violent	81	3.4
Non-violent	651	27.5
Domestic Viol.	55	NA

Emergency/Fire

Director.....................Vincent Vitiello

Public School District

(for school year 2004-2005 except as noted)

South Orange-Maplewood School District
525 Academy St
Maplewood, NJ 07040
973-378-9630

Superintendent	Peter Horoschak
Grade plan	K-12
Enrollment	6,295.0
Students per teacher	11.6
Per pupil expenditure	$12,484
Median faculty salary	$59,615
Median administrator salary	$114,559
Grade 12 enrollment	462.0
High school graduation rate	95.7%

Assessment test results
(percent scoring at proficient or advanced level)

	Language	Math
Grade 3	84.1%	83.0%
Grade 8	76.3%	71.7%
High school	89.5%	83.8%

SAT

Percent tested	89%
Average SAT math score	528
Average SAT verbal score	511

No Child Left Behind, 2003-04

Attendence rate (target = 90%)	96.0%
Drop rate	1.7%
Highly-qualified teachers	82.2%
District needs improvement?(AYP)	No

Municipal Finance

Fiscal Year 2005

Total tax levy	$77,567,614
County levy	13,193,826
County taxes	12,917,481
County library	0
County health	0
County open space	276,346
School levy	45,088,392
Local muni. budget	19,285,396
Misc. revenues	9,118,565
Total aid	$2,568,370
CMPTRA	1,035,241
Muni. block grant	94,742
Energy tax receipts	1,348,387
Homeland security	90,000

Fiscal Year 2006

Total aid	$2,568,369
CMPTRA	988,047
Muni. block grant	94,742
Energy tax receipts	1,395,580
Homeland security	90,000

Taxes

	2003	2004	2005
General tax rate per $100	3.42	3.610	3.790
Net valuation taxable	$2,044,957,900	$2,046,176,400	$2,047,664,500
State equalized value	$2,480,540,878	$2,738,623,446	$3,084,761,223
County equalization ratio	93.07	93.07	74.70

Demographics & Socio-Economic Characteristics
(2000 U.S. Census, except as noted)

Population
1980*	9,179
1990*	8,431
2000	8,193
Male	3,861
Female	4,332
2004 (estimate)*	8,627
Persons per sq. mi. of land	6,134

Race & Hispanic Origin, 2000
Race
White	7,843
Black/African American	71
Amer. Indian/Alaska Natv.	2
Asian	128
Natv. Hawaiian/Pac. Islander	6
Other Race	75
Two or more races	68
Hispanic origin, total	222
Mexican	39
Puerto Rican	74
Cuban	13
Other Hispanic	96

Age & Nativity, 2000
Under 5 years	298
18 years and over	6,935
21 years and over	6,800
65 years and over	2,365
85 years and over	255
Median Age	49.8
Native born	7,586
Foreign born	607

Educational Attainment, 2000
Population 25 years and over	6,668
0-8 yrs of school	2.0%
High School grad or higher	88.3%
Bachelor's degree or higher	36.5%
Graduate degree	13.4%

Income & Poverty, 1999
Per capita income	$33,566
Median household income	$45,876
Median family income	$63,917
Persons in poverty	594
H'holds receiving public assistance	47
H'holds receiving social security	1,734

Households, 2000
Total households	3,984
With persons under 18	725
With persons over 65	1,707
Family households	2,303
One-person households	1,440
Persons per household	2.06
Persons per family	2.67

Labor & Employment
Total civilian labor force, 2004**	4,657
Unemployment rate	3.7%
Total civilian labor force, 2000	3,981
Unemployment rate	5.6%

Employed persons 16 years and over by occupation, 2000
Managers & professionals	1,415
Service occupations	783
Sales & office occupations	1,198
Farming, fishing & forestry	0
Construction & maintenance	220
Production & transportation	142
Self-employed persons	361

*US Census Bureau
**New Jersey Department of Labor

General Information
City of Margate
1 S Washington Ave
Margate, NJ 08402
609-822-2605

Web site	www.margate-nj.com
Land area (sq. miles)	1.41
Water area (sq. miles)	0.18
Type of government	City
Form of government	Comm.

Government
Legislative Districts
US Congressional	2
State Legislative	2

Local Officials, 2006
Mayor	Vaughan M. Reale
Admin/Manager	NA
Clerk	Thomas Hiltner
Finance Dir/Treas	Charles F. Beirne
Engineer	Remington & Vernick
Attorney	Mary Siracusa
Tax assessor	Andy Bednarek
Tax collector	NA
Building officer	Jim Galantino
Zoning officer	Roger Rubin
Public Works	Frank Ricciotti

Housing & Construction
Housing Units, 2000*
Total	7,006
Median rent	$739
Median SF home value	$189,300

New Privately Owned Housing Units Authorized by Building Permit
	Units	Value
Total, 2004	106	$17,619,807
Single family	55	$11,503,115
Total, 2005	60	$13,284,890
Single family	31	$8,667,420

Real Property Valuation - parcels, 2005
	Number	Valuation
Total		$3,272,772,300
Vacant	305	88,172,700
Residential	6,327	3,084,114,800
Commercial	186	90,992,300
Industrial	0	0
Apartments	13	9,492,500
Farm land	0	0
Farm homestead	0	0

Average Property Value & Tax, 2005
Residential value	$487,453
Property tax	$5,474
FAIR rebate	$774

Public Library
Margate City Public Library
8100 Atlantic Ave
Margate City, NJ 08402
609-822-4700

Director ... James Cahill

Library statistics, 2004
	Total	per capita
Volumes	45,116	5.51
Expenditure	$731,473	$89.28

Public Safety
Police
Chief	David Wolfson
Number of officers, 2004	37

Crime, 2004	Number	Rate
Total	138	16.6
Violent	8	1
Non-violent	130	15.6
Domestic Viol.	94	NA

Emergency/Fire
Director ... John Kelley

Public School District
(for school year 2004-2005 except as noted)

Margate City School District
8103 Winchester Ave
Margate City, NJ 08402
609-822-1686

Superintendent	Dominick Potena
Grade plan	K-12
Enrollment	591.0
Students per teacher	9.5
Per pupil expenditure	$14,646
Median faculty salary	$51,962
Median administrator salary	$88,500
Grade 12 enrollment	NA
High school graduation rate	NA

Assessment test results
(percent scoring at proficient or advanced level)
	Language	Math
Grade 3	95.0%	98.3%
Grade 8	83.0%	78.5%
High school	NA	NA

SAT
Percent tested	NA
Average SAT math score	NA
Average SAT verbal score	NA

No Child Left Behind, 2003-04
Attendence rate (target = 90%)	94.1%
Drop rate	NA
Highly-qualified teachers	95.8%
District needs improvement?(AYP)	No

Municipal Finance
Fiscal Year 2005
Total tax levy	$36,768,066
County levy	9,659,214
County taxes	8,670,264
County library	0
County health	472,587
County open space	516,363
School levy	10,911,203
Local muni. budget	16,197,649
Misc. revenues	4,220,671
Total aid	$967,515
CMPTRA	61,714
Muni. block grant	36,892
Energy tax receipts	818,909
Homeland security	50,000

Fiscal Year 2006
Total aid	$967,515
CMPTRA	33,052
Muni. block grant	36,892
Energy tax receipts	847,571
Homeland security	50,000

Taxes
	2003	2004	2005
General tax rate per $100	2.33	2.506	1.124
Net valuation taxable	$1,310,112,532	$1,329,746,104	$3,274,070,521
State equalized value	$2,085,170,352	$2,568,249,761	$3,192,346,452
County equalization ratio	78.16	62.83	127.00

Demographics & Socio-Economic Characteristics
(2000 U.S. Census, except as noted)

Population
1980*	17,560
1990*	27,974
2000	36,398
Male	18,048
Female	18,350
2004 (estimate)*	39,780
Persons per sq. mi. of land	1,300

Race & Hispanic Origin, 2000
Race
White	30,487
Black/African American	752
Amer. Indian/Alaska Natv.	17
Asian	4,612
Natv. Hawaiian/Pac. Islander	5
Other Race	171
Two or more races	354
Hispanic origin, total	1,051
Mexican	123
Puerto Rican	350
Cuban	107
Other Hispanic	471

Age & Nativity, 2000
Under 5 years	2,723
18 years and over	25,409
21 years and over	24,466
65 years and over	3,207
85 years and over	248
Median Age	37.6
Native born	30,782
Foreign born	5,621

Educational Attainment, 2000
Population 25 years and over	23,453
0-8 yrs of school	2.1%
High School grad or higher	94.0%
Bachelor's degree or higher	52.3%
Graduate degree	22.6%

Income & Poverty, 1999
Per capita income	$38,635
Median household income	$101,322
Median family income	$107,894
Persons in poverty	1,256
H'holds receiving public assistance	74
H'holds receiving social security	2,313

Households, 2000
Total households	11,478
With persons under 18	5,925
With persons over 65	2,245
Family households	10,167
One-person households	1,110
Persons per household	3.15
Persons per family	3.38

Labor & Employment
Total civilian labor force, 2004**	15,697
Unemployment rate	3.3%
Total civilian labor force, 2000	17,945
Unemployment rate	3.3%

Employed persons 16 years and over by occupation, 2000
Managers & professionals	9,569
Service occupations	1,095
Sales & office occupations	4,973
Farming, fishing & forestry	0
Construction & maintenance	724
Production & transportation	993
Self-employed persons	1,059

*US Census Bureau
**New Jersey Department of Labor

General Information
Township of Marlboro
1979 Township Dr
Marlboro, NJ 07746
732-536-0200

Web site	www.marlboro-nj.gov
Land area (sq. miles)	30.59
Water area (sq. miles)	0
Type of government	Township
Form of government	MC '50

Government

Legislative Districts
US Congressional	6, 12
State Legislative	12

Local Officials, 2006
Mayor	Robert Kleinberg
Admin/Manager	Judith Tiernan
Clerk	Alida DeGaeta
Finance Dir/Treas	Ulrich Steinberg
Engineer	Birdsall Eng./J. Priol
Attorney	Andrew Bayer
Tax assessor	Walter Kosul
Tax collector	Shirley Giaquinto
Building officer	Joseph Labruzza
Zoning officer	Sarah Paris
Public Works	Robert DiMarco

Housing & Construction

Housing Units, 2000*
Total	11,896
Median rent	$1,334
Median SF home value	$286,300

New Privately Owned Housing Units
Authorized by Building Permit
	Units	Value
Total, 2004	151	$29,715,125
Single family	151	$29,715,125
Total, 2005	138	$27,857,052
Single family	123	$27,444,052

Real Property Valuation - parcels, 2005
	Number	Valuation
Total		$3,012,105,850
Vacant	896	57,950,900
Residential	12,454	2,720,795,700
Commercial	211	172,691,600
Industrial	28	42,131,400
Apartments	2	2,965,200
Farm land	80	14,787,100
Farm homestead	151	783,950

Average Property Value & Tax, 2005
Residential value	$215,913
Property tax	$8,289
FAIR rebate	$547

Public Library
Marlboro Library†
1 Library Ct
Marlboro, NJ 07746
732-536-9406

Branch Librarian	Jennifer King

Library statistics, 2004
	Total	per capita
Volumes	NA	NA
Expenditure	NA	NA

†Branch of County Library

Public Safety
Police
Chief	Robert Holmes
Number of officers, 2004	76

Crime, 2004	Number	Rate
Total	400	10.3
Violent	15	0.4
Non-violent	385	9.9
Domestic Viol.	178	NA

Emergency/Fire
Director	NA

Public School District
(for school year 2004-2005 except as noted)

Marlboro Township School District
1980 Township Drive
Marlboro, NJ 07746
732-972-2015

Superintendent	David Abbott
Grade plan	K-8
Enrollment	6,012.0
Students per teacher	12.9
Per pupil expenditure	$9,898
Median faculty salary	$44,450
Median administrator salary	$104,987
Grade 12 enrollment	NA
High school graduation rate	NA

Assessment test results
(percent scoring at proficient or advanced level)
	Language	Math
Grade 3	93.7%	92.4%
Grade 8	88.8%	79.4%
High school	NA	NA

SAT
Percent tested	NA
Average SAT math score	NA
Average SAT verbal score	NA

No Child Left Behind, 2003-04
Attendence rate (target = 90%)	96.0%
Drop rate	NA
Highly-qualified teachers	96.8%
District needs improvement?(AYP)	No

Municipal Finance

Fiscal Year 2005
Total tax levy	$115,840,675
County levy	19,828,587
County taxes	17,506,215
County library	964,317
County health	319,231
County open space	1,038,824
School levy	79,927,748
Local muni. budget	16,084,340
Misc. revenues	12,769,501
Total aid	$3,333,494
CMPTRA	884,758
Muni. block grant	142,717
Energy tax receipts	2,166,019
Homeland security	140,000

Fiscal Year 2006
Total aid	$3,333,494
CMPTRA	808,947
Muni. block grant	142,717
Energy tax receipts	2,241,830
Homeland security	140,000

Taxes
	2003	2004	2005
General tax rate per $100	3.53	3.635	3.840
Net valuation taxable	$2,865,467,222	$2,943,126,361	$3,017,281,871
State equalized value	$5,049,281,448	$5,696,176,531	$6,370,949,897
County equalization ratio	63.74	56.75	51.62

Demographics & Socio-Economic Characteristics
(2000 U.S. Census, except as noted)

Population
1980*	8,837
1990*	9,270
2000	8,910
Male	4,400
Female	4,510
2004 (estimate)*	8,919
Persons per sq. mi. of land	3,913

Race & Hispanic Origin, 2000
Race
White	7,337
Black/African American	582
Amer. Indian/Alaska Natv.	2
Asian	712
Natv. Hawaiian/Pac. Islander	2
Other Race	110
Two or more races	165
Hispanic origin, total	575
Mexican	112
Puerto Rican	242
Cuban	51
Other Hispanic	170

Age & Nativity, 2000
Under 5 years	562
18 years and over	6,900
21 years and over	6,627
65 years and over	935
85 years and over	90
Median Age	36.4
Native born	7,641
Foreign born	1,336

Educational Attainment, 2000
Population 25 years and over	6,256
0-8 yrs of school	3.9%
High School grad or higher	88.4%
Bachelor's degree or higher	30.4%
Graduate degree	11.5%

Income & Poverty, 1999
Per capita income	$30,320
Median household income	$63,594
Median family income	$72,183
Persons in poverty	485
H'holds receiving public assistance	46
H'holds receiving social security	831

Households, 2000
Total households	3,531
With persons under 18	1,153
With persons over 65	715
Family households	2,375
One-person households	904
Persons per household	2.52
Persons per family	3.07

Labor & Employment
Total civilian labor force, 2004**	6,122
Unemployment rate	4.2%
Total civilian labor force, 2000	4,928
Unemployment rate	4.8%

Employed persons 16 years and over by occupation, 2000
Managers & professionals	1,970
Service occupations	596
Sales & office occupations	1,322
Farming, fishing & forestry	0
Construction & maintenance	384
Production & transportation	418
Self-employed persons	225

*US Census Bureau
**New Jersey Department of Labor

General Information
Matawan Borough
201 Broad St
Matawan, NJ 07747
732-566-3898
Web site	www.matawanborough.com
Land area (sq. miles)	2.28
Water area (sq. miles)	0.12
Type of government	Borough
Form of government	B

Government

Legislative Districts
US Congressional	6
State Legislative	13

Local Officials, 2006
Mayor	Mary Aufseeser
Admin/Manager	James Roberts
Clerk	Jean Montfort
Finance Dir/Treas	Monica Antista
Engineer	William White
Attorney	David Barry
Tax assessor	Eric Zanetti
Tax collector	Peggy Warren
Building officer	Paul Reinhold
Zoning officer	Paul Reinhold
Public Works	Anthony Bucco

Housing & Construction

Housing Units, 2000*
Total	3,640
Median rent	$808
Median SF home value	$178,500

New Privately Owned Housing Units Authorized by Building Permit
	Units	Value
Total, 2004	2	$565,700
Single family	2	$565,700
Total, 2005	42	$6,787,950
Single family	42	$6,787,950

Real Property Valuation - parcels, 2005
	Number	Valuation
Total		$428,617,634
Vacant	130	3,337,375
Residential	2,298	329,617,159
Commercial	143	63,213,900
Industrial	9	4,356,200
Apartments	16	28,093,000
Farm land	0	0
Farm homestead	0	0

Average Property Value & Tax, 2005
Residential value	$143,437
Property tax	$6,770
FAIR rebate	$654

Public Library
Matawan-Aberdeen Public Library†
165 Main St
Matawan, NJ 07747
732-583-9100
Director	Susan Pike

Library statistics, 2004
	Total	per capita
Volumes	89,918	3.41
Expenditure	$636,215	$24.13

†Joint Library with Aberdeen Twp

Public Safety

Police
Chief	NA
Number of officers, 2004	22

Crime, 2004	Number	Rate
Total	113	12.7
Violent	6	0.7
Non-violent	107	12.1
Domestic Viol.	93	NA

Emergency/Fire
Director	Joe Lopes

Public School District
(for school year 2004-2005 except as noted)

Matawan-Aberdeen Regional School District
One Crest Way
Aberdeen, NJ 07747
732-290-2705
Superintendent	Bruce Quinn
Grade plan	K-12
Enrollment	3,839.5
Students per teacher	11.1
Per pupil expenditure	$12,895
Median faculty salary	$50,700
Median administrator salary	$105,944
Grade 12 enrollment	215.0
High school graduation rate	96.5%

Assessment test results
(percent scoring at proficient or advanced level)
	Language	Math
Grade 3	93.4%	88.9%
Grade 8	74.9%	68.7%
High school	86.5%	77.4%

SAT
Percent tested	76%
Average SAT math score	504
Average SAT verbal score	499

No Child Left Behind, 2003-04
Attendence rate (target = 90%)	94.7%
Drop rate	0.5%
Highly-qualified teachers	98.9%
District needs improvement?(AYP)	No

Municipal Finance

Fiscal Year 2005
Total tax levy	$20,278,451
County levy	2,420,418
County taxes	2,246,149
County library	0
County health	40,987
County open space	133,282
School levy	13,272,977
Local muni. budget	4,585,056
Misc. revenues	3,485,188
Total aid	$1,995,083
CMPTRA	429,435
Muni. block grant	40,562
Energy tax receipts	1,475,086
Homeland security	50,000

Fiscal Year 2006
Total aid	$1,995,083
CMPTRA	377,807
Muni. block grant	40,562
Energy tax receipts	1,526,714
Homeland security	50,000

Taxes
	2003	2004	2005
General tax rate per $100	4.20	4.602	4.721
Net valuation taxable	$427,304,729	$425,938,019	$429,613,084
State equalized value	$659,624,466	$742,185,934	$873,552,428
County equalization ratio	72.2	64.78	57.23

Demographics & Socio-Economic Characteristics

(2000 U.S. Census, except as noted)

Population

1980*	4,577
1990*	6,648
2000	6,928
Male	5,093
Female	1,835
2000 (revised)	7,374
2004 (estimate)*	7,542
Persons per sq. mi. of land	81

Race & Hispanic Origin, 2000

Race

White	4,062
Black/African American	2,285
Amer. Indian/Alaska Natv.	54
Asian	19
Natv. Hawaiian/Pac. Islander	1
Other Race	307
Two or more races	200
Hispanic origin, total	634
Mexican	15
Puerto Rican	404
Cuban	51
Other Hispanic	164

Age & Nativity, 2000

Under 5 years	200
18 years and over	6,036
21 years and over	5,914
65 years and over	443
85 years and over	39
Median Age	36
Native born	6,710
Foreign born	218

Educational Attainment, 2000

Population 25 years and over	5,704
0-8 yrs of school	7.4%
High School grad or higher	62.8%
Bachelor's degree or higher	4.7%
Graduate degree	1.1%

Income & Poverty, 1999

Per capita income	$17,141
Median household income	$43,182
Median family income	$46,987
Persons in poverty	287
H'holds receiving public assistance	26
H'holds receiving social security	394

Households, 2000

Total households	1,332
With persons under 18	483
With persons over 65	327
Family households	1,012
One-person households	258
Persons per household	2.68
Persons per family	3.03

Labor & Employment

Total civilian labor force, 2004**	1,911
Unemployment rate	4.4%
Total civilian labor force, 2000	1,777
Unemployment rate	5.7%

Employed persons 16 years and over by occupation, 2000

Managers & professionals	385
Service occupations	345
Sales & office occupations	328
Farming, fishing & forestry	11
Construction & maintenance	228
Production & transportation	379
Self-employed persons	72

*US Census Bureau
**New Jersey Department of Labor

General Information

Township of Maurice River
PO Box 218
590 Main St
Leesburg, NJ 08327
856-785-1120

Web site	www.mauricerivertwp.org
Land area (sq. miles)	93.41
Water area (sq. miles)	2.31
Type of government	Township
Form of government	TC

Government

Legislative Districts

US Congressional	2
State Legislative	1

Local Officials, 2006

Mayor	Ronald D. Riggins Sr.
Admin/Manager	NA
Clerk	J. Roy Oliver
Finance Dir/Treas	Sharon Lloyd
Engineer	Kent Schellinger
Attorney	Edward Duffy
Tax assessor	Michelle Sharp
Tax collector	J. Roy Oliver
Building officer	Gordon Gross
Zoning officer	Gordon Gross
Public Works	NA

Housing & Construction

Housing Units, 2000*

Total	1,461
Median rent	$613
Median SF home value	$84,100

New Privately Owned Housing Units
Authorized by Building Permit

	Units	Value
Total, 2004	9	$1,124,017
Single family	9	$1,124,017
Total, 2005	10	$846,411
Single family	10	$846,411

Real Property Valuation - parcels, 2005

	Number	Valuation
Total		$138,691,800
Vacant	2,182	10,083,700
Residential	1,385	108,735,100
Commercial	40	6,201,300
Industrial	26	7,601,100
Apartments	1	125,100
Farm land	30	4,267,100
Farm homestead	82	1,678,400

Average Property Value & Tax, 2005

Residential value	$75,265
Property tax	$2,504
FAIR rebate	$610

Public Library

No public municipal library.

Library statistics, 2004

	Total	per capita
Volumes	NA	NA
Expenditure	NA	NA

Public Safety

Police

Chief	State
Number of officers, 2004	0

Crime, 2004	Number	Rate
Total	72	9.5
Violent	6	0.8
Non-violent	66	8.7
Domestic Viol.	31	NA

Emergency/Fire

Director	NA

Public School District

(for school year 2004-2005 except as noted)

Maurice River Township School District
S Delsea Dr
Port Elizabeth, NJ 08348
856-825-7411

Superintendent	John Saporito
Grade plan	K-12
Enrollment	408.0
Students per teacher	10.1
Per pupil expenditure	$11,275
Median faculty salary	$44,227
Median administrator salary	$90,827
Grade 12 enrollment	NA
High school graduation rate	NA

Assessment test results

(percent scoring at proficient or advanced level)

	Language	Math
Grade 3	80.5%	90.2%
Grade 8	56.6%	62.3%
High school	NA	NA

SAT

Percent tested	NA
Average SAT math score	NA
Average SAT verbal score	NA

No Child Left Behind, 2003-04

Attendence rate (target = 90%)	94.7%
Drop rate	NA
Highly-qualified teachers	80.9%
District needs improvement?(AYP)	No

Municipal Finance

Fiscal Year 2005

Total tax levy	$4,644,926
County levy	1,992,128
County taxes	1,892,109
County library	0
County health	80,803
County open space	19,217
School levy	2,373,540
Local muni. budget	279,258
Misc. revenues	3,309,712
Total aid	$945,170
CMPTRA	455,887
Muni. block grant	29,090
Energy tax receipts	460,193
Homeland security	0

Fiscal Year 2006

Total aid	$945,171
CMPTRA	439,781
Muni. block grant	29,090
Energy tax receipts	476,300
Homeland security	NA

Taxes

	2003	2004	2005
General tax rate per $100	2.98	3.091	3.329
Net valuation taxable	$137,441,315	$138,022,554	$139,626,797
State equalized value	$176,071,375	$187,486,036	$217,521,105
County equalization ratio	83.82	78.06	73.47

Demographics & Socio-Economic Characteristics
(2000 U.S. Census, except as noted)

Population
1980*	9,895
1990*	9,473
2000	9,523
Male	4,428
Female	5,095
2004 (estimate)*	9,505
Persons per sq. mi. of land	7,312

Race & Hispanic Origin, 2000
Race
White	8,054
Black/African American	266
Amer. Indian/Alaska Natv.	7
Asian	682
Natv. Hawaiian/Pac. Islander	1
Other Race	315
Two or more races	198
Hispanic origin, total	1,115
Mexican	27
Puerto Rican	301
Cuban	106
Other Hispanic	681

Age & Nativity, 2000
Under 5 years	618
18 years and over	7,514
21 years and over	7,262
65 years and over	1,670
85 years and over	263
Median Age	40.2
Native born	7,728
Foreign born	1,795

Educational Attainment, 2000
Population 25 years and over	7,053
0-8 yrs of school	4.0%
High School grad or higher	87.6%
Bachelor's degree or higher	31.2%
Graduate degree	10.1%

Income & Poverty, 1999
Per capita income	$28,117
Median household income	$62,113
Median family income	$73,419
Persons in poverty	311
H'holds receiving public assistance	58
H'holds receiving social security	1,273

Households, 2000
Total households	3,710
With persons under 18	1,161
With persons over 65	1,239
Family households	2,626
One-person households	923
Persons per household	2.56
Persons per family	3.09

Labor & Employment
Total civilian labor force, 2004**	5,462
Unemployment rate	3.7%
Total civilian labor force, 2000	5,116
Unemployment rate	3.5%

Employed persons 16 years and over by occupation, 2000
Managers & professionals	1,858
Service occupations	422
Sales & office occupations	1,864
Farming, fishing & forestry	4
Construction & maintenance	377
Production & transportation	413
Self-employed persons	253

*US Census Bureau
**New Jersey Department of Labor

General Information
Borough of Maywood
15 Park Ave
Maywood, NJ 07607
201-845-2900
Web site	www.maywoodnj.org
Land area (sq. miles)	1.30
Water area (sq. miles)	0
Type of government	Borough
Form of government	B

Government

Legislative Districts
US Congressional	9
State Legislative	37

Local Officials, 2006
Mayor	Thomas H. Richards
Admin/Manager	Jack Terhune
Clerk	Jean M. Pelligra
Finance Dir/Treas	Charles Cuccia
Engineer	Michael Neglia
Attorney	William Rupp
Tax assessor	George Reggo
Tax collector	NA
Building officer	George Gorgeou
Zoning officer	Harry Hillenius
Public Works	Donald Cooke

Housing & Construction

Housing Units, 2000*
Total	3,777
Median rent	$880
Median SF home value	$197,900

New Privately Owned Housing Units Authorized by Building Permit
	Units	Value
Total, 2004	1	$160,100
Single family	1	$160,100
Total, 2005	1	$9,000
Single family	1	$9,000

Real Property Valuation - parcels, 2005
	Number	Valuation
Total		$617,156,500
Vacant	62	3,159,200
Residential	2,731	488,007,600
Commercial	106	51,209,400
Industrial	27	51,320,400
Apartments	15	23,459,900
Farm land	0	0
Farm homestead	0	0

Average Property Value & Tax, 2005
Residential value	$178,692
Property tax	$6,501
FAIR rebate	$627

Public Library
Maywood Public Library
459 Maywood Ave
Maywood, NJ 07607
201-845-2915
Director	Diane Rhodes

Library statistics, 2004
	Total	per capita
Volumes	63,366	6.65
Expenditure	$382,902	$40.21

Public Safety
Police
Chief	David Pegg
Number of officers, 2004	24

Crime, 2004	Number	Rate
Total	116	12.2
Violent	2	0.2
Non-violent	114	12
Domestic Viol.	55	NA

Emergency/Fire
Director	Glenn Mohring

Public School District
(for school year 2004-2005 except as noted)

Maywood School District
452 Maywood Ave
Maywood, NJ 07607
201-845-9114
Superintendent	Robert Otnisky
Grade plan	K-12
Enrollment	801.0
Students per teacher	11.2
Per pupil expenditure	$12,433
Median faculty salary	$47,000
Median administrator salary	$101,521
Grade 12 enrollment	NA
High school graduation rate	NA

Assessment test results
(percent scoring at proficient or advanced level)
	Language	Math
Grade 3	94.1%	93.1%
Grade 8	79.4%	70.1%
High school	NA	NA

SAT
Percent tested	NA
Average SAT math score	NA
Average SAT verbal score	NA

No Child Left Behind, 2003-04
Attendence rate (target = 90%)	96.4%
Drop rate	NA
Highly-qualified teachers	96.2%
District needs improvement?(AYP)	No

Municipal Finance

Fiscal Year 2005
Total tax levy	$22,469,732
County levy	2,092,269
County taxes	1,987,390
County library	0
County health	0
County open space	104,879
School levy	12,412,881
Local muni. budget	7,964,582
Misc. revenues	3,980,226
Total aid	$1,447,726
CMPTRA	415,381
Muni. block grant	41,727
Energy tax receipts	940,618
Homeland security	50,000

Fiscal Year 2006
Total aid	$1,447,726
CMPTRA	382,459
Muni. block grant	41,727
Energy tax receipts	973,540
Homeland security	50,000

Taxes
	2003	2004	2005
General tax rate per $100	3.26	3.450	3.640
Net valuation taxable	$618,284,029	$618,588,964	$617,665,199
State equalized value	$936,652,066	$1,043,801,770	$1,176,281,087
County equalization ratio	73.7	66.01	59.24

Demographics & Socio-Economic Characteristics
(2000 U.S. Census, except as noted)

Population
1980*	4,958
1990*	4,462
2000	4,173
Male	2,043
Female	2,130
2004 (estimate)*	4,202
Persons per sq. mi. of land	3,487

Race & Hispanic Origin, 2000
Race
White	4,103
Black/African American	18
Amer. Indian/Alaska Natv.	5
Asian	20
Natv. Hawaiian/Pac. Islander	0
Other Race	4
Two or more races	23
Hispanic origin, total	41
Mexican	2
Puerto Rican	13
Cuban	18
Other Hispanic	8

Age & Nativity, 2000
Under 5 years	261
18 years and over	3,106
21 years and over	2,988
65 years and over	516
85 years and over	31
Median Age	40.3
Native born	4,102
Foreign born	71

Educational Attainment, 2000
Population 25 years and over	2,910
0-8 yrs of school	1.2%
High School grad or higher	95.2%
Bachelor's degree or higher	50.1%
Graduate degree	14.0%

Income & Poverty, 1999
Per capita income	$31,382
Median household income	$77,536
Median family income	$83,695
Persons in poverty	89
H'holds receiving public assistance	7
H'holds receiving social security	392

Households, 2000
Total households	1,527
With persons under 18	592
With persons over 65	363
Family households	1,239
One-person households	231
Persons per household	2.73
Persons per family	3.04

Labor & Employment
Total civilian labor force, 2004**	12,310
Unemployment rate	4.3%
Total civilian labor force, 2000	2,346
Unemployment rate	1.5%

Employed persons 16 years and over by occupation, 2000
Managers & professionals	1,124
Service occupations	218
Sales & office occupations	735
Farming, fishing & forestry	0
Construction & maintenance	96
Production & transportation	137
Self-employed persons	134

*US Census Bureau
**New Jersey Department of Labor

General Information
Borough of Medford Lakes
Cabin Circle
Medford Lakes, NJ 08055
609-654-8898

Web site	www.medfordlakes.com
Land area (sq. miles)	1.21
Water area (sq. miles)	0.10
Type of government	Borough
Form of government	CM '23

Government

Legislative Districts
US Congressional	3
State Legislative	8

Local Officials, 2006
Mayor	David D. Wasson
Admin/Manager	Richard J. Knight
Clerk	Richard J. Knight
Finance Dir/Treas	Donna Condo
Engineer	Alaimo Group
Attorney	Peter Lange Jr.
Tax assessor	Douglas Kolton
Tax collector	NA
Building officer	Thomas Heck
Zoning officer	Thomas Heck
Public Works	Pat McCorriston Sr.

Housing & Construction

Housing Units, 2000*
Total	1,555
Median rent	$920
Median SF home value	$161,100

New Privately Owned Housing Units
Authorized by Building Permit
	Units	Value
Total, 2004	4	$1,803,000
Single family	4	$1,803,000
Total, 2005	4	$1,681,014
Single family	4	$1,681,014

Real Property Valuation - parcels, 2005
	Number	Valuation
Total		$231,731,300
Vacant	36	1,051,500
Residential	1,540	227,264,500
Commercial	15	3,415,300
Industrial	0	0
Apartments	0	0
Farm land	0	0
Farm homestead	0	0

Average Property Value & Tax, 2005
Residential value	$147,574
Property tax	$6,915
FAIR rebate	$554

Public Library
No public municipal library.

Library statistics, 2004
	Total	per capita
Volumes	NA	NA
Expenditure	NA	NA

Public Safety

Police
Chief	Frank Martine
Number of officers, 2004	7

Crime, 2004	Number	Rate
Total	26	6.2
Violent	4	1
Non-violent	22	5.2
Domestic Viol.	12	NA

Emergency/Fire
Director	Mark McIntosh

Public School District
(for school year 2004-2005 except as noted)

Medford Lakes Borough School District
135 Mudjekeewis Trail
Medford Lakes, NJ 08055
609-654-0991

Superintendent	Diane Bacher
Grade plan	K-8
Enrollment	535.0
Students per teacher	11.5
Per pupil expenditure	$10,235
Median faculty salary	$46,650
Median administrator salary	$84,000
Grade 12 enrollment	NA
High school graduation rate	NA

Assessment test results
(percent scoring at proficient or advanced level)
	Language	Math
Grade 3	98.2%	98.3%
Grade 8	93.4%	78.7%
High school	NA	NA

SAT
Percent tested	NA
Average SAT math score	NA
Average SAT verbal score	NA

No Child Left Behind, 2003-04
Attendance rate (target = 90%)	95.6%
Drop rate	NA
Highly-qualified teachers	100%
District needs improvement?(AYP)	No

Municipal Finance

Fiscal Year 2005
Total tax levy	$10,867,124
County levy	1,670,154
County taxes	1,401,084
County library	122,677
County health	0
County open space	146,393
School levy	6,949,748
Local muni. budget	2,247,222
Misc. revenues	1,649,872
Total aid	$454,594
CMPTRA	193,075
Muni. block grant	19,524
Energy tax receipts	216,995
Homeland security	25,000

Fiscal Year 2006
Total aid	$454,594
CMPTRA	185,480
Muni. block grant	19,524
Energy tax receipts	224,590
Homeland security	25,000

Taxes
	2003	2004	2005
General tax rate per $100	4.24	4.376	4.686
Net valuation taxable	$230,887,334	$231,695,655	$231,932,824
State equalized value	$318,158,101	$365,078,165	$413,206,528
County equalization ratio	79.18	72.57	63.44

Demographics & Socio-Economic Characteristics
(2000 U.S. Census, except as noted)

Population
1980*	17,471
1990*	20,526
2000	22,253
Male	10,779
Female	11,474
2004 (estimate)*	23,568
Persons per sq. mi. of land	599

Race & Hispanic Origin, 2000
Race
White	21,527
Black/African American	170
Amer. Indian/Alaska Natv.	26
Asian	327
Natv. Hawaiian/Pac. Islander	9
Other Race	63
Two or more races	131
Hispanic origin, total	252
Mexican	37
Puerto Rican	99
Cuban	18
Other Hispanic	98

Age & Nativity, 2000
Under 5 years	1,416
18 years and over	16,279
21 years and over	15,684
65 years and over	2,387
85 years and over	430
Median Age	40
Native born	21,375
Foreign born	878

Educational Attainment, 2000
Population 25 years and over	15,045
0-8 yrs of school	1.2%
High School grad or higher	94.8%
Bachelor's degree or higher	49.9%
Graduate degree	18.5%

Income & Poverty, 1999
Per capita income	$38,641
Median household income	$83,059
Median family income	$97,135
Persons in poverty	410
H'holds receiving public assistance	67
H'holds receiving social security	1,720

Households, 2000
Total households	7,946
With persons under 18	3,188
With persons over 65	1,628
Family households	6,287
One-person households	1,383
Persons per household	2.77
Persons per family	3.16

Labor & Employment
Total civilian labor force, 2004**	3,035
Unemployment rate	3.5%
Total civilian labor force, 2000	11,619
Unemployment rate	2.2%

Employed persons 16 years and over by occupation, 2000
Managers & professionals	6,249
Service occupations	1,007
Sales & office occupations	2,992
Farming, fishing & forestry	8
Construction & maintenance	559
Production & transportation	549
Self-employed persons	770

*US Census Bureau
**New Jersey Department of Labor

General Information
Township of Medford
17 North Main St
Medford, NJ 08055
609-654-2608
Web site	www.medfordtownship.com
Land area (sq. miles)	39.32
Water area (sq. miles)	0.49
Type of government	Township
Form of government	CM '50

Government
Legislative Districts
US Congressional	3
State Legislative	8

Local Officials, 2006
Mayor	Lisa Post
Admin/Manager	Mike Achey (Actg)
Clerk	Joyce Frenia
Finance Dir/Treas	Katherine Burger
Engineer	Christopher Noll
Attorney	Richard Hunt
Tax assessor	Gilbert Goble
Tax collector	Joan Schifferdecker
Building officer	Edwin Brown Jr.
Zoning officer	Dennis Funaro
Public Works	George Snyder

Housing & Construction
Housing Units, 2000*
Total	8,147
Median rent	$947
Median SF home value	$213,600

New Privately Owned Housing Units
Authorized by Building Permit
	Units	Value
Total, 2004	29	$4,431,438
Single family	29	$4,431,438
Total, 2005	27	$5,968,775
Single family	27	$5,968,775

Real Property Valuation - parcels, 2005
	Number	Valuation
Total		$1,737,768,600
Vacant	723	21,187,300
Residential	7,610	1,508,864,000
Commercial	325	145,992,900
Industrial	10	8,842,900
Apartments	7	29,815,900
Farm land	101	20,565,900
Farm homestead	178	2,499,700

Average Property Value & Tax, 2005
Residential value	$194,063
Property tax	$7,662
FAIR rebate	$522

Public Library
Pinelands Branch Library†
39 Allen Ave
Medford, NJ 08055
609-654-6113
Branch Librarian	Judy Aley

Library statistics, 2004
	Total	per capita
Volumes	NA	NA
Expenditure	NA	NA

†Branch of County Library

Public Safety
Police
Chief	James Kehoe
Number of officers, 2004	43

Crime, 2004	Number	Rate
Total	296	12.7
Violent	10	0.4
Non-violent	286	12.2
Domestic Viol.	176	NA

Emergency/Fire
Director	NA

Public School District
(for school year 2004-2005 except as noted)

Medford Township School District
128 Route 70
Medford, NJ 08055
609-654-6416
Superintendent	Joseph J. Del Rossi
Grade plan	K-8
Enrollment	3,029.0
Students per teacher	12.6
Per pupil expenditure	$11,742
Median faculty salary	$49,800
Median administrator salary	$98,500
Grade 12 enrollment	NA
High school graduation rate	NA

Assessment test results
(percent scoring at proficient or advanced level)
	Language	Math
Grade 3	93.6%	90.3%
Grade 8	89.5%	85.6%
High school	NA	NA

SAT
Percent tested	NA
Average SAT math score	NA
Average SAT verbal score	NA

No Child Left Behind, 2003-04
Attendence rate (target = 90%)	96.2%
Drop rate	NA
Highly-qualified teachers	98.6%
District needs improvement?(AYP)	No

Municipal Finance
Fiscal Year 2005
Total tax levy	$68,790,947
County levy	11,759,523
County taxes	9,865,004
County library	863,769
County health	0
County open space	1,030,750
School levy	48,337,179
Local muni. budget	8,694,245
Misc. revenues	9,401,603
Total aid	$2,819,464
CMPTRA	862,329
Muni. block grant	89,815
Energy tax receipts	1,704,558
Homeland security	90,000

Fiscal Year 2006
Total aid	$2,819,464
CMPTRA	802,669
Muni. block grant	89,815
Energy tax receipts	1,764,218
Homeland security	90,000

Taxes
	2003	2004	2005
General tax rate per $100	3.53	3.809	3.949
Net valuation taxable	$1,699,367,220	$1,729,843,604	$1,742,325,078
State equalized value	$2,249,923,501	$2,553,387,146	$2,853,931,332
County equalization ratio	83.43	75.53	67.68

Demographics & Socio-Economic Characteristics
(2000 U.S. Census, except as noted)

Population
1980*	4,899
1990*	4,890
2000	5,097
Male	2,410
Female	2,687
2004 (estimate)*	5,160
Persons per sq. mi. of land	857

Race & Hispanic Origin, 2000
Race
White	4,951
Black/African American	23
Amer. Indian/Alaska Natv.	1
Asian	72
Natv. Hawaiian/Pac. Islander	3
Other Race	14
Two or more races	33
Hispanic origin, total	125
Mexican	11
Puerto Rican	23
Cuban	3
Other Hispanic	88

Age & Nativity, 2000
Under 5 years	351
18 years and over	3,730
21 years and over	3,600
65 years and over	857
85 years and over	150
Median Age	41.9
Native born	4,681
Foreign born	416

Educational Attainment, 2000
Population 25 years and over	3,489
0-8 yrs of school	0.7%
High School grad or higher	95.3%
Bachelor's degree or higher	62.2%
Graduate degree	27.8%

Income & Poverty, 1999
Per capita income	$48,629
Median household income	$110,348
Median family income	$129,812
Persons in poverty	200
H'holds receiving public assistance	0
H'holds receiving social security	514

Households, 2000
Total households	1,781
With persons under 18	666
With persons over 65	514
Family households	1,380
One-person households	332
Persons per household	2.72
Persons per family	3.13

Labor & Employment
Total civilian labor force, 2004**	2,794
Unemployment rate	1.5%
Total civilian labor force, 2000	2,274
Unemployment rate	1.2%

Employed persons 16 years and over by occupation, 2000
Managers & professionals	1,240
Service occupations	135
Sales & office occupations	728
Farming, fishing & forestry	14
Construction & maintenance	73
Production & transportation	57
Self-employed persons	230

*US Census Bureau
**New Jersey Department of Labor

General Information
Borough of Mendham
2 West Main St
Mendham, NJ 07945
973-543-7152
Web site	www.mendhamnj.org
Land area (sq. miles)	6.02
Water area (sq. miles)	0.02
Type of government	Borough
Form of government	B

Government
Legislative Districts
US Congressional	11
State Legislative	16

Local Officials, 2006
Mayor	Richard Kraft
Admin/Manager	Ralph Blakeslee
Clerk	Maureen Massey
Finance Dir/Treas	Susan Giordano
Engineer	Paul Ferriero
Attorney	John Jansen
Tax assessor	Ernest DelGuercio
Tax collector	Rosalie Lauerman
Building officer	Joseph Alicino
Zoning officer	Geoff Price
Public Works	Thomas Miller

Housing & Construction
Housing Units, 2000*
Total	1,828
Median rent	$1,186
Median SF home value	$397,000

New Privately Owned Housing Units Authorized by Building Permit
	Units	Value
Total, 2004	6	$6,322,000
Single family	6	$6,322,000
Total, 2005	3	$2,883,167
Single family	3	$2,883,167

Real Property Valuation - parcels, 2005
	Number	Valuation
Total		$625,026,215
Vacant	42	7,851,304
Residential	1,631	544,056,600
Commercial	86	55,412,000
Industrial	0	0
Apartments	4	1,443,900
Farm land	19	15,421,400
Farm homestead	53	841,011

Average Property Value & Tax, 2005
Residential value	$323,573
Property tax	$9,999
FAIR rebate	$629

Public Library
Mendham Free Public Library
10 Hilltop Rd
Mendham, NJ 07945
973-543-4152
Director	Kathie O'Dowd

Library statistics, 2004
	Total	per capita
Volumes	37,990	7.45
Expenditure	$306,843	$60.20

Public Safety
Police
Chief	John Taylor
Number of officers, 2004	11

Crime, 2004	Number	Rate
Total	41	8
Violent	1	0.2
Non-violent	40	7.8
Domestic Viol.	9	NA

Emergency/Fire
Director	Michael Orgera

Public School District
(for school year 2004-2005 except as noted)

Mendham Borough School District
12 Hilltop Rd
Mendham, NJ 07945
973-543-2295
Superintendent	Janie P. Edmonds
Grade plan	K-8
Enrollment	672.0
Students per teacher	10.4
Per pupil expenditure	$10,781
Median faculty salary	$46,782
Median administrator salary	$97,850
Grade 12 enrollment	NA
High school graduation rate	NA

Assessment test results
(percent scoring at proficient or advanced level)
	Language	Math
Grade 3	95.6%	98.6%
Grade 8	97.6%	89.2%
High school	NA	NA

SAT
Percent tested	NA
Average SAT math score	NA
Average SAT verbal score	NA

No Child Left Behind, 2003-04
Attendence rate (target = 90%)	96.4%
Drop rate	NA
Highly-qualified teachers	90.5%
District needs improvement?(AYP)	No

Municipal Finance
Fiscal Year 2005
Total tax levy	$19,351,802
County levy	3,220,763
County taxes	2,638,213
County library	0
County health	0
County open space	582,550
School levy	12,792,306
Local muni. budget	3,338,732
Misc. revenues	2,158,901
Total aid	$768,482
CMPTRA	166,968
Muni. block grant	21,397
Energy tax receipts	530,117
Homeland security	50,000

Fiscal Year 2006
Total aid	$768,483
CMPTRA	148,414
Muni. block grant	21,397
Energy tax receipts	548,672
Homeland security	50,000

Taxes
	2003	2004	2005
General tax rate per $100	2.75	2.940	3.100
Net valuation taxable	$617,934,292	$619,289,542	$626,250,185
State equalized value	$1,116,009,196	$1,195,292,825	$1,269,254,530
County equalization ratio	61.34	55.37	51.76

Demographics & Socio-Economic Characteristics
(2000 U.S. Census, except as noted)

Population
1980*	4,488
1990*	4,537
2000	5,400
Male	2,656
Female	2,744
2004 (estimate)*	5,625
Persons per sq. mi. of land	315

Race & Hispanic Origin, 2000
Race
White	5,179
Black/African American	50
Amer. Indian/Alaska Natv.	5
Asian	109
Natv. Hawaiian/Pac. Islander	0
Other Race	19
Two or more races	38
Hispanic origin, total	82
Mexican	10
Puerto Rican	9
Cuban	12
Other Hispanic	51

Age & Nativity, 2000
Under 5 years	423
18 years and over	3,674
21 years and over	3,569
65 years and over	582
85 years and over	44
Median Age	40.3
Native born	4,993
Foreign born	407

Educational Attainment, 2000
Population 25 years and over	3,467
0-8 yrs of school	0.9%
High School grad or higher	97.9%
Bachelor's degree or higher	71.3%
Graduate degree	34.6%

Income & Poverty, 1999
Per capita income	$61,460
Median household income	$136,174
Median family income	$146,254
Persons in poverty	96
H'holds receiving public assistance	0
H'holds receiving social security	406

Households, 2000
Total households	1,788
With persons under 18	853
With persons over 65	382
Family households	1,539
One-person households	198
Persons per household	3.01
Persons per family	3.27

Labor & Employment
Total civilian labor force, 2004**	2,565
Unemployment rate	1.9%
Total civilian labor force, 2000	2,355
Unemployment rate	1.1%

Employed persons 16 years and over by occupation, 2000
Managers & professionals	1,405
Service occupations	134
Sales & office occupations	605
Farming, fishing & forestry	0
Construction & maintenance	110
Production & transportation	75
Self-employed persons	205

*US Census Bureau
**New Jersey Department of Labor

General Information
Township of Mendham
Township Hall
Box 520
Brookside, NJ 07926
973-543-4555
Web site	www.mendhamtownship.org
Land area (sq. miles)	17.86
Water area (sq. miles)	0.12
Type of government	Township
Form of government	TC

Government

Legislative Districts
US Congressional	11
State Legislative	25

Local Officials, 2006
Mayor	Richard H. Krieg
Admin/Manager	Stephen Mountain
Clerk	Penny Newell
Finance Dir/Treas	Heather Webster
Engineer	Thomas Lemanowicz
Attorney	Christopher Falcon
Tax assessor	Ernest DelGuercio
Tax collector	NA
Building officer	Russ Heiney
Zoning officer	NA
Public Works	NA

Housing & Construction

Housing Units, 2000*
Total	1,849
Median rent	$1,139
Median SF home value	$556,200

New Privately Owned Housing Units
Authorized by Building Permit

	Units	Value
Total, 2004	0	$50,000
Single family	0	$50,000
Total, 2005	5	$4,952,875
Single family	5	$4,952,875

Real Property Valuation - parcels, 2005
	Number	Valuation
Total		$2,114,823,400
Vacant	104	46,891,100
Residential	1,929	1,953,835,900
Commercial	7	11,650,600
Industrial	1	3,000
Apartments	1	6,830,600
Farm land	60	94,200,900
Farm homestead	96	1,411,300

Average Property Value & Tax, 2005
Residential value	$965,554
Property tax	$13,431
FAIR rebate	$592

Public Library
Mendham Twp Library
Municipal Bldg Cherry Ln
Brookside, NJ 07926
973-543-4018
Director	(Vacant)

Library statistics, 2004
	Total	per capita
Volumes	38,495	7.13
Expenditure	$237,664	$44.01

Public Safety

Police
Chief	Thomas Costanza
Number of officers, 2004	15

Crime, 2004	Number	Rate
Total	47	8.4
Violent	5	0.9
Non-violent	42	7.5
Domestic Viol.	2	NA

Emergency/Fire
Director	Samuel Tolley (Chief)

Public School District
(for school year 2004-2005 except as noted)

Mendham Township School District
West Main St
Brookside, NJ 07926
973-543-7107
Superintendent	Christine Johnson
Grade plan	K-8
Enrollment	905.0
Students per teacher	9.7
Per pupil expenditure	$13,452
Median faculty salary	$47,770
Median administrator salary	$105,000
Grade 12 enrollment	NA
High school graduation rate	NA

Assessment test results
(percent scoring at proficient or advanced level)
	Language	Math
Grade 3	97.0%	92.0%
Grade 8	90.4%	85.7%
High school	NA	NA

SAT
Percent tested	NA
Average SAT math score	NA
Average SAT verbal score	NA

No Child Left Behind, 2003-04
Attendence rate (target = 90%)	96.5%
Drop rate	NA
Highly-qualified teachers	94.5%
District needs improvement?(AYP)	No

Municipal Finance

Fiscal Year 2005
Total tax levy	$29,435,961
County levy	4,703,504
County taxes	3,852,820
County library	0
County health	0
County open space	850,683
School levy	19,361,125
Local muni. budget	5,371,332
Misc. revenues	2,967,891
Total aid	$695,393
CMPTRA	105,204
Muni. block grant	21,174
Energy tax receipts	490,956
Homeland security	50,000

Fiscal Year 2006
Total aid	$695,393
CMPTRA	88,021
Muni. block grant	21,174
Energy tax receipts	508,139
Homeland security	50,000

Taxes
	2003	2004	2005
General tax rate per $100	2.70	2.810	1.400
Net valuation taxable	$968,511,020	$986,134,422	$2,116,183,594
State equalized value	$1,601,109,307	$1,741,308,073	$1,974,051,860
County equalization ratio	65.09	60.49	119.74

Demographics & Socio-Economic Characteristics
(2000 U.S. Census, except as noted)

Population
1980*	3,972
1990*	4,095
2000	3,801
Male	1,791
Female	2,010
2004 (estimate)*	3,816
Persons per sq. mi. of land	6,342

Race & Hispanic Origin, 2000
Race
White	3,265
Black/African American	282
Amer. Indian/Alaska Natv.	11
Asian	80
Natv. Hawaiian/Pac. Islander	0
Other Race	108
Two or more races	55
Hispanic origin, total	208
Mexican	4
Puerto Rican	138
Cuban	7
Other Hispanic	59

Age & Nativity, 2000
Under 5 years	250
18 years and over	2,825
21 years and over	2,719
65 years and over	526
85 years and over	62
Median Age	37.2
Native born	3,651
Foreign born	150

Educational Attainment, 2000
Population 25 years and over	2,531
0-8 yrs of school	3.1%
High School grad or higher	81.8%
Bachelor's degree or higher	27.7%
Graduate degree	8.1%

Income & Poverty, 1999
Per capita income	$25,589
Median household income	$49,392
Median family income	$60,652
Persons in poverty	259
H'holds receiving public assistance	36
H'holds receiving social security	391

Households, 2000
Total households	1,524
With persons under 18	524
With persons over 65	398
Family households	946
One-person households	488
Persons per household	2.48
Persons per family	3.19

Labor & Employment
Total civilian labor force, 2004**	2,173
Unemployment rate	4.1%
Total civilian labor force, 2000	2,026
Unemployment rate	3.3%

Employed persons 16 years and over by occupation, 2000
Managers & professionals	704
Service occupations	233
Sales & office occupations	644
Farming, fishing & forestry	0
Construction & maintenance	186
Production & transportation	193
Self-employed persons	150

*US Census Bureau
**New Jersey Department of Labor

General Information
Borough of Merchantville
1 W Maple Ave
Merchantville, NJ 08109
856-662-2474
Web site	merchantvillenj.com
Land area (sq. miles)	0.60
Water area (sq. miles)	0
Type of government	Borough
Form of government	B

Government

Legislative Districts
US Congressional	3
State Legislative	7

Local Officials, 2006
Mayor	Patrick Brennan
Admin/Manager	John Fry
Clerk	Oren R. Thomas IV
Finance Dir/Treas	Susan Walker
Engineer	Edward Vernick
Attorney	Timothy Higgins
Tax assessor	John Dymond
Tax collector	John Fry
Building officer	William Joseph
Zoning officer	Walt Sikerski
Public Works	Daniel Beckett

Housing & Construction

Housing Units, 2000*
Total	1,607
Median rent	$642
Median SF home value	$122,200

New Privately Owned Housing Units
Authorized by Building Permit
	Units	Value
Total, 2004	9	$798,552
Single family	9	$798,552
Total, 2005	9	$798,552
Single family	9	$798,552

Real Property Valuation - parcels, 2005
	Number	Valuation
Total		$158,328,600
Vacant	54	901,600
Residential	1,076	131,411,400
Commercial	85	17,332,600
Industrial	0	0
Apartments	24	8,683,000
Farm land	0	0
Farm homestead	0	0

Average Property Value & Tax, 2005
Residential value	$122,130
Property tax	$5,383
FAIR rebate	$532

Public Library
Merchantville Library†
130 S Centre St
Merchantville, NJ 08109
856-665-3128
Branch Librarian	Mimi Cirillo

Library statistics, 2004
	Total	per capita
Volumes	NA	NA
Expenditure	NA	NA

†Branch of county library

Public Safety

Police
Chief	Wayne Bauer
Number of officers, 2004	13

Crime, 2004	Number	Rate
Total	90	23.6
Violent	10	2.6
Non-violent	80	21
Domestic Viol.	14	NA

Emergency/Fire
Director	Roy Adair

Public School District
(for school year 2004-2005 except as noted)

Merchantville School District
130 S Centre St
Merchantville, NJ 08109
856-663-1091
Administrator	Christian Swanson
Grade plan	K-12
Enrollment	371.0
Students per teacher	12.3
Per pupil expenditure	$11,966
Median faculty salary	$62,685
Median administrator salary	$90,228
Grade 12 enrollment	NA
High school graduation rate	NA

Assessment test results
(percent scoring at proficient or advanced level)
	Language	Math
Grade 3	91.1%	97.0%
Grade 8	78.8%	75.8%
High school	NA	NA

SAT
Percent tested	NA
Average SAT math score	NA
Average SAT verbal score	NA

No Child Left Behind, 2003-04
Attendence rate (target = 90%)	94.5%
Drop rate	NA
Highly-qualified teachers	100%
District needs improvement?(AYP)	No

Municipal Finance

Fiscal Year 2005
Total tax levy	$7,196,123
County levy	1,698,459
County taxes	1,565,375
County library	112,559
County health	0
County open space	20,525
School levy	3,891,477
Local muni. budget	1,606,187
Misc. revenues	2,526,298
Total aid	$859,811
CMPTRA	480,631
Muni. block grant	17,918
Energy tax receipts	336,262
Homeland security	25,000

Fiscal Year 2006
Total aid	$859,811
CMPTRA	468,862
Muni. block grant	17,918
Energy tax receipts	348,031
Homeland security	25,000

Taxes
	2003	2004	2005
General tax rate per $100	4.17	4.225	4.408
Net valuation taxable	$163,571,570	$163,230,247	$163,279,412
State equalized value	$181,202,581	$203,818,571	$231,930,983
County equalization ratio	97.33	90.27	79.50

Demographics & Socio-Economic Characteristics
(2000 U.S. Census, except as noted)

Population
1980*	13,762
1990*	12,804
2000	12,840
Male	6,137
Female	6,703
2004 (estimate)*	13,335
Persons per sq. mi. of land	4,865

Race & Hispanic Origin, 2000
Race
White	10,835
Black/African American	681
Amer. Indian/Alaska Natv.	13
Asian	928
Natv. Hawaiian/Pac. Islander	0
Other Race	144
Two or more races	239
Hispanic origin, total	508
Mexican	50
Puerto Rican	188
Cuban	51
Other Hispanic	219

Age & Nativity, 2000
Under 5 years	847
18 years and over	9,849
21 years and over	9,531
65 years and over	1,910
85 years and over	173
Median Age	39.5
Native born	11,020
Foreign born	1,820

Educational Attainment, 2000
Population 25 years and over	9,254
0-8 yrs of school	2.3%
High School grad or higher	92.1%
Bachelor's degree or higher	49.2%
Graduate degree	19.8%

Income & Poverty, 1999
Per capita income	$36,749
Median household income	$75,546
Median family income	$85,022
Persons in poverty	500
H'holds receiving public assistance	40
H'holds receiving social security	1,322

Households, 2000
Total households	4,992
With persons under 18	1,726
With persons over 65	1,377
Family households	3,583
One-person households	1,150
Persons per household	2.57
Persons per family	3.05

Labor & Employment
Total civilian labor force, 2004**	7,979
Unemployment rate	2.8%
Total civilian labor force, 2000	7,058
Unemployment rate	4.4%

Employed persons 16 years and over by occupation, 2000
Managers & professionals	3,593
Service occupations	482
Sales & office occupations	1,864
Farming, fishing & forestry	0
Construction & maintenance	282
Production & transportation	523
Self-employed persons	337

*US Census Bureau
**New Jersey Department of Labor

General Information
Borough of Metuchen
500 Main St
Metuchen, NJ 08840
732-632-8540

Web site	www.metuchennj.org
Land area (sq. miles)	2.74
Water area (sq. miles)	0
Type of government	Borough
Form of government	B

Government

Legislative Districts
US Congressional	6
State Legislative	18

Local Officials, 2006
Mayor	Edmund O'Brien
Admin/Manager	William Boerth
Clerk	Bozena Lacina
Finance Dir/Treas	Rebecca Cuthbert
Engineer	David Hoder
Attorney	David Frizell
Tax assessor	Walker Matlack
Tax collector	NA
Building officer	James Gyug
Zoning officer	Fany Ayala
Public Works	NA

Housing & Construction

Housing Units, 2000*
Total	5,104
Median rent	$873
Median SF home value	$194,900

New Privately Owned Housing Units Authorized by Building Permit
	Units	Value
Total, 2004	41	$4,095,696
Single family	23	$3,085,601
Total, 2005	14	$2,378,381
Single family	12	$2,192,100

Real Property Valuation - parcels, 2005
	Number	Valuation
Total		$952,405,700
Vacant	142	11,629,600
Residential	4,543	770,745,700
Commercial	356	111,299,600
Industrial	57	39,150,400
Apartments	18	19,580,400
Farm land	0	0
Farm homestead	0	0

Average Property Value & Tax, 2005
Residential value	$169,656
Property tax	$6,466
FAIR rebate	$598

Public Library
Metuchen Public Library
480 Middlesex Ave
Metuchen, NJ 08840
732-632-8526

Director | Melody Kokola

Library statistics, 2004
	Total	per capita
Volumes	80,341	6.26
Expenditure	$663,927	$51.71

Public Safety
Police
Chief	James Keane
Number of officers, 2004	28

Crime, 2004	Number	Rate
Total	219	16.5
Violent	14	1.1
Non-violent	205	15.4
Domestic Viol.	80	NA

Emergency/Fire
Director | Robert Donnan

Public School District
(for school year 2004-2005 except as noted)

Metuchen School District
16 Simpson Place
Metuchen, NJ 08840
732-321-8700
Superintendent	T. Pollifrone-Sinatra
Grade plan	K-12
Enrollment	1,889.5
Students per teacher	10.3
Per pupil expenditure	$12,896
Median faculty salary	$59,700
Median administrator salary	$93,730
Grade 12 enrollment	150.0
High school graduation rate	98.6%

Assessment test results
(percent scoring at proficient or advanced level)
	Language	Math
Grade 3	96.5%	93.7%
Grade 8	87.1%	76.0%
High school	96.0%	88.4%

SAT
Percent tested	79%
Average SAT math score	559
Average SAT verbal score	543

No Child Left Behind, 2003-04
Attendence rate (target = 90%)	95.6%
Drop rate	0%
Highly-qualified teachers	100%
District needs improvement?(AYP)	No

Municipal Finance
Fiscal Year 2005
Total tax levy	$36,507,688
County levy	5,301,157
County taxes	4,799,982
County library	0
County health	0
County open space	501,175
School levy	24,696,110
Local muni. budget	6,510,421
Misc. revenues	5,966,217
Total aid	$2,007,782
CMPTRA	791,905
Muni. block grant	56,027
Energy tax receipts	1,089,850
Homeland security	70,000

Fiscal Year 2006
Total aid	$2,007,782
CMPTRA	753,760
Muni. block grant	56,027
Energy tax receipts	1,127,995
Homeland security	70,000

Taxes
	2003	2004	2005
General tax rate per $100	3.40	3.560	3.820
Net valuation taxable	$949,104,496	$958,027,296	$957,841,188
State equalized value	$1,525,646,192	$1,687,265,701	$1,930,742,165
County equalization ratio	70.53	62.21	56.63

Demographics & Socio-Economic Characteristics

(2000 U.S. Census, except as noted)

Population

1980*	11,373
1990*	14,771
2000	16,405
Male	7,908
Female	8,497
2004 (estimate)*	16,724
Persons per sq. mi. of land	235

Race & Hispanic Origin, 2000

Race

White	13,979
Black/African American	1,781
Amer. Indian/Alaska Natv.	37
Asian	236
Natv. Hawaiian/Pac. Islander	4
Other Race	108
Two or more races	260
Hispanic origin, total	347
Mexican	27
Puerto Rican	173
Cuban	15
Other Hispanic	132

Age & Nativity, 2000

Under 5 years	933
18 years and over	12,360
21 years and over	11,823
65 years and over	2,925
85 years and over	483
Median Age	39.8
Native born	15,906
Foreign born	499

Educational Attainment, 2000

Population 25 years and over	11,252
0-8 yrs of school	6.0%
High School grad or higher	77.8%
Bachelor's degree or higher	16.5%
Graduate degree	4.5%

Income & Poverty, 1999

Per capita income	$19,805
Median household income	$41,533
Median family income	$49,030
Persons in poverty	1,580
H'holds receiving public assistance	203
H'holds receiving social security	2,081

Households, 2000

Total households	6,009
With persons under 18	2,101
With persons over 65	1,797
Family households	4,216
One-person households	1,481
Persons per household	2.58
Persons per family	3.08

Labor & Employment

Total civilian labor force, 2004**	9,175
Unemployment rate	7.2%
Total civilian labor force, 2000	7,610
Unemployment rate	7.1%

Employed persons 16 years and over by occupation, 2000

Managers & professionals	1,916
Service occupations	1,672
Sales & office occupations	1,811
Farming, fishing & forestry	68
Construction & maintenance	976
Production & transportation	628
Self-employed persons	568

*US Census Bureau
**New Jersey Department of Labor

General Information

Township of Middle
Cape May Courthouse
33 Mechanic St
Middle, NJ 08210
609-465-8732

Web site	www.middletownship.com
Land area (sq. miles)	71.27
Water area (sq. miles)	11.83
Type of government	Township
Form of government	TC

Government

Legislative Districts

US Congressional	2
State Legislative	1

Local Officials, 2006

Mayor	F. Nate Doughty
Admin/Manager	James Alexis
Clerk	James Alexis
Finance Dir/Treas	Tracey Taverner
Engineer	Vincent Orlando
Attorney	James Pickering
Tax assessor	Joseph Ravitz
Tax collector	Sandy Beasley
Building officer	Ralph James
Zoning officer	David May
Public Works	Richard Ceglarski

Housing & Construction

Housing Units, 2000*

Total	7,510
Median rent	$677
Median SF home value	$116,200

New Privately Owned Housing Units
Authorized by Building Permit

	Units	Value
Total, 2004	232	$26,443,667
Single family	230	$26,247,259
Total, 2005	192	$25,515,529
Single family	186	$25,011,529

Real Property Valuation - parcels, 2005

	Number	Valuation
Total		$1,071,039,800
Vacant	4,067	71,526,100
Residential	6,739	740,610,600
Commercial	493	247,651,200
Industrial	4	2,381,000
Apartments	10	2,159,100
Farm land	51	5,866,400
Farm homestead	86	845,400

Average Property Value & Tax, 2005

Residential value	$108,638
Property tax	$3,047
FAIR rebate	$590

Public Library

No public municipal library.

Library statistics, 2004

	Total	per capita
Volumes	NA	NA
Expenditure	NA	NA

Public Safety

Police

Chief	Joseph Evangelista
Number of officers, 2004	50

Crime, 2004	Number	Rate
Total	765	45.3
Violent	82	4.9
Non-violent	683	40.5
Domestic Viol.	186	NA

Emergency/Fire

Director	NA

Public School District

(for school year 2004-2005 except as noted)

Middle Township School District
216 S Main St
Cape May Court House, NJ 08210
609-465-1800

Superintendent	Michael Kopakowski
Grade plan	K-12
Enrollment	2,945.0
Students per teacher	11.3
Per pupil expenditure	$11,839
Median faculty salary	$49,390
Median administrator salary	$92,015
Grade 12 enrollment	230.5
High school graduation rate	86.3%

Assessment test results

(percent scoring at proficient or advanced level)

	Language	Math
Grade 3	72.3%	77.9%
Grade 8	62.2%	57.9%
High school	79.4%	73.7%

SAT

Percent tested	62%
Average SAT math score	534
Average SAT verbal score	516

No Child Left Behind, 2003-04

Attendance rate (target = 90%)	93.0%
Drop rate	2.8%
Highly-qualified teachers	95.9%
District needs improvement?(AYP)	Yes

Municipal Finance

Fiscal Year 2005

Total tax levy	$30,157,325
County levy	4,521,650
County taxes	3,801,582
County library	535,479
County health	0
County open space	184,589
School levy	19,024,668
Local muni. budget	6,611,007
Misc. revenues	10,189,607
Total aid	$4,242,590
CMPTRA	415,988
Muni. block grant	64,633
Energy tax receipts	3,691,969
Homeland security	70,000

Fiscal Year 2006

Total aid	$4,242,591
CMPTRA	286,770
Muni. block grant	64,633
Energy tax receipts	3,821,188
Homeland security	70,000

Taxes

	2003	2004	2005
General tax rate per $100	2.72	2.730	2.810
Net valuation taxable	$990,495,617	$1,024,189,578	$1,075,205,749
State equalized value	$1,379,520,358	$1,751,464,461	$2,281,361,657
County equalization ratio	81.2	71.80	58.35

Demographics & Socio-Economic Characteristics
(2000 U.S. Census, except as noted)

Population
1980*	13,480
1990*	13,055
2000	13,717
Male	6,682
Female	7,035
2004 (estimate)*	13,967
Persons per sq. mi. of land	3,993

Race & Hispanic Origin, 2000
Race
White	11,970
Black/African American	461
Amer. Indian/Alaska Natv.	18
Asian	570
Natv. Hawaiian/Pac. Islander	3
Other Race	440
Two or more races	255
Hispanic origin, total	1,235
Mexican	48
Puerto Rican	244
Cuban	27
Other Hispanic	916

Age & Nativity, 2000
Under 5 years	914
18 years and over	10,411
21 years and over	10,030
65 years and over	1,942
85 years and over	168
Median Age	38
Native born	11,973
Foreign born	1,744

Educational Attainment, 2000
Population 25 years and over	9,538
0-8 yrs of school	4.3%
High School grad or higher	85.4%
Bachelor's degree or higher	23.4%
Graduate degree	6.3%

Income & Poverty, 1999
Per capita income	$27,834
Median household income	$60,723
Median family income	$70,343
Persons in poverty	499
H'holds receiving public assistance	65
H'holds receiving social security	1,558

Households, 2000
Total households	5,048
With persons under 18	1,849
With persons over 65	1,451
Family households	3,739
One-person households	1,097
Persons per household	2.71
Persons per family	3.17

Labor & Employment
Total civilian labor force, 2004**	8,370
Unemployment rate	3.4%
Total civilian labor force, 2000	7,259
Unemployment rate	2.9%

Employed persons 16 years and over by occupation, 2000
Managers & professionals	2,460
Service occupations	794
Sales & office occupations	2,148
Farming, fishing & forestry	0
Construction & maintenance	698
Production & transportation	947
Self-employed persons	350

*US Census Bureau
**New Jersey Department of Labor

General Information
Borough of Middlesex
1200 Mountain Ave
Middlesex, NJ 08846
732-356-7400
Web site	www.middlesexboro-nj.gov
Land area (sq. miles)	3.50
Water area (sq. miles)	0.02
Type of government	Borough
Form of government	Mayor-Council

Government
Legislative Districts
US Congressional	6
State Legislative	22

Local Officials, 2006
Mayor	Gerald D'Angelo
Admin/Manager	Ronald Dobies
Clerk	Kathleen Anello
Finance Dir/Treas	Andrea Corcoran
Engineer	T & M Associats
Attorney	Edward J. Johnson
Tax assessor	Burnham Hobbs
Tax collector	Tonya Hubosky
Building officer	William Murphy
Zoning officer	Daniel Coppola
Public Works	Jerry Schaefer

Housing & Construction
Housing Units, 2000*
Total	5,130
Median rent	$830
Median SF home value	$164,200

New Privately Owned Housing Units
Authorized by Building Permit
	Units	Value
Total, 2004	9	$1,872,811
Single family	9	$1,872,811
Total, 2005	6	$814,390
Single family	6	$814,390

Real Property Valuation - parcels, 2005
	Number	Valuation
Total		$495,908,000
Vacant	174	5,166,600
Residential	4,163	383,941,500
Commercial	201	35,501,600
Industrial	148	61,453,300
Apartments	5	9,845,000
Farm land	0	0
Farm homestead	0	0

Average Property Value & Tax, 2005
Residential value	$92,227
Property tax	$5,393
FAIR rebate	$604

Public Library
Middlesex Public Library
1300 Mountain Ave
Middlesex, NJ 08846
732-356-6602
Director	May Ho

Library statistics, 2004
	Total	per capita
Volumes	68,695	5.01
Expenditure	$449,354	$32.76

Public Safety
Police
Chief	James Benson
Number of officers, 2004	31

Crime, 2004	Number	Rate
Total	145	10.4
Violent	16	1.1
Non-violent	129	9.2
Domestic Viol.	46	NA

Emergency/Fire
Director	Edward Winters

Public School District
(for school year 2004-2005 except as noted)

Middlesex Borough School District
300 Kennedy Dr
Middlesex, NJ 08846
732-317-6000
Superintendent	James Baker
Grade plan	K-12
Enrollment	2,088.5
Students per teacher	10.5
Per pupil expenditure	$11,097
Median faculty salary	$49,112
Median administrator salary	$79,999
Grade 12 enrollment	155.0
High school graduation rate	97.9%

Assessment test results
(percent scoring at proficient or advanced level)
	Language	Math
Grade 3	82.8%	84.3%
Grade 8	76.0%	58.5%
High school	82.9%	76.1%

SAT
Percent tested	69%
Average SAT math score	510
Average SAT verbal score	480

No Child Left Behind, 2003-04
Attendance rate (target = 90%)	95.5%
Drop rate	0.5%
Highly-qualified teachers	100%
District needs improvement?(AYP)	No

Municipal Finance
Fiscal Year 2005
Total tax levy	$29,038,135
County levy	3,934,007
County taxes	3,563,613
County library	0
County health	0
County open space	370,394
School levy	17,396,589
Local muni. budget	7,707,540
Misc. revenues	6,094,541
Total aid	$2,444,669
CMPTRA	1,189,365
Muni. block grant	57,124
Energy tax receipts	1,128,180
Homeland security	70,000

Fiscal Year 2006
Total aid	$2,444,668
CMPTRA	1,149,878
Muni. block grant	57,124
Energy tax receipts	1,167,666
Homeland security	70,000

Taxes
	2003	2004	2005
General tax rate per $100	5.40	5.530	5.850
Net valuation taxable	$494,964,344	$496,320,195	$496,611,033
State equalized value	$1,059,200,394	$1,236,008,193	$1,407,627,645
County equalization ratio	53.26	46.73	40.12

Demographics & Socio-Economic Characteristics
(2000 U.S. Census, except as noted)

Population
1980*	62,574
1990*	68,183
2000	66,327
Male	32,267
Female	34,060
2000 (revised)	67,119
2004 (estimate)*	68,185
Persons per sq. mi. of land	1,658

Race & Hispanic Origin, 2000
Race
White	62,819
Black/African American	803
Amer. Indian/Alaska Natv.	46
Asian	1,717
Natv. Hawaiian/Pac. Islander	17
Other Race	353
Two or more races	572
Hispanic origin, total	2,265
Mexican	116
Puerto Rican	1,087
Cuban	188
Other Hispanic	874

Age & Nativity, 2000
Under 5 years	4,510
18 years and over	48,886
21 years and over	46,945
65 years and over	8,487
85 years and over	996
Median Age	38.8
Native born	62,069
Foreign born	4,258

Educational Attainment, 2000
Population 25 years and over	44,664
0-8 yrs of school	2.7%
High School grad or higher	90.7%
Bachelor's degree or higher	35.0%
Graduate degree	12.6%

Income & Poverty, 1999
Per capita income	$34,196
Median household income	$75,566
Median family income	$86,124
Persons in poverty	2,049
H'holds receiving public assistance	228
H'holds receiving social security	6,448

Households, 2000
Total households	23,236
With persons under 18	9,311
With persons over 65	6,165
Family households	18,109
One-person households	4,397
Persons per household	2.84
Persons per family	3.27

Labor & Employment
Total civilian labor force, 2004**	39,244
Unemployment rate	4.1%
Total civilian labor force, 2000	33,728
Unemployment rate	3.4%

Employed persons 16 years and over by occupation, 2000
Managers & professionals	13,619
Service occupations	3,571
Sales & office occupations	9,952
Farming, fishing & forestry	66
Construction & maintenance	2,679
Production & transportation	2,710
Self-employed persons	1,587

*US Census Bureau
**New Jersey Department of Labor

General Information
Township of Middletown
1 Kings Highway
Middletown, NJ 07748
732-615-2000
Web site	www.middletownnj.org
Land area (sq. miles)	41.12
Water area (sq. miles)	18.23
Type of government	Township
Form of government	TC

Government

Legislative Districts
US Congressional	6, 12
State Legislative	13

Local Officials, 2006
Mayor	Thomas G. Hall
Admin/Manager	Robert Czech
Clerk	Heidi R. Abs
Finance Dir/Treas	Robert Roth
Engineer	Robert Bucco
Attorney	Dowd & Reilly
Tax assessor	Charles Heck
Tax collector	Robert Kapral
Building officer	Joseph Kachinsky
Zoning officer	Mariann Hanko
Public Works	Lawrence Werger

Housing & Construction

Housing Units, 2000*
Total	23,841
Median rent	$836
Median SF home value	$210,700

New Privately Owned Housing Units
Authorized by Building Permit
	Units	Value
Total, 2004	196	$22,906,393
Single family	191	$22,758,068
Total, 2005	76	$15,652,890
Single family	76	$15,652,890

Real Property Valuation - parcels, 2005
	Number	Valuation
Total		$4,901,230,038
Vacant	1,186	48,092,060
Residential	21,841	4,103,775,578
Commercial	591	661,326,000
Industrial	2	1,152,500
Apartments	12	45,413,800
Farm land	77	40,970,800
Farm homestead	144	499,300

Average Property Value & Tax, 2005
Residential value	$186,685
Property tax	$6,400
FAIR rebate	$534

Public Library
Middletown Twp Public Library
55 New Monmouth Rd
Middletown, NJ 07748
732-671-3700
Director	Susan O'Neal

Library statistics, 2004
	Total	per capita
Volumes	180,872	2.73
Expenditure	$2,687,174	$40.51

Public Safety

Police
Chief	Robert Oches
Number of officers, 2004	104

Crime, 2004	Number	Rate
Total	764	11.5
Violent	66	1
Non-violent	698	10.5
Domestic Viol.	273	NA

Emergency/Fire
Director	Peter Lucyek

Public School District
(for school year 2004-2005 except as noted)

Middletown Township School District
59 Tindall Rd
Middletown, NJ 07748
732-671-3850
Superintendent	David Witmer
Grade plan	K-12
Enrollment	10,272.0
Students per teacher	11.6
Per pupil expenditure	$11,714
Median faculty salary	$56,524
Median administrator salary	$112,885
Grade 12 enrollment	671.5
High school graduation rate	NA

Assessment test results
(percent scoring at proficient or advanced level)
	Language	Math
Grade 3	92.1%	91.5%
Grade 8	84.8%	77.2%
High school	91.4%	84.1%

SAT
Percent tested	NA
Average SAT math score	NA
Average SAT verbal score	NA

No Child Left Behind, 2003-04
Attendence rate (target = 90%)	93.8%
Drop rate	0.3%
Highly-qualified teachers	96.2%
District needs improvement?(AYP)	No

Municipal Finance

Fiscal Year 2005
Total tax levy	$168,307,264
County levy	29,430,708
County taxes	27,782,121
County library	0
County health	0
County open space	1,648,587
School levy	106,060,412
Local muni. budget	32,816,144
Misc. revenues	25,147,655
Total aid	$8,263,450
CMPTRA	2,126,048
Muni. block grant	298,346
Energy tax receipts	5,691,301
Homeland security	140,000

Fiscal Year 2006
Total aid	$8,263,450
CMPTRA	1,926,053
Muni. block grant	298,346
Energy tax receipts	5,890,496
Homeland security	140,000

Taxes
	2003	2004	2005
General tax rate per $100	3.21	3.324	3.429
Net valuation taxable	$4,822,943,763	$4,865,593,966	$4,909,216,446
State equalized value	$8,129,013,590	$9,182,924,624	$10,356,996,722
County equalization ratio	68.7	59.33	52.94

Demographics & Socio-Economic Characteristics

(2000 U.S. Census, except as noted)

Population
1980*	7,381
1990*	7,047
2000	6,947
Male	3,388
Female	3,559
2004 (estimate)*	6,953
Persons per sq. mi. of land	4,443

Race & Hispanic Origin, 2000
Race
White	6,656
Black/African American	30
Amer. Indian/Alaska Natv.	4
Asian	154
Natv. Hawaiian/Pac. Islander	1
Other Race	53
Two or more races	49
Hispanic origin, total	256
Mexican	13
Puerto Rican	50
Cuban	22
Other Hispanic	171

Age & Nativity, 2000
Under 5 years	508
18 years and over	5,258
21 years and over	5,083
65 years and over	1,015
85 years and over	111
Median Age	38.8
Native born	6,381
Foreign born	566

Educational Attainment, 2000
Population 25 years and over	4,867
0-8 yrs of school	3.4%
High School grad or higher	93.1%
Bachelor's degree or higher	38.9%
Graduate degree	10.7%

Income & Poverty, 1999
Per capita income	$32,284
Median household income	$76,462
Median family income	$83,926
Persons in poverty	141
H'holds receiving public assistance	14
H'holds receiving social security	742

Households, 2000
Total households	2,613
With persons under 18	909
With persons over 65	739
Family households	1,884
One-person households	617
Persons per household	2.65
Persons per family	3.19

Labor & Employment
Total civilian labor force, 2004**	4,080
Unemployment rate	3.8%
Total civilian labor force, 2000	3,806
Unemployment rate	1.7%

Employed persons 16 years and over by occupation, 2000
Managers & professionals	1,625
Service occupations	437
Sales & office occupations	1,081
Farming, fishing & forestry	0
Construction & maintenance	344
Production & transportation	253
Self-employed persons	205

*US Census Bureau
**New Jersey Department of Labor

General Information
Borough of Midland Park
280 Godwin Ave
Midland Park, NJ 07432
201-445-5720

Web site	mpnj.com
Land area (sq. miles)	1.56
Water area (sq. miles)	0
Type of government	Borough
Form of government	B

Government

Legislative Districts
US Congressional	5
State Legislative	40

Local Officials, 2006
Mayor	Ester Vierheilig
Admin/Manager	Michelle Dugan
Clerk	Adeline Hanna
Finance Dir/Treas	Michelle Dugan
Engineer	Vollmer Assoc.
Attorney	Robert Regan
Tax assessor	Marie Merolla
Tax collector	Michelle Dugan
Building officer	John Wittekind
Zoning officer	NA
Public Works	Rudy Gnehm

Housing & Construction

Housing Units, 2000*
Total	2,650
Median rent	$1,044
Median SF home value	$256,500

New Privately Owned Housing Units Authorized by Building Permit
	Units	Value
Total, 2004	18	$2,507,691
Single family	9	$2,438,341
Total, 2005	2	$450,250
Single family	2	$450,250

Real Property Valuation - parcels, 2005
	Number	Valuation
Total		$853,908,600
Vacant	40	5,775,700
Residential	2,199	676,571,800
Commercial	134	118,222,400
Industrial	39	42,033,700
Apartments	4	11,305,000
Farm land	0	0
Farm homestead	0	0

Average Property Value & Tax, 2005
Residential value	$307,672
Property tax	$7,807
FAIR rebate	$596

Public Library
Midland Park Mem Library
250 Godwin Ave
Midland Park, NJ 07432
201-444-2390

Director ... Jean Scott

Library statistics, 2004
	Total	per capita
Volumes	53,086	7.64
Expenditure	$442,624	$63.71

Public Safety

Police
Chief	Robert Klinger
Number of officers, 2004	14

Crime, 2004	Number	Rate
Total	63	9.1
Violent	2	0.3
Non-violent	61	8.8
Domestic Viol.	23	NA

Emergency/Fire
Director ... Pete Hook

Public School District
(for school year 2004-2005 except as noted)

Midland Park Borough School District
31 Highland Ave
Midland Park, NJ 07432
201-444-1400

Superintendent	August DePreker
Grade plan	K-12
Enrollment	1,101.0
Students per teacher	10.5
Per pupil expenditure	$13,240
Median faculty salary	$56,564
Median administrator salary	$117,522
Grade 12 enrollment	73.5
High school graduation rate	96.0%

Assessment test results
(percent scoring at proficient or advanced level)
	Language	Math
Grade 3	94.9%	86.1%
Grade 8	82.6%	73.9%
High school	92.1%	90.6%

SAT
Percent tested	98%
Average SAT math score	543
Average SAT verbal score	534

No Child Left Behind, 2003-04
Attendence rate (target = 90%)	96.0%
Drop rate	1.3%
Highly-qualified teachers	73.2%
District needs improvement?(AYP)	No

Municipal Finance

Fiscal Year 2005
Total tax levy	$21,694,644
County levy	2,073,714
County taxes	1,969,922
County library	0
County health	0
County open space	103,792
School levy	14,012,906
Local muni. budget	5,608,025
Misc. revenues	2,621,185
Total aid	$849,113
CMPTRA	343,548
Muni. block grant	30,835
Energy tax receipts	424,730
Homeland security	50,000

Fiscal Year 2006
Total aid	$849,114
CMPTRA	328,683
Muni. block grant	30,835
Energy tax receipts	439,596
Homeland security	50,000

Taxes
	2003	2004	2005
General tax rate per $100	2.27	2.430	2.540
Net valuation taxable	$845,842,817	$849,021,120	$855,006,629
State equalized value	$932,983,473	$1,017,534,162	$1,151,059,005
County equalization ratio	99.34	90.66	83.42

Demographics & Socio-Economic Characteristics
(2000 U.S. Census, except as noted)

Population

1980*	1,368
1990*	1,273
2000	1,195
Male	606
Female	589
2004 (estimate)*	1,208
Persons per sq. mi. of land	1,049

Race & Hispanic Origin, 2000

Race

White	1,166
Black/African American	2
Amer. Indian/Alaska Natv.	2
Asian	5
Natv. Hawaiian/Pac. Islander	4
Other Race	1
Two or more races	15
Hispanic origin, total	24
Mexican	10
Puerto Rican	2
Cuban	1
Other Hispanic	11

Age & Nativity, 2000

Under 5 years	70
18 years and over	892
21 years and over	863
65 years and over	163
85 years and over	15
Median Age	38.7
Native born	1,163
Foreign born	32

Educational Attainment, 2000

Population 25 years and over	846
0-8 yrs of school	3.1%
High School grad or higher	88.5%
Bachelor's degree or higher	26.2%
Graduate degree	6.5%

Income & Poverty, 1999

Per capita income	$25,039
Median household income	$54,519
Median family income	$62,167
Persons in poverty	44
H'holds receiving public assistance	12
H'holds receiving social security	133

Households, 2000

Total households	469
With persons under 18	165
With persons over 65	122
Family households	323
One-person households	127
Persons per household	2.55
Persons per family	3.11

Labor & Employment

Total civilian labor force, 2004**	811
Unemployment rate	3.6%
Total civilian labor force, 2000	631
Unemployment rate	3.6%

Employed persons 16 years and over by occupation, 2000

Managers & professionals	197
Service occupations	63
Sales & office occupations	178
Farming, fishing & forestry	0
Construction & maintenance	79
Production & transportation	91
Self-employed persons	61

*US Census Bureau
**New Jersey Department of Labor

General Information
Borough of Milford
30 Water St
Milford, NJ 08848
908-995-4323

Web site	NA
Land area (sq. miles)	1.15
Water area (sq. miles)	0.07
Type of government	Borough
Form of government	B

Government

Legislative Districts

US Congressional	7
State Legislative	23

Local Officials, 2006

Mayor	James A. Gallos
Admin/Manager	NA
Clerk	Karen Dysart
Finance Dir/Treas	Dawn Merante
Engineer	Robert Clerico
Attorney	Todd L. Bolig
Tax assessor	David Gill
Tax collector	NA
Building officer	DCA
Zoning officer	NA
Public Works	NA

Housing & Construction

Housing Units, 2000*

Total	484
Median rent	$794
Median SF home value	$153,800

New Privately Owned Housing Units Authorized by Building Permit

	Units	Value
Total, 2004	NA	NA
Single family	NA	NA
Total, 2005	5	$777,238
Single family	5	$777,238

Real Property Valuation - parcels, 2005

	Number	Valuation
Total		$118,085,170
Vacant	63	2,959,200
Residential	404	89,689,000
Commercial	43	12,439,670
Industrial	4	8,318,800
Apartments	1	3,238,200
Farm land	4	1,408,500
Farm homestead	8	31,800

Average Property Value & Tax, 2005

Residential value	$217,769
Property tax	$5,548
FAIR rebate	$591

Public Library
Milford Public Library
40 Frenchtown Rd
Milford, NJ 08848
908-995-4072

Director | Nancy Beisel

Library statistics, 2004

	Total	per capita
Volumes	18,883	15.80
Expenditure	$53,976	$45.17

Public Safety

Police

Chief	NA
Number of officers, 2004	0

Crime, 2004	Number	Rate
Total	22	18.3
Violent	2	1.7
Non-violent	20	16.7
Domestic Viol.	8	NA

Emergency/Fire

Director | Douglas Sloyer

Public School District
(for school year 2004-2005 except as noted)

Milford Borough School District
7 Hillside Ave
Milford, NJ 08848
908-995-4349

Administrator	Brian Bolig
Grade plan	K-8
Enrollment	116.0
Students per teacher	9.8
Per pupil expenditure	$15,558
Median faculty salary	$47,495
Median administrator salary	$92,808
Grade 12 enrollment	NA
High school graduation rate	NA

Assessment test results
(percent scoring at proficient or advanced level)

	Language	Math
Grade 3	75.0%	75.0%
Grade 8	NA	NA
High school	NA	NA

SAT

Percent tested	NA
Average SAT math score	NA
Average SAT verbal score	NA

No Child Left Behind, 2003-04

Attendence rate (target = 90%)	94.4%
Drop rate	NA
Highly-qualified teachers	100%
District needs improvement?(AYP)	No

Municipal Finance

Fiscal Year 2005

Total tax levy	$3,015,608
County levy	495,842
County taxes	453,172
County library	0
County health	0
County open space	42,670
School levy	1,992,633
Local muni. budget	527,132
Misc. revenues	828,855
Total aid	$417,889
CMPTRA	257,718
Muni. block grant	5,570
Energy tax receipts	154,601
Homeland security	0

Fiscal Year 2006

Total aid	$417,889
CMPTRA	252,307
Muni. block grant	5,570
Energy tax receipts	160,012
Homeland security	NA

Taxes

	2003	2004	2005
General tax rate per $100	2.20	2.530	2.550
Net valuation taxable	$112,795,841	$118,534,017	$118,377,206
State equalized value	$107,783,890	$117,120,590	$128,824,906
County equalization ratio	99.43	90.95	87.58

Demographics & Socio-Economic Characteristics
(2000 U.S. Census, except as noted)

Population
1980*	19,543
1990*	18,630
2000	19,765
Male	9,584
Female	10,181
2004 (estimate)*	19,585
Persons per sq. mi. of land	2,087

Race & Hispanic Origin, 2000
Race
White	17,573
Black/African American	217
Amer. Indian/Alaska Natv.	10
Asian	1,660
Natv. Hawaiian/Pac. Islander	6
Other Race	85
Two or more races	214
Hispanic origin, total	404
Mexican	48
Puerto Rican	64
Cuban	35
Other Hispanic	257

Age & Nativity, 2000
Under 5 years	1,720
18 years and over	13,789
21 years and over	13,502
65 years and over	2,581
85 years and over	304
Median Age	39.2
Native born	16,866
Foreign born	2,899

Educational Attainment, 2000
Population 25 years and over	13,190
0-8 yrs of school	1.2%
High School grad or higher	96.6%
Bachelor's degree or higher	74.0%
Graduate degree	38.4%

Income & Poverty, 1999
Per capita income	$76,796
Median household income	$130,848
Median family income	$158,888
Persons in poverty	288
H'holds receiving public assistance	50
H'holds receiving social security	1,711

Households, 2000
Total households	7,015
With persons under 18	3,158
With persons over 65	1,784
Family households	5,604
One-person households	1,224
Persons per household	2.82
Persons per family	3.19

Labor & Employment
Total civilian labor force, 2004**	11,426
Unemployment rate	2.3%
Total civilian labor force, 2000	8,956
Unemployment rate	1.8%

Employed persons 16 years and over by occupation, 2000
Managers & professionals	5,761
Service occupations	421
Sales & office occupations	2,167
Farming, fishing & forestry	0
Construction & maintenance	170
Production & transportation	280
Self-employed persons	799

*US Census Bureau
**New Jersey Department of Labor

General Information
Township of Millburn
375 Millburn Ave
Millburn, NJ 07041
973-564-7000
Web site	www.twp.millburn.nj.us
Land area (sq. miles)	9.38
Water area (sq. miles)	0.52
Type of government	Township
Form of government	TC

Government
Legislative Districts
US Congressional	11
State Legislative	21

Local Officials, 2006
Mayor	Daniel Baer
Admin/Manager	Timothy Gordon
Clerk	Joanne Monarque
Finance Dir/Treas	Jason Gabloff
Engineer	W. Thomas Watkinson
Attorney	Roger Clapp
Tax assessor	Ernest Del Gurcio
Tax collector	Gerald Viturello
Building officer	Phil Kehoe
Zoning officer	NA
Public Works	Peter Gallitelli

Housing & Construction
Housing Units, 2000*
Total	7,158
Median rent	$1,114
Median SF home value	$549,000

New Privately Owned Housing Units Authorized by Building Permit
	Units	Value
Total, 2004	30	$17,090,400
Single family	30	$17,090,400
Total, 2005	43	$24,051,472
Single family	43	$24,051,472

Real Property Valuation - parcels, 2005
	Number	Valuation
Total		$5,956,178,200
Vacant	90	38,494,800
Residential	6,164	4,769,923,800
Commercial	232	1,056,553,000
Industrial	30	38,646,400
Apartments	20	52,560,200
Farm land	0	0
Farm homestead	0	0

Average Property Value & Tax, 2005
Residential value	$773,836
Property tax	$15,860
FAIR rebate	$618

Public Library
Millburn Public Library
200 Glen Ave
Millburn, NJ 07041
973-376-1006
Director	William Swinson

Library statistics, 2004
	Total	per capita
Volumes	102,246	5.17
Expenditure	$2,369,167	$119.87

Public Safety
Police
Chief	Paul Boegershausen
Number of officers, 2004	50

Crime, 2004	Number	Rate
Total	676	34.4
Violent	18	0.9
Non-violent	658	33.5
Domestic Viol.	75	NA

Emergency/Fire
Director	J. Michael Roberts

Public School District
(for school year 2004-2005 except as noted)

Millburn Township School District
434 Millburn Ave
Millburn, NJ 07041
973-376-3600
Superintendent	Richard Brodow
Grade plan	K-12
Enrollment	4,437.0
Students per teacher	10.6
Per pupil expenditure	$12,908
Median faculty salary	$65,050
Median administrator salary	$113,558
Grade 12 enrollment	254.0
High school graduation rate	99.6%

Assessment test results
(percent scoring at proficient or advanced level)
	Language	Math
Grade 3	97.9%	95.2%
Grade 8	93.1%	89.6%
High school	97.0%	94.0%

SAT
Percent tested	105%
Average SAT math score	630
Average SAT verbal score	602

No Child Left Behind, 2003-04
Attendence rate (target = 90%)	94.9%
Drop rate	0.1%
Highly-qualified teachers	96.1%
District needs improvement?(AYP)	No

Municipal Finance
Fiscal Year 2005
Total tax levy	$122,204,561
County levy	33,566,201
County taxes	32,862,654
County library	0
County health	0
County open space	703,547
School levy	60,678,422
Local muni. budget	27,959,939
Misc. revenues	11,192,429
Total aid	$3,354,832
CMPTRA	662,927
Muni. block grant	81,519
Energy tax receipts	2,512,750
Homeland security	70,000

Fiscal Year 2006
Total aid	$3,354,832
CMPTRA	574,981
Muni. block grant	81,519
Energy tax receipts	2,600,696
Homeland security	70,000

Taxes
	2003	2004	2005
General tax rate per $100	1.86	1.960	2.050
Net valuation taxable	$5,927,251,143	$5,938,155,735	$5,962,668,369
State equalized value	$6,441,264,011	$6,978,293,557	$7,608,355,709
County equalization ratio	99.95	99.95	85.08

Demographics & Socio-Economic Characteristics
(2000 U.S. Census, except as noted)

Population
1980*	530
1990*	450
2000	410
Male	204
Female	206
2004 (estimate)*	431
Persons per sq. mi. of land	575

Race & Hispanic Origin, 2000
Race
White	400
Black/African American	4
Amer. Indian/Alaska Natv.	0
Asian	4
Natv. Hawaiian/Pac. Islander	0
Other Race	0
Two or more races	2
Hispanic origin, total	13
Mexican	0
Puerto Rican	10
Cuban	0
Other Hispanic	3

Age & Nativity, 2000
Under 5 years	17
18 years and over	331
21 years and over	323
65 years and over	70
85 years and over	10
Median Age	45.6
Native born	398
Foreign born	19

Educational Attainment, 2000
Population 25 years and over	305
0-8 yrs of school	2.0%
High School grad or higher	91.5%
Bachelor's degree or higher	39.0%
Graduate degree	16.4%

Income & Poverty, 1999
Per capita income	$30,694
Median household income	$76,353
Median family income	$83,118
Persons in poverty	19
H'holds receiving public assistance	2
H'holds receiving social security	44

Households, 2000
Total households	169
With persons under 18	47
With persons over 65	51
Family households	127
One-person households	32
Persons per household	2.43
Persons per family	2.79

Labor & Employment
Total civilian labor force, 2004**	338
Unemployment rate	2.7%
Total civilian labor force, 2000	245
Unemployment rate	2.0%

Employed persons 16 years and over by occupation, 2000
Managers & professionals	127
Service occupations	20
Sales & office occupations	51
Farming, fishing & forestry	0
Construction & maintenance	23
Production & transportation	19
Self-employed persons	21

*US Census Bureau
**New Jersey Department of Labor

General Information
Borough of Millstone
1353 Main St
Millstone, NJ 08844
908-281-6893

Web site	www.millstoneboro.org
Land area (sq. miles)	0.75
Water area (sq. miles)	0
Type of government	Borough
Form of government	B

Government

Legislative Districts
US Congressional	7
State Legislative	16

Local Officials, 2006
Mayor	Mary Patrick
Admin/Manager	NA
Clerk	Gregory Bonin
Finance Dir/Treas	Gregory Della Pia
Engineer	James DeMuro
Attorney	Steven Offen
Tax assessor	Marcia Sudano
Tax collector	Diane Schubach
Building officer	State of New Jersey
Zoning officer	Dan Devoti
Public Works	NA

Housing & Construction

Housing Units, 2000*
Total	173
Median rent	$875
Median SF home value	$205,400

New Privately Owned Housing Units
Authorized by Building Permit
	Units	Value
Total, 2004	0	$0
Single family	0	$0
Total, 2005	0	$0
Single family	0	$0

Real Property Valuation - parcels, 2005
	Number	Valuation
Total		$49,116,100
Vacant	11	395,900
Residential	155	45,090,800
Commercial	10	3,510,100
Industrial	0	0
Apartments	0	0
Farm land	0	0
Farm homestead	9	119,300

Average Property Value & Tax, 2005
Residential value	$275,671
Property tax	$5,933
FAIR rebate	$636

Public Library

No public municipal library.

Library statistics, 2004
	Total	per capita
Volumes	NA	NA
Expenditure	NA	NA

Public Safety

Police
Chief	NA
Number of officers, 2004	0

Crime, 2004	Number	Rate
Total	3	7.3
Violent	0	0
Non-violent	3	7.3
Domestic Viol.	2	NA

Emergency/Fire
Director	NA

Public School District
(for school year 2004-2005 except as noted)

Millstone Borough School District†
PO Box 854
Somerville, NJ 08876

†No schools in district - sends children to Hillsborough schools.

Grade plan	NA
Enrollment	NA
Students per teacher	NA
Per pupil expenditure	NA
Median faculty salary	NA

Assessment test results
(percent scoring at proficient or advanced level)
	Language	Math
Grade 3	NA	NA
Grade 8	NA	NA
High school	NA	NA

SAT
Percent tested	NA
Average SAT math score	NA
Average SAT verbal score	NA

No Child Left Behind, 2003-04
Attendence rate (target = 90%)	NA
Drop rate	NA
Highly-qualified teachers	NA
District needs improvement?(AYP)	NA

Municipal Finance

Fiscal Year 2005
Total tax levy	$1,058,546
County levy	194,169
County taxes	160,869
County library	17,832
County health	0
County open space	15,468
School levy	504,446
Local muni. budget	359,931
Misc. revenues	174,593
Total aid	$88,925
CMPTRA	21,460
Muni. block grant	1,969
Energy tax receipts	65,496
Homeland security	0

Fiscal Year 2006
Total aid	$88,925
CMPTRA	19,167
Muni. block grant	1,969
Energy tax receipts	67,789
Homeland security	NA

Taxes
	2003	2004	2005
General tax rate per $100	2.09	2.130	2.160
Net valuation taxable	$40,198,121	$40,359,764	$49,185,299
State equalized value	$46,742,001	$51,358,680	$51,422,163
County equalization ratio	112.1	86.00	95.63

Demographics & Socio-Economic Characteristics
(2000 U.S. Census, except as noted)

Population
1980*	3,926
1990*	5,069
2000	8,970
Male	4,472
Female	4,498
2004 (estimate)*	9,882
Persons per sq. mi. of land	269

Race & Hispanic Origin, 2000
Race
White	8,237
Black/African American	274
Amer. Indian/Alaska Natv.	9
Asian	308
Natv. Hawaiian/Pac. Islander	3
Other Race	55
Two or more races	84
Hispanic origin, total	315
Mexican	41
Puerto Rican	130
Cuban	35
Other Hispanic	109

Age & Nativity, 2000
Under 5 years	758
18 years and over	6,028
21 years and over	5,818
65 years and over	538
85 years and over	60
Median Age	37.1
Native born	8,374
Foreign born	596

Educational Attainment, 2000
Population 25 years and over	5,624
0-8 yrs of school	2.7%
High School grad or higher	92.2%
Bachelor's degree or higher	42.7%
Graduate degree	16.1%

Income & Poverty, 1999
Per capita income	$37,285
Median household income	$94,561
Median family income	$96,116
Persons in poverty	434
H'holds receiving public assistance	36
H'holds receiving social security	377

Households, 2000
Total households	2,708
With persons under 18	1,477
With persons over 65	366
Family households	2,426
One-person households	204
Persons per household	3.28
Persons per family	3.46

Labor & Employment
Total civilian labor force, 2004**	3,029
Unemployment rate	3.9%
Total civilian labor force, 2000	4,337
Unemployment rate	2.5%

Employed persons 16 years and over by occupation, 2000
Managers & professionals	2,184
Service occupations	391
Sales & office occupations	1,138
Farming, fishing & forestry	37
Construction & maintenance	272
Production & transportation	207
Self-employed persons	356

*US Census Bureau
**New Jersey Department of Labor

General Information
Township of Millstone
PO Box 240
Perrinville, NJ 08535
732-446-4249 or 462
Web site	www.millstone.nj.us
Land area (sq. miles)	36.76
Water area (sq. miles)	0.42
Type of government	Township
Form of government	TC

Government

Legislative Districts
US Congressional	4
State Legislative	12

Local Officials, 2006
Mayor	Nancy A. Grbelja
Admin/Manager	James Pickering Jr.
Clerk	Maria Dellasala
Finance Dir/Treas	Amanda Salerno
Engineer	Matt Shafai
Attorney	Duane Davison
Tax assessor	Thomas Davis
Tax collector	Shari Phillips
Building officer	Henry Salerno
Zoning officer	Pat Hynes
Public Works	Allan Boyce

Housing & Construction

Housing Units, 2000*
Total	2,797
Median rent	$941
Median SF home value	$319,500

New Privately Owned Housing Units Authorized by Building Permit
	Units	Value
Total, 2004	64	$14,934,502
Single family	64	$14,934,502
Total, 2005	34	$9,353,536
Single family	34	$9,353,536

Real Property Valuation - parcels, 2005
	Number	Valuation
Total		$1,319,534,100
Vacant	430	48,970,300
Residential	2,906	1,149,034,100
Commercial	76	44,217,200
Industrial	4	3,925,900
Apartments	0	0
Farm land	241	68,948,200
Farm homestead	444	4,438,400

Average Property Value & Tax, 2005
Residential value	$344,320
Property tax	$7,964
FAIR rebate	$563

Public Library

No public municipal library.

Library statistics, 2004
	Total	per capita
Volumes	NA	NA
Expenditure	NA	NA

Public Safety

Police
Chief	(State)
Number of officers, 2004	0

Crime, 2004	Number	Rate
Total	79	8.1
Violent	4	0.4
Non-violent	75	7.7
Domestic Viol.	15	NA

Emergency/Fire
Director	Joe Carbin

Public School District
(for school year 2004-2005 except as noted)

Millstone Township School District
18 Schoolhouse Lane
Clarksburg, NJ 08510
732-446-0890
Superintendent	William Setaro
Grade plan	K-12
Enrollment	1,711.0
Students per teacher	11.9
Per pupil expenditure	$10,213
Median faculty salary	$44,800
Median administrator salary	$119,135
Grade 12 enrollment	NA
High school graduation rate	NA

Assessment test results
(percent scoring at proficient or advanced level)
	Language	Math
Grade 3	91.1%	89.5%
Grade 8	88.3%	75.2%
High school	NA	NA

SAT
Percent tested	NA
Average SAT math score	NA
Average SAT verbal score	NA

No Child Left Behind, 2003-04
Attendence rate (target = 90%)	95.4%
Drop rate	NA
Highly-qualified teachers	99.5%
District needs improvement?(AYP)	No

Municipal Finance

Fiscal Year 2005
Total tax levy	$30,579,506
County levy	5,483,256
County taxes	4,841,041
County library	266,664
County health	88,278
County open space	287,272
School levy	23,244,900
Local muni. budget	1,851,350
Misc. revenues	5,503,407
Total aid	$1,105,989
CMPTRA	194,106
Muni. block grant	35,172
Energy tax receipts	876,711
Homeland security	0

Fiscal Year 2006
Total aid	$1,105,988
CMPTRA	163,421
Muni. block grant	35,172
Energy tax receipts	907,395
Homeland security	NA

Taxes
	2003	2004	2005
General tax rate per $100	2.01	2.096	2.315
Net valuation taxable	$1,232,062,847	$1,267,240,840	$1,322,024,153
State equalized value	$1,349,318,637	$1,546,920,963	$1,797,449,562
County equalization ratio	100.46	91.31	81.89

Demographics & Socio-Economic Characteristics
(2000 U.S. Census, except as noted)

Population
1980*	7,136
1990*	6,968
2000	7,000
Male	3,377
Female	3,623
2004 (estimate)*	7,148
Persons per sq. mi. of land	4,546

Race & Hispanic Origin, 2000
Race
White	6,570
Black/African American	53
Amer. Indian/Alaska Natv.	11
Asian	215
Natv. Hawaiian/Pac. Islander	0
Other Race	81
Two or more races	70
Hispanic origin, total	261
Mexican	16
Puerto Rican	67
Cuban	25
Other Hispanic	153

Age & Nativity, 2000
Under 5 years	387
18 years and over	5,399
21 years and over	5,200
65 years and over	1,098
85 years and over	121
Median Age	39.9
Native born	6,470
Foreign born	530

Educational Attainment, 2000
Population 25 years and over	4,918
0-8 yrs of school	4.4%
High School grad or higher	86.9%
Bachelor's degree or higher	27.2%
Graduate degree	7.4%

Income & Poverty, 1999
Per capita income	$29,996
Median household income	$68,429
Median family income	$77,869
Persons in poverty	158
H'holds receiving public assistance	34
H'holds receiving social security	799

Households, 2000
Total households	2,627
With persons under 18	882
With persons over 65	794
Family households	1,945
One-person households	561
Persons per household	2.66
Persons per family	3.12

Labor & Employment
Total civilian labor force, 2004**	4,015
Unemployment rate	2.8%
Total civilian labor force, 2000	3,754
Unemployment rate	3.7%

Employed persons 16 years and over by occupation, 2000
Managers & professionals	1,393
Service occupations	475
Sales & office occupations	1,077
Farming, fishing & forestry	0
Construction & maintenance	336
Production & transportation	334
Self-employed persons	120

*US Census Bureau
**New Jersey Department of Labor

General Information
Borough of Milltown
39 Washington Ave
Milltown, NJ 08850
732-828-2100

Web site	www.milltownnj.org
Land area (sq. miles)	1.57
Water area (sq. miles)	0.03
Type of government	Borough
Form of government	B

Government

Legislative Districts
US Congressional	6
State Legislative	17

Local Officials, 2006
Mayor	Gloria Bradford
Admin/Manager	Denise Biancamono
Clerk	Michael Januszka
Finance Dir/Treas	Denise Biancamono
Engineer	Michael McClelland
Attorney	Patrick Diegnan Jr.
Tax assessor	Eldo Magnani
Tax collector	NA
Building officer	Steven Curtis
Zoning officer	NA
Public Works	Rich Williams

Housing & Construction

Housing Units, 2000*
Total	2,670
Median rent	$753
Median SF home value	$178,400

New Privately Owned Housing Units
Authorized by Building Permit
	Units	Value
Total, 2004	4	$539,875
Single family	4	$539,875
Total, 2005	3	$351,438
Single family	3	$351,438

Real Property Valuation - parcels, 2005
	Number	Valuation
Total		$465,379,600
Vacant	57	5,968,800
Residential	2,383	394,699,400
Commercial	97	53,889,000
Industrial	5	8,927,400
Apartments	5	1,895,000
Farm land	0	0
Farm homestead	0	0

Average Property Value & Tax, 2005
Residential value	$165,631
Property tax	$5,858
FAIR rebate	$843

Public Library
Milltown Public Library
20 W Church St
Milltown, NJ 08850
732-247-2270

Director............... Bonnie Goldstein

Library statistics, 2004
	Total	per capita
Volumes	36,270	5.18
Expenditure	$224,343	$32.05

Public Safety
Police
Chief	Raymond Geipel
Number of officers, 2004	16

Crime, 2004	Number	Rate
Total	157	21.9
Violent	11	1.5
Non-violent	146	20.3
Domestic Viol.	49	NA

Emergency/Fire
Director..................... Dave Petry

Public School District
(for school year 2004-2005 except as noted)

Milltown School District
80 Violet Terrace
Milltown, NJ 08850
732-828-8620

Superintendent	Linda Madison
Grade plan	K-12
Enrollment	669.0
Students per teacher	10.9
Per pupil expenditure	$11,585
Median faculty salary	$42,501
Median administrator salary	$94,500
Grade 12 enrollment	NA
High school graduation rate	NA

Assessment test results
(percent scoring at proficient or advanced level)
	Language	Math
Grade 3	92.1%	89.5%
Grade 8	83.8%	79.7%
High school	NA	NA

SAT
Percent tested	NA
Average SAT math score	NA
Average SAT verbal score	NA

No Child Left Behind, 2003-04
Attendence rate (target = 90%)	95.6%
Drop rate	NA
Highly-qualified teachers	93.7%
District needs improvement?(AYP)	No

Municipal Finance

Fiscal Year 2005
Total tax levy	$16,472,780
County levy	2,456,335
County taxes	2,225,096
County library	0
County health	0
County open space	231,239
School levy	10,500,117
Local muni. budget	3,516,328
Misc. revenues	4,183,297
Total aid	$659,460
CMPTRA	368,184
Muni. block grant	30,490
Energy tax receipts	210,786
Homeland security	50,000

Fiscal Year 2006
Total aid	$659,461
CMPTRA	360,807
Muni. block grant	30,490
Energy tax receipts	218,164
Homeland security	50,000

Taxes
	2003	2004	2005
General tax rate per $100	3.26	3.390	3.540
Net valuation taxable	$463,351,758	$464,692,199	$465,740,454
State equalized value	$669,100,012	$772,011,132	$848,497,821
County equalization ratio	77.39	69.25	60.17

Demographics & Socio-Economic Characteristics

(2000 U.S. Census, except as noted)

Population

1980*	24,815
1990*	25,992
2000	26,847
Male	12,678
Female	14,169
2004 (estimate)*	27,611
Persons per sq. mi. of land	652

Race & Hispanic Origin, 2000

Race

White	20,438
Black/African American	4,025
Amer. Indian/Alaska Natv.	139
Asian	216
Natv. Hawaiian/Pac. Islander	8
Other Race	1,384
Two or more races	637
Hispanic origin, total	2,998
Mexican	168
Puerto Rican	2,392
Cuban	14
Other Hispanic	424

Age & Nativity, 2000

Under 5 years	1,871
18 years and over	19,349
21 years and over	18,311
65 years and over	3,460
85 years and over	393
Median Age	35
Native born	26,261
Foreign born	586

Educational Attainment, 2000

Population 25 years and over	16,998
0-8 yrs of school	7.8%
High School grad or higher	74.1%
Bachelor's degree or higher	12.2%
Graduate degree	3.2%

Income & Poverty, 1999

Per capita income	$18,632
Median household income	$40,378
Median family income	$46,093
Persons in poverty	4,034
H'holds receiving public assistance	555
H'holds receiving social security	2,818

Households, 2000

Total households	10,043
With persons under 18	3,978
With persons over 65	2,559
Family households	7,011
One-person households	2,519
Persons per household	2.65
Persons per family	3.15

Labor & Employment

Total civilian labor force, 2004**	13,432
Unemployment rate	5.8%
Total civilian labor force, 2000	13,003
Unemployment rate	9.3%

Employed persons 16 years and over by occupation, 2000

Managers & professionals	2,927
Service occupations	2,345
Sales & office occupations	2,884
Farming, fishing & forestry	27
Construction & maintenance	1,270
Production & transportation	2,338
Self-employed persons	606

*US Census Bureau
**New Jersey Department of Labor

General Information

City of Millville
PO Box 609
12 S High St
Millville, NJ 08332
856-825-7000

Web site	www.millvillenj.gov
Land area (sq. miles)	42.35
Water area (sq. miles)	2.19
Type of government	City
Form of government	Comm.

Government

Legislative Districts

US Congressional	2
State Legislative	1

Local Officials, 2006

Mayor	James Quinn
Admin/Manager	Lewis Thompson
Clerk	Lewis Thompson
Finance Dir/Treas	Ronald Charlesworth
Engineer	John Knoop
Attorney	Richard McCarthy
Tax assessor	Ralph Lane
Tax collector	Suzanne Olah
Building officer	Milton Truxton
Zoning officer	Tom Ayres
Public Works	John Hollingshead

Housing & Construction

Housing Units, 2000*

Total	10,652
Median rent	$589
Median SF home value	$86,700

New Privately Owned Housing Units Authorized by Building Permit

	Units	Value
Total, 2004	129	$12,571,415
Single family	127	$12,563,814
Total, 2005	151	$13,503,325
Single family	149	$13,495,724

Real Property Valuation - parcels, 2005

	Number	Valuation
Total		$1,346,628,180
Vacant	1,242	46,708,000
Residential	7,754	923,432,000
Commercial	385	191,871,680
Industrial	65	132,217,700
Apartments	38	42,599,500
Farm land	45	8,342,400
Farm homestead	132	1,456,900

Average Property Value & Tax, 2005

Residential value	$117,282
Property tax	$2,743
FAIR rebate	$601

Public Library

Millville Public Library
210 Buck St
Millville, NJ 08332
856-825-7087

Director............. Norman Gluckman

Library statistics, 2004

	Total	per capita
Volumes	43,892	1.63
Expenditure	$640,116	$23.84

Public Safety

Police

Chief	Ronald Harvey
Number of officers, 2004	71

Crime, 2004	Number	Rate
Total	1,787	65.9
Violent	213	7.9
Non-violent	1,574	58
Domestic Viol.	709	NA

Emergency/Fire

Director...................... Kurt Hess

Public School District

(for school year 2004-2005 except as noted)

Millville School District
PO Box 5010
Millville, NJ 08332
856-327-7575

Superintendent	Shelly Schneider
Grade plan	K-12
Enrollment	6,043.0
Students per teacher	10.1
Per pupil expenditure	$13,937
Median faculty salary	$56,595
Median administrator salary	$88,055
Grade 12 enrollment	419.5
High school graduation rate	78.4%

Assessment test results

(percent scoring at proficient or advanced level)

	Language	Math
Grade 3	64.4%	61.3%
Grade 8	46.5%	36.8%
High school	67.8%	60.3%

SAT

Percent tested	32%
Average SAT math score	506
Average SAT verbal score	501

No Child Left Behind, 2003-04

Attendence rate (target = 90%)	91.9%
Drop rate	7.1%
Highly-qualified teachers	93.8%
District needs improvement?(AYP)	No

Municipal Finance

Fiscal Year 2005

Total tax levy	$31,639,082
County levy	11,042,456
County taxes	10,482,578
County library	0
County health	452,310
County open space	107,568
School levy	8,991,505
Local muni. budget	11,605,121
Misc. revenues	12,831,663
Total aid	$5,288,351
CMPTRA	2,208,251
Muni. block grant	113,733
Energy tax receipts	2,876,367
Homeland security	90,000

Fiscal Year 2006

Total aid	$5,288,350
CMPTRA	2,107,578
Muni. block grant	113,733
Energy tax receipts	2,977,039
Homeland security	90,000

Taxes

	2003	2004	2005
General tax rate per $100	4.11	4.257	2.340
Net valuation taxable	$669,887,491	$684,072,886	$1,352,978,038
State equalized value	$964,838,673	$1,042,492,124	$1,315,358,777
County equalization ratio	71.71	69.43	128.52

Demographics & Socio-Economic Characteristics

(2000 U.S. Census, except as noted)

Population

1980*	3,325
1990*	3,333
2000	3,679
Male	1,787
Female	1,892
2004 (estimate)*	3,683
Persons per sq. mi. of land	1,230

Race & Hispanic Origin, 2000

Race

White	3,326
Black/African American	126
Amer. Indian/Alaska Natv.	4
Asian	92
Natv. Hawaiian/Pac. Islander	3
Other Race	66
Two or more races	62
Hispanic origin, total	319
Mexican	13
Puerto Rican	105
Cuban	19
Other Hispanic	182

Age & Nativity, 2000

Under 5 years	312
18 years and over	2,778
21 years and over	2,696
65 years and over	487
85 years and over	30
Median Age	37.6
Native born	3,257
Foreign born	422

Educational Attainment, 2000

Population 25 years and over	2,626
0-8 yrs of school	2.2%
High School grad or higher	90.9%
Bachelor's degree or higher	28.2%
Graduate degree	9.2%

Income & Poverty, 1999

Per capita income	$27,119
Median household income	$64,643
Median family income	$67,467
Persons in poverty	206
H'holds receiving public assistance	20
H'holds receiving social security	414

Households, 2000

Total households	1,365
With persons under 18	499
With persons over 65	349
Family households	1,041
One-person households	264
Persons per household	2.7
Persons per family	3.08

Labor & Employment

Total civilian labor force, 2004**	2,101
Unemployment rate	4.7%
Total civilian labor force, 2000	1,885
Unemployment rate	3.4%

Employed persons 16 years and over by occupation, 2000

Managers & professionals	737
Service occupations	180
Sales & office occupations	524
Farming, fishing & forestry	7
Construction & maintenance	199
Production & transportation	173
Self-employed persons	28

*US Census Bureau
**New Jersey Department of Labor

General Information

Township of Mine Hill
10 Baker St
Mine Hill, NJ 07803
973-366-9031

Web site	NA
Land area (sq. miles)	2.99
Water area (sq. miles)	0.01
Type of government	Township
Form of government	Faulkner E

Government

Legislative Districts

US Congressional	11
State Legislative	25

Local Officials, 2006

Mayor	Richard Leary
Admin/Manager	Barry Lewis
Clerk	Patricia Korpos
Finance Dir/Treas	Janice Congleton
Engineer	Paul Sterbenz
Attorney	Stephen N. Severud
Tax assessor	Joseph Ferraris
Tax collector	NA
Building officer	Steve Kaplan
Zoning officer	NA
Public Works	NA

Housing & Construction

Housing Units, 2000*

Total	1,388
Median rent	$1,192
Median SF home value	$161,900

New Privately Owned Housing Units
Authorized by Building Permit

	Units	Value
Total, 2004	2	$302,200
Single family	2	$302,200
Total, 2005	3	$329,100
Single family	3	$329,100

Real Property Valuation - parcels, 2005

	Number	Valuation
Total		$224,095,600
Vacant	133	7,062,000
Residential	1,336	190,605,900
Commercial	51	14,372,300
Industrial	8	11,678,300
Apartments	1	358,500
Farm land	0	0
Farm homestead	2	18,600

Average Property Value & Tax, 2005

Residential value	$142,470
Property tax	$5,490
FAIR rebate	$561

Public Library

No public municipal library.

Library statistics, 2004

	Total	per capita
Volumes	NA	NA
Expenditure	NA	NA

Public Safety

Police

Chief	NA
Number of officers, 2004	0

Crime, 2004	Number	Rate
Total	38	10.3
Violent	4	1.1
Non-violent	34	9.2
Domestic Viol.	29	NA

Emergency/Fire

Director	Jerry Coviello

Public School District

(for school year 2004-2005 except as noted)

Mine Hill Township School District
Canfield Ave
Mine Hill, NJ 07803
973-366-0590

Superintendent	C. Dan Blachford
Grade plan	K-12
Enrollment	371.0
Students per teacher	11.7
Per pupil expenditure	$11,638
Median faculty salary	$43,772
Median administrator salary	$96,680
Grade 12 enrollment	NA
High school graduation rate	NA

Assessment test results

(percent scoring at proficient or advanced level)

	Language	Math
Grade 3	97.5%	92.5%
Grade 8	NA	NA
High school	NA	NA

SAT

Percent tested	NA
Average SAT math score	NA
Average SAT verbal score	NA

No Child Left Behind, 2003-04

Attendence rate (target = 90%)	96.1%
Drop rate	NA
Highly-qualified teachers	93.9%
District needs improvement?(AYP)	No

Municipal Finance

Fiscal Year 2005

Total tax levy	$8,646,128
County levy	1,041,163
County taxes	852,860
County library	0
County health	0
County open space	188,303
School levy	5,584,715
Local muni. budget	2,020,250
Misc. revenues	1,627,804
Total aid	$441,077
CMPTRA	189,913
Muni. block grant	14,584
Energy tax receipts	211,580
Homeland security	25,000

Fiscal Year 2006

Total aid	$441,077
CMPTRA	182,508
Muni. block grant	14,584
Energy tax receipts	218,985
Homeland security	25,000

Taxes

	2003	2004	2005
General tax rate per $100	3.38	3.720	3.860
Net valuation taxable	$224,332,454	$224,174,654	$224,358,342
State equalized value	$345,392,539	$388,541,897	$446,662,039
County equalization ratio	73.46	64.95	57.66

Demographics & Socio-Economic Characteristics
(2000 U.S. Census, except as noted)

Population
1980*	3,318
1990*	3,303
2000	3,595
Male	1,684
Female	1,911
2004 (estimate)*	3,634
Persons per sq. mi. of land	3,391

Race & Hispanic Origin, 2000
Race
White	3,511
Black/African American	19
Amer. Indian/Alaska Natv.	0
Asian	31
Natv. Hawaiian/Pac. Islander	0
Other Race	12
Two or more races	22
Hispanic origin, total	68
Mexican	5
Puerto Rican	23
Cuban	10
Other Hispanic	30

Age & Nativity, 2000
Under 5 years	206
18 years and over	2,864
21 years and over	2,812
65 years and over	732
85 years and over	70
Median Age	44.6
Native born	3,382
Foreign born	213

Educational Attainment, 2000
Population 25 years and over	2,737
0-8 yrs of school	2.2%
High School grad or higher	94.3%
Bachelor's degree or higher	48.8%
Graduate degree	19.0%

Income & Poverty, 1999
Per capita income	$52,862
Median household income	$80,484
Median family income	$93,401
Persons in poverty	68
H'holds receiving public assistance	28
H'holds receiving social security	497

Households, 2000
Total households	1,633
With persons under 18	413
With persons over 65	538
Family households	976
One-person households	574
Persons per household	2.2
Persons per family	2.89

Labor & Employment
Total civilian labor force, 2004**	2,181
Unemployment rate	2.6%
Total civilian labor force, 2000	1,952
Unemployment rate	3.8%

Employed persons 16 years and over by occupation, 2000
Managers & professionals	1,031
Service occupations	126
Sales & office occupations	507
Farming, fishing & forestry	0
Construction & maintenance	125
Production & transportation	89
Self-employed persons	182

*US Census Bureau
**New Jersey Department of Labor

General Information
Borough of Monmouth Beach
22 Beach Rd
Monmouth Beach, NJ 07750
732-229-2204
Web site	www.monmouthbeach.us
Land area (sq. miles)	1.07
Water area (sq. miles)	0.85
Type of government	Borough
Form of government	Comm.

Government
Legislative Districts
US Congressional	6
State Legislative	11

Local Officials, 2006
Mayor	Susan Howard
Admin/Manager	NA
Clerk	Bonnie Moore
Finance Dir/Treas	James Fuller
Engineer	Richard Schulz
Attorney	Dennis Collins
Tax assessor	Timothy Anfuso
Tax collector	James Fuller
Building officer	Theodore Lewis
Zoning officer	NA
Public Works	NA

Housing & Construction
Housing Units, 2000*
Total	1,969
Median rent	$1,037
Median SF home value	$342,000

New Privately Owned Housing Units Authorized by Building Permit
	Units	Value
Total, 2004	16	$5,420,330
Single family	16	$5,420,330
Total, 2005	11	$4,257,556
Single family	11	$4,257,556

Real Property Valuation - parcels, 2005
	Number	Valuation
Total		$1,223,357,300
Vacant	86	14,116,300
Residential	1,997	1,178,555,900
Commercial	34	30,685,100
Industrial	0	0
Apartments	0	0
Farm land	0	0
Farm homestead	0	0

Average Property Value & Tax, 2005
Residential value	$590,163
Property tax	$6,010
FAIR rebate	$442

Public Library
Monmouth Beach Library
18 Willow Ave
Monmouth Beach, NJ 07750
732-229-1187
Director................. Nancy Leporatti

Library statistics, 2004
	Total	per capita
Volumes	40,828	11.36
Expenditure	$92,845	$25.83

Public Safety
Police
Chief	Richard White
Number of officers, 2004	10

Crime, 2004	Number	Rate
Total	31	8.6
Violent	0	0
Non-violent	31	8.6
Domestic Viol.	2	NA

Emergency/Fire
Director.................... James Cook

Public School District
(for school year 2004-2005 except as noted)

Monmouth Beach School District
7 Hastings Place
Monmouth Beach, NJ 07750
732-222-6139
Superintendent	Neil Frankenfield
Grade plan	K-8
Enrollment	322.0
Students per teacher	11.4
Per pupil expenditure	$11,345
Median faculty salary	$43,622
Median administrator salary	$95,227
Grade 12 enrollment	NA
High school graduation rate	NA

Assessment test results
(percent scoring at proficient or advanced level)
	Language	Math
Grade 3	96.9%	93.8%
Grade 8	84.8%	72.7%
High school	NA	NA

SAT
Percent tested	NA
Average SAT math score	NA
Average SAT verbal score	NA

No Child Left Behind, 2003-04
Attendence rate (target = 90%)	95.5%
Drop rate	NA
Highly-qualified teachers	100%
District needs improvement?(AYP)	No

Municipal Finance
Fiscal Year 2005
Total tax levy	$12,462,972
County levy	3,141,165
County taxes	2,818,643
County library	155,262
County health	0
County open space	167,260
School levy	6,180,405
Local muni. budget	3,141,402
Misc. revenues	2,266,243
Total aid	$438,337
CMPTRA	86,818
Muni. block grant	14,453
Energy tax receipts	312,066
Homeland security	25,000

Fiscal Year 2006
Total aid	$438,338
CMPTRA	75,896
Muni. block grant	14,453
Energy tax receipts	322,989
Homeland security	25,000

Taxes
	2003	2004	2005
General tax rate per $100	3.07	3.137	1.019
Net valuation taxable	$366,728,630	$373,632,423	$1,223,756,327
State equalized value	$784,614,099	$935,189,664	$1,202,827,135
County equalization ratio	56.02	46.74	130.14

Demographics & Socio-Economic Characteristics

(2000 U.S. Census, except as noted)

Population

1980*	21,639
1990*	26,703
2000	28,967
Male	13,988
Female	14,979
2004 (estimate)*	30,960
Persons per sq. mi. of land	665

Race & Hispanic Origin, 2000

Race

White	24,573
Black/African American	3,231
Amer. Indian/Alaska Natv.	72
Asian	356
Natv. Hawaiian/Pac. Islander	9
Other Race	286
Two or more races	440
Hispanic origin, total	785
Mexican	96
Puerto Rican	486
Cuban	24
Other Hispanic	179

Age & Nativity, 2000

Under 5 years	1,908
18 years and over	21,540
21 years and over	20,553
65 years and over	3,737
85 years and over	331
Median Age	37.1
Native born	28,131
Foreign born	836

Educational Attainment, 2000

Population 25 years and over	19,377
0-8 yrs of school	4.4%
High School grad or higher	80.2%
Bachelor's degree or higher	15.9%
Graduate degree	4.0%

Income & Poverty, 1999

Per capita income	$20,488
Median household income	$50,037
Median family income	$56,810
Persons in poverty	1,769
H'holds receiving public assistance	174
H'holds receiving social security	3,029

Households, 2000

Total households	10,521
With persons under 18	3,996
With persons over 65	2,742
Family households	7,848
One-person households	2,214
Persons per household	2.73
Persons per family	3.18

Labor & Employment

Total civilian labor force, 2004**	16,078
Unemployment rate	4.2%
Total civilian labor force, 2000	14,596
Unemployment rate	5.1%

Employed persons 16 years and over by occupation, 2000

Managers & professionals	3,692
Service occupations	2,237
Sales & office occupations	4,399
Farming, fishing & forestry	26
Construction & maintenance	1,588
Production & transportation	1,908
Self-employed persons	710

*US Census Bureau
**New Jersey Department of Labor

General Information

Township of Monroe
125 Virginia Ave
Williamstown, NJ 08094
856-728-9800

Web site	www.monroetownshipnj.org
Land area (sq. miles)	46.55
Water area (sq. miles)	0.38
Type of government	Township
Form of government	MC '50

Government

Legislative Districts

US Congressional	1
State Legislative	4

Local Officials, 2006

Mayor	Michael Gabbianelli
Admin/Manager	Kevin Heydel
Clerk	Susan McCormick
Finance Dir/Treas	Jeff Coles
Engineer	Adams, Rehman et al
Attorney	Charles Fiore
Tax assessor	Bruce Coyle
Tax collector	Alma Alexander
Building officer	Michael DePalma
Zoning officer	Fred Weikel
Public Works	Vincent J. Agnesino

Housing & Construction

Housing Units, 2000*

Total	11,069
Median rent	$621
Median SF home value	$114,200

New Privately Owned Housing Units Authorized by Building Permit

	Units	Value
Total, 2004	242	$24,793,846
Single family	242	$24,793,846
Total, 2005	247	$30,260,768
Single family	247	$30,260,768

Real Property Valuation - parcels, 2005

	Number	Valuation
Total		$1,308,058,020
Vacant	1,899	36,799,600
Residential	9,732	1,092,572,000
Commercial	370	138,389,520
Industrial	16	6,211,100
Apartments	14	16,215,800
Farm land	148	15,833,900
Farm homestead	345	2,036,100

Average Property Value & Tax, 2005

Residential value	$108,624
Property tax	$4,690
FAIR rebate	$559

Public Library

Monroe Twp. Public Library
306 S Main St
Williamstown, NJ 08094
856-629-1212

Director................. Elizabeth Lillie

Library statistics, 2004

	Total	per capita
Volumes	71,948	2.48
Expenditure	$814,036	$28.10

Public Safety

Police

Chief	Dominic Christopher
Number of officers, 2004	65

Crime, 2004	Number	Rate
Total	639	21
Violent	64	2.1
Non-violent	575	18.9
Domestic Viol.	324	NA

Emergency/Fire

Director............ Salvatore Tomarchio

Public School District

(for school year 2004-2005 except as noted)

Monroe Township School District
75 E Academy St
Williamstown, NJ 08094
856-629-6400

Superintendent	Robert E. Terrill
Grade plan	K-12
Enrollment	5,485.0
Students per teacher	13.1
Per pupil expenditure	$9,997
Median faculty salary	$46,750
Median administrator salary	$96,323
Grade 12 enrollment	292.5
High school graduation rate	92.6%

Assessment test results

(percent scoring at proficient or advanced level)

	Language	Math
Grade 3	90.4%	89.9%
Grade 8	77.9%	61.9%
High school	91.0%	81.8%

SAT

Percent tested	72%
Average SAT math score	484
Average SAT verbal score	479

No Child Left Behind, 2003-04

Attendence rate (target = 90%)	94.1%
Drop rate	1.5%
Highly-qualified teachers	97.3%
District needs improvement?(AYP)	No

Municipal Finance

Fiscal Year 2005

Total tax levy	$56,776,179
County levy	11,758,756
County taxes	11,025,207
County library	0
County health	0
County open space	733,549
School levy	31,002,406
Local muni. budget	14,015,017
Misc. revenues	14,320,795
Total aid	$5,610,939
CMPTRA	1,600,684
Muni. block grant	116,844
Energy tax receipts	3,607,119
Homeland security	90,000

Fiscal Year 2006

Total aid	$5,660,939
CMPTRA	1,474,435
Muni. block grant	116,844
Energy tax receipts	3,733,368
Homeland security	140,000

Taxes

	2003	2004	2005
General tax rate per $100	3.66	3.927	4.318
Net valuation taxable	$1,213,330,149	$1,268,584,218	$1,315,085,296
State equalized value	$1,546,037,397	$1,766,184,681	$2,100,104,273
County equalization ratio	84.99	78.48	71.70

Demographics & Socio-Economic Characteristics
(2000 U.S. Census, except as noted)

Population
1980*	15,858
1990*	22,255
2000	27,999
Male	12,845
Female	15,154
2004 (estimate)*	32,621
Persons per sq. mi. of land	778

Race & Hispanic Origin, 2000
Race
White	26,127
Black/African American	820
Amer. Indian/Alaska Natv.	16
Asian	655
Natv. Hawaiian/Pac. Islander	24
Other Race	189
Two or more races	168
Hispanic origin, total	666
Mexican	63
Puerto Rican	295
Cuban	57
Other Hispanic	251

Age & Nativity, 2000
Under 5 years	1,109
18 years and over	23,521
21 years and over	22,893
65 years and over	12,185
85 years and over	1,380
Median Age	58.9
Native born	25,737
Foreign born	2,262

Educational Attainment, 2000
Population 25 years and over	22,394
0-8 yrs of school	2.9%
High School grad or higher	90.0%
Bachelor's degree or higher	29.5%
Graduate degree	10.1%

Income & Poverty, 1999
Per capita income	$31,772
Median household income	$53,306
Median family income	$68,479
Persons in poverty	908
H'holds receiving public assistance	66
H'holds receiving social security	7,971

Households, 2000
Total households	12,536
With persons under 18	2,148
With persons over 65	8,107
Family households	8,233
One-person households	4,006
Persons per household	2.15
Persons per family	2.7

Labor & Employment
Total civilian labor force, 2004**	9,680
Unemployment rate	5.5%
Total civilian labor force, 2000	10,058
Unemployment rate	5.0%

Employed persons 16 years and over by occupation, 2000
Managers & professionals	3,794
Service occupations	1,006
Sales & office occupations	2,945
Farming, fishing & forestry	34
Construction & maintenance	815
Production & transportation	961
Self-employed persons	617

*US Census Bureau
**New Jersey Department of Labor

General Information
Township of Monroe
1 Municipal Plaza
Monroe Township, NJ 08831
732-521-4400

Web site	NA
Land area (sq. miles)	41.94
Water area (sq. miles)	0.10
Type of government	Township
Form of government	MC '50

Government
Legislative Districts
US Congressional	12
State Legislative	14

Local Officials, 2006
Mayor	Richard Pucci
Admin/Manager	Wayne Hamilton
Clerk	Sharon Doerfler
Finance Dir/Treas	Wendy Matson
Engineer	Ernest Feist
Attorney	Joel Shain
Tax assessor	Mitchell Elias
Tax collector	Dolores Schauer
Building officer	Ronald Appleby
Zoning officer	NA
Public Works	Wayne Horbatt

Housing & Construction
Housing Units, 2000*
Total	13,259
Median rent	$877
Median SF home value	$174,100

New Privately Owned Housing Units Authorized by Building Permit
	Units	Value
Total, 2004	704	$111,792,796
Single family	704	$111,792,79
Total, 2005	634	$89,104,241
Single family	634	$89,104,241

Real Property Valuation - parcels, 2005
	Number	Valuation
Total		$3,099,782,200
Vacant	3,409	207,390,900
Residential	14,901	2,381,593,600
Commercial	188	212,707,400
Industrial	46	231,148,000
Apartments	3	29,159,300
Farm land	181	33,152,100
Farm homestead	379	4,630,900

Average Property Value & Tax, 2005
Residential value	$156,167
Property tax	$4,556
FAIR rebate	$662

Public Library
Monroe Township Library
4 Municipal Plaza
Monroe Twp., NJ 08831
732-521-5000

Director	Irene Goldberg

Library statistics, 2004
	Total	per capita
Volumes	94,753	3.38
Expenditure	$2,087,893	$74.57

Public Safety
Police
Chief	John Kraivec
Number of officers, 2004	45

Crime, 2004	Number	Rate
Total	214	6.8
Violent	15	0.5
Non-violent	199	6.3
Domestic Viol.	24	NA

Emergency/Fire
Director	NA

Public School District
(for school year 2004-2005 except as noted)

Monroe Township School District
423 Buckelew Ave
Monroe Township, NJ 08831
732-521-2111

Superintendent	Ralph Ferrie
Grade plan	K-12
Enrollment	4,302.0
Students per teacher	10.8
Per pupil expenditure	$12,153
Median faculty salary	$50,090
Median administrator salary	$104,507
Grade 12 enrollment	293.5
High school graduation rate	97.6%

Assessment test results
(percent scoring at proficient or advanced level)
	Language	Math
Grade 3	92.3%	87.9%
Grade 8	87.4%	69.6%
High school	88.5%	83.3%

SAT
Percent tested	77%
Average SAT math score	535
Average SAT verbal score	508

No Child Left Behind, 2003-04
Attendence rate (target = 90%)	95.5%
Drop rate	0.2%
Highly-qualified teachers	98.6%
District needs improvement?(AYP)	No

Municipal Finance
Fiscal Year 2005
Total tax levy	$90,615,787
County levy	15,980,856
County taxes	14,476,145
County library	0
County health	0
County open space	1,504,711
School levy	56,429,006
Local muni. budget	18,205,925
Misc. revenues	14,784,532
Total aid	$3,178,706
CMPTRA	857,923
Muni. block grant	109,785
Energy tax receipts	2,070,998
Homeland security	140,000

Fiscal Year 2006
Total aid	$3,178,706
CMPTRA	785,438
Muni. block grant	109,785
Energy tax receipts	2,143,483
Homeland security	140,000

Taxes
	2003	2004	2005
General tax rate per $100	2.73	2.900	2.920
Net valuation taxable	$2,666,496,065	$2,860,228,577	$3,105,831,277
State equalized value	$4,057,976,054	$4,622,221,647	$5,512,657,574
County equalization ratio	71.35	65.72	61.83

Demographics & Socio-Economic Characteristics
(2000 U.S. Census, except as noted)

Population

1980*	2,066
1990*	2,832
2000	3,412
Male	1,764
Female	1,648
2004 (estimate)*	3,729
Persons per sq. mi. of land	85

Race & Hispanic Origin, 2000
Race

White	3,250
Black/African American	61
Amer. Indian/Alaska Natv.	6
Asian	23
Natv. Hawaiian/Pac. Islander	0
Other Race	37
Two or more races	35
Hispanic origin, total	112
Mexican	9
Puerto Rican	39
Cuban	12
Other Hispanic	52

Age & Nativity, 2000

Under 5 years	241
18 years and over	2,485
21 years and over	2,377
65 years and over	378
85 years and over	22
Median Age	37
Native born	3,278
Foreign born	134

Educational Attainment, 2000

Population 25 years and over	2,262
0-8 yrs of school	5.4%
High School grad or higher	80.2%
Bachelor's degree or higher	14.5%
Graduate degree	6.0%

Income & Poverty, 1999

Per capita income	$20,676
Median household income	$45,368
Median family income	$50,833
Persons in poverty	406
H'holds receiving public assistance	47
H'holds receiving social security	337

Households, 2000

Total households	1,286
With persons under 18	481
With persons over 65	281
Family households	911
One-person households	298
Persons per household	2.65
Persons per family	3.14

Labor & Employment

Total civilian labor force, 2004**	1,701
Unemployment rate	5.3%
Total civilian labor force, 2000	1,638
Unemployment rate	5.7%

Employed persons 16 years and over by occupation, 2000

Managers & professionals	397
Service occupations	252
Sales & office occupations	441
Farming, fishing & forestry	0
Construction & maintenance	262
Production & transportation	193
Self-employed persons	147

*US Census Bureau
**New Jersey Department of Labor

General Information
Township of Montague
277 Clove Rd
Montague, NJ 07827
973-293-7300

Web site	NA
Land area (sq. miles)	44.01
Water area (sq. miles)	1.33
Type of government	Township
Form of government	TC

Government

Legislative Districts

US Congressional	5
State Legislative	24

Local Officials, 2006

Mayor	Paul Brislin
Admin/Manager	NA
Clerk	Dianna Francisco
Finance Dir/Treas	Gail Magura
Engineer	Jack O'Krepky
Attorney	Stephen Edelstein
Tax assessor	David Poe
Tax collector	NA
Building officer	Donald Stambough
Zoning officer	Wayne Rumsey
Public Works	NA

Housing & Construction

Housing Units, 2000*

Total	1,588
Median rent	$806
Median SF home value	$129,400

New Privately Owned Housing Units
Authorized by Building Permit

	Units	Value
Total, 2004	59	$5,300,340
Single family	59	$5,300,340
Total, 2005	46	$6,283,052
Single family	44	$6,211,052

Real Property Valuation - parcels, 2005

	Number	Valuation
Total		$208,097,210
Vacant	1,006	16,244,800
Residential	1,570	159,613,500
Commercial	58	21,310,900
Industrial	6	2,136,600
Apartments	2	420,000
Farm land	55	7,371,600
Farm homestead	154	999,810

Average Property Value & Tax, 2005

Residential value	$93,163
Property tax	$2,816
FAIR rebate	$575

Public Library

No public municipal library.

Library statistics, 2004

	Total	per capita
Volumes	NA	NA
Expenditure	NA	NA

Public Safety

Police

Chief	(State)
Number of officers, 2004	0

Crime, 2004	Number	Rate
Total	83	23.1
Violent	5	1.4
Non-violent	78	21.7
Domestic Viol.	60	NA

Emergency/Fire

Director	David Coss

Public School District
(for school year 2004-2005 except as noted)

Montague School District
475 Route 206
Montague, NJ 07827
973-293-7131

Administrator	Janice Hodge
Grade plan	K-12
Enrollment	320.0
Students per teacher	9.0
Per pupil expenditure	$11,876
Median faculty salary	$48,812
Median administrator salary	$78,000
Grade 12 enrollment	NA
High school graduation rate	NA

Assessment test results
(percent scoring at proficient or advanced level)

	Language	Math
Grade 3	76.9%	84.7%
Grade 8	NA	NA
High school	NA	NA

SAT

Percent tested	NA
Average SAT math score	NA
Average SAT verbal score	NA

No Child Left Behind, 2003-04

Attendence rate (target = 90%)	95.5%
Drop rate	NA
Highly-qualified teachers	100%
District needs improvement?(AYP)	No

Municipal Finance

Fiscal Year 2005

Total tax levy	$6,319,364
County levy	1,401,836
County taxes	1,189,765
County library	102,578
County health	48,287
County open space	61,207
School levy	4,348,451
Local muni. budget	569,077
Misc. revenues	1,290,517
Total aid	$370,477
CMPTRA	100,417
Muni. block grant	13,379
Energy tax receipts	256,681
Homeland security	0

Fiscal Year 2006

Total aid	$370,476
CMPTRA	91,433
Muni. block grant	13,379
Energy tax receipts	265,664
Homeland security	NA

Taxes

	2003	2004	2005
General tax rate per $100	2.87	2.880	3.030
Net valuation taxable	$197,203,941	$201,626,745	$209,069,369
State equalized value	$257,547,265	$293,760,169	$378,680,255
County equalization ratio	93.68	76.57	68.52

Demographics & Socio-Economic Characteristics
(2000 U.S. Census, except as noted)

Population
1980*	38,321
1990*	37,729
2000	38,977
Male	18,053
Female	20,924
2000 (revised)	38,658
2004 (estimate)*	38,298
Persons per sq. mi. of land	6,076

Race & Hispanic Origin, 2000
Race
White	23,297
Black/African American	12,497
Amer. Indian/Alaska Natv.	73
Asian	1,228
Natv. Hawaiian/Pac. Islander	14
Other Race	688
Two or more races	1,180
Hispanic origin, total	1,995
Mexican	183
Puerto Rican	584
Cuban	171
Other Hispanic	1,057

Age & Nativity, 2000
Under 5 years	2,716
18 years and over	29,013
21 years and over	27,887
65 years and over	4,665
85 years and over	786
Median Age	37.5
Native born	33,389
Foreign born	5,679

Educational Attainment, 2000
Population 25 years and over	26,652
0-8 yrs of school	3.0%
High School grad or higher	92.0%
Bachelor's degree or higher	57.4%
Graduate degree	27.1%

Income & Poverty, 1999
Per capita income	$44,870
Median household income	$74,894
Median family income	$96,252
Persons in poverty	2,149
H'holds receiving public assistance	369
H'holds receiving social security	3,197

Households, 2000
Total households	15,020
With persons under 18	5,574
With persons over 65	3,271
Family households	9,682
One-person households	4,396
Persons per household	2.53
Persons per family	3.16

Labor & Employment
Total civilian labor force, 2004**	9,062
Unemployment rate	1.5%
Total civilian labor force, 2000	21,484
Unemployment rate	5.0%

Employed persons 16 years and over by occupation, 2000
Managers & professionals	11,898
Service occupations	2,120
Sales & office occupations	4,833
Farming, fishing & forestry	0
Construction & maintenance	561
Production & transportation	1,002
Self-employed persons	1,532

*US Census Bureau
**New Jersey Department of Labor

General Information
Township of Montclair
205 Claremont Ave
Montclair, NJ 07042
973-744-1400
Web site	www.to.montclair.nj.us
Land area (sq. miles)	6.30
Water area (sq. miles)	0
Type of government	Township
Form of government	CM '50

Government

Legislative Districts
US Congressional	8, 10
State Legislative	34

Local Officials, 2006
Mayor	Edward Remsen
Admin/Manager	Joseph M. Hartnett
Clerk	Linda S. Wanat
Finance Dir/Treas	Dianne Marus
Engineer	Kimberli Craft
Attorney	Alan Trembulak
Tax assessor	Joan Kozeniesky
Tax collector	Maureen Montesano
Building officer	Anthony Montuori
Zoning officer	Karen Kadus
Public Works	Steve Wood

Housing & Construction

Housing Units, 2000*
Total	15,531
Median rent	$866
Median SF home value	$317,500

New Privately Owned Housing Units
Authorized by Building Permit
	Units	Value
Total, 2004	33	$3,849,805
Single family	12	$2,714,591
Total, 2005	65	$11,636,616
Single family	25	$8,396,772

Real Property Valuation - parcels, 2005
	Number	Valuation
Total		$2,770,668,100
Vacant	172	11,095,600
Residential	9,438	2,387,199,500
Commercial	542	239,062,000
Industrial	3	1,955,700
Apartments	163	131,355,300
Farm land	0	0
Farm homestead	0	0

Average Property Value & Tax, 2005
Residential value	$252,935
Property tax	$12,870
FAIR rebate	$574

Public Library
Montclair Public Library
50 South Fullerton Ave
Montclair, NJ 07042
973-744-0500
Director	NA

Library statistics, 2004
	Total	per capita
Volumes	214,381	5.50
Expenditure	$3,843,287	$98.60

Public Safety
Police
Chief	David Sabagh
Number of officers, 2004	110

Crime, 2004	Number	Rate
Total	1,173	30.4
Violent	144	3.7
Non-violent	1,029	26.7
Domestic Viol.	193	NA

Emergency/Fire
Director	Kevin Allen

Public School District
(for school year 2004-2005 except as noted)

Montclair School District
22 Valley Rd
Montclair, NJ 07042
973-509-4010
Superintendent	Frank Alverez
Grade plan	K-12
Enrollment	6,580.0
Students per teacher	10.6
Per pupil expenditure	$12,892
Median faculty salary	$56,011
Median administrator salary	$103,177
Grade 12 enrollment	441.0
High school graduation rate	99.1%

Assessment test results
(percent scoring at proficient or advanced level)
	Language	Math
Grade 3	91.4%	91.4%
Grade 8	78.2%	64.7%
High school	88.6%	80.2%

SAT
Percent tested	86%
Average SAT math score	542
Average SAT verbal score	541

No Child Left Behind, 2003-04
Attendance rate (target = 90%)	95.2%
Drop rate	0.1%
Highly-qualified teachers	95%
District needs improvement?(AYP)	No

Municipal Finance

Fiscal Year 2005
Total tax levy	$141,218,639
County levy	26,673,060
County taxes	26,114,622
County library	0
County health	0
County open space	558,438
School levy	82,414,227
Local muni. budget	32,131,352
Misc. revenues	21,215,867
Total aid	$4,263,614
CMPTRA	1,728,068
Muni. block grant	164,031
Energy tax receipts	2,231,515
Homeland security	140,000

Fiscal Year 2006
Total aid	$4,263,614
CMPTRA	1,649,965
Muni. block grant	164,031
Energy tax receipts	2,309,618
Homeland security	140,000

Taxes
	2003	2004	2005
General tax rate per $100	4.67	4.910	5.090
Net valuation taxable	$2,749,296,294	$2,769,222,845	$2,775,430,506
State equalized value	$4,949,228,252	$5,541,995,243	$6,145,771,714
County equalization ratio	64.73	64.73	49.92

Demographics & Socio-Economic Characteristics

(2000 U.S. Census, except as noted)

Population

1980*	7,360
1990*	9,612
2000	17,481
Male	8,624
Female	8,857
2004 (estimate)*	22,287
Persons per sq. mi. of land	683

Race & Hispanic Origin, 2000

Race

White	14,781
Black/African American	361
Amer. Indian/Alaska Natv.	15
Asian	2,011
Natv. Hawaiian/Pac. Islander	2
Other Race	80
Two or more races	231
Hispanic origin, total	387
Mexican	76
Puerto Rican	96
Cuban	47
Other Hispanic	168

Age & Nativity, 2000

Under 5 years	1,514
18 years and over	11,722
21 years and over	11,395
65 years and over	1,189
85 years and over	94
Median Age	36.8
Native born	14,934
Foreign born	2,531

Educational Attainment, 2000

Population 25 years and over	11,032
0-8 yrs of school	1.4%
High School grad or higher	97.3%
Bachelor's degree or higher	70.2%
Graduate degree	34.8%

Income & Poverty, 1999

Per capita income	$48,699
Median household income	$118,850
Median family income	$129,150
Persons in poverty	261
H'holds receiving public assistance	22
H'holds receiving social security	878

Households, 2000

Total households	5,803
With persons under 18	3,006
With persons over 65	839
Family households	4,783
One-person households	823
Persons per household	2.99
Persons per family	3.33

Labor & Employment

Total civilian labor force, 2004**	6,303
Unemployment rate	2.2%
Total civilian labor force, 2000	8,711
Unemployment rate	2.1%

Employed persons 16 years and over by occupation, 2000

Managers & professionals	5,947
Service occupations	384
Sales & office occupations	1,714
Farming, fishing & forestry	21
Construction & maintenance	249
Production & transportation	217
Self-employed persons	446

*US Census Bureau
**New Jersey Department of Labor

General Information

Township of Montgomery
2261 Route 206
Belle Mead, NJ 08502
908-359-8211

Web site	www.twp.montgomery.nj.us
Land area (sq. miles)	32.62
Water area (sq. miles)	0
Type of government	Township
Form of government	TC

Government

Legislative Districts

US Congressional	7
State Legislative	16

Local Officials, 2006

Mayor	Louise Wilson
Admin/Manager	Donato Nieman
Clerk	Donna Kukla
Finance Dir/Treas	Randy Bahr
Engineer	Gail Smith
Attorney	Kristina Hadinger
Tax assessor	Eleanor Blake
Tax collector	Randy Bahr
Building officer	John Marold
Zoning officer	Joe Palmer
Public Works	Arthur Villano

Housing & Construction

Housing Units, 2000*

Total	6,130
Median rent	$1,196
Median SF home value	$348,500

New Privately Owned Housing Units Authorized by Building Permit

	Units	Value
Total, 2004	60	$8,659,326
Single family	60	$8,659,326
Total, 2005	17	$2,143,850
Single family	17	$2,143,850

Real Property Valuation - parcels, 2005

	Number	Valuation
Total		$3,754,675,432
Vacant	532	98,119,700
Residential	6,237	3,204,571,700
Commercial	160	318,381,180
Industrial	1	3,112,900
Apartments	9	74,229,800
Farm land	97	54,270,300
Farm homestead	201	1,989,852

Average Property Value & Tax, 2005

Residential value	$498,068
Property tax	$10,942
FAIR rebate	$477

Public Library

No public municipal library.

Library statistics, 2004

	Total	per capita
Volumes	NA	NA
Expenditure	NA	NA

Public Safety

Police

Chief	Michael Beltranena (Dir)
Number of officers, 2004	26

Crime, 2004	Number	Rate
Total	212	10.1
Violent	4	0.2
Non-violent	208	9.9
Domestic Viol.	72	NA

Emergency/Fire

Director	NA

Public School District

(for school year 2004-2005 except as noted)

Montgomery Township School District
1014 Route 601
Skillman, NJ 08558
609-466-7601

Superintendent	Stuart Schnur
Grade plan	K-12
Enrollment	4,899.0
Students per teacher	12.4
Per pupil expenditure	$10,261
Median faculty salary	$47,205
Median administrator salary	$105,250
Grade 12 enrollment	264.0
High school graduation rate	99.6%

Assessment test results

(percent scoring at proficient or advanced level)

	Language	Math
Grade 3	93.7%	93.1%
Grade 8	94.0%	88.1%
High school	98.3%	96.8%

SAT

Percent tested	102%
Average SAT math score	627
Average SAT verbal score	617

No Child Left Behind, 2003-04

Attendence rate (target = 90%)	95.9%
Drop rate	0.1%
Highly-qualified teachers	94.9%
District needs improvement?(AYP)	No

Municipal Finance

Fiscal Year 2005

Total tax levy	$82,609,677
County levy	14,249,304
County taxes	11,805,402
County library	1,308,649
County health	0
County open space	1,135,252
School levy	58,423,351
Local muni. budget	9,937,022
Misc. revenues	22,824,211
Total aid	$2,032,809
CMPTRA	422,773
Muni. block grant	68,543
Energy tax receipts	1,471,493
Homeland security	70,000

Fiscal Year 2006

Total aid	$2,052,810
CMPTRA	371,271
Muni. block grant	68,543
Energy tax receipts	1,522,996
Homeland security	90,000

Taxes

	2003	2004	2005
General tax rate per $100	2.30	2.450	2.200
Net valuation taxable	$2,988,237,026	$3,048,033,805	$3,760,460,580
State equalized value	$3,397,268,106	$3,655,427,363	$4,247,188,367
County equalization ratio	103	87.96	99.43

Demographics & Socio-Economic Characteristics
(2000 U.S. Census, except as noted)

Population
1980*	7,318
1990*	6,946
2000	7,034
Male	3,466
Female	3,568
2004 (estimate)*	7,321
Persons per sq. mi. of land	1,842

Race & Hispanic Origin, 2000
Race
White	6,527
Black/African American	31
Amer. Indian/Alaska Natv.	6
Asian	377
Natv. Hawaiian/Pac. Islander	0
Other Race	44
Two or more races	49
Hispanic origin, total	217
Mexican	36
Puerto Rican	41
Cuban	36
Other Hispanic	104

Age & Nativity, 2000
Under 5 years	490
18 years and over	5,209
21 years and over	5,043
65 years and over	884
85 years and over	75
Median Age	39.7
Native born	6,111
Foreign born	923

Educational Attainment, 2000
Population 25 years and over	4,818
0-8 yrs of school	0.9%
High School grad or higher	95.0%
Bachelor's degree or higher	55.3%
Graduate degree	20.0%

Income & Poverty, 1999
Per capita income	$45,448
Median household income	$93,031
Median family income	$104,047
Persons in poverty	62
H'holds receiving public assistance	0
H'holds receiving social security	567

Households, 2000
Total households	2,509
With persons under 18	984
With persons over 65	626
Family households	2,000
One-person households	437
Persons per household	2.8
Persons per family	3.18

Labor & Employment
Total civilian labor force, 2004**	4,132
Unemployment rate	3.0%
Total civilian labor force, 2000	3,698
Unemployment rate	2.8%

Employed persons 16 years and over by occupation, 2000
Managers & professionals	1,989
Service occupations	300
Sales & office occupations	1,023
Farming, fishing & forestry	0
Construction & maintenance	125
Production & transportation	159
Self-employed persons	169

*US Census Bureau
**New Jersey Department of Labor

General Information
Borough of Montvale
12 Mercedes Dr
Montvale, NJ 07645
201-391-5700

Web site	www.montvale.org
Land area (sq. miles)	3.97
Water area (sq. miles)	0
Type of government	Borough
Form of government	B

Government

Legislative Districts
US Congressional	5
State Legislative	39

Local Officials, 2006
Mayor	George Barry Zeller
Admin/Manager	John Doyle
Clerk	Marueen Iarossi-Alwan
Finance Dir/Treas	Carl Bello
Engineer	Boswell Engineering
Attorney	Russell Huntington
Tax assessor	Michael Leposky
Tax collector	Alice Lee
Building officer	Raymond Dressler
Zoning officer	NA
Public Works	Robert Culvert

Housing & Construction

Housing Units, 2000*
Total	2,590
Median rent	$1,116
Median SF home value	$346,400

New Privately Owned Housing Units Authorized by Building Permit
	Units	Value
Total, 2004	11	$3,662,076
Single family	11	$3,662,076
Total, 2005	19	$6,329,625
Single family	19	$6,329,625

Real Property Valuation - parcels, 2005
	Number	Valuation
Total		$1,093,949,800
Vacant	86	11,640,900
Residential	2,453	699,500,500
Commercial	114	367,170,700
Industrial	6	7,749,600
Apartments	1	7,000,000
Farm land	3	832,300
Farm homestead	13	55,800

Average Property Value & Tax, 2005
Residential value	$283,681
Property tax	$7,747
FAIR rebate	$591

Public Library
Montvale Public Library
12 Mercedes Dr
Montvale, NJ 07645
201-391-5090

Director . . . . Susan Ruttenber

Library statistics, 2004
	Total	per capita
Volumes	53,118	7.55
Expenditure	$569,703	$80.99

Public Safety

Police
Chief	Joseph Marigliani
Number of officers, 2004	22

Crime, 2004	Number	Rate
Total	75	10.3
Violent	9	1.2
Non-violent	66	9.1
Domestic Viol.	6	NA

Emergency/Fire
Director . . . . Clinton Miller (Chief)

Public School District
(for school year 2004-2005 except as noted)

Montvale School District
47 Spring Valley Rd
Montvale, NJ 07645
201-391-1662

Superintendent	Susan King
Grade plan	K-8
Enrollment	1,035.0
Students per teacher	11.0
Per pupil expenditure	$11,662
Median faculty salary	$49,558
Median administrator salary	$111,060
Grade 12 enrollment	NA
High school graduation rate	NA

Assessment test results
(percent scoring at proficient or advanced level)
	Language	Math
Grade 3	97.1%	92.1%
Grade 8	92.1%	86.7%
High school	NA	NA

SAT
Percent tested	NA
Average SAT math score	NA
Average SAT verbal score	NA

No Child Left Behind, 2003-04
Attendence rate (target = 90%)	96.7%
Drop rate	NA
Highly-qualified teachers	99%
District needs improvement?(AYP)	No

Municipal Finance

Fiscal Year 2005
Total tax levy	$29,917,785
County levy	3,475,777
County taxes	3,301,960
County library	0
County health	0
County open space	173,817
School levy	18,625,142
Local muni. budget	7,816,867
Misc. revenues	6,118,752
Total aid	$1,685,021
CMPTRA	275,107
Muni. block grant	30,393
Energy tax receipts	1,329,521
Homeland security	50,000

Fiscal Year 2006
Total aid	$1,685,021
CMPTRA	228,573
Muni. block grant	30,393
Energy tax receipts	1,376,055
Homeland security	50,000

Taxes
	2003	2004	2005
General tax rate per $100	2.49	2.590	2.740
Net valuation taxable	$1,094,412,996	$1,098,515,536	$1,095,570,257
State equalized value	$1,577,873,408	$1,735,161,439	$1,920,368,549
County equalization ratio	71.77	69.36	63.27

Demographics & Socio-Economic Characteristics

(2000 U.S. Census, except as noted)

Population

1980*	14,290
1990*	15,600
2000	20,839
Male	10,138
Female	10,701
2004 (estimate)*	21,368
Persons per sq. mi. of land	1,132

Race & Hispanic Origin, 2000

Race
White	17,703
Black/African American	193
Amer. Indian/Alaska Natv.	9
Asian	2,619
Natv. Hawaiian/Pac. Islander	4
Other Race	74
Two or more races	237
Hispanic origin, total	531
Mexican	69
Puerto Rican	158
Cuban	75
Other Hispanic	229

Age & Nativity, 2000

Under 5 years	1,435
18 years and over	15,597
21 years and over	15,126
65 years and over	2,256
85 years and over	233
Median Age	38.9
Native born	17,251
Foreign born	3,588

Educational Attainment, 2000

Population 25 years and over	14,445
0-8 yrs of school	1.9%
High School grad or higher	93.5%
Bachelor's degree or higher	51.2%
Graduate degree	20.4%

Income & Poverty, 1999

Per capita income	$43,341
Median household income	$94,557
Median family income	$105,394
Persons in poverty	794
H'holds receiving public assistance	78
H'holds receiving social security	1,403

Households, 2000

Total households	7,380
With persons under 18	2,858
With persons over 65	1,542
Family households	5,869
One-person households	1,225
Persons per household	2.8
Persons per family	3.17

Labor & Employment

Total civilian labor force, 2004**	9,616
Unemployment rate	4.8%
Total civilian labor force, 2000	11,412
Unemployment rate	2.0%

Employed persons 16 years and over by occupation, 2000
Managers & professionals	6,023
Service occupations	686
Sales & office occupations	3,205
Farming, fishing & forestry	0
Construction & maintenance	638
Production & transportation	637
Self-employed persons	783

*US Census Bureau
**New Jersey Department of Labor

General Information

Township of Montville
195 Changebridge Rd
Montville, NJ 07045
973-331-3300

Web site	www.montvillenj.org
Land area (sq. miles)	18.87
Water area (sq. miles)	0.26
Type of government	Township
Form of government	SC

Government

Legislative Districts

US Congressional	11
State Legislative	26

Local Officials, 2006

Mayor	Stephen Moscone
Admin/Manager	Joseph Rompala
Clerk	Gertrude Atkinson
Finance Dir/Treas	Frances Vanderhoof
Engineer	Anthony Barile Jr.
Attorney	Martin Murphy
Tax assessor	Thomas Lenhardt
Tax collector	Francine Novak
Building officer	Brian Laird
Zoning officer	Linda White
Public Works	Anthony Barile Jr.

Housing & Construction

Housing Units, 2000*

Total	7,541
Median rent	$1,186
Median SF home value	$346,600

New Privately Owned Housing Units Authorized by Building Permit

	Units	Value
Total, 2004	34	$13,890,609
Single family	34	$13,890,609
Total, 2005	49	$28,093,610
Single family	49	$28,093,610

Real Property Valuation - parcels, 2005

	Number	Valuation
Total		$2,787,918,700
Vacant	419	62,991,400
Residential	6,900	2,240,814,100
Commercial	280	155,641,400
Industrial	80	269,354,600
Apartments	5	52,558,100
Farm land	22	6,362,200
Farm homestead	41	196,900

Average Property Value & Tax, 2005

Residential value	$322,866
Property tax	$8,845
FAIR rebate	$562

Public Library

Montville Twp Public Library
90 Horseneck Rd
Montville, NJ 07045
973-402-0900

Director................Patty Anderson

Library statistics, 2004

	Total	per capita
Volumes	112,595	5.4
Expenditure	$1,211,290	$58.13

Public Safety

Police

Chief	Richard Cook
Number of officers, 2004	40

Crime, 2004	Number	Rate
Total	224	10.6
Violent	7	0.3
Non-violent	217	10.2
Domestic Viol.	74	NA

Emergency/Fire

Director..........................NA

Public School District

(for school year 2004-2005 except as noted)

Montville Township School District
328 Changebridge Rd
Pine Brook, NJ 07058
973-808-8580

Superintendent	Catherine Mozak (Int)
Grade plan	K-12
Enrollment	3,991.0
Students per teacher	11.6
Per pupil expenditure	$12,246
Median faculty salary	$51,600
Median administrator salary	$112,200
Grade 12 enrollment	258.5
High school graduation rate	98.8%

Assessment test results

(percent scoring at proficient or advanced level)

	Language	Math
Grade 3	96.0%	92.6%
Grade 8	94.9%	83.5%
High school	92.1%	90.5%

SAT

Percent tested	87%
Average SAT math score	586
Average SAT verbal score	562

No Child Left Behind, 2003-04

Attendance rate (target = 90%)	95.7%
Drop rate	0.3%
Highly-qualified teachers	100%
District needs improvement?(AYP)	No

Municipal Finance

Fiscal Year 2005

Total tax levy	$76,489,646
County levy	11,494,834
County taxes	9,415,694
County library	0
County health	0
County open space	2,079,140
School levy	49,717,769
Local muni. budget	15,277,043
Misc. revenues	9,854,967
Total aid	$2,993,403
CMPTRA	539,167
Muni. block grant	81,710
Energy tax receipts	2,280,834
Homeland security	90,000

Fiscal Year 2006

Total aid	$2,993,404
CMPTRA	459,338
Muni. block grant	81,710
Energy tax receipts	2,360,664
Homeland security	90,000

Taxes

	2003	2004	2005
General tax rate per $100	2.36	2.530	2.740
Net valuation taxable	$2,750,430,325	$2,771,533,100	$2,792,190,798
State equalized value	$3,859,711,374	$4,284,728,743	$4,676,253,221
County equalization ratio	79.35	71.26	64.64

Demographics & Socio-Economic Characteristics

(2000 U.S. Census, except as noted)

Population

1980*	2,706
1990*	2,817
2000	2,754
Male	1,355
Female	1,399
2004 (estimate)*	2,816
Persons per sq. mi. of land	1,632

Race & Hispanic Origin, 2000

Race
White	2,359
Black/African American	26
Amer. Indian/Alaska Natv.	3
Asian	183
Natv. Hawaiian/Pac. Islander	0
Other Race	81
Two or more races	102
Hispanic origin, total	349
Mexican	22
Puerto Rican	88
Cuban	72
Other Hispanic	167

Age & Nativity, 2000

Under 5 years	131
18 years and over	2,179
21 years and over	2,090
65 years and over	422
85 years and over	35
Median Age	40.4
Native born	2,151
Foreign born	603

Educational Attainment, 2000

Population 25 years and over	1,982
0-8 yrs of school	10.0%
High School grad or higher	72.9%
Bachelor's degree or higher	13.2%
Graduate degree	3.2%

Income & Poverty, 1999

Per capita income	$24,654
Median household income	$50,571
Median family income	$62,163
Persons in poverty	104
H'holds receiving public assistance	19
H'holds receiving social security	322

Households, 2000

Total households	1,041
With persons under 18	333
With persons over 65	328
Family households	708
One-person households	289
Persons per household	2.65
Persons per family	3.27

Labor & Employment

Total civilian labor force, 2004**	1,683
Unemployment rate	4.5%
Total civilian labor force, 2000	1,426
Unemployment rate	2.5%

Employed persons 16 years and over by occupation, 2000
Managers & professionals	312
Service occupations	176
Sales & office occupations	513
Farming, fishing & forestry	0
Construction & maintenance	134
Production & transportation	255
Self-employed persons	66

*US Census Bureau
**New Jersey Department of Labor

General Information

Borough of Moonachie
70 Moonachie Rd
Moonachie, NJ 07074
201-641-1813

Web site	www.moonachie.net
Land area (sq. miles)	1.73
Water area (sq. miles)	0
Type of government	Borough
Form of government	B

Government

Legislative Districts

US Congressional	9
State Legislative	36

Local Officials, 2006

Mayor	Frederick Dressel
Admin/Manager	Paul Hansen
Clerk	Jean Finch
Finance Dir/Treas	Paul Hansen
Engineer	Kevin Boswell
Attorney	Frank Migliorino
Tax assessor	Paul Barbire
Tax collector	NA
Building officer	Robert Connell
Zoning officer	Robert Connell
Public Works	NA

Housing & Construction

Housing Units, 2000*

Total	1,074
Median rent	$851
Median SF home value	$192,900

New Privately Owned Housing Units Authorized by Building Permit

	Units	Value
Total, 2004	4	$639,000
Single family	4	$639,000
Total, 2005	8	$1,806,000
Single family	8	$1,806,000

Real Property Valuation - parcels, 2005

	Number	Valuation
Total		$803,385,700
Vacant	27	12,722,300
Residential	592	225,168,000
Commercial	40	73,732,800
Industrial	140	491,762,600
Apartments	0	0
Farm land	0	0
Farm homestead	0	0

Average Property Value & Tax, 2005

Residential value	$380,351
Property tax	$5,113
FAIR rebate	$666

Public Library

No public municipal library.

Library statistics, 2004

	Total	per capita
Volumes	NA	NA
Expenditure	NA	NA

Public Safety

Police

Chief	Michael McGahn
Number of officers, 2004	19

Crime, 2004	Number	Rate
Total	91	32.1
Violent	3	1.1
Non-violent	88	31
Domestic Viol.	37	NA

Emergency/Fire

Director	James O'Neill

Public School District

(for school year 2004-2005 except as noted)

Moonachie School District
20 W Park St
Moonachie, NJ 07074
201-641-5833

Superintendent	Mark Solimo
Grade plan	K-12
Enrollment	286.0
Students per teacher	10.1
Per pupil expenditure	$14,956
Median faculty salary	$66,163
Median administrator salary	$105,375
Grade 12 enrollment	NA
High school graduation rate	NA

Assessment test results

(percent scoring at proficient or advanced level)
	Language	Math
Grade 3	78.1%	90.7%
Grade 8	66.7%	51.8%
High school	NA	NA

SAT

Percent tested	NA
Average SAT math score	NA
Average SAT verbal score	NA

No Child Left Behind, 2003-04

Attendance rate (target = 90%)	95.0%
Drop rate	NA
Highly-qualified teachers	100%
District needs improvement?(AYP)	No

Municipal Finance

Fiscal Year 2005

Total tax levy	$10,808,823
County levy	1,314,455
County taxes	1,248,646
County library	0
County health	0
County open space	65,808
School levy	5,734,368
Local muni. budget	3,760,000
Misc. revenues	2,745,157
Total aid	$651,443
CMPTRA	163,765
Muni. block grant	12,327
Energy tax receipts	450,351
Homeland security	25,000

Fiscal Year 2006

Total aid	$651,443
CMPTRA	148,003
Muni. block grant	12,327
Energy tax receipts	466,113
Homeland security	25,000

Taxes

	2003	2004	2005
General tax rate per $100	2.46	2.530	1.350
Net valuation taxable	$399,748,693	$401,789,178	$804,097,900
State equalized value	$562,471,779	$650,349,424	$732,930,362
County equalization ratio	69.17	71.07	123.69

Demographics & Socio-Economic Characteristics

(2000 U.S. Census, except as noted)

Population

1980*	15,596
1990*	16,116
2000	19,017
Male	8,974
Female	10,043
2004 (estimate)*	20,041
Persons per sq. mi. of land	1,357

Race & Hispanic Origin, 2000

Race

White	16,962
Black/African American	1,082
Amer. Indian/Alaska Natv.	30
Asian	621
Natv. Hawaiian/Pac. Islander	1
Other Race	81
Two or more races	240
Hispanic origin, total	332
Mexican	49
Puerto Rican	140
Cuban	26
Other Hispanic	117

Age & Nativity, 2000

Under 5 years	1,218
18 years and over	13,797
21 years and over	13,363
65 years and over	3,120
85 years and over	557
Median Age	40.9
Native born	17,906
Foreign born	1,111

Educational Attainment, 2000

Population 25 years and over	12,946
0-8 yrs of school	2.7%
High School grad or higher	92.5%
Bachelor's degree or higher	52.5%
Graduate degree	23.2%

Income & Poverty, 1999

Per capita income	$42,154
Median household income	$78,826
Median family income	$94,844
Persons in poverty	634
H'holds receiving public assistance	71
H'holds receiving social security	2,048

Households, 2000

Total households	6,971
With persons under 18	2,697
With persons over 65	2,005
Family households	5,273
One-person households	1,461
Persons per household	2.68
Persons per family	3.13

Labor & Employment

Total civilian labor force, 2004**	9,457
Unemployment rate	2.9%
Total civilian labor force, 2000	8,973
Unemployment rate	3.0%

Employed persons 16 years and over by occupation, 2000

Managers & professionals	4,877
Service occupations	599
Sales & office occupations	2,279
Farming, fishing & forestry	12
Construction & maintenance	347
Production & transportation	590
Self-employed persons	711

*US Census Bureau
**New Jersey Department of Labor

General Information

Township of Moorestown
111 West Second St
Moorestown, NJ 08057
856-235-0912

Web site	www.moorestown.nj.us
Land area (sq. miles)	14.77
Water area (sq. miles)	0.16
Type of government	Township
Form of government	CM '50

Government

Legislative Districts

US Congressional	3
State Legislative	8

Local Officials, 2006

Mayor	Kevin E. Aberant
Admin/Manager	John Terry
Clerk	Patricia Hunt
Finance Dir/Treas	Thomas Merchel
Engineer	Remington & Venick
Attorney	David M. Serlin
Tax assessor	Dennis Bianchini
Tax collector	NA
Building officer	Steven Holmes
Zoning officer	Peter D. Clifford
Public Works	NA

Housing & Construction

Housing Units, 2000*

Total	7,211
Median rent	$843
Median SF home value	$254,900

New Privately Owned Housing Units Authorized by Building Permit

	Units	Value
Total, 2004	37	$11,496,322
Single family	37	$11,496,322
Total, 2005	61	$17,164,413
Single family	61	$17,164,413

Real Property Valuation - parcels, 2005

	Number	Valuation
Total		$1,908,400,200
Vacant	395	27,257,000
Residential	6,407	1,372,142,900
Commercial	254	279,085,700
Industrial	83	170,559,300
Apartments	23	40,013,200
Farm land	43	18,629,600
Farm homestead	111	712,500

Average Property Value & Tax, 2005

Residential value	$210,625
Property tax	$8,465
FAIR rebate	$613

Public Library

Moorestown Public Library
111 West Second St
Moorestown, NJ 08075
856-234-0333

Director ... Deborah Dennis

Library statistics, 2004

	Total	per capita
Volumes	130,487	6.86
Expenditure	$1,487,077	$78.20

Public Safety

Police

Chief	Harry Johnson
Number of officers, 2004	39

Crime, 2004	Number	Rate
Total	461	23.1
Violent	25	1.3
Non-violent	436	21.9
Domestic Viol.	52	NA

Emergency/Fire

Director ... D. Constantine/W. Ruggiano

Public School District

(for school year 2004-2005 except as noted)

Moorestown Township School District
803 N Stanwick Rd
Moorestown, NJ 08057
856-778-6600

Superintendent	Paul Kadri
Grade plan	K-12
Enrollment	4,242.0
Students per teacher	12.1
Per pupil expenditure	$11,389
Median faculty salary	$52,794
Median administrator salary	$101,035
Grade 12 enrollment	275.0
High school graduation rate	94.8%

Assessment test results

(percent scoring at proficient or advanced level)

	Language	Math
Grade 3	95.2%	94.3%
Grade 8	88.8%	88.8%
High school	94.1%	93.0%

SAT

Percent tested	94%
Average SAT math score	569
Average SAT verbal score	554

No Child Left Behind, 2003-04

Attendance rate (target = 90%)	96.0%
Drop rate	0.6%
Highly-qualified teachers	97.3%
District needs improvement?(AYP)	No

Municipal Finance

Fiscal Year 2005

Total tax levy	$77,087,499
County levy	14,074,130
County taxes	12,742,722
County library	0
County health	0
County open space	1,331,408
School levy	51,361,867
Local muni. budget	11,651,502
Misc. revenues	10,396,529
Total aid	$2,604,223
CMPTRA	1,059,852
Muni. block grant	74,566
Energy tax receipts	1,399,805
Homeland security	70,000

Fiscal Year 2006

Total aid	$2,604,223
CMPTRA	1,010,859
Muni. block grant	74,566
Energy tax receipts	1,448,798
Homeland security	70,000

Taxes

	2003	2004	2005
General tax rate per $100	3.59	3.832	4.020
Net valuation taxable	$1,849,459,245	$1,892,079,021	$1,918,047,214
State equalized value	$3,047,387,123	$3,260,928,819	$3,672,309,428
County equalization ratio	67.09	60.69	57.90

Demographics & Socio-Economic Characteristics
(2000 U.S. Census, except as noted)

Population
1980*	5,305
1990*	5,219
2000	5,236
Male	2,512
Female	2,724
2004 (estimate)*	5,563
Persons per sq. mi. of land	2,145

Race & Hispanic Origin, 2000
Race
White	4,865
Black/African American	70
Amer. Indian/Alaska Natv.	3
Asian	226
Natv. Hawaiian/Pac. Islander	5
Other Race	21
Two or more races	46
Hispanic origin, total	141
Mexican	28
Puerto Rican	31
Cuban	13
Other Hispanic	69

Age & Nativity, 2000
Under 5 years	379
18 years and over	4,003
21 years and over	3,913
65 years and over	848
85 years and over	127
Median Age	40.7
Native born	4,730
Foreign born	506

Educational Attainment, 2000
Population 25 years and over	3,777
0-8 yrs of school	1.9%
High School grad or higher	94.3%
Bachelor's degree or higher	51.0%
Graduate degree	21.5%

Income & Poverty, 1999
Per capita income	$36,553
Median household income	$84,806
Median family income	$98,333
Persons in poverty	124
H'holds receiving public assistance	0
H'holds receiving social security	573

Households, 2000
Total households	1,955
With persons under 18	679
With persons over 65	547
Family households	1,478
One-person households	386
Persons per household	2.63
Persons per family	3.05

Labor & Employment
Total civilian labor force, 2004**	3,336
Unemployment rate	2.9%
Total civilian labor force, 2000	2,728
Unemployment rate	3.1%

Employed persons 16 years and over by occupation, 2000
Managers & professionals	1,496
Service occupations	235
Sales & office occupations	669
Farming, fishing & forestry	0
Construction & maintenance	147
Production & transportation	96
Self-employed persons	168

*US Census Bureau
**New Jersey Department of Labor

General Information
Borough of Morris Plains
531 Speedwell Ave
Morris Plains, NJ 07950
973-538-2224
Web site	www.morrisplainsboro.org
Land area (sq. miles)	2.59
Water area (sq. miles)	0.02
Type of government	Borough
Form of government	B

Government

Legislative Districts
US Congressional	11
State Legislative	26

Local Officials, 2006
Mayor	Frank J. Druetzler
Admin/Manager	NA
Clerk	June Uhrin
Finance Dir/Treas	David Banks
Engineer	Leon C. Hall
Attorney	Gail Fraser
Tax assessor	Allan W. Adams
Tax collector	Ana Noguera
Building officer	Edward Easse
Zoning officer	Donald Salerno
Public Works	Joseph Signorelli Jr.

Housing & Construction

Housing Units, 2000*
Total	1,994
Median rent	$1,045
Median SF home value	$282,500

New Privately Owned Housing Units Authorized by Building Permit
	Units	Value
Total, 2004	49	$6,241,764
Single family	6	$4,151,232
Total, 2005	57	$7,071,965
Single family	8	$4,689,732

Real Property Valuation - parcels, 2005
	Number	Valuation
Total		$778,995,750
Vacant	78	4,506,500
Residential	2,051	452,844,450
Commercial	95	259,227,200
Industrial	3	52,005,000
Apartments	1	10,412,600
Farm land	0	0
Farm homestead	0	0

Average Property Value & Tax, 2005
Residential value	$220,792
Property tax	$6,145
FAIR rebate	$603

Public Library
Morris Plains Public Library
77 Glenbrook Rd
Morris Plains, NJ 07950
973-538-2599
Director	Lynn Schwager-Miles

Library statistics, 2004
	Total	per capita
Volumes	23,485	4.49
Expenditure	$111,436	$21.28

Public Safety

Police
Chief	Douglas Scherzer
Number of officers, 2004	17

Crime, 2004	Number	Rate
Total	127	23
Violent	6	1.1
Non-violent	121	21.9
Domestic Viol.	19	NA

Emergency/Fire
Director	Michael Geary

Public School District
(for school year 2004-2005 except as noted)

Morris Plains School District
500 Speedwell Ave
Morris Plains, NJ 07950
973-538-1650
Superintendent	Fred Ferrone (Int)
Grade plan	K-12
Enrollment	580.0
Students per teacher	10.1
Per pupil expenditure	$15,484
Median faculty salary	$45,006
Median administrator salary	$104,313
Grade 12 enrollment	NA
High school graduation rate	NA

Assessment test results
(percent scoring at proficient or advanced level)
	Language	Math
Grade 3	93.7%	95.3%
Grade 8	96.3%	88.9%
High school	NA	NA

SAT
Percent tested	NA
Average SAT math score	NA
Average SAT verbal score	NA

No Child Left Behind, 2003-04
Attendence rate (target = 90%)	96.4%
Drop rate	NA
Highly-qualified teachers	98.8%
District needs improvement?(AYP)	No

Municipal Finance

Fiscal Year 2005
Total tax levy	$21,712,336
County levy	3,484,553
County taxes	2,854,340
County library	0
County health	0
County open space	630,213
School levy	11,095,179
Local muni. budget	7,132,605
Misc. revenues	3,426,836
Total aid	$949,716
CMPTRA	363,281
Muni. block grant	22,837
Energy tax receipts	513,598
Homeland security	50,000

Fiscal Year 2006
Total aid	$949,716
CMPTRA	345,305
Muni. block grant	22,837
Energy tax receipts	531,574
Homeland security	50,000

Taxes
	2003	2004	2005
General tax rate per $100	2.50	2.660	2.790
Net valuation taxable	$774,340,075	$780,042,814	$780,183,032
State equalized value	$1,134,896,783	$1,295,868,800	$1,360,626,146
County equalization ratio	78.29	68.23	60.15

Demographics & Socio-Economic Characteristics
(2000 U.S. Census, except as noted)

Population
1980*	18,486
1990*	19,952
2000	21,796
Male	10,287
Female	11,509
2000 (revised)	21,427
2004 (estimate)*	21,412
Persons per sq. mi. of land	1,359

Race & Hispanic Origin, 2000
Race
White	19,317
Black/African American	1,189
Amer. Indian/Alaska Natv.	33
Asian	849
Natv. Hawaiian/Pac. Islander	3
Other Race	199
Two or more races	206
Hispanic origin, total	830
Mexican	62
Puerto Rican	157
Cuban	56
Other Hispanic	555

Age & Nativity, 2000
Under 5 years	1,563
18 years and over	16,846
21 years and over	16,247
65 years and over	3,356
85 years and over	457
Median Age	40.9
Native born	19,460
Foreign born	2,336

Educational Attainment, 2000
Population 25 years and over	15,565
0-8 yrs of school	1.9%
High School grad or higher	95.1%
Bachelor's degree or higher	63.6%
Graduate degree	29.6%

Income & Poverty, 1999
Per capita income	$54,782
Median household income	$101,902
Median family income	$116,866
Persons in poverty	802
H'holds receiving public assistance	49
H'holds receiving social security	2,075

Households, 2000
Total households	8,116
With persons under 18	2,639
With persons over 65	2,088
Family households	5,953
One-person households	1,766
Persons per household	2.55
Persons per family	2.99

Labor & Employment
Total civilian labor force, 2004**	12,452
Unemployment rate	2.8%
Total civilian labor force, 2000	11,579
Unemployment rate	4.2%

Employed persons 16 years and over by occupation, 2000
Managers & professionals	6,956
Service occupations	736
Sales & office occupations	2,660
Farming, fishing & forestry	0
Construction & maintenance	407
Production & transportation	330
Self-employed persons	820

*US Census Bureau
**New Jersey Department of Labor

General Information
Township of Morris
PO Box 7603
50 Woodland Ave
Convent Station, NJ 07961
973-326-7430
Web site	www.morristwp.com
Land area (sq. miles)	15.76
Water area (sq. miles)	0.05
Type of government	Township
Form of government	TC

Government

Legislative Districts
US Congressional	11
State Legislative	25

Local Officials, 2006
Mayor	Robert E. Nace
Admin/Manager	Fred Rossi
Clerk	Cathleen Amelio
Finance Dir/Treas	Julia Hasbrouck
Engineer	James Slate
Attorney	John Mills III
Tax assessor	Sue Aceto
Tax collector	Audrey Adams
Building officer	Albert Mastrobatista
Zoning officer	NA
Public Works	Joseph Giordano

Housing & Construction

Housing Units, 2000*
Total	8,298
Median rent	$1,040
Median SF home value	$350,400

New Privately Owned Housing Units Authorized by Building Permit
	Units	Value
Total, 2004	13	$4,790,228
Single family	13	$4,790,228
Total, 2005	14	$5,005,842
Single family	14	$5,005,842

Real Property Valuation - parcels, 2005
	Number	Valuation
Total		$3,831,652,350
Vacant	247	23,771,850
Residential	7,595	2,964,962,000
Commercial	141	630,688,800
Industrial	21	175,028,100
Apartments	4	31,165,000
Farm land	6	5,987,800
Farm homestead	9	48,800

Average Property Value & Tax, 2005
Residential value	$389,928
Property tax	$7,995
FAIR rebate	$595

Public Library
Joint Library of Morristown & Morris Twp†
1 Miller Rd
Morristown, NJ 07960
973-538-6161
Director	Susan Gulick

Library statistics, 2004
	Total	per capita
Volumes	185,070	4.59
Expenditure	$2,424,056	$60.09

†Joint Library with Morristown

Public Safety
Police
Chief	Michael Loughman
Number of officers, 2004	40

Crime, 2004	Number	Rate
Total	192	9
Violent	25	1.2
Non-violent	167	7.8
Domestic Viol.	89	NA

Emergency/Fire
Director	Craig Goss

Public School District
(for school year 2004-2005 except as noted)

Morris School District
31 Hazel St
Morristown, NJ 07960
973-292-2300
Superintendent	Thomas Ficarra
Grade plan	K-12
Enrollment	4,563.0
Students per teacher	9.5
Per pupil expenditure	$16,710
Median faculty salary	$61,672
Median administrator salary	$109,530
Grade 12 enrollment	374.0
High school graduation rate	97.1%

Assessment test results
(percent scoring at proficient or advanced level)
	Language	Math
Grade 3	84.9%	92.0%
Grade 8	80.6%	70.6%
High school	84.6%	78.3%

SAT
Percent tested	81%
Average SAT math score	529
Average SAT verbal score	513

No Child Left Behind, 2003-04
Attendence rate (target = 90%)	95.4%
Drop rate	1.6%
Highly-qualified teachers	95.8%
District needs improvement?(AYP)	Yes

Municipal Finance

Fiscal Year 2005
Total tax levy	$78,658,749
County levy	12,388,445
County taxes	10,146,195
County library	0
County health	0
County open space	2,242,251
School levy	46,687,020
Local muni. budget	19,583,284
Misc. revenues	9,141,882
Total aid	$4,694,868
CMPTRA	2,666,034
Muni. block grant	87,303
Energy tax receipts	1,851,531
Homeland security	90,000

Fiscal Year 2006
Total aid	$4,694,868
CMPTRA	2,601,230
Muni. block grant	87,303
Energy tax receipts	1,916,335
Homeland security	90,000

Taxes
	2003	2004	2005
General tax rate per $100	1.87	2.030	2.060
Net valuation taxable	$3,909,084,355	$3,836,672,971	$3,836,370,667
State equalized value	$4,436,595,568	$4,668,596,999	$5,062,510,777
County equalization ratio	93.52	88.11	82.16

Demographics & Socio-Economic Characteristics
(2000 U.S. Census, except as noted)

Population
1980*	16,614
1990*	16,189
2000	18,544
Male	9,302
Female	9,242
2004 (estimate)*	18,842
Persons per sq. mi. of land	6,405

Race & Hispanic Origin, 2000
Race
White	12,452
Black/African American	3,144
Amer. Indian/Alaska Natv.	41
Asian	700
Natv. Hawaiian/Pac. Islander	12
Other Race	1,572
Two or more races	623
Hispanic origin, total	5,034
Mexican	139
Puerto Rican	286
Cuban	50
Other Hispanic	4,559

Age & Nativity, 2000
Under 5 years	1,026
18 years and over	15,140
21 years and over	14,576
65 years and over	2,292
85 years and over	406
Median Age	35
Native born	12,528
Foreign born	6,016

Educational Attainment, 2000
Population 25 years and over	13,604
0-8 yrs of school	7.6%
High School grad or higher	83.0%
Bachelor's degree or higher	39.3%
Graduate degree	16.0%

Income & Poverty, 1999
Per capita income	$30,086
Median household income	$57,563
Median family income	$66,419
Persons in poverty	2,069
H'holds receiving public assistance	125
H'holds receiving social security	1,565

Households, 2000
Total households	7,252
With persons under 18	1,875
With persons over 65	1,574
Family households	3,700
One-person households	2,805
Persons per household	2.43
Persons per family	3.19

Labor & Employment
Total civilian labor force, 2004**	10,716
Unemployment rate	5.1%
Total civilian labor force, 2000	10,747
Unemployment rate	3.4%

Employed persons 16 years and over by occupation, 2000
Managers & professionals	4,303
Service occupations	2,226
Sales & office occupations	2,144
Farming, fishing & forestry	42
Construction & maintenance	722
Production & transportation	947
Self-employed persons	387

*US Census Bureau
**New Jersey Department of Labor

General Information
Town of Morristown
PO Box 914
200 South St
Morristown, NJ 07963
973-292-6627

Web site	NA
Land area (sq. miles)	2.94
Water area (sq. miles)	0.06
Type of government	Town
Form of government	MC '50

Government

Legislative Districts
US Congressional	11
State Legislative	25

Local Officials, 2006
Mayor	Donald Crestiello
Admin/Manager	Eric Maurer
Clerk	Matthew Stechauner
Finance Dir/Treas	Bob Calise
Engineer	Jeffrey Hartke
Attorney	Peter Wolfson
Tax assessor	Thomas Harraka
Tax collector	NA
Building officer	Jim Silance
Zoning officer	NA
Public Works	NA

Housing & Construction

Housing Units, 2000*
Total	7,615
Median rent	$914
Median SF home value	$224,400

New Privately Owned Housing Units
Authorized by Building Permit
	Units	Value
Total, 2004	24	$2,862,286
Single family	8	$996,105
Total, 2005	18	$1,872,750
Single family	7	$1,430,069

Real Property Valuation - parcels, 2005
	Number	Valuation
Total		$2,225,308,082
Vacant	137	22,030,900
Residential	3,345	1,184,769,182
Commercial	549	821,217,000
Industrial	10	11,665,100
Apartments	74	185,625,900
Farm land	0	0
Farm homestead	0	0

Average Property Value & Tax, 2005
Residential value	$354,191
Property tax	$7,483
FAIR rebate	$590

Public Library
Joint Library of Morristown & Morris Twp†
1 Miller Rd
Morristown, NJ 07960
973-538-6161

Director	Susan Gulick

Library statistics, 2004
	Total	per capita
Volumes	185,070	4.59
Expenditure	$2,424,056	$60.09

†Joint Library with Morris Twp

Public Safety

Police
Chief	Peter Demnitz
Number of officers, 2004	58

Crime, 2004	Number	Rate
Total	867	46.1
Violent	132	7
Non-violent	735	39.1
Domestic Viol.	229	NA

Emergency/Fire
Director	David Barter

Public School District
(for school year 2004-2005 except as noted)

Morris School District
31 Hazel St
Morristown, NJ 07960
973-292-2300

Superintendent	Thomas Ficarra
Grade plan	K-12
Enrollment	4,563.0
Students per teacher	9.5
Per pupil expenditure	$16,710
Median faculty salary	$61,672
Median administrator salary	$109,530
Grade 12 enrollment	374.0
High school graduation rate	97.1%

Assessment test results
(percent scoring at proficient or advanced level)
	Language	Math
Grade 3	84.9%	92.0%
Grade 8	80.6%	70.6%
High school	84.6%	78.3%

SAT
Percent tested	81%
Average SAT math score	529
Average SAT verbal score	513

No Child Left Behind, 2003-04
Attendence rate (target = 90%)	95.4%
Drop rate	1.6%
Highly-qualified teachers	95.8%
District needs improvement?(AYP)	Yes

Municipal Finance

Fiscal Year 2005
Total tax levy	$47,441,866
County levy	5,880,231
County taxes	4,816,749
County library	0
County health	0
County open space	1,063,481
School levy	20,891,168
Local muni. budget	20,670,468
Misc. revenues	12,397,953
Total aid	$3,865,228
CMPTRA	1,463,993
Muni. block grant	72,711
Energy tax receipts	2,258,524
Homeland security	70,000

Fiscal Year 2006
Total aid	$3,865,228
CMPTRA	1,384,944
Muni. block grant	72,711
Energy tax receipts	2,337,573
Homeland security	70,000

Taxes
	2003	2004	2005
General tax rate per $100	3.22	2.030	2.120
Net valuation taxable	$1,287,349,995	$2,226,892,763	$2,245,556,075
State equalized value	$1,946,107,324	$2,180,874,010	$2,450,410,383
County equalization ratio	72.21	112.83	102.13

Demographics & Socio-Economic Characteristics

(2000 U.S. Census, except as noted)

Population

1980*	4,251
1990*	3,630
2000	4,663
Male	2,216
Female	2,447
2004 (estimate)*	5,139
Persons per sq. mi. of land	2,432

Race & Hispanic Origin, 2000

Race

White	4,263
Black/African American	85
Amer. Indian/Alaska Natv.	9
Asian	178
Natv. Hawaiian/Pac. Islander	2
Other Race	59
Two or more races	67
Hispanic origin, total	212
Mexican	16
Puerto Rican	68
Cuban	15
Other Hispanic	113

Age & Nativity, 2000

Under 5 years	310
18 years and over	3,634
21 years and over	3,526
65 years and over	496
85 years and over	30
Median Age	37.9
Native born	4,207
Foreign born	456

Educational Attainment, 2000

Population 25 years and over	3,408
0-8 yrs of school	2.4%
High School grad or higher	90.4%
Bachelor's degree or higher	35.9%
Graduate degree	11.2%

Income & Poverty, 1999

Per capita income	$32,222
Median household income	$67,213
Median family income	$79,514
Persons in poverty	153
H'holds receiving public assistance	22
H'holds receiving social security	392

Households, 2000

Total households	1,918
With persons under 18	576
With persons over 65	374
Family households	1,263
One-person households	535
Persons per household	2.42
Persons per family	2.99

Labor & Employment

Total civilian labor force, 2004**	2,385
Unemployment rate	4.5%
Total civilian labor force, 2000	2,738
Unemployment rate	3.0%

Employed persons 16 years and over by occupation, 2000

Managers & professionals	999
Service occupations	276
Sales & office occupations	870
Farming, fishing & forestry	0
Construction & maintenance	266
Production & transportation	246
Self-employed persons	188

*US Census Bureau
**New Jersey Department of Labor

General Information

Borough of Mount Arlington
419 Howard Blvd
Mount Arlington, NJ 07856
973-398-6832

Web site	www.ci.mount-arlington.nj.us
Land area (sq. miles)	2.11
Water area (sq. miles)	0.72
Type of government	Borough
Form of government	B

Government

Legislative Districts

US Congressional	11
State Legislative	25

Local Officials, 2006

Mayor	Arthur R. Ondish
Admin/Manager	JoAnne Sendler
Clerk	Linda DeSantis
Finance Dir/Treas	Allan Dickinson
Engineer	Daren Phil
Attorney	Joseph Bell
Tax assessor	John Marchione
Tax collector	Patricia Simari
Building officer	Sandor Nyari
Zoning officer	Al Thomson
Public Works	Paul Nelson

Housing & Construction

Housing Units, 2000*

Total	2,039
Median rent	$831
Median SF home value	$183,700

New Privately Owned Housing Units Authorized by Building Permit

	Units	Value
Total, 2004	92	$4,505,222
Single family	68	$4,086,398
Total, 2005	193	$8,244,371
Single family	30	$2,667,951

Real Property Valuation - parcels, 2005

	Number	Valuation
Total		$627,458,300
Vacant	233	12,274,600
Residential	1,805	517,190,600
Commercial	47	82,796,400
Industrial	1	234,200
Apartments	6	14,950,200
Farm land	0	0
Farm homestead	16	12,300

Average Property Value & Tax, 2005

Residential value	$284,021
Property tax	$5,041
FAIR rebate	$530

Public Library

Mt Arlington Public Library
404 Howard Blvd
Mt Arlington, NJ 07856
973-398-1516

Director..................James Garland

Library statistics, 2004

	Total	per capita
Volumes	24,063	5.16
Expenditure	$210,058	$45.05

Public Safety

Police

Chief	Richard Peterson
Number of officers, 2004	12

Crime, 2004	Number	Rate
Total	75	14.9
Violent	2	0.4
Non-violent	73	14.6
Domestic Viol.	50	NA

Emergency/Fire

Director....................Tom Perillo

Public School District

(for school year 2004-2005 except as noted)

Mount Arlington School District
446 Howard Blvd
Mount Arlington, NJ 07856
973-398-6400

Superintendent	Jane Jameson
Grade plan	K-12
Enrollment	434.0
Students per teacher	10.0
Per pupil expenditure	$12,414
Median faculty salary	$49,197
Median administrator salary	$76,500
Grade 12 enrollment	NA
High school graduation rate	NA

Assessment test results

(percent scoring at proficient or advanced level)

	Language	Math
Grade 3	66.7%	80.5%
Grade 8	73.3%	72.9%
High school	NA	NA

SAT

Percent tested	NA
Average SAT math score	NA
Average SAT verbal score	NA

No Child Left Behind, 2003-04

Attendance rate (target = 90%)	93.5%
Drop rate	NA
Highly-qualified teachers	91.7%
District needs improvement?(AYP)	No

Municipal Finance

Fiscal Year 2005

Total tax levy	$11,151,501
County levy	1,633,163
County taxes	1,337,556
County library	0
County health	0
County open space	295,607
School levy	7,210,429
Local muni. budget	2,307,909
Misc. revenues	4,778,968
Total aid	$505,042
CMPTRA	162,144
Muni. block grant	18,284
Energy tax receipts	299,614
Homeland security	25,000

Fiscal Year 2006

Total aid	$530,041
CMPTRA	151,657
Muni. block grant	18,284
Energy tax receipts	310,100
Homeland security	50,000

Taxes

	2003	2004	2005
General tax rate per $100	3.21	1.660	1.780
Net valuation taxable	$297,721,157	$627,587,110	$628,328,490
State equalized value	$512,428,842	$616,808,993	$684,081,100
County equalization ratio	63.89	115.39	101.75

Demographics & Socio-Economic Characteristics
(2000 U.S. Census, except as noted)

Population
1980*	4,863
1990*	4,517
2000	4,495
Male	2,173
Female	2,322
2004 (estimate)*	4,470
Persons per sq. mi. of land	5,072

Race & Hispanic Origin, 2000
Race
White	4,383
Black/African American	18
Amer. Indian/Alaska Natv.	3
Asian	28
Natv. Hawaiian/Pac. Islander	1
Other Race	29
Two or more races	33
Hispanic origin, total	89
Mexican	5
Puerto Rican	67
Cuban	5
Other Hispanic	12

Age & Nativity, 2000
Under 5 years	257
18 years and over	3,491
21 years and over	3,345
65 years and over	804
85 years and over	72
Median Age	39.6
Native born	4,395
Foreign born	100

Educational Attainment, 2000
Population 25 years and over	3,184
0-8 yrs of school	5.5%
High School grad or higher	78.5%
Bachelor's degree or higher	13.3%
Graduate degree	3.4%

Income & Poverty, 1999
Per capita income	$21,150
Median household income	$44,824
Median family income	$59,468
Persons in poverty	219
H'holds receiving public assistance	39
H'holds receiving social security	671

Households, 2000
Total households	1,818
With persons under 18	541
With persons over 65	620
Family households	1,175
One-person households	556
Persons per household	2.46
Persons per family	3.13

Labor & Employment
Total civilian labor force, 2004**	2,382
Unemployment rate	3.5%
Total civilian labor force, 2000	2,286
Unemployment rate	5.5%

Employed persons 16 years and over by occupation, 2000
Managers & professionals	672
Service occupations	218
Sales & office occupations	669
Farming, fishing & forestry	0
Construction & maintenance	259
Production & transportation	342
Self-employed persons	53

*US Census Bureau
**New Jersey Department of Labor

General Information
Borough of Mount Ephraim
121 S Black Horse Pike
Mount Ephraim, NJ 08059
856-931-1546
Web site	www.mountephraim-nj.com
Land area (sq. miles)	0.88
Water area (sq. miles)	0.01
Type of government	Borough
Form of government	Comm.

Government
Legislative Districts
US Congressional	1
State Legislative	5

Local Officials, 2006
Mayor	Michael P. Reader
Admin/Manager	NA
Clerk	Mildred Salamone
Finance Dir/Treas	Dorothea Jones
Engineer	Remington & Vernick
Attorney	Charles Shimberg
Tax assessor	Steve Kessler
Tax collector	Marie Darlington
Building officer	Robert Scouler
Zoning officer	Daniel Christy
Public Works	Joseph Ciano

Housing & Construction
Housing Units, 2000*
Total	1,881
Median rent	$542
Median SF home value	$94,000

New Privately Owned Housing Units Authorized by Building Permit
	Units	Value
Total, 2004	6	$411,878
Single family	6	$411,878
Total, 2005	4	$274,584
Single family	4	$274,584

Real Property Valuation - parcels, 2005
	Number	Valuation
Total		$171,126,600
Vacant	77	1,558,800
Residential	1,584	145,249,100
Commercial	100	20,234,200
Industrial	3	741,200
Apartments	8	3,343,300
Farm land	0	0
Farm homestead	0	0

Average Property Value & Tax, 2005
Residential value	$91,698
Property tax	$4,085
FAIR rebate	$629

Public Library
Mount Ephraim Library
130 Bell Rd
Mt. Ephraim, NJ 08059
856-931-6606
Director	Gloria Marsh

Library statistics, 2004
	Total	per capita
Volumes	NA	NA
Expenditure	NA	NA

Public Safety
Police
Chief	Christopher Ferrari
Number of officers, 2004	12

Crime, 2004	Number	Rate
Total	219	48.7
Violent	20	4.4
Non-violent	199	44.3
Domestic Viol.	116	NA

Emergency/Fire
Director	Mario Scullan

Public School District
(for school year 2004-2005 except as noted)

Mount Ephraim Borough School District
125 S Black Horse Pike
Mount Ephraim, NJ 08059
856-931-1634
Administrator	Richard Serfling
Grade plan	K-12
Enrollment	457.0
Students per teacher	12.8
Per pupil expenditure	$10,086
Median faculty salary	$45,757
Median administrator salary	$102,356
Grade 12 enrollment	NA
High school graduation rate	NA

Assessment test results
(percent scoring at proficient or advanced level)
	Language	Math
Grade 3	81.6%	89.5%
Grade 8	79.0%	84.2%
High school	NA	NA

SAT
Percent tested	NA
Average SAT math score	NA
Average SAT verbal score	NA

No Child Left Behind, 2003-04
Attendence rate (target = 90%)	95.1%
Drop rate	NA
Highly-qualified teachers	100%
District needs improvement?(AYP)	No

Municipal Finance
Fiscal Year 2005
Total tax levy	$7,641,054
County levy	1,782,936
County taxes	1,643,257
County library	118,136
County health	0
County open space	21,542
School levy	3,700,618
Local muni. budget	2,157,500
Misc. revenues	2,016,213
Total aid	$590,227
CMPTRA	263,576
Muni. block grant	19,765
Energy tax receipts	281,886
Homeland security	25,000

Fiscal Year 2006
Total aid	$590,227
CMPTRA	253,710
Muni. block grant	19,765
Energy tax receipts	291,752
Homeland security	25,000

Taxes
	2003	2004	2005
General tax rate per $100	3.85	3.994	4.456
Net valuation taxable	$170,304,176	$170,750,302	$171,510,075
State equalized value	$190,560,788	$213,163,026	$252,443,443
County equalization ratio	97.38	89.37	80.06

Demographics & Socio-Economic Characteristics
(2000 U.S. Census, except as noted)

Population
1980*	10,818
1990*	10,639
2000	10,728
Male	5,356
Female	5,372
2004 (estimate)*	10,738
Persons per sq. mi. of land	3,754

Race & Hispanic Origin, 2000
Race
White	7,368
Black/African American	2,314
Amer. Indian/Alaska Natv.	45
Asian	147
Natv. Hawaiian/Pac. Islander	7
Other Race	512
Two or more races	335
Hispanic origin, total	942
Mexican	71
Puerto Rican	638
Cuban	15
Other Hispanic	218

Age & Nativity, 2000
Under 5 years	706
18 years and over	7,905
21 years and over	7,467
65 years and over	1,335
85 years and over	153
Median Age	35
Native born	10,127
Foreign born	618

Educational Attainment, 2000
Population 25 years and over	6,955
0-8 yrs of school	4.5%
High School grad or higher	77.9%
Bachelor's degree or higher	18.6%
Graduate degree	4.2%

Income & Poverty, 1999
Per capita income	$19,672
Median household income	$43,284
Median family income	$52,000
Persons in poverty	1,023
H'holds receiving public assistance	180
H'holds receiving social security	1,095

Households, 2000
Total households	3,903
With persons under 18	1,430
With persons over 65	982
Family households	2,585
One-person households	1,063
Persons per household	2.64
Persons per family	3.2

Labor & Employment
Total civilian labor force, 2004**	5,770
Unemployment rate	6.9%
Total civilian labor force, 2000	5,163
Unemployment rate	6.4%

Employed persons 16 years and over by occupation, 2000
Managers & professionals	1,317
Service occupations	839
Sales & office occupations	1,349
Farming, fishing & forestry	20
Construction & maintenance	452
Production & transportation	854
Self-employed persons	238

*US Census Bureau
**New Jersey Department of Labor

General Information
Township of Mount Holly
23 Washington St
Mount Holly, NJ 08060
609-267-0170
Web site	www.mountholly.info
Land area (sq. miles)	2.86
Water area (sq. miles)	0.02
Type of government	Township
Form of government	CM '50

Government

Legislative Districts
US Congressional	3
State Legislative	7

Local Officials, 2006
Mayor	Jules Thiessen
Admin/Manager	Arthur Liston
Clerk	Kathleen D. Hoffman
Finance Dir/Treas	Christina Chambers
Engineer	Richard Alaimo Assoc.
Attorney	Brian Guest
Tax assessor	Leo Midure
Tax collector	Maryann Zanone
Building officer	Thomas Casey
Zoning officer	Thomas Casey
Public Works	Rick Jankowski

Housing & Construction

Housing Units, 2000*
Total	4,248
Median rent	$719
Median SF home value	$98,200

New Privately Owned Housing Units Authorized by Building Permit
	Units	Value
Total, 2004	0	$715,500
Single family	0	$715,500
Total, 2005	14	$1,654,800
Single family	14	$1,654,800

Real Property Valuation - parcels, 2005
	Number	Valuation
Total		$319,303,000
Vacant	181	5,096,400
Residential	3,164	252,580,800
Commercial	210	44,469,300
Industrial	12	4,847,700
Apartments	40	12,151,900
Farm land	1	142,700
Farm homestead	3	14,200

Average Property Value & Tax, 2005
Residential value	$79,758
Property tax	$3,110
FAIR rebate	$597

Public Library
Mount Holly Public Library
307 High St
Mount Holly, NJ 08060
609-267-7111
Director	Michael Eck

Library statistics, 2004
	Total	per capita
Volumes	11,564	1.08
Expenditure	$92,368	$8.61

Public Safety

Police
Chief	Steve Martin
Number of officers, 2004	26

Crime, 2004	Number	Rate
Total	458	42.5
Violent	52	4.8
Non-violent	406	37.7
Domestic Viol.	309	NA

Emergency/Fire
Director	Ian Bruce

Public School District
(for school year 2004-2005 except as noted)

Mount Holly Township School District
330 Levis Drive
Mount Holly, NJ 08060
609-267-7108
Superintendent	Paul Spaventa
Grade plan	K-8
Enrollment	1,122.0
Students per teacher	10.2
Per pupil expenditure	$13,900
Median faculty salary	$66,053
Median administrator salary	$87,640
Grade 12 enrollment	NA
High school graduation rate	NA

Assessment test results
(percent scoring at proficient or advanced level)
	Language	Math
Grade 3	66.7%	68.2%
Grade 8	62.0%	50.0%
High school	NA	NA

SAT
Percent tested	NA
Average SAT math score	NA
Average SAT verbal score	NA

No Child Left Behind, 2003-04
Attendance rate (target = 90%)	93.7%
Drop rate	NA
Highly-qualified teachers	100%
District needs improvement?(AYP)	No

Municipal Finance

Fiscal Year 2005
Total tax levy	$12,651,247
County levy	2,150,848
County taxes	1,804,329
County library	157,988
County health	0
County open space	188,531
School levy	7,749,674
Local muni. budget	2,750,726
Misc. revenues	5,186,529
Total aid	$2,051,874
CMPTRA	1,150,442
Muni. block grant	46,552
Energy tax receipts	784,880
Homeland security	70,000

Fiscal Year 2006
Total aid	$2,051,874
CMPTRA	1,122,971
Muni. block grant	46,552
Energy tax receipts	812,351
Homeland security	70,000

Taxes
	2003	2004	2005
General tax rate per $100	3.40	3.647	3.900
Net valuation taxable	$327,329,323	$325,315,157	$324,441,701
State equalized value	$421,490,243	$467,280,239	$550,367,601
County equalization ratio	86.06	77.66	69.23

Demographics & Socio-Economic Characteristics
(2000 U.S. Census, except as noted)

Population
1980*	17,614
1990*	30,270
2000	40,221
Male	18,983
Female	21,238
2004 (estimate)*	40,682
Persons per sq. mi. of land	1,866

Race & Hispanic Origin, 2000
Race
White	35,034
Black/African American	2,785
Amer. Indian/Alaska Natv.	38
Asian	1,529
Natv. Hawaiian/Pac. Islander	12
Other Race	256
Two or more races	567
Hispanic origin, total	901
Mexican	110
Puerto Rican	407
Cuban	60
Other Hispanic	324

Age & Nativity, 2000
Under 5 years	2,460
18 years and over	30,916
21 years and over	30,015
65 years and over	5,905
85 years and over	413
Median Age	38.9
Native born	37,444
Foreign born	2,777

Educational Attainment, 2000
Population 25 years and over	28,924
0-8 yrs of school	2.2%
High School grad or higher	92.1%
Bachelor's degree or higher	42.1%
Graduate degree	14.1%

Income & Poverty, 1999
Per capita income	$32,245
Median household income	$63,750
Median family income	$76,288
Persons in poverty	1,243
H'holds receiving public assistance	96
H'holds receiving social security	4,311

Households, 2000
Total households	16,570
With persons under 18	5,279
With persons over 65	4,065
Family households	11,062
One-person households	4,630
Persons per household	2.41
Persons per family	2.98

Labor & Employment
Total civilian labor force, 2004**	20,397
Unemployment rate	2.5%
Total civilian labor force, 2000	21,688
Unemployment rate	3.0%

Employed persons 16 years and over by occupation, 2000
Managers & professionals	10,417
Service occupations	1,930
Sales & office occupations	6,352
Farming, fishing & forestry	23
Construction & maintenance	1,015
Production & transportation	1,294
Self-employed persons	739

*US Census Bureau
**New Jersey Department of Labor

General Information
Township of Mount Laurel
100 Mount Laurel Rd
Mount Laurel, NJ 08054
856-234-0001

Web site	www.mountlaurel.com
Land area (sq. miles)	21.81
Water area (sq. miles)	0.12
Type of government	Township
Form of government	Council Manager

Government

Legislative Districts
US Congressional	3
State Legislative	8

Local Officials, 2006
Mayor	Peter McCaffrey
Admin/Manager	Patricia Halbe
Clerk	Patricia Halbe
Finance Dir/Treas	Linda Lewis
Engineer	William Long
Attorney	Michael Mouber
Tax assessor	Terry Paglione
Tax collector	Margaret Odell
Building officer	Raymond Holshue Jr.
Zoning officer	NA
Public Works	Everett Johnson

Housing & Construction

Housing Units, 2000*
Total	17,163
Median rent	$939
Median SF home value	$161,900

New Privately Owned Housing Units
Authorized by Building Permit
	Units	Value
Total, 2004	70	$6,280,036
Single family	70	$6,280,036
Total, 2005	5	$372,509
Single family	5	$372,509

Real Property Valuation - parcels, 2005
	Number	Valuation
Total		$3,263,586,800
Vacant	1,107	88,800,300
Residential	15,946	2,201,934,900
Commercial	398	800,401,400
Industrial	50	112,193,800
Apartments	7	51,942,000
Farm land	25	7,730,900
Farm homestead	65	583,500

Average Property Value & Tax, 2005
Residential value	$137,563
Property tax	$4,685
FAIR rebate	$586

Public Library
Mount Laurel Public Library
100 Walt Whitman Ave
Mount Laurel, NJ 08054
856-234-7319

Director.................Joan Bernstein

Library statistics, 2004
	Total	per capita
Volumes	95,155	2.37
Expenditure	$1,403,919	$34.91

Public Safety

Police
Chief	Dennis Moffett
Number of officers, 2004	68

Crime, 2004	Number	Rate
Total	838	20.7
Violent	45	1.1
Non-violent	793	19.6
Domestic Viol.	208	NA

Emergency/Fire
Director..................Robert Gallos

Public School District
(for school year 2004-2005 except as noted)

Mount Laurel Township School District
330 Moorestown-Mount Laurel Rd
Mount Laurel, NJ 08054
856-235-3387

Superintendent	Antoinette Rath
Grade plan	K-8
Enrollment	4,552.0
Students per teacher	11.4
Per pupil expenditure	$10,606
Median faculty salary	$48,350
Median administrator salary	$94,595
Grade 12 enrollment	NA
High school graduation rate	NA

Assessment test results
(percent scoring at proficient or advanced level)
	Language	Math
Grade 3	94.1%	90.9%
Grade 8	85.0%	70.1%
High school	NA	NA

SAT
Percent tested	NA
Average SAT math score	NA
Average SAT verbal score	NA

No Child Left Behind, 2003-04
Attendence rate (target = 90%)	96.2%
Drop rate	NA
Highly-qualified teachers	87.2%
District needs improvement?(AYP)	No

Municipal Finance

Fiscal Year 2005
Total tax levy	$111,466,286
County levy	19,744,812
County taxes	17,876,907
County library	0
County health	0
County open space	1,867,905
School levy	75,061,871
Local muni. budget	16,659,603
Misc. revenues	17,090,000
Total aid	$4,008,901
CMPTRA	1,011,585
Muni. block grant	157,707
Energy tax receipts	2,699,609
Homeland security	140,000

Fiscal Year 2006
Total aid	$4,008,901
CMPTRA	917,099
Muni. block grant	157,707
Energy tax receipts	2,794,095
Homeland security	140,000

Taxes
	2003	2004	2005
General tax rate per $100	3.13	3.213	3.407
Net valuation taxable	$3,152,177,879	$3,228,260,573	$3,273,254,101
State equalized value	$3,999,210,707	$4,597,178,509	$5,175,923,626
County equalization ratio	88.38	78.82	70.15

Demographics & Socio-Economic Characteristics

(2000 U.S. Census, except as noted)

Population

1980*	18,748
1990*	21,282
2000	24,193
Male	12,119
Female	12,074
2004 (estimate)*	25,718
Persons per sq. mi. of land	847

Race & Hispanic Origin, 2000

Race

White	20,974
Black/African American	918
Amer. Indian/Alaska Natv.	40
Asian	1,452
Natv. Hawaiian/Pac. Islander	2
Other Race	369
Two or more races	438
Hispanic origin, total	1,445
Mexican	102
Puerto Rican	466
Cuban	86
Other Hispanic	791

Age & Nativity, 2000

Under 5 years	2,108
18 years and over	17,525
21 years and over	16,896
65 years and over	1,542
85 years and over	123
Median Age	34.1
Native born	21,059
Foreign born	3,134

Educational Attainment, 2000

Population 25 years and over	15,764
0-8 yrs of school	2.4%
High School grad or higher	91.9%
Bachelor's degree or higher	36.5%
Graduate degree	11.2%

Income & Poverty, 1999

Per capita income	$28,691
Median household income	$64,515
Median family income	$75,189
Persons in poverty	735
H'holds receiving public assistance	67
H'holds receiving social security	1,267

Households, 2000

Total households	9,068
With persons under 18	3,696
With persons over 65	1,219
Family households	6,372
One person households	2,150
Persons per household	2.66
Persons per family	3.22

Labor & Employment

Total civilian labor force, 2004**	14,216
Unemployment rate	3.7%
Total civilian labor force, 2000	13,589
Unemployment rate	3.8%

Employed persons 16 years and over by occupation, 2000

Managers & professionals	5,728
Service occupations	1,403
Sales & office occupations	3,424
Farming, fishing & forestry	25
Construction & maintenance	1,031
Production & transportation	1,463
Self-employed persons	603

*US Census Bureau
**New Jersey Department of Labor

General Information

Township of Mount Olive
PO Box 450
204 Flanders-Drakestown Rd
Budd Lake, NJ 07828
973-691-0900

Web site	www.mountolivetownship.com
Land area (sq. miles)	30.35
Water area (sq. miles)	0.70
Type of government	Township
Form of government	MC '50

Government

Legislative Districts

US Congressional	11
State Legislative	24

Local Officials, 2006

Mayor	Richard De La Roche
Admin/Manager	Ricky Prill
Clerk	Lisa Lashway
Finance Dir/Treas	Sherry Jenkins
Engineer	Eugene Buczynski
Attorney	John Dorsey
Tax assessor	John Marchione
Tax collector	Rose Barsanti
Building officer	Gary Lindsay
Zoning officer	Jay Holler
Public Works	Tim Quinn

Housing & Construction

Housing Units, 2000*

Total	9,311
Median rent	$800
Median SF home value	$197,800

New Privately Owned Housing Units
Authorized by Building Permit

	Units	Value
Total, 2004	110	$15,966,222
Single family	110	$15,966,222
Total, 2005	95	$12,803,630
Single family	95	$12,803,630

Real Property Valuation - parcels, 2005

	Number	Valuation
Total		$1,981,184,100
Vacant	990	64,936,100
Residential	6,053	1,178,432,500
Commercial	328	266,405,500
Industrial	60	317,578,200
Apartments	6	145,725,000
Farm land	32	6,929,100
Farm homestead	96	1,177,700

Average Property Value & Tax, 2005

Residential value	$191,838
Property tax	$6,788
FAIR rebate	$463

Public Library

Mount Olive Public Library
202 Flanders-Drakestown Rd
Flanders, NJ 07836
973-691-8686

Director	Rita Hilbert

Library statistics, 2004

	Total	per capita
Volumes	82,643	3.42
Expenditure	$766,255	$31.67

Public Safety

Police

Chief	Edward Katona
Number of officers, 2004	51

Crime, 2004	Number	Rate
Total	321	12.6
Violent	17	0.7
Non-violent	304	11.9
Domestic Viol.	149	NA

Emergency/Fire

Director	NA

Public School District

(for school year 2004-2005 except as noted)

Mount Olive Township School District
89 Route 46
Budd Lake, NJ 07828
973-691-4008

Superintendent	Rosalie LaMonte
Grade plan	K-12
Enrollment	4,833.5
Students per teacher	11.6
Per pupil expenditure	$12,340
Median faculty salary	$52,247
Median administrator salary	$98,506
Grade 12 enrollment	266.5
High school graduation rate	97.4%

Assessment test results

(percent scoring at proficient or advanced level)

	Language	Math
Grade 3	87.7%	85.5%
Grade 8	88.9%	81.7%
High school	88.7%	83.0%

SAT

Percent tested	80%
Average SAT math score	535
Average SAT verbal score	514

No Child Left Behind, 2003-04

Attendence rate (target = 90%)	95.3%
Drop rate	0.5%
Highly-qualified teachers	94.1%
District needs improvement?(AYP)	No

Municipal Finance

Fiscal Year 2005

Total tax levy	$70,264,799
County levy	7,487,839
County taxes	6,133,598
County library	0
County health	0
County open space	1,354,241
School levy	48,554,478
Local muni. budget	14,222,482
Misc. revenues	8,676,725
Total aid	$2,744,662
CMPTRA	971,617
Muni. block grant	94,861
Energy tax receipts	1,579,019
Homeland security	90,000

Fiscal Year 2006

Total aid	$2,744,663
CMPTRA	916,352
Muni. block grant	94,861
Energy tax receipts	1,634,285
Homeland security	90,000

Taxes

	2003	2004	2005
General tax rate per $100	3.05	3.240	3.540
Net valuation taxable	$1,934,299,613	$2,003,135,532	$1,985,836,832
State equalized value	$2,403,752,470	$2,835,364,913	$3,326,359,853
County equalization ratio	87.64	80.47	70.60

Demographics & Socio-Economic Characteristics
(2000 U.S. Census, except as noted)

Population
1980*	4,153
1990*	3,847
2000	4,256
Male	2,119
Female	2,137
2004 (estimate)*	4,324
Persons per sq. mi. of land	1,618

Race & Hispanic Origin, 2000
Race
White	3,960
Black/African American	16
Amer. Indian/Alaska Natv.	0
Asian	220
Natv. Hawaiian/Pac. Islander	3
Other Race	22
Two or more races	35
Hispanic origin, total	72
Mexican	10
Puerto Rican	18
Cuban	11
Other Hispanic	33

Age & Nativity, 2000
Under 5 years	317
18 years and over	2,738
21 years and over	2,676
65 years and over	386
85 years and over	14
Median Age	39.4
Native born	3,839
Foreign born	417

Educational Attainment, 2000
Population 25 years and over	2,624
0-8 yrs of school	0.8%
High School grad or higher	98.4%
Bachelor's degree or higher	76.1%
Graduate degree	35.2%

Income & Poverty, 1999
Per capita income	$65,086
Median household income	$141,757
Median family income	$153,227
Persons in poverty	85
H'holds receiving public assistance	0
H'holds receiving social security	242

Households, 2000
Total households	1,330
With persons under 18	724
With persons over 65	266
Family households	1,187
One-person households	122
Persons per household	3.2
Persons per family	3.41

Labor & Employment
Total civilian labor force, 2004**	2,080
Unemployment rate	2.8%
Total civilian labor force, 2000	1,819
Unemployment rate	1.0%

Employed persons 16 years and over by occupation, 2000
Managers & professionals	1,239
Service occupations	108
Sales & office occupations	356
Farming, fishing & forestry	0
Construction & maintenance	52
Production & transportation	46
Self-employed persons	156

*US Census Bureau
**New Jersey Department of Labor

General Information
Borough of Mountain Lakes
400 Boulevard
Mountain Lakes, NJ 07046
973-334-3131

Web site	NA
Land area (sq. miles)	2.67
Water area (sq. miles)	0.22
Type of government	Borough
Form of government	CM '50

Government

Legislative Districts
US Congressional	11
State Legislative	25

Local Officials, 2006
Mayor	Stephen H. Shaw
Admin/Manager	Gary Webb
Clerk	Christina Whitaker
Finance Dir/Treas	Dana Mooney
Engineer	Bill Ryden
Attorney	Martin Murphy
Tax assessor	Rick DelGuercio
Tax collector	NA
Building officer	Joseph Montemarano
Zoning officer	Dan Hagberg
Public Works	NA

Housing & Construction

Housing Units, 2000*
Total	1,357
Median rent	$1,804
Median SF home value	$488,900

New Privately Owned Housing Units
Authorized by Building Permit
	Units	Value
Total, 2004	9	$1,401,558
Single family	9	$1,401,558
Total, 2005	8	$1,243,208
Single family	8	$1,243,208

Real Property Valuation - parcels, 2005
	Number	Valuation
Total		$639,107,351
Vacant	36	2,347,650
Residential	1,354	585,216,500
Commercial	69	49,059,100
Industrial	4	2,482,901
Apartments	0	0
Farm land	0	0
Farm homestead	3	1,200

Average Property Value & Tax, 2005
Residential value	$431,258
Property tax	$15,199
FAIR rebate	$564

Public Library
Mountain Lakes Public Library
9 Elm Rd
Mountain Lakes, NJ 07046
973-334-5095

Director................Margaret Bulfer

Library statistics, 2004
	Total	per capita
Volumes	39,953	9.39
Expenditure	$217,375	$51.07

Public Safety

Police
Chief	Robert Tovo
Number of officers, 2004	14

Crime, 2004	Number	Rate
Total	93	21.6
Violent	1	0.2
Non-violent	92	21.4
Domestic Viol.	0	NA

Emergency/Fire
Director....................Tom Miller

Public School District
(for school year 2004-2005 except as noted)

Mountain Lakes School District
400 Blvd
Mountain Lakes, NJ 07046
973-334-8280

Superintendent	John Kazmark
Grade plan	K-12
Enrollment	1,453.0
Students per teacher	7.6
Per pupil expenditure	$16,102
Median faculty salary	$56,085
Median administrator salary	$108,544
Grade 12 enrollment	159.5
High school graduation rate	99.4%

Assessment test results
(percent scoring at proficient or advanced level)
	Language	Math
Grade 3	100%	92.6%
Grade 8	95.5%	90.9%
High school	97.5%	92.5%

SAT
Percent tested	100%
Average SAT math score	604
Average SAT verbal score	582

No Child Left Behind, 2003-04
Attendence rate (target = 90%)	95.3%
Drop rate	0%
Highly-qualified teachers	99.1%
District needs improvement?(AYP)	No

Municipal Finance

Fiscal Year 2005
Total tax levy	$22,553,163
County levy	3,003,808
County taxes	2,460,544
County library	0
County health	0
County open space	543,264
School levy	16,071,662
Local muni. budget	3,477,693
Misc. revenues	3,106,752
Total aid	$628,278
CMPTRA	160,495
Muni. block grant	16,834
Energy tax receipts	425,949
Homeland security	25,000

Fiscal Year 2006
Total aid	$628,278
CMPTRA	145,587
Muni. block grant	16,834
Energy tax receipts	440,857
Homeland security	25,000

Taxes
	2003	2004	2005
General tax rate per $100	3.08	3.360	3.530
Net valuation taxable	$630,961,930	$635,453,858	$639,917,067
State equalized value	$1,028,462,804	$1,119,224,743	$1,293,807,252
County equalization ratio	66.03	61.35	56.74

Demographics & Socio-Economic Characteristics

(2000 U.S. Census, except as noted)

Population

1980*	7,118
1990*	6,657
2000	6,602
Male	3,112
Female	3,490
2004 (estimate)*	6,660
Persons per sq. mi. of land	1,655

Race & Hispanic Origin, 2000

Race

White	6,278
Black/African American	62
Amer. Indian/Alaska Natv.	6
Asian	185
Natv. Hawaiian/Pac. Islander	4
Other Race	18
Two or more races	49
Hispanic origin, total	199
Mexican	16
Puerto Rican	32
Cuban	48
Other Hispanic	103

Age & Nativity, 2000

Under 5 years	405
18 years and over	5,210
21 years and over	5,102
65 years and over	1,644
85 years and over	252
Median Age	46.4
Native born	5,726
Foreign born	876

Educational Attainment, 2000

Population 25 years and over	4,931
0-8 yrs of school	2.5%
High School grad or higher	92.6%
Bachelor's degree or higher	47.9%
Graduate degree	21.9%

Income & Poverty, 1999

Per capita income	$47,474
Median household income	$97,195
Median family income	$105,773
Persons in poverty	187
H'holds receiving public assistance	35
H'holds receiving social security	1,022

Households, 2000

Total households	2,434
With persons under 18	745
With persons over 65	990
Family households	1,925
One-person households	436
Persons per household	2.6
Persons per family	2.95

Labor & Employment

Total civilian labor force, 2004**	3,445
Unemployment rate	3.2%
Total civilian labor force, 2000	2,952
Unemployment rate	2.5%

Employed persons 16 years and over by occupation, 2000

Managers & professionals	1,519
Service occupations	289
Sales & office occupations	794
Farming, fishing & forestry	0
Construction & maintenance	160
Production & transportation	116
Self-employed persons	235

*US Census Bureau
**New Jersey Department of Labor

General Information

Borough of Mountainside
1385 Route 22
Mountainside, NJ 07092
908-232-2400

Web site	www.mountainside-nj.com
Land area (sq. miles)	4.02
Water area (sq. miles)	0.03
Type of government	Borough
Form of government	B

Government

Legislative Districts

US Congressional	7
State Legislative	21

Local Officials, 2006

Mayor	Robert Viglianti
Admin/Manager	James Debbie Jr.
Clerk	Martha DeJesus (Actg)
Finance Dir/Treas	Dianne Marus
Engineer	Mike Disko
Attorney	John Post
Tax assessor	Eldo Magnani
Tax collector	NA
Building officer	Jerry Eger
Zoning officer	Stephanie Trano
Public Works	NA

Housing & Construction

Housing Units, 2000*

Total	2,478
Median rent	$950
Median SF home value	$346,100

New Privately Owned Housing Units Authorized by Building Permit

	Units	Value
Total, 2004	NA	NA
Single family	NA	NA
Total, 2005	21	$5,529,023
Single family	21	$5,529,023

Real Property Valuation - parcels, 2005

	Number	Valuation
Total		$483,163,400
Vacant	99	6,853,600
Residential	2,385	383,295,800
Commercial	101	62,868,900
Industrial	56	30,145,100
Apartments	0	0
Farm land	0	0
Farm homestead	0	0

Average Property Value & Tax, 2005

Residential value	$160,711
Property tax	$7,090
FAIR rebate	$669

Public Library

Mountainside Public Library
Constitution Plaza
Mountainside, NJ 07092
908-233-0115

Director	Miriam Bein

Library statistics, 2004

	Total	per capita
Volumes	52,440	7.94
Expenditure	$463,053	$70.14

Public Safety

Police

Chief	James Debbie Jr.
Number of officers, 2004	22

Crime, 2004	Number	Rate
Total	68	10.2
Violent	4	0.6
Non-violent	64	9.6
Domestic Viol.	5	NA

Emergency/Fire

Director	Robert Farley

Public School District

(for school year 2004-2005 except as noted)

Mountainside School District
1497 Woodacres Drive
Mountainside, NJ 07092
908-232-3232

Superintendent	Richard O'Malley
Grade plan	K-12
Enrollment	622.0
Students per teacher	9.6
Per pupil expenditure	$11,924
Median faculty salary	$46,273
Median administrator salary	$89,341
Grade 12 enrollment	NA
High school graduation rate	NA

Assessment test results

(percent scoring at proficient or advanced level)

	Language	Math
Grade 3	97.1%	100%
Grade 8	91.7%	81.1%
High school	NA	NA

SAT

Percent tested	NA
Average SAT math score	NA
Average SAT verbal score	NA

No Child Left Behind, 2003-04

Attendance rate (target = 90%)	95.7%
Drop rate	NA
Highly-qualified teachers	88.1%
District needs improvement?(AYP)	No

Municipal Finance

Fiscal Year 2005

Total tax levy	$21,334,283
County levy	6,072,368
County taxes	5,832,224
County library	0
County health	0
County open space	240,144
School levy	10,378,833
Local muni. budget	4,883,082
Misc. revenues	4,162,196
Total aid	$1,194,156
CMPTRA	425,110
Muni. block grant	29,128
Energy tax receipts	689,918
Homeland security	50,000

Fiscal Year 2006

Total aid	$1,194,156
CMPTRA	400,963
Muni. block grant	29,128
Energy tax receipts	714,065
Homeland security	50,000

Taxes

	2003	2004	2005
General tax rate per $100	4.07	4.310	4.412
Net valuation taxable	$479,081,634	$480,806,843	$483,573,794
State equalized value	$1,308,251,322	$1,488,942,182	$1,677,910,458
County equalization ratio	40.78	35.83	30.50

Demographics & Socio-Economic Characteristics
(2000 U.S. Census, except as noted)

Population
1980*	5,243
1990*	5,896
2000	5,912
Male	2,975
Female	2,937
2004 (estimate)*	6,070
Persons per sq. mi. of land	107

Race & Hispanic Origin, 2000
Race
White	4,764
Black/African American	371
Amer. Indian/Alaska Natv.	16
Asian	49
Natv. Hawaiian/Pac. Islander	7
Other Race	509
Two or more races	196
Hispanic origin, total	975
Mexican	86
Puerto Rican	766
Cuban	3
Other Hispanic	120

Age & Nativity, 2000
Under 5 years	354
18 years and over	4,318
21 years and over	4,105
65 years and over	630
85 years and over	42
Median Age	37
Native born	5,696
Foreign born	216

Educational Attainment, 2000
Population 25 years and over	3,949
0-8 yrs of school	9.9%
High School grad or higher	78.5%
Bachelor's degree or higher	13.4%
Graduate degree	3.7%

Income & Poverty, 1999
Per capita income	$19,764
Median household income	$50,417
Median family income	$55,143
Persons in poverty	462
H'holds receiving public assistance	27
H'holds receiving social security	557

Households, 2000
Total households	2,044
With persons under 18	842
With persons over 65	474
Family households	1,537
One-person households	396
Persons per household	2.87
Persons per family	3.3

Labor & Employment
Total civilian labor force, 2004**	3,122
Unemployment rate	7.3%
Total civilian labor force, 2000	2,957
Unemployment rate	6.3%

Employed persons 16 years and over by occupation, 2000
Managers & professionals	603
Service occupations	679
Sales & office occupations	680
Farming, fishing & forestry	49
Construction & maintenance	478
Production & transportation	282
Self-employed persons	112

*US Census Bureau
**New Jersey Department of Labor

General Information
Township of Mullica
PO Box 317
Elwood, NJ 08217
609-561-0064
Web site	mullicatownship.org
Land area (sq. miles)	56.58
Water area (sq. miles)	0.36
Type of government	Township
Form of government	MC '50

Government

Legislative Districts
US Congressional	2
State Legislative	2

Local Officials, 2006
Mayor	Kathy Chasey
Admin/Manager	NA
Clerk	Kimberly Johnson
Finance Dir/Treas	Dawn Stollenwerk
Engineer	Dave Wood
Attorney	Tim Maguire
Tax assessor	Gerard Mead
Tax collector	Burt Cappuccio
Building officer	Robert Lemon
Zoning officer	Tom Sandman
Public Works	Pete Berenato

Housing & Construction

Housing Units, 2000*
Total	2,176
Median rent	$733
Median SF home value	$109,000

New Privately Owned Housing Units Authorized by Building Permit
	Units	Value
Total, 2004	35	$2,922,002
Single family	35	$2,922,002
Total, 2005	23	$2,666,002
Single family	23	$2,666,002

Real Property Valuation - parcels, 2005
	Number	Valuation
Total		$275,693,900
Vacant	2,026	16,643,400
Residential	2,112	231,445,800
Commercial	85	15,615,300
Industrial	3	2,471,800
Apartments	2	515,400
Farm land	56	6,163,900
Farm homestead	176	2,838,300

Average Property Value & Tax, 2005
Residential value	$102,397
Property tax	$3,351
FAIR rebate	$560

Public Library
No public municipal library.

Library statistics, 2004
	Total	per capita
Volumes	NA	NA
Expenditure	NA	NA

Public Safety

Police
Chief	Jimmie Davis
Number of officers, 2004	14

Crime, 2004	Number	Rate
Total	116	19.2
Violent	10	1.7
Non-violent	106	17.6
Domestic Viol.	54	NA

Emergency/Fire
Director	Gary Franklin

Public School District
(for school year 2004-2005 except as noted)

Mullica Township School District
PO Box 318
Elwood, NJ 08217
609-561-3868
Superintendent	David Dunlevy
Grade plan	K-8
Enrollment	859.0
Students per teacher	12.2
Per pupil expenditure	$10,014
Median faculty salary	$53,930
Median administrator salary	$96,031
Grade 12 enrollment	NA
High school graduation rate	NA

Assessment test results
(percent scoring at proficient or advanced level)
	Language	Math
Grade 3	84.1%	82.6%
Grade 8	89.2%	82.3%
High school	NA	NA

SAT
Percent tested	NA
Average SAT math score	NA
Average SAT verbal score	NA

No Child Left Behind, 2003-04
Attendence rate (target = 90%)	94.5%
Drop rate	NA
Highly-qualified teachers	88.9%
District needs improvement?(AYP)	No

Municipal Finance

Fiscal Year 2005
Total tax levy	$9,068,378
County levy	1,570,944
County taxes	1,282,611
County library	142,048
County health	69,905
County open space	76,380
School levy	4,931,018
Local muni. budget	2,566,417
Misc. revenues	2,004,676
Total aid	$723,528
CMPTRA	301,577
Muni. block grant	25,799
Energy tax receipts	338,238
Homeland security	50,000

Fiscal Year 2006
Total aid	$723,528
CMPTRA	289,739
Muni. block grant	25,799
Energy tax receipts	350,076
Homeland security	50,000

Taxes
	2003	2004	2005
General tax rate per $100	3.11	3.157	3.273
Net valuation taxable	$269,552,706	$272,469,852	$277,143,039
State equalized value	$338,506,475	$374,070,858	$453,144,276
County equalization ratio	85.64	79.63	72.72

Demographics & Socio-Economic Characteristics
(2000 U.S. Census, except as noted)

Population

1980*	3,552
1990*	3,413
2000	3,205
Male	1,596
Female	1,609
2004 (estimate)*	3,208
Persons per sq. mi. of land	3,222

Race & Hispanic Origin, 2000
Race

White	3,152
Black/African American	3
Amer. Indian/Alaska Natv.	8
Asian	8
Natv. Hawaiian/Pac. Islander	1
Other Race	17
Two or more races	16
Hispanic origin, total	46
Mexican	7
Puerto Rican	29
Cuban	3
Other Hispanic	7

Age & Nativity, 2000

Under 5 years	181
18 years and over	2,360
21 years and over	2,209
65 years and over	402
85 years and over	28
Median Age	36.7
Native born	3,177
Foreign born	28

Educational Attainment, 2000

Population 25 years and over	2,065
0-8 yrs of school	4.9%
High School grad or higher	76.7%
Bachelor's degree or higher	7.0%
Graduate degree	1.2%

Income & Poverty, 1999

Per capita income	$18,048
Median household income	$48,534
Median family income	$51,535
Persons in poverty	242
H'holds receiving public assistance	19
H'holds receiving social security	315

Households, 2000

Total households	1,111
With persons under 18	472
With persons over 65	292
Family households	865
One-person households	207
Persons per household	2.86
Persons per family	3.24

Labor & Employment

Total civilian labor force, 2004**	1,958
Unemployment rate	9.8%
Total civilian labor force, 2000	1,652
Unemployment rate	5.4%

Employed persons 16 years and over by occupation, 2000

Managers & professionals	292
Service occupations	293
Sales & office occupations	396
Farming, fishing & forestry	4
Construction & maintenance	254
Production & transportation	324
Self-employed persons	26

*US Census Bureau
**New Jersey Department of Labor

General Information
Borough of National Park
7 S Grove Ave
National Park, NJ 08063
856-845-3891

Web site	NA
Land area (sq. miles)	1.00
Water area (sq. miles)	0.44
Type of government	Borough
Form of government	B

Government

Legislative Districts

US Congressional	1
State Legislative	3

Local Officials, 2006

Mayor	Patricia Koloski
Admin/Manager	Robert Dougherty Jr.
Clerk	Robert Dougherty Jr.
Finance Dir/Treas	George Damminger
Engineer	Edwin Steck
Attorney	Thomas G. Campo
Tax assessor	Roy Duffield
Tax collector	NA
Building officer	William Cattell
Zoning officer	NA
Public Works	NA

Housing & Construction

Housing Units, 2000*

Total	1,165
Median rent	$647
Median SF home value	$92,800

New Privately Owned Housing Units Authorized by Building Permit

	Units	Value
Total, 2004	8	$736,400
Single family	8	$736,400
Total, 2005	4	$175,395
Single family	4	$175,395

Real Property Valuation - parcels, 2005

	Number	Valuation
Total		$95,742,400
Vacant	124	1,671,000
Residential	1,076	89,099,600
Commercial	33	4,336,000
Industrial	0	0
Apartments	4	635,800
Farm land	0	0
Farm homestead	0	0

Average Property Value & Tax, 2005

Residential value	$82,806
Property tax	$3,672
FAIR rebate	$627

Public Library

No public municipal library.

Library statistics, 2004

	Total	per capita
Volumes	NA	NA
Expenditure	NA	NA

Public Safety

Police

Chief	Lin T. Couch
Number of officers, 2004	8

Crime, 2004	Number	Rate
Total	55	17.2
Violent	7	2.2
Non-violent	48	15
Domestic Viol.	22	NA

Emergency/Fire

Director	Dennis Kappler

Public School District
(for school year 2004-2005 except as noted)

National Park Borough School District
516 Lakehurst Ave
National Park, NJ 08063
856-845-6876

Superintendent	Raymond Bider
Grade plan	K-6
Enrollment	373.0
Students per teacher	14.0
Per pupil expenditure	$10,816
Median faculty salary	$48,550
Median administrator salary	$93,450
Grade 12 enrollment	NA
High school graduation rate	NA

Assessment test results
(percent scoring at proficient or advanced level)

	Language	Math
Grade 3	74.3%	82.4%
Grade 8	NA	NA
High school	NA	NA

SAT

Percent tested	NA
Average SAT math score	NA
Average SAT verbal score	NA

No Child Left Behind, 2003-04

Attendence rate (target = 90%)	95.0%
Drop rate	NA
Highly-qualified teachers	90.9%
District needs improvement?(AYP)	No

Municipal Finance

Fiscal Year 2005

Total tax levy	$4,251,414
County levy	807,486
County taxes	708,036
County library	52,325
County health	0
County open space	47,125
School levy	2,622,828
Local muni. budget	821,100
Misc. revenues	1,638,677
Total aid	$589,603
CMPTRA	159,143
Muni. block grant	14,934
Energy tax receipts	390,526
Homeland security	25,000

Fiscal Year 2006

Total aid	$589,604
CMPTRA	145,475
Muni. block grant	14,934
Energy tax receipts	404,195
Homeland security	25,000

Taxes

	2003	2004	2005
General tax rate per $100	4.05	4.043	4.435
Net valuation taxable	$95,001,661	$95,432,461	$95,873,122
State equalized value	$111,113,054	$117,219,926	$134,032,045
County equalization ratio	88.54	85.50	81.39

Demographics & Socio-Economic Characteristics
(2000 U.S. Census, except as noted)

Population
1980*	5,276
1990*	4,997
2000	5,218
Male	2,436
Female	2,782
2004 (estimate)*	5,373
Persons per sq. mi. of land	5,913

Race & Hispanic Origin, 2000
Race
White	4,351
Black/African American	497
Amer. Indian/Alaska Natv.	12
Asian	142
Natv. Hawaiian/Pac. Islander	0
Other Race	110
Two or more races	106
Hispanic origin, total	277
Mexican	69
Puerto Rican	145
Cuban	11
Other Hispanic	52

Age & Nativity, 2000
Under 5 years	304
18 years and over	4,096
21 years and over	3,964
65 years and over	854
85 years and over	141
Median Age	39.8
Native born	4,801
Foreign born	417

Educational Attainment, 2000
Population 25 years and over	3,771
0-8 yrs of school	5.0%
High School grad or higher	82.0%
Bachelor's degree or higher	16.9%
Graduate degree	4.6%

Income & Poverty, 1999
Per capita income	$22,191
Median household income	$43,451
Median family income	$46,393
Persons in poverty	279
H'holds receiving public assistance	19
H'holds receiving social security	636

Households, 2000
Total households	2,221
With persons under 18	644
With persons over 65	582
Family households	1,331
One-person households	743
Persons per household	2.29
Persons per family	2.96

Labor & Employment
Total civilian labor force, 2004**	3,021
Unemployment rate	3.2%
Total civilian labor force, 2000	2,640
Unemployment rate	4.1%

Employed persons 16 years and over by occupation, 2000
Managers & professionals	690
Service occupations	436
Sales & office occupations	675
Farming, fishing & forestry	7
Construction & maintenance	366
Production & transportation	359
Self-employed persons	54

*US Census Bureau
**New Jersey Department of Labor

General Information
Borough of Neptune City
106 W Sylvania Ave
Neptune City, NJ 07753
732-776-7224

Web site	www.neptunecitynj.com
Land area (sq. miles)	0.91
Water area (sq. miles)	0
Type of government	Borough
Form of government	B

Government

Legislative Districts
US Congressional	6
State Legislative	11

Local Officials, 2006
Mayor	Thomas Arnone
Admin/Manager	Joel Popkin
Clerk	Joel Popkin
Finance Dir/Treas	J. Popkin/W. Folk
Engineer	Matt Shafai
Attorney	Mark Aikins
Tax assessor	Stephen Walters
Tax collector	Joel Popkin
Building officer	William Doolittle
Zoning officer	William Doolittle
Public Works	Gerrit DeVos

Housing & Construction

Housing Units, 2000*
Total	2,342
Median rent	$705
Median SF home value	$124,100

New Privately Owned Housing Units
Authorized by Building Permit
	Units	Value
Total, 2004	16	$1,440,110
Single family	16	$1,440,110
Total, 2005	108	$1,300,821
Single family	9	$993,125

Real Property Valuation - parcels, 2005
	Number	Valuation
Total		$434,772,500
Vacant	84	7,003,600
Residential	1,468	304,049,600
Commercial	104	82,584,100
Industrial	9	11,376,500
Apartments	9	29,758,700
Farm land	0	0
Farm homestead	0	0

Average Property Value & Tax, 2005
Residential value	$207,118
Property tax	$4,285
FAIR rebate	$605

Public Library
Neptune City Public Library
106 W Sylvania Ave
Neptune City, NJ 07753
732-988-8866

Director	Patricia Scott

Library statistics, 2004
	Total	per capita
Volumes	NA	NA
Expenditure	NA	NA

Public Safety

Police
Chief	William Geschke
Number of officers, 2004	17

Crime, 2004	Number	Rate
Total	231	44.5
Violent	16	3.1
Non-violent	215	41.4
Domestic Viol.	45	NA

Emergency/Fire
Director	James Hewitson

Public School District
(for school year 2004-2005 except as noted)

Neptune City School District
210 W Sylvania Ave
Neptune City, NJ 07753
732-775-5319

Superintendent	Robert J. Shafer
Grade plan	K-12
Enrollment	417.0
Students per teacher	11.5
Per pupil expenditure	$10,697
Median faculty salary	$38,255
Median administrator salary	$94,700
Grade 12 enrollment	NA
High school graduation rate	NA

Assessment test results
(percent scoring at proficient or advanced level)
	Language	Math
Grade 3	81.0%	69.0%
Grade 8	88.5%	82.6%
High school	NA	NA

SAT
Percent tested	NA
Average SAT math score	NA
Average SAT verbal score	NA

No Child Left Behind, 2003-04
Attendence rate (target = 90%)	94.8%
Drop rate	NA
Highly-qualified teachers	100%
District needs improvement?(AYP)	No

Municipal Finance

Fiscal Year 2005
Total tax levy	$9,004,930
County levy	1,520,858
County taxes	1,342,731
County library	73,963
County health	24,485
County open space	79,679
School levy	4,435,381
Local muni. budget	3,048,691
Misc. revenues	2,146,168
Total aid	$738,514
CMPTRA	282,780
Muni. block grant	21,865
Energy tax receipts	383,869
Homeland security	50,000

Fiscal Year 2006
Total aid	$738,514
CMPTRA	269,345
Muni. block grant	21,865
Energy tax receipts	397,304
Homeland security	50,000

Taxes
	2003	2004	2005
General tax rate per $100	3.82	1.937	2.070
Net valuation taxable	$216,476,197	$434,312,710	$435,229,523
State equalized value	$360,673,437	$444,252,268	$490,897,274
County equalization ratio	72.56	119.39	97.76

Demographics & Socio-Economic Characteristics

(2000 U.S. Census, except as noted)

Population

1980*	28,366
1990*	28,148
2000	27,690
Male	12,890
Female	14,800
2004 (estimate)*	28,207
Persons per sq. mi. of land	3,430

Race & Hispanic Origin, 2000

Race

White	15,485
Black/African American	10,567
Amer. Indian/Alaska Natv.	46
Asian	325
Natv. Hawaiian/Pac. Islander	12
Other Race	547
Two or more races	708
Hispanic origin, total	1,537
Mexican	296
Puerto Rican	791
Cuban	46
Other Hispanic	404

Age & Nativity, 2000

Under 5 years	1,657
18 years and over	21,292
21 years and over	20,477
65 years and over	4,639
85 years and over	784
Median Age	39.4
Native born	25,663
Foreign born	2,027

Educational Attainment, 2000

Population 25 years and over	19,450
0-8 yrs of school	4.8%
High School grad or higher	84.0%
Bachelor's degree or higher	23.5%
Graduate degree	8.1%

Income & Poverty, 1999

Per capita income	$22,569
Median household income	$46,250
Median family income	$57,735
Persons in poverty	3,150
H'holds receiving public assistance	409
H'holds receiving social security	3,314

Households, 2000

Total households	10,907
With persons under 18	3,422
With persons over 65	3,062
Family households	6,802
One-person households	3,437
Persons per household	2.46
Persons per family	3.14

Labor & Employment

Total civilian labor force, 2004**	16,555
Unemployment rate	4.9%
Total civilian labor force, 2000	13,943
Unemployment rate	7.1%

Employed persons 16 years and over by occupation, 2000

Managers & professionals	4,769
Service occupations	2,086
Sales & office occupations	3,678
Farming, fishing & forestry	14
Construction & maintenance	976
Production & transportation	1,425
Self-employed persons	611

*US Census Bureau
**New Jersey Department of Labor

General Information

Township of Neptune
PO Box 1125
Neptune, NJ 07754
732-988-5200

Web site	www.neptuntownship.org
Land area (sq. miles)	8.22
Water area (sq. miles)	0.54
Type of government	Township
Form of government	TC

Government

Legislative Districts

US Congressional	6
State Legislative	11

Local Officials, 2006

Mayor	Thomas J. Catley
Admin/Manager	Philip Huhn
Clerk	Richard Cuttrell
Finance Dir/Treas	Michael Bascom
Engineer	Gerald Freda
Attorney	Donald Beekman
Tax assessor	Bernard Haney
Tax collector	Michael Bascom
Building officer	William Doolittle
Zoning officer	Richad Gardella
Public Works	Wayne Rode

Housing & Construction

Housing Units, 2000*

Total	12,217
Median rent	$658
Median SF home value	$138,100

New Privately Owned Housing Units Authorized by Building Permit

	Units	Value
Total, 2004	248	$4,935,776
Single family	7	$3,353,420
Total, 2005	102	$6,687,699
Single family	46	$6,531,128

Real Property Valuation - parcels, 2005

	Number	Valuation
Total		$2,905,340,600
Vacant	459	48,213,400
Residential	9,505	2,273,627,700
Commercial	428	430,072,900
Industrial	62	74,698,500
Apartments	78	78,061,000
Farm land	2	651,000
Farm homestead	3	16,100

Average Property Value & Tax, 2005

Residential value	$239,130
Property tax	$4,561
FAIR rebate	$661

Public Library

Neptune Public Library
25 Neptune Blvd
Neptune, NJ 07753
732-775-8241

Director . . . . Marian Bauman

Library statistics, 2004

	Total	per capita
Volumes	87,316	3.15
Expenditure	$1,424,745	$51.45

Public Safety

Police

Chief	Howard O'Neil
Number of officers, 2004	74

Crime, 2004	Number	Rate
Total	1,539	54.2
Violent	136	4.8
Non-violent	1,403	49.4
Domestic Viol.	505	NA

Emergency/Fire

Director . . . . Kenneth Northrup

Public School District

(for school year 2004-2005 except as noted)

Neptune Township School District
3301B Route 66
Neptune, NJ 07753
732-776-2000

Superintendent	David Mooij
Grade plan	K-12
Enrollment	4,218.0
Students per teacher	11.0
Per pupil expenditure	$14,761
Median faculty salary	$50,535
Median administrator salary	$100,729
Grade 12 enrollment	232.5
High school graduation rate	96.9%

Assessment test results

(percent scoring at proficient or advanced level)

	Language	Math
Grade 3	69.5%	67.0%
Grade 8	52.1%	36.8%
High school	72.3%	65.9%

SAT

Percent tested	72%
Average SAT math score	445
Average SAT verbal score	429

No Child Left Behind, 2003-04

Attendence rate (target = 90%)	92.6%
Drop rate	0.2%
Highly-qualified teachers	99.7%
District needs improvement?(AYP)	No

Municipal Finance

Fiscal Year 2005

Total tax levy	$55,552,745
County levy	9,565,003
County taxes	8,876,504
County library	0
County health	161,884
County open space	526,615
School levy	28,085,097
Local muni. budget	17,902,645
Misc. revenues	13,741,464
Total aid	$6,728,697
CMPTRA	3,630,816
Muni. block grant	123,166
Energy tax receipts	2,884,715
Homeland security	90,000

Fiscal Year 2006

Total aid	$6,728,697
CMPTRA	3,529,851
Muni. block grant	123,166
Energy tax receipts	2,985,680
Homeland security	90,000

Taxes

	2003	2004	2005
General tax rate per $100	3.49	1.795	1.908
Net valuation taxable	$1,379,011,719	$2,898,878,732	$2,912,345,753
State equalized value	$2,460,324,209	$2,947,093,545	$3,456,379,958
County equalization ratio	67.71	116.67	98.36

Demographics & Socio-Economic Characteristics

(2000 U.S. Census, except as noted)

Population

1980*	3,557
1990*	3,311
2000	2,580
Male	1,267
Female	1,313
2000 (revised)	3,236
2004 (estimate)*	3,296
Persons per sq. mi. of land	3,918

Race & Hispanic Origin, 2000

Race

White	2,433
Black/African American	31
Amer. Indian/Alaska Natv.	1
Asian	43
Natv. Hawaiian/Pac. Islander	0
Other Race	37
Two or more races	35
Hispanic origin, total	184
Mexican	21
Puerto Rican	38
Cuban	12
Other Hispanic	113

Age & Nativity, 2000

Under 5 years	148
18 years and over	1,987
21 years and over	1,895
65 years and over	377
85 years and over	47
Median Age	37.8
Native born	2,311
Foreign born	269

Educational Attainment, 2000

Population 25 years and over	1,817
0-8 yrs of school	7.9%
High School grad or higher	84.8%
Bachelor's degree or higher	22.0%
Graduate degree	6.2%

Income & Poverty, 1999

Per capita income	$23,472
Median household income	$55,000
Median family income	$65,833
Persons in poverty	80
H'holds receiving public assistance	12
H'holds receiving social security	276

Households, 2000

Total households	1,008
With persons under 18	328
With persons over 65	283
Family households	681
One-person households	265
Persons per household	2.56
Persons per family	3.1

Labor & Employment

Total civilian labor force, 2004**	2,089
Unemployment rate	4.1%
Total civilian labor force, 2000	1,425
Unemployment rate	2.9%

Employed persons 16 years and over by occupation, 2000

Managers & professionals	434
Service occupations	253
Sales & office occupations	370
Farming, fishing & forestry	0
Construction & maintenance	131
Production & transportation	196
Self-employed persons	96

*US Census Bureau
**New Jersey Department of Labor

General Information

Borough of Netcong
23 Maple Ave
Netcong, NJ 07857
973-347-0252

Web site	www.netcong.org
Land area (sq. miles)	0.84
Water area (sq. miles)	0.06
Type of government	Borough
Form of government	B

Government

Legislative Districts

US Congressional	11
State Legislative	24

Local Officials, 2006

Mayor	Nicholas Pompilio
Admin/Manager	Marvin Joss
Clerk	Dolores Dalessandro
Finance Dir/Treas	Anna Madonna
Engineer	Robert Guerin
Attorney	Anthony Bucco
Tax assessor	Marvin Joss
Tax collector	Dolores Dalessandro
Building officer	Barrie Krause
Zoning officer	Barrie Krause
Public Works	Bobby Olivo

Housing & Construction

Housing Units, 2000*

Total	1,043
Median rent	$764
Median SF home value	$147,400

New Privately Owned Housing Units Authorized by Building Permit

	Units	Value
Total, 2004	4	$487,025
Single family	4	$487,025
Total, 2005	5	$607,518
Single family	5	$607,518

Real Property Valuation - parcels, 2005

	Number	Valuation
Total		$176,220,900
Vacant	42	2,536,700
Residential	814	117,883,500
Commercial	77	24,191,100
Industrial	6	11,034,300
Apartments	3	20,575,300
Farm land	0	0
Farm homestead	0	0

Average Property Value & Tax, 2005

Residential value	$144,820
Property tax	$5,131
FAIR rebate	$642

Public Library

No public municipal library.

Library statistics, 2004

	Total	per capita
Volumes	NA	NA
Expenditure	NA	NA

Public Safety

Police

Chief	Robert Weisert (Dir)
Number of officers, 2004	9

Crime, 2004	Number	Rate
Total	121	36.9
Violent	8	2.4
Non-violent	113	34.4
Domestic Viol.	55	NA

Emergency/Fire

Director	Pete Schroeder

Public School District

(for school year 2004-2005 except as noted)

Netcong School District
26 College Rd
Netcong, NJ 07857
973-347-0020

Superintendent	James Grube
Grade plan	K-8
Enrollment	282.0
Students per teacher	9.1
Per pupil expenditure	$11,817
Median faculty salary	$57,820
Median administrator salary	$75,000
Grade 12 enrollment	NA
High school graduation rate	NA

Assessment test results

(percent scoring at proficient or advanced level)

	Language	Math
Grade 3	89.2%	89.2%
Grade 8	80.7%	78.2%
High school	NA	NA

SAT

Percent tested	NA
Average SAT math score	NA
Average SAT verbal score	NA

No Child Left Behind, 2003-04

Attendance rate (target = 90%)	94.7%
Drop rate	NA
Highly-qualified teachers	80.9%
District needs improvement?(AYP)	No

Municipal Finance

Fiscal Year 2005

Total tax levy	$6,325,571
County levy	704,870
County taxes	577,388
County library	0
County health	0
County open space	127,482
School levy	4,005,690
Local muni. budget	1,615,010
Misc. revenues	1,587,540
Total aid	$622,081
CMPTRA	318,581
Muni. block grant	14,487
Energy tax receipts	264,013
Homeland security	25,000

Fiscal Year 2006

Total aid	$622,081
CMPTRA	309,341
Muni. block grant	14,487
Energy tax receipts	273,253
Homeland security	25,000

Taxes

	2003	2004	2005
General tax rate per $100	3.19	3.390	3.550
Net valuation taxable	$179,369,300	$178,223,589	$178,521,829
State equalized value	$238,491,291	$262,356,282	$293,863,093
County equalization ratio	87.2	75.21	67.62

Demographics & Socio-Economic Characteristics
(2000 U.S. Census, except as noted)

Population

1980*	41,442
1990*	41,711
2000	48,573
Male	24,085
Female	24,488
2000 (revised)	48,591
2004 (estimate)*	50,010
Persons per sq. mi. of land	9,568

Race & Hispanic Origin, 2000

Race

White	23,701
Black/African American	11,185
Amer. Indian/Alaska Natv.	224
Asian	2,584
Natv. Hawaiian/Pac. Islander	40
Other Race	8,780
Two or more races	2,059
Hispanic origin, total	18,947
Mexican	7,364
Puerto Rican	3,178
Cuban	254
Other Hispanic	8,151

Age & Nativity, 2000

Under 5 years	3,394
18 years and over	38,824
21 years and over	31,338
65 years and over	3,146
85 years and over	389
Median Age	23.6
Native born	32,358
Foreign born	16,215

Educational Attainment, 2000

Population 25 years and over	22,088
0-8 yrs of school	21.6%
High School grad or higher	62.6%
Bachelor's degree or higher	19.2%
Graduate degree	7.5%

Income & Poverty, 1999

Per capita income	$14,308
Median household income	$36,080
Median family income	$38,222
Persons in poverty	11,454
H'holds receiving public assistance	741
H'holds receiving social security	2,396

Households, 2000

Total households	13,057
With persons under 18	4,576
With persons over 65	2,429
Family households	7,202
One-person households	3,178
Persons per household	3.23
Persons per family	3.69

Labor & Employment

Total civilian labor force, 2004**	24,259
Unemployment rate	7.9%
Total civilian labor force, 2000	26,652
Unemployment rate	10.6%

Employed persons 16 years and over by occupation, 2000

Managers & professionals	5,929
Service occupations	5,327
Sales & office occupations	6,307
Farming, fishing & forestry	108
Construction & maintenance	1,099
Production & transportation	5,062
Self-employed persons	448

*US Census Bureau
**New Jersey Department of Labor

General Information
City of New Brunswick
City Hall
78 Bayard St
New Brunswick, NJ 08901
732-745-5004

Web site	www.cityofnewbrunswick.org
Land area (sq. miles)	5.23
Water area (sq. miles)	0.52
Type of government	City
Form of government	MC '50

Government

Legislative Districts

US Congressional	6
State Legislative	17

Local Officials, 2006

Mayor	James Cahill
Admin/Manager	Thomas Loughlin
Clerk	Daniel Torrisi
Finance Dir/Treas	Douglas Petix
Engineer	(Vacant)
Attorney	William Hamilton
Tax assessor	Philip Duchesneau
Tax collector	Marilyn Chetrancola
Building officer	William Schrum
Zoning officer	NA
Public Works	Steve Zarecki

Housing & Construction

Housing Units, 2000*

Total	13,893
Median rent	$837
Median SF home value	$122,600

New Privately Owned Housing Units Authorized by Building Permit

	Units	Value
Total, 2004	222	$33,301,266
Single family	30	$1,476,707
Total, 2005	226	$32,856,289
Single family	29	$1,435,617

Real Property Valuation - parcels, 2005

	Number	Valuation
Total		$1,281,855,300
Vacant	956	25,345,000
Residential	5,328	600,142,200
Commercial	697	377,687,800
Industrial	90	134,627,300
Apartments	228	144,053,000
Farm land	0	0
Farm homestead	0	0

Average Property Value & Tax, 2005

Residential value	$112,639
Property tax	$4,554
FAIR rebate	$514

Public Library
New Brunswick Public Library
60 Livingston Ave
New Brunswick, NJ 08901
732-745-5271

Director....................Robert Belvin

Library statistics, 2004

	Total	per capita
Volumes	83,108	1.71
Expenditure	$1,490,603	$30.69

Public Safety

Police

Chief	Joseph Catanese
Number of officers, 2004	135

Crime, 2004	Number	Rate
Total	2,308	46.3
Violent	352	7.1
Non-violent	1,956	39.3
Domestic Viol.	684	NA

Emergency/Fire

Director.............Robert McLaughlin

Public School District
(for school year 2004-2005 except as noted)

New Brunswick School District
PO Box 2683
New Brunswick, NJ 08903
732-745-5300

Superintendent	Richard Kaplan
Grade plan	K-12
Enrollment	6,736.0
Students per teacher	9.4
Per pupil expenditure	$15,283
Median faculty salary	$55,153
Median administrator salary	$98,413
Grade 12 enrollment	257.0
High school graduation rate	NA

Assessment test results
(percent scoring at proficient or advanced level)

	Language	Math
Grade 3	56.6%	65.4%
Grade 8	46.1%	43.2%
High school	60.8%	63.9%

SAT

Percent tested	54%
Average SAT math score	451
Average SAT verbal score	414

No Child Left Behind, 2003-04

Attendence rate (target = 90%)	94.3%
Drop rate	6%
Highly-qualified teachers	96.5%
District needs improvement?(AYP)	Yes

Municipal Finance

Fiscal Year 2005

Total tax levy	$53,325,526
County levy	7,862,153
County taxes	7,120,303
County library	0
County health	0
County open space	741,850
School levy	25,495,665
Local muni. budget	19,967,708
Misc. revenues	39,403,638
Total aid	$16,472,832
CMPTRA	13,833,415
Muni. block grant	190,456
Energy tax receipts	2,308,961
Homeland security	140,000

Fiscal Year 2006

Total aid	$16,472,833
CMPTRA	13,752,602
Muni. block grant	190,456
Energy tax receipts	2,389,775
Homeland security	140,000

Taxes

	2003	2004	2005
General tax rate per $100	3.75	3.970	4.050
Net valuation taxable	$1,327,328,817	$1,303,466,279	$1,318,918,764
State equalized value	$2,031,418,453	$2,416,687,618	$2,869,085,847
County equalization ratio	75.23	65.34	53.07

Demographics & Socio-Economic Characteristics
(2000 U.S. Census, except as noted)

Population
1980*	14,258
1990*	9,546
2000	9,744
Male	7,802
Female	1,942
2004 (estimate)*	9,815
Persons per sq. mi. of land	440

Race & Hispanic Origin, 2000
Race
White	6,249
Black/African American	2,816
Amer. Indian/Alaska Natv.	41
Asian	143
Natv. Hawaiian/Pac. Islander	8
Other Race	259
Two or more races	228
Hispanic origin, total	1,890
Mexican	227
Puerto Rican	928
Cuban	77
Other Hispanic	658

Age & Nativity, 2000
Under 5 years	408
18 years and over	8,331
21 years and over	7,807
65 years and over	125
85 years and over	3
Median Age	32.1
Native born	9,498
Foreign born	336

Educational Attainment, 2000
Population 25 years and over	6,700
0-8 yrs of school	6.2%
High School grad or higher	74.1%
Bachelor's degree or higher	14.6%
Graduate degree	3.3%

Income & Poverty, 1999
Per capita income	$12,140
Median household income	$44,386
Median family income	$45,511
Persons in poverty	146
H'holds receiving public assistance	5
H'holds receiving social security	48

Households, 2000
Total households	1,162
With persons under 18	723
With persons over 65	41
Family households	991
One-person households	159
Persons per household	3.14
Persons per family	3.46

Labor & Employment
Total civilian labor force, 2004**	958
Unemployment rate	2.6%
Total civilian labor force, 2000	950
Unemployment rate	3.4%

Employed persons 16 years and over by occupation, 2000
Managers & professionals	356
Service occupations	197
Sales & office occupations	216
Farming, fishing & forestry	0
Construction & maintenance	70
Production & transportation	79
Self-employed persons	38

*US Census Bureau
**New Jersey Department of Labor

General Information
Township of New Hanover
PO Box 159
Cookstown, NJ 08511
609-758-2172

Web site	NA
Land area (sq. miles)	22.28
Water area (sq. miles)	0.10
Type of government	Township
Form of government	TC

Government
Legislative Districts
US Congressional	3
State Legislative	30

Local Officials, 2006
Mayor	Dennis Roohr
Admin/Manager	Jeffrey Urbanik
Clerk	Jeffrey Urbanik
Finance Dir/Treas	Dawn Robertson
Engineer	Richard Tangel
Attorney	Anthony Drollas
Tax assessor	Ed Burek
Tax collector	NA
Building officer	Michael Malloy
Zoning officer	NA
Public Works	NA

Housing & Construction
Housing Units, 2000*
Total	1,381
Median rent	$906
Median SF home value	$133,200

New Privately Owned Housing Units Authorized by Building Permit
	Units	Value
Total, 2004	4	$425,750
Single family	4	$425,750
Total, 2005	0	$0
Single family	0	$0

Real Property Valuation - parcels, 2005
	Number	Valuation
Total		$53,709,900
Vacant	71	2,542,400
Residential	215	34,565,000
Commercial	24	12,153,400
Industrial	1	88,000
Apartments	0	0
Farm land	18	3,738,000
Farm homestead	33	623,100

Average Property Value & Tax, 2005
Residential value	$141,888
Property tax	$2,815
FAIR rebate	$524

Public Library
No public municipal library.

Library statistics, 2004
	Total	per capita
Volumes	NA	NA
Expenditure	NA	NA

Public Safety
Police
Chief	Gary Timmons
Number of officers, 2004	3

Crime, 2004	Number	Rate
Total	25	2.6
Violent	2	0.2
Non-violent	23	2.4
Domestic Viol.	8	NA

Emergency/Fire
Director	Charles Wilkins

Public School District
(for school year 2004-2005 except as noted)

New Hanover Township School District
122 Fort Dix St
Wrightstown, NJ 08562
609-723-2139

Superintendent	George Pratt
Grade plan	K-12
Enrollment	150.0
Students per teacher	7.7
Per pupil expenditure	$16,987
Median faculty salary	$44,418
Median administrator salary	$72,500
Grade 12 enrollment	NA
High school graduation rate	NA

Assessment test results
(percent scoring at proficient or advanced level)
	Language	Math
Grade 3	80.0%	73.3%
Grade 8	75.0%	75.0%
High school	NA	NA

SAT
Percent tested	NA
Average SAT math score	NA
Average SAT verbal score	NA

No Child Left Behind, 2003-04
Attendance rate (target = 90%)	94.9%
Drop rate	NA
Highly-qualified teachers	88.9%
District needs improvement?(AYP)	No

Municipal Finance
Fiscal Year 2005
Total tax levy	$1,171,247
County levy	280,996
County taxes	235,730
County library	20,638
County health	0
County open space	24,628
School levy	890,251
Local muni. budget	0
Misc. revenues	2,167,996
Total aid	$1,088,635
CMPTRA	709,883
Muni. block grant	41,770
Energy tax receipts	336,982
Homeland security	0

Fiscal Year 2006
Total aid	$1,088,635
CMPTRA	698,088
Muni. block grant	41,770
Energy tax receipts	348,777
Homeland security	NA

Taxes
	2003	2004	2005
General tax rate per $100	2.03	1.859	2.140
Net valuation taxable	$52,281,402	$52,232,433	$54,734,695
State equalized value	$47,960,189	$58,538,346	$67,515,351
County equalization ratio	115.16	109.01	88.99

Demographics & Socio-Economic Characteristics
(2000 U.S. Census, except as noted)

Population
1980*	16,876
1990*	15,990
2000	16,400
Male	7,900
Female	8,500
2004 (estimate)*	16,397
Persons per sq. mi. of land	7,098

Race & Hispanic Origin, 2000
Race
White	12,888
Black/African American	429
Amer. Indian/Alaska Natv.	19
Asian	2,420
Natv. Hawaiian/Pac. Islander	4
Other Race	305
Two or more races	335
Hispanic origin, total	1,326
Mexican	47
Puerto Rican	328
Cuban	190
Other Hispanic	761

Age & Nativity, 2000
Under 5 years	1,050
18 years and over	12,895
21 years and over	12,512
65 years and over	2,888
85 years and over	404
Median Age	39.9
Native born	12,334
Foreign born	4,066

Educational Attainment, 2000
Population 25 years and over	11,853
0-8 yrs of school	4.6%
High School grad or higher	87.6%
Bachelor's degree or higher	32.4%
Graduate degree	11.2%

Income & Poverty, 1999
Per capita income	$29,064
Median household income	$59,118
Median family income	$77,216
Persons in poverty	543
H'holds receiving public assistance	98
H'holds receiving social security	1,870

Households, 2000
Total households	6,346
With persons under 18	1,996
With persons over 65	1,954
Family households	4,275
One-person households	1,817
Persons per household	2.54
Persons per family	3.18

Labor & Employment
Total civilian labor force, 2004**	9,349
Unemployment rate	5.2%
Total civilian labor force, 2000	8,748
Unemployment rate	3.7%

Employed persons 16 years and over by occupation, 2000
Managers & professionals	3,509
Service occupations	830
Sales & office occupations	2,815
Farming, fishing & forestry	0
Construction & maintenance	589
Production & transportation	681
Self-employed persons	406

*US Census Bureau
**New Jersey Department of Labor

General Information
Borough of New Milford
930 River Rd
New Milford, NJ 07646
201-967-5044

Web site	www.newmilfordboro.com
Land area (sq. miles)	2.31
Water area (sq. miles)	0
Type of government	Borough
Form of government	B

Government
Legislative Districts
US Congressional	9
State Legislative	39

Local Officials, 2006
Mayor	Frank DeBari
Admin/Manager	Kathy Sayers
Clerk	Kathy Sayers
Finance Dir/Treas	Gene Vinci
Engineer	Stephen Boswell
Attorney	S. Greg Moscaritolo
Tax assessor	Barbara Potash
Tax collector	Denise Amoroso
Building officer	Douglas Baker
Zoning officer	Karl Schaffenberger
Public Works	NA

Housing & Construction
Housing Units, 2000*
Total	6,437
Median rent	$763
Median SF home value	$223,400

New Privately Owned Housing Units Authorized by Building Permit
	Units	Value
Total, 2004	12	$2,437,075
Single family	12	$2,437,075
Total, 2005	17	$3,913,658
Single family	17	$3,913,658

Real Property Valuation - parcels, 2005
	Number	Valuation
Total		$1,923,776,300
Vacant	48	4,918,700
Residential	4,191	1,697,641,700
Commercial	76	88,954,500
Industrial	2	3,736,200
Apartments	14	128,525,200
Farm land	0	0
Farm homestead	0	0

Average Property Value & Tax, 2005
Residential value	$405,068
Property tax	$7,244
FAIR rebate	$612

Public Library
New Milford Public Library
200 Dahlia Ave
New Milford, NJ 07646
201-262-1797

Director | Terri McColl

Library statistics, 2004
	Total	per capita
Volumes	56,247	3.43
Expenditure	$758,222	$46.23

Public Safety
Police
Chief	Frank Papapietro
Number of officers, 2004	36

Crime, 2004	Number	Rate
Total	145	8.9
Violent	7	0.4
Non-violent	138	8.4
Domestic Viol.	100	NA

Emergency/Fire
Director | James Tufaro

Public School District
(for school year 2004-2005 except as noted)

New Milford School District
145 Madison Ave
New Milford, NJ 07646
201-261-2952

Superintendent	Elaine Baldwin
Grade plan	K-12
Enrollment	1,980.5
Students per teacher	11.9
Per pupil expenditure	$11,821
Median faculty salary	$45,650
Median administrator salary	$96,737
Grade 12 enrollment	123.5
High school graduation rate	98.4%

Assessment test results
(percent scoring at proficient or advanced level)
	Language	Math
Grade 3	92.6%	87.1%
Grade 8	81.5%	78.1%
High school	96.7%	86.0%

SAT
Percent tested	85%
Average SAT math score	539
Average SAT verbal score	515

No Child Left Behind, 2003-04
Attendence rate (target = 90%)	97.6%
Drop rate	0%
Highly-qualified teachers	97.8%
District needs improvement?(AYP)	No

Municipal Finance
Fiscal Year 2005
Total tax levy	$34,417,599
County levy	3,203,662
County taxes	3,043,503
County library	0
County health	0
County open space	160,159
School levy	20,938,828
Local muni. budget	10,275,109
Misc. revenues	4,136,883
Total aid	$2,232,597
CMPTRA	709,961
Muni. block grant	69,967
Energy tax receipts	1,382,669
Homeland security	70,000

Fiscal Year 2006
Total aid	$2,232,597
CMPTRA	661,568
Muni. block grant	69,967
Energy tax receipts	1,431,062
Homeland security	70,000

Taxes
	2003	2004	2005
General tax rate per $100	3.16	3.280	1.790
Net valuation taxable	$988,474,788	$992,588,345	$1,924,645,190
State equalized value	$1,437,572,408	$1,591,323,129	$1,821,028,659
County equalization ratio	77.02	68.76	120.37

Demographics & Socio-Economic Characteristics
(2000 U.S. Census, except as noted)

Population
1980*	12,426
1990*	11,439
2000	11,907
Male	5,770
Female	6,137
2004 (estimate)*	11,981
Persons per sq. mi. of land	3,257

Race & Hispanic Origin, 2000
Race
White	10,689
Black/African American	105
Amer. Indian/Alaska Natv.	4
Asian	905
Natv. Hawaiian/Pac. Islander	3
Other Race	81
Two or more races	120
Hispanic origin, total	417
Mexican	37
Puerto Rican	57
Cuban	44
Other Hispanic	279

Age & Nativity, 2000
Under 5 years	934
18 years and over	8,771
21 years and over	8,545
65 years and over	1,821
85 years and over	212
Median Age	39
Native born	9,774
Foreign born	2,133

Educational Attainment, 2000
Population 25 years and over	8,319
0-8 yrs of school	2.3%
High School grad or higher	95.1%
Bachelor's degree or higher	58.1%
Graduate degree	27.6%

Income & Poverty, 1999
Per capita income	$42,995
Median household income	$90,964
Median family income	$105,013
Persons in poverty	212
H'holds receiving public assistance	0
H'holds receiving social security	1,275

Households, 2000
Total households	4,404
With persons under 18	1,709
With persons over 65	1,215
Family households	3,309
One-person households	944
Persons per household	2.67
Persons per family	3.13

Labor & Employment
Total civilian labor force, 2004**	6,533
Unemployment rate	2.2%
Total civilian labor force, 2000	6,189
Unemployment rate	3.3%

Employed persons 16 years and over by occupation, 2000
Managers & professionals	3,601
Service occupations	437
Sales & office occupations	1,440
Farming, fishing & forestry	0
Construction & maintenance	314
Production & transportation	195
Self-employed persons	368

*US Census Bureau
**New Jersey Department of Labor

General Information
Borough of New Providence
360 Elkwood Ave
New Providence, NJ 07974
908-665-1400
Web site	www.newprov.org
Land area (sq. miles)	3.68
Water area (sq. miles)	0
Type of government	Borough
Form of government	B

Government
Legislative Districts
US Congressional	7
State Legislative	21

Local Officials, 2006
Mayor	Allen Morgan
Admin/Manager	Douglas Marvin
Clerk	Wendi Barry
Finance Dir/Treas	Ken DeRoberts
Engineer	Andrew Hipolit
Attorney	Carl Woodward
Tax assessor	Pat Spychala
Tax collector	NA
Building officer	Keith Lynch
Zoning officer	NA
Public Works	NA

Housing & Construction
Housing Units, 2000*
Total	4,485
Median rent	$941
Median SF home value	$317,100

New Privately Owned Housing Units Authorized by Building Permit
	Units	Value
Total, 2004	6	$1,159,000
Single family	6	$1,159,000
Total, 2005	15	$2,300,419
Single family	13	$2,081,669

Real Property Valuation - parcels, 2005
	Number	Valuation
Total		$1,302,529,400
Vacant	112	13,958,800
Residential	3,633	1,017,117,000
Commercial	128	154,948,500
Industrial	13	79,518,600
Apartments	16	36,986,500
Farm land	0	0
Farm homestead	0	0

Average Property Value & Tax, 2005
Residential value	$279,966
Property tax	$9,071
FAIR rebate	$609

Public Library
New Providence Memorial Library
377 Elkwood Ave
New Providence, NJ 07974
908-665-0311
Director . . . . James Keehbler

Library statistics, 2004
	Total	per capita
Volumes	69,457	5.83
Expenditure	$627,498	$52.70

Public Safety
Police
Chief	Anthony Buccelli
Number of officers, 2004	26

Crime, 2004	Number	Rate
Total	107	8.9
Violent	7	0.6
Non-violent	100	8.3
Domestic Viol.	48	NA

Emergency/Fire
Director . . . . Crdig Stapfer

Public School District
(for school year 2004-2005 except as noted)

New Providence School District
356 Elkwood Ave
New Providence, NJ 07974
908-464-9050
Superintendent	Ann Marie Inzano
Grade plan	K-12
Enrollment	2,188.5
Students per teacher	11.0
Per pupil expenditure	$11,293
Median faculty salary	$52,930
Median administrator salary	$105,617
Grade 12 enrollment	155.0
High school graduation rate	100.0%

Assessment test results
(percent scoring at proficient or advanced level)
	Language	Math
Grade 3	92.6%	97.2%
Grade 8	95.8%	95.1%
High school	95.6%	92.4%

SAT
Percent tested	99%
Average SAT math score	592
Average SAT verbal score	574

No Child Left Behind, 2003-04
Attendence rate (target = 90%)	96.0%
Drop rate	0%
Highly-qualified teachers	96.8%
District needs improvement?(AYP)	No

Municipal Finance
Fiscal Year 2005
Total tax levy	$42,352,914
County levy	8,121,377
County taxes	7,800,324
County library	0
County health	0
County open space	321,053
School levy	25,282,549
Local muni. budget	8,948,988
Misc. revenues	5,562,911
Total aid	$1,843,336
CMPTRA	636,594
Muni. block grant	50,054
Energy tax receipts	1,086,688
Homeland security	70,000

Fiscal Year 2006
Total aid	$1,843,336
CMPTRA	598,560
Muni. block grant	50,054
Energy tax receipts	1,124,722
Homeland security	70,000

Taxes
	2003	2004	2005
General tax rate per $100	2.89	3.090	3.240
Net valuation taxable	$1,313,491,948	$1,313,619,220	$1,307,203,407
State equalized value	$1,859,153,500	$1,977,037,837	$2,213,348,132
County equalization ratio	71.74	64.49	61.30

Demographics & Socio-Economic Characteristics
(2000 U.S. Census, except as noted)

Population
1980*	329,248
1990*	275,221
2000	273,546
Male	132,701
Female	140,845
2000 (revised)	272,537
2004 (estimate)*	280,451
Persons per sq. mi. of land	11,785

Race & Hispanic Origin, 2000
Race
White	72,537
Black/African American	146,250
Amer. Indian/Alaska Natv.	1,005
Asian	3,263
Natv. Hawaiian/Pac. Islander	135
Other Race	38,430
Two or more races	11,926
Hispanic origin, total	80,622
Mexican	2,295
Puerto Rican	39,650
Cuban	2,962
Other Hispanic	35,715

Age & Nativity, 2000
Under 5 years	21,293
18 years and over	197,127
21 years and over	183,103
65 years and over	25,306
85 years and over	2,722
Median Age	30.8
Native born	207,489
Foreign born	66,057

Educational Attainment, 2000
Population 25 years and over	164,298
0-8 yrs of school	18.1%
High School grad or higher	57.9%
Bachelor's degree or higher	9.0%
Graduate degree	3.0%

Income & Poverty, 1999
Per capita income	$13,009
Median household income	$26,913
Median family income	$30,781
Persons in poverty	74,263
H'holds receiving public assistance	11,515
H'holds receiving social security	21,956

Households, 2000
Total households	91,382
With persons under 18	39,255
With persons over 65	19,077
Family households	61,999
One-person households	24,331
Persons per household	2.85
Persons per family	3.43

Labor & Employment
Total civilian labor force, 2004**	20,350
Unemployment rate	3.6%
Total civilian labor force, 2000	108,256
Unemployment rate	16.1%

Employed persons 16 years and over by occupation, 2000
Managers & professionals	17,168
Service occupations	19,796
Sales & office occupations	24,985
Farming, fishing & forestry	134
Construction & maintenance	9,455
Production & transportation	19,281
Self-employed persons	2,707

*US Census Bureau
**New Jersey Department of Labor

General Information
City of Newark
920 Broad St
Newark, NJ 07102
973-733-6400

Web site	www.ci.newark.nj.us
Land area (sq. miles)	23.80
Water area (sq. miles)	2.17
Type of government	City
Form of government	MC '50

Government

Legislative Districts
US Congressional	10, 13
State Legislative	27, 28, 29

Local Officials, 2006
Mayor	Sharpe James
Admin/Manager	Richard Monteilh
Clerk	Robert P. Marasco
Finance Dir/Treas	Daniel Gonzalez
Engineer	James Adam
Attorney	JoAnne Watson
Tax assessor	Evelyn Laccitiello
Tax collector	NA
Building officer	John Anstiss
Zoning officer	NA
Public Works	NA

Housing & Construction

Housing Units, 2000*
Total	100,141
Median rent	$586
Median SF home value	$119,000

New Privately Owned Housing Units
Authorized by Building Permit
	Units	Value
Total, 2004	1,662	$96,663,841
Single family	128	$5,808,006
Total, 2005	2,064	$146,035,698
Single family	374	$26,128,333

Real Property Valuation - parcels, 2005
	Number	Valuation
Total		$10,790,618,200
Vacant	4,734	436,849,900
Residential	27,809	4,612,558,500
Commercial	5,712	3,833,371,700
Industrial	980	1,163,103,000
Apartments	1,243	744,735,100
Farm land	0	0
Farm homestead	0	0

Average Property Value & Tax, 2005
Residential value	$165,866
Property tax	$3,809
FAIR rebate	$647

Public Library
Newark Public Library
5 Washington St
Newark, NJ 07101
973-733-7800

Director .... Wilma Grey

Library statistics, 2004
	Total	per capita
Volumes	1,577,554	5.77
Expenditure	$15,649,952	$57.21

Public Safety

Police
Chief	Robert Rankin
Number of officers, 2004	1282

Crime, 2004	Number	Rate
Total	17,035	61.3
Violent	2,984	10.7
Non-violent	14,051	50.6
Domestic Viol.	1,978	NA

Emergency/Fire
Director .... Lowell F. Jones

Public School District
(for school year 2004-2005 except as noted)

Newark School District
2 Cedar St
Newark, NJ 07102
973-733-7333

Superintendent	Marion Bolden
Grade plan	K-12
Enrollment	41,458.0
Students per teacher	9.4
Per pupil expenditure	$16,506
Median faculty salary	$76,213
Median administrator salary	$105,471
Grade 12 enrollment	1,923.0
High school graduation rate	NA

Assessment test results
(percent scoring at proficient or advanced level)
	Language	Math
Grade 3	58.3%	62.9%
Grade 8	47.1%	30.3%
High school	52.4%	37.4%

SAT
Percent tested	NA
Average SAT math score	NA
Average SAT verbal score	NA

No Child Left Behind, 2003-04
Attendence rate (target = 90%)	91.0%
Drop rate	3.3%
Highly-qualified teachers	80.9%
District needs improvement?(AYP)	Yes

Municipal Finance

Fiscal Year 2005
Total tax levy	$250,341,149
County levy	57,527,923
County taxes	56,309,522
County library	0
County health	0
County open space	1,218,401
School levy	82,206,190
Local muni. budget	110,607,035
Misc. revenues	452,932,557
Total aid	$111,553,952
CMPTRA	84,524,136
Muni. block grant	1,204,261
Energy tax receipts	25,685,555
Homeland security	140,000

Fiscal Year 2006
Total aid	$111,553,952
CMPTRA	83,625,141
Muni. block grant	1,204,261
Energy tax receipts	26,584,550
Homeland security	140,000

Taxes
	2003	2004	2005
General tax rate per $100	2.16	2.220	2.300
Net valuation taxable	$10,790,782,068	$10,796,617,895	$10,900,573,643
State equalized value	$10,001,651,745	$11,395,648,225	$13,475,798,792
County equalization ratio	137.01	137.01	94.69

Demographics & Socio-Economic Characteristics
(2000 U.S. Census, except as noted)

Population
1980*	1,563
1990*	1,592
2000	1,616
Male	744
Female	872
2004 (estimate)*	1,653
Persons per sq. mi. of land	973

Race & Hispanic Origin, 2000
Race
White	1,537
Black/African American	21
Amer. Indian/Alaska Natv.	11
Asian	9
Natv. Hawaiian/Pac. Islander	0
Other Race	17
Two or more races	21
Hispanic origin, total	62
Mexican	12
Puerto Rican	32
Cuban	3
Other Hispanic	15

Age & Nativity, 2000
Under 5 years	93
18 years and over	1,222
21 years and over	1,169
65 years and over	230
85 years and over	27
Median Age	38.8
Native born	1,561
Foreign born	55

Educational Attainment, 2000
Population 25 years and over	1,115
0-8 yrs of school	5.6%
High School grad or higher	83.5%
Bachelor's degree or higher	15.7%
Graduate degree	3.7%

Income & Poverty, 1999
Per capita income	$21,063
Median household income	$51,875
Median family income	$59,934
Persons in poverty	105
H'holds receiving public assistance	9
H'holds receiving social security	178

Households, 2000
Total households	596
With persons under 18	221
With persons over 65	163
Family households	471
One-person households	105
Persons per household	2.71
Persons per family	3.04

Labor & Employment
Total civilian labor force, 2004**	1,034
Unemployment rate	4.2%
Total civilian labor force, 2000	877
Unemployment rate	4.8%

Employed persons 16 years and over by occupation, 2000
Managers & professionals	229
Service occupations	117
Sales & office occupations	248
Farming, fishing & forestry	2
Construction & maintenance	122
Production & transportation	117
Self-employed persons	47

*US Census Bureau
**New Jersey Department of Labor

General Information
Borough of Newfield
PO Box 856
18 Catawba Ave
Newfield, NJ 08344
856-697-1100
Web site	www.newfieldboro.com
Land area (sq. miles)	1.70
Water area (sq. miles)	0
Type of government	Borough
Form of government	B

Government

Legislative Districts
US Congressional	2
State Legislative	4

Local Officials, 2006
Mayor	Richard Westergaard
Admin/Manager	NA
Clerk	Toni Van Camp
Finance Dir/Treas	Robert Scharle
Engineer	Federici & Aikin
Attorney	John Eastlack
Tax assessor	Timothy Mead
Tax collector	Penny Carre
Building officer	Raymond Martilini
Zoning officer	NA
Public Works	NA

Housing & Construction

Housing Units, 2000*
Total	620
Median rent	$711
Median SF home value	$103,200

New Privately Owned Housing Units Authorized by Building Permit
	Units	Value
Total, 2004	4	$436,500
Single family	4	$436,500
Total, 2005	4	$449,250
Single family	4	$449,250

Real Property Valuation - parcels, 2005
	Number	Valuation
Total		$59,524,600
Vacant	92	1,358,400
Residential	558	49,422,300
Commercial	33	4,172,000
Industrial	11	2,817,700
Apartments	4	671,000
Farm land	8	969,600
Farm homestead	20	113,600

Average Property Value & Tax, 2005
Residential value	$85,702
Property tax	$3,821
FAIR rebate	$622

Public Library
Newfield Public Library
115 Catawba Ave
Newfield, NJ 08344
856-697-0415
Manager	Susan Mounier

Library statistics, 2004
	Total	per capita
Volumes	21,222	13.13
Expenditure	$29,053	$17.98

Public Safety
Police
Chief	Vincent Parisi
Number of officers, 2004	5

Crime, 2004	Number	Rate
Total	18	11.1
Violent	0	0
Non-violent	18	11.1
Domestic Viol.	16	NA

Emergency/Fire
Director	Robert Cesare

Public School District
(for school year 2004-2005 except as noted)

Newfield School District
1122 Almond Rd
Pittsgrove, NJ 08318
Superintendent	NA
Grade plan	NA
Enrollment	NA
Students per teacher	NA
Per pupil expenditure	NA
Median faculty salary	NA
Median administrator salary	NA
Grade 12 enrollment	NA
High school graduation rate	NA

Assessment test results
(percent scoring at proficient or advanced level)
	Language	Math
Grade 3	NA	NA
Grade 8	NA	NA
High school	NA	NA

SAT
Percent tested	NA
Average SAT math score	NA
Average SAT verbal score	NA

No Child Left Behind, 2003-04
Attendence rate (target = 90%)	NA
Drop rate	NA
Highly-qualified teachers	NA
District needs improvement?(AYP)	NA

Municipal Finance

Fiscal Year 2005
Total tax levy	$2,665,318
County levy	578,909
County taxes	507,645
County library	37,517
County health	0
County open space	33,747
School levy	1,515,645
Local muni. budget	570,764
Misc. revenues	717,812
Total aid	$194,824
CMPTRA	101,488
Muni. block grant	6,966
Energy tax receipts	86,370
Homeland security	0

Fiscal Year 2006
Total aid	$194,824
CMPTRA	98,465
Muni. block grant	6,966
Energy tax receipts	89,393
Homeland security	NA

Taxes
	2003	2004	2005
General tax rate per $100	3.98	4.192	4.459
Net valuation taxable	$62,101,313	$59,033,535	$59,775,582
State equalized value	$80,494,249	$82,679,839	$98,073,145
County equalization ratio	80.15	77.15	71.30

Demographics & Socio-Economic Characteristics
(2000 U.S. Census, except as noted)

Population
1980*	7,748
1990*	7,521
2000	8,244
Male	3,951
Female	4,293
2004 (estimate)*	8,382
Persons per sq. mi. of land	2,706

Race & Hispanic Origin, 2000
Race
White	7,582
Black/African American	281
Amer. Indian/Alaska Natv.	11
Asian	162
Natv. Hawaiian/Pac. Islander	1
Other Race	96
Two or more races	111
Hispanic origin, total	313
Mexican	50
Puerto Rican	129
Cuban	20
Other Hispanic	114

Age & Nativity, 2000
Under 5 years	522
18 years and over	6,271
21 years and over	5,992
65 years and over	1,284
85 years and over	225
Median Age	37.6
Native born	7,569
Foreign born	675

Educational Attainment, 2000
Population 25 years and over	5,690
0-8 yrs of school	4.7%
High School grad or higher	83.6%
Bachelor's degree or higher	19.2%
Graduate degree	6.7%

Income & Poverty, 1999
Per capita income	$20,577
Median household income	$41,667
Median family income	$56,484
Persons in poverty	882
H'holds receiving public assistance	98
H'holds receiving social security	1,049

Households, 2000
Total households	3,258
With persons under 18	1,042
With persons over 65	892
Family households	1,942
One-person households	1,093
Persons per household	2.39
Persons per family	3.12

Labor & Employment
Total civilian labor force, 2004**	4,456
Unemployment rate	4.9%
Total civilian labor force, 2000	4,152
Unemployment rate	3.3%

Employed persons 16 years and over by occupation, 2000
Managers & professionals	1,318
Service occupations	661
Sales & office occupations	1,202
Farming, fishing & forestry	0
Construction & maintenance	303
Production & transportation	532
Self-employed persons	184

*US Census Bureau
**New Jersey Department of Labor

General Information
Town of Newton
39 Trinity St
Newton, NJ 07860
973-383-3521
Web site	www.newtontownhall.com
Land area (sq. miles)	3.10
Water area (sq. miles)	0.01
Type of government	Town
Form of government	CM '50

Government

Legislative Districts
US Congressional	5
State Legislative	24

Local Officials, 2006
Mayor	Philip J. Diglio
Admin/Manager	Colin Connelly
Clerk	Lorraine Read
Finance Dir/Treas	Eileen Kithcart
Engineer	Harold Pellow
Attorney	Sanford Hollander
Tax assessor	Scott Holzhauer
Tax collector	Linda Roth
Building officer	Robert Bittle
Zoning officer	T. Linda Paolucci
Public Works	Christopher Bond

Housing & Construction

Housing Units, 2000*
Total	3,425
Median rent	$697
Median SF home value	$136,100

New Privately Owned Housing Units Authorized by Building Permit
	Units	Value
Total, 2004	32	$2,265,066
Single family	9	$2,238,316
Total, 2005	6	$594,029
Single family	1	$287,212

Real Property Valuation - parcels, 2005
	Number	Valuation
Total		$375,544,600
Vacant	88	4,386,700
Residential	1,932	245,341,000
Commercial	238	91,956,700
Industrial	12	10,204,400
Apartments	28	23,285,100
Farm land	2	313,300
Farm homestead	9	57,400

Average Property Value & Tax, 2005
Residential value	$126,429
Property tax	$5,347
FAIR rebate	$573

Public Library
Dennis Mem. Branch Library†
101 Main St
Newton, NJ 07860
973-383-4810
Branch Librarian	Debbie Mole

Library statistics, 2004
	Total	per capita
Volumes	NA	NA
Expenditure	NA	NA

†Branch of County Library

Public Safety

Police
Chief	John Tomasula
Number of officers, 2004	23

Crime, 2004	Number	Rate
Total	199	23.7
Violent	10	1.2
Non-violent	189	22.5
Domestic Viol.	108	NA

Emergency/Fire
Director	Rich Dayermanjian

Public School District
(for school year 2004-2005 except as noted)

Newton School District
57 Trinity St
Newton, NJ 07860
973-383-7392
Administrator	Mark Miller
Grade plan	K-12
Enrollment	1,746.0
Students per teacher	10.4
Per pupil expenditure	$10,891
Median faculty salary	$52,670
Median administrator salary	$101,237
Grade 12 enrollment	170.0
High school graduation rate	94.5%

Assessment test results
(percent scoring at proficient or advanced level)
	Language	Math
Grade 3	88.2%	86.3%
Grade 8	81.9%	75.0%
High school	89.6%	82.3%

SAT
Percent tested	68%
Average SAT math score	548
Average SAT verbal score	539

No Child Left Behind, 2003-04
Attendance rate (target = 90%)	93.8%
Drop rate	0.4%
Highly-qualified teachers	100%
District needs improvement?(AYP)	No

Municipal Finance

Fiscal Year 2005
Total tax levy	$16,054,340
County levy	2,577,039
County taxes	2,187,169
County library	188,543
County health	88,727
County open space	112,601
School levy	9,146,005
Local muni. budget	4,331,296
Misc. revenues	3,388,704
Total aid	$1,428,243
CMPTRA	543,853
Muni. block grant	32,910
Energy tax receipts	801,480
Homeland security	50,000

Fiscal Year 2006
Total aid	$1,428,244
CMPTRA	515,802
Muni. block grant	32,910
Energy tax receipts	829,532
Homeland security	50,000

Taxes
	2003	2004	2005
General tax rate per $100	3.70	3.950	4.230
Net valuation taxable	$368,354,572	$376,392,139	$379,632,623
State equalized value	$479,940,810	$550,698,347	$651,394,343
County equalization ratio	90.53	76.75	68.09

Demographics & Socio-Economic Characteristics
(2000 U.S. Census, except as noted)

Population
1980*	16,587
1990*	13,790
2000	15,181
Male	7,137
Female	8,044
2004 (estimate)*	15,254
Persons per sq. mi. of land	5,909

Race & Hispanic Origin, 2000
Race
White	13,603
Black/African American	70
Amer. Indian/Alaska Natv.	22
Asian	852
Natv. Hawaiian/Pac. Islander	2
Other Race	348
Two or more races	284
Hispanic origin, total	1,605
Mexican	56
Puerto Rican	390
Cuban	241
Other Hispanic	918

Age & Nativity, 2000
Under 5 years	686
18 years and over	12,445
21 years and over	12,003
65 years and over	2,942
85 years and over	361
Median Age	40.9
Native born	11,880
Foreign born	3,301

Educational Attainment, 2000
Population 25 years and over	11,252
0-8 yrs of school	6.9%
High School grad or higher	82.1%
Bachelor's degree or higher	19.5%
Graduate degree	5.2%

Income & Poverty, 1999
Per capita income	$24,441
Median household income	$51,787
Median family income	$62,483
Persons in poverty	773
H'holds receiving public assistance	114
H'holds receiving social security	2,254

Households, 2000
Total households	6,392
With persons under 18	1,669
With persons over 65	2,186
Family households	4,129
One-person households	1,977
Persons per household	2.37
Persons per family	3

Labor & Employment
Total civilian labor force, 2004**	7,861
Unemployment rate	4.3%
Total civilian labor force, 2000	7,851
Unemployment rate	4.0%

Employed persons 16 years and over by occupation, 2000
Managers & professionals	2,262
Service occupations	1,047
Sales & office occupations	2,654
Farming, fishing & forestry	0
Construction & maintenance	637
Production & transportation	939
Self-employed persons	301

*US Census Bureau
**New Jersey Department of Labor

General Information
Borough of North Arlington
214 Ridge Rd
North Arlington, NJ 07031
201-991-6060
Web site	www.northarlington.org
Land area (sq. miles)	2.58
Water area (sq. miles)	0.04
Type of government	Borough
Form of government	B

Government

Legislative Districts
US Congressional	9
State Legislative	36

Local Officials, 2006
Mayor	Russell Pitman
Admin/Manager	NA
Clerk	Martin Gobbo
Finance Dir/Treas	Judith Tutela
Engineer	Michael Neglia
Attorney	Joseph Mariniello
Tax assessor	Denis McGuire
Tax collector	NA
Building officer	Robert Kairys
Zoning officer	James Pacente
Public Works	NA

Housing & Construction

Housing Units, 2000*
Total	6,529
Median rent	$763
Median SF home value	$183,300

New Privately Owned Housing Units Authorized by Building Permit
	Units	Value
Total, 2004	13	$1,482,800
Single family	7	$1,240,200
Total, 2005	5	$531,000
Single family	5	$531,000

Real Property Valuation - parcels, 2005
	Number	Valuation
Total		$804,290,200
Vacant	66	11,998,700
Residential	3,723	659,644,200
Commercial	190	69,944,100
Industrial	52	25,247,800
Apartments	38	37,455,400
Farm land	0	0
Farm homestead	0	0

Average Property Value & Tax, 2005
Residential value	$177,181
Property tax	$6,462
FAIR rebate	$688

Public Library
N. Arlington Public Library
210 Ridge Rd
N. Arlington, NJ 07031
201-955-5640
Director	Maria Puszkar

Library statistics, 2004
	Total	per capita
Volumes	87,554	5.77
Expenditure	$574,972	$37.87

Public Safety

Police
Chief	Louis Ghione
Number of officers, 2004	35

Crime, 2004	Number	Rate
Total	151	9.9
Violent	13	0.9
Non-violent	138	9.1
Domestic Viol.	112	NA

Emergency/Fire
Director	Mark Cunningham

Public School District
(for school year 2004-2005 except as noted)

North Arlington School District
222 Ridge Rd
North Arlington, NJ 07031
201-991-6800
Superintendent	Oliver Stringham
Grade plan	K-12
Enrollment	1,550.5
Students per teacher	11.6
Per pupil expenditure	$10,913
Median faculty salary	$42,079
Median administrator salary	$99,395
Grade 12 enrollment	116.5
High school graduation rate	92.3%

Assessment test results
(percent scoring at proficient or advanced level)
	Language	Math
Grade 3	91.5%	89.7%
Grade 8	84.6%	71.1%
High school	70.3%	68.2%

SAT
Percent tested	78%
Average SAT math score	483
Average SAT verbal score	451

No Child Left Behind, 2003-04
Attendence rate (target = 90%)	94.8%
Drop rate	2.2%
Highly-qualified teachers	93.8%
District needs improvement?(AYP)	No

Municipal Finance

Fiscal Year 2005
Total tax levy	$29,366,649
County levy	2,650,013
County taxes	2,517,522
County library	0
County health	0
County open space	132,491
School levy	16,780,343
Local muni. budget	9,936,293
Misc. revenues	7,643,113
Total aid	$1,502,211
CMPTRA	456,338
Muni. block grant	60,341
Energy tax receipts	915,532
Homeland security	70,000

Fiscal Year 2006
Total aid	$1,502,211
CMPTRA	424,294
Muni. block grant	60,341
Energy tax receipts	947,576
Homeland security	70,000

Taxes
	2003	2004	2005
General tax rate per $100	3.37	3.490	3.650
Net valuation taxable	$796,546,091	$798,549,999	$805,206,400
State equalized value	$1,120,317,990	$1,308,417,330	$1,543,132,235
County equalization ratio	79.85	71.10	61.00

Demographics & Socio-Economic Characteristics
(2000 U.S. Census, except as noted)

Population
1980*	47,019
1990*	48,414
2000	58,092
Male	27,758
Female	30,334
2004 (estimate)*	58,004
Persons per sq. mi. of land	11,163

Race & Hispanic Origin, 2000
Race
White	39,131
Black/African American	1,581
Amer. Indian/Alaska Natv.	235
Asian	3,756
Natv. Hawaiian/Pac. Islander	28
Other Race	9,023
Two or more races	4,338
Hispanic origin, total	33,260
Mexican	553
Puerto Rican	4,535
Cuban	7,635
Other Hispanic	20,537

Age & Nativity, 2000
Under 5 years	3,713
18 years and over	44,887
21 years and over	42,885
65 years and over	8,028
85 years and over	1,220
Median Age	35.9
Native born	30,990
Foreign born	27,216

Educational Attainment, 2000
Population 25 years and over	39,719
0-8 yrs of school	15.4%
High School grad or higher	68.7%
Bachelor's degree or higher	19.6%
Graduate degree	7.1%

Income & Poverty, 1999
Per capita income	$20,058
Median household income	$40,844
Median family income	$46,172
Persons in poverty	6,397
H'holds receiving public assistance	669
H'holds receiving social security	5,701

Households, 2000
Total households	21,236
With persons under 18	7,481
With persons over 65	5,809
Family households	14,242
One-person households	5,890
Persons per household	2.7
Persons per family	3.33

Labor & Employment
Total civilian labor force, 2004**	27,252
Unemployment rate	5.1%
Total civilian labor force, 2000	27,526
Unemployment rate	8.1%

Employed persons 16 years and over by occupation, 2000
Managers & professionals	6,796
Service occupations	3,653
Sales & office occupations	7,958
Farming, fishing & forestry	29
Construction & maintenance	1,685
Production & transportation	5,168
Self-employed persons	1,257

*US Census Bureau
**New Jersey Department of Labor

General Information
Township of North Bergen
4233 Kennedy Blvd
North Bergen, NJ 07047
201-392-2000

Web site	www.northbergen.org
Land area (sq. miles)	5.20
Water area (sq. miles)	0.42
Type of government	Township
Form of government	Comm.

Government
Legislative Districts
US Congressional	9, 13
State Legislative	32

Local Officials, 2006
Mayor	Nicholas Sacco
Admin/Manager	Christopher Pianese
Clerk	Carol Ann Fontana
Finance Dir/Treas	Robert Pittfield
Engineer	Rick McGrath
Attorney	Herb Klitzner
Tax assessor	Paul Sadlon
Tax collector	Denise Zambardino
Building officer	Brian Ribbaro
Zoning officer	NA
Public Works	Frank Gargiulo

Housing & Construction
Housing Units, 2000*
Total	22,009
Median rent	$733
Median SF home value	$162,600

New Privately Owned Housing Units
Authorized by Building Permit
	Units	Value
Total, 2004	333	$7,322,470
Single family	15	$2,234,078
Total, 2005	372	$15,671,973
Single family	26	$3,799,024

Real Property Valuation - parcels, 2005
	Number	Valuation
Total		$2,453,161,200
Vacant	423	54,858,600
Residential	9,910	1,280,782,800
Commercial	660	626,467,600
Industrial	223	308,396,300
Apartments	174	182,655,900
Farm land	0	0
Farm homestead	0	0

Average Property Value & Tax, 2005
Residential value	$129,241
Property tax	$4,959
FAIR rebate	$623

Public Library
N. Bergen Public Library
8411 Bergenline Ave
North Bergen, NJ 07047
201-869-4715

Director ... Sai Rao

Library statistics, 2004
	Total	per capita
Volumes	226,100	3.89
Expenditure	$893,036	$15.37

Public Safety
Police
Chief	William Galvin
Number of officers, 2004	111

Crime, 2004	Number	Rate
Total	1,402	24
Violent	110	1.9
Non-violent	1,292	22.1
Domestic Viol.	617	NA

Emergency/Fire
Director ... Michael DeOrio

Public School District
(for school year 2004-2005 except as noted)

North Bergen School District
7317 Kennedy Blvd
North Bergen, NJ 07047
201-295-2706

Superintendent	Peter Fischbach
Grade plan	K-12
Enrollment	7,540.0
Students per teacher	13.9
Per pupil expenditure	$10,350
Median faculty salary	$58,800
Median administrator salary	$132,505
Grade 12 enrollment	456.0
High school graduation rate	85.8%

Assessment test results
(percent scoring at proficient or advanced level)
	Language	Math
Grade 3	76.5%	77.6%
Grade 8	74.2%	66.1%
High school	82.8%	77.7%

SAT
Percent tested	72%
Average SAT math score	447
Average SAT verbal score	428

No Child Left Behind, 2003-04
Attendence rate (target = 90%)	94.4%
Drop rate	1.9%
Highly-qualified teachers	95%
District needs improvement?(AYP)	No

Municipal Finance
Fiscal Year 2005
Total tax levy	$100,106,860
County levy	21,611,399
County taxes	21,200,580
County library	0
County health	0
County open space	410,819
School levy	35,893,117
Local muni. budget	42,602,344
Misc. revenues	22,157,636
Total aid	$9,323,696
CMPTRA	5,677,658
Muni. block grant	227,780
Energy tax receipts	3,278,258
Homeland security	140,000

Fiscal Year 2006
Total aid	$9,323,696
CMPTRA	5,562,919
Muni. block grant	227,780
Energy tax receipts	3,392,997
Homeland security	140,000

Taxes
	2003	2004	2005
General tax rate per $100	3.83	3.958	4.071
Net valuation taxable	$2,349,087,397	$2,379,353,705	$2,459,049,775
State equalized value	$3,329,205,495	$3,932,680,631	$4,794,403,929
County equalization ratio	77.26	70.56	60.42

Demographics & Socio-Economic Characteristics

(2000 U.S. Census, except as noted)

Population

1980*	22,220
1990*	31,287
2000	36,287
Male	18,021
Female	18,266
2004 (estimate)*	38,872
Persons per sq. mi. of land	3,233

Race & Hispanic Origin, 2000

Race

White	22,763
Black/African American	5,542
Amer. Indian/Alaska Natv.	63
Asian	5,152
Natv. Hawaiian/Pac. Islander	10
Other Race	1,707
Two or more races	1,050
Hispanic origin, total	3,775
Mexican	522
Puerto Rican	1,316
Cuban	161
Other Hispanic	1,776

Age & Nativity, 2000

Under 5 years	2,437
18 years and over	27,934
21 years and over	26,806
65 years and over	3,615
85 years and over	328
Median Age	35.4
Native born	27,424
Foreign born	8,863

Educational Attainment, 2000

Population 25 years and over	25,089
0-8 yrs of school	4.9%
High School grad or higher	85.8%
Bachelor's degree or higher	37.0%
Graduate degree	14.3%

Income & Poverty, 1999

Per capita income	$28,431
Median household income	$61,325
Median family income	$70,812
Persons in poverty	1,661
H'holds receiving public assistance	377
H'holds receiving social security	2,932

Households, 2000

Total households	13,635
With persons under 18	4,817
With persons over 65	2,772
Family households	9,363
One-person households	3,339
Persons per household	2.58
Persons per family	3.12

Labor & Employment

Total civilian labor force, 2004**	20,319
Unemployment rate	2.7%
Total civilian labor force, 2000	19,586
Unemployment rate	3.6%

Employed persons 16 years and over by occupation, 2000

Managers & professionals	8,736
Service occupations	1,763
Sales & office occupations	5,365
Farming, fishing & forestry	0
Construction & maintenance	990
Production & transportation	2,022
Self-employed persons	816

*US Census Bureau
**New Jersey Department of Labor

General Information

Township of North Brunswick
710 Hermann Rd
North Brunswick, NJ 08902
732-247-0922

Web site	www.northbrunswickonline.com
Land area (sq. miles)	12.02
Water area (sq. miles)	0.23
Type of government	Township
Form of government	MCA

Government

Legislative Districts

US Congressional	6
State Legislative	17

Local Officials, 2006

Mayor	Francis Womack III
Admin/Manager	Robert Lombard
Clerk	Lisa Russo
Finance Dir/Treas	R. Lombard (Actg)
Engineer	CME Assoc.
Attorney	Ronald Gordon
Tax assessor	Dianne Walker
Tax collector	NA
Building officer	Tom Paun
Zoning officer	Michael Proietti
Public Works	NA

Housing & Construction

Housing Units, 2000*

Total	13,932
Median rent	$907
Median SF home value	$179,400

New Privately Owned Housing Units Authorized by Building Permit

	Units	Value
Total, 2004	209	$11,239,652
Single family	146	$8,275,252
Total, 2005	277	$16,622,445
Single family	79	$7,528,045

Real Property Valuation - parcels, 2005

	Number	Valuation
Total		$2,457,728,500
Vacant	1,125	70,297,000
Residential	9,497	1,478,975,000
Commercial	354	382,024,400
Industrial	58	350,486,700
Apartments	30	173,989,300
Farm land	8	1,785,100
Farm homestead	10	171,000

Average Property Value & Tax, 2005

Residential value	$155,585
Property tax	$5,817
FAIR rebate	$528

Public Library

N. Brunswick Public Library
880 Hermann Rd
North Brunswick, NJ 08902
732-246-3545

Director................Cheryl McBride

Library statistics, 2004

	Total	per capita
Volumes	137,794	3.80
Expenditure	$1,166,853	$32.16

Public Safety

Police

Chief	Kenneth McCormick
Number of officers, 2004	81

Crime, 2004	Number	Rate
Total	994	25.9
Violent	79	2.1
Non-violent	915	23.8
Domestic Viol.	178	NA

Emergency/Fire

Director.................Craig Snediker

Public School District

(for school year 2004-2005 except as noted)

North Brunswick Township School District
PO Box 6016
North Brunswick, NJ 08902
732-289-3030

Superintendent	Robert Rimmer
Grade plan	K-12
Enrollment	5,458.5
Students per teacher	12.1
Per pupil expenditure	$11,012
Median faculty salary	$48,123
Median administrator salary	$99,761
Grade 12 enrollment	409.0
High school graduation rate	96.0%

Assessment test results

(percent scoring at proficient or advanced level)

	Language	Math
Grade 3	81.2%	81.2%
Grade 8	78.7%	64.2%
High school	86.5%	82.6%

SAT

Percent tested	79%
Average SAT math score	535
Average SAT verbal score	515

No Child Left Behind, 2003-04

Attendance rate (target = 90%)	94.9%
Drop rate	1.4%
Highly-qualified teachers	99%
District needs improvement?(AYP)	No

Municipal Finance

Fiscal Year 2005

Total tax levy	$92,046,755
County levy	11,545,754
County taxes	10,461,701
County library	0
County health	0
County open space	1,084,052
School levy	59,573,781
Local muni. budget	20,927,220
Misc. revenues	16,972,618
Total aid	$6,110,307
CMPTRA	2,315,879
Muni. block grant	142,282
Energy tax receipts	3,507,493
Homeland security	140,000

Fiscal Year 2006

Total aid	$6,110,307
CMPTRA	2,193,117
Muni. block grant	142,282
Energy tax receipts	3,630,255
Homeland security	140,000

Taxes

	2003	2004	2005
General tax rate per $100	3.33	3.540	3.740
Net valuation taxable	$2,439,166,006	$2,452,322,703	$2,462,025,809
State equalized value	$3,275,367,270	$3,525,474,267	$3,967,809,523
County equalization ratio	82.18	74.47	69.52

Demographics & Socio-Economic Characteristics

(2000 U.S. Census, except as noted)

Population

1980*	5,832
1990*	6,706
2000	7,375
Male	3,999
Female	3,376
2004 (estimate)*	7,354
Persons per sq. mi. of land	2,458

Race & Hispanic Origin, 2000

Race

White	5,873
Black/African American	1,070
Amer. Indian/Alaska Natv.	2
Asian	347
Natv. Hawaiian/Pac. Islander	0
Other Race	19
Two or more races	64
Hispanic origin, total	159
Mexican	19
Puerto Rican	21
Cuban	39
Other Hispanic	80

Age & Nativity, 2000

Under 5 years	431
18 years and over	5,673
21 years and over	5,441
65 years and over	801
85 years and over	48
Median Age	37.3
Native born	6,740
Foreign born	635

Educational Attainment, 2000

Population 25 years and over	4,919
0-8 yrs of school	0.7%
High School grad or higher	92.6%
Bachelor's degree or higher	58.2%
Graduate degree	29.1%

Income & Poverty, 1999

Per capita income	$48,249
Median household income	$117,395
Median family income	$125,465
Persons in poverty	75
H'holds receiving public assistance	0
H'holds receiving social security	507

Households, 2000

Total households	2,070
With persons under 18	904
With persons over 65	538
Family households	1,835
One-person households	198
Persons per household	3.02
Persons per family	3.23

Labor & Employment

Total civilian labor force, 2004**	110,944
Unemployment rate	10.1%
Total civilian labor force, 2000	3,196
Unemployment rate	2.4%

Employed persons 16 years and over by occupation, 2000

Managers & professionals	1,967
Service occupations	141
Sales & office occupations	854
Farming, fishing & forestry	0
Construction & maintenance	79
Production & transportation	77
Self-employed persons	320

*US Census Bureau
**New Jersey Department of Labor

General Information

Borough of North Caldwell
Gould Ave
North Caldwell, NJ 07006
973-228-6410

Web site	www.northcaldwell.org
Land area (sq. miles)	2.99
Water area (sq. miles)	0
Type of government	Borough
Form of government	B

Government

Legislative Districts

US Congressional	11
State Legislative	27

Local Officials, 2006

Mayor	Melvin Levine
Admin/Manager	John Kosko
Clerk	Geraldine Gibian
Finance Dir/Treas	John Kosko
Engineer	Frank Zichelli
Attorney	David Paris
Tax assessor	Nathan Peraino
Tax collector	NA
Building officer	Ronald Young
Zoning officer	NA
Public Works	NA

Housing & Construction

Housing Units, 2000*

Total	2,108
Median rent	$1,759
Median SF home value	$399,000

New Privately Owned Housing Units Authorized by Building Permit

	Units	Value
Total, 2004	6	$1,660,446
Single family	6	$1,660,446
Total, 2005	7	$4,593,382
Single family	7	$4,593,382

Real Property Valuation - parcels, 2005

	Number	Valuation
Total		$357,234,840
Vacant	56	4,201,100
Residential	2,100	346,397,640
Commercial	13	5,797,600
Industrial	2	739,600
Apartments	0	0
Farm land	1	94,900
Farm homestead	1	4,000

Average Property Value & Tax, 2005

Residential value	$164,875
Property tax	$11,895
FAIR rebate	$592

Public Library

No public municipal library.

Library statistics, 2004

	Total	per capita
Volumes	NA	NA
Expenditure	NA	NA

Public Safety

Police

Chief	Joseph Clark
Number of officers, 2004	15

Crime, 2004	Number	Rate
Total	27	3.7
Violent	1	0.1
Non-violent	26	3.5
Domestic Viol.	3	NA

Emergency/Fire

Director	John D'Ascensio

Public School District

(for school year 2004-2005 except as noted)

North Caldwell School District
132 Gould Ave
North Caldwell, NJ 07006
973-228-6439

Superintendent	Carolyn Hartley
Grade plan	K-6
Enrollment	620.0
Students per teacher	10.4
Per pupil expenditure	$11,819
Median faculty salary	$44,446
Median administrator salary	$91,000
Grade 12 enrollment	NA
High school graduation rate	NA

Assessment test results

(percent scoring at proficient or advanced level)

	Language	Math
Grade 3	95.1%	88.5%
Grade 8	NA	NA
High school	NA	NA

SAT

Percent tested	NA
Average SAT math score	NA
Average SAT verbal score	NA

No Child Left Behind, 2003-04

Attendance rate (target = 90%)	96.1%
Drop rate	NA
Highly-qualified teachers	97.3%
District needs improvement?(AYP)	No

Municipal Finance

Fiscal Year 2005

Total tax levy	$25,786,302
County levy	6,523,049
County taxes	6,386,472
County library	0
County health	0
County open space	136,577
School levy	15,139,596
Local muni. budget	4,123,658
Misc. revenues	3,029,012
Total aid	$729,002
CMPTRA	197,729
Muni. block grant	29,344
Energy tax receipts	451,929
Homeland security	50,000

Fiscal Year 2006

Total aid	$729,002
CMPTRA	181,912
Muni. block grant	29,344
Energy tax receipts	467,746
Homeland security	50,000

Taxes

	2003	2004	2005
General tax rate per $100	6.76	6.990	7.220
Net valuation taxable	$346,795,579	$351,497,234	$357,412,392
State equalized value	$1,217,253,700	$1,334,889,805	$1,513,817,840
County equalization ratio	31.75	31.75	26.32

Demographics & Socio-Economic Characteristics
(2000 U.S. Census, except as noted)

Population
1980*	8,177
1990*	7,987
2000	7,920
Male	3,737
Female	4,183
2004 (estimate)*	8,812
Persons per sq. mi. of land	2,560

Race & Hispanic Origin, 2000
Race
White	7,526
Black/African American	114
Amer. Indian/Alaska Natv.	5
Asian	79
Natv. Hawaiian/Pac. Islander	0
Other Race	75
Two or more races	121
Hispanic origin, total	308
Mexican	14
Puerto Rican	59
Cuban	36
Other Hispanic	199

Age & Nativity, 2000
Under 5 years	436
18 years and over	6,360
21 years and over	6,055
65 years and over	1,551
85 years and over	246
Median Age	40.5
Native born	6,858
Foreign born	1,062

Educational Attainment, 2000
Population 25 years and over	5,580
0-8 yrs of school	4.9%
High School grad or higher	88.1%
Bachelor's degree or higher	33.8%
Graduate degree	9.7%

Income & Poverty, 1999
Per capita income	$30,322
Median household income	$74,700
Median family income	$80,936
Persons in poverty	298
H'holds receiving public assistance	21
H'holds receiving social security	1,002

Households, 2000
Total households	2,626
With persons under 18	807
With persons over 65	977
Family households	2,076
One-person households	465
Persons per household	2.79
Persons per family	3.18

Labor & Employment
Total civilian labor force, 2004**	4,420
Unemployment rate	4.2%
Total civilian labor force, 2000	4,383
Unemployment rate	3.5%

Employed persons 16 years and over by occupation, 2000
Managers & professionals	1,818
Service occupations	725
Sales & office occupations	996
Farming, fishing & forestry	8
Construction & maintenance	398
Production & transportation	283
Self-employed persons	241

*US Census Bureau
**New Jersey Department of Labor

General Information
Borough of North Haledon
103 Overlook Ave
North Haledon, NJ 07508
973-427-7793

Web site	NA
Land area (sq. miles)	3.44
Water area (sq. miles)	0.03
Type of government	Borough
Form of government	B

Government

Legislative Districts
US Congressional	5, 8
State Legislative	35

Local Officials, 2006
Mayor	Randolph George
Admin/Manager	Lucille Debiak
Clerk	Lucille Debiak
Finance Dir/Treas	Laura Leibowitz
Engineer	Boswell McClave
Attorney	James Segreto
Tax assessor	Michael Barker
Tax collector	NA
Building officer	Philip Cheff
Zoning officer	James Booth
Public Works	NA

Housing & Construction

Housing Units, 2000*
Total	2,675
Median rent	$891
Median SF home value	$237,900

New Privately Owned Housing Units Authorized by Building Permit
	Units	Value
Total, 2004	117	$15,543,950
Single family	117	$15,543,950
Total, 2005	11	$4,483,855
Single family	11	$4,483,855

Real Property Valuation - parcels, 2005
	Number	Valuation
Total		$411,267,500
Vacant	262	13,246,700
Residential	2,716	378,280,700
Commercial	84	17,225,800
Industrial	6	2,147,700
Apartments	0	0
Farm land	2	354,800
Farm homestead	3	11,800

Average Property Value & Tax, 2005
Residential value	$139,129
Property tax	$7,170
FAIR rebate	$649

Public Library
N. Haledon Public Library
129 Overlook Ave
North Haledon, NJ 07508
973-427-6213

Director ..... Susan Serico

Library statistics, 2004
	Total	per capita
Volumes	26,892	3.40
Expenditure	$297,897	$37.61

Public Safety

Police
Chief	Robert Bracco
Number of officers, 2004	18

Crime, 2004	Number	Rate
Total	88	10.6
Violent	6	0.7
Non-violent	82	9.8
Domestic Viol.	59	NA

Emergency/Fire
Director ..... Joseph Foti

Public School District
(for school year 2004-2005 except as noted)

North Haledon School District
515 High Mountain Rd
North Haledon, NJ 07508
973-427-8993

Administrator	Charles Ferraro
Grade plan	K-8
Enrollment	637.0
Students per teacher	11.0
Per pupil expenditure	$9,989
Median faculty salary	$57,295
Median administrator salary	$110,001
Grade 12 enrollment	NA
High school graduation rate	NA

Assessment test results
(percent scoring at proficient or advanced level)
	Language	Math
Grade 3	97.2%	97.3%
Grade 8	86.5%	77.9%
High school	NA	NA

SAT
Percent tested	NA
Average SAT math score	NA
Average SAT verbal score	NA

No Child Left Behind, 2003-04
Attendance rate (target = 90%)	96.2%
Drop rate	NA
Highly-qualified teachers	100%
District needs improvement?(AYP)	No

Municipal Finance

Fiscal Year 2005
Total tax levy	$21,214,220
County levy	6,104,188
County taxes	5,988,135
County library	0
County health	0
County open space	116,053
School levy	9,022,818
Local muni. budget	6,087,214
Misc. revenues	3,152,492
Total aid	$936,940
CMPTRA	410,898
Muni. block grant	34,948
Energy tax receipts	439,966
Homeland security	50,000

Fiscal Year 2006
Total aid	$936,940
CMPTRA	395,499
Muni. block grant	34,948
Energy tax receipts	455,365
Homeland security	50,000

Taxes
	2003	2004	2005
General tax rate per $100	5.05	5.040	5.160
Net valuation taxable	$363,613,924	$390,764,673	$411,634,453
State equalized value	$901,373,138	$1,099,632,724	$1,283,149,791
County equalization ratio	45.78	40.34	35.51

Demographics & Socio-Economic Characteristics
(2000 U.S. Census, except as noted)

Population
1980*	9,050
1990*	9,994
2000	7,347
Male	3,682
Female	3,665
2004 (estimate)*	7,582
Persons per sq. mi. of land	437

Race & Hispanic Origin, 2000
Race
White	5,924
Black/African American	805
Amer. Indian/Alaska Natv.	35
Asian	156
Natv. Hawaiian/Pac. Islander	4
Other Race	160
Two or more races	263
Hispanic origin, total	423
Mexican	107
Puerto Rican	154
Cuban	21
Other Hispanic	141

Age & Nativity, 2000
Under 5 years	818
18 years and over	4,879
21 years and over	4,646
65 years and over	452
85 years and over	17
Median Age	28.7
Native born	6,967
Foreign born	358

Educational Attainment, 2000
Population 25 years and over	4,156
0-8 yrs of school	2.9%
High School grad or higher	87.0%
Bachelor's degree or higher	13.3%
Graduate degree	3.3%

Income & Poverty, 1999
Per capita income	$17,580
Median household income	$39,988
Median family income	$45,553
Persons in poverty	387
H'holds receiving public assistance	58
H'holds receiving social security	426

Households, 2000
Total households	2,498
With persons under 18	1,351
With persons over 65	350
Family households	2,020
One-person households	388
Persons per household	2.94
Persons per family	3.29

Labor & Employment
Total civilian labor force, 2004**	4,294
Unemployment rate	6.0%
Total civilian labor force, 2000	3,000
Unemployment rate	4.8%

Employed persons 16 years and over by occupation, 2000
Managers & professionals	767
Service occupations	389
Sales & office occupations	827
Farming, fishing & forestry	27
Construction & maintenance	379
Production & transportation	467
Self-employed persons	236

*US Census Bureau
**New Jersey Department of Labor

General Information
Township of North Hanover
41 Schoolhouse Rd
Jacobstown, NJ 08562
609-758-2522

Web site	www.northhanover.us
Land area (sq. miles)	17.34
Water area (sq. miles)	0.04
Type of government	Township
Form of government	TC

Government

Legislative Districts
US Congressional	4
State Legislative	30

Local Officials, 2006
Mayor	Willliam Tilton
Admin/Manager	NA
Clerk	Elaine Kennedy
Finance Dir/Treas	Veronica Gitto
Engineer	Maser Consulting
Attorney	Mark Roselli
Tax assessor	Donald Kosul
Tax collector	Dawn Mitchell
Building officer	Jeffrey Jones
Zoning officer	Benjamin Palombi
Public Works	Wayne Wharton

Housing & Construction

Housing Units, 2000*
Total	2,670
Median rent	$648
Median SF home value	$175,000

New Privately Owned Housing Units Authorized by Building Permit
	Units	Value
Total, 2004	23	$3,495,693
Single family	23	$3,495,693
Total, 2005	15	$2,936,467
Single family	15	$2,936,467

Real Property Valuation - parcels, 2005
	Number	Valuation
Total		$218,927,700
Vacant	114	4,657,100
Residential	934	159,428,750
Commercial	60	27,205,400
Industrial	0	0
Apartments	10	7,346,300
Farm land	85	17,230,300
Farm homestead	174	3,059,850

Average Property Value & Tax, 2005
Residential value	$146,650
Property tax	$3,734
FAIR rebate	$535

Public Library

No public municipal library.

Library statistics, 2004
	Total	per capita
Volumes	NA	NA
Expenditure	NA	NA

Public Safety

Police
Chief	Mark Keubler
Number of officers, 2004	8

Crime, 2004	Number	Rate
Total	74	9.8
Violent	6	0.8
Non-violent	68	9
Domestic Viol.	53	NA

Emergency/Fire
Director	Steve Taylor

Public School District
(for school year 2004-2005 except as noted)

North Hanover Township School District
46 Schoolhouse Rd
Wrightstown,NJ, NJ 08562
609-723-3050

Superintendent	Richard Carson
Grade plan	K-6
Enrollment	1,318.0
Students per teacher	9.3
Per pupil expenditure	$12,767
Median faculty salary	$48,625
Median administrator salary	$95,000
Grade 12 enrollment	NA
High school graduation rate	NA

Assessment test results
(percent scoring at proficient or advanced level)
	Language	Math
Grade 3	87.9%	79.0%
Grade 8	NA	NA
High school	NA	NA

SAT
Percent tested	NA
Average SAT math score	NA
Average SAT verbal score	NA

No Child Left Behind, 2003-04
Attendence rate (target = 90%)	95.0%
Drop rate	NA
Highly-qualified teachers	96.5%
District needs improvement?(AYP)	No

Municipal Finance

Fiscal Year 2005
Total tax levy	$5,761,189
County levy	1,404,496
County taxes	1,178,213
County library	103,169
County health	0
County open space	123,114
School levy	3,704,429
Local muni. budget	652,263
Misc. revenues	2,601,325
Total aid	$1,155,915
CMPTRA	340,122
Muni. block grant	43,731
Energy tax receipts	722,062
Homeland security	50,000

Fiscal Year 2006
Total aid	$1,155,915
CMPTRA	314,850
Muni. block grant	43,731
Energy tax receipts	747,334
Homeland security	50,000

Taxes
	2003	2004	2005
General tax rate per $100	2.45	2.529	2.625
Net valuation taxable	$211,326,570	$214,006,182	$219,617,043
State equalized value	$267,637,500	$299,090,303	$360,264,178
County equalization ratio	88.53	78.96	71.48

Demographics & Socio-Economic Characteristics
(2000 U.S. Census, except as noted)

Population
1980*	19,108
1990*	18,820
2000	21,103
Male	10,409
Female	10,694
2004 (estimate)*	21,135
Persons per sq. mi. of land	7,576

Race & Hispanic Origin, 2000
Race
White	13,307
Black/African American	2,824
Amer. Indian/Alaska Natv.	59
Asian	1,064
Natv. Hawaiian/Pac. Islander	17
Other Race	2,887
Two or more races	945
Hispanic origin, total	6,916
Mexican	332
Puerto Rican	787
Cuban	93
Other Hispanic	5,704

Age & Nativity, 2000
Under 5 years	1,654
18 years and over	15,664
21 years and over	14,959
65 years and over	1,996
85 years and over	282
Median Age	33.7
Native born	14,123
Foreign born	6,980

Educational Attainment, 2000
Population 25 years and over	13,863
0-8 yrs of school	8.3%
High School grad or higher	80.7%
Bachelor's degree or higher	26.5%
Graduate degree	9.3%

Income & Poverty, 1999
Per capita income	$22,791
Median household income	$55,322
Median family income	$62,875
Persons in poverty	1,340
H'holds receiving public assistance	112
H'holds receiving social security	1,413

Households, 2000
Total households	7,202
With persons under 18	2,899
With persons over 65	1,410
Family households	5,086
One-person households	1,673
Persons per household	2.9
Persons per family	3.4

Labor & Employment
Total civilian labor force, 2004**	13,486
Unemployment rate	4.1%
Total civilian labor force, 2000	11,554
Unemployment rate	5.1%

Employed persons 16 years and over by occupation, 2000
Managers & professionals	3,386
Service occupations	1,389
Sales & office occupations	2,908
Farming, fishing & forestry	29
Construction & maintenance	955
Production & transportation	2,300
Self-employed persons	561

*US Census Bureau
**New Jersey Department of Labor

General Information
Borough of North Plainfield
263 Somerset St
North Plainfield, NJ 07060
908-769-2900
Web site	www.northplainfield.org
Land area (sq. miles)	2.79
Water area (sq. miles)	0
Type of government	Borough
Form of government	MC '50

Government
Legislative Districts
US Congressional	7
State Legislative	22

Local Officials, 2006
Mayor	Janice Allen
Admin/Manager	David Hollod
Clerk	Gloria Pflueger
Finance Dir/Treas	Patrick DeBlasio
Engineer	Daniel Swayze
Attorney	Eric Bernstein
Tax assessor	Eugene Flaherty
Tax collector	Constance Ludden
Building officer	John Kapp
Zoning officer	James Rodino
Public Works	James Rodino

Housing & Construction
Housing Units, 2000*
Total	7,393
Median rent	$828
Median SF home value	$150,100

New Privately Owned Housing Units
Authorized by Building Permit
	Units	Value
Total, 2004	3	$793,200
Single family	3	$793,200
Total, 2005	2	$404,400
Single family	2	$404,400

Real Property Valuation - parcels, 2005
	Number	Valuation
Total		$836,343,175
Vacant	89	2,910,900
Residential	4,966	652,604,700
Commercial	244	118,305,475
Industrial	3	1,505,800
Apartments	36	61,016,300
Farm land	0	0
Farm homestead	0	0

Average Property Value & Tax, 2005
Residential value	$131,415
Property tax	$6,330
FAIR rebate	$534

Public Library
N. Plainfield Branch Library†
6 Rockview Ave
North Plainfield, NJ 07060
908-755-7909
Director	Richard Stevens

Library statistics, 2004
	Total	per capita
Volumes	NA	NA
Expenditure	NA	NA

†Branch of County Library

Public Safety
Police
Chief	William Parenti
Number of officers, 2004	48

Crime, 2004	Number	Rate
Total	546	25.9
Violent	62	2.9
Non-violent	484	22.9
Domestic Viol.	239	NA

Emergency/Fire
Director	William F. Eaton

Public School District
(for school year 2004-2005 except as noted)

North Plainfield Borough School District
33 Mountain Ave
North Plainfield, NJ 07060
908-769-6060
Superintendent	Marilyn Birnbaum
Grade plan	K-12
Enrollment	3,247.0
Students per teacher	10.0
Per pupil expenditure	$11,512
Median faculty salary	$46,990
Median administrator salary	$116,082
Grade 12 enrollment	193.0
High school graduation rate	96.9%

Assessment test results
(percent scoring at proficient or advanced level)
	Language	Math
Grade 3	68.3%	63.3%
Grade 8	43.9%	35.1%
High school	72.9%	52.5%

SAT
Percent tested	66%
Average SAT math score	487
Average SAT verbal score	478

No Child Left Behind, 2003-04
Attendence rate (target = 90%)	95.1%
Drop rate	0.8%
Highly-qualified teachers	94%
District needs improvement?(AYP)	Yes

Municipal Finance
Fiscal Year 2005
Total tax levy	$40,327,490
County levy	5,124,368
County taxes	4,245,529
County library	470,607
County health	0
County open space	408,232
School levy	24,572,043
Local muni. budget	10,631,080
Misc. revenues	5,256,676
Total aid	$2,082,911
CMPTRA	949,024
Muni. block grant	82,745
Energy tax receipts	961,142
Homeland security	90,000

Fiscal Year 2006
Total aid	$2,082,911
CMPTRA	915,384
Muni. block grant	82,745
Energy tax receipts	994,782
Homeland security	90,000

Taxes
	2003	2004	2005
General tax rate per $100	3.92	4.300	4.820
Net valuation taxable	$834,167,799	$834,979,108	$837,171,163
State equalized value	$1,176,375,404	$1,352,439,745	$1,609,325,573
County equalization ratio	81.43	70.91	61.71

Demographics & Socio-Economic Characteristics
(2000 U.S. Census, except as noted)

Population
1980*	4,714
1990*	5,017
2000	4,935
Male	2,369
Female	2,566
2004 (estimate)*	4,801
Persons per sq. mi. of land	2,719

Race & Hispanic Origin, 2000
Race
White	4,768
Black/African American	40
Amer. Indian/Alaska Natv.	4
Asian	28
Natv. Hawaiian/Pac. Islander	1
Other Race	38
Two or more races	56
Hispanic origin, total	96
Mexican	3
Puerto Rican	64
Cuban	0
Other Hispanic	29

Age & Nativity, 2000
Under 5 years	195
18 years and over	4,086
21 years and over	3,956
65 years and over	1,168
85 years and over	112
Median Age	47.2
Native born	4,706
Foreign born	229

Educational Attainment, 2000
Population 25 years and over	3,807
0-8 yrs of school	5.1%
High School grad or higher	82.3%
Bachelor's degree or higher	13.4%
Graduate degree	3.8%

Income & Poverty, 1999
Per capita income	$19,656
Median household income	$32,582
Median family income	$46,250
Persons in poverty	575
H'holds receiving public assistance	67
H'holds receiving social security	991

Households, 2000
Total households	2,309
With persons under 18	476
With persons over 65	869
Family households	1,394
One-person households	804
Persons per household	2.14
Persons per family	2.73

Labor & Employment
Total civilian labor force, 2004**	3,018
Unemployment rate	13.7%
Total civilian labor force, 2000	2,285
Unemployment rate	13.7%

Employed persons 16 years and over by occupation, 2000
Managers & professionals	561
Service occupations	466
Sales & office occupations	624
Farming, fishing & forestry	12
Construction & maintenance	200
Production & transportation	110
Self-employed persons	108

*US Census Bureau
**New Jersey Department of Labor

General Information
City of North Wildwood
901 Atlantic Ave
North Wildwood, NJ 08260
609-522-2030

Web site	www.northwildwood.com
Land area (sq. miles)	1.77
Water area (sq. miles)	0.36
Type of government	City
Form of government	C

Government

Legislative Districts
US Congressional	2
State Legislative	1

Local Officials, 2006
Mayor	William J. Henfey
Admin/Manager	Ray Townsend
Clerk	Janet Harkins
Finance Dir/Treas	Ross Versaggi
Engineer	Ralph Petrella Jr.
Attorney	William Kaufmann
Tax assessor	Joseph Gallagher
Tax collector	Todd Burkey
Building officer	Mario Zaccaria
Zoning officer	NA
Public Works	Harry Wozunk

Housing & Construction

Housing Units, 2000*
Total	7,411
Median rent	$634
Median SF home value	$129,600

New Privately Owned Housing Units
Authorized by Building Permit
	Units	Value
Total, 2004	235	$19,314,683
Single family	65	$6,827,807
Total, 2005	351	$44,091,995
Single family	53	$8,625,870

Real Property Valuation - parcels, 2005
	Number	Valuation
Total		$794,533,800
Vacant	191	10,820,200
Residential	6,093	645,436,400
Commercial	260	118,183,700
Industrial	0	0
Apartments	98	20,093,500
Farm land	0	0
Farm homestead	0	0

Average Property Value & Tax, 2005
Residential value	$105,931
Property tax	$2,708
FAIR rebate	$796

Public Library
No public municipal library.

Library statistics, 2004
	Total	per capita
Volumes	NA	NA
Expenditure	NA	NA

Public Safety
Police
Chief	Robert Matteucci
Number of officers, 2004	29

Crime, 2004	Number	Rate
Total	313	64.5
Violent	24	4.9
Non-violent	289	59.5
Domestic Viol.	68	NA

Emergency/Fire
Director	Paul Evangelista

Public School District
(for school year 2004-2005 except as noted)

North Wildwood City School District
1201 Atlantic Ave
North Wildwood, NJ 08260
609-522-6885

Superintendent	Michael Buccialia
Grade plan	K-12
Enrollment	341.5
Students per teacher	7.1
Per pupil expenditure	$17,034
Median faculty salary	$47,298
Median administrator salary	$73,789
Grade 12 enrollment	NA
High school graduation rate	NA

Assessment test results
(percent scoring at proficient or advanced level)
	Language	Math
Grade 3	91.2%	100%
Grade 8	62.5%	60.0%
High school	NA	NA

SAT
Percent tested	NA
Average SAT math score	NA
Average SAT verbal score	NA

No Child Left Behind, 2003-04
Attendence rate (target = 90%)	92.2%
Drop rate	NA
Highly-qualified teachers	99%
District needs improvement?(AYP)	No

Municipal Finance

Fiscal Year 2005
Total tax levy	$20,321,535
County levy	4,112,067
County taxes	3,456,725
County library	487,347
County health	0
County open space	167,995
School levy	5,763,582
Local muni. budget	10,445,887
Misc. revenues	8,650,705
Total aid	$659,945
CMPTRA	195,703
Muni. block grant	21,952
Energy tax receipts	417,290
Homeland security	25,000

Fiscal Year 2006
Total aid	$659,945
CMPTRA	181,098
Muni. block grant	21,952
Energy tax receipts	431,895
Homeland security	25,000

Taxes
	2003	2004	2005
General tax rate per $100	2.62	2.580	2.560
Net valuation taxable	$688,182,456	$731,084,474	$794,912,099
State equalized value	$1,204,801,218	$1,544,433,059	$1,975,918,715
County equalization ratio	72.06	57.12	47.32

Demographics & Socio-Economic Characteristics

(2000 U.S. Census, except as noted)

Population

1980*	7,795
1990*	7,305
2000	7,725
Male	3,679
Female	4,046
2004 (estimate)*	8,054
Persons per sq. mi. of land	2,351

Race & Hispanic Origin, 2000

Race

White	7,070
Black/African American	205
Amer. Indian/Alaska Natv.	8
Asian	193
Natv. Hawaiian/Pac. Islander	6
Other Race	140
Two or more races	103
Hispanic origin, total	338
Mexican	18
Puerto Rican	90
Cuban	14
Other Hispanic	216

Age & Nativity, 2000

Under 5 years	417
18 years and over	5,755
21 years and over	5,578
65 years and over	1,373
85 years and over	182
Median Age	40.4
Native born	7,284
Foreign born	441

Educational Attainment, 2000

Population 25 years and over	5,374
0-8 yrs of school	3.4%
High School grad or higher	87.5%
Bachelor's degree or higher	22.5%
Graduate degree	5.0%

Income & Poverty, 1999

Per capita income	$25,059
Median household income	$56,875
Median family income	$62,896
Persons in poverty	420
H'holds receiving public assistance	21
H'holds receiving social security	897

Households, 2000

Total households	2,824
With persons under 18	1,068
With persons over 65	879
Family households	2,110
One-person households	597
Persons per household	2.66
Persons per family	3.11

Labor & Employment

Total civilian labor force, 2004**	4,125
Unemployment rate	2.7%
Total civilian labor force, 2000	3,947
Unemployment rate	3.3%

Employed persons 16 years and over by occupation, 2000

Managers & professionals	1,171
Service occupations	1,104
Sales & office occupations	959
Farming, fishing & forestry	0
Construction & maintenance	307
Production & transportation	277
Self-employed persons	247

*US Census Bureau
**New Jersey Department of Labor

General Information

City of Northfield
1600 Shore Rd
Northfield, NJ 08225
609-641-2832

Web site	www.northfield-nj.com
Land area (sq. miles)	3.43
Water area (sq. miles)	0.02
Type of government	City
Form of government	C

Government

Legislative Districts

US Congressional	2
State Legislative	2

Local Officials, 2006

Mayor	Frank Perri Jr.
Admin/Manager	Jeffrey Bruckler
Clerk	Carol A. Raph
Finance Dir/Treas	Marilyn Dolcy
Engineer	Matt Doran
Attorney	Keith Bonchi
Tax assessor	Mark Sykes
Tax collector	Cindy Ruffo
Building officer	Richard Stevens
Zoning officer	Michael Dattalo
Public Works	NA

Housing & Construction

Housing Units, 2000*

Total	2,922
Median rent	$783
Median SF home value	$128,100

New Privately Owned Housing Units Authorized by Building Permit

	Units	Value
Total, 2004	18	$2,103,689
Single family	18	$2,103,689
Total, 2005	40	$4,450,126
Single family	40	$4,450,126

Real Property Valuation - parcels, 2005

	Number	Valuation
Total		$530,431,500
Vacant	291	17,428,100
Residential	3,049	394,253,600
Commercial	212	117,850,600
Industrial	0	0
Apartments	3	542,900
Farm land	1	352,700
Farm homestead	1	3,600

Average Property Value & Tax, 2005

Residential value	$129,265
Property tax	$4,710
FAIR rebate	$604

Public Library

Otto Bruyns Public Library
241 West Mill Rd
Northfield, NJ 08225
856-646-4476

Director............ Margaret Derescavage

Library statistics, 2004

	Total	per capita
Volumes	28,579	3.70
Expenditure	$182,262	$23.59

Public Safety

Police

Chief	Robert Carty (Actg)
Number of officers, 2004	21

Crime, 2004	Number	Rate
Total	131	16.5
Violent	11	1.4
Non-violent	120	15.1
Domestic Viol.	68	NA

Emergency/Fire

Director............ Henry Martinelli

Public School District

(for school year 2004-2005 except as noted)

Northfield City School District
2000 New Rd
Northfield, NJ 08225
609-407-4000

Superintendent	Richard Stepura
Grade plan	K-8
Enrollment	1,219.0
Students per teacher	14.5
Per pupil expenditure	$8,798
Median faculty salary	$44,341
Median administrator salary	$85,000
Grade 12 enrollment	NA
High school graduation rate	NA

Assessment test results

(percent scoring at proficient or advanced level)

	Language	Math
Grade 3	84.6%	85.5%
Grade 8	79.4%	72.5%
High school	NA	NA

SAT

Percent tested	NA
Average SAT math score	NA
Average SAT verbal score	NA

No Child Left Behind, 2003-04

Attendence rate (target = 90%)	94.6%
Drop rate	NA
Highly-qualified teachers	100%
District needs improvement?(AYP)	No

Municipal Finance

Fiscal Year 2005

Total tax levy	$19,374,458
County levy	2,986,572
County taxes	2,680,819
County library	0
County health	146,109
County open space	159,643
School levy	11,011,856
Local muni. budget	5,376,030
Misc. revenues	4,664,014
Total aid	$960,520
CMPTRA	361,131
Muni. block grant	31,965
Energy tax receipts	517,424
Homeland security	50,000

Fiscal Year 2006

Total aid	$960,520
CMPTRA	343,021
Muni. block grant	31,965
Energy tax receipts	535,534
Homeland security	50,000

Taxes

	2003	2004	2005
General tax rate per $100	3.32	3.515	3.644
Net valuation taxable	$515,393,312	$528,078,932	$531,748,155
State equalized value	$685,545,773	$789,058,861	$965,410,594
County equalization ratio	86.63	75.18	66.86

Demographics & Socio-Economic Characteristics

(2000 U.S. Census, except as noted)

Population

1980*	5,046
1990*	4,563
2000	4,460
Male	2,222
Female	2,238
2004 (estimate)*	4,571
Persons per sq. mi. of land	3,465

Race & Hispanic Origin, 2000

Race

White	3,698
Black/African American	34
Amer. Indian/Alaska Natv.	3
Asian	627
Natv. Hawaiian/Pac. Islander	0
Other Race	52
Two or more races	46
Hispanic origin, total	211
Mexican	3
Puerto Rican	36
Cuban	47
Other Hispanic	125

Age & Nativity, 2000

Under 5 years	256
18 years and over	3,458
21 years and over	3,328
65 years and over	713
85 years and over	70
Median Age	40.2
Native born	3,586
Foreign born	866

Educational Attainment, 2000

Population 25 years and over	3,190
0-8 yrs of school	4.3%
High School grad or higher	87.2%
Bachelor's degree or higher	29.6%
Graduate degree	10.8%

Income & Poverty, 1999

Per capita income	$28,206
Median household income	$72,500
Median family income	$81,153
Persons in poverty	171
H'holds receiving public assistance	31
H'holds receiving social security	512

Households, 2000

Total households	1,575
With persons under 18	572
With persons over 65	520
Family households	1,237
One-person households	291
Persons per household	2.83
Persons per family	3.21

Labor & Employment

Total civilian labor force, 2004**	2,971
Unemployment rate	2.3%
Total civilian labor force, 2000	2,456
Unemployment rate	2.3%

Employed persons 16 years and over by occupation, 2000

Managers & professionals	987
Service occupations	343
Sales & office occupations	674
Farming, fishing & forestry	0
Construction & maintenance	258
Production & transportation	137
Self-employed persons	82

*US Census Bureau
**New Jersey Department of Labor

General Information

Borough of Northvale
116 Paris Ave
Northvale, NJ 07647
201-767-3330

Web site	www.boroughofnorthvale.com
Land area (sq. miles)	1.32
Water area (sq. miles)	0
Type of government	Borough
Form of government	B

Government

Legislative Districts

US Congressional	5
State Legislative	39

Local Officials, 2006

Mayor	John E. Rooney
Admin/Manager	NA
Clerk	Wanda Worner
Finance Dir/Treas	Ann-Marie Mancuso
Engineer	Louis Raimondi
Attorney	Dwight deStefan
Tax assessor	John Guercio
Tax collector	Suzanne Burroughs
Building officer	Nick Lepore
Zoning officer	NA
Public Works	Edward Keegan

Housing & Construction

Housing Units, 2000*

Total	1,596
Median rent	$871
Median SF home value	$246,100

New Privately Owned Housing Units Authorized by Building Permit

	Units	Value
Total, 2004	8	$1,577,212
Single family	8	$1,577,212
Total, 2005	11	$2,248,484
Single family	11	$2,248,484

Real Property Valuation - parcels, 2005

	Number	Valuation
Total		$475,408,600
Vacant	70	5,809,500
Residential	1,424	316,692,200
Commercial	79	42,365,600
Industrial	59	110,541,300
Apartments	0	0
Farm land	0	0
Farm homestead	0	0

Average Property Value & Tax, 2005

Residential value	$222,396
Property tax	$7,289
FAIR rebate	$619

Public Library

Northvale Public Library
116 Paris Ave
Northvale, NJ 07647
201-768-4784

Director ... Virginia Beckman

Library statistics, 2004

	Total	per capita
Volumes	35,037	7.86
Expenditure	$221,254	$49.61

Public Safety

Police

Chief	Edward Giannotti
Number of officers, 2004	15

Crime, 2004	Number	Rate
Total	34	7.5
Violent	0	0
Non-violent	34	7.5
Domestic Viol.	10	NA

Emergency/Fire

Director	Joseph DeSena

Public School District

(for school year 2004-2005 except as noted)

Northvale School District
441 Tappan Rd
Northvale, NJ 07647
201-768-8484

Superintendent	Sylvan Hershey
Grade plan	K-8
Enrollment	604.0
Students per teacher	12.4
Per pupil expenditure	$10,984
Median faculty salary	$54,733
Median administrator salary	$101,500
Grade 12 enrollment	NA
High school graduation rate	NA

Assessment test results

(percent scoring at proficient or advanced level)

	Language	Math
Grade 3	92.2%	83.1%
Grade 8	91.2%	82.7%
High school	NA	NA

SAT

Percent tested	NA
Average SAT math score	NA
Average SAT verbal score	NA

No Child Left Behind, 2003-04

Attendance rate (target = 90%)	96.7%
Drop rate	NA
Highly-qualified teachers	71.6%
District needs improvement?(AYP)	No

Municipal Finance

Fiscal Year 2005

Total tax levy	$15,596,977
County levy	1,605,691
County taxes	1,525,411
County library	0
County health	0
County open space	80,280
School levy	9,926,078
Local muni. budget	4,065,208
Misc. revenues	2,693,939
Total aid	$839,532
CMPTRA	373,380
Muni. block grant	19,966
Energy tax receipts	421,186
Homeland security	25,000

Fiscal Year 2006

Total aid	$839,532
CMPTRA	358,639
Muni. block grant	19,966
Energy tax receipts	435,927
Homeland security	25,000

Taxes

	2003	2004	2005
General tax rate per $100	2.95	3.120	3.280
Net valuation taxable	$471,610,603	$473,468,790	$475,861,687
State equalized value	$695,180,724	$789,375,708	$859,421,504
County equalization ratio	79.58	67.84	59.95

Demographics & Socio-Economic Characteristics
(2000 U.S. Census, except as noted)

Population
1980*	4,413
1990*	4,858
2000	5,751
Male	2,704
Female	3,047
2004 (estimate)*	6,223
Persons per sq. mi. of land	2,263

Race & Hispanic Origin, 2000
Race
White	4,478
Black/African American	48
Amer. Indian/Alaska Natv.	1
Asian	1,092
Natv. Hawaiian/Pac. Islander	0
Other Race	54
Two or more races	78
Hispanic origin, total	172
Mexican	9
Puerto Rican	26
Cuban	39
Other Hispanic	98

Age & Nativity, 2000
Under 5 years	320
18 years and over	4,269
21 years and over	4,104
65 years and over	896
85 years and over	186
Median Age	40.8
Native born	4,465
Foreign born	1,286

Educational Attainment, 2000
Population 25 years and over	3,900
0-8 yrs of school	2.8%
High School grad or higher	91.0%
Bachelor's degree or higher	42.8%
Graduate degree	14.2%

Income & Poverty, 1999
Per capita income	$40,039
Median household income	$92,447
Median family income	$100,329
Persons in poverty	271
H'holds receiving public assistance	15
H'holds receiving social security	436

Households, 2000
Total households	1,857
With persons under 18	799
With persons over 65	484
Family households	1,563
One-person households	254
Persons per household	2.97
Persons per family	3.26

Labor & Employment
Total civilian labor force, 2004**	2,671
Unemployment rate	1.9%
Total civilian labor force, 2000	2,654
Unemployment rate	4.1%

Employed persons 16 years and over by occupation, 2000
Managers & professionals	1,288
Service occupations	291
Sales & office occupations	688
Farming, fishing & forestry	0
Construction & maintenance	161
Production & transportation	118
Self-employed persons	263

*US Census Bureau
**New Jersey Department of Labor

General Information
Borough of Norwood
455 Broadway
Norwood, NJ 07648
201-767-7200

Web site	www.norwoodboro.org
Land area (sq. miles)	2.75
Water area (sq. miles)	0.01
Type of government	Borough
Form of government	B

Government

Legislative Districts
US Congressional	5
State Legislative	39

Local Officials, 2006
Mayor	Michael Kaplan
Admin/Manager	Lorraine McMackin
Clerk	Lorraine McMackin
Finance Dir/Treas	Maureen Neville
Engineer	Joseph Neglia
Attorney	Andrew Fede
Tax assessor	John Guercio
Tax collector	Maureen Neville
Building officer	Nick Lapore (Actg)
Zoning officer	NA
Public Works	NA

Housing & Construction

Housing Units, 2000*
Total	1,888
Median rent	$1,086
Median SF home value	$345,100

New Privately Owned Housing Units Authorized by Building Permit
	Units	Value
Total, 2004	21	$5,923,710
Single family	21	$5,923,710
Total, 2005	20	$6,796,123
Single family	20	$6,796,123

Real Property Valuation - parcels, 2005
	Number	Valuation
Total		$726,231,000
Vacant	77	7,983,000
Residential	1,785	620,563,200
Commercial	53	37,222,200
Industrial	42	50,865,200
Apartments	1	9,573,800
Farm land	0	0
Farm homestead	1	23,600

Average Property Value & Tax, 2005
Residential value	$347,473
Property tax	$9,583
FAIR rebate	$626

Public Library
Norwood Public Library
198 Summit St
Norwood, NJ 07648
201-768-9555

Director.................David Beckman

Library statistics, 2004
	Total	per capita
Volumes	26,393	4.59
Expenditure	$247,925	$43.11

Public Safety
Police
Chief	Jeffrey Krapels
Number of officers, 2004	14

Crime, 2004	Number	Rate
Total	49	8
Violent	6	1
Non-violent	43	7
Domestic Viol.	0	NA

Emergency/Fire
Director.................Robert Abbott

Public School District
(for school year 2004-2005 except as noted)

Norwood School District
177 Summit St
Norwood, NJ 07648
201-768-6363

Superintendent	Andrew Rose
Grade plan	K-8
Enrollment	639.0
Students per teacher	12.7
Per pupil expenditure	$11,091
Median faculty salary	$53,250
Median administrator salary	$118,052
Grade 12 enrollment	NA
High school graduation rate	NA

Assessment test results
(percent scoring at proficient or advanced level)
	Language	Math
Grade 3	98.5%	96.9%
Grade 8	88.2%	87.1%
High school	NA	NA

SAT
Percent tested	NA
Average SAT math score	NA
Average SAT verbal score	NA

No Child Left Behind, 2003-04
Attendence rate (target = 90%)	95.7%
Drop rate	NA
Highly-qualified teachers	98.2%
District needs improvement?(AYP)	No

Municipal Finance

Fiscal Year 2005
Total tax levy	$20,046,753
County levy	2,211,835
County taxes	2,101,262
County library	0
County health	0
County open space	110,574
School levy	12,997,355
Local muni. budget	4,837,563
Misc. revenues	2,277,876
Total aid	$847,056
CMPTRA	172,439
Muni. block grant	22,550
Energy tax receipts	596,333
Homeland security	50,000

Fiscal Year 2006
Total aid	$847,056
CMPTRA	151,567
Muni. block grant	22,550
Energy tax receipts	617,205
Homeland security	50,000

Taxes
	2003	2004	2005
General tax rate per $100	2.60	2.670	2.760
Net valuation taxable	$696,938,279	$716,727,386	$726,919,386
State equalized value	$968,373,321	$1,087,510,379	$1,246,218,731
County equalization ratio	77.86	71.97	65.88

Demographics & Socio-Economic Characteristics
(2000 U.S. Census, except as noted)

Population
1980*	28,998
1990*	27,099
2000	27,362
Male	12,912
Female	14,450
2004 (estimate)*	27,875
Persons per sq. mi. of land	8,275

Race & Hispanic Origin, 2000
Race
White	24,064
Black/African American	511
Amer. Indian/Alaska Natv.	15
Asian	1,943
Natv. Hawaiian/Pac. Islander	10
Other Race	480
Two or more races	339
Hispanic origin, total	1,830
Mexican	72
Puerto Rican	585
Cuban	178
Other Hispanic	995

Age & Nativity, 2000
Under 5 years	1,510
18 years and over	21,396
21 years and over	20,686
65 years and over	4,402
85 years and over	476
Median Age	39.3
Native born	23,350
Foreign born	4,012

Educational Attainment, 2000
Population 25 years and over	19,689
0-8 yrs of school	4.4%
High School grad or higher	86.5%
Bachelor's degree or higher	32.9%
Graduate degree	10.5%

Income & Poverty, 1999
Per capita income	$28,039
Median household income	$59,634
Median family income	$73,264
Persons in poverty	1,312
H'holds receiving public assistance	128
H'holds receiving social security	3,273

Households, 2000
Total households	10,884
With persons under 18	3,401
With persons over 65	3,261
Family households	7,371
One-person households	3,036
Persons per household	2.51
Persons per family	3.11

Labor & Employment
Total civilian labor force, 2004**	2,994
Unemployment rate	1.4%
Total civilian labor force, 2000	14,709
Unemployment rate	3.8%

Employed persons 16 years and over by occupation, 2000
Managers & professionals	5,815
Service occupations	1,578
Sales & office occupations	4,460
Farming, fishing & forestry	0
Construction & maintenance	1,048
Production & transportation	1,254
Self-employed persons	736

*US Census Bureau
**New Jersey Department of Labor

General Information
Township of Nutley
1 Kennedy Dr
Nutley, NJ 07110
973-284-4951

Web site	NA
Land area (sq. miles)	3.37
Water area (sq. miles)	0.06
Type of government	Township
Form of government	Comm.

Government

Legislative Districts
US Congressional	8
State Legislative	36

Local Officials, 2006
Mayor	Joanne Cocchiola
Admin/Manager	NA
Clerk	Evelyn Rosario
Finance Dir/Treas	Rosemary Costa
Engineer	Pennoni Assoc.
Attorney	Kevin Harkins
Tax assessor	George Librizzi
Tax collector	NA
Building officer	William Spiezio
Zoning officer	NA
Public Works	NA

Housing & Construction

Housing Units, 2000*
Total	11,118
Median rent	$814
Median SF home value	$190,500

New Privately Owned Housing Units
Authorized by Building Permit
	Units	Value
Total, 2004	0	$8,500
Single family	0	$8,500
Total, 2005	9	$1,219,041
Single family	6	$1,190,041

Real Property Valuation - parcels, 2005
	Number	Valuation
Total		$517,141,500
Vacant	192	1,674,300
Residential	8,262	386,726,300
Commercial	448	40,693,900
Industrial	33	68,394,900
Apartments	68	19,652,100
Farm land	0	0
Farm homestead	0	0

Average Property Value & Tax, 2005
Residential value	$46,808
Property tax	$7,327
FAIR rebate	$596

Public Library
Nutley Public Library
93 Booth Dr
Nutley, NJ 07110
973-667-0405
Director.................. JoAnn Tropiano

Library statistics, 2004
	Total	per capita
Volumes	84,755	3.10
Expenditure	$1,130,134	$41.30

Public Safety

Police
Chief	John Holland
Number of officers, 2004	63

Crime, 2004	Number	Rate
Total	403	14.3
Violent	42	1.5
Non-violent	361	12.9
Domestic Viol.	146	NA

Emergency/Fire
Director.................. Thomas Peters

Public School District
(for school year 2004-2005 except as noted)

Nutley School District
375 Bloomfield Ave
Nutley, NJ 07110
973-661-8798
Superintendent	Joseph Zarra
Grade plan	K-12
Enrollment	4,253.0
Students per teacher	13.1
Per pupil expenditure	$9,959
Median faculty salary	$59,524
Median administrator salary	$105,028
Grade 12 enrollment	292.0
High school graduation rate	96.0%

Assessment test results
(percent scoring at proficient or advanced level)
	Language	Math
Grade 3	93.9%	92.0%
Grade 8	80.2%	71.8%
High school	89.3%	87.4%

SAT
Percent tested	88%
Average SAT math score	525
Average SAT verbal score	510

No Child Left Behind, 2003-04
Attendence rate (target = 90%)	94.9%
Drop rate	0.9%
Highly-qualified teachers	100%
District needs improvement?(AYP)	No

Municipal Finance

Fiscal Year 2005
Total tax levy	$81,090,119
County levy	16,835,016
County taxes	16,482,514
County library	0
County health	0
County open space	352,502
School levy	38,612,253
Local muni. budget	25,642,850
Misc. revenues	11,784,674
Total aid	$3,492,659
CMPTRA	1,529,720
Muni. block grant	118,576
Energy tax receipts	1,754,363
Homeland security	90,000

Fiscal Year 2006
Total aid	$3,492,659
CMPTRA	1,468,317
Muni. block grant	118,576
Energy tax receipts	1,815,766
Homeland security	90,000

Taxes
	2003	2004	2005
General tax rate per $100	13.75	14.170	15.660
Net valuation taxable	$512,703,027	$518,787,337	$518,053,700
State equalized value	$2,832,613,409	$3,487,586,526	$3,912,792,296
County equalization ratio	21.21	21.21	14.85

Demographics & Socio-Economic Characteristics

(2000 U.S. Census, except as noted)

Population

1980*	13,443
1990*	11,997
2000	12,466
Male	6,090
Female	6,376
2004 (estimate)*	13,707
Persons per sq. mi. of land	1,593

Race & Hispanic Origin, 2000

Race
White	11,813
Black/African American	97
Amer. Indian/Alaska Natv.	8
Asian	337
Natv. Hawaiian/Pac. Islander	1
Other Race	87
Two or more races	123
Hispanic origin, total	483
Mexican	49
Puerto Rican	146
Cuban	62
Other Hispanic	226

Age & Nativity, 2000

Under 5 years	970
18 years and over	9,294
21 years and over	9,012
65 years and over	1,584
85 years and over	193
Median Age	38.9
Native born	11,316
Foreign born	1,150

Educational Attainment, 2000

Population 25 years and over	8,707
0-8 yrs of school	2.6%
High School grad or higher	92.5%
Bachelor's degree or higher	41.4%
Graduate degree	14.8%

Income & Poverty, 1999

Per capita income	$35,252
Median household income	$86,629
Median family income	$93,695
Persons in poverty	206
H'holds receiving public assistance	57
H'holds receiving social security	959

Households, 2000

Total households	4,255
With persons under 18	1,730
With persons over 65	992
Family households	3,567
One-person households	545
Persons per household	2.88
Persons per family	3.15

Labor & Employment

Total civilian labor force, 2004**	7,354
Unemployment rate	2.7%
Total civilian labor force, 2000	6,847
Unemployment rate	2.9%

Employed persons 16 years and over by occupation, 2000
Managers & professionals	3,151
Service occupations	531
Sales & office occupations	1,988
Farming, fishing & forestry	0
Construction & maintenance	580
Production & transportation	399
Self-employed persons	390

*US Census Bureau
**New Jersey Department of Labor

General Information

Borough of Oakland
One Municipal Plaza
Oakland, NJ 07436
201-337-8111

Web site	www.oakland-nj.org
Land area (sq. miles)	8.60
Water area (sq. miles)	0.15
Type of government	Borough
Form of government	B

Government

Legislative Districts

US Congressional	5
State Legislative	40

Local Officials, 2006

Mayor	John P. Szabo Jr.
Admin/Manager	Charles M. Smiley Jr.
Clerk	Lisa Duncan
Finance Dir/Treas	Steven Schwager
Engineer	James Kelly
Attorney	Brian Chewcaskie
Tax assessor	Scott Holzhauer
Tax collector	Alice Li
Building officer	Joseph Montemarano
Zoning officer	Robert Porrino
Public Works	Anthony Marcucilli

Housing & Construction

Housing Units, 2000*

Total	4,345
Median rent	$1,173
Median SF home value	$245,300

New Privately Owned Housing Units Authorized by Building Permit

	Units	Value
Total, 2004	8	$2,460,939
Single family	8	$2,460,939
Total, 2005	2	$1,141,700
Single family	2	$1,141,700

Real Property Valuation - parcels, 2005

	Number	Valuation
Total		$2,522,361,600
Vacant	198	57,551,100
Residential	4,411	2,113,284,400
Commercial	139	174,470,800
Industrial	57	172,170,700
Apartments	0	0
Farm land	5	4,855,200
Farm homestead	9	29,400

Average Property Value & Tax, 2005

Residential value	$478,125
Property tax	$7,972
FAIR rebate	$540

Public Library

Oakland Public Library
Municipal Plaza
Oakland, NJ 07436
201-337-3742

Director	Thomas Coyle

Library statistics, 2004

	Total	per capita
Volumes	58,100	4.66
Expenditure	$679,041	$54.47

Public Safety

Police

Chief	James O'Connor
Number of officers, 2004	30

Crime, 2004	Number	Rate
Total	118	8.7
Violent	8	0.6
Non-violent	110	8.1
Domestic Viol.	59	NA

Emergency/Fire

Director	Steven Milano

Public School District

(for school year 2004-2005 except as noted)

Oakland School District
315 Ramapo Valley Rd
Oakland, NJ 07436
201-337-6156

Superintendent	Richard Heflich
Grade plan	K-8
Enrollment	1,700.0
Students per teacher	11.2
Per pupil expenditure	$12,486
Median faculty salary	$50,740
Median administrator salary	$126,059
Grade 12 enrollment	NA
High school graduation rate	NA

Assessment test results

(percent scoring at proficient or advanced level)
	Language	Math
Grade 3	97.4%	92.7%
Grade 8	96.1%	87.9%
High school	NA	NA

SAT

Percent tested	NA
Average SAT math score	NA
Average SAT verbal score	NA

No Child Left Behind, 2003-04

Attendence rate (target = 90%)	95.5%
Drop rate	NA
Highly-qualified teachers	99%
District needs improvement?(AYP)	No

Municipal Finance

Fiscal Year 2005

Total tax levy	$42,093,270
County levy	4,184,808
County taxes	3,974,395
County library	0
County health	0
County open space	210,413
School levy	28,330,142
Local muni. budget	9,578,321
Misc. revenues	4,872,836
Total aid	$1,822,433
CMPTRA	569,092
Muni. block grant	52,495
Energy tax receipts	1,130,846
Homeland security	70,000

Fiscal Year 2006

Total aid	$1,822,433
CMPTRA	529,512
Muni. block grant	52,495
Energy tax receipts	1,170,426
Homeland security	70,000

Taxes

	2003	2004	2005
General tax rate per $100	3.11	3.350	1.670
Net valuation taxable	$1,176,505,001	$1,176,976,017	$2,524,648,350
State equalized value	$1,872,521,090	$2,070,167,428	$2,382,867,721
County equalization ratio	69.58	62.83	120.33

Demographics & Socio-Economic Characteristics
(2000 U.S. Census, except as noted)

Population
1980*	4,223
1990*	4,430
2000	4,188
Male	2,036
Female	2,152
2004 (estimate)*	4,129
Persons per sq. mi. of land	6,728

Race & Hispanic Origin, 2000
Race
White	4,017
Black/African American	48
Amer. Indian/Alaska Natv.	9
Asian	40
Natv. Hawaiian/Pac. Islander	1
Other Race	35
Two or more races	38
Hispanic origin, total	97
Mexican	2
Puerto Rican	75
Cuban	1
Other Hispanic	19

Age & Nativity, 2000
Under 5 years	247
18 years and over	3,233
21 years and over	3,114
65 years and over	703
85 years and over	85
Median Age	38
Native born	4,104
Foreign born	64

Educational Attainment, 2000
Population 25 years and over	2,889
0-8 yrs of school	4.8%
High School grad or higher	82.5%
Bachelor's degree or higher	19.3%
Graduate degree	5.5%

Income & Poverty, 1999
Per capita income	$24,157
Median household income	$44,364
Median family income	$55,434
Persons in poverty	271
H'holds receiving public assistance	29
H'holds receiving social security	563

Households, 2000
Total households	1,791
With persons under 18	516
With persons over 65	542
Family households	1,067
One-person households	614
Persons per household	2.34
Persons per family	3.07

Labor & Employment
Total civilian labor force, 2004**	2,325
Unemployment rate	3.1%
Total civilian labor force, 2000	2,219
Unemployment rate	3.6%

Employed persons 16 years and over by occupation, 2000
Managers & professionals	696
Service occupations	251
Sales & office occupations	726
Farming, fishing & forestry	0
Construction & maintenance	271
Production & transportation	195
Self-employed persons	87

*US Census Bureau
**New Jersey Department of Labor

General Information
Borough of Oaklyn
500 White Horse Pike
Oaklyn, NJ 08107
856-858-2457
Web site	www.oaklyn-nj.com
Land area (sq. miles)	0.61
Water area (sq. miles)	0.08
Type of government	Borough
Form of government	B

Government
Legislative Districts
US Congressional	1
State Legislative	6

Local Officials, 2006
Mayor	Michael LaMaina
Admin/Manager	NA
Clerk	Marie Hawkins
Finance Dir/Treas	Denise O'Kane & J. Brun
Engineer	Key Engineers
Attorney	Timothy Higgins
Tax assessor	Anthony Leone
Tax collector	Judy Pierce
Building officer	Dan Scriboni
Zoning officer	Jack Moore
Public Works	Rich Hawco

Housing & Construction
Housing Units, 2000*
Total	1,893
Median rent	$540
Median SF home value	$98,200

New Privately Owned Housing Units Authorized by Building Permit
	Units	Value
Total, 2004	0	$0
Single family	0	$0
Total, 2005	0	$0
Single family	0	$0

Real Property Valuation - parcels, 2005
	Number	Valuation
Total		$159,160,300
Vacant	22	1,067,600
Residential	1,335	133,331,400
Commercial	73	16,218,000
Industrial	2	672,700
Apartments	18	7,870,600
Farm land	0	0
Farm homestead	0	0

Average Property Value & Tax, 2005
Residential value	$99,874
Property tax	$4,524
FAIR rebate	$573

Public Library
Oaklyn Memorial Library
602 Newton Ave
Oaklyn, NJ 08107
856-858-8226
Director	Ann Marie Latini

Library statistics, 2004
	Total	per capita
Volumes	25,581	6.11
Expenditure	$55,138	$13.17

Public Safety
Police
Chief	Jon Shelly
Number of officers, 2004	15

Crime, 2004	Number	Rate
Total	159	38.3
Violent	15	3.6
Non-violent	144	34.6
Domestic Viol.	38	NA

Emergency/Fire
Director	Fred Bartling

Public School District
(for school year 2004-2005 except as noted)

Oaklyn Borough School District
Kendall Blvd
Oaklyn, NJ 08107
856-858-1731
Superintendent	Tommie Stringer
Grade plan	K-12
Enrollment	532.0
Students per teacher	13.2
Per pupil expenditure	$9,939
Median faculty salary	$38,980
Median administrator salary	$80,066
Grade 12 enrollment	NA
High school graduation rate	NA

Assessment test results
(percent scoring at proficient or advanced level)
	Language	Math
Grade 3	74.6%	74.6%
Grade 8	75.0%	50.0%
High school	NA	NA

SAT
Percent tested	NA
Average SAT math score	NA
Average SAT verbal score	NA

No Child Left Behind, 2003-04
Attendence rate (target = 90%)	94.0%
Drop rate	0%
Highly-qualified teachers	NA
District needs improvement?(AYP)	No

Municipal Finance
Fiscal Year 2005
Total tax levy	$7,220,202
County levy	1,700,332
County taxes	1,567,007
County library	112,763
County health	0
County open space	20,563
School levy	3,542,770
Local muni. budget	1,977,100
Misc. revenues	1,678,200
Total aid	$503,762
CMPTRA	223,084
Muni. block grant	19,384
Energy tax receipts	236,294
Homeland security	25,000

Fiscal Year 2006
Total aid	$503,761
CMPTRA	214,813
Muni. block grant	19,384
Energy tax receipts	244,564
Homeland security	25,000

Taxes
	2003	2004	2005
General tax rate per $100	3.80	3.960	4.531
Net valuation taxable	$158,738,463	$159,123,454	$159,383,689
State equalized value	$180,487,167	$204,139,677	$231,696,015
County equalization ratio	96.45	87.95	77.92

Demographics & Socio-Economic Characteristics
(2000 U.S. Census, except as noted)

Population
1980*	13,949
1990*	15,512
2000	15,378
Male	7,129
Female	8,249
2004 (estimate)*	15,506
Persons per sq. mi. of land	2,241

Race & Hispanic Origin, 2000
Race
White	14,389
Black/African American	663
Amer. Indian/Alaska Natv.	18
Asian	86
Natv. Hawaiian/Pac. Islander	10
Other Race	80
Two or more races	132
Hispanic origin, total	306
Mexican	60
Puerto Rican	140
Cuban	15
Other Hispanic	91

Age & Nativity, 2000
Under 5 years	529
18 years and over	12,862
21 years and over	12,510
65 years and over	3,989
85 years and over	580
Median Age	47.8
Native born	14,817
Foreign born	561

Educational Attainment, 2000
Population 25 years and over	11,981
0-8 yrs of school	2.6%
High School grad or higher	89.5%
Bachelor's degree or higher	33.5%
Graduate degree	10.3%

Income & Poverty, 1999
Per capita income	$33,217
Median household income	$44,158
Median family income	$61,731
Persons in poverty	1,031
H'holds receiving public assistance	80
H'holds receiving social security	2,962

Households, 2000
Total households	7,464
With persons under 18	1,370
With persons over 65	2,815
Family households	4,007
One-person households	3,015
Persons per household	2.02
Persons per family	2.71

Labor & Employment
Total civilian labor force, 2004**	10,779
Unemployment rate	4.2%
Total civilian labor force, 2000	7,979
Unemployment rate	6.0%

Employed persons 16 years and over by occupation, 2000
Managers & professionals	2,871
Service occupations	1,427
Sales & office occupations	2,217
Farming, fishing & forestry	36
Construction & maintenance	499
Production & transportation	454
Self-employed persons	612

*US Census Bureau
**New Jersey Department of Labor

General Information
City of Ocean
861 Asbury Ave
Ocean, NJ 08226
609-399-6111
Web site	www.ocean-city.nj.us
Land area (sq. miles)	6.92
Water area (sq. miles)	4.16
Type of government	City
Form of government	MC '50

Government
Legislative Districts
US Congressional	2
State Legislative	1

Local Officials, 2006
Mayor	Henry Knight
Admin/Manager	Richard Deaney
Clerk	Cindy Griffith
Finance Dir/Treas	John Hansen
Engineer	George Savastano
Attorney	Gerald Corcoran
Tax assessor	Joseph Elliott
Tax collector	Gary Hink
Building officer	Patrick Newton
Zoning officer	Ken Jones
Public Works	George Savastano

Housing & Construction
Housing Units, 2000*
Total	20,298
Median rent	$722
Median SF home value	$224,700

New Privately Owned Housing Units Authorized by Building Permit
	Units	Value
Total, 2004	500	$88,767,023
Single family	117	$31,340,608
Total, 2005	534	$104,792,199
Single family	154	$45,920,095

Real Property Valuation - parcels, 2005
	Number	Valuation
Total		$7,769,332,300
Vacant	1,042	204,309,400
Residential	16,386	7,169,452,500
Commercial	558	366,767,700
Industrial	2	533,600
Apartments	44	28,269,100
Farm land	0	0
Farm homestead	0	0

Average Property Value & Tax, 2005
Residential value	$437,535
Property tax	$4,192
FAIR rebate	$761

Public Library
Ocean City Free Pub Library
1735 Simpson Ave
Ocean City, NJ 08226
609-399-2434
Director	Chirs Maloney

Library statistics, 2004
	Total	per capita
Volumes	90,673	5.9
Expenditure	$1,909,425	$124.17

Public Safety
Police
Chief	Robert Blevin
Number of officers, 2004	64

Crime, 2004	Number	Rate
Total	1,026	65.9
Violent	40	2.6
Non-violent	986	63.4
Domestic Viol.	157	NA

Emergency/Fire
Director	Joseph Foglio

Public School District
(for school year 2004-2005 except as noted)

Ocean City School District
501 Atlantic Ave
Ocean City, NJ 08226
609-399-5150
Superintendent	David H. Moyer
Grade plan	K-12
Enrollment	2,156.0
Students per teacher	9.0
Per pupil expenditure	$16,841
Median faculty salary	$81,102
Median administrator salary	$98,471
Grade 12 enrollment	308.5
High school graduation rate	95.7%

Assessment test results
(percent scoring at proficient or advanced level)
	Language	Math
Grade 3	85.1%	90.5%
Grade 8	82.0%	73.0%
High school	88.2%	83.3%

SAT
Percent tested	77%
Average SAT math score	515
Average SAT verbal score	497

No Child Left Behind, 2003-04
Attendence rate (target = 90%)	96.7%
Drop rate	1.7%
Highly-qualified teachers	99.6%
District needs improvement?(AYP)	No

Municipal Finance
Fiscal Year 2005
Total tax levy	$74,481,036
County levy	20,354,733
County taxes	19,412,198
County library	0
County health	0
County open space	942,535
School levy	20,601,713
Local muni. budget	33,524,589
Misc. revenues	18,266,496
Total aid	$2,520,297
CMPTRA	110,153
Muni. block grant	67,876
Energy tax receipts	2,272,268
Homeland security	70,000

Fiscal Year 2006
Total aid	$2,520,296
CMPTRA	30,623
Muni. block grant	67,876
Energy tax receipts	2,351,797
Homeland security	70,000

Taxes
	2003	2004	2005
General tax rate per $100	0.97	0.970	0.960
Net valuation taxable	$7,411,270,164	$7,549,955,663	$7,774,231,834
State equalized value	$7,591,181,157	$9,123,667,746	$11,340,965,476
County equalization ratio	118.42	97.63	82.74

Demographics & Socio-Economic Characteristics
(2000 U.S. Census, except as noted)

Population
1980*	1,385
1990*	2,078
2000	2,076
Male	977
Female	1,099
2004 (estimate)*	2,117
Persons per sq. mi. of land	4,843

Race & Hispanic Origin, 2000
Race
White	2,004
Black/African American	20
Amer. Indian/Alaska Natv.	3
Asian	20
Natv. Hawaiian/Pac. Islander	0
Other Race	11
Two or more races	18
Hispanic origin, total	49
Mexican	7
Puerto Rican	29
Cuban	1
Other Hispanic	12

Age & Nativity, 2000
Under 5 years	144
18 years and over	1,536
21 years and over	1,462
65 years and over	300
85 years and over	28
Median Age	37
Native born	2,065
Foreign born	11

Educational Attainment, 2000
Population 25 years and over	1,393
0-8 yrs of school	4.7%
High School grad or higher	81.3%
Bachelor's degree or higher	7.3%
Graduate degree	0.6%

Income & Poverty, 1999
Per capita income	$19,239
Median household income	$41,067
Median family income	$50,847
Persons in poverty	213
H'holds receiving public assistance	9
H'holds receiving social security	216

Households, 2000
Total households	832
With persons under 18	305
With persons over 65	221
Family households	547
One-person households	234
Persons per household	2.5
Persons per family	3.06

Labor & Employment
Total civilian labor force, 2004**	1,205
Unemployment rate	7.1%
Total civilian labor force, 2000	1,071
Unemployment rate	4.3%

Employed persons 16 years and over by occupation, 2000
Managers & professionals	215
Service occupations	171
Sales & office occupations	318
Farming, fishing & forestry	0
Construction & maintenance	188
Production & transportation	133
Self-employed persons	45

*US Census Bureau
**New Jersey Department of Labor

General Information
Borough of Ocean Gate
151 E Longport Ave CN-100
Ocean Gate, NJ 08740
732-269-3166

Web site	NA
Land area (sq. miles)	0.44
Water area (sq. miles)	0
Type of government	Borough
Form of government	B

Government

Legislative Districts
US Congressional	3
State Legislative	9

Local Officials, 2006
Mayor	Peter Terranova
Admin/Manager	Richard J. Napelitaro
Clerk	Diane Cripps
Finance Dir/Treas	Elizabeth V. Barger
Engineer	Chris Theodos
Attorney	Donna Conoshenti
Tax assessor	Scott Pezarras
Tax collector	NA
Building officer	Ocean County Const.
Zoning officer	Paul E. Buton Jr.
Public Works	NA

Housing & Construction

Housing Units, 2000*
Total	1,152
Median rent	$819
Median SF home value	$101,500

New Privately Owned Housing Units
Authorized by Building Permit
	Units	Value
Total, 2004	2	$193,000
Single family	2	$193,000
Total, 2005	17	$971,570
Single family	17	$971,570

Real Property Valuation - parcels, 2005
	Number	Valuation
Total		$256,415,600
Vacant	41	3,628,900
Residential	1,036	246,829,600
Commercial	13	4,683,100
Industrial	0	0
Apartments	3	1,274,000
Farm land	0	0
Farm homestead	0	0

Average Property Value & Tax, 2005
Residential value	$238,253
Property tax	$3,921
FAIR rebate	$615

Public Library

No public municipal library.

Library statistics, 2004
	Total	per capita
Volumes	NA	NA
Expenditure	NA	NA

Public Safety
Police
Chief	Daryl Maffia
Number of officers, 2004	7

Crime, 2004	Number	Rate
Total	38	18
Violent	7	3.3
Non-violent	31	14.7
Domestic Viol.	48	NA

Emergency/Fire
Director	Larry Murray

Public School District
(for school year 2004-2005 except as noted)

Ocean Gate School District
126 W Arverne Ave
Ocean Gate, NJ 08740
732-269-3023

Superintendent	Toni Mullins
Grade plan	K-6
Enrollment	165.0
Students per teacher	9.4
Per pupil expenditure	$10,468
Median faculty salary	$37,110
Median administrator salary	$79,613
Grade 12 enrollment	NA
High school graduation rate	NA

Assessment test results
(percent scoring at proficient or advanced level)
	Language	Math
Grade 3	92.8%	85.8%
Grade 8	NA	NA
High school	NA	NA

SAT
Percent tested	NA
Average SAT math score	NA
Average SAT verbal score	NA

No Child Left Behind, 2003-04
Attendence rate (target = 90%)	93.4%
Drop rate	NA
Highly-qualified teachers	100%
District needs improvement?(AYP)	No

Municipal Finance

Fiscal Year 2005
Total tax levy	$4,222,673
County levy	747,884
County taxes	630,113
County library	66,199
County health	28,059
County open space	23,514
School levy	2,211,492
Local muni. budget	1,263,297
Misc. revenues	949,869
Total aid	$236,001
CMPTRA	90,359
Muni. block grant	9,093
Energy tax receipts	111,549
Homeland security	25,000

Fiscal Year 2006
Total aid	$236,002
CMPTRA	86,455
Muni. block grant	9,093
Energy tax receipts	115,454
Homeland security	25,000

Taxes
	2003	2004	2005
General tax rate per $100	3.24	3.695	1.646
Net valuation taxable	$98,883,008	$99,681,270	$256,604,156
State equalized value	$157,356,792	$195,065,347	$238,524,034
County equalization ratio	77.1	62.84	131.20

Demographics & Socio-Economic Characteristics
(2000 U.S. Census, except as noted)

Population
1980*	23,570
1990*	25,058
2000	26,959
Male	12,983
Female	13,976
2004 (estimate)*	27,379
Persons per sq. mi. of land	2,481

Race & Hispanic Origin, 2000
Race
White	22,738
Black/African American	1,529
Amer. Indian/Alaska Natv.	40
Asian	1,689
Natv. Hawaiian/Pac. Islander	20
Other Race	425
Two or more races	518
Hispanic origin, total	1,215
Mexican	148
Puerto Rican	335
Cuban	63
Other Hispanic	669

Age & Nativity, 2000
Under 5 years	1,698
18 years and over	20,088
21 years and over	19,285
65 years and over	3,275
85 years and over	294
Median Age	38.4
Native born	22,719
Foreign born	4,240

Educational Attainment, 2000
Population 25 years and over	18,333
0-8 yrs of school	2.4%
High School grad or higher	90.2%
Bachelor's degree or higher	39.1%
Graduate degree	16.1%

Income & Poverty, 1999
Per capita income	$30,581
Median household income	$62,058
Median family income	$74,572
Persons in poverty	1,350
H'holds receiving public assistance	118
H'holds receiving social security	2,439

Households, 2000
Total households	10,254
With persons under 18	3,822
With persons over 65	2,421
Family households	7,338
One-person households	2,456
Persons per household	2.63
Persons per family	3.14

Labor & Employment
Total civilian labor force, 2004**	15,659
Unemployment rate	3.9%
Total civilian labor force, 2000	13,946
Unemployment rate	4.2%

Employed persons 16 years and over by occupation, 2000
Managers & professionals	5,559
Service occupations	1,696
Sales & office occupations	4,261
Farming, fishing & forestry	14
Construction & maintenance	824
Production & transportation	1,009
Self-employed persons	822

*US Census Bureau
**New Jersey Department of Labor

General Information
Township of Ocean
399 Monmouth Rd
Oakhurst, NJ 07755
732-531-5000

Web site	www.oceantwp.org
Land area (sq. miles)	11.03
Water area (sq. miles)	0.09
Type of government	Township
Form of government	CM '50

Government
Legislative Districts
US Congressional	6
State Legislative	11

Local Officials, 2006
Mayor	William Larkin
Admin/Manager	David Kochel
Clerk	Deborah Smith
Finance Dir/Treas	Stephen Gallagher
Engineer	Francis Mullen
Attorney	Martin J. Arbus
Tax assessor	Edward Mullane
Tax collector	Stephen Gallagher
Building officer	Paul Vitale
Zoning officer	Jerry Donlon
Public Works	William Taylor

Housing & Construction
Housing Units, 2000*
Total	10,756
Median rent	$689
Median SF home value	$198,900

New Privately Owned Housing Units Authorized by Building Permit
	Units	Value
Total, 2004	248	$28,192,900
Single family	128	$19,692,900
Total, 2005	88	$11,162,610
Single family	88	$11,162,610

Real Property Valuation - parcels, 2005
	Number	Valuation
Total		$4,508,094,200
Vacant	873	128,139,000
Residential	7,951	3,540,957,600
Commercial	375	636,902,500
Industrial	5	7,047,700
Apartments	15	194,035,400
Farm land	1	1,008,800
Farm homestead	3	3,200

Average Property Value & Tax, 2005
Residential value	$445,180
Property tax	$7,030
FAIR rebate	$572

Public Library
Ocean Twp. Public Library†
601 Deal Rd
Oakhurst, NJ 07755
732-531-5092
Branch Librarian . . . . Deborah Bagchi

Library statistics, 2004
	Total	per capita
Volumes	NA	NA
Expenditure	NA	NA

†Branch of County Library

Public Safety
Police
Chief	Antonio Amodio
Number of officers, 2004	60

Crime, 2004	Number	Rate
Total	706	25.5
Violent	42	1.5
Non-violent	664	24
Domestic Viol.	159	NA

Emergency/Fire
Director . . . . E. Alexander/K. Kenlien

Public School District
(for school year 2004-2005 except as noted)

Ocean Township School District
163 Monmouth Rd
Oakhurst, NJ 07755
732-531-5600

Superintendent	Thomas Pagano
Grade plan	K-12
Enrollment	4,447.0
Students per teacher	11.6
Per pupil expenditure	$11,976
Median faculty salary	$61,760
Median administrator salary	$105,800
Grade 12 enrollment	328.0
High school graduation rate	98.5%

Assessment test results
(percent scoring at proficient or advanced level)
	Language	Math
Grade 3	91.2%	86.8%
Grade 8	81.2%	75.7%
High school	92.8%	91.1%

SAT
Percent tested	94%
Average SAT math score	543
Average SAT verbal score	522

No Child Left Behind, 2003-04
Attendence rate (target = 90%)	95.8%
Drop rate	0.1%
Highly-qualified teachers	84.5%
District needs improvement?(AYP)	No

Municipal Finance
Fiscal Year 2005
Total tax levy	$71,252,991
County levy	12,566,304
County taxes	11,276,046
County library	621,132
County health	0
County open space	669,126
School levy	45,851,626
Local muni. budget	12,835,061
Misc. revenues	12,963,420
Total aid	$3,474,742
CMPTRA	1,072,598
Muni. block grant	109,645
Energy tax receipts	2,202,499
Homeland security	90,000

Fiscal Year 2006
Total aid	$3,474,742
CMPTRA	995,511
Muni. block grant	109,645
Energy tax receipts	2,279,586
Homeland security	90,000

Taxes
	2003	2004	2005
General tax rate per $100	3.40	3.521	1.580
Net valuation taxable	$1,847,775,351	$1,883,962,297	$4,512,324,619
State equalized value	$3,180,883,717	$3,704,615,768	$4,751,816,153
County equalization ratio	66.01	58.09	120.12

Demographics & Socio-Economic Characteristics
(2000 U.S. Census, except as noted)

Population
1980*	3,731
1990*	5,416
2000	6,450
Male	3,201
Female	3,249
2004 (estimate)*	7,492
Persons per sq. mi. of land	360

Race & Hispanic Origin, 2000
Race
White	6,278
Black/African American	48
Amer. Indian/Alaska Natv.	10
Asian	27
Natv. Hawaiian/Pac. Islander	2
Other Race	23
Two or more races	62
Hispanic origin, total	200
Mexican	29
Puerto Rican	77
Cuban	32
Other Hispanic	62

Age & Nativity, 2000
Under 5 years	373
18 years and over	4,807
21 years and over	4,585
65 years and over	888
85 years and over	87
Median Age	37.7
Native born	6,358
Foreign born	92

Educational Attainment, 2000
Population 25 years and over	4,369
0-8 yrs of school	2.5%
High School grad or higher	86.2%
Bachelor's degree or higher	15.7%
Graduate degree	5.0%

Income & Poverty, 1999
Per capita income	$22,830
Median household income	$46,461
Median family income	$55,379
Persons in poverty	502
H'holds receiving public assistance	23
H'holds receiving social security	767

Households, 2000
Total households	2,446
With persons under 18	885
With persons over 65	647
Family households	1,745
One-person households	571
Persons per household	2.61
Persons per family	3.08

Labor & Employment
Total civilian labor force, 2004**	3,165
Unemployment rate	5.0%
Total civilian labor force, 2000	3,177
Unemployment rate	6.9%

Employed persons 16 years and over by occupation, 2000
Managers & professionals	745
Service occupations	568
Sales & office occupations	685
Farming, fishing & forestry	0
Construction & maintenance	645
Production & transportation	315
Self-employed persons	222

*US Census Bureau
**New Jersey Department of Labor

General Information
Township of Ocean
50 Railroad Ave
Waretown, NJ 08758
609-693-3302

Web site	www.oceantwp.com
Land area (sq. miles)	20.80
Water area (sq. miles)	11.23
Type of government	Township
Form of government	TC

Government

Legislative Districts
US Congressional	3
State Legislative	9

Local Officials, 2006
Mayor	Daniel Van Pelt
Admin/Manager	NA
Clerk	Dorothy Horner
Finance Dir/Treas	Christine Thorne
Engineer	Alaimo Associates
Attorney	Gregory McGuckin
Tax assessor	Martin Lynch
Tax collector	NA
Building officer	Larry Leonard
Zoning officer	NA
Public Works	NA

Housing & Construction

Housing Units, 2000*
Total	2,981
Median rent	$833
Median SF home value	$104,800

New Privately Owned Housing Units
Authorized by Building Permit

	Units	Value
Total, 2004	178	$19,169,109
Single family	178	$19,169,109
Total, 2005	212	$26,764,594
Single family	212	$26,764,594

Real Property Valuation - parcels, 2005
	Number	Valuation
Total		$1,092,022,400
Vacant	1,155	102,904,300
Residential	3,418	930,601,400
Commercial	118	55,087,100
Industrial	1	574,600
Apartments	0	0
Farm land	5	2,490,400
Farm homestead	93	364,600

Average Property Value & Tax, 2005
Residential value	$265,157
Property tax	$3,610
FAIR rebate	$832

Public Library
Waretown Branch Library†
112 Main St
Waretown, NJ 08758
609-693-5133

Branch Librarian	Kelly Ann Pernel

Library statistics, 2004
	Total	per capita
Volumes	NA	NA
Expenditure	NA	NA

†Branch of County Library

Public Safety

Police
Chief	Kenneth Flatt
Number of officers, 2004	16

Crime, 2004	Number	Rate
Total	115	15.9
Violent	10	1.4
Non-violent	105	14.6
Domestic Viol.	49	NA

Emergency/Fire
Director	Matthew Ambrosino

Public School District
(for school year 2004-2005 except as noted)

Ocean Township School District
64 Railroad Ave
Waretown, NJ 08758
609-693-3329

Superintendent	Donald Bochicchio
Grade plan	K-12
Enrollment	614.0
Students per teacher	9.8
Per pupil expenditure	$12,801
Median faculty salary	$46,746
Median administrator salary	$77,024
Grade 12 enrollment	NA
High school graduation rate	NA

Assessment test results
(percent scoring at proficient or advanced level)
	Language	Math
Grade 3	83.5%	78.1%
Grade 8	NA	NA
High school	NA	NA

SAT
Percent tested	NA
Average SAT math score	NA
Average SAT verbal score	NA

No Child Left Behind, 2003-04
Attendence rate (target = 90%)	94.6%
Drop rate	NA
Highly-qualified teachers	100%
District needs improvement?(AYP)	No

Municipal Finance

Fiscal Year 2005
Total tax levy	$14,887,918
County levy	3,118,066
County taxes	2,627,052
County library	275,992
County health	116,982
County open space	98,040
School levy	7,986,898
Local muni. budget	3,782,954
Misc. revenues	5,622,423
Total aid	$872,108
CMPTRA	207,587
Muni. block grant	25,291
Energy tax receipts	583,960
Homeland security	50,000

Fiscal Year 2006
Total aid	$872,109
CMPTRA	187,149
Muni. block grant	25,291
Energy tax receipts	604,399
Homeland security	50,000

Taxes
	2003	2004	2005
General tax rate per $100	3.26	3.277	1.362
Net valuation taxable	$389,830,170	$430,607,250	$1,093,513,551
State equalized value	$595,433,282	$765,290,068	$1,037,390,713
County equalization ratio	77.46	65.47	134.07

Demographics & Socio-Economic Characteristics
(2000 U.S. Census, except as noted)

Population
1980*	5,888
1990*	6,146
2000	5,807
Male	2,875
Female	2,932
2004 (estimate)*	5,832
Persons per sq. mi. of land	1,810

Race & Hispanic Origin, 2000
Race
White	5,558
Black/African American	114
Amer. Indian/Alaska Natv.	4
Asian	46
Natv. Hawaiian/Pac. Islander	1
Other Race	32
Two or more races	52
Hispanic origin, total	120
Mexican	24
Puerto Rican	39
Cuban	12
Other Hispanic	45

Age & Nativity, 2000
Under 5 years	347
18 years and over	4,384
21 years and over	4,104
65 years and over	827
85 years and over	82
Median Age	40.5
Native born	5,595
Foreign born	220

Educational Attainment, 2000
Population 25 years and over	3,891
0-8 yrs of school	3.1%
High School grad or higher	90.6%
Bachelor's degree or higher	35.7%
Graduate degree	10.8%

Income & Poverty, 1999
Per capita income	$33,356
Median household income	$71,458
Median family income	$85,038
Persons in poverty	149
H'holds receiving public assistance	7
H'holds receiving social security	635

Households, 2000
Total households	2,043
With persons under 18	762
With persons over 65	613
Family households	1,555
One-person households	443
Persons per household	2.71
Persons per family	3.18

Labor & Employment
Total civilian labor force, 2004**	3,468
Unemployment rate	4.0%
Total civilian labor force, 2000	2,798
Unemployment rate	2.3%

Employed persons 16 years and over by occupation, 2000
Managers & professionals	1,221
Service occupations	223
Sales & office occupations	875
Farming, fishing & forestry	0
Construction & maintenance	221
Production & transportation	194
Self-employed persons	159

*US Census Bureau
**New Jersey Department of Labor

General Information
Borough of Oceanport
PO Box 370
222 Monmouth Blvd
Oceanport, NJ 07757
732-222-8221

Web site	www.oceanportboro.com
Land area (sq. miles)	3.22
Water area (sq. miles)	0.63
Type of government	Borough
Form of government	B

Government

Legislative Districts
US Congressional	12
State Legislative	12

Local Officials, 2006
Mayor	Lucille A. Chaump
Admin/Manager	NA
Clerk	Kimberly Jungfer
Finance Dir/Treas	Annette David
Engineer	Thomas Rospos
Attorney	Scott Arnette
Tax assessor	Helen Ward
Tax collector	Cynthia Cortale
Building officer	Walter Joyce
Zoning officer	NA
Public Works	Demitrio Zarate

Housing & Construction

Housing Units, 2000*
Total	2,114
Median rent	$672
Median SF home value	$231,400

New Privately Owned Housing Units Authorized by Building Permit
	Units	Value
Total, 2004	19	$2,366,058
Single family	19	$2,366,058
Total, 2005	13	$3,492,236
Single family	13	$3,492,236

Real Property Valuation - parcels, 2005
	Number	Valuation
Total		$491,453,800
Vacant	114	7,842,800
Residential	1,965	418,695,100
Commercial	31	64,462,600
Industrial	0	0
Apartments	1	256,500
Farm land	1	188,400
Farm homestead	1	8,400

Average Property Value & Tax, 2005
Residential value	$212,972
Property tax	$7,009
FAIR rebate	$588

Public Library
Oceanport Library†
Monmouth Blvd & Myrtle Ave
Oceanport, NJ 07757
732-229-2626

Branch Librarian ..... Michele Blake

Library statistics, 2004
	Total	per capita
Volumes	NA	NA
Expenditure	NA	NA

†Branch of County Library

Public Safety

Police
Chief	Harold Sutton
Number of officers, 2004	14

Crime, 2004	Number	Rate
Total	74	12.4
Violent	3	0.5
Non-violent	71	11.9
Domestic Viol.	12	NA

Emergency/Fire
Director ..... Scott Sirianni

Public School District
(for school year 2004-2005 except as noted)

Oceanport Borough School District
Wolf Hill Ave
Oceanport, NJ 07757
732-544-8588

Superintendent	James DiGiovanna
Grade plan	K-8
Enrollment	758.0
Students per teacher	11.5
Per pupil expenditure	$9,466
Median faculty salary	$47,275
Median administrator salary	$97,635
Grade 12 enrollment	NA
High school graduation rate	NA

Assessment test results
(percent scoring at proficient or advanced level)
	Language	Math
Grade 3	91.9%	85.0%
Grade 8	89.7%	81.4%
High school	NA	NA

SAT
Percent tested	NA
Average SAT math score	NA
Average SAT verbal score	NA

No Child Left Behind, 2003-04
Attendence rate (target = 90%)	94.9%
Drop rate	NA
Highly-qualified teachers	100%
District needs improvement?(AYP)	No

Municipal Finance

Fiscal Year 2005
Total tax levy	$16,186,387
County levy	3,244,766
County taxes	2,864,730
County library	157,801
County health	52,239
County open space	169,996
School levy	9,599,151
Local muni. budget	3,342,469
Misc. revenues	1,947,345
Total aid	$816,516
CMPTRA	257,949
Muni. block grant	26,893
Energy tax receipts	481,674
Homeland security	50,000

Fiscal Year 2006
Total aid	$816,516
CMPTRA	241,090
Muni. block grant	26,893
Energy tax receipts	498,533
Homeland security	50,000

Taxes
	2003	2004	2005
General tax rate per $100	3.01	3.181	3.291
Net valuation taxable	$490,338,528	$494,893,142	$491,851,779
State equalized value	$856,486,512	$957,747,739	$1,088,408,451
County equalization ratio	68.19	57.25	51.65

Demographics & Socio-Economic Characteristics
(2000 U.S. Census, except as noted)

Population
1980*	2,737
1990*	2,722
2000	2,638
Male	1,335
Female	1,303
2004 (estimate)*	2,643
Persons per sq. mi. of land	1,157

Race & Hispanic Origin, 2000
Race
White	2,573
Black/African American	4
Amer. Indian/Alaska Natv.	1
Asian	19
Natv. Hawaiian/Pac. Islander	0
Other Race	7
Two or more races	34
Hispanic origin, total	110
Mexican	33
Puerto Rican	38
Cuban	5
Other Hispanic	34

Age & Nativity, 2000
Under 5 years	185
18 years and over	1,860
21 years and over	1,760
65 years and over	212
85 years and over	16
Median Age	35
Native born	2,480
Foreign born	158

Educational Attainment, 2000
Population 25 years and over	1,668
0-8 yrs of school	2.7%
High School grad or higher	89.3%
Bachelor's degree or higher	20.0%
Graduate degree	5.9%

Income & Poverty, 1999
Per capita income	$24,305
Median household income	$60,313
Median family income	$70,521
Persons in poverty	150
H'holds receiving public assistance	5
H'holds receiving social security	187

Households, 2000
Total households	881
With persons under 18	400
With persons over 65	162
Family households	705
One-person households	146
Persons per household	2.99
Persons per family	3.38

Labor & Employment
Total civilian labor force, 2004**	1,714
Unemployment rate	3.1%
Total civilian labor force, 2000	1,418
Unemployment rate	2.6%

Employed persons 16 years and over by occupation, 2000
Managers & professionals	465
Service occupations	152
Sales & office occupations	406
Farming, fishing & forestry	0
Construction & maintenance	141
Production & transportation	217
Self-employed persons	43

*US Census Bureau
**New Jersey Department of Labor

General Information
Borough of Ogdensburg
14 Highland Ave
Ogdensburg, NJ 07439
973-827-3444

Web site	NA
Land area (sq. miles)	2.28
Water area (sq. miles)	0.02
Type of government	Borough
Form of government	B

Government
Legislative Districts
US Congressional	5, 11
State Legislative	24

Local Officials, 2006
Mayor	Jacquie Pietrodangelo
Admin/Manager	NA
Clerk	Phyllis Drouin
Finance Dir/Treas	M. LaStarza (Int)
Engineer	Eugene Buczynski
Attorney	Sanford Hollander
Tax assessor	Kathleen Keib
Tax collector	NA
Building officer	Jan Op't Hof
Zoning officer	NA
Public Works	NA

Housing & Construction
Housing Units, 2000*
Total	903
Median rent	$775
Median SF home value	$141,600

New Privately Owned Housing Units Authorized by Building Permit
	Units	Value
Total, 2004	0	$0
Single family	0	$0
Total, 2005	2	$480,000
Single family	2	$480,000

Real Property Valuation - parcels, 2005
	Number	Valuation
Total		$115,049,550
Vacant	51	3,180,300
Residential	799	101,795,750
Commercial	29	7,047,600
Industrial	3	1,646,200
Apartments	3	734,000
Farm land	3	624,600
Farm homestead	4	21,100

Average Property Value & Tax, 2005
Residential value	$126,796
Property tax	$5,539
FAIR rebate	$537

Public Library
No public municipal library.

Library statistics, 2004
	Total	per capita
Volumes	NA	NA
Expenditure	NA	NA

Public Safety
Police
Chief	George Lott
Number of officers, 2004	7

Crime, 2004	Number	Rate
Total	9	3.4
Violent	1	0.4
Non-violent	8	3
Domestic Viol.	33	NA

Emergency/Fire
Director	Michael Franek

Public School District
(for school year 2004-2005 except as noted)

Ogdensburg Borough School District
100 Main St
Ogdensburg, NJ 07439
973-827-7126

Administrator	John Petrelli
Grade plan	K-8
Enrollment	376.0
Students per teacher	10.7
Per pupil expenditure	$11,110
Median faculty salary	$51,100
Median administrator salary	$71,866
Grade 12 enrollment	NA
High school graduation rate	NA

Assessment test results
(percent scoring at proficient or advanced level)
	Language	Math
Grade 3	81.0%	61.9%
Grade 8	84.0%	66.0%
High school	NA	NA

SAT
Percent tested	NA
Average SAT math score	NA
Average SAT verbal score	NA

No Child Left Behind, 2003-04
Attendence rate (target = 90%)	95.6%
Drop rate	NA
Highly-qualified teachers	93.4%
District needs improvement?(AYP)	No

Municipal Finance
Fiscal Year 2005
Total tax levy	$5,040,678
County levy	787,931
County taxes	692,580
County library	59,703
County health	0
County open space	35,648
School levy	2,645,199
Local muni. budget	1,607,548
Misc. revenues	975,159
Total aid	$317,349
CMPTRA	204,899
Muni. block grant	11,911
Energy tax receipts	75,539
Homeland security	25,000

Fiscal Year 2006
Total aid	$317,349
CMPTRA	202,255
Muni. block grant	11,911
Energy tax receipts	78,183
Homeland security	25,000

Taxes
	2003	2004	2005
General tax rate per $100	3.77	3.960	4.370
Net valuation taxable	$116,237,593	$115,566,501	$115,381,319
State equalized value	$158,729,473	$176,454,814	$194,736,403
County equalization ratio	93.06	73.23	65.42

Demographics & Socio-Economic Characteristics
(2000 U.S. Census, except as noted)

Population
1980*	51,515
1990*	56,475
2000	60,456
Male	29,549
Female	30,907
2004 (estimate)*	64,151
Persons per sq. mi. of land	1,684

Race & Hispanic Origin, 2000
Race
White	48,049
Black/African American	3,207
Amer. Indian/Alaska Natv.	94
Asian	6,544
Natv. Hawaiian/Pac. Islander	27
Other Race	1,133
Two or more races	1,402
Hispanic origin, total	4,578
Mexican	439
Puerto Rican	2,002
Cuban	377
Other Hispanic	1,760

Age & Nativity, 2000
Under 5 years	4,252
18 years and over	44,822
21 years and over	43,002
65 years and over	6,370
85 years and over	695
Median Age	36.5
Native born	49,341
Foreign born	11,115

Educational Attainment, 2000
Population 25 years and over	40,677
0-8 yrs of school	3.5%
High School grad or higher	88.4%
Bachelor's degree or higher	29.5%
Graduate degree	8.9%

Income & Poverty, 1999
Per capita income	$26,814
Median household income	$64,707
Median family income	$74,045
Persons in poverty	2,547
H'holds receiving public assistance	253
H'holds receiving social security	4,765

Households, 2000
Total households	21,438
With persons under 18	8,643
With persons over 65	4,524
Family households	15,959
One-person households	4,527
Persons per household	2.8
Persons per family	3.3

Labor & Employment
Total civilian labor force, 2004**	35,374
Unemployment rate	4.0%
Total civilian labor force, 2000	31,618
Unemployment rate	4.7%

Employed persons 16 years and over by occupation, 2000
Managers & professionals	11,218
Service occupations	3,373
Sales & office occupations	9,469
Farming, fishing & forestry	21
Construction & maintenance	2,794
Production & transportation	3,265
Self-employed persons	1,097

*US Census Bureau
**New Jersey Department of Labor

General Information
Township of Old Bridge
1 Old Bridge Plaza
Old Bridge, NJ 08857
732-721-5600
Web site	www.oldbridge.com
Land area (sq. miles)	38.09
Water area (sq. miles)	2.57
Type of government	Township
Form of government	MC '50

Government

Legislative Districts
US Congressional	6
State Legislative	13

Local Officials, 2006
Mayor	James T. Phillips
Admin/Manager	Michael Jacobs
Clerk	Rose-Marie Saracino
Finance Dir/Treas	Himanshu Shah
Engineer	James Cleary
Attorney	Jerome J. Convery
Tax assessor	Brian Enright
Tax collector	Kathleen Silber
Building officer	Alex Tucciarone
Zoning officer	NA
Public Works	Rocco Donatelli

Housing & Construction

Housing Units, 2000*
Total	21,896
Median rent	$770
Median SF home value	$162,800

New Privately Owned Housing Units Authorized by Building Permit
	Units	Value
Total, 2004	313	$30,794,780
Single family	196	$24,476,898
Total, 2005	623	$70,098,291
Single family	305	$51,704,564

Real Property Valuation - parcels, 2005
	Number	Valuation
Total		$3,259,675,000
Vacant	1,480	125,358,600
Residential	17,197	2,556,402,600
Commercial	434	331,672,100
Industrial	57	50,634,500
Apartments	27	185,974,100
Farm land	37	5,885,400
Farm homestead	118	3,747,700

Average Property Value & Tax, 2005
Residential value	$147,857
Property tax	$5,424
FAIR rebate	$571

Public Library
Old Bridge Public Library
One Old Bridge Plaza
Old Bridge, NJ 08857
732-721-5600
Director	Margery Cyr

Library statistics, 2004
	Total	per capita
Volumes	166,884	2.76
Expenditure	$2,069,383	$34.23

Public Safety

Police
Chief	Thomas Collow
Number of officers, 2004	103

Crime, 2004	Number	Rate
Total	1,110	17.4
Violent	58	0.9
Non-violent	1,052	16.5
Domestic Viol.	467	NA

Emergency/Fire
Director	NA

Public School District
(for school year 2004-2005 except as noted)

Old Bridge Township School District
4207 Route 516
Matawan, NJ 07747
732-290-3976
Superintendent	Simon Bosco
Grade plan	K-12
Enrollment	10,008.0
Students per teacher	13.2
Per pupil expenditure	$10,916
Median faculty salary	$55,167
Median administrator salary	$111,320
Grade 12 enrollment	711.5
High school graduation rate	94.2%

Assessment test results
(percent scoring at proficient or advanced level)
	Language	Math
Grade 3	88.0%	85.6%
Grade 8	77.3%	64.8%
High school	84.2%	76.6%

SAT
Percent tested	75%
Average SAT math score	519
Average SAT verbal score	492

No Child Left Behind, 2003-04
Attendence rate (target = 90%)	95.1%
Drop rate	1.1%
Highly-qualified teachers	98.5%
District needs improvement?(AYP)	No

Municipal Finance

Fiscal Year 2005
Total tax levy	$119,782,994
County levy	18,436,916
County taxes	16,707,978
County library	0
County health	0
County open space	1,728,938
School levy	75,877,413
Local muni. budget	25,468,665
Misc. revenues	24,251,684
Total aid	$8,544,546
CMPTRA	4,379,405
Muni. block grant	247,195
Energy tax receipts	3,777,946
Homeland security	140,000

Fiscal Year 2006
Total aid	$8,544,546
CMPTRA	4,247,177
Muni. block grant	247,195
Energy tax receipts	3,910,174
Homeland security	140,000

Taxes
	2003	2004	2005
General tax rate per $100	3.43	3.590	3.670
Net valuation taxable	$3,162,773,038	$3,196,717,300	$3,265,492,900
State equalized value	$4,772,556,267	$5,545,031,142	$6,334,612,803
County equalization ratio	75.6	66.27	57.60

Demographics & Socio-Economic Characteristics
(2000 U.S. Census, except as noted)

Population
1980*	4,168
1990*	4,254
2000	5,482
Male	2,632
Female	2,850
2004 (estimate)*	5,869
Persons per sq. mi. of land	1,817

Race & Hispanic Origin, 2000
Race
White	4,533
Black/African American	33
Amer. Indian/Alaska Natv.	3
Asian	857
Natv. Hawaiian/Pac. Islander	0
Other Race	24
Two or more races	32
Hispanic origin, total	151
Mexican	14
Puerto Rican	28
Cuban	36
Other Hispanic	73

Age & Nativity, 2000
Under 5 years	346
18 years and over	4,004
21 years and over	3,844
65 years and over	798
85 years and over	110
Median Age	41
Native born	4,562
Foreign born	920

Educational Attainment, 2000
Population 25 years and over	3,708
0-8 yrs of school	1.8%
High School grad or higher	93.5%
Bachelor's degree or higher	49.4%
Graduate degree	18.3%

Income & Poverty, 1999
Per capita income	$48,367
Median household income	$102,127
Median family income	$106,772
Persons in poverty	94
H'holds receiving public assistance	16
H'holds receiving social security	519

Households, 2000
Total households	1,778
With persons under 18	780
With persons over 65	478
Family households	1,542
One-person households	215
Persons per household	3.02
Persons per family	3.28

Labor & Employment
Total civilian labor force, 2004**	2,351
Unemployment rate	1.7%
Total civilian labor force, 2000	2,607
Unemployment rate	3.0%

Employed persons 16 years and over by occupation, 2000
Managers & professionals	1,389
Service occupations	188
Sales & office occupations	775
Farming, fishing & forestry	0
Construction & maintenance	86
Production & transportation	92
Self-employed persons	197

*US Census Bureau
**New Jersey Department of Labor

General Information
Borough of Old Tappan
227 Old Tappan Rd
Old Tappan, NJ 07675
201-664-1849

Web site	www.oldtappan.net
Land area (sq. miles)	3.23
Water area (sq. miles)	0.85
Type of government	Borough
Form of government	B

Government

Legislative Districts
US Congressional	5
State Legislative	39

Local Officials, 2006
Mayor	Victor Polce
Admin/Manager	Gregory Hart
Clerk	Gregory Hart
Finance Dir/Treas	Christine Cauvet
Engineer	Thomas Skrable
Attorney	Allen Bell
Tax assessor	Irwin Sabin
Tax collector	Christine Cauvet
Building officer	Peiro Abballe
Zoning officer	Nicholas Pappas
Public Works	Arthur Lake

Housing & Construction

Housing Units, 2000*
Total	1,804
Median rent	$940
Median SF home value	$436,900

New Privately Owned Housing Units Authorized by Building Permit
	Units	Value
Total, 2004	23	$8,606,119
Single family	23	$8,606,119
Total, 2005	49	$7,290,294
Single family	49	$7,290,294

Real Property Valuation - parcels, 2005
	Number	Valuation
Total		$1,209,148,100
Vacant	82	36,747,400
Residential	1,902	1,105,903,400
Commercial	53	65,354,100
Industrial	0	0
Apartments	1	331,800
Farm land	3	801,500
Farm homestead	1	9,900

Average Property Value & Tax, 2005
Residential value	$581,142
Property tax	$10,932
FAIR rebate	$596

Public Library
Old Tappan Public Library
56 Russell Ave
Old Tappan, NJ 07675
201-664-3499

Director	Susan Meeske

Library statistics, 2004
	Total	per capita
Volumes	40,572	7.40
Expenditure	$333,867	$60.90

Public Safety

Police
Chief	Joseph Fasulo
Number of officers, 2004	13

Crime, 2004	Number	Rate
Total	32	5.5
Violent	2	0.3
Non-violent	30	5.2
Domestic Viol.	5	NA

Emergency/Fire
Director	Kevin Dorney

Public School District
(for school year 2004-2005 except as noted)

Old Tappan School District
T. Baldwin Demarest School
Old Tappan, NJ 07675
201-664-7231

Superintendent	Patricia Lennon
Grade plan	K-8
Enrollment	814.0
Students per teacher	11.7
Per pupil expenditure	$11,647
Median faculty salary	$58,032
Median administrator salary	$117,000
Grade 12 enrollment	NA
High school graduation rate	NA

Assessment test results
(percent scoring at proficient or advanced level)
	Language	Math
Grade 3	93.4%	91.6%
Grade 8	97.7%	88.5%
High school	NA	NA

SAT
Percent tested	NA
Average SAT math score	NA
Average SAT verbal score	NA

No Child Left Behind, 2003-04
Attendence rate (target = 90%)	95.0%
Drop rate	NA
Highly-qualified teachers	97.2%
District needs improvement?(AYP)	No

Municipal Finance

Fiscal Year 2005
Total tax levy	$22,765,326
County levy	2,813,986
County taxes	2,672,217
County library	0
County health	0
County open space	141,769
School levy	16,898,286
Local muni. budget	3,053,054
Misc. revenues	3,441,369
Total aid	$1,746,065
CMPTRA	104,424
Muni. block grant	21,495
Energy tax receipts	1,531,606
Homeland security	50,000

Fiscal Year 2006
Total aid	$1,746,066
CMPTRA	50,818
Muni. block grant	21,495
Energy tax receipts	1,585,213
Homeland security	50,000

Taxes
	2003	2004	2005
General tax rate per $100	1.73	1.810	1.890
Net valuation taxable	$1,146,195,128	$1,179,143,283	$1,210,174,760
State equalized value	$1,221,305,411	$1,379,724,594	$1,587,530,841
County equalization ratio	102.56	93.85	85.45

Demographics & Socio-Economic Characteristics
(2000 U.S. Census, except as noted)

Population
1980*	1,847
1990*	1,683
2000	1,798
Male	909
Female	889
2004 (estimate)*	1,812
Persons per sq. mi. of land	91

Race & Hispanic Origin, 2000
Race
White	1,561
Black/African American	173
Amer. Indian/Alaska Natv.	5
Asian	3
Natv. Hawaiian/Pac. Islander	0
Other Race	36
Two or more races	20
Hispanic origin, total	75
Mexican	27
Puerto Rican	29
Cuban	0
Other Hispanic	19

Age & Nativity, 2000
Under 5 years	98
18 years and over	1,355
21 years and over	1,292
65 years and over	213
85 years and over	22
Median Age	39.1
Native born	1,755
Foreign born	43

Educational Attainment, 2000
Population 25 years and over	1,236
0-8 yrs of school	5.6%
High School grad or higher	81.9%
Bachelor's degree or higher	10.9%
Graduate degree	3.2%

Income & Poverty, 1999
Per capita income	$22,495
Median household income	$57,589
Median family income	$64,091
Persons in poverty	146
H'holds receiving public assistance	7
H'holds receiving social security	179

Households, 2000
Total households	654
With persons under 18	235
With persons over 65	152
Family households	517
One-person households	111
Persons per household	2.74
Persons per family	3.07

Labor & Employment
Total civilian labor force, 2004**	847
Unemployment rate	3.9%
Total civilian labor force, 2000	950
Unemployment rate	5.9%

Employed persons 16 years and over by occupation, 2000
Managers & professionals	230
Service occupations	96
Sales & office occupations	250
Farming, fishing & forestry	5
Construction & maintenance	111
Production & transportation	202
Self-employed persons	60

*US Census Bureau
**New Jersey Department of Labor

General Information
Township of Oldmans
PO Box 416
Pedricktown, NJ 08067
856-299-0780

Web site	NA
Land area (sq. miles)	19.97
Water area (sq. miles)	0.33
Type of government	Township
Form of government	TC

Government

Legislative Districts
US Congressional	2
State Legislative	3

Local Officials, 2006
Mayor	Harry A. Moore
Admin/Manager	NA
Clerk	Susan Miller
Finance Dir/Treas	Helen Moore
Engineer	John Bickel
Attorney	John Hoffman
Tax assessor	Michael Raio
Tax collector	Margie L. Schieber
Building officer	Jeryl Goff
Zoning officer	Susan Miller
Public Works	NA

Housing & Construction

Housing Units, 2000*
Total	694
Median rent	$714
Median SF home value	$104,300

New Privately Owned Housing Units Authorized by Building Permit
	Units	Value
Total, 2004	7	$984,872
Single family	7	$984,872
Total, 2005	3	$525,872
Single family	3	$525,872

Real Property Valuation - parcels, 2005
	Number	Valuation
Total		$110,583,640
Vacant	219	2,976,000
Residential	573	52,674,200
Commercial	42	6,020,500
Industrial	15	35,155,870
Apartments	0	0
Farm land	109	10,581,500
Farm homestead	259	3,175,570

Average Property Value & Tax, 2005
Residential value	$67,127
Property tax	$2,530
FAIR rebate	$624

Public Library

No public municipal library.

Library statistics, 2004
	Total	per capita
Volumes	NA	NA
Expenditure	NA	NA

Public Safety
Police
Chief	NA
Number of officers, 2004	0

Crime, 2004	Number	Rate
Total	62	34.4
Violent	6	3.3
Non-violent	56	31.1
Domestic Viol.	8	NA

Emergency/Fire
Director	Gary Moore

Public School District
(for school year 2004-2005 except as noted)

Oldmans Township School District
10 Freed Rd
Pedricktown, NJ 08067
856-299-4240

Administrator	Stephen Combs
Grade plan	K-12
Enrollment	248.0
Students per teacher	10.5
Per pupil expenditure	$12,753
Median faculty salary	$57,943
Median administrator salary	$83,300
Grade 12 enrollment	NA
High school graduation rate	NA

Assessment test results
(percent scoring at proficient or advanced level)
	Language	Math
Grade 3	72.7%	77.3%
Grade 8	54.5%	63.7%
High school	NA	NA

SAT
Percent tested	NA
Average SAT math score	NA
Average SAT verbal score	NA

No Child Left Behind, 2003-04
Attendence rate (target = 90%)	97.0%
Drop rate	NA
Highly-qualified teachers	100%
District needs improvement?(AYP)	No

Municipal Finance

Fiscal Year 2005
Total tax levy	$4,184,072
County levy	1,605,616
County taxes	1,573,760
County library	0
County health	0
County open space	31,857
School levy	2,423,393
Local muni. budget	155,062
Misc. revenues	1,101,020
Total aid	$338,492
CMPTRA	113,895
Muni. block grant	7,365
Energy tax receipts	217,232
Homeland security	0

Fiscal Year 2006
Total aid	$338,491
CMPTRA	106,291
Muni. block grant	7,365
Energy tax receipts	224,835
Homeland security	NA

Taxes
	2003	2004	2005
General tax rate per $100	3.34	3.549	3.770
Net valuation taxable	$110,088,869	$110,072,050	$110,995,461
State equalized value	$143,662,885	$156,395,955	$163,493,093
County equalization ratio	82.7	76.63	70.29

Demographics & Socio-Economic Characteristics

(2000 U.S. Census, except as noted)

Population

1980*	8,658
1990*	8,024
2000	8,047
Male	3,849
Female	4,198
2004 (estimate)*	8,041
Persons per sq. mi. of land	3,316

Race & Hispanic Origin, 2000

Race
White	7,248
Black/African American	39
Amer. Indian/Alaska Natv.	3
Asian	651
Natv. Hawaiian/Pac. Islander	1
Other Race	26
Two or more races	79
Hispanic origin, total	249
Mexican	12
Puerto Rican	72
Cuban	64
Other Hispanic	101

Age & Nativity, 2000

Under 5 years	509
18 years and over	6,020
21 years and over	5,852
65 years and over	1,337
85 years and over	182
Median Age	41.5
Native born	6,976
Foreign born	1,071

Educational Attainment, 2000

Population 25 years and over	5,617
0-8 yrs of school	1.8%
High School grad or higher	94.9%
Bachelor's degree or higher	51.8%
Graduate degree	21.4%

Income & Poverty, 1999

Per capita income	$39,520
Median household income	$91,014
Median family income	$102,842
Persons in poverty	193
H'holds receiving public assistance	17
H'holds receiving social security	784

Households, 2000

Total households	2,789
With persons under 18	1,097
With persons over 65	858
Family households	2,300
One-person households	438
Persons per household	2.83
Persons per family	3.17

Labor & Employment

Total civilian labor force, 2004**	4,608
Unemployment rate	3.0%
Total civilian labor force, 2000	3,980
Unemployment rate	2.9%

Employed persons 16 years and over by occupation, 2000
Managers & professionals	2,189
Service occupations	234
Sales & office occupations	1,124
Farming, fishing & forestry	0
Construction & maintenance	124
Production & transportation	194
Self-employed persons	270

*US Census Bureau
**New Jersey Department of Labor

General Information

Borough of Oradell
355 Kinderkamack Rd
Oradell, NJ 07649
201-261-8200

Web site	www.oradell.org
Land area (sq. miles)	2.42
Water area (sq. miles)	0.13
Type of government	Borough
Form of government	B

Government

Legislative Districts

US Congressional	5
State Legislative	39

Local Officials, 2006

Mayor	Frederick LaMonica
Admin/Manager	James McCue
Clerk	Ivana Malec
Finance Dir/Treas	James McCue
Engineer	Boswell McClave
Attorney	Raymond Wiss
Tax assessor	James Anzevino
Tax collector	Patricia Burns
Building officer	Melvin Streeter
Zoning officer	NA
Public Works	Mark DiGennaro

Housing & Construction

Housing Units, 2000*

Total	2,833
Median rent	$957
Median SF home value	$330,900

New Privately Owned Housing Units
Authorized by Building Permit

	Units	Value
Total, 2004	6	$1,350,920
Single family	6	$1,350,920
Total, 2005	5	$1,134,116
Single family	5	$1,134,116

Real Property Valuation - parcels, 2005

	Number	Valuation
Total		$837,082,100
Vacant	25	2,219,100
Residential	2,640	729,239,000
Commercial	94	101,714,700
Industrial	1	187,100
Apartments	5	3,722,200
Farm land	0	0
Farm homestead	0	0

Average Property Value & Tax, 2005

Residential value	$276,227
Property tax	$9,817
FAIR rebate	$611

Public Library

Oradell Public Library
375 Kinderkamack Rd
Oradell, NJ 07649
201-262-2613

Director	Lori Barnes

Library statistics, 2004

	Total	per capita
Volumes	73,978	9.19
Expenditure	$765,172	$95.09

Public Safety

Police

Chief	Rhynie Emanuel
Number of officers, 2004	23

Crime, 2004	Number	Rate
Total	70	8.7
Violent	3	0.4
Non-violent	67	8.3
Domestic Viol.	18	NA

Emergency/Fire

Director	David Gangemi

Public School District

(for school year 2004-2005 except as noted)

Oradell School District
350 Prospect Ave
Oradell, NJ 07649
201-261-1153

Superintendent	Jeffrey Mohre
Grade plan	K-6
Enrollment	747.0
Students per teacher	12.8
Per pupil expenditure	$10,148
Median faculty salary	$43,032
Median administrator salary	$105,304
Grade 12 enrollment	NA
High school graduation rate	NA

Assessment test results

(percent scoring at proficient or advanced level)
	Language	Math
Grade 3	100%	92.8%
Grade 8	NA	NA
High school	NA	NA

SAT

Percent tested	NA
Average SAT math score	NA
Average SAT verbal score	NA

No Child Left Behind, 2003-04

Attendence rate (target = 90%)	96.4%
Drop rate	NA
Highly-qualified teachers	100%
District needs improvement?(AYP)	No

Municipal Finance

Fiscal Year 2005

Total tax levy	$29,779,050
County levy	3,005,961
County taxes	2,855,595
County library	0
County health	0
County open space	150,367
School levy	19,598,553
Local muni. budget	7,174,536
Misc. revenues	4,392,049
Total aid	$1,161,329
CMPTRA	242,429
Muni. block grant	35,110
Energy tax receipts	819,690
Homeland security	50,000

Fiscal Year 2006

Total aid	$1,161,330
CMPTRA	213,740
Muni. block grant	35,110
Energy tax receipts	848,380
Homeland security	50,000

Taxes

	2003	2004	2005
General tax rate per $100	3.24	3.410	3.560
Net valuation taxable	$834,087,061	$835,456,756	$837,944,713
State equalized value	$1,353,378,324	$1,496,742,471	$1,696,931,375
County equalization ratio	66.35	61.63	55.79

Demographics & Socio-Economic Characteristics

(2000 U.S. Census, except as noted)

Population

1980*	31,136
1990*	29,925
2000	32,868
Male	15,199
Female	17,669
2000 (revised)	32,799
2004 (estimate)*	32,388
Persons per sq. mi. of land	14,686

Race & Hispanic Origin, 2000

Race

White	4,337
Black/African American	24,685
Amer. Indian/Alaska Natv.	113
Asian	415
Natv. Hawaiian/Pac. Islander	33
Other Race	1,712
Two or more races	1,573
Hispanic origin, total	4,097
Mexican	387
Puerto Rican	538
Cuban	38
Other Hispanic	3,134

Age & Nativity, 2000

Under 5 years	2,810
18 years and over	23,760
21 years and over	22,469
65 years and over	3,562
85 years and over	504
Median Age	32.5
Native born	22,575
Foreign born	10,293

Educational Attainment, 2000

Population 25 years and over	20,628
0-8 yrs of school	10.0%
High School grad or higher	72.2%
Bachelor's degree or higher	16.7%
Graduate degree	6.3%

Income & Poverty, 1999

Per capita income	$16,861
Median household income	$35,759
Median family income	$40,852
Persons in poverty	6,078
H'holds receiving public assistance	885
H'holds receiving social security	2,699

Households, 2000

Total households	11,885
With persons under 18	4,783
With persons over 65	2,693
Family households	7,647
One-person households	3,589
Persons per household	2.73
Persons per family	3.38

Labor & Employment

Total civilian labor force, 2004**	13,864
Unemployment rate	3.4%
Total civilian labor force, 2000	15,403
Unemployment rate	11.0%

Employed persons 16 years and over by occupation, 2000

Managers & professionals	3,513
Service occupations	3,170
Sales & office occupations	3,975
Farming, fishing & forestry	23
Construction & maintenance	1,061
Production & transportation	1,968
Self-employed persons	491

*US Census Bureau
**New Jersey Department of Labor

General Information

Township of Orange City
29 North Day St
Orange City, NJ 07050
973-266-4005

Web site	www.ci.orange.nj.us
Land area (sq. miles)	2.21
Water area (sq. miles)	0
Type of government	Township
Form of government	MC '50

Government

Legislative Districts

US Congressional	10
State Legislative	27

Local Officials, 2006

Mayor	Mims Hackett Jr.
Admin/Manager	Jewel V. Thompson
Clerk	Dwight Mitchell
Finance Dir/Treas	Jack Kelly
Engineer	Paul Lasek
Attorney	Marvin Braker
Tax assessor	Barbara Phillips
Tax collector	NA
Building officer	Robert Corrado
Zoning officer	Curtiss Webb
Public Works	NA

Housing & Construction

Housing Units, 2000*

Total	12,665
Median rent	$687
Median SF home value	$131,400

New Privately Owned Housing Units
Authorized by Building Permit

	Units	Value
Total, 2004	81	$5,823,700
Single family	4	$558,960
Total, 2005	109	$7,058,066
Single family	7	$890,360

Real Property Valuation - parcels, 2005

	Number	Valuation
Total		$109,834,000
Vacant	357	1,416,800
Residential	4,143	63,127,800
Commercial	416	21,430,700
Industrial	56	3,976,200
Apartments	172	19,882,500
Farm land	0	0
Farm homestead	0	0

Average Property Value & Tax, 2005

Residential value	$15,237
Property tax	$5,754
FAIR rebate	$598

Public Library

Orange Public Library
348 Main St
Orange, NJ 07050
973-673-0153

Director . . . . Doris Walker

Library statistics, 2004

	Total	per capita
Volumes	200,760	6.11
Expenditure	$1,050,334	$31.96

Public Safety

Police

Chief	Edward Lucas
Number of officers, 2004	109

Crime, 2004	Number	Rate
Total	2,094	64.3
Violent	382	11.7
Non-violent	1,712	52.6
Domestic Viol.	409	NA

Emergency/Fire

Director . . . . Allen Barnhardt

Public School District

(for school year 2004-2005 except as noted)

City Of Orange Township School District
451 Lincoln Ave
Orange, NJ 07050
973-677-4000

Superintendent	Nathan Parker
Grade plan	K-12
Enrollment	4,678.0
Students per teacher	9.2
Per pupil expenditure	$14,952
Median faculty salary	$46,232
Median administrator salary	$80,997
Grade 12 enrollment	201.0
High school graduation rate	70.8%

Assessment test results
(percent scoring at proficient or advanced level)

	Language	Math
Grade 3	71.2%	73.3%
Grade 8	31.4%	20.0%
High school	52.2%	33.2%

SAT

Percent tested	80%
Average SAT math score	379
Average SAT verbal score	366

No Child Left Behind, 2003-04

Attendence rate (target = 90%)	94.1%
Drop rate	4%
Highly-qualified teachers	50.7%
District needs improvement?(AYP)	No

Municipal Finance

Fiscal Year 2005

Total tax levy	$41,544,688
County levy	5,394,992
County taxes	5,281,923
County library	0
County health	0
County open space	113,069
School levy	9,646,298
Local muni. budget	26,503,398
Misc. revenues	27,233,599
Total aid	$10,234,171
CMPTRA	7,871,054
Muni. block grant	130,942
Energy tax receipts	2,092,175
Homeland security	140,000

Fiscal Year 2006

Total aid	$10,234,171
CMPTRA	7,797,828
Muni. block grant	130,942
Energy tax receipts	2,165,401
Homeland security	140,000

Taxes

	2003	2004	2005
General tax rate per $100	32.80	35.430	37.770
Net valuation taxable	$106,786,600	$106,871,550	$110,007,639
State equalized value	$956,012,534	$1,077,448,317	$1,304,954,199
County equalization ratio	12.3	12.30	9.90

Demographics & Socio-Economic Characteristics
(2000 U.S. Census, except as noted)

Population
1980*	1,659
1990*	1,790
2000	2,307
Male	1,137
Female	1,170
2004 (estimate)*	2,625
Persons per sq. mi. of land	442

Race & Hispanic Origin, 2000
Race
White	2,228
Black/African American	28
Amer. Indian/Alaska Natv.	5
Asian	12
Natv. Hawaiian/Pac. Islander	0
Other Race	15
Two or more races	19
Hispanic origin, total	80
Mexican	2
Puerto Rican	38
Cuban	4
Other Hispanic	36

Age & Nativity, 2000
Under 5 years	163
18 years and over	1,673
21 years and over	1,621
65 years and over	261
85 years and over	32
Median Age	36.4
Native born	2,223
Foreign born	84

Educational Attainment, 2000
Population 25 years and over	1,568
0-8 yrs of school	6.1%
High School grad or higher	82.1%
Bachelor's degree or higher	19.8%
Graduate degree	5.0%

Income & Poverty, 1999
Per capita income	$23,515
Median household income	$53,359
Median family income	$63,750
Persons in poverty	92
H'holds receiving public assistance	22
H'holds receiving social security	214

Households, 2000
Total households	886
With persons under 18	340
With persons over 65	209
Family households	618
One-person households	233
Persons per household	2.6
Persons per family	3.18

Labor & Employment
Total civilian labor force, 2004**	1,073
Unemployment rate	4.5%
Total civilian labor force, 2000	1,219
Unemployment rate	6.8%

Employed persons 16 years and over by occupation, 2000
Managers & professionals	346
Service occupations	194
Sales & office occupations	281
Farming, fishing & forestry	4
Construction & maintenance	139
Production & transportation	172
Self-employed persons	63

*US Census Bureau
**New Jersey Department of Labor

General Information
Township of Oxford
PO Box 119
11 Green St
Oxford, NJ 07863
908-453-3098

Web site	NA
Land area (sq. miles)	5.94
Water area (sq. miles)	0.08
Type of government	Township
Form of government	TC

Government

Legislative Districts
US Congressional	5
State Legislative	23

Local Officials, 2006
Mayor	N. Angelo Accetturo
Admin/Manager	NA
Clerk	Sheila L. Oberly
Finance Dir/Treas	Peter Kowalick
Engineer	Michael Finelli
Attorney	Michael Lavery
Tax assessor	Michael Schmidt
Tax collector	NA
Building officer	DCA
Zoning officer	NA
Public Works	NA

Housing & Construction

Housing Units, 2000*
Total	938
Median rent	$665
Median SF home value	$125,200

New Privately Owned Housing Units Authorized by Building Permit
	Units	Value
Total, 2004	13	$1,263,834
Single family	13	$1,263,834
Total, 2005	5	$421,543
Single family	5	$421,543

Real Property Valuation - parcels, 2005
	Number	Valuation
Total		$117,429,458
Vacant	213	3,094,500
Residential	840	101,881,600
Commercial	27	4,756,700
Industrial	4	4,694,600
Apartments	0	0
Farm land	17	2,752,900
Farm homestead	53	249,158

Average Property Value & Tax, 2005
Residential value	$114,368
Property tax	$4,176
FAIR rebate	$513

Public Library
Oxford Public Library
42 Washington Ave
Oxford, NJ 07863
908-453-2625

Librarian	Shirley Halsted

Library statistics, 2004
	Total	per capita
Volumes	NA	NA
Expenditure	NA	NA

Public Safety

Police
Chief	Charles Lilly (OIC)
Number of officers, 2004	4

Crime, 2004	Number	Rate
Total	10	3.8
Violent	1	0.4
Non-violent	9	3.4
Domestic Viol.	19	NA

Emergency/Fire
Director	Richard Calabrese

Public School District
(for school year 2004-2005 except as noted)

Oxford Township School District
17 Kent St
Oxford, NJ 07863
908-453-4101

Administrator	Dennis Wolf
Grade plan	K-12
Enrollment	325.0
Students per teacher	10.4
Per pupil expenditure	$11,284
Median faculty salary	$41,200
Median administrator salary	$84,000
Grade 12 enrollment	NA
High school graduation rate	NA

Assessment test results
(percent scoring at proficient or advanced level)
	Language	Math
Grade 3	76.6%	73.3%
Grade 8	80.6%	67.8%
High school	NA	NA

SAT
Percent tested	NA
Average SAT math score	NA
Average SAT verbal score	NA

No Child Left Behind, 2003-04
Attendence rate (target = 90%)	95.7%
Drop rate	NA
Highly-qualified teachers	100%
District needs improvement?(AYP)	No

Municipal Finance

Fiscal Year 2005
Total tax levy	$4,309,742
County levy	1,177,796
County taxes	972,986
County library	94,277
County health	0
County open space	110,533
School levy	2,789,626
Local muni. budget	342,320
Misc. revenues	1,796,209
Total aid	$297,865
CMPTRA	115,073
Muni. block grant	9,046
Energy tax receipts	148,746
Homeland security	25,000

Fiscal Year 2006
Total aid	$297,865
CMPTRA	109,867
Muni. block grant	9,046
Energy tax receipts	153,952
Homeland security	25,000

Taxes
	2003	2004	2005
General tax rate per $100	3.01	3.250	3.660
Net valuation taxable	$116,831,765	$117,551,928	$118,041,191
State equalized value	$162,041,283	$181,900,166	$205,289,028
County equalization ratio	82.22	72.10	64.49

Demographics & Socio-Economic Characteristics

(2000 U.S. Census, except as noted)

Population

1980*	13,732
1990*	14,536
2000	17,073
Male	8,497
Female	8,576
2004 (estimate)*	18,301
Persons per sq. mi. of land	15,127

Race & Hispanic Origin, 2000

Race
White	8,241
Black/African American	235
Amer. Indian/Alaska Natv.	32
Asian	7,016
Natv. Hawaiian/Pac. Islander	5
Other Race	991
Two or more races	553
Hispanic origin, total	2,813
Mexican	86
Puerto Rican	293
Cuban	279
Other Hispanic	2,155

Age & Nativity, 2000

Under 5 years	1,152
18 years and over	13,761
21 years and over	13,182
65 years and over	2,061
85 years and over	222
Median Age	35.6
Native born	7,348
Foreign born	9,725

Educational Attainment, 2000

Population 25 years and over	12,173
0-8 yrs of school	11.4%
High School grad or higher	79.3%
Bachelor's degree or higher	30.6%
Graduate degree	7.5%

Income & Poverty, 1999

Per capita income	$22,607
Median household income	$48,015
Median family income	$54,503
Persons in poverty	1,659
H'holds receiving public assistance	137
H'holds receiving social security	1,373

Households, 2000

Total households	6,247
With persons under 18	2,083
With persons over 65	1,537
Family households	4,445
One-person households	1,429
Persons per household	2.73
Persons per family	3.2

Labor & Employment

Total civilian labor force, 2004**	8,584
Unemployment rate	5.0%
Total civilian labor force, 2000	8,874
Unemployment rate	4.3%

Employed persons 16 years and over by occupation, 2000
Managers & professionals	2,809
Service occupations	1,405
Sales & office occupations	2,498
Farming, fishing & forestry	0
Construction & maintenance	674
Production & transportation	1,107
Self-employed persons	482

*US Census Bureau
**New Jersey Department of Labor

General Information

Borough of Palisades Park
275 Broad Ave
Palisades Park, NJ 07650
201-585-4100

Web site	NA
Land area (sq. miles)	1.21
Water area (sq. miles)	0.06
Type of government	Borough
Form of government	B

Government

Legislative Districts

US Congressional	9
State Legislative	37

Local Officials, 2006

Mayor	James Rotlindo
Admin/Manager	NA
Clerk	Martin A. Gobbo
Finance Dir/Treas	Roy Riggitano
Engineer	Steven Collazuol
Attorney	Joseph Mariniello
Tax assessor	Jim Anzevino
Tax collector	NA
Building officer	Anthony Pollotta
Zoning officer	NA
Public Works	NA

Housing & Construction

Housing Units, 2000*

Total	6,386
Median rent	$903
Median SF home value	$231,700

New Privately Owned Housing Units Authorized by Building Permit

	Units	Value
Total, 2004	255	$32,448,058
Single family	23	$3,675,000
Total, 2005	221	$30,914,700
Single family	43	$6,233,500

Real Property Valuation - parcels, 2005

	Number	Valuation
Total		$982,565,500
Vacant	89	12,998,900
Residential	3,128	741,428,900
Commercial	200	107,939,500
Industrial	41	50,405,200
Apartments	79	69,793,000
Farm land	0	0
Farm homestead	0	0

Average Property Value & Tax, 2005

Residential value	$237,030
Property tax	$6,885
FAIR rebate	$657

Public Library

Palisades Park Public Library
257 Second St
Palisades Park, NJ 07650
201-585-4150

Director ... Terrie McColl

Library statistics, 2004

	Total	per capita
Volumes	47,826	2.80
Expenditure	$497,219	$29.12

Public Safety

Police

Chief	Michael Vietri
Number of officers, 2004	33

Crime, 2004	Number	Rate
Total	190	10.6
Violent	15	0.8
Non-violent	175	9.7
Domestic Viol.	103	NA

Emergency/Fire

Director ... Howie Donovan

Public School District

(for school year 2004-2005 except as noted)

Palisades Park School District
270 First St
Palisades Park, NJ 07650
201-947-3560

Superintendent	Mark Hayes
Grade plan	K-12
Enrollment	1,520.0
Students per teacher	11.7
Per pupil expenditure	$11,165
Median faculty salary	$44,500
Median administrator salary	$105,716
Grade 12 enrollment	95.0
High school graduation rate	94.1%

Assessment test results

(percent scoring at proficient or advanced level)
	Language	Math
Grade 3	74.2%	75.0%
Grade 8	66.4%	60.0%
High school	69.3%	77.2%

SAT

Percent tested	86%
Average SAT math score	523
Average SAT verbal score	451

No Child Left Behind, 2003-04

Attendence rate (target = 90%)	95.2%
Drop rate	1.5%
Highly-qualified teachers	89.1%
District needs improvement?(AYP)	No

Municipal Finance

Fiscal Year 2005

Total tax levy	$28,552,331
County levy	3,437,836
County taxes	3,264,680
County library	0
County health	0
County open space	173,156
School levy	15,854,069
Local muni. budget	9,260,426
Misc. revenues	6,459,380
Total aid	$1,370,437
CMPTRA	555,597
Muni. block grant	66,944
Energy tax receipts	677,896
Homeland security	70,000

Fiscal Year 2006

Total aid	$1,370,437
CMPTRA	531,871
Muni. block grant	66,944
Energy tax receipts	701,622
Homeland security	70,000

Taxes

	2003	2004	2005
General tax rate per $100	2.86	2.860	2.910
Net valuation taxable	$894,355,836	$935,637,476	$982,964,792
State equalized value	$1,436,485,442	$1,641,127,387	$1,958,877,625
County equalization ratio	68.85	62.26	57.00

Demographics & Socio-Economic Characteristics
(2000 U.S. Census, except as noted)

Population
1980*	7,085
1990*	7,056
2000	7,091
Male	3,421
Female	3,670
2004 (estimate)*	7,672
Persons per sq. mi. of land	3,881

Race & Hispanic Origin, 2000
Race
White	5,743
Black/African American	1,017
Amer. Indian/Alaska Natv.	21
Asian	99
Natv. Hawaiian/Pac. Islander	3
Other Race	100
Two or more races	108
Hispanic origin, total	229
Mexican	19
Puerto Rican	146
Cuban	13
Other Hispanic	51

Age & Nativity, 2000
Under 5 years	413
18 years and over	5,508
21 years and over	5,296
65 years and over	960
85 years and over	86
Median Age	38
Native born	6,798
Foreign born	293

Educational Attainment, 2000
Population 25 years and over	5,068
0-8 yrs of school	3.2%
High School grad or higher	85.1%
Bachelor's degree or higher	21.8%
Graduate degree	6.1%

Income & Poverty, 1999
Per capita income	$23,454
Median household income	$51,150
Median family income	$57,192
Persons in poverty	295
H'holds receiving public assistance	45
H'holds receiving social security	705

Households, 2000
Total households	3,004
With persons under 18	894
With persons over 65	733
Family households	1,852
One-person households	962
Persons per household	2.36
Persons per family	3.02

Labor & Employment
Total civilian labor force, 2004**	4,578
Unemployment rate	5.3%
Total civilian labor force, 2000	4,053
Unemployment rate	4.7%

Employed persons 16 years and over by occupation, 2000
Managers & professionals	1,258
Service occupations	485
Sales & office occupations	1,248
Farming, fishing & forestry	5
Construction & maintenance	394
Production & transportation	473
Self-employed persons	204

*US Census Bureau
**New Jersey Department of Labor

General Information
Borough of Palmyra
20 W Broad St
Palmyra, NJ 08065
856-829-6100
Web site	www.boroughofpalmyra.com
Land area (sq. miles)	1.98
Water area (sq. miles)	0.44
Type of government	Borough
Form of government	B

Government

Legislative Districts
US Congressional	1
State Legislative	7

Local Officials, 2006
Mayor	John J. Gural Jr.
Admin/Manager	Marianne Hulme
Clerk	Pamela Scott
Finance Dir/Treas	Marianne Hulme
Engineer	Land Engineering
Attorney	Ted Rosenburg
Tax assessor	Karen Davis
Tax collector	Marianne Hulme
Building officer	Matthew O'Hara
Zoning officer	Matthew O'Hara
Public Works	Brian McCleary

Housing & Construction

Housing Units, 2000*
Total	3,219
Median rent	$818
Median SF home value	$110,500

New Privately Owned Housing Units Authorized by Building Permit
	Units	Value
Total, 2004	10	$626,138
Single family	10	$626,138
Total, 2005	10	$628,192
Single family	10	$628,192

Real Property Valuation - parcels, 2005
	Number	Valuation
Total		$313,499,550
Vacant	154	3,991,700
Residential	2,778	270,263,750
Commercial	112	19,428,500
Industrial	25	6,250,400
Apartments	46	13,356,200
Farm land	0	0
Farm homestead	6	209,000

Average Property Value & Tax, 2005
Residential value	$97,153
Property tax	$3,581
FAIR rebate	$585

Public Library
Riverton Free Library
306 Main St
Riverton, NJ 08077
856-829-2476
Director	Michael Robinson

Library statistics, 2004
	Total	per capita
Volumes	NA	NA
Expenditure	NA	NA

Public Safety

Police
Chief	Richard K. Dreby
Number of officers, 2004	17

Crime, 2004	Number	Rate
Total	172	22.5
Violent	11	1.4
Non-violent	161	21
Domestic Viol.	78	NA

Emergency/Fire
Director	Alan Zimmerman

Public School District
(for school year 2004-2005 except as noted)

Palmyra Borough School District
301 Delaware Ave
Palmyra, NJ 08065
856-786-2963
Superintendent	Walter Rudder (Int)
Grade plan	K-12
Enrollment	1,073.0
Students per teacher	11.0
Per pupil expenditure	$10,142
Median faculty salary	$43,049
Median administrator salary	$80,095
Grade 12 enrollment	89.0
High school graduation rate	93.7%

Assessment test results
(percent scoring at proficient or advanced level)
	Language	Math
Grade 3	88.0%	94.0%
Grade 8	70.1%	49.4%
High school	81.1%	74.6%

SAT
Percent tested	74%
Average SAT math score	492
Average SAT verbal score	512

No Child Left Behind, 2003-04
Attendence rate (target = 90%)	94.8%
Drop rate	1.6%
Highly-qualified teachers	97.1%
District needs improvement?(AYP)	No

Municipal Finance

Fiscal Year 2005
Total tax levy	$11,571,088
County levy	1,965,013
County taxes	1,648,440
County library	144,335
County health	0
County open space	172,238
School levy	6,244,721
Local muni. budget	3,361,354
Misc. revenues	3,040,106
Total aid	$834,096
CMPTRA	352,157
Muni. block grant	30,875
Energy tax receipts	401,064
Homeland security	50,000

Fiscal Year 2006
Total aid	$834,097
CMPTRA	338,120
Muni. block grant	30,875
Energy tax receipts	415,102
Homeland security	50,000

Taxes
	2003	2004	2005
General tax rate per $100	3.39	3.503	3.687
Net valuation taxable	$313,431,420	$313,811,392	$313,959,790
State equalized value	$382,373,332	$428,266,861	$484,505,849
County equalization ratio	88.73	81.97	73.24

Demographics & Socio-Economic Characteristics
(2000 U.S. Census, except as noted)

Population
1980*	26,474
1990*	25,067
2000	25,737
Male	12,497
Female	13,240
2004 (estimate)*	26,624
Persons per sq. mi. of land	2,542

Race & Hispanic Origin, 2000
Race
White	20,380
Black/African American	291
Amer. Indian/Alaska Natv.	12
Asian	4,434
Natv. Hawaiian/Pac. Islander	3
Other Race	229
Two or more races	388
Hispanic origin, total	1,253
Mexican	60
Puerto Rican	211
Cuban	285
Other Hispanic	697

Age & Nativity, 2000
Under 5 years	1,331
18 years and over	19,755
21 years and over	19,117
65 years and over	5,531
85 years and over	824
Median Age	42.9
Native born	19,275
Foreign born	6,462

Educational Attainment, 2000
Population 25 years and over	18,264
0-8 yrs of school	5.8%
High School grad or higher	86.2%
Bachelor's degree or higher	38.7%
Graduate degree	14.3%

Income & Poverty, 1999
Per capita income	$29,295
Median household income	$76,918
Median family income	$84,406
Persons in poverty	803
H'holds receiving public assistance	21
H'holds receiving social security	2,809

Households, 2000
Total households	8,082
With persons under 18	3,182
With persons over 65	2,989
Family households	6,779
One-person households	1,164
Persons per household	3.0
Persons per family	3.32

Labor & Employment
Total civilian labor force, 2004**	13,772
Unemployment rate	3.3%
Total civilian labor force, 2000	12,069
Unemployment rate	2.3%

Employed persons 16 years and over by occupation, 2000
Managers & professionals	5,206
Service occupations	1,073
Sales & office occupations	3,932
Farming, fishing & forestry	0
Construction & maintenance	736
Production & transportation	846
Self-employed persons	806

*US Census Bureau
**New Jersey Department of Labor

General Information
Borough of Paramus
One Jockish Square
Paramus, NJ 07652
201-265-2100

Web site	www.paramusborough.org
Land area (sq. miles)	10.47
Water area (sq. miles)	0
Type of government	Borough
Form of government	B

Government

Legislative Districts
US Congressional	5
State Legislative	38

Local Officials, 2006
Mayor	James Tedesco III
Admin/Manager	NA
Clerk	Ian Shore
Finance Dir/Treas	Joseph Citro
Engineer	Boswell Engineering
Attorney	Dewnis Oury
Tax assessor	James Anzevino
Tax collector	NA
Building officer	Peter Wells
Zoning officer	NA
Public Works	NA

Housing & Construction

Housing Units, 2000*
Total	8,209
Median rent	$1,483
Median SF home value	$284,800

New Privately Owned Housing Units Authorized by Building Permit
	Units	Value
Total, 2004	36	$10,645,640
Single family	32	$10,010,640
Total, 2005	61	$18,448,666
Single family	46	$18,438,517

Real Property Valuation - parcels, 2005
	Number	Valuation
Total		$6,824,573,600
Vacant	127	158,796,700
Residential	8,108	3,578,172,800
Commercial	412	2,955,286,100
Industrial	30	113,790,400
Apartments	1	17,025,400
Farm land	4	1,479,800
Farm homestead	4	22,400

Average Property Value & Tax, 2005
Residential value	$441,099
Property tax	$6,469
FAIR rebate	$647

Public Library
Paramus Public Library
E 116 Century Rd
Paramus, NJ 07652
201-599-1302
Director	Leonard LoPinto

Library statistics, 2004
	Total	per capita
Volumes	100,906	3.92
Expenditure	$2,134,777	$82.95

Public Safety
Police
Chief	Fred Corrubia
Number of officers, 2004	98

Crime, 2004	Number	Rate
Total	2,198	82.9
Violent	85	3.2
Non-violent	2,113	79.7
Domestic Viol.	137	NA

Emergency/Fire
Director	Kevin Sheehan (Dept Chief)

Public School District
(for school year 2004-2005 except as noted)

Paramus School District
145 Spring Valley Rd
Paramus, NJ 07652
201-261-7800
Superintendent	Janice Dime
Grade plan	K-12
Enrollment	4,285.0
Students per teacher	11.0
Per pupil expenditure	$13,425
Median faculty salary	$49,237
Median administrator salary	$108,652
Grade 12 enrollment	299.5
High school graduation rate	98.3%

Assessment test results
(percent scoring at proficient or advanced level)
	Language	Math
Grade 3	93.8%	91.1%
Grade 8	89.2%	81.2%
High school	93.2%	88.0%

SAT
Percent tested	93%
Average SAT math score	570
Average SAT verbal score	532

No Child Left Behind, 2003-04
Attendence rate (target = 90%)	97.1%
Drop rate	0.3%
Highly-qualified teachers	79.5%
District needs improvement?(AYP)	No

Municipal Finance

Fiscal Year 2005
Total tax levy	$100,172,246
County levy	14,497,219
County taxes	13,769,467
County library	0
County health	0
County open space	727,752
School levy	56,664,174
Local muni. budget	29,010,853
Misc. revenues	15,122,323
Total aid	$5,613,387
CMPTRA	2,390,443
Muni. block grant	109,410
Energy tax receipts	3,023,534
Homeland security	90,000

Fiscal Year 2006
Total aid	$5,613,387
CMPTRA	2,284,619
Muni. block grant	109,410
Energy tax receipts	3,129,358
Homeland security	90,000

Taxes
	2003	2004	2005
General tax rate per $100	2.44	1.370	1.470
Net valuation taxable	$3,460,466,493	$6,838,732,453	$6,830,307,119
State equalized value	$6,271,233,224	$7,201,360,464	$8,201,617,578
County equalization ratio	65.16	107.98	94.96

Demographics & Socio-Economic Characteristics

(2000 U.S. Census, except as noted)

Population

1980*	8,515
1990*	8,102
2000	8,708
Male	4,178
Female	4,530
2004 (estimate)*	8,970
Persons per sq. mi. of land	3,454

Race & Hispanic Origin, 2000

Race

White	8,140
Black/African American	75
Amer. Indian/Alaska Natv.	12
Asian	336
Natv. Hawaiian/Pac. Islander	2
Other Race	64
Two or more races	79
Hispanic origin, total	463
Mexican	233
Puerto Rican	52
Cuban	38
Other Hispanic	140

Age & Nativity, 2000

Under 5 years	599
18 years and over	6,664
21 years and over	6,470
65 years and over	1,408
85 years and over	253
Median Age	40.9
Native born	7,510
Foreign born	1,198

Educational Attainment, 2000

Population 25 years and over	6,293
0-8 yrs of school	2.5%
High School grad or higher	91.4%
Bachelor's degree or higher	45.0%
Graduate degree	17.3%

Income & Poverty, 1999

Per capita income	$40,351
Median household income	$86,632
Median family income	$97,294
Persons in poverty	260
H'holds receiving public assistance	33
H'holds receiving social security	863

Households, 2000

Total households	3,161
With persons under 18	1,110
With persons over 65	839
Family households	2,389
One-person households	673
Persons per household	2.67
Persons per family	3.12

Labor & Employment

Total civilian labor force, 2004**	4,819
Unemployment rate	4.0%
Total civilian labor force, 2000	4,480
Unemployment rate	1.5%

Employed persons 16 years and over by occupation, 2000

Managers & professionals	2,082
Service occupations	493
Sales & office occupations	1,365
Farming, fishing & forestry	0
Construction & maintenance	272
Production & transportation	200
Self-employed persons	295

*US Census Bureau
**New Jersey Department of Labor

General Information

Borough of Park Ridge
55 Park Ave
Park Ridge, NJ 07656
201-573-1800

Web site	www.parkridgeboro.com
Land area (sq. miles)	2.60
Water area (sq. miles)	0.04
Type of government	Borough
Form of government	B

Government

Legislative Districts

US Congressional	5
State Legislative	39

Local Officials, 2006

Mayor	Donald Ruschman
Admin/Manager	Gene Vinci
Clerk	Karen Hughes
Finance Dir/Treas	Ann Kilmartin
Engineer	Brooker Engineering
Attorney	John D'Anton
Tax assessor	Robert Campora
Tax collector	Ann Kilmartin
Building officer	Nick Saluzzi
Zoning officer	Nancy Russell
Public Works	Buddy Roehrer

Housing & Construction

Housing Units, 2000*

Total	3,258
Median rent	$996
Median SF home value	$307,000

New Privately Owned Housing Units Authorized by Building Permit

	Units	Value
Total, 2004	17	$4,183,209
Single family	15	$4,033,877
Total, 2005	18	$4,938,659
Single family	16	$4,789,327

Real Property Valuation - parcels, 2005

	Number	Valuation
Total		$1,685,016,100
Vacant	90	19,316,100
Residential	2,859	1,443,325,000
Commercial	100	205,431,700
Industrial	3	3,379,800
Apartments	9	13,563,500
Farm land	0	0
Farm homestead	0	0

Average Property Value & Tax, 2005

Residential value	$504,836
Property tax	$8,063
FAIR rebate	$608

Public Library

Park Ridge Library
51 Park Ave
Park Ridge, NJ 07656
201-391-5151

Director	Christina Doto

Library statistics, 2004

	Total	per capita
Volumes	47,429	5.45
Expenditure	$470,250	$54.00

Public Safety

Police

Chief	Richard Oppenheimer
Number of officers, 2004	17

Crime, 2004	Number	Rate
Total	45	5.1
Violent	0	0
Non-violent	45	5.1
Domestic Viol.	13	NA

Emergency/Fire

Director	Tom Derienzo

Public School District

(for school year 2004-2005 except as noted)

Park Ridge School District
2 Park Ave
Park Ridge, NJ 07656
201-573-6000

Superintendent	Patricia Johnson
Grade plan	K-12
Enrollment	1,313.0
Students per teacher	10.9
Per pupil expenditure	$12,934
Median faculty salary	$55,886
Median administrator salary	$106,956
Grade 12 enrollment	66.5
High school graduation rate	100.0%

Assessment test results

(percent scoring at proficient or advanced level)

	Language	Math
Grade 3	95.8%	97.5%
Grade 8	81.1%	91.0%
High school	94.1%	88.3%

SAT

Percent tested	84%
Average SAT math score	561
Average SAT verbal score	546

No Child Left Behind, 2003-04

Attendance rate (target = 90%)	95.8%
Drop rate	0%
Highly-qualified teachers	98.7%
District needs improvement?(AYP)	No

Municipal Finance

Fiscal Year 2005

Total tax levy	$26,938,163
County levy	3,112,328
County taxes	2,954,302
County library	0
County health	0
County open space	158,026
School levy	16,992,876
Local muni. budget	6,832,960
Misc. revenues	3,287,362
Total aid	$643,167
CMPTRA	260,821
Muni. block grant	35,452
Energy tax receipts	295,296
Homeland security	50,000

Fiscal Year 2006

Total aid	$643,166
CMPTRA	250,485
Muni. block grant	35,452
Energy tax receipts	305,631
Homeland security	50,000

Taxes

	2003	2004	2005
General tax rate per $100	2.47	1.510	1.600
Net valuation taxable	$941,937,069	$1,681,943,905	$1,686,617,247
State equalized value	$1,374,488,646	$1,572,019,150	$1,770,726,769
County equalization ratio	73.86	121.29	107.00

Demographics & Socio-Economic Characteristics
(2000 U.S. Census, except as noted)

Population
1980*	49,868
1990*	48,478
2000	50,649
Male	25,039
Female	25,610
2004 (estimate)*	51,639
Persons per sq. mi. of land	2,157

Race & Hispanic Origin, 2000
Race
White	37,620
Black/African American	1,574
Amer. Indian/Alaska Natv.	61
Asian	9,145
Natv. Hawaiian/Pac. Islander	28
Other Race	963
Two or more races	1,258
Hispanic origin, total	3,535
Mexican	221
Puerto Rican	709
Cuban	228
Other Hispanic	2,377

Age & Nativity, 2000
Under 5 years	3,065
18 years and over	40,034
21 years and over	38,731
65 years and over	5,691
85 years and over	572
Median Age	37.6
Native born	37,064
Foreign born	13,585

Educational Attainment, 2000
Population 25 years and over	36,644
0-8 yrs of school	3.5%
High School grad or higher	89.9%
Bachelor's degree or higher	43.0%
Graduate degree	15.4%

Income & Poverty, 1999
Per capita income	$32,220
Median household income	$68,133
Median family income	$81,041
Persons in poverty	1,918
H'holds receiving public assistance	256
H'holds receiving social security	3,992

Households, 2000
Total households	19,624
With persons under 18	6,184
With persons over 65	4,141
Family households	13,160
One-person households	5,321
Persons per household	2.53
Persons per family	3.13

Labor & Employment
Total civilian labor force, 2004**	32,942
Unemployment rate	3.2%
Total civilian labor force, 2000	29,230
Unemployment rate	2.9%

Employed persons 16 years and over by occupation, 2000
Managers & professionals	13,363
Service occupations	2,548
Sales & office occupations	8,115
Farming, fishing & forestry	18
Construction & maintenance	1,722
Production & transportation	2,623
Self-employed persons	1,304

*US Census Bureau
**New Jersey Department of Labor

General Information
Township of Parsippany-Troy Hills
1001 Parsippany Blvd
Parsippany, NJ 07054
973-263-4350
Web site	www.parsippany.net
Land area (sq. miles)	23.94
Water area (sq. miles)	1.48
Type of government	Township
Form of government	MC Plan E '66

Government
Legislative Districts
US Congressional	11
State Legislative	26

Local Officials, 2006
Mayor	Michael M. Luther
Admin/Manager	Jasmine Lim
Clerk	Judith Silver
Finance Dir/Treas	Ruby Malcolm
Engineer	Michael Pucilowski
Attorney	Alfred C. DeCotiis
Tax assessor	Daniel Cassese
Tax collector	Frank Ogrodnik
Building officer	Ronald Bauer
Zoning officer	NA
Public Works	NA

Housing & Construction
Housing Units, 2000*
Total	20,066
Median rent	$823
Median SF home value	$234,100

New Privately Owned Housing Units
Authorized by Building Permit
	Units	Value
Total, 2004	29	$3,795,280
Single family	27	$3,739,580
Total, 2005	48	$7,582,647
Single family	48	$7,582,647

Real Property Valuation - parcels, 2005
	Number	Valuation
Total		$7,761,011,100
Vacant	660	143,482,400
Residential	13,276	4,121,676,500
Commercial	592	2,715,594,800
Industrial	61	325,849,900
Apartments	34	454,078,000
Farm land	1	326,400
Farm homestead	1	3,100

Average Property Value & Tax, 2005
Residential value	$310,438
Property tax	$5,879
FAIR rebate	$540

Public Library
Parsippany-Troy Hills Public Libr
292 Parsippany Rd
Parsippany, NJ 07054
973-887-5150
Director	Jayne Beline

Library statistics, 2004
	Total	per capita
Volumes	186,750	3.69
Expenditure	$2,585,636	$51.05

Public Safety
Police
Chief	Michael Filippello
Number of officers, 2004	109

Crime, 2004	Number	Rate
Total	868	16.9
Violent	35	0.7
Non-violent	833	16.3
Domestic Viol.	225	NA

Emergency/Fire
Director	NA

Public School District
(for school year 2004-2005 except as noted)

Parsippany-Troy Hills Township Dist.
PO Box 52
Parsippany, NJ 07054
973-263-7250
Superintendent	James Dwyer (Int)
Grade plan	K-12
Enrollment	6,754.5
Students per teacher	10.3
Per pupil expenditure	$14,039
Median faculty salary	$55,865
Median administrator salary	$104,990
Grade 12 enrollment	530.0
High school graduation rate	NA

Assessment test results
(percent scoring at proficient or advanced level)
	Language	Math
Grade 3	89.1%	91.0%
Grade 8	83.4%	78.5%
High school	84.2%	84.2%

SAT
Percent tested	NA
Average SAT math score	NA
Average SAT verbal score	NA

No Child Left Behind, 2003-04
Attendence rate (target = 90%)	96.2%
Drop rate	0.9%
Highly-qualified teachers	98.4%
District needs improvement?(AYP)	No

Municipal Finance
Fiscal Year 2005
Total tax levy	$147,204,320
County levy	20,080,313
County taxes	16,447,817
County library	0
County health	0
County open space	3,632,496
School levy	93,398,563
Local muni. budget	33,725,444
Misc. revenues	20,403,882
Total aid	$6,256,777
CMPTRA	2,875,433
Muni. block grant	212,124
Energy tax receipts	2,974,042
Homeland security	140,000

Fiscal Year 2006
Total aid	$6,256,778
CMPTRA	2,771,342
Muni. block grant	212,124
Energy tax receipts	3,078,134
Homeland security	140,000

Taxes
	2003	2004	2005
General tax rate per $100	1.72	1.810	1.900
Net valuation taxable	$7,821,180,431	$7,861,372,866	$7,773,465,557
State equalized value	$6,923,236,639	$7,632,027,402	$8,644,868,280
County equalization ratio	124.06	112.97	103.01

Demographics & Socio-Economic Characteristics
(2000 U.S. Census, except as noted)

Population
1980*	52,463
1990*	58,041
2000	67,861
Male	33,852
Female	34,009
2004 (estimate)*	68,662
Persons per sq. mi. of land	22,062

Race & Hispanic Origin, 2000
Race
White	24,044
Black/African American	9,385
Amer. Indian/Alaska Natv.	531
Asian	3,740
Natv. Hawaiian/Pac. Islander	29
Other Race	26,709
Two or more races	3,423
Hispanic origin, total	42,387
Mexican	13,346
Puerto Rican	9,122
Cuban	654
Other Hispanic	19,265

Age & Nativity, 2000
Under 5 years	6,525
18 years and over	46,962
21 years and over	43,331
65 years and over	5,513
85 years and over	757
Median Age	28.6
Native born	36,760
Foreign born	31,101

Educational Attainment, 2000
Population 25 years and over	38,437
0-8 yrs of school	23.2%
High School grad or higher	55.5%
Bachelor's degree or higher	13.7%
Graduate degree	5.1%

Income & Poverty, 1999
Per capita income	$12,874
Median household income	$33,594
Median family income	$34,935
Persons in poverty	14,249
H'holds receiving public assistance	1,238
H'holds receiving social security	4,274

Households, 2000
Total households	19,458
With persons under 18	9,532
With persons over 65	4,228
Family households	14,456
One-person households	3,945
Persons per household	3.46
Persons per family	3.93

Labor & Employment
Total civilian labor force, 2004**	29,459
Unemployment rate	9.2%
Total civilian labor force, 2000	28,589
Unemployment rate	10.3%

Employed persons 16 years and over by occupation, 2000
Managers & professionals	4,608
Service occupations	4,452
Sales & office occupations	6,038
Farming, fishing & forestry	82
Construction & maintenance	1,857
Production & transportation	8,601
Self-employed persons	762

*US Census Bureau
**New Jersey Department of Labor

General Information
City of Passaic
330 Passaic St
Passaic, NJ 07055
973-365-5500

Web site	www.cityofpassaic.com
Land area (sq. miles)	3.11
Water area (sq. miles)	0.10
Type of government	City
Form of government	MC '50

Government

Legislative Districts
US Congressional	8
State Legislative	36

Local Officials, 2006
Mayor	Samuel Rivera
Admin/Manager	Greg Hill
Clerk	Amada D. Curling
Finance Dir/Treas	Jose L. Agosto
Engineer	Donald Schlechter
Attorney	Donald Scarinci
Tax assessor	Thomas Poalillo
Tax collector	Carrie Malak
Building officer	John Miskovsky
Zoning officer	Ricardo Fernandez
Public Works	Theodore Evans

Housing & Construction

Housing Units, 2000*
Total	20,194
Median rent	$677
Median SF home value	$153,000

New Privately Owned Housing Units
Authorized by Building Permit
	Units	Value
Total, 2004	52	$2,834,445
Single family	14	$1,125,089
Total, 2005	53	$4,346,027
Single family	8	$1,363,455

Real Property Valuation - parcels, 2005
	Number	Valuation
Total		$1,347,708,100
Vacant	250	5,169,700
Residential	6,181	789,124,300
Commercial	1,175	301,459,500
Industrial	124	97,632,000
Apartments	405	154,322,600
Farm land	0	0
Farm homestead	0	0

Average Property Value & Tax, 2005
Residential value	$127,669
Property tax	$6,007
FAIR rebate	$609

Public Library
Passaic Public Library
195 Gregory Ave
Passaic, NJ 07055
973-779-0474

Director .... Alan Bobwski

Library statistics, 2004
	Total	per capita
Volumes	113,049	1.67
Expenditure	$1,373,242	$20.24

Public Safety

Police
Chief	Stanley Jarensky
Number of officers, 2004	164

Crime, 2004	Number	Rate
Total	2,698	39.4
Violent	683	10
Non-violent	2,015	29.4
Domestic Viol.	701	NA

Emergency/Fire
Director .... Timothy Zayatz

Public School District
(for school year 2004-2005 except as noted)

Passaic City School District
101 Passaic Ave
Passaic, NJ 07055
973-470-5201

Administrator	Robert Holster
Grade plan	K-12
Enrollment	12,151.0
Students per teacher	11.1
Per pupil expenditure	$14,732
Median faculty salary	$51,970
Median administrator salary	$101,866
Grade 12 enrollment	472.0
High school graduation rate	67.1%

Assessment test results
(percent scoring at proficient or advanced level)
	Language	Math
Grade 3	59.9%	59.7%
Grade 8	39.2%	25.5%
High school	56.0%	46.7%

SAT
Percent tested	47%
Average SAT math score	426
Average SAT verbal score	394

No Child Left Behind, 2003-04
Attendence rate (target = 90%)	94.3%
Drop rate	7%
Highly-qualified teachers	91.3%
District needs improvement?(AYP)	No

Municipal Finance

Fiscal Year 2005
Total tax levy	$63,779,287
County levy	12,121,000
County taxes	11,890,419
County library	0
County health	0
County open space	230,581
School levy	13,887,710
Local muni. budget	37,770,577
Misc. revenues	25,528,484
Total aid	$15,355,203
CMPTRA	12,524,446
Muni. block grant	266,085
Energy tax receipts	2,424,672
Homeland security	140,000

Fiscal Year 2006
Total aid	$15,355,203
CMPTRA	12,439,582
Muni. block grant	266,085
Energy tax receipts	2,509,536
Homeland security	140,000

Taxes
	2003	2004	2005
General tax rate per $100	4.37	4.550	4.710
Net valuation taxable	$1,351,233,809	$1,358,227,100	$1,355,558,400
State equalized value	$1,926,481,051	$2,237,484,438	$2,705,165,436
County equalization ratio	80.47	70.14	60.53

Demographics & Socio-Economic Characteristics
(2000 U.S. Census, except as noted)

Population
1980*	137,970
1990*	140,891
2000	149,222
Male	72,473
Female	76,749
2004 (estimate)*	150,869
Persons per sq. mi. of land	17,870

Race & Hispanic Origin, 2000
Race
White	45,913
Black/African American	49,095
Amer. Indian/Alaska Natv.	901
Asian	2,831
Natv. Hawaiian/Pac. Islander	84
Other Race	41,184
Two or more races	9,214
Hispanic origin, total	74,774
Mexican	5,004
Puerto Rican	24,013
Cuban	858
Other Hispanic	44,899

Age & Nativity, 2000
Under 5 years	12,578
18 years and over	104,785
21 years and over	97,577
65 years and over	12,399
85 years and over	1,356
Median Age	30.5
Native born	100,298
Foreign born	48,924

Educational Attainment, 2000
Population 25 years and over	88,077
0-8 yrs of school	18.1%
High School grad or higher	58.5%
Bachelor's degree or higher	8.2%
Graduate degree	2.8%

Income & Poverty, 1999
Per capita income	$13,257
Median household income	$32,778
Median family income	$35,420
Persons in poverty	32,474
H'holds receiving public assistance	3,874
H'holds receiving social security	10,102

Households, 2000
Total households	44,710
With persons under 18	21,997
With persons over 65	9,801
Family households	33,351
One-person households	9,143
Persons per household	3.25
Persons per family	3.71

Labor & Employment
Total civilian labor force, 2004**	69,687
Unemployment rate	9.2%
Total civilian labor force, 2000	60,463
Unemployment rate	13.1%

Employed persons 16 years and over by occupation, 2000
Managers & professionals	8,774
Service occupations	10,640
Sales & office occupations	14,529
Farming, fishing & forestry	84
Construction & maintenance	4,114
Production & transportation	14,404
Self-employed persons	1,390

*US Census Bureau
**New Jersey Department of Labor

General Information
City of Paterson
155 Market St
Paterson, NJ 07505
973-321-1500
Web site	www.patcity.com
Land area (sq. miles)	8.44
Water area (sq. miles)	0.29
Type of government	City
Form of government	MC '50

Government
Legislative Districts
US Congressional	8
State Legislative	35

Local Officials, 2006
Mayor	Jose Torres
Admin/Manager	Eli Burgos
Clerk	Jane Williams-Warren
Finance Dir/Treas	Marge Cherone
Engineer	Frederick Margron
Attorney	Susan Champion
Tax assessor	J. Krieger/C. Parmelli
Tax collector	NA
Building officer	L. Vildshteyn/R. Morabi
Zoning officer	James Peloso
Public Works	Manny Ojeda

Housing & Construction
Housing Units, 2000*
Total	47,169
Median rent	$696
Median SF home value	$137,500

New Privately Owned Housing Units Authorized by Building Permit
	Units	Value
Total, 2004	7	$591,300
Single family	7	$516,300
Total, 2005	1	$73,757
Single family	1	$73,757

Real Property Valuation - parcels, 2005
	Number	Valuation
Total		$573,166,346
Vacant	2,380	9,553,380
Residential	17,555	364,174,765
Commercial	2,368	118,308,010
Industrial	422	42,712,663
Apartments	495	38,417,528
Farm land	0	0
Farm homestead	0	0

Average Property Value & Tax, 2005
Residential value	$20,745
Property tax	$5,182
FAIR rebate	$610

Public Library
Paterson Free Public Library
250 Broadway
Paterson, NJ 07501
973-321-1223
Director	Cindy Czesak

Library statistics, 2004
	Total	per capita
Volumes	192,172	1.29
Expenditure	$2,639,398	$17.69

Public Safety
Police
Chief	Lawrence Spagnola
Number of officers, 2004	399

Crime, 2004	Number	Rate
Total	5,871	38.9
Violent	1,219	8.1
Non-violent	4,652	30.9
Domestic Viol.	2,177	NA

Emergency/Fire
Director	Michael Postorino

Public School District
(for school year 2004-2005 except as noted)

Paterson School District
33-35 Church St
Paterson, NJ 07505
973-321-0980
Superintendent	Michael Glascoe
Grade plan	K-12
Enrollment	26,256.0
Students per teacher	9.1
Per pupil expenditure	$14,280
Median faculty salary	$46,500
Median administrator salary	$105,000
Grade 12 enrollment	1,141.0
High school graduation rate	NA

Assessment test results
(percent scoring at proficient or advanced level)
	Language	Math
Grade 3	61.9%	60.4%
Grade 8	46.1%	36.3%
High school	53.8%	47.2%

SAT
Percent tested	NA
Average SAT math score	NA
Average SAT verbal score	NA

No Child Left Behind, 2003-04
Attendence rate (target = 90%)	92.6%
Drop rate	9.5%
Highly-qualified teachers	93.5%
District needs improvement?(AYP)	Yes

Municipal Finance
Fiscal Year 2005
Total tax levy	$143,602,479
County levy	25,911,848
County taxes	25,407,914
County library	0
County health	0
County open space	503,934
School levy	36,202,974
Local muni. budget	81,487,658
Misc. revenues	96,782,133
Total aid	$40,082,038
CMPTRA	33,638,341
Muni. block grant	616,491
Energy tax receipts	5,686,877
Homeland security	140,000

Fiscal Year 2006
Total aid	$40,082,038
CMPTRA	33,439,300
Muni. block grant	616,491
Energy tax receipts	5,885,918
Homeland security	140,000

Taxes
	2003	2004	2005
General tax rate per $100	22.97	23.490	24.990
Net valuation taxable	$580,180,828	$577,831,453	$574,851,402
State equalized value	$4,297,635,763	$4,975,109,665	$6,038,355,063
County equalization ratio	15.49	13.50	11.58

Demographics & Socio-Economic Characteristics
(2000 U.S. Census, except as noted)

Population

1980*	6,944
1990*	6,577
2000	6,160
Male	2,885
Female	3,275
2004 (estimate)*	6,110
Persons per sq. mi. of land	3,115

Race & Hispanic Origin, 2000

Race

White	3,915
Black/African American	1,949
Amer. Indian/Alaska Natv.	15
Asian	20
Natv. Hawaiian/Pac. Islander	6
Other Race	81
Two or more races	174
Hispanic origin, total	268
Mexican	36
Puerto Rican	159
Cuban	4
Other Hispanic	69

Age & Nativity, 2000

Under 5 years	463
18 years and over	4,387
21 years and over	4,138
65 years and over	854
85 years and over	86
Median Age	34.3
Native born	5,921
Foreign born	239

Educational Attainment, 2000

Population 25 years and over	3,813
0-8 yrs of school	7.2%
High School grad or higher	75.4%
Bachelor's degree or higher	6.0%
Graduate degree	1.9%

Income & Poverty, 1999

Per capita income	$16,368
Median household income	$35,569
Median family income	$41,359
Persons in poverty	1,084
H'holds receiving public assistance	77
H'holds receiving social security	714

Households, 2000

Total households	2,353
With persons under 18	908
With persons over 65	658
Family households	1,615
One-person households	633
Persons per household	2.61
Persons per family	3.15

Labor & Employment

Total civilian labor force, 2004**	3,344
Unemployment rate	10.3%
Total civilian labor force, 2000	2,874
Unemployment rate	11.1%

Employed persons 16 years and over by occupation, 2000

Managers & professionals	395
Service occupations	488
Sales & office occupations	799
Farming, fishing & forestry	12
Construction & maintenance	281
Production & transportation	579
Self-employed persons	62

*US Census Bureau
**New Jersey Department of Labor

General Information
Borough of Paulsboro
1211 Delaware St
Paulsboro, NJ 08066
856-423-1500

Web site	www.paulsboronj.org
Land area (sq. miles)	1.96
Water area (sq. miles)	0.66
Type of government	Borough
Form of government	B

Government

Legislative Districts

US Congressional	1
State Legislative	3

Local Officials, 2006

Mayor	John Burzichelli
Admin/Manager	John Salvatore
Clerk	Kathy VanScoy
Finance Dir/Treas	John Salvatore
Engineer	Remington & Vernick
Attorney	Michael Angelini
Tax assessor	Robyn Hammond
Tax collector	Barbara Sockwell
Building officer	Phil Zimm
Zoning officer	Marc Kamp
Public Works	NA

Housing & Construction

Housing Units, 2000*

Total	2,628
Median rent	$570
Median SF home value	$78,600

New Privately Owned Housing Units
Authorized by Building Permit

	Units	Value
Total, 2004	0	$58,000
Single family	0	$58,000
Total, 2005	0	$372,700
Single family	0	$372,700

Real Property Valuation - parcels, 2005

	Number	Valuation
Total		$272,458,000
Vacant	208	2,808,200
Residential	1,974	139,128,400
Commercial	147	63,086,000
Industrial	8	60,548,900
Apartments	13	6,867,500
Farm land	0	0
Farm homestead	1	19,000

Average Property Value & Tax, 2005

Residential value	$70,454
Property tax	$2,467
FAIR rebate	$680

Public Library
Gill Memorial Library
Broad and Commerce Sts
Paulsboro, NJ 08066
856-423-5155

Librarian	Violet Valentin

Library statistics, 2004

	Total	per capita
Volumes	21,563	3.50
Expenditure	$122,253	$19.85

Public Safety

Police

Chief	Kenneth Ridinger
Number of officers, 2004	20

Crime, 2004	Number	Rate
Total	303	49.5
Violent	43	7
Non-violent	260	42.5
Domestic Viol.	194	NA

Emergency/Fire

Director	Gary Stevenson

Public School District
(for school year 2004-2005 except as noted)

Paulsboro School District
662 N Delaware St
Paulsboro, NJ 08066
856-423-5515

Superintendent	Frank Scambia
Grade plan	K-12
Enrollment	1,458.5
Students per teacher	11.4
Per pupil expenditure	$12,111
Median faculty salary	$64,509
Median administrator salary	$89,989
Grade 12 enrollment	101.0
High school graduation rate	84.1%

Assessment test results
(percent scoring at proficient or advanced level)

	Language	Math
Grade 3	66.6%	57.3%
Grade 8	51.2%	53.9%
High school	83.2%	72.5%

SAT

Percent tested	66%
Average SAT math score	452
Average SAT verbal score	449

No Child Left Behind, 2003-04

Attendence rate (target = 90%)	92.0%
Drop rate	2.4%
Highly-qualified teachers	96%
District needs improvement?(AYP)	No

Municipal Finance

Fiscal Year 2005

Total tax levy	$9,611,154
County levy	2,017,984
County taxes	1,892,193
County library	0
County health	0
County open space	125,791
School levy	3,916,170
Local muni. budget	3,677,000
Misc. revenues	2,942,431
Total aid	$874,959
CMPTRA	567,863
Muni. block grant	28,779
Energy tax receipts	228,317
Homeland security	50,000

Fiscal Year 2006

Total aid	$874,959
CMPTRA	559,872
Muni. block grant	28,779
Energy tax receipts	236,308
Homeland security	50,000

Taxes

	2003	2004	2005
General tax rate per $100	3.22	3.361	3.502
Net valuation taxable	$274,217,694	$274,065,538	$274,517,014
State equalized value	$291,039,794	$310,084,975	$332,264,602
County equalization ratio	95.95	94.22	88.30

Demographics & Socio-Economic Characteristics
(2000 U.S. Census, except as noted)

Population
1980*	2,038
1990*	2,111
2000	2,433
Male	1,203
Female	1,230
2004 (estimate)*	2,468
Persons per sq. mi. of land	426

Race & Hispanic Origin, 2000
Race
White	2,298
Black/African American	76
Amer. Indian/Alaska Natv.	2
Asian	30
Natv. Hawaiian/Pac. Islander	0
Other Race	17
Two or more races	10
Hispanic origin, total	92
Mexican	18
Puerto Rican	8
Cuban	3
Other Hispanic	63

Age & Nativity, 2000
Under 5 years	183
18 years and over	1,801
21 years and over	1,740
65 years and over	296
85 years and over	38
Median Age	39.5
Native born	2,138
Foreign born	295

Educational Attainment, 2000
Population 25 years and over	1,694
0-8 yrs of school	3.3%
High School grad or higher	92.9%
Bachelor's degree or higher	56.9%
Graduate degree	19.2%

Income & Poverty, 1999
Per capita income	$56,542
Median household income	$99,499
Median family income	$118,770
Persons in poverty	101
H'holds receiving public assistance	0
H'holds receiving social security	224

Households, 2000
Total households	840
With persons under 18	325
With persons over 65	202
Family households	647
One-person households	152
Persons per household	2.71
Persons per family	3.11

Labor & Employment
Total civilian labor force, 2004**	1,375
Unemployment rate	2.4%
Total civilian labor force, 2000	1,318
Unemployment rate	5.0%

Employed persons 16 years and over by occupation, 2000
Managers & professionals	648
Service occupations	160
Sales & office occupations	331
Farming, fishing & forestry	9
Construction & maintenance	56
Production & transportation	48
Self-employed persons	94

*US Census Bureau
**New Jersey Department of Labor

General Information
Borough of Peapack & Gladstone
PO Box 218
1 School St
Peapack, NJ 07977
908-234-2250
Web site	www.peapack-gladstone-nj.gov
Land area (sq. miles)	5.80
Water area (sq. miles)	0
Type of government	Borough
Form of government	B

Government

Legislative Districts
US Congressional	7
State Legislative	16

Local Officials, 2006
Mayor	Vincent Girardy
Admin/Manager	Margaret Gould
Clerk	Margaret Gould
Finance Dir/Treas	Mary Robinson
Engineer	William Ryden
Attorney	Sharon Moore
Tax assessor	Edward Kerwin
Tax collector	NA
Building officer	Joseph Alicino
Zoning officer	Len Taylor
Public Works	John O'Neill

Housing & Construction

Housing Units, 2000*
Total	871
Median rent	$1,132
Median SF home value	$461,500

New Privately Owned Housing Units
Authorized by Building Permit
	Units	Value
Total, 2004	2	$925,000
Single family	2	$925,000
Total, 2005	1	$2,700,000
Single family	1	$2,700,000

Real Property Valuation - parcels, 2005
	Number	Valuation
Total		$755,561,900
Vacant	40	11,713,600
Residential	732	504,830,900
Commercial	42	168,751,000
Industrial	1	7,325,000
Apartments	8	4,736,100
Farm land	29	57,612,400
Farm homestead	99	592,900

Average Property Value & Tax, 2005
Residential value	$608,212
Property tax	$10,691
FAIR rebate	$606

Public Library
Peapack Gladstone Branch†
School St
Peapack, NJ 07977
908-234-0598
Branch Librarian	Cecelia Butler

Library statistics, 2004
	Total	per capita
Volumes	NA	NA
Expenditure	NA	NA

†Branch of County Library

Public Safety

Police
Chief	Gregory Skinner
Number of officers, 2004	7

Crime, 2004	Number	Rate
Total	21	8.6
Violent	0	0
Non-violent	21	8.6
Domestic Viol.	4	NA

Emergency/Fire
Director	Douglas Fagan

Public School District
(for school year 2004-2005 except as noted)

Sends children to Somerset Hills Regional school district (see Bernardsville Borough).
Grade plan	NA
Enrollment	NA
Students per teacher	NA
Per pupil expenditure	NA
Median faculty salary	NA
Median administrator salary	NA
Grade 12 enrollment	NA
High school graduation rate	NA

Assessment test results
(percent scoring at proficient or advanced level)
	Language	Math
Grade 3	NA	NA
Grade 8	NA	NA
High school	NA	NA

SAT
Percent tested	NA
Average SAT math score	NA
Average SAT verbal score	NA

No Child Left Behind, 2003-04
Attendence rate (target = 90%)	NA
Drop rate	NA
Highly-qualified teachers	NA
District needs improvement?(AYP)	NA

Municipal Finance

Fiscal Year 2005
Total tax levy	$13,296,683
County levy	2,833,928
County taxes	2,347,882
County library	260,263
County health	0
County open space	225,783
School levy	6,725,076
Local muni. budget	3,737,680
Misc. revenues	2,200,950
Total aid	$352,398
CMPTRA	50,841
Muni. block grant	9,540
Energy tax receipts	267,017
Homeland security	25,000

Fiscal Year 2006
Total aid	$352,397
CMPTRA	41,495
Muni. block grant	9,540
Energy tax receipts	276,362
Homeland security	25,000

Taxes
	2003	2004	2005
General tax rate per $100	1.56	1.850	1.760
Net valuation taxable	$679,898,867	$673,858,563	$756,473,045
State equalized value	$743,546,442	$740,504,153	$821,538,928
County equalization ratio	96.05	91.44	100.61

Demographics & Socio-Economic Characteristics

(2000 U.S. Census, except as noted)

Population

1980*	1,198
1990*	1,367
2000	1,210
Male	614
Female	596
2004 (estimate)*	1,325
Persons per sq. mi. of land	2,228

Race & Hispanic Origin, 2000

Race

White	949
Black/African American	154
Amer. Indian/Alaska Natv.	8
Asian	29
Natv. Hawaiian/Pac. Islander	0
Other Race	33
Two or more races	37
Hispanic origin, total	104
Mexican	15
Puerto Rican	60
Cuban	2
Other Hispanic	27

Age & Nativity, 2000

Under 5 years	83
18 years and over	886
21 years and over	832
65 years and over	108
85 years and over	8
Median Age	33.9
Native born	1,130
Foreign born	80

Educational Attainment, 2000

Population 25 years and over	767
0-8 yrs of school	4.2%
High School grad or higher	83.7%
Bachelor's degree or higher	15.5%
Graduate degree	4.3%

Income & Poverty, 1999

Per capita income	$18,909
Median household income	$44,063
Median family income	$48,500
Persons in poverty	94
H'holds receiving public assistance	23
H'holds receiving social security	93

Households, 2000

Total households	470
With persons under 18	189
With persons over 65	82
Family households	317
One-person households	124
Persons per household	2.56
Persons per family	3.06

Labor & Employment

Total civilian labor force, 2004**	835
Unemployment rate	4.5%
Total civilian labor force, 2000	648
Unemployment rate	4.3%

Employed persons 16 years and over by occupation, 2000

Managers & professionals	146
Service occupations	137
Sales & office occupations	163
Farming, fishing & forestry	0
Construction & maintenance	76
Production & transportation	98
Self-employed persons	49

*US Census Bureau
**New Jersey Department of Labor

General Information

Borough of Pemberton
50 Egbert St
Pemberton, NJ 08068
609-894-8222

Web site	www.pembertonborough.us
Land area (sq. miles)	0.59
Water area (sq. miles)	0.02
Type of government	Borough
Form of government	B

Government

Legislative Districts

US Congressional	3
State Legislative	8

Local Officials, 2006

Mayor	F. Lyman Simpkins
Admin/Manager	NA
Clerk	Donna Mull
Finance Dir/Treas	Donna Mull
Engineer	Richard Acaimo & Asso.
Attorney	Schulze & Rupinski
Tax assessor	Edward Burek
Tax collector	Harold Griffin
Building officer	Harry Wetterskog
Zoning officer	NA
Public Works	Raymond Downs

Housing & Construction

Housing Units, 2000*

Total	513
Median rent	$641
Median SF home value	$113,300

New Privately Owned Housing Units
Authorized by Building Permit

	Units	Value
Total, 2004	3	$184,274
Single family	3	$184,274
Total, 2005	3	$192,850
Single family	3	$192,850

Real Property Valuation - parcels, 2005

	Number	Valuation
Total		$43,950,100
Vacant	52	2,614,300
Residential	333	31,136,600
Commercial	49	7,311,900
Industrial	0	0
Apartments	10	2,753,800
Farm land	1	122,700
Farm homestead	5	10,800

Average Property Value & Tax, 2005

Residential value	$92,152
Property tax	$3,500
FAIR rebate	$546

Public Library

No public municipal library.

Library statistics, 2004

	Total	per capita
Volumes	NA	NA
Expenditure	NA	NA

Public Safety

Police

Chief	Joseph Conlin
Number of officers, 2004	5

Crime, 2004	Number	Rate
Total	41	32.9
Violent	4	3.2
Non-violent	37	29.6
Domestic Viol.	25	NA

Emergency/Fire

Director	Chas Bozoski

Public School District

(for school year 2004-2005 except as noted)

Pemberton Borough School District
50 Egbert St
Pemberton, NJ 08068
609-894-2261

Superintendent	Charles Smith
Grade plan	K-12
Enrollment	95.0
Students per teacher	9.0
Per pupil expenditure	$14,070
Median faculty salary	$50,105
Median administrator salary	$59,280
Grade 12 enrollment	NA
High school graduation rate	NA

Assessment test results
(percent scoring at proficient or advanced level)

	Language	Math
Grade 3	100%	100%
Grade 8	NA	NA
High school	NA	NA

SAT

Percent tested	NA
Average SAT math score	NA
Average SAT verbal score	NA

No Child Left Behind, 2003-04

Attendence rate (target = 90%)	93.6%
Drop rate	NA
Highly-qualified teachers	100%
District needs improvement?(AYP)	No

Municipal Finance

Fiscal Year 2005

Total tax levy	$1,699,672
County levy	286,428
County taxes	240,283
County library	21,039
County health	0
County open space	25,106
School levy	1,099,845
Local muni. budget	313,399
Misc. revenues	668,601
Total aid	$178,240
CMPTRA	103,420
Muni. block grant	5,982
Energy tax receipts	43,838
Homeland security	25,000

Fiscal Year 2006

Total aid	$178,240
CMPTRA	101,886
Muni. block grant	5,982
Energy tax receipts	45,372
Homeland security	25,000

Taxes

	2003	2004	2005
General tax rate per $100	3.74	3.612	3.799
Net valuation taxable	$38,202,565	$40,801,804	$44,746,637
State equalized value	$48,877,386	$56,812,263	$71,548,828
County equalization ratio	85.17	78.16	71.39

Demographics & Socio-Economic Characteristics
(2000 U.S. Census, except as noted)

Population
1980*	29,720
1990*	31,342
2000	28,691
Male	14,148
Female	14,543
2000 (revised)	28,569
2004 (estimate)*	28,967
Persons per sq. mi. of land	470

Race & Hispanic Origin, 2000
Race
White	18,946
Black/African American	6,632
Amer. Indian/Alaska Natv.	132
Asian	913
Natv. Hawaiian/Pac. Islander	23
Other Race	828
Two or more races	1,217
Hispanic origin, total	2,477
Mexican	225
Puerto Rican	1,560
Cuban	44
Other Hispanic	648

Age & Nativity, 2000
Under 5 years	1,925
18 years and over	20,770
21 years and over	19,594
65 years and over	2,793
85 years and over	189
Median Age	34.4
Native born	26,607
Foreign born	2,043

Educational Attainment, 2000
Population 25 years and over	18,049
0-8 yrs of school	4.5%
High School grad or higher	80.0%
Bachelor's degree or higher	9.4%
Graduate degree	2.5%

Income & Poverty, 1999
Per capita income	$19,238
Median household income	$47,394
Median family income	$52,860
Persons in poverty	2,612
H'holds receiving public assistance	418
H'holds receiving social security	2,164

Households, 2000
Total households	10,050
With persons under 18	4,277
With persons over 65	2,009
Family households	7,484
One-person households	2,048
Persons per household	2.8
Persons per family	3.22

Labor & Employment
Total civilian labor force, 2004**	17,065
Unemployment rate	5.9%
Total civilian labor force, 2000	13,931
Unemployment rate	6.1%

Employed persons 16 years and over by occupation, 2000
Managers & professionals	2,806
Service occupations	3,013
Sales & office occupations	3,769
Farming, fishing & forestry	51
Construction & maintenance	1,319
Production & transportation	2,129
Self-employed persons	566

*US Census Bureau
**New Jersey Department of Labor

General Information
Township of Pemberton
500 Pemberton-Browns Mills
Pemberton, NJ 08068
609-894-8201
Web site	www.pemberton-twp.com
Land area (sq. miles)	61.68
Water area (sq. miles)	0.82
Type of government	Township
Form of government	MC'50

Government

Legislative Districts
US Congressional	3
State Legislative	8

Local Officials, 2006
Mayor	Robert McCullough
Admin/Manager	David W. Thompson
Clerk	Mary Ann Young
Finance Dir/Treas	Linda Eden
Engineer	Richard Alaimo
Attorney	Kenneth Domzalski
Tax assessor	Karen McMahon
Tax collector	C. Anne Doyle
Building officer	Robert Benasch
Zoning officer	R. Benash/E. Donelson/C. Fisher
Public Works	Phil Sager

Housing & Construction

Housing Units, 2000*
Total	10,778
Median rent	$670
Median SF home value	$98,300

New Privately Owned Housing Units
Authorized by Building Permit
	Units	Value
Total, 2004	35	$2,702,496
Single family	30	$2,702,495
Total, 2005	65	$9,537,724
Single family	65	$9,537,724

Real Property Valuation - parcels, 2005
	Number	Valuation
Total		$848,499,820
Vacant	3,077	18,769,200
Residential	7,908	733,607,200
Commercial	147	53,589,720
Industrial	5	4,321,700
Apartments	14	18,876,300
Farm land	140	15,846,400
Farm homestead	276	3,489,300

Average Property Value & Tax, 2005
Residential value	$90,066
Property tax	$2,918
FAIR rebate	$562

Public Library
No public municipal library.

Library statistics, 2004
	Total	per capita
Volumes	NA	NA
Expenditure	NA	NA

Public Safety
Police
Chief	Stephen Emery
Number of officers, 2004	52

Crime, 2004	Number	Rate
Total	608	21
Violent	62	2.1
Non-violent	546	18.9
Domestic Viol.	344	NA

Emergency/Fire
Director	NA

Public School District
(for school year 2004-2005 except as noted)

Pemberton Township School District
One Egbert St
Pemberton, NJ 08068
609-893-8141
Superintendent	Mark Cowell
Grade plan	K-12
Enrollment	5,562.0
Students per teacher	8.9
Per pupil expenditure	$15,978
Median faculty salary	$67,477
Median administrator salary	$107,085
Grade 12 enrollment	305.0
High school graduation rate	86.2%

Assessment test results
(percent scoring at proficient or advanced level)
	Language	Math
Grade 3	82.0%	84.8%
Grade 8	63.3%	42.9%
High school	79.7%	61.8%

SAT
Percent tested	51%
Average SAT math score	454
Average SAT verbal score	455

No Child Left Behind, 2003-04
Attendence rate (target = 90%)	93.0%
Drop rate	1.8%
Highly-qualified teachers	98.2%
District needs improvement?(AYP)	No

Municipal Finance

Fiscal Year 2005
Total tax levy	$27,597,912
County levy	5,033,512
County taxes	4,222,516
County library	369,766
County health	0
County open space	441,229
School levy	10,844,995
Local muni. budget	11,719,406
Misc. revenues	9,130,649
Total aid	$3,850,959
CMPTRA	1,950,709
Muni. block grant	137,142
Energy tax receipts	1,663,429
Homeland security	90,000

Fiscal Year 2006
Total aid	$3,850,959
CMPTRA	1,892,489
Muni. block grant	137,142
Energy tax receipts	1,721,649
Homeland security	90,000

Taxes
	2003	2004	2005
General tax rate per $100	2.92	2.982	3.244
Net valuation taxable	$841,214,216	$846,855,002	$851,697,405
State equalized value	$963,479,803	$1,098,570,613	$1,284,805,257
County equalization ratio	94.8	87.31	77.01

Demographics & Socio-Economic Characteristics

(2000 U.S. Census, except as noted)

Population

1980*	2,109
1990*	2,537
2000	2,696
Male	1,293
Female	1,403
2004 (estimate)*	2,713
Persons per sq. mi. of land	2,819

Race & Hispanic Origin, 2000

Race

White	2,560
Black/African American	71
Amer. Indian/Alaska Natv.	0
Asian	27
Natv. Hawaiian/Pac. Islander	0
Other Race	11
Two or more races	27
Hispanic origin, total	32
Mexican	4
Puerto Rican	4
Cuban	2
Other Hispanic	22

Age & Nativity, 2000

Under 5 years	173
18 years and over	1,922
21 years and over	1,859
65 years and over	405
85 years and over	51
Median Age	41.3
Native born	2,539
Foreign born	157

Educational Attainment, 2000

Population 25 years and over	1,781
0-8 yrs of school	0.4%
High School grad or higher	97.1%
Bachelor's degree or higher	69.5%
Graduate degree	33.0%

Income & Poverty, 1999

Per capita income	$45,843
Median household income	$90,366
Median family income	$107,089
Persons in poverty	64
H'holds receiving public assistance	0
H'holds receiving social security	269

Households, 2000

Total households	1,013
With persons under 18	417
With persons over 65	293
Family households	762
One-person households	223
Persons per household	2.66
Persons per family	3.14

Labor & Employment

Total civilian labor force, 2004**	1,463
Unemployment rate	1.6%
Total civilian labor force, 2000	1,338
Unemployment rate	2.6%

Employed persons 16 years and over by occupation, 2000

Managers & professionals	837
Service occupations	60
Sales & office occupations	315
Farming, fishing & forestry	0
Construction & maintenance	43
Production & transportation	48
Self-employed persons	120

*US Census Bureau
**New Jersey Department of Labor

General Information

Borough of Pennington
30 N Main St
Pennington, NJ 08534
609-737-0276

Web site	www.penningtonboro.org
Land area (sq. miles)	0.96
Water area (sq. miles)	0
Type of government	Borough
Form of government	B

Government

Legislative Districts

US Congressional	12
State Legislative	15

Local Officials, 2006

Mayor	James E. Benton
Admin/Manager	Eugene Dunworth Jr.
Clerk	Betty Sterling
Finance Dir/Treas	Sandra Webb
Engineer	Donald Fetzer
Attorney	Walter Bliss
Tax assessor	Antoinette Sost
Tax collector	Irene Billings
Building officer	John Hall
Zoning officer	John Flemming
Public Works	William J. Wittkop

Housing & Construction

Housing Units, 2000*

Total	1,040
Median rent	$881
Median SF home value	$283,800

New Privately Owned Housing Units Authorized by Building Permit

	Units	Value
Total, 2004	3	$972,200
Single family	3	$972,200
Total, 2005	1	$240,000
Single family	1	$240,000

Real Property Valuation - parcels, 2005

	Number	Valuation
Total		$226,842,800
Vacant	58	1,145,300
Residential	853	197,211,900
Commercial	58	25,470,500
Industrial	2	2,086,200
Apartments	4	928,900
Farm land	0	0
Farm homestead	0	0

Average Property Value & Tax, 2005

Residential value	$231,198
Property tax	$9,328
FAIR rebate	$597

Public Library

Pennington Public Library
30 N Main St
Pennington, NJ 08534
609-737-0404

Director ... Kathleen Doyle

Library statistics, 2004

	Total	per capita
Volumes	24,054	8.92
Expenditure	$140,321	$52.05

Public Safety

Police

Chief	NA
Number of officers, 2004	6

Crime, 2004	Number	Rate
Total	31	11.5
Violent	0	0
Non-violent	31	11.5
Domestic Viol.	1	NA

Emergency/Fire

Director ... Stewart Schwab

Public School District

(for school year 2004-2005 except as noted)

Sends children to Hopewell Valley Regional school district (see Appendix A).

Grade plan	NA
Enrollment	NA
Students per teacher	NA
Per pupil expenditure	NA
Median faculty salary	NA
Median administrator salary	NA
Grade 12 enrollment	NA
High school graduation rate	NA

Assessment test results

(percent scoring at proficient or advanced level)

	Language	Math
Grade 3	NA	NA
Grade 8	NA	NA
High school	NA	NA

SAT

Percent tested	NA
Average SAT math score	NA
Average SAT verbal score	NA

No Child Left Behind, 2003-04

Attendence rate (target = 90%)	NA
Drop rate	NA
Highly-qualified teachers	NA
District needs improvement?(AYP)	NA

Municipal Finance

Fiscal Year 2005

Total tax levy	$9,200,894
County levy	2,237,064
County taxes	2,118,067
County library	0
County health	0
County open space	118,997
School levy	5,303,463
Local muni. budget	1,660,367
Misc. revenues	1,234,192
Total aid	$300,700
CMPTRA	99,041
Muni. block grant	11,101
Energy tax receipts	165,558
Homeland security	25,000

Fiscal Year 2006

Total aid	$300,700
CMPTRA	93,246
Muni. block grant	11,101
Energy tax receipts	171,353
Homeland security	25,000

Taxes

	2003	2004	2005
General tax rate per $100	3.72	3.830	4.040
Net valuation taxable	$224,457,622	$225,536,364	$228,041,075
State equalized value	$364,971,743	$391,669,443	$433,620,603
County equalization ratio	67.99	61.50	57.44

Demographics & Socio-Economic Characteristics
(2000 U.S. Census, except as noted)

Population
1980*	5,760
1990*	5,228
2000	4,886
Male	2,252
Female	2,634
2004 (estimate)*	4,807
Persons per sq. mi. of land	5,190

Race & Hispanic Origin, 2000
Race
White	2,387
Black/African American	1,942
Amer. Indian/Alaska Natv.	18
Asian	14
Natv. Hawaiian/Pac. Islander	8
Other Race	397
Two or more races	120
Hispanic origin, total	845
Mexican	147
Puerto Rican	580
Cuban	15
Other Hispanic	103

Age & Nativity, 2000
Under 5 years	412
18 years and over	3,275
21 years and over	3,062
65 years and over	576
85 years and over	57
Median Age	30.9
Native born	4,704
Foreign born	176

Educational Attainment, 2000
Population 25 years and over	2,803
0-8 yrs of school	14.4%
High School grad or higher	65.6%
Bachelor's degree or higher	7.5%
Graduate degree	1.6%

Income & Poverty, 1999
Per capita income	$13,330
Median household income	$26,227
Median family income	$34,076
Persons in poverty	1,020
H'holds receiving public assistance	118
H'holds receiving social security	606

Households, 2000
Total households	1,827
With persons under 18	799
With persons over 65	471
Family households	1,232
One-person households	513
Persons per household	2.67
Persons per family	3.26

Labor & Employment
Total civilian labor force, 2004**	2,144
Unemployment rate	11.9%
Total civilian labor force, 2000	2,140
Unemployment rate	15.3%

Employed persons 16 years and over by occupation, 2000
Managers & professionals	349
Service occupations	368
Sales & office occupations	431
Farming, fishing & forestry	24
Construction & maintenance	150
Production & transportation	490
Self-employed persons	73

*US Census Bureau
**New Jersey Department of Labor

General Information
Borough of Penns Grove
PO Box 527
Penns Grove, NJ 08069
856-299-0098

Web site	NA
Land area (sq. miles)	0.93
Water area (sq. miles)	0
Type of government	Borough
Form of government	B

Government
Legislative Districts
US Congressional	2
State Legislative	3

Local Officials, 2006
Mayor	John A. Washington
Admin/Manager	NA
Clerk	Sharon R. Williams
Finance Dir/Treas	Stephen Labb
Engineer	Mark Brunermer
Attorney	Benjamin Telsey
Tax assessor	Marie Proccaci
Tax collector	Tom Freeman
Building officer	Jeryl Goff
Zoning officer	Till Lerro
Public Works	NA

Housing & Construction
Housing Units, 2000*
Total	2,075
Median rent	$526
Median SF home value	$72,900

New Privately Owned Housing Units Authorized by Building Permit
	Units	Value
Total, 2004	2	$72,000
Single family	2	$72,000
Total, 2005	4	$340,494
Single family	4	$340,494

Real Property Valuation - parcels, 2005
	Number	Valuation
Total		$88,674,300
Vacant	341	2,469,600
Residential	1,215	69,719,100
Commercial	107	14,312,300
Industrial	0	0
Apartments	12	2,173,300
Farm land	0	0
Farm homestead	0	0

Average Property Value & Tax, 2005
Residential value	$57,382
Property tax	$2,919
FAIR rebate	$586

Public Library
Penns Grove-Carneys Point Library†
222 S Broad St
Penns Grove, NJ 08069
856-299-4255

Director	Barbara Hunt

Library statistics, 2004
	Total	per capita
Volumes	NA	NA
Expenditure	NA	NA

†Joint Library with Carneys Point

Public Safety
Police
Chief	Gary Doubledee
Number of officers, 2004	16

Crime, 2004	Number	Rate
Total	240	49.6
Violent	33	6.8
Non-violent	207	42.8
Domestic Viol.	108	NA

Emergency/Fire
Director	Joseph Grasso

Public School District
(for school year 2004-2005 except as noted)

Penns Grove-Carneys Pt. Reg. School Dist.
100 Iona Ave
Penns Grove, NJ 08069
856-299-4250

Superintendent	Joseph A. Massare
Grade plan	K-12
Enrollment	2,302.5
Students per teacher	10.9
Per pupil expenditure	$11,135
Median faculty salary	$49,835
Median administrator salary	$85,223
Grade 12 enrollment	116.0
High school graduation rate	85.4%

Assessment test results
(percent scoring at proficient or advanced level)
	Language	Math
Grade 3	70.0%	75.0%
Grade 8	48.0%	35.2%
High school	77.9%	64.1%

SAT
Percent tested	63%
Average SAT math score	469
Average SAT verbal score	469

No Child Left Behind, 2003-04
Attendence rate (target = 90%)	92.9%
Drop rate	2.7%
Highly-qualified teachers	96.2%
District needs improvement?(AYP)	No

Municipal Finance
Fiscal Year 2005
Total tax levy	$4,583,369
County levy	1,254,483
County taxes	1,229,592
County library	0
County health	0
County open space	24,891
School levy	1,956,453
Local muni. budget	1,372,432
Misc. revenues	4,123,450
Total aid	$1,661,471
CMPTRA	1,366,632
Muni. block grant	22,876
Energy tax receipts	246,963
Homeland security	25,000

Fiscal Year 2006
Total aid	$1,661,470
CMPTRA	1,357,988
Muni. block grant	22,876
Energy tax receipts	255,606
Homeland security	25,000

Taxes
	2003	2004	2005
General tax rate per $100	4.51	4.793	5.087
Net valuation taxable	$93,022,987	$90,059,258	$90,113,832
State equalized value	$117,186,932	$122,639,098	$132,872,061
County equalization ratio	77.59	79.38	73.09

Demographics & Socio-Economic Characteristics

(2000 U.S. Census, except as noted)

Population

1980*	33,775
1990*	34,738
2000	35,737
Male	17,116
Female	18,621
2000 (revised)	35,757
2004 (estimate)*	35,625
Persons per sq. mi. of land	3,382

Race & Hispanic Origin, 2000

Race

White	21,479
Black/African American	8,641
Amer. Indian/Alaska Natv.	124
Asian	1,636
Natv. Hawaiian/Pac. Islander	7
Other Race	2,954
Two or more races	896
Hispanic origin, total	5,126
Mexican	218
Puerto Rican	3,629
Cuban	32
Other Hispanic	1,247

Age & Nativity, 2000

Under 5 years	2,212
18 years and over	25,925
21 years and over	24,634
65 years and over	5,065
85 years and over	608
Median Age	36.1
Native born	32,881
Foreign born	2,822

Educational Attainment, 2000

Population 25 years and over	22,983
0-8 yrs of school	6.2%
High School grad or higher	77.2%
Bachelor's degree or higher	15.4%
Graduate degree	4.8%

Income & Poverty, 1999

Per capita income	$19,004
Median household income	$47,538
Median family income	$52,760
Persons in poverty	2,807
H'holds receiving public assistance	331
H'holds receiving social security	3,651

Households, 2000

Total households	12,389
With persons under 18	5,120
With persons over 65	3,436
Family households	9,097
One-person households	2,865
Persons per household	2.83
Persons per family	3.34

Labor & Employment

Total civilian labor force, 2004**	18,223
Unemployment rate	3.9%
Total civilian labor force, 2000	16,881
Unemployment rate	5.4%

Employed persons 16 years and over by occupation, 2000

Managers & professionals	4,447
Service occupations	2,553
Sales & office occupations	4,967
Farming, fishing & forestry	5
Construction & maintenance	1,292
Production & transportation	2,699
Self-employed persons	542

*US Census Bureau
**New Jersey Department of Labor

General Information

Township of Pennsauken
5605 N Crescent Blvd
Pennsauken, NJ 08110
856-665-1000

Web site	www.twp.pennsauken.nj.us
Land area (sq. miles)	10.53
Water area (sq. miles)	1.65
Type of government	Township
Form of government	TC

Government

Legislative Districts

US Congressional	1
State Legislative	7

Local Officials, 2006

Mayor	Greg Schofield
Admin/Manager	Bob Cummings
Clerk	Patricia Gudis
Finance Dir/Treas	Ronald Crane
Engineer	Dennis O'Rourke
Attorney	Dave Luthman
Tax assessor	John Dymond
Tax collector	NA
Building officer	Gary Burgin
Zoning officer	NA
Public Works	NA

Housing & Construction

Housing Units, 2000*

Total	12,945
Median rent	$584
Median SF home value	$95,300

New Privately Owned Housing Units
Authorized by Building Permit

	Units	Value
Total, 2004	12	$959,692
Single family	12	$959,692
Total, 2005	94	$7,747,050
Single family	15	$1,483,050

Real Property Valuation - parcels, 2005

	Number	Valuation
Total		$1,614,293,200
Vacant	297	16,644,000
Residential	10,963	981,220,100
Commercial	777	511,958,600
Industrial	29	82,591,300
Apartments	45	21,879,200
Farm land	0	0
Farm homestead	0	0

Average Property Value & Tax, 2005

Residential value	$89,503
Property tax	$3,346
FAIR rebate	$585

Public Library

Pennsauken Free Pub Library
5605 Crescent Blvd
Pennsauken, NJ 08110
856-665-5959

Director.....................Richard Thau

Library statistics, 2004

	Total	per capita
Volumes	105,692	2.96
Expenditure	$826,644	$23.13

Public Safety

Police

Chief	John Coffey
Number of officers, 2004	86

Crime, 2004	Number	Rate
Total	1,482	41.3
Violent	159	4.4
Non-violent	1,323	36.9
Domestic Viol.	448	NA

Emergency/Fire

Director.................North Figueroa

Public School District

(for school year 2004-2005 except as noted)

Pennsauken Township School District
1695 Hylton Rd
Pennsauken, NJ 08110
856-662-8505

Superintendent	Jim Chapman
Grade plan	K-12
Enrollment	5,992.0
Students per teacher	12.4
Per pupil expenditure	$11,376
Median faculty salary	$56,225
Median administrator salary	$104,594
Grade 12 enrollment	422.0
High school graduation rate	80.0%

Assessment test results

(percent scoring at proficient or advanced level)

	Language	Math
Grade 3	76.9%	71.7%
Grade 8	52.7%	47.1%
High school	63.8%	50.3%

SAT

Percent tested	61%
Average SAT math score	453
Average SAT verbal score	447

No Child Left Behind, 2003-04

Attendance rate (target = 90%)	93.5%
Drop rate	5.9%
Highly-qualified teachers	95.8%
District needs improvement?(AYP)	No

Municipal Finance

Fiscal Year 2005

Total tax levy	$60,507,614
County levy	14,837,222
County taxes	14,643,987
County library	0
County health	0
County open space	193,236
School levy	32,695,242
Local muni. budget	12,975,150
Misc. revenues	16,994,850
Total aid	$7,433,355
CMPTRA	2,992,018
Muni. block grant	152,002
Energy tax receipts	4,149,335
Homeland security	140,000

Fiscal Year 2006

Total aid	$7,433,354
CMPTRA	2,846,791
Muni. block grant	152,002
Energy tax receipts	4,294,561
Homeland security	140,000

Taxes

	2003	2004	2005
General tax rate per $100	3.38	3.557	3.739
Net valuation taxable	$1,632,825,960	$1,626,623,253	$1,618,484,615
State equalized value	$1,770,960,911	$1,903,461,029	$2,152,240,180
County equalization ratio	97.21	92.20	85.42

Demographics & Socio-Economic Characteristics

(2000 U.S. Census, except as noted)

Population

1980*	13,848
1990*	13,794
2000	13,194
Male	6,337
Female	6,857
2004 (estimate)*	13,194
Persons per sq. mi. of land	571

Race & Hispanic Origin, 2000

Race

White	12,756
Black/African American	127
Amer. Indian/Alaska Natv.	21
Asian	127
Natv. Hawaiian/Pac. Islander	2
Other Race	51
Two or more races	110
Hispanic origin, total	211
Mexican	45
Puerto Rican	102
Cuban	6
Other Hispanic	58

Age & Nativity, 2000

Under 5 years	758
18 years and over	10,134
21 years and over	9,689
65 years and over	2,047
85 years and over	189
Median Age	39.3
Native born	12,817
Foreign born	428

Educational Attainment, 2000

Population 25 years and over	9,260
0-8 yrs of school	4.4%
High School grad or higher	82.0%
Bachelor's degree or higher	13.6%
Graduate degree	2.6%

Income & Poverty, 1999

Per capita income	$22,717
Median household income	$47,250
Median family income	$57,340
Persons in poverty	653
H'holds receiving public assistance	131
H'holds receiving social security	1,789

Households, 2000

Total households	5,317
With persons under 18	1,730
With persons over 65	1,499
Family households	3,712
One-person households	1,380
Persons per household	2.47
Persons per family	2.98

Labor & Employment

Total civilian labor force, 2004**	6,836
Unemployment rate	3.9%
Total civilian labor force, 2000	6,821
Unemployment rate	4.5%

Employed persons 16 years and over by occupation, 2000

Managers & professionals	1,843
Service occupations	936
Sales & office occupations	1,794
Farming, fishing & forestry	23
Construction & maintenance	754
Production & transportation	1,163
Self-employed persons	224

*US Census Bureau
**New Jersey Department of Labor

General Information

Township of Pennsville
90 North Broadway
Pennsville, NJ 08070
856-678-3089

Web site	www.pennsville.org
Land area (sq. miles)	23.10
Water area (sq. miles)	1.71
Type of government	Township
Form of government	TC

Government

Legislative Districts

US Congressional	2
State Legislative	3

Local Officials, 2006

Mayor	Thomas H. Strong Sr.
Admin/Manager	Jack Lynch
Clerk	Cynthia Dalessio
Finance Dir/Treas	John Willadsen
Engineer	Mark Brunermer
Attorney	Walter Ray
Tax assessor	Randal Shidner
Tax collector	Nancy McCarthy
Building officer	Tony Dariano
Zoning officer	Robert Chambers
Public Works	Jack Lynch

Housing & Construction

Housing Units, 2000*

Total	5,623
Median rent	$640
Median SF home value	$103,700

New Privately Owned Housing Units Authorized by Building Permit

	Units	Value
Total, 2004	39	$3,135,067
Single family	39	$3,135,067
Total, 2005	53	$5,629,146
Single family	53	$5,629,146

Real Property Valuation - parcels, 2005

	Number	Valuation
Total		$730,121,000
Vacant	836	15,643,500
Residential	4,541	460,183,800
Commercial	187	76,339,300
Industrial	4	151,654,300
Apartments	14	17,513,000
Farm land	49	6,724,800
Farm homestead	217	2,062,300

Average Property Value & Tax, 2005

Residential value	$97,151
Property tax	$3,599
FAIR rebate	$685

Public Library

Pennsville Pub Library
190 S Broadway
Pennsville, NJ 08070
856-678-5473

Director | Richard Blocksom

Library statistics, 2004

	Total	per capita
Volumes	43,523	3.30
Expenditure	$192,998	$14.63

Public Safety

Police

Chief	Patrick McCaffery
Number of officers, 2004	23

Crime, 2004	Number	Rate
Total	326	24.8
Violent	14	1.1
Non-violent	312	23.7
Domestic Viol.	306	NA

Emergency/Fire

Director | L. Zimmerman/J. Hoffman

Public School District

(for school year 2004-2005 except as noted)

Pennsville Township School District
30 Church St
Pennsville, NJ 08070
856-540-6210

Superintendent	Mark Jones
Grade plan	K-12
Enrollment	2,062.0
Students per teacher	11.0
Per pupil expenditure	$11,584
Median faculty salary	$47,252
Median administrator salary	$87,322
Grade 12 enrollment	118.0
High school graduation rate	87.4%

Assessment test results

(percent scoring at proficient or advanced level)

	Language	Math
Grade 3	77.5%	81.6%
Grade 8	77.0%	59.9%
High school	79.5%	60.4%

SAT

Percent tested	75%
Average SAT math score	474
Average SAT verbal score	482

No Child Left Behind, 2003-04

Attendence rate (target = 90%)	94.3%
Drop rate	0.9%
Highly-qualified teachers	99.8%
District needs improvement?(AYP)	No

Municipal Finance

Fiscal Year 2005

Total tax levy	$27,129,392
County levy	9,224,663
County taxes	9,041,199
County library	0
County health	0
County open space	183,463
School levy	15,549,404
Local muni. budget	2,355,325
Misc. revenues	10,707,402
Total aid	$7,000,195
CMPTRA	2,647,795
Muni. block grant	60,358
Energy tax receipts	4,222,042
Homeland security	70,000

Fiscal Year 2006

Total aid	$7,000,195
CMPTRA	2,500,023
Muni. block grant	60,358
Energy tax receipts	4,369,814
Homeland security	70,000

Taxes

	2003	2004	2005
General tax rate per $100	3.18	3.415	3.705
Net valuation taxable	$723,673,780	$721,289,873	$732,315,311
State equalized value	$764,740,336	$843,985,011	$879,869,411
County equalization ratio	96.68	94.63	85.42

Demographics & Socio-Economic Characteristics

(2000 U.S. Census, except as noted)

Population

1980*	13,776
1990*	12,844
2000	13,888
Male	6,688
Female	7,200
2004 (estimate)*	15,192
Persons per sq. mi. of land	2,150

Race & Hispanic Origin, 2000

Race
White	13,416
Black/African American	41
Amer. Indian/Alaska Natv.	17
Asian	265
Natv. Hawaiian/Pac. Islander	0
Other Race	69
Two or more races	80
Hispanic origin, total	408
Mexican	29
Puerto Rican	144
Cuban	42
Other Hispanic	193

Age & Nativity, 2000

Under 5 years	947
18 years and over	10,293
21 years and over	9,912
65 years and over	1,956
85 years and over	206
Median Age	38.9
Native born	12,904
Foreign born	984

Educational Attainment, 2000

Population 25 years and over	9,495
0-8 yrs of school	2.4%
High School grad or higher	92.8%
Bachelor's degree or higher	37.5%
Graduate degree	11.4%

Income & Poverty, 1999

Per capita income	$31,892
Median household income	$72,729
Median family income	$84,487
Persons in poverty	414
H'holds receiving public assistance	43
H'holds receiving social security	1,460

Households, 2000

Total households	5,026
With persons under 18	1,849
With persons over 65	1,414
Family households	3,828
One-person households	1,052
Persons per household	2.76
Persons per family	3.23

Labor & Employment

Total civilian labor force, 2004**	7,890
Unemployment rate	3.7%
Total civilian labor force, 2000	7,243
Unemployment rate	3.7%

Employed persons 16 years and over by occupation, 2000
Managers & professionals	3,057
Service occupations	701
Sales & office occupations	2,263
Farming, fishing & forestry	7
Construction & maintenance	466
Production & transportation	484
Self-employed persons	358

*US Census Bureau
**New Jersey Department of Labor

General Information

Township of Pequannock
530 Newton-Pompton Tpke
Pompton Plains, NJ 07444
973-835-5700

Web site	www.pequannocktownship.org
Land area (sq. miles)	7.07
Water area (sq. miles)	0.14
Type of government	Township
Form of government	CM '50

Government

Legislative Districts

US Congressional	11
State Legislative	26

Local Officials, 2006

Mayor	Ruth Spellman
Admin/Manager	Kevin Boyle
Clerk	Dolores Sweeney
Finance Dir/Treas	David Hollberg
Engineer	Fred Herrmann
Attorney	Michael Hubner
Tax assessor	Robert Sweeney
Tax collector	Lori Tarnogursky
Building officer	Robert Grant
Zoning officer	NA
Public Works	Matt Pinto

Housing & Construction

Housing Units, 2000*

Total	5,097
Median rent	$787
Median SF home value	$246,100

New Privately Owned Housing Units Authorized by Building Permit

	Units	Value
Total, 2004	165	$12,975,230
Single family	13	$2,375,230
Total, 2005	266	$23,615,311
Single family	12	$2,620,574

Real Property Valuation - parcels, 2005

	Number	Valuation
Total		$1,184,343,047
Vacant	148	10,448,700
Residential	4,759	923,347,600
Commercial	224	142,716,500
Industrial	13	13,642,000
Apartments	2	87,568,100
Farm land	19	6,325,900
Farm homestead	24	294,247

Average Property Value & Tax, 2005

Residential value	$193,109
Property tax	$6,278
FAIR rebate	$628

Public Library

Pequannock Twp Pub Library
477 Newark-Pompton Tpke
Pompton Plains, NJ 07444
973-835-7460
Director............Rosemary Garwood

Library statistics, 2004

	Total	per capita
Volumes	78,633	5.66
Expenditure	$887,468	$63.90

Public Safety

Police

Chief	Brian Spring
Number of officers, 2004	26

Crime, 2004	Number	Rate
Total	194	13.4
Violent	5	0.3
Non-violent	189	13
Domestic Viol.	57	NA

Emergency/Fire

Director...........H. Reeves/D. Hollberg

Public School District

(for school year 2004-2005 except as noted)

Pequannock Township School District
538 Newark-Pompton Turnpike
Pompton Plains, NJ 07444
973-616-6040

Superintendent	Jerry Cichellli
Grade plan	K-12
Enrollment	2,506.5
Students per teacher	11.2
Per pupil expenditure	$10,744
Median faculty salary	$51,250
Median administrator salary	$105,084
Grade 12 enrollment	174.5
High school graduation rate	100.0%

Assessment test results

(percent scoring at proficient or advanced level)
	Language	Math
Grade 3	92.9%	93.0%
Grade 8	85.2%	80.6%
High school	92.4%	88.4%

SAT

Percent tested	90%
Average SAT math score	517
Average SAT verbal score	509

No Child Left Behind, 2003-04

Attendance rate (target = 90%)	96.4%
Drop rate	0%
Highly-qualified teachers	50.9%
District needs improvement?(AYP)	No

Municipal Finance

Fiscal Year 2005

Total tax levy	$38,545,742
County levy	5,567,796
County taxes	4,560,804
County library	0
County health	0
County open space	1,006,992
School levy	25,710,240
Local muni. budget	7,267,707
Misc. revenues	5,391,335
Total aid	$1,701,627
CMPTRA	604,180
Muni. block grant	56,201
Energy tax receipts	971,246
Homeland security	70,000

Fiscal Year 2006

Total aid	$1,701,626
CMPTRA	570,186
Muni. block grant	56,201
Energy tax receipts	1,005,239
Homeland security	70,000

Taxes

	2003	2004	2005
General tax rate per $100	3.06	3.110	3.260
Net valuation taxable	$1,123,900,439	$1,163,511,353	$1,185,606,531
State equalized value	$1,771,595,900	$2,047,673,820	$2,318,354,578
County equalization ratio	70.06	63.44	56.79

Demographics & Socio-Economic Characteristics
(2000 U.S. Census, except as noted)

Population
1980*	38,951
1990*	41,967
2000	47,303
Male	23,441
Female	23,862
2004 (estimate)*	48,823
Persons per sq. mi. of land	10,210

Race & Hispanic Origin, 2000
Race
White	21,951
Black/African American	4,749
Amer. Indian/Alaska Natv.	330
Asian	723
Natv. Hawaiian/Pac. Islander	60
Other Race	16,834
Two or more races	2,656
Hispanic origin, total	33,033
Mexican	3,056
Puerto Rican	13,145
Cuban	918
Other Hispanic	15,914

Age & Nativity, 2000
Under 5 years	3,805
18 years and over	33,831
21 years and over	31,558
65 years and over	4,820
85 years and over	599
Median Age	31.2
Native born	30,408
Foreign born	16,895

Educational Attainment, 2000
Population 25 years and over	28,309
0-8 yrs of school	23.7%
High School grad or higher	55.7%
Bachelor's degree or higher	9.7%
Graduate degree	3.4%

Income & Poverty, 1999
Per capita income	$14,989
Median household income	$37,608
Median family income	$40,740
Persons in poverty	8,190
H'holds receiving public assistance	760
H'holds receiving social security	3,694

Households, 2000
Total households	14,562
With persons under 18	6,727
With persons over 65	3,493
Family households	10,768
One-person households	2,993
Persons per household	3.2
Persons per family	3.63

Labor & Employment
Total civilian labor force, 2004**	23,716
Unemployment rate	9.8%
Total civilian labor force, 2000	20,970
Unemployment rate	10.8%

Employed persons 16 years and over by occupation, 2000
Managers & professionals	3,267
Service occupations	3,252
Sales & office occupations	4,667
Farming, fishing & forestry	15
Construction & maintenance	1,636
Production & transportation	5,861
Self-employed persons	528

*US Census Bureau
**New Jersey Department of Labor

General Information
City of Perth Amboy
260 High St
Perth Amboy, NJ 08861
732-826-0290

Web site	www.ci.perthamboy.nj.us
Land area (sq. miles)	4.78
Water area (sq. miles)	1.20
Type of government	City
Form of government	Faulkner Plan B - MC

Government

Legislative Districts
US Congressional	13
State Legislative	19

Local Officials, 2006
Mayor	Joseph Vas
Admin/Manager	Donald Perlee
Clerk	Elaine M. Jasko
Finance Dir/Treas	Jill Goldy
Engineer	Michael Carr
Attorney	Frank G. Capece
Tax assessor	William Wheeler
Tax collector	Steven Davis
Building officer	NA
Zoning officer	Jamie Rios
Public Works	Kenneth Schwartz

Housing & Construction

Housing Units, 2000*
Total	15,236
Median rent	$732
Median SF home value	$126,200

New Privately Owned Housing Units Authorized by Building Permit
	Units	Value
Total, 2004	56	$2,659,173
Single family	51	$875,501
Total, 2005	178	$10,683,568
Single family	21	$2,155,856

Real Property Valuation - parcels, 2005
	Number	Valuation
Total		$1,392,803,350
Vacant	447	35,984,700
Residential	7,283	817,780,150
Commercial	803	203,522,500
Industrial	137	213,500,900
Apartments	151	122,015,100
Farm land	0	0
Farm homestead	0	0

Average Property Value & Tax, 2005
Residential value	$112,286
Property tax	$3,766
FAIR rebate	$636

Public Library
Perth Amboy Public Library
196 Jefferson St
Perth Amboy, NJ 08861
732-826-2600

Director...................Patricia Gandy

Library statistics, 2004
	Total	per capita
Volumes	173,939	3.68
Expenditure	$1,185,522	$25.06

Public Safety

Police
Chief	Michael Kohut
Number of officers, 2004	123

Crime, 2004	Number	Rate
Total	1,182	24.4
Violent	154	3.2
Non-violent	1,028	21.2
Domestic Viol.	337	NA

Emergency/Fire
Director............. Lawrence Cattano

Public School District
(for school year 2004-2005 except as noted)

Perth Amboy School District
178 Barracks St
Perth Amboy, NJ 08861
732-376-6279

Superintendent	John Rodecker
Grade plan	K-12
Enrollment	9,336.0
Students per teacher	10.6
Per pupil expenditure	$14,075
Median faculty salary	$46,350
Median administrator salary	$103,562
Grade 12 enrollment	432.5
High school graduation rate	90.6%

Assessment test results
(percent scoring at proficient or advanced level)
	Language	Math
Grade 3	64.2%	76.4%
Grade 8	44.6%	31.2%
High school	61.5%	52.1%

SAT
Percent tested	50%
Average SAT math score	438
Average SAT verbal score	411

No Child Left Behind, 2003-04
Attendence rate (target = 90%)	93.6%
Drop rate	2.7%
Highly-qualified teachers	97.6%
District needs improvement?(AYP)	No

Municipal Finance

Fiscal Year 2005
Total tax levy	$46,820,711
County levy	7,694,123
County taxes	6,969,317
County library	0
County health	0
County open space	724,806
School levy	16,813,422
Local muni. budget	22,313,166
Misc. revenues	29,849,841
Total aid	$11,584,492
CMPTRA	9,401,117
Muni. block grant	185,476
Energy tax receipts	1,857,899
Homeland security	140,000

Fiscal Year 2006
Total aid	$11,584,492
CMPTRA	9,336,091
Muni. block grant	185,476
Energy tax receipts	1,922,925
Homeland security	140,000

Taxes
	2003	2004	2005
General tax rate per $100	3.07	3.140	3.360
Net valuation taxable	$1,388,088,512	$1,382,943,542	$1,396,003,183
State equalized value	$2,006,488,164	$2,342,744,129	$2,777,563,038
County equalization ratio	82.22	69.18	58.96

Demographics & Socio-Economic Characteristics
(2000 U.S. Census, except as noted)

Population
1980*	16,647
1990*	15,757
2000	15,166
Male	7,226
Female	7,940
2004 (estimate)*	15,070
Persons per sq. mi. of land	4,674

Race & Hispanic Origin, 2000
Race
White	13,928
Black/African American	527
Amer. Indian/Alaska Natv.	18
Asian	126
Natv. Hawaiian/Pac. Islander	2
Other Race	306
Two or more races	259
Hispanic origin, total	816
Mexican	120
Puerto Rican	374
Cuban	30
Other Hispanic	292

Age & Nativity, 2000
Under 5 years	1,090
18 years and over	11,128
21 years and over	10,553
65 years and over	2,311
85 years and over	271
Median Age	36
Native born	14,537
Foreign born	629

Educational Attainment, 2000
Population 25 years and over	9,913
0-8 yrs of school	7.9%
High School grad or higher	71.3%
Bachelor's degree or higher	9.2%
Graduate degree	2.3%

Income & Poverty, 1999
Per capita income	$18,452
Median household income	$37,368
Median family income	$46,925
Persons in poverty	2,009
H'holds receiving public assistance	306
H'holds receiving social security	2,014

Households, 2000
Total households	6,044
With persons under 18	2,120
With persons over 65	1,751
Family households	3,945
One-person households	1,793
Persons per household	2.49
Persons per family	3.08

Labor & Employment
Total civilian labor force, 2004**	9,165
Unemployment rate	6.4%
Total civilian labor force, 2000	7,320
Unemployment rate	5.9%

Employed persons 16 years and over by occupation, 2000
Managers & professionals	1,382
Service occupations	1,304
Sales & office occupations	2,032
Farming, fishing & forestry	9
Construction & maintenance	597
Production & transportation	1,566
Self-employed persons	238

*US Census Bureau
**New Jersey Department of Labor

General Information
Town of Phillipsburg
675 Corliss Ave
Phillipsburg, NJ 08865
908-454-5500

Web site	www.phillipsburgnj.org
Land area (sq. miles)	3.22
Water area (sq. miles)	0.11
Type of government	Town
Form of government	MC '50

Government

Legislative Districts
US Congressional	5
State Legislative	23

Local Officials, 2006
Mayor	Harry Wyant
Admin/Manager	Michele Broubalow
Clerk	Michele Broubalow
Finance Dir/Treas	Joseph Hriczak
Engineer	Eugene Buczynski
Attorney	Joel Kobert
Tax assessor	Lydia Zdrodowski
Tax collector	Joseph Hriczak
Building officer	Kevin Duddy
Zoning officer	John Fritts
Public Works	Dennis Viscomi

Housing & Construction

Housing Units, 2000*
Total	6,651
Median rent	$600
Median SF home value	$90,000

New Privately Owned Housing Units
Authorized by Building Permit
	Units	Value
Total, 2004	NA	NA
Single family	NA	NA
Total, 2005	10	$1,112,196
Single family	10	$1,112,196

Real Property Valuation - parcels, 2005
	Number	Valuation
Total		$551,278,260
Vacant	159	5,500,700
Residential	4,467	396,714,700
Commercial	326	85,552,000
Industrial	33	43,944,150
Apartments	38	19,533,100
Farm land	0	0
Farm homestead	2	33,610

Average Property Value & Tax, 2005
Residential value	$88,778
Property tax	$2,940
FAIR rebate	$636

Public Library
Phillipsburg Public Library
200 Frost Ave
Phillipsburg, NJ 08865
908-454-3712

Director..................Patricia Lawson

Library statistics, 2004
	Total	per capita
Volumes	94,367	6.22
Expenditure	$1,225,659	$80.82

Public Safety

Police
Chief	Robert Mirabelli
Number of officers, 2004	37

Crime, 2004	Number	Rate
Total	290	19.1
Violent	27	1.8
Non-violent	263	17.3
Domestic Viol.	549	NA

Emergency/Fire
Director...................Richard Hay

Public School District
(for school year 2004-2005 except as noted)

Phillipsburg School District
445 Marshall St
Phillipsburg, NJ 08865
908-454-3400

Superintendent	H. Gordon Pethick
Grade plan	K-12
Enrollment	3,481.0
Students per teacher	8.6
Per pupil expenditure	$14,163
Median faculty salary	$52,480
Median administrator salary	$87,272
Grade 12 enrollment	333.5
High school graduation rate	88.3%

Assessment test results
(percent scoring at proficient or advanced level)
	Language	Math
Grade 3	70.9%	74.3%
Grade 8	62.6%	53.0%
High school	85.1%	75.4%

SAT
Percent tested	65%
Average SAT math score	506
Average SAT verbal score	498

No Child Left Behind, 2003-04
Attendence rate (target = 90%)	92.4%
Drop rate	2%
Highly-qualified teachers	100%
District needs improvement?(AYP)	No

Municipal Finance

Fiscal Year 2005
Total tax levy	$18,359,339
County levy	4,439,865
County taxes	3,988,334
County library	0
County health	0
County open space	451,531
School levy	6,354,522
Local muni. budget	7,564,952
Misc. revenues	6,523,071
Total aid	$2,571,724
CMPTRA	1,632,198
Muni. block grant	68,948
Energy tax receipts	800,578
Homeland security	70,000

Fiscal Year 2006
Total aid	$2,571,724
CMPTRA	1,604,177
Muni. block grant	68,948
Energy tax receipts	828,599
Homeland security	70,000

Taxes
	2003	2004	2005
General tax rate per $100	2.99	3.140	3.320
Net valuation taxable	$551,980,450	$552,264,724	$554,463,875
State equalized value	$644,084,539	$731,668,103	$850,274,306
County equalization ratio	93.61	85.70	75.36

Demographics & Socio-Economic Characteristics
(2000 U.S. Census, except as noted)

Population

1980*	2,810
1990*	3,250
2000	3,923
Male	2,029
Female	1,894
2004 (estimate)*	4,124
Persons per sq. mi. of land	118

Race & Hispanic Origin, 2000

Race

White	3,320
Black/African American	478
Amer. Indian/Alaska Natv.	11
Asian	36
Natv. Hawaiian/Pac. Islander	2
Other Race	42
Two or more races	34
Hispanic origin, total	117
Mexican	24
Puerto Rican	51
Cuban	0
Other Hispanic	42

Age & Nativity, 2000

Under 5 years	168
18 years and over	2,989
21 years and over	2,811
65 years and over	566
85 years and over	112
Median Age	40
Native born	3,864
Foreign born	65

Educational Attainment, 2000

Population 25 years and over	2,709
0-8 yrs of school	3.0%
High School grad or higher	87.7%
Bachelor's degree or higher	22.8%
Graduate degree	6.7%

Income & Poverty, 1999

Per capita income	$27,400
Median household income	$66,042
Median family income	$71,629
Persons in poverty	120
H'holds receiving public assistance	5
H'holds receiving social security	315

Households, 2000

Total households	1,216
With persons under 18	473
With persons over 65	317
Family households	995
One-person households	181
Persons per household	2.91
Persons per family	3.24

Labor & Employment

Total civilian labor force, 2004**	1,637
Unemployment rate	1.0%
Total civilian labor force, 2000	1,895
Unemployment rate	4.2%

Employed persons 16 years and over by occupation, 2000

Managers & professionals	691
Service occupations	237
Sales & office occupations	396
Farming, fishing & forestry	24
Construction & maintenance	201
Production & transportation	266
Self-employed persons	228

*US Census Bureau
**New Jersey Department of Labor

General Information

Township of Pilesgrove
1180 Route 40
Pilesgrove, NJ 08098
856-769-3222

Web site	NA
Land area (sq. miles)	34.91
Water area (sq. miles)	0.14
Type of government	Township
Form of government	TC

Government

Legislative Districts

US Congressional	2
State Legislative	3

Local Officials, 2006

Mayor	Ernest A. Bickford
Admin/Manager	Maureen R. Abdill
Clerk	Maureen Abdill
Finance Dir/Treas	Ruth Moynihan
Engineer	Carl Gaskill
Attorney	William L. Horner
Tax assessor	Randall Shidner
Tax collector	NA
Building officer	James N. Kates
Zoning officer	James N. Kates
Public Works	NA

Housing & Construction

Housing Units, 2000*

Total	1,261
Median rent	$590
Median SF home value	$158,400

New Privately Owned Housing Units
Authorized by Building Permit

	Units	Value
Total, 2004	101	$7,748,805
Single family	82	$7,698,805
Total, 2005	56	$7,156,277
Single family	56	$7,156,277

Real Property Valuation - parcels, 2005

	Number	Valuation
Total		$255,879,200
Vacant	263	7,217,100
Residential	1,122	171,711,900
Commercial	65	28,952,000
Industrial	2	1,343,000
Apartments	3	377,600
Farm land	233	39,353,200
Farm homestead	455	6,924,400

Average Property Value & Tax, 2005

Residential value	$113,276
Property tax	$3,854
FAIR rebate	$620

Public Library

Woodstown-Pilesgrove Library†
14 School Ln
Woodstown, NJ 08098
856-769-0098

Librarian	Betty Lou Wiest

Library statistics, 2004

	Total	per capita
Volumes	NA	NA
Expenditure	NA	NA

†Joint Library with Woodstown

Public Safety

Police

Chief	NA
Number of officers, 2004	0

Crime, 2004	Number	Rate
Total	89	22
Violent	7	1.7
Non-violent	82	20.2
Domestic Viol.	23	NA

Emergency/Fire

Director	Carlo Castagliuolo Jr.

Public School District
(for school year 2004-2005 except as noted)

Woodstown-Pilesgrove Reg. School District
135 E Ave
Woodstown, NJ 08098
856-769-1664

Superintendent	Robert Bumpus
Grade plan	K-12
Enrollment	1,581.0
Students per teacher	11.6
Per pupil expenditure	$10,541
Median faculty salary	$61,252
Median administrator salary	$89,683
Grade 12 enrollment	131.0
High school graduation rate	95.1%

Assessment test results
(percent scoring at proficient or advanced level)

	Language	Math
Grade 3	84.8%	82.6%
Grade 8	80.8%	70.0%
High school	89.6%	82.6%

SAT

Percent tested	66%
Average SAT math score	518
Average SAT verbal score	510

No Child Left Behind, 2003-04

Attendence rate (target = 90%)	94.3%
Drop rate	0.6%
Highly-qualified teachers	98.4%
District needs improvement?(AYP)	No

Municipal Finance

Fiscal Year 2005

Total tax levy	$8,743,295
County levy	3,649,550
County taxes	3,577,071
County library	0
County health	0
County open space	72,479
School levy	5,016,657
Local muni. budget	77,088
Misc. revenues	2,463,676
Total aid	$622,839
CMPTRA	181,099
Muni. block grant	15,382
Energy tax receipts	426,358
Homeland security	0

Fiscal Year 2006

Total aid	$622,838
CMPTRA	166,176
Muni. block grant	15,382
Energy tax receipts	441,280
Homeland security	NA

Taxes

	2003	2004	2005
General tax rate per $100	2.91	3.134	3.403
Net valuation taxable	$243,430,501	$249,276,144	$256,960,051
State equalized value	$301,461,921	$349,728,419	$395,140,783
County equalization ratio	89.24	80.75	71.17

Demographics & Socio-Economic Characteristics
(2000 U.S. Census, except as noted)

Population
1980*	1,796
1990*	1,954
2000	1,950
Male	940
Female	1,010
2004 (estimate)*	2,020
Persons per sq. mi. of land	3,243

Race & Hispanic Origin, 2000
Race
White	1,919
Black/African American	5
Amer. Indian/Alaska Natv.	1
Asian	12
Natv. Hawaiian/Pac. Islander	0
Other Race	4
Two or more races	9
Hispanic origin, total	46
Mexican	2
Puerto Rican	21
Cuban	11
Other Hispanic	12

Age & Nativity, 2000
Under 5 years	101
18 years and over	1,507
21 years and over	1,454
65 years and over	337
85 years and over	38
Median Age	41.6
Native born	1,899
Foreign born	51

Educational Attainment, 2000
Population 25 years and over	1,398
0-8 yrs of school	1.7%
High School grad or higher	90.7%
Bachelor's degree or higher	32.6%
Graduate degree	11.5%

Income & Poverty, 1999
Per capita income	$26,487
Median household income	$57,366
Median family income	$67,404
Persons in poverty	68
H'holds receiving public assistance	2
H'holds receiving social security	259

Households, 2000
Total households	767
With persons under 18	254
With persons over 65	247
Family households	558
One-person households	172
Persons per household	2.54
Persons per family	3.01

Labor & Employment
Total civilian labor force, 2004**	1,247
Unemployment rate	4.2%
Total civilian labor force, 2000	1,015
Unemployment rate	3.8%

Employed persons 16 years and over by occupation, 2000
Managers & professionals	381
Service occupations	136
Sales & office occupations	268
Farming, fishing & forestry	0
Construction & maintenance	125
Production & transportation	66
Self-employed persons	54

*US Census Bureau
**New Jersey Department of Labor

General Information
Borough of Pine Beach
599 Pennsylvania Ave
Pine Beach, NJ 08741
732-349-6425
Web site	www.pinebeachborough.us
Land area (sq. miles)	0.62
Water area (sq. miles)	0.01
Type of government	Borough
Form of government	B

Government

Legislative Districts
US Congressional	3
State Legislative	9

Local Officials, 2006
Mayor	Russell Corby
Admin/Manager	Charlene Carney
Clerk	Charlene Carney
Finance Dir/Treas	Mary Jane Steib
Engineer	John Mallon
Attorney	Steven Secare
Tax assessor	Richard Kenny
Tax collector	Christine Dehnz
Building officer	Anthony Avello
Zoning officer	John Tilton
Public Works	NA

Housing & Construction

Housing Units, 2000*
Total	872
Median rent	$858
Median SF home value	$149,100

New Privately Owned Housing Units
Authorized by Building Permit
	Units	Value
Total, 2004	7	$981,250
Single family	7	$981,250
Total, 2005	7	$1,121,000
Single family	7	$1,121,000

Real Property Valuation - parcels, 2005
	Number	Valuation
Total		$282,922,200
Vacant	36	5,066,500
Residential	861	270,786,800
Commercial	18	7,068,900
Industrial	0	0
Apartments	0	0
Farm land	0	0
Farm homestead	0	0

Average Property Value & Tax, 2005
Residential value	$314,503
Property tax	$4,157
FAIR rebate	$635

Public Library
No public municipal library.

Library statistics, 2004
	Total	per capita
Volumes	NA	NA
Expenditure	NA	NA

Public Safety
Police
Chief	Glenn Jones
Number of officers, 2004	6

Crime, 2004	Number	Rate
Total	31	15.5
Violent	2	1
Non-violent	29	14.5
Domestic Viol.	16	NA

Emergency/Fire
Director	Kevin Simon

Public School District
(for school year 2004-2005 except as noted)

Sends children to Toms River Regional school district (see South Toms River Borough).

Grade plan	NA
Enrollment	NA
Students per teacher	NA
Per pupil expenditure	NA
Median faculty salary	NA
Median administrator salary	NA
Grade 12 enrollment	NA
High school graduation rate	NA

Assessment test results
(percent scoring at proficient or advanced level)
	Language	Math
Grade 3	NA	NA
Grade 8	NA	NA
High school	NA	NA

SAT
Percent tested	NA
Average SAT math score	NA
Average SAT verbal score	NA

No Child Left Behind, 2003-04
Attendence rate (target = 90%)	NA
Drop rate	NA
Highly-qualified teachers	NA
District needs improvement?(AYP)	NA

Municipal Finance

Fiscal Year 2005
Total tax levy	$3,742,119
County levy	847,353
County taxes	713,918
County library	75,003
County health	31,791
County open space	26,641
School levy	1,782,412
Local muni. budget	1,112,353
Misc. revenues	2,427,637
Total aid	$310,530
CMPTRA	79,501
Muni. block grant	8,551
Energy tax receipts	197,478
Homeland security	25,000

Fiscal Year 2006
Total aid	$310,530
CMPTRA	72,589
Muni. block grant	8,551
Energy tax receipts	204,390
Homeland security	25,000

Taxes
	2003	2004	2005
General tax rate per $100	2.63	2.575	1.322
Net valuation taxable	$124,792,383	$126,218,974	$283,085,464
State equalized value	$178,990,796	$218,548,867	$255,931,167
County equalization ratio	76.85	69.72	127.75

Demographics & Socio-Economic Characteristics
(2000 U.S. Census, except as noted)

Population
1980*	8,684
1990*	9,854
2000	10,880
Male	5,161
Female	5,719
2004 (estimate)*	11,221
Persons per sq. mi. of land	2,855

Race & Hispanic Origin, 2000
Race
White	8,355
Black/African American	1,996
Amer. Indian/Alaska Natv.	30
Asian	153
Natv. Hawaiian/Pac. Islander	2
Other Race	132
Two or more races	212
Hispanic origin, total	396
Mexican	47
Puerto Rican	252
Cuban	16
Other Hispanic	81

Age & Nativity, 2000
Under 5 years	811
18 years and over	7,917
21 years and over	7,499
65 years and over	923
85 years and over	74
Median Age	33.3
Native born	10,530
Foreign born	389

Educational Attainment, 2000
Population 25 years and over	6,959
0-8 yrs of school	4.1%
High School grad or higher	80.7%
Bachelor's degree or higher	13.8%
Graduate degree	3.8%

Income & Poverty, 1999
Per capita income	$18,613
Median household income	$42,035
Median family income	$50,040
Persons in poverty	768
H'holds receiving public assistance	93
H'holds receiving social security	892

Households, 2000
Total households	4,214
With persons under 18	1,687
With persons over 65	743
Family households	2,742
One-person households	1,172
Persons per household	2.58
Persons per family	3.18

Labor & Employment
Total civilian labor force, 2004**	5,575
Unemployment rate	6.5%
Total civilian labor force, 2000	5,844
Unemployment rate	5.9%

Employed persons 16 years and over by occupation, 2000
Managers & professionals	1,423
Service occupations	966
Sales & office occupations	1,732
Farming, fishing & forestry	4
Construction & maintenance	719
Production & transportation	653
Self-employed persons	237

*US Census Bureau
**New Jersey Department of Labor

General Information
Borough of Pine Hill
45 W Seventh Ave
Pine Hill, NJ 08021
856-783-7400
Web site	www.pinehillboronj.com
Land area (sq. miles)	3.93
Water area (sq. miles)	0.03
Type of government	Borough
Form of government	B

Government

Legislative Districts
US Congressional	1
State Legislative	6

Local Officials, 2006
Mayor	Fred Costantino
Admin/Manager	NA
Clerk	Joan A. Schneebele
Finance Dir/Treas	Thomas Cardis
Engineer	Michael Meyer
Attorney	John Kearney
Tax assessor	Michael Raio
Tax collector	Diane May
Building officer	Raymond Hallworth
Zoning officer	Neil Clark
Public Works	David Flynn

Housing & Construction

Housing Units, 2000*
Total	4,444
Median rent	$627
Median SF home value	$88,500

New Privately Owned Housing Units Authorized by Building Permit
	Units	Value
Total, 2004	48	$3,472,328
Single family	48	$3,472,328
Total, 2005	28	$2,156,921
Single family	28	$2,156,921

Real Property Valuation - parcels, 2005
	Number	Valuation
Total		$271,935,720
Vacant	278	7,076,920
Residential	3,007	242,489,300
Commercial	46	7,546,300
Industrial	3	772,800
Apartments	6	13,788,900
Farm land	3	244,800
Farm homestead	5	16,700

Average Property Value & Tax, 2005
Residential value	$80,513
Property tax	$4,114
FAIR rebate	$502

Public Library
No public municipal library.

Library statistics, 2004
	Total	per capita
Volumes	NA	NA
Expenditure	NA	NA

Public Safety
Police
Chief	Kenneth Cheeseman
Number of officers, 2004	22

Crime, 2004	Number	Rate
Total	305	27.5
Violent	42	3.8
Non-violent	263	23.7
Domestic Viol.	216	NA

Emergency/Fire
Director	Richard Wright Sr. (Chief)

Public School District
(for school year 2004-2005 except as noted)

Pine Hill Borough School District
1003 Turnerville Rd
Pine Hill, NJ 08021
856-783-6900
Superintendent	Kenneth Koczur
Grade plan	K-12
Enrollment	2,282.0
Students per teacher	10.5
Per pupil expenditure	$12,121
Median faculty salary	$68,701
Median administrator salary	$95,262
Grade 12 enrollment	174.0
High school graduation rate	80.9%

Assessment test results
(percent scoring at proficient or advanced level)
	Language	Math
Grade 3	68.0%	86.0%
Grade 8	57.1%	49.0%
High school	82.0%	66.9%

SAT
Percent tested	62%
Average SAT math score	474
Average SAT verbal score	468

No Child Left Behind, 2003-04
Attendence rate (target = 90%)	92.7%
Drop rate	2.1%
Highly-qualified teachers	98.9%
District needs improvement?(AYP)	No

Municipal Finance

Fiscal Year 2005
Total tax levy	$13,927,085
County levy	3,059,664
County taxes	2,819,964
County library	202,732
County health	0
County open space	36,969
School levy	8,011,076
Local muni. budget	2,856,345
Misc. revenues	3,664,942
Total aid	$1,237,447
CMPTRA	548,724
Muni. block grant	43,118
Energy tax receipts	575,605
Homeland security	70,000

Fiscal Year 2006
Total aid	$1,237,446
CMPTRA	528,577
Muni. block grant	43,118
Energy tax receipts	595,751
Homeland security	70,000

Taxes
	2003	2004	2005
General tax rate per $100	4.78	4.763	5.110
Net valuation taxable	$262,666,004	$268,270,998	$272,574,180
State equalized value	$317,076,296	$362,895,202	$423,580,699
County equalization ratio	88.72	82.84	73.87

Demographics & Socio-Economic Characteristics
(2000 U.S. Census, except as noted)

Population
1980*	23
1990*	19
2000	20
Male	12
Female	8
2004 (estimate)*	22
Persons per sq. mi. of land	23

Race & Hispanic Origin, 2000
Race
White	20
Black/African American	0
Amer. Indian/Alaska Natv.	0
Asian	0
Natv. Hawaiian/Pac. Islander	0
Other Race	0
Two or more races	0
Hispanic origin, total	0
Mexican	0
Puerto Rican	0
Cuban	0
Other Hispanic	0

Age & Nativity, 2000
Under 5 years	0
18 years and over	15
21 years and over	15
65 years and over	8
85 years and over	0
Median Age	58.5
Native born	16
Foreign born	0

Educational Attainment, 2000
Population 25 years and over	12
0-8 yrs of school	0.0%
High School grad or higher	83.3%
Bachelor's degree or higher	0.0%
Graduate degree	0.0%

Income & Poverty, 1999
Per capita income	$23,981
Median household income	$31,875
Median family income	$65,625
Persons in poverty	0
H'holds receiving public assistance	2
H'holds receiving social security	6

Households, 2000
Total households	8
With persons under 18	2
With persons over 65	5
Family households	7
One-person households	1
Persons per household	2.5
Persons per family	2.71

Labor & Employment
Total civilian labor force, 2004**	10
Unemployment rate	0.0%
Total civilian labor force, 2000	5
Unemployment rate	0.0%

Employed persons 16 years and over by occupation, 2000
Managers & professionals	2
Service occupations	0
Sales & office occupations	2
Farming, fishing & forestry	0
Construction & maintenance	0
Production & transportation	1
Self-employed persons	0

*US Census Bureau
**New Jersey Department of Labor

General Information
Borough of Pine Valley
1 Club Road
Pine Valley, NJ 08021
856-783-7078

Web site	NA
Land area (sq. miles)	0.95
Water area (sq. miles)	0.01
Type of government	Borough
Form of government	Comm.

Government

Legislative Districts
US Congressional	1
State Legislative	6

Local Officials, 2006
Mayor	William Carson Jr.
Admin/Manager	NA
Clerk	Patricia M. Porter
Finance Dir/Treas	Patricia McConney
Engineer	William Underwood
Attorney	Joseph Betley
Tax assessor	Christine Wahl
Tax collector	Patricia McConney
Building officer	Richard Wright
Zoning officer	NA
Public Works	NA

Housing & Construction

Housing Units, 2000*
Total	21
Median rent	$-
Median SF home value	$325,000

New Privately Owned Housing Units
Authorized by Building Permit
	Units	Value
Total, 2004	0	$0
Single family	0	$0
Total, 2005	1	$551,500
Single family	1	$551,500

Real Property Valuation - parcels, 2005
	Number	Valuation
Total		$34,004,800
Vacant	6	4,596,400
Residential	23	5,322,700
Commercial	16	24,085,700
Industrial	0	0
Apartments	0	0
Farm land	0	0
Farm homestead	0	0

Average Property Value & Tax, 2005
Residential value	$231,422
Property tax	$3,512
FAIR rebate	$650

Public Library

No public municipal library.

Library statistics, 2004
	Total	per capita
Volumes	NA	NA
Expenditure	NA	NA

Public Safety

Police
Chief	Timothy Kemble
Number of officers, 2004	4

Crime, 2004	Number	Rate
Total	2	+
Violent	0	+
Non-violent	2	+
Domestic Viol.	0	NA

Emergency/Fire
Director	NA

Public School District
(for school year 2004-2005 except as noted)

Pine Valley School District†
Pine Valley Golf Club
Clementon, NJ 08021

†No schools or pupils in district.

Grade plan	NA
Enrollment	NA
Students per teacher	NA
Per pupil expenditure	NA
Median faculty salary	NA

Assessment test results
(percent scoring at proficient or advanced level)
	Language	Math
Grade 3	NA	NA
Grade 8	NA	NA
High school	NA	NA

SAT
Percent tested	NA
Average SAT math score	NA
Average SAT verbal score	NA

No Child Left Behind, 2003-04
Attendence rate (target = 90%)	NA
Drop rate	NA
Highly-qualified teachers	NA
District needs improvement?(AYP)	NA

Municipal Finance

Fiscal Year 2005
Total tax levy	$517,089
County levy	283,006
County taxes	260,835
County library	18,752
County health	0
County open space	3,419
School levy	0
Local muni. budget	234,083
Misc. revenues	132,877
Total aid	$2,669
CMPTRA	313
Muni. block grant	83
Energy tax receipts	2,273
Homeland security	0

Fiscal Year 2006
Total aid	$2,669
CMPTRA	233
Muni. block grant	83
Energy tax receipts	2,353
Homeland security	NA

Taxes
	2003	2004	2005
General tax rate per $100	1.66	1.593	1.518
Net valuation taxable	$34,168,146	$34,080,252	$34,072,602
State equalized value	$31,121,364	$32,675,203	$33,368,526
County equalization ratio	100	100.00	100.00

Demographics & Socio-Economic Characteristics
(2000 U.S. Census, except as noted)

Population
1980*	42,223
1990*	47,089
2000	50,482
Male	24,979
Female	25,503
2000 (revised)	50,558
2004 (estimate)*	52,412
Persons per sq. mi. of land	2,791

Race & Hispanic Origin, 2000
Race
White	24,642
Black/African American	10,254
Amer. Indian/Alaska Natv.	104
Asian	12,519
Natv. Hawaiian/Pac. Islander	13
Other Race	1,553
Two or more races	1,397
Hispanic origin, total	4,002
Mexican	185
Puerto Rican	1,060
Cuban	202
Other Hispanic	2,555

Age & Nativity, 2000
Under 5 years	3,127
18 years and over	39,430
21 years and over	35,541
65 years and over	4,374
85 years and over	361
Median Age	33.3
Native born	35,430
Foreign born	15,052

Educational Attainment, 2000
Population 25 years and over	32,118
0-8 yrs of school	4.0%
High School grad or higher	88.5%
Bachelor's degree or higher	40.5%
Graduate degree	16.6%

Income & Poverty, 1999
Per capita income	$26,321
Median household income	$68,721
Median family income	$75,218
Persons in poverty	1,769
H'holds receiving public assistance	259
H'holds receiving social security	3,136

Households, 2000
Total households	16,500
With persons under 18	6,264
With persons over 65	3,288
Family households	12,325
One-person households	3,219
Persons per household	2.84
Persons per family	3.29

Labor & Employment
Total civilian labor force, 2004**	30,126
Unemployment rate	4.1%
Total civilian labor force, 2000	27,973
Unemployment rate	5.7%

Employed persons 16 years and over by occupation, 2000
Managers & professionals	12,068
Service occupations	2,310
Sales & office occupations	7,223
Farming, fishing & forestry	12
Construction & maintenance	1,545
Production & transportation	3,230
Self-employed persons	701

*US Census Bureau
**New Jersey Department of Labor

General Information
Township of Piscataway
Municipal Complex
455 Hoes Ln
Piscataway, NJ 08854
732-562-2300

Web site	www.piscatawaynj.org
Land area (sq. miles)	18.78
Water area (sq. miles)	0.20
Type of government	Township
Form of government	MC '50

Government

Legislative Districts
US Congressional	6
State Legislative	17

Local Officials, 2006
Mayor	Brian Wahler
Admin/Manager	Lyn Evers
Clerk	Ann Nolan
Finance Dir/Treas	Ulrick Steinberg (Actg)
Engineer	Richard Kosenski
Attorney	James Clarkin III
Tax assessor	Joan Dambach
Tax collector	NA
Building officer	Joseph Hoff
Zoning officer	NA
Public Works	NA

Housing & Construction

Housing Units, 2000*
Total	16,946
Median rent	$829
Median SF home value	$170,800

New Privately Owned Housing Units Authorized by Building Permit
	Units	Value
Total, 2004	145	$13,576,555
Single family	82	$8,257,055
Total, 2005	230	$22,656,535
Single family	154	$15,557,435

Real Property Valuation - parcels, 2005
	Number	Valuation
Total		$2,253,101,900
Vacant	726	36,287,000
Residential	12,600	1,386,888,200
Commercial	224	171,504,500
Industrial	196	543,852,300
Apartments	20	110,431,000
Farm land	17	3,916,100
Farm homestead	16	222,800

Average Property Value & Tax, 2005
Residential value	$109,949
Property tax	$5,304
FAIR rebate	$527

Public Library
Piscataway Twp Libraries
500 Hoes Ln
Piscataway, NJ 08854
732-463-1633

Director .... Anne Roman

Library statistics, 2004
	Total	per capita
Volumes	153,947	3.05
Expenditure	$2,809,740	$55.66

Public Safety

Police
Chief	Kevin Harris
Number of officers, 2004	90

Crime, 2004	Number	Rate
Total	857	16.5
Violent	31	0.6
Non-violent	826	15.9
Domestic Viol.	294	NA

Emergency/Fire
Director .... Robert Gorr

Public School District
(for school year 2004-2005 except as noted)

Piscataway Township School District
PO Box 1332
Piscataway, NJ 08855
732-572-2289

Superintendent	Robert Copeland
Grade plan	K-12
Enrollment	6,842.0
Students per teacher	12.1
Per pupil expenditure	$11,770
Median faculty salary	$60,360
Median administrator salary	$106,375
Grade 12 enrollment	516.5
High school graduation rate	97.6%

Assessment test results
(percent scoring at proficient or advanced level)
	Language	Math
Grade 3	91.5%	88.6%
Grade 8	71.9%	57.5%
High school	87.2%	78.4%

SAT
Percent tested	80%
Average SAT math score	504
Average SAT verbal score	481

No Child Left Behind, 2003-04
Attendence rate (target = 90%)	95.5%
Drop rate	0.8%
Highly-qualified teachers	97.5%
District needs improvement?(AYP)	No

Municipal Finance

Fiscal Year 2005
Total tax levy	$109,173,935
County levy	15,716,004
County taxes	14,236,120
County library	0
County health	0
County open space	1,479,884
School levy	70,258,875
Local muni. budget	23,199,056
Misc. revenues	17,633,394
Total aid	$7,962,118
CMPTRA	3,469,812
Muni. block grant	206,047
Energy tax receipts	4,146,259
Homeland security	140,000

Fiscal Year 2006
Total aid	$7,962,118
CMPTRA	3,324,693
Muni. block grant	206,047
Energy tax receipts	4,291,378
Homeland security	140,000

Taxes
	2003	2004	2005
General tax rate per $100	4.34	4.610	4.830
Net valuation taxable	$2,269,809,488	$2,264,105,961	$2,263,104,481
State equalized value	$4,414,254,158	$4,953,614,356	$5,807,299,156
County equalization ratio	57.75	51.42	45.58

Demographics & Socio-Economic Characteristics
(2000 U.S. Census, except as noted)

Population

1980*	9,744
1990*	9,365
2000	9,331
Male	4,338
Female	4,993
2004 (estimate)*	9,271
Persons per sq. mi. of land	4,042

Race & Hispanic Origin, 2000

Race

White	9,066
Black/African American	85
Amer. Indian/Alaska Natv.	11
Asian	58
Natv. Hawaiian/Pac. Islander	1
Other Race	21
Two or more races	89
Hispanic origin, total	132
Mexican	36
Puerto Rican	49
Cuban	8
Other Hispanic	39

Age & Nativity, 2000

Under 5 years	542
18 years and over	6,977
21 years and over	6,628
65 years and over	1,404
85 years and over	248
Median Age	38.1
Native born	9,125
Foreign born	206

Educational Attainment, 2000

Population 25 years and over	6,219
0-8 yrs of school	3.4%
High School grad or higher	87.9%
Bachelor's degree or higher	31.7%
Graduate degree	10.3%

Income & Poverty, 1999

Per capita income	$22,133
Median household income	$49,743
Median family income	$59,419
Persons in poverty	526
H'holds receiving public assistance	32
H'holds receiving social security	955

Households, 2000

Total households	3,473
With persons under 18	1,263
With persons over 65	898
Family households	2,431
One-person households	903
Persons per household	2.6
Persons per family	3.15

Labor & Employment

Total civilian labor force, 2004**	5,678
Unemployment rate	3.8%
Total civilian labor force, 2000	4,892
Unemployment rate	9.6%

Employed persons 16 years and over by occupation, 2000

Managers & professionals	1,891
Service occupations	494
Sales & office occupations	1,074
Farming, fishing & forestry	4
Construction & maintenance	452
Production & transportation	507
Self-employed persons	278

*US Census Bureau
**New Jersey Department of Labor

General Information

Borough of Pitman
110 South Broadway
Pitman, NJ 08071
856-589-3522

Web site	NA
Land area (sq. miles)	2.29
Water area (sq. miles)	0.03
Type of government	Borough
Form of government	B

Government

Legislative Districts

US Congressional	2
State Legislative	4

Local Officials, 2006

Mayor	Alice Polocz
Admin/Manager	Caren Andrews
Clerk	Caren Andrews
Finance Dir/Treas	Stephen Considine
Engineer	Tim Kernan
Attorney	William Rozanski III
Tax assessor	Ronald Fijalkowski
Tax collector	Beth A. Walls
Building officer	Jeffrey Kier
Zoning officer	NA
Public Works	Chris Walsh

Housing & Construction

Housing Units, 2000*

Total	3,653
Median rent	$654
Median SF home value	$118,500

New Privately Owned Housing Units
Authorized by Building Permit

	Units	Value
Total, 2004	0	$119,475
Single family	0	$119,475
Total, 2005	1	$183,000
Single family	1	$183,000

Real Property Valuation - parcels, 2005

	Number	Valuation
Total		$378,630,600
Vacant	64	2,179,000
Residential	2,983	321,392,900
Commercial	138	24,282,600
Industrial	4	22,074,500
Apartments	12	8,501,800
Farm land	1	189,700
Farm homestead	3	10,100

Average Property Value & Tax, 2005

Residential value	$107,637
Property tax	$4,452
FAIR rebate	$573

Public Library

McCowan Memorial Library
15 Pitman Ave
Pitman, NJ 08071
856-589-1656

Director.................Sharon Furgason

Library statistics, 2004

	Total	per capita
Volumes	39,712	4.26
Expenditure	$285,640	$30.61

Public Safety

Police

Chief	Scott Campbell
Number of officers, 2004	15

Crime, 2004	Number	Rate
Total	112	12.1
Violent	1	0.1
Non-violent	111	12
Domestic Viol.	110	NA

Emergency/Fire

Director....................Tony Gresko

Public School District
(for school year 2004-2005 except as noted)

Pitman School District
420 Hudson Ave
Pitman, NJ 08071
856-589-2145

Superintendent	Thomas Shulte
Grade plan	K-12
Enrollment	1,574.0
Students per teacher	9.8
Per pupil expenditure	$12,101
Median faculty salary	$54,453
Median administrator salary	$92,861
Grade 12 enrollment	123.5
High school graduation rate	86.7%

Assessment test results
(percent scoring at proficient or advanced level)

	Language	Math
Grade 3	81.0%	79.0%
Grade 8	81.8%	84.9%
High school	93.1%	89.6%

SAT

Percent tested	69%
Average SAT math score	534
Average SAT verbal score	517

No Child Left Behind, 2003-04

Attendence rate (target = 90%)	94.9%
Drop rate	2.3%
Highly-qualified teachers	98.7%
District needs improvement?(AYP)	No

Municipal Finance

Fiscal Year 2005

Total tax levy	$15,682,598
County levy	3,282,910
County taxes	3,078,247
County library	0
County health	0
County open space	204,663
School levy	9,207,381
Local muni. budget	3,192,307
Misc. revenues	3,190,180
Total aid	$1,040,414
CMPTRA	588,186
Muni. block grant	40,978
Energy tax receipts	361,250
Homeland security	50,000

Fiscal Year 2006

Total aid	$1,040,414
CMPTRA	575,542
Muni. block grant	40,978
Energy tax receipts	373,894
Homeland security	50,000

Taxes

	2003	2004	2005
General tax rate per $100	3.81	3.899	4.137
Net valuation taxable	$376,442,965	$377,743,596	$379,133,910
State equalized value	$448,627,059	$506,150,674	$578,036,149
County equalization ratio	87.68	83.91	74.60

Demographics & Socio-Economic Characteristics
(2000 U.S. Census, except as noted)

Population
1980*	6,954
1990*	8,121
2000	8,893
Male	4,403
Female	4,490
2004 (estimate)*	9,262
Persons per sq. mi. of land	205

Race & Hispanic Origin, 2000
Race
White	7,838
Black/African American	715
Amer. Indian/Alaska Natv.	34
Asian	52
Natv. Hawaiian/Pac. Islander	4
Other Race	115
Two or more races	135
Hispanic origin, total	303
Mexican	25
Puerto Rican	188
Cuban	1
Other Hispanic	89

Age & Nativity, 2000
Under 5 years	472
18 years and over	6,523
21 years and over	6,140
65 years and over	1,014
85 years and over	108
Median Age	38.1
Native born	8,719
Foreign born	174

Educational Attainment, 2000
Population 25 years and over	5,827
0-8 yrs of school	8.4%
High School grad or higher	78.8%
Bachelor's degree or higher	16.4%
Graduate degree	4.4%

Income & Poverty, 1999
Per capita income	$21,624
Median household income	$56,687
Median family income	$63,266
Persons in poverty	434
H'holds receiving public assistance	46
H'holds receiving social security	746

Households, 2000
Total households	3,020
With persons under 18	1,288
With persons over 65	667
Family households	2,421
One-person households	490
Persons per household	2.9
Persons per family	3.23

Labor & Employment
Total civilian labor force, 2004**	3,898
Unemployment rate	4.7%
Total civilian labor force, 2000	4,656
Unemployment rate	6.3%

Employed persons 16 years and over by occupation, 2000
Managers & professionals	1,240
Service occupations	637
Sales & office occupations	983
Farming, fishing & forestry	24
Construction & maintenance	618
Production & transportation	863
Self-employed persons	275

*US Census Bureau
**New Jersey Department of Labor

General Information
Township of Pittsgrove
989 Centerton Rd
Pittsgrove, NJ 08318
856-358-2300

Web site	www.pittsgrovetownship.com
Land area (sq. miles)	45.19
Water area (sq. miles)	0.74
Type of government	Township
Form of government	TC

Government

Legislative Districts
US Congressional	2
State Legislative	3

Local Officials, 2006
Mayor	Peter Voros
Admin/Manager	David A. Mulford Jr
Clerk	Constance Garton
Finance Dir/Treas	Donna Jacobs
Engineer	Mark Brunermer
Attorney	Benjamin C. Telsey
Tax assessor	Lisa Perella
Tax collector	Daniel O'Brien Jr.
Building officer	James Grasso
Zoning officer	Robert Berducci
Public Works	Harry E. Snyder

Housing & Construction

Housing Units, 2000*
Total	3,155
Median rent	$728
Median SF home value	$125,600

New Privately Owned Housing Units Authorized by Building Permit
	Units	Value
Total, 2004	63	$7,127,115
Single family	63	$7,127,115
Total, 2005	48	$4,457,261
Single family	48	$4,457,261

Real Property Valuation - parcels, 2005
	Number	Valuation
Total		$571,758,400
Vacant	571	25,341,000
Residential	2,482	437,510,900
Commercial	79	55,643,000
Industrial	0	0
Apartments	0	0
Farm land	271	48,001,200
Farm homestead	603	5,262,300

Average Property Value & Tax, 2005
Residential value	$143,525
Property tax	$3,705
FAIR rebate	$565

Public Library
No public municipal library.

Library statistics, 2004
	Total	per capita
Volumes	NA	NA
Expenditure	NA	NA

Public Safety

Police
Chief	NA
Number of officers, 2004	0

Crime, 2004	Number	Rate
Total	104	11.3
Violent	10	1.1
Non-violent	94	10.2
Domestic Viol.	112	NA

Emergency/Fire
Director	NA

Public School District
(for school year 2004-2005 except as noted)

Pittsgrove Township School District
1076 Almond Rd
Pittsgrove, NJ 08318
856-358-3094

Superintendent	Loren Thomas
Grade plan	K-12
Enrollment	1,919.0
Students per teacher	12.0
Per pupil expenditure	$10,565
Median faculty salary	$52,800
Median administrator salary	$81,000
Grade 12 enrollment	147.0
High school graduation rate	95.3%

Assessment test results
(percent scoring at proficient or advanced level)
	Language	Math
Grade 3	82.2%	79.1%
Grade 8	68.5%	69.7%
High school	81.3%	70.4%

SAT
Percent tested	64%
Average SAT math score	503
Average SAT verbal score	497

No Child Left Behind, 2003-04
Attendence rate (target = 90%)	94.4%
Drop rate	1%
Highly-qualified teachers	95.4%
District needs improvement?(AYP)	No

Municipal Finance

Fiscal Year 2005
Total tax levy	$14,812,305
County levy	5,210,012
County taxes	5,104,874
County library	0
County health	0
County open space	105,138
School levy	8,121,960
Local muni. budget	1,480,333
Misc. revenues	2,784,381
Total aid	$995,244
CMPTRA	401,699
Muni. block grant	35,535
Energy tax receipts	558,010
Homeland security	0

Fiscal Year 2006
Total aid	$995,245
CMPTRA	382,169
Muni. block grant	35,535
Energy tax receipts	577,541
Homeland security	NA

Taxes
	2003	2004	2005
General tax rate per $100	4.09	2.320	2.582
Net valuation taxable	$293,102,146	$582,588,556	$573,778,274
State equalized value	$465,093,853	$531,932,833	$587,165,651
County equalization ratio	69.24	122.59	109.56

Demographics & Socio-Economic Characteristics
(2000 U.S. Census, except as noted)

Population

1980*	45,555
1990*	46,567
2000	47,829
Male	23,393
Female	24,436
2004 (estimate)*	47,987
Persons per sq. mi. of land	7,948

Race & Hispanic Origin, 2000
Race

White	10,258
Black/African American	29,550
Amer. Indian/Alaska Natv.	195
Asian	447
Natv. Hawaiian/Pac. Islander	46
Other Race	5,156
Two or more races	2,177
Hispanic origin, total	12,033
Mexican	807
Puerto Rican	1,782
Cuban	145
Other Hispanic	9,299

Age & Nativity, 2000

Under 5 years	3,770
18 years and over	34,662
21 years and over	32,669
65 years and over	4,402
85 years and over	566
Median Age	32.8
Native born	36,502
Foreign born	11,327

Educational Attainment, 2000

Population 25 years and over	29,821
0-8 yrs of school	12.3%
High School grad or higher	70.6%
Bachelor's degree or higher	18.5%
Graduate degree	6.2%

Income & Poverty, 1999

Per capita income	$19,052
Median household income	$46,683
Median family income	$50,774
Persons in poverty	7,476
H'holds receiving public assistance	892
H'holds receiving social security	3,573

Households, 2000

Total households	15,137
With persons under 18	6,748
With persons over 65	3,195
Family households	10,898
One-person households	3,194
Persons per household	3.1
Persons per family	3.49

Labor & Employment

Total civilian labor force, 2004**	25,609
Unemployment rate	7.2%
Total civilian labor force, 2000	24,966
Unemployment rate	7.9%

Employed persons 16 years and over by occupation, 2000

Managers & professionals	5,518
Service occupations	4,059
Sales & office occupations	6,272
Farming, fishing & forestry	33
Construction & maintenance	1,935
Production & transportation	5,180
Self-employed persons	639

*US Census Bureau
**New Jersey Department of Labor

General Information
City of Plainfield
515 Watchung Ave
Plainfield, NJ 07060
908-753-3000

Web site	www.plainfield.com
Land area (sq. miles)	6.04
Water area (sq. miles)	0
Type of government	City
Form of government	SC

Government

Legislative Districts

US Congressional	6
State Legislative	22

Local Officials, 2006

Mayor	Sharon Robinson-Briggs
Admin/Manager	Carton McGee (Actg)
Clerk	Laddie Wyatt
Finance Dir/Treas	Pete Sepelya
Engineer	Robert Bucco
Attorney	Daniel Williamson
Tax assessor	Tracy Bennett
Tax collector	NA
Building officer	Jocelyn Pringley
Zoning officer	NA
Public Works	Jennifer Wenson-Maier

Housing & Construction

Housing Units, 2000*

Total	16,180
Median rent	$726
Median SF home value	$137,500

New Privately Owned Housing Units Authorized by Building Permit

	Units	Value
Total, 2004	14	$1,655,000
Single family	14	$1,655,000
Total, 2005	19	$1,934,214
Single family	17	$1,674,214

Real Property Valuation - parcels, 2005

	Number	Valuation
Total		$1,274,886,700
Vacant	354	8,658,200
Residential	9,126	1,025,288,700
Commercial	661	147,637,700
Industrial	64	27,520,400
Apartments	115	65,776,400
Farm land	0	0
Farm homestead	1	5,300

Average Property Value & Tax, 2005

Residential value	$112,336
Property tax	$5,800
FAIR rebate	$584

Public Library
Plainfield Public Library
800 Park Ave
Plainfield, NJ 07060
908-757-1111

Director..................Joseph DaRold

Library statistics, 2004

	Total	per capita
Volumes	194,691	4.07
Expenditure	$2,263,872	$47.33

Public Safety

Police

Chief	Edward Santiago
Number of officers, 2004	151

Crime, 2004	Number	Rate
Total	2,145	44.7
Violent	553	11.5
Non-violent	1,592	33.1
Domestic Viol.	946	NA

Emergency/Fire

Director	Cecil Allen

Public School District
(for school year 2004-2005 except as noted)

Plainfield School District
504 Madison Ave
Plainfield, NJ 07060
908-731-4335

Superintendent	Paula Howard (Actg)
Grade plan	K-12
Enrollment	7,570.0
Students per teacher	10.2
Per pupil expenditure	$13,067
Median faculty salary	$59,055
Median administrator salary	$102,400
Grade 12 enrollment	286.5
High school graduation rate	81.1%

Assessment test results
(percent scoring at proficient or advanced level)

	Language	Math
Grade 3	66.6%	52.1%
Grade 8	42.9%	32.7%
High school	60.0%	34.6%

SAT

Percent tested	73%
Average SAT math score	399
Average SAT verbal score	398

No Child Left Behind, 2003-04

Attendence rate (target = 90%)	93.5%
Drop rate	8.7%
Highly-qualified teachers	96%
District needs improvement?(AYP)	Yes

Municipal Finance

Fiscal Year 2005

Total tax levy	$66,213,699
County levy	8,991,692
County taxes	8,635,251
County library	0
County health	0
County open space	356,440
School levy	17,820,457
Local muni. budget	39,401,551
Misc. revenues	22,946,395
Total aid	$9,794,093
CMPTRA	6,852,436
Muni. block grant	203,806
Energy tax receipts	2,597,851
Homeland security	140,000

Fiscal Year 2006

Total aid	$9,794,092
CMPTRA	6,761,511
Muni. block grant	203,806
Energy tax receipts	2,688,775
Homeland security	140,000

Taxes

	2003	2004	2005
General tax rate per $100	4.45	4.164	5.163
Net valuation taxable	$1,288,963,880	$1,285,165,952	$1,282,552,245
State equalized value	$1,936,253,387	$2,268,210,553	$2,686,535,913
County equalization ratio	70.51	63.73	54.42

Demographics & Socio-Economic Characteristics

(2000 U.S. Census, except as noted)

Population

1980*	5,605
1990*	14,213
2000	20,215
Male	10,229
Female	9,986
2004 (estimate)*	21,300
Persons per sq. mi. of land	1,799

Race & Hispanic Origin, 2000

Race
White	11,765
Black/African American	1,533
Amer. Indian/Alaska Natv.	20
Asian	6,168
Natv. Hawaiian/Pac. Islander	2
Other Race	275
Two or more races	452
Hispanic origin, total	937
Mexican	79
Puerto Rican	284
Cuban	77
Other Hispanic	497

Age & Nativity, 2000

Under 5 years	1,428
18 years and over	15,239
21 years and over	14,873
65 years and over	853
85 years and over	83
Median Age	32.9
Native born	13,244
Foreign born	6,971

Educational Attainment, 2000

Population 25 years and over	13,947
0-8 yrs of school	0.9%
High School grad or higher	97.3%
Bachelor's degree or higher	70.3%
Graduate degree	31.7%

Income & Poverty, 1999

Per capita income	$38,982
Median household income	$72,097
Median family income	$88,783
Persons in poverty	601
H'holds receiving public assistance	57
H'holds receiving social security	589

Households, 2000

Total households	8,742
With persons under 18	2,991
With persons over 65	644
Family households	5,123
One-person households	2,966
Persons per household	2.3
Persons per family	3.06

Labor & Employment

Total civilian labor force, 2004**	10,919
Unemployment rate	3.0%
Total civilian labor force, 2000	12,412
Unemployment rate	2.3%

Employed persons 16 years and over by occupation, 2000
Managers & professionals	8,389
Service occupations	619
Sales & office occupations	2,479
Farming, fishing & forestry	0
Construction & maintenance	252
Production & transportation	389
Self-employed persons	316

*US Census Bureau
**New Jersey Department of Labor

General Information

Township of Plainsboro
641 Plainsboro Rd
Plainsboro, NJ 08536
609-799-0909

Web site	www.plainsboronj.com
Land area (sq. miles)	11.84
Water area (sq. miles)	0.41
Type of government	Township
Form of government	TC

Government

Legislative Districts

US Congressional	12
State Legislative	14

Local Officials, 2006

Mayor	Peter Cantu
Admin/Manager	Robert Sheehan
Clerk	Patricia Hullfish
Finance Dir/Treas	Wendy Wulstein
Engineer	Mike McClelland
Attorney	Joseph Stonaker
Tax assessor	Jean Jacobson
Tax collector	Judith Scheideler
Building officer	Tom Boyd
Zoning officer	Ron Yake
Public Works	NA

Housing & Construction

Housing Units, 2000*

Total	9,133
Median rent	$942
Median SF home value	$257,100

New Privately Owned Housing Units Authorized by Building Permit

	Units	Value
Total, 2004	47	$5,778,436
Single family	47	$5,778,436
Total, 2005	49	$7,378,684
Single family	49	$7,378,684

Real Property Valuation - parcels, 2005

	Number	Valuation
Total		$3,618,761,600
Vacant	493	73,530,100
Residential	5,065	1,999,645,000
Commercial	88	1,192,978,700
Industrial	4	61,863,700
Apartments	17	279,740,000
Farm land	16	10,065,500
Farm homestead	67	938,600

Average Property Value & Tax, 2005

Residential value	$389,825
Property tax	$7,537
FAIR rebate	$418

Public Library

Plainsboro Free Public Library
641 Plainsboro Rd
Plainsboro, NJ 08536
609-275-2897
Director . . . . Virginia Baeckler

Library statistics, 2004

	Total	per capita
Volumes	82,049	4.06
Expenditure	$1,060,764	$52.47

Public Safety

Police

Chief	NA
Number of officers, 2004	32

Crime, 2004	Number	Rate
Total	189	9
Violent	11	0.5
Non-violent	178	8.5
Domestic Viol.	87	NA

Emergency/Fire

Director . . . . Brian Stultz

Public School District

(for school year 2004-2005 except as noted)

West Windsor-Plainsboro Reg. School Dist.
PO Box 505
Princeton Junction, NJ 08550
609-716-5000

Administrator	Robert Loretan
Grade plan	K-12
Enrollment	9,097.0
Students per teacher	11.1
Per pupil expenditure	$12,653
Median faculty salary	$56,100
Median administrator salary	$104,475
Grade 12 enrollment	644.0
High school graduation rate	NA

Assessment test results

(percent scoring at proficient or advanced level)
	Language	Math
Grade 3	96.2%	96.0%
Grade 8	91.6%	88.8%
High school	95.7%	94.4%

SAT

Percent tested	NA
Average SAT math score	NA
Average SAT verbal score	NA

No Child Left Behind, 2003-04

Attendence rate (target = 90%)	96.5%
Drop rate	0.3%
Highly-qualified teachers	98.6%
District needs improvement?(AYP)	No

Municipal Finance

Fiscal Year 2005

Total tax levy	$70,106,154
County levy	10,947,470
County taxes	9,917,117
County library	0
County health	0
County open space	1,030,353
School levy	51,350,195
Local muni. budget	7,808,489
Misc. revenues	10,727,005
Total aid	$2,293,895
CMPTRA	494,676
Muni. block grant	79,263
Energy tax receipts	1,629,956
Homeland security	90,000

Fiscal Year 2006

Total aid	$2,293,895
CMPTRA	437,627
Muni. block grant	79,263
Energy tax receipts	1,687,005
Homeland security	90,000

Taxes

	2003	2004	2005
General tax rate per $100	2.81	3.140	1.940
Net valuation taxable	$2,106,073,808	$2,059,259,922	$3,626,167,479
State equalized value	$3,013,412,231	$3,341,310,999	$3,674,673,165
County equalization ratio	87.13	70.79	104.86

Demographics & Socio-Economic Characteristics
(2000 U.S. Census, except as noted)

Population
1980*	13,435
1990*	16,027
2000	19,012
Male	8,925
Female	10,087
2004 (estimate)*	19,113
Persons per sq. mi. of land	3,309

Race & Hispanic Origin, 2000
Race
White	4,755
Black/African American	10,969
Amer. Indian/Alaska Natv.	54
Asian	371
Natv. Hawaiian/Pac. Islander	5
Other Race	2,084
Two or more races	774
Hispanic origin, total	4,158
Mexican	451
Puerto Rican	2,085
Cuban	61
Other Hispanic	1,561

Age & Nativity, 2000
Under 5 years	1,481
18 years and over	13,234
21 years and over	12,481
65 years and over	2,124
85 years and over	373
Median Age	32.7
Native born	16,639
Foreign born	2,457

Educational Attainment, 2000
Population 25 years and over	11,583
0-8 yrs of school	7.5%
High School grad or higher	70.1%
Bachelor's degree or higher	10.2%
Graduate degree	3.1%

Income & Poverty, 1999
Per capita income	$17,668
Median household income	$36,913
Median family income	$40,016
Persons in poverty	2,939
H'holds receiving public assistance	286
H'holds receiving social security	1,705

Households, 2000
Total households	6,402
With persons under 18	2,838
With persons over 65	1,421
Family households	4,365
One-person households	1,568
Persons per household	2.9
Persons per family	3.44

Labor & Employment
Total civilian labor force, 2004**	8,720
Unemployment rate	9.4%
Total civilian labor force, 2000	8,500
Unemployment rate	10.2%

Employed persons 16 years and over by occupation, 2000
Managers & professionals	1,347
Service occupations	2,979
Sales & office occupations	1,979
Farming, fishing & forestry	33
Construction & maintenance	466
Production & transportation	833
Self-employed persons	140

*US Census Bureau
**New Jersey Department of Labor

General Information
City of Pleasantville
18 North First St
Pleasantville, NJ 08232
609-484-3600
Web site	www.pleasantville-nj.org
Land area (sq. miles)	5.78
Water area (sq. miles)	1.55
Type of government	City
Form of government	C

Government

Legislative Districts
US Congressional	2
State Legislative	2

Local Officials, 2006
Mayor	Ralph Peterson Sr.
Admin/Manager	NA
Clerk	Gloria V. Griffin
Finance Dir/Treas	Ted Freedman
Engineer	Remington & Vernick
Attorney	Alfred Scerni Jr.
Tax assessor	Brian Vigue
Tax collector	Flor Roman
Building officer	Kevin Cain
Zoning officer	Kevin Cain
Public Works	Robert Oglesby

Housing & Construction

Housing Units, 2000*
Total	7,042
Median rent	$715
Median SF home value	$86,500

New Privately Owned Housing Units Authorized by Building Permit
	Units	Value
Total, 2004	36	$2,233,153
Single family	36	$2,233,153
Total, 2005	92	$7,821,432
Single family	92	$7,821,432

Real Property Valuation - parcels, 2005
	Number	Valuation
Total		$533,508,000
Vacant	449	12,548,400
Residential	5,030	353,226,300
Commercial	341	96,395,100
Industrial	82	44,431,600
Apartments	24	26,906,600
Farm land	0	0
Farm homestead	0	0

Average Property Value & Tax, 2005
Residential value	$70,224
Property tax	$2,925
FAIR rebate	$565

Public Library
Pleasantville Branch Library†
132 W Washington Ave
Pleasantville, NJ 08232
609-641-1778
Branch Librarian	Pamela Saunders

Library statistics, 2004
	Total	per capita
Volumes	NA	NA
Expenditure	NA	NA

†Branch of County Library

Public Safety

Police
Chief	Duane Comeaux
Number of officers, 2004	57

Crime, 2004	Number	Rate
Total	933	49.1
Violent	193	10.1
Non-violent	740	38.9
Domestic Viol.	402	NA

Emergency/Fire
Director	Leroy Borden

Public School District
(for school year 2004-2005 except as noted)

Pleasantville School District
PO Box 960
Pleasantville, NJ 08232
609-383-6800
Superintendent	Gail Brooks
Grade plan	K-12
Enrollment	3,725.0
Students per teacher	8.2
Per pupil expenditure	$14,828
Median faculty salary	$41,073
Median administrator salary	$93,655
Grade 12 enrollment	190.0
High school graduation rate	78.7%

Assessment test results
(percent scoring at proficient or advanced level)
	Language	Math
Grade 3	69.7%	72.6%
Grade 8	42.2%	27.8%
High school	61.5%	31.3%

SAT
Percent tested	34%
Average SAT math score	404
Average SAT verbal score	365

No Child Left Behind, 2003-04
Attendence rate (target = 90%)	91.4%
Drop rate	3%
Highly-qualified teachers	84.5%
District needs improvement?(AYP)	No

Municipal Finance

Fiscal Year 2005
Total tax levy	$22,775,889
County levy	3,050,376
County taxes	2,490,142
County library	276,001
County health	135,825
County open space	148,407
School levy	7,172,732
Local muni. budget	12,552,781
Misc. revenues	7,677,369
Total aid	$2,662,950
CMPTRA	1,368,240
Muni. block grant	74,546
Energy tax receipts	1,150,164
Homeland security	70,000

Fiscal Year 2006
Total aid	$2,662,950
CMPTRA	1,327,985
Muni. block grant	74,546
Energy tax receipts	1,190,419
Homeland security	70,000

Taxes
	2003	2004	2005
General tax rate per $100	3.75	3.804	4.166
Net valuation taxable	$536,991,073	$540,133,515	$546,811,685
State equalized value	$633,244,190	$720,195,280	$841,896,359
County equalization ratio	92.21	94.80	74.49

Demographics & Socio-Economic Characteristics
(2000 U.S. Census, except as noted)

Population
1980*	4,674
1990*	6,005
2000	7,275
Male	3,620
Female	3,655
2004 (estimate)*	8,045
Persons per sq. mi. of land	201

Race & Hispanic Origin, 2000
Race
White	6,831
Black/African American	167
Amer. Indian/Alaska Natv.	10
Asian	53
Natv. Hawaiian/Pac. Islander	1
Other Race	99
Two or more races	114
Hispanic origin, total	280
Mexican	103
Puerto Rican	132
Cuban	17
Other Hispanic	28

Age & Nativity, 2000
Under 5 years	501
18 years and over	5,204
21 years and over	4,960
65 years and over	621
85 years and over	49
Median Age	36
Native born	6,940
Foreign born	335

Educational Attainment, 2000
Population 25 years and over	4,720
0-8 yrs of school	5.5%
High School grad or higher	84.2%
Bachelor's degree or higher	17.4%
Graduate degree	4.2%

Income & Poverty, 1999
Per capita income	$22,433
Median household income	$61,357
Median family income	$62,255
Persons in poverty	367
H'holds receiving public assistance	73
H'holds receiving social security	539

Households, 2000
Total households	2,510
With persons under 18	1,116
With persons over 65	465
Family households	2,002
One-person households	400
Persons per household	2.9
Persons per family	3.22

Labor & Employment
Total civilian labor force, 2004**	4,218
Unemployment rate	3.5%
Total civilian labor force, 2000	3,871
Unemployment rate	3.2%

Employed persons 16 years and over by occupation, 2000
Managers & professionals	1,133
Service occupations	475
Sales & office occupations	1,028
Farming, fishing & forestry	43
Construction & maintenance	504
Production & transportation	563
Self-employed persons	182

*US Census Bureau
**New Jersey Department of Labor

General Information
Township of Plumsted
121 Evergreen Rd
New Egypt, NJ 08533
609-758-2241
Web site	www.plumsted.org
Land area (sq. miles)	40.02
Water area (sq. miles)	0.20
Type of government	Township
Form of government	TC

Government
Legislative Districts
US Congressional	4
State Legislative	30

Local Officials, 2006
Mayor	Ronald S. Dancer
Admin/Manager	Richard Kachmar
Clerk	Dorothy Hendrickson
Finance Dir/Treas	June Madden
Engineer	John Mallon
Attorney	Gilmore & Monahan
Tax assessor	Maureen Francis
Tax collector	Danielle Peacock
Building officer	Glenn Riccardi
Zoning officer	NA
Public Works	NA

Housing & Construction
Housing Units, 2000*
Total	2,628
Median rent	$697
Median SF home value	$150,800

New Privately Owned Housing Units
Authorized by Building Permit
	Units	Value
Total, 2004	20	$3,179,110
Single family	20	$3,179,110
Total, 2005	38	$4,356,879
Single family	36	$4,315,879

Real Property Valuation - parcels, 2005
	Number	Valuation
Total		$406,041,100
Vacant	346	9,166,400
Residential	2,354	349,810,200
Commercial	90	20,464,800
Industrial	8	4,070,000
Apartments	8	1,625,000
Farm land	107	18,741,800
Farm homestead	141	2,162,900

Average Property Value & Tax, 2005
Residential value	$141,071
Property tax	$4,247
FAIR rebate	$607

Public Library
Plumsted Branch Library†
119 Evergreen Rd
New Egypt, NJ 08533
609-758-7888
Branch Librarian	Barbara Rothlein

Library statistics, 2004
	Total	per capita
Volumes	NA	NA
Expenditure	NA	NA

†Branch of County Library

Public Safety
Police
Chief	Michael Lynch
Number of officers, 2004	9

Crime, 2004	Number	Rate
Total	68	8.5
Violent	7	0.9
Non-violent	61	7.6
Domestic Viol.	43	NA

Emergency/Fire
Director	Tim Byrne

Public School District
(for school year 2004-2005 except as noted)

Plumsted Township School District
y17 Evergreen Rd
New Egypt, NJ 08533
609-758-6800
Superintendent	Gerald North
Grade plan	K-12
Enrollment	1,774.5
Students per teacher	11.1
Per pupil expenditure	$9,784
Median faculty salary	$40,427
Median administrator salary	$93,938
Grade 12 enrollment	120.0
High school graduation rate	96.7%

Assessment test results
(percent scoring at proficient or advanced level)
	Language	Math
Grade 3	77.9%	73.4%
Grade 8	72.7%	70.6%
High school	85.6%	78.2%

SAT
Percent tested	64%
Average SAT math score	511
Average SAT verbal score	507

No Child Left Behind, 2003-04
Attendence rate (target = 90%)	95.3%
Drop rate	0.9%
Highly-qualified teachers	97.9%
District needs improvement?(AYP)	No

Municipal Finance
Fiscal Year 2005
Total tax levy	$12,279,413
County levy	2,652,312
County taxes	2,234,650
County library	234,768
County health	99,508
County open space	83,386
School levy	9,039,688
Local muni. budget	587,413
Misc. revenues	2,931,782
Total aid	$716,878
CMPTRA	206,832
Muni. block grant	28,525
Energy tax receipts	431,400
Homeland security	50,000

Fiscal Year 2006
Total aid	$716,878
CMPTRA	191,733
Muni. block grant	28,525
Energy tax receipts	446,499
Homeland security	50,000

Taxes
	2003	2004	2005
General tax rate per $100	2.80	2.830	3.011
Net valuation taxable	$397,120,866	$402,845,660	$407,878,861
State equalized value	$590,602,121	$684,648,046	$788,324,045
County equalization ratio	75.39	67.24	58.71

Demographics & Socio-Economic Characteristics
(2000 U.S. Census, except as noted)

Population
1980*	3,856
1990*	3,591
2000	3,416
Male	1,693
Female	1,723
2004 (estimate)*	3,427
Persons per sq. mi. of land	257

Race & Hispanic Origin, 2000
Race
White	3,348
Black/African American	15
Amer. Indian/Alaska Natv.	1
Asian	10
Natv. Hawaiian/Pac. Islander	0
Other Race	22
Two or more races	20
Hispanic origin, total	69
Mexican	5
Puerto Rican	20
Cuban	5
Other Hispanic	39

Age & Nativity, 2000
Under 5 years	221
18 years and over	2,621
21 years and over	2,538
65 years and over	546
85 years and over	48
Median Age	39.8
Native born	3,346
Foreign born	70

Educational Attainment, 2000
Population 25 years and over	2,428
0-8 yrs of school	3.5%
High School grad or higher	86.1%
Bachelor's degree or higher	17.4%
Graduate degree	5.8%

Income & Poverty, 1999
Per capita income	$24,754
Median household income	$52,188
Median family income	$60,208
Persons in poverty	148
H'holds receiving public assistance	5
H'holds receiving social security	365

Households, 2000
Total households	1,341
With persons under 18	434
With persons over 65	399
Family households	990
One-person households	295
Persons per household	2.54
Persons per family	2.99

Labor & Employment
Total civilian labor force, 2004**	2,324
Unemployment rate	2.4%
Total civilian labor force, 2000	1,851
Unemployment rate	2.9%

Employed persons 16 years and over by occupation, 2000
Managers & professionals	629
Service occupations	236
Sales & office occupations	506
Farming, fishing & forestry	6
Construction & maintenance	243
Production & transportation	177
Self-employed persons	146

*US Census Bureau
**New Jersey Department of Labor

General Information
Township of Pohatcong
50 Municipal Dr
Phillipsburg, NJ 08865
908-454-6121

Web site	www.pohatcong.com
Land area (sq. miles)	13.33
Water area (sq. miles)	0.28
Type of government	Township
Form of government	TC

Government

Legislative Districts
US Congressional	5
State Legislative	23

Local Officials, 2006
Mayor	Stephen Babinsky
Admin/Manager	NA
Clerk	Wanda Kutzman
Finance Dir/Treas	Peter Kowalick
Engineer	Gwen Steckel
Attorney	Kevin Benbrook
Tax assessor	Michael Schmidt
Tax collector	Carrie Rochelle
Building officer	Wayne Degan
Zoning officer	Rich McIntyre
Public Works	NA

Housing & Construction

Housing Units, 2000*
Total	1,411
Median rent	$717
Median SF home value	$135,100

New Privately Owned Housing Units Authorized by Building Permit
	Units	Value
Total, 2004	9	$1,174,753
Single family	9	$1,174,753
Total, 2005	10	$1,529,306
Single family	10	$1,529,306

Real Property Valuation - parcels, 2005
	Number	Valuation
Total		$338,719,400
Vacant	128	5,290,800
Residential	1,233	202,748,700
Commercial	55	95,142,800
Industrial	5	5,636,800
Apartments	2	399,300
Farm land	108	26,929,200
Farm homestead	204	2,571,800

Average Property Value & Tax, 2005
Residential value	$142,881
Property tax	$4,218
FAIR rebate	$615

Public Library

No public municipal library.

Library statistics, 2004
	Total	per capita
Volumes	NA	NA
Expenditure	NA	NA

Public Safety

Police
Chief	Paul Hager
Number of officers, 2004	11

Crime, 2004	Number	Rate
Total	207	60.2
Violent	16	4.7
Non-violent	191	55.6
Domestic Viol.	10	NA

Emergency/Fire
Director	Don Freeman

Public School District
(for school year 2004-2005 except as noted)

Pohatcong Township School District
240 Route 519
Phillipsburg, NJ 08865
908-859-8155

Administrator	Frank Jiorle
Grade plan	K-12
Enrollment	373.0
Students per teacher	11.4
Per pupil expenditure	$10,883
Median faculty salary	$41,327
Median administrator salary	$71,321
Grade 12 enrollment	NA
High school graduation rate	NA

Assessment test results
(percent scoring at proficient or advanced level)
	Language	Math
Grade 3	90.2%	71.4%
Grade 8	88.9%	93.3%
High school	NA	NA

SAT
Percent tested	NA
Average SAT math score	NA
Average SAT verbal score	NA

No Child Left Behind, 2003-04
Attendence rate (target = 90%)	95.5%
Drop rate	NA
Highly-qualified teachers	91.3%
District needs improvement?(AYP)	No

Municipal Finance

Fiscal Year 2005
Total tax levy	$10,020,976
County levy	2,434,143
County taxes	2,012,350
County library	194,158
County health	0
County open space	227,635
School levy	5,013,663
Local muni. budget	2,573,170
Misc. revenues	1,946,317
Total aid	$525,175
CMPTRA	207,177
Muni. block grant	15,713
Energy tax receipts	277,285
Homeland security	25,000

Fiscal Year 2006
Total aid	$525,175
CMPTRA	197,472
Muni. block grant	15,713
Energy tax receipts	286,990
Homeland security	25,000

Taxes
	2003	2004	2005
General tax rate per $100	2.60	2.720	2.960
Net valuation taxable	$336,697,721	$338,328,840	$339,468,198
State equalized value	$331,721,893	$376,198,158	$407,573,776
County equalization ratio	112.94	101.50	89.91

Demographics & Socio-Economic Characteristics
(2000 U.S. Census, except as noted)

Population
1980*	5,415
1990*	5,112
2000	5,314
Male	2,678
Female	2,636
2004 (estimate)*	5,408
Persons per sq. mi. of land	3,761

Race & Hispanic Origin, 2000
Race
White	5,098
Black/African American	28
Amer. Indian/Alaska Natv.	18
Asian	54
Natv. Hawaiian/Pac. Islander	1
Other Race	78
Two or more races	37
Hispanic origin, total	234
Mexican	120
Puerto Rican	33
Cuban	8
Other Hispanic	73

Age & Nativity, 2000
Under 5 years	234
18 years and over	4,292
21 years and over	4,150
65 years and over	1,012
85 years and over	141
Median Age	42.6
Native born	5,008
Foreign born	306

Educational Attainment, 2000
Population 25 years and over	3,926
0-8 yrs of school	3.8%
High School grad or higher	87.1%
Bachelor's degree or higher	34.1%
Graduate degree	11.6%

Income & Poverty, 1999
Per capita income	$27,853
Median household income	$51,105
Median family income	$61,250
Persons in poverty	325
H'holds receiving public assistance	46
H'holds receiving social security	802

Households, 2000
Total households	2,317
With persons under 18	570
With persons over 65	742
Family households	1,317
One-person households	841
Persons per household	2.25
Persons per family	2.96

Labor & Employment
Total civilian labor force, 2004**	3,404
Unemployment rate	3.3%
Total civilian labor force, 2000	2,617
Unemployment rate	5.2%

Employed persons 16 years and over by occupation, 2000
Managers & professionals	918
Service occupations	396
Sales & office occupations	742
Farming, fishing & forestry	65
Construction & maintenance	206
Production & transportation	153
Self-employed persons	108

*US Census Bureau
**New Jersey Department of Labor

General Information
Borough of Point Pleasant Beach
416 New Jersey Ave
Point Pleasant Beach, NJ 08742
732-892-1118
Web site	www.pointpleasantbeach.org
Land area (sq. miles)	1.44
Water area (sq. miles)	0.28
Type of government	Borough
Form of government	B

Government
Legislative Districts
US Congressional	4
State Legislative	10

Local Officials, 2006
Mayor	Thomas Vogel
Admin/Manager	Christine Riehl
Clerk	Maryann Ellsworth
Finance Dir/Treas	Christine Riehl
Engineer	Raymond Savacool
Attorney	Sean Gertner
Tax assessor	Carey Rowe
Tax collector	Christine Riehl
Building officer	Michael Gardner
Zoning officer	Elaine Petrillo
Public Works	Robert Meany

Housing & Construction
Housing Units, 2000*
Total	3,558
Median rent	$777
Median SF home value	$223,600

New Privately Owned Housing Units Authorized by Building Permit
	Units	Value
Total, 2004	14	$2,192,750
Single family	14	$2,192,750
Total, 2005	17	$2,923,550
Single family	17	$2,923,550

Real Property Valuation - parcels, 2005
	Number	Valuation
Total		$664,451,400
Vacant	184	21,871,200
Residential	2,700	486,563,600
Commercial	273	148,032,600
Industrial	0	0
Apartments	13	7,984,000
Farm land	0	0
Farm homestead	0	0

Average Property Value & Tax, 2005
Residential value	$180,209
Property tax	$5,051
FAIR rebate	$576

Public Library
Point Pleasant Beach Branch†
710 McLean Ave
Point Pleasant Bea, NJ 08742
732-892-4575
Branch Librarian	Edith Alberts

Library statistics, 2004
	Total	per capita
Volumes	NA	NA
Expenditure	NA	NA

†Branch of County Library

Public Safety
Police
Chief	Daniel DePolo
Number of officers, 2004	26

Crime, 2004	Number	Rate
Total	274	50.7
Violent	18	3.3
Non-violent	256	47.4
Domestic Viol.	154	NA

Emergency/Fire
Director	Joseph Michigan

Public School District
(for school year 2004-2005 except as noted)

Point Pleasant Beach School District
Cook's Lane and Niblick St
Point Pleasant Beach, NJ 08742
732-899-8840
Superintendent	John Ravally
Grade plan	K-12
Enrollment	898.0
Students per teacher	10.2
Per pupil expenditure	$11,426
Median faculty salary	$47,614
Median administrator salary	$102,125
Grade 12 enrollment	106.0
High school graduation rate	95.3%

Assessment test results
(percent scoring at proficient or advanced level)
	Language	Math
Grade 3	98.1%	92.3%
Grade 8	82.7%	75.0%
High school	92.7%	88.5%

SAT
Percent tested	86%
Average SAT math score	533
Average SAT verbal score	520

No Child Left Behind, 2003-04
Attendence rate (target = 90%)	93.5%
Drop rate	0.5%
Highly-qualified teachers	100%
District needs improvement?(AYP)	No

Municipal Finance
Fiscal Year 2005
Total tax levy	$18,630,649
County levy	5,696,628
County taxes	4,799,542
County library	504,233
County health	213,726
County open space	179,127
School levy	8,813,283
Local muni. budget	4,120,738
Misc. revenues	5,169,248
Total aid	$869,704
CMPTRA	195,076
Muni. block grant	22,369
Energy tax reccipts	602,259
Homeland security	50,000

Fiscal Year 2006
Total aid	$869,705
CMPTRA	173,997
Muni. block grant	22,369
Energy tax receipts	623,339
Homeland security	50,000

Taxes
	2003	2004	2005
General tax rate per $100	2.60	2.721	2.803
Net valuation taxable	$654,881,109	$661,457,125	$664,743,186
State equalized value	$1,272,602,233	$1,477,349,086	$1,847,021,912
County equalization ratio	59.41	51.46	44.76

Demographics & Socio-Economic Characteristics

(2000 U.S. Census, except as noted)

Population

1980*	17,747
1990*	18,177
2000	19,306
Male	9,279
Female	10,027
2004 (estimate)*	19,821
Persons per sq. mi. of land	5,607

Race & Hispanic Origin, 2000

Race

White	18,887
Black/African American	56
Amer. Indian/Alaska Natv.	27
Asian	105
Natv. Hawaiian/Pac. Islander	2
Other Race	96
Two or more races	133
Hispanic origin, total	465
Mexican	171
Puerto Rican	117
Cuban	35
Other Hispanic	142

Age & Nativity, 2000

Under 5 years	1,150
18 years and over	14,729
21 years and over	14,193
65 years and over	2,883
85 years and over	412
Median Age	39.4
Native born	18,713
Foreign born	593

Educational Attainment, 2000

Population 25 years and over	13,447
0-8 yrs of school	2.6%
High School grad or higher	88.5%
Bachelor's degree or higher	27.8%
Graduate degree	7.7%

Income & Poverty, 1999

Per capita income	$25,715
Median household income	$55,987
Median family income	$64,798
Persons in poverty	616
H'holds receiving public assistance	86
H'holds receiving social security	2,079

Households, 2000

Total households	7,560
With persons under 18	2,566
With persons over 65	1,982
Family households	5,228
One-person households	1,941
Persons per household	2.52
Persons per family	3.06

Labor & Employment

Total civilian labor force, 2004**	12,115
Unemployment rate	3.8%
Total civilian labor force, 2000	10,105
Unemployment rate	3.7%

Employed persons 16 years and over by occupation, 2000

Managers & professionals	3,511
Service occupations	1,532
Sales & office occupations	2,806
Farming, fishing & forestry	18
Construction & maintenance	1,017
Production & transportation	846
Self-employed persons	619

*US Census Bureau
**New Jersey Department of Labor

General Information

Borough of Point Pleasant
PO Box 25
2233 Bridge Ave
Point Pleasant, NJ 08742
732-892-3434

Web site	www.ptboro.com
Land area (sq. miles)	3.53
Water area (sq. miles)	0.63
Type of government	Borough
Form of government	B

Government

Legislative Districts

US Congressional	4
State Legislative	10

Local Officials, 2006

Mayor	Martin Konkus
Admin/Manager	David Maffei
Clerk	David Maffei
Finance Dir/Treas	Judith Block
Engineer	Schoor DePalma
Attorney	Jerry Dasti
Tax assessor	Richard Kenny
Tax collector	Bernadine Pierce
Building officer	Michael Gardner
Zoning officer	NA
Public Works	Dennis Sears

Housing & Construction

Housing Units, 2000*

Total	8,350
Median rent	$859
Median SF home value	$160,100

New Privately Owned Housing Units Authorized by Building Permit

	Units	Value
Total, 2004	64	$9,337,593
Single family	64	$9,337,593
Total, 2005	42	$7,012,716
Single family	42	$7,012,716

Real Property Valuation - parcels, 2005

	Number	Valuation
Total		$1,348,890,400
Vacant	238	17,907,100
Residential	7,527	1,207,638,100
Commercial	303	109,000,500
Industrial	0	0
Apartments	15	14,344,700
Farm land	0	0
Farm homestead	0	0

Average Property Value & Tax, 2005

Residential value	$160,441
Property tax	$5,166
FAIR rebate	$485

Public Library

Point Pleasant Branch Library†
834 Beaver Dam Rd
Point Pleasant, NJ 08742
732-295-1555

Branch Librarian ....Barbara Kaden

Library statistics, 2004

	Total	per capita
Volumes	NA	NA
Expenditure	NA	NA

†Branch of County Library

Public Safety

Police

Chief	Raymond Hilling
Number of officers, 2004	32

Crime, 2004	Number	Rate
Total	347	17.5
Violent	14	0.7
Non-violent	333	16.8
Domestic Viol.	150	NA

Emergency/Fire

Director	NA

Public School District

(for school year 2004-2005 except as noted)

Point Pleasant Borough School District
2100 Panther Path
Point Pleasant, NJ 08742
732-701-1900

Superintendent	Robert Ciliento
Grade plan	K-12
Enrollment	3,149.0
Students per teacher	12.3
Per pupil expenditure	$9,550
Median faculty salary	$46,230
Median administrator salary	$100,079
Grade 12 enrollment	208.5
High school graduation rate	99.0%

Assessment test results

(percent scoring at proficient or advanced level)

	Language	Math
Grade 3	97.1%	97.1%
Grade 8	84.3%	81.7%
High school	97.4%	80.0%

SAT

Percent tested	89%
Average SAT math score	506
Average SAT verbal score	511

No Child Left Behind, 2003-04

Attendence rate (target = 90%)	94.3%
Drop rate	0%
Highly-qualified teachers	100%
District needs improvement?(AYP)	No

Municipal Finance

Fiscal Year 2005

Total tax levy	$43,512,862
County levy	9,984,852
County taxes	8,412,511
County library	883,816
County health	374,607
County open space	313,918
School levy	24,722,511
Local muni. budget	8,805,499
Misc. revenues	5,597,236
Total aid	$1,741,222
CMPTRA	579,896
Muni. block grant	79,537
Energy tax receipts	1,011,789
Homeland security	70,000

Fiscal Year 2006

Total aid	$1,741,221
CMPTRA	544,483
Muni. block grant	79,537
Energy tax receipts	1,047,201
Homeland security	70,000

Taxes

	2003	2004	2005
General tax rate per $100	2.92	3.026	3.220
Net valuation taxable	$1,341,454,580	$1,347,821,089	$1,351,395,959
State equalized value	$2,212,161,247	$2,601,174,017	$3,030,035,783
County equalization ratio	70.63	60.64	51.76

Demographics & Socio-Economic Characteristics
(2000 U.S. Census, except as noted)

Population
1980*	10,660
1990*	10,539
2000	10,640
Male	5,119
Female	5,521
2004 (estimate)*	11,389
Persons per sq. mi. of land	3,838

Race & Hispanic Origin, 2000
Race
White	9,896
Black/African American	129
Amer. Indian/Alaska Natv.	20
Asian	322
Natv. Hawaiian/Pac. Islander	1
Other Race	167
Two or more races	105
Hispanic origin, total	611
Mexican	180
Puerto Rican	148
Cuban	62
Other Hispanic	221

Age & Nativity, 2000
Under 5 years	738
18 years and over	8,061
21 years and over	7,754
65 years and over	1,425
85 years and over	146
Median Age	37.2
Native born	9,542
Foreign born	1,098

Educational Attainment, 2000
Population 25 years and over	7,297
0-8 yrs of school	5.0%
High School grad or higher	88.8%
Bachelor's degree or higher	28.4%
Graduate degree	7.9%

Income & Poverty, 1999
Per capita income	$26,802
Median household income	$65,648
Median family income	$74,701
Persons in poverty	343
H'holds receiving public assistance	34
H'holds receiving social security	1,159

Households, 2000
Total households	3,949
With persons under 18	1,424
With persons over 65	1,081
Family households	2,805
One-person households	939
Persons per household	2.69
Persons per family	3.24

Labor & Employment
Total civilian labor force, 2004**	6,062
Unemployment rate	3.0%
Total civilian labor force, 2000	5,932
Unemployment rate	4.0%

Employed persons 16 years and over by occupation, 2000
Managers & professionals	2,225
Service occupations	648
Sales & office occupations	1,559
Farming, fishing & forestry	0
Construction & maintenance	604
Production & transportation	660
Self-employed persons	196

*US Census Bureau
**New Jersey Department of Labor

General Information
Borough of Pompton Lakes
25 Lenox Ave
Pompton Lakes, NJ 07442
973-835-0143
Web site	www.pomptonlakesgov.com
Land area (sq. miles)	2.97
Water area (sq. miles)	0.19
Type of government	Borough
Form of government	B

Government

Legislative Districts
US Congressional	8
State Legislative	26

Local Officials, 2006
Mayor	John Murrin
Admin/Manager	Lawrence Pollex
Clerk	Carol Kehoe
Finance Dir/Treas	Lawrence Pollex
Engineer	Alaimo Group
Attorney	Kenneth Petrie
Tax assessor	Michael Barker
Tax collector	Gail Bado
Building officer	Barbara Polito
Zoning officer	Barbara Polito
Public Works	Ben Steltzer

Housing & Construction

Housing Units, 2000*
Total	4,024
Median rent	$933
Median SF home value	$180,100

New Privately Owned Housing Units Authorized by Building Permit
	Units	Value
Total, 2004	0	$0
Single family	0	$0
Total, 2005	1	$112,800
Single family	1	$112,800

Real Property Valuation - parcels, 2005
	Number	Valuation
Total		$638,100,200
Vacant	57	3,442,400
Residential	3,688	545,289,300
Commercial	168	59,424,700
Industrial	5	17,498,600
Apartments	8	12,445,200
Farm land	0	0
Farm homestead	0	0

Average Property Value & Tax, 2005
Residential value	$147,855
Property tax	$6,865
FAIR rebate	$547

Public Library
Emanuel Einstein Public Library
333 Wanaque Ave
Pompton Lakes, NJ 07442
973-835-0482
Director	Margaret Freathy

Library statistics, 2004
	Total	per capita
Volumes	38,043	3.58
Expenditure	$316,535	$29.75

Public Safety

Police
Chief	Albert Ekkers
Number of officers, 2004	25

Crime, 2004	Number	Rate
Total	150	13.5
Violent	12	1.1
Non-violent	138	12.4
Domestic Viol.	67	NA

Emergency/Fire
Director	Dean Cioppa

Public School District
(for school year 2004-2005 except as noted)

Pompton Lakes School District
237 Van Ave
Pompton Lakes, NJ 07442
973-835-4334
Administrator	Terrance Brennan
Grade plan	K-12
Enrollment	1,840.5
Students per teacher	11.2
Per pupil expenditure	$11,863
Median faculty salary	$51,465
Median administrator salary	$117,302
Grade 12 enrollment	164.0
High school graduation rate	96.4%

Assessment test results
(percent scoring at proficient or advanced level)
	Language	Math
Grade 3	87.2%	83.2%
Grade 8	77.7%	69.0%
High school	88.5%	83.2%

SAT
Percent tested	76%
Average SAT math score	500
Average SAT verbal score	487

No Child Left Behind, 2003-04
Attendence rate (target = 90%)	94.1%
Drop rate	0.8%
Highly-qualified teachers	97%
District needs improvement?(AYP)	No

Municipal Finance

Fiscal Year 2005
Total tax levy	$29,655,616
County levy	5,999,979
County taxes	5,885,830
County library	0
County health	0
County open space	114,149
School levy	17,591,545
Local muni. budget	6,064,093
Misc. revenues	4,324,211
Total aid	$1,449,003
CMPTRA	675,491
Muni. block grant	46,115
Energy tax receipts	657,397
Homeland security	70,000

Fiscal Year 2006
Total aid	$1,449,003
CMPTRA	652,483
Muni. block grant	46,115
Energy tax receipts	680,405
Homeland security	70,000

Taxes
	2003	2004	2005
General tax rate per $100	4.18	4.350	4.650
Net valuation taxable	$612,470,882	$631,091,253	$638,686,330
State equalized value	$964,521,074	$1,118,116,350	$1,291,057,873
County equalization ratio	72.89	63.50	56.41

Demographics & Socio-Economic Characteristics
(2000 U.S. Census, except as noted)

Population
1980*	837
1990*	992
2000	1,037
Male	510
Female	527
2004 (estimate)*	1,140
Persons per sq. mi. of land	150

Race & Hispanic Origin, 2000
Race
White	986
Black/African American	17
Amer. Indian/Alaska Natv.	4
Asian	6
Natv. Hawaiian/Pac. Islander	0
Other Race	7
Two or more races	17
Hispanic origin, total	11
Mexican	0
Puerto Rican	7
Cuban	0
Other Hispanic	4

Age & Nativity, 2000
Under 5 years	58
18 years and over	788
21 years and over	746
65 years and over	124
85 years and over	17
Median Age	41.3
Native born	985
Foreign born	47

Educational Attainment, 2000
Population 25 years and over	707
0-8 yrs of school	3.4%
High School grad or higher	90.5%
Bachelor's degree or higher	27.7%
Graduate degree	7.5%

Income & Poverty, 1999
Per capita income	$24,369
Median household income	$65,833
Median family income	$70,714
Persons in poverty	36
H'holds receiving public assistance	3
H'holds receiving social security	85

Households, 2000
Total households	365
With persons under 18	146
With persons over 65	92
Family households	289
One-person households	61
Persons per household	2.82
Persons per family	3.17

Labor & Employment
Total civilian labor force, 2004**	545
Unemployment rate	3.3%
Total civilian labor force, 2000	578
Unemployment rate	4.2%

Employed persons 16 years and over by occupation, 2000
Managers & professionals	161
Service occupations	89
Sales & office occupations	153
Farming, fishing & forestry	7
Construction & maintenance	79
Production & transportation	65
Self-employed persons	64

*US Census Bureau
**New Jersey Department of Labor

General Information
City of Port Republic
143 Main St
Port Republic, NJ 08241
609-652-1501

Web site	NA
Land area (sq. miles)	7.62
Water area (sq. miles)	1.05
Type of government	City
Form of government	C

Government
Legislative Districts
US Congressional	2
State Legislative	2

Local Officials, 2006
Mayor	Gary Giberson
Admin/Manager	NA
Clerk	Lucy Samuelsen
Finance Dir/Treas	Karen Thomas
Engineer	Doran Eng.
Attorney	Sal Perillo
Tax assessor	Brian Vigue
Tax collector	NA
Building officer	Kevin Cain
Zoning officer	NA
Public Works	NA

Housing & Construction
Housing Units, 2000*
Total	389
Median rent	$790
Median SF home value	$155,700

New Privately Owned Housing Units
Authorized by Building Permit
	Units	Value
Total, 2004	25	$3,366,313
Single family	25	$3,366,313
Total, 2005	23	$3,072,001
Single family	23	$3,072,001

Real Property Valuation - parcels, 2005
	Number	Valuation
Total		$68,564,000
Vacant	121	2,904,900
Residential	433	62,346,200
Commercial	10	2,171,000
Industrial	0	0
Apartments	0	0
Farm land	6	1,068,700
Farm homestead	7	73,200

Average Property Value & Tax, 2005
Residential value	$141,862
Property tax	$3,993
FAIR rebate	$525

Public Library
No public municipal library.

Library statistics, 2004
	Total	per capita
Volumes	NA	NA
Expenditure	NA	NA

Public Safety
Police
Chief	NA
Number of officers, 2004	0

Crime, 2004	Number	Rate
Total	9	8.4
Violent	2	1.9
Non-violent	7	6.5
Domestic Viol.	3	NA

Emergency/Fire
Director	John Yochim

Public School District
(for school year 2004-2005 except as noted)

Port Republic School District
137 Pomona Ave
Port Republic, NJ 08241
609-652-7377

Administrator	Rose Anne Fiore
Grade plan	K-12
Enrollment	131.0
Students per teacher	8.3
Per pupil expenditure	$12,938
Median faculty salary	$52,669
Median administrator salary	$75,915
Grade 12 enrollment	NA
High school graduation rate	NA

Assessment test results
(percent scoring at proficient or advanced level)
	Language	Math
Grade 3	93.3%	80.0%
Grade 8	83.4%	58.3%
High school	NA	NA

SAT
Percent tested	NA
Average SAT math score	NA
Average SAT verbal score	NA

No Child Left Behind, 2003-04
Attendence rate (target = 90%)	94.2%
Drop rate	NA
Highly-qualified teachers	100%
District needs improvement?(AYP)	No

Municipal Finance
Fiscal Year 2005
Total tax levy	$1,941,869
County levy	445,490
County taxes	363,724
County library	40,282
County health	19,824
County open space	21,660
School levy	1,131,843
Local muni. budget	364,536
Misc. revenues	1,064,052
Total aid	$222,552
CMPTRA	32,455
Muni. block grant	4,341
Energy tax receipts	185,756
Homeland security	0

Fiscal Year 2006
Total aid	$222,553
CMPTRA	25,954
Muni. block grant	4,341
Energy tax receipts	192,258
Homeland security	NA

Taxes
	2003	2004	2005
General tax rate per $100	2.53	2.651	2.815
Net valuation taxable	$65,851,538	$67,826,259	$68,987,910
State equalized value	$84,980,692	$106,115,154	$119,770,677
County equalization ratio	86.12	77.49	63.73

Demographics & Socio-Economic Characteristics
(2000 U.S. Census, except as noted)

Population
1980*	12,035
1990*	12,016
2000	14,203
Male	7,380
Female	6,823
2000 (revised)	13,568
2004 (estimate)*	13,590
Persons per sq. mi. of land	7,354

Race & Hispanic Origin, 2000
Race
White	11,399
Black/African American	908
Amer. Indian/Alaska Natv.	40
Asian	1,060
Natv. Hawaiian/Pac. Islander	20
Other Race	355
Two or more races	421
Hispanic origin, total	1,009
Mexican	340
Puerto Rican	113
Cuban	30
Other Hispanic	526

Age & Nativity, 2000
Under 5 years	446
18 years and over	12,774
21 years and over	9,644
65 years and over	1,321
85 years and over	264
Median Age	24.7
Native born	12,191
Foreign born	2,012

Educational Attainment, 2000
Population 25 years and over	7,148
0-8 yrs of school	4.8%
High School grad or higher	89.4%
Bachelor's degree or higher	60.1%
Graduate degree	39.6%

Income & Poverty, 1999
Per capita income	$27,292
Median household income	$67,346
Median family income	$102,957
Persons in poverty	656
H'holds receiving public assistance	16
H'holds receiving social security	811

Households, 2000
Total households	3,326
With persons under 18	780
With persons over 65	819
Family households	1,693
One-person households	1,334
Persons per household	2.2
Persons per family	2.92

Labor & Employment
Total civilian labor force, 2004**	6,975
Unemployment rate	2.6%
Total civilian labor force, 2000	9,999
Unemployment rate	42.3%

Employed persons 16 years and over by occupation, 2000
Managers & professionals	3,620
Service occupations	1,076
Sales & office occupations	801
Farming, fishing & forestry	12
Construction & maintenance	133
Production & transportation	126
Self-employed persons	232

*US Census Bureau
**New Jersey Department of Labor

General Information
Borough of Princeton
PO Box 390
Princeton, NJ 08542
609-924-3118
Web site	www.princetonboro.org
Land area (sq. miles)	1.85
Water area (sq. miles)	0
Type of government	Borough
Form of government	B

Government

Legislative Districts
US Congressional	12
State Legislative	15

Local Officials, 2006
Mayor	Mildred T. Trotman
Admin/Manager	Robert W. Bruschi
Clerk	Andrea L. Quinty
Finance Dir/Treas	Decimus W. Marsh
Engineer	Carl Peters
Attorney	Michael J. Herbert
Tax assessor	Neal Snyder
Tax collector	NA
Building officer	Martin Vogt
Zoning officer	Frank Slimak
Public Works	Wayne Carr

Housing & Construction

Housing Units, 2000*
Total	3,495
Median rent	$920
Median SF home value	$343,500

New Privately Owned Housing Units Authorized by Building Permit
	Units	Value
Total, 2004	6	$1,279,711
Single family	4	$955,211
Total, 2005	16	$5,462,909
Single family	14	$5,162,909

Real Property Valuation - parcels, 2005
	Number	Valuation
Total		$997,308,900
Vacant	143	15,975,100
Residential	2,039	711,590,600
Commercial	200	223,229,500
Industrial	0	0
Apartments	44	46,513,700
Farm land	0	0
Farm homestead	0	0

Average Property Value & Tax, 2005
Residential value	$348,990
Property tax	$12,636
FAIR rebate	$665

Public Library
Princeton Public Library†
65 Witherspoon St
Princeton, NJ 08540
609-924-9529
Director	Leslie Burger

Library statistics, 2004
	Total	per capita
Volumes	131,856	4.36
Expenditure	$3,760,211	$124.39

†Joint Library with Princeton Twp

Public Safety

Police
Chief	Anthony V. Federico
Number of officers, 2004	33

Crime, 2004	Number	Rate
Total	502	37
Violent	23	1.7
Non-violent	479	35.3
Domestic Viol.	42	NA

Emergency/Fire
Director	Patrick McAvenia

Public School District
(for school year 2004-2005 except as noted)

Princeton Regional School District
25 Valley Rd
Princeton, NJ 08540
609-806-4220
Superintendent	Judith A. Wilson
Grade plan	K-12
Enrollment	3,276.0
Students per teacher	10.1
Per pupil expenditure	$14,645
Median faculty salary	$56,165
Median administrator salary	$113,051
Grade 12 enrollment	258.0
High school graduation rate	96.6%

Assessment test results
(percent scoring at proficient or advanced level)
	Language	Math
Grade 3	93.4%	90.2%
Grade 8	87.8%	90.2%
High school	91.3%	86.8%

SAT
Percent tested	99%
Average SAT math score	616
Average SAT verbal score	599

No Child Left Behind, 2003-04
Attendence rate (target = 90%)	96.3%
Drop rate	0%
Highly-qualified teachers	100%
District needs improvement?(AYP)	No

Municipal Finance

Fiscal Year 2005
Total tax levy	$36,243,361
County levy	10,358,935
County taxes	9,808,000
County library	0
County health	0
County open space	550,935
School levy	16,875,494
Local muni. budget	9,008,932
Misc. revenues	13,035,347
Total aid	$1,442,384
CMPTRA	466,738
Muni. block grant	55,690
Energy tax receipts	849,956
Homeland security	70,000

Fiscal Year 2006
Total aid	$1,442,384
CMPTRA	436,989
Muni. block grant	55,690
Energy tax receipts	879,705
Homeland security	70,000

Taxes
	2003	2004	2005
General tax rate per $100	3.06	3.350	3.630
Net valuation taxable	$1,008,758,681	$999,000,350	$1,000,992,410
State equalized value	$1,690,279,291	$1,823,248,321	$1,957,739,898
County equalization ratio	67.95	59.68	54.69

Demographics & Socio-Economic Characteristics
(2000 U.S. Census, except as noted)

Population
1980*	13,683
1990*	13,198
2000	16,027
Male	7,750
Female	8,277
2000 (revised)	16,662
2004 (estimate)*	17,349
Persons per sq. mi. of land	1,059

Race & Hispanic Origin, 2000
Race
White	12,807
Black/African American	852
Amer. Indian/Alaska Natv.	20
Asian	1,599
Natv. Hawaiian/Pac. Islander	8
Other Race	338
Two or more races	403
Hispanic origin, total	847
Mexican	309
Puerto Rican	70
Cuban	23
Other Hispanic	445

Age & Nativity, 2000
Under 5 years	821
18 years and over	12,121
21 years and over	11,804
65 years and over	2,463
85 years and over	228
Median Age	40.8
Native born	11,962
Foreign born	4,065

Educational Attainment, 2000
Population 25 years and over	11,355
0-8 yrs of school	2.6%
High School grad or higher	94.2%
Bachelor's degree or higher	75.9%
Graduate degree	48.2%

Income & Poverty, 1999
Per capita income	$56,360
Median household income	$94,580
Median family income	$123,098
Persons in poverty	897
H'holds receiving public assistance	45
H'holds receiving social security	1,482

Households, 2000
Total households	6,044
With persons under 18	2,121
With persons over 65	1,658
Family households	4,358
One-person households	1,243
Persons per household	2.57
Persons per family	2.98

Labor & Employment
Total civilian labor force, 2004**	7,596
Unemployment rate	2.9%
Total civilian labor force, 2000	7,990
Unemployment rate	0.8%

Employed persons 16 years and over by occupation, 2000
Managers & professionals	5,629
Service occupations	676
Sales & office occupations	1,252
Farming, fishing & forestry	12
Construction & maintenance	113
Production & transportation	243
Self-employed persons	940

*US Census Bureau
**New Jersey Department of Labor

General Information
Township of Princeton
400 Witherspoon St
Princeton, NJ 08540
609-924-5176
Web site	www.princetontwp.org
Land area (sq. miles)	16.38
Water area (sq. miles)	0.23
Type of government	Township
Form of government	TC

Government

Legislative Districts
US Congressional	12
State Legislative	15

Local Officials, 2006
Mayor	Phyllis Marchand
Admin/Manager	James Pascale
Clerk	Linda McDermott
Finance Dir/Treas	Kathryn Shaddow
Engineer	Robert Kiser
Attorney	Edwin Schmierer
Tax assessor	Neal Snyder
Tax collector	NA
Building officer	John Pettenati
Zoning officer	NA
Public Works	NA

Housing & Construction

Housing Units, 2000*
Total	6,224
Median rent	$748
Median SF home value	$417,000

New Privately Owned Housing Units
Authorized by Building Permit
	Units	Value
Total, 2004	16	$10,788,041
Single family	16	$10,788,041
Total, 2005	80	$15,979,450
Single family	12	$6,394,450

Real Property Valuation - parcels, 2005
	Number	Valuation
Total		$2,377,758,510
Vacant	357	43,360,400
Residential	4,893	2,045,750,800
Commercial	111	185,088,400
Industrial	3	6,137,500
Apartments	7	78,150,100
Farm land	19	18,926,200
Farm homestead	46	345,110

Average Property Value & Tax, 2005
Residential value	$414,273
Property tax	$13,222
FAIR rebate	$618

Public Library
Princeton Public Library†
65 Witherspoon St
Princeton, NJ 08540
609-924-9529
Director	Leslie Burger

Library statistics, 2004
	Total	per capita
Volumes	131,856	4.36
Expenditure	$3,760,211	$124.39

†Joint Library with Princeton Boro

Public Safety

Police
Chief	Mark V. Emann
Number of officers, 2004	34

Crime, 2004	Number	Rate
Total	183	10.6
Violent	6	0.3
Non-violent	177	10.3
Domestic Viol.	67	NA

Emergency/Fire
Director	Patrick McAvania

Public School District
(for school year 2004-2005 except as noted)

Princeton Regional School District
25 Valley Rd
Princeton, NJ 08540
609-806-4220
Superintendent	Judith A. Wilson
Grade plan	K-12
Enrollment	3,276.0
Students per teacher	10.1
Per pupil expenditure	$14,645
Median faculty salary	$56,165
Median administrator salary	$113,051
Grade 12 enrollment	258.0
High school graduation rate	96.6%

Assessment test results
(percent scoring at proficient or advanced level)
	Language	Math
Grade 3	93.4%	90.2%
Grade 8	87.8%	90.2%
High school	91.3%	86.8%

SAT
Percent tested	99%
Average SAT math score	616
Average SAT verbal score	599

No Child Left Behind, 2003-04
Attendence rate (target = 90%)	96.3%
Drop rate	0%
Highly-qualified teachers	100%
District needs improvement?(AYP)	No

Municipal Finance

Fiscal Year 2005
Total tax levy	$75,954,615
County levy	22,793,919
County taxes	21,581,664
County library	0
County health	0
County open space	1,212,255
School levy	36,488,533
Local muni. budget	16,672,163
Misc. revenues	13,490,376
Total aid	$2,130,219
CMPTRA	540,130
Muni. block grant	62,842
Energy tax receipts	1,457,247
Homeland security	70,000

Fiscal Year 2006
Total aid	$2,130,219
CMPTRA	489,126
Muni. block grant	62,842
Energy tax receipts	1,508,251
Homeland security	70,000

Taxes
	2003	2004	2005
General tax rate per $100	2.79	2.940	3.200
Net valuation taxable	$2,336,446,160	$2,351,050,872	$2,379,755,105
State equalized value	$3,605,070,452	$3,985,296,235	$4,454,801,769
County equalization ratio	71.09	64.81	58.97

Demographics & Socio-Economic Characteristics
(2000 U.S. Census, except as noted)

Population
1980*	5,142
1990*	5,053
2000	5,779
Male	2,750
Female	3,029
2004 (estimate)*	5,802
Persons per sq. mi. of land	12,092

Race & Hispanic Origin, 2000
Race
White	3,535
Black/African American	789
Amer. Indian/Alaska Natv.	24
Asian	182
Natv. Hawaiian/Pac. Islander	4
Other Race	792
Two or more races	453
Hispanic origin, total	2,211
Mexican	41
Puerto Rican	706
Cuban	43
Other Hispanic	1,421

Age & Nativity, 2000
Under 5 years	443
18 years and over	4,070
21 years and over	3,831
65 years and over	510
85 years and over	54
Median Age	30.9
Native born	3,955
Foreign born	1,824

Educational Attainment, 2000
Population 25 years and over	3,433
0-8 yrs of school	14.9%
High School grad or higher	68.3%
Bachelor's degree or higher	12.4%
Graduate degree	3.2%

Income & Poverty, 1999
Per capita income	$16,410
Median household income	$46,434
Median family income	$49,405
Persons in poverty	575
H'holds receiving public assistance	30
H'holds receiving social security	440

Households, 2000
Total households	1,822
With persons under 18	904
With persons over 65	380
Family households	1,432
One-person households	309
Persons per household	3.17
Persons per family	3.56

Labor & Employment
Total civilian labor force, 2004**	2,893
Unemployment rate	4.2%
Total civilian labor force, 2000	2,712
Unemployment rate	6.1%

Employed persons 16 years and over by occupation, 2000
Managers & professionals	564
Service occupations	445
Sales & office occupations	818
Farming, fishing & forestry	0
Construction & maintenance	227
Production & transportation	492
Self-employed persons	34

*US Census Bureau
**New Jersey Department of Labor

General Information
Borough of Prospect Park
106 Brown Ave
Prospect Park, NJ 07508
973-790-7902

Web site	www.prospectpark.net
Land area (sq. miles)	0.48
Water area (sq. miles)	0
Type of government	Borough
Form of government	B

Government

Legislative Districts
US Congressional	8
State Legislative	35

Local Officials, 2006
Mayor	Mohamed T. Khairullah
Admin/Manager	(Vacant)
Clerk	Yancy Wazirmas
Finance Dir/Treas	Stephen Sanzari
Engineer	Boswell Engineeering
Attorney	Schwartz Simon et al
Tax assessor	Rose Farrell
Tax collector	Stephen Sanzari
Building officer	David Heerema
Zoning officer	NA
Public Works	Ken Valt

Housing & Construction

Housing Units, 2000*
Total	1,889
Median rent	$852
Median SF home value	$137,600

New Privately Owned Housing Units Authorized by Building Permit
	Units	Value
Total, 2004	0	$0
Single family	0	$0
Total, 2005	2	$300,000
Single family	2	$300,000

Real Property Valuation - parcels, 2005
	Number	Valuation
Total		$180,305,450
Vacant	25	3,090,200
Residential	1,083	159,916,200
Commercial	58	14,541,650
Industrial	2	2,757,400
Apartments	0	0
Farm land	0	0
Farm homestead	0	0

Average Property Value & Tax, 2005
Residential value	$147,660
Property tax	$6,541
FAIR rebate	$568

Public Library

No public municipal library.

Library statistics, 2004
	Total	per capita
Volumes	NA	NA
Expenditure	NA	NA

Public Safety

Police
Chief	Frank Franco
Number of officers, 2004	16

Crime, 2004	Number	Rate
Total	147	25.4
Violent	11	1.9
Non-violent	136	23.5
Domestic Viol.	51	NA

Emergency/Fire
Director	Douglas Struyk

Public School District
(for school year 2004-2005 except as noted)

Prospect Park School District
290 N 8th St
Prospect Park, NJ 07508
973-720-1982

Administrator	James Barriale
Grade plan	K-8
Enrollment	809.0
Students per teacher	11.4
Per pupil expenditure	$10,406
Median faculty salary	$46,500
Median administrator salary	$91,432
Grade 12 enrollment	NA
High school graduation rate	NA

Assessment test results
(percent scoring at proficient or advanced level)
	Language	Math
Grade 3	80.9%	66.7%
Grade 8	58.2%	39.1%
High school	NA	NA

SAT
Percent tested	NA
Average SAT math score	NA
Average SAT verbal score	NA

No Child Left Behind, 2003-04
Attendance rate (target = 90%)	95.7%
Drop rate	NA
Highly-qualified teachers	92.4%
District needs improvement?(AYP)	No

Municipal Finance

Fiscal Year 2005
Total tax levy	$7,998,549
County levy	1,549,613
County taxes	1,520,104
County library	0
County health	0
County open space	29,509
School levy	4,068,421
Local muni. budget	2,380,515
Misc. revenues	1,945,028
Total aid	$546,715
CMPTRA	307,365
Muni. block grant	22,660
Energy tax receipts	166,690
Homeland security	50,000

Fiscal Year 2006
Total aid	$546,715
CMPTRA	301,531
Muni. block grant	22,660
Energy tax receipts	172,524
Homeland security	50,000

Taxes
	2003	2004	2005
General tax rate per $100	3.57	3.890	4.430
Net valuation taxable	$180,137,860	$180,412,560	$180,574,550
State equalized value	$249,602,134	$292,926,162	$341,673,699
County equalization ratio	82.49	72.17	61.55

Demographics & Socio-Economic Characteristics

(2000 U.S. Census, except as noted)

Population

1980*	2,887
1990*	2,511
2000	2,786
Male	1,391
Female	1,395
2004 (estimate)*	2,828
Persons per sq. mi. of land	117

Race & Hispanic Origin, 2000

Race

White	2,286
Black/African American	403
Amer. Indian/Alaska Natv.	30
Asian	9
Natv. Hawaiian/Pac. Islander	0
Other Race	20
Two or more races	38
Hispanic origin, total	42
Mexican	7
Puerto Rican	14
Cuban	1
Other Hispanic	20

Age & Nativity, 2000

Under 5 years	161
18 years and over	2,128
21 years and over	2,034
65 years and over	441
85 years and over	50
Median Age	39
Native born	2,737
Foreign born	49

Educational Attainment, 2000

Population 25 years and over	1,931
0-8 yrs of school	10.9%
High School grad or higher	72.1%
Bachelor's degree or higher	10.3%
Graduate degree	2.2%

Income & Poverty, 1999

Per capita income	$18,921
Median household income	$41,193
Median family income	$48,272
Persons in poverty	258
H'holds receiving public assistance	34
H'holds receiving social security	365

Households, 2000

Total households	1,074
With persons under 18	357
With persons over 65	324
Family households	779
One-person households	244
Persons per household	2.56
Persons per family	3.02

Labor & Employment

Total civilian labor force, 2004**	1,089
Unemployment rate	9.5%
Total civilian labor force, 2000	1,294
Unemployment rate	8.8%

Employed persons 16 years and over by occupation, 2000

Managers & professionals	291
Service occupations	188
Sales & office occupations	267
Farming, fishing & forestry	17
Construction & maintenance	158
Production & transportation	259
Self-employed persons	63

*US Census Bureau
**New Jersey Department of Labor

General Information

Township of Quinton
PO Box 65
Quinton, NJ 08072
856-935-2325

Web site	NA
Land area (sq. miles)	24.17
Water area (sq. miles)	0.37
Type of government	Township
Form of government	TC

Government

Legislative Districts

US Congressional	2
State Legislative	3

Local Officials, 2006

Mayor	Joseph Donelson
Admin/Manager	NA
Clerk	Marty Uzdanovics
Finance Dir/Treas	Jill Elwell
Engineer	J & B Engel Engineers
Attorney	Gary Salber
Tax assessor	Joseph Harasta
Tax collector	NA
Building officer	Wayne Serfass
Zoning officer	Donna Bradway
Public Works	NA

Housing & Construction

Housing Units, 2000*

Total	1,133
Median rent	$668
Median SF home value	$101,300

New Privately Owned Housing Units Authorized by Building Permit

	Units	Value
Total, 2004	11	$1,852,000
Single family	11	$1,852,000
Total, 2005	10	$1,733,500
Single family	10	$1,733,500

Real Property Valuation - parcels, 2005

	Number	Valuation
Total		$118,544,300
Vacant	359	4,685,800
Residential	819	81,936,900
Commercial	54	10,497,900
Industrial	0	0
Apartments	1	302,600
Farm land	147	17,506,800
Farm homestead	375	3,614,300

Average Property Value & Tax, 2005

Residential value	$71,651
Property tax	$2,293
FAIR rebate	$547

Public Library

No public municipal library.

Library statistics, 2004

	Total	per capita
Volumes	NA	NA
Expenditure	NA	NA

Public Safety

Police

Chief	NA
Number of officers, 2004	0

Crime, 2004	Number	Rate
Total	43	15.3
Violent	2	0.7
Non-violent	41	14.6
Domestic Viol.	12	NA

Emergency/Fire

Director	Patrick Foster

Public School District

(for school year 2004-2005 except as noted)

Quinton Township School District
PO Box 365
Quinton, NJ 08072
856-935-2379

Administrator	Donna Agnew
Grade plan	K-12
Enrollment	360.0
Students per teacher	10.8
Per pupil expenditure	$10,903
Median faculty salary	$43,742
Median administrator salary	$63,440
Grade 12 enrollment	NA
High school graduation rate	NA

Assessment test results

(percent scoring at proficient or advanced level)

	Language	Math
Grade 3	81.6%	89.5%
Grade 8	76.3%	68.4%
High school	NA	NA

SAT

Percent tested	NA
Average SAT math score	NA
Average SAT verbal score	NA

No Child Left Behind, 2003-04

Attendence rate (target = 90%)	95.2%
Drop rate	NA
Highly-qualified teachers	100%
District needs improvement?(AYP)	No

Municipal Finance

Fiscal Year 2005

Total tax levy	$3,818,003
County levy	1,387,172
County taxes	1,359,278
County library	0
County health	0
County open space	27,894
School levy	2,144,051
Local muni. budget	286,781
Misc. revenues	1,321,219
Total aid	$443,490
CMPTRA	140,371
Muni. block grant	10,987
Energy tax receipts	289,265
Homeland security	0

Fiscal Year 2006

Total aid	$443,490
CMPTRA	130,247
Muni. block grant	10,987
Energy tax receipts	299,389
Homeland security	NA

Taxes

	2003	2004	2005
General tax rate per $100	2.84	2.948	3.200
Net valuation taxable	$118,829,773	$119,317,851	$119,319,569
State equalized value	$127,897,721	$138,327,481	$149,974,320
County equalization ratio	97.41	82.91	86.17

Demographics & Socio-Economic Characteristics
(2000 U.S. Census, except as noted)

Population
1980*	26,723
1990*	25,325
2000	26,500
Male	12,639
Female	13,861
2004 (estimate)*	27,578
Persons per sq. mi. of land	6,913

Race & Hispanic Origin, 2000
Race
White	15,950
Black/African American	7,173
Amer. Indian/Alaska Natv.	42
Asian	950
Natv. Hawaiian/Pac. Islander	14
Other Race	1,489
Two or more races	882
Hispanic origin, total	3,675
Mexican	424
Puerto Rican	887
Cuban	216
Other Hispanic	2,148

Age & Nativity, 2000
Under 5 years	1,660
18 years and over	20,170
21 years and over	19,300
65 years and over	3,836
85 years and over	430
Median Age	37.1
Native born	21,947
Foreign born	4,553

Educational Attainment, 2000
Population 25 years and over	18,140
0-8 yrs of school	6.7%
High School grad or higher	81.5%
Bachelor's degree or higher	18.6%
Graduate degree	5.5%

Income & Poverty, 1999
Per capita income	$22,481
Median household income	$50,729
Median family income	$61,931
Persons in poverty	1,864
H'holds receiving public assistance	342
H'holds receiving social security	3,019

Households, 2000
Total households	10,028
With persons under 18	3,448
With persons over 65	2,883
Family households	6,727
One-person households	2,806
Persons per household	2.63
Persons per family	3.24

Labor & Employment
Total civilian labor force, 2004**	13,898
Unemployment rate	4.4%
Total civilian labor force, 2000	13,495
Unemployment rate	6.6%

Employed persons 16 years and over by occupation, 2000
Managers & professionals	3,862
Service occupations	1,683
Sales & office occupations	3,924
Farming, fishing & forestry	0
Construction & maintenance	1,206
Production & transportation	1,930
Self-employed persons	427

*US Census Bureau
**New Jersey Department of Labor

General Information
City of Rahway
City Hall Plaza
Rahway, NJ 07065
732-827-2000

Web site	www.cityofrahway.com
Land area (sq. miles)	3.99
Water area (sq. miles)	0.05
Type of government	City
Form of government	MC '50

Government

Legislative Districts
US Congressional	10
State Legislative	22

Local Officials, 2006
Mayor	James Kennedy
Admin/Manager	Robert Gorman
Clerk	Jean Kuc
Finance Dir/Treas	F. Ruggiero
Engineer	Ludwig Bohler
Attorney	Louis N. Rainone
Tax assessor	William Marbach
Tax collector	Sally DiRini
Building officer	Richard Watkins
Zoning officer	Lenore Slothower
Public Works	Tom Newbery

Housing & Construction

Housing Units, 2000*
Total	10,381
Median rent	$732
Median SF home value	$142,600

New Privately Owned Housing Units Authorized by Building Permit
	Units	Value
Total, 2004	82	$4,645,466
Single family	11	$1,250,209
Total, 2005	120	$10,824,159
Single family	73	$8,862,010

Real Property Valuation - parcels, 2005
	Number	Valuation
Total		$1,489,814,200
Vacant	278	13,847,100
Residential	7,021	935,684,200
Commercial	380	126,427,300
Industrial	90	375,830,700
Apartments	74	38,024,900
Farm land	0	0
Farm homestead	0	0

Average Property Value & Tax, 2005
Residential value	$133,269
Property tax	$5,515
FAIR rebate	$615

Public Library
Rahway Public Library
3 City Hall Plaza
Rahway, NJ 07065
732-340-1551

Director ... Gail Miller

Library statistics, 2004
	Total	per capita
Volumes	78,197	2.95
Expenditure	$1,265,039	$47.74

Public Safety

Police
Chief	Edward Hudak
Number of officers, 2004	80

Crime, 2004	Number	Rate
Total	768	28.7
Violent	93	3.5
Non-violent	675	25.2
Domestic Viol.	624	NA

Emergency/Fire
Director ... Harold Stahl

Public School District
(for school year 2004-2005 except as noted)

Rahway School District
Rahway Middle School
Rahway, NJ 07065
732-396-1020

Superintendent	William Petrino
Grade plan	K-12
Enrollment	3,997.0
Students per teacher	12.1
Per pupil expenditure	$11,023
Median faculty salary	$48,897
Median administrator salary	$104,022
Grade 12 enrollment	223.5
High school graduation rate	84.8%

Assessment test results
(percent scoring at proficient or advanced level)
	Language	Math
Grade 3	76.7%	77.2%
Grade 8	63.1%	52.9%
High school	79.5%	64.9%

SAT
Percent tested	76%
Average SAT math score	460
Average SAT verbal score	442

No Child Left Behind, 2003-04
Attendence rate (target = 90%)	93.8%
Drop rate	2.8%
Highly-qualified teachers	92.9%
District needs improvement?(AYP)	No

Municipal Finance

Fiscal Year 2005
Total tax levy	$61,885,413
County levy	9,508,403
County taxes	9,132,985
County library	0
County health	0
County open space	375,419
School levy	29,290,694
Local muni. budget	23,086,316
Misc. revenues	16,414,737
Total aid	$5,203,003
CMPTRA	3,363,600
Muni. block grant	110,814
Energy tax receipts	1,638,589
Homeland security	90,000

Fiscal Year 2006
Total aid	$5,203,002
CMPTRA	3,306,249
Muni. block grant	110,814
Energy tax receipts	1,695,939
Homeland security	90,000

Taxes
	2003	2004	2005
General tax rate per $100	3.74	3.872	4.139
Net valuation taxable	$1,474,634,426	$1,495,552,117	$1,495,515,100
State equalized value	$1,916,603,101	$2,254,654,297	$2,684,946,320
County equalization ratio	82.03	71.45	60.39

Demographics & Socio-Economic Characteristics
(2000 U.S. Census, except as noted)

Population
1980*	12,899
1990*	13,228
2000	14,351
Male	6,928
Female	7,423
2004 (estimate)*	14,601
Persons per sq. mi. of land	2,628

Race & Hispanic Origin, 2000
Race
White	13,148
Black/African American	112
Amer. Indian/Alaska Natv.	14
Asian	840
Natv. Hawaiian/Pac. Islander	1
Other Race	78
Two or more races	158
Hispanic origin, total	420
Mexican	82
Puerto Rican	81
Cuban	36
Other Hispanic	221

Age & Nativity, 2000
Under 5 years	1,088
18 years and over	10,474
21 years and over	10,173
65 years and over	1,614
85 years and over	171
Median Age	38.6
Native born	12,641
Foreign born	1,710

Educational Attainment, 2000
Population 25 years and over	9,729
0-8 yrs of school	2.0%
High School grad or higher	95.5%
Bachelor's degree or higher	54.5%
Graduate degree	19.9%

Income & Poverty, 1999
Per capita income	$41,964
Median household income	$88,187
Median family income	$104,036
Persons in poverty	276
H'holds receiving public assistance	62
H'holds receiving social security	1,193

Households, 2000
Total households	5,313
With persons under 18	2,054
With persons over 65	1,185
Family households	3,945
One-person households	1,200
Persons per household	2.68
Persons per family	3.18

Labor & Employment
Total civilian labor force, 2004**	7,599
Unemployment rate	3.4%
Total civilian labor force, 2000	7,510
Unemployment rate	3.0%

Employed persons 16 years and over by occupation, 2000
Managers & professionals	3,917
Service occupations	505
Sales & office occupations	2,139
Farming, fishing & forestry	6
Construction & maintenance	411
Production & transportation	310
Self-employed persons	383

*US Census Bureau
**New Jersey Department of Labor

General Information
Borough of Ramsey
33 N Central Ave
Ramsey, NJ 07446
201-825-3400

Web site	NA
Land area (sq. miles)	5.56
Water area (sq. miles)	0.05
Type of government	Borough
Form of government	B

Government

Legislative Districts
US Congressional	5
State Legislative	39

Local Officials, 2006
Mayor	Richard Muti
Admin/Manager	Nicholas Saros
Clerk	Meredith Bendian
Finance Dir/Treas	Richard Mathieson
Engineer	Harold Reed
Attorney	NA
Tax assessor	Angela Mattiace
Tax collector	NA
Building officer	Robert Connell
Zoning officer	NA
Public Works	NA

Housing & Construction

Housing Units, 2000*
Total	5,400
Median rent	$1,120
Median SF home value	$329,700

New Privately Owned Housing Units
Authorized by Building Permit
	Units	Value
Total, 2004	12	$3,068,497
Single family	12	$3,068,497
Total, 2005	121	$17,984,606
Single family	121	$17,984,606

Real Property Valuation - parcels, 2005
	Number	Valuation
Total		$2,715,365,200
Vacant	185	39,670,800
Residential	5,041	2,116,832,400
Commercial	218	419,457,400
Industrial	27	124,301,100
Apartments	6	15,103,500
Farm land	0	0
Farm homestead	0	0

Average Property Value & Tax, 2005
Residential value	$419,923
Property tax	$8,544
FAIR rebate	$541

Public Library
Ramsey Free Public Library
30 Wyckoff Ave
Ramsey, NJ 07446
201-327-1445
Director .... Wendy Bloom

Library statistics, 2004
	Total	per capita
Volumes	78,039	5.44
Expenditure	$867,992	$60.48

Public Safety
Police
Chief	Bryan Gurney
Number of officers, 2004	37

Crime, 2004	Number	Rate
Total	202	13.9
Violent	15	1
Non-violent	187	12.9
Domestic Viol.	80	NA

Emergency/Fire
Director	Thomas Lanning

Public School District
(for school year 2004-2005 except as noted)

Ramsey School District
266 E Main St
Ramsey, NJ 07446
201-785-2300
Superintendent	Roy Montessano
Grade plan	K-12
Enrollment	3,008.5
Students per teacher	11.3
Per pupil expenditure	$12,691
Median faculty salary	$50,705
Median administrator salary	$116,261
Grade 12 enrollment	187.5
High school graduation rate	100.0%

Assessment test results
(percent scoring at proficient or advanced level)
	Language	Math
Grade 3	97.7%	98.2%
Grade 8	93.5%	87.6%
High school	95.9%	97.4%

SAT
Percent tested	102%
Average SAT math score	577
Average SAT verbal score	558

No Child Left Behind, 2003-04
Attendence rate (target = 90%)	95.8%
Drop rate	0.1%
Highly-qualified teachers	95.7%
District needs improvement?(AYP)	No

Municipal Finance

Fiscal Year 2005
Total tax levy	$55,458,377
County levy	5,734,870
County taxes	5,447,502
County library	0
County health	0
County open space	287,367
School levy	37,533,026
Local muni. budget	12,190,481
Misc. revenues	7,180,326
Total aid	$2,123,995
CMPTRA	515,669
Muni. block grant	57,882
Energy tax receipts	1,480,444
Homeland security	70,000

Fiscal Year 2006
Total aid	$2,123,994
CMPTRA	463,853
Muni. block grant	57,882
Energy tax receipts	1,532,259
Homeland security	70,000

Taxes
	2003	2004	2005
General tax rate per $100	1.81	1.910	2.040
Net valuation taxable	$2,699,432,309	$2,712,440,996	$2,725,566,472
State equalized value	$2,516,249,356	$2,849,855,473	$3,214,869,630
County equalization ratio	118.62	107.28	95.16

Demographics & Socio-Economic Characteristics
(2000 U.S. Census, except as noted)

Population
1980*	17,828
1990*	19,974
2000	24,847
Male	12,317
Female	12,530
2004 (estimate)*	25,734
Persons per sq. mi. of land	1,228

Race & Hispanic Origin, 2000
Race
White	21,293
Black/African American	572
Amer. Indian/Alaska Natv.	15
Asian	2,272
Natv. Hawaiian/Pac. Islander	5
Other Race	326
Two or more races	364
Hispanic origin, total	1,208
Mexican	130
Puerto Rican	257
Cuban	81
Other Hispanic	740

Age & Nativity, 2000
Under 5 years	1,885
18 years and over	17,469
21 years and over	16,902
65 years and over	1,817
85 years and over	172
Median Age	36.5
Native born	20,849
Foreign born	3,998

Educational Attainment, 2000
Population 25 years and over	16,253
0-8 yrs of school	1.3%
High School grad or higher	95.7%
Bachelor's degree or higher	59.4%
Graduate degree	25.7%

Income & Poverty, 1999
Per capita income	$43,072
Median household income	$97,589
Median family income	$115,722
Persons in poverty	356
H'holds receiving public assistance	49
H'holds receiving social security	1,398

Households, 2000
Total households	8,679
With persons under 18	3,929
With persons over 65	1,341
Family households	6,806
One-person households	1,562
Persons per household	2.86
Persons per family	3.28

Labor & Employment
Total civilian labor force, 2004**	12,269
Unemployment rate	3.4%
Total civilian labor force, 2000	13,155
Unemployment rate	2.2%

Employed persons 16 years and over by occupation, 2000
Managers & professionals	7,575
Service occupations	957
Sales & office occupations	3,019
Farming, fishing & forestry	0
Construction & maintenance	584
Production & transportation	731
Self-employed persons	1,013

*US Census Bureau
**New Jersey Department of Labor

General Information
Township of Randolph
502 Millbrook Ave
Randolph, NJ 07869
973-989-7100

Web site	www.randolfnj.org
Land area (sq. miles)	20.96
Water area (sq. miles)	0.12
Type of government	Township
Form of government	CM '50

Government

Legislative Districts
US Congressional	11
State Legislative	25

Local Officials, 2006
Mayor	Gary C. Algeier
Admin/Manager	John Lovell
Clerk	Donna M. Luciani (Actg)
Finance Dir/Treas	Michael Soccio
Engineer	Carl Bressan
Attorney	Ed Buzak
Tax assessor	Barbara Gothie
Tax collector	Lisa Combes
Building officer	Frank Howard
Zoning officer	Barrie Krause
Public Works	Bill Kerwick

Housing & Construction

Housing Units, 2000*
Total	8,903
Median rent	$875
Median SF home value	$329,800

New Privately Owned Housing Units Authorized by Building Permit
	Units	Value
Total, 2004	21	$3,233,301
Single family	21	$3,233,301
Total, 2005	35	$7,203,210
Single family	35	$7,203,210

Real Property Valuation - parcels, 2005
	Number	Valuation
Total		$2,850,469,700
Vacant	350	38,824,700
Residential	7,159	2,358,838,300
Commercial	250	227,225,500
Industrial	49	113,492,200
Apartments	16	102,620,400
Farm land	24	9,263,400
Farm homestead	49	205,200

Average Property Value & Tax, 2005
Residential value	$327,281
Property tax	$8,773
FAIR rebate	$489

Public Library
Randolph Twp Public Library
28 Calais Rd
Randolph, NJ 07869
973-895-3556

Director ... Anita Freeman

Library statistics, 2004
	Total	per capita
Volumes	98,824	3.98
Expenditure	$1,168,956	$47.05

Public Safety

Police
Chief	Dean Kazaba
Number of officers, 2004	39

Crime, 2004	Number	Rate
Total	265	10.4
Violent	12	0.5
Non-violent	253	9.9
Domestic Viol.	204	NA

Emergency/Fire
Director ... Mark Forstenhausler

Public School District
(for school year 2004-2005 except as noted)

Randolph Township School District
2 Emery Ave
Randolph, NJ 07869
973-361-0808

Superintendent	Max R. Riley
Grade plan	K-12
Enrollment	5,495.0
Students per teacher	11.2
Per pupil expenditure	$11,029
Median faculty salary	$47,800
Median administrator salary	$100,802
Grade 12 enrollment	355.0
High school graduation rate	98.1%

Assessment test results
(percent scoring at proficient or advanced level)
	Language	Math
Grade 3	91.8%	90.9%
Grade 8	89.2%	82.8%
High school	93.8%	91.4%

SAT
Percent tested	94%
Average SAT math score	583
Average SAT verbal score	563

No Child Left Behind, 2003-04
Attendence rate (target = 90%)	94.8%
Drop rate	0.6%
Highly-qualified teachers	97.8%
District needs improvement?(AYP)	No

Municipal Finance

Fiscal Year 2005
Total tax levy	$76,538,788
County levy	10,377,916
County taxes	8,500,860
County library	0
County health	0
County open space	1,877,057
School levy	51,884,452
Local muni. budget	14,276,420
Misc. revenues	15,647,925
Total aid	$2,623,855
CMPTRA	912,543
Muni. block grant	97,426
Energy tax receipts	1,507,342
Homeland security	90,000

Fiscal Year 2006
Total aid	$2,623,856
CMPTRA	859,787
Muni. block grant	97,426
Energy tax receipts	1,560,099
Homeland security	90,000

Taxes
	2003	2004	2005
General tax rate per $100	2.47	2.580	2.690
Net valuation taxable	$2,792,666,136	$2,822,450,864	$2,855,284,138
State equalized value	$3,498,266,486	$3,848,579,363	$4,313,769,660
County equalization ratio	87.41	79.83	73.30

Demographics & Socio-Economic Characteristics
(2000 U.S. Census, except as noted)

Population
1980*	6,128
1990*	5,798
2000	6,338
Male	3,042
Female	3,296
2004 (estimate)*	6,401
Persons per sq. mi. of land	3,145

Race & Hispanic Origin, 2000
Race
White	5,561
Black/African American	59
Amer. Indian/Alaska Natv.	5
Asian	518
Natv. Hawaiian/Pac. Islander	10
Other Race	104
Two or more races	81
Hispanic origin, total	533
Mexican	43
Puerto Rican	63
Cuban	13
Other Hispanic	414

Age & Nativity, 2000
Under 5 years	460
18 years and over	4,922
21 years and over	4,757
65 years and over	1,026
85 years and over	128
Median Age	37.6
Native born	4,858
Foreign born	1,480

Educational Attainment, 2000
Population 25 years and over	4,557
0-8 yrs of school	10.0%
High School grad or higher	77.3%
Bachelor's degree or higher	27.0%
Graduate degree	9.1%

Income & Poverty, 1999
Per capita income	$26,420
Median household income	$51,122
Median family income	$59,962
Persons in poverty	406
H'holds receiving public assistance	47
H'holds receiving social security	715

Households, 2000
Total households	2,556
With persons under 18	817
With persons over 65	758
Family households	1,671
One-person households	740
Persons per household	2.48
Persons per family	3.08

Labor & Employment
Total civilian labor force, 2004**	4,038
Unemployment rate	4.4%
Total civilian labor force, 2000	3,217
Unemployment rate	4.3%

Employed persons 16 years and over by occupation, 2000
Managers & professionals	1,132
Service occupations	457
Sales & office occupations	837
Farming, fishing & forestry	0
Construction & maintenance	271
Production & transportation	382
Self-employed persons	116

*US Census Bureau
**New Jersey Department of Labor

General Information
Borough of Raritan
22 First St
Raritan, NJ 08869
908-231-1300

Web site	NA
Land area (sq. miles)	2.04
Water area (sq. miles)	0
Type of government	Borough
Form of government	B

Government

Legislative Districts
US Congressional	11
State Legislative	16

Local Officials, 2006
Mayor	Anthony Hudak
Admin/Manager	Daniel Jaxel
Clerk	Pam Huefner
Finance Dir/Treas	Carolyn Gara
Engineer	Stanley Schrek
Attorney	Paul Rizzo
Tax assessor	Catherine Gantner
Tax collector	NA
Building officer	Louis Gara
Zoning officer	NA
Public Works	NA

Housing & Construction

Housing Units, 2000*
Total	2,644
Median rent	$801
Median SF home value	$182,500

New Privately Owned Housing Units Authorized by Building Permit
	Units	Value
Total, 2004	9	$1,016,364
Single family	5	$737,364
Total, 2005	246	$24,729,392
Single family	4	$589,892

Real Property Valuation - parcels, 2005
	Number	Valuation
Total		$1,127,701,744
Vacant	42	10,361,600
Residential	1,904	608,188,134
Commercial	175	202,898,295
Industrial	15	304,355,115
Apartments	4	1,898,600
Farm land	0	0
Farm homestead	0	0

Average Property Value & Tax, 2005
Residential value	$319,427
Property tax	$5,611
FAIR rebate	$659

Public Library
Raritan Public Library
54 E Somerset St
Raritan, NJ 08869
908-725-0413
Director................Jackie Widows

Library statistics, 2004
	Total	per capita
Volumes	45,773	7.22
Expenditure	$265,356	$41.87

Public Safety
Police
Chief	Michael Sniscak
Number of officers, 2004	18

Crime, 2004	Number	Rate
Total	141	22.2
Violent	8	1.3
Non-violent	133	20.9
Domestic Viol.	55	NA

Emergency/Fire
Director................Carl Memoli

Public School District
(for school year 2004-2005 except as noted)

Bridgewater-Raritan Regional School Dist.
836 Newmans Lane
Bridgewater, NJ 08807
908-685-2777
Superintendent	Walter Mahler
Grade plan	K-12
Enrollment	8,777.0
Students per teacher	10.9
Per pupil expenditure	$11,750
Median faculty salary	$48,530
Median administrator salary	$109,956
Grade 12 enrollment	520.5
High school graduation rate	98.3%

Assessment test results
(percent scoring at proficient or advanced level)
	Language	Math
Grade 3	92.8%	92.1%
Grade 8	87.3%	77.8%
High school	92.1%	87.7%

SAT
Percent tested	93%
Average SAT math score	578
Average SAT verbal score	543

No Child Left Behind, 2003-04
Attendence rate (target = 90%)	95.5%
Drop rate	0.5%
Highly-qualified teachers	96.9%
District needs improvement?(AYP)	No

Municipal Finance

Fiscal Year 2005
Total tax levy	$19,856,269
County levy	3,730,402
County taxes	3,403,163
County library	0
County health	0
County open space	327,239
School levy	10,849,473
Local muni. budget	5,276,394
Misc. revenues	2,819,609
Total aid	$1,023,721
CMPTRA	478,695
Muni. block grant	25,370
Energy tax receipts	469,656
Homeland security	50,000

Fiscal Year 2006
Total aid	$1,023,721
CMPTRA	462,257
Muni. block grant	25,370
Energy tax receipts	486,094
Homeland security	50,000

Taxes
	2003	2004	2005
General tax rate per $100	2.88	3.260	1.760
Net valuation taxable	$569,382,528	$572,357,098	$1,130,418,017
State equalized value	$970,317,873	$1,048,865,816	$1,157,740,697
County equalization ratio	72.46	58.68	104.86

Demographics & Socio-Economic Characteristics
(2000 U.S. Census, except as noted)

Population
1980*	8,292
1990*	15,616
2000	19,809
Male	9,606
Female	10,203
2004 (estimate)*	22,362
Persons per sq. mi. of land	591

Race & Hispanic Origin, 2000
Race
White	18,466
Black/African American	244
Amer. Indian/Alaska Natv.	17
Asian	693
Natv. Hawaiian/Pac. Islander	2
Other Race	135
Two or more races	252
Hispanic origin, total	552
Mexican	86
Puerto Rican	173
Cuban	80
Other Hispanic	213

Age & Nativity, 2000
Under 5 years	1,431
18 years and over	14,010
21 years and over	13,570
65 years and over	1,770
85 years and over	251
Median Age	37.4
Native born	18,188
Foreign born	1,621

Educational Attainment, 2000
Population 25 years and over	13,086
0-8 yrs of school	1.8%
High School grad or higher	94.3%
Bachelor's degree or higher	48.3%
Graduate degree	17.7%

Income & Poverty, 1999
Per capita income	$38,919
Median household income	$85,996
Median family income	$96,336
Persons in poverty	399
H'holds receiving public assistance	69
H'holds receiving social security	1,169

Households, 2000
Total households	6,939
With persons under 18	3,083
With persons over 65	1,167
Family households	5,389
One-person households	1,263
Persons per household	2.81
Persons per family	3.24

Labor & Employment
Total civilian labor force, 2004**	10,669
Unemployment rate	2.9%
Total civilian labor force, 2000	10,655
Unemployment rate	1.4%

Employed persons 16 years and over by occupation, 2000
Managers & professionals	5,508
Service occupations	945
Sales & office occupations	2,628
Farming, fishing & forestry	17
Construction & maintenance	686
Production & transportation	717
Self-employed persons	811

*US Census Bureau
**New Jersey Department of Labor

General Information
Township of Raritan
1 Municipal Dr
Flemington, NJ 08822
908-806-6100
Web site	www.raritan-township.com
Land area (sq. miles)	37.84
Water area (sq. miles)	0.07
Type of government	Township
Form of government	TC

Government
Legislative Districts
US Congressional	7
State Legislative	23

Local Officials, 2006
Mayor	Peter Kinsella
Admin/Manager	Allan Pietrefesa
Clerk	Dorothy Gooditis
Finance Dir/Treas	Allan Pietrefesa
Engineer	Frederick Coppola
Attorney	John Belardo
Tax assessor	Richard Vinchur
Tax collector	Nancy Spooner
Building officer	Peter Ball
Zoning officer	NA
Public Works	Dirk Struening

Housing & Construction
Housing Units, 2000*
Total	7,094
Median rent	$971
Median SF home value	$248,300

New Privately Owned Housing Units
Authorized by Building Permit
	Units	Value
Total, 2004	171	$25,013,514
Single family	150	$23,235,814
Total, 2005	75	$16,432,611
Single family	75	$16,432,611

Real Property Valuation - parcels, 2005
	Number	Valuation
Total		$2,190,406,500
Vacant	781	58,921,800
Residential	7,508	1,772,932,500
Commercial	237	246,015,300
Industrial	27	58,902,300
Apartments	3	6,112,000
Farm land	158	38,560,100
Farm homestead	295	8,962,500

Average Property Value & Tax, 2005
Residential value	$228,360
Property tax	$7,328
FAIR rebate	$489

Public Library
Hunterdon County Library
314 State Route 12
Flemington, NJ 08822
908-788-1444
Director	Janet Friend

Library statistics, 2004
	Total	per capita
Volumes	NA	NA
Expenditure	NA	NA

Public Safety
Police
Chief	Frederick Brown
Number of officers, 2004	36

Crime, 2004	Number	Rate
Total	245	11.3
Violent	8	0.4
Non-violent	237	10.9
Domestic Viol.	155	NA

Emergency/Fire
Director	Mark Bishop

Public School District
(for school year 2004-2005 except as noted)

Flemington-Raritan Regional School Dist.
50 Court St
Flemington, NJ 08822
908-284-7561
Superintendent	Jack Farr
Grade plan	K-8
Enrollment	3,555.0
Students per teacher	11.4
Per pupil expenditure	$11,042
Median faculty salary	$47,520
Median administrator salary	$100,477
Grade 12 enrollment	NA
High school graduation rate	NA

Assessment test results
(percent scoring at proficient or advanced level)
	Language	Math
Grade 3	92.2%	91.6%
Grade 8	88.3%	78.1%
High school	NA	NA

SAT
Percent tested	NA
Average SAT math score	NA
Average SAT verbal score	NA

No Child Left Behind, 2003-04
Attendence rate (target = 90%)	96.2%
Drop rate	NA
Highly-qualified teachers	100%
District needs improvement?(AYP)	No

Municipal Finance
Fiscal Year 2005
Total tax levy	$70,452,982
County levy	14,221,715
County taxes	12,075,055
County library	1,010,379
County health	0
County open space	1,136,281
School levy	49,490,762
Local muni. budget	6,740,506
Misc. revenues	9,647,090
Total aid	$2,985,210
CMPTRA	702,016
Muni. block grant	77,672
Energy tax receipts	2,115,522
Homeland security	90,000

Fiscal Year 2006
Total aid	$2,985,211
CMPTRA	627,973
Muni. block grant	77,672
Energy tax receipts	2,189,566
Homeland security	90,000

Taxes
	2003	2004	2005
General tax rate per $100	2.99	3.100	3.210
Net valuation taxable	$2,015,064,653	$2,090,438,349	$2,195,501,325
State equalized value	$2,806,496,731	$3,185,655,249	$3,611,615,932
County equalization ratio	66.98	64.34	58.25

Demographics & Socio-Economic Characteristics
(2000 U.S. Census, except as noted)

Population
1980*	10,855
1990*	13,400
2000	15,803
Male	7,782
Female	8,021
2004 (estimate)*	16,401
Persons per sq. mi. of land	344

Race & Hispanic Origin, 2000
Race
White	15,035
Black/African American	120
Amer. Indian/Alaska Natv.	10
Asian	405
Natv. Hawaiian/Pac. Islander	0
Other Race	84
Two or more races	149
Hispanic origin, total	324
Mexican	34
Puerto Rican	103
Cuban	35
Other Hispanic	152

Age & Nativity, 2000
Under 5 years	1,171
18 years and over	11,618
21 years and over	11,279
65 years and over	1,542
85 years and over	147
Median Age	39
Native born	14,684
Foreign born	1,119

Educational Attainment, 2000
Population 25 years and over	10,767
0-8 yrs of school	1.4%
High School grad or higher	94.6%
Bachelor's degree or higher	48.2%
Graduate degree	18.8%

Income & Poverty, 1999
Per capita income	$41,000
Median household income	$95,356
Median family income	$106,343
Persons in poverty	255
H'holds receiving public assistance	72
H'holds receiving social security	1,174

Households, 2000
Total households	5,676
With persons under 18	2,221
With persons over 65	1,137
Family households	4,413
One-person households	1,032
Persons per household	2.77
Persons per family	3.18

Labor & Employment
Total civilian labor force, 2004**	9,309
Unemployment rate	3.1%
Total civilian labor force, 2000	8,784
Unemployment rate	2.3%

Employed persons 16 years and over by occupation, 2000
Managers & professionals	4,476
Service occupations	565
Sales & office occupations	2,320
Farming, fishing & forestry	17
Construction & maintenance	532
Production & transportation	676
Self-employed persons	517

*US Census Bureau
**New Jersey Department of Labor

General Information
Township of Readington
509 Route 523
Whitehouse Station, NJ 08889
908-534-4051
Web site . . . www.township.readington.nj.us	
Land area (sq. miles)	47.69
Water area (sq. miles)	0.12
Type of government	Township
Form of government	TC

Government
Legislative Districts
US Congressional	7
State Legislative	23

Local Officials, 2006
Mayor	Gerard Shamey
Admin/Manager	Vita Mekovetz
Clerk	Vita Mekovetz
Finance Dir/Treas	Vita Mekovetz
Engineer	Clay McEldowney
Attorney	Sharon Dragan
Tax assessor	Mary Mastro
Tax collector	Bonnie Holborow
Building officer	Michael Kovonuk
Zoning officer	John Barczyk
Public Works	Scott Jesseman

Housing & Construction
Housing Units, 2000*
Total	5,794
Median rent	$937
Median SF home value	$289,700

New Privately Owned Housing Units Authorized by Building Permit
	Units	Value
Total, 2004	28	$7,472,338
Single family	28	$7,472,338
Total, 2005	20	$5,127,243
Single family	20	$5,127,243

Real Property Valuation - parcels, 2005
	Number	Valuation
Total		$2,790,405,629
Vacant	266	39,301,400
Residential	5,506	2,105,634,700
Commercial	250	486,627,050
Industrial	15	23,027,200
Apartments	4	2,067,600
Farm land	318	129,024,400
Farm homestead	496	4,723,279

Average Property Value & Tax, 2005
Residential value	$351,609
Property tax	$7,736
FAIR rebate	$530

Public Library
Readington Township Library†
105 Route 523
Whitehouse Station, NJ 08889
908-534-4421
Branch Librarian	Karen Konn

Library statistics, 2004
	Total	per capita
Volumes	NA	NA
Expenditure	NA	NA

†Branch of County Library

Public Safety
Police
Chief	James Paganessi
Number of officers, 2004	24

Crime, 2004	Number	Rate
Total	177	10.8
Violent	10	0.6
Non-violent	167	10.2
Domestic Viol.	76	NA

Emergency/Fire
Director	NA

Public School District
(for school year 2004-2005 except as noted)

Readington Township School District
PO Box 807
Whitehouse Station, NJ 08889
908-534-2195
Superintendent	James Sheerin (Int)
Grade plan	K-8
Enrollment	2,241.0
Students per teacher	11.1
Per pupil expenditure	$11,228
Median faculty salary	$47,752
Median administrator salary	$106,300
Grade 12 enrollment	NA
High school graduation rate	NA

Assessment test results
(percent scoring at proficient or advanced level)
	Language	Math
Grade 3	91.5%	90.2%
Grade 8	89.6%	88.0%
High school	NA	NA

SAT
Percent tested	NA
Average SAT math score	NA
Average SAT verbal score	NA

No Child Left Behind, 2003-04
Attendence rate (target = 90%)	96.2%
Drop rate	NA
Highly-qualified teachers	99.5%
District needs improvement?(AYP)	No

Municipal Finance
Fiscal Year 2005
Total tax levy	$61,520,718
County levy	12,151,625
County taxes	10,317,419
County library	863,310
County health	0
County open space	970,896
School levy	39,818,641
Local muni. budget	9,550,451
Misc. revenues	6,116,428
Total aid	$2,019,541
CMPTRA	483,421
Muni. block grant	61,964
Energy tax receipts	1,404,156
Homeland security	70,000

Fiscal Year 2006
Total aid	$2,019,541
CMPTRA	434,276
Muni. block grant	61,964
Energy tax receipts	1,453,301
Homeland security	70,000

Taxes
	2003	2004	2005
General tax rate per $100	1.96	2.070	2.210
Net valuation taxable	$2,772,401,241	$2,791,395,384	$2,796,354,190
State equalized value	$2,640,130,693	$2,916,534,287	$3,282,105,857
County equalization ratio	99.14	95.74	86.62

Demographics & Socio-Economic Characteristics
(2000 U.S. Census, except as noted)

Population
1980*	12,031
1990*	10,636
2000	11,844
Male	5,670
Female	6,174
2004 (estimate)*	11,940
Persons per sq. mi. of land	6,693

Race & Hispanic Origin, 2000
Race
White	8,077
Black/African American	2,375
Amer. Indian/Alaska Natv.	41
Asian	259
Natv. Hawaiian/Pac. Islander	10
Other Race	797
Two or more races	285
Hispanic origin, total	2,027
Mexican	1,171
Puerto Rican	296
Cuban	24
Other Hispanic	536

Age & Nativity, 2000
Under 5 years	682
18 years and over	9,770
21 years and over	9,376
65 years and over	2,173
85 years and over	479
Median Age	37.5
Native born	10,073
Foreign born	1,771

Educational Attainment, 2000
Population 25 years and over	8,737
0-8 yrs of school	8.7%
High School grad or higher	81.6%
Bachelor's degree or higher	31.9%
Graduate degree	10.6%

Income & Poverty, 1999
Per capita income	$26,265
Median household income	$47,282
Median family income	$63,333
Persons in poverty	1,363
H'holds receiving public assistance	89
H'holds receiving social security	1,582

Households, 2000
Total households	5,201
With persons under 18	1,126
With persons over 65	1,478
Family households	2,504
One-person households	2,233
Persons per household	2.2
Persons per family	2.99

Labor & Employment
Total civilian labor force, 2004**	6,369
Unemployment rate	5.2%
Total civilian labor force, 2000	6,354
Unemployment rate	5.7%

Employed persons 16 years and over by occupation, 2000
Managers & professionals	2,194
Service occupations	1,166
Sales & office occupations	1,788
Farming, fishing & forestry	10
Construction & maintenance	388
Production & transportation	444
Self-employed persons	333

*US Census Bureau
**New Jersey Department of Labor

General Information
Borough of Red Bank
90 Monmouth St
Red Bank, NJ 07701
732-530-2740
Web site	www.redbanknj.org
Land area (sq. miles)	1.78
Water area (sq. miles)	0.37
Type of government	Borough
Form of government	B

Government
Legislative Districts
US Congressional	6
State Legislative	12

Local Officials, 2006
Mayor	Edward McKenna Jr.
Admin/Manager	Stanley Sickels
Clerk	Carol Vivona
Finance Dir/Treas	Terence Whalen
Engineer	Richard Kosenski
Attorney	Kenneth Pringle
Tax assessor	Mitchell Ellias
Tax collector	Terence Whalen
Building officer	James Williams
Zoning officer	Donna Barr
Public Works	Gary Watson

Housing & Construction
Housing Units, 2000*
Total	5,450
Median rent	$813
Median SF home value	$178,900

New Privately Owned Housing Units
Authorized by Building Permit
	Units	Value
Total, 2004	32	$5,324,226
Single family	32	$5,324,226
Total, 2005	3	$243,540
Single family	3	$243,540

Real Property Valuation - parcels, 2005
	Number	Valuation
Total		$959,795,000
Vacant	129	12,932,100
Residential	3,343	595,638,800
Commercial	491	256,379,900
Industrial	58	23,662,400
Apartments	27	71,181,800
Farm land	0	0
Farm homestead	0	0

Average Property Value & Tax, 2005
Residential value	$178,175
Property tax	$5,742
FAIR rebate	$538

Public Library
Red Bank Public Library
84 West Front St
Red Bank, NJ 07701
732-842-0690
Director .... Deborah Griffin-Sadel

Library statistics, 2004
	Total	per capita
Volumes	47,092	3.98
Expenditure	$649,977	$54.88

Public Safety
Police
Chief	Mark Fitzgerald
Number of officers, 2004	39

Crime, 2004	Number	Rate
Total	329	27.9
Violent	43	3.6
Non-violent	286	24.3
Domestic Viol.	143	NA

Emergency/Fire
Director .... Larry Brooks

Public School District
(for school year 2004-2005 except as noted)

Red Bank School District
76 Branch Ave
Red Bank, NJ 07701
732-758-1507
Superintendent	Robert Mahon (Int)
Grade plan	K-8
Enrollment	793.0
Students per teacher	9.2
Per pupil expenditure	$12,442
Median faculty salary	$43,190
Median administrator salary	$95,790
Grade 12 enrollment	NA
High school graduation rate	NA

Assessment test results
(percent scoring at proficient or advanced level)
	Language	Math
Grade 3	76.8%	89.8%
Grade 8	57.7%	62.0%
High school	NA	NA

SAT
Percent tested	NA
Average SAT math score	NA
Average SAT verbal score	NA

No Child Left Behind, 2003-04
Attendence rate (target = 90%)	94.7%
Drop rate	NA
Highly-qualified teachers	97.2%
District needs improvement?(AYP)	No

Municipal Finance
Fiscal Year 2005
Total tax levy	$31,103,886
County levy	5,028,964
County taxes	4,747,257
County library	0
County health	0
County open space	281,707
School levy	18,433,394
Local muni. budget	7,641,528
Misc. revenues	8,132,859
Total aid	$2,718,510
CMPTRA	723,561
Muni. block grant	46,540
Energy tax receipts	1,878,409
Homeland security	70,000

Fiscal Year 2006
Total aid	$2,718,510
CMPTRA	657,817
Muni. block grant	46,540
Energy tax receipts	1,944,153
Homeland security	70,000

Taxes
	2003	2004	2005
General tax rate per $100	2.97	3.076	3.223
Net valuation taxable	$956,668,706	$963,776,234	$965,104,265
State equalized value	$1,309,070,479	$1,570,202,760	$1,913,370,866
County equalization ratio	81.07	73.08	61.22

Demographics & Socio-Economic Characteristics
(2000 U.S. Census, except as noted)

Population
1980*	10,294
1990*	9,996
2000	10,830
Male	5,240
Female	5,590
2004 (estimate)*	11,005
Persons per sq. mi. of land	4,217

Race & Hispanic Origin, 2000
Race
White	8,217
Black/African American	83
Amer. Indian/Alaska Natv.	9
Asian	1,887
Natv. Hawaiian/Pac. Islander	4
Other Race	379
Two or more races	251
Hispanic origin, total	1,494
Mexican	30
Puerto Rican	244
Cuban	361
Other Hispanic	859

Age & Nativity, 2000
Under 5 years	567
18 years and over	8,465
21 years and over	8,192
65 years and over	1,853
85 years and over	230
Median Age	39.5
Native born	7,184
Foreign born	3,646

Educational Attainment, 2000
Population 25 years and over	7,737
0-8 yrs of school	7.3%
High School grad or higher	78.8%
Bachelor's degree or higher	26.0%
Graduate degree	6.7%

Income & Poverty, 1999
Per capita income	$25,558
Median household income	$54,081
Median family income	$66,330
Persons in poverty	709
H'holds receiving public assistance	88
H'holds receiving social security	1,356

Households, 2000
Total households	4,020
With persons under 18	1,385
With persons over 65	1,367
Family households	2,967
One-person households	925
Persons per household	2.69
Persons per family	3.19

Labor & Employment
Total civilian labor force, 2004**	5,693
Unemployment rate	3.4%
Total civilian labor force, 2000	5,162
Unemployment rate	3.6%

Employed persons 16 years and over by occupation, 2000
Managers & professionals	1,787
Service occupations	770
Sales & office occupations	1,353
Farming, fishing & forestry	0
Construction & maintenance	480
Production & transportation	585
Self-employed persons	308

*US Census Bureau
**New Jersey Department of Labor

General Information
Borough of Ridgefield
604 Broad Ave
Ridgefield, NJ 07657
201-943-5215
Web site	ridgefieldboro.com
Land area (sq. miles)	2.61
Water area (sq. miles)	0.26
Type of government	Borough
Form of government	B

Government

Legislative Districts
US Congressional	9
State Legislative	38

Local Officials, 2006
Mayor	Anthony Suarez
Admin/Manager	Roberta Stern
Clerk	Stewart Veale
Finance Dir/Treas	Joseph Iannaconi Jr.
Engineer	Schoor DePalma
Attorney	Stephen Pellino
Tax assessor	George Reggo
Tax collector	Frank Berardo
Building officer	Armand Marini III
Zoning officer	James Russell
Public Works	Nick Gambardella

Housing & Construction

Housing Units, 2000*
Total	4,120
Median rent	$903
Median SF home value	$239,100

New Privately Owned Housing Units Authorized by Building Permit
	Units	Value
Total, 2004	32	$4,871,758
Single family	10	$1,735,358
Total, 2005	24	$4,242,502
Single family	16	$3,060,448

Real Property Valuation - parcels, 2005
	Number	Valuation
Total		$1,852,790,500
Vacant	99	67,089,500
Residential	2,498	1,242,774,600
Commercial	211	243,342,100
Industrial	87	232,995,500
Apartments	14	66,588,800
Farm land	0	0
Farm homestead	0	0

Average Property Value & Tax, 2005
Residential value	$497,508
Property tax	$5,788
FAIR rebate	$687

Public Library
Ridgefield Public Library
527 Morse Ave
Ridgefield, NJ 07657
201-941-0192
Director	Jane Forte

Library statistics, 2004
	Total	per capita
Volumes	44,547	4.11
Expenditure	$401,955	$37.11

Public Safety

Police
Chief	John Bogovich
Number of officers, 2004	29

Crime, 2004	Number	Rate
Total	110	10.1
Violent	9	0.8
Non-violent	101	9.2
Domestic Viol.	56	NA

Emergency/Fire
Director	Michael Kees

Public School District
(for school year 2004-2005 except as noted)

Ridgefield School District
555 Chestnut St
Ridgefield, NJ 07657
201-945-9236
Superintendent	Richard Brockel
Grade plan	K-12
Enrollment	1,948.5
Students per teacher	10.1
Per pupil expenditure	$12,641
Median faculty salary	$48,324
Median administrator salary	$95,010
Grade 12 enrollment	124.5
High school graduation rate	97.8%

Assessment test results
(percent scoring at proficient or advanced level)
	Language	Math
Grade 3	88.9%	86.5%
Grade 8	73.9%	70.0%
High school	83.4%	79.6%

SAT
Percent tested	80%
Average SAT math score	572
Average SAT verbal score	497

No Child Left Behind, 2003-04
Attendence rate (target = 90%)	94.8%
Drop rate	0.8%
Highly-qualified teachers	93.5%
District needs improvement?(AYP)	No

Municipal Finance

Fiscal Year 2005
Total tax levy	$21,570,991
County levy	3,153,371
County taxes	2,995,107
County library	0
County health	0
County open space	158,264
School levy	10,924,449
Local muni. budget	7,493,171
Misc. revenues	9,803,270
Total aid	$6,009,397
CMPTRA	170,903
Muni. block grant	43,739
Energy tax receipts	5,724,755
Homeland security	70,000

Fiscal Year 2006
Total aid	$6,038,860
CMPTRA	0
Muni. block grant	43,739
Energy tax receipts	5,925,121
Homeland security	70,000

Taxes
	2003	2004	2005
General tax rate per $100	1.90	2.170	1.170
Net valuation taxable	$807,854,885	$808,053,433	$1,854,169,156
State equalized value	$1,408,885,394	$1,556,185,263	$1,708,439,285
County equalization ratio	69.09	57.34	118.43

Demographics & Socio-Economic Characteristics
(2000 U.S. Census, except as noted)

Population
1980*	12,738
1990*	12,454
2000	12,873
Male	6,150
Female	6,723
2004 (estimate)*	12,822
Persons per sq. mi. of land	7,406

Race & Hispanic Origin, 2000
Race
White	10,067
Black/African American	528
Amer. Indian/Alaska Natv.	28
Asian	1,011
Natv. Hawaiian/Pac. Islander	4
Other Race	837
Two or more races	398
Hispanic origin, total	2,863
Mexican	64
Puerto Rican	491
Cuban	513
Other Hispanic	1,795

Age & Nativity, 2000
Under 5 years	755
18 years and over	9,995
21 years and over	9,615
65 years and over	1,655
85 years and over	163
Median Age	37.2
Native born	9,792
Foreign born	3,081

Educational Attainment, 2000
Population 25 years and over	9,024
0-8 yrs of school	5.1%
High School grad or higher	85.1%
Bachelor's degree or higher	26.1%
Graduate degree	8.3%

Income & Poverty, 1999
Per capita income	$24,290
Median household income	$51,825
Median family income	$62,414
Persons in poverty	865
H'holds receiving public assistance	83
H'holds receiving social security	1,280

Households, 2000
Total households	5,012
With persons under 18	1,588
With persons over 65	1,263
Family households	3,243
One-person households	1,484
Persons per household	2.56
Persons per family	3.24

Labor & Employment
Total civilian labor force, 2004**	7,685
Unemployment rate	4.2%
Total civilian labor force, 2000	6,852
Unemployment rate	4.1%

Employed persons 16 years and over by occupation, 2000
Managers & professionals	2,115
Service occupations	848
Sales & office occupations	2,290
Farming, fishing & forestry	0
Construction & maintenance	517
Production & transportation	801
Self-employed persons	253

*US Census Bureau
**New Jersey Department of Labor

General Information
Village of Ridgefield Park
234 Main St
Ridgefield Park, NJ 07660
201-641-4950
Web site	www.ci.ridgefield-park.nj.us
Land area (sq. miles)	1.73
Water area (sq. miles)	0.19
Type of government	Village
Form of government	Comm.

Government

Legislative Districts
US Congressional	9
State Legislative	37

Local Officials, 2006
Mayor	George Fosdick
Admin/Manager	NA
Clerk	Sarah Warlikowski
Finance Dir/Treas	D. Heck/P. Hansen
Engineer	Boswell Engineering
Attorney	Martin Durkin
Tax assessor	Paul Barbire
Tax collector	NA
Building officer	Douglas Hansen
Zoning officer	James Russell
Public Works	Alan O'Grady

Housing & Construction

Housing Units, 2000*
Total	5,134
Median rent	$848
Median SF home value	$171,300

New Privately Owned Housing Units Authorized by Building Permit
	Units	Value
Total, 2004	0	$0
Single family	0	$0
Total, 2005	1	$159,000
Single family	1	$159,000

Real Property Valuation - parcels, 2005
	Number	Valuation
Total		$867,005,650
Vacant	57	22,153,600
Residential	2,822	550,464,800
Commercial	167	191,625,950
Industrial	38	32,328,400
Apartments	43	70,432,900
Farm land	0	0
Farm homestead	0	0

Average Property Value & Tax, 2005
Residential value	$195,062
Property tax	$7,186
FAIR rebate	$599

Public Library
Ridgefield Park Public Library
107 Cedar St
Ridgefield Pk, NJ 07660
201-641-0689
Director .... Eileen Mackesy-Karpoff

Library statistics, 2004
	Total	per capita
Volumes	56,296	4.37
Expenditure	$526,720	$40.92

Public Safety

Police
Chief	Dieter Ahrlich
Number of officers, 2004	29

Crime, 2004	Number	Rate
Total	168	13.1
Violent	12	0.9
Non-violent	156	12.2
Domestic Viol.	40	NA

Emergency/Fire
Director	Stephen Dembski

Public School District
(for school year 2004-2005 except as noted)

Ridgefield Park School District
712 Lincoln Ave
Ridgefield Park, NJ 07660
201-807-2638
Superintendent	John Richardson
Grade plan	K-12
Enrollment	1,928.0
Students per teacher	10.4
Per pupil expenditure	$12,244
Median faculty salary	$50,561
Median administrator salary	$105,250
Grade 12 enrollment	168.0
High school graduation rate	94.9%

Assessment test results
(percent scoring at proficient or advanced level)
	Language	Math
Grade 3	94.9%	94.9%
Grade 8	76.4%	64.4%
High school	89.7%	75.5%

SAT
Percent tested	82%
Average SAT math score	471
Average SAT verbal score	454

No Child Left Behind, 2003-04
Attendence rate (target = 90%)	95.2%
Drop rate	1.6%
Highly-qualified teachers	100%
District needs improvement?(AYP)	No

Municipal Finance

Fiscal Year 2005
Total tax levy	$31,977,082
County levy	2,461,885
County taxes	2,338,098
County library	0
County health	0
County open space	123,787
School levy	18,911,564
Local muni. budget	10,603,633
Misc. revenues	4,307,443
Total aid	$1,634,246
CMPTRA	726,573
Muni. block grant	54,494
Energy tax receipts	783,179
Homeland security	70,000

Fiscal Year 2006
Total aid	$1,634,245
CMPTRA	699,161
Muni. block grant	54,494
Energy tax receipts	810,590
Homeland security	70,000

Taxes
	2003	2004	2005
General tax rate per $100	3.08	3.350	3.690
Net valuation taxable	$892,771,899	$885,270,499	$867,961,464
State equalized value	$1,085,965,088	$1,255,121,330	$1,401,972,967
County equalization ratio	95.37	82.21	70.50

Demographics & Socio-Economic Characteristics
(2000 U.S. Census, except as noted)

Population

1980*	25,208
1990*	24,152
2000	24,936
Male	12,002
Female	12,934
2004 (estimate)*	24,916
Persons per sq. mi. of land	4,306

Race & Hispanic Origin, 2000
Race

White	21,899
Black/African American	409
Amer. Indian/Alaska Natv.	11
Asian	2,162
Natv. Hawaiian/Pac. Islander	0
Other Race	148
Two or more races	307
Hispanic origin, total	942
Mexican	110
Puerto Rican	173
Cuban	134
Other Hispanic	525

Age & Nativity, 2000

Under 5 years	1,938
18 years and over	17,461
21 years and over	16,918
65 years and over	3,031
85 years and over	418
Median Age	38.6
Native born	20,931
Foreign born	4,005

Educational Attainment, 2000

Population 25 years and over	16,407
0-8 yrs of school	1.8%
High School grad or higher	95.9%
Bachelor's degree or higher	66.7%
Graduate degree	29.0%

Income & Poverty, 1999

Per capita income	$51,658
Median household income	$104,286
Median family income	$121,848
Persons in poverty	741
H'holds receiving public assistance	112
H'holds receiving social security	2,091

Households, 2000

Total households	8,603
With persons under 18	3,910
With persons over 65	2,101
Family households	6,777
One-person households	1,592
Persons per household	2.87
Persons per family	3.3

Labor & Employment

Total civilian labor force, 2004**	13,033
Unemployment rate	2.8%
Total civilian labor force, 2000	11,791
Unemployment rate	3.1%

Employed persons 16 years and over by occupation, 2000

Managers & professionals	7,029
Service occupations	755
Sales & office occupations	2,973
Farming, fishing & forestry	0
Construction & maintenance	379
Production & transportation	290
Self-employed persons	965

*US Census Bureau
**New Jersey Department of Labor

General Information

Village of Ridgewood
131 N Maple Ave
Ridgewood, NJ 07451
201-670-5500

Web site	ridgewoodnj.net
Land area (sq. miles)	5.79
Water area (sq. miles)	0.05
Type of government	Village
Form of government	CM '50

Government

Legislative Districts

US Congressional	5
State Legislative	40

Local Officials, 2006

Mayor	David Pfund
Admin/Manager	James Ten Hoeve
Clerk	Heather Mailander
Finance Dir/Treas	S. Sanzari/D. Stikna
Engineer	Christopher Rutishauser
Attorney	(Vacant)
Tax assessor	Michael Barker
Tax collector	Mary Jo Gilmour
Building officer	Anthony Merlino
Zoning officer	Anthony Merlino
Public Works	Christopher Rutishauser

Housing & Construction

Housing Units, 2000*

Total	8,802
Median rent	$1,220
Median SF home value	$387,200

New Privately Owned Housing Units
Authorized by Building Permit

	Units	Value
Total, 2004	17	$6,457,787
Single family	15	$6,148,787
Total, 2005	13	$4,240,857
Single family	13	$4,240,857

Real Property Valuation - parcels, 2005

	Number	Valuation
Total		$3,896,269,100
Vacant	99	12,207,800
Residential	7,438	3,477,133,000
Commercial	326	347,364,700
Industrial	0	0
Apartments	27	59,563,600
Farm land	0	0
Farm homestead	0	0

Average Property Value & Tax, 2005

Residential value	$467,482
Property tax	$11,966
FAIR rebate	$578

Public Library

Ridgewood Public Library
125 North Maple Ave
Ridgewood, NJ 07450
201-670-5600

Director .... Nancy Greene

Library statistics, 2004

	Total	per capita
Volumes	130,394	5.23
Expenditure	$2,116,166	$84.86

Public Safety

Police

Chief	William Corcoran
Number of officers, 2004	46

Crime, 2004	Number	Rate
Total	212	8.5
Violent	6	0.2
Non-violent	206	8.3
Domestic Viol.	102	NA

Emergency/Fire

Director .... James Bombace

Public School District
(for school year 2004-2005 except as noted)

Ridgewood Village School District
49 Cottage Place
Ridgewood, NJ 07451
201-670-2700

Superintendent	John Porter
Grade plan	K-12
Enrollment	5,452.0
Students per teacher	12.2
Per pupil expenditure	$12,183
Median faculty salary	$65,055
Median administrator salary	$116,812
Grade 12 enrollment	377.0
High school graduation rate	96.9%

Assessment test results
(percent scoring at proficient or advanced level)

	Language	Math
Grade 3	96.3%	95.4%
Grade 8	92.1%	90.8%
High school	95.1%	93.8%

SAT

Percent tested	103%
Average SAT math score	597
Average SAT verbal score	571

No Child Left Behind, 2003-04

Attendence rate (target = 90%)	95.8%
Drop rate	0.8%
Highly-qualified teachers	100%
District needs improvement?(AYP)	No

Municipal Finance

Fiscal Year 2005

Total tax levy	$99,882,270
County levy	10,370,928
County taxes	9,852,165
County library	0
County health	0
County open space	518,763
School levy	66,380,039
Local muni. budget	23,131,303
Misc. revenues	12,675,111
Total aid	$2,750,310
CMPTRA	904,160
Muni. block grant	105,682
Energy tax receipts	1,650,468
Homeland security	90,000

Fiscal Year 2006

Total aid	$2,750,309
CMPTRA	846,393
Muni. block grant	105,682
Energy tax receipts	1,708,234
Homeland security	90,000

Taxes

	2003	2004	2005
General tax rate per $100	2.34	2.460	2.560
Net valuation taxable	$3,863,576,558	$3,881,555,577	$3,902,027,619
State equalized value	$4,703,075,542	$5,149,927,784	$5,761,151,069
County equalization ratio	91	82.15	75.34

Demographics & Socio-Economic Characteristics
(2000 U.S. Census, except as noted)

Population
1980*	12,625
1990*	12,623
2000	12,396
Male	6,201
Female	6,195
2004 (estimate)*	12,769
Persons per sq. mi. of land	506

Race & Hispanic Origin, 2000
Race
White	11,636
Black/African American	199
Amer. Indian/Alaska Natv.	179
Asian	148
Natv. Hawaiian/Pac. Islander	1
Other Race	83
Two or more races	150
Hispanic origin, total	527
Mexican	40
Puerto Rican	195
Cuban	61
Other Hispanic	231

Age & Nativity, 2000
Under 5 years	935
18 years and over	8,978
21 years and over	8,638
65 years and over	982
85 years and over	98
Median Age	37.4
Native born	11,322
Foreign born	1,074

Educational Attainment, 2000
Population 25 years and over	8,192
0-8 yrs of school	1.1%
High School grad or higher	91.5%
Bachelor's degree or higher	39.2%
Graduate degree	11.7%

Income & Poverty, 1999
Per capita income	$31,341
Median household income	$81,636
Median family income	$85,108
Persons in poverty	342
H'holds receiving public assistance	23
H'holds receiving social security	759

Households, 2000
Total households	4,108
With persons under 18	1,832
With persons over 65	691
Family households	3,446
One-person households	496
Persons per household	3.0
Persons per family	3.28

Labor & Employment
Total civilian labor force, 2004**	7,454
Unemployment rate	4.6%
Total civilian labor force, 2000	6,877
Unemployment rate	3.8%

Employed persons 16 years and over by occupation, 2000
Managers & professionals	2,950
Service occupations	544
Sales & office occupations	1,878
Farming, fishing & forestry	0
Construction & maintenance	715
Production & transportation	531
Self-employed persons	500

*US Census Bureau
**New Jersey Department of Labor

General Information
Borough of Ringwood
60 Margaret King Ave
Ringwood, NJ 07456
973-962-7037
Web site	www.ringwoodnj.net
Land area (sq. miles)	25.25
Water area (sq. miles)	2.78
Type of government	Borough
Form of government	Faulkner Plan E

Government
Legislative Districts
US Congressional	5
State Legislative	40

Local Officials, 2006
Mayor	Joanne Atlas
Admin/Manager	Kenneth L. Hetrick
Clerk	Kelley Rohde
Finance Dir/Treas	Gail Bado
Engineer	Edward Haack
Attorney	Joseph J. Maraziti Jr.
Tax assessor	Richard Motyka
Tax collector	NA
Building officer	William Fleck
Zoning officer	NA
Public Works	Willard Bierwas

Housing & Construction
Housing Units, 2000*
Total	4,221
Median rent	$1,137
Median SF home value	$193,400

New Privately Owned Housing Units
Authorized by Building Permit
	Units	Value
Total, 2004	42	$8,121,409
Single family	42	$8,121,409
Total, 2005	33	$7,133,527
Single family	33	$7,133,527

Real Property Valuation - parcels, 2005
	Number	Valuation
Total		$857,200,190
Vacant	333	43,162,200
Residential	4,263	766,121,860
Commercial	49	28,564,000
Industrial	22	16,224,300
Apartments	0	0
Farm land	14	2,987,500
Farm homestead	45	140,330

Average Property Value & Tax, 2005
Residential value	$177,870
Property tax	$7,679
FAIR rebate	$498

Public Library
Ringwood Public Library
30 Cannici Dr
Ringwood, NJ 07456
973-962-6256
Director	Andrea Cahoon

Library statistics, 2004
	Total	per capita
Volumes	51,480	4.15
Expenditure	$580,695	$46.85

Public Safety
Police
Chief	Bernard Lombardo
Number of officers, 2004	23

Crime, 2004	Number	Rate
Total	87	6.8
Violent	9	0.7
Non-violent	78	6.1
Domestic Viol.	61	NA

Emergency/Fire
Director	NA

Public School District
(for school year 2004-2005 except as noted)

Ringwood School District
121 Carletondale Rd
Ringwood, NJ 07456
973-962-7028
Administrator	Patrick Martin
Grade plan	K-8
Enrollment	1,419.0
Students per teacher	12.3
Per pupil expenditure	$11,972
Median faculty salary	$60,537
Median administrator salary	$95,242
Grade 12 enrollment	NA
High school graduation rate	NA

Assessment test results
(percent scoring at proficient or advanced level)
	Language	Math
Grade 3	92.7%	87.2%
Grade 8	82.4%	76.1%
High school	NA	NA

SAT
Percent tested	NA
Average SAT math score	NA
Average SAT verbal score	NA

No Child Left Behind, 2003-04
Attendance rate (target = 90%)	95.2%
Drop rate	NA
Highly-qualified teachers?	99.2%
District needs improvement?(AYP)	No

Municipal Finance
Fiscal Year 2005
Total tax levy	$37,070,031
County levy	8,019,021
County taxes	7,866,356
County library	0
County health	0
County open space	152,666
School levy	21,739,612
Local muni. budget	7,311,397
Misc. revenues	6,104,985
Total aid	$2,192,927
CMPTRA	488,471
Muni. block grant	55,234
Energy tax receipts	1,579,222
Homeland security	70,000

Fiscal Year 2006
Total aid	$2,192,927
CMPTRA	433,198
Muni. block grant	55,234
Energy tax receipts	1,634,495
Homeland security	70,000

Taxes
	2003	2004	2005
General tax rate per $100	3.97	4.160	4.320
Net valuation taxable	$827,108,040	$840,316,190	$858,640,051
State equalized value	$1,302,737,502	$1,493,140,322	$1,673,109,998
County equalization ratio	70.78	63.49	56.23

Demographics & Socio-Economic Characteristics

(2000 U.S. Census, except as noted)

Population

1980*	11,111
1990*	10,603
2000	10,946
Male	5,211
Female	5,735
2004 (estimate)*	10,966
Persons per sq. mi. of land	5,815

Race & Hispanic Origin, 2000

Race
White	9,208
Black/African American	116
Amer. Indian/Alaska Natv.	9
Asian	1,379
Natv. Hawaiian/Pac. Islander	1
Other Race	89
Two or more races	144
Hispanic origin, total	581
Mexican	32
Puerto Rican	141
Cuban	113
Other Hispanic	295

Age & Nativity, 2000

Under 5 years	781
18 years and over	8,312
21 years and over	8,075
65 years and over	1,859
85 years and over	265
Median Age	40
Native born	8,602
Foreign born	2,344

Educational Attainment, 2000

Population 25 years and over	7,807
0-8 yrs of school	2.3%
High School grad or higher	93.6%
Bachelor's degree or higher	45.4%
Graduate degree	16.4%

Income & Poverty, 1999

Per capita income	$33,188
Median household income	$71,792
Median family income	$80,422
Persons in poverty	338
H'holds receiving public assistance	65
H'holds receiving social security	1,321

Households, 2000

Total households	4,165
With persons under 18	1,501
With persons over 65	1,331
Family households	3,105
One-person households	947
Persons per household	2.62
Persons per family	3.11

Labor & Employment

Total civilian labor force, 2004**	6,091
Unemployment rate	2.7%
Total civilian labor force, 2000	5,498
Unemployment rate	2.9%

Employed persons 16 years and over by occupation, 2000
Managers & professionals	2,722
Service occupations	467
Sales & office occupations	1,600
Farming, fishing & forestry	0
Construction & maintenance	271
Production & transportation	281
Self-employed persons	298

*US Census Bureau
**New Jersey Department of Labor

General Information

Borough of River Edge
705 Kinderkamack Rd
River Edge, NJ 07661
201-599-6300

Web site	www.riveredgenj.org
Land area (sq. miles)	1.89
Water area (sq. miles)	0.02
Type of government	Borough
Form of government	B

Government

Legislative Districts

US Congressional	9
State Legislative	39

Local Officials, 2006

Mayor	Margaret Watkins
Admin/Manager	Alan Negreann
Clerk	Denise A. Dondiego
Finance Dir/Treas	Alan Negreann
Engineer	Robert Costa
Attorney	William Lindsley
Tax assessor	Frank Bucino
Tax collector	NA
Building officer	Robert Byrnes
Zoning officer	NA
Public Works	NA

Housing & Construction

Housing Units, 2000*

Total	4,210
Median rent	$969
Median SF home value	$252,700

New Privately Owned Housing Units Authorized by Building Permit

	Units	Value
Total, 2004	8	$995,713
Single family	8	$995,713
Total, 2005	13	$3,670,515
Single family	8	$1,490,615

Real Property Valuation - parcels, 2005

	Number	Valuation
Total		$1,611,517,800
Vacant	33	6,710,100
Residential	3,215	1,399,533,700
Commercial	124	121,381,000
Industrial	5	12,836,500
Apartments	15	71,056,500
Farm land	0	0
Farm homestead	0	0

Average Property Value & Tax, 2005

Residential value	$435,314
Property tax	$8,383
FAIR rebate	$609

Public Library

River Edge Free Public Library
675 Elm Ave
River Edge, NJ 07661
201-261-1663

Director...............Daragh O'Connor

Library statistics, 2004

	Total	per capita
Volumes	73,508	6.72
Expenditure	$700,953	$64.04

Public Safety

Police

Chief	Ronald Starace
Number of officers, 2004	22

Crime, 2004	Number	Rate
Total	124	11.3
Violent	7	0.6
Non-violent	117	10.7
Domestic Viol.	65	NA

Emergency/Fire

Director.....................Dave Stucke

Public School District

(for school year 2004-2005 except as noted)

River Edge School District
410 Bogert Rd
River Edge, NJ 07661
201-261-3404

Superintendent	Erica Steinbauer
Grade plan	K-6
Enrollment	1,076.0
Students per teacher	13.1
Per pupil expenditure	$9,179
Median faculty salary	$50,031
Median administrator salary	$109,000
Grade 12 enrollment	NA
High school graduation rate	NA

Assessment test results

(percent scoring at proficient or advanced level)
	Language	Math
Grade 3	94.0%	85.4%
Grade 8	NA	NA
High school	NA	NA

SAT

Percent tested	NA
Average SAT math score	NA
Average SAT verbal score	NA

No Child Left Behind, 2003-04

Attendance rate (target = 90%)	96.5%
Drop rate	NA
Highly-qualified teachers	79.7%
District needs improvement?(AYP)	No

Municipal Finance

Fiscal Year 2005

Total tax levy	$31,177,728
County levy	2,870,539
County taxes	2,726,968
County library	0
County health	0
County open space	143,571
School levy	20,069,368
Local muni. budget	8,237,821
Misc. revenues	4,538,356
Total aid	$1,486,148
CMPTRA	472,614
Muni. block grant	46,396
Energy tax receipts	897,138
Homeland security	70,000

Fiscal Year 2006

Total aid	$1,486,148
CMPTRA	441,214
Muni. block grant	46,396
Energy tax receipts	928,538
Homeland security	70,000

Taxes

	2003	2004	2005
General tax rate per $100	3.36	3.600	1.930
Net valuation taxable	$829,369,971	$831,474,489	$1,619,016,446
State equalized value	$1,265,827,184	$1,424,251,415	$1,619,826,359
County equalization ratio	73.76	65.52	113.06

Demographics & Socio-Economic Characteristics

(2000 U.S. Census, except as noted)

Population

1980*	9,489
1990*	9,410
2000	9,449
Male	4,560
Female	4,889
2004 (estimate)*	9,812
Persons per sq. mi. of land	2,407

Race & Hispanic Origin, 2000

Race

White	8,724
Black/African American	55
Amer. Indian/Alaska Natv.	0
Asian	557
Natv. Hawaiian/Pac. Islander	2
Other Race	41
Two or more races	70
Hispanic origin, total	304
Mexican	14
Puerto Rican	56
Cuban	74
Other Hispanic	160

Age & Nativity, 2000

Under 5 years	654
18 years and over	6,876
21 years and over	6,657
65 years and over	1,263
85 years and over	123
Median Age	40.3
Native born	8,361
Foreign born	1,088

Educational Attainment, 2000

Population 25 years and over	6,454
0-8 yrs of school	1.4%
High School grad or higher	94.3%
Bachelor's degree or higher	48.5%
Graduate degree	18.5%

Income & Poverty, 1999

Per capita income	$40,709
Median household income	$95,129
Median family income	$105,919
Persons in poverty	261
H'holds receiving public assistance	19
H'holds receiving social security	815

Households, 2000

Total households	3,275
With persons under 18	1,372
With persons over 65	866
Family households	2,677
One-person households	503
Persons per household	2.87
Persons per family	3.22

Labor & Employment

Total civilian labor force, 2004**	5,470
Unemployment rate	3.4%
Total civilian labor force, 2000	4,468
Unemployment rate	2.3%

Employed persons 16 years and over by occupation, 2000

Managers & professionals	2,295
Service occupations	306
Sales & office occupations	1,282
Farming, fishing & forestry	0
Construction & maintenance	190
Production & transportation	293
Self-employed persons	357

*US Census Bureau
**New Jersey Department of Labor

General Information

Township of River Vale
406 River Vale Rd
River Vale, NJ 07675
201-664-2346

Web site	www.rivervale.nj.org
Land area (sq. miles)	4.08
Water area (sq. miles)	0.23
Type of government	Township
Form of government	MC '50

Government

Legislative Districts

US Congressional	5
State Legislative	39

Local Officials, 2006

Mayor	George Paschalis
Admin/Manager	Bibi Stewart Garvin
Clerk	Wanda Worner
Finance Dir/Treas	Roy Rossow
Engineer	Joe Zaniello
Attorney	John N. Carbone
Tax assessor	Denis McGuire
Tax collector	Kunjesh Trivedi
Building officer	Nick Lepore
Zoning officer	NA
Public Works	Richard Campanelli

Housing & Construction

Housing Units, 2000*

Total	3,312
Median rent	$1,119
Median SF home value	$350,300

New Privately Owned Housing Units Authorized by Building Permit

	Units	Value
Total, 2004	4	$1,215,000
Single family	4	$1,215,000
Total, 2005	17	$5,265,550
Single family	17	$5,265,550

Real Property Valuation - parcels, 2005

	Number	Valuation
Total		$997,755,967
Vacant	82	17,305,250
Residential	3,285	925,278,767
Commercial	40	49,623,550
Industrial	0	0
Apartments	3	4,834,400
Farm land	1	714,000
Farm homestead	0	0

Average Property Value & Tax, 2005

Residential value	$281,668
Property tax	$9,460
FAIR rebate	$589

Public Library

River Vale Public Library
412 Rivervale Rd
River Vale, NJ 07675
201-391-2460

Director ..... Holly Deni

Library statistics, 2004

	Total	per capita
Volumes	47,825	5.06
Expenditure	$531,100	$56.21

Public Safety

Police

Chief	Aaron Back
Number of officers, 2004	21

Crime, 2004	Number	Rate
Total	39	4
Violent	12	1.2
Non-violent	27	2.8
Domestic Viol.	15	NA

Emergency/Fire

Director ..... John Tobin

Public School District

(for school year 2004-2005 except as noted)

River Vale School District
609 Westwood Ave
River Vale, NJ 07675
201-358-4020

Superintendent	David Verducci
Grade plan	K-8
Enrollment	1,377.0
Students per teacher	11.7
Per pupil expenditure	$10,986
Median faculty salary	$51,745
Median administrator salary	$117,500
Grade 12 enrollment	NA
High school graduation rate	NA

Assessment test results

(percent scoring at proficient or advanced level)

	Language	Math
Grade 3	95.6%	90.1%
Grade 8	88.3%	86.2%
High school	NA	NA

SAT

Percent tested	NA
Average SAT math score	NA
Average SAT verbal score	NA

No Child Left Behind, 2003-04

Attendence rate (target = 90%)	91.1%
Drop rate	NA
Highly-qualified teachers	96.4%
District needs improvement?(AYP)	No

Municipal Finance

Fiscal Year 2005

Total tax levy	$33,532,244
County levy	3,469,144
County taxes	3,295,692
County library	0
County health	0
County open space	173,452
School levy	23,606,542
Local muni. budget	6,456,558
Misc. revenues	2,945,884
Total aid	$1,141,833
CMPTRA	313,859
Muni. block grant	41,175
Energy tax receipts	713,440
Homeland security	50,000

Fiscal Year 2006

Total aid	$1,141,833
CMPTRA	288,889
Muni. block grant	41,175
Energy tax receipts	738,410
Homeland security	50,000

Taxes

	2003	2004	2005
General tax rate per $100	2.92	3.160	3.360
Net valuation taxable	$982,018,940	$991,084,457	$998,392,262
State equalized value	$1,535,124,183	$1,719,471,449	$1,933,744,455
County equalization ratio	70.12	63.97	57.62

Demographics & Socio-Economic Characteristics
(2000 U.S. Census, except as noted)

Population
1980*	2,530
1990*	2,370
2000	2,498
Male	1,211
Female	1,287
2004 (estimate)*	2,633
Persons per sq. mi. of land	1,281

Race & Hispanic Origin, 2000
Race
White	2,333
Black/African American	27
Amer. Indian/Alaska Natv.	1
Asian	68
Natv. Hawaiian/Pac. Islander	0
Other Race	40
Two or more races	29
Hispanic origin, total	110
Mexican	15
Puerto Rican	39
Cuban	7
Other Hispanic	49

Age & Nativity, 2000
Under 5 years	152
18 years and over	1,911
21 years and over	1,827
65 years and over	302
85 years and over	21
Median Age	37.2
Native born	2,270
Foreign born	228

Educational Attainment, 2000
Population 25 years and over	1,724
0-8 yrs of school	2.1%
High School grad or higher	89.2%
Bachelor's degree or higher	30.9%
Graduate degree	8.4%

Income & Poverty, 1999
Per capita income	$31,187
Median household income	$71,083
Median family income	$79,557
Persons in poverty	132
H'holds receiving public assistance	7
H'holds receiving social security	241

Households, 2000
Total households	919
With persons under 18	313
With persons over 65	228
Family households	672
One-person households	194
Persons per household	2.68
Persons per family	3.14

Labor & Employment
Total civilian labor force, 2004**	1,492
Unemployment rate	5.0%
Total civilian labor force, 2000	1,464
Unemployment rate	4.4%

Employed persons 16 years and over by occupation, 2000
Managers & professionals	506
Service occupations	120
Sales & office occupations	475
Farming, fishing & forestry	0
Construction & maintenance	157
Production & transportation	142
Self-employed persons	71

*US Census Bureau
**New Jersey Department of Labor

General Information
Borough of Riverdale
Box 6
91 Newark-Pompton Tpke
Riverdale, NJ 07457
973-835-4060
Web site	www.riverdalenj.com
Land area (sq. miles)	2.06
Water area (sq. miles)	0.01
Type of government	Borough
Form of government	B

Government
Legislative Districts
US Congressional	11
State Legislative	26

Local Officials, 2006
Mayor	William Budesheim
Admin/Manager	NA
Clerk	Carol Talerico
Finance Dir/Treas	C. Talerico/K. Sesholtz
Engineer	Paul Darmofalski
Attorney	Robert Oostdyk
Tax assessor	Joseph De Stefano
Tax collector	Maryann Murphy
Building officer	Joseph Montemarano
Zoning officer	Linda Roetman
Public Works	Walter Mahon

Housing & Construction
Housing Units, 2000*
Total	940
Median rent	$951
Median SF home value	$210,200

New Privately Owned Housing Units
Authorized by Building Permit
	Units	Value
Total, 2004	4	$462,330
Single family	4	$462,330
Total, 2005	944	$24,098,031
Single family	20	$2,740,650

Real Property Valuation - parcels, 2005
	Number	Valuation
Total		$655,629,300
Vacant	103	75,865,800
Residential	1,087	385,679,200
Commercial	104	144,102,100
Industrial	26	48,343,700
Apartments	4	1,634,600
Farm land	0	0
Farm homestead	1	3,900

Average Property Value & Tax, 2005
Residential value	$354,488
Property tax	$4,441
FAIR rebate	$600

Public Library
Riverdale Public Library
93 Newark-Pompton Turnpike
Riverdale, NJ 07457
973-835-5044
Director	Abby Sanner

Library statistics, 2004
	Total	per capita
Volumes	15,909	6.37
Expenditure	$194,495	$77.86

Public Safety
Police
Chief	Thomas Soules
Number of officers, 2004	17

Crime, 2004	Number	Rate
Total	68	26.1
Violent	1	0.4
Non-violent	67	25.7
Domestic Viol.	18	NA

Emergency/Fire
Director	Patrick Cleary

Public School District
(for school year 2004-2005 except as noted)

Riverdale School District
52 Newark-Pompton Turnpike
Riverdale, NJ 07457
973-839-1304
Superintendent	Betty Ann Wyks
Grade plan	K-12
Enrollment	271.0
Students per teacher	11.6
Per pupil expenditure	$11,896
Median faculty salary	$46,500
Median administrator salary	$94,000
Grade 12 enrollment	NA
High school graduation rate	NA

Assessment test results
(percent scoring at proficient or advanced level)
	Language	Math
Grade 3	86.2%	93.1%
Grade 8	70.0%	67.5%
High school	NA	NA

SAT
Percent tested	NA
Average SAT math score	NA
Average SAT verbal score	NA

No Child Left Behind, 2003-04
Attendence rate (target = 90%)	96.4%
Drop rate	NA
Highly-qualified teachers	100%
District needs improvement?(AYP)	No

Municipal Finance
Fiscal Year 2005
Total tax levy	$8,310,937
County levy	1,408,910
County taxes	1,154,097
County library	0
County health	0
County open space	254,813
School levy	4,578,837
Local muni. budget	2,323,191
Misc. revenues	3,298,461
Total aid	$657,140
CMPTRA	238,482
Muni. block grant	10,370
Energy tax receipts	383,288
Homeland security	25,000

Fiscal Year 2006
Total aid	$657,140
CMPTRA	225,067
Muni. block grant	10,370
Energy tax receipts	396,703
Homeland security	25,000

Taxes
	2003	2004	2005
General tax rate per $100	2.31	2.420	1.260
Net valuation taxable	$317,919,778	$336,569,158	$663,440,749
State equalized value	$459,886,848	$515,155,651	$625,238,666
County equalization ratio	79.11	69.13	126.81

Demographics & Socio-Economic Characteristics
(2000 U.S. Census, except as noted)

Population
1980*	7,941
1990*	7,974
2000	7,911
Male	3,936
Female	3,975
2004 (estimate)*	8,007
Persons per sq. mi. of land	5,260

Race & Hispanic Origin, 2000
Race
White	7,137
Black/African American	351
Amer. Indian/Alaska Natv.	11
Asian	33
Natv. Hawaiian/Pac. Islander	1
Other Race	180
Two or more races	198
Hispanic origin, total	325
Mexican	37
Puerto Rican	150
Cuban	2
Other Hispanic	136

Age & Nativity, 2000
Under 5 years	515
18 years and over	5,931
21 years and over	5,638
65 years and over	1,089
85 years and over	126
Median Age	35.6
Native born	7,105
Foreign born	806

Educational Attainment, 2000
Population 25 years and over	5,234
0-8 yrs of school	9.8%
High School grad or higher	75.6%
Bachelor's degree or higher	11.5%
Graduate degree	3.0%

Income & Poverty, 1999
Per capita income	$18,758
Median household income	$43,358
Median family income	$52,479
Persons in poverty	642
H'holds receiving public assistance	59
H'holds receiving social security	867

Households, 2000
Total households	2,978
With persons under 18	1,091
With persons over 65	806
Family households	1,992
One-person households	814
Persons per household	2.64
Persons per family	3.21

Labor & Employment
Total civilian labor force, 2004**	4,719
Unemployment rate	6.5%
Total civilian labor force, 2000	4,199
Unemployment rate	3.9%

Employed persons 16 years and over by occupation, 2000
Managers & professionals	804
Service occupations	570
Sales & office occupations	1,240
Farming, fishing & forestry	14
Construction & maintenance	651
Production & transportation	756
Self-employed persons	188

*US Census Bureau
**New Jersey Department of Labor

General Information
Township of Riverside
PO Box 188
Riverside, NJ 08075
856-461-1460

Web site	NA
Land area (sq. miles)	1.52
Water area (sq. miles)	0.10
Type of government	Township
Form of government	TC

Government

Legislative Districts
US Congressional	3
State Legislative	7

Local Officials, 2006
Mayor	Charles F. Hilton Jr.
Admin/Manager	Eric Berry
Clerk	Susan M. Dydek
Finance Dir/Treas	Deborah Crowe
Engineer	Alaimo Assoc.
Attorney	Douglas Heinold
Tax assessor	Carl Cicali
Tax collector	Nancy Elmeaze
Building officer	Leonard Mason
Zoning officer	NA
Public Works	NA

Housing & Construction

Housing Units, 2000*
Total	3,118
Median rent	$670
Median SF home value	$100,400

New Privately Owned Housing Units Authorized by Building Permit
	Units	Value
Total, 2004	16	$1,343,622
Single family	16	$1,343,622
Total, 2005	16	$1,359,825
Single family	16	$1,359,825

Real Property Valuation - parcels, 2005
	Number	Valuation
Total		$450,034,550
Vacant	93	3,880,700
Residential	2,446	374,420,450
Commercial	170	44,416,000
Industrial	15	13,830,500
Apartments	25	13,486,900
Farm land	0	0
Farm homestead	0	0

Average Property Value & Tax, 2005
Residential value	$153,075
Property tax	$3,571
FAIR rebate	$605

Public Library
Riverside Public Library
10 Franklin St
Riverside, NJ 08075
856-461-6922

Director	Jean Bowker

Library statistics, 2004
	Total	per capita
Volumes	30,925	3.91
Expenditure	$57,274	$7.24

Public Safety

Police
Chief	Paul Tursi
Number of officers, 2004	14

Crime, 2004	Number	Rate
Total	161	20.1
Violent	33	4.1
Non-violent	128	16
Domestic Viol.	159	NA

Emergency/Fire
Director	Jeff Conard

Public School District
(for school year 2004-2005 except as noted)

Riverside Township School District
112 E Washington St
Riverside, NJ 08075
856-461-1255
Superintendent	Robert H. Goldschmidt
Grade plan	K-12
Enrollment	1,419.0
Students per teacher	11.8
Per pupil expenditure	$10,632
Median faculty salary	$50,808
Median administrator salary	$80,675
Grade 12 enrollment	108.0
High school graduation rate	90.6%

Assessment test results
(percent scoring at proficient or advanced level)
	Language	Math
Grade 3	78.5%	82.4%
Grade 8	62.7%	45.1%
High school	77.6%	68.2%

SAT
Percent tested	58%
Average SAT math score	479
Average SAT verbal score	467

No Child Left Behind, 2003-04
Attendence rate (target = 90%)	93.2%
Drop rate	2.7%
Highly-qualified teachers	100%
District needs improvement?(AYP)	No

Municipal Finance

Fiscal Year 2005
Total tax levy	$10,541,617
County levy	1,652,492
County taxes	1,386,266
County library	121,380
County health	0
County open space	144,846
School levy	6,339,925
Local muni. budget	2,549,200
Misc. revenues	3,085,300
Total aid	$1,182,632
CMPTRA	538,536
Muni. block grant	34,892
Energy tax receipts	559,204
Homeland security	50,000

Fiscal Year 2006
Total aid	$1,182,632
CMPTRA	518,964
Muni. block grant	34,892
Energy tax receipts	578,776
Homeland security	50,000

Taxes
	2003	2004	2005
General tax rate per $100	2.97	3.153	2.334
Net valuation taxable	$267,319,840	$273,400,196	$451,887,327
State equalized value	$310,764,752	$354,497,959	$420,008,669
County equalization ratio	90.41	86.02	127.29

Demographics & Socio-Economic Characteristics
(2000 U.S. Census, except as noted)

Population
1980*	3,068
1990*	2,775
2000	2,759
Male	1,309
Female	1,450
2004 (estimate)*	2,754
Persons per sq. mi. of land	4,198

Race & Hispanic Origin, 2000
Race
White	2,644
Black/African American	49
Amer. Indian/Alaska Natv.	3
Asian	23
Natv. Hawaiian/Pac. Islander	0
Other Race	8
Two or more races	32
Hispanic origin, total	30
Mexican	4
Puerto Rican	8
Cuban	2
Other Hispanic	16

Age & Nativity, 2000
Under 5 years	165
18 years and over	2,158
21 years and over	2,100
65 years and over	532
85 years and over	105
Median Age	41.8
Native born	2,687
Foreign born	72

Educational Attainment, 2000
Population 25 years and over	2,036
0-8 yrs of school	2.4%
High School grad or higher	89.8%
Bachelor's degree or higher	36.2%
Graduate degree	12.6%

Income & Poverty, 1999
Per capita income	$30,223
Median household income	$58,977
Median family income	$68,125
Persons in poverty	82
H'holds receiving public assistance	9
H'holds receiving social security	309

Households, 2000
Total households	1,066
With persons under 18	344
With persons over 65	293
Family households	746
One-person households	270
Persons per household	2.48
Persons per family	3

Labor & Employment
Total civilian labor force, 2004**	1,723
Unemployment rate	1.7%
Total civilian labor force, 2000	1,382
Unemployment rate	2.2%

Employed persons 16 years and over by occupation, 2000
Managers & professionals	642
Service occupations	84
Sales & office occupations	381
Farming, fishing & forestry	0
Construction & maintenance	110
Production & transportation	135
Self-employed persons	121

*US Census Bureau
**New Jersey Department of Labor

General Information
Borough of Riverton
505A Howard St
Riverton, NJ 08077
856-829-0120

Web site	www.riverton-nj.com
Land area (sq. miles)	0.66
Water area (sq. miles)	0.29
Type of government	Borough
Form of government	B

Government

Legislative Districts
US Congressional	1
State Legislative	7

Local Officials, 2006
Mayor	Robert Martin
Admin/Manager	NA
Clerk	Mary Longbottom
Finance Dir/Treas	Betty Boyle
Engineer	Richard Arango
Attorney	Bruce Gunn
Tax assessor	Tom Davis
Tax collector	NA
Building officer	Ed Schaefer
Zoning officer	(Vacant)
Public Works	NA

Housing & Construction

Housing Units, 2000*
Total	1,113
Median rent	$695
Median SF home value	$153,600

New Privately Owned Housing Units Authorized by Building Permit
	Units	Value
Total, 2004	2	$400,000
Single family	2	$400,000
Total, 2005	1	$200,000
Single family	1	$200,000

Real Property Valuation - parcels, 2005
	Number	Valuation
Total		$130,966,500
Vacant	23	855,300
Residential	875	118,077,400
Commercial	48	7,728,000
Industrial	1	932,000
Apartments	12	3,373,800
Farm land	0	0
Farm homestead	0	0

Average Property Value & Tax, 2005
Residential value	$134,946
Property tax	$6,476
FAIR rebate	$590

Public Library
Riverton Free Library
306 Main St
Riverton, NJ 08077
856-829-2476

Director	Michael Robinson

Library statistics, 2004
	Total	per capita
Volumes	NA	NA
Expenditure	NA	NA

Public Safety
Police
Chief	Robert Norcross
Number of officers, 2004	6

Crime, 2004	Number	Rate
Total	58	21
Violent	5	1.8
Non-violent	53	19.2
Domestic Viol.	12	NA

Emergency/Fire
Director	Scott Reed

Public School District
(for school year 2004-2005 except as noted)

Riverton Borough School District
600 Fifth St
Riverton, NJ 08077
856-829-0087

Superintendent	Mary Ellen Eck
Grade plan	K-12
Enrollment	219.0
Students per teacher	8.6
Per pupil expenditure	$11,540
Median faculty salary	$46,963
Median administrator salary	$71,063
Grade 12 enrollment	NA
High school graduation rate	NA

Assessment test results
(percent scoring at proficient or advanced level)
	Language	Math
Grade 3	100.0%	95.7%
Grade 8	82.8%	58.6%
High school	NA	NA

SAT
Percent tested	NA
Average SAT math score	NA
Average SAT verbal score	NA

No Child Left Behind, 2003-04
Attendance rate (target = 90%)	95.5%
Drop rate	NA
Highly-qualified teachers	100%
District needs improvement?(AYP)	No

Municipal Finance

Fiscal Year 2005
Total tax levy	$6,292,113
County levy	916,590
County taxes	768,923
County library	67,326
County health	0
County open space	80,341
School levy	3,698,225
Local muni. budget	1,677,298
Misc. revenues	1,408,830
Total aid	$360,189
CMPTRA	141,388
Muni. block grant	12,142
Energy tax receipts	181,659
Homeland security	25,000

Fiscal Year 2006
Total aid	$360,189
CMPTRA	135,030
Muni. block grant	12,142
Energy tax receipts	188,017
Homeland security	25,000

Taxes
	2003	2004	2005
General tax rate per $100	4.11	4.486	4.800
Net valuation taxable	$131,010,321	$131,108,448	$131,106,426
State equalized value	$181,832,507	$200,232,150	$232,705,761
County equalization ratio	79.95	72.05	65.45

Demographics & Socio-Economic Characteristics
(2000 U.S. Census, except as noted)

Population
1980*	5,603
1990*	5,587
2000	5,528
Male	2,525
Female	3,003
2004 (estimate)*	5,734
Persons per sq. mi. of land	5,485

Race & Hispanic Origin, 2000
Race
White	4,980
Black/African American	25
Amer. Indian/Alaska Natv.	2
Asian	333
Natv. Hawaiian/Pac. Islander	0
Other Race	112
Two or more races	76
Hispanic origin, total	474
Mexican	20
Puerto Rican	105
Cuban	68
Other Hispanic	281

Age & Nativity, 2000
Under 5 years	312
18 years and over	4,497
21 years and over	4,359
65 years and over	1,319
85 years and over	320
Median Age	43.2
Native born	4,640
Foreign born	888

Educational Attainment, 2000
Population 25 years and over	4,197
0-8 yrs of school	5.1%
High School grad or higher	85.3%
Bachelor's degree or higher	23.7%
Graduate degree	7.6%

Income & Poverty, 1999
Per capita income	$25,054
Median household income	$60,818
Median family income	$74,016
Persons in poverty	153
H'holds receiving public assistance	41
H'holds receiving social security	785

Households, 2000
Total households	2,061
With persons under 18	577
With persons over 65	775
Family households	1,394
One-person households	563
Persons per household	2.52
Persons per family	3.12

Labor & Employment
Total civilian labor force, 2004**	3,074
Unemployment rate	3.4%
Total civilian labor force, 2000	2,784
Unemployment rate	4.1%

Employed persons 16 years and over by occupation, 2000
Managers & professionals	1,002
Service occupations	357
Sales & office occupations	851
Farming, fishing & forestry	0
Construction & maintenance	152
Production & transportation	307
Self-employed persons	126

*US Census Bureau
**New Jersey Department of Labor

General Information
Township of Rochelle Park
151 W Passaic St
Rochelle Park, NJ 07662
201-587-7730

Web site	rochelleparknj.gov
Land area (sq. miles)	1.05
Water area (sq. miles)	0
Type of government	Township
Form of government	TC

Government

Legislative Districts
US Congressional	5
State Legislative	37

Local Officials, 2006
Mayor	Phyllis Strohmeyer
Admin/Manager	Michael Mariniello Jr.
Clerk	Virginia De Maria
Finance Dir/Treas	Michael Mariniello Jr.
Engineer	Kenneth Job
Attorney	Joseph Rotolo
Tax assessor	George Reggo
Tax collector	Roy Riggitano
Building officer	Richard Bolan
Zoning officer	Richard Bolan
Public Works	Brian Koenig

Housing & Construction

Housing Units, 2000*
Total	2,111
Median rent	$842
Median SF home value	$190,600

New Privately Owned Housing Units
Authorized by Building Permit
	Units	Value
Total, 2004	67	$1,539,131
Single family	5	$773,700
Total, 2005	86	$1,608,080
Single family	5	$608,080

Real Property Valuation - parcels, 2005
	Number	Valuation
Total		$668,635,700
Vacant	57	9,564,400
Residential	1,721	391,230,600
Commercial	130	221,611,800
Industrial	23	24,498,800
Apartments	4	21,730,100
Farm land	0	0
Farm homestead	0	0

Average Property Value & Tax, 2005
Residential value	$227,327
Property tax	$4,951
FAIR rebate	$651

Public Library
Rochelle Park Public Library
151 W Passaic St
Rochelle Park, NJ 07662
201-587-8850

Director..................Judith Sands

Library statistics, 2004
	Total	per capita
Volumes	12,904	2.33
Expenditure	$211,962	$38.34

Public Safety

Police
Chief	Richard Zavinsky
Number of officers, 2004	20

Crime, 2004	Number	Rate
Total	104	18.8
Violent	3	0.5
Non-violent	101	18.3
Domestic Viol.	5	NA

Emergency/Fire
Director..................Darryl DeMott

Public School District
(for school year 2004-2005 except as noted)

Rochelle Park School District
300 Rochelle Ave
Rochelle Park, NJ 07662
201-843-3120
Superintendent	C. Lauren Schoen
Grade plan	K-12
Enrollment	481.0
Students per teacher	9.7
Per pupil expenditure	$12,254
Median faculty salary	$67,816
Median administrator salary	$94,340
Grade 12 enrollment	NA
High school graduation rate	NA

Assessment test results
(percent scoring at proficient or advanced level)
	Language	Math
Grade 3	87.2%	80.9%
Grade 8	81.1%	81.1%
High school	NA	NA

SAT
Percent tested	NA
Average SAT math score	NA
Average SAT verbal score	NA

No Child Left Behind, 2003-04
Attendence rate (target = 90%)	96.4%
Drop rate	NA
Highly-qualified teachers	100%
District needs improvement?(AYP)	No

Municipal Finance

Fiscal Year 2005
Total tax levy	$15,119,587
County levy	1,570,530
County taxes	1,491,221
County library	0
County health	0
County open space	79,310
School levy	7,696,191
Local muni. budget	5,852,866
Misc. revenues	2,887,420
Total aid	$1,100,693
CMPTRA	598,710
Muni. block grant	24,447
Energy tax receipts	427,536
Homeland security	50,000

Fiscal Year 2006
Total aid	$1,100,693
CMPTRA	583,747
Muni. block grant	24,447
Energy tax receipts	442,499
Homeland security	50,000

Taxes
	2003	2004	2005
General tax rate per $100	2.06	2.140	2.180
Net valuation taxable	$682,906,094	$696,633,036	$694,238,894
State equalized value	$746,998,571	$791,338,733	$890,163,988
County equalization ratio	98.52	91.42	87.63

Demographics & Socio-Economic Characteristics

(2000 U.S. Census, except as noted)

Population

1980*	6,852
1990*	6,243
2000	6,473
Male	3,148
Female	3,325
2004 (estimate)*	6,437
Persons per sq. mi. of land	3,082

Race & Hispanic Origin, 2000

Race

White	5,680
Black/African American	91
Amer. Indian/Alaska Natv.	13
Asian	412
Natv. Hawaiian/Pac. Islander	2
Other Race	193
Two or more races	82
Hispanic origin, total	608
Mexican	57
Puerto Rican	158
Cuban	16
Other Hispanic	377

Age & Nativity, 2000

Under 5 years	435
18 years and over	4,968
21 years and over	4,783
65 years and over	770
85 years and over	63
Median Age	37.8
Native born	5,476
Foreign born	997

Educational Attainment, 2000

Population 25 years and over	4,552
0-8 yrs of school	3.4%
High School grad or higher	89.7%
Bachelor's degree or higher	28.7%
Graduate degree	7.6%

Income & Poverty, 1999

Per capita income	$26,500
Median household income	$61,002
Median family income	$66,997
Persons in poverty	322
H'holds receiving public assistance	39
H'holds receiving social security	476

Households, 2000

Total households	2,445
With persons under 18	881
With persons over 65	585
Family households	1,709
One-person households	582
Persons per household	2.64
Persons per family	3.16

Labor & Employment

Total civilian labor force, 2004**	3,975
Unemployment rate	4.6%
Total civilian labor force, 2000	3,714
Unemployment rate	4.6%

Employed persons 16 years and over by occupation, 2000

Managers & professionals	1,278
Service occupations	386
Sales & office occupations	1,149
Farming, fishing & forestry	13
Construction & maintenance	254
Production & transportation	463
Self-employed persons	156

*US Census Bureau
**New Jersey Department of Labor

General Information

Borough of Rockaway
1 East Main St
Rockaway, NJ 07866
973-627-2000

Web site	www.rockawayborough.com
Land area (sq. miles)	2.09
Water area (sq. miles)	0.02
Type of government	Borough
Form of government	B

Government

Legislative Districts

US Congressional	11
State Legislative	25

Local Officials, 2006

Mayor	Mary Lockwood
Admin/Manager	NA
Clerk	Sheila Seifert
Finance Dir/Treas	John Doherty
Engineer	Michael Spillane
Attorney	Edward Wacks
Tax assessor	Bernard Murdoch
Tax collector	NA
Building officer	Joseph Montemarano
Zoning officer	Barrie Krause
Public Works	NA

Housing & Construction

Housing Units, 2000*

Total	2,491
Median rent	$875
Median SF home value	$187,200

New Privately Owned Housing Units
Authorized by Building Permit

	Units	Value
Total, 2004	1	$215,000
Single family	1	$215,000
Total, 2005	0	$0
Single family	0	$0

Real Property Valuation - parcels, 2005

	Number	Valuation
Total		$766,106,400
Vacant	78	9,051,900
Residential	1,905	555,860,800
Commercial	198	154,113,100
Industrial	13	24,756,900
Apartments	22	22,323,700
Farm land	0	0
Farm homestead	0	0

Average Property Value & Tax, 2005

Residential value	$291,790
Property tax	$5,654
FAIR rebate	$565

Public Library

Rockaway Borough Library
82 East Main St
Rockaway, NJ 07866
973-627-5709

Director	Edna Puleo

Library statistics, 2004

	Total	per capita
Volumes	29,019	4.48
Expenditure	$215,770	$33.33

Public Safety

Police

Chief	Gary Farina
Number of officers, 2004	14

Crime, 2004	Number	Rate
Total	79	12.3
Violent	5	0.8
Non-violent	74	11.5
Domestic Viol.	45	NA

Emergency/Fire

Director	Robert Hopler

Public School District

(for school year 2004-2005 except as noted)

Rockaway Borough School District
103 E Main St
Rockaway, NJ 07866
973-625-8601

Superintendent	Emil Suarez
Grade plan	K-8
Enrollment	621.0
Students per teacher	12.8
Per pupil expenditure	$10,798
Median faculty salary	$49,569
Median administrator salary	$100,673
Grade 12 enrollment	NA
High school graduation rate	NA

Assessment test results

(percent scoring at proficient or advanced level)

	Language	Math
Grade 3	85.5%	89.8%
Grade 8	85.5%	70.2%
High school	NA	NA

SAT

Percent tested	NA
Average SAT math score	NA
Average SAT verbal score	NA

No Child Left Behind, 2003-04

Attendence rate (target = 90%)	95.7%
Drop rate	NA
Highly-qualified teachers	100%
District needs improvement?(AYP)	No

Municipal Finance

Fiscal Year 2005

Total tax levy	$14,863,828
County levy	1,928,463
County taxes	1,579,654
County library	0
County health	0
County open space	348,810
School levy	9,820,642
Local muni. budget	3,114,723
Misc. revenues	2,698,594
Total aid	$873,413
CMPTRA	441,857
Muni. block grant	27,317
Energy tax receipts	354,239
Homeland security	50,000

Fiscal Year 2006

Total aid	$873,414
CMPTRA	429,459
Muni. block grant	27,317
Energy tax receipts	366,638
Homeland security	50,000

Taxes

	2003	2004	2005
General tax rate per $100	2.96	1.830	1.940
Net valuation taxable	$446,916,418	$771,600,033	$767,065,591
State equalized value	$632,578,086	$723,484,418	$796,041,502
County equalization ratio	84.98	121.63	106.66

Demographics & Socio-Economic Characteristics
(2000 U.S. Census, except as noted)

Population
1980*	19,850
1990*	19,572
2000	22,930
Male	11,329
Female	11,601
2004 (estimate)*	25,244
Persons per sq. mi. of land	590

Race & Hispanic Origin, 2000
Race
White	20,375
Black/African American	565
Amer. Indian/Alaska Natv.	23
Asian	1,295
Natv. Hawaiian/Pac. Islander	4
Other Race	367
Two or more races	301
Hispanic origin, total	1,440
Mexican	127
Puerto Rican	455
Cuban	109
Other Hispanic	749

Age & Nativity, 2000
Under 5 years	1,771
18 years and over	16,715
21 years and over	16,164
65 years and over	2,162
85 years and over	162
Median Age	37
Native born	19,892
Foreign born	3,038

Educational Attainment, 2000
Population 25 years and over	15,488
0-8 yrs of school	2.2%
High School grad or higher	93.0%
Bachelor's degree or higher	41.4%
Graduate degree	12.4%

Income & Poverty, 1999
Per capita income	$33,184
Median household income	$80,939
Median family income	$89,281
Persons in poverty	551
H'holds receiving public assistance	51
H'holds receiving social security	1,722

Households, 2000
Total households	8,108
With persons under 18	3,392
With persons over 65	1,586
Family households	6,381
One-person households	1,376
Persons per household	2.82
Persons per family	3.21

Labor & Employment
Total civilian labor force, 2004**	12,606
Unemployment rate	3.3%
Total civilian labor force, 2000	12,706
Unemployment rate	3.3%

Employed persons 16 years and over by occupation, 2000
Managers & professionals	5,842
Service occupations	1,209
Sales & office occupations	3,469
Farming, fishing & forestry	0
Construction & maintenance	763
Production & transportation	1,004
Self-employed persons	603

*US Census Bureau
**New Jersey Department of Labor

General Information
Township of Rockaway
65 Mt Hope Rd
Rockaway, NJ 07866
973-627-7200
Web site	www.rockawaytownship.org
Land area (sq. miles)	42.82
Water area (sq. miles)	3.17
Type of government	Township
Form of government	MC '50

Government

Legislative Districts
US Congressional	11
State Legislative	25

Local Officials, 2006
Mayor	Louis Sceusi
Admin/Manager	Steve Levinson
Clerk	Mary Cilurso
Finance Dir/Treas	Charles Wood
Engineer	Lisa Ryden
Attorney	Edward Buzak
Tax assessor	Mark Burek
Tax collector	Lorraine Benderoth
Building officer	Andy Sanfilippo
Zoning officer	Dennis Creran
Public Works	Ed Hollenbeck

Housing & Construction

Housing Units, 2000*
Total	8,506
Median rent	$948
Median SF home value	$206,200

New Privately Owned Housing Units Authorized by Building Permit
	Units	Value
Total, 2004	138	$9,833,077
Single family	49	$9,435,458
Total, 2005	186	$20,531,413
Single family	31	$9,555,901

Real Property Valuation - parcels, 2005
	Number	Valuation
Total		$2,919,150,300
Vacant	578	90,804,800
Residential	8,640	2,130,423,600
Commercial	164	467,819,900
Industrial	47	193,367,600
Apartments	8	32,887,700
Farm land	10	3,613,000
Farm homestead	36	233,700

Average Property Value & Tax, 2005
Residential value	$245,581
Property tax	$6,968
FAIR rebate	$558

Public Library
Rockaway Township Library
61 Mount Hope Rd
Rockaway, NJ 07866
973-627-2344
Director . . . . Jeanette Cohn

Library statistics, 2004
	Total	per capita
Volumes	120,643	5.26
Expenditure	$1,046,288	$45.63

Public Safety

Police
Chief	Walter Kimble
Number of officers, 2004	55

Crime, 2004	Number	Rate
Total	419	16.7
Violent	21	0.8
Non-violent	398	15.9
Domestic Viol.	163	NA

Emergency/Fire
Director . . . . Clifford Graner

Public School District
(for school year 2004-2005 except as noted)

Rockaway Township School District
PO Box 500
Hibernia, NJ 07842
973-627-8200
Superintendent	Arthur Travlos
Grade plan	K-8
Enrollment	2,813.0
Students per teacher	9.1
Per pupil expenditure	$13,785
Median faculty salary	$49,624
Median administrator salary	$103,397
Grade 12 enrollment	NA
High school graduation rate	NA

Assessment test results
(percent scoring at proficient or advanced level)
	Language	Math
Grade 3	88.9%	88.8%
Grade 8	87.7%	75.7%
High school	NA	NA

SAT
Percent tested	NA
Average SAT math score	NA
Average SAT verbal score	NA

No Child Left Behind, 2003-04
Attendence rate (target = 90%)	96.1%
Drop rate	NA
Highly-qualified teachers	100%
District needs improvement?(AYP)	No

Municipal Finance

Fiscal Year 2005
Total tax levy	$82,922,528
County levy	9,108,997
County taxes	7,458,664
County library	0
County health	0
County open space	1,650,332
School levy	55,090,632
Local muni. budget	18,722,900
Misc. revenues	10,190,580
Total aid	$2,322,707
CMPTRA	918,681
Muni. block grant	89,909
Energy tax receipts	1,049,700
Homeland security	90,000

Fiscal Year 2006
Total aid	$2,322,707
CMPTRA	881,941
Muni. block grant	89,909
Energy tax receipts	1,086,440
Homeland security	90,000

Taxes
	2003	2004	2005
General tax rate per $100	2.50	2.670	2.840
Net valuation taxable	$2,903,678,338	$2,928,373,613	$2,922,353,434
State equalized value	$3,101,889,048	$3,466,912,951	$4,162,896,630
County equalization ratio	104.82	93.61	84.45

Demographics & Socio-Economic Characteristics
(2000 U.S. Census, except as noted)

Population
1980*	192
1990*	270
2000	391
Male	191
Female	200
2004 (estimate)*	396
Persons per sq. mi. of land	407

Race & Hispanic Origin, 2000
Race
White	351
Black/African American	13
Amer. Indian/Alaska Natv.	1
Asian	15
Natv. Hawaiian/Pac. Islander	0
Other Race	4
Two or more races	7
Hispanic origin, total	19
Mexican	3
Puerto Rican	2
Cuban	6
Other Hispanic	8

Age & Nativity, 2000
Under 5 years	18
18 years and over	288
21 years and over	280
65 years and over	125
85 years and over	60
Median Age	49.1
Native born	319
Foreign born	80

Educational Attainment, 2000
Population 25 years and over	277
0-8 yrs of school	13.4%
High School grad or higher	78.7%
Bachelor's degree or higher	28.9%
Graduate degree	12.6%

Income & Poverty, 1999
Per capita income	$48,935
Median household income	$152,262
Median family income	$157,816
Persons in poverty	68
H'holds receiving public assistance	3
H'holds receiving social security	15

Households, 2000
Total households	74
With persons under 18	29
With persons over 65	20
Family households	58
One-person households	8
Persons per household	3.04
Persons per family	3.4

Labor & Employment
Total civilian labor force, 2004**	87
Unemployment rate	0.0%
Total civilian labor force, 2000	114
Unemployment rate	0.0%

Employed persons 16 years and over by occupation, 2000
Managers & professionals	68
Service occupations	9
Sales & office occupations	30
Farming, fishing & forestry	2
Construction & maintenance	3
Production & transportation	2
Self-employed persons	6

*US Census Bureau
**New Jersey Department of Labor

General Information
Borough of Rockleigh
26 Rockleigh Rd
Rockleigh, NJ 07647
201-768-4217

Web site	www.rockleigh.org
Land area (sq. miles)	0.97
Water area (sq. miles)	0
Type of government	Borough
Form of government	B

Government

Legislative Districts
US Congressional	5
State Legislative	39

Local Officials, 2006
Mayor	Nicholas Langella
Admin/Manager	William J. McGuire
Clerk	William J. McGuire
Finance Dir/Treas	Anne Murphy
Engineer	Neglia Engineering
Attorney	John Hall
Tax assessor	Raymond Damiano
Tax collector	Anne Murphy
Building officer	William McGuire
Zoning officer	William McGuire
Public Works	NA

Housing & Construction

Housing Units, 2000*
Total	80
Median rent	$2,001
Median SF home value	$937,500

New Privately Owned Housing Units Authorized by Building Permit
	Units	Value
Total, 2004	0	$0
Single family	0	$0
Total, 2005	0	$0
Single family	0	$0

Real Property Valuation - parcels, 2005
	Number	Valuation
Total		$117,259,000
Vacant	11	2,418,700
Residential	72	51,663,100
Commercial	4	8,927,400
Industrial	12	54,249,800
Apartments	0	0
Farm land	0	0
Farm homestead	0	0

Average Property Value & Tax, 2005
Residential value	$717,543
Property tax	$9,507
FAIR rebate	$535

Public Library
No public municipal library.

Library statistics, 2004
	Total	per capita
Volumes	NA	NA
Expenditure	NA	NA

Public Safety

Police
Chief	Bruce Tietjen
Number of officers, 2004	0

Crime, 2004	Number	Rate
Total	9	22.7
Violent	5	12.6
Non-violent	4	10.1
Domestic Viol.	1	NA

Emergency/Fire
Director	Mike Malhame

Public School District
(for school year 2004-2005 except as noted)

Rockleigh School District†
Box 343
Closter, NJ 07624

†No schools in district - sends children to Northvale and Northern Valley Regional schools (see Appendix A).

Grade plan	NA
Enrollment	NA
Students per teacher	NA
Per pupil expenditure	NA
Median faculty salary	NA

Assessment test results
(percent scoring at proficient or advanced level)
	Language	Math
Grade 3	NA	NA
Grade 8	NA	NA
High school	NA	NA

SAT
Percent tested	NA
Average SAT math score	NA
Average SAT verbal score	NA

No Child Left Behind, 2003-04
Attendence rate (target = 90%)	NA
Drop rate	NA
Highly-qualified teachers	NA
District needs improvement?(AYP)	NA

Municipal Finance

Fiscal Year 2005
Total tax levy	$1,555,784
County levy	383,502
County taxes	364,330
County library	0
County health	0
County open space	19,172
School levy	365,990
Local muni. budget	806,292
Misc. revenues	582,281
Total aid	$155,710
CMPTRA	44,249
Muni. block grant	1,533
Energy tax receipts	84,928
Homeland security	25,000

Fiscal Year 2006
Total aid	$155,710
CMPTRA	41,276
Muni. block grant	1,533
Energy tax receipts	87,901
Homeland security	25,000

Taxes
	2003	2004	2005
General tax rate per $100	1.42	1.380	1.330
Net valuation taxable	$118,993,980	$119,000,304	$117,424,841
State equalized value	$167,455,643	$190,310,181	$200,110,499
County equalization ratio	64.76	71.06	62.49

Demographics & Socio-Economic Characteristics
(2000 U.S. Census, except as noted)

Population
1980*	717
1990*	693
2000	662
Male	328
Female	334
2004 (estimate)*	665
Persons per sq. mi. of land	986

Race & Hispanic Origin, 2000
Race
White	630
Black/African American	9
Amer. Indian/Alaska Natv.	0
Asian	3
Natv. Hawaiian/Pac. Islander	4
Other Race	6
Two or more races	10
Hispanic origin, total	26
Mexican	3
Puerto Rican	13
Cuban	3
Other Hispanic	7

Age & Nativity, 2000
Under 5 years	38
18 years and over	528
21 years and over	521
65 years and over	114
85 years and over	15
Median Age	43.8
Native born	585
Foreign born	73

Educational Attainment, 2000
Population 25 years and over	523
0-8 yrs of school	2.1%
High School grad or higher	96.0%
Bachelor's degree or higher	59.7%
Graduate degree	29.1%

Income & Poverty, 1999
Per capita income	$48,357
Median household income	$79,469
Median family income	$100,314
Persons in poverty	18
H'holds receiving public assistance	3
H'holds receiving social security	84

Households, 2000
Total households	284
With persons under 18	71
With persons over 65	89
Family households	190
One-person households	79
Persons per household	2.33
Persons per family	2.82

Labor & Employment
Total civilian labor force, 2004**	492
Unemployment rate	4.0%
Total civilian labor force, 2000	386
Unemployment rate	2.6%

Employed persons 16 years and over by occupation, 2000
Managers & professionals	230
Service occupations	30
Sales & office occupations	70
Farming, fishing & forestry	0
Construction & maintenance	25
Production & transportation	21
Self-employed persons	40

*US Census Bureau
**New Jersey Department of Labor

General Information
Borough of Rocky Hill
PO Box 188
Rocky Hill, NJ 08553
609-924-7445
Web site	www.rockyhill-nj.gov
Land area (sq. miles)	0.67
Water area (sq. miles)	0
Type of government	Borough
Form of government	B

Government

Legislative Districts
US Congressional	7
State Legislative	16

Local Officials, 2006
Mayor	George Morren
Admin/Manager	NA
Clerk	Raymond Whitlock Jr.
Finance Dir/Treas	C. Ross Bobal
Engineer	Neil Van Cleef
Attorney	Albert Cruz
Tax assessor	George Sopko
Tax collector	Donna Griffiths
Building officer	DCA
Zoning officer	Lewrence Reffaelli
Public Works	NA

Housing & Construction

Housing Units, 2000*
Total	295
Median rent	$914
Median SF home value	$271,400

New Privately Owned Housing Units Authorized by Building Permit
	Units	Value
Total, 2004	0	$0
Single family	0	$0
Total, 2005	0	$0
Single family	0	$0

Real Property Valuation - parcels, 2005
	Number	Valuation
Total		$61,776,200
Vacant	9	275,600
Residential	256	54,274,300
Commercial	13	3,451,000
Industrial	1	3,185,000
Apartments	2	569,400
Farm land	0	0
Farm homestead	3	20,900

Average Property Value & Tax, 2005
Residential value	$209,634
Property tax	$5,395
FAIR rebate	$677

Public Library
Mary Jacobs Branch Library†
64 Washington St
Rocky Hill, NJ 08553
609-924-7073
Branch Librarian	Helen Morris

Library statistics, 2004
	Total	per capita
Volumes	NA	NA
Expenditure	NA	NA

†Branch of County Library

Public Safety

Police
Chief	NA
Number of officers, 2004	0

Crime, 2004	Number	Rate
Total	9	13.6
Violent	0	0
Non-violent	9	13.6
Domestic Viol.	0	NA

Emergency/Fire
Director	Todd Harris

Public School District
(for school year 2004-2005 except as noted)

Rocky Hill Borough School District
PO Box Q
Rocky Hill, NJ 08553
Superintendent	NA
Grade plan	NA
Enrollment	NA
Students per teacher	NA
Per pupil expenditure	NA
Median faculty salary	NA
Median administrator salary	NA
Grade 12 enrollment	NA
High school graduation rate	NA

Assessment test results
(percent scoring at proficient or advanced level)
	Language	Math
Grade 3	NA	NA
Grade 8	NA	NA
High school	NA	NA

SAT
Percent tested	NA
Average SAT math score	NA
Average SAT verbal score	NA

No Child Left Behind, 2003-04
Attendence rate (target = 90%)	NA
Drop rate	NA
Highly-qualified teachers	NA
District needs improvement?(AYP)	NA

Municipal Finance

Fiscal Year 2005
Total tax levy	$1,592,523
County levy	399,244
County taxes	330,773
County library	36,665
County health	0
County open space	31,806
School levy	805,312
Local muni. budget	387,967
Misc. revenues	494,999
Total aid	$113,075
CMPTRA	50,128
Muni. block grant	3,032
Energy tax receipts	59,915
Homeland security	0

Fiscal Year 2006
Total aid	$113,075
CMPTRA	48,031
Muni. block grant	3,032
Energy tax receipts	62,012
Homeland security	NA

Taxes
	2003	2004	2005
General tax rate per $100	2.33	2.440	2.580
Net valuation taxable	$61,303,207	$61,710,513	$61,881,553
State equalized value	$95,891,142	$104,098,881	$120,815,215
County equalization ratio	70.46	63.93	59.26

Demographics & Socio-Economic Characteristics
(2000 U.S. Census, except as noted)

Population

1980*	835
1990*	884
2000	933
Male	449
Female	484
2004 (estimate)*	931
Persons per sq. mi. of land	476

Race & Hispanic Origin, 2000

Race
White	830
Black/African American	24
Amer. Indian/Alaska Natv.	0
Asian	19
Natv. Hawaiian/Pac. Islander	1
Other Race	21
Two or more races	38
Hispanic origin, total	42
Mexican	4
Puerto Rican	19
Cuban	0
Other Hispanic	19

Age & Nativity, 2000

Under 5 years	49
18 years and over	674
21 years and over	641
65 years and over	113
85 years and over	14
Median Age	40.4
Native born	848
Foreign born	80

Educational Attainment, 2000

Population 25 years and over	584
0-8 yrs of school	3.8%
High School grad or higher	93.0%
Bachelor's degree or higher	44.2%
Graduate degree	17.8%

Income & Poverty, 1999

Per capita income	$24,892
Median household income	$61,979
Median family income	$67,019
Persons in poverty	40
H'holds receiving public assistance	2
H'holds receiving social security	80

Households, 2000

Total households	337
With persons under 18	138
With persons over 65	86
Family households	258
One-person households	63
Persons per household	2.77
Persons per family	3.17

Labor & Employment

Total civilian labor force, 2004**	558
Unemployment rate	2.9%
Total civilian labor force, 2000	496
Unemployment rate	4.4%

Employed persons 16 years and over by occupation, 2000
Managers & professionals	221
Service occupations	45
Sales & office occupations	97
Farming, fishing & forestry	0
Construction & maintenance	66
Production & transportation	45
Self-employed persons	27

*US Census Bureau
**New Jersey Department of Labor

General Information
Borough of Roosevelt
PO Box 128
33 N Rochdale Ave
Roosevelt, NJ 08555
609-448-0539

Web site	NA
Land area (sq. miles)	1.96
Water area (sq. miles)	0
Type of government	Borough
Form of government	B

Government

Legislative Districts

US Congressional	4
State Legislative	30

Local Officials, 2006

Mayor	Neil Marko
Admin/Manager	Harold Klein
Clerk	Krystyna Bieracka-Olejn
Finance Dir/Treas	A. Debevec/G. Lang
Engineer	Carmela Roberts
Attorney	Ira Karasick
Tax assessor	Michael L. Ticktin
Tax collector	NA
Building officer	Robert Ward
Zoning officer	NA
Public Works	NA

Housing & Construction

Housing Units, 2000*

Total	351
Median rent	$809
Median SF home value	$134,100

New Privately Owned Housing Units Authorized by Building Permit

	Units	Value
Total, 2004	0	$0
Single family	0	$0
Total, 2005	8	$3,909,821
Single family	8	$3,909,821

Real Property Valuation - parcels, 2005

	Number	Valuation
Total		$35,635,110
Vacant	3	216,400
Residential	307	31,869,400
Commercial	4	697,160
Industrial	3	503,100
Apartments	1	990,300
Farm land	8	1,178,000
Farm homestead	12	180,750

Average Property Value & Tax, 2005

Residential value	$100,471
Property tax	$4,711
FAIR rebate	$590

Public Library

No public municipal library.

Library statistics, 2004

	Total	per capita
Volumes	NA	NA
Expenditure	NA	NA

Public Safety

Police

Chief	NA
Number of officers, 2004	0

Crime, 2004	Number	Rate
Total	0	0
Violent	0	0
Non-violent	0	0
Domestic Viol.	1	NA

Emergency/Fire

Director	Kim Dexheimer

Public School District
(for school year 2004-2005 except as noted)

Roosevelt Borough School District
School Lane
Roosevelt, NJ 08555
609-448-2798

Superintendent	Dale Weinbach
Grade plan	K-12
Enrollment	85.0
Students per teacher	8.0
Per pupil expenditure	$12,592
Median faculty salary	$37,883
Median administrator salary	$89,500
Grade 12 enrollment	NA
High school graduation rate	NA

Assessment test results
(percent scoring at proficient or advanced level)

	Language	Math
Grade 3	92.9%	100%
Grade 8	NA	NA
High school	NA	NA

SAT

Percent tested	NA
Average SAT math score	NA
Average SAT verbal score	NA

No Child Left Behind, 2003-04

Attendence rate (target = 90%)	96.5%
Drop rate	NA
Highly-qualified teachers	100%
District needs improvement?(AYP)	No

Municipal Finance

Fiscal Year 2005

Total tax levy	$1,673,795
County levy	221,120
County taxes	195,222
County library	10,754
County health	3,560
County open space	11,585
School levy	1,203,912
Local muni. budget	248,763
Misc. revenues	487,577
Total aid	$119,466
CMPTRA	53,498
Muni. block grant	3,868
Energy tax receipts	62,100
Homeland security	0

Fiscal Year 2006

Total aid	$119,466
CMPTRA	51,324
Muni. block grant	3,868
Energy tax receipts	64,274
Homeland security	NA

Taxes

	2003	2004	2005
General tax rate per $100	4.63	4.625	4.690
Net valuation taxable	$35,640,198	$35,618,482	$35,693,588
State equalized value	$51,031,211	$64,873,056	$75,589,979
County equalization ratio	76.57	69.84	54.85

Demographics & Socio-Economic Characteristics
(2000 U.S. Census, except as noted)

Population
1980*	5,330
1990*	4,847
2000	5,298
Male	2,448
Female	2,850
2004 (estimate)*	5,341
Persons per sq. mi. of land	1,476

Race & Hispanic Origin, 2000
Race
White	4,950
Black/African American	38
Amer. Indian/Alaska Natv.	2
Asian	250
Natv. Hawaiian/Pac. Islander	0
Other Race	23
Two or more races	35
Hispanic origin, total	121
Mexican	11
Puerto Rican	23
Cuban	12
Other Hispanic	75

Age & Nativity, 2000
Under 5 years	314
18 years and over	4,207
21 years and over	4,107
65 years and over	1,044
85 years and over	92
Median Age	44
Native born	4,694
Foreign born	604

Educational Attainment, 2000
Population 25 years and over	3,988
0-8 yrs of school	2.4%
High School grad or higher	92.2%
Bachelor's degree or higher	46.5%
Graduate degree	18.8%

Income & Poverty, 1999
Per capita income	$41,415
Median household income	$82,499
Median family income	$93,957
Persons in poverty	88
H'holds receiving public assistance	9
H'holds receiving social security	794

Households, 2000
Total households	2,142
With persons under 18	587
With persons over 65	768
Family households	1,525
One-person households	550
Persons per household	2.47
Persons per family	2.99

Labor & Employment
Total civilian labor force, 2004**	2,659
Unemployment rate	2.5%
Total civilian labor force, 2000	2,760
Unemployment rate	2.7%

Employed persons 16 years and over by occupation, 2000
Managers & professionals	1,416
Service occupations	193
Sales & office occupations	840
Farming, fishing & forestry	0
Construction & maintenance	161
Production & transportation	75
Self-employed persons	169

*US Census Bureau
**New Jersey Department of Labor

General Information
Borough of Roseland
19 Harrison Ave
Roseland, NJ 07068
973-226-8080
Web site	www.roselandnj.org
Land area (sq. miles)	3.62
Water area (sq. miles)	0
Type of government	Borough
Form of government	B

Government
Legislative Districts
US Congressional	11
State Legislative	27

Local Officials, 2006
Mayor	Michael Pacio Jr.
Admin/Manager	Thomas Kaczynski
Clerk	Thomas Kaczynski
Finance Dir/Treas	Maureen Chumacas
Engineer	Ralph Tango Jr.
Attorney	David Fox
Tax assessor	Kevin Dillon
Tax collector	Maureen Chumacas
Building officer	Leonard Mendola
Zoning officer	Gail Tynan
Public Works	NA

Housing & Construction
Housing Units, 2000*
Total	2,187
Median rent	$1,266
Median SF home value	$292,700

New Privately Owned Housing Units
Authorized by Building Permit
	Units	Value
Total, 2004	58	$9,287,334
Single family	58	$9,287,334
Total, 2005	34	$5,818,797
Single family	34	$5,818,797

Real Property Valuation - parcels, 2005
	Number	Valuation
Total		$263,384,141
Vacant	175	3,827,800
Residential	1,938	120,485,141
Commercial	63	118,630,900
Industrial	24	12,819,900
Apartments	1	7,616,900
Farm land	0	0
Farm homestead	1	3,500

Average Property Value & Tax, 2005
Residential value	$62,140
Property tax	$6,294
FAIR rebate	$629

Public Library
Roseland Free Public Library
20 Roseland Ave
Roseland, NJ 07068
973-226-8636
Director	Judith Lind

Library statistics, 2004
	Total	per capita
Volumes	52,704	9.95
Expenditure	$492,157	$92.89

Public Safety
Police
Chief	Richard McDonough
Number of officers, 2004	28

Crime, 2004	Number	Rate
Total	86	16.2
Violent	7	1.3
Non-violent	79	14.9
Domestic Viol.	55	NA

Emergency/Fire
Director	Kent Yates

Public School District
(for school year 2004-2005 except as noted)

Roseland School District
Noecker School
Roseland, NJ 07068
973-226-1296
Superintendent	Richard Sierchio (Actg)
Grade plan	K-6
Enrollment	451.0
Students per teacher	11.6
Per pupil expenditure	$11,026
Median faculty salary	$55,928
Median administrator salary	$107,364
Grade 12 enrollment	NA
High school graduation rate	NA

Assessment test results
(percent scoring at proficient or advanced level)
	Language	Math
Grade 3	95.2%	95.2%
Grade 8	NA	NA
High school	NA	NA

SAT
Percent tested	NA
Average SAT math score	NA
Average SAT verbal score	NA

No Child Left Behind, 2003-04
Attendence rate (target = 90%)	96.5%
Drop rate	NA
Highly-qualified teachers	100%
District needs improvement?(AYP)	No

Municipal Finance
Fiscal Year 2005
Total tax levy	$26,711,131
County levy	6,648,422
County taxes	6,509,217
County library	0
County health	0
County open space	139,205
School levy	11,834,346
Local muni. budget	8,228,363
Misc. revenues	3,929,243
Total aid	$1,233,374
CMPTRA	298,180
Muni. block grant	21,209
Energy tax receipts	863,985
Homeland security	50,000

Fiscal Year 2006
Total aid	$1,233,375
CMPTRA	267,941
Muni. block grant	21,209
Energy tax receipts	894,225
Homeland security	50,000

Taxes
	2003	2004	2005
General tax rate per $100	9.35	9.530	10.130
Net valuation taxable	$265,481,539	$269,103,097	$263,730,528
State equalized value	$1,307,146,918	$1,403,631,001	$1,798,980,409
County equalization ratio	21.56	21.56	19.15

Demographics & Socio-Economic Characteristics

(2000 U.S. Census, except as noted)

Population

1980*	20,641
1990*	20,314
2000	21,274
Male	9,950
Female	11,324
2004 (estimate)*	21,415
Persons per sq. mi. of land	8,102

Race & Hispanic Origin, 2000

Race

White	7,570
Black/African American	10,917
Amer. Indian/Alaska Natv.	67
Asian	577
Natv. Hawaiian/Pac. Islander	15
Other Race	1,291
Two or more races	837
Hispanic origin, total	3,641
Mexican	597
Puerto Rican	876
Cuban	230
Other Hispanic	1,938

Age & Nativity, 2000

Under 5 years	1,410
18 years and over	15,841
21 years and over	14,948
65 years and over	2,562
85 years and over	268
Median Age	35.3
Native born	16,396
Foreign born	4,878

Educational Attainment, 2000

Population 25 years and over	14,017
0-8 yrs of school	6.2%
High School grad or higher	77.6%
Bachelor's degree or higher	17.3%
Graduate degree	4.8%

Income & Poverty, 1999

Per capita income	$21,269
Median household income	$51,254
Median family income	$58,841
Persons in poverty	1,582
H'holds receiving public assistance	258
H'holds receiving social security	2,024

Households, 2000

Total households	7,520
With persons under 18	2,916
With persons over 65	1,984
Family households	5,223
One-person households	1,895
Persons per household	2.82
Persons per family	3.41

Labor & Employment

Total civilian labor force, 2004**	11,229
Unemployment rate	6.4%
Total civilian labor force, 2000	10,970
Unemployment rate	6.6%

Employed persons 16 years and over by occupation, 2000

Managers & professionals	2,567
Service occupations	1,608
Sales & office occupations	3,456
Farming, fishing & forestry	5
Construction & maintenance	686
Production & transportation	1,925
Self-employed persons	369

*US Census Bureau
**New Jersey Department of Labor

General Information

Borough of Roselle
210 Chestnut St
Roselle, NJ 07203
908-245-5600

Web site	www.boroughofroselle.com
Land area (sq. miles)	2.64
Water area (sq. miles)	0.01
Type of government	Borough
Form of government	B

Government

Legislative Districts

US Congressional	10
State Legislative	20

Local Officials, 2006

Mayor	Garrett B. Smith
Admin/Manager	David Brown II
Clerk	Rhona Bluestien
Finance Dir/Treas	Kenneth Blum Jr.
Engineer	Frank Koczur
Attorney	Dwayne Warren
Tax assessor	Pamela Steele
Tax collector	Mary Testori
Building officer	Jeff Guy
Zoning officer	Rodney Smith
Public Works	Carl Bowles

Housing & Construction

Housing Units, 2000*

Total	7,870
Median rent	$700
Median SF home value	$129,200

New Privately Owned Housing Units Authorized by Building Permit

	Units	Value
Total, 2004	8	$583,830
Single family	2	$234,780
Total, 2005	8	$797,620
Single family	2	$426,420

Real Property Valuation - parcels, 2005

	Number	Valuation
Total		$781,073,301
Vacant	78	4,359,500
Residential	5,172	605,936,001
Commercial	233	83,849,900
Industrial	88	39,435,000
Apartments	49	47,492,900
Farm land	0	0
Farm homestead	0	0

Average Property Value & Tax, 2005

Residential value	$117,157
Property tax	$7,086
FAIR rebate	$576

Public Library

Roselle Free Public Library
104 W Fourth Ave
Roselle, NJ 07203
908-245-5809

Director	Keith McCoy

Library statistics, 2004

	Total	per capita
Volumes	44,337	2.08
Expenditure	$542,050	$25.48

Public Safety

Police

Chief	Peter De Rose
Number of officers, 2004	56

Crime, 2004	Number	Rate
Total	580	27.1
Violent	67	3.1
Non-violent	513	23.9
Domestic Viol.	174	NA

Emergency/Fire

Director	Robert Hill

Public School District

(for school year 2004-2005 except as noted)

Roselle Borough School District
710 Locust St
Roselle, NJ 07203
908-298-2040

Superintendent	Darlene Roberto
Grade plan	K-12
Enrollment	2,934.0
Students per teacher	10.9
Per pupil expenditure	$14,328
Median faculty salary	$45,201
Median administrator salary	$88,892
Grade 12 enrollment	162.0
High school graduation rate	98.2%

Assessment test results

(percent scoring at proficient or advanced level)

	Language	Math
Grade 3	70.6%	77.5%
Grade 8	34.3%	24.3%
High school	64.7%	34.4%

SAT

Percent tested	66%
Average SAT math score	392
Average SAT verbal score	390

No Child Left Behind, 2003-04

Attendence rate (target = 90%)	93.2%
Drop rate	0.6%
Highly-qualified teachers	96.5%
District needs improvement?(AYP)	No

Municipal Finance

Fiscal Year 2005

Total tax levy	$47,481,872
County levy	5,067,236
County taxes	4,866,517
County library	0
County health	0
County open space	200,719
School levy	21,207,859
Local muni. budget	21,206,777
Misc. revenues	9,546,123
Total aid	$3,219,105
CMPTRA	1,809,047
Muni. block grant	88,887
Energy tax receipts	1,231,171
Homeland security	90,000

Fiscal Year 2006

Total aid	$3,219,105
CMPTRA	1,765,056
Muni. block grant	88,887
Energy tax receipts	1,274,262
Homeland security	90,000

Taxes

	2003	2004	2005
General tax rate per $100	5.17	5.552	6.049
Net valuation taxable	$779,764,110	$782,029,476	$785,028,946
State equalized value	$1,034,993,509	$1,248,119,058	$1,454,295,936
County equalization ratio	83.44	72.88	58.78

Demographics & Socio-Economic Characteristics
(2000 U.S. Census, except as noted)

Population
1980*	13,377
1990*	12,805
2000	13,281
Male	6,469
Female	6,812
2004 (estimate)*	13,296
Persons per sq. mi. of land	10,868

Race & Hispanic Origin, 2000
Race
White	10,740
Black/African American	322
Amer. Indian/Alaska Natv.	14
Asian	1,214
Natv. Hawaiian/Pac. Islander	2
Other Race	650
Two or more races	339
Hispanic origin, total	2,170
Mexican	242
Puerto Rican	423
Cuban	275
Other Hispanic	1,230

Age & Nativity, 2000
Under 5 years	781
18 years and over	10,328
21 years and over	9,904
65 years and over	1,680
85 years and over	209
Median Age	36.7
Native born	9,993
Foreign born	3,288

Educational Attainment, 2000
Population 25 years and over	9,095
0-8 yrs of school	5.5%
High School grad or higher	82.9%
Bachelor's degree or higher	25.6%
Graduate degree	7.7%

Income & Poverty, 1999
Per capita income	$24,101
Median household income	$53,717
Median family income	$63,403
Persons in poverty	571
H'holds receiving public assistance	96
H'holds receiving social security	1,265

Households, 2000
Total households	5,137
With persons under 18	1,665
With persons over 65	1,260
Family households	3,415
One-person households	1,448
Persons per household	2.58
Persons per family	3.22

Labor & Employment
Total civilian labor force, 2004**	7,551
Unemployment rate	4.5%
Total civilian labor force, 2000	7,488
Unemployment rate	4.6%

Employed persons 16 years and over by occupation, 2000
Managers & professionals	2,480
Service occupations	1,036
Sales & office occupations	2,190
Farming, fishing & forestry	0
Construction & maintenance	530
Production & transportation	908
Self-employed persons	224

*US Census Bureau
**New Jersey Department of Labor

General Information
Borough of Roselle Park
110 E Westfield Ave
Roselle Park, NJ 07204
908-245-6222

Web site	NA
Land area (sq. miles)	1.22
Water area (sq. miles)	0
Type of government	Borough
Form of government	B

Government

Legislative Districts
US Congressional	7
State Legislative	21

Local Officials, 2006
Mayor	Joseph DeIorio
Admin/Manager	NA
Clerk	Doreen Cali
Finance Dir/Treas	Kenneth Blum
Engineer	Ed Dec
Attorney	William Lane
Tax assessor	Paul Endler
Tax collector	NA
Building officer	John Risso
Zoning officer	NA
Public Works	NA

Housing & Construction

Housing Units, 2000*
Total	5,258
Median rent	$785
Median SF home value	$157,700

New Privately Owned Housing Units Authorized by Building Permit
	Units	Value
Total, 2004	1	$125,000
Single family	1	$125,000
Total, 2005	7	$569,730
Single family	7	$569,730

Real Property Valuation - parcels, 2005
	Number	Valuation
Total		$290,558,200
Vacant	31	433,000
Residential	3,311	232,845,200
Commercial	180	25,497,500
Industrial	24	5,897,800
Apartments	35	25,884,700
Farm land	0	0
Farm homestead	0	0

Average Property Value & Tax, 2005
Residential value	$70,325
Property tax	$6,397
FAIR rebate	$593

Public Library
Veteran's Memorial Library
404 Chestnut St
Roselle Park, NJ 07204
908-245-2456

Director................Susan Calantone

Library statistics, 2004
	Total	per capita
Volumes	63,470	4.78
Expenditure	$431,479	$32.49

Public Safety

Police
Chief	Warren Wielgus
Number of officers, 2004	34

Crime, 2004	Number	Rate
Total	243	18.3
Violent	24	1.8
Non-violent	219	16.5
Domestic Viol.	65	NA

Emergency/Fire
Director............Robert Tobe (Chief)

Public School District
(for school year 2004-2005 except as noted)

Roselle Park School District
510 Chestnut St
Roselle Park, NJ 07204
908-245-1197

Superintendent	Patrick Spagnoletti
Grade plan	K-12
Enrollment	2,074.0
Students per teacher	10.8
Per pupil expenditure	$10,903
Median faculty salary	$47,719
Median administrator salary	$94,950
Grade 12 enrollment	145.5
High school graduation rate	99.0%

Assessment test results
(percent scoring at proficient or advanced level)
	Language	Math
Grade 3	85.7%	78.6%
Grade 8	69.3%	49.4%
High school	80.8%	77.7%

SAT
Percent tested	76%
Average SAT math score	498
Average SAT verbal score	467

No Child Left Behind, 2003-04
Attendence rate (target = 90%)	95.6%
Drop rate	0%
Highly-qualified teachers	99.2%
District needs improvement?(AYP)	No

Municipal Finance

Fiscal Year 2005
Total tax levy	$26,448,439
County levy	3,825,641
County taxes	3,674,606
County library	0
County health	0
County open space	151,035
School levy	14,643,512
Local muni. budget	7,979,287
Misc. revenues	3,761,895
Total aid	$1,472,817
CMPTRA	700,898
Muni. block grant	56,031
Energy tax receipts	645,888
Homeland security	70,000

Fiscal Year 2006
Total aid	$1,472,817
CMPTRA	678,292
Muni. block grant	56,031
Energy tax receipts	668,494
Homeland security	70,000

Taxes
	2003	2004	2005
General tax rate per $100	7.96	8.478	9.096
Net valuation taxable	$290,512,851	$290,549,428	$290,771,295
State equalized value	$812,168,999	$919,481,104	$1,057,734,794
County equalization ratio	39.83	33.36	28.98

Demographics & Socio-Economic Characteristics
(2000 U.S. Census, except as noted)

Population
1980*	18,878
1990*	20,429
2000	23,883
Male	11,674
Female	12,209
2000 (revised)	23,227
2004 (estimate)*	23,854
Persons per sq. mi. of land	1,116

Race & Hispanic Origin, 2000
Race
White	22,110
Black/African American	456
Amer. Indian/Alaska Natv.	35
Asian	855
Natv. Hawaiian/Pac. Islander	17
Other Race	162
Two or more races	248
Hispanic origin, total	1,154
Mexican	77
Puerto Rican	393
Cuban	103
Other Hispanic	581

Age & Nativity, 2000
Under 5 years	1,705
18 years and over	17,438
21 years and over	16,751
65 years and over	2,363
85 years and over	253
Median Age	37.5
Native born	21,470
Foreign born	2,413

Educational Attainment, 2000
Population 25 years and over	16,150
0-8 yrs of school	3.3%
High School grad or higher	90.0%
Bachelor's degree or higher	33.9%
Graduate degree	10.0%

Income & Poverty, 1999
Per capita income	$30,174
Median household income	$72,982
Median family income	$83,409
Persons in poverty	642
H'holds receiving public assistance	107
H'holds receiving social security	1,908

Households, 2000
Total households	8,364
With persons under 18	3,524
With persons over 65	1,711
Family households	6,534
One-person households	1,501
Persons per household	2.84
Persons per family	3.25

Labor & Employment
Total civilian labor force, 2004**	12,467
Unemployment rate	3.3%
Total civilian labor force, 2000	13,018
Unemployment rate	3.0%

Employed persons 16 years and over by occupation, 2000
Managers & professionals	5,430
Service occupations	1,319
Sales & office occupations	3,772
Farming, fishing & forestry	9
Construction & maintenance	1,121
Production & transportation	974
Self-employed persons	701

*US Census Bureau
**New Jersey Department of Labor

General Information
Roxbury Township
1715 Route 46
Ledgewood, NJ 07852
973-448-2000

Web site	NA
Land area (sq. miles)	21.37
Water area (sq. miles)	0.53
Type of government	Township
Form of government	CM '50

Government

Legislative Districts
US Congressional	11
State Legislative	25

Local Officials, 2006
Mayor	Martin Schmidt
Admin/Manager	Christopher Raths
Clerk	Betty Lou DeCroce
Finance Dir/Treas	Lisa Palmieri
Engineer	Mike Kobylarz
Attorney	Tony Bucco Jr.
Tax assessor	Lora Corica
Tax collector	Arlene Ehehalt
Building officer	Russel Brown
Zoning officer	Tom Potere
Public Works	Rick Blood

Housing & Construction

Housing Units, 2000*
Total	8,550
Median rent	$759
Median SF home value	$207,400

New Privately Owned Housing Units Authorized by Building Permit
	Units	Value
Total, 2004	20	$4,051,255
Single family	20	$4,051,255
Total, 2005	100	$4,540,129
Single family	52	$3,907,717

Real Property Valuation - parcels, 2005
	Number	Valuation
Total		$2,041,854,200
Vacant	488	41,677,700
Residential	7,753	1,593,736,100
Commercial	397	320,210,300
Industrial	44	70,532,900
Apartments	13	10,934,900
Farm land	16	4,571,300
Farm homestead	32	191,000

Average Property Value & Tax, 2005
Residential value	$204,743
Property tax	$6,541
FAIR rebate	$518

Public Library
Roxbury Public Library
103 Main St
Succasunna, NJ 07876
973-584-2400

Director	Mary Romance

Library statistics, 2004
	Total	per capita
Volumes	75,797	3.17
Expenditure	$1,152,229	$48.24

Public Safety
Police
Chief	Mark Noll
Number of officers, 2004	48

Crime, 2004	Number	Rate
Total	365	15.4
Violent	26	1.1
Non-violent	339	14.3
Domestic Viol.	110	NA

Emergency/Fire
Director	Joe Lang Jr.

Public School District
(for school year 2004-2005 except as noted)

Roxbury Township School District
42 N Hillside Ave
Succasunna, NJ 07876
973-584-6867

Superintendent	Dennis Mack
Grade plan	K-12
Enrollment	4,533.0
Students per teacher	11.3
Per pupil expenditure	$11,513
Median faculty salary	$56,094
Median administrator salary	$103,957
Grade 12 enrollment	353.0
High school graduation rate	95.4%

Assessment test results
(percent scoring at proficient or advanced level)
	Language	Math
Grade 3	94.4%	92.8%
Grade 8	79.7%	72.2%
High school	89.1%	75.6%

SAT
Percent tested	79%
Average SAT math score	532
Average SAT verbal score	529

No Child Left Behind, 2003-04
Attendence rate (target = 90%)	95.9%
Drop rate	0.8%
Highly-qualified teachers	100%
District needs improvement?(AYP)	No

Municipal Finance

Fiscal Year 2005
Total tax levy	$65,454,761
County levy	8,242,680
County taxes	6,751,883
County library	0
County health	0
County open space	1,490,797
School levy	41,754,565
Local muni. budget	15,457,516
Misc. revenues	7,190,723
Total aid	$2,912,417
CMPTRA	1,182,178
Muni. block grant	93,646
Energy tax receipts	1,546,593
Homeland security	90,000

Fiscal Year 2006
Total aid	$2,912,417
CMPTRA	1,128,047
Muni. block grant	93,646
Energy tax receipts	1,600,724
Homeland security	90,000

Taxes
	2003	2004	2005
General tax rate per $100	2.78	2.970	3.200
Net valuation taxable	$2,034,688,517	$2,040,875,553	$2,048,814,719
State equalized value	$2,642,452,619	$3,070,123,508	$3,517,882,416
County equalization ratio	84.26	77.00	66.39

Demographics & Socio-Economic Characteristics
(2000 U.S. Census, except as noted)

Population
1980*	7,623
1990*	6,701
2000	7,137
Male	3,457
Female	3,680
2004 (estimate)*	7,271
Persons per sq. mi. of land	1,392

Race & Hispanic Origin, 2000
Race
White	6,978
Black/African American	17
Amer. Indian/Alaska Natv.	4
Asian	76
Natv. Hawaiian/Pac. Islander	0
Other Race	26
Two or more races	36
Hispanic origin, total	99
Mexican	25
Puerto Rican	19
Cuban	20
Other Hispanic	35

Age & Nativity, 2000
Under 5 years	528
18 years and over	4,862
21 years and over	4,729
65 years and over	914
85 years and over	92
Median Age	39.2
Native born	6,845
Foreign born	292

Educational Attainment, 2000
Population 25 years and over	4,630
0-8 yrs of school	0.3%
High School grad or higher	97.1%
Bachelor's degree or higher	63.9%
Graduate degree	24.9%

Income & Poverty, 1999
Per capita income	$73,692
Median household income	$120,865
Median family income	$140,668
Persons in poverty	228
H'holds receiving public assistance	12
H'holds receiving social security	642

Households, 2000
Total households	2,452
With persons under 18	1,116
With persons over 65	651
Family households	1,989
One-person households	412
Persons per household	2.91
Persons per family	3.29

Labor & Employment
Total civilian labor force, 2004**	3,687
Unemployment rate	2.0%
Total civilian labor force, 2000	3,047
Unemployment rate	2.6%

Employed persons 16 years and over by occupation, 2000
Managers & professionals	1,763
Service occupations	154
Sales & office occupations	844
Farming, fishing & forestry	0
Construction & maintenance	134
Production & transportation	74
Self-employed persons	204

*US Census Bureau
**New Jersey Department of Labor

General Information
Borough of Rumson
80 East River Rd
Rumson, NJ 07760
732-842-3300

Web site	rumsonboro.com
Land area (sq. miles)	5.22
Water area (sq. miles)	2.01
Type of government	Borough
Form of government	B

Government

Legislative Districts
US Congressional	12
State Legislative	11

Local Officials, 2006
Mayor	John E. Ekdahl
Admin/Manager	Thomas S. Rogers
Clerk	Thomas S. Rogers
Finance Dir/Treas	Helen Graves
Engineer	C. Bernard Blum Jr.
Attorney	Martin Barger
Tax assessor	Peter Barnett
Tax collector	Melissa E. Gonzalez
Building officer	Paul Reinhold Jr.
Zoning officer	Frederick Andre
Public Works	Mark T. Wellner

Housing & Construction

Housing Units, 2000*
Total	2,610
Median rent	$1,187
Median SF home value	$455,300

New Privately Owned Housing Units
Authorized by Building Permit
	Units	Value
Total, 2004	43	$19,894,820
Single family	43	$19,894,820
Total, 2005	33	$18,262,553
Single family	33	$18,262,553

Real Property Valuation - parcels, 2005
	Number	Valuation
Total		$2,776,209,300
Vacant	35	13,070,000
Residential	2,458	2,656,044,000
Commercial	71	103,472,000
Industrial	0	0
Apartments	4	3,597,600
Farm land	0	0
Farm homestead	4	25,700

Average Property Value & Tax, 2005
Residential value	$1,078,826
Property tax	$14,264
FAIR rebate	$547

Public Library
Oceanic Free Library
Ave Of Two Rivers
Rumson, NJ 07760
732-842-2692

Director .... Ann Wissel

Library statistics, 2004
	Total	per capita
Volumes	24,556	3.44
Expenditure	$162,616	$22.78

Public Safety

Police
Chief	Rick Tobias (OIC)
Number of officers, 2004	17

Crime, 2004	Number	Rate
Total	89	12.2
Violent	1	0.1
Non-violent	88	12
Domestic Viol.	8	NA

Emergency/Fire
Director .... Joe Ward

Public School District
(for school year 2004-2005 except as noted)

Rumson Borough School District
Forrest Ave
Rumson, NJ 07760
732-842-4747

Superintendent	Richard Noonan
Grade plan	K-8
Enrollment	987.0
Students per teacher	11.2
Per pupil expenditure	$10,700
Median faculty salary	$48,630
Median administrator salary	$89,352
Grade 12 enrollment	NA
High school graduation rate	NA

Assessment test results
(percent scoring at proficient or advanced level)
	Language	Math
Grade 3	94.5%	94.5%
Grade 8	95.0%	89.2%
High school	NA	NA

SAT
Percent tested	NA
Average SAT math score	NA
Average SAT verbal score	NA

No Child Left Behind, 2003-04
Attendence rate (target = 90%)	95.4%
Drop rate	NA
Highly-qualified teachers	98.3%
District needs improvement?(AYP)	No

Municipal Finance

Fiscal Year 2005
Total tax levy	$36,724,413
County levy	8,986,670
County taxes	8,064,012
County library	444,231
County health	0
County open space	478,427
School levy	19,949,878
Local muni. budget	7,787,865
Misc. revenues	4,620,190
Total aid	$946,214
CMPTRA	161,086
Muni. block grant	29,321
Energy tax receipts	705,807
Homeland security	50,000

Fiscal Year 2006
Total aid	$946,215
CMPTRA	136,383
Muni. block grant	29,321
Energy tax receipts	730,511
Homeland security	50,000

Taxes
	2003	2004	2005
General tax rate per $100	3.05	1.255	1.323
Net valuation taxable	$1,036,473,658	$2,743,977,511	$2,777,584,506
State equalized value	$2,237,637,431	$2,671,610,268	$3,079,703,411
County equalization ratio	54.2	121.37	102.71

Demographics & Socio-Economic Characteristics
(2000 U.S. Census, except as noted)

Population
1980*	9,461
1990*	9,042
2000	8,533
Male	4,103
Female	4,430
2004 (estimate)*	8,511
Persons per sq. mi. of land	4,074

Race & Hispanic Origin, 2000
Race
White	7,831
Black/African American	321
Amer. Indian/Alaska Natv.	9
Asian	132
Natv. Hawaiian/Pac. Islander	1
Other Race	104
Two or more races	135
Hispanic origin, total	306
Mexican	81
Puerto Rican	170
Cuban	4
Other Hispanic	51

Age & Nativity, 2000
Under 5 years	489
18 years and over	6,557
21 years and over	6,243
65 years and over	1,332
85 years and over	118
Median Age	37.8
Native born	8,182
Foreign born	351

Educational Attainment, 2000
Population 25 years and over	5,803
0-8 yrs of school	5.5%
High School grad or higher	78.6%
Bachelor's degree or higher	12.6%
Graduate degree	3.4%

Income & Poverty, 1999
Per capita income	$19,143
Median household income	$41,126
Median family income	$50,127
Persons in poverty	474
H'holds receiving public assistance	17
H'holds receiving social security	1,138

Households, 2000
Total households	3,376
With persons under 18	1,145
With persons over 65	1,001
Family households	2,274
One-person households	938
Persons per household	2.52
Persons per family	3.08

Labor & Employment
Total civilian labor force, 2004**	4,837
Unemployment rate	4.5%
Total civilian labor force, 2000	4,434
Unemployment rate	6.1%

Employed persons 16 years and over by occupation, 2000
Managers & professionals	1,071
Service occupations	662
Sales & office occupations	1,376
Farming, fishing & forestry	0
Construction & maintenance	406
Production & transportation	648
Self-employed persons	149

*US Census Bureau
**New Jersey Department of Labor

General Information
Borough of Runnemede
24 N Black Horse Pike
Runnemede, NJ 08078
856-939-5161

Web site	NA
Land area (sq. miles)	2.09
Water area (sq. miles)	0.03
Type of government	Borough
Form of government	B

Government
Legislative Districts
US Congressional	1
State Legislative	5

Local Officials, 2006
Mayor	Virginia Betteridge
Admin/Manager	NA
Clerk	Joyce Pinto
Finance Dir/Treas	Dean Ciminera
Engineer	Steven Bach
Attorney	Michael Albano
Tax assessor	Ronald Aaronson
Tax collector	NA
Building officer	Chris Mecca
Zoning officer	NA
Public Works	NA

Housing & Construction
Housing Units, 2000*
Total	3,510
Median rent	$598
Median SF home value	$97,800

New Privately Owned Housing Units Authorized by Building Permit
	Units	Value
Total, 2004	16	$1,372,300
Single family	16	$1,372,300
Total, 2005	8	$685,000
Single family	8	$685,000

Real Property Valuation - parcels, 2005
	Number	Valuation
Total		$332,476,700
Vacant	82	2,930,400
Residential	2,577	253,501,100
Commercial	158	44,497,800
Industrial	13	13,249,700
Apartments	21	18,297,700
Farm land	0	0
Farm homestead	0	0

Average Property Value & Tax, 2005
Residential value	$98,371
Property tax	$4,418
FAIR rebate	$636

Public Library
Runnemede Public Library
Broadway & Black Horse Pike
Runnemede, NJ 08078
856-939-4688

Director ... Kathleen Vasinda

Library statistics, 2004
	Total	per capita
Volumes	23,226	2.72
Expenditure	$188,903	$22.14

Public Safety
Police
Chief	Mark Diano
Number of officers, 2004	20

Crime, 2004	Number	Rate
Total	361	42.3
Violent	31	3.6
Non-violent	330	38.6
Domestic Viol.	61	NA

Emergency/Fire
Director	Patrick Moriarty

Public School District
(for school year 2004-2005 except as noted)

Runnemede Borough School District
505 W Third Ave
Runnemede, NJ 08078
856-931-5365

Superintendent	Joseph Sweeney
Grade plan	K-8
Enrollment	789.0
Students per teacher	10.5
Per pupil expenditure	$12,054
Median faculty salary	$53,500
Median administrator salary	$92,000
Grade 12 enrollment	NA
High school graduation rate	NA

Assessment test results
(percent scoring at proficient or advanced level)
	Language	Math
Grade 3	86.5%	87.8%
Grade 8	65.9%	38.3%
High school	NA	NA

SAT
Percent tested	NA
Average SAT math score	NA
Average SAT verbal score	NA

No Child Left Behind, 2003-04
Attendance rate (target = 90%)	95.1%
Drop rate	NA
Highly-qualified teachers	93.5%
District needs improvement?(AYP)	No

Municipal Finance
Fiscal Year 2005
Total tax levy	$15,001,740
County levy	3,144,989
County taxes	3,104,260
County library	0
County health	0
County open space	40,729
School levy	8,730,546
Local muni. budget	3,126,206
Misc. revenues	3,293,794
Total aid	$1,270,861
CMPTRA	551,180
Muni. block grant	39,565
Energy tax receipts	630,116
Homeland security	50,000

Fiscal Year 2006
Total aid	$1,270,861
CMPTRA	529,176
Muni. block grant	39,565
Energy tax receipts	652,170
Homeland security	50,000

Taxes
	2003	2004	2005
General tax rate per $100	4.00	4.305	4.491
Net valuation taxable	$331,298,139	$330,913,721	$334,052,693
State equalized value	$371,285,598	$400,888,392	$471,559,420
County equalization ratio	95.24	89.23	82.47

Demographics & Socio-Economic Characteristics
(2000 U.S. Census, except as noted)

Population
1980*	19,068
1990*	17,790
2000	18,110
Male	8,699
Female	9,411
2004 (estimate)*	18,084
Persons per sq. mi. of land	6,442

Race & Hispanic Origin, 2000
Race
White	14,849
Black/African American	489
Amer. Indian/Alaska Natv.	8
Asian	2,054
Natv. Hawaiian/Pac. Islander	5
Other Race	337
Two or more races	368
Hispanic origin, total	1,555
Mexican	88
Puerto Rican	348
Cuban	280
Other Hispanic	839

Age & Nativity, 2000
Under 5 years	946
18 years and over	14,349
21 years and over	13,818
65 years and over	2,637
85 years and over	328
Median Age	38.8
Native born	14,466
Foreign born	3,644

Educational Attainment, 2000
Population 25 years and over	12,997
0-8 yrs of school	3.7%
High School grad or higher	88.3%
Bachelor's degree or higher	40.3%
Graduate degree	14.0%

Income & Poverty, 1999
Per capita income	$30,495
Median household income	$63,820
Median family income	$78,120
Persons in poverty	668
H'holds receiving public assistance	111
H'holds receiving social security	1,970

Households, 2000
Total households	7,055
With persons under 18	2,165
With persons over 65	1,976
Family households	4,672
One-person households	1,998
Persons per household	2.52
Persons per family	3.16

Labor & Employment
Total civilian labor force, 2004**	10,221
Unemployment rate	3.8%
Total civilian labor force, 2000	9,815
Unemployment rate	4.6%

Employed persons 16 years and over by occupation, 2000
Managers & professionals	4,191
Service occupations	984
Sales & office occupations	2,834
Farming, fishing & forestry	0
Construction & maintenance	603
Production & transportation	751
Self-employed persons	484

*US Census Bureau
**New Jersey Department of Labor

General Information
Borough of Rutherford
176 Park Ave
Rutherford, NJ 07070
201-460-3000
Web site	www.rutherford-nj.com
Land area (sq. miles)	2.81
Water area (sq. miles)	0.12
Type of government	Borough
Form of government	B

Government

Legislative Districts
US Congressional	9
State Legislative	36

Local Officials, 2006
Mayor	Bernadette McPherson
Admin/Manager	Timothy F. Stafford
Clerk	Mary Kriston
Finance Dir/Treas	Ed Cortright
Engineer	Matthew Neuls
Attorney	Anne Marie Rizzuto
Tax assessor	Frank Bucino
Tax collector	NA
Building officer	John Uhl
Zoning officer	NA
Public Works	NA

Housing & Construction

Housing Units, 2000*
Total	7,214
Median rent	$832
Median SF home value	$218,300

New Privately Owned Housing Units Authorized by Building Permit
	Units	Value
Total, 2004	4	$349,700
Single family	2	$167,700
Total, 2005	17	$2,542,250
Single family	13	$1,962,250

Real Property Valuation - parcels, 2005
	Number	Valuation
Total		$1,243,153,000
Vacant	97	25,678,300
Residential	4,947	931,416,700
Commercial	236	185,037,700
Industrial	25	53,181,400
Apartments	36	47,838,900
Farm land	0	0
Farm homestead	0	0

Average Property Value & Tax, 2005
Residential value	$188,279
Property tax	$6,967
FAIR rebate	$597

Public Library
Rutherford Public Library
150 Park Ave
Rutherford, NJ 07070
201-939-8600
Director	Jane Fisher

Library statistics, 2004
	Total	per capita
Volumes	126,252	6.97
Expenditure	$1,220,386	$67.39

Public Safety

Police
Chief	Steven Nienstedt
Number of officers, 2004	40

Crime, 2004	Number	Rate
Total	341	18.9
Violent	11	0.6
Non-violent	330	18.3
Domestic Viol.	90	NA

Emergency/Fire
Director	Tom Verdino

Public School District
(for school year 2004-2005 except as noted)

Rutherford School District
176 Park Ave
Rutherford, NJ 07070
201-939-1717
Superintendent	Leslie Conlon
Grade plan	K-12
Enrollment	2,285.5
Students per teacher	11.4
Per pupil expenditure	$12,120
Median faculty salary	$64,162
Median administrator salary	$108,524
Grade 12 enrollment	199.5
High school graduation rate	99.5%

Assessment test results
(percent scoring at proficient or advanced level)
	Language	Math
Grade 3	88.7%	85.4%
Grade 8	88.9%	76.9%
High school	92.6%	87.7%

SAT
Percent tested	89%
Average SAT math score	516
Average SAT verbal score	502

No Child Left Behind, 2003-04
Attendence rate (target = 90%)	95.8%
Drop rate	0.1%
Highly-qualified teachers	97.6%
District needs improvement?(AYP)	No

Municipal Finance

Fiscal Year 2005
Total tax levy	$46,333,181
County levy	4,298,432
County taxes	4,083,469
County library	0
County health	0
County open space	214,963
School levy	28,434,857
Local muni. budget	13,599,892
Misc. revenues	10,367,089
Total aid	$1,946,215
CMPTRA	764,148
Muni. block grant	77,844
Energy tax receipts	1,034,223
Homeland security	70,000

Fiscal Year 2006
Total aid	$1,946,216
CMPTRA	727,951
Muni. block grant	77,844
Energy tax receipts	1,070,421
Homeland security	70,000

Taxes
	2003	2004	2005
General tax rate per $100	3.41	3.520	3.710
Net valuation taxable	$1,239,463,552	$1,247,664,465	$1,252,104,081
State equalized value	$1,908,334,953	$2,134,742,519	$2,469,633,296
County equalization ratio	74.46	64.95	58.25

Demographics & Socio-Economic Characteristics
(2000 U.S. Census, except as noted)

Population
1980*	14,084
1990*	13,296
2000	13,155
Male	6,210
Female	6,945
2004 (estimate)*	13,236
Persons per sq. mi. of land	4,860

Race & Hispanic Origin, 2000
Race
White	11,936
Black/African American	183
Amer. Indian/Alaska Natv.	5
Asian	623
Natv. Hawaiian/Pac. Islander	0
Other Race	223
Two or more races	185
Hispanic origin, total	825
Mexican	19
Puerto Rican	198
Cuban	87
Other Hispanic	521

Age & Nativity, 2000
Under 5 years	744
18 years and over	10,499
21 years and over	10,124
65 years and over	2,368
85 years and over	266
Median Age	40.3
Native born	11,043
Foreign born	2,112

Educational Attainment, 2000
Population 25 years and over	9,703
0-8 yrs of school	4.6%
High School grad or higher	85.3%
Bachelor's degree or higher	25.2%
Graduate degree	6.1%

Income & Poverty, 1999
Per capita income	$27,561
Median household income	$63,545
Median family income	$73,205
Persons in poverty	434
H'holds receiving public assistance	34
H'holds receiving social security	1,605

Households, 2000
Total households	5,062
With persons under 18	1,518
With persons over 65	1,645
Family households	3,579
One-person households	1,263
Persons per household	2.58
Persons per family	3.11

Labor & Employment
Total civilian labor force, 2004**	7,727
Unemployment rate	5.1%
Total civilian labor force, 2000	6,953
Unemployment rate	5.2%

Employed persons 16 years and over by occupation, 2000
Managers & professionals	2,335
Service occupations	714
Sales & office occupations	2,187
Farming, fishing & forestry	0
Construction & maintenance	604
Production & transportation	752
Self-employed persons	272

*US Census Bureau
**New Jersey Department of Labor

General Information
Township of Saddle Brook
93 Market St
Saddle Brook, NJ 07663
201-843-7100 or 587

Web site	NA
Land area (sq. miles)	2.72
Water area (sq. miles)	0.01
Type of government	Township
Form of government	MC '50

Government
Legislative Districts
US Congressional	9
State Legislative	38

Local Officials, 2006
Mayor	Louis D'Arminio
Admin/Manager	Robert Elia
Clerk	Peter Lo Dico
Finance Dir/Treas	Thomas Kane
Engineer	Birdsall Engineering
Attorney	Anthony Suarez
Tax assessor	Arthur Carlson
Tax collector	NA
Building officer	John Sistaro
Zoning officer	NA
Public Works	NA

Housing & Construction
Housing Units, 2000*
Total	5,161
Median rent	$887
Median SF home value	$198,600

New Privately Owned Housing Units
Authorized by Building Permit

	Units	Value
Total, 2004	NA	NA
Single family	NA	NA
Total, 2005	149	$6,106,020
Single family	105	$5,590,969

Real Property Valuation - parcels, 2005
	Number	Valuation
Total		$1,162,311,754
Vacant	114	11,094,900
Residential	4,056	753,011,600
Commercial	124	207,253,500
Industrial	79	161,373,454
Apartments	7	29,578,300
Farm land	0	0
Farm homestead	0	0

Average Property Value & Tax, 2005
Residential value	$185,654
Property tax	$5,447
FAIR rebate	$657

Public Library
Saddle Brook Public Library
340 Mayhill St
Saddle Brook, NJ 07663
201-843-3287
Director .... Alma Henderson

Library statistics, 2004
	Total	per capita
Volumes	66,365	5.04
Expenditure	$477,888	$36.33

Public Safety
Police
Chief	Robert Kugler
Number of officers, 2004	34

Crime, 2004	Number	Rate
Total	490	37.3
Violent	17	1.3
Non-violent	473	36
Domestic Viol.	59	NA

Emergency/Fire
Director .... John La Barbera

Public School District
(for school year 2004-2005 except as noted)

Saddle Brook Township School District
355 Mayhill St
Saddle Brook, NJ 07663
201-843-2133

Superintendent	Harry Groveman
Grade plan	K-12
Enrollment	1,710.5
Students per teacher	12.3
Per pupil expenditure	$11,595
Median faculty salary	$56,015
Median administrator salary	$105,756
Grade 12 enrollment	124.0
High school graduation rate	96.9%

Assessment test results
(percent scoring at proficient or advanced level)
	Language	Math
Grade 3	84.8%	87.0%
Grade 8	77.6%	65.7%
High school	92.3%	82.2%

SAT
Percent tested	76%
Average SAT math score	485
Average SAT verbal score	468

No Child Left Behind, 2003-04
Attendence rate (target = 90%)	94.5%
Drop rate	1.2%
Highly-qualified teachers	98.2%
District needs improvement?(AYP)	No

Municipal Finance
Fiscal Year 2005
Total tax levy	$34,131,606
County levy	3,508,210
County taxes	3,332,685
County library	0
County health	0
County open space	175,524
School levy	20,265,310
Local muni. budget	10,358,086
Misc. revenues	3,888,200
Total aid	$1,996,193
CMPTRA	704,476
Muni. block grant	58,179
Energy tax receipts	1,163,538
Homeland security	70,000

Fiscal Year 2006
Total aid	$1,996,193
CMPTRA	663,752
Muni. block grant	58,179
Energy tax receipts	1,204,262
Homeland security	70,000

Taxes
	2003	2004	2005
General tax rate per $100	2.61	2.750	2.940
Net valuation taxable	$1,150,054,981	$1,153,990,034	$1,163,358,395
State equalized value	$1,603,534,552	$1,723,588,719	$2,088,989,756
County equalization ratio	78.99	71.72	66.93

Demographics & Socio-Economic Characteristics
(2000 U.S. Census, except as noted)

Population

1980*	2,763
1990*	2,950
2000	3,201
Male	1,541
Female	1,660
2004 (estimate)*	3,743
Persons per sq. mi. of land	751

Race & Hispanic Origin, 2000
Race

White	2,876
Black/African American	24
Amer. Indian/Alaska Natv.	0
Asian	229
Natv. Hawaiian/Pac. Islander	1
Other Race	26
Two or more races	45
Hispanic origin, total	82
Mexican	12
Puerto Rican	18
Cuban	22
Other Hispanic	30

Age & Nativity, 2000

Under 5 years	165
18 years and over	2,482
21 years and over	2,400
65 years and over	653
85 years and over	127
Median Age	46.9
Native born	2,638
Foreign born	563

Educational Attainment, 2000

Population 25 years and over	2,335
0-8 yrs of school	2.8%
High School grad or higher	93.7%
Bachelor's degree or higher	60.6%
Graduate degree	31.9%

Income & Poverty, 1999

Per capita income	$85,934
Median household income	$134,289
Median family income	$152,169
Persons in poverty	111
H'holds receiving public assistance	0
H'holds receiving social security	340

Households, 2000

Total households	1,118
With persons under 18	368
With persons over 65	378
Family households	927
One-person households	159
Persons per household	2.77
Persons per family	3.05

Labor & Employment

Total civilian labor force, 2004**	1,565
Unemployment rate	2.0%
Total civilian labor force, 2000	1,344
Unemployment rate	3.2%

Employed persons 16 years and over by occupation, 2000

Managers & professionals	843
Service occupations	69
Sales & office occupations	304
Farming, fishing & forestry	0
Construction & maintenance	32
Production & transportation	53
Self-employed persons	182

*US Census Bureau
**New Jersey Department of Labor

General Information

Borough of Saddle River
100 E Allendale Rd
Saddle River, NJ 07458
201-327-2609

Web site	www.saddleriver.org
Land area (sq. miles)	4.98
Water area (sq. miles)	0
Type of government	Borough
Form of government	B

Government

Legislative Districts

US Congressional	5
State Legislative	39

Local Officials, 2006

Mayor	Conrad Caruso
Admin/Manager	Charles Cuccia
Clerk	Marie Macari
Finance Dir/Treas	Charles Cuccia
Engineer	Charles Wilde
Attorney	Harry Norton Jr.
Tax assessor	Stuart Stolarz
Tax collector	Linda Canavan
Building officer	John Scialla
Zoning officer	John Scialla
Public Works	NA

Housing & Construction

Housing Units, 2000*

Total	1,183
Median rent	$1,451
Median SF home value	$970,100

New Privately Owned Housing Units
Authorized by Building Permit

	Units	Value
Total, 2004	18	$17,021,769
Single family	18	$17,021,769
Total, 2005	17	$14,441,278
Single family	17	$14,441,278

Real Property Valuation - parcels, 2005

	Number	Valuation
Total		$2,003,544,600
Vacant	110	69,898,700
Residential	1,214	1,887,185,900
Commercial	18	37,594,800
Industrial	0	0
Apartments	0	0
Farm land	6	8,762,800
Farm homestead	10	102,400

Average Property Value & Tax, 2005

Residential value	$1,541,902
Property tax	$11,936
FAIR rebate	$678

Public Library

No public municipal library.

Library statistics, 2004

	Total	per capita
Volumes	NA	NA
Expenditure	NA	NA

Public Safety

Police

Chief	Timothy McWilliams
Number of officers, 2004	17

Crime, 2004	Number	Rate
Total	30	8.1
Violent	2	0.5
Non-violent	28	7.6
Domestic Viol.	3	NA

Emergency/Fire

Director	Glen Dowson

Public School District
(for school year 2004-2005 except as noted)

Saddle River School District
97 E Allendale Rd
Saddle River, NJ 07458
201-327-0727

Superintendent	David Goldblatt
Grade plan	K-12
Enrollment	199.0
Students per teacher	8.0
Per pupil expenditure	$15,826
Median faculty salary	$50,754
Median administrator salary	$114,815
Grade 12 enrollment	NA
High school graduation rate	NA

Assessment test results
(percent scoring at proficient or advanced level)

	Language	Math
Grade 3	100%	96.8%
Grade 8	NA	NA
High school	NA	NA

SAT

Percent tested	NA
Average SAT math score	NA
Average SAT verbal score	NA

No Child Left Behind, 2003-04

Attendence rate (target = 90%)	95.2%
Drop rate	NA
Highly-qualified teachers	100%
District needs improvement?(AYP)	No

Municipal Finance

Fiscal Year 2005

Total tax levy	$15,516,806
County levy	4,076,632
County taxes	3,871,431
County library	0
County health	0
County open space	205,201
School levy	5,974,947
Local muni. budget	5,465,228
Misc. revenues	2,560,661
Total aid	$532,727
CMPTRA	52,134
Muni. block grant	12,908
Energy tax receipts	442,685
Homeland security	25,000

Fiscal Year 2006

Total aid	$532,727
CMPTRA	36,640
Muni. block grant	12,908
Energy tax receipts	458,179
Homeland security	25,000

Taxes

	2003	2004	2005
General tax rate per $100	0.72	0.750	0.780
Net valuation taxable	$1,884,001,016	$1,947,604,824	$2,004,522,124
State equalized value	$1,817,481,204	$1,994,043,256	$2,185,003,405
County equalization ratio	113.41	103.66	97.67

Demographics & Socio-Economic Characteristics
(2000 U.S. Census, except as noted)

Population
1980*	6,959
1990*	6,883
2000	5,857
Male	2,615
Female	3,242
2004 (estimate)*	5,787
Persons per sq. mi. of land	2,218

Race & Hispanic Origin, 2000
Race
White	2,194
Black/African American	3,325
Amer. Indian/Alaska Natv.	35
Asian	14
Natv. Hawaiian/Pac. Islander	0
Other Race	81
Two or more races	208
Hispanic origin, total	286
Mexican	25
Puerto Rican	191
Cuban	8
Other Hispanic	62

Age & Nativity, 2000
Under 5 years	518
18 years and over	4,044
21 years and over	3,801
65 years and over	821
85 years and over	83
Median Age	33.5
Native born	5,761
Foreign born	45

Educational Attainment, 2000
Population 25 years and over	3,385
0-8 yrs of school	12.1%
High School grad or higher	67.8%
Bachelor's degree or higher	7.9%
Graduate degree	1.8%

Income & Poverty, 1999
Per capita income	$13,559
Median household income	$25,846
Median family income	$29,699
Persons in poverty	1,531
H'holds receiving public assistance	182
H'holds receiving social security	791

Households, 2000
Total households	2,383
With persons under 18	901
With persons over 65	647
Family households	1,464
One-person households	813
Persons per household	2.43
Persons per family	3.1

Labor & Employment
Total civilian labor force, 2004**	2,724
Unemployment rate	12.0%
Total civilian labor force, 2000	2,209
Unemployment rate	10.3%

Employed persons 16 years and over by occupation, 2000
Managers & professionals	403
Service occupations	425
Sales & office occupations	449
Farming, fishing & forestry	0
Construction & maintenance	201
Production & transportation	503
Self-employed persons	44

*US Census Bureau
**New Jersey Department of Labor

General Information
City of Salem
17 New Market St
Salem, NJ 08079
856-935-0372

Web site	NA
Land area (sq. miles)	2.61
Water area (sq. miles)	0.19
Type of government	City
Form of government	SC

Government

Legislative Districts
US Congressional	2
State Legislative	3

Local Officials, 2006
Mayor	Earl Gage
Admin/Manager	Barbara Wright
Clerk	Barbara Wright
Finance Dir/Treas	David Crescenzi
Engineer	Albert A. Fralinger Jr.
Attorney	David Puma
Tax assessor	Henry N. Nelson
Tax collector	David Crescenzi
Building officer	Wayne Serfass
Zoning officer	Henry N. Nelsom
Public Works	NA

Housing & Construction

Housing Units, 2000*
Total	2,863
Median rent	$444
Median SF home value	$74,300

New Privately Owned Housing Units Authorized by Building Permit
	Units	Value
Total, 2004	6	$246,156
Single family	6	$246,156
Total, 2005	5	$204,289
Single family	5	$204,289

Real Property Valuation - parcels, 2005
	Number	Valuation
Total		$114,894,125
Vacant	273	1,387,625
Residential	1,564	68,262,025
Commercial	138	26,920,275
Industrial	15	9,620,800
Apartments	9	8,446,750
Farm land	3	103,200
Farm homestead	9	153,450

Average Property Value & Tax, 2005
Residential value	$43,494
Property tax	$2,341
FAIR rebate	$656

Public Library
Salem Free Public Library
112 W Broadway
Salem, NJ 08079
856-935-0526

Director	NA

Library statistics, 2004
	Total	per capita
Volumes	39,790	6.79
Expenditure	$147,420	$25.17

Public Safety

Police
Chief	Ronald Sorrell
Number of officers, 2004	46

Crime, 2004	Number	Rate
Total	420	72.5
Violent	72	12.4
Non-violent	348	60.1
Domestic Viol.	248	NA

Emergency/Fire
Director	John Ayars

Public School District
(for school year 2004-2005 except as noted)

Salem City School District
51 New Market St
Salem, NJ 08079
856-935-3800

Superintendent	Margaret Nicolosi
Grade plan	K-12
Enrollment	1,519.5
Students per teacher	8.6
Per pupil expenditure	$13,927
Median faculty salary	$43,825
Median administrator salary	$71,888
Grade 12 enrollment	117.0
High school graduation rate	88.1%

Assessment test results
(percent scoring at proficient or advanced level)
	Language	Math
Grade 3	53.6%	64.7%
Grade 8	31.8%	30.3%
High school	70.8%	52.0%

SAT
Percent tested	53%
Average SAT math score	464
Average SAT verbal score	462

No Child Left Behind, 2003-04
Attendence rate (target = 90%)	91.8%
Drop rate	3%
Highly-qualified teachers	94.7%
District needs improvement?(AYP)	No

Municipal Finance

Fiscal Year 2005
Total tax levy	$6,294,613
County levy	1,580,480
County taxes	1,549,125
County library	0
County health	0
County open space	31,355
School levy	2,412,787
Local muni. budget	2,301,346
Misc. revenues	5,672,388
Total aid	$1,995,892
CMPTRA	1,439,621
Muni. block grant	30,118
Energy tax receipts	476,153
Homeland security	50,000

Fiscal Year 2006
Total aid	$1,995,893
CMPTRA	1,422,956
Muni. block grant	30,118
Energy tax receipts	492,819
Homeland security	50,000

Taxes
	2003	2004	2005
General tax rate per $100	4.34	5.162	5.383
Net valuation taxable	$117,477,608	$117,213,488	$116,955,845
State equalized value	$144,463,364	$151,413,597	$162,011,144
County equalization ratio	84.18	81.32	77.08

Demographics & Socio-Economic Characteristics
(2000 U.S. Census, except as noted)

Population
1980*	1,485
1990*	1,732
2000	1,825
Male	919
Female	906
2004 (estimate)*	1,905
Persons per sq. mi. of land	45

Race & Hispanic Origin, 2000
Race
White	1,786
Black/African American	7
Amer. Indian/Alaska Natv.	3
Asian	8
Natv. Hawaiian/Pac. Islander	2
Other Race	1
Two or more races	18
Hispanic origin, total	24
Mexican	0
Puerto Rican	10
Cuban	5
Other Hispanic	9

Age & Nativity, 2000
Under 5 years	101
18 years and over	1,365
21 years and over	1,312
65 years and over	244
85 years and over	33
Median Age	40.4
Native born	1,761
Foreign born	68

Educational Attainment, 2000
Population 25 years and over	1,249
0-8 yrs of school	2.6%
High School grad or higher	87.4%
Bachelor's degree or higher	24.7%
Graduate degree	7.6%

Income & Poverty, 1999
Per capita income	$23,854
Median household income	$55,667
Median family income	$65,774
Persons in poverty	99
H'holds receiving public assistance	8
H'holds receiving social security	201

Households, 2000
Total households	693
With persons under 18	257
With persons over 65	183
Family households	504
One-person households	158
Persons per household	2.63
Persons per family	3.12

Labor & Employment
Total civilian labor force, 2004**	1,055
Unemployment rate	3.5%
Total civilian labor force, 2000	954
Unemployment rate	3.2%

Employed persons 16 years and over by occupation, 2000
Managers & professionals	314
Service occupations	128
Sales & office occupations	240
Farming, fishing & forestry	2
Construction & maintenance	118
Production & transportation	121
Self-employed persons	84

*US Census Bureau
**New Jersey Department of Labor

General Information
Township of Sandyston
133 County Route 645
Sandyston, NJ 07826
973-948-3520
Web site	www.sandystontownship.com
Land area (sq. miles)	42.61
Water area (sq. miles)	0.70
Type of government	Township
Form of government	TC

Government

Legislative Districts
US Congressional	5
State Legislative	24

Local Officials, 2006
Mayor	Fred MacDonald
Admin/Manager	NA
Clerk	Betsy Cuneo
Finance Dir/Treas	Jerry Orr
Engineer	Harold Pellow
Attorney	Christopher Quinn
Tax assessor	Robert W. Pastor
Tax collector	Beverly Bathgate
Building officer	John deJager
Zoning officer	NA
Public Works	NA

Housing & Construction

Housing Units, 2000*
Total	907
Median rent	$860
Median SF home value	$144,800

New Privately Owned Housing Units
Authorized by Building Permit
	Units	Value
Total, 2004	11	$1,449,272
Single family	11	$1,449,272
Total, 2005	12	$1,411,100
Single family	12	$1,411,100

Real Property Valuation - parcels, 2005
	Number	Valuation
Total		$132,671,700
Vacant	203	7,137,200
Residential	826	103,795,400
Commercial	51	10,012,300
Industrial	5	1,398,000
Apartments	0	0
Farm land	59	9,173,000
Farm homestead	167	1,155,800

Average Property Value & Tax, 2005
Residential value	$105,691
Property tax	$3,087
FAIR rebate	$559

Public Library
No public municipal library.

Library statistics, 2004
	Total	per capita
Volumes	NA	NA
Expenditure	NA	NA

Public Safety

Police
Chief	NA
Number of officers, 2004	0

Crime, 2004	Number	Rate
Total	16	8.4
Violent	2	1.1
Non-violent	14	7.4
Domestic Viol.	9	NA

Emergency/Fire
Director	Alan Delea

Public School District
(for school year 2004-2005 except as noted)

Sandyston-Walpack Township School Dist.
100 Route 560
Layton, NJ 07851
973-948-4450
Administrator	Glenn Sumpman
Grade plan	K-6
Enrollment	178.0
Students per teacher	9.6
Per pupil expenditure	$12,965
Median faculty salary	$50,233
Median administrator salary	$110,000
Grade 12 enrollment	NA
High school graduation rate	NA

Assessment test results
(percent scoring at proficient or advanced level)
	Language	Math
Grade 3	100.0%	94.6%
Grade 8	NA	NA
High school	NA	NA

SAT
Percent tested	NA
Average SAT math score	NA
Average SAT verbal score	NA

No Child Left Behind, 2003-04
Attendence rate (target = 90%)	95.4%
Drop rate	NA
Highly-qualified teachers	100%
District needs improvement?(AYP)	No

Municipal Finance

Fiscal Year 2005
Total tax levy	$3,889,986
County levy	892,342
County taxes	757,348
County library	65,297
County health	30,738
County open space	38,959
School levy	2,665,766
Local muni. budget	331,878
Misc. revenues	1,329,385
Total aid	$250,279
CMPTRA	76,909
Muni. block grant	7,579
Energy tax receipts	165,791
Homeland security	0

Fiscal Year 2006
Total aid	$250,278
CMPTRA	71,106
Muni. block grant	7,579
Energy tax receipts	171,593
Homeland security	NA

Taxes
	2003	2004	2005
General tax rate per $100	2.80	2.840	2.930
Net valuation taxable	$130,168,154	$132,093,396	$133,181,089
State equalized value	$163,466,224	$191,946,392	$222,264,835
County equalization ratio	93.62	79.63	68.72

Demographics & Socio-Economic Characteristics
(2000 U.S. Census, except as noted)

Population
1980*	29,969
1990*	34,986
2000	40,377
Male	19,803
Female	20,574
2004 (estimate)*	42,663
Persons per sq. mi. of land	2,683

Race & Hispanic Origin, 2000
Race
White	30,875
Black/African American	3,481
Amer. Indian/Alaska Natv.	53
Asian	4,265
Natv. Hawaiian/Pac. Islander	8
Other Race	855
Two or more races	840
Hispanic origin, total	2,942
Mexican	105
Puerto Rican	1,365
Cuban	194
Other Hispanic	1,278

Age & Nativity, 2000
Under 5 years	2,712
18 years and over	30,863
21 years and over	29,654
65 years and over	5,004
85 years and over	488
Median Age	36.5
Native born	32,279
Foreign born	8,098

Educational Attainment, 2000
Population 25 years and over	27,872
0-8 yrs of school	4.7%
High School grad or higher	85.6%
Bachelor's degree or higher	24.9%
Graduate degree	7.4%

Income & Poverty, 1999
Per capita income	$24,736
Median household income	$58,919
Median family income	$66,266
Persons in poverty	1,905
H'holds receiving public assistance	220
H'holds receiving social security	3,906

Households, 2000
Total households	14,955
With persons under 18	5,505
With persons over 65	3,639
Family households	10,923
One-person households	3,342
Persons per household	2.68
Persons per family	3.17

Labor & Employment
Total civilian labor force, 2004**	21,707
Unemployment rate	3.6%
Total civilian labor force, 2000	20,837
Unemployment rate	4.4%

Employed persons 16 years and over by occupation, 2000
Managers & professionals	7,066
Service occupations	2,360
Sales & office occupations	6,232
Farming, fishing & forestry	21
Construction & maintenance	1,847
Production & transportation	2,397
Self-employed persons	656

*US Census Bureau
**New Jersey Department of Labor

General Information
Borough of Sayreville
167 Main St
Sayreville, NJ 08872
732-390-7000

Web site	www.sayreville.com
Land area (sq. miles)	15.90
Water area (sq. miles)	2.85
Type of government	Borough
Form of government	B

Government
Legislative Districts
US Congressional	6
State Legislative	19

Local Officials, 2006
Mayor	Kennedy O'Brien
Admin/Manager	Jeffry Bertrand
Clerk	Theresa Farbaniec
Finance Dir/Treas	Wayne Kronowski
Engineer	David Samuel
Attorney	Weiner Lesniak LLP
Tax assessor	Joseph Kupsch Jr.
Tax collector	Donna Brodzinski
Building officer	Michael Gianotto
Zoning officer	Andrew Mashanski
Public Works	NA

Housing & Construction
Housing Units, 2000*
Total	15,235
Median rent	$795
Median SF home value	$153,400

New Privately Owned Housing Units
Authorized by Building Permit

	Units	Value
Total, 2004	187	$13,819,202
Single family	187	$13,819,202
Total, 2005	59	$9,430,883
Single family	59	$9,430,883

Real Property Valuation - parcels, 2005
	Number	Valuation
Total		$2,239,697,700
Vacant	632	71,059,600
Residential	11,758	1,661,331,100
Commercial	430	182,346,800
Industrial	37	174,670,800
Apartments	22	150,136,800
Farm land	1	143,900
Farm homestead	2	8,700

Average Property Value & Tax, 2005
Residential value	$141,270
Property tax	$4,767
FAIR rebate	$574

Public Library
Sayreville Public Library
1050 Washington Rd
Parlin, NJ 08859
732-727-0212

Director	Joseph Lyons

Library statistics, 2004
	Total	per capita
Volumes	96,760	2.40
Expenditure	$914,750	$22.66

Public Safety
Police
Chief	John Garbowski
Number of officers, 2004	84

Crime, 2004	Number	Rate
Total	864	20.5
Violent	86	2
Non-violent	778	18.5
Domestic Viol.	240	NA

Emergency/Fire
Director	Stamatis Bratsano

Public School District
(for school year 2004-2005 except as noted)

Sayreville School District
PO Box 997
Sayreville, NJ 08872
732-525-5224

Superintendent	Frank Alfano
Grade plan	K-12
Enrollment	5,715.0
Students per teacher	12.4
Per pupil expenditure	$10,391
Median faculty salary	$46,400
Median administrator salary	$105,849
Grade 12 enrollment	405.0
High school graduation rate	96.0%

Assessment test results
(percent scoring at proficient or advanced level)
	Language	Math
Grade 3	86.1%	87.0%
Grade 8	79.3%	69.5%
High school	85.7%	81.9%

SAT
Percent tested	75%
Average SAT math score	498
Average SAT verbal score	482

No Child Left Behind, 2003-04
Attendence rate (target = 90%)	94.6%
Drop rate	0.8%
Highly-qualified teachers	94.8%
District needs improvement?(AYP)	No

Municipal Finance
Fiscal Year 2005
Total tax levy	$75,730,725
County levy	12,135,843
County taxes	10,993,320
County library	0
County health	0
County open space	1,142,523
School levy	46,494,994
Local muni. budget	17,099,888
Misc. revenues	25,717,665
Total aid	$12,151,523
CMPTRA	2,143,874
Muni. block grant	158,319
Energy tax receipts	9,709,330
Homeland security	140,000

Fiscal Year 2006
Total aid	$12,151,524
CMPTRA	1,804,048
Muni. block grant	158,319
Energy tax receipts	10,049,157
Homeland security	140,000

Taxes
	2003	2004	2005
General tax rate per $100	3.18	3.290	3.380
Net valuation taxable	$2,152,390,660	$2,198,709,688	$2,244,382,465
State equalized value	$3,233,760,006	$3,701,640,877	$4,273,386,262
County equalization ratio	75.07	66.56	59.34

Demographics & Socio-Economic Characteristics
(2000 U.S. Census, except as noted)

Population
1980*	20,774
1990*	21,160
2000	22,732
Male	10,890
Female	11,842
2004 (estimate)*	23,027
Persons per sq. mi. of land	2,536

Race & Hispanic Origin, 2000
Race
White	17,931
Black/African American	2,568
Amer. Indian/Alaska Natv.	21
Asian	1,648
Natv. Hawaiian/Pac. Islander	3
Other Race	216
Two or more races	345
Hispanic origin, total	895
Mexican	53
Puerto Rican	229
Cuban	106
Other Hispanic	507

Age & Nativity, 2000
Under 5 years	1,777
18 years and over	16,967
21 years and over	16,528
65 years and over	3,214
85 years and over	344
Median Age	38.6
Native born	19,155
Foreign born	3,577

Educational Attainment, 2000
Population 25 years and over	15,911
0-8 yrs of school	2.8%
High School grad or higher	92.0%
Bachelor's degree or higher	49.7%
Graduate degree	19.9%

Income & Poverty, 1999
Per capita income	$39,913
Median household income	$81,599
Median family income	$96,238
Persons in poverty	674
H'holds receiving public assistance	131
H'holds receiving social security	2,125

Households, 2000
Total households	8,349
With persons under 18	3,179
With persons over 65	2,262
Family households	6,291
One-person households	1,737
Persons per household	2.71
Persons per family	3.16

Labor & Employment
Total civilian labor force, 2004**	12,012
Unemployment rate	3.1%
Total civilian labor force, 2000	11,822
Unemployment rate	2.6%

Employed persons 16 years and over by occupation, 2000
Managers & professionals	6,381
Service occupations	811
Sales & office occupations	3,139
Farming, fishing & forestry	0
Construction & maintenance	533
Production & transportation	656
Self-employed persons	567

*US Census Bureau
**New Jersey Department of Labor

General Information
Township of Scotch Plains
430 Park Ave
Scotch Plains, NJ 07076
908-322-6700
Web site	www.scotchplainsnj.com
Land area (sq. miles)	9.08
Water area (sq. miles)	0.01
Type of government	Township
Form of government	CM '50

Government

Legislative Districts
US Congressional	7
State Legislative	22

Local Officials, 2006
Mayor	Martin Marks
Admin/Manager	Thomas Atkins
Clerk	Barbara Riepe
Finance Dir/Treas	Lori Mzajeski
Engineer	Edward Gottko
Attorney	(Vacant)
Tax assessor	Michael Ross
Tax collector	NA
Building officer	Robert LaCosta
Zoning officer	NA
Public Works	NA

Housing & Construction

Housing Units, 2000*
Total	8,479
Median rent	$985
Median SF home value	$258,800

New Privately Owned Housing Units
Authorized by Building Permit
	Units	Value
Total, 2004	136	$12,750,093
Single family	136	$12,750,093
Total, 2005	72	$12,768,001
Single family	72	$12,768,001

Real Property Valuation - parcels, 2005
	Number	Valuation
Total		$973,632,100
Vacant	346	8,610,700
Residential	7,192	864,529,500
Commercial	246	64,400,300
Industrial	26	5,737,800
Apartments	8	29,240,400
Farm land	4	1,098,900
Farm homestead	4	14,500

Average Property Value & Tax, 2005
Residential value	$120,142
Property tax	$8,984
FAIR rebate	$599

Public Library
Scotch Plains Public Library
1927 Bartle Ave
Scotch Plains, NJ 07076
908-322-5007
Director	Meg Kolaya

Library statistics, 2004
	Total	per capita
Volumes	77,386	3.40
Expenditure	$1,050,483	$46.21

Public Safety
Police
Chief	Brian Mahoney
Number of officers, 2004	43

Crime, 2004	Number	Rate
Total	274	11.9
Violent	20	0.9
Non-violent	254	11.1
Domestic Viol.	77	NA

Emergency/Fire
Director	Mark Zyla

Public School District
(for school year 2004-2005 except as noted)

Scotch Plains-Fanwood School District
Evergreen Ave & Cedar St
Scotch Plains, NJ 07076
908-232-6161
Superintendent	Carol Choye
Grade plan	K-12
Enrollment	5,048.0
Students per teacher	12.3
Per pupil expenditure	$11,962
Median faculty salary	$52,325
Median administrator salary	$113,500
Grade 12 enrollment	346.0
High school graduation rate	100.0%

Assessment test results
(percent scoring at proficient or advanced level)
	Language	Math
Grade 3	93.5%	91.9%
Grade 8	83.3%	83.5%
High school	91.6%	88.7%

SAT
Percent tested	93%
Average SAT math score	548
Average SAT verbal score	526

No Child Left Behind, 2003-04
Attendence rate (target = 90%)	96.3%
Drop rate	0.1%
Highly-qualified teachers	97.7%
District needs improvement?(AYP)	No

Municipal Finance

Fiscal Year 2005
Total tax levy	$72,878,397
County levy	12,907,232
County taxes	12,397,543
County library	0
County health	0
County open space	509,689
School levy	46,807,320
Local muni. budget	13,163,845
Misc. revenues	7,856,594
Total aid	$3,127,677
CMPTRA	1,119,150
Muni. block grant	92,545
Energy tax receipts	1,825,982
Homeland security	90,000

Fiscal Year 2006
Total aid	$3,127,677
CMPTRA	1,055,241
Muni. block grant	92,545
Energy tax receipts	1,889,891
Homeland security	90,000

Taxes
	2003	2004	2005
General tax rate per $100	6.67	7.057	7.478
Net valuation taxable	$965,222,348	$970,949,697	$974,583,717
State equalized value	$2,895,956,640	$3,174,754,661	$3,584,346,146
County equalization ratio	37.2	33.27	28.71

Demographics & Socio-Economic Characteristics

(2000 U.S. Census, except as noted)

Population

1980*	1,812
1990*	1,693
2000	1,818
Male	951
Female	867
2004 (estimate)*	1,819
Persons per sq. mi. of land	2,848

Race & Hispanic Origin, 2000

Race

White	1,716
Black/African American	32
Amer. Indian/Alaska Natv.	0
Asian	41
Natv. Hawaiian/Pac. Islander	0
Other Race	16
Two or more races	13
Hispanic origin, total	82
Mexican	37
Puerto Rican	16
Cuban	5
Other Hispanic	24

Age & Nativity, 2000

Under 5 years	59
18 years and over	1,615
21 years and over	1,592
65 years and over	196
85 years and over	32
Median Age	40.2
Native born	1,608
Foreign born	217

Educational Attainment, 2000

Population 25 years and over	1,488
0-8 yrs of school	2.8%
High School grad or higher	91.4%
Bachelor's degree or higher	47.0%
Graduate degree	18.5%

Income & Poverty, 1999

Per capita income	$45,066
Median household income	$65,563
Median family income	$72,031
Persons in poverty	138
H'holds receiving public assistance	21
H'holds receiving social security	164

Households, 2000

Total households	1,003
With persons under 18	127
With persons over 65	159
Family households	402
One-person households	455
Persons per household	1.81
Persons per family	2.51

Labor & Employment

Total civilian labor force, 2004**	1,253
Unemployment rate	3.8%
Total civilian labor force, 2000	1,208
Unemployment rate	5.1%

Employed persons 16 years and over by occupation, 2000

Managers & professionals	558
Service occupations	114
Sales & office occupations	341
Farming, fishing & forestry	12
Construction & maintenance	63
Production & transportation	78
Self-employed persons	56

*US Census Bureau
**New Jersey Department of Labor

General Information

Borough of Sea Bright
1167 Ocean Ave
Sea Bright, NJ 07760
732-842-0099

Web site	seabrightnj.org
Land area (sq. miles)	0.64
Water area (sq. miles)	0.49
Type of government	Borough
Form of government	B

Government

Legislative Districts

US Congressional	6
State Legislative	11

Local Officials, 2006

Mayor	Jo-Ann Kalaka-Adams
Admin/Manager	NA
Clerk	Maryann Smeltzer
Finance Dir/Treas	Michael Bascom
Engineer	David Hoder
Attorney	Scott Arnette
Tax assessor	Timothy Anfuso
Tax collector	Patricia Spahr
Building officer	Edward Wheeler
Zoning officer	NA
Public Works	David Bahrle

Housing & Construction

Housing Units, 2000*

Total	1,202
Median rent	$906
Median SF home value	$227,600

New Privately Owned Housing Units Authorized by Building Permit

	Units	Value
Total, 2004	11	$5,367,110
Single family	11	$5,367,110
Total, 2005	20	$9,545,605
Single family	20	$9,545,605

Real Property Valuation - parcels, 2005

	Number	Valuation
Total		$500,826,100
Vacant	174	17,381,000
Residential	1,026	380,880,800
Commercial	74	96,249,300
Industrial	0	0
Apartments	7	6,315,000
Farm land	0	0
Farm homestead	0	0

Average Property Value & Tax, 2005

Residential value	$371,229
Property tax	$4,878
FAIR rebate	$795

Public Library

J.W. Ross/Seabright Library
1097 Ocean Ave
Seabright, NJ 07760
732-758-9554

Director... Joan Walsh

Library statistics, 2004

	Total	per capita
Volumes	NA	NA
Expenditure	NA	NA

Public Safety

Police

Chief	William Moore
Number of officers, 2004	10

Crime, 2004	Number	Rate
Total	31	17.3
Violent	0	0
Non-violent	31	17.3
Domestic Viol.	0	NA

Emergency/Fire

Director... Matthew Clemmenson

Public School District

(for school year 2004-2005 except as noted)

Sea Bright School District†
PO Box 3125
Sea Bright, NJ 07760
732-477-4052

†No schools in district - sends children to Oceanport Borough and Shore Regional schools (see Appendix A).

Grade plan	NA
Enrollment	NA
Students per teacher	NA
Per pupil expenditure	NA
Median faculty salary	NA

Assessment test results

(percent scoring at proficient or advanced level)

	Language	Math
Grade 3	NA	NA
Grade 8	NA	NA
High school	NA	NA

SAT

Percent tested	NA
Average SAT math score	NA
Average SAT verbal score	NA

No Child Left Behind, 2003-04

Attendence rate (target = 90%)	NA
Drop rate	NA
Highly-qualified teachers	NA
District needs improvement?(AYP)	NA

Municipal Finance

Fiscal Year 2005

Total tax levy	$6,586,829
County levy	1,681,110
County taxes	1,508,502
County library	83,100
County health	0
County open space	89,508
School levy	2,035,553
Local muni. budget	2,870,167
Misc. revenues	1,408,355
Total aid	$260,981
CMPTRA	71,004
Muni. block grant	7,408
Energy tax receipts	157,569
Homeland security	25,000

Fiscal Year 2006

Total aid	$260,981
CMPTRA	65,489
Muni. block grant	7,408
Energy tax receipts	163,084
Homeland security	25,000

Taxes

	2003	2004	2005
General tax rate per $100	3.02	1.279	1.315
Net valuation taxable	$199,040,562	$500,223,181	$501,226,608
State equalized value	$386,786,945	$501,827,678	$628,891,604
County equalization ratio	60.99	128.92	99.68

Demographics & Socio-Economic Characteristics
(2000 U.S. Census, except as noted)

Population
1980*	2,650
1990*	2,099
2000	2,148
Male	1,001
Female	1,147
2004 (estimate)*	2,097
Persons per sq. mi. of land	1,979

Race & Hispanic Origin, 2000
Race
White	2,129
Black/African American	2
Amer. Indian/Alaska Natv.	0
Asian	6
Natv. Hawaiian/Pac. Islander	0
Other Race	1
Two or more races	10
Hispanic origin, total	30
Mexican	3
Puerto Rican	7
Cuban	1
Other Hispanic	19

Age & Nativity, 2000
Under 5 years	96
18 years and over	1,716
21 years and over	1,678
65 years and over	591
85 years and over	87
Median Age	50.3
Native born	2,083
Foreign born	65

Educational Attainment, 2000
Population 25 years and over	1,622
0-8 yrs of school	1.0%
High School grad or higher	96.5%
Bachelor's degree or higher	58.6%
Graduate degree	23.3%

Income & Poverty, 1999
Per capita income	$63,871
Median household income	$86,104
Median family income	$102,680
Persons in poverty	75
H'holds receiving public assistance	4
H'holds receiving social security	400

Households, 2000
Total households	942
With persons under 18	199
With persons over 65	412
Family households	637
One-person households	279
Persons per household	2.28
Persons per family	2.83

Labor & Employment
Total civilian labor force, 2004**	1,106
Unemployment rate	3.0%
Total civilian labor force, 2000	940
Unemployment rate	2.9%

Employed persons 16 years and over by occupation, 2000
Managers & professionals	520
Service occupations	76
Sales & office occupations	285
Farming, fishing & forestry	0
Construction & maintenance	14
Production & transportation	18
Self-employed persons	89

*US Census Bureau
**New Jersey Department of Labor

General Information
Borough of Sea Girt
4th & Baltimore Blvd
Sea Girt, NJ 08750
732-449-9433

Web site	www.seagirtboro.com
Land area (sq. miles)	1.06
Water area (sq. miles)	0.39
Type of government	Borough
Form of government	B

Government

Legislative Districts
US Congressional	6
State Legislative	11

Local Officials, 2006
Mayor	Edward Ahern
Admin/Manager	NA
Clerk	Patricia Allen
Finance Dir/Treas	Patricia Allen
Engineer	Leon Avakian
Attorney	William Burns
Tax assessor	Mary Lou Hartman
Tax collector	Patricia Allen
Building officer	Albert Ratz
Zoning officer	Jim Quigley
Public Works	Kevin Thompson

Housing & Construction

Housing Units, 2000*
Total	1,285
Median rent	$1,095
Median SF home value	$549,300

New Privately Owned Housing Units Authorized by Building Permit
	Units	Value
Total, 2004	24	$9,113,569
Single family	24	$9,113,569
Total, 2005	30	$8,513,208
Single family	30	$8,513,208

Real Property Valuation - parcels, 2005
	Number	Valuation
Total		$1,911,681,300
Vacant	30	34,487,600
Residential	1,225	1,838,215,700
Commercial	43	38,978,000
Industrial	0	0
Apartments	0	0
Farm land	0	0
Farm homestead	0	0

Average Property Value & Tax, 2005
Residential value	$1,500,584
Property tax	$9,496
FAIR rebate	$584

Public Library
Sea Girt Library
Railroad Station at the Plaza
Sea Girt, NJ 08750
732-449-1099

Librarian ... Anne Ryan

Library statistics, 2004
	Total	per capita
Volumes	NA	NA
Expenditure	NA	NA

Public Safety

Police
Chief	Edward J. Sidley
Number of officers, 2004	13

Crime, 2004	Number	Rate
Total	18	8.2
Violent	3	1.4
Non-violent	15	6.8
Domestic Viol.	0	NA

Emergency/Fire
Director ... Edward J. Sidley

Public School District
(for school year 2004-2005 except as noted)

Sea Girt Borough School District
Bell Place
Sea Girt, NJ 08750
732-449-3422

Superintendent	John Gibbs III
Grade plan	K-12
Enrollment	180.0
Students per teacher	10.2
Per pupil expenditure	$13,782
Median faculty salary	$50,389
Median administrator salary	$110,144
Grade 12 enrollment	NA
High school graduation rate	NA

Assessment test results
(percent scoring at proficient or advanced level)
	Language	Math
Grade 3	100%	100%
Grade 8	96.1%	96.1%
High school	NA	NA

SAT
Percent tested	NA
Average SAT math score	NA
Average SAT verbal score	NA

No Child Left Behind, 2003-04
Attendance rate (target = 90%)	95.7%
Drop rate	NA
Highly-qualified teachers	100%
District needs improvement?(AYP)	No

Municipal Finance

Fiscal Year 2005
Total tax levy	$12,099,226
County levy	4,999,031
County taxes	4,485,750
County library	247,093
County health	0
County open space	266,188
School levy	3,335,195
Local muni. budget	3,765,000
Misc. revenues	1,241,053
Total aid	$323,941
CMPTRA	102,007
Muni. block grant	9,185
Energy tax receipts	187,749
Homeland security	25,000

Fiscal Year 2006
Total aid	$323,941
CMPTRA	95,436
Muni. block grant	9,185
Energy tax receipts	194,320
Homeland security	25,000

Taxes
	2003	2004	2005
General tax rate per $100	1.87	1.907	0.633
Net valuation taxable	$594,457,539	$600,383,449	$1,912,007,914
State equalized value	$1,244,416,033	$1,456,993,623	$1,699,562,590
County equalization ratio	54.76	47.77	127.78

Demographics & Socio-Economic Characteristics

(2000 U.S. Census, except as noted)

Population

1980*	2,644
1990*	2,692
2000	2,835
Male	1,354
Female	1,481
2004 (estimate)*	2,976
Persons per sq. mi. of land	1,351

Race & Hispanic Origin, 2000

Race

White	2,775
Black/African American	8
Amer. Indian/Alaska Natv.	11
Asian	10
Natv. Hawaiian/Pac. Islander	1
Other Race	2
Two or more races	28
Hispanic origin, total	30
Mexican	15
Puerto Rican	10
Cuban	2
Other Hispanic	3

Age & Nativity, 2000

Under 5 years	94
18 years and over	2,391
21 years and over	2,340
65 years and over	768
85 years and over	78
Median Age	51.3
Native born	2,730
Foreign born	94

Educational Attainment, 2000

Population 25 years and over	2,176
0-8 yrs of school	3.4%
High School grad or higher	85.2%
Bachelor's degree or higher	28.3%
Graduate degree	9.8%

Income & Poverty, 1999

Per capita income	$28,754
Median household income	$45,708
Median family income	$62,847
Persons in poverty	214
H'holds receiving public assistance	0
H'holds receiving social security	584

Households, 2000

Total households	1,370
With persons under 18	235
With persons over 65	552
Family households	795
One-person households	512
Persons per household	2.07
Persons per family	2.71

Labor & Employment

Total civilian labor force, 2004**	1,561
Unemployment rate	7.6%
Total civilian labor force, 2000	1,372
Unemployment rate	6.5%

Employed persons 16 years and over by occupation, 2000

Managers & professionals	445
Service occupations	247
Sales & office occupations	373
Farming, fishing & forestry	0
Construction & maintenance	141
Production & transportation	77
Self-employed persons	89

*US Census Bureau
**New Jersey Department of Labor

General Information

City of Sea Isle
4416 Landis Ave
Sea Isle, NJ 08243
609-263-4461

Web site	NA
Land area (sq. miles)	2.20
Water area (sq. miles)	0.35
Type of government	City
Form of government	Comm.

Government

Legislative Districts

US Congressional	2
State Legislative	1

Local Officials, 2006

Mayor	Leonard Desiderio
Admin/Manager	NA
Clerk	Theresa Tighe
Finance Dir/Treas	James Terruso
Engineer	Andrew Previti
Attorney	Paul Baldini
Tax assessor	Joseph Berrodin Jr.
Tax collector	Paula Doll
Building officer	Robert Bowman
Zoning officer	NA
Public Works	John Manganaro

Housing & Construction

Housing Units, 2000*

Total	6,622
Median rent	$717
Median SF home value	$280,100

New Privately Owned Housing Units Authorized by Building Permit

	Units	Value
Total, 2004	237	$30,396,279
Single family	169	$22,164,000
Total, 2005	237	$39,381,184
Single family	237	$39,381,184

Real Property Valuation - parcels, 2005

	Number	Valuation
Total		$3,496,543,800
Vacant	506	123,236,900
Residential	5,824	3,278,212,800
Commercial	156	95,094,100
Industrial	0	0
Apartments	0	0
Farm land	0	0
Farm homestead	0	0

Average Property Value & Tax, 2005

Residential value	$562,880
Property tax	$3,200
FAIR rebate	$735

Public Library

Sea Isle City Branch Library†
125 JF Kennedy Blvd
Sea Isle City, NJ 08243
609-263-8485

Branch Librarian . . . . Donna MacBride

Library statistics, 2004

	Total	per capita
Volumes	NA	NA
Expenditure	NA	NA

†Branch of County Library

Public Safety

Police

Chief	William Kennedy
Number of officers, 2004	20

Crime, 2004	Number	Rate
Total	261	88.3
Violent	21	7.1
Non-violent	240	81.2
Domestic Viol.	21	NA

Emergency/Fire

Director . . . . John Mazurie

Public School District

(for school year 2004-2005 except as noted)

Sea isle City School District
4501 Park Rd
Sea Isle City, NJ 08243
609-263-8461

Superintendent	Joanne Smith
Grade plan	K-12
Enrollment	107.5
Students per teacher	5.4
Per pupil expenditure	$20,532
Median faculty salary	$61,513
Median administrator salary	$82,025
Grade 12 enrollment	NA
High school graduation rate	NA

Assessment test results

(percent scoring at proficient or advanced level)

	Language	Math
Grade 3	NA	NA
Grade 8	78.6%	100.0%
High school	NA	NA

SAT

Percent tested	NA
Average SAT math score	NA
Average SAT verbal score	NA

No Child Left Behind, 2003-04

Attendence rate (target = 90%)	94.2%
Drop rate	NA
Highly-qualified teachers	93.9%
District needs improvement?(AYP)	No

Municipal Finance

Fiscal Year 2005

Total tax levy	$19,887,342
County levy	8,352,141
County taxes	7,022,050
County library	989,123
County health	0
County open space	340,968
School levy	3,296,483
Local muni. budget	8,238,717
Misc. revenues	6,649,170
Total aid	$327,745
CMPTRA	0
Muni. block grant	11,779
Energy tax receipts	339,609
Homeland security	25,000

Fiscal Year 2006

Total aid	$339,631
CMPTRA	0
Muni. block grant	11,779
Energy tax receipts	302,852
Homeland security	25,000

Taxes

	2003	2004	2005
General tax rate per $100	1.69	0.560	0.570
Net valuation taxable	$1,077,482,303	$3,447,162,457	$3,498,256,661
State equalized value	$2,548,444,425	$3,355,928,930	$4,211,215,434
County equalization ratio	49.57	132.95	102.72

Demographics & Socio-Economic Characteristics
(2000 U.S. Census, except as noted)

Population
1980*	1,802
1990*	2,366
2000	3,155
Male	1,627
Female	1,528
2004 (estimate)*	3,194
Persons per sq. mi. of land	5,226

Race & Hispanic Origin, 2000
Race
White	2,838
Black/African American	127
Amer. Indian/Alaska Natv.	20
Asian	27
Natv. Hawaiian/Pac. Islander	0
Other Race	37
Two or more races	106
Hispanic origin, total	306
Mexican	102
Puerto Rican	113
Cuban	5
Other Hispanic	86

Age & Nativity, 2000
Under 5 years	238
18 years and over	2,419
21 years and over	2,293
65 years and over	348
85 years and over	33
Median Age	33.3
Native born	2,917
Foreign born	238

Educational Attainment, 2000
Population 25 years and over	2,052
0-8 yrs of school	5.0%
High School grad or higher	76.3%
Bachelor's degree or higher	15.6%
Graduate degree	3.6%

Income & Poverty, 1999
Per capita income	$18,665
Median household income	$25,963
Median family income	$27,197
Persons in poverty	753
H'holds receiving public assistance	87
H'holds receiving social security	359

Households, 2000
Total households	1,408
With persons under 18	400
With persons over 65	260
Family households	692
One-person households	564
Persons per household	2.17
Persons per family	2.93

Labor & Employment
Total civilian labor force, 2004**	1,489
Unemployment rate	10.5%
Total civilian labor force, 2000	1,590
Unemployment rate	7.5%

Employed persons 16 years and over by occupation, 2000
Managers & professionals	325
Service occupations	412
Sales & office occupations	374
Farming, fishing & forestry	10
Construction & maintenance	165
Production & transportation	184
Self-employed persons	61

*US Census Bureau
**New Jersey Department of Labor

General Information
Borough of Seaside Heights
PO Box 38
Seaside Heights, NJ 08751
732-793-9100
Web site	www.seaside-heightsnj.org
Land area (sq. miles)	0.61
Water area (sq. miles)	0.15
Type of government	Borough
Form of government	B

Government
Legislative Districts
US Congressional	3
State Legislative	10

Local Officials, 2006
Mayor	P Kenneth Hershey
Admin/Manager	John Camera
Clerk	John Camera (Actg.)
Finance Dir/Treas	Barbara Risley
Engineer	O'Donnell & Stanton
Attorney	George Gilmore
Tax assessor	Carey Rowe
Tax collector	Christine Sierfeld
Building officer	James Erdman
Zoning officer	Kenneth Roberts
Public Works	Louis DiGuilio

Housing & Construction
Housing Units, 2000*
Total	2,840
Median rent	$635
Median SF home value	$124,400

New Privately Owned Housing Units Authorized by Building Permit
	Units	Value
Total, 2004	41	$4,486,000
Single family	8	$440,000
Total, 2005	32	$3,538,667
Single family	27	$2,911,000

Real Property Valuation - parcels, 2005
	Number	Valuation
Total		$228,418,400
Vacant	96	6,362,900
Residential	1,565	126,613,500
Commercial	171	84,544,100
Industrial	0	0
Apartments	67	10,897,900
Farm land	0	0
Farm homestead	0	0

Average Property Value & Tax, 2005
Residential value	$80,903
Property tax	$2,851
FAIR rebate	$679

Public Library
No public municipal library.

Library statistics, 2004
	Total	per capita
Volumes	NA	NA
Expenditure	NA	NA

Public Safety
Police
Chief	Thomas Boyd
Number of officers, 2004	20

Crime, 2004	Number	Rate
Total	338	106.3
Violent	79	24.8
Non-violent	259	81.4
Domestic Viol.	184	NA

Emergency/Fire
Director	William Rumbolo

Public School District
(for school year 2004-2005 except as noted)

Seaside Heights Borough School District
1200 Bay Blvd
Seaside Heights, NJ 08751
732-793-8485
Superintendent	Michael Ritacco
Grade plan	K-6
Enrollment	284.0
Students per teacher	NA
Per pupil expenditure	$12,300
Median faculty salary	$42,760
Median administrator salary	NA
Grade 12 enrollment	NA
High school graduation rate	NA

Assessment test results
(percent scoring at proficient or advanced level)
	Language	Math
Grade 3	81.8%	81.0%
Grade 8	NA	NA
High school	NA	NA

SAT
Percent tested	NA
Average SAT math score	NA
Average SAT verbal score	NA

No Child Left Behind, 2003-04
Attendence rate (target = 90%)	90.6%
Drop rate	NA
Highly-qualified teachers	100%
District needs improvement?(AYP)	No

Municipal Finance
Fiscal Year 2005
Total tax levy	$8,056,754
County levy	1,791,646
County taxes	1,509,511
County library	158,590
County health	67,218
County open space	56,327
School levy	4,121,834
Local muni. budget	2,143,275
Misc. revenues	6,861,116
Total aid	$253,313
CMPTRA	66,103
Muni. block grant	12,371
Energy tax receipts	149,839
Homeland security	25,000

Fiscal Year 2006
Total aid	$253,314
CMPTRA	60,859
Muni. block grant	12,371
Energy tax receipts	155,084
Homeland security	25,000

Taxes
	2003	2004	2005
General tax rate per $100	3.09	3.235	3.525
Net valuation taxable	$223,166,808	$224,786,597	$228,602,161
State equalized value	$360,411,512	$458,486,603	$637,485,112
County equalization ratio	75.55	61.92	49.00

Demographics & Socio-Economic Characteristics
(2000 U.S. Census, except as noted)

Population

1980*	1,795
1990*	1,871
2000	2,263
Male	1,106
Female	1,157
2004 (estimate)*	2,302
Persons per sq. mi. of land	3,542

Race & Hispanic Origin, 2000
Race

White	2,213
Black/African American	6
Amer. Indian/Alaska Natv.	8
Asian	14
Natv. Hawaiian/Pac. Islander	2
Other Race	4
Two or more races	16
Hispanic origin, total	52
Mexican	7
Puerto Rican	18
Cuban	2
Other Hispanic	25

Age & Nativity, 2000

Under 5 years	107
18 years and over	1,938
21 years and over	1,889
65 years and over	568
85 years and over	79
Median Age	46.8
Native born	2,176
Foreign born	90

Educational Attainment, 2000

Population 25 years and over	1,819
0-8 yrs of school	4.5%
High School grad or higher	88.0%
Bachelor's degree or higher	33.8%
Graduate degree	11.8%

Income & Poverty, 1999

Per capita income	$30,090
Median household income	$45,380
Median family income	$58,636
Persons in poverty	195
H'holds receiving public assistance	20
H'holds receiving social security	490

Households, 2000

Total households	1,127
With persons under 18	197
With persons over 65	404
Family households	606
One-person households	437
Persons per household	2.01
Persons per family	2.61

Labor & Employment

Total civilian labor force, 2004**	1,240
Unemployment rate	5.2%
Total civilian labor force, 2000	1,140
Unemployment rate	5.7%

Employed persons 16 years and over by occupation, 2000

Managers & professionals	382
Service occupations	149
Sales & office occupations	336
Farming, fishing & forestry	0
Construction & maintenance	121
Production & transportation	87
Self-employed persons	120

*US Census Bureau
**New Jersey Department of Labor

General Information
Borough of Seaside Park
PO Box B
1701 N Ocean Ave
Seaside Park, NJ 08752
732-793-3700

Web site	wwwseasideparknj.org
Land area (sq. miles)	0.65
Water area (sq. miles)	0.11
Type of government	Borough
Form of government	B

Government

Legislative Districts

US Congressional	3
State Legislative	10

Local Officials, 2006

Mayor	Robert W. Matthies
Admin/Manager	Jay Delaney
Clerk	Jay Delaney
Finance Dir/Treas	Ella Rice
Engineer	John Walsh
Attorney	William Hiering Jr.
Tax assessor	Dennis Raftery
Tax collector	NA
Building officer	NA
Zoning officer	Geoffrey Schwartz
Public Works	NA

Housing & Construction

Housing Units, 2000*

Total	2,811
Median rent	$718
Median SF home value	$215,100

New Privately Owned Housing Units
Authorized by Building Permit

	Units	Value
Total, 2004	16	$3,281,483
Single family	14	$3,146,750
Total, 2005	21	$5,325,409
Single family	19	$5,190,676

Real Property Valuation - parcels, 2005

	Number	Valuation
Total		$679,529,200
Vacant	42	10,070,400
Residential	1,870	611,073,100
Commercial	53	51,457,200
Industrial	0	0
Apartments	17	6,928,500
Farm land	0	0
Farm homestead	0	0

Average Property Value & Tax, 2005

Residential value	$326,777
Property tax	$5,525
FAIR rebate	$627

Public Library

No public municipal library.

Library statistics, 2004

	Total	per capita
Volumes	NA	NA
Expenditure	NA	NA

Public Safety
Police

Chief	William Beining
Number of officers, 2004	15

Crime, 2004	Number	Rate
Total	50	21.8
Violent	5	2.2
Non-violent	45	19.6
Domestic Viol.	28	NA

Emergency/Fire

Director	Robert Cadwell

Public School District
(for school year 2004-2005 except as noted)

Seaside Park Borough School District
Central & Fourth Aves
Seaside Park, NJ 08752
732-793-0177

Superintendent	Theresa Hamilton
Grade plan	K-6
Enrollment	113.0
Students per teacher	8.4
Per pupil expenditure	$12,376
Median faculty salary	$38,606
Median administrator salary	$65,316
Grade 12 enrollment	NA
High school graduation rate	NA

Assessment test results
(percent scoring at proficient or advanced level)

	Language	Math
Grade 3	88.9%	83.4%
Grade 8	NA	NA
High school	NA	NA

SAT

Percent tested	NA
Average SAT math score	NA
Average SAT verbal score	NA

No Child Left Behind, 2003-04

Attendence rate (target = 90%)	94.0%
Drop rate	NA
Highly-qualified teachers	100%
District needs improvement?(AYP)	No

Municipal Finance

Fiscal Year 2005

Total tax levy	$11,494,640
County levy	3,412,450
County taxes	2,875,066
County library	302,050
County health	128,029
County open space	107,305
School levy	4,175,079
Local muni. budget	3,907,111
Misc. revenues	3,710,860
Total aid	$283,954
CMPTRA	29,673
Muni. block grant	8,873
Energy tax receipts	220,408
Homeland security	25,000

Fiscal Year 2006

Total aid	$283,954
CMPTRA	21,959
Muni. block grant	8,873
Energy tax receipts	228,122
Homeland security	25,000

Taxes

	2003	2004	2005
General tax rate per $100	1.46	1.544	1.691
Net valuation taxable	$677,284,002	$678,274,331	$679,901,640
State equalized value	$723,439,438	$890,301,701	$1,080,409,407
County equalization ratio	115.8	93.62	76.17

Demographics & Socio-Economic Characteristics
(2000 U.S. Census, except as noted)

Population
1980*	13,719
1990*	14,061
2000	15,931
Male	7,879
Female	8,052
2004 (estimate)*	15,663
Persons per sq. mi. of land	2,661

Race & Hispanic Origin, 2000
Race
White	12,512
Black/African American	709
Amer. Indian/Alaska Natv.	18
Asian	1,880
Natv. Hawaiian/Pac. Islander	7
Other Race	445
Two or more races	360
Hispanic origin, total	1,953
Mexican	47
Puerto Rican	521
Cuban	376
Other Hispanic	1,009

Age & Nativity, 2000
Under 5 years	825
18 years and over	12,866
21 years and over	12,430
65 years and over	2,571
85 years and over	311
Median Age	39.5
Native born	12,593
Foreign born	3,246

Educational Attainment, 2000
Population 25 years and over	11,780
0-8 yrs of school	6.2%
High School grad or higher	82.2%
Bachelor's degree or higher	29.1%
Graduate degree	10.5%

Income & Poverty, 1999
Per capita income	$31,684
Median household income	$59,800
Median family income	$72,568
Persons in poverty	1,149
H'holds receiving public assistance	81
H'holds receiving social security	1,934

Households, 2000
Total households	6,214
With persons under 18	1,718
With persons over 65	1,876
Family households	3,948
One-person households	1,962
Persons per household	2.41
Persons per family	3.08

Labor & Employment
Total civilian labor force, 2004**	7,979
Unemployment rate	2.6%
Total civilian labor force, 2000	7,889
Unemployment rate	5.7%

Employed persons 16 years and over by occupation, 2000
Managers & professionals	3,032
Service occupations	673
Sales & office occupations	2,436
Farming, fishing & forestry	6
Construction & maintenance	550
Production & transportation	744
Self-employed persons	393

*US Census Bureau
**New Jersey Department of Labor

General Information
Town of Secaucus
1203 Paterson Plank Rd
Secaucus, NJ 07094
201-330-2000
Web site	www.townofsecaucus.net
Land area (sq. miles)	5.89
Water area (sq. miles)	0.63
Type of government	Town
Form of government	T

Government

Legislative Districts
US Congressional	9
State Legislative	32

Local Officials, 2006
Mayor	Dennis Elwell
Admin/Manager	Anthony Iacono
Clerk	Michael Marra
Finance Dir/Treas	Margaret Barkala
Engineer	Gerald Perricone
Attorney	Frank Leanza
Tax assessor	E. Giunta/M. Jaeger
Tax collector	Alan Bartolozzi
Building officer	Vincent Prieto
Zoning officer	Vincent Prieto
Public Works	Michael Gonnelli

Housing & Construction

Housing Units, 2000*
Total	6,385
Median rent	$850
Median SF home value	$209,400

New Privately Owned Housing Units Authorized by Building Permit
	Units	Value
Total, 2004	107	$9,171,241
Single family	97	$8,100,032
Total, 2005	111	$10,211,404
Single family	109	$9,997,162

Real Property Valuation - parcels, 2005
	Number	Valuation
Total		$2,478,305,550
Vacant	340	80,154,800
Residential	4,461	711,852,250
Commercial	226	763,724,600
Industrial	156	905,737,700
Apartments	11	16,836,200
Farm land	0	0
Farm homestead	0	0

Average Property Value & Tax, 2005
Residential value	$159,572
Property tax	$4,563
FAIR rebate	$621

Public Library
Secaucus Public Library
1379 Paterson Plank Rd
Secaucus, NJ 07094
201-330-2083
Director..............Katherine Steffens

Library statistics, 2004
	Total	per capita
Volumes	98,382	6.18
Expenditure	$1,046,445	$65.69

Public Safety

Police
Chief	Dennis Corcoran
Number of officers, 2004	59

Crime, 2004	Number	Rate
Total	725	46.1
Violent	18	1.1
Non-violent	707	44.9
Domestic Viol.	195	NA

Emergency/Fire
Director..............Raymond Cieciuch

Public School District
(for school year 2004-2005 except as noted)

Secaucus School District
20 Centre Ave
Secaucus, NJ 07094
201-974-2004
Superintendent	Constantino Scerbo
Grade plan	K-12
Enrollment	1,909.5
Students per teacher	11.6
Per pupil expenditure	$13,267
Median faculty salary	$55,023
Median administrator salary	$107,070
Grade 12 enrollment	127.0
High school graduation rate	93.4%

Assessment test results
(percent scoring at proficient or advanced level)
	Language	Math
Grade 3	92.3%	97.7%
Grade 8	79.9%	65.0%
High school	92.1%	84.8%

SAT
Percent tested	78%
Average SAT math score	503
Average SAT verbal score	457

No Child Left Behind, 2003-04
Attendence rate (target = 90%)	95.1%
Drop rate	2%
Highly-qualified teachers	99.5%
District needs improvement?(AYP)	No

Municipal Finance

Fiscal Year 2005
Total tax levy	$70,995,280
County levy	19,299,050
County taxes	18,933,942
County library	0
County health	0
County open space	365,109
School levy	25,701,672
Local muni. budget	25,994,558
Misc. revenues	12,017,927
Total aid	$2,554,225
CMPTRA	938,190
Muni. block grant	62,466
Energy tax receipts	1,483,569
Homeland security	70,000

Fiscal Year 2006
Total aid	$2,554,225
CMPTRA	886,265
Muni. block grant	62,466
Energy tax receipts	1,535,494
Homeland security	70,000

Taxes
	2003	2004	2005
General tax rate per $100	2.68	2.745	2.860
Net valuation taxable	$2,487,159,656	$2,507,940,973	$2,482,969,997
State equalized value	$3,087,721,485	$3,658,189,408	$3,912,037,178
County equalization ratio	87.79	80.55	68.51

Demographics & Socio-Economic Characteristics

(2000 U.S. Census, except as noted)

Population

1980*	4,537
1990*	5,765
2000	6,462
Male	3,239
Female	3,223
2004 (estimate)*	6,827
Persons per sq. mi. of land	152

Race & Hispanic Origin, 2000

Race

White	6,284
Black/African American	53
Amer. Indian/Alaska Natv.	7
Asian	43
Natv. Hawaiian/Pac. Islander	0
Other Race	20
Two or more races	55
Hispanic origin, total	68
Mexican	17
Puerto Rican	23
Cuban	9
Other Hispanic	19

Age & Nativity, 2000

Under 5 years	442
18 years and over	4,564
21 years and over	4,339
65 years and over	386
85 years and over	24
Median Age	37.3
Native born	6,330
Foreign born	132

Educational Attainment, 2000

Population 25 years and over	4,134
0-8 yrs of school	1.4%
High School grad or higher	92.3%
Bachelor's degree or higher	37.1%
Graduate degree	10.9%

Income & Poverty, 1999

Per capita income	$30,934
Median household income	$77,457
Median family income	$82,534
Persons in poverty	168
H'holds receiving public assistance	14
H'holds receiving social security	388

Households, 2000

Total households	2,132
With persons under 18	1,002
With persons over 65	292
Family households	1,821
One-person households	243
Persons per household	3.03
Persons per family	3.29

Labor & Employment

Total civilian labor force, 2004**	3,386
Unemployment rate	3.1%
Total civilian labor force, 2000	3,586
Unemployment rate	2.7%

Employed persons 16 years and over by occupation, 2000

Managers & professionals	1,470
Service occupations	448
Sales & office occupations	1,014
Farming, fishing & forestry	5
Construction & maintenance	296
Production & transportation	256
Self-employed persons	245

*US Census Bureau
**New Jersey Department of Labor

General Information

Township of Shamong
105 Willow Grove Rd
Shamong, NJ 08088
609-268-2377

Web site	www.shamong.net
Land area (sq. miles)	44.81
Water area (sq. miles)	0.25
Type of government	Township
Form of government	TC

Government

Legislative Districts

US Congressional	3
State Legislative	8

Local Officials, 2006

Mayor	Jonathan Shevele
Admin/Manager	Susan Onorato
Clerk	Susan Onorato
Finance Dir/Treas	Kathleen Phelan
Engineer	Melanie Adamson
Attorney	Douglas L. Heinold
Tax assessor	James Renwick
Tax collector	Kathryn Taylor
Building officer	Dan McGonigle
Zoning officer	Charles Schmidt
Public Works	NA

Housing & Construction

Housing Units, 2000*

Total	2,175
Median rent	$764
Median SF home value	$191,900

New Privately Owned Housing Units
Authorized by Building Permit

	Units	Value
Total, 2004	26	$4,833,092
Single family	26	$4,833,092
Total, 2005	21	$4,180,982
Single family	21	$4,180,982

Real Property Valuation - parcels, 2005

	Number	Valuation
Total		$398,831,600
Vacant	230	5,163,850
Residential	1,940	367,840,900
Commercial	42	8,007,700
Industrial	8	1,654,000
Apartments	0	0
Farm land	95	14,631,400
Farm homestead	179	1,533,750

Average Property Value & Tax, 2005

Residential value	$174,316
Property tax	$0
FAIR rebate	$461

Public Library

No public municipal library.

Library statistics, 2004

	Total	per capita
Volumes	NA	NA
Expenditure	NA	NA

Public Safety

Police

Chief	NA
Number of officers, 2004	0

Crime, 2004	Number	Rate
Total	38	5.6
Violent	1	0.1
Non-violent	37	5.5
Domestic Viol.	4	NA

Emergency/Fire

Director	Jim White

Public School District

(for school year 2004-2005 except as noted)

Shamong Township School District
295 Indian Mills Rd
Shamong, NJ 08088
609-268-0120

Superintendent	Thomas Christianson
Grade plan	K-8
Enrollment	958.0
Students per teacher	11.7
Per pupil expenditure	$11,464
Median faculty salary	$65,540
Median administrator salary	$87,842
Grade 12 enrollment	NA
High school graduation rate	NA

Assessment test results

(percent scoring at proficient or advanced level)

	Language	Math
Grade 3	93.8%	91.2%
Grade 8	85.9%	80.4%
High school	NA	NA

SAT

Percent tested	NA
Average SAT math score	NA
Average SAT verbal score	NA

No Child Left Behind, 2003-04

Attendance rate (target = 90%)	95.7%
Drop rate	NA
Highly-qualified teachers	100%
District needs improvement?(AYP)	No

Municipal Finance

Fiscal Year 2005

Total tax levy	$13,613,586
County levy	2,754,663
County taxes	2,310,875
County library	202,335
County health	0
County open space	241,454
School levy	10,782,157
Local muni. budget	76,766
Misc. revenues	2,707,775
Total aid	$710,297
CMPTRA	264,290
Muni. block grant	25,338
Energy tax receipts	420,399
Homeland security	0

Fiscal Year 2006

Total aid	$710,297
CMPTRA	249,576
Muni. block grant	35,558
Energy tax receipts	435,113
Homeland security	NA

Taxes

	2003	2004	2005
General tax rate per $100	3.15	3.226	3.405
Net valuation taxable	$387,027,885	$393,238,724	$400,234,661
State equalized value	$513,503,894	$590,223,836	$660,017,581
County equalization ratio	82.55	75.37	66.53

Demographics & Socio-Economic Characteristics
(2000 U.S. Census, except as noted)

Population
1980*	604
1990*	408
2000	534
Male	251
Female	283
2004 (estimate)*	622
Persons per sq. mi. of land	520

Race & Hispanic Origin, 2000
Race
White	508
Black/African American	14
Amer. Indian/Alaska Natv.	3
Asian	0
Natv. Hawaiian/Pac. Islander	0
Other Race	0
Two or more races	9
Hispanic origin, total	16
Mexican	7
Puerto Rican	9
Cuban	0
Other Hispanic	0

Age & Nativity, 2000
Under 5 years	34
18 years and over	403
21 years and over	390
65 years and over	84
85 years and over	7
Median Age	39.8
Native born	528
Foreign born	8

Educational Attainment, 2000
Population 25 years and over	341
0-8 yrs of school	4.4%
High School grad or higher	76.8%
Bachelor's degree or higher	14.1%
Graduate degree	3.5%

Income & Poverty, 1999
Per capita income	$16,880
Median household income	$49,191
Median family income	$54,219
Persons in poverty	31
H'holds receiving public assistance	0
H'holds receiving social security	49

Households, 2000
Total households	194
With persons under 18	72
With persons over 65	59
Family households	152
One-person households	35
Persons per household	2.75
Persons per family	3.09

Labor & Employment
Total civilian labor force, 2004**	192
Unemployment rate	4.8%
Total civilian labor force, 2000	293
Unemployment rate	5.1%

Employed persons 16 years and over by occupation, 2000
Managers & professionals	71
Service occupations	27
Sales & office occupations	61
Farming, fishing & forestry	8
Construction & maintenance	45
Production & transportation	66
Self-employed persons	7

*US Census Bureau
**New Jersey Department of Labor

General Information
Borough of Shiloh
PO Box 349
Shiloh, NJ 08353
856-455-3054
Email	shilohclerk@snip.net
Land area (sq. miles)	1.20
Water area (sq. miles)	0
Type of government	Borough
Form of government	B

Government

Legislative Districts
US Congressional	2
State Legislative	3

Local Officials, 2006
Mayor	Howard Scull Jr.
Admin/Manager	NA
Clerk	Ronald Campbell Sr.
Finance Dir/Treas	Jeanne Wilford
Engineer	Michael Fralinger
Attorney	Theodore Baker
Tax assessor	Lois Mazza
Tax collector	Elizabeth Wallender
Building officer	Pete Mattee
Zoning officer	Michael Morroni
Public Works	NA

Housing & Construction

Housing Units, 2000*
Total	204
Median rent	$558
Median SF home value	$97,600

New Privately Owned Housing Units
Authorized by Building Permit
	Units	Value
Total, 2004	7	$675,104
Single family	7	$675,104
Total, 2005	5	$535,819
Single family	5	$535,819

Real Property Valuation - parcels, 2005
	Number	Valuation
Total		$18,927,800
Vacant	10	247,700
Residential	183	15,859,700
Commercial	13	1,077,400
Industrial	0	0
Apartments	0	0
Farm land	11	1,408,600
Farm homestead	25	334,400

Average Property Value & Tax, 2005
Residential value	$77,856
Property tax	$2,820
FAIR rebate	$636

Public Library
No public municipal library.

Library statistics, 2004
	Total	per capita
Volumes	NA	NA
Expenditure	NA	NA

Public Safety
Police
Chief	NA
Number of officers, 2004	0

Crime, 2004	Number	Rate
Total	7	11.7
Violent	0	0
Non-violent	7	11.7
Domestic Viol.	4	NA

Emergency/Fire
Director	Ronald Dubois

Public School District
(for school year 2004-2005 except as noted)

Shiloh School District
Main St
Shiloh, NJ 08353
856-451-5424
Superintendent	David Hitchner
Grade plan	K-8
Enrollment	77.0
Students per teacher	11.7
Per pupil expenditure	$10,141
Median faculty salary	$34,125
Median administrator salary	$30,000
Grade 12 enrollment	NA
High school graduation rate	NA

Assessment test results
(percent scoring at proficient or advanced level)
	Language	Math
Grade 3	NA	NA
Grade 8	NA	NA
High school	NA	NA

SAT
Percent tested	NA
Average SAT math score	NA
Average SAT verbal score	NA

No Child Left Behind, 2003-04
Attendance rate (target = 90%)	96.7%
Drop rate	NA
Highly-qualified teachers	100%
District needs improvement?(AYP)	No

Municipal Finance

Fiscal Year 2005
Total tax levy	$691,647
County levy	224,039
County taxes	212,824
County library	0
County health	9,061
County open space	2,155
School levy	387,644
Local muni. budget	79,963
Misc. revenues	149,745
Total aid	$48,648
CMPTRA	23,555
Muni. block grant	2,094
Energy tax receipts	22,999
Homeland security	0

Fiscal Year 2006
Total aid	$48,648
CMPTRA	22,750
Muni. block grant	2,094
Energy tax receipts	23,804
Homeland security	NA

Taxes
	2003	2004	2005
General tax rate per $100	3.70	3.417	3.625
Net valuation taxable	$18,627,827	$18,679,878	$19,094,488
State equalized value	$19,791,571	$20,937,905	$25,167,376
County equalization ratio	92.2	94.12	89.12

Demographics & Socio-Economic Characteristics
(2000 U.S. Census, except as noted)

Population
1980*	1,427
1990*	1,352
2000	1,384
Male	666
Female	718
2004 (estimate)*	1,418
Persons per sq. mi. of land	2,040

Race & Hispanic Origin, 2000
Race
White	1,333
Black/African American	4
Amer. Indian/Alaska Natv.	10
Asian	12
Natv. Hawaiian/Pac. Islander	0
Other Race	15
Two or more races	10
Hispanic origin, total	80
Mexican	52
Puerto Rican	5
Cuban	3
Other Hispanic	20

Age & Nativity, 2000
Under 5 years	47
18 years and over	1,179
21 years and over	1,146
65 years and over	372
85 years and over	45
Median Age	50.5
Native born	1,318
Foreign born	77

Educational Attainment, 2000
Population 25 years and over	1,079
0-8 yrs of school	2.4%
High School grad or higher	89.0%
Bachelor's degree or higher	25.4%
Graduate degree	9.4%

Income & Poverty, 1999
Per capita income	$27,870
Median household income	$42,098
Median family income	$60,417
Persons in poverty	114
H'holds receiving public assistance	3
H'holds receiving social security	291

Households, 2000
Total households	664
With persons under 18	111
With persons over 65	268
Family households	396
One-person households	238
Persons per household	2.08
Persons per family	2.65

Labor & Employment
Total civilian labor force, 2004**	803
Unemployment rate	4.4%
Total civilian labor force, 2000	696
Unemployment rate	6.6%

Employed persons 16 years and over by occupation, 2000
Managers & professionals	219
Service occupations	128
Sales & office occupations	173
Farming, fishing & forestry	3
Construction & maintenance	77
Production & transportation	50
Self-employed persons	92

*US Census Bureau
**New Jersey Department of Labor

General Information
Borough of Ship Bottom
1621 Long Beach Blvd
Ship Bottom, NJ 08008
609-494-2171

Web site	shipbottom.org
Land area (sq. miles)	0.70
Water area (sq. miles)	0.30
Type of government	Borough
Form of government	B

Government

Legislative Districts
US Congressional	3
State Legislative	9

Local Officials, 2006
Mayor	William Huelsenbeck
Admin/Manager	T. Richard Bethea
Clerk	Kathleen Wells
Finance Dir/Treas	T. Richard Bethea
Engineer	Owen, Little & Assoc
Attorney	Christopher Conners
Tax assessor	William Procacci
Tax collector	T. Richard Bethea
Building officer	Frank Zappavigna
Zoning officer	NA
Public Works	NA

Housing & Construction

Housing Units, 2000*
Total	2,218
Median rent	$783
Median SF home value	$236,000

New Privately Owned Housing Units Authorized by Building Permit
	Units	Value
Total, 2004	12	$1,304,793
Single family	12	$1,304,793
Total, 2005	24	$5,564,883
Single family	24	$5,564,883

Real Property Valuation - parcels, 2005
	Number	Valuation
Total		$1,046,636,100
Vacant	69	25,395,400
Residential	1,778	888,728,500
Commercial	156	125,420,600
Industrial	0	0
Apartments	8	7,091,600
Farm land	0	0
Farm homestead	0	0

Average Property Value & Tax, 2005
Residential value	$499,847
Property tax	$4,371
FAIR rebate	$767

Public Library

No public municipal library.

Library statistics, 2004
	Total	per capita
Volumes	NA	NA
Expenditure	NA	NA

Public Safety

Police
Chief	Paul Sharkey
Number of officers, 2004	11

Crime, 2004	Number	Rate
Total	99	69.8
Violent	3	2.1
Non-violent	96	67.7
Domestic Viol.	15	NA

Emergency/Fire
Director	Frederick Traut

Public School District
(for school year 2004-2005 except as noted)

Sends children to Long Beach Island school district (see Appendix A).
Grade plan	NA
Enrollment	NA
Students per teacher	NA
Per pupil expenditure	NA
Median faculty salary	NA
Median administrator salary	NA
Grade 12 enrollment	NA
High school graduation rate	NA

Assessment test results
(percent scoring at proficient or advanced level)
	Language	Math
Grade 3	NA	NA
Grade 8	NA	NA
High school	NA	NA

SAT
Percent tested	NA
Average SAT math score	NA
Average SAT verbal score	NA

No Child Left Behind, 2003-04
Attendence rate (target = 90%)	NA
Drop rate	NA
Highly-qualified teachers	NA
District needs improvement?(AYP)	NA

Municipal Finance

Fiscal Year 2005
Total tax levy	$9,155,618
County levy	3,531,372
County taxes	3,091,251
County library	324,761
County health	0
County open space	115,360
School levy	2,984,596
Local muni. budget	2,639,650
Misc. revenues	2,297,850
Total aid	$291,488
CMPTRA	0
Muni. block grant	5,916
Energy tax receipts	260,572
Homeland security	25,000

Fiscal Year 2006
Total aid	$300,608
CMPTRA	0
Muni. block grant	5,916
Energy tax receipts	269,692
Homeland security	25,000

Taxes
	2003	2004	2005
General tax rate per $100	1.93	2.125	0.875
Net valuation taxable	$414,233,219	$422,845,293	$1,046,996,207
State equalized value	$787,815,175	$946,340,947	$1,148,148,050
County equalization ratio	62.18	52.58	109.23

Demographics & Socio-Economic Characteristics
(2000 U.S. Census, except as noted)

Population
1980*	2,962
1990*	3,096
2000	3,590
Male	1,781
Female	1,809
2004 (estimate)*	3,731
Persons per sq. mi. of land	1,691

Race & Hispanic Origin, 2000
Race
White	3,468
Black/African American	19
Amer. Indian/Alaska Natv.	0
Asian	60
Natv. Hawaiian/Pac. Islander	0
Other Race	13
Two or more races	30
Hispanic origin, total	69
Mexican	16
Puerto Rican	13
Cuban	8
Other Hispanic	32

Age & Nativity, 2000
Under 5 years	310
18 years and over	2,485
21 years and over	2,412
65 years and over	431
85 years and over	43
Median Age	38.4
Native born	3,325
Foreign born	265

Educational Attainment, 2000
Population 25 years and over	2,367
0-8 yrs of school	2.7%
High School grad or higher	91.0%
Bachelor's degree or higher	48.7%
Graduate degree	19.6%

Income & Poverty, 1999
Per capita income	$38,218
Median household income	$86,911
Median family income	$92,719
Persons in poverty	37
H'holds receiving public assistance	13
H'holds receiving social security	290

Households, 2000
Total households	1,207
With persons under 18	567
With persons over 65	301
Family households	1,016
One-person households	156
Persons per household	2.96
Persons per family	3.27

Labor & Employment
Total civilian labor force, 2004**	1,802
Unemployment rate	2.0%
Total civilian labor force, 2000	1,686
Unemployment rate	2.7%

Employed persons 16 years and over by occupation, 2000
Managers & professionals	832
Service occupations	137
Sales & office occupations	516
Farming, fishing & forestry	0
Construction & maintenance	83
Production & transportation	72
Self-employed persons	152

*US Census Bureau
**New Jersey Department of Labor

General Information
Borough of Shrewsbury
419 Sycamore Ave
Shrewsbury, NJ 07702
732-741-4200
Web site	www.shrewsburyboro.com
Land area (sq. miles)	2.21
Water area (sq. miles)	0.02
Type of government	Borough
Form of government	B

Government
Legislative Districts
US Congressional	12
State Legislative	12

Local Officials, 2006
Mayor	Emilia Siciliano
Admin/Manager	Tom Seaman
Clerk	Lynn Spillane
Finance Dir/Treas	Thomas Seaman
Engineer	Cranmen Engr.
Attorney	Martin Barger
Tax assessor	Stephen Walters
Tax collector	Thomas Seaman
Building officer	Cary Costa
Zoning officer	Jerome Donlon
Public Works	Robert Wentway

Housing & Construction
Housing Units, 2000*
Total	1,223
Median rent	$898
Median SF home value	$258,300

New Privately Owned Housing Units
Authorized by Building Permit
	Units	Value
Total, 2004	33	$4,616,759
Single family	33	$4,616,759
Total, 2005	18	$3,768,723
Single family	18	$3,768,723

Real Property Valuation - parcels, 2005
	Number	Valuation
Total		$789,527,700
Vacant	45	7,395,600
Residential	1,276	494,432,700
Commercial	170	286,909,800
Industrial	0	0
Apartments	0	0
Farm land	1	778,700
Farm homestead	1	10,900

Average Property Value & Tax, 2005
Residential value	$387,192
Property tax	$8,331
FAIR rebate	$568

Public Library
Eastern Branch Library†
1001 Rte 35
Shrewsbury, NJ 07702
732-842-5995
Branch Librarian	Janet Kranis

Library statistics, 2004
	Total	per capita
Volumes	NA	NA
Expenditure	NA	NA

†Branch of County Library

Public Safety
Police
Chief	John Wilson III
Number of officers, 2004	15

Crime, 2004	Number	Rate
Total	97	26
Violent	5	1.3
Non-violent	92	24.7
Domestic Viol.	4	NA

Emergency/Fire
Director	Ed Magenheimer

Public School District
(for school year 2004-2005 except as noted)

Shrewsbury Borough School District
20 Obre Place
Shrewsbury, NJ 07702
732-747-0882
Superintendent	Lawrence Ambrosino
Grade plan	K-8
Enrollment	526.0
Students per teacher	11.1
Per pupil expenditure	$9,483
Median faculty salary	$44,340
Median administrator salary	$90,000
Grade 12 enrollment	NA
High school graduation rate	NA

Assessment test results
(percent scoring at proficient or advanced level)
	Language	Math
Grade 3	100%	88.1%
Grade 8	96.5%	85.7%
High school	NA	NA

SAT
Percent tested	NA
Average SAT math score	NA
Average SAT verbal score	NA

No Child Left Behind, 2003-04
Attendence rate (target = 90%)	96.3%
Drop rate	NA
Highly-qualified teachers	100%
District needs improvement?(AYP)	No

Municipal Finance
Fiscal Year 2005
Total tax levy	$17,027,399
County levy	2,872,261
County taxes	2,577,351
County library	141,974
County health	0
County open space	152,936
School levy	9,012,003
Local muni. budget	5,143,135
Misc. revenues	2,114,937
Total aid	$569,367
CMPTRA	138,878
Muni. block grant	14,076
Energy tax receipts	391,413
Homeland security	25,000

Fiscal Year 2006
Total aid	$569,367
CMPTRA	125,179
Muni. block grant	14,076
Energy tax receipts	405,112
Homeland security	25,000

Taxes
	2003	2004	2005
General tax rate per $100	1.98	2.064	2.152
Net valuation taxable	$786,763,315	$791,987,690	$791,332,531
State equalized value	$751,804,410	$857,506,381	$965,510,653
County equalization ratio	67.17	104.65	92.34

Demographics & Socio-Economic Characteristics

(2000 U.S. Census, except as noted)

Population

1980*	995
1990*	1,098
2000	1,098
Male	530
Female	568
2004 (estimate)*	1,090
Persons per sq. mi. of land	11,540

Race & Hispanic Origin, 2000

Race

White	733
Black/African American	183
Amer. Indian/Alaska Natv.	0
Asian	110
Natv. Hawaiian/Pac. Islander	0
Other Race	31
Two or more races	41
Hispanic origin, total	73
Mexican	22
Puerto Rican	19
Cuban	0
Other Hispanic	32

Age & Nativity, 2000

Under 5 years	82
18 years and over	872
21 years and over	838
65 years and over	119
85 years and over	16
Median Age	34.9
Native born	905
Foreign born	193

Educational Attainment, 2000

Population 25 years and over	770
0-8 yrs of school	6.9%
High School grad or higher	82.5%
Bachelor's degree or higher	20.4%
Graduate degree	5.7%

Income & Poverty, 1999

Per capita income	$23,574
Median household income	$36,875
Median family income	$42,500
Persons in poverty	96
H'holds receiving public assistance	10
H'holds receiving social security	90

Households, 2000

Total households	521
With persons under 18	143
With persons over 65	102
Family households	255
One-person households	206
Persons per household	2.1
Persons per family	2.89

Labor & Employment

Total civilian labor force, 2004**	733
Unemployment rate	4.0%
Total civilian labor force, 2000	689
Unemployment rate	7.0%

Employed persons 16 years and over by occupation, 2000

Managers & professionals	192
Service occupations	79
Sales & office occupations	232
Farming, fishing & forestry	0
Construction & maintenance	48
Production & transportation	90
Self-employed persons	20

*US Census Bureau
**New Jersey Department of Labor

General Information

Shrewsbury Township
1979 Crawford St
Shrewsbury, NJ 07724
732-542-0675

Web site	NA
Land area (sq. miles)	0.09
Water area (sq. miles)	0
Type of government	Township
Form of government	TC

Government

Legislative Districts

US Congressional	12
State Legislative	12

Local Officials, 2006

Mayor	Albert Klose
Admin/Manager	Jan Delonardo
Clerk	Jan Delonardo
Finance Dir/Treas	Adeline Schmidt
Engineer	Richard Maser
Attorney	Gene Anthony
Tax assessor	Stephen Walters
Tax collector	NA
Building officer	Joseph Muzetska
Zoning officer	NA
Public Works	NA

Housing & Construction

Housing Units, 2000*

Total	546
Median rent	$825
Median SF home value	$61,100

New Privately Owned Housing Units Authorized by Building Permit

	Units	Value
Total, 2004	0	$0
Single family	0	$0
Total, 2005	0	$0
Single family	0	$0

Real Property Valuation - parcels, 2005

	Number	Valuation
Total		$27,238,100
Vacant	0	0
Residential	122	9,103,800
Commercial	0	0
Industrial	0	0
Apartments	269	18,134,300
Farm land	0	0
Farm homestead	0	0

Average Property Value & Tax, 2005

Residential value	$74,621
Property tax	$3,705
FAIR rebate	$597

Public Library

Eastern Branch Library†
1001 Rte 35
Shrewsbury, NJ 07702
732-842-5995

Branch Librarian .... Janet Kranis

Library statistics, 2004

	Total	per capita
Volumes	NA	NA
Expenditure	NA	NA

†Branch of County Library

Public Safety

Police

Chief	NA
Number of officers, 2004	0

Crime, 2004	Number	Rate
Total	10	9.2
Violent	1	0.9
Non-violent	9	8.3
Domestic Viol.	3	NA

Emergency/Fire

Director	NA

Public School District

(for school year 2004-2005 except as noted)

Tinton Falls School District
658 Tinton Ave
Tinton Falls, NJ 07724
732-460-2404

Superintendent	Leonard Kelpsh
Grade plan	K-8
Enrollment	1,768.0
Students per teacher	12.8
Per pupil expenditure	$12,937
Median faculty salary	$51,588
Median administrator salary	$94,262
Grade 12 enrollment	NA
High school graduation rate	NA

Assessment test results

(percent scoring at proficient or advanced level)

	Language	Math
Grade 3	92.7%	90.3%
Grade 8	81.7%	77.5%
High school	NA	NA

SAT

Percent tested	NA
Average SAT math score	NA
Average SAT verbal score	NA

No Child Left Behind, 2003-04

Attendance rate (target = 90%)	95.6%
Drop rate	NA
Highly-qualified teachers	98.1%
District needs improvement?(AYP)	No

Municipal Finance

Fiscal Year 2005

Total tax levy	$1,355,527
County levy	184,161
County taxes	165,252
County library	9,103
County health	0
County open space	9,806
School levy	690,791
Local muni. budget	480,575
Misc. revenues	239,648
Total aid	$123,448
CMPTRA	74,001
Muni. block grant	4,804
Energy tax receipts	44,643
Homeland security	0

Fiscal Year 2006

Total aid	$123,449
CMPTRA	72,439
Muni. block grant	4,804
Energy tax receipts	46,206
Homeland security	NA

Taxes

	2003	2004	2005
General tax rate per $100	4.20	4.487	4.965
Net valuation taxable	$27,264,596	$27,288,601	$27,304,436
State equalized value	$44,894,774	$55,121,467	$63,117,050
County equalization ratio	72.8	60.73	46.46

Demographics & Socio-Economic Characteristics
(2000 U.S. Census, except as noted)

Population
1980*	5,900
1990*	5,440
2000	5,192
Male	2,541
Female	2,651
2004 (estimate)*	5,162
Persons per sq. mi. of land	3,757

Race & Hispanic Origin, 2000
Race
White	3,912
Black/African American	917
Amer. Indian/Alaska Natv.	11
Asian	168
Natv. Hawaiian/Pac. Islander	1
Other Race	56
Two or more races	127
Hispanic origin, total	202
Mexican	14
Puerto Rican	105
Cuban	5
Other Hispanic	78

Age & Nativity, 2000
Under 5 years	274
18 years and over	4,033
21 years and over	3,868
65 years and over	801
85 years and over	64
Median Age	39
Native born	4,850
Foreign born	348

Educational Attainment, 2000
Population 25 years and over	3,722
0-8 yrs of school	2.8%
High School grad or higher	84.5%
Bachelor's degree or higher	16.7%
Graduate degree	6.9%

Income & Poverty, 1999
Per capita income	$21,259
Median household income	$46,898
Median family income	$54,200
Persons in poverty	283
H'holds receiving public assistance	64
H'holds receiving social security	659

Households, 2000
Total households	2,068
With persons under 18	661
With persons over 65	599
Family households	1,380
One-person households	613
Persons per household	2.51
Persons per family	3.11

Labor & Employment
Total civilian labor force, 2004**	2,976
Unemployment rate	3.8%
Total civilian labor force, 2000	2,743
Unemployment rate	4.7%

Employed persons 16 years and over by occupation, 2000
Managers & professionals	802
Service occupations	367
Sales & office occupations	765
Farming, fishing & forestry	0
Construction & maintenance	261
Production & transportation	418
Self-employed persons	92

*US Census Bureau
**New Jersey Department of Labor

General Information
Borough of Somerdale
105 Kennedy Blvd
Somerdale, NJ 08083
856-783-6320

Web site	NA
Land area (sq. miles)	1.37
Water area (sq. miles)	0
Type of government	Borough
Form of government	B

Government

Legislative Districts
US Congressional	1
State Legislative	5

Local Officials, 2006
Mayor	Gary Passanante
Admin/Manager	Victor Cantillo
Clerk	Regina J. White
Finance Dir/Treas	Victor Cantillo
Engineer	Charles Riebel
Attorney	John Kearney
Tax assessor	Thomas Davis
Tax collector	Virginia Knecht
Building officer	Steve Murray
Zoning officer	NA
Public Works	Donald Wharton

Housing & Construction

Housing Units, 2000*
Total	2,168
Median rent	$544
Median SF home value	$97,700

New Privately Owned Housing Units
Authorized by Building Permit
	Units	Value
Total, 2004	4	$285,800
Single family	4	$285,800
Total, 2005	6	$698,750
Single family	6	$698,750

Real Property Valuation - parcels, 2005
	Number	Valuation
Total		$191,535,800
Vacant	109	1,923,800
Residential	1,683	146,368,900
Commercial	123	27,479,600
Industrial	30	8,881,700
Apartments	7	6,881,800
Farm land	0	0
Farm homestead	0	0

Average Property Value & Tax, 2005
Residential value	$86,969
Property tax	$4,184
FAIR rebate	$641

Public Library
No public municipal library.

Library statistics, 2004
	Total	per capita
Volumes	NA	NA
Expenditure	NA	NA

Public Safety
Police
Chief	Anthony Campbell
Number of officers, 2004	14

Crime, 2004	Number	Rate
Total	133	25.7
Violent	15	2.9
Non-violent	118	22.8
Domestic Viol.	18	NA

Emergency/Fire
Director	Brian Alexander

Public School District
(for school year 2004-2005 except as noted)

Somerdale Borough School District
301 Grace St
Somerdale, NJ 08083
856-783-2933

Superintendent	Debra Bruner
Grade plan	K-8
Enrollment	504.0
Students per teacher	11.1
Per pupil expenditure	$10,547
Median faculty salary	$45,963
Median administrator salary	$75,000
Grade 12 enrollment	NA
High school graduation rate	NA

Assessment test results
(percent scoring at proficient or advanced level)
	Language	Math
Grade 3	97.8%	86.7%
Grade 8	76.0%	64.0%
High school	NA	NA

SAT
Percent tested	NA
Average SAT math score	NA
Average SAT verbal score	NA

No Child Left Behind, 2003-04
Attendence rate (target = 90%)	94.3%
Drop rate	NA
Highly-qualified teachers	79.7%
District needs improvement?(AYP)	No

Municipal Finance

Fiscal Year 2005
Total tax levy	$9,233,464
County levy	1,876,079
County taxes	1,726,395
County library	126,599
County health	0
County open space	23,086
School levy	5,318,221
Local muni. budget	2,039,164
Misc. revenues	2,324,836
Total aid	$753,654
CMPTRA	304,650
Muni. block grant	23,804
Energy tax receipts	375,200
Homeland security	50,000

Fiscal Year 2006
Total aid	$753,654
CMPTRA	291,518
Muni. block grant	23,804
Energy tax receipts	388,332
Homeland security	50,000

Taxes
	2003	2004	2005
General tax rate per $100	4.46	4.591	4.811
Net valuation taxable	$194,823,090	$194,884,047	$191,938,059
State equalized value	$219,370,668	$232,941,331	$263,796,123
County equalization ratio	94.2	88.81	83.63

Demographics & Socio-Economic Characteristics
(2000 U.S. Census, except as noted)

Population

1980*	10,330
1990*	11,216
2000	11,614
Male	5,460
Female	6,154
2004 (estimate)*	11,731
Persons per sq. mi. of land	2,912

Race & Hispanic Origin, 2000
Race

White	9,948
Black/African American	814
Amer. Indian/Alaska Natv.	29
Asian	368
Natv. Hawaiian/Pac. Islander	4
Other Race	261
Two or more races	190
Hispanic origin, total	696
Mexican	132
Puerto Rican	332
Cuban	10
Other Hispanic	222

Age & Nativity, 2000

Under 5 years	699
18 years and over	8,899
21 years and over	8,571
65 years and over	1,748
85 years and over	245
Median Age	38.4
Native born	10,667
Foreign born	947

Educational Attainment, 2000

Population 25 years and over	8,090
0-8 yrs of school	3.8%
High School grad or higher	84.2%
Bachelor's degree or higher	19.8%
Graduate degree	5.1%

Income & Poverty, 1999

Per capita income	$22,229
Median household income	$42,222
Median family income	$51,868
Persons in poverty	799
H'holds receiving public assistance	97
H'holds receiving social security	1,391

Households, 2000

Total households	4,920
With persons under 18	1,564
With persons over 65	1,248
Family households	2,952
One-person households	1,621
Persons per household	2.32
Persons per family	2.97

Labor & Employment

Total civilian labor force, 2004**	6,470
Unemployment rate	3.8%
Total civilian labor force, 2000	6,124
Unemployment rate	6.0%

Employed persons 16 years and over by occupation, 2000

Managers & professionals	1,569
Service occupations	1,691
Sales & office occupations	1,452
Farming, fishing & forestry	40
Construction & maintenance	573
Production & transportation	433
Self-employed persons	308

*US Census Bureau
**New Jersey Department of Labor

General Information
City of Somers Point
One West New Jersey Ave
Somers Point, NJ 08244
609-927-9088

Web site	www.somerspoint-nj.com
Land area (sq. miles)	4.03
Water area (sq. miles)	1.14
Type of government	City
Form of government	C

Government

Legislative Districts

US Congressional	2
State Legislative	1

Local Officials, 2006

Mayor	Dan Reilly
Admin/Manager	W. E. Swain
Clerk	Carol Degrassi
Finance Dir/Treas	John Hanson
Engineer	Roger McLernon
Attorney	Roger Steedle
Tax assessor	Diane Hesley
Tax collector	Lynn MacEwan
Building officer	Burton Federman
Zoning officer	NA
Public Works	Richard Gray

Housing & Construction

Housing Units, 2000*

Total	5,402
Median rent	$639
Median SF home value	$122,000

New Privately Owned Housing Units
Authorized by Building Permit

	Units	Value
Total, 2004	NA	NA
Single family	NA	NA
Total, 2005	22	$3,276,092
Single family	22	$3,276,092

Real Property Valuation - parcels, 2005

	Number	Valuation
Total		$670,920,900
Vacant	195	16,389,900
Residential	3,723	456,075,200
Commercial	265	157,464,200
Industrial	0	0
Apartments	16	40,991,600
Farm land	0	0
Farm homestead	0	0

Average Property Value & Tax, 2005

Residential value	$122,502
Property tax	$4,113
FAIR rebate	$603

Public Library
Somers Point Branch Library†
747 Shore Rd
Somers Point, NJ 08244
609-927-7113

Branch Librarian	Mary Jane Bolden

Library statistics, 2004

	Total	per capita
Volumes	NA	NA
Expenditure	NA	NA

†Branch of county library

Public Safety

Police

Chief	Orville Mathis
Number of officers, 2004	28

Crime, 2004	Number	Rate
Total	392	33.7
Violent	44	3.8
Non-violent	348	30
Domestic Viol.	273	NA

Emergency/Fire

Director	Michael Sweeney

Public School District
(for school year 2004-2005 except as noted)

Somers Point School District
Jordan Rd School
Somers Point, NJ 08244
609-927-3043

Superintendent	Gerald Toscano
Grade plan	K-8
Enrollment	1,220.0
Students per teacher	11.7
Per pupil expenditure	$9,290
Median faculty salary	$41,803
Median administrator salary	$92,029
Grade 12 enrollment	NA
High school graduation rate	NA

Assessment test results
(percent scoring at proficient or advanced level)

	Language	Math
Grade 3	78.7%	80.9%
Grade 8	79.2%	58.1%
High school	NA	NA

SAT

Percent tested	NA
Average SAT math score	NA
Average SAT verbal score	NA

No Child Left Behind, 2003-04

Attendance rate (target = 90%)	93.6%
Drop rate	NA
Highly-qualified teachers	100%
District needs improvement?(AYP)	No

Municipal Finance

Fiscal Year 2005

Total tax levy	$22,617,284
County levy	4,083,367
County taxes	3,333,243
County library	369,552
County health	181,863
County open space	198,709
School levy	12,738,013
Local muni. budget	5,795,904
Misc. revenues	4,519,822
Total aid	$1,377,312
CMPTRA	609,060
Muni. block grant	49,078
Energy tax receipts	649,174
Homeland security	70,000

Fiscal Year 2006

Total aid	$1,377,312
CMPTRA	586,339
Muni. block grant	49,078
Energy tax receipts	671,895
Homeland security	70,000

Taxes

	2003	2004	2005
General tax rate per $100	3.14	3.147	3.358
Net valuation taxable	$647,068,442	$676,586,322	$673,666,921
State equalized value	$812,797,942	$994,383,266	$1,278,305,353
County equalization ratio	83.58	79.61	67.94

Demographics & Socio-Economic Characteristics
(2000 U.S. Census, except as noted)

Population
1980*	11,973
1990*	11,632
2000	12,423
Male	6,249
Female	6,174
2004 (estimate)*	12,434
Persons per sq. mi. of land	5,267

Race & Hispanic Origin, 2000
Race
White	8,847
Black/African American	1,606
Amer. Indian/Alaska Natv.	23
Asian	913
Natv. Hawaiian/Pac. Islander	3
Other Race	634
Two or more races	397
Hispanic origin, total	2,112
Mexican	278
Puerto Rican	402
Cuban	46
Other Hispanic	1,386

Age & Nativity, 2000
Under 5 years	869
18 years and over	9,698
21 years and over	9,285
65 years and over	1,738
85 years and over	229
Median Age	35.6
Native born	9,674
Foreign born	2,807

Educational Attainment, 2000
Population 25 years and over	8,603
0-8 yrs of school	6.6%
High School grad or higher	81.9%
Bachelor's degree or higher	31.5%
Graduate degree	10.6%

Income & Poverty, 1999
Per capita income	$23,310
Median household income	$51,237
Median family income	$60,422
Persons in poverty	926
H'holds receiving public assistance	153
H'holds receiving social security	1,430

Households, 2000
Total households	4,743
With persons under 18	1,472
With persons over 65	1,210
Family households	2,891
One-person households	1,489
Persons per household	2.49
Persons per family	3.15

Labor & Employment
Total civilian labor force, 2004**	8,129
Unemployment rate	5.9%
Total civilian labor force, 2000	6,495
Unemployment rate	5.0%

Employed persons 16 years and over by occupation, 2000
Managers & professionals	2,313
Service occupations	1,015
Sales & office occupations	1,601
Farming, fishing & forestry	0
Construction & maintenance	535
Production & transportation	705
Self-employed persons	281

*US Census Bureau
**New Jersey Department of Labor

General Information
Borough of Somerville
25 West End Ave
Somerville, NJ 08876
908-725-2300

Web site	www.somervillenj.org
Land area (sq. miles)	2.36
Water area (sq. miles)	0
Type of government	Borough
Form of government	B

Government

Legislative Districts
US Congressional	11
State Legislative	16

Local Officials, 2006
Mayor	Brian Gallagher
Admin/Manager	Ralph Sternadori
Clerk	Ralph Sternadori
Finance Dir/Treas	Janet Kelk
Engineer	(County)
Attorney	Jermy Solomon
Tax assessor	Frank Betts
Tax collector	Janet Kelk
Building officer	Frank Vuosa
Zoning officer	NA
Public Works	Peter Hendershot

Housing & Construction

Housing Units, 2000*
Total	4,882
Median rent	$822
Median SF home value	$156,700

New Privately Owned Housing Units Authorized by Building Permit
	Units	Value
Total, 2004	8	$1,029,400
Single family	8	$1,029,400
Total, 2005	10	$1,893,550
Single family	10	$1,893,550

Real Property Valuation - parcels, 2005
	Number	Valuation
Total		$649,182,300
Vacant	69	4,367,800
Residential	2,648	391,768,700
Commercial	414	199,806,800
Industrial	14	11,328,800
Apartments	31	41,910,200
Farm land	0	0
Farm homestead	0	0

Average Property Value & Tax, 2005
Residential value	$147,949
Property tax	$6,335
FAIR rebate	$603

Public Library
Somerville Mem. Public Library
35 West End Ave
Somerville, NJ 08876
908-725-1336

Director	Melissa Banks

Library statistics, 2004
	Total	per capita
Volumes	55,820	4.49
Expenditure	$638,416	$51.39

Public Safety
Police
Chief	Dennis Manning
Number of officers, 2004	32

Crime, 2004	Number	Rate
Total	291	23.5
Violent	40	3.2
Non-violent	251	20.3
Domestic Viol.	94	NA

Emergency/Fire
Director	Bruce Kessler

Public School District
(for school year 2004-2005 except as noted)

Somerville Borough School District
51 W Cliff St
Somerville, NJ 08876
908-218-4101

Superintendent	Carolyn Leary
Grade plan	K-12
Enrollment	2,192.0
Students per teacher	11.1
Per pupil expenditure	$12,771
Median faculty salary	$57,830
Median administrator salary	$95,000
Grade 12 enrollment	242.5
High school graduation rate	96.8%

Assessment test results
(percent scoring at proficient or advanced level)
	Language	Math
Grade 3	85.2%	77.4%
Grade 8	87.1%	72.5%
High school	89.5%	81.4%

SAT
Percent tested	85%
Average SAT math score	550
Average SAT verbal score	534

No Child Left Behind, 2003-04
Attendance rate (target = 90%)	95.8%
Drop rate	0.8%
Highly-qualified teachers	90.9%
District needs improvement?(AYP)	No

Municipal Finance

Fiscal Year 2005
Total tax levy	$28,107,464
County levy	3,397,800
County taxes	3,099,742
County library	0
County health	0
County open space	298,058
School levy	17,355,243
Local muni. budget	7,354,421
Misc. revenues	6,266,148
Total aid	$1,943,133
CMPTRA	713,851
Muni. block grant	50,897
Energy tax receipts	1,108,385
Homeland security	70,000

Fiscal Year 2006
Total aid	$1,943,133
CMPTRA	675,057
Muni. block grant	50,897
Energy tax receipts	1,147,179
Homeland security	70,000

Taxes
	2003	2004	2005
General tax rate per $100	3.87	4.160	4.290
Net valuation taxable	$661,375,728	$652,393,071	$656,457,956
State equalized value	$902,655,559	$978,402,433	$1,099,963,063
County equalization ratio	86.47	73.27	66.38

Demographics & Socio-Economic Characteristics
(2000 U.S. Census, except as noted)

Population

1980*	8,322
1990*	7,863
2000	7,913
Male	3,865
Female	4,048
2004 (estimate)*	8,008
Persons per sq. mi. of land	5,163

Race & Hispanic Origin, 2000
Race

White	7,456
Black/African American	68
Amer. Indian/Alaska Natv.	15
Asian	109
Natv. Hawaiian/Pac. Islander	2
Other Race	135
Two or more races	128
Hispanic origin, total	534
Mexican	28
Puerto Rican	236
Cuban	21
Other Hispanic	249

Age & Nativity, 2000

Under 5 years	474
18 years and over	5,990
21 years and over	5,741
65 years and over	1,073
85 years and over	124
Median Age	36.7
Native born	7,204
Foreign born	709

Educational Attainment, 2000

Population 25 years and over	5,393
0-8 yrs of school	5.4%
High School grad or higher	81.1%
Bachelor's degree or higher	12.5%
Graduate degree	3.2%

Income & Poverty, 1999

Per capita income	$23,598
Median household income	$50,529
Median family income	$62,029
Persons in poverty	582
H'holds receiving public assistance	86
H'holds receiving social security	1,058

Households, 2000

Total households	2,967
With persons under 18	1,045
With persons over 65	839
Family households	2,042
One-person households	768
Persons per household	2.65
Persons per family	3.22

Labor & Employment

Total civilian labor force, 2004**	4,544
Unemployment rate	2.3%
Total civilian labor force, 2000	3,893
Unemployment rate	4.2%

Employed persons 16 years and over by occupation, 2000

Managers & professionals	847
Service occupations	593
Sales & office occupations	1,258
Farming, fishing & forestry	0
Construction & maintenance	422
Production & transportation	610
Self-employed persons	108

*US Census Bureau
**New Jersey Department of Labor

General Information
City of South Amboy
140 N Broadway
South Amboy, NJ 08879
732-727-4600

Web site	NA
Land area (sq. miles)	1.55
Water area (sq. miles)	1.15
Type of government	City
Form of government	MC '50

Government

Legislative Districts

US Congressional	6
State Legislative	19

Local Officials, 2006

Mayor	John O'Leary Jr.
Admin/Manager	Camille Tooker
Clerk	Kathleen Vigilante
Finance Dir/Treas	Terance O'Neill
Engineer	James Cleary
Attorney	John Lanza
Tax assessor	Brian Enright
Tax collector	NA
Building officer	Thomas Kelly
Zoning officer	NA
Public Works	NA

Housing & Construction

Housing Units, 2000*

Total	3,110
Median rent	$767
Median SF home value	$138,500

New Privately Owned Housing Units
Authorized by Building Permit

	Units	Value
Total, 2004	1	$116,984
Single family	1	$116,984
Total, 2005	2	$233,968
Single family	2	$233,968

Real Property Valuation - parcels, 2005

	Number	Valuation
Total		$823,152,800
Vacant	121	39,006,700
Residential	2,504	666,408,100
Commercial	158	85,035,700
Industrial	12	26,889,500
Apartments	8	5,812,800
Farm land	0	0
Farm homestead	0	0

Average Property Value & Tax, 2005

Residential value	$266,137
Property tax	$4,167
FAIR rebate	$596

Public Library
Dowdell Public Library
100 Hoffman Plaza
South Amboy, NJ 08879
732-721-6060

Director .... Elaine Gaber

Library statistics, 2004

	Total	per capita
Volumes	51,802	6.55
Expenditure	$313,516	$39.62

Public Safety

Police

Chief	James Wallis
Number of officers, 2004	22

Crime, 2004	Number	Rate
Total	167	20.8
Violent	20	2.5
Non-violent	147	18.3
Domestic Viol.	64	NA

Emergency/Fire

Director .... Clarkson Jensen

Public School District
(for school year 2004-2005 except as noted)

South Amboy School District
240 John St
South Amboy, NJ 08879
732-525-2102

Superintendent	Robert Sheedy
Grade plan	K-12
Enrollment	1,139.5
Students per teacher	10.6
Per pupil expenditure	$11,125
Median faculty salary	$54,904
Median administrator salary	$98,604
Grade 12 enrollment	65.0
High school graduation rate	88.6%

Assessment test results
(percent scoring at proficient or advanced level)

	Language	Math
Grade 3	78.9%	77.7%
Grade 8	65.5%	52.9%
High school	89.9%	73.9%

SAT

Percent tested	54%
Average SAT math score	470
Average SAT verbal score	444

No Child Left Behind, 2003-04

Attendence rate (target = 90%)	95.1%
Drop rate	1.9%
Highly-qualified teachers	93.5%
District needs improvement?(AYP)	No

Municipal Finance

Fiscal Year 2005

Total tax levy	$12,904,389
County levy	2,152,611
County taxes	1,949,941
County library	0
County health	0
County open space	202,670
School levy	7,209,324
Local muni. budget	3,542,454
Misc. revenues	9,388,885
Total aid	$4,529,819
CMPTRA	411,094
Muni. block grant	34,354
Energy tax receipts	4,034,371
Homeland security	50,000

Fiscal Year 2006

Total aid	$4,529,819
CMPTRA	269,891
Muni. block grant	34,354
Energy tax receipts	4,175,574
Homeland security	50,000

Taxes

	2003	2004	2005
General tax rate per $100	5.34	6.400	1.570
Net valuation taxable	$190,543,200	$206,978,000	$824,098,308
State equalized value	$534,783,048	$648,833,391	$853,192,161
County equalization ratio	43.92	35.63	121.18

Demographics & Socio-Economic Characteristics
(2000 U.S. Census, except as noted)

Population
1980*	4,331
1990*	4,185
2000	4,492
Male	2,303
Female	2,189
2004 (estimate)*	4,507
Persons per sq. mi. of land	5,785

Race & Hispanic Origin, 2000
Race
White	3,504
Black/African American	349
Amer. Indian/Alaska Natv.	12
Asian	184
Natv. Hawaiian/Pac. Islander	2
Other Race	295
Two or more races	146
Hispanic origin, total	1,028
Mexican	276
Puerto Rican	173
Cuban	3
Other Hispanic	576

Age & Nativity, 2000
Under 5 years	285
18 years and over	3,437
21 years and over	3,274
65 years and over	472
85 years and over	64
Median Age	35.1
Native born	3,495
Foreign born	997

Educational Attainment, 2000
Population 25 years and over	3,061
0-8 yrs of school	7.2%
High School grad or higher	78.5%
Bachelor's degree or higher	17.8%
Graduate degree	6.6%

Income & Poverty, 1999
Per capita income	$21,131
Median household income	$48,984
Median family income	$58,214
Persons in poverty	299
H'holds receiving public assistance	56
H'holds receiving social security	438

Households, 2000
Total households	1,632
With persons under 18	575
With persons over 65	364
Family households	1,104
One-person households	409
Persons per household	2.75
Persons per family	3.31

Labor & Employment
Total civilian labor force, 2004**	2,971
Unemployment rate	6.5%
Total civilian labor force, 2000	2,426
Unemployment rate	5.3%

Employed persons 16 years and over by occupation, 2000
Managers & professionals	544
Service occupations	382
Sales & office occupations	688
Farming, fishing & forestry	17
Construction & maintenance	212
Production & transportation	454
Self-employed persons	49

*US Census Bureau
**New Jersey Department of Labor

General Information
Borough of South Bound Brook
12 Main St
South Bound Brook, NJ 08880
732-356-0258
Web site	www.southboundbrook.com
Land area (sq. miles)	0.78
Water area (sq. miles)	0
Type of government	Borough
Form of government	B

Government

Legislative Districts
US Congressional	7
State Legislative	16

Local Officials, 2006
Mayor	Tom Ormosi
Admin/Manager	Donald Kazar
Clerk	Donald Kazar
Finance Dir/Treas	Randy Bahr
Engineer	Thomas Herits
Attorney	William Cooper
Tax assessor	Barbara Flaherty
Tax collector	NA
Building officer	William Boyle
Zoning officer	William Boyle
Public Works	NA

Housing & Construction

Housing Units, 2000*
Total	1,676
Median rent	$818
Median SF home value	$132,800

New Privately Owned Housing Units Authorized by Building Permit
	Units	Value
Total, 2004	8	$570,050
Single family	2	$264,050
Total, 2005	121	$8,908,000
Single family	44	$4,530,400

Real Property Valuation - parcels, 2005
	Number	Valuation
Total		$164,104,845
Vacant	34	652,600
Residential	1,119	141,157,745
Commercial	40	11,709,100
Industrial	1	201,300
Apartments	10	10,384,100
Farm land	0	0
Farm homestead	0	0

Average Property Value & Tax, 2005
Residential value	$126,146
Property tax	$6,112
FAIR rebate	$575

Public Library
Contracts with Bound Brook Library

Library statistics, 2004
	Total	per capita
Volumes	NA	NA
Expenditure	NA	NA

Public Safety

Police
Chief	Robert Verry
Number of officers, 2004	12

Crime, 2004	Number	Rate
Total	15	3.3
Violent	5	1.1
Non-violent	10	2.2
Domestic Viol.	43	NA

Emergency/Fire
Director	Michael Tomaro

Public School District
(for school year 2004-2005 except as noted)

South Bound Brook Borough School Dist.
122 Elizabeth St
South Bound Brook, NJ 08880
732-356-0018
Superintendent	Carol Rosevear
Grade plan	K-12
Enrollment	497.0
Students per teacher	10.4
Per pupil expenditure	$11,356
Median faculty salary	$54,755
Median administrator salary	$96,330
Grade 12 enrollment	NA
High school graduation rate	NA

Assessment test results
(percent scoring at proficient or advanced level)
	Language	Math
Grade 3	66.0%	63.0%
Grade 8	73.2%	41.4%
High school	NA	NA

SAT
Percent tested	NA
Average SAT math score	NA
Average SAT verbal score	NA

No Child Left Behind, 2003-04
Attendence rate (target = 90%)	95.3%
Drop rate	NA
Highly-qualified teachers	100%
District needs improvement?(AYP)	No

Municipal Finance

Fiscal Year 2005
Total tax levy	$7,975,073
County levy	875,744
County taxes	798,921
County library	0
County health	0
County open space	76,823
School levy	4,664,283
Local muni. budget	2,435,046
Misc. revenues	2,879,803
Total aid	$637,252
CMPTRA	323,747
Muni. block grant	18,313
Energy tax receipts	270,192
Homeland security	25,000

Fiscal Year 2006
Total aid	$637,251
CMPTRA	314,290
Muni. block grant	18,313
Energy tax receipts	279,648
Homeland security	25,000

Taxes
	2003	2004	2005
General tax rate per $100	4.12	4.530	4.850
Net valuation taxable	$165,232,544	$164,627,051	$164,585,321
State equalized value	$232,166,003	$253,913,133	$294,586,220
County equalization ratio	80.92	71.17	64.76

Demographics & Socio-Economic Characteristics
(2000 U.S. Census, except as noted)

Population
1980*	17,127
1990*	25,792
2000	37,734
Male	18,281
Female	19,453
2004 (estimate)*	40,318
Persons per sq. mi. of land	987

Race & Hispanic Origin, 2000
Race
White	26,600
Black/African American	2,975
Amer. Indian/Alaska Natv.	48
Asian	6,808
Natv. Hawaiian/Pac. Islander	14
Other Race	518
Two or more races	771
Hispanic origin, total	1,918
Mexican	190
Puerto Rican	700
Cuban	141
Other Hispanic	887

Age & Nativity, 2000
Under 5 years	3,042
18 years and over	27,005
21 years and over	26,084
65 years and over	2,761
85 years and over	252
Median Age	35
Native born	29,578
Foreign born	8,156

Educational Attainment, 2000
Population 25 years and over	24,872
0-8 yrs of school	1.9%
High School grad or higher	93.3%
Bachelor's degree or higher	49.0%
Graduate degree	20.0%

Income & Poverty, 1999
Per capita income	$32,104
Median household income	$78,737
Median family income	$86,891
Persons in poverty	1,156
H'holds receiving public assistance	85
H'holds receiving social security	1,876

Households, 2000
Total households	13,428
With persons under 18	6,002
With persons over 65	2,031
Family households	10,083
One-person households	2,627
Persons per household	2.8
Persons per family	3.27

Labor & Employment
Total civilian labor force, 2004**	17,051
Unemployment rate	3.1%
Total civilian labor force, 2000	20,797
Unemployment rate	3.4%

Employed persons 16 years and over by occupation, 2000
Managers & professionals	10,822
Service occupations	1,608
Sales & office occupations	5,268
Farming, fishing & forestry	0
Construction & maintenance	1,090
Production & transportation	1,305
Self-employed persons	757

*US Census Bureau
**New Jersey Department of Labor

General Information
Township of South Brunswick
PO Box 190
540 Ridge Road
Monmouth Junction, NJ 08852
732-329-4000

Web site	www.sbtnj.net
Land area (sq. miles)	40.86
Water area (sq. miles)	0.24
Type of government	Township
Form of government	TC

Government

Legislative Districts
US Congressional	12
State Legislative	14

Local Officials, 2006
Mayor	Frank Gambatese
Admin/Manager	Matthew U. Watkins
Clerk	Barbara Nyitrai
Finance Dir/Treas	Joseph Monzo
Engineer	Jay Cornell
Attorney	Donald Sears
Tax assessor	Keith Fasanella
Tax collector	Wendy Bukowski
Building officer	Jim Dowgin (Actg)
Zoning officer	Joe Pawlak
Public Works	Raymond Olsen

Housing & Construction

Housing Units, 2000*
Total	13,862
Median rent	$969
Median SF home value	$202,000

New Privately Owned Housing Units
Authorized by Building Permit
	Units	Value
Total, 2004	129	$14,943,838
Single family	129	$14,943,838
Total, 2005	188	$20,513,376
Single family	188	$20,513,376

Real Property Valuation - parcels, 2005
	Number	Valuation
Total		$3,789,346,100
Vacant	926	114,339,000
Residential	11,527	2,195,018,100
Commercial	315	293,707,400
Industrial	181	1,055,921,700
Apartments	19	99,965,000
Farm land	100	24,453,800
Farm homestead	299	5,941,100

Average Property Value & Tax, 2005
Residential value	$186,112
Property tax	$6,240
FAIR rebate	$467

Public Library
S. Brunswick Pub Library
110 Kingston Lane
So Brunswick, NJ 08852
732-329-4000

Director	Lorraine Jackson

Library statistics, 2004
	Total	per capita
Volumes	147,731	3.92
Expenditure	$2,331,734	$61.79

Public Safety

Police
Chief	Raymong Hayducka
Number of officers, 2004	78

Crime, 2004	Number	Rate
Total	537	13.4
Violent	33	0.8
Non-violent	504	12.5
Domestic Viol.	142	NA

Emergency/Fire
Director	Robert Davidson

Public School District
(for school year 2004-2005 except as noted)

South Brunswick Township School District
4 Executive Dr
Monmouth Junction, NJ 08852
732-297-7800

Superintendent	Gary P. McCartney
Grade plan	K-12
Enrollment	8,564.0
Students per teacher	11.4
Per pupil expenditure	$11,645
Median faculty salary	$48,295
Median administrator salary	$88,000
Grade 12 enrollment	571.0
High school graduation rate	94.0%

Assessment test results
(percent scoring at proficient or advanced level)
	Language	Math
Grade 3	87.4%	90.7%
Grade 8	88.3%	75.0%
High school	92.6%	85.8%

SAT
Percent tested	83%
Average SAT math score	552
Average SAT verbal score	532

No Child Left Behind, 2003-04
Attendence rate (target = 90%)	95.3%
Drop rate	0.8%
Highly-qualified teachers	98%
District needs improvement?(AYP)	No

Municipal Finance

Fiscal Year 2005
Total tax levy	$127,417,687
County levy	18,225,625
County taxes	16,506,937
County library	0
County health	0
County open space	1,718,688
School levy	87,913,818
Local muni. budget	21,278,243
Misc. revenues	23,626,964
Total aid	$6,720,287
CMPTRA	975,139
Muni. block grant	147,956
Energy tax receipts	5,456,205
Homeland security	140,000

Fiscal Year 2006
Total aid	$6,720,288
CMPTRA	784,172
Muni. block grant	147,956
Energy tax receipts	5,647,173
Homeland security	140,000

Taxes
	2003	2004	2005
General tax rate per $100	2.96	3.140	3.360
Net valuation taxable	$3,844,330,441	$3,873,609,036	$3,800,163,189
State equalized value	$5,272,706,681	$5,944,509,388	$6,592,927,115
County equalization ratio	80.39	72.91	65.09

Demographics & Socio-Economic Characteristics
(2000 U.S. Census, except as noted)

Population
1980*	2,229
1990*	2,106
2000	2,249
Male	1,082
Female	1,167
2004 (estimate)*	2,325
Persons per sq. mi. of land	3,268

Race & Hispanic Origin, 2000
Race
White	1,865
Black/African American	49
Amer. Indian/Alaska Natv.	5
Asian	129
Natv. Hawaiian/Pac. Islander	7
Other Race	142
Two or more races	52
Hispanic origin, total	339
Mexican	13
Puerto Rican	53
Cuban	22
Other Hispanic	251

Age & Nativity, 2000
Under 5 years	128
18 years and over	1,807
21 years and over	1,730
65 years and over	372
85 years and over	32
Median Age	37.7
Native born	1,640
Foreign born	612

Educational Attainment, 2000
Population 25 years and over	1,664
0-8 yrs of school	9.9%
High School grad or higher	75.9%
Bachelor's degree or higher	13.7%
Graduate degree	4.4%

Income & Poverty, 1999
Per capita income	$27,128
Median household income	$57,917
Median family income	$66,071
Persons in poverty	159
H'holds receiving public assistance	3
H'holds receiving social security	276

Households, 2000
Total households	811
With persons under 18	258
With persons over 65	268
Family households	594
One-person households	187
Persons per household	2.77
Persons per family	3.27

Labor & Employment
Total civilian labor force, 2004**	1,235
Unemployment rate	5.9%
Total civilian labor force, 2000	1,178
Unemployment rate	4.9%

Employed persons 16 years and over by occupation, 2000
Managers & professionals	305
Service occupations	102
Sales & office occupations	421
Farming, fishing & forestry	0
Construction & maintenance	143
Production & transportation	149
Self-employed persons	51

*US Census Bureau
**New Jersey Department of Labor

General Information
Township of South Hackensack
227 Phillips Ave
South Hackensack, NJ 07606
201-440-1815

Web site	NA
Land area (sq. miles)	0.71
Water area (sq. miles)	0.02
Type of government	Township
Form of government	TC

Government

Legislative Districts
US Congressional	9
State Legislative	38

Local Officials, 2006
Mayor	Robyn Scholz
Admin/Manager	NA
Clerk	Linda LoPiccolo
Finance Dir/Treas	L. D'Ambrosio/R. Giotis
Engineer	Boswell McClave
Attorney	David Nasta
Tax assessor	George Reggo
Tax collector	Rosemarie Giotis
Building officer	James Riley
Zoning officer	Ray DeRiso
Public Works	Larry Paladino

Housing & Construction

Housing Units, 2000*
Total	830
Median rent	$984
Median SF home value	$183,600

New Privately Owned Housing Units Authorized by Building Permit
	Units	Value
Total, 2004	4	$230,000
Single family	0	$0
Total, 2005	2	$115,000
Single family	0	$0

Real Property Valuation - parcels, 2005
	Number	Valuation
Total		$384,517,100
Vacant	63	8,995,400
Residential	511	115,105,700
Commercial	55	45,104,600
Industrial	168	215,311,400
Apartments	0	0
Farm land	0	0
Farm homestead	0	0

Average Property Value & Tax, 2005
Residential value	$225,256
Property tax	$5,609
FAIR rebate	$769

Public Library

No public municipal library.

Library statistics, 2004
	Total	per capita
Volumes	NA	NA
Expenditure	NA	NA

Public Safety

Police
Chief	Mike Frew
Number of officers, 2004	19

Crime, 2004	Number	Rate
Total	79	34.3
Violent	14	6.1
Non-violent	65	28.2
Domestic Viol.	12	NA

Emergency/Fire
Director	James Riley

Public School District
(for school year 2004-2005 except as noted)

South Hackensack School District
Dyer Ave
South Hackensack, NJ 07606
201-440-2783

Superintendent	William DeFabiis
Grade plan	K-12
Enrollment	245.0
Students per teacher	10.8
Per pupil expenditure	$14,059
Median faculty salary	$47,200
Median administrator salary	$126,396
Grade 12 enrollment	NA
High school graduation rate	NA

Assessment test results
(percent scoring at proficient or advanced level)
	Language	Math
Grade 3	83.3%	83.3%
Grade 8	72.2%	57.9%
High school	NA	NA

SAT
Percent tested	NA
Average SAT math score	NA
Average SAT verbal score	NA

No Child Left Behind, 2003-04
Attendence rate (target = 90%)	95.8%
Drop rate	NA
Highly-qualified teachers	93.2%
District needs improvement?(AYP)	No

Municipal Finance

Fiscal Year 2005
Total tax levy	$10,011,623
County levy	934,619
County taxes	887,679
County library	0
County health	0
County open space	46,940
School levy	4,167,345
Local muni. budget	4,909,659
Misc. revenues	1,901,856
Total aid	$707,184
CMPTRA	325,400
Muni. block grant	9,215
Energy tax receipts	347,569
Homeland security	25,000

Fiscal Year 2006
Total aid	$707,184
CMPTRA	313,236
Muni. block grant	9,215
Energy tax receipts	359,733
Homeland security	25,000

Taxes
	2003	2004	2005
General tax rate per $100	2.33	2.490	2.610
Net valuation taxable	$385,191,611	$384,400,329	$384,936,698
State equalized value	$452,740,492	$454,938,729	$501,807,715
County equalization ratio	98.19	65.08	84.48

Demographics & Socio-Economic Characteristics
(2000 U.S. Census, except as noted)

Population
1980*	1,486
1990*	1,919
2000	2,417
Male	1,223
Female	1,194
2004 (estimate)*	2,845
Persons per sq. mi. of land	180

Race & Hispanic Origin, 2000
Race
White	2,250
Black/African American	91
Amer. Indian/Alaska Natv.	1
Asian	7
Natv. Hawaiian/Pac. Islander	1
Other Race	53
Two or more races	14
Hispanic origin, total	83
Mexican	42
Puerto Rican	29
Cuban	2
Other Hispanic	10

Age & Nativity, 2000
Under 5 years	155
18 years and over	1,767
21 years and over	1,684
65 years and over	226
85 years and over	20
Median Age	38.4
Native born	2,307
Foreign born	110

Educational Attainment, 2000
Population 25 years and over	1,604
0-8 yrs of school	4.4%
High School grad or higher	86.3%
Bachelor's degree or higher	27.2%
Graduate degree	9.5%

Income & Poverty, 1999
Per capita income	$25,968
Median household income	$68,491
Median family income	$76,390
Persons in poverty	193
H'holds receiving public assistance	11
H'holds receiving social security	202

Households, 2000
Total households	800
With persons under 18	350
With persons over 65	166
Family households	663
One-person households	107
Persons per household	2.94
Persons per family	3.25

Labor & Employment
Total civilian labor force, 2004**	1,211
Unemployment rate	2.8%
Total civilian labor force, 2000	1,246
Unemployment rate	4.3%

Employed persons 16 years and over by occupation, 2000
Managers & professionals	477
Service occupations	97
Sales & office occupations	298
Farming, fishing & forestry	11
Construction & maintenance	171
Production & transportation	139
Self-employed persons	100

*US Census Bureau
**New Jersey Department of Labor

General Information
Township of South Harrison
PO Box 113
664 Harrisonville Rd
Harrisonville, NJ 08039
856-769-3737
Web site	www.southharrison-nj.org
Land area (sq. miles)	15.80
Water area (sq. miles)	0.02
Type of government	Township
Form of government	TC

Government

Legislative Districts
US Congressional	2
State Legislative	3

Local Officials, 2006
Mayor	James McCall
Admin/Manager	NA
Clerk	Nancy Kearns
Finance Dir/Treas	Thomas Sager
Engineer	Chris Perks
Attorney	William Horner
Tax assessor	Thomas Colavecchio
Tax collector	Maria Berkett
Building officer	Jeff Kier
Zoning officer	Joseph Wille
Public Works	NA

Housing & Construction

Housing Units, 2000*
Total	829
Median rent	$656
Median SF home value	$188,900

New Privately Owned Housing Units
Authorized by Building Permit
	Units	Value
Total, 2004	19	$1,859,600
Single family	19	$1,859,600
Total, 2005	30	$4,269,817
Single family	30	$4,269,817

Real Property Valuation - parcels, 2005
	Number	Valuation
Total		$188,618,600
Vacant	181	7,180,300
Residential	761	146,242,900
Commercial	15	5,334,400
Industrial	0	0
Apartments	0	0
Farm land	139	27,009,200
Farm homestead	221	2,851,800

Average Property Value & Tax, 2005
Residential value	$151,828
Property tax	$4,855
FAIR rebate	$523

Public Library

No public municipal library.

Library statistics, 2004
	Total	per capita
Volumes	NA	NA
Expenditure	NA	NA

Public Safety

Police
Chief	Warren Mabey
Number of officers, 2004	4

Crime, 2004	Number	Rate
Total	24	8.8
Violent	2	0.7
Non-violent	22	8.1
Domestic Viol.	9	NA

Emergency/Fire
Director	Phil Clifford

Public School District
(for school year 2004-2005 except as noted)

South Harrison Township School District
904 Mullica Hill Rd
Harrisonville, NJ 08039
856-769-0855
Administrator	David Datz
Grade plan	K-6
Enrollment	275.0
Students per teacher	12.2
Per pupil expenditure	$11,986
Median faculty salary	$41,193
Median administrator salary	$68,030
Grade 12 enrollment	NA
High school graduation rate	NA

Assessment test results
(percent scoring at proficient or advanced level)
	Language	Math
Grade 3	92.9%	95.3%
Grade 8	NA	NA
High school	NA	NA

SAT
Percent tested	NA
Average SAT math score	NA
Average SAT verbal score	NA

No Child Left Behind, 2003-04
Attendence rate (target = 90%)	96.0%
Drop rate	NA
Highly-qualified teachers	100%
District needs improvement?(AYP)	No

Municipal Finance

Fiscal Year 2005
Total tax levy	$6,049,504
County levy	1,752,774
County taxes	1,536,992
County library	113,589
County health	0
County open space	102,193
School levy	4,111,780
Local muni. budget	184,951
Misc. revenues	1,607,979
Total aid	$206,268
CMPTRA	100,650
Muni. block grant	9,477
Energy tax receipts	96,141
Homeland security	0

Fiscal Year 2006
Total aid	$206,268
CMPTRA	97,285
Muni. block grant	9,477
Energy tax receipts	99,506
Homeland security	NA

Taxes
	2003	2004	2005
General tax rate per $100	3.08	3.122	3.198
Net valuation taxable	$167,007,997	$178,384,197	$189,189,543
State equalized value	$208,109,654	$239,237,739	$270,928,746
County equalization ratio	85.54	80.25	74.50

Demographics & Socio-Economic Characteristics
(2000 U.S. Census, except as noted)

Population
1980*	15,864
1990*	16,390
2000	16,964
Male	8,142
Female	8,822
2004 (estimate)*	16,788
Persons per sq. mi. of land	5,884

Race & Hispanic Origin, 2000
Race
White	10,248
Black/African American	5,309
Amer. Indian/Alaska Natv.	16
Asian	660
Natv. Hawaiian/Pac. Islander	5
Other Race	266
Two or more races	460
Hispanic origin, total	837
Mexican	92
Puerto Rican	266
Cuban	60
Other Hispanic	419

Age & Nativity, 2000
Under 5 years	988
18 years and over	13,187
21 years and over	11,413
65 years and over	2,024
85 years and over	289
Median Age	34.7
Native born	14,095
Foreign born	2,869

Educational Attainment, 2000
Population 25 years and over	10,351
0-8 yrs of school	2.4%
High School grad or higher	93.4%
Bachelor's degree or higher	57.4%
Graduate degree	29.2%

Income & Poverty, 1999
Per capita income	$41,035
Median household income	$83,611
Median family income	$107,641
Persons in poverty	791
H'holds receiving public assistance	89
H'holds receiving social security	1,474

Households, 2000
Total households	5,522
With persons under 18	2,010
With persons over 65	1,464
Family households	3,768
One-person households	1,393
Persons per household	2.69
Persons per family	3.26

Labor & Employment
Total civilian labor force, 2004**	8,615
Unemployment rate	2.4%
Total civilian labor force, 2000	9,422
Unemployment rate	4.2%

Employed persons 16 years and over by occupation, 2000
Managers & professionals	4,791
Service occupations	1,135
Sales & office occupations	2,411
Farming, fishing & forestry	0
Construction & maintenance	231
Production & transportation	462
Self-employed persons	704

*US Census Bureau
**New Jersey Department of Labor

General Information
Township of South Orange Village
Village Hall
101 S Orange Ave
South Orange Village, NJ 07079
973-378-7715

Web site	www.sourthorange.org
Land area (sq. miles)	2.85
Water area (sq. miles)	0
Type of government	Township
Form of government	SC

Government

Legislative Districts
US Congressional	10
State Legislative	27

Local Officials, 2006
Mayor	William Calabrese
Admin/Manager	John Gross
Clerk	Marjorie Smith
Finance Dir/Treas	John Gross
Engineer	Salvatore Renda
Attorney	Edwin Matthews
Tax assessor	Ellen Foye Malgieri
Tax collector	Aderonke Zaccheus
Building officer	Anthony Grenci
Zoning officer	Salvatore Renda
Public Works	Mario Luciani

Housing & Construction

Housing Units, 2000*
Total	5,671
Median rent	$879
Median SF home value	$274,600

New Privately Owned Housing Units Authorized by Building Permit
	Units	Value
Total, 2004	16	$3,759,450
Single family	16	$3,759,450
Total, 2005	3	$5,136,401
Single family	0	$4,786,401

Real Property Valuation - parcels, 2005
	Number	Valuation
Total		$1,001,243,500
Vacant	99	6,027,000
Residential	4,287	892,786,700
Commercial	179	71,098,300
Industrial	6	1,383,600
Apartments	26	29,947,900
Farm land	0	0
Farm homestead	0	0

Average Property Value & Tax, 2005
Residential value	$208,254
Property tax	$12,120
FAIR rebate	$554

Public Library
South Orange Public Library
65 Scotland Rd
South Orange, NJ 07079
973-762-0230
Director . . . . Melissa Kopecky

Library statistics, 2004
	Total	per capita
Volumes	95,946	5.66
Expenditure	$1,000,731	$58.99

Public Safety

Police
Chief	James Chelel
Number of officers, 2004	54

Crime, 2004	Number	Rate
Total	580	34.3
Violent	69	4.1
Non-violent	511	30.2
Domestic Viol.	43	NA

Emergency/Fire
Director . . . . .Jeff Markey

Public School District
(for school year 2004-2005 except as noted)

South Orange-Maplewood School District
525 Academy St
Maplewood, NJ 07040
973-378-9630
Superintendent	Peter Horoschak
Grade plan	K-12
Enrollment	6,295.0
Students per teacher	11.6
Per pupil expenditure	$12,484
Median faculty salary	$59,615
Median administrator salary	$114,559
Grade 12 enrollment	462.0
High school graduation rate	95.7%

Assessment test results
(percent scoring at proficient or advanced level)
	Language	Math
Grade 3	84.1%	83.0%
Grade 8	76.3%	71.7%
High school	89.5%	83.8%

SAT
Percent tested	89%
Average SAT math score	528
Average SAT verbal score	511

No Child Left Behind, 2003-04
Attendence rate (target = 90%)	96.0%
Drop rate	1.7%
Highly-qualified teachers	82.2%
District needs improvement?(AYP)	No

Municipal Finance

Fiscal Year 2005
Total tax levy	$58,447,107
County levy	9,785,875
County taxes	9,580,989
County library	0
County health	0
County open space	204,885
School levy	32,596,156
Local muni. budget	16,065,076
Misc. revenues	12,367,522
Total aid	$2,079,915
CMPTRA	635,623
Muni. block grant	71,717
Energy tax receipts	1,302,575
Homeland security	70,000

Fiscal Year 2006
Total aid	$2,079,915
CMPTRA	590,033
Muni. block grant	71,717
Energy tax receipts	1,348,165
Homeland security	70,000

Taxes
	2003	2004	2005
General tax rate per $100	5.28	5.560	5.820
Net valuation taxable	$998,898,325	$999,301,923	$1,004,248,560
State equalized value	$1,801,114,903	$2,028,027,585	$2,339,814,911
County equalization ratio	62.94	62.94	49.19

Demographics & Socio-Economic Characteristics

(2000 U.S. Census, except as noted)

Population

1980*	20,521
1990*	20,489
2000	21,810
Male	10,690
Female	11,120
2004 (estimate)*	23,034
Persons per sq. mi. of land	2,756

Race & Hispanic Origin, 2000

Race

White	16,956
Black/African American	1,866
Amer. Indian/Alaska Natv.	49
Asian	1,652
Natv. Hawaiian/Pac. Islander	1
Other Race	759
Two or more races	527
Hispanic origin, total	1,888
Mexican	131
Puerto Rican	517
Cuban	99
Other Hispanic	1,141

Age & Nativity, 2000

Under 5 years	1,344
18 years and over	16,325
21 years and over	15,649
65 years and over	3,071
85 years and over	281
Median Age	38
Native born	18,589
Foreign born	3,221

Educational Attainment, 2000

Population 25 years and over	14,940
0-8 yrs of school	5.4%
High School grad or higher	84.3%
Bachelor's degree or higher	24.0%
Graduate degree	6.7%

Income & Poverty, 1999

Per capita income	$25,270
Median household income	$67,466
Median family income	$72,745
Persons in poverty	727
H'holds receiving public assistance	105
H'holds receiving social security	2,030

Households, 2000

Total households	7,151
With persons under 18	2,948
With persons over 65	2,049
Family households	5,858
One-person households	1,094
Persons per household	3.01
Persons per family	3.35

Labor & Employment

Total civilian labor force, 2004**	12,680
Unemployment rate	4.0%
Total civilian labor force, 2000	11,348
Unemployment rate	3.1%

Employed persons 16 years and over by occupation, 2000

Managers & professionals	4,126
Service occupations	1,178
Sales & office occupations	3,065
Farming, fishing & forestry	5
Construction & maintenance	946
Production & transportation	1,671
Self-employed persons	465

*US Census Bureau
**New Jersey Department of Labor

General Information

Borough of South Plainfield
2480 Plainfield Ave
South Plainfield, NJ 07080
908-754-9000

Web site	www.southplainfieldnj.com
Land area (sq. miles)	8.36
Water area (sq. miles)	0.04
Type of government	Borough
Form of government	B

Government

Legislative Districts

US Congressional	7
State Legislative	18

Local Officials, 2006

Mayor	Daniel Gallagher
Admin/Manager	Vincent Buttiglieri
Clerk	Vincent Buttiglieri
Finance Dir/Treas	Glenn Cullen
Engineer	David Samuels
Attorney	Patrick Diegnan
Tax assessor	Gary Toth
Tax collector	Richard Lorentzen
Building officer	John Pabst
Zoning officer	John Pabst
Public Works	Joseph Glowacki

Housing & Construction

Housing Units, 2000*

Total	7,307
Median rent	$976
Median SF home value	$165,800

New Privately Owned Housing Units
Authorized by Building Permit

	Units	Value
Total, 2004	39	$4,680,360
Single family	29	$4,634,526
Total, 2005	23	$3,866,322
Single family	23	$3,866,322

Real Property Valuation - parcels, 2005

	Number	Valuation
Total		$1,405,582,000
Vacant	415	23,444,600
Residential	7,116	841,669,400
Commercial	220	158,534,800
Industrial	316	361,450,700
Apartments	2	20,400,000
Farm land	0	0
Farm homestead	13	82,500

Average Property Value & Tax, 2005

Residential value	$118,074
Property tax	$4,779
FAIR rebate	$572

Public Library

South Plainfield Public Library
2484 Plainfield Ave
South Plainfield, NJ 07080
908-754-7885

Director................ Sunnie Randolph

Library statistics, 2004

	Total	per capita
Volumes	52,271	2.40
Expenditure	$750,451	$34.41

Public Safety

Police

Chief	John Ferraro
Number of officers, 2004	54

Crime, 2004	Number	Rate
Total	472	20.6
Violent	48	2.1
Non-violent	424	18.5
Domestic Viol.	140	NA

Emergency/Fire

Director............. Lawrence DelNegro

Public School District

(for school year 2004-2005 except as noted)

South Plainfield School District
125 Jackson Ave
South Plainfield, NJ 07080
908-754-4620

Superintendent	Robert Rosado
Grade plan	K-12
Enrollment	3,857.0
Students per teacher	11.0
Per pupil expenditure	$10,950
Median faculty salary	$57,751
Median administrator salary	$99,831
Grade 12 enrollment	309.0
High school graduation rate	97.0%

Assessment test results

(percent scoring at proficient or advanced level)

	Language	Math
Grade 3	90.2%	86.2%
Grade 8	78.6%	70.2%
High school	88.6%	77.0%

SAT

Percent tested	75%
Average SAT math score	510
Average SAT verbal score	496

No Child Left Behind, 2003-04

Attendence rate (target = 90%)	95.4%
Drop rate	0.6%
Highly-qualified teachers	99.7%
District needs improvement?(AYP)	No

Municipal Finance

Fiscal Year 2005

Total tax levy	$57,033,414
County levy	9,143,809
County taxes	8,282,874
County library	0
County health	0
County open space	860,935
School levy	35,088,696
Local muni. budget	12,800,910
Misc. revenues	10,031,393
Total aid	$3,707,431
CMPTRA	1,534,959
Muni. block grant	89,653
Energy tax receipts	1,992,819
Homeland security	90,000

Fiscal Year 2006

Total aid	$3,707,431
CMPTRA	1,465,210
Muni. block grant	89,653
Energy tax receipts	2,062,568
Homeland security	90,000

Taxes

	2003	2004	2005
General tax rate per $100	3.69	3.780	4.050
Net valuation taxable	$1,416,306,929	$1,426,370,782	$1,409,031,502
State equalized value	$2,533,190,715	$2,909,194,119	$3,158,555,261
County equalization ratio	60.78	55.91	48.96

Demographics & Socio-Economic Characteristics
(2000 U.S. Census, except as noted)

Population
1980*	14,361
1990*	13,692
2000	15,322
Male	7,574
Female	7,748
2004 (estimate)*	16,025
Persons per sq. mi. of land	5,694

Race & Hispanic Origin, 2000
Race
White	12,801
Black/African American	929
Amer. Indian/Alaska Natv.	18
Asian	542
Natv. Hawaiian/Pac. Islander	8
Other Race	587
Two or more races	437
Hispanic origin, total	1,480
Mexican	248
Puerto Rican	435
Cuban	53
Other Hispanic	744

Age & Nativity, 2000
Under 5 years	1,008
18 years and over	11,793
21 years and over	11,266
65 years and over	2,231
85 years and over	260
Median Age	36.4
Native born	11,290
Foreign born	4,032

Educational Attainment, 2000
Population 25 years and over	10,547
0-8 yrs of school	11.6%
High School grad or higher	76.5%
Bachelor's degree or higher	20.9%
Graduate degree	6.4%

Income & Poverty, 1999
Per capita income	$23,684
Median household income	$52,324
Median family income	$62,869
Persons in poverty	744
H'holds receiving public assistance	80
H'holds receiving social security	1,615

Households, 2000
Total households	5,606
With persons under 18	1,976
With persons over 65	1,624
Family households	3,985
One-person households	1,306
Persons per household	2.72
Persons per family	3.23

Labor & Employment
Total civilian labor force, 2004**	7,946
Unemployment rate	5.1%
Total civilian labor force, 2000	7,920
Unemployment rate	6.1%

Employed persons 16 years and over by occupation, 2000
Managers & professionals	2,037
Service occupations	889
Sales & office occupations	2,141
Farming, fishing & forestry	0
Construction & maintenance	1,223
Production & transportation	1,148
Self-employed persons	341

*US Census Bureau
**New Jersey Department of Labor

General Information
Borough of South River
48 Washington St
South River, NJ 08882
732-257-1999

Web site	www.southrivernj.org
Land area (sq. miles)	2.81
Water area (sq. miles)	0.13
Type of government	Borough
Form of government	B

Government

Legislative Districts
US Congressional	6
State Legislative	18

Local Officials, 2006
Mayor	Robert Szegeti
Admin/Manager	Joseph D. Kunz
Clerk	Albert Seaman
Finance Dir/Treas	Kanthiah Sivananthan
Engineer	David Samuel
Attorney	Frederick Roselli
Tax assessor	Michael Frangella
Tax collector	NA
Building officer	David Wroblewski
Zoning officer	David Wroblewski
Public Works	NA

Housing & Construction

Housing Units, 2000*
Total	5,769
Median rent	$745
Median SF home value	$149,600

New Privately Owned Housing Units
Authorized by Building Permit
	Units	Value
Total, 2004	NA	NA
Single family	NA	NA
Total, 2005	44	$3,393,378
Single family	8	$861,376

Real Property Valuation - parcels, 2005
	Number	Valuation
Total		$426,946,300
Vacant	272	3,545,100
Residential	4,406	365,193,100
Commercial	198	26,019,400
Industrial	28	22,637,500
Apartments	14	9,551,200
Farm land	0	0
Farm homestead	0	0

Average Property Value & Tax, 2005
Residential value	$82,885
Property tax	$4,279
FAIR rebate	$622

Public Library
South River Public Library
55 Appleby Ave
South River, NJ 08882
732-254-2488
Director .... Andrea Londensky

Library statistics, 2004
	Total	per capita
Volumes	47,884	3.13
Expenditure	$410,065	$26.76

Public Safety

Police
Chief	Wesley Bomba
Number of officers, 2004	30

Crime, 2004	Number	Rate
Total	272	17
Violent	26	1.6
Non-violent	246	15.3
Domestic Viol.	202	NA

Emergency/Fire
Director .... Gerald Murphy

Public School District
(for school year 2004-2005 except as noted)

South River School District
15 Montgomery St
South River, NJ 08882
732-613-4000

Superintendent	Ronald Grygo
Grade plan	K-12
Enrollment	2,167.5
Students per teacher	12.7
Per pupil expenditure	$8,947
Median faculty salary	$40,870
Median administrator salary	$80,880
Grade 12 enrollment	149.0
High school graduation rate	92.9%

Assessment test results
(percent scoring at proficient or advanced level)
	Language	Math
Grade 3	67.7%	64.9%
Grade 8	66.2%	56.1%
High school	84.7%	81.6%

SAT
Percent tested	62%
Average SAT math score	475
Average SAT verbal score	466

No Child Left Behind, 2003-04
Attendence rate (target = 90%)	93.7%
Drop rate	1.3%
Highly-qualified teachers	98.5%
District needs improvement?(AYP)	No

Municipal Finance

Fiscal Year 2005
Total tax levy	$22,061,149
County levy	3,850,523
County taxes	3,488,031
County library	0
County health	0
County open space	362,492
School levy	11,906,170
Local muni. budget	6,304,457
Misc. revenues	6,670,028
Total aid	$1,209,136
CMPTRA	708,521
Muni. block grant	60,078
Energy tax receipts	370,537
Homeland security	70,000

Fiscal Year 2006
Total aid	$1,209,136
CMPTRA	695,552
Muni. block grant	60,078
Energy tax receipts	383,506
Homeland security	70,000

Taxes
	2003	2004	2005
General tax rate per $100	4.45	4.660	5.170
Net valuation taxable	$423,818,033	$425,827,666	$427,361,228
State equalized value	$1,059,810,035	$1,208,401,437	$1,383,493,778
County equalization ratio	45.95	39.99	35.21

Demographics & Socio-Economic Characteristics
(2000 U.S. Census, except as noted)

Population
1980*	3,954
1990*	3,869
2000	3,634
Male	1,752
Female	1,882
2004 (estimate)*	3,699
Persons per sq. mi. of land	3,188

Race & Hispanic Origin, 2000
Race
White	2,637
Black/African American	769
Amer. Indian/Alaska Natv.	5
Asian	25
Natv. Hawaiian/Pac. Islander	0
Other Race	91
Two or more races	107
Hispanic origin, total	337
Mexican	39
Puerto Rican	238
Cuban	5
Other Hispanic	55

Age & Nativity, 2000
Under 5 years	253
18 years and over	2,467
21 years and over	2,306
65 years and over	328
85 years and over	22
Median Age	31.9
Native born	3,513
Foreign born	95

Educational Attainment, 2000
Population 25 years and over	2,201
0-8 yrs of school	5.9%
High School grad or higher	74.0%
Bachelor's degree or higher	5.6%
Graduate degree	1.4%

Income & Poverty, 1999
Per capita income	$16,292
Median household income	$43,468
Median family income	$45,375
Persons in poverty	452
H'holds receiving public assistance	18
H'holds receiving social security	294

Households, 2000
Total households	1,073
With persons under 18	545
With persons over 65	252
Family households	902
One-person households	134
Persons per household	3.39
Persons per family	3.63

Labor & Employment
Total civilian labor force, 2004**	2,355
Unemployment rate	6.6%
Total civilian labor force, 2000	1,773
Unemployment rate	8.0%

Employed persons 16 years and over by occupation, 2000
Managers & professionals	274
Service occupations	365
Sales & office occupations	511
Farming, fishing & forestry	9
Construction & maintenance	236
Production & transportation	237
Self-employed persons	54

*US Census Bureau
**New Jersey Department of Labor

General Information
Borough of South Toms River
144 Mill St
South Toms River, NJ 08757
732-349-0403

Web site	NA
Land area (sq. miles)	1.16
Water area (sq. miles)	0.06
Type of government	Borough
Form of government	B

Government

Legislative Districts
US Congressional	3
State Legislative	10

Local Officials, 2006
Mayor	George Greitz Jr.
Admin/Manager	NA
Clerk	Elizabeth Silvestri
Finance Dir/Treas	Steve Gallagher
Engineer	Michael O'Donnell
Attorney	Gregory McGuckin
Tax assessor	Dennis Raftery
Tax collector	NA
Building officer	County Insp
Zoning officer	Jim Richardson
Public Works	NA

Housing & Construction

Housing Units, 2000*
Total	1,123
Median rent	$756
Median SF home value	$85,600

New Privately Owned Housing Units
Authorized by Building Permit

	Units	Value
Total, 2004	6	$499,211
Single family	6	$499,211
Total, 2005	9	$784,387
Single family	9	$784,387

Real Property Valuation - parcels, 2005
	Number	Valuation
Total		$94,947,600
Vacant	86	2,526,800
Residential	1,078	78,961,400
Commercial	49	13,381,400
Industrial	1	78,000
Apartments	0	0
Farm land	0	0
Farm homestead	0	0

Average Property Value & Tax, 2005
Residential value	$73,248
Property tax	$2,768
FAIR rebate	$799

Public Library

No public municipal library.

Library statistics, 2004
	Total	per capita
Volumes	NA	NA
Expenditure	NA	NA

Public Safety

Police
Chief	Andrew Izatt
Number of officers, 2004	12

Crime, 2004	Number	Rate
Total	105	28.4
Violent	14	3.8
Non-violent	91	24.6
Domestic Viol.	80	NA

Emergency/Fire
Director	NA

Public School District
(for school year 2004-2005 except as noted)

Toms River Regional School District
1144 Hooper Ave
Toms River, NJ 08753
732-505-5510

Superintendent	Michael J. Ritacco
Grade plan	K-12
Enrollment	17,948.0
Students per teacher	13.9
Per pupil expenditure	$9,788
Median faculty salary	$45,761
Median administrator salary	$106,500
Grade 12 enrollment	1,195.0
High school graduation rate	NA

Assessment test results
(percent scoring at proficient or advanced level)
	Language	Math
Grade 3	90.9%	89.2%
Grade 8	78.5%	69.8%
High school	89.1%	77.7%

SAT
Percent tested	NA
Average SAT math score	NA
Average SAT verbal score	NA

No Child Left Behind, 2003-04
Attendance rate (target = 90%)	93.5%
Drop rate	1.9%
Highly-qualified teachers	98%
District needs improvement?(AYP)	No

Municipal Finance

Fiscal Year 2005
Total tax levy	$3,597,799
County levy	662,624
County taxes	558,279
County library	58,652
County health	24,860
County open space	20,833
School levy	1,357,926
Local muni. budget	1,577,249
Misc. revenues	1,117,298
Total aid	$485,884
CMPTRA	237,880
Muni. block grant	16,930
Energy tax receipts	206,074
Homeland security	25,000

Fiscal Year 2006
Total aid	$485,885
CMPTRA	230,668
Muni. block grant	16,930
Energy tax receipts	213,287
Homeland security	25,000

Taxes
	2003	2004	2005
General tax rate per $100	3.26	3.595	3.779
Net valuation taxable	$94,511,376	$94,760,326	$95,207,256
State equalized value	$140,141,423	$171,776,481	$213,086,965
County equalization ratio	77.12	67.44	55.07

Demographics & Socio-Economic Characteristics
(2000 U.S. Census, except as noted)

Population
1980*	8,008
1990*	10,202
2000	10,388
Male	4,856
Female	5,532
2004 (estimate)*	10,952
Persons per sq. mi. of land	249

Race & Hispanic Origin, 2000
Race
White	10,086
Black/African American	125
Amer. Indian/Alaska Natv.	29
Asian	65
Natv. Hawaiian/Pac. Islander	0
Other Race	31
Two or more races	52
Hispanic origin, total	134
Mexican	34
Puerto Rican	63
Cuban	5
Other Hispanic	32

Age & Nativity, 2000
Under 5 years	411
18 years and over	8,534
21 years and over	8,285
65 years and over	3,295
85 years and over	426
Median Age	49.7
Native born	9,977
Foreign born	356

Educational Attainment, 2000
Population 25 years and over	7,951
0-8 yrs of school	3.9%
High School grad or higher	83.7%
Bachelor's degree or higher	18.0%
Graduate degree	6.1%

Income & Poverty, 1999
Per capita income	$26,977
Median household income	$44,419
Median family income	$57,419
Persons in poverty	399
H'holds receiving public assistance	51
H'holds receiving social security	2,303

Households, 2000
Total households	4,574
With persons under 18	1,001
With persons over 65	2,284
Family households	3,047
One-person households	1,369
Persons per household	2.26
Persons per family	2.79

Labor & Employment
Total civilian labor force, 2004**	4,639
Unemployment rate	4.5%
Total civilian labor force, 2000	4,546
Unemployment rate	4.9%

Employed persons 16 years and over by occupation, 2000
Managers & professionals	1,382
Service occupations	616
Sales & office occupations	1,187
Farming, fishing & forestry	14
Construction & maintenance	494
Production & transportation	628
Self-employed persons	324

*US Census Bureau
**New Jersey Department of Labor

General Information
Township of Southampton
5 Retreat Rd
Southampton, NJ 08088
609-859-2736
Web site	www.southamptonnj.org
Land area (sq. miles)	44.03
Water area (sq. miles)	0.24
Type of government	Township
Form of government	TC

Government

Legislative Districts
US Congressional	3
State Legislative	8

Local Officials, 2006
Mayor	James Young
Admin/Manager	John Lipsett
Clerk	John Lipsett
Finance Dir/Treas	Nancy Gower
Engineer	Richard Alaimo Associat
Attorney	Brian Guest
Tax assessor	Dennis DeKlerk
Tax collector	NA
Building officer	Daniel McGonigle
Zoning officer	NA
Public Works	Charles Oatman

Housing & Construction

Housing Units, 2000*
Total	4,751
Median rent	$724
Median SF home value	$113,200

New Privately Owned Housing Units Authorized by Building Permit
	Units	Value
Total, 2004	18	$4,348,801
Single family	18	$4,348,801
Total, 2005	80	$15,791,016
Single family	80	$15,791,016

Real Property Valuation - parcels, 2005
	Number	Valuation
Total		$717,365,300
Vacant	560	20,135,300
Residential	4,315	600,156,700
Commercial	142	45,829,500
Industrial	23	7,205,800
Apartments	0	0
Farm land	190	37,806,300
Farm homestead	366	6,231,700

Average Property Value & Tax, 2005
Residential value	$129,542
Property tax	$3,893
FAIR rebate	$821

Public Library
Keen Memorial Library
94 Main St
Vincentown, NJ 08088
609-859-3598
Director	Lynn French

Library statistics, 2004
	Total	per capita
Volumes	20,326	1.96
Expenditure	$77,275	$7.44

Public Safety

Police
Chief	NA
Number of officers, 2004	0

Crime, 2004	Number	Rate
Total	120	11
Violent	12	1.1
Non-violent	108	9.9
Domestic Viol.	30	NA

Emergency/Fire
Director	NA

Public School District
(for school year 2004-2005 except as noted)

Southampton Township School District
177 Main St
Southampton, NJ 08088
609-859-2256
Superintendent	Michael Harris
Grade plan	K-8
Enrollment	829.0
Students per teacher	10.4
Per pupil expenditure	$12,428
Median faculty salary	$64,750
Median administrator salary	$99,500
Grade 12 enrollment	NA
High school graduation rate	NA

Assessment test results
(percent scoring at proficient or advanced level)
	Language	Math
Grade 3	93.8%	92.6%
Grade 8	91.2%	75.7%
High school	NA	NA

SAT
Percent tested	NA
Average SAT math score	NA
Average SAT verbal score	NA

No Child Left Behind, 2003-04
Attendence rate (target = 90%)	92.5%
Drop rate	NA
Highly-qualified teachers	96%
District needs improvement?(AYP)	No

Municipal Finance

Fiscal Year 2005
Total tax levy	$21,638,226
County levy	4,317,477
County taxes	3,621,895
County library	317,135
County health	0
County open space	378,447
School levy	15,374,354
Local muni. budget	1,946,395
Misc. revenues	3,381,012
Total aid	$1,658,330
CMPTRA	351,041
Muni. block grant	44,641
Energy tax receipts	1,149,247
Homeland security	0

Fiscal Year 2006
Total aid	$1,658,331
CMPTRA	310,818
Muni. block grant	44,641
Energy tax receipts	1,189,471
Homeland security	NA

Taxes
	2003	2004	2005
General tax rate per $100	2.57	2.780	3.005
Net valuation taxable	$702,809,609	$709,912,815	$720,109,519
State equalized value	$807,363,135	$931,115,554	$1,088,600,936
County equalization ratio	101.74	87.05	76.16

Demographics & Socio-Economic Characteristics
(2000 U.S. Census, except as noted)

Population
1980*	13,333
1990*	15,157
2000	18,080
Male	8,915
Female	9,165
2000 (revised)	18,013
2004 (estimate)*	19,256
Persons per sq. mi. of land	515

Race & Hispanic Origin, 2000
Race
White	17,481
Black/African American	52
Amer. Indian/Alaska Natv.	12
Asian	252
Natv. Hawaiian/Pac. Islander	5
Other Race	81
Two or more races	197
Hispanic origin, total	459
Mexican	81
Puerto Rican	106
Cuban	55
Other Hispanic	217

Age & Nativity, 2000
Under 5 years	1,381
18 years and over	12,544
21 years and over	12,108
65 years and over	1,491
85 years and over	179
Median Age	37.8
Native born	16,841
Foreign born	1,266

Educational Attainment, 2000
Population 25 years and over	11,764
0-8 yrs of school	1.7%
High School grad or higher	94.8%
Bachelor's degree or higher	50.2%
Graduate degree	17.6%

Income & Poverty, 1999
Per capita income	$36,910
Median household income	$89,835
Median family income	$100,658
Persons in poverty	279
H'holds receiving public assistance	29
H'holds receiving social security	1,226

Households, 2000
Total households	6,225
With persons under 18	2,851
With persons over 65	1,120
Family households	5,032
One-person households	1,005
Persons per household	2.9
Persons per family	3.28

Labor & Employment
Total civilian labor force, 2004**	9,579
Unemployment rate	3.8%
Total civilian labor force, 2000	9,248
Unemployment rate	2.2%

Employed persons 16 years and over by occupation, 2000
Managers & professionals	4,520
Service occupations	760
Sales & office occupations	2,541
Farming, fishing & forestry	0
Construction & maintenance	539
Production & transportation	681
Self-employed persons	543

*US Census Bureau
**New Jersey Department of Labor

General Information
Township of Sparta
65 Main St
Sparta, NJ 07871
973-729-4493

Web site	spartanj.net
Land area (sq. miles)	37.39
Water area (sq. miles)	1.83
Type of government	Township
Form of government	CM '50

Government

Legislative Districts
US Congressional	5, 11
State Legislative	24

Local Officials, 2006
Mayor	Ailish Hambel
Admin/Manager	Henry Underhill
Clerk	Miriam Tower
Finance Dir/Treas	Michael Guerino
Engineer	Charles Ryan
Attorney	Laddey, Clark & Ryan
Tax assessor	Joseph Ferraris
Tax collector	NA
Building officer	Jan Opt'Hof
Zoning officer	NA
Public Works	NA

Housing & Construction

Housing Units, 2000*
Total	6,590
Median rent	$777
Median SF home value	$222,700

New Privately Owned Housing Units
Authorized by Building Permit
	Units	Value
Total, 2004	50	$14,082,700
Single family	48	$13,666,700
Total, 2005	75	$19,944,239
Single family	75	$19,944,239

Real Property Valuation - parcels, 2005
	Number	Valuation
Total		$2,304,804,300
Vacant	976	64,949,800
Residential	6,641	2,027,559,200
Commercial	240	147,655,200
Industrial	45	40,201,200
Apartments	3	5,040,400
Farm land	48	18,372,600
Farm homestead	171	1,025,900

Average Property Value & Tax, 2005
Residential value	$297,796
Property tax	$8,071
FAIR rebate	$491

Public Library
Sparta Public Library
22 Woodport Rd
Sparta, NJ 07871
973-729-3101

Director	Carol Boutilier

Library statistics, 2004
	Total	per capita
Volumes	63,863	3.53
Expenditure	$852,565	$47.16

Public Safety
Police
Chief	Ernest Reigstad
Number of officers, 2004	35

Crime, 2004	Number	Rate
Total	95	4.9
Violent	4	0.2
Non-violent	91	4.7
Domestic Viol.	65	NA

Emergency/Fire
Director	Marc Ricciardi

Public School District
(for school year 2004-2005 except as noted)

Sparta Township School District
18 Mohawk Ave
Sparta, NJ 07871
973-729-7886

Administrator	Thomas Mortan
Grade plan	K-12
Enrollment	4,012.0
Students per teacher	12.6
Per pupil expenditure	$10,790
Median faculty salary	$58,185
Median administrator salary	$103,007
Grade 12 enrollment	237.0
High school graduation rate	97.5%

Assessment test results
(percent scoring at proficient or advanced level)
	Language	Math
Grade 3	95.9%	94.8%
Grade 8	91.2%	84.5%
High school	95.7%	91.9%

SAT
Percent tested	94%
Average SAT math score	533
Average SAT verbal score	526

No Child Left Behind, 2003-04
Attendence rate (target = 90%)	94.8%
Drop rate	0.6%
Highly-qualified teachers	99%
District needs improvement?(AYP)	No

Municipal Finance
Fiscal Year 2005
Total tax levy	$62,632,147
County levy	11,514,349
County taxes	10,950,516
County library	0
County health	0
County open space	563,834
School levy	39,353,963
Local muni. budget	11,763,835
Misc. revenues	9,285,041
Total aid	$1,774,360
CMPTRA	664,656
Muni. block grant	70,892
Energy tax receipts	939,484
Homeland security	70,000

Fiscal Year 2006
Total aid	$1,774,360
CMPTRA	631,774
Muni. block grant	70,892
Energy tax receipts	972,366
Homeland security	70,000

Taxes
	2003	2004	2005
General tax rate per $100	2.52	2.620	2.720
Net valuation taxable	$2,212,814,159	$2,268,903,072	$2,310,861,087
State equalized value	$2,454,863,722	$2,773,628,479	$3,068,465,127
County equalization ratio	110.44	90.14	81.76

Demographics & Socio-Economic Characteristics
(2000 U.S. Census, except as noted)

Population
1980*	7,840
1990*	7,983
2000	7,880
Male	3,810
Female	4,070
2004 (estimate)*	8,215
Persons per sq. mi. of land	3,534

Race & Hispanic Origin, 2000
Race
White	7,391
Black/African American	122
Amer. Indian/Alaska Natv.	6
Asian	230
Natv. Hawaiian/Pac. Islander	1
Other Race	58
Two or more races	72
Hispanic origin, total	345
Mexican	13
Puerto Rican	138
Cuban	55
Other Hispanic	139

Age & Nativity, 2000
Under 5 years	472
18 years and over	6,117
21 years and over	5,876
65 years and over	1,369
85 years and over	117
Median Age	39.7
Native born	7,259
Foreign born	621

Educational Attainment, 2000
Population 25 years and over	5,650
0-8 yrs of school	4.7%
High School grad or higher	83.2%
Bachelor's degree or higher	18.1%
Graduate degree	4.0%

Income & Poverty, 1999
Per capita income	$25,247
Median household income	$55,833
Median family income	$73,062
Persons in poverty	336
H'holds receiving public assistance	44
H'holds receiving social security	1,091

Households, 2000
Total households	3,099
With persons under 18	985
With persons over 65	1,047
Family households	2,163
One-person households	821
Persons per household	2.54
Persons per family	3.1

Labor & Employment
Total civilian labor force, 2004**	4,766
Unemployment rate	5.4%
Total civilian labor force, 2000	4,146
Unemployment rate	3.6%

Employed persons 16 years and over by occupation, 2000
Managers & professionals	1,112
Service occupations	452
Sales & office occupations	1,246
Farming, fishing & forestry	0
Construction & maintenance	530
Production & transportation	656
Self-employed persons	147

*US Census Bureau
**New Jersey Department of Labor

General Information
Borough of Spotswood
77 Summerhill Rd
Spotswood, NJ 08884
732-251-0700
Web site	www.spotswoodboro.com
Land area (sq. miles)	2.32
Water area (sq. miles)	0.17
Type of government	Borough
Form of government	MC Plan B

Government

Legislative Districts
US Congressional	6
State Legislative	18

Local Officials, 2006
Mayor	Barry Zagnit
Admin/Manager	Ronald Fasanello
Clerk	Patricia DeStefano
Finance Dir/Treas	Barbara Petren
Engineer	David Samuel
Attorney	Gary Schwartz
Tax assessor	Patricia Williams
Tax collector	Sandra Conover
Building officer	Bob Simonelli
Zoning officer	NA
Public Works	Patricia Pacyna

Housing & Construction

Housing Units, 2000*
Total	3,158
Median rent	$704
Median SF home value	$155,100

New Privately Owned Housing Units Authorized by Building Permit
	Units	Value
Total, 2004	19	$2,332,795
Single family	19	$2,332,795
Total, 2005	25	$3,536,808
Single family	25	$3,536,808

Real Property Valuation - parcels, 2005
	Number	Valuation
Total		$733,998,300
Vacant	265	9,923,900
Residential	2,507	628,954,700
Commercial	56	56,690,200
Industrial	5	30,792,200
Apartments	3	7,637,300
Farm land	0	0
Farm homestead	0	0

Average Property Value & Tax, 2005
Residential value	$250,879
Property tax	$5,330
FAIR rebate	$561

Public Library
Spotswood Public Library
548 Main St
Spotswood, NJ 08884
732-251-1515
Director................Mary Faith Chmiel

Library statistics, 2004
	Total	per capita
Volumes	30,210	3.83
Expenditure	$235,369	$29.87

Public Safety

Police
Chief	Karl Martins
Number of officers, 2004	19

Crime, 2004	Number	Rate
Total	102	12.4
Violent	13	1.6
Non-violent	89	10.8
Domestic Viol.	64	NA

Emergency/Fire
Director................Jason Michaels

Public School District
(for school year 2004-2005 except as noted)

Spotswood School District
105 Summerhill Rd
Spotswood, NJ 08884
732-723-2236
Superintendent	John Krewer
Grade plan	K-12
Enrollment	1,652.0
Students per teacher	10.4
Per pupil expenditure	$11,481
Median faculty salary	$44,006
Median administrator salary	$96,091
Grade 12 enrollment	188.0
High school graduation rate	96.2%

Assessment test results
(percent scoring at proficient or advanced level)
	Language	Math
Grade 3	89.3%	83.2%
Grade 8	77.1%	78.1%
High school	90.9%	85.0%

SAT
Percent tested	65%
Average SAT math score	506
Average SAT verbal score	489

No Child Left Behind, 2003-04
Attendence rate (target = 90%)	94.6%
Drop rate	0.6%
Highly-qualified teachers	100%
District needs improvement?(AYP)	No

Municipal Finance

Fiscal Year 2005
Total tax levy	$15,658,276
County levy	2,141,816
County taxes	1,940,103
County library	0
County health	0
County open space	201,713
School levy	9,517,480
Local muni. budget	3,998,981
Misc. revenues	3,296,302
Total aid	$1,134,815
CMPTRA	607,893
Muni. block grant	34,931
Energy tax receipts	441,991
Homeland security	50,000

Fiscal Year 2006
Total aid	$1,134,815
CMPTRA	592,423
Muni. block grant	34,931
Energy tax receipts	457,461
Homeland security	50,000

Taxes
	2003	2004	2005
General tax rate per $100	6.81	7.060	2.130
Net valuation taxable	$207,744,997	$210,605,878	$736,976,729
State equalized value	$586,850,274	$659,419,553	$748,960,090
County equalization ratio	41.1	35.40	110.12

Demographics & Socio-Economic Characteristics

(2000 U.S. Census, except as noted)

Population

1980*	4,215
1990*	3,499
2000	3,567
Male	1,650
Female	1,917
2004 (estimate)*	3,557
Persons per sq. mi. of land	2,716

Race & Hispanic Origin, 2000

Race

White	3,523
Black/African American	12
Amer. Indian/Alaska Natv.	0
Asian	10
Natv. Hawaiian/Pac. Islander	0
Other Race	4
Two or more races	18
Hispanic origin, total	26
Mexican	5
Puerto Rican	11
Cuban	4
Other Hispanic	6

Age & Nativity, 2000

Under 5 years	205
18 years and over	2,790
21 years and over	2,725
65 years and over	897
85 years and over	133
Median Age	47.7
Native born	3,499
Foreign born	68

Educational Attainment, 2000

Population 25 years and over	2,600
0-8 yrs of school	0.5%
High School grad or higher	96.5%
Bachelor's degree or higher	59.5%
Graduate degree	26.6%

Income & Poverty, 1999

Per capita income	$59,445
Median household income	$89,885
Median family income	$103,405
Persons in poverty	91
H'holds receiving public assistance	4
H'holds receiving social security	602

Households, 2000

Total households	1,463
With persons under 18	359
With persons over 65	627
Family households	983
One-person households	431
Persons per household	2.43
Persons per family	3.03

Labor & Employment

Total civilian labor force, 2004**	1,839
Unemployment rate	1.4%
Total civilian labor force, 2000	1,488
Unemployment rate	4.5%

Employed persons 16 years and over by occupation, 2000

Managers & professionals	757
Service occupations	142
Sales & office occupations	421
Farming, fishing & forestry	0
Construction & maintenance	67
Production & transportation	34
Self-employed persons	122

*US Census Bureau
**New Jersey Department of Labor

General Information

Borough of Spring Lake
5th & Warren Aves
Spring Lake, NJ 07762
732-449-0800

Web site	springlakeboro.org
Land area (sq. miles)	1.31
Water area (sq. miles)	0.40
Type of government	Borough
Form of government	B

Government

Legislative Districts

US Congressional	6
State Legislative	11

Local Officials, 2006

Mayor	Thomas Byrne III
Admin/Manager	Thomas Ferguson
Clerk	Mary Anne Coogan
Finance Dir/Treas	Susan Schreck
Engineer	T & M Associates
Attorney	Joseph J. Colao Jr.
Tax assessor	Brian Enright
Tax collector	Susan M. Schreck
Building officer	Sandy Ratz
Zoning officer	NA
Public Works	Frank Phillips

Housing & Construction

Housing Units, 2000*

Total	1,930
Median rent	$1,420
Median SF home value	$638,200

New Privately Owned Housing Units
Authorized by Building Permit

	Units	Value
Total, 2004	23	$13,053,645
Single family	23	$13,053,645
Total, 2005	24	$10,704,750
Single family	24	$10,704,750

Real Property Valuation - parcels, 2005

	Number	Valuation
Total		$3,325,508,800
Vacant	40	41,355,900
Residential	1,887	3,128,856,100
Commercial	103	152,188,100
Industrial	1	599,100
Apartments	1	2,509,600
Farm land	0	0
Farm homestead	0	0

Average Property Value & Tax, 2005

Residential value	$1,658,111
Property tax	$9,429
FAIR rebate	$763

Public Library

Spring Lake Public Library
1501 3rd Ave
Spring Lake, NJ 07762
732-449-6654

Director............Kateri Quinn

Library statistics, 2004

	Total	per capita
Volumes	NA	NA
Expenditure	NA	NA

Public Safety

Police

Chief	Robert Dawson Jr.
Number of officers, 2004	14

Crime, 2004	Number	Rate
Total	108	29.4
Violent	1	0.3
Non-violent	107	29.1
Domestic Viol.	10	NA

Emergency/Fire

Director...............Thomas Mullaney

Public School District

(for school year 2004-2005 except as noted)

Spring Lake School District
411 Tuttle Ave
Spring Lake, NJ 07762
732-449-6380

Superintendent	William Palmer
Grade plan	K-12
Enrollment	286.5
Students per teacher	9.6
Per pupil expenditure	$13,952
Median faculty salary	$43,400
Median administrator salary	$90,489
Grade 12 enrollment	NA
High school graduation rate	NA

Assessment test results

(percent scoring at proficient or advanced level)

	Language	Math
Grade 3	94.7%	94.7%
Grade 8	91.1%	91.2%
High school	NA	NA

SAT

Percent tested	NA
Average SAT math score	NA
Average SAT verbal score	NA

No Child Left Behind, 2003-04

Attendence rate (target = 90%)	94.9%
Drop rate	NA
Highly-qualified teachers	100%
District needs improvement?(AYP)	No

Municipal Finance

Fiscal Year 2005

Total tax levy	$18,932,710
County levy	8,221,578
County taxes	7,761,032
County library	0
County health	0
County open space	460,546
School levy	5,431,862
Local muni. budget	5,279,270
Misc. revenues	2,841,848
Total aid	$389,528
CMPTRA	23,749
Muni. block grant	15,310
Energy tax receipts	325,469
Homeland security	25,000

Fiscal Year 2006

Total aid	$389,527
CMPTRA	12,357
Muni. block grant	15,310
Energy tax receipts	336,860
Homeland security	25,000

Taxes

	2003	2004	2005
General tax rate per $100	1.54	1.581	0.569
Net valuation taxable	$1,112,737,529	$1,147,606,180	$3,329,471,072
State equalized value	$2,242,970,226	$2,534,410,806	$3,121,281,590
County equalization ratio	56.1	49.61	128.72

Demographics & Socio-Economic Characteristics
(2000 U.S. Census, except as noted)

Population
1980*	5,424
1990*	5,341
2000	5,227
Male	2,346
Female	2,881
2004 (estimate)*	5,190
Persons per sq. mi. of land	3,920

Race & Hispanic Origin, 2000
Race
White	5,085
Black/African American	58
Amer. Indian/Alaska Natv.	1
Asian	19
Natv. Hawaiian/Pac. Islander	1
Other Race	35
Two or more races	28
Hispanic origin, total	111
Mexican	15
Puerto Rican	29
Cuban	16
Other Hispanic	51

Age & Nativity, 2000
Under 5 years	215
18 years and over	4,347
21 years and over	4,239
65 years and over	1,545
85 years and over	210
Median Age	48.3
Native born	5,021
Foreign born	206

Educational Attainment, 2000
Population 25 years and over	4,079
0-8 yrs of school	4.1%
High School grad or higher	89.4%
Bachelor's degree or higher	38.5%
Graduate degree	12.0%

Income & Poverty, 1999
Per capita income	$35,093
Median household income	$51,330
Median family income	$64,345
Persons in poverty	392
H'holds receiving public assistance	19
H'holds receiving social security	1,088

Households, 2000
Total households	2,511
With persons under 18	472
With persons over 65	1,115
Family households	1,359
One-person households	1,048
Persons per household	2.04
Persons per family	2.82

Labor & Employment
Total civilian labor force, 2004**	3,051
Unemployment rate	5.1%
Total civilian labor force, 2000	2,337
Unemployment rate	7.2%

Employed persons 16 years and over by occupation, 2000
Managers & professionals	977
Service occupations	341
Sales & office occupations	631
Farming, fishing & forestry	0
Construction & maintenance	101
Production & transportation	119
Self-employed persons	213

*US Census Bureau
**New Jersey Department of Labor

General Information
Borough of Spring Lake Heights
555 Brighton Ave
Spring Lake Heights, NJ 07762
732-449-3500
Web site	www.springlakehts.com
Land area (sq. miles)	1.32
Water area (sq. miles)	0.02
Type of government	Borough
Form of government	B

Government

Legislative Districts
US Congressional	4, 6
State Legislative	11

Local Officials, 2006
Mayor	Elwood L. Malick
Admin/Manager	NA
Clerk	Elise McCann (Actg)
Finance Dir/Treas	Wendy Matson
Engineer	William T. Birdsall
Attorney	William Kelly
Tax assessor	Mitchell Elias
Tax collector	Mary Grace Neuhaus
Building officer	Sandy Ratz
Zoning officer	NA
Public Works	Art Herner

Housing & Construction

Housing Units, 2000*
Total	2,950
Median rent	$877
Median SF home value	$218,600

New Privately Owned Housing Units Authorized by Building Permit
	Units	Value
Total, 2004	33	$5,756,336
Single family	33	$5,756,336
Total, 2005	25	$5,025,269
Single family	25	$5,025,269

Real Property Valuation - parcels, 2005
	Number	Valuation
Total		$711,446,800
Vacant	56	6,926,700
Residential	2,115	591,479,800
Commercial	79	73,132,100
Industrial	0	0
Apartments	9	39,908,200
Farm land	0	0
Farm homestead	0	0

Average Property Value & Tax, 2005
Residential value	$279,659
Property tax	$4,705
FAIR rebate	$584

Public Library

No public municipal library.

Library statistics, 2004
	Total	per capita
Volumes	NA	NA
Expenditure	NA	NA

Public Safety

Police
Chief	Mark Steets
Number of officers, 2004	12

Crime, 2004	Number	Rate
Total	46	8.8
Violent	1	0.2
Non-violent	45	8.6
Domestic Viol.	0	NA

Emergency/Fire
Director	Eric Bennett

Public School District
(for school year 2004-2005 except as noted)

Spring Lake Heights Borough School Dist.
1110 Highway 71
Spring Lake Heights, NJ 07762
732-449-6149
Superintendent	Linda Martensen
Grade plan	K-12
Enrollment	394.0
Students per teacher	9.9
Per pupil expenditure	$10,591
Median faculty salary	$47,750
Median administrator salary	$77,141
Grade 12 enrollment	NA
High school graduation rate	NA

Assessment test results
(percent scoring at proficient or advanced level)
	Language	Math
Grade 3	76.9%	84.6%
Grade 8	86.6%	69.3%
High school	NA	NA

SAT
Percent tested	NA
Average SAT math score	NA
Average SAT verbal score	NA

No Child Left Behind, 2003-04
Attendence rate (target = 90%)	95.2%
Drop rate	NA
Highly-qualified teachers	100%
District needs improvement?(AYP)	No

Municipal Finance

Fiscal Year 2005
Total tax levy	$11,975,172
County levy	2,959,182
County taxes	2,655,339
County library	146,269
County health	0
County open space	157,573
School levy	6,169,808
Local muni. budget	2,846,182
Misc. revenues	1,661,851
Total aid	$608,334
CMPTRA	157,135
Muni. block grant	23,370
Energy tax receipts	377,829
Homeland security	50,000

Fiscal Year 2006
Total aid	$608,334
CMPTRA	143,911
Muni. block grant	23,370
Energy tax receipts	391,053
Homeland security	50,000

Taxes
	2003	2004	2005
General tax rate per $100	1.62	1.714	1.683
Net valuation taxable	$703,517,770	$706,972,972	$711,852,970
State equalized value	$780,299,213	$878,986,023	$1,045,766,079
County equalization ratio	97.44	90.16	80.42

Demographics & Socio-Economic Characteristics

(2000 U.S. Census, except as noted)

Population

1980*	1,691
1990*	3,028
2000	3,227
Male	1,614
Female	1,613
2004 (estimate)*	3,543
Persons per sq. mi. of land	118

Race & Hispanic Origin, 2000

Race

White	2,967
Black/African American	104
Amer. Indian/Alaska Natv.	10
Asian	85
Natv. Hawaiian/Pac. Islander	0
Other Race	7
Two or more races	54
Hispanic origin, total	57
Mexican	5
Puerto Rican	28
Cuban	4
Other Hispanic	20

Age & Nativity, 2000

Under 5 years	180
18 years and over	2,394
21 years and over	2,310
65 years and over	346
85 years and over	28
Median Age	39.3
Native born	3,015
Foreign born	212

Educational Attainment, 2000

Population 25 years and over	2,206
0-8 yrs of school	3.4%
High School grad or higher	87.3%
Bachelor's degree or higher	26.4%
Graduate degree	8.3%

Income & Poverty, 1999

Per capita income	$29,322
Median household income	$69,268
Median family income	$72,292
Persons in poverty	116
H'holds receiving public assistance	5
H'holds receiving social security	283

Households, 2000

Total households	1,098
With persons under 18	439
With persons over 65	244
Family households	907
One-person households	146
Persons per household	2.93
Persons per family	3.22

Labor & Employment

Total civilian labor force, 2004**	1,883
Unemployment rate	3.6%
Total civilian labor force, 2000	1,710
Unemployment rate	3.8%

Employed persons 16 years and over by occupation, 2000

Managers & professionals	600
Service occupations	180
Sales & office occupations	530
Farming, fishing & forestry	15
Construction & maintenance	153
Production & transportation	167
Self-employed persons	151

*US Census Bureau
**New Jersey Department of Labor

General Information

Township of Springfield
PO Box 119
2159 Jacksonville-Jobstown Rd
Jobstown, NJ 08041
609-723-2464

Web site	www.springfieldtownship.org
Land area (sq. miles)	30.03
Water area (sq. miles)	0.01
Type of government	Township
Form of government	TC

Government

Legislative Districts

US Congressional	4
State Legislative	8

Local Officials, 2006

Mayor	William Pettit Sr.
Admin/Manager	J. Paul Keller
Clerk	Caryn Hoyer
Finance Dir/Treas	Judith Schetler
Engineer	Raymond Worrell II
Attorney	Dennis McInerney
Tax assessor	John Schwager
Tax collector	Dawn Mitchell
Building officer	Tom Casey
Zoning officer	Bernard Dunn
Public Works	NA

Housing & Construction

Housing Units, 2000*

Total	1,138
Median rent	$541
Median SF home value	$185,400

New Privately Owned Housing Units Authorized by Building Permit

	Units	Value
Total, 2004	13	$2,130,480
Single family	13	$2,130,480
Total, 2005	15	$2,266,606
Single family	15	$2,266,606

Real Property Valuation - parcels, 2005

	Number	Valuation
Total		$428,547,003
Vacant	120	8,580,660
Residential	1,004	317,304,800
Commercial	78	46,738,980
Industrial	0	0
Apartments	0	0
Farm land	151	49,095,100
Farm homestead	334	6,827,463

Average Property Value & Tax, 2005

Residential value	$242,251
Property tax	$4,838
FAIR rebate	$550

Public Library

No public municipal library.

Library statistics, 2004

	Total	per capita
Volumes	NA	NA
Expenditure	NA	NA

Public Safety

Police

Chief	Kenneth Gerber
Number of officers, 2004	9

Crime, 2004	Number	Rate
Total	52	14.8
Violent	4	1.1
Non-violent	48	13.7
Domestic Viol.	16	NA

Emergency/Fire

Director	NA

Public School District

(for school year 2004-2005 except as noted)

Springfield Township School District
2146 Jacksonville Rd
Jobstown, NJ 08041
609-723-2479

Superintendent	Helena J. Sullivan
Grade plan	K-6
Enrollment	313.0
Students per teacher	11.4
Per pupil expenditure	$11,539
Median faculty salary	$47,019
Median administrator salary	$82,851
Grade 12 enrollment	NA
High school graduation rate	NA

Assessment test results

(percent scoring at proficient or advanced level)

	Language	Math
Grade 3	90.7%	95.4%
Grade 8	NA	NA
High school	NA	NA

SAT

Percent tested	NA
Average SAT math score	NA
Average SAT verbal score	NA

No Child Left Behind, 2003-04

Attendence rate (target = 90%)	96.1%
Drop rate	NA
Highly-qualified teachers	100%
District needs improvement?(AYP)	No

Municipal Finance

Fiscal Year 2005

Total tax levy	$8,583,443
County levy	1,687,015
County taxes	1,415,214
County library	123,924
County health	0
County open space	147,877
School levy	5,666,619
Local muni. budget	1,229,809
Misc. revenues	2,126,145
Total aid	$609,211
CMPTRA	165,896
Muni. block grant	13,249
Energy tax receipts	405,066
Homeland security	25,000

Fiscal Year 2006

Total aid	$609,210
CMPTRA	151,718
Muni. block grant	13,249
Energy tax receipts	419,243
Homeland security	25,000

Taxes

	2003	2004	2005
General tax rate per $100	3.47	3.530	1.999
Net valuation taxable	$219,452,688	$224,912,939	$429,773,825
State equalized value	$323,724,278	$368,290,813	$419,947,064
County equalization ratio	76.24	67.79	116.48

Demographics & Socio-Economic Characteristics
(2000 U.S. Census, except as noted)

Population
1980*	13,955
1990*	13,420
2000	14,429
Male	6,805
Female	7,624
2004 (estimate)*	14,788
Persons per sq. mi. of land	2,872

Race & Hispanic Origin, 2000
Race
White	12,946
Black/African American	537
Amer. Indian/Alaska Natv.	3
Asian	676
Natv. Hawaiian/Pac. Islander	0
Other Race	139
Two or more races	128
Hispanic origin, total	597
Mexican	20
Puerto Rican	78
Cuban	48
Other Hispanic	451

Age & Nativity, 2000
Under 5 years	893
18 years and over	11,463
21 years and over	11,164
65 years and over	2,972
85 years and over	390
Median Age	42.1
Native born	11,492
Foreign born	2,937

Educational Attainment, 2000
Population 25 years and over	10,991
0-8 yrs of school	3.9%
High School grad or higher	90.3%
Bachelor's degree or higher	46.7%
Graduate degree	16.8%

Income & Poverty, 1999
Per capita income	$36,754
Median household income	$73,790
Median family income	$85,725
Persons in poverty	453
H'holds receiving public assistance	30
H'holds receiving social security	1,981

Households, 2000
Total households	6,001
With persons under 18	1,707
With persons over 65	2,153
Family households	4,015
One-person households	1,724
Persons per household	2.4
Persons per family	2.98

Labor & Employment
Total civilian labor force, 2004**	7,529
Unemployment rate	2.9%
Total civilian labor force, 2000	7,706
Unemployment rate	1.5%

Employed persons 16 years and over by occupation, 2000
Managers & professionals	3,771
Service occupations	749
Sales & office occupations	2,095
Farming, fishing & forestry	8
Construction & maintenance	438
Production & transportation	526
Self-employed persons	630

*US Census Bureau
**New Jersey Department of Labor

General Information
Township of Springfield
100 Mountain Ave
Springfield, NJ 07081
973-912-2200
Web site	www.springfield-nj.com
Land area (sq. miles)	5.15
Water area (sq. miles)	0
Type of government	Township
Form of government	TC

Government
Legislative Districts
US Congressional	7
State Legislative	21

Local Officials, 2006
Mayor	Clara Harelik
Admin/Manager	Edward J. Fanning
Clerk	Kathleen Wisniewski
Finance Dir/Treas	Marie Sedlak
Engineer	Robert Kirkpatrick
Attorney	Bruce Bergen
Tax assessor	Ed Galente
Tax collector	Corinne Eckmann
Building officer	John Risso
Zoning officer	Richard Coan
Public Works	Ken Homlish

Housing & Construction
Housing Units, 2000*
Total	6,204
Median rent	$1,018
Median SF home value	$250,500

New Privately Owned Housing Units Authorized by Building Permit
	Units	Value
Total, 2004	28	$2,891,430
Single family	8	$1,264,430
Total, 2005	35	$3,557,584
Single family	10	$1,523,834

Real Property Valuation - parcels, 2005
	Number	Valuation
Total		$1,090,063,100
Vacant	84	5,977,700
Residential	4,778	754,423,700
Commercial	243	222,173,900
Industrial	69	54,612,700
Apartments	16	52,635,900
Farm land	1	203,700
Farm homestead	4	35,500

Average Property Value & Tax, 2005
Residential value	$157,771
Property tax	$7,622
FAIR rebate	$617

Public Library
Springfield Public Library
66 Mountain Ave
Springfield, NJ 07081
973-376-4930
Director	Susan Permahos

Library statistics, 2004
	Total	per capita
Volumes	73,371	5.08
Expenditure	$860,645	$59.65

Public Safety
Police
Chief	William Chisholm
Number of officers, 2004	41

Crime, 2004	Number	Rate
Total	307	20.8
Violent	11	0.7
Non-violent	296	20.1
Domestic Viol.	79	NA

Emergency/Fire
Director	Donald Schwerdt

Public School District
(for school year 2004-2005 except as noted)

Springfield School District
Springfield Public Schools
Springfield, NJ 07081
973-376-1025
Superintendent	Michael A. Davino
Grade plan	K-12
Enrollment	2,093.0
Students per teacher	11.1
Per pupil expenditure	$13,056
Median faculty salary	$55,058
Median administrator salary	$106,426
Grade 12 enrollment	134.0
High school graduation rate	99.2%

Assessment test results
(percent scoring at proficient or advanced level)
	Language	Math
Grade 3	86.8%	91.0%
Grade 8	84.1%	79.9%
High school	89.8%	84.1%

SAT
Percent tested	88%
Average SAT math score	530
Average SAT verbal score	512

No Child Left Behind, 2003-04
Attendence rate (target = 90%)	94.9%
Drop rate	0.4%
Highly-qualified teachers	96.8%
District needs improvement?(AYP)	No

Municipal Finance
Fiscal Year 2005
Total tax levy	$52,709,940
County levy	9,509,132
County taxes	9,132,984
County library	0
County health	0
County open space	376,148
School levy	27,438,043
Local muni. budget	15,762,765
Misc. revenues	6,052,908
Total aid	$2,405,971
CMPTRA	964,257
Muni. block grant	58,721
Energy tax receipts	1,312,993
Homeland security	70,000

Fiscal Year 2006
Total aid	$2,405,972
CMPTRA	918,303
Muni. block grant	58,721
Energy tax receipts	1,358,948
Homeland security	70,000

Taxes
	2003	2004	2005
General tax rate per $100	4.33	4.551	4.831
Net valuation taxable	$1,082,997,000	$1,089,763,100	$1,091,083,600
State equalized value	$2,085,895,609	$2,306,540,835	$2,532,103,968
County equalization ratio	56.05	50.49	43.83

Demographics & Socio-Economic Characteristics
(2000 U.S. Census, except as noted)

Population
1980*	10,385
1990*	13,325
2000	22,532
Male	10,924
Female	11,608
2004 (estimate)*	24,944
Persons per sq. mi. of land	536

Race & Hispanic Origin, 2000
Race
White	21,808
Black/African American	166
Amer. Indian/Alaska Natv.	21
Asian	217
Natv. Hawaiian/Pac. Islander	7
Other Race	114
Two or more races	199
Hispanic origin, total	542
Mexican	88
Puerto Rican	202
Cuban	55
Other Hispanic	197

Age & Nativity, 2000
Under 5 years	1,466
18 years and over	17,180
21 years and over	16,554
65 years and over	4,244
85 years and over	485
Median Age	40.3
Native born	21,533
Foreign born	984

Educational Attainment, 2000
Population 25 years and over	16,012
0-8 yrs of school	2.7%
High School grad or higher	84.9%
Bachelor's degree or higher	18.7%
Graduate degree	4.5%

Income & Poverty, 1999
Per capita income	$25,397
Median household income	$52,269
Median family income	$59,072
Persons in poverty	899
H'holds receiving public assistance	69
H'holds receiving social security	3,156

Households, 2000
Total households	8,535
With persons under 18	2,885
With persons over 65	2,756
Family households	6,433
One-person households	1,755
Persons per household	2.61
Persons per family	3.01

Labor & Employment
Total civilian labor force, 2004**	7,830
Unemployment rate	5.2%
Total civilian labor force, 2000	10,559
Unemployment rate	4.6%

Employed persons 16 years and over by occupation, 2000
Managers & professionals	3,154
Service occupations	1,613
Sales & office occupations	2,913
Farming, fishing & forestry	35
Construction & maintenance	1,411
Production & transportation	948
Self-employed persons	772

*US Census Bureau
**New Jersey Department of Labor

General Information
Township of Stafford
260 E Bay Ave
Manahawkin, NJ 08050
609-597-1000
Web site	www.twp.stafford.nj.us
Land area (sq. miles)	46.53
Water area (sq. miles)	8.29
Type of government	Township
Form of government	SM '50

Government

Legislative Districts
US Congressional	3
State Legislative	9

Local Officials, 2006
Mayor	Carl W. Block
Admin/Manager	Paul Shives
Clerk	Bernadette Park
Finance Dir/Treas	Suzanne Babcock
Engineer	John Walsh
Attorney	George Gilmore
Tax assessor	James Mancini
Tax collector	Margaret Bevilacqua
Building officer	Robert Gaestel
Zoning officer	Martha Kremer
Public Works	Ronald Cop

Housing & Construction

Housing Units, 2000*
Total	11,522
Median rent	$848
Median SF home value	$139,100

New Privately Owned Housing Units
Authorized by Building Permit
	Units	Value
Total, 2004	318	$32,816,147
Single family	318	$32,816,147
Total, 2005	315	$39,989,871
Single family	231	$27,472,492

Real Property Valuation - parcels, 2005
	Number	Valuation
Total		$4,091,394,300
Vacant	1,958	181,471,900
Residential	12,055	3,542,196,500
Commercial	370	357,989,000
Industrial	1	3,834,600
Apartments	3	4,230,600
Farm land	6	1,573,200
Farm homestead	20	98,500

Average Property Value & Tax, 2005
Residential value	$293,358
Property tax	$4,361
FAIR rebate	$567

Public Library
Stafford Branch Library†
129 N Main St
Manahawkin, NJ 08050
609-597-3381
Branch Librarian	Sharon Osborn

Library statistics, 2004
	Total	per capita
Volumes	NA	NA
Expenditure	NA	NA

†Branch of County Library

Public Safety
Police
Chief	Thomas Conroy
Number of officers, 2004	52

Crime, 2004	Number	Rate
Total	662	27.2
Violent	43	1.8
Non-violent	619	25.5
Domestic Viol.	140	NA

Emergency/Fire
Director	Edward Hazelton

Public School District
(for school year 2004-2005 except as noted)

Stafford Township School District
775 E Bay Ave
Manahawkin, NJ 08050
609-978-5700
Superintendent	Ronald Meinders
Grade plan	K-6
Enrollment	2,476.0
Students per teacher	11.9
Per pupil expenditure	$10,104
Median faculty salary	$41,196
Median administrator salary	$84,558
Grade 12 enrollment	NA
High school graduation rate	NA

Assessment test results
(percent scoring at proficient or advanced level)
	Language	Math
Grade 3	88.0%	78.9%
Grade 8	NA	NA
High school	NA	NA

SAT
Percent tested	NA
Average SAT math score	NA
Average SAT verbal score	NA

No Child Left Behind, 2003-04
Attendence rate (target = 90%)	95.0%
Drop rate	NA
Highly-qualified teachers	100%
District needs improvement?(AYP)	No

Municipal Finance

Fiscal Year 2005
Total tax levy	$60,926,472
County levy	13,419,728
County taxes	11,306,490
County library	1,187,861
County health	503,476
County open space	421,902
School levy	26,818,571
Local muni. budget	20,688,173
Misc. revenues	9,380,904
Total aid	$3,527,177
CMPTRA	385,702
Muni. block grant	88,348
Energy tax receipts	2,726,630
Homeland security	90,000

Fiscal Year 2006
Total aid	$3,527,177
CMPTRA	290,270
Muni. block grant	88,348
Energy tax receipts	2,822,062
Homeland security	90,000

Taxes
	2003	2004	2005
General tax rate per $100	2.44	2.648	1.487
Net valuation taxable	$2,025,698,761	$2,093,243,847	$4,098,047,731
State equalized value	$2,784,848,448	$3,426,601,854	$4,163,836,345
County equalization ratio	87.56	72.74	116.81

Demographics & Socio-Economic Characteristics
(2000 U.S. Census, except as noted)

Population
1980*	3,638
1990*	3,393
2000	3,584
Male	1,700
Female	1,884
2004 (estimate)*	3,709
Persons per sq. mi. of land	1,980

Race & Hispanic Origin, 2000
Race
White	3,353
Black/African American	48
Amer. Indian/Alaska Natv.	2
Asian	55
Natv. Hawaiian/Pac. Islander	3
Other Race	50
Two or more races	73
Hispanic origin, total	145
Mexican	9
Puerto Rican	52
Cuban	5
Other Hispanic	79

Age & Nativity, 2000
Under 5 years	249
18 years and over	2,686
21 years and over	2,588
65 years and over	268
85 years and over	23
Median Age	36.8
Native born	3,338
Foreign born	183

Educational Attainment, 2000
Population 25 years and over	2,433
0-8 yrs of school	0.9%
High School grad or higher	91.8%
Bachelor's degree or higher	32.3%
Graduate degree	7.5%

Income & Poverty, 1999
Per capita income	$27,535
Median household income	$63,059
Median family income	$73,203
Persons in poverty	77
H'holds receiving public assistance	4
H'holds receiving social security	239

Households, 2000
Total households	1,384
With persons under 18	501
With persons over 65	198
Family households	979
One-person households	317
Persons per household	2.58
Persons per family	3.1

Labor & Employment
Total civilian labor force, 2004**	2,394
Unemployment rate	3.9%
Total civilian labor force, 2000	2,066
Unemployment rate	3.2%

Employed persons 16 years and over by occupation, 2000
Managers & professionals	813
Service occupations	173
Sales & office occupations	693
Farming, fishing & forestry	0
Construction & maintenance	125
Production & transportation	196
Self-employed persons	63

*US Census Bureau
**New Jersey Department of Labor

General Information
Borough of Stanhope
77 Main St
Stanhope, NJ 07874
973-347-0159

Web site	NA
Land area (sq. miles)	1.87
Water area (sq. miles)	0.34
Type of government	Borough
Form of government	B

Government

Legislative Districts
US Congressional	11
State Legislative	24

Local Officials, 2006
Mayor	Diana Kuncken
Admin/Manager	Teri Massood
Clerk	Robin Kline
Finance Dir/Treas	(Vacant)
Engineer	E. Keller, Omland Eng.
Attorney	Richard Stein
Tax assessor	Maureen Kaman
Tax collector	NA
Building officer	Thomas Pershouse
Zoning officer	Arlene Fisher
Public Works	NA

Housing & Construction

Housing Units, 2000*
Total	1,419
Median rent	$965
Median SF home value	$151,100

New Privately Owned Housing Units
Authorized by Building Permit
	Units	Value
Total, 2004	3	$547,000
Single family	3	$547,000
Total, 2005	0	$0
Single family	0	$0

Real Property Valuation - parcels, 2005
	Number	Valuation
Total		$168,652,300
Vacant	174	1,834,700
Residential	1,360	152,249,100
Commercial	50	9,866,000
Industrial	4	3,111,800
Apartments	8	1,572,500
Farm land	0	0
Farm homestead	11	18,200

Average Property Value & Tax, 2005
Residential value	$111,063
Property tax	$5,703
FAIR rebate	$497

Public Library
E. Louise Childs Branch Library†
21 Sparta Rd
Stanhope, NJ 07874
973-770-1000
Branch Librarian .... Victoria Larson

Library statistics, 2004
	Total	per capita
Volumes	NA	NA
Expenditure	NA	NA

†Branch of County Library

Public Safety

Police
Chief	Steven Pittigher
Number of officers, 2004	7

Crime, 2004	Number	Rate
Total	31	8.4
Violent	5	1.4
Non-violent	26	7
Domestic Viol.	28	NA

Emergency/Fire
Director	Ed Frenenski

Public School District
(for school year 2004-2005 except as noted)

Stanhope Borough School District
24 Valley Rd
Stanhope, NJ 07874
973-347-0008

Administrator	Nicholas P. Brown
Grade plan	K-8
Enrollment	333.0
Students per teacher	12.5
Per pupil expenditure	$10,689
Median faculty salary	$53,401
Median administrator salary	$78,025
Grade 12 enrollment	NA
High school graduation rate	NA

Assessment test results
(percent scoring at proficient or advanced level)
	Language	Math
Grade 3	100%	90.3%
Grade 8	71.1%	55.6%
High school	NA	NA

SAT
Percent tested	NA
Average SAT math score	NA
Average SAT verbal score	NA

No Child Left Behind, 2003-04
Attendence rate (target = 90%)	95.4%
Drop rate	NA
Highly-qualified teachers	79.1%
District needs improvement?(AYP)	No

Municipal Finance

Fiscal Year 2005
Total tax levy	$8,675,292
County levy	1,431,532
County taxes	1,258,313
County library	108,488
County health	0
County open space	64,731
School levy	4,962,163
Local muni. budget	2,281,596
Misc. revenues	1,281,868
Total aid	$360,228
CMPTRA	193,451
Muni. block grant	14,847
Energy tax receipts	126,930
Homeland security	25,000

Fiscal Year 2006
Total aid	$360,228
CMPTRA	189,008
Muni. block grant	14,847
Energy tax receipts	131,373
Homeland security	25,000

Taxes
	2003	2004	2005
General tax rate per $100	4.57	4.900	5.140
Net valuation taxable	$164,524,991	$166,719,025	$168,931,999
State equalized value	$263,197,874	$316,338,730	$357,150,104
County equalization ratio	80.64	62.51	52.56

Demographics & Socio-Economic Characteristics

(2000 U.S. Census, except as noted)

Population

1980*	3,887
1990*	4,253
2000	4,267
Male	2,105
Female	2,162
2004 (estimate)*	4,384
Persons per sq. mi. of land	162

Race & Hispanic Origin, 2000

Race

White	4,180
Black/African American	7
Amer. Indian/Alaska Natv.	9
Asian	20
Natv. Hawaiian/Pac. Islander	0
Other Race	10
Two or more races	41
Hispanic origin, total	89
Mexican	4
Puerto Rican	31
Cuban	7
Other Hispanic	47

Age & Nativity, 2000

Under 5 years	265
18 years and over	3,072
21 years and over	2,909
65 years and over	360
85 years and over	32
Median Age	37.2
Native born	4,127
Foreign born	140

Educational Attainment, 2000

Population 25 years and over	2,797
0-8 yrs of school	2.5%
High School grad or higher	92.2%
Bachelor's degree or higher	27.1%
Graduate degree	8.4%

Income & Poverty, 1999

Per capita income	$24,933
Median household income	$63,750
Median family income	$71,563
Persons in poverty	120
H'holds receiving public assistance	0
H'holds receiving social security	324

Households, 2000

Total households	1,494
With persons under 18	653
With persons over 65	272
Family households	1,155
One-person households	258
Persons per household	2.85
Persons per family	3.27

Labor & Employment

Total civilian labor force, 2004**	2,663
Unemployment rate	7.5%
Total civilian labor force, 2000	2,373
Unemployment rate	1.3%

Employed persons 16 years and over by occupation, 2000

Managers & professionals	793
Service occupations	236
Sales & office occupations	632
Farming, fishing & forestry	0
Construction & maintenance	387
Production & transportation	294
Self-employed persons	185

*US Census Bureau
**New Jersey Department of Labor

General Information

Stillwater Township
964 Stillwater Rd
Newton, NJ 07860
973-383-9484

Web site	www.stillwaternj.us
Land area (sq. miles)	27.12
Water area (sq. miles)	1.26
Type of government	Township
Form of government	TC

Government

Legislative Districts

US Congressional	5
State Legislative	24

Local Officials, 2006

Mayor	Alfred P. Fuoco
Admin/Manager	NA
Clerk	Karen Reinertsen (Actg)
Finance Dir/Treas	Beth Barile
Engineer	Michael G. Vreeland
Attorney	Richard Clark
Tax assessor	David Poe
Tax collector	Donna Clouse
Building officer	Charles O'Connor
Zoning officer	NA
Public Works	Bill Ryker

Housing & Construction

Housing Units, 2000*

Total	2,030
Median rent	$760
Median SF home value	$152,400

New Privately Owned Housing Units
Authorized by Building Permit

	Units	Value
Total, 2004	14	$2,168,918
Single family	14	$2,168,918
Total, 2005	14	$2,840,985
Single family	14	$2,840,985

Real Property Valuation - parcels, 2005

	Number	Valuation
Total		$243,784,900
Vacant	415	7,069,700
Residential	1,671	202,521,700
Commercial	46	8,930,700
Industrial	1	408,900
Apartments	0	0
Farm land	132	23,536,900
Farm homestead	239	1,317,000

Average Property Value & Tax, 2005

Residential value	$106,722
Property tax	$3,976
FAIR rebate	$497

Public Library

No public municipal library.

Library statistics, 2004

	Total	per capita
Volumes	NA	NA
Expenditure	NA	NA

Public Safety

Police

Chief	Anthony Kozlowski
Number of officers, 2004	3

Crime, 2004	Number	Rate
Total	17	3.9
Violent	1	0.2
Non-violent	16	3.6
Domestic Viol.	5	NA

Emergency/Fire

Director	NA

Public School District

(for school year 2004-2005 except as noted)

Stillwater Township School District
PO Box 12
Stillwater, NJ 07875
973-383-6171

Administrator	S. William Shelton
Grade plan	K-6
Enrollment	403.0
Students per teacher	9.1
Per pupil expenditure	$12,516
Median faculty salary	$61,575
Median administrator salary	$89,758
Grade 12 enrollment	NA
High school graduation rate	NA

Assessment test results

(percent scoring at proficient or advanced level)

	Language	Math
Grade 3	96.4%	98.2%
Grade 8	NA	NA
High school	NA	NA

SAT

Percent tested	NA
Average SAT math score	NA
Average SAT verbal score	NA

No Child Left Behind, 2003-04

Attendence rate (target = 90%)	95.9%
Drop rate	NA
Highly-qualified teachers	100%
District needs improvement?(AYP)	No

Municipal Finance

Fiscal Year 2005

Total tax levy	$9,105,894
County levy	1,888,910
County taxes	1,603,155
County library	138,218
County health	65,065
County open space	82,472
School levy	5,819,628
Local muni. budget	1,397,356
Misc. revenues	2,022,467
Total aid	$429,202
CMPTRA	157,699
Muni. block grant	18,610
Energy tax receipts	227,893
Homeland security	25,000

Fiscal Year 2006

Total aid	$429,202
CMPTRA	149,723
Muni. block grant	18,610
Energy tax receipts	235,869
Homeland security	25,000

Taxes

	2003	2004	2005
General tax rate per $100	3.55	3.640	3.730
Net valuation taxable	$242,464,775	$243,524,912	$244,394,774
State equalized value	$364,773,244	$408,817,188	$487,521,991
County equalization ratio	83.56	66.47	59.50

Demographics & Socio-Economic Characteristics
(2000 U.S. Census, except as noted)

Population
1980*	643
1990*	629
2000	560
Male	262
Female	298
2004 (estimate)*	562
Persons per sq. mi. of land	1,030

Race & Hispanic Origin, 2000
Race
White	552
Black/African American	0
Amer. Indian/Alaska Natv.	0
Asian	5
Natv. Hawaiian/Pac. Islander	0
Other Race	0
Two or more races	3
Hispanic origin, total	3
Mexican	0
Puerto Rican	0
Cuban	1
Other Hispanic	2

Age & Nativity, 2000
Under 5 years	38
18 years and over	441
21 years and over	432
65 years and over	83
85 years and over	8
Median Age	40.6
Native born	549
Foreign born	8

Educational Attainment, 2000
Population 25 years and over	415
0-8 yrs of school	4.3%
High School grad or higher	86.7%
Bachelor's degree or higher	31.1%
Graduate degree	12.3%

Income & Poverty, 1999
Per capita income	$25,712
Median household income	$51,406
Median family income	$65,000
Persons in poverty	11
H'holds receiving public assistance	5
H'holds receiving social security	77

Households, 2000
Total households	246
With persons under 18	71
With persons over 65	62
Family households	148
One-person households	75
Persons per household	2.28
Persons per family	2.94

Labor & Employment
Total civilian labor force, 2004**	418
Unemployment rate	2.3%
Total civilian labor force, 2000	318
Unemployment rate	1.3%

Employed persons 16 years and over by occupation, 2000
Managers & professionals	125
Service occupations	30
Sales & office occupations	81
Farming, fishing & forestry	0
Construction & maintenance	29
Production & transportation	49
Self-employed persons	26

*US Census Bureau
**New Jersey Department of Labor

General Information
Borough of Stockton
PO Box M
2 South Main St
Stockton, NJ 08559
609-397-0070
Email	stocktonboro@snip.net
Land area (sq. miles)	0.55
Water area (sq. miles)	0.06
Type of government	Borough
Form of government	B

Government

Legislative Districts
US Congressional	12
State Legislative	23

Local Officials, 2006
Mayor	Gregg Rackin
Admin/Manager	NA
Clerk	Michele Hovan
Finance Dir/Treas	Elaine Vanselous
Engineer	Hopewell Valley Eng.
Attorney	John Bennett
Tax assessor	Richard Vinchur
Tax collector	NA
Building officer	Jeffrey Klein
Zoning officer	Robert Miller
Public Works	NA

Housing & Construction

Housing Units, 2000*
Total	258
Median rent	$850
Median SF home value	$188,500

New Privately Owned Housing Units Authorized by Building Permit
	Units	Value
Total, 2004	1	$151,100
Single family	1	$151,100
Total, 2005	0	$0
Single family	0	$0

Real Property Valuation - parcels, 2005
	Number	Valuation
Total		$42,491,400
Vacant	21	1,107,000
Residential	203	33,786,000
Commercial	27	6,404,800
Industrial	1	162,400
Apartments	2	579,100
Farm land	2	427,500
Farm homestead	6	24,600

Average Property Value & Tax, 2005
Residential value	$161,773
Property tax	$5,077
FAIR rebate	$617

Public Library

No public municipal library.

Library statistics, 2004
	Total	per capita
Volumes	NA	NA
Expenditure	NA	NA

Public Safety

Police
Chief	NA
Number of officers, 2004	0

Crime, 2004	Number	Rate
Total	5	8.9
Violent	0	0
Non-violent	5	8.9
Domestic Viol.	0	NA

Emergency/Fire
Director	Paul Steffanelli

Public School District
(for school year 2004-2005 except as noted)

Stockton Borough School District
19 S Main St
Stockton, NJ 08559
609-397-2012
Administrator	Suzanne Ivans
Grade plan	K-6
Enrollment	54.0
Students per teacher	9.6
Per pupil expenditure	$8,184
Median faculty salary	$29,150
Median administrator salary	$51,990
Grade 12 enrollment	NA
High school graduation rate	NA

Assessment test results
(percent scoring at proficient or advanced level)
	Language	Math
Grade 3	NA	NA
Grade 8	NA	NA
High school	NA	NA

SAT
Percent tested	NA
Average SAT math score	NA
Average SAT verbal score	NA

No Child Left Behind, 2003-04
Attendence rate (target = 90%)	95.9%
Drop rate	NA
Highly-qualified teachers	100%
District needs improvement?(AYP)	No

Municipal Finance

Fiscal Year 2005
Total tax levy	$1,336,307
County levy	328,602
County taxes	279,003
County library	23,345
County health	0
County open space	26,253
School levy	782,242
Local muni. budget	225,463
Misc. revenues	301,604
Total aid	$66,243
CMPTRA	26,671
Muni. block grant	2,752
Energy tax receipts	36,820
Homeland security	0

Fiscal Year 2006
Total aid	$66,244
CMPTRA	25,383
Muni. block grant	2,752
Energy tax receipts	38,109
Homeland security	NA

Taxes
	2003	2004	2005
General tax rate per $100	2.99	2.960	3.140
Net valuation taxable	$42,370,103	$42,361,850	$42,577,168
State equalized value	$63,685,710	$74,983,073	$82,770,544
County equalization ratio	66.03	61.12	48.88

Demographics & Socio-Economic Characteristics

(2000 U.S. Census, except as noted)

Population

1980*	1,187
1990*	1,025
2000	1,128
Male	518
Female	610
2004 (estimate)*	1,087
Persons per sq. mi. of land	767

Race & Hispanic Origin, 2000

Race

White	1,114
Black/African American	9
Amer. Indian/Alaska Natv.	0
Asian	0
Natv. Hawaiian/Pac. Islander	0
Other Race	2
Two or more races	3
Hispanic origin, total	5
Mexican	0
Puerto Rican	2
Cuban	0
Other Hispanic	3

Age & Nativity, 2000

Under 5 years	27
18 years and over	989
21 years and over	973
65 years and over	437
85 years and over	44
Median Age	57.5
Native born	1,104
Foreign born	24

Educational Attainment, 2000

Population 25 years and over	954
0-8 yrs of school	1.6%
High School grad or higher	93.9%
Bachelor's degree or higher	43.8%
Graduate degree	18.7%

Income & Poverty, 1999

Per capita income	$46,427
Median household income	$51,471
Median family income	$67,250
Persons in poverty	39
H'holds receiving public assistance	5
H'holds receiving social security	291

Households, 2000

Total households	596
With persons under 18	75
With persons over 65	317
Family households	331
One-person households	240
Persons per household	1.89
Persons per family	2.5

Labor & Employment

Total civilian labor force, 2004**	528
Unemployment rate	4.1%
Total civilian labor force, 2000	486
Unemployment rate	4.9%

Employed persons 16 years and over by occupation, 2000

Managers & professionals	203
Service occupations	61
Sales & office occupations	146
Farming, fishing & forestry	3
Construction & maintenance	27
Production & transportation	22
Self-employed persons	49

*US Census Bureau
**New Jersey Department of Labor

General Information

Borough of Stone Harbor
9508 Second Ave
Stone Harbor, NJ 08247
609-368-5102

Web site	www.stone-harbor.nj.us
Land area (sq. miles)	1.42
Water area (sq. miles)	0.57
Type of government	Borough
Form of government	B

Government

Legislative Districts

US Congressional	2
State Legislative	1

Local Officials, 2006

Mayor	Suzanne Walters
Admin/Manager	Kenneth Hawk
Clerk	Suzanne Stanford
Finance Dir/Treas	James Nicola
Engineer	Marc DeBlasio
Attorney	Michael Donohue
Tax assessor	Harry Supple Jr.
Tax collector	Kathryn McClure
Building officer	Michael Koochembere
Zoning officer	Joanne Mascia
Public Works	Greg Sheeran

Housing & Construction

Housing Units, 2000*

Total	3,428
Median rent	$669
Median SF home value	$445,300

New Privately Owned Housing Units Authorized by Building Permit

	Units	Value
Total, 2004	36	$12,394,036
Single family	36	$12,394,036
Total, 2005	57	$24,850,653
Single family	57	$24,850,653

Real Property Valuation - parcels, 2005

	Number	Valuation
Total		$3,566,477,000
Vacant	66	81,338,200
Residential	2,868	3,342,567,200
Commercial	196	137,472,800
Industrial	0	0
Apartments	3	5,098,800
Farm land	0	0
Farm homestead	0	0

Average Property Value & Tax, 2005

Residential value	$1,165,470
Property tax	$5,148
FAIR rebate	$879

Public Library

Stone Harbor Branch Library†
95th & Second Ave
Stone Harbor, NJ 08247
609-368-6809
Branch Librarian.. Geraldine M. Fridmann

Library statistics, 2004

	Total	per capita
Volumes	NA	NA
Expenditure	NA	NA

†Branch of County Library

Public Safety

Police

Chief	William Toland
Number of officers, 2004	18

Crime, 2004	Number	Rate
Total	85	76.5
Violent	3	2.7
Non-violent	82	73.8
Domestic Viol.	5	NA

Emergency/Fire

Director	Roger Stanford

Public School District

(for school year 2004-2005 except as noted)

Stone Harbor School District
275 93rd St
Stone Harbor, NJ 08247
609-368-4413

Principal	David Rauenzahn
Grade plan	K-12
Enrollment	81.0
Students per teacher	6.8
Per pupil expenditure	$16,327
Median faculty salary	$56,131
Median administrator salary	$100,940
Grade 12 enrollment	NA
High school graduation rate	NA

Assessment test results

(percent scoring at proficient or advanced level)

	Language	Math
Grade 3	NA	NA
Grade 8	100.0%	81.8%
High school	NA	NA

SAT

Percent tested	NA
Average SAT math score	NA
Average SAT verbal score	NA

No Child Left Behind, 2003-04

Attendance rate (target = 90%)	94.9%
Drop rate	NA
Highly-qualified teachers	87.5%
District needs improvement?(AYP)	No

Municipal Finance

Fiscal Year 2005

Total tax levy	$15,755,391
County levy	7,173,942
County taxes	6,031,406
County library	849,657
County health	0
County open space	292,880
School levy	2,016,076
Local muni. budget	6,565,372
Misc. revenues	3,012,606
Total aid	$245,187
CMPTRA	0
Muni. block grant	4,485
Energy tax receipts	248,950
Homeland security	25,000

Fiscal Year 2006

Total aid	$253,901
CMPTRA	0
Muni. block grant	4,485
Energy tax receipts	224,416
Homeland security	25,000

Taxes

	2003	2004	2005
General tax rate per $100	0.78	0.790	0.450
Net valuation taxable	$1,801,888,963	$1,816,535,993	$3,567,039,533
State equalized value	$2,460,588,506	$2,908,058,193	$3,855,425,349
County equalization ratio	82.56	78.23	122.00

Demographics & Socio-Economic Characteristics
(2000 U.S. Census, except as noted)

Population
1980*	1,365
1990*	1,437
2000	1,429
Male	703
Female	726
2004 (estimate)*	1,523
Persons per sq. mi. of land	82

Race & Hispanic Origin, 2000
Race
White	1,335
Black/African American	50
Amer. Indian/Alaska Natv.	23
Asian	3
Natv. Hawaiian/Pac. Islander	0
Other Race	12
Two or more races	6
Hispanic origin, total	24
Mexican	2
Puerto Rican	12
Cuban	0
Other Hispanic	10

Age & Nativity, 2000
Under 5 years	74
18 years and over	1,093
21 years and over	1,044
65 years and over	207
85 years and over	12
Median Age	40.7
Native born	1,405
Foreign born	29

Educational Attainment, 2000
Population 25 years and over	975
0-8 yrs of school	5.9%
High School grad or higher	83.1%
Bachelor's degree or higher	18.9%
Graduate degree	5.8%

Income & Poverty, 1999
Per capita income	$20,925
Median household income	$52,500
Median family income	$58,583
Persons in poverty	96
H'holds receiving public assistance	9
H'holds receiving social security	149

Households, 2000
Total households	536
With persons under 18	182
With persons over 65	143
Family households	425
One-person households	96
Persons per household	2.67
Persons per family	3.01

Labor & Employment
Total civilian labor force, 2004**	806
Unemployment rate	3.7%
Total civilian labor force, 2000	746
Unemployment rate	4.4%

Employed persons 16 years and over by occupation, 2000
Managers & professionals	231
Service occupations	94
Sales & office occupations	150
Farming, fishing & forestry	13
Construction & maintenance	98
Production & transportation	127
Self-employed persons	44

*US Census Bureau
**New Jersey Department of Labor

General Information
Township of Stow Creek
474 Macanippuck Rd
Bridgeton, NJ 08302
856-451-8822
Web site	NA
Land area (sq. miles)	18.45
Water area (sq. miles)	0.42
Type of government	Township
Form of government	TC

Government
Legislative Districts
US Congressional	2
State Legislative	3

Local Officials, 2006
Mayor	Dale Cruzan Sr.
Admin/Manager	NA
Clerk	Bruce Porter
Finance Dir/Treas	Ron Campbell
Engineer	J. Michael Fralinger
Attorney	Thomas Farnoly
Tax assessor	Donna Harris
Tax collector	Roberta DiGiuseppi
Building officer	Robert Young
Zoning officer	NA
Public Works	NA

Housing & Construction
Housing Units, 2000*
Total	560
Median rent	$620
Median SF home value	$114,400

New Privately Owned Housing Units Authorized by Building Permit
	Units	Value
Total, 2004	3	$370,000
Single family	3	$370,000
Total, 2005	4	$646,000
Single family	4	$646,000

Real Property Valuation - parcels, 2005
	Number	Valuation
Total		$75,712,200
Vacant	51	823,000
Residential	362	43,662,000
Commercial	14	2,708,600
Industrial	0	0
Apartments	0	0
Farm land	171	25,042,400
Farm homestead	347	3,476,200

Average Property Value & Tax, 2005
Residential value	$66,485
Property tax	$1,874
FAIR rebate	$559

Public Library
No public municipal library.

Library statistics, 2004
	Total	per capita
Volumes	NA	NA
Expenditure	NA	NA

Public Safety
Police
Chief	NA
Number of officers, 2004	0

Crime, 2004	Number	Rate
Total	15	10
Violent	3	2
Non-violent	12	8
Domestic Viol.	8	NA

Emergency/Fire
Director	Max Dilks

Public School District
(for school year 2004-2005 except as noted)

Stow Creek Township School District
11 Gum Tree Corner Rd
Bridgeton, NJ 08302
856-455-1717
Administrator	Donna Levick
Grade plan	K-8
Enrollment	138.0
Students per teacher	10.3
Per pupil expenditure	$11,764
Median faculty salary	$37,318
Median administrator salary	$74,289
Grade 12 enrollment	NA
High school graduation rate	NA

Assessment test results
(percent scoring at proficient or advanced level)
	Language	Math
Grade 3	76.9%	69.3%
Grade 8	81.3%	68.8%
High school	NA	NA

SAT
Percent tested	NA
Average SAT math score	NA
Average SAT verbal score	NA

No Child Left Behind, 2003-04
Attendence rate (target = 90%)	95.7%
Drop rate	NA
Highly-qualified teachers	82.2%
District needs improvement?(AYP)	No

Municipal Finance
Fiscal Year 2005
Total tax levy	$2,150,002
County levy	837,882
County taxes	795,937
County library	0
County health	33,886
County open space	8,059
School levy	1,243,660
Local muni. budget	68,460
Misc. revenues	489,345
Total aid	$193,484
CMPTRA	84,988
Muni. block grant	6,287
Energy tax receipts	102,209
Homeland security	0

Fiscal Year 2006
Total aid	$193,484
CMPTRA	81,411
Muni. block grant	6,287
Energy tax receipts	105,786
Homeland security	NA

Taxes
	2003	2004	2005
General tax rate per $100	2.25	2.362	2.821
Net valuation taxable	$73,971,704	$74,470,906	$76,278,901
State equalized value	$68,683,105	$77,877,540	$85,437,837
County equalization ratio	104.67	107.70	95.59

Demographics & Socio-Economic Characteristics
(2000 U.S. Census, except as noted)

Population
1980*	8,005
1990*	7,614
2000	7,271
Male	3,544
Female	3,727
2004 (estimate)*	7,201
Persons per sq. mi. of land	4,559

Race & Hispanic Origin, 2000
Race
White	6,439
Black/African American	480
Amer. Indian/Alaska Natv.	9
Asian	173
Natv. Hawaiian/Pac. Islander	1
Other Race	63
Two or more races	106
Hispanic origin, total	277
Mexican	105
Puerto Rican	92
Cuban	7
Other Hispanic	73

Age & Nativity, 2000
Under 5 years	447
18 years and over	5,476
21 years and over	5,222
65 years and over	1,150
85 years and over	116
Median Age	37.7
Native born	6,885
Foreign born	386

Educational Attainment, 2000
Population 25 years and over	4,910
0-8 yrs of school	4.5%
High School grad or higher	86.3%
Bachelor's degree or higher	20.0%
Graduate degree	4.5%

Income & Poverty, 1999
Per capita income	$21,748
Median household income	$50,977
Median family income	$57,500
Persons in poverty	327
H'holds receiving public assistance	52
H'holds receiving social security	802

Households, 2000
Total households	2,736
With persons under 18	953
With persons over 65	747
Family households	1,907
One-person households	705
Persons per household	2.61
Persons per family	3.18

Labor & Employment
Total civilian labor force, 2004**	4,278
Unemployment rate	4.1%
Total civilian labor force, 2000	3,660
Unemployment rate	3.7%

Employed persons 16 years and over by occupation, 2000
Managers & professionals	1,288
Service occupations	483
Sales & office occupations	1,181
Farming, fishing & forestry	13
Construction & maintenance	271
Production & transportation	289
Self-employed persons	133

*US Census Bureau
**New Jersey Department of Labor

General Information
Borough of Stratford
307 Union Ave
Stratford, NJ 08084
856-783-0600
Web site	www.stratfordnj.org
Land area (sq. miles)	1.58
Water area (sq. miles)	0
Type of government	Borough
Form of government	B

Government
Legislative Districts
US Congressional	1
State Legislative	5

Local Officials, 2006
Mayor	Thomas Angelucci
Admin/Manager	John Keenan Jr.
Clerk	John Keenan Jr.
Finance Dir/Treas	John Fabritiis
Engineer	Clancy & Assoc
Attorney	Jeffrey Baron
Tax assessor	Richard Arrowood
Tax collector	NA
Building officer	Chris Mecca
Zoning officer	Frank Gagliard Jr.
Public Works	Ken Ryker

Housing & Construction
Housing Units, 2000*
Total	2,849
Median rent	$594
Median SF home value	$114,000

New Privately Owned Housing Units
Authorized by Building Permit
	Units	Value
Total, 2004	2	$145,300
Single family	2	$145,300
Total, 2005	1	$78,000
Single family	1	$78,000

Real Property Valuation - parcels, 2005
	Number	Valuation
Total		$285,921,200
Vacant	33	991,500
Residential	2,112	221,322,200
Commercial	111	51,888,300
Industrial	0	0
Apartments	11	11,719,200
Farm land	0	0
Farm homestead	0	0

Average Property Value & Tax, 2005
Residential value	$104,793
Property tax	$4,813
FAIR rebate	$628

Public Library
Stratford Public Library
303 Union Ave
Stratford, NJ 08084
856-783-0602
Director	Ruth Roderick

Library statistics, 2004
	Total	per capita
Volumes	38,841	5.34
Expenditure	$112,355	$15.45

Public Safety
Police
Chief	Ronald Morello
Number of officers, 2004	13

Crime, 2004	Number	Rate
Total	174	24
Violent	18	2.5
Non-violent	156	21.5
Domestic Viol.	79	NA

Emergency/Fire
Director	Michael Meyers

Public School District
(for school year 2004-2005 except as noted)

Stratford Borough School District
111 Warwick Rd
Stratford, NJ 08084
856-783-2555
Superintendent	Albert Brown
Grade plan	K-8
Enrollment	863.0
Students per teacher	11.3
Per pupil expenditure	$10,147
Median faculty salary	$46,245
Median administrator salary	$79,255
Grade 12 enrollment	NA
High school graduation rate	NA

Assessment test results
(percent scoring at proficient or advanced level)
	Language	Math
Grade 3	76.0%	74.7%
Grade 8	71.7%	58.9%
High school	NA	NA

SAT
Percent tested	NA
Average SAT math score	NA
Average SAT verbal score	NA

No Child Left Behind, 2003-04
Attendence rate (target = 90%)	97.2%
Drop rate	NA
Highly-qualified teachers	98.3%
District needs improvement?(AYP)	No

Municipal Finance
Fiscal Year 2005
Total tax levy	$13,169,143
County levy	2,732,870
County taxes	2,697,487
County library	0
County health	0
County open space	35,383
School levy	8,250,773
Local muni. budget	2,185,500
Misc. revenues	2,790,395
Total aid	$1,066,202
CMPTRA	420,727
Muni. block grant	33,317
Energy tax receipts	562,158
Homeland security	50,000

Fiscal Year 2006
Total aid	$1,066,202
CMPTRA	401,051
Muni. block grant	33,317
Energy tax receipts	581,834
Homeland security	50,000

Taxes
	2003	2004	2005
General tax rate per $100	4.14	4.347	4.594
Net valuation taxable	$285,916,964	$286,247,199	$286,714,550
State equalized value	$328,112,192	$351,017,492	$403,709,589
County equalization ratio	93.81	87.14	81.50

Demographics & Socio-Economic Characteristics
(2000 U.S. Census, except as noted)

Population
1980*	21,071
1990*	19,757
2000	21,131
Male	10,225
Female	10,906
2004 (estimate)*	21,267
Persons per sq. mi. of land	3,513

Race & Hispanic Origin, 2000
Race
White	18,546
Black/African American	914
Amer. Indian/Alaska Natv.	19
Asian	941
Natv. Hawaiian/Pac. Islander	3
Other Race	360
Two or more races	348
Hispanic origin, total	2,150
Mexican	162
Puerto Rican	207
Cuban	159
Other Hispanic	1,622

Age & Nativity, 2000
Under 5 years	1,815
18 years and over	15,434
21 years and over	15,071
65 years and over	2,769
85 years and over	349
Median Age	37.3
Native born	17,262
Foreign born	3,869

Educational Attainment, 2000
Population 25 years and over	14,517
0-8 yrs of school	2.8%
High School grad or higher	92.4%
Bachelor's degree or higher	61.6%
Graduate degree	30.0%

Income & Poverty, 1999
Per capita income	$62,598
Median household income	$92,964
Median family income	$117,053
Persons in poverty	895
H'holds receiving public assistance	74
H'holds receiving social security	1,985

Households, 2000
Total households	7,897
With persons under 18	2,908
With persons over 65	2,054
Family households	5,610
One-person households	1,887
Persons per household	2.67
Persons per family	3.18

Labor & Employment
Total civilian labor force, 2004**	10,722
Unemployment rate	2.5%
Total civilian labor force, 2000	10,473
Unemployment rate	2.5%

Employed persons 16 years and over by occupation, 2000
Managers & professionals	5,983
Service occupations	1,079
Sales & office occupations	2,287
Farming, fishing & forestry	11
Construction & maintenance	358
Production & transportation	498
Self-employed persons	761

*US Census Bureau
**New Jersey Department of Labor

General Information
City of Summit
512 Springfield Ave
Summit, NJ 07901
908-273-6400

Web site	www.cityofsummit.org
Land area (sq. miles)	6.05
Water area (sq. miles)	0.02
Type of government	City
Form of government	C

Government

Legislative Districts
US Congressional	7
State Legislative	21

Local Officials, 2006
Mayor	Jordan Glatt
Admin/Manager	Christopher Cotter
Clerk	David Hughes
Finance Dir/Treas	Ronald Angelo
Engineer	Andy Hipolit
Attorney	Barry Osmun
Tax assessor	Victor Lupi
Tax collector	Carolyn Brattlof
Building officer	Tony Doyle
Zoning officer	Christa Anderson
Public Works	Paul Cascais

Housing & Construction

Housing Units, 2000*
Total	8,146
Median rent	$1,078
Median SF home value	$469,200

New Privately Owned Housing Units Authorized by Building Permit
	Units	Value
Total, 2004	42	$3,235,501
Single family	42	$3,235,501
Total, 2005	23	$5,874,595
Single family	21	$5,693,475

Real Property Valuation - parcels, 2005
	Number	Valuation
Total		$3,062,924,500
Vacant	124	15,387,600
Residential	5,992	2,415,514,900
Commercial	388	322,967,000
Industrial	11	238,177,900
Apartments	48	70,877,100
Farm land	0	0
Farm homestead	0	0

Average Property Value & Tax, 2005
Residential value	$403,123
Property tax	$11,749
FAIR rebate	$643

Public Library
Summit Free Public Library
75 Maple St
Summit, NJ 07901
908-273-0350

Director................... Glenn Devitt

Library statistics, 2004
	Total	per capita
Volumes	123,993	5.87
Expenditure	$1,913,838	$90.57

Public Safety

Police
Chief	Robert Lucid
Number of officers, 2004	48

Crime, 2004	Number	Rate
Total	386	18.2
Violent	14	0.7
Non-violent	372	17.5
Domestic Viol.	133	NA

Emergency/Fire
Director...............Christopher Cotter

Public School District
(for school year 2004-2005 except as noted)

Summit City School District
90 Maple St
Summit, NJ 07901
908-273-3023

Superintendent	Carolyn Deacon
Grade plan	K-12
Enrollment	3,625.5
Students per teacher	10.7
Per pupil expenditure	$12,473
Median faculty salary	$56,003
Median administrator salary	$111,974
Grade 12 enrollment	223.0
High school graduation rate	98.2%

Assessment test results
(percent scoring at proficient or advanced level)
	Language	Math
Grade 3	95.2%	92.8%
Grade 8	89.7%	83.1%
High school	95.1%	93.8%

SAT
Percent tested	92%
Average SAT math score	580
Average SAT verbal score	564

No Child Left Behind, 2003-04
Attendence rate (target = 90%)	96.1%
Drop rate	0.1%
Highly-qualified teachers	99.6%
District needs improvement?(AYP)	No

Municipal Finance

Fiscal Year 2005
Total tax levy	$89,392,682
County levy	22,592,807
County taxes	21,699,848
County library	0
County health	0
County open space	892,959
School levy	46,243,868
Local muni. budget	20,556,008
Misc. revenues	14,975,656
Total aid	$4,078,736
CMPTRA	708,047
Muni. block grant	86,451
Energy tax receipts	3,194,238
Homeland security	90,000

Fiscal Year 2006
Total aid	$4,078,735
CMPTRA	596,248
Muni. block grant	86,451
Energy tax receipts	3,306,036
Homeland security	90,000

Taxes
	2003	2004	2005
General tax rate per $100	2.62	2.758	2.915
Net valuation taxable	$3,032,377,938	$3,052,497,402	$3,067,049,487
State equalized value	$5,046,393,640	$5,598,949,786	$6,164,923,592
County equalization ratio	59.67	55.68	51.73

Demographics & Socio-Economic Characteristics

(2000 U.S. Census, except as noted)

Population

1980*	1,571
1990*	1,375
2000	1,442
Male	685
Female	757
2004 (estimate)*	1,517
Persons per sq. mi. of land	2,094

Race & Hispanic Origin, 2000

Race
White	1,414
Black/African American	2
Amer. Indian/Alaska Natv.	3
Asian	5
Natv. Hawaiian/Pac. Islander	6
Other Race	8
Two or more races	4
Hispanic origin, total	28
Mexican	15
Puerto Rican	1
Cuban	1
Other Hispanic	11

Age & Nativity, 2000

Under 5 years	39
18 years and over	1,263
21 years and over	1,230
65 years and over	492
85 years and over	58
Median Age	53.4
Native born	1,385
Foreign born	46

Educational Attainment, 2000

Population 25 years and over	1,202
0-8 yrs of school	3.2%
High School grad or higher	87.5%
Bachelor's degree or higher	26.0%
Graduate degree	6.4%

Income & Poverty, 1999

Per capita income	$26,632
Median household income	$38,190
Median family income	$50,268
Persons in poverty	107
H'holds receiving public assistance	2
H'holds receiving social security	352

Households, 2000

Total households	706
With persons under 18	102
With persons over 65	343
Family households	421
One-person households	246
Persons per household	2.04
Persons per family	2.61

Labor & Employment

Total civilian labor force, 2004**	771
Unemployment rate	2.1%
Total civilian labor force, 2000	615
Unemployment rate	4.2%

Employed persons 16 years and over by occupation, 2000
Managers & professionals	191
Service occupations	91
Sales & office occupations	209
Farming, fishing & forestry	5
Construction & maintenance	45
Production & transportation	48
Self-employed persons	77

*US Census Bureau
**New Jersey Department of Labor

General Information

Borough of Surf City
813 Boulevard
Surf City, NJ 08008
609-494-3064

Web site	NA
Land area (sq. miles)	0.72
Water area (sq. miles)	0.20
Type of government	Borough
Form of government	B

Government

Legislative Districts

US Congressional	3
State Legislative	9

Local Officials, 2006

Mayor	Leonard Connors Jr.
Admin/Manager	Mary Madonna
Clerk	Mary Madonna
Finance Dir/Treas	David Pawlishak
Engineer	Frank Little
Attorney	Christopher Connors
Tax assessor	William Procacci
Tax collector	NA
Building officer	Frank Zappavigna
Zoning officer	Pamela Michniewicz
Public Works	NA

Housing & Construction

Housing Units, 2000*

Total	2,621
Median rent	$738
Median SF home value	$230,200

New Privately Owned Housing Units
Authorized by Building Permit

	Units	Value
Total, 2004	34	$7,963,800
Single family	34	$7,963,800
Total, 2005	38	$11,224,200
Single family	38	$11,224,200

Real Property Valuation - parcels, 2005

	Number	Valuation
Total		$1,460,750,100
Vacant	42	18,846,400
Residential	2,102	1,358,922,900
Commercial	95	82,980,800
Industrial	0	0
Apartments	0	0
Farm land	0	0
Farm homestead	0	0

Average Property Value & Tax, 2005

Residential value	$646,490
Property tax	$4,997
FAIR rebate	$645

Public Library

Long Beach Island Branch Library†
217 S Central Ave
Surf City, NJ 08008
609-494-2480

Branch Librarian	Elise Weber

Library statistics, 2004

	Total	per capita
Volumes	NA	NA
Expenditure	NA	NA

†Branch of County Library

Public Safety

Police

Chief	William Collins
Number of officers, 2004	11

Crime, 2004	Number	Rate
Total	30	20.1
Violent	1	0.7
Non-violent	29	19.4
Domestic Viol.	11	NA

Emergency/Fire

Director	B. Stasik

Public School District

(for school year 2004-2005 except as noted)

Sends children to Long Beach Island school district (see Appendix A).

Grade plan	NA
Enrollment	NA
Students per teacher	NA
Per pupil expenditure	NA
Median faculty salary	NA
Median administrator salary	NA
Grade 12 enrollment	NA
High school graduation rate	NA

Assessment test results

(percent scoring at proficient or advanced level)

	Language	Math
Grade 3	NA	NA
Grade 8	NA	NA
High school	NA	NA

SAT

Percent tested	NA
Average SAT math score	NA
Average SAT verbal score	NA

No Child Left Behind, 2003-04

Attendence rate (target = 90%)	NA
Drop rate	NA
Highly-qualified teachers	NA
District needs improvement?(AYP)	NA

Municipal Finance

Fiscal Year 2005

Total tax levy	$11,303,112
County levy	4,642,207
County taxes	4,063,637
County library	426,912
County health	0
County open space	151,658
School levy	3,850,655
Local muni. budget	2,810,250
Misc. revenues	1,994,450
Total aid	$212,023
CMPTRA	6,297
Muni. block grant	6,017
Energy tax receipts	174,709
Homeland security	25,000

Fiscal Year 2006

Total aid	$212,023
CMPTRA	182
Muni. block grant	6,017
Energy tax receipts	180,824
Homeland security	25,000

Taxes

	2003	2004	2005
General tax rate per $100	1.94	2.106	0.773
Net valuation taxable	$505,194,136	$515,509,621	$1,462,298,371
State equalized value	$1,051,830,389	$1,234,619,654	$1,521,800,782
County equalization ratio	57.05	48.03	115.84

Demographics & Socio-Economic Characteristics
(2000 U.S. Census, except as noted)

Population
1980*	2,418
1990*	2,201
2000	2,145
Male	1,025
Female	1,120
2004 (estimate)*	2,186
Persons per sq. mi. of land	3,667

Race & Hispanic Origin, 2000
Race
White	2,066
Black/African American	24
Amer. Indian/Alaska Natv.	2
Asian	26
Natv. Hawaiian/Pac. Islander	0
Other Race	8
Two or more races	19
Hispanic origin, total	55
Mexican	6
Puerto Rican	28
Cuban	2
Other Hispanic	19

Age & Nativity, 2000
Under 5 years	133
18 years and over	1,632
21 years and over	1,552
65 years and over	273
85 years and over	27
Median Age	36.1
Native born	2,111
Foreign born	34

Educational Attainment, 2000
Population 25 years and over	1,446
0-8 yrs of school	4.2%
High School grad or higher	75.0%
Bachelor's degree or higher	10.7%
Graduate degree	2.5%

Income & Poverty, 1999
Per capita income	$18,866
Median household income	$36,172
Median family income	$45,250
Persons in poverty	235
H'holds receiving public assistance	45
H'holds receiving social security	250

Households, 2000
Total households	903
With persons under 18	287
With persons over 65	219
Family households	513
One-person households	317
Persons per household	2.36
Persons per family	3.12

Labor & Employment
Total civilian labor force, 2004**	1,301
Unemployment rate	6.7%
Total civilian labor force, 2000	1,093
Unemployment rate	3.3%

Employed persons 16 years and over by occupation, 2000
Managers & professionals	184
Service occupations	238
Sales & office occupations	279
Farming, fishing & forestry	8
Construction & maintenance	111
Production & transportation	237
Self-employed persons	34

*US Census Bureau
**New Jersey Department of Labor

General Information
Borough of Sussex
2 Main St
Sussex, NJ 07461
973-875-4831

Web site	NA
Land area (sq. miles)	0.60
Water area (sq. miles)	0.02
Type of government	Borough
Form of government	B

Government
Legislative Districts
US Congressional	5
State Legislative	24

Local Officials, 2006
Mayor	Katherine Little
Admin/Manager	NA
Clerk	Vito D. Gadaleta
Finance Dir/Treas	Grant Rome
Engineer	Robert Guerin
Attorney	Michael Hanifan
Tax assessor	John Dyksen
Tax collector	NA
Building officer	Nick Frasche
Zoning officer	NA
Public Works	NA

Housing & Construction
Housing Units, 2000*
Total	961
Median rent	$667
Median SF home value	$122,500

New Privately Owned Housing Units
Authorized by Building Permit
	Units	Value
Total, 2004	6	$831,080
Single family	6	$831,080
Total, 2005	10	$1,470,647
Single family	10	$1,470,647

Real Property Valuation - parcels, 2005
	Number	Valuation
Total		$78,198,800
Vacant	42	828,300
Residential	464	52,967,800
Commercial	70	16,615,600
Industrial	3	496,100
Apartments	5	6,896,000
Farm land	1	373,900
Farm homestead	4	21,100

Average Property Value & Tax, 2005
Residential value	$113,224
Property tax	$4,047
FAIR rebate	$608

Public Library
Sussex-Wantage Branch Library†
69 Route 639
Wantage, NJ 07461
973-875-3940

Branch Librarian .... Nancy Helmer

Library statistics, 2004
	Total	per capita
Volumes	NA	NA
Expenditure	NA	NA

†Branch of County Library

Public Safety
Police
Chief	NA
Number of officers, 2004	0

Crime, 2004	Number	Rate
Total	47	21.6
Violent	4	1.8
Non-violent	43	19.7
Domestic Viol.	56	NA

Emergency/Fire
Director .... Bob Stormes

Public School District
(for school year 2004-2005 except as noted)

Sussex-Wantage Regional School District
31 Ryan Rd
Wantage, NJ 07461
973-875-3175
Superintendent	Anthony Mistretta (Int)
Grade plan	K-8
Enrollment	1,726.0
Students per teacher	10.6
Per pupil expenditure	$12,048
Median faculty salary	$58,230
Median administrator salary	$94,256
Grade 12 enrollment	NA
High school graduation rate	NA

Assessment test results
(percent scoring at proficient or advanced level)
	Language	Math
Grade 3	79.4%	78.2%
Grade 8	80.6%	67.8%
High school	NA	NA

SAT
Percent tested	NA
Average SAT math score	NA
Average SAT verbal score	NA

No Child Left Behind, 2003-04
Attendence rate (target = 90%)	94.9%
Drop rate	NA
Highly-qualified teachers	91.9%
District needs improvement?(AYP)	No

Municipal Finance
Fiscal Year 2005
Total tax levy	$2,840,319
County levy	504,525
County taxes	428,198
County library	36,914
County health	17,369
County open space	22,044
School levy	1,885,833
Local muni. budget	449,961
Misc. revenues	708,273
Total aid	$279,622
CMPTRA	160,618
Muni. block grant	9,631
Energy tax receipts	109,373
Homeland security	0

Fiscal Year 2006
Total aid	$279,623
CMPTRA	156,790
Muni. block grant	9,631
Energy tax receipts	113,202
Homeland security	NA

Taxes
	2003	2004	2005
General tax rate per $100	3.48	3.610	3.580
Net valuation taxable	$78,702,727	$79,308,748	$79,468,917
State equalized value	$99,347,042	$108,797,502	$127,599,417
County equalization ratio	90.39	79.22	72.55

Demographics & Socio-Economic Characteristics
(2000 U.S. Census, except as noted)

Population
1980*	2,031
1990*	2,024
2000	2,055
Male	1,009
Female	1,046
2004 (estimate)*	2,054
Persons per sq. mi. of land	2,829

Race & Hispanic Origin, 2000
Race
White	1,581
Black/African American	339
Amer. Indian/Alaska Natv.	1
Asian	7
Natv. Hawaiian/Pac. Islander	0
Other Race	69
Two or more races	58
Hispanic origin, total	175
Mexican	10
Puerto Rican	126
Cuban	1
Other Hispanic	38

Age & Nativity, 2000
Under 5 years	153
18 years and over	1,492
21 years and over	1,406
65 years and over	258
85 years and over	38
Median Age	35.9
Native born	1,992
Foreign born	63

Educational Attainment, 2000
Population 25 years and over	1,355
0-8 yrs of school	8.8%
High School grad or higher	81.1%
Bachelor's degree or higher	14.2%
Graduate degree	4.9%

Income & Poverty, 1999
Per capita income	$20,857
Median household income	$49,286
Median family income	$58,721
Persons in poverty	198
H'holds receiving public assistance	28
H'holds receiving social security	220

Households, 2000
Total households	771
With persons under 18	300
With persons over 65	209
Family households	529
One-person households	200
Persons per household	2.66
Persons per family	3.22

Labor & Employment
Total civilian labor force, 2004**	1,252
Unemployment rate	7.1%
Total civilian labor force, 2000	1,006
Unemployment rate	5.1%

Employed persons 16 years and over by occupation, 2000
Managers & professionals	281
Service occupations	108
Sales & office occupations	295
Farming, fishing & forestry	9
Construction & maintenance	98
Production & transportation	164
Self-employed persons	26

*US Census Bureau
**New Jersey Department of Labor

General Information
Borough of Swedesboro
PO Box 56
Swedesboro, NJ 08085
856-467-0202
Web site	NA
Land area (sq. miles)	0.73
Water area (sq. miles)	0.03
Type of government	Borough
Form of government	B

Government
Legislative Districts
US Congressional	2
State Legislative	3

Local Officials, 2006
Mayor	Thomas W. Fromm
Admin/Manager	NA
Clerk	Dolores Connors
Finance Dir/Treas	Joanne Mitcho
Engineer	Bowman & Co.
Attorney	Timothy W. Chell
Tax assessor	Horace Spoto
Tax collector	NA
Building officer	George Davis
Zoning officer	NA
Public Works	NA

Housing & Construction
Housing Units, 2000*
Total	860
Median rent	$642
Median SF home value	$98,400

New Privately Owned Housing Units
Authorized by Building Permit
	Units	Value
Total, 2004	0	$129,300
Single family	0	$129,300
Total, 2005	2	$231,000
Single family	2	$231,000

Real Property Valuation - parcels, 2005
	Number	Valuation
Total		$71,949,500
Vacant	69	1,457,500
Residential	622	54,566,700
Commercial	78	13,759,700
Industrial	4	902,800
Apartments	8	1,000,700
Farm land	1	236,600
Farm homestead	4	25,500

Average Property Value & Tax, 2005
Residential value	$87,208
Property tax	$3,770
FAIR rebate	$592

Public Library
Swedesboro Public Library†
442 Kings Hwy
Swedesboro, NJ 08085
856-467-0111
Director	Marge Dombrosky

Library statistics, 2004
	Total	per capita
Volumes	10,870	5.29
Expenditure	$21,980	$10.70

†Joint library with Woolwich Twp.

Public Safety
Police
Chief	William Dupper Jr.
Number of officers, 2004	7

Crime, 2004	Number	Rate
Total	72	35.1
Violent	6	2.9
Non-violent	66	32.2
Domestic Viol.	22	NA

Emergency/Fire
Director	Edward Barber

Public School District
(for school year 2004-2005 except as noted)

Swedesboro-Woolwich School District
15 Fredrick Blvd
Woolwich Township, NJ 08085
856-241-1136
Superintendent	Richard Fisher
Grade plan	K-6
Enrollment	1,058.0
Students per teacher	10.3
Per pupil expenditure	$10,104
Median faculty salary	$36,720
Median administrator salary	$83,637
Grade 12 enrollment	NA
High school graduation rate	NA

Assessment test results
(percent scoring at proficient or advanced level)
	Language	Math
Grade 3	88.6%	85.9%
Grade 8	NA	NA
High school	NA	NA

SAT
Percent tested	NA
Average SAT math score	NA
Average SAT verbal score	NA

No Child Left Behind, 2003-04
Attendence rate (target = 90%)	95.0%
Drop rate	NA
Highly-qualified teachers	100%
District needs improvement?(AYP)	No

Municipal Finance
Fiscal Year 2005
Total tax levy	$3,202,028
County levy	659,834
County taxes	578,608
County library	42,761
County health	0
County open space	38,465
School levy	1,738,228
Local muni. budget	803,966
Misc. revenues	997,912
Total aid	$412,947
CMPTRA	256,824
Muni. block grant	8,856
Energy tax receipts	122,267
Homeland security	25,000

Fiscal Year 2006
Total aid	$412,946
CMPTRA	252,544
Muni. block grant	8,856
Energy tax receipts	126,546
Homeland security	25,000

Taxes
	2003	2004	2005
General tax rate per $100	3.88	4.134	4.324
Net valuation taxable	$73,473,245	$74,344,028	$74,067,833
State equalized value	$86,024,172	$93,961,737	$106,373,450
County equalization ratio	87.91	85.41	78.56

Demographics & Socio-Economic Characteristics
(2000 U.S. Census, except as noted)

Population
1980*	6,236
1990*	7,360
2000	7,170
Male	3,632
Female	3,538
2000 (revised)	7,167
2004 (estimate)*	7,349
Persons per sq. mi. of land	149

Race & Hispanic Origin, 2000
Race
White	6,904
Black/African American	150
Amer. Indian/Alaska Natv.	7
Asian	52
Natv. Hawaiian/Pac. Islander	0
Other Race	22
Two or more races	35
Hispanic origin, total	106
Mexican	10
Puerto Rican	61
Cuban	8
Other Hispanic	27

Age & Nativity, 2000
Under 5 years	384
18 years and over	5,166
21 years and over	4,897
65 years and over	502
85 years and over	47
Median Age	38.1
Native born	7,012
Foreign born	158

Educational Attainment, 2000
Population 25 years and over	4,651
0-8 yrs of school	1.7%
High School grad or higher	92.7%
Bachelor's degree or higher	30.6%
Graduate degree	10.0%

Income & Poverty, 1999
Per capita income	$27,874
Median household income	$76,432
Median family income	$86,729
Persons in poverty	144
H'holds receiving public assistance	28
H'holds receiving social security	510

Households, 2000
Total households	2,346
With persons under 18	1,040
With persons over 65	389
Family households	2,011
One-person households	268
Persons per household	3.03
Persons per family	3.28

Labor & Employment
Total civilian labor force, 2004**	4,657
Unemployment rate	2.8%
Total civilian labor force, 2000	3,994
Unemployment rate	2.0%

Employed persons 16 years and over by occupation, 2000
Managers & professionals	1,630
Service occupations	357
Sales & office occupations	1,147
Farming, fishing & forestry	12
Construction & maintenance	398
Production & transportation	369
Self-employed persons	233

*US Census Bureau
**New Jersey Department of Labor

General Information
Township of Tabernacle
163 Carranza Rd
Tabernacle, NJ 08088
609-268-1220
Web site . www.townshipoftabernacle-nj.gov	
Land area (sq. miles)	49.46
Water area (sq. miles)	0.06
Type of government	Township
Form of government	TC

Government
Legislative Districts
US Congressional	3
State Legislative	8

Local Officials, 2006
Mayor	Richard Franzen
Admin/Manager	Douglas Cramer
Clerk	LaShawn Ruffin
Finance Dir/Treas	Terry Henry
Engineer	Ray Worrell
Attorney	Peter Lange
Tax assessor	Dennis DeKlerk
Tax collector	Terry W. Henry
Building officer	Frank Robert Perri
Zoning officer	Frank Robert Perri
Public Works	Douglas Cramer

Housing & Construction
Housing Units, 2000*
Total	2,385
Median rent	$761
Median SF home value	$171,700

New Privately Owned Housing Units
Authorized by Building Permit
	Units	Value
Total, 2004	15	$1,960,450
Single family	15	$1,960,450
Total, 2005	22	$5,508,779
Single family	22	$5,508,779

Real Property Valuation - parcels, 2005
	Number	Valuation
Total		$386,226,650
Vacant	286	6,938,000
Residential	2,262	357,397,800
Commercial	52	9,492,700
Industrial	3	433,600
Apartments	0	0
Farm land	75	10,171,300
Farm homestead	184	1,793,250

Average Property Value & Tax, 2005
Residential value	$146,848
Property tax	$5,368
FAIR rebate	$483

Public Library
No public municipal library.

Library statistics, 2004
	Total	per capita
Volumes	NA	NA
Expenditure	NA	NA

Public Safety
Police
Chief	NA
Number of officers, 2004	0

Crime, 2004	Number	Rate
Total	68	9.3
Violent	6	0.8
Non-violent	62	8.5
Domestic Viol.	13	NA

Emergency/Fire
Director	Al Freeman

Public School District
(for school year 2004-2005 except as noted)

Tabernacle Township School District
132 New Rd
Tabernacle, NJ 08088
609-268-0153
Superintendent	Berenice Blum-Bart
Grade plan	K-8
Enrollment	1,066.0
Students per teacher	13.8
Per pupil expenditure	$12,141
Median faculty salary	$69,340
Median administrator salary	$98,208
Grade 12 enrollment	NA
High school graduation rate	NA

Assessment test results
(percent scoring at proficient or advanced level)
	Language	Math
Grade 3	87.6%	89.3%
Grade 8	83.9%	71.2%
High school	NA	NA

SAT
Percent tested	NA
Average SAT math score	NA
Average SAT verbal score	NA

No Child Left Behind, 2003-04
Attendence rate (target = 90%)	95.9%
Drop rate	NA
Highly-qualified teachers	95.9%
District needs improvement?(AYP)	No

Municipal Finance
Fiscal Year 2005
Total tax levy	$14,144,848
County levy	2,748,041
County taxes	2,305,318
County library	201,851
County health	0
County open space	240,872
School levy	10,204,833
Local muni. budget	1,191,974
Misc. revenues	1,909,620
Total aid	$802,457
CMPTRA	246,797
Muni. block grant	32,204
Energy tax receipts	523,308
Homeland security	0

Fiscal Year 2006
Total aid	$802,457
CMPTRA	228,481
Muni. block grant	32,204
Energy tax receipts	541,624
Homeland security	NA

Taxes
	2003	2004	2005
General tax rate per $100	3.26	3.413	3.656
Net valuation taxable	$379,238,300	$382,854,760	$386,982,411
State equalized value	$515,479,543	$594,744,284	$673,364,209
County equalization ratio	81.1	73.57	64.32

Demographics & Socio-Economic Characteristics

(2000 U.S. Census, except as noted)

Population

1980*	9
1990*	35
2000	24
Male	12
Female	12
2004 (estimate)*	30
Persons per sq. mi. of land	118

Race & Hispanic Origin, 2000

Race
White	22
Black/African American	2
Amer. Indian/Alaska Natv.	0
Asian	0
Natv. Hawaiian/Pac. Islander	0
Other Race	0
Two or more races	0
Hispanic origin, total	0
Mexican	0
Puerto Rican	0
Cuban	0
Other Hispanic	0

Age & Nativity, 2000

Under 5 years	1
18 years and over	15
21 years and over	13
65 years and over	2
85 years and over	0
Median Age	38.5
Native born	22
Foreign born	1

Educational Attainment, 2000

Population 25 years and over	9
0-8 yrs of school	0.0%
High School grad or higher	88.9%
Bachelor's degree or higher	33.3%
Graduate degree	22.2%

Income & Poverty, 1999

Per capita income	$14,600
Median household income	$58,750
Median family income	$36,875
Persons in poverty	5
H'holds receiving public assistance	1
H'holds receiving social security	1

Households, 2000

Total households	7
With persons under 18	4
With persons over 65	2
Family households	7
One-person households	0
Persons per household	3.43
Persons per family	3.43

Labor & Employment

Total civilian labor force, 2004**	24
Unemployment rate	0.0%
Total civilian labor force, 2000	9
Unemployment rate	0.0%

Employed persons 16 years and over by occupation, 2000
Managers & professionals	4
Service occupations	2
Sales & office occupations	0
Farming, fishing & forestry	0
Construction & maintenance	1
Production & transportation	2
Self-employed persons	4

*US Census Bureau
**New Jersey Department of Labor

General Information

Borough of Tavistock
PO Box 8988
Turnersville, NJ 08012
856-429-0039

Web site	NA
Land area (sq. miles)	0.25
Water area (sq. miles)	0
Type of government	Borough
Form of government	Comm.

Government

Legislative Districts

US Congressional	1
State Legislative	6

Local Officials, 2006

Mayor	George Buff III
Admin/Manager	Theresa Lappe
Clerk	Theresa Lappe
Finance Dir/Treas	Mary Breslin
Engineer	Edward Vernick
Attorney	Matthew S. Wolf
Tax assessor	Steven Kessler
Tax collector	NA
Building officer	NA
Zoning officer	NA
Public Works	NA

Housing & Construction

Housing Units, 2000*

Total	7
Median rent	$675
Median SF home value	$137,500

New Privately Owned Housing Units
Authorized by Building Permit

	Units	Value
Total, 2004	NA	NA
Single family	NA	NA
Total, 2005	0	$0
Single family	0	$0

Real Property Valuation - parcels, 2005

	Number	Valuation
Total		$16,555,200
Vacant	0	0
Residential	3	4,550,000
Commercial	2	12,005,200
Industrial	0	0
Apartments	0	0
Farm land	0	0
Farm homestead	0	0

Average Property Value & Tax, 2005

Residential value	$1,516,667
Property tax	$21,168
FAIR rebate	$0

Public Library

No public municipal library.

Library statistics, 2004

	Total	per capita
Volumes	NA	NA
Expenditure	NA	NA

Public Safety

Police

Chief	NA
Number of officers, 2004	0

Crime, 2004	Number	Rate
Total	2	+
Violent	0	+
Non-violent	2	+
Domestic Viol.	0	NA

Emergency/Fire

Director	NA

Public School District

(for school year 2004-2005 except as noted)

Tavistock Borough School District†
PO Box 8988
Turnersville, NJ 08012

†No schools in district - sends children to Haddonfield Borough schools.

Grade plan	NA
Enrollment	NA
Students per teacher	NA
Per pupil expenditure	NA
Median faculty salary	NA

Assessment test results

(percent scoring at proficient or advanced level)
	Language	Math
Grade 3	NA	NA
Grade 8	NA	NA
High school	NA	NA

SAT

Percent tested	NA
Average SAT math score	NA
Average SAT verbal score	NA

No Child Left Behind, 2003-04

Attendence rate (target = 90%)	NA
Drop rate	NA
Highly-qualified teachers	NA
District needs improvement?(AYP)	NA

Municipal Finance

Fiscal Year 2005

Total tax levy	$231,093
County levy	137,512
County taxes	126,739
County library	9,111
County health	0
County open space	1,661
School levy	15,024
Local muni. budget	78,557
Misc. revenues	28,823
Total aid	$3,986
CMPTRA	2,848
Muni. block grant	94
Energy tax receipts	1,044
Homeland security	0

Fiscal Year 2006

Total aid	$3,987
CMPTRA	2,812
Muni. block grant	94
Energy tax receipts	1,081
Homeland security	NA

Taxes

	2003	2004	2005
General tax rate per $100	3.94	8.559	1.396
Net valuation taxable	$3,353,320	$3,353,121	$16,557,646
State equalized value	$3,325,717	$3,339,442	$10,201,248
County equalization ratio	100	100.00	100.00

Demographics & Socio-Economic Characteristics
(2000 U.S. Census, except as noted)

Population
1980*	39,007
1990*	37,825
2000	39,260
Male	18,584
Female	20,676
2004 (estimate)*	39,853
Persons per sq. mi. of land	6,584

Race & Hispanic Origin, 2000
Race
White	22,082
Black/African American	11,298
Amer. Indian/Alaska Natv.	59
Asian	2,798
Natv. Hawaiian/Pac. Islander	11
Other Race	1,633
Two or more races	1,379
Hispanic origin, total	4,103
Mexican	151
Puerto Rican	1,132
Cuban	329
Other Hispanic	2,491

Age & Nativity, 2000
Under 5 years	2,521
18 years and over	29,139
21 years and over	27,538
65 years and over	5,584
85 years and over	826
Median Age	38.4
Native born	29,825
Foreign born	9,435

Educational Attainment, 2000
Population 25 years and over	26,054
0-8 yrs of school	3.6%
High School grad or higher	89.7%
Bachelor's degree or higher	47.9%
Graduate degree	23.0%

Income & Poverty, 1999
Per capita income	$32,212
Median household income	$74,903
Median family income	$84,791
Persons in poverty	1,596
H'holds receiving public assistance	302
H'holds receiving social security	4,020

Households, 2000
Total households	13,418
With persons under 18	5,202
With persons over 65	4,075
Family households	10,071
One-person households	2,838
Persons per household	2.86
Persons per family	3.34

Labor & Employment
Total civilian labor force, 2004**	22,332
Unemployment rate	4.3%
Total civilian labor force, 2000	20,106
Unemployment rate	4.7%

Employed persons 16 years and over by occupation, 2000
Managers & professionals	10,185
Service occupations	1,794
Sales & office occupations	5,137
Farming, fishing & forestry	0
Construction & maintenance	805
Production & transportation	1,230
Self-employed persons	1,268

*US Census Bureau
**New Jersey Department of Labor

General Information
Township of Teaneck
818 Teaneck Rd
Teaneck, NJ 07666
201-837-4811
Web site	www.teanecknjgov.org
Land area (sq. miles)	6.05
Water area (sq. miles)	0.20
Type of government	Township
Form of government	CM '50

Government

Legislative Districts
US Congressional	9
State Legislative	37

Local Officials, 2006
Mayor	Jacqueline Kates
Admin/Manager	Helene Fall
Clerk	Robyn LaMorte
Finance Dir/Treas	Anthony Bianchi
Engineer	Charles McKearnin
Attorney	Stanley Turitz
Tax assessor	James Tighe
Tax collector	Milene Quijano
Building officer	Steven Gluck
Zoning officer	NA
Public Works	Charles McKearnin

Housing & Construction

Housing Units, 2000*
Total	13,719
Median rent	$873
Median SF home value	$208,800

New Privately Owned Housing Units
Authorized by Building Permit
	Units	Value
Total, 2004	19	$5,934,600
Single family	19	$5,934,600
Total, 2005	94	$5,460,400
Single family	9	$2,689,400

Real Property Valuation - parcels, 2005
	Number	Valuation
Total		$2,633,228,700
Vacant	141	14,132,600
Residential	11,148	2,214,425,400
Commercial	380	272,815,200
Industrial	16	24,341,200
Apartments	57	107,514,300
Farm land	0	0
Farm homestead	0	0

Average Property Value & Tax, 2005
Residential value	$198,639
Property tax	$8,695
FAIR rebate	$587

Public Library
Teaneck Public Library
840 Teaneck Rd
Teaneck, NJ 07666
201-837-4171
Director	Michael McCue

Library statistics, 2004
	Total	per capita
Volumes	108,102	2.75
Expenditure	$2,296,875	$58.50

Public Safety
Police
Chief	Paul Tiernan
Number of officers, 2004	97

Crime, 2004	Number	Rate
Total	822	20.6
Violent	75	1.9
Non-violent	747	18.8
Domestic Viol.	281	NA

Emergency/Fire
Director	John Bauer

Public School District
(for school year 2004-2005 except as noted)

Teaneck School District
1 Merrison St
Teaneck, NJ 07666
201-833-5510
Superintendent	John Czeterko
Grade plan	K-12
Enrollment	4,254.0
Students per teacher	10.5
Per pupil expenditure	$15,326
Median faculty salary	$69,137
Median administrator salary	$105,547
Grade 12 enrollment	294.5
High school graduation rate	94.4%

Assessment test results
(percent scoring at proficient or advanced level)
	Language	Math
Grade 3	81.2%	75.9%
Grade 8	79.1%	61.4%
High school	81.4%	71.3%

SAT
Percent tested	89%
Average SAT math score	494
Average SAT verbal score	481

No Child Left Behind, 2003-04
Attendence rate (target = 90%)	95.1%
Drop rate	2.1%
Highly-qualified teachers	95.9%
District needs improvement?(AYP)	No

Municipal Finance

Fiscal Year 2005
Total tax levy	$115,400,935
County levy	9,086,467
County taxes	8,632,150
County library	0
County health	0
County open space	454,317
School levy	67,837,399
Local muni. budget	38,477,069
Misc. revenues	13,643,566
Total aid	$4,489,188
CMPTRA	1,670,258
Muni. block grant	165,510
Energy tax receipts	2,513,420
Homeland security	140,000

Fiscal Year 2006
Total aid	$4,489,187
CMPTRA	1,582,288
Muni. block grant	165,510
Energy tax receipts	2,601,389
Homeland security	140,000

Taxes
	2003	2004	2005
General tax rate per $100	3.99	4.180	4.380
Net valuation taxable	$2,587,617,759	$2,602,345,852	$2,636,350,451
State equalized value	$3,998,791,159	$4,472,821,418	$5,034,085,261
County equalization ratio	72.48	64.71	58.15

Demographics & Socio-Economic Characteristics
(2000 U.S. Census, except as noted)

Population
1980*	13,552
1990*	13,326
2000	13,806
Male	6,649
Female	7,157
2004 (estimate)*	14,214
Persons per sq. mi. of land	3,082

Race & Hispanic Origin, 2000
Race
White	10,601
Black/African American	132
Amer. Indian/Alaska Natv.	13
Asian	2,634
Natv. Hawaiian/Pac. Islander	3
Other Race	193
Two or more races	230
Hispanic origin, total	642
Mexican	42
Puerto Rican	99
Cuban	98
Other Hispanic	403

Age & Nativity, 2000
Under 5 years	904
18 years and over	9,900
21 years and over	9,561
65 years and over	2,092
85 years and over	294
Median Age	40.9
Native born	9,862
Foreign born	3,944

Educational Attainment, 2000
Population 25 years and over	9,173
0-8 yrs of school	2.5%
High School grad or higher	93.5%
Bachelor's degree or higher	62.1%
Graduate degree	33.4%

Income & Poverty, 1999
Per capita income	$53,170
Median household income	$90,931
Median family income	$111,029
Persons in poverty	718
H'holds receiving public assistance	50
H'holds receiving social security	1,340

Households, 2000
Total households	4,774
With persons under 18	2,154
With persons over 65	1,399
Family households	3,868
One-person households	801
Persons per household	2.86
Persons per family	3.21

Labor & Employment
Total civilian labor force, 2004**	6,788
Unemployment rate	2.4%
Total civilian labor force, 2000	6,559
Unemployment rate	3.6%

Employed persons 16 years and over by occupation, 2000
Managers & professionals	3,690
Service occupations	487
Sales & office occupations	1,650
Farming, fishing & forestry	8
Construction & maintenance	172
Production & transportation	314
Self-employed persons	621

*US Census Bureau
**New Jersey Department of Labor

General Information
Borough of Tenafly
100 Riveredge Rd
Tenafly, NJ 07670
201-568-6100

Web site	www.tenaflynj.org
Land area (sq. miles)	4.61
Water area (sq. miles)	0.58
Type of government	Borough
Form of government	B

Government
Legislative Districts
US Congressional	5
State Legislative	37

Local Officials, 2006
Mayor	Peter S. Rustin
Admin/Manager	Joseph Di Giacomo
Clerk	Nancy Hatten
Finance Dir/Treas	Karen Palermo
Engineer	David Hals
Attorney	William McClure
Tax assessor	Carol Byrne
Tax collector	Lily Tom
Building officer	(Vacant)
Zoning officer	Frank Mottola
Public Works	NA

Housing & Construction
Housing Units, 2000*
Total	4,897
Median rent	$1,186
Median SF home value	$403,600

New Privately Owned Housing Units Authorized by Building Permit
	Units	Value
Total, 2004	89	$15,126,587
Single family	24	$11,906,237
Total, 2005	49	$17,056,655
Single family	35	$15,889,780

Real Property Valuation - parcels, 2005
	Number	Valuation
Total		$2,875,390,900
Vacant	147	23,180,100
Residential	4,243	2,629,588,700
Commercial	179	176,942,200
Industrial	15	15,196,400
Apartments	8	30,483,500
Farm land	0	0
Farm homestead	0	0

Average Property Value & Tax, 2005
Residential value	$619,748
Property tax	$13,313
FAIR rebate	$616

Public Library
Tenafly Public Library
100 River Edge Rd
Tenafly, NJ 07670
201-568-8680

Director .... Stephen Wechtler

Library statistics, 2004
	Total	per capita
Volumes	78,165	5.66
Expenditure	$1,011,799	$73.29

Public Safety
Police
Chief	Michael Bruno
Number of officers, 2004	32

Crime, 2004	Number	Rate
Total	128	9.1
Violent	8	0.6
Non-violent	120	8.5
Domestic Viol.	36	NA

Emergency/Fire
Director .... Richard Philpott

Public School District
(for school year 2004-2005 except as noted)

Tenafly School District
500 Tenafly Rd
Tenafly, NJ 07670
201-816-4501

Superintendent	Morton Sherman
Grade plan	K-12
Enrollment	3,173.0
Students per teacher	10.5
Per pupil expenditure	$13,562
Median faculty salary	$58,678
Median administrator salary	$119,524
Grade 12 enrollment	245.0
High school graduation rate	99.6%

Assessment test results
(percent scoring at proficient or advanced level)
	Language	Math
Grade 3	97.4%	96.2%
Grade 8	91.7%	84.4%
High school	96.9%	94.3%

SAT
Percent tested	98%
Average SAT math score	636
Average SAT verbal score	580

No Child Left Behind, 2003-04
Attendence rate (target = 90%)	96.4%
Drop rate	0%
Highly-qualified teachers	98.6%
District needs improvement?(AYP)	No

Municipal Finance
Fiscal Year 2005
Total tax levy	$61,799,500
County levy	6,169,091
County taxes	5,860,025
County library	0
County health	0
County open space	309,065
School levy	40,115,159
Local muni. budget	15,515,250
Misc. revenues	4,746,056
Total aid	$1,656,793
CMPTRA	418,595
Muni. block grant	58,310
Energy tax receipts	1,109,888
Homeland security	70,000

Fiscal Year 2006
Total aid	$1,656,793
CMPTRA	379,749
Muni. block grant	58,310
Energy tax receipts	1,148,734
Homeland security	70,000

Taxes
	2003	2004	2005
General tax rate per $100	1.91	2.040	2.150
Net valuation taxable	$2,828,649,526	$2,848,105,848	$2,876,948,670
State equalized value	$2,756,162,453	$3,054,144,991	$3,456,209,358
County equalization ratio	116.36	102.63	93.25

Demographics & Socio-Economic Characteristics
(2000 U.S. Census, except as noted)

Population
1980*	19
1990*	22
2000	18
Male	9
Female	9
2004 (estimate)*	18
Persons per sq. mi. of land	16

Race & Hispanic Origin, 2000
Race
White	15
Black/African American	0
Amer. Indian/Alaska Natv.	0
Asian	0
Natv. Hawaiian/Pac. Islander	0
Other Race	0
Two or more races	3
Hispanic origin, total	0
Mexican	0
Puerto Rican	0
Cuban	0
Other Hispanic	0

Age & Nativity, 2000
Under 5 years	3
18 years and over	12
21 years and over	11
65 years and over	1
85 years and over	0
Median Age	33
Native born	16
Foreign born	0

Educational Attainment, 2000
Population 25 years and over	10
0-8 yrs of school	0.0%
High School grad or higher	100.0%
Bachelor's degree or higher	50.0%
Graduate degree	0.0%

Income & Poverty, 1999
Per capita income	$72,613
Median household income	$44,167
Median family income	$43,750
Persons in poverty	0
H'holds receiving public assistance	0
H'holds receiving social security	3

Households, 2000
Total households	7
With persons under 18	3
With persons over 65	1
Family households	5
One-person households	1
Persons per household	2.57
Persons per family	3

Labor & Employment
Total civilian labor force, 2004**	18
Unemployment rate	0.0%
Total civilian labor force, 2000	13
Unemployment rate	0.0%

Employed persons 16 years and over by occupation, 2000
Managers & professionals	3
Service occupations	0
Sales & office occupations	6
Farming, fishing & forestry	0
Construction & maintenance	4
Production & transportation	0
Self-employed persons	0

*US Census Bureau
**New Jersey Department of Labor

General Information
Borough of Teterboro
Municipal Building
510 Route 46 West
Teterboro, NJ 07608
201-288-1200

Web site	NA
Land area (sq. miles)	1.11
Water area (sq. miles)	0
Type of government	Borough
Form of government	CM '23

Government
Legislative Districts
US Congressional	9
State Legislative	38

Local Officials, 2006
Mayor	John Watt
Admin/Manager	Paul Busch
Clerk	Nadine Conn
Finance Dir/Treas	Rosemary McClave
Engineer	Boswell McClave Eng.
Attorney	David Bole
Tax assessor	James Hall
Tax collector	NA
Building officer	Joseph Marra
Zoning officer	NA
Public Works	NA

Housing & Construction
Housing Units, 2000*
Total	8
Median rent	$738
Median SF home value	$-

New Privately Owned Housing Units Authorized by Building Permit
	Units	Value
Total, 2004	0	$0
Single family	0	$0
Total, 2005	0	$0
Single family	0	$0

Real Property Valuation - parcels, 2005
	Number	Valuation
Total		$313,527,500
Vacant	7	930,600
Residential	7	1,080,700
Commercial	6	2,563,400
Industrial	58	307,928,600
Apartments	1	1,024,200
Farm land	0	0
Farm homestead	0	0

Average Property Value & Tax, 2005
Residential value	$154,386
Property tax	$1,532
FAIR rebate	$0

Public Library

No public municipal library.

Library statistics, 2004
	Total	per capita
Volumes	NA	NA
Expenditure	NA	NA

Public Safety
Police
Chief	NA
Number of officers, 2004	0

Crime, 2004	Number	Rate
Total	22	+
Violent	2	+
Non-violent	20	+
Domestic Viol.	2	NA

Emergency/Fire
Director	NA

Public School District
(for school year 2004-2005 except as noted)

Teterboro School District
Municipal Building
Teterboro, NJ 07608
Superintendent	NA
Grade plan	NA
Enrollment	NA
Students per teacher	NA
Per pupil expenditure	NA
Median faculty salary	NA
Median administrator salary	NA
Grade 12 enrollment	NA
High school graduation rate	NA

Assessment test results
(percent scoring at proficient or advanced level)
	Language	Math
Grade 3	NA	NA
Grade 8	NA	NA
High school	NA	NA

SAT
Percent tested	NA
Average SAT math score	NA
Average SAT verbal score	NA

No Child Left Behind, 2003-04
Attendence rate (target = 90%)	NA
Drop rate	NA
Highly-qualified teachers	NA
District needs improvement?(AYP)	NA

Municipal Finance
Fiscal Year 2005
Total tax levy	$3,123,938
County levy	580,269
County taxes	551,261
County library	0
County health	0
County open space	29,009
School levy	247,973
Local muni. budget	2,295,695
Misc. revenues	1,978,011
Total aid	$259,201
CMPTRA	132,939
Muni. block grant	96
Energy tax receipts	101,166
Homeland security	25,000

Fiscal Year 2006
Total aid	$259,201
CMPTRA	129,398
Muni. block grant	96
Energy tax receipts	104,707
Homeland security	25,000

Taxes
	2003	2004	2005
General tax rate per $100	1.36	0.960	1.000
Net valuation taxable	$232,017,995	$314,977,627	$314,726,170
State equalized value	$222,260,748	$278,612,566	$337,363,244
County equalization ratio	101.54	141.94	113.11

Demographics & Socio-Economic Characteristics
(2000 U.S. Census, except as noted)

Population
1980*	4,094
1990*	4,803
2000	5,541
Male	2,729
Female	2,812
2004 (estimate)*	5,998
Persons per sq. mi. of land	190

Race & Hispanic Origin, 2000
Race
White	5,365
Black/African American	29
Amer. Indian/Alaska Natv.	0
Asian	104
Natv. Hawaiian/Pac. Islander	0
Other Race	15
Two or more races	28
Hispanic origin, total	85
Mexican	8
Puerto Rican	16
Cuban	15
Other Hispanic	46

Age & Nativity, 2000
Under 5 years	373
18 years and over	4,091
21 years and over	3,989
65 years and over	623
85 years and over	43
Median Age	42.6
Native born	5,268
Foreign born	273

Educational Attainment, 2000
Population 25 years and over	3,886
0-8 yrs of school	1.7%
High School grad or higher	95.7%
Bachelor's degree or higher	58.9%
Graduate degree	25.6%

Income & Poverty, 1999
Per capita income	$65,470
Median household income	$135,649
Median family income	$150,189
Persons in poverty	152
H'holds receiving public assistance	0
H'holds receiving social security	441

Households, 2000
Total households	1,986
With persons under 18	747
With persons over 65	441
Family households	1,663
One-person households	249
Persons per household	2.79
Persons per family	3.05

Labor & Employment
Total civilian labor force, 2004**	2,958
Unemployment rate	3.3%
Total civilian labor force, 2000	2,814
Unemployment rate	1.8%

Employed persons 16 years and over by occupation, 2000
Managers & professionals	1,814
Service occupations	193
Sales & office occupations	559
Farming, fishing & forestry	28
Construction & maintenance	98
Production & transportation	71
Self-employed persons	382

*US Census Bureau
**New Jersey Department of Labor

General Information
Township of Tewksbury
169 Old Turnpike Rd
Califon, NJ 07830
908-439-0022
Web site	www.tewksburytwp.net
Land area (sq. miles)	31.63
Water area (sq. miles)	0.02
Type of government	Township
Form of government	TC

Government

Legislative Districts
US Congressional	7
State Legislative	24

Local Officials, 2006
Mayor	William J. Voyce
Admin/Manager	Jesse Landon
Clerk	Roberta Brassard
Finance Dir/Treas	Judie McGrorey
Engineer	Andrew Holt
Attorney	Judy Kopen
Tax assessor	Mark Whitt
Tax collector	NA
Building officer	Charles Rogers
Zoning officer	Randall Benson
Public Works	NA

Housing & Construction

Housing Units, 2000*
Total	2,052
Median rent	$1,388
Median SF home value	$461,200

New Privately Owned Housing Units
Authorized by Building Permit
	Units	Value
Total, 2004	37	$7,987,359
Single family	37	$7,987,359
Total, 2005	31	$9,645,583
Single family	21	$9,246,583

Real Property Valuation - parcels, 2005
	Number	Valuation
Total		$1,296,952,700
Vacant	182	20,666,000
Residential	1,890	1,007,121,600
Commercial	40	58,315,200
Industrial	1	2,862,100
Apartments	0	0
Farm land	331	204,405,100
Farm homestead	554	3,582,700

Average Property Value & Tax, 2005
Residential value	$413,545
Property tax	$9,068
FAIR rebate	$574

Public Library
Tewksbury Township Library
31 Old Turnpike Rd
Oldwick, NJ 08858
908-439-3761
Director	Judie Garey

Library statistics, 2004
	Total	per capita
Volumes	21,343	3.85
Expenditure	$72,601	$13.10

Public Safety

Police
Chief	Russel O'Dell
Number of officers, 2004	11

Crime, 2004	Number	Rate
Total	33	5.6
Violent	0	0
Non-violent	33	5.6
Domestic Viol.	18	NA

Emergency/Fire
Director	Jeff Hayes

Public School District
(for school year 2004-2005 except as noted)

Tewksbury Township School District
173 Old Turnpike Rd
Califon, NJ 07830
908-439-2010
Superintendent	Gayle Carrick
Grade plan	K-8
Enrollment	719.0
Students per teacher	10.0
Per pupil expenditure	$14,000
Median faculty salary	$49,380
Median administrator salary	$101,968
Grade 12 enrollment	NA
High school graduation rate	NA

Assessment test results
(percent scoring at proficient or advanced level)
	Language	Math
Grade 3	97.4%	98.7%
Grade 8	93.4%	90.8%
High school	NA	NA

SAT
Percent tested	NA
Average SAT math score	NA
Average SAT verbal score	NA

No Child Left Behind, 2003-04
Attendence rate (target = 90%)	96.1%
Drop rate	NA
Highly-qualified teachers	97.8%
District needs improvement?(AYP)	No

Municipal Finance

Fiscal Year 2005
Total tax levy	$28,491,696
County levy	6,154,549
County taxes	5,225,577
County library	437,243
County health	0
County open space	491,729
School levy	17,643,210
Local muni. budget	4,693,937
Misc. revenues	5,263,843
Total aid	$808,587
CMPTRA	212,338
Muni. block grant	21,726
Energy tax receipts	524,523
Homeland security	50,000

Fiscal Year 2006
Total aid	$808,587
CMPTRA	193,980
Muni. block grant	21,726
Energy tax receipts	542,881
Homeland security	50,000

Taxes
	2003	2004	2005
General tax rate per $100	1.96	2.100	2.200
Net valuation taxable	$1,229,489,930	$1,267,521,498	$1,299,362,841
State equalized value	$1,352,276,650	$1,484,650,978	$1,650,823,073
County equalization ratio	92.86	89.21	79.58

Demographics & Socio-Economic Characteristics
(2000 U.S. Census, except as noted)

Population
1980*	7,740
1990*	12,361
2000	15,053
Male	7,157
Female	7,896
2004 (estimate)*	16,206
Persons per sq. mi. of land	1,040

Race & Hispanic Origin, 2000
Race
White	11,862
Black/African American	1,963
Amer. Indian/Alaska Natv.	36
Asian	747
Natv. Hawaiian/Pac. Islander	2
Other Race	157
Two or more races	286
Hispanic origin, total	707
Mexican	122
Puerto Rican	305
Cuban	49
Other Hispanic	231

Age & Nativity, 2000
Under 5 years	1,184
18 years and over	11,215
21 years and over	10,908
65 years and over	1,633
85 years and over	203
Median Age	36.8
Native born	13,557
Foreign born	1,498

Educational Attainment, 2000
Population 25 years and over	10,457
0-8 yrs of school	1.9%
High School grad or higher	92.7%
Bachelor's degree or higher	42.3%
Graduate degree	14.5%

Income & Poverty, 1999
Per capita income	$31,520
Median household income	$68,697
Median family income	$79,773
Persons in poverty	577
H'holds receiving public assistance	61
H'holds receiving social security	1,173

Households, 2000
Total households	5,883
With persons under 18	2,145
With persons over 65	1,122
Family households	3,977
One-person households	1,602
Persons per household	2.51
Persons per family	3.11

Labor & Employment
Total civilian labor force, 2004**	7,534
Unemployment rate	3.2%
Total civilian labor force, 2000	8,088
Unemployment rate	4.1%

Employed persons 16 years and over by occupation, 2000
Managers & professionals	3,570
Service occupations	869
Sales & office occupations	2,396
Farming, fishing & forestry	22
Construction & maintenance	376
Production & transportation	524
Self-employed persons	386

*US Census Bureau
**New Jersey Department of Labor

General Information
Borough of Tinton Falls
556 Tinton Ave
Tinton Falls, NJ 07724
732-542-3400
Web site	www.tintonfalls.com
Land area (sq. miles)	15.59
Water area (sq. miles)	0.03
Type of government	Borough
Form of government	MC '50

Government

Legislative Districts
US Congressional	12
State Legislative	12

Local Officials, 2006
Mayor	Peter Maclearie
Admin/Manager	W. Bryan Dempsey
Clerk	Karen Mount-Taylor
Finance Dir/Treas	Stephen Pfeffer
Engineer	Birdsall Engineering
Attorney	James E. Berube Jr.
Tax assessor	Scott Imbriaco
Tax collector	Carol Hussey
Building officer	Robert Corby
Zoning officer	Lori Paone
Public Works	John Bucciero

Housing & Construction

Housing Units, 2000*
Total	6,211
Median rent	$1,198
Median SF home value	$187,900

New Privately Owned Housing Units
Authorized by Building Permit
	Units	Value
Total, 2004	63	$5,747,370
Single family	63	$5,747,370
Total, 2005	67	$7,859,654
Single family	39	$5,680,836

Real Property Valuation - parcels, 2005
	Number	Valuation
Total		$1,243,428,447
Vacant	942	36,489,704
Residential	5,903	897,285,943
Commercial	148	190,298,500
Industrial	16	16,401,300
Apartments	3	99,635,200
Farm land	19	3,108,800
Farm homestead	37	209,000

Average Property Value & Tax, 2005
Residential value	$151,093
Property tax	$5,161
FAIR rebate	$580

Public Library
Tinton Falls Public Library
664 Tinton Ave
Tinton Falls, NJ 07724
732-542-3110
Director	Rosemary Tunnicliffe

Library statistics, 2004
	Total	per capita
Volumes	37,705	2.50
Expenditure	$120,800	$8.02

Public Safety

Police
Chief	Gerald M. Turning Sr.
Number of officers, 2004	40

Crime, 2004	Number	Rate
Total	289	18.1
Violent	14	0.9
Non-violent	275	17.2
Domestic Viol.	101	NA

Emergency/Fire
Director	NA

Public School District
(for school year 2004-2005 except as noted)

Tinton Falls School District
658 Tinton Ave
Tinton Falls, NJ 07724
732-460-2404
Superintendent	Leonard Kelpsh
Grade plan	K-8
Enrollment	1,768.0
Students per teacher	12.8
Per pupil expenditure	$12,937
Median faculty salary	$51,588
Median administrator salary	$94,262
Grade 12 enrollment	NA
High school graduation rate	NA

Assessment test results
(percent scoring at proficient or advanced level)
	Language	Math
Grade 3	92.7%	90.3%
Grade 8	81.7%	77.5%
High school	NA	NA

SAT
Percent tested	NA
Average SAT math score	NA
Average SAT verbal score	NA

No Child Left Behind, 2003-04
Attendence rate (target = 90%)	95.6%
Drop rate	NA
Highly-qualified teachers	98.1%
District needs improvement?(AYP)	No

Municipal Finance

Fiscal Year 2005
Total tax levy	$42,538,082
County levy	7,468,642
County taxes	6,701,808
County library	369,185
County health	0
County open space	397,648
School levy	27,459,445
Local muni. budget	7,609,996
Misc. revenues	11,177,235
Total aid	$2,057,377
CMPTRA	555,519
Muni. block grant	59,023
Energy tax receipts	1,372,835
Homeland security	70,000

Fiscal Year 2006
Total aid	$2,057,376
CMPTRA	507,469
Muni. block grant	59,023
Energy tax receipts	1,420,884
Homeland security	70,000

Taxes
	2003	2004	2005
General tax rate per $100	3.21	3.413	3.416
Net valuation taxable	$1,140,791,925	$1,189,589,422	$1,245,289,313
State equalized value	$1,765,658,451	$2,134,674,218	$2,503,597,332
County equalization ratio	74.02	64.61	55.68

Demographics & Socio-Economic Characteristics
(2000 U.S. Census, except as noted)

Population
1980*	11,448
1990*	10,177
2000	9,892
Male	4,672
Female	5,220
2004 (estimate)*	10,360
Persons per sq. mi. of land	2,592

Race & Hispanic Origin, 2000
Race
White	9,239
Black/African American	111
Amer. Indian/Alaska Natv.	2
Asian	224
Natv. Hawaiian/Pac. Islander	0
Other Race	195
Two or more races	121
Hispanic origin, total	630
Mexican	5
Puerto Rican	253
Cuban	30
Other Hispanic	342

Age & Nativity, 2000
Under 5 years	444
18 years and over	8,085
21 years and over	7,808
65 years and over	2,113
85 years and over	257
Median Age	42.7
Native born	8,533
Foreign born	1,313

Educational Attainment, 2000
Population 25 years and over	7,402
0-8 yrs of school	11.9%
High School grad or higher	74.7%
Bachelor's degree or higher	17.8%
Graduate degree	4.1%

Income & Poverty, 1999
Per capita income	$26,561
Median household income	$60,408
Median family income	$69,354
Persons in poverty	398
H'holds receiving public assistance	0
H'holds receiving social security	1,369

Households, 2000
Total households	3,539
With persons under 18	1,028
With persons over 65	1,385
Family households	2,645
One-person households	770
Persons per household	2.63
Persons per family	3.09

Labor & Employment
Total civilian labor force, 2004**	5,244
Unemployment rate	3.2%
Total civilian labor force, 2000	5,129
Unemployment rate	3.5%

Employed persons 16 years and over by occupation, 2000
Managers & professionals	1,330
Service occupations	702
Sales & office occupations	1,544
Farming, fishing & forestry	0
Construction & maintenance	539
Production & transportation	832
Self-employed persons	188

*US Census Bureau
**New Jersey Department of Labor

General Information
Borough of Totowa
537 Totowa Rd
Totowa, NJ 07512
973-956-1000

Web site	NA
Land area (sq. miles)	4.00
Water area (sq. miles)	0.05
Type of government	Borough
Form of government	B

Government

Legislative Districts
US Congressional	8
State Legislative	35

Local Officials, 2006
Mayor	John Coiro
Admin/Manager	NA
Clerk	Joseph Wassel
Finance Dir/Treas	J. Iandiorio/J. Ten Hoeve
Engineer	Alaimo Group
Attorney	Kristin M. Corrado
Tax assessor	Curt Masklee
Tax collector	NA
Building officer	Allan Burghardt
Zoning officer	NA
Public Works	NA

Housing & Construction

Housing Units, 2000*
Total	3,630
Median rent	$935
Median SF home value	$197,500

New Privately Owned Housing Units
Authorized by Building Permit
	Units	Value
Total, 2004	118	$17,306,193
Single family	118	$17,306,193
Total, 2005	47	$7,399,321
Single family	47	$7,399,321

Real Property Valuation - parcels, 2005
	Number	Valuation
Total		$1,175,241,100
Vacant	119	12,624,100
Residential	3,383	634,068,400
Commercial	223	321,028,500
Industrial	66	206,968,800
Apartments	0	0
Farm land	1	550,800
Farm homestead	1	500

Average Property Value & Tax, 2005
Residential value	$187,373
Property tax	$5,776
FAIR rebate	$685

Public Library
Dwight D Eisenhower Library
537 Totowa Rd
Totowa, NJ 07512
973-790-3265

Director	Joan Krautheim

Library statistics, 2004
	Total	per capita
Volumes	46,978	4.75
Expenditure	$505,971	$51.15

Public Safety

Police
Chief	Robert Coyle
Number of officers, 2004	28

Crime, 2004	Number	Rate
Total	327	32.6
Violent	11	1.1
Non-violent	316	31.5
Domestic Viol.	15	NA

Emergency/Fire
Director	Larry Sperling

Public School District
(for school year 2004-2005 except as noted)

Totowa School District
10 Crews St
Totowa, NJ 07512
973-956-0010

Administrator	Vincent Varcadipane
Grade plan	K-8
Enrollment	902.0
Students per teacher	10.8
Per pupil expenditure	$11,576
Median faculty salary	$58,088
Median administrator salary	$101,493
Grade 12 enrollment	NA
High school graduation rate	NA

Assessment test results
(percent scoring at proficient or advanced level)
	Language	Math
Grade 3	88.5%	87.6%
Grade 8	89.4%	71.2%
High school	NA	NA

SAT
Percent tested	NA
Average SAT math score	NA
Average SAT verbal score	NA

No Child Left Behind, 2003-04
Attendence rate (target = 90%)	96.6%
Drop rate	NA
Highly-qualified teachers	93.2%
District needs improvement?(AYP)	No

Municipal Finance

Fiscal Year 2005
Total tax levy	$36,278,789
County levy	10,405,091
County taxes	10,206,642
County library	0
County health	0
County open space	198,449
School levy	17,659,743
Local muni. budget	8,213,955
Misc. revenues	4,870,109
Total aid	$1,849,962
CMPTRA	580,188
Muni. block grant	44,531
Energy tax receipts	1,155,243
Homeland security	70,000

Fiscal Year 2006
Total aid	$1,849,962
CMPTRA	539,754
Muni. block grant	44,531
Energy tax receipts	1,195,677
Homeland security	70,000

Taxes
	2003	2004	2005
General tax rate per $100	2.71	2.910	3.090
Net valuation taxable	$1,107,246,027	$1,142,650,091	$1,176,878,670
State equalized value	$1,592,472,353	$1,913,344,191	$2,100,069,004
County equalization ratio	82.88	69.53	59.68

Demographics & Socio-Economic Characteristics
(2000 U.S. Census, except as noted)

Population
1980*	92,124
1990*	88,675
2000	85,403
Male	42,180
Female	43,223
2004 (estimate)*	85,379
Persons per sq. mi. of land	11,150

Race & Hispanic Origin, 2000
Race
White	27,802
Black/African American	44,465
Amer. Indian/Alaska Natv.	300
Asian	716
Natv. Hawaiian/Pac. Islander	199
Other Race	9,190
Two or more races	2,731
Hispanic origin, total	18,391
Mexican	925
Puerto Rican	8,952
Cuban	200
Other Hispanic	8,314

Age & Nativity, 2000
Under 5 years	6,468
18 years and over	61,757
21 years and over	58,165
65 years and over	9,716
85 years and over	1,201
Median Age	32.2
Native born	73,234
Foreign born	12,024

Educational Attainment, 2000
Population 25 years and over	53,021
0-8 yrs of school	12.2%
High School grad or higher	62.4%
Bachelor's degree or higher	9.2%
Graduate degree	3.5%

Income & Poverty, 1999
Per capita income	$14,621
Median household income	$31,074
Median family income	$36,681
Persons in poverty	17,222
H'holds receiving public assistance	2,255
H'holds receiving social security	7,836

Households, 2000
Total households	29,437
With persons under 18	11,659
With persons over 65	7,490
Family households	18,695
One-person households	8,756
Persons per household	2.75
Persons per family	3.38

Labor & Employment
Total civilian labor force, 2004**	44,959
Unemployment rate	9.0%
Total civilian labor force, 2000	36,283
Unemployment rate	10.5%

Employed persons 16 years and over by occupation, 2000
Managers & professionals	6,980
Service occupations	8,390
Sales & office occupations	8,973
Farming, fishing & forestry	99
Construction & maintenance	2,731
Production & transportation	5,297
Self-employed persons	936

*US Census Bureau
**New Jersey Department of Labor

General Information
City of Trenton
319 East State St
Trenton, NJ 08608
609-989-3185
Web site	www.ci.trenton.nj.us
Land area (sq. miles)	7.66
Water area (sq. miles)	0.49
Type of government	City
Form of government	MC '50

Government

Legislative Districts
US Congressional	4
State Legislative	15

Local Officials, 2006
Mayor	Douglas H. Palmer
Admin/Manager	Jane Feigenbaum
Clerk	Anthony J. Conti
Finance Dir/Treas	Chris Stankiewicz
Engineer	Frank Chiacchio
Attorney	R. Denise Lyles
Tax assessor	Patricia Hice
Tax collector	NA
Building officer	Leonard Pucciatti
Zoning officer	NA
Public Works	NA

Housing & Construction

Housing Units, 2000*
Total	33,843
Median rent	$604
Median SF home value	$65,500

New Privately Owned Housing Units Authorized by Building Permit
	Units	Value
Total, 2004	5	$71,500
Single family	5	$71,500
Total, 2005	7	$988,400
Single family	7	$988,400

Real Property Valuation - parcels, 2005
	Number	Valuation
Total		$1,900,273,595
Vacant	1,184	21,986,110
Residential	20,918	1,295,070,360
Commercial	2,140	496,337,825
Industrial	91	43,270,700
Apartments	161	43,608,600
Farm land	0	0
Farm homestead	0	0

Average Property Value & Tax, 2005
Residential value	$61,912
Property tax	$2,512
FAIR rebate	$646

Public Library
Trenton Public Library
120 Academy St
Trenton, NJ 08608
609-392-7188
Director.............Irene Percelli (Actg)

Library statistics, 2004
	Total	per capita
Volumes	407,649	4.77
Expenditure	$3,545,936	$41.52

Public Safety

Police
Chief	Joseph Santiago
Number of officers, 2004	356

Crime, 2004	Number	Rate
Total	5,324	62.4
Violent	1,364	16
Non-violent	3,960	46.4
Domestic Viol.	1,820	NA

Emergency/Fire
Director.............Dennis Keenan Jr.

Public School District
(for school year 2004-2005 except as noted)

Trenton School District
108 N Clinton Ave
Trenton, NJ 08609
609-656-4900
Superintendent	James Lytle
Grade plan	K-12
Enrollment	12,216.0
Students per teacher	10.6
Per pupil expenditure	$14,483
Median faculty salary	$66,790
Median administrator salary	$98,875
Grade 12 enrollment	546.0
High school graduation rate	NA

Assessment test results
(percent scoring at proficient or advanced level)
	Language	Math
Grade 3	62.8%	58.3%
Grade 8	23.6%	12.7%
High school	51.5%	30.5%

SAT
Percent tested	NA
Average SAT math score	NA
Average SAT verbal score	NA

No Child Left Behind, 2003-04
Attendence rate (target = 90%)	91.0%
Drop rate	5.4%
Highly-qualified teachers?	38.5%
District needs improvement?(AYP)	Yes

Municipal Finance

Fiscal Year 2005
Total tax levy	$77,857,900
County levy	11,900,871
County taxes	11,267,875
County library	0
County health	0
County open space	632,997
School levy	23,250,114
Local muni. budget	42,706,915
Misc. revenues	123,037,571
Total aid	$53,195,061
CMPTRA	48,020,685
Muni. block grant	388,012
Energy tax receipts	4,645,659
Homeland security	140,000

Fiscal Year 2006
Total aid	$53,195,062
CMPTRA	47,858,087
Muni. block grant	388,012
Energy tax receipts	4,808,258
Homeland security	140,000

Taxes
	2003	2004	2005
General tax rate per $100	3.98	4.020	4.060
Net valuation taxable	$1,883,665,278	$1,899,865,910	$1,918,990,947
State equalized value	$1,949,156,952	$2,007,411,884	$2,333,119,692
County equalization ratio	99.4	96.64	94.59

Demographics & Socio-Economic Characteristics
(2000 U.S. Census, except as noted)

Population
1980*	2,472
1990*	3,048
2000	3,517
Male	1,749
Female	1,768
2004 (estimate)*	3,600
Persons per sq. mi. of land	984

Race & Hispanic Origin, 2000
Race
White	3,408
Black/African American	14
Amer. Indian/Alaska Natv.	10
Asian	19
Natv. Hawaiian/Pac. Islander	0
Other Race	19
Two or more races	47
Hispanic origin, total	109
Mexican	55
Puerto Rican	32
Cuban	4
Other Hispanic	18

Age & Nativity, 2000
Under 5 years	209
18 years and over	2,708
21 years and over	2,579
65 years and over	591
85 years and over	62
Median Age	39.2
Native born	3,349
Foreign born	94

Educational Attainment, 2000
Population 25 years and over	2,408
0-8 yrs of school	4.4%
High School grad or higher	84.6%
Bachelor's degree or higher	13.5%
Graduate degree	4.3%

Income & Poverty, 1999
Per capita income	$20,118
Median household income	$40,042
Median family income	$49,528
Persons in poverty	273
H'holds receiving public assistance	30
H'holds receiving social security	569

Households, 2000
Total households	1,477
With persons under 18	441
With persons over 65	452
Family households	921
One-person households	467
Persons per household	2.38
Persons per family	3.02

Labor & Employment
Total civilian labor force, 2004**	1,857
Unemployment rate	6.3%
Total civilian labor force, 2000	1,634
Unemployment rate	6.3%

Employed persons 16 years and over by occupation, 2000
Managers & professionals	435
Service occupations	256
Sales & office occupations	420
Farming, fishing & forestry	15
Construction & maintenance	236
Production & transportation	169
Self-employed persons	83

*US Census Bureau
**New Jersey Department of Labor

General Information
Borough of Tuckerton
140 E Main St
Tuckerton, NJ 08087
609-296-2701
Web site	tuckertonborough.com
Land area (sq. miles)	3.66
Water area (sq. miles)	0.12
Type of government	Borough
Form of government	B

Government

Legislative Districts
US Congressional	3
State Legislative	9

Local Officials, 2006
Mayor	Kevin Quinlan
Admin/Manager	NA
Clerk	Grace Di Elmo
Finance Dir/Treas	Laura Giovene
Engineer	John Hess
Attorney	Christopher Connors
Tax assessor	Fredrick Millman
Tax collector	E. J. Mary King
Building officer	Phil Read
Zoning officer	Al Revy
Public Works	Carl R. Hewitt Jr.

Housing & Construction

Housing Units, 2000*
Total	1,971
Median rent	$747
Median SF home value	$105,900

New Privately Owned Housing Units
Authorized by Building Permit
	Units	Value
Total, 2004	112	$5,552,067
Single family	112	$5,552,067
Total, 2005	35	$3,168,824
Single family	14	$1,968,823

Real Property Valuation - parcels, 2005
	Number	Valuation
Total		$405,554,600
Vacant	211	24,011,200
Residential	1,559	335,205,000
Commercial	94	37,989,400
Industrial	0	0
Apartments	2	8,349,000
Farm land	0	0
Farm homestead	0	0

Average Property Value & Tax, 2005
Residential value	$215,013
Property tax	$3,636
FAIR rebate	$901

Public Library
Tuckerton Branch Library†
380 Bay Ave
Tuckerton, NJ 08087
609-296-1470
Branch Librarian	Rita Oakes

Library statistics, 2004
	Total	per capita
Volumes	NA	NA
Expenditure	NA	NA

†Branch of County Library

Public Safety
Police
Chief	Charles Robinson
Number of officers, 2004	10

Crime, 2004	Number	Rate
Total	69	19.1
Violent	4	1.1
Non-violent	65	18
Domestic Viol.	30	NA

Emergency/Fire
Director	Tom McAndrew

Public School District
(for school year 2004-2005 except as noted)

Tuckerton Borough School District
Marine St
Tuckerton, NJ 08087
609-294-2681
Administrator	Robert Gray Jr.
Grade plan	K-6
Enrollment	299.0
Students per teacher	9.3
Per pupil expenditure	$9,705
Median faculty salary	$38,017
Median administrator salary	$60,603
Grade 12 enrollment	NA
High school graduation rate	NA

Assessment test results
(percent scoring at proficient or advanced level)
	Language	Math
Grade 3	97.7%	95.4%
Grade 8	NA	NA
High school	NA	NA

SAT
Percent tested	NA
Average SAT math score	NA
Average SAT verbal score	NA

No Child Left Behind, 2003-04
Attendence rate (target = 90%)	94.0%
Drop rate	NA
Highly-qualified teachers	100%
District needs improvement?(AYP)	No

Municipal Finance
Fiscal Year 2005
Total tax levy	$6,871,649
County levy	1,262,771
County taxes	1,063,914
County library	111,777
County health	47,379
County open space	39,702
School levy	3,857,800
Local muni. budget	1,751,077
Misc. revenues	1,987,356
Total aid	$476,186
CMPTRA	136,766
Muni. block grant	13,790
Energy tax receipts	300,630
Homeland security	25,000

Fiscal Year 2006
Total aid	$476,186
CMPTRA	126,244
Muni. block grant	13,790
Energy tax receipts	311,152
Homeland security	25,000

Taxes
	2003	2004	2005
General tax rate per $100	3.53	3.638	1.692
Net valuation taxable	$169,344,003	$171,890,664	$406,327,209
State equalized value	$264,063,625	$326,294,902	$421,108,103
County equalization ratio	82.02	64.13	123.36

Demographics & Socio-Economic Characteristics
(2000 U.S. Census, except as noted)

Population
1980*	6,354
1990*	6,156
2000	6,649
Male	3,358
Female	3,291
2004 (estimate)*	6,750
Persons per sq. mi. of land	3,599

Race & Hispanic Origin, 2000
Race
White	6,280
Black/African American	58
Amer. Indian/Alaska Natv.	13
Asian	82
Natv. Hawaiian/Pac. Islander	0
Other Race	90
Two or more races	126
Hispanic origin, total	538
Mexican	77
Puerto Rican	318
Cuban	49
Other Hispanic	94

Age & Nativity, 2000
Under 5 years	483
18 years and over	4,713
21 years and over	4,454
65 years and over	498
85 years and over	32
Median Age	34.4
Native born	6,310
Foreign born	339

Educational Attainment, 2000
Population 25 years and over	4,167
0-8 yrs of school	4.8%
High School grad or higher	79.0%
Bachelor's degree or higher	8.5%
Graduate degree	2.0%

Income & Poverty, 1999
Per capita income	$20,973
Median household income	$59,946
Median family income	$65,179
Persons in poverty	319
H'holds receiving public assistance	24
H'holds receiving social security	552

Households, 2000
Total households	2,143
With persons under 18	1,038
With persons over 65	388
Family households	1,722
One-person households	332
Persons per household	3.09
Persons per family	3.44

Labor & Employment
Total civilian labor force, 2004**	3,572
Unemployment rate	6.1%
Total civilian labor force, 2000	3,418
Unemployment rate	5.5%

Employed persons 16 years and over by occupation, 2000
Managers & professionals	737
Service occupations	458
Sales & office occupations	948
Farming, fishing & forestry	0
Construction & maintenance	530
Production & transportation	557
Self-employed persons	89

*US Census Bureau
**New Jersey Department of Labor

General Information
Borough of Union Beach
650 Poole Ave
Union Beach, NJ 07735
732-264-2277
Web site	www.unionbeach.net
Land area (sq. miles)	1.88
Water area (sq. miles)	0.06
Type of government	Borough
Form of government	B

Government

Legislative Districts
US Congressional	6
State Legislative	13

Local Officials, 2006
Mayor	Richard Ellison
Admin/Manager	NA
Clerk	Mary Sabik
Finance Dir/Treas	Joseph Faccone
Engineer	Edward Broberg
Attorney	Robert McLeod
Tax assessor	Judy Cannon
Tax collector	NA
Building officer	Paul Reinhold
Zoning officer	NA
Public Works	NA

Housing & Construction

Housing Units, 2000*
Total	2,229
Median rent	$1,002
Median SF home value	$132,800

New Privately Owned Housing Units
Authorized by Building Permit
	Units	Value
Total, 2004	14	$1,061,876
Single family	6	$501,876
Total, 2005	7	$580,279
Single family	7	$580,279

Real Property Valuation - parcels, 2005
	Number	Valuation
Total		$440,487,600
Vacant	126	7,986,200
Residential	2,129	373,686,200
Commercial	56	14,195,800
Industrial	5	44,428,600
Apartments	1	190,800
Farm land	0	0
Farm homestead	0	0

Average Property Value & Tax, 2005
Residential value	$175,522
Property tax	$4,391
FAIR rebate	$533

Public Library
Union Beach Mem. Library
810 Union Ave
Union Beach, NJ 07735
732-264-3792
Director	NA

Library statistics, 2004
	Total	per capita
Volumes	NA	NA
Expenditure	NA	NA

Public Safety

Police
Chief	Michael Kelly
Number of officers, 2004	15

Crime, 2004	Number	Rate
Total	101	15
Violent	14	2.1
Non-violent	87	12.9
Domestic Viol.	65	NA

Emergency/Fire
Director	Jerry Ortiz

Public School District
(for school year 2004-2005 except as noted)

Union Beach Borough School District
1207 Florance Ave
Union Beach, NJ 07735
732-264-5405
Superintendent	Arthur Waltz
Grade plan	K-12
Enrollment	915.0
Students per teacher	12.4
Per pupil expenditure	$10,616
Median faculty salary	$46,470
Median administrator salary	$80,000
Grade 12 enrollment	NA
High school graduation rate	NA

Assessment test results
(percent scoring at proficient or advanced level)
	Language	Math
Grade 3	78.3%	79.8%
Grade 8	67.0%	61.7%
High school	NA	NA

SAT
Percent tested	NA
Average SAT math score	NA
Average SAT verbal score	NA

No Child Left Behind, 2003-04
Attendence rate (target = 90%)	93.1%
Drop rate	NA
Highly-qualified teachers	95.5%
District needs improvement?(AYP)	No

Municipal Finance

Fiscal Year 2005
Total tax levy	$11,032,587
County levy	1,692,444
County taxes	1,494,414
County library	82,251
County health	27,772
County open space	88,007
School levy	5,629,888
Local muni. budget	3,710,255
Misc. revenues	2,753,947
Total aid	$962,563
CMPTRA	371,826
Muni. block grant	26,937
Energy tax receipts	513,800
Homeland security	50,000

Fiscal Year 2006
Total aid	$962,563
CMPTRA	353,843
Muni. block grant	26,937
Energy tax receipts	531,783
Homeland security	50,000

Taxes
	2003	2004	2005
General tax rate per $100	2.37	2.455	2.502
Net valuation taxable	$439,187,258	$439,099,778	$440,980,606
State equalized value	$407,863,353	$476,820,481	$553,508,982
County equalization ratio	82.63	107.68	92.08

Demographics & Socio-Economic Characteristics
(2000 U.S. Census, except as noted)

Population
1980*	55,593
1990*	58,012
2000	67,088
Male	33,639
Female	33,449
2004 (estimate)*	66,167
Persons per sq. mi. of land	52,251

Race & Hispanic Origin, 2000
Race
White	39,167
Black/African American	2,442
Amer. Indian/Alaska Natv.	467
Asian	1,441
Natv. Hawaiian/Pac. Islander	54
Other Race	18,911
Two or more races	4,606
Hispanic origin, total	55,226
Mexican	2,752
Puerto Rican	7,388
Cuban	10,296
Other Hispanic	34,790

Age & Nativity, 2000
Under 5 years	4,945
18 years and over	50,117
21 years and over	47,197
65 years and over	6,694
85 years and over	739
Median Age	32.5
Native born	27,710
Foreign born	39,378

Educational Attainment, 2000
Population 25 years and over	42,677
0-8 yrs of school	24.9%
High School grad or higher	54.4%
Bachelor's degree or higher	12.5%
Graduate degree	5.4%

Income & Poverty, 1999
Per capita income	$13,997
Median household income	$30,642
Median family income	$32,246
Persons in poverty	14,244
H'holds receiving public assistance	1,495
H'holds receiving social security	4,894

Households, 2000
Total households	22,872
With persons under 18	9,473
With persons over 65	5,097
Family households	16,067
One-person households	5,259
Persons per household	2.92
Persons per family	3.4

Labor & Employment
Total civilian labor force, 2004**	31,150
Unemployment rate	7.4%
Total civilian labor force, 2000	29,551
Unemployment rate	12.4%

Employed persons 16 years and over by occupation, 2000
Managers & professionals	4,436
Service occupations	4,969
Sales & office occupations	6,315
Farming, fishing & forestry	35
Construction & maintenance	2,038
Production & transportation	8,081
Self-employed persons	1,029

*US Census Bureau
**New Jersey Department of Labor

General Information
City of Union
3715 Palisade Ave
Union, NJ 07087
201-348-5755

Web site	www.ucnj.com
Land area (sq. miles)	1.27
Water area (sq. miles)	0
Type of government	City
Form of government	Comm.

Government

Legislative Districts
US Congressional	13
State Legislative	33

Local Officials, 2006
Mayor	Brian P. Stack
Admin/Manager	NA
Clerk	Michael Licameli
Finance Dir/Treas	Douglas Gutch
Engineer	Schoor Depalma
Attorney	Donald Scarinci
Tax assessor	Salvatore Bonaccorsi
Tax collector	NA
Building officer	Martin Martinetti
Zoning officer	NA
Public Works	NA

Housing & Construction

Housing Units, 2000*
Total	23,741
Median rent	$658
Median SF home value	$141,000

New Privately Owned Housing Units Authorized by Building Permit
	Units	Value
Total, 2004	97	$6,453,200
Single family	8	$870,500
Total, 2005	71	$6,693,800
Single family	0	$0

Real Property Valuation - parcels, 2005
	Number	Valuation
Total		$1,406,255,850
Vacant	209	20,588,300
Residential	4,925	647,442,650
Commercial	1,372	431,228,300
Industrial	110	38,633,400
Apartments	709	268,363,200
Farm land	0	0
Farm homestead	0	0

Average Property Value & Tax, 2005
Residential value	$131,460
Property tax	$5,509
FAIR rebate	$678

Public Library
Union City Public Library
324 43rd St
Union City, NJ 07087
201-866-7500

Director	Rita Mann

Library statistics, 2004
	Total	per capita
Volumes	66,009	0.98
Expenditure	$765,099	$11.40

Public Safety

Police
Chief	Charles Everett
Number of officers, 2004	176

Crime, 2004	Number	Rate
Total	1,936	29.1
Violent	323	4.9
Non-violent	1,613	24.2
Domestic Viol.	596	NA

Emergency/Fire
Director	NA

Public School District
(for school year 2004-2005 except as noted)

Union City School District
3912 Bergen Turnpike
Union City, NJ 07087
201-348-5851

Superintendent	Stanley Sanger
Grade plan	K-12
Enrollment	10,150.0
Students per teacher	10.9
Per pupil expenditure	$14,258
Median faculty salary	$49,783
Median administrator salary	$115,339
Grade 12 enrollment	610.0
High school graduation rate	NA

Assessment test results
(percent scoring at proficient or advanced level)
	Language	Math
Grade 3	76.4%	81.8%
Grade 8	63.0%	62.2%
High school	64.1%	56.3%

SAT
Percent tested	NA
Average SAT math score	NA
Average SAT verbal score	NA

No Child Left Behind, 2003-04
Attendence rate (target = 90%)	95.2%
Drop rate	7.8%
Highly-qualified teachers	95.8%
District needs improvement?(AYP)	No

Municipal Finance

Fiscal Year 2005
Total tax levy	$66,346,121
County levy	12,569,308
County taxes	12,331,061
County library	0
County health	0
County open space	238,247
School levy	15,807,969
Local muni. budget	37,968,844
Misc. revenues	40,419,687
Total aid	$18,845,274
CMPTRA	16,556,315
Muni. block grant	263,054
Energy tax receipts	1,885,905
Homeland security	140,000

Fiscal Year 2006
Total aid	$18,845,274
CMPTRA	16,490,308
Muni. block grant	263,054
Energy tax receipts	1,951,912
Homeland security	140,000

Taxes
	2003	2004	2005
General tax rate per $100	4.44	4.556	4.682
Net valuation taxable	$1,390,207,639	$1,413,668,713	$1,417,116,686
State equalized value	$1,960,524,100	$2,339,494,252	$2,851,915,247
County equalization ratio	82.19	70.91	60.21

Demographics & Socio-Economic Characteristics
(2000 U.S. Census, except as noted)

Population
1980*	3,971
1990*	5,078
2000	6,160
Male	2,557
Female	3,603
2004 (estimate)*	6,400
Persons per sq. mi. of land	337

Race & Hispanic Origin, 2000
Race
White	5,041
Black/African American	823
Amer. Indian/Alaska Natv.	11
Asian	98
Natv. Hawaiian/Pac. Islander	1
Other Race	98
Two or more races	88
Hispanic origin, total	316
Mexican	15
Puerto Rican	159
Cuban	38
Other Hispanic	104

Age & Nativity, 2000
Under 5 years	278
18 years and over	4,980
21 years and over	4,842
65 years and over	404
85 years and over	25
Median Age	37.6
Native born	5,818
Foreign born	342

Educational Attainment, 2000
Population 25 years and over	4,591
0-8 yrs of school	9.8%
High School grad or higher	77.1%
Bachelor's degree or higher	31.9%
Graduate degree	11.6%

Income & Poverty, 1999
Per capita income	$29,535
Median household income	$81,089
Median family income	$102,146
Persons in poverty	69
H'holds receiving public assistance	9
H'holds receiving social security	287

Households, 2000
Total households	1,666
With persons under 18	621
With persons over 65	275
Family households	1,163
One-person households	405
Persons per household	2.61
Persons per family	3.18

Labor & Employment
Total civilian labor force, 2004**	2,668
Unemployment rate	2.4%
Total civilian labor force, 2000	2,386
Unemployment rate	3.0%

Employed persons 16 years and over by occupation, 2000
Managers & professionals	1,272
Service occupations	157
Sales & office occupations	565
Farming, fishing & forestry	9
Construction & maintenance	174
Production & transportation	138
Self-employed persons	190

*US Census Bureau
**New Jersey Department of Labor

General Information
Township of Union
140 Perryville Rd
Hampton, NJ 08827
908-735-8027
Web site	www.uniontwp-hcnj.org
Land area (sq. miles)	18.97
Water area (sq. miles)	1.62
Type of government	Township
Form of government	TC

Government

Legislative Districts
US Congressional	7
State Legislative	23

Local Officials, 2006
Mayor	Bruce Rossi
Admin/Manager	NA
Clerk	K. Judith Fabian
Finance Dir/Treas	Grace Brennan
Engineer	Robert C. Bogart
Attorney	J. Peter Jost
Tax assessor	Robert McN. Vance
Tax collector	John Earley
Building officer	John W Leonard
Zoning officer	NA
Public Works	NA

Housing & Construction

Housing Units, 2000*
Total	1,725
Median rent	$973
Median SF home value	$285,200

New Privately Owned Housing Units Authorized by Building Permit
	Units	Value
Total, 2004	16	$4,487,460
Single family	16	$4,487,460
Total, 2005	15	$4,552,292
Single family	15	$4,552,292

Real Property Valuation - parcels, 2005
	Number	Valuation
Total		$654,883,118
Vacant	121	18,052,753
Residential	1,670	490,224,800
Commercial	66	100,639,700
Industrial	6	14,192,100
Apartments	1	230,900
Farm land	90	30,377,650
Farm homestead	157	1,165,215

Average Property Value & Tax, 2005
Residential value	$268,960
Property tax	$6,274
FAIR rebate	$488

Public Library

No public municipal library.

Library statistics, 2004
	Total	per capita
Volumes	NA	NA
Expenditure	NA	NA

Public Safety

Police
Chief	NA
Number of officers, 2004	11

Crime, 2004	Number	Rate
Total	49	7.7
Violent	1	0.2
Non-violent	48	7.5
Domestic Viol.	13	NA

Emergency/Fire
Director	Dan VanFossen

Public School District
(for school year 2004-2005 except as noted)

Union Township School District
165 Perryville Rd
Hampton, NJ 08827
908-735-5511
Administrator	John Sico Jr.
Grade plan	K-8
Enrollment	600.0
Students per teacher	10.2
Per pupil expenditure	$10,545
Median faculty salary	$47,770
Median administrator salary	$92,000
Grade 12 enrollment	NA
High school graduation rate	NA

Assessment test results
(percent scoring at proficient or advanced level)
	Language	Math
Grade 3	95.7%	95.6%
Grade 8	89.6%	88.3%
High school	NA	NA

SAT
Percent tested	NA
Average SAT math score	NA
Average SAT verbal score	NA

No Child Left Behind, 2003-04
Attendence rate (target = 90%)	96.0%
Drop rate	NA
Highly-qualified teachers	87.5%
District needs improvement?(AYP)	No

Municipal Finance

Fiscal Year 2005
Total tax levy	$15,315,691
County levy	3,230,390
County taxes	2,742,782
County library	229,504
County health	0
County open space	258,103
School levy	11,654,820
Local muni. budget	430,482
Misc. revenues	2,525,097
Total aid	$570,020
CMPTRA	212,222
Muni. block grant	24,154
Energy tax receipts	333,644
Homeland security	0

Fiscal Year 2006
Total aid	$570,020
CMPTRA	200,545
Muni. block grant	24,154
Energy tax receipts	345,321
Homeland security	NA

Taxes
	2003	2004	2005
General tax rate per $100	2.07	2.200	2.340
Net valuation taxable	$644,384,218	$646,885,385	$656,558,506
State equalized value	$692,067,681	$751,177,610	$836,593,407
County equalization ratio	91.28	86.80	76.61

Demographics & Socio-Economic Characteristics

(2000 U.S. Census, except as noted)

Population

1980*	50,184
1990*	50,024
2000	54,405
Male	25,446
Female	28,959
2004 (estimate)*	55,636
Persons per sq. mi. of land	6,103

Race & Hispanic Origin, 2000

Race

White	36,809
Black/African American	10,752
Amer. Indian/Alaska Natv.	80
Asian	4,201
Natv. Hawaiian/Pac. Islander	13
Other Race	1,329
Two or more races	1,221
Hispanic origin, total	4,861
Mexican	113
Puerto Rican	1,398
Cuban	666
Other Hispanic	2,684

Age & Nativity, 2000

Under 5 years	2,994
18 years and over	42,286
21 years and over	39,998
65 years and over	9,427
85 years and over	1,391
Median Age	38.7
Native born	41,045
Foreign born	13,360

Educational Attainment, 2000

Population 25 years and over	37,595
0-8 yrs of school	8.0%
High School grad or higher	80.9%
Bachelor's degree or higher	26.5%
Graduate degree	8.4%

Income & Poverty, 1999

Per capita income	$24,768
Median household income	$59,173
Median family income	$68,707
Persons in poverty	2,212
H'holds receiving public assistance	439
H'holds receiving social security	6,707

Households, 2000

Total households	19,534
With persons under 18	6,824
With persons over 65	6,827
Family households	14,164
One-person households	4,656
Persons per household	2.71
Persons per family	3.25

Labor & Employment

Total civilian labor force, 2004**	26,969
Unemployment rate	3.8%
Total civilian labor force, 2000	27,371
Unemployment rate	4.5%

Employed persons 16 years and over by occupation, 2000

Managers & professionals	9,906
Service occupations	3,150
Sales & office occupations	8,130
Farming, fishing & forestry	0
Construction & maintenance	2,071
Production & transportation	2,878
Self-employed persons	1,089

*US Census Bureau
**New Jersey Department of Labor

General Information

Township of Union
1976 Morris Ave
Union, NJ 07083
908-688-2800

Web site	NA
Land area (sq. miles)	9.12
Water area (sq. miles)	0
Type of government	Township
Form of government	TC

Government

Legislative Districts

US Congressional	7, 10
State Legislative	20

Local Officials, 2006

Mayor	Peter Capodice
Admin/Manager	Frank Bradley
Clerk	Eileen Birch
Finance Dir/Treas	Debra Cyburt
Engineer	Robert Bucco Jr.
Attorney	Daniel Antonelli
Tax assessor	Paul Parsons
Tax collector	Terri Magnusson
Building officer	Richard Malanda
Zoning officer	NA
Public Works	NA

Housing & Construction

Housing Units, 2000*

Total	20,001
Median rent	$844
Median SF home value	$172,900

New Privately Owned Housing Units Authorized by Building Permit

	Units	Value
Total, 2004	47	$3,171,918
Single family	13	$1,524,632
Total, 2005	37	$3,684,881
Single family	21	$2,166,595

Real Property Valuation - parcels, 2005

	Number	Valuation
Total		$1,062,586,400
Vacant	211	6,160,100
Residential	16,075	733,541,200
Commercial	708	197,028,500
Industrial	213	104,566,600
Apartments	49	21,290,000
Farm land	0	0
Farm homestead	0	0

Average Property Value & Tax, 2005

Residential value	$45,632
Property tax	$5,906
FAIR rebate	$605

Public Library

Union Free Public Library
1980 Morris Ave
Union, NJ 07083
908-851-5450

Director................ Laurie Sansone

Library statistics, 2004

	Total	per capita
Volumes	165,343	3.04
Expenditure	$1,821,659	$33.48

Public Safety

Police

Chief	Thomas Kraemer
Number of officers, 2004	138

Crime, 2004	Number	Rate
Total	1,881	33.8
Violent	200	3.6
Non-violent	1,681	30.2
Domestic Viol.	374	NA

Emergency/Fire

Director................ Frederic Fretz

Public School District

(for school year 2004-2005 except as noted)

Union Township School District
2369 Morris Ave
Union, NJ 07083
908-851-6420

Superintendent	Theodore Jakubowski
Grade plan	K-12
Enrollment	7,866.0
Students per teacher	12.5
Per pupil expenditure	$11,698
Median faculty salary	$53,874
Median administrator salary	$106,995
Grade 12 enrollment	592.5
High school graduation rate	98.2%

Assessment test results

(percent scoring at proficient or advanced level)

	Language	Math
Grade 3	78.3%	80.4%
Grade 8	64.9%	51.6%
High school	77.5%	66.4%

SAT

Percent tested	69%
Average SAT math score	482
Average SAT verbal score	469

No Child Left Behind, 2003-04

Attendence rate (target = 90%)	94.8%
Drop rate	0.2%
Highly-qualified teachers	92%
District needs improvement?(AYP)	No

Municipal Finance

Fiscal Year 2005

Total tax levy	$137,804,411
County levy	23,650,233
County taxes	22,714,826
County library	0
County health	0
County open space	935,407
School levy	66,102,634
Local muni. budget	48,051,544
Misc. revenues	19,987,221
Total aid	$7,971,857
CMPTRA	3,533,647
Muni. block grant	218,889
Energy tax receipts	4,079,321
Homeland security	140,000

Fiscal Year 2006

Total aid	$7,971,858
CMPTRA	3,390,871
Muni. block grant	218,889
Energy tax receipts	4,222,098
Homeland security	140,000

Taxes

	2003	2004	2005
General tax rate per $100	11.40	12.184	12.942
Net valuation taxable	$1,067,902,142	$1,070,034,775	$1,064,799,976
State equalized value	$5,023,058,053	$5,629,682,576	$6,304,321,942
County equalization ratio	22.63	19.55	17.21

Demographics & Socio-Economic Characteristics
(2000 U.S. Census, except as noted)

Population
1980*	6,810
1990*	6,927
2000	7,556
Male	3,663
Female	3,893
2004 (estimate)*	7,834
Persons per sq. mi. of land	252

Race & Hispanic Origin, 2000
Race
White	5,725
Black/African American	1,240
Amer. Indian/Alaska Natv.	61
Asian	231
Natv. Hawaiian/Pac. Islander	1
Other Race	138
Two or more races	160
Hispanic origin, total	343
Mexican	25
Puerto Rican	267
Cuban	6
Other Hispanic	45

Age & Nativity, 2000
Under 5 years	519
18 years and over	5,455
21 years and over	5,179
65 years and over	1,074
85 years and over	117
Median Age	37.5
Native born	7,314
Foreign born	242

Educational Attainment, 2000
Population 25 years and over	4,910
0-8 yrs of school	5.3%
High School grad or higher	81.1%
Bachelor's degree or higher	15.6%
Graduate degree	4.3%

Income & Poverty, 1999
Per capita income	$18,884
Median household income	$47,861
Median family income	$51,472
Persons in poverty	1,032
H'holds receiving public assistance	193
H'holds receiving social security	930

Households, 2000
Total households	2,757
With persons under 18	1,088
With persons over 65	783
Family households	2,126
One-person households	551
Persons per household	2.73
Persons per family	3.12

Labor & Employment
Total civilian labor force, 2004**	3,741
Unemployment rate	6.2%
Total civilian labor force, 2000	3,576
Unemployment rate	7.3%

Employed persons 16 years and over by occupation, 2000
Managers & professionals	982
Service occupations	508
Sales & office occupations	938
Farming, fishing & forestry	36
Construction & maintenance	229
Production & transportation	622
Self-employed persons	255

*US Census Bureau
**New Jersey Department of Labor

General Information
Township of Upper Deerfield
PO Box 5098
Seabrook, NJ 08302
856-451-3811

Web site	NA
Land area (sq. miles)	31.10
Water area (sq. miles)	0.14
Type of government	Township
Form of government	TC

Government

Legislative Districts
US Congressional	2
State Legislative	3

Local Officials, 2006
Mayor	C. Kenneth Hill
Admin/Manager	Roy Spoltore
Clerk	Roy Spoltore
Finance Dir/Treas	Ruth Moynihan
Engineer	Brian Murphy
Attorney	Theodore Baker
Tax assessor	Kevin Maloney
Tax collector	Andrea Penny
Building officer	Fred Froelich
Zoning officer	NA
Public Works	Terry O'Neill

Housing & Construction

Housing Units, 2000*
Total	2,881
Median rent	$535
Median SF home value	$116,000

New Privately Owned Housing Units Authorized by Building Permit
	Units	Value
Total, 2004	20	$3,537,161
Single family	20	$3,537,161
Total, 2005	41	$12,061,975
Single family	41	$12,061,975

Real Property Valuation - parcels, 2005
	Number	Valuation
Total		$397,856,800
Vacant	374	12,052,300
Residential	2,379	267,994,600
Commercial	103	55,838,200
Industrial	2	11,644,500
Apartments	8	13,822,100
Farm land	214	29,397,100
Farm homestead	448	7,108,000

Average Property Value & Tax, 2005
Residential value	$97,313
Property tax	$3,125
FAIR rebate	$646

Public Library
No public municipal library.

Library statistics, 2004
	Total	per capita
Volumes	NA	NA
Expenditure	NA	NA

Public Safety

Police
Chief	NA
Number of officers, 2004	0

Crime, 2004	Number	Rate
Total	242	31.5
Violent	21	2.7
Non-violent	221	28.8
Domestic Viol.	152	NA

Emergency/Fire
Director	NA

Public School District
(for school year 2004-2005 except as noted)

Upper Deerfield Township School District
1369 Highway #77
Seabrook, NJ 08302
856-455-2267

Superintendent	Philip Exley
Grade plan	K-8
Enrollment	982.0
Students per teacher	10.6
Per pupil expenditure	$11,641
Median faculty salary	$44,769
Median administrator salary	$89,853
Grade 12 enrollment	NA
High school graduation rate	NA

Assessment test results
(percent scoring at proficient or advanced level)
	Language	Math
Grade 3	50.0%	54.9%
Grade 8	76.9%	60.5%
High school	NA	NA

SAT
Percent tested	NA
Average SAT math score	NA
Average SAT verbal score	NA

No Child Left Behind, 2003-04
Attendence rate (target = 90%)	94.5%
Drop rate	NA
Highly-qualified teachers	100%
District needs improvement?(AYP)	No

Municipal Finance

Fiscal Year 2005
Total tax levy	$12,827,335
County levy	4,827,542
County taxes	4,585,872
County library	0
County health	195,239
County open space	46,432
School levy	7,999,793
Local muni. budget	0
Misc. revenues	3,844,822
Total aid	$1,840,136
CMPTRA	384,544
Muni. block grant	30,310
Energy tax receipts	1,425,282
Homeland security	0

Fiscal Year 2006
Total aid	$1,840,136
CMPTRA	334,659
Muni. block grant	30,310
Energy tax receipts	1,475,167
Homeland security	NA

Taxes
	2003	2004	2005
General tax rate per $100	2.70	2.878	3.214
Net valuation taxable	$384,445,670	$391,223,338	$399,407,924
State equalized value	$395,398,200	$442,830,912	$502,021,021
County equalization ratio	99.69	97.23	88.30

Demographics & Socio-Economic Characteristics
(2000 U.S. Census, except as noted)

Population
1980*	2,750
1990*	3,277
2000	4,282
Male	2,159
Female	2,123
2004 (estimate)*	5,996
Persons per sq. mi. of land	128

Race & Hispanic Origin, 2000
Race
White	4,055
Black/African American	45
Amer. Indian/Alaska Natv.	6
Asian	60
Natv. Hawaiian/Pac. Islander	0
Other Race	36
Two or more races	80
Hispanic origin, total	151
Mexican	57
Puerto Rican	54
Cuban	3
Other Hispanic	37

Age & Nativity, 2000
Under 5 years	342
18 years and over	3,091
21 years and over	2,990
65 years and over	404
85 years and over	40
Median Age	38.4
Native born	4,051
Foreign born	231

Educational Attainment, 2000
Population 25 years and over	2,829
0-8 yrs of school	3.1%
High School grad or higher	88.8%
Bachelor's degree or higher	36.3%
Graduate degree	9.6%

Income & Poverty, 1999
Per capita income	$29,387
Median household income	$71,250
Median family income	$78,334
Persons in poverty	173
H'holds receiving public assistance	5
H'holds receiving social security	309

Households, 2000
Total households	1,437
With persons under 18	642
With persons over 65	287
Family households	1,199
One-person households	168
Persons per household	2.96
Persons per family	3.24

Labor & Employment
Total civilian labor force, 2004**	2,038
Unemployment rate	3.1%
Total civilian labor force, 2000	2,285
Unemployment rate	2.7%

Employed persons 16 years and over by occupation, 2000
Managers & professionals	915
Service occupations	326
Sales & office occupations	538
Farming, fishing & forestry	69
Construction & maintenance	196
Production & transportation	179
Self-employed persons	169

*US Census Bureau
**New Jersey Department of Labor

General Information
Township of Upper Freehold
PO Box 89
314 Rt 539
Cream Ridge, NJ 08514
609-758-7738
Web site	www.uftnj.com
Land area (sq. miles)	46.86
Water area (sq. miles)	0.27
Type of government	Township
Form of government	TC

Government

Legislative Districts
US Congressional	4
State Legislative	30

Local Officials, 2006
Mayor	Stephen J. Fleischacker
Admin/Manager	Barbara Bascom
Clerk	Barbara Bascom
Finance Dir/Treas	Dianne Kelly
Engineer	Glenn Gerken
Attorney	Granville D. Magee
Tax assessor	Steve Walters
Tax collector	NA
Building officer	Ron Gafgen
Zoning officer	Ron Gafgen
Public Works	NA

Housing & Construction

Housing Units, 2000*
Total	1,501
Median rent	$743
Median SF home value	$255,500

New Privately Owned Housing Units
Authorized by Building Permit
	Units	Value
Total, 2004	151	$20,681,473
Single family	151	$20,681,473
Total, 2005	62	$16,090,457
Single family	62	$16,090,457

Real Property Valuation - parcels, 2005
	Number	Valuation
Total		$590,534,800
Vacant	355	23,171,700
Residential	1,823	460,054,000
Commercial	54	17,360,100
Industrial	16	6,572,400
Apartments	1	188,400
Farm land	297	73,285,100
Farm homestead	513	9,903,100

Average Property Value & Tax, 2005
Residential value	$201,180
Property tax	$6,177
FAIR rebate	$532

Public Library

No public municipal library.

Library statistics, 2004
	Total	per capita
Volumes	NA	NA
Expenditure	NA	NA

Public Safety
Police
Chief	NA
Number of officers, 2004	0

Crime, 2004	Number	Rate
Total	59	9.7
Violent	4	0.7
Non-violent	55	9
Domestic Viol.	7	NA

Emergency/Fire
Director	NA

Public School District
(for school year 2004-2005 except as noted)

Upper Freehold Regional School Dist.
27 High St
Allentown, NJ 08501
609-259-7292
Superintendent	Robert Connelly
Grade plan	K-12
Enrollment	2,109.5
Students per teacher	12.7
Per pupil expenditure	$10,829
Median faculty salary	$48,372
Median administrator salary	$95,000
Grade 12 enrollment	206.5
High school graduation rate	97.7%

Assessment test results
(percent scoring at proficient or advanced level)
	Language	Math
Grade 3	90.5%	85.0%
Grade 8	87.7%	81.5%
High school	88.4%	79.8%

SAT
Percent tested	84%
Average SAT math score	499
Average SAT verbal score	493

No Child Left Behind, 2003-04
Attendence rate (target = 90%)	95.1%
Drop rate	0.9%
Highly-qualified teachers	89.1%
District needs improvement?(AYP)	No

Municipal Finance

Fiscal Year 2005
Total tax levy	$18,179,672
County levy	3,093,269
County taxes	2,775,664
County library	152,894
County health	0
County open space	164,711
School levy	13,507,649
Local muni. budget	1,578,754
Misc. revenues	5,461,089
Total aid	$734,401
CMPTRA	192,844
Muni. block grant	16,790
Energy tax receipts	524,767
Homeland security	0

Fiscal Year 2006
Total aid	$734,401
CMPTRA	174,477
Muni. block grant	16,790
Energy tax receipts	543,134
Homeland security	NA

Taxes
	2003	2004	2005
General tax rate per $100	2.82	2.968	3.071
Net valuation taxable	$504,188,966	$546,042,393	$592,108,242
State equalized value	$718,013,338	$851,397,800	$1,006,815,579
County equalization ratio	78.88	70.22	64.06

Demographics & Socio-Economic Characteristics
(2000 U.S. Census, except as noted)

Population
1980*	3,139
1990*	3,140
2000	3,468
Male	1,728
Female	1,740
2004 (estimate)*	3,606
Persons per sq. mi. of land	89

Race & Hispanic Origin, 2000
Race
White	3,289
Black/African American	75
Amer. Indian/Alaska Natv.	18
Asian	11
Natv. Hawaiian/Pac. Islander	0
Other Race	45
Two or more races	30
Hispanic origin, total	109
Mexican	41
Puerto Rican	32
Cuban	0
Other Hispanic	36

Age & Nativity, 2000
Under 5 years	190
18 years and over	2,591
21 years and over	2,462
65 years and over	477
85 years and over	67
Median Age	38.9
Native born	3,342
Foreign born	126

Educational Attainment, 2000
Population 25 years and over	2,299
0-8 yrs of school	6.7%
High School grad or higher	81.9%
Bachelor's degree or higher	19.1%
Graduate degree	5.8%

Income & Poverty, 1999
Per capita income	$21,732
Median household income	$53,813
Median family income	$56,768
Persons in poverty	288
H'holds receiving public assistance	18
H'holds receiving social security	294

Households, 2000
Total households	1,207
With persons under 18	452
With persons over 65	299
Family households	960
One-person households	204
Persons per household	2.8
Persons per family	3.13

Labor & Employment
Total civilian labor force, 2004**	1,540
Unemployment rate	1.8%
Total civilian labor force, 2000	1,728
Unemployment rate	3.2%

Employed persons 16 years and over by occupation, 2000
Managers & professionals	528
Service occupations	244
Sales & office occupations	410
Farming, fishing & forestry	36
Construction & maintenance	178
Production & transportation	277
Self-employed persons	136

*US Census Bureau
**New Jersey Department of Labor

General Information
Township of Upper Pittsgrove
431 Route 77
Elmer, NJ 08318
856-358-8500
Web site	NA
Land area (sq. miles)	40.39
Water area (sq. miles)	0.07
Type of government	Township
Form of government	TC

Government

Legislative Districts
US Congressional	2
State Legislative	3

Local Officials, 2006
Mayor	Jack Cimprich
Admin/Manager	NA
Clerk	Alan Newkirk
Finance Dir/Treas	Alan Newkirk
Engineer	J. Michael Fralinger
Attorney	William Horner
Tax assessor	Edwin F. Kay
Tax collector	Susan DeFrancesco
Building officer	(State)
Zoning officer	L. Andrew Hoglen
Public Works	Barry Foote

Housing & Construction

Housing Units, 2000*
Total	1,250
Median rent	$646
Median SF home value	$127,000

New Privately Owned Housing Units
Authorized by Building Permit
	Units	Value
Total, 2004	5	$444,320
Single family	5	$444,320
Total, 2005	7	$712,550
Single family	7	$712,550

Real Property Valuation - parcels, 2005
	Number	Valuation
Total		$148,810,355
Vacant	140	3,019,200
Residential	846	85,020,500
Commercial	66	12,625,500
Industrial	0	0
Apartments	0	0
Farm land	340	41,267,000
Farm homestead	682	6,878,155

Average Property Value & Tax, 2005
Residential value	$60,143
Property tax	$2,271
FAIR rebate	$560

Public Library

No public municipal library.

Library statistics, 2004
	Total	per capita
Volumes	NA	NA
Expenditure	NA	NA

Public Safety

Police
Chief	NA
Number of officers, 2004	0

Crime, 2004	Number	Rate
Total	50	14
Violent	6	1.7
Non-violent	44	12.3
Domestic Viol.	19	NA

Emergency/Fire
Director	NA

Public School District
(for school year 2004-2005 except as noted)

Upper Pittsgrove Township School Dist.
235 Pine Tavern Rd
Monroeville, NJ 08343
856-358-8163
Superintendent	Robert Bazzel
Grade plan	K-12
Enrollment	438.0
Students per teacher	14.6
Per pupil expenditure	$10,056
Median faculty salary	$48,150
Median administrator salary	$57,750
Grade 12 enrollment	NA
High school graduation rate	NA

Assessment test results
(percent scoring at proficient or advanced level)
	Language	Math
Grade 3	88.4%	83.7%
Grade 8	79.3%	81.2%
High school	NA	NA

SAT
Percent tested	NA
Average SAT math score	NA
Average SAT verbal score	NA

No Child Left Behind, 2003-04
Attendence rate (target = 90%)	95.3%
Drop rate	NA
Highly-qualified teachers	94.3%
District needs improvement?(AYP)	No

Municipal Finance

Fiscal Year 2005
Total tax levy	$5,654,941
County levy	2,544,519
County taxes	2,494,064
County library	0
County health	0
County open space	50,456
School levy	3,035,572
Local muni. budget	74,850
Misc. revenues	1,660,658
Total aid	$642,542
CMPTRA	184,455
Muni. block grant	13,739
Energy tax receipts	444,348
Homeland security	0

Fiscal Year 2006
Total aid	$642,542
CMPTRA	168,903
Muni. block grant	13,739
Energy tax receipts	459,900
Homeland security	NA

Taxes
	2003	2004	2005
General tax rate per $100	3.24	3.418	3.776
Net valuation taxable	$146,764,100	$148,686,175	$149,791,337
State equalized value	$211,933,718	$248,083,916	$267,915,108
County equalization ratio	73.29	69.25	59.74

Demographics & Socio-Economic Characteristics
(2000 U.S. Census, except as noted)

Population
1980*	7,958
1990*	7,198
2000	7,741
Male	3,813
Female	3,928
2004 (estimate)*	8,362
Persons per sq. mi. of land	1,580

Race & Hispanic Origin, 2000
Race
White	7,063
Black/African American	72
Amer. Indian/Alaska Natv.	2
Asian	486
Natv. Hawaiian/Pac. Islander	1
Other Race	40
Two or more races	77
Hispanic origin, total	169
Mexican	15
Puerto Rican	33
Cuban	37
Other Hispanic	84

Age & Nativity, 2000
Under 5 years	594
18 years and over	5,368
21 years and over	5,233
65 years and over	882
85 years and over	50
Median Age	40.1
Native born	6,801
Foreign born	940

Educational Attainment, 2000
Population 25 years and over	5,147
0-8 yrs of school	1.3%
High School grad or higher	96.6%
Bachelor's degree or higher	59.9%
Graduate degree	25.5%

Income & Poverty, 1999
Per capita income	$57,239
Median household income	$127,635
Median family income	$132,401
Persons in poverty	52
H'holds receiving public assistance	0
H'holds receiving social security	585

Households, 2000
Total households	2,497
With persons under 18	1,203
With persons over 65	609
Family households	2,242
One-person households	210
Persons per household	3.09
Persons per family	3.27

Labor & Employment
Total civilian labor force, 2004**	3,847
Unemployment rate	2.5%
Total civilian labor force, 2000	3,523
Unemployment rate	4.2%

Employed persons 16 years and over by occupation, 2000
Managers & professionals	2,057
Service occupations	123
Sales & office occupations	986
Farming, fishing & forestry	0
Construction & maintenance	127
Production & transportation	83
Self-employed persons	319

*US Census Bureau
**New Jersey Department of Labor

General Information
Borough of Upper Saddle River
376 W Saddle River Rd
Upper Saddle River, NJ 07458
201-327-2196
Web site	www.usrtoday.com
Land area (sq. miles)	5.29
Water area (sq. miles)	0
Type of government	Borough
Form of government	B

Government
Legislative Districts
US Congressional	5
State Legislative	39

Local Officials, 2006
Mayor	Kenneth Gabbert
Admin/Manager	Michael Mariniello
Clerk	Rose Vido
Finance Dir/Treas	Michael Mariniello
Engineer	David Hals
Attorney	Robert Regan
Tax assessor	Marie Merolla
Tax collector	Jeff Krop
Building officer	Allen Brown
Zoning officer	Robert Schortau
Public Works	NA

Housing & Construction
Housing Units, 2000*
Total	2,560
Median rent	$1,929
Median SF home value	$603,900

New Privately Owned Housing Units Authorized by Building Permit
	Units	Value
Total, 2004	66	$22,832,926
Single family	66	$22,832,926
Total, 2005	26	$16,520,929
Single family	26	$16,520,929

Real Property Valuation - parcels, 2005
	Number	Valuation
Total		$2,046,904,200
Vacant	89	25,957,700
Residential	2,560	1,787,710,600
Commercial	68	200,068,200
Industrial	4	6,217,700
Apartments	2	26,950,000
Farm land	0	0
Farm homestead	0	0

Average Property Value & Tax, 2005
Residential value	$698,324
Property tax	$12,353
FAIR rebate	$603

Public Library
Upper Saddle River Public Library
245 Lake St
Upper Saddle River, NJ 07458
201-327-2583
Director . . . . Barbara Kruger

Library statistics, 2004
	Total	per capita
Volumes	63,811	8.24
Expenditure	$851,486	$110.00

Public Safety
Police
Chief	Theodore Preusch
Number of officers, 2004	18

Crime, 2004	Number	Rate
Total	47	5.7
Violent	2	0.2
Non-violent	45	5.5
Domestic Viol.	6	NA

Emergency/Fire
Director . . . . James Levine

Public School District
(for school year 2004-2005 except as noted)

Upper Saddle River School District
395 W Saddle River Rd
Upper Saddle River, NJ 07458
201-961-6502
Superintendent	Joyce Snider
Grade plan	K-8
Enrollment	1,398.0
Students per teacher	11.9
Per pupil expenditure	$11,792
Median faculty salary	$52,000
Median administrator salary	$93,000
Grade 12 enrollment	NA
High school graduation rate	NA

Assessment test results
(percent scoring at proficient or advanced level)
	Language	Math
Grade 3	93.6%	93.0%
Grade 8	94.2%	89.8%
High school	NA	NA

SAT
Percent tested	NA
Average SAT math score	NA
Average SAT verbal score	NA

No Child Left Behind, 2003-04
Attendence rate (target = 90%)	95.9%
Drop rate	NA
Highly-qualified teachers	98.1%
District needs improvement?(AYP)	No

Municipal Finance
Fiscal Year 2005
Total tax levy	$36,237,028
County levy	4,768,506
County taxes	4,529,484
County library	0
County health	0
County open space	239,022
School levy	26,003,426
Local muni. budget	5,465,097
Misc. revenues	4,331,952
Total aid	$1,277,348
CMPTRA	291,366
Muni. block grant	31,496
Energy tax receipts	904,486
Homeland security	50,000

Fiscal Year 2006
Total aid	$1,277,348
CMPTRA	259,709
Muni. block grant	31,496
Energy tax receipts	936,143
Homeland security	50,000

Taxes
	2003	2004	2005
General tax rate per $100	1.61	1.720	1.770
Net valuation taxable	$1,979,488,298	$2,013,077,348	$2,048,429,129
State equalized value	$2,121,410,672	$2,344,326,429	$2,586,727,022
County equalization ratio	99.69	93.31	85.86

Demographics & Socio-Economic Characteristics
(2000 U.S. Census, except as noted)

Population
1980*	6,713
1990*	10,681
2000	12,115
Male	5,837
Female	6,278
2004 (estimate)*	11,985
Persons per sq. mi. of land	190

Race & Hispanic Origin, 2000
Race
White	11,823
Black/African American	83
Amer. Indian/Alaska Natv.	15
Asian	74
Natv. Hawaiian/Pac. Islander	7
Other Race	23
Two or more races	90
Hispanic origin, total	155
Mexican	40
Puerto Rican	66
Cuban	2
Other Hispanic	47

Age & Nativity, 2000
Under 5 years	736
18 years and over	8,648
21 years and over	8,294
65 years and over	1,472
85 years and over	130
Median Age	38.4
Native born	11,800
Foreign born	315

Educational Attainment, 2000
Population 25 years and over	7,928
0-8 yrs of school	2.0%
High School grad or higher	91.2%
Bachelor's degree or higher	32.4%
Graduate degree	8.8%

Income & Poverty, 1999
Per capita income	$27,498
Median household income	$60,942
Median family income	$68,824
Persons in poverty	417
H'holds receiving public assistance	9
H'holds receiving social security	1,133

Households, 2000
Total households	4,266
With persons under 18	1,775
With persons over 65	1,053
Family households	3,365
One-person households	744
Persons per household	2.84
Persons per family	3.23

Labor & Employment
Total civilian labor force, 2004**	7,362
Unemployment rate	4.3%
Total civilian labor force, 2000	6,149
Unemployment rate	2.5%

Employed persons 16 years and over by occupation, 2000
Managers & professionals	2,506
Service occupations	1,038
Sales & office occupations	1,415
Farming, fishing & forestry	43
Construction & maintenance	627
Production & transportation	368
Self-employed persons	546

*US Census Bureau
**New Jersey Department of Labor

General Information
Upper Township
PO Box 205
Tuckahoe, NJ 08250
609-628-2011
Web site	www.uppertownship.com
Land area (sq. miles)	63.15
Water area (sq. miles)	5.32
Type of government	Township
Form of government	TC

Government

Legislative Districts
US Congressional	2
State Legislative	1

Local Officials, 2006
Mayor	Richard Palombo
Admin/Manager	NA
Clerk	Wanda Gaglione
Finance Dir/Treas	Patricia Garbutt
Engineer	Paul Dietrich
Attorney	Daniel J. Young
Tax assessor	Kristen Errickson
Tax collector	NA
Building officer	Edward Kenney
Zoning officer	Shelley Lea
Public Works	NA

Housing & Construction

Housing Units, 2000*
Total	5,472
Median rent	$827
Median SF home value	$161,700

New Privately Owned Housing Units
Authorized by Building Permit
	Units	Value
Total, 2004	55	$4,070,017
Single family	55	$4,070,017
Total, 2005	48	$3,833,737
Single family	48	$3,833,737

Real Property Valuation - parcels, 2005
	Number	Valuation
Total		$891,448,200
Vacant	2,069	54,234,800
Residential	4,610	724,477,800
Commercial	275	96,088,300
Industrial	1	11,148,100
Apartments	5	794,300
Farm land	31	4,074,800
Farm homestead	84	630,100

Average Property Value & Tax, 2005
Residential value	$154,475
Property tax	$3,931
FAIR rebate	$537

Public Library
Upper Cape Branch Library†
2050 Rte 631
Petersburg, NJ 08270
609-628-2607
Branch Librarian	Beth Dusman

Library statistics, 2004
	Total	per capita
Volumes	NA	NA
Expenditure	NA	NA

†Branch of County Library

Public Safety

Police
Chief	NA
Number of officers, 2004	0

Crime, 2004	Number	Rate
Total	179	15
Violent	8	0.7
Non-violent	171	14.3
Domestic Viol.	62	NA

Emergency/Fire
Director	NA

Public School District
(for school year 2004-2005 except as noted)

Upper Township School District
525 Perry Rd
Petersburg, NJ 08270
609-628-3513
Superintendent	Laurence A. Hobdell
Grade plan	K-12
Enrollment	1,699.0
Students per teacher	11.3
Per pupil expenditure	$10,880
Median faculty salary	$58,611
Median administrator salary	$90,901
Grade 12 enrollment	NA
High school graduation rate	NA

Assessment test results
(percent scoring at proficient or advanced level)
	Language	Math
Grade 3	85.2%	83.4%
Grade 8	83.2%	78.4%
High school	NA	NA

SAT
Percent tested	NA
Average SAT math score	NA
Average SAT verbal score	NA

No Child Left Behind, 2003-04
Attendence rate (target = 90%)	94.7%
Drop rate	NA
Highly-qualified teachers	97%
District needs improvement?(AYP)	No

Municipal Finance

Fiscal Year 2005
Total tax levy	$22,800,978
County levy	3,608,307
County taxes	3,033,748
County library	427,269
County health	0
County open space	147,290
School levy	19,192,671
Local muni. budget	0
Misc. revenues	10,859,084
Total aid	$6,556,440
CMPTRA	58,284
Muni. block grant	47,503
Energy tax receipts	6,445,124
Homeland security	0

Fiscal Year 2006
Total aid	$6,723,735
CMPTRA	0
Muni. block grant	47,503
Energy tax receipts	6,670,703
Homeland security	NA

Taxes
	2003	2004	2005
General tax rate per $100	2.16	2.230	2.550
Net valuation taxable	$853,992,932	$866,994,723	$895,903,081
State equalized value	$1,188,577,498	$1,422,752,387	$1,678,349,721
County equalization ratio	81.4	71.85	60.79

Demographics & Socio-Economic Characteristics
(2000 U.S. Census, except as noted)

Population
1980*	11,704
1990*	11,005
2000	12,910
Male	6,152
Female	6,758
2004 (estimate)*	12,831
Persons per sq. mi. of land	5,986

Race & Hispanic Origin, 2000
Race
White	9,953
Black/African American	379
Amer. Indian/Alaska Natv.	24
Asian	962
Natv. Hawaiian/Pac. Islander	4
Other Race	1,210
Two or more races	378
Hispanic origin, total	2,213
Mexican	365
Puerto Rican	629
Cuban	44
Other Hispanic	1,175

Age & Nativity, 2000
Under 5 years	721
18 years and over	10,328
21 years and over	9,996
65 years and over	2,550
85 years and over	309
Median Age	40.6
Native born	9,938
Foreign born	2,972

Educational Attainment, 2000
Population 25 years and over	9,470
0-8 yrs of school	6.7%
High School grad or higher	80.3%
Bachelor's degree or higher	21.4%
Graduate degree	7.7%

Income & Poverty, 1999
Per capita income	$22,631
Median household income	$42,478
Median family income	$52,701
Persons in poverty	894
H'holds receiving public assistance	107
H'holds receiving social security	1,910

Households, 2000
Total households	5,480
With persons under 18	1,403
With persons over 65	1,915
Family households	3,256
One-person households	1,837
Persons per household	2.35
Persons per family	3.02

Labor & Employment
Total civilian labor force, 2004**	6,256
Unemployment rate	3.7%
Total civilian labor force, 2000	6,530
Unemployment rate	6.1%

Employed persons 16 years and over by occupation, 2000
Managers & professionals	1,859
Service occupations	2,329
Sales & office occupations	1,452
Farming, fishing & forestry	23
Construction & maintenance	320
Production & transportation	347
Self-employed persons	330

*US Census Bureau
**New Jersey Department of Labor

General Information
City of Ventnor
6201 Atlantic Ave
Ventnor, NJ 08406
609-823-7900
Web site	www.ventnorcity.org
Land area (sq. miles)	2.14
Water area (sq. miles)	1.40
Type of government	City
Form of government	Comm.

Government
Legislative Districts
US Congressional	2
State Legislative	2

Local Officials, 2006
Mayor	Tim Kreischer
Admin/Manager	Andrew McCrosson Jr.
Clerk	Sandra M. Biagi
Finance Dir/Treas	William Johnson
Engineer	Richard Carter
Attorney	John Scott Abbott
Tax assessor	William Johnson
Tax collector	Julie Harron
Building officer	Jimmie Agnesino
Zoning officer	Jimmie Agnesino
Public Works	David Smith

Housing & Construction
Housing Units, 2000*
Total	8,009
Median rent	$729
Median SF home value	$129,700

New Privately Owned Housing Units Authorized by Building Permit
	Units	Value
Total, 2004	18	$5,200,499
Single family	18	$5,200,499
Total, 2005	16	$5,853,047
Single family	16	$5,853,047

Real Property Valuation - parcels, 2005
	Number	Valuation
Total		$1,287,037,900
Vacant	173	31,118,500
Residential	6,199	1,180,867,300
Commercial	134	62,948,500
Industrial	2	1,559,100
Apartments	33	10,544,500
Farm land	0	0
Farm homestead	0	0

Average Property Value & Tax, 2005
Residential value	$190,493
Property tax	$5,269
FAIR rebate	$673

Public Library
Ventnor Community Library†
6500 Atlantic Ave
Ventnor City, NJ 08406
609-823-4614
Branch Librarian	Ellen Eisen

Library statistics, 2004
	Total	per capita
Volumes	NA	NA
Expenditure	NA	NA

†Branch of County Library

Public Safety
Police
Chief	Stanley Wodazak
Number of officers, 2004	39

Crime, 2004	Number	Rate
Total	330	25.8
Violent	20	1.6
Non-violent	310	24.3
Domestic Viol.	307	NA

Emergency/Fire
Director	Bert Sabo

Public School District
(for school year 2004-2005 except as noted)

Ventnor City School District
400 N Lafayette Ave
Ventnor, NJ 08406
609-487-7918
Superintendent	Carmine Bonanni
Grade plan	K-12
Enrollment	1,077.0
Students per teacher	10.5
Per pupil expenditure	$10,443
Median faculty salary	$48,246
Median administrator salary	$74,222
Grade 12 enrollment	NA
High school graduation rate	NA

Assessment test results
(percent scoring at proficient or advanced level)
	Language	Math
Grade 3	74.0%	73.1%
Grade 8	60.8%	54.3%
High school	NA	NA

SAT
Percent tested	NA
Average SAT math score	NA
Average SAT verbal score	NA

No Child Left Behind, 2003-04
Attendence rate (target = 90%)	94.8%
Drop rate	NA
Highly-qualified teachers	100%
District needs improvement?(AYP)	No

Municipal Finance
Fiscal Year 2005
Total tax levy	$35,654,401
County levy	7,244,242
County taxes	5,912,320
County library	656,177
County health	322,917
County open space	352,828
School levy	14,741,841
Local muni. budget	13,668,318
Misc. revenues	6,071,243
Total aid	$913,713
CMPTRA	236,174
Muni. block grant	50,620
Energy tax receipts	556,919
Homeland security	70,000

Fiscal Year 2006
Total aid	$913,714
CMPTRA	216,682
Muni. block grant	50,620
Energy tax receipts	576,412
Homeland security	70,000

Taxes
	2003	2004	2005
General tax rate per $100	2.36	2.534	2.766
Net valuation taxable	$1,298,510,865	$1,286,094,162	$1,289,108,275
State equalized value	$1,429,920,565	$1,756,962,560	$2,146,367,424
County equalization ratio	116.08	90.81	73.16

Demographics & Socio-Economic Characteristics
(2000 U.S. Census, except as noted)

Population
1980*	16,302
1990*	21,211
2000	24,686
Male	12,505
Female	12,181
2004 (estimate)*	25,553
Persons per sq. mi. of land	374

Race & Hispanic Origin, 2000
Race
White	23,837
Black/African American	188
Amer. Indian/Alaska Natv.	22
Asian	173
Natv. Hawaiian/Pac. Islander	7
Other Race	195
Two or more races	264
Hispanic origin, total	889
Mexican	62
Puerto Rican	352
Cuban	85
Other Hispanic	390

Age & Nativity, 2000
Under 5 years	1,643
18 years and over	17,126
21 years and over	16,349
65 years and over	1,566
85 years and over	144
Median Age	35.4
Native born	23,431
Foreign born	1,255

Educational Attainment, 2000
Population 25 years and over	15,485
0-8 yrs of school	2.0%
High School grad or higher	92.8%
Bachelor's degree or higher	25.3%
Graduate degree	7.7%

Income & Poverty, 1999
Per capita income	$25,250
Median household income	$67,566
Median family income	$72,609
Persons in poverty	717
H'holds receiving public assistance	130
H'holds receiving social security	1,384

Households, 2000
Total households	8,368
With persons under 18	3,932
With persons over 65	1,168
Family households	6,607
One-person households	1,359
Persons per household	2.95
Persons per family	3.35

Labor & Employment
Total civilian labor force, 2004**	12,920
Unemployment rate	4.8%
Total civilian labor force, 2000	13,184
Unemployment rate	4.8%

Employed persons 16 years and over by occupation, 2000
Managers & professionals	4,313
Service occupations	1,559
Sales & office occupations	3,554
Farming, fishing & forestry	22
Construction & maintenance	1,587
Production & transportation	1,511
Self-employed persons	788

*US Census Bureau
**New Jersey Department of Labor

General Information
Township of Vernon
21 Church St
Vernon, NJ 07462
973-764-4055
Web site	www.vernontwp.com
Land area (sq. miles)	68.39
Water area (sq. miles)	2.14
Type of government	Township
Form of government	TC

Government
Legislative Districts
US Congressional	5
State Legislative	24

Local Officials, 2006
Mayor	Janet Morrison
Admin/Manager	Don Teolis
Clerk	Patricia Lycosky
Finance Dir/Treas	Monica Goscicki
Engineer	Lou Kneip
Attorney	Joseph Ragno
Tax assessor	Lynne Schweighardt
Tax collector	NA
Building officer	Thomas Pinand
Zoning officer	Lou Kneip
Public Works	Dave Pullis

Housing & Construction
Housing Units, 2000*
Total	9,994
Median rent	$930
Median SF home value	$150,800

New Privately Owned Housing Units
Authorized by Building Permit
	Units	Value
Total, 2004	30	$4,206,609
Single family	25	$3,620,106
Total, 2005	52	$6,112,643
Single family	52	$6,112,643

Real Property Valuation - parcels, 2005
	Number	Valuation
Total		$1,447,920,794
Vacant	2,700	54,116,782
Residential	10,325	1,254,741,600
Commercial	301	106,966,112
Industrial	21	8,130,300
Apartments	3	1,117,700
Farm land	118	21,056,100
Farm homestead	192	1,792,200

Average Property Value & Tax, 2005
Residential value	$119,476
Property tax	$4,410
FAIR rebate	$477

Public Library
Vernon Branch Library†
66 Rte 94
Vernon, NJ 07462
973-827-8095
Branch Librarian	Jacqueline Oregero

Library statistics, 2004
	Total	per capita
Volumes	NA	NA
Expenditure	NA	NA

†Branch of County Library

Public Safety
Police
Chief	Roy Wherry
Number of officers, 2004	30

Crime, 2004	Number	Rate
Total	398	15.6
Violent	16	0.6
Non-violent	382	15
Domestic Viol.	150	NA

Emergency/Fire
Director	NA

Public School District
(for school year 2004-2005 except as noted)
Vernon Township School District
539 Route 515
Vernon, NJ 07462
973-764-2900
Administrator	Anthony Macerino
Grade plan	K-12
Enrollment	5,324.0
Students per teacher	12.4
Per pupil expenditure	$11,233
Median faculty salary	$69,764
Median administrator salary	$98,427
Grade 12 enrollment	421.5
High school graduation rate	92.4%

Assessment test results
(percent scoring at proficient or advanced level)
	Language	Math
Grade 3	90.8%	87.9%
Grade 8	79.8%	73.8%
High school	91.2%	87.5%

SAT
Percent tested	80%
Average SAT math score	525
Average SAT verbal score	517

No Child Left Behind, 2003-04
Attendence rate (target = 90%)	94.7%
Drop rate	1.8%
Highly-qualified teachers	98.2%
District needs improvement?(AYP)	No

Municipal Finance
Fiscal Year 2005
Total tax levy	$53,709,155
County levy	10,258,769
County taxes	9,017,439
County library	777,463
County health	0
County open space	463,867
School levy	32,702,467
Local muni. budget	10,747,919
Misc. revenues	9,258,079
Total aid	$2,891,216
CMPTRA	715,096
Muni. block grant	96,794
Energy tax receipts	1,694,871
Homeland security	90,000

Fiscal Year 2006
Total aid	$2,891,217
CMPTRA	655,776
Muni. block grant	96,794
Energy tax receipts	1,754,192
Homeland security	90,000

Taxes
	2003	2004	2005
General tax rate per $100	3.48	3.640	3.700
Net valuation taxable	$1,436,407,756	$1,445,897,910	$1,454,972,223
State equalized value	$1,999,454,003	$2,293,121,226	$2,590,762,505
County equalization ratio	85.86	71.84	62.93

Demographics & Socio-Economic Characteristics
(2000 U.S. Census, except as noted)

Population
1980*	14,166
1990*	13,597
2000	13,533
Male	6,376
Female	7,157
2004 (estimate)*	13,315
Persons per sq. mi. of land	4,838

Race & Hispanic Origin, 2000
Race
White	12,585
Black/African American	207
Amer. Indian/Alaska Natv.	3
Asian	462
Natv. Hawaiian/Pac. Islander	8
Other Race	96
Two or more races	172
Hispanic origin, total	467
Mexican	38
Puerto Rican	127
Cuban	72
Other Hispanic	230

Age & Nativity, 2000
Under 5 years	888
18 years and over	10,490
21 years and over	10,236
65 years and over	2,614
85 years and over	385
Median Age	41.4
Native born	12,223
Foreign born	1,310

Educational Attainment, 2000
Population 25 years and over	9,980
0-8 yrs of school	2.6%
High School grad or higher	92.4%
Bachelor's degree or higher	49.5%
Graduate degree	18.4%

Income & Poverty, 1999
Per capita income	$41,202
Median household income	$74,619
Median family income	$97,673
Persons in poverty	441
H'holds receiving public assistance	38
H'holds receiving social security	1,921

Households, 2000
Total households	5,585
With persons under 18	1,694
With persons over 65	1,954
Family households	3,695
One-person households	1,678
Persons per household	2.42
Persons per family	3.06

Labor & Employment
Total civilian labor force, 2004**	6,996
Unemployment rate	1.7%
Total civilian labor force, 2000	6,975
Unemployment rate	2.0%

Employed persons 16 years and over by occupation, 2000
Managers & professionals	3,314
Service occupations	676
Sales & office occupations	2,020
Farming, fishing & forestry	0
Construction & maintenance	271
Production & transportation	352
Self-employed persons	572

*US Census Bureau
**New Jersey Department of Labor

General Information
Township of Verona
600 Bloomfield Ave
Verona, NJ 07044
973-239-3220

Web site	veronanj.org
Land area (sq. miles)	2.75
Water area (sq. miles)	0.02
Type of government	Township
Form of government	CM '50

Government
Legislative Districts
US Congressional	8
State Legislative	40

Local Officials, 2006
Mayor	Jay Sniatkowski
Admin/Manager	Joseph A. Martin
Clerk	Evelyn Hill
Finance Dir/Treas	Dee Trimmer
Engineer	James Helb
Attorney	Paul J. Giblin
Tax assessor	Romeo Longo
Tax collector	Dee Trimmer
Building officer	Tom Jacobson
Zoning officer	NA
Public Works	NA

Housing & Construction
Housing Units, 2000*
Total	5,719
Median rent	$867
Median SF home value	$237,900

New Privately Owned Housing Units Authorized by Building Permit
	Units	Value
Total, 2004	4	$699,000
Single family	4	$699,000
Total, 2005	7	$1,951,250
Single family	7	$1,951,250

Real Property Valuation - parcels, 2005
	Number	Valuation
Total		$501,754,000
Vacant	66	3,012,500
Residential	4,823	438,881,300
Commercial	183	48,144,300
Industrial	6	2,193,100
Apartments	13	9,522,800
Farm land	0	0
Farm homestead	0	0

Average Property Value & Tax, 2005
Residential value	$90,998
Property tax	$7,555
FAIR rebate	$613

Public Library
Verona Public Library
17 Gould St
Verona, NJ 07044
973-857-4848
Director.................. James Thomas

Library statistics, 2004
	Total	per capita
Volumes	63,000	4.72
Expenditure	$641,045	$47.37

Public Safety
Police
Chief	Douglas Huber
Number of officers, 2004	28

Crime, 2004	Number	Rate
Total	194	14.5
Violent	12	0.9
Non-violent	182	13.6
Domestic Viol.	14	NA

Emergency/Fire
Director.............. Harvey Goodman

Public School District
(for school year 2004-2005 except as noted)

Verona Township School Dist.
121 Fairview Ave
Verona, NJ 07044
973-239-2100

Superintendent	Earl Kim
Grade plan	K-12
Enrollment	2,059.5
Students per teacher	11.6
Per pupil expenditure	$10,860
Median faculty salary	$54,489
Median administrator salary	$104,273
Grade 12 enrollment	152.0
High school graduation rate	98.7%

Assessment test results
(percent scoring at proficient or advanced level)
	Language	Math
Grade 3	93.4%	91.6%
Grade 8	87.9%	80.0%
High school	91.9%	88.5%

SAT
Percent tested	98%
Average SAT math score	552
Average SAT verbal score	541

No Child Left Behind, 2003-04
Attendence rate (target = 90%)	95.8%
Drop rate	0.3%
Highly-qualified teachers	98.9%
District needs improvement?(AYP)	No

Municipal Finance
Fiscal Year 2005
Total tax levy	$41,688,706
County levy	9,178,587
County taxes	8,986,381
County library	0
County health	0
County open space	192,206
School levy	22,243,858
Local muni. budget	10,266,261
Misc. revenues	5,598,226
Total aid	$1,636,743
CMPTRA	678,067
Muni. block grant	59,496
Energy tax receipts	829,180
Homeland security	70,000

Fiscal Year 2006
Total aid	$1,636,743
CMPTRA	649,046
Muni. block grant	59,496
Energy tax receipts	858,201
Homeland security	70,000

Taxes
	2003	2004	2005
General tax rate per $100	7.63	7.950	8.310
Net valuation taxable	$500,229,500	$501,211,900	$502,114,400
State equalized value	$1,694,544,377	$1,902,434,046	$2,117,732,602
County equalization ratio	33.08	33.08	26.33

Demographics & Socio-Economic Characteristics
(2000 U.S. Census, except as noted)

Population
1980*	1,043
1990*	1,314
2000	1,546
Male	743
Female	803
2004 (estimate)*	1,533
Persons per sq. mi. of land	10,494

Race & Hispanic Origin, 2000
Race
White	794
Black/African American	331
Amer. Indian/Alaska Natv.	1
Asian	84
Natv. Hawaiian/Pac. Islander	0
Other Race	236
Two or more races	100
Hispanic origin, total	783
Mexican	32
Puerto Rican	213
Cuban	2
Other Hispanic	536

Age & Nativity, 2000
Under 5 years	117
18 years and over	1,137
21 years and over	1,079
65 years and over	84
85 years and over	3
Median Age	31.9
Native born	979
Foreign born	567

Educational Attainment, 2000
Population 25 years and over	984
0-8 yrs of school	8.7%
High School grad or higher	70.1%
Bachelor's degree or higher	10.2%
Graduate degree	1.2%

Income & Poverty, 1999
Per capita income	$20,616
Median household income	$44,375
Median family income	$43,594
Persons in poverty	130
H'holds receiving public assistance	27
H'holds receiving social security	87

Households, 2000
Total households	564
With persons under 18	251
With persons over 65	65
Family households	382
One-person households	142
Persons per household	2.74
Persons per family	3.21

Labor & Employment
Total civilian labor force, 2004**	916
Unemployment rate	6.7%
Total civilian labor force, 2000	827
Unemployment rate	3.3%

Employed persons 16 years and over by occupation, 2000
Managers & professionals	108
Service occupations	193
Sales & office occupations	241
Farming, fishing & forestry	0
Construction & maintenance	70
Production & transportation	188
Self-employed persons	14

*US Census Bureau
**New Jersey Department of Labor

General Information
Borough of Victory Gardens
337 S Salem St
Victory Gardens, NJ 07801
973-366-5312

Web site	NA
Land area (sq. miles)	0.15
Water area (sq. miles)	0
Type of government	Borough
Form of government	B

Government

Legislative Districts
US Congressional	11
State Legislative	25

Local Officials, 2006
Mayor	Nanette Courtine
Admin/Manager	Deborah Evans
Clerk	Deborah Evans
Finance Dir/Treas	Charles Wood
Engineer	Schorr DePalma
Attorney	Tom Zelante
Tax assessor	Mark Burec
Tax collector	NA
Building officer	Gerald Hartman
Zoning officer	Jim Benton
Public Works	NA

Housing & Construction

Housing Units, 2000*
Total	588
Median rent	$834
Median SF home value	$117,100

New Privately Owned Housing Units Authorized by Building Permit
	Units	Value
Total, 2004	0	$0
Single family	0	$0
Total, 2005	0	$0
Single family	0	$0

Real Property Valuation - parcels, 2005
	Number	Valuation
Total		$39,746,000
Vacant	2	51,000
Residential	292	25,657,700
Commercial	25	8,065,300
Industrial	0	0
Apartments	2	5,972,000
Farm land	0	0
Farm homestead	0	0

Average Property Value & Tax, 2005
Residential value	$87,869
Property tax	$3,594
FAIR rebate	$553

Public Library
No public municipal library.

Library statistics, 2004
	Total	per capita
Volumes	NA	NA
Expenditure	NA	NA

Public Safety

Police
Chief	(State)
Number of officers, 2004	0

Crime, 2004	Number	Rate
Total	23	15
Violent	1	0.7
Non-violent	22	14.4
Domestic Viol.	13	NA

Emergency/Fire
Director	Larry Gallelo

Public School District
(for school year 2004-2005 except as noted)

Victory Gardens School District†
23 Franklin Rd
Dover, NJ 07801

†No schools in district - sends children to Dover Town schools.

Grade plan	NA
Enrollment	NA
Students per teacher	NA
Per pupil expenditure	NA
Median faculty salary	NA

Assessment test results
(percent scoring at proficient or advanced level)
	Language	Math
Grade 3	NA	NA
Grade 8	NA	NA
High school	NA	NA

SAT
Percent tested	NA
Average SAT math score	NA
Average SAT verbal score	NA

No Child Left Behind, 2003-04
Attendence rate (target = 90%)	NA
Drop rate	NA
Highly-qualified teachers	NA
District needs improvement?(AYP)	NA

Municipal Finance

Fiscal Year 2005
Total tax levy	$1,626,707
County levy	273,718
County taxes	224,214
County library	0
County health	0
County open space	49,504
School levy	679,890
Local muni. budget	673,100
Misc. revenues	796,194
Total aid	$114,286
CMPTRA	77,912
Muni. block grant	6,062
Energy tax receipts	30,312
Homeland security	0

Fiscal Year 2006
Total aid	$114,286
CMPTRA	76,851
Muni. block grant	6,062
Energy tax receipts	31,373
Homeland security	NA

Taxes
	2003	2004	2005
General tax rate per $100	3.10	3.300	4.090
Net valuation taxable	$39,787,623	$39,791,777	$39,775,297
State equalized value	$66,356,943	$102,663,688	$98,283,412
County equalization ratio	65.96	59.96	38.73

Demographics & Socio-Economic Characteristics
(2000 U.S. Census, except as noted)

Population
1980*	53,753
1990*	54,780
2000	56,271
Male	26,967
Female	29,304
2000 (revised)	55,825
2004 (estimate)*	58,009
Persons per sq. mi. of land	844

Race & Hispanic Origin, 2000
Race
White	37,964
Black/African American	7,664
Amer. Indian/Alaska Natv.	304
Asian	655
Natv. Hawaiian/Pac. Islander	43
Other Race	7,881
Two or more races	1,760
Hispanic origin, total	16,880
Mexican	1,365
Puerto Rican	13,284
Cuban	232
Other Hispanic	1,999

Age & Nativity, 2000
Under 5 years	3,477
18 years and over	41,808
21 years and over	39,639
65 years and over	7,976
85 years and over	1,080
Median Age	36.5
Native born	51,686
Foreign born	4,585

Educational Attainment, 2000
Population 25 years and over	37,333
0-8 yrs of school	14.2%
High School grad or higher	67.8%
Bachelor's degree or higher	14.3%
Graduate degree	4.8%

Income & Poverty, 1999
Per capita income	$18,797
Median household income	$40,076
Median family income	$47,909
Persons in poverty	7,560
H'holds receiving public assistance	1,040
H'holds receiving social security	5,807

Households, 2000
Total households	19,930
With persons under 18	7,694
With persons over 65	5,488
Family households	14,201
One-person households	4,731
Persons per household	2.7
Persons per family	3.17

Labor & Employment
Total civilian labor force, 2004**	27,550
Unemployment rate	6.5%
Total civilian labor force, 2000	27,593
Unemployment rate	10.7%

Employed persons 16 years and over by occupation, 2000
Managers & professionals	6,467
Service occupations	4,437
Sales & office occupations	6,045
Farming, fishing & forestry	488
Construction & maintenance	2,378
Production & transportation	4,818
Self-employed persons	1,211

*US Census Bureau
**New Jersey Department of Labor

General Information
City of Vineland
PO Box 1508
Vineland, NJ 08362
856-794-4000

Web site	www.ci.vineland.nj.us
Land area (sq. miles)	68.69
Water area (sq. miles)	0.29
Type of government	City
Form of government	MC '50

Government

Legislative Districts
US Congressional	2
State Legislative	1

Local Officials, 2006
Mayor	Perry Barse
Admin/Manager	Paul Trivellini
Clerk	Keith Petrosky
Finance Dir/Treas	Mary Ann Chalow
Engineer	David Battistini
Attorney	Richard Tonetta
Tax assessor	Donald Seifrit
Tax collector	Carmen DiGiorgio
Building officer	Kevin Kirchner
Zoning officer	Patrick Finley
Public Works	Joe Bond

Housing & Construction

Housing Units, 2000*
Total	20,958
Median rent	$638
Median SF home value	$97,200

New Privately Owned Housing Units
Authorized by Building Permit
	Units	Value
Total, 2004	114	$14,620,965
Single family	114	$14,620,965
Total, 2005	139	$17,519,611
Single family	125	$15,691,611

Real Property Valuation - parcels, 2005
	Number	Valuation
Total		$1,859,049,000
Vacant	1,544	33,736,400
Residential	14,554	1,310,667,700
Commercial	1,267	358,609,600
Industrial	85	65,756,900
Apartments	69	53,012,200
Farm land	400	32,986,100
Farm homestead	670	4,280,100

Average Property Value & Tax, 2005
Residential value	$86,373
Property tax	$3,105
FAIR rebate	$603

Public Library
Vineland Public Library
1058 E Landis Ave
Vineland, NJ 08360
856-794-4244

Director . . . . Gloria Urban

Library statistics, 2004
	Total	per capita
Volumes	88,097	1.57
Expenditure	$1,491,266	$26.50

Public Safety

Police
Chief	Mario Brunetta
Number of officers, 2004	149

Crime, 2004	Number	Rate
Total	3,371	59.1
Violent	449	7.9
Non-violent	2,922	51.2
Domestic Viol.	1,576	NA

Emergency/Fire
Director . . . . Peter Finley

Public School District
(for school year 2004-2005 except as noted)

Vineland City School District
625 Plum St
Vineland, NJ 08360
856-794-6700

Superintendent	Clarence Hoover
Grade plan	K-12
Enrollment	9,680.0
Students per teacher	9.2
Per pupil expenditure	$15,410
Median faculty salary	$46,212
Median administrator salary	$94,499
Grade 12 enrollment	603.5
High school graduation rate	91.5%

Assessment test results
(percent scoring at proficient or advanced level)
	Language	Math
Grade 3	77.2%	82.9%
Grade 8	50.1%	44.1%
High school	69.2%	57.7%

SAT
Percent tested	52%
Average SAT math score	470
Average SAT verbal score	459

No Child Left Behind, 2003-04
Attendence rate (target = 90%)	92.3%
Drop rate	4.1%
Highly-qualified teachers	90.6%
District needs improvement?(AYP)	No

Municipal Finance

Fiscal Year 2005
Total tax levy	$67,215,154
County levy	27,062,515
County taxes	26,790,697
County library	0
County health	0
County open space	271,818
School levy	18,921,676
Local muni. budget	21,230,963
Misc. revenues	28,841,158
Total aid	$8,251,391
CMPTRA	4,347,766
Muni. block grant	239,699
Energy tax receipts	3,518,933
Homeland security	140,000

Fiscal Year 2006
Total aid	$8,251,391
CMPTRA	4,224,603
Muni. block grant	239,699
Energy tax receipts	3,642,096
Homeland security	140,000

Taxes
	2003	2004	2005
General tax rate per $100	3.09	3.156	3.597
Net valuation taxable	$1,776,892,861	$1,819,713,131	$1,869,730,783
State equalized value	$2,298,994,515	$2,575,758,479	$2,919,629,580
County equalization ratio	83.25	77.29	70.51

Demographics & Socio-Economic Characteristics
(2000 U.S. Census, except as noted)

Population
1980*	12,919
1990*	24,559
2000	28,126
Male	13,505
Female	14,621
2004 (estimate)*	28,742
Persons per sq. mi. of land	2,477

Race & Hispanic Origin, 2000
Race
White	22,011
Black/African American	2,249
Amer. Indian/Alaska Natv.	38
Asian	3,217
Natv. Hawaiian/Pac. Islander	8
Other Race	156
Two or more races	447
Hispanic origin, total	694
Mexican	102
Puerto Rican	301
Cuban	52
Other Hispanic	239

Age & Nativity, 2000
Under 5 years	1,767
18 years and over	20,699
21 years and over	19,960
65 years and over	3,075
85 years and over	628
Median Age	37.2
Native born	24,364
Foreign born	3,762

Educational Attainment, 2000
Population 25 years and over	18,961
0-8 yrs of school	2.8%
High School grad or higher	91.2%
Bachelor's degree or higher	46.2%
Graduate degree	20.0%

Income & Poverty, 1999
Per capita income	$33,635
Median household income	$68,402
Median family income	$86,873
Persons in poverty	1,551
H'holds receiving public assistance	102
H'holds receiving social security	1,897

Households, 2000
Total households	10,489
With persons under 18	4,047
With persons over 65	1,969
Family households	7,072
One-person households	2,826
Persons per household	2.6
Persons per family	3.23

Labor & Employment
Total civilian labor force, 2004**	14,285
Unemployment rate	2.2%
Total civilian labor force, 2000	14,938
Unemployment rate	3.2%

Employed persons 16 years and over by occupation, 2000
Managers & professionals	7,809
Service occupations	1,477
Sales & office occupations	3,902
Farming, fishing & forestry	29
Construction & maintenance	492
Production & transportation	745
Self-employed persons	870

*US Census Bureau
**New Jersey Department of Labor

General Information
Township of Voorhees
620 Berlin Rd
Voorhees, NJ 08043
856-429-7757
Web site	www.voorhees-nj.com
Land area (sq. miles)	11.60
Water area (sq. miles)	0.03
Type of government	Township
Form of government	TC

Government

Legislative Districts
US Congressional	1
State Legislative	6

Local Officials, 2006
Mayor	Michael R. Mignogna
Admin/Manager	Lawrence Spellman
Clerk	Jeanette Schelberg
Finance Dir/Treas	Dean Ciminera
Engineer	Environmental Resolutions
Attorney	Howard Long
Tax assessor	Michael Kane
Tax collector	Jennifer Barnes
Building officer	Charles Bogardus
Zoning officer	Agnes Jones
Public Works	John Maurer

Housing & Construction

Housing Units, 2000*
Total	11,084
Median rent	$864
Median SF home value	$179,500

New Privately Owned Housing Units
Authorized by Building Permit
	Units	Value
Total, 2004	116	$16,471,400
Single family	116	$16,471,400
Total, 2005	277	$33,895,255
Single family	125	$16,967,728

Real Property Valuation - parcels, 2005
	Number	Valuation
Total		$1,588,467,894
Vacant	785	31,870,330
Residential	8,279	1,104,972,088
Commercial	412	362,995,600
Industrial	30	16,400,100
Apartments	16	71,309,900
Farm land	8	836,700
Farm homestead	18	83,176

Average Property Value & Tax, 2005
Residential value	$133,187
Property tax	$7,086
FAIR rebate	$495

Public Library
Camden County Library
203 Laurel Rd
Voorhees, NJ 08043
856-772-1636
Director	Claudia Sumler

Library statistics, 2004
	Total	per capita
Volumes	NA	NA
Expenditure	NA	NA

Public Safety

Police
Chief	Keith Hummel
Number of officers, 2004	50

Crime, 2004	Number	Rate
Total	887	31.1
Violent	70	2.5
Non-violent	817	28.6
Domestic Viol.	218	NA

Emergency/Fire
Director	James Pacifico

Public School District
(for school year 2004-2005 except as noted)

Voorhees Township School District
329 Route 73
Voorhees, NJ 08043
856-751-8446
Superintendent	Raymond Brosel Jr.
Grade plan	K-8
Enrollment	3,436.0
Students per teacher	11.8
Per pupil expenditure	$11,726
Median faculty salary	$70,988
Median administrator salary	$113,712
Grade 12 enrollment	NA
High school graduation rate	NA

Assessment test results
(percent scoring at proficient or advanced level)
	Language	Math
Grade 3	95.5%	93.0%
Grade 8	88.2%	81.7%
High school	NA	NA

SAT
Percent tested	NA
Average SAT math score	NA
Average SAT verbal score	NA

No Child Left Behind, 2003-04
Attendance rate (target = 90%)	96.0%
Drop rate	NA
Highly-qualified teachers	99.5%
District needs improvement?(AYP)	No

Municipal Finance

Fiscal Year 2005
Total tax levy	$84,691,801
County levy	23,237,853
County taxes	21,415,326
County library	1,541,442
County health	0
County open space	281,085
School levy	49,517,313
Local muni. budget	11,936,635
Misc. revenues	9,724,529
Total aid	$3,092,953
CMPTRA	1,045,150
Muni. block grant	110,283
Energy tax receipts	1,847,520
Homeland security	90,000

Fiscal Year 2006
Total aid	$3,092,953
CMPTRA	980,487
Muni. block grant	110,283
Energy tax receipts	1,912,183
Homeland security	90,000

Taxes
	2003	2004	2005
General tax rate per $100	4.86	5.134	5.321
Net valuation taxable	$1,587,916,906	$1,575,650,035	$1,591,897,612
State equalized value	$2,559,917,630	$2,772,104,363	$3,082,683,215
County equalization ratio	69.02	62.03	56.78

Demographics & Socio-Economic Characteristics

(2000 U.S. Census, except as noted)

Population

1980*	10,802
1990*	9,757
2000	9,622
Male	4,683
Female	4,939
2004 (estimate)*	9,664
Persons per sq. mi. of land	4,636

Race & Hispanic Origin, 2000

Race
White	8,918
Black/African American	57
Amer. Indian/Alaska Natv.	4
Asian	435
Natv. Hawaiian/Pac. Islander	0
Other Race	126
Two or more races	82
Hispanic origin, total	511
Mexican	36
Puerto Rican	105
Cuban	27
Other Hispanic	343

Age & Nativity, 2000

Under 5 years	734
18 years and over	7,170
21 years and over	6,963
65 years and over	1,459
85 years and over	114
Median Age	38.1
Native born	8,434
Foreign born	1,188

Educational Attainment, 2000

Population 25 years and over	6,676
0-8 yrs of school	2.2%
High School grad or higher	92.2%
Bachelor's degree or higher	36.7%
Graduate degree	9.8%

Income & Poverty, 1999

Per capita income	$30,733
Median household income	$75,532
Median family income	$82,208
Persons in poverty	199
H'holds receiving public assistance	59
H'holds receiving social security	1,018

Households, 2000

Total households	3,428
With persons under 18	1,316
With persons over 65	1,041
Family households	2,678
One-person households	641
Persons per household	2.81
Persons per family	3.22

Labor & Employment

Total civilian labor force, 2004**	6,000
Unemployment rate	4.6%
Total civilian labor force, 2000	5,085
Unemployment rate	1.9%

Employed persons 16 years and over by occupation, 2000
Managers & professionals	2,153
Service occupations	623
Sales & office occupations	1,522
Farming, fishing & forestry	0
Construction & maintenance	384
Production & transportation	304
Self-employed persons	315

*US Census Bureau
**New Jersey Department of Labor

General Information

Borough of Waldwick
63 Franklin Turnpike
Waldwick, NJ 07463
201-652-5300

Web site	www.waldwickpd.org
Land area (sq. miles)	2.08
Water area (sq. miles)	0.01
Type of government	Borough
Form of government	B

Government

Legislative Districts

US Congressional	5
State Legislative	39

Local Officials, 2006

Mayor	Rick Vander Wende
Admin/Manager	Gary Kratz
Clerk	Paula Jaegge
Finance Dir/Treas	MaryAnn Viviani
Engineer	Dennis O'Brien
Attorney	Thomas Herton
Tax assessor	Angela Mattiace
Tax collector	NA
Building officer	Joseph Mysliwiec
Zoning officer	Joseph Mysliwiec
Public Works	Joseph Agugliaro

Housing & Construction

Housing Units, 2000*

Total	3,495
Median rent	$1,127
Median SF home value	$229,400

New Privately Owned Housing Units Authorized by Building Permit

	Units	Value
Total, 2004	NA	NA
Single family	NA	NA
Total, 2005	15	$2,422,180
Single family	15	$2,422,180

Real Property Valuation - parcels, 2005

	Number	Valuation
Total		$1,534,828,700
Vacant	122	19,616,200
Residential	3,297	1,371,936,400
Commercial	123	112,843,900
Industrial	20	30,432,200
Apartments	0	0
Farm land	0	0
Farm homestead	0	0

Average Property Value & Tax, 2005

Residential value	$416,117
Property tax	$7,504
FAIR rebate	$604

Public Library

Waldwick Public Library
19-21 E Prospect St
Waldwick, NJ 07463
201-652-5104

Director	Patricia Boyd

Library statistics, 2004

	Total	per capita
Volumes	40,517	4.21
Expenditure	$446,186	$46.37

Public Safety

Police

Chief	Mark Messner
Number of officers, 2004	19

Crime, 2004	Number	Rate
Total	79	8.2
Violent	5	0.5
Non-violent	74	7.7
Domestic Viol.	33	NA

Emergency/Fire

Director	Joseph Alvarez

Public School District

(for school year 2004-2005 except as noted)

Waldwick School District
155 Summit Ave
Waldwick, NJ 07463
201-445-3131

Superintendent	Gregg Hauser (Int)
Grade plan	K-12
Enrollment	1,515.5
Students per teacher	10.8
Per pupil expenditure	$12,453
Median faculty salary	$51,035
Median administrator salary	$110,452
Grade 12 enrollment	93.0
High school graduation rate	98.9%

Assessment test results

(percent scoring at proficient or advanced level)
	Language	Math
Grade 3	90.8%	83.1%
Grade 8	89.7%	82.3%
High school	88.7%	88.3%

SAT

Percent tested	91%
Average SAT math score	530
Average SAT verbal score	498

No Child Left Behind, 2003-04

Attendence rate (target = 90%)	96.0%
Drop rate	0.5%
Highly-qualified teachers	97%
District needs improvement?(AYP)	No

Municipal Finance

Fiscal Year 2005

Total tax levy	$27,692,562
County levy	2,563,514
County taxes	2,435,246
County library	0
County health	0
County open space	128,268
School levy	18,570,788
Local muni. budget	6,558,260
Misc. revenues	4,830,061
Total aid	$3,086,422
CMPTRA	406,302
Muni. block grant	42,693
Energy tax receipts	2,587,427
Homeland security	50,000

Fiscal Year 2006

Total aid	$3,086,422
CMPTRA	315,742
Muni. block grant	42,693
Energy tax receipts	2,677,987
Homeland security	50,000

Taxes

	2003	2004	2005
General tax rate per $100	3.44	3.740	1.810
Net valuation taxable	$682,188,401	$685,626,585	$1,535,620,331
State equalized value	$1,126,466,977	$1,269,028,255	$1,489,880,985
County equalization ratio	67.28	60.56	120.04

Demographics & Socio-Economic Characteristics

(2000 U.S. Census, except as noted)

Population

1980*	18,952
1990*	20,244
2000	25,261
Male	12,155
Female	13,106
2004 (estimate)*	26,267
Persons per sq. mi. of land	858

Race & Hispanic Origin, 2000

Race

White	24,526
Black/African American	155
Amer. Indian/Alaska Natv.	26
Asian	319
Natv. Hawaiian/Pac. Islander	9
Other Race	80
Two or more races	146
Hispanic origin, total	391
Mexican	60
Puerto Rican	128
Cuban	43
Other Hispanic	160

Age & Nativity, 2000

Under 5 years	1,671
18 years and over	18,887
21 years and over	18,255
65 years and over	3,641
85 years and over	450
Median Age	40.3
Native born	24,243
Foreign born	1,018

Educational Attainment, 2000

Population 25 years and over	17,618
0-8 yrs of school	2.1%
High School grad or higher	91.6%
Bachelor's degree or higher	38.9%
Graduate degree	13.9%

Income & Poverty, 1999

Per capita income	$32,954
Median household income	$73,989
Median family income	$83,795
Persons in poverty	569
H'holds receiving public assistance	91
H'holds receiving social security	2,575

Households, 2000

Total households	9,437
With persons under 18	3,361
With persons over 65	2,508
Family households	6,931
One-person households	2,140
Persons per household	2.64
Persons per family	3.14

Labor & Employment

Total civilian labor force, 2004**	12,158
Unemployment rate	3.8%
Total civilian labor force, 2000	12,820
Unemployment rate	4.0%

Employed persons 16 years and over by occupation, 2000

Managers & professionals	5,470
Service occupations	1,190
Sales & office occupations	3,395
Farming, fishing & forestry	56
Construction & maintenance	1,238
Production & transportation	954
Self-employed persons	955

*US Census Bureau
**New Jersey Department of Labor

General Information

Township of Wall
2700 Allaire Rd
Wall, NJ 07719
732-449-8444

Web site	www.wallnj.com
Land area (sq. miles)	30.62
Water area (sq. miles)	0.80
Type of government	Township
Form of government	TC

Government

Legislative Districts

US Congressional	4
State Legislative	11

Local Officials, 2006

Mayor	Mary L. Burn
Admin/Manager	Joseph Verruni
Clerk	Lorraine Kubacz
Finance Dir/Treas	Stephen Mayer
Engineer	Matt Zahorsky
Attorney	Roger McLaughlin
Tax assessor	Denise Siegel
Tax collector	Theresa Vola
Building officer	Paul Rabenda
Zoning officer	Matt Zahorsky
Public Works	Ken Critchlow

Housing & Construction

Housing Units, 2000*

Total	9,957
Median rent	$818
Median SF home value	$234,700

New Privately Owned Housing Units Authorized by Building Permit

	Units	Value
Total, 2004	92	$15,941,152
Single family	74	$8,990,152
Total, 2005	214	$23,463,667
Single family	121	$20,981,667

Real Property Valuation - parcels, 2005

	Number	Valuation
Total		$3,688,534,825
Vacant	532	98,274,600
Residential	9,090	2,809,175,700
Commercial	582	575,742,725
Industrial	86	154,250,000
Apartments	8	24,318,700
Farm land	59	25,888,900
Farm homestead	86	884,200

Average Property Value & Tax, 2005

Residential value	$306,240
Property tax	$6,574
FAIR rebate	$582

Public Library

Wall Public Library†
2700 Allaire Rd
Wall, NJ 07719
732-449-8877

Branch Librarian	Pamela Sawall

Library statistics, 2004

	Total	per capita
Volumes	NA	NA
Expenditure	NA	NA

†Branch of County Library

Public Safety

Police

Chief	Roy Hall
Number of officers, 2004	71

Crime, 2004	Number	Rate
Total	421	16.2
Violent	30	1.2
Non-violent	391	15
Domestic Viol.	128	NA

Emergency/Fire

Director	NA

Public School District

(for school year 2004-2005 except as noted)

Wall Township School District
PO Box 1199
Wall, NJ 07719
732-556-2000

Superintendent	James Habel
Grade plan	K-12
Enrollment	4,315.5
Students per teacher	11.5
Per pupil expenditure	$11,664
Median faculty salary	$42,715
Median administrator salary	$111,926
Grade 12 enrollment	303.0
High school graduation rate	92.3%

Assessment test results

(percent scoring at proficient or advanced level)

	Language	Math
Grade 3	92.4%	92.6%
Grade 8	78.3%	74.7%
High school	90.9%	83.0%

SAT

Percent tested	83%
Average SAT math score	521
Average SAT verbal score	515

No Child Left Behind, 2003-04

Attendence rate (target = 90%)	95.1%
Drop rate	1.5%
Highly-qualified teachers	93.7%
District needs improvement?(AYP)	No

Municipal Finance

Fiscal Year 2005

Total tax levy	$79,304,777
County levy	16,036,602
County taxes	14,158,344
County library	779,921
County health	258,176
County open space	840,161
School levy	46,101,408
Local muni. budget	17,166,767
Misc. revenues	10,828,992
Total aid	$4,542,445
CMPTRA	643,579
Muni. block grant	99,049
Energy tax receipts	3,701,028
Homeland security	90,000

Fiscal Year 2006

Total aid	$4,542,445
CMPTRA	514,043
Muni. block grant	99,049
Energy tax receipts	3,830,564
Homeland security	90,000

Taxes

	2003	2004	2005
General tax rate per $100	2.04	2.108	2.147
Net valuation taxable	$3,616,357,722	$3,653,841,058	$3,694,395,414
State equalized value	$4,127,319,929	$4,672,393,559	$5,343,354,663
County equalization ratio	98.97	87.62	78.17

Demographics & Socio-Economic Characteristics
(2000 U.S. Census, except as noted)

Population
1980*	10,741
1990*	10,828
2000	11,583
Male	5,582
Female	6,001
2004 (estimate)*	11,558
Persons per sq. mi. of land	11,607

Race & Hispanic Origin, 2000
Race
White	10,147
Black/African American	309
Amer. Indian/Alaska Natv.	11
Asian	577
Natv. Hawaiian/Pac. Islander	2
Other Race	269
Two or more races	268
Hispanic origin, total	776
Mexican	37
Puerto Rican	252
Cuban	66
Other Hispanic	421

Age & Nativity, 2000
Under 5 years	611
18 years and over	9,451
21 years and over	9,083
65 years and over	1,757
85 years and over	220
Median Age	38.2
Native born	6,849
Foreign born	4,734

Educational Attainment, 2000
Population 25 years and over	8,434
0-8 yrs of school	11.9%
High School grad or higher	72.4%
Bachelor's degree or higher	17.0%
Graduate degree	6.4%

Income & Poverty, 1999
Per capita income	$24,431
Median household income	$45,656
Median family income	$55,291
Persons in poverty	729
H'holds receiving public assistance	82
H'holds receiving social security	1,381

Households, 2000
Total households	4,752
With persons under 18	1,307
With persons over 65	1,342
Family households	3,043
One-person households	1,415
Persons per household	2.44
Persons per family	3.05

Labor & Employment
Total civilian labor force, 2004**	6,578
Unemployment rate	7.3%
Total civilian labor force, 2000	6,269
Unemployment rate	5.9%

Employed persons 16 years and over by occupation, 2000
Managers & professionals	1,848
Service occupations	782
Sales & office occupations	1,711
Farming, fishing & forestry	0
Construction & maintenance	740
Production & transportation	1,118
Self-employed persons	272

*US Census Bureau
**New Jersey Department of Labor

General Information
Borough of Wallington
24 Union Blvd
Wallington, NJ 07057
973-777-0318

Web site	www.wallington-nj.gov
Land area (sq. miles)	1.00
Water area (sq. miles)	0.04
Type of government	Borough
Form of government	B

Government

Legislative Districts
US Congressional	9
State Legislative	36

Local Officials, 2006
Mayor	Walter Wargacki
Admin/Manager	Witold Baginski
Clerk	Witold Baginski
Finance Dir/Treas	Alice Czykier
Engineer	Kenneth Job
Attorney	Kenneth Slomienski
Tax assessor	Stuart Stolarz
Tax collector	Alice Czykier
Building officer	Nick Melfi
Zoning officer	NA
Public Works	Robert Siery

Housing & Construction

Housing Units, 2000*
Total	4,906
Median rent	$756
Median SF home value	$201,800

New Privately Owned Housing Units Authorized by Building Permit
	Units	Value
Total, 2004	4	$371,000
Single family	0	$0
Total, 2005	4	$660,500
Single family	2	$475,000

Real Property Valuation - parcels, 2005
	Number	Valuation
Total		$525,780,500
Vacant	57	4,683,200
Residential	2,122	382,615,000
Commercial	154	65,264,900
Industrial	39	29,412,700
Apartments	33	43,804,700
Farm land	0	0
Farm homestead	0	0

Average Property Value & Tax, 2005
Residential value	$180,309
Property tax	$5,641
FAIR rebate	$739

Public Library
JFK Memorial Library
92 Hathaway St
Wallington, NJ 07057
973-471-1692
Director............. Marianne Williams

Library statistics, 2004
	Total	per capita
Volumes	39,897	3.44
Expenditure	$242,285	$20.92

Public Safety
Police
Chief	Anthony Denevento (Dir)
Number of officers, 2004	25

Crime, 2004	Number	Rate
Total	216	18.7
Violent	15	1.3
Non-violent	201	17.4
Domestic Viol.	48	NA

Emergency/Fire
Director................Matthew Palmer

Public School District
(for school year 2004-2005 except as noted)

Wallington School District
Jefferson School
Wallington, NJ 07057
973-777-4421

Superintendent	Frank Cocchiola Jr.
Grade plan	K-12
Enrollment	1,090.5
Students per teacher	11.4
Per pupil expenditure	$10,156
Median faculty salary	$48,910
Median administrator salary	$98,461
Grade 12 enrollment	74.0
High school graduation rate	91.4%

Assessment test results
(percent scoring at proficient or advanced level)
	Language	Math
Grade 3	87.4%	83.5%
Grade 8	80.2%	55.9%
High school	78.4%	80.4%

SAT
Percent tested	72%
Average SAT math score	479
Average SAT verbal score	464

No Child Left Behind, 2003-04
Attendence rate (target = 90%)	95.1%
Drop rate	0.8%
Highly-qualified teachers	93.2%
District needs improvement?(AYP)	No

Municipal Finance
Fiscal Year 2005
Total tax levy	$16,464,915
County levy	1,677,971
County taxes	1,594,010
County library	0
County health	0
County open space	83,962
School levy	9,668,902
Local muni. budget	5,118,042
Misc. revenues	3,810,986
Total aid	$994,341
CMPTRA	451,321
Muni. block grant	47,380
Energy tax receipts	425,640
Homeland security	70,000

Fiscal Year 2006
Total aid	$994,340
CMPTRA	436,423
Muni. block grant	47,380
Energy tax receipts	440,537
Homeland security	70,000

Taxes
	2003	2004	2005
General tax rate per $100	2.72	2.910	3.130
Net valuation taxable	$524,546,788	$525,416,421	$526,270,097
State equalized value	$727,123,355	$832,850,362	$950,804,150
County equalization ratio	82.17	72.14	63.06

Demographics & Socio-Economic Characteristics
(2000 U.S. Census, except as noted)

Population
1980*	150
1990*	67
2000	41
Male	20
Female	21
2004 (estimate)*	41
Persons per sq. mi. of land	2

Race & Hispanic Origin, 2000
Race
White	41
Black/African American	0
Amer. Indian/Alaska Natv.	0
Asian	0
Natv. Hawaiian/Pac. Islander	0
Other Race	0
Two or more races	0
Hispanic origin, total	0
Mexican	0
Puerto Rican	0
Cuban	0
Other Hispanic	0

Age & Nativity, 2000
Under 5 years	0
18 years and over	33
21 years and over	33
65 years and over	11
85 years and over	1
Median Age	49.3
Native born	37
Foreign born	0

Educational Attainment, 2000
Population 25 years and over	37
0-8 yrs of school	0.0%
High School grad or higher	62.2%
Bachelor's degree or higher	0.0%
Graduate degree	0.0%

Income & Poverty, 1999
Per capita income	$17,624
Median household income	$22,250
Median family income	$22,250
Persons in poverty	0
H'holds receiving public assistance	0
H'holds receiving social security	14

Households, 2000
Total households	20
With persons under 18	4
With persons over 65	7
Family households	12
One-person households	8
Persons per household	2.05
Persons per family	2.75

Labor & Employment
Total civilian labor force, 2004**	41
Unemployment rate	0.0%
Total civilian labor force, 2000	18
Unemployment rate	0.0%

Employed persons 16 years and over by occupation, 2000
Managers & professionals	0
Service occupations	10
Sales & office occupations	0
Farming, fishing & forestry	0
Construction & maintenance	8
Production & transportation	0
Self-employed persons	0

*US Census Bureau
**New Jersey Department of Labor

General Information
Township of Walpack
Box 94
Walpack Center
Walpack, NJ 07881
908-841-9576

Web site	NA
Land area (sq. miles)	24.07
Water area (sq. miles)	0.65
Type of government	Township
Form of government	TC

Government
Legislative Districts
US Congressional	5
State Legislative	24

Local Officials, 2006
Mayor	Raymond Fuller
Admin/Manager	NA
Clerk	Betsy Cuneo
Finance Dir/Treas	Michelle Lastarza
Engineer	NA
Attorney	Richard Clark
Tax assessor	John Dykson
Tax collector	Terry Beshada
Building officer	Greg Chontow
Zoning officer	NA
Public Works	NA

Housing & Construction
Housing Units, 2000*
Total	34
Median rent	$400
Median SF home value	$275,000

New Privately Owned Housing Units Authorized by Building Permit
	Units	Value
Total, 2004	0	$0
Single family	0	$0
Total, 2005	0	$0
Single family	0	$0

Real Property Valuation - parcels, 2005
	Number	Valuation
Total		$2,331,700
Vacant	7	85,100
Residential	8	645,250
Commercial	2	1,077,400
Industrial	0	0
Apartments	0	0
Farm land	4	422,000
Farm homestead	9	101,950

Average Property Value & Tax, 2005
Residential value	$43,953
Property tax	$576
FAIR rebate	$824

Public Library
No public municipal library.

Library statistics, 2004
	Total	per capita
Volumes	NA	NA
Expenditure	NA	NA

Public Safety
Police
Chief	NA
Number of officers, 2004	0

Crime, 2004	Number	Rate
Total	0	+
Violent	0	+
Non-violent	0	+
Domestic Viol.	0	NA

Emergency/Fire
Director	NA

Public School District
(for school year 2004-2005 except as noted)

Sandyston-Walpack Township School Dist.
100 Route 560
Layton, NJ 07851
973-948-4450

Administrator	Glenn Sumpman
Grade plan	K-6
Enrollment	178.0
Students per teacher	9.6
Per pupil expenditure	$12,965
Median faculty salary	$50,233
Median administrator salary	$110,000
Grade 12 enrollment	NA
High school graduation rate	NA

Assessment test results
(percent scoring at proficient or advanced level)
	Language	Math
Grade 3	100%	94.6%
Grade 8	NA	NA
High school	NA	NA

SAT
Percent tested	NA
Average SAT math score	NA
Average SAT verbal score	NA

No Child Left Behind, 2003-04
Attendance rate (target = 90%)	95.4%
Drop rate	NA
Highly-qualified teachers	100%
District needs improvement?(AYP)	No

Municipal Finance
Fiscal Year 2005
Total tax levy	$31,559
County levy	10,880
County taxes	9,004
County library	908
County health	427
County open space	542
School levy	20,679
Local muni. budget	0
Misc. revenues	129,572
Total aid	$41,155
CMPTRA	2,404
Muni. block grant	293
Energy tax receipts	38,458
Homeland security	0

Fiscal Year 2006
Total aid	$41,155
CMPTRA	1,058
Muni. block grant	293
Energy tax receipts	39,804
Homeland security	NA

Taxes
	2003	2004	2005
General tax rate per $100	1.74	1.530	1.320
Net valuation taxable	$2,404,887	$2,408,949	$2,408,266
State equalized value	$2,509,011	$2,520,867	$2,523,859
County equalization ratio	95	95.85	95.42

Demographics & Socio-Economic Characteristics
(2000 U.S. Census, except as noted)

Population
1980*	10,025
1990*	9,711
2000	10,266
Male	4,956
Female	5,310
2004 (estimate)*	10,440
Persons per sq. mi. of land	1,309

Race & Hispanic Origin, 2000
Race
White	9,308
Black/African American	155
Amer. Indian/Alaska Natv.	35
Asian	372
Natv. Hawaiian/Pac. Islander	3
Other Race	211
Two or more races	182
Hispanic origin, total	554
Mexican	69
Puerto Rican	179
Cuban	44
Other Hispanic	262

Age & Nativity, 2000
Under 5 years	689
18 years and over	7,765
21 years and over	7,470
65 years and over	1,233
85 years and over	247
Median Age	37.6
Native born	8,973
Foreign born	1,293

Educational Attainment, 2000
Population 25 years and over	7,162
0-8 yrs of school	6.2%
High School grad or higher	84.2%
Bachelor's degree or higher	22.3%
Graduate degree	7.7%

Income & Poverty, 1999
Per capita income	$25,403
Median household income	$66,113
Median family income	$71,127
Persons in poverty	330
H'holds receiving public assistance	64
H'holds receiving social security	841

Households, 2000
Total households	3,444
With persons under 18	1,401
With persons over 65	687
Family households	2,689
One-person households	575
Persons per household	2.86
Persons per family	3.23

Labor & Employment
Total civilian labor force, 2004**	5,328
Unemployment rate	4.6%
Total civilian labor force, 2000	5,675
Unemployment rate	3.6%

Employed persons 16 years and over by occupation, 2000
Managers & professionals	1,712
Service occupations	871
Sales & office occupations	1,763
Farming, fishing & forestry	0
Construction & maintenance	473
Production & transportation	650
Self-employed persons	210

*US Census Bureau
**New Jersey Department of Labor

General Information
Borough of Wanaque
579 Ringwood Ave
Wanaque, NJ 07465
973-839-3000

Web site	www.wanaqueborough.com
Land area (sq. miles)	7.98
Water area (sq. miles)	1.23
Type of government	Borough
Form of government	B

Government

Legislative Districts
US Congressional	5
State Legislative	40

Local Officials, 2006
Mayor	Thomas Balunis
Admin/Manager	Thomas Carroll
Clerk	Katherine Falone
Finance Dir/Treas	Mary Ann Brindisi
Engineer	Mike Cristaldi
Attorney	Tony Fiorello
Tax assessor	Brian Townsend
Tax collector	Laurel Matthews
Building officer	Jeff Brusco
Zoning officer	Jeff Brusco
Public Works	Donald Babcock

Housing & Construction

Housing Units, 2000*
Total	3,500
Median rent	$946
Median SF home value	$172,100

New Privately Owned Housing Units
Authorized by Building Permit
	Units	Value
Total, 2004	87	$6,369,702
Single family	10	$872,330
Total, 2005	235	$20,442,892
Single family	1	$87,233

Real Property Valuation - parcels, 2005
	Number	Valuation
Total		$496,598,484
Vacant	240	25,063,200
Residential	3,119	413,565,074
Commercial	102	43,334,120
Industrial	20	12,895,390
Apartments	4	1,600,100
Farm land	1	127,300
Farm homestead	3	13,300

Average Property Value & Tax, 2005
Residential value	$132,472
Property tax	$6,681
FAIR rebate	$522

Public Library
Wanaque Public Library
616 Ringwood Ave
Wanaque, NJ 07465
973-839-4434

Director .... Richard Mariconda

Library statistics, 2004
	Total	per capita
Volumes	32,875	3.20
Expenditure	$322,375	$31.40

Public Safety
Police
Chief	Jack Reno
Number of officers, 2004	22

Crime, 2004	Number	Rate
Total	148	14.2
Violent	13	1.2
Non-violent	135	13
Domestic Viol.	92	NA

Emergency/Fire
Director .... Scott Montegari

Public School District
(for school year 2004-2005 except as noted)

Wanaque School District
547 Ringwood Ave
Wanaque, NJ 07465
973-835-8202

Administrator	Andrew Luciani
Grade plan	K-8
Enrollment	1,034.0
Students per teacher	12.1
Per pupil expenditure	$10,847
Median faculty salary	$67,228
Median administrator salary	$92,000
Grade 12 enrollment	NA
High school graduation rate	NA

Assessment test results
(percent scoring at proficient or advanced level)
	Language	Math
Grade 3	87.0%	86.0%
Grade 8	63.6%	61.0%
High school	NA	NA

SAT
Percent tested	NA
Average SAT math score	NA
Average SAT verbal score	NA

No Child Left Behind, 2003-04
Attendence rate (target = 90%)	96.2%
Drop rate	NA
Highly-qualified teachers	99%
District needs improvement?(AYP)	No

Municipal Finance

Fiscal Year 2005
Total tax levy	$25,089,378
County levy	4,949,249
County taxes	4,855,040
County library	0
County health	0
County open space	94,209
School levy	14,518,553
Local muni. budget	5,621,576
Misc. revenues	3,369,565
Total aid	$1,286,299
CMPTRA	561,169
Muni. block grant	42,492
Energy tax receipts	612,638
Homeland security	70,000

Fiscal Year 2006
Total aid	$1,286,299
CMPTRA	539,727
Muni. block grant	42,492
Energy tax receipts	634,080
Homeland security	70,000

Taxes
	2003	2004	2005
General tax rate per $100	4.54	4.820	5.050
Net valuation taxable	$496,801,034	$497,122,502	$497,452,440
State equalized value	$854,343,997	$937,382,538	$1,070,941,744
County equalization ratio	65.55	58.15	52.99

Demographics & Socio-Economic Characteristics
(2000 U.S. Census, except as noted)

Population
1980*	7,268
1990*	9,487
2000	10,387
Male	5,113
Female	5,274
2004 (estimate)*	11,315
Persons per sq. mi. of land	169

Race & Hispanic Origin, 2000
Race
White	10,086
Black/African American	67
Amer. Indian/Alaska Natv.	6
Asian	70
Natv. Hawaiian/Pac. Islander	1
Other Race	43
Two or more races	114
Hispanic origin, total	300
Mexican	23
Puerto Rican	130
Cuban	34
Other Hispanic	113

Age & Nativity, 2000
Under 5 years	701
18 years and over	7,337
21 years and over	6,975
65 years and over	916
85 years and over	97
Median Age	36.3
Native born	9,895
Foreign born	492

Educational Attainment, 2000
Population 25 years and over	6,565
0-8 yrs of school	4.0%
High School grad or higher	84.6%
Bachelor's degree or higher	19.5%
Graduate degree	7.7%

Income & Poverty, 1999
Per capita income	$22,488
Median household income	$58,440
Median family income	$65,339
Persons in poverty	508
H'holds receiving public assistance	102
H'holds receiving social security	826

Households, 2000
Total households	3,441
With persons under 18	1,592
With persons over 65	667
Family households	2,857
One-person households	467
Persons per household	3.02
Persons per family	3.33

Labor & Employment
Total civilian labor force, 2004**	5,547
Unemployment rate	3.4%
Total civilian labor force, 2000	5,261
Unemployment rate	4.4%

Employed persons 16 years and over by occupation, 2000
Managers & professionals	1,597
Service occupations	759
Sales & office occupations	1,353
Farming, fishing & forestry	51
Construction & maintenance	658
Production & transportation	610
Self-employed persons	384

*US Census Bureau
**New Jersey Department of Labor

General Information
Township of Wantage
888 Route 23
Wantage, NJ 07461
973-875-7192
Web site	www.wantagetwp.com
Land area (sq. miles)	67.12
Water area (sq. miles)	0.42
Type of government	Township
Form of government	TC

Government

Legislative Districts
US Congressional	5
State Legislative	24

Local Officials, 2006
Mayor	Jeff Parrott
Admin/Manager	Jim Doherty
Clerk	Jim Doherty
Finance Dir/Treas	Michelle Lastarza
Engineer	Harold Pellow
Attorney	Richard Clark
Tax assessor	Melissa Rockwell
Tax collector	NA
Building officer	Ed Vanderberg
Zoning officer	NA
Public Works	NA

Housing & Construction

Housing Units, 2000*
Total	3,663
Median rent	$768
Median SF home value	$154,200

New Privately Owned Housing Units Authorized by Building Permit
	Units	Value
Total, 2004	61	$11,702,646
Single family	61	$11,702,646
Total, 2005	79	$12,254,487
Single family	79	$12,254,487

Real Property Valuation - parcels, 2005
	Number	Valuation
Total		$630,602,585
Vacant	536	21,454,000
Residential	3,353	482,019,645
Commercial	124	50,224,500
Industrial	2	575,500
Apartments	3	3,242,600
Farm land	398	62,988,200
Farm homestead	754	10,098,140

Average Property Value & Tax, 2005
Residential value	$119,824
Property tax	$4,429
FAIR rebate	$518

Public Library
Sussex-Wantage Branch Library†
69 Route 639
Wantage, NJ 07461
973-875-3940
Branch Librarian | Nancy Helmer

Library statistics, 2004
	Total	per capita
Volumes	NA	NA
Expenditure	NA	NA

†Branch of County Library

Public Safety
Police
Chief	NA
Number of officers, 2004	0

Crime, 2004	Number	Rate
Total	90	8.1
Violent	11	1
Non-violent	79	7.1
Domestic Viol.	96	NA

Emergency/Fire
Director	Scott Haggerty

Public School District
(for school year 2004-2005 except as noted)

Sussex-Wantage Regional School District
31 Ryan Rd
Wantage, NJ 07461
973-875-3175
Superintendent	Anthony Mistretta (Int)
Grade plan	K-8
Enrollment	1,726.0
Students per teacher	10.6
Per pupil expenditure	$12,048
Median faculty salary	$58,230
Median administrator salary	$94,256
Grade 12 enrollment	NA
High school graduation rate	NA

Assessment test results
(percent scoring at proficient or advanced level)
	Language	Math
Grade 3	79.4%	78.2%
Grade 8	80.6%	67.8%
High school	NA	NA

SAT
Percent tested	NA
Average SAT math score	NA
Average SAT verbal score	NA

No Child Left Behind, 2003-04
Attendance rate (target = 90%)	94.9%
Drop rate	NA
Highly-qualified teachers	91.9%
District needs improvement?(AYP)	No

Municipal Finance

Fiscal Year 2005
Total tax levy	$23,390,840
County levy	4,639,832
County taxes	3,937,954
County library	339,384
County health	159,657
County open space	202,837
School levy	16,648,415
Local muni. budget	2,102,593
Misc. revenues	3,774,487
Total aid	$1,082,638
CMPTRA	512,002
Muni. block grant	41,513
Energy tax receipts	524,564
Homeland security	0

Fiscal Year 2006
Total aid	$1,082,638
CMPTRA	493,643
Muni. block grant	41,513
Energy tax receipts	542,923
Homeland security	NA

Taxes
	2003	2004	2005
General tax rate per $100	3.43	3.670	3.700
Net valuation taxable	$599,546,939	$613,612,824	$632,828,623
State equalized value	$846,817,710	$980,900,761	$1,092,025,234
County equalization ratio	84.43	70.80	62.46

Demographics & Socio-Economic Characteristics
(2000 U.S. Census, except as noted)

Population
1980*	9,805
1990*	10,830
2000	14,259
Male	7,099
Female	7,160
2004 (estimate)*	15,531
Persons per sq. mi. of land	790

Race & Hispanic Origin, 2000
Race
White	12,303
Black/African American	180
Amer. Indian/Alaska Natv.	5
Asian	1,521
Natv. Hawaiian/Pac. Islander	8
Other Race	59
Two or more races	183
Hispanic origin, total	455
Mexican	33
Puerto Rican	66
Cuban	76
Other Hispanic	280

Age & Nativity, 2000
Under 5 years	1,019
18 years and over	10,027
21 years and over	9,708
65 years and over	1,598
85 years and over	151
Median Age	39.4
Native born	12,018
Foreign born	2,241

Educational Attainment, 2000
Population 25 years and over	9,396
0-8 yrs of school	2.4%
High School grad or higher	93.4%
Bachelor's degree or higher	58.2%
Graduate degree	28.4%

Income & Poverty, 1999
Per capita income	$49,475
Median household income	$103,677
Median family income	$121,264
Persons in poverty	299
H'holds receiving public assistance	17
H'holds receiving social security	1,046

Households, 2000
Total households	4,629
With persons under 18	2,147
With persons over 65	1,079
Family households	3,937
One-person households	565
Persons per household	3.05
Persons per family	3.33

Labor & Employment
Total civilian labor force, 2004**	7,028
Unemployment rate	4.4%
Total civilian labor force, 2000	6,936
Unemployment rate	1.6%

Employed persons 16 years and over by occupation, 2000
Managers & professionals	3,947
Service occupations	554
Sales & office occupations	1,598
Farming, fishing & forestry	5
Construction & maintenance	345
Production & transportation	374
Self-employed persons	585

*US Census Bureau
**New Jersey Department of Labor

General Information
Township of Warren
46 Mountain Blvd
Warren, NJ 07059
908-753-8000

Web site	www.warrennj.org
Land area (sq. miles)	19.67
Water area (sq. miles)	0
Type of government	Township
Form of government	TC

Government

Legislative Districts
US Congressional	7
State Legislative	21

Local Officials, 2006
Mayor	Carolann Garafola
Admin/Manager	Mark Krane
Clerk	Patricia DiRocco
Finance Dir/Treas	Shaw Boswell
Engineer	Christian Kastrud
Attorney	John Belardo
Tax assessor	Edward Kerwin Jr.
Tax collector	Loree Saums
Building officer	Jeffrey Heiss
Zoning officer	John Chadwick
Public Works	Douglas Buro

Housing & Construction

Housing Units, 2000*
Total	4,718
Median rent	$1,135
Median SF home value	$427,200

New Privately Owned Housing Units Authorized by Building Permit
	Units	Value
Total, 2004	45	$12,229,965
Single family	45	$12,229,965
Total, 2005	27	$9,501,528
Single family	27	$9,501,528

Real Property Valuation - parcels, 2005
	Number	Valuation
Total		$3,909,598,800
Vacant	457	81,998,000
Residential	4,909	3,118,738,500
Commercial	194	633,593,000
Industrial	12	45,913,500
Apartments	0	0
Farm land	50	29,093,000
Farm homestead	98	262,800

Average Property Value & Tax, 2005
Residential value	$622,928
Property tax	$10,271
FAIR rebate	$568

Public Library
Warren Twp. Branch Library†
42 Mountain Blvd
Warren, NJ 07059
908-754-5554

Branch Director............ Elaine Whiting

Library statistics, 2004
	Total	per capita
Volumes	NA	NA
Expenditure	NA	NA

†Branch of County Library

Public Safety

Police
Chief	William Stahl
Number of officers, 2004	27

Crime, 2004	Number	Rate
Total	163	10.6
Violent	7	0.5
Non-violent	156	10.2
Domestic Viol.	20	NA

Emergency/Fire
Director	Timothy McGowan

Public School District
(for school year 2004-2005 except as noted)

Warren Township School District
213 Mount Horeb Rd
Warren, NJ 07059
732-560-8700

Superintendent	James Crisfield
Grade plan	K-8
Enrollment	2,255.0
Students per teacher	9.3
Per pupil expenditure	$13,124
Median faculty salary	$49,432
Median administrator salary	$108,076
Grade 12 enrollment	NA
High school graduation rate	NA

Assessment test results
(percent scoring at proficient or advanced level)
	Language	Math
Grade 3	95.9%	97.6%
Grade 8	93.2%	86.0%
High school	NA	NA

SAT
Percent tested	NA
Average SAT math score	NA
Average SAT verbal score	NA

No Child Left Behind, 2003-04
Attendance rate (target = 90%)	96.4%
Drop rate	NA
Highly-qualified teachers	95.9%
District needs improvement?(AYP)	No

Municipal Finance

Fiscal Year 2005
Total tax levy	$64,564,371
County levy	14,564,982
County taxes	12,066,776
County library	1,337,678
County health	0
County open space	1,160,528
School levy	41,935,543
Local muni. budget	8,063,846
Misc. revenues	6,375,434
Total aid	$1,797,156
CMPTRA	261,890
Muni. block grant	55,910
Energy tax receipts	1,409,356
Homeland security	70,000

Fiscal Year 2006
Total aid	$1,797,155
CMPTRA	212,562
Muni. block grant	55,910
Energy tax receipts	1,458,683
Homeland security	70,000

Taxes
	2003	2004	2005
General tax rate per $100	1.70	1.800	1.650
Net valuation taxable	$3,306,354,841	$3,356,730,153	$3,915,902,784
State equalized value	$3,506,952,525	$3,785,684,641	$4,317,899,199
County equalization ratio	101.8	94.28	101.26

Demographics & Socio-Economic Characteristics

(2000 U.S. Census, except as noted)

Population

1980*	6,429
1990*	6,474
2000	6,712
Male	3,340
Female	3,372
2004 (estimate)*	6,885
Persons per sq. mi. of land	3,518

Race & Hispanic Origin, 2000

Race
White	6,138
Black/African American	261
Amer. Indian/Alaska Natv.	8
Asian	97
Natv. Hawaiian/Pac. Islander	1
Other Race	108
Two or more races	99
Hispanic origin, total	280
Mexican	27
Puerto Rican	130
Cuban	18
Other Hispanic	105

Age & Nativity, 2000

Under 5 years	444
18 years and over	4,932
21 years and over	4,716
65 years and over	715
85 years and over	97
Median Age	35.2
Native born	6,120
Foreign born	592

Educational Attainment, 2000

Population 25 years and over	4,414
0-8 yrs of school	4.3%
High School grad or higher	83.4%
Bachelor's degree or higher	22.7%
Graduate degree	7.9%

Income & Poverty, 1999

Per capita income	$23,166
Median household income	$47,000
Median family income	$61,379
Persons in poverty	375
H'holds receiving public assistance	31
H'holds receiving social security	654

Households, 2000

Total households	2,724
With persons under 18	975
With persons over 65	578
Family households	1,685
One-person households	862
Persons per household	2.46
Persons per family	3.15

Labor & Employment

Total civilian labor force, 2004**	4,057
Unemployment rate	4.2%
Total civilian labor force, 2000	3,629
Unemployment rate	3.3%

Employed persons 16 years and over by occupation, 2000
Managers & professionals	1,176
Service occupations	494
Sales & office occupations	906
Farming, fishing & forestry	0
Construction & maintenance	399
Production & transportation	534
Self-employed persons	180

*US Census Bureau
**New Jersey Department of Labor

General Information

Borough of Washington
100 Belvidere Ave
Washington, NJ 07882
908-689-3600

Web site	www.washingtonboro-nj.org
Land area (sq. miles)	1.96
Water area (sq. miles)	0
Type of government	Borough
Form of government	CM '50

Government

Legislative Districts

US Congressional	5
State Legislative	23

Local Officials, 2006

Mayor	Marianne Van Deursen
Admin/Manager	Richard J. Sheola
Clerk	Linda Hendershot
Finance Dir/Treas	Kay Stasyshan
Engineer	Robert Miller
Attorney	Richard Cushing
Tax assessor	Athan Efstathiou
Tax collector	NA
Building officer	Chuck Herring
Zoning officer	Rudolph Bescherer
Public Works	NA

Housing & Construction

Housing Units, 2000*

Total	2,876
Median rent	$697
Median SF home value	$119,000

New Privately Owned Housing Units Authorized by Building Permit

	Units	Value
Total, 2004	30	$3,329,579
Single family	30	$3,329,579
Total, 2005	10	$1,195,293
Single family	10	$1,195,293

Real Property Valuation - parcels, 2005

	Number	Valuation
Total		$370,906,860
Vacant	81	3,672,800
Residential	1,905	276,846,160
Commercial	174	49,158,100
Industrial	14	16,803,900
Apartments	19	23,983,000
Farm land	1	437,600
Farm homestead	4	5,300

Average Property Value & Tax, 2005

Residential value	$145,024
Property tax	$5,083
FAIR rebate	$534

Public Library

Washington Public Library
20 West Carlton Ave
Washington, NJ 07882
908-689-0201

Director	Barbara Rose

Library statistics, 2004

	Total	per capita
Volumes	47,306	7.05
Expenditure	$281,049	$41.87

Public Safety

Police

Chief	G. Cortellesi
Number of officers, 2004	12

Crime, 2004	Number	Rate
Total	144	21.1
Violent	10	1.5
Non-violent	134	19.6
Domestic Viol.	130	NA

Emergency/Fire

Director	Kurt Klausfelder

Public School District

(for school year 2004-2005 except as noted)

Washington Borough School District
300 W Stewart St
Washington, NJ 07882
908-689-0241

Superintendent	Lance Rozsa
Grade plan	K-6
Enrollment	506.0
Students per teacher	9.8
Per pupil expenditure	$11,638
Median faculty salary	$53,435
Median administrator salary	$76,000
Grade 12 enrollment	NA
High school graduation rate	NA

Assessment test results

(percent scoring at proficient or advanced level)
	Language	Math
Grade 3	74.6%	69.0%
Grade 8	NA	NA
High school	NA	NA

SAT

Percent tested	NA
Average SAT math score	NA
Average SAT verbal score	NA

No Child Left Behind, 2003-04

Attendence rate (target = 90%)	94.4%
Drop rate	NA
Highly-qualified teachers	100%
District needs improvement?(AYP)	No

Municipal Finance

Fiscal Year 2005

Total tax levy	$13,109,887
County levy	2,692,665
County taxes	2,418,953
County library	0
County health	0
County open space	273,711
School levy	7,258,521
Local muni. budget	3,158,701
Misc. revenues	2,434,736
Total aid	$897,116
CMPTRA	413,836
Muni. block grant	28,328
Energy tax receipts	404,952
Homeland security	50,000

Fiscal Year 2006

Total aid	$897,115
CMPTRA	399,662
Muni. block grant	28,328
Energy tax receipts	419,125
Homeland security	50,000

Taxes

	2003	2004	2005
General tax rate per $100	3.05	3.200	3.510
Net valuation taxable	$358,271,644	$369,316,499	$374,055,293
State equalized value	$387,572,094	$446,355,054	$505,411,827
County equalization ratio	104.67	92.44	82.60

Demographics & Socio-Economic Characteristics
(2000 U.S. Census, except as noted)

Population
1980*	9,550
1990*	9,245
2000	8,938
Male	4,291
Female	4,647
2004 (estimate)*	9,623
Persons per sq. mi. of land	3,306

Race & Hispanic Origin, 2000
Race
White	8,229
Black/African American	88
Amer. Indian/Alaska Natv.	4
Asian	498
Natv. Hawaiian/Pac. Islander	0
Other Race	39
Two or more races	80
Hispanic origin, total	299
Mexican	21
Puerto Rican	85
Cuban	83
Other Hispanic	110

Age & Nativity, 2000
Under 5 years	606
18 years and over	6,905
21 years and over	6,730
65 years and over	1,512
85 years and over	92
Median Age	41.8
Native born	7,672
Foreign born	1,266

Educational Attainment, 2000
Population 25 years and over	6,489
0-8 yrs of school	2.3%
High School grad or higher	94.0%
Bachelor's degree or higher	44.8%
Graduate degree	16.6%

Income & Poverty, 1999
Per capita income	$39,248
Median household income	$83,694
Median family income	$88,017
Persons in poverty	216
H'holds receiving public assistance	19
H'holds receiving social security	994

Households, 2000
Total households	3,219
With persons under 18	1,147
With persons over 65	1,069
Family households	2,688
One-person households	468
Persons per household	2.77
Persons per family	3.07

Labor & Employment
Total civilian labor force, 2004**	5,688
Unemployment rate	2.4%
Total civilian labor force, 2000	4,772
Unemployment rate	3.8%

Employed persons 16 years and over by occupation, 2000
Managers & professionals	3,441
Service occupations	388
Sales & office occupations	1,447
Farming, fishing & forestry	0
Construction & maintenance	260
Production & transportation	153
Self-employed persons	240

*US Census Bureau
**New Jersey Department of Labor

General Information
Township of Washington
350 Hudson Ave
Township of Washington, NJ 07676
201-664-4425
Web site	www.twpofwashington.org
Land area (sq. miles)	2.91
Water area (sq. miles)	0.05
Type of government	Township
Form of government	MC '50

Government
Legislative Districts
US Congressional	5
State Legislative	39

Local Officials, 2006
Mayor	Rudolph J. Wenzel
Admin/Manager	Agnes Smith
Clerk	Mary Ann Ozment
Finance Dir/Treas	Jacqueline Do
Engineer	Azzolina, Feury, et al
Attorney	Kenneth Poller
Tax assessor	Raymond Damiano
Tax collector	NA
Building officer	John Scialla
Zoning officer	NA
Public Works	NA

Housing & Construction
Housing Units, 2000*
Total	3,245
Median rent	$1,909
Median SF home value	$287,800

New Privately Owned Housing Units Authorized by Building Permit
	Units	Value
Total, 2004	37	$2,564,083
Single family	37	$2,564,083
Total, 2005	25	$3,305,873
Single family	25	$3,305,873

Real Property Valuation - parcels, 2005
	Number	Valuation
Total		$846,213,800
Vacant	83	3,974,700
Residential	3,337	835,229,400
Commercial	11	7,009,700
Industrial	0	0
Apartments	0	0
Farm land	0	0
Farm homestead	0	0

Average Property Value & Tax, 2005
Residential value	$250,293
Property tax	$7,864
FAIR rebate	$635

Public Library
Washington Twp Public Library
144 Woodfield Rd
Township of Washington, NJ 07676
201-664-4586
Director	Juliette Sobon

Library statistics, 2004
	Total	Per Capita
Volumes	36,109	4.04
Expenditure	$387,499	$43.35

Public Safety
Police
Chief	William Cicchetti
Number of officers, 2004	24

Crime, 2004	Number	Rate
Total	42	4.4
Violent	2	0.2
Non-violent	40	4.2
Domestic Viol.	3	NA

Emergency/Fire
Director	Rio Fasciano

Public School District
(for school year 2004-2005 except as noted)

Westwood Regional School District
701 Ridgewood Rd
Township of Washington, NJ 07676
201-664-2765
Superintendent	Roy Montesano
Grade plan	K-12
Enrollment	2,641.0
Students per teacher	10.9
Per pupil expenditure	$13,071
Median faculty salary	$48,659
Median administrator salary	$113,303
Grade 12 enrollment	160.0
High school graduation rate	98.1%

Assessment test results
(percent scoring at proficient or advanced level)
	Language	Math
Grade 3	97.0%	92.0%
Grade 8	84.0%	77.7%
High school	95.1%	88.7%

SAT
Percent tested	81%
Average SAT math score	538
Average SAT verbal score	503

No Child Left Behind, 2003-04
Attendence rate (target = 90%)	96.2%
Drop rate	1.2%
Highly-qualified teachers	97.8%
District needs improvement?(AYP)	No

Municipal Finance
Fiscal Year 2005
Total tax levy	$26,599,753
County levy	3,031,782
County taxes	2,880,162
County library	0
County health	0
County open space	151,621
School levy	16,692,314
Local muni. budget	6,875,657
Misc. revenues	3,049,799
Total aid	$1,043,932
CMPTRA	272,146
Muni. block grant	40,453
Energy tax receipts	681,333
Homeland security	50,000

Fiscal Year 2006
Total aid	$1,043,932
CMPTRA	248,300
Muni. block grant	40,153
Energy tax receipts	705,179
Homeland security	50,000

Taxes
	2003	2004	2005
General tax rate per $100	2.76	3.010	3.150
Net valuation taxable	$826,960,650	$833,612,138	$846,636,302
State equalized value	$1,346,622,130	$1,492,197,728	$1,702,123,647
County equalization ratio	68.12	61.41	55.85

Demographics & Socio-Economic Characteristics

(2000 U.S. Census, except as noted)

Population

1980*	808
1990*	805
2000	621
Male	298
Female	323
2004 (estimate)*	640
Persons per sq. mi. of land	6

Race & Hispanic Origin, 2000

Race
White	519
Black/African American	18
Amer. Indian/Alaska Natv.	0
Asian	2
Natv. Hawaiian/Pac. Islander	0
Other Race	75
Two or more races	7
Hispanic origin, total	106
Mexican	3
Puerto Rican	96
Cuban	0
Other Hispanic	7

Age & Nativity, 2000

Under 5 years	29
18 years and over	439
21 years and over	420
65 years and over	151
85 years and over	58
Median Age	40.8
Native born	572
Foreign born	7

Educational Attainment, 2000

Population 25 years and over	384
0-8 yrs of school	21.1%
High School grad or higher	55.7%
Bachelor's degree or higher	12.2%
Graduate degree	2.9%

Income & Poverty, 1999

Per capita income	$13,977
Median household income	$41,250
Median family income	$42,188
Persons in poverty	68
H'holds receiving public assistance	11
H'holds receiving social security	46

Households, 2000

Total households	160
With persons under 18	63
With persons over 65	48
Family households	113
One-person households	39
Persons per household	2.76
Persons per family	3.27

Labor & Employment

Total civilian labor force, 2004**	401
Unemployment rate	5.8%
Total civilian labor force, 2000	174
Unemployment rate	2.9%

Employed persons 16 years and over by occupation, 2000
Managers & professionals	34
Service occupations	26
Sales & office occupations	27
Farming, fishing & forestry	30
Construction & maintenance	9
Production & transportation	43
Self-employed persons	10

*US Census Bureau
**New Jersey Department of Labor

General Information

Township of Washington
1018 River Rd
Egg Harbor, NJ 08215
609-965-3242

Web site	NA
Land area (sq. miles)	100.14
Water area (sq. miles)	2.72
Type of government	Township
Form of government	TC

Government

Legislative Districts

US Congressional	2
State Legislative	9

Local Officials, 2006

Mayor	Daniel James
Admin/Manager	NA
Clerk	Paul Kain
Finance Dir/Treas	John Cicalese
Engineer	Kris Kluk
Attorney	Peter H. Nelson
Tax assessor	Jay Renwick
Tax collector	Victoria Boras
Building officer	DCA
Zoning officer	NA
Public Works	NA

Housing & Construction

Housing Units, 2000*

Total	171
Median rent	$500
Median SF home value	$95,000

New Privately Owned Housing Units Authorized by Building Permit

	Units	Value
Total, 2004	3	$205,784
Single family	3	$205,784
Total, 2005	4	$385,785
Single family	4	$385,785

Real Property Valuation - parcels, 2005

	Number	Valuation
Total		$46,097,650
Vacant	178	2,053,400
Residential	342	35,274,050
Commercial	15	4,187,500
Industrial	3	951,200
Apartments	1	84,200
Farm land	17	2,436,100
Farm homestead	22	1,111,200

Average Property Value & Tax, 2005

Residential value	$99,959
Property tax	$2,795
FAIR rebate	$558

Public Library

No public municipal library.

Library statistics, 2004

	Total	per capita
Volumes	NA	NA
Expenditure	NA	NA

Public Safety

Police

Chief	NA
Number of officers, 2004	0

Crime, 2004	Number	Rate
Total	13	20.4
Violent	1	1.6
Non-violent	12	18.8
Domestic Viol.	3	NA

Emergency/Fire

Director	L. Forand/W. Homiller

Public School District

(for school year 2004-2005 except as noted)

Washington Township School District
2436 Route 563
Egg Harbor, NJ 08215
609-965-3520

Superintendent	L. David Rhine
Grade plan	K-12
Enrollment	102.0
Students per teacher	6.9
Per pupil expenditure	$13,295
Median faculty salary	$38,526
Median administrator salary	$81,902
Grade 12 enrollment	NA
High school graduation rate	NA

Assessment test results

(percent scoring at proficient or advanced level)
	Language	Math
Grade 3	NA	NA
Grade 8	84.6%	69.3%
High school	NA	NA

SAT

Percent tested	NA
Average SAT math score	NA
Average SAT verbal score	NA

No Child Left Behind, 2003-04

Attendance rate (target = 90%)	94.7%
Drop rate	NA
Highly-qualified teachers	92.9%
District needs improvement?(AYP)	No

Municipal Finance

Fiscal Year 2005

Total tax levy	$1,294,654
County levy	405,903
County taxes	340,510
County library	29,815
County health	0
County open space	35,578
School levy	888,752
Local muni. budget	0
Misc. revenues	1,483,692
Total aid	$154,228
CMPTRA	60,311
Muni. block grant	3,523
Energy tax receipts	67,829
Homeland security	0

Fiscal Year 2006

Total aid	$154,228
CMPTRA	57,937
Muni. block grant	3,523
Energy tax receipts	70,203
Homeland security	NA

Taxes

	2003	2004	2005
General tax rate per $100	2.31	2.655	2.798
Net valuation taxable	$46,424,644	$46,640,352	$46,302,896
State equalized value	$71,753,700	$88,139,230	$90,665,549
County equalization ratio	83.5	64.70	52.79

Demographics & Socio-Economic Characteristics

(2000 U.S. Census, except as noted)

Population

1980*	27,878
1990*	41,960
2000	47,114
Male	22,834
Female	24,280
2004 (estimate)*	50,878
Persons per sq. mi. of land	2,381

Race & Hispanic Origin, 2000

Race

White	42,497
Black/African American	2,286
Amer. Indian/Alaska Natv.	39
Asian	1,558
Natv. Hawaiian/Pac. Islander	6
Other Race	252
Two or more races	476
Hispanic origin, total	955
Mexican	138
Puerto Rican	464
Cuban	53
Other Hispanic	300

Age & Nativity, 2000

Under 5 years	2,901
18 years and over	33,571
21 years and over	31,831
65 years and over	4,233
85 years and over	491
Median Age	36
Native born	44,834
Foreign born	2,280

Educational Attainment, 2000

Population 25 years and over	29,876
0-8 yrs of school	2.0%
High School grad or higher	89.9%
Bachelor's degree or higher	30.4%
Graduate degree	8.8%

Income & Poverty, 1999

Per capita income	$25,705
Median household income	$66,546
Median family income	$74,661
Persons in poverty	1,518
H'holds receiving public assistance	145
H'holds receiving social security	3,435

Households, 2000

Total households	15,609
With persons under 18	7,198
With persons over 65	3,016
Family households	12,659
One-person households	2,405
Persons per household	3.0
Persons per family	3.38

Labor & Employment

Total civilian labor force, 2004**	27,404
Unemployment rate	3.6%
Total civilian labor force, 2000	25,153
Unemployment rate	3.6%

Employed persons 16 years and over by occupation, 2000

Managers & professionals	9,895
Service occupations	3,025
Sales & office occupations	7,523
Farming, fishing & forestry	9
Construction & maintenance	1,713
Production & transportation	2,075
Self-employed persons	1,050

*US Census Bureau
**New Jersey Department of Labor

General Information

Township of Washington
523 Egg Harbor Rd
Sewell, NJ 08080
856-589-0520

Web site	www.twp.washington.nj.us
Land area (sq. miles)	21.37
Water area (sq. miles)	0.12
Type of government	Township
Form of government	MC'50

Government

Legislative Districts

US Congressional	1
State Legislative	4

Local Officials, 2006

Mayor	Paul D. Moriarty
Admin/Manager	Debra Fourre
Clerk	Jennica Bileci
Finance Dir/Treas	Debra Fourre
Engineer	Remington & Vernick
Attorney	John Eastlack
Tax assessor	Leo Miduri
Tax collector	Penny Carre
Building officer	Tom Krwawecz
Zoning officer	NA
Public Works	James McKeever

Housing & Construction

Housing Units, 2000*

Total	16,020
Median rent	$833
Median SF home value	$140,700

New Privately Owned Housing Units Authorized by Building Permit

	Units	Value
Total, 2004	67	$8,940,745
Single family	67	$8,940,745
Total, 2005	64	$8,937,791
Single family	64	$8,937,791

Real Property Valuation - parcels, 2005

	Number	Valuation
Total		$2,511,920,300
Vacant	547	33,868,400
Residential	16,020	2,056,678,800
Commercial	735	370,029,400
Industrial	12	5,945,200
Apartments	8	39,750,300
Farm land	37	4,938,900
Farm homestead	87	709,300

Average Property Value & Tax, 2005

Residential value	$127,733
Property tax	$5,103
FAIR rebate	$519

Public Library

Margaret E. Heggan Public Library
208 East Holly Ave
Hurffville, NJ 08080
856-589-3334

Director.................. Linda Snyder

Library statistics, 2004

	Total	per capita
Volumes	71,750	1.52
Expenditure	$1,028,309	$21.83

Public Safety

Police

Chief	Charles Billingham
Number of officers, 2004	85

Crime, 2004	Number	Rate
Total	1,345	26.7
Violent	97	1.9
Non-violent	1,248	24.8
Domestic Viol.	468	NA

Emergency/Fire

Director.......................... NA

Public School District

(for school year 2004-2005 except as noted)

Washington Township School District
206 E Holly Ave
Sewell, NJ 08080
856-589-6644

Superintendent	Cheryl Simone
Grade plan	K-12
Enrollment	9,413.0
Students per teacher	11.0
Per pupil expenditure	$11,381
Median faculty salary	$50,315
Median administrator salary	$99,443
Grade 12 enrollment	719.0
High school graduation rate	95.9%

Assessment test results

(percent scoring at proficient or advanced level)

	Language	Math
Grade 3	92.5%	89.4%
Grade 8	83.4%	69.2%
High school	95.3%	88.2%

SAT

Percent tested	80%
Average SAT math score	516
Average SAT verbal score	502

No Child Left Behind, 2003-04

Attendence rate (target = 90%)	95.4%
Drop rate	1.6%
Highly-qualified teachers	96.4%
District needs improvement?(AYP)	No

Municipal Finance

Fiscal Year 2005

Total tax levy	$100,566,199
County levy	23,857,631
County taxes	22,369,790
County library	0
County health	0
County open space	1,487,841
School levy	55,648,563
Local muni. budget	21,060,005
Misc. revenues	15,882,326
Total aid	$4,486,242
CMPTRA	1,885,190
Muni. block grant	184,735
Energy tax receipts	2,276,317
Homeland security	140,000

Fiscal Year 2006

Total aid	$4,486,241
CMPTRA	1,805,518
Muni. block grant	104,707
Energy tax receipts	2,355,988
Homeland security	140,000

Taxes

	2003	2004	2005
General tax rate per $100	3.63	3.755	3.995
Net valuation taxable	$2,439,894,724	$2,488,704,452	$2,517,398,028
State equalized value	$3,186,905,334	$3,668,066,071	$4,225,949,350
County equalization ratio	82.87	76.56	67.79

Demographics & Socio-Economic Characteristics
(2000 U.S. Census, except as noted)

Population
1980*	3,487
1990*	5,815
2000	10,275
Male	4,908
Female	5,367
2004 (estimate)*	11,445
Persons per sq. mi. of land	559

Race & Hispanic Origin, 2000
Race
White	9,350
Black/African American	297
Amer. Indian/Alaska Natv.	14
Asian	443
Natv. Hawaiian/Pac. Islander	0
Other Race	57
Two or more races	114
Hispanic origin, total	279
Mexican	29
Puerto Rican	95
Cuban	34
Other Hispanic	121

Age & Nativity, 2000
Under 5 years	945
18 years and over	7,590
21 years and over	7,450
65 years and over	995
85 years and over	61
Median Age	37.3
Native born	9,382
Foreign born	893

Educational Attainment, 2000
Population 25 years and over	7,241
0-8 yrs of school	3.0%
High School grad or higher	92.3%
Bachelor's degree or higher	46.9%
Graduate degree	15.3%

Income & Poverty, 1999
Per capita income	$35,529
Median household income	$71,377
Median family income	$90,878
Persons in poverty	381
H'holds receiving public assistance	26
H'holds receiving social security	863

Households, 2000
Total households	4,074
With persons under 18	1,519
With persons over 65	765
Family households	2,815
One-person households	1,074
Persons per household	2.52
Persons per family	3.09

Labor & Employment
Total civilian labor force, 2004**	3,960
Unemployment rate	2.2%
Total civilian labor force, 2000	5,605
Unemployment rate	2.3%

Employed persons 16 years and over by occupation, 2000
Managers & professionals	3,144
Service occupations	344
Sales & office occupations	1,437
Farming, fishing & forestry	0
Construction & maintenance	254
Production & transportation	296
Self-employed persons	204

*US Census Bureau
**New Jersey Department of Labor

General Information
Township of Washington
1117 Route 130
Robbinsville, NJ 08691
609-259-7082
Web site	www.washington-twp.org
Land area (sq. miles)	20.48
Water area (sq. miles)	0.02
Type of government	Township
Form of government	Mayor-Council

Government

Legislative Districts
US Congressional	4
State Legislative	30

Local Officials, 2006
Mayor	David Fried
Admin/Manager	Mary Caffrey
Clerk	Michele Auletta
Finance Dir/Treas	NA
Engineer	Jack West
Attorney	Mark Roselli
Tax assessor	Gregory Busa
Tax collector	Janice Garcia
Building officer	Jack West
Zoning officer	Jack West
Public Works	Bing Colarocco

Housing & Construction

Housing Units, 2000*
Total	4,163
Median rent	$788
Median SF home value	$216,500

New Privately Owned Housing Units Authorized by Building Permit
	Units	Value
Total, 2004	113	$13,188,083
Single family	111	$12,963,083
Total, 2005	147	$21,399,929
Single family	147	$21,399,929

Real Property Valuation - parcels, 2005
	Number	Valuation
Total		$934,409,858
Vacant	539	33,492,390
Residential	4,268	716,570,200
Commercial	146	67,059,050
Industrial	17	99,793,000
Apartments	1	3,002,000
Farm land	79	11,859,900
Farm homestead	226	2,633,318

Average Property Value & Tax, 2005
Residential value	$160,036
Property tax	$6,800
FAIR rebate	$484

Public Library
Washington Twp Brnch Libr†
42 Allentown Robbinsville Rd
Robbinsville, NJ 08691
609-259-2150
Branch Librarian .... Ann Marie Ehrenberg

Library statistics, 2004
	Total	per capita
Volumes	NA	NA
Expenditure	NA	NA

†Branch of County Library

Public Safety

Police
Chief	Martin Masseroni
Number of officers, 2004	27

Crime, 2004	Number	Rate
Total	123	11.1
Violent	11	1
Non-violent	112	10.1
Domestic Viol.	85	NA

Emergency/Fire
Director	Kevin Brink

Public School District
(for school year 2004-2005 except as noted)

Washington Township School District
155 Robbinsville-Edinburg Rd
Robbinsville, NJ 08691
609-632-0910
Superintendent	John J. Szabo
Grade plan	K-12
Enrollment	1,726.0
Students per teacher	10.6
Per pupil expenditure	$10,889
Median faculty salary	$43,000
Median administrator salary	$100,913
Grade 12 enrollment	NA
High school graduation rate	NA

Assessment test results
(percent scoring at proficient or advanced level)
	Language	Math
Grade 3	91.1%	80.2%
Grade 8	87.8%	76.5%
High school	NA	NA

SAT
Percent tested	NA
Average SAT math score	NA
Average SAT verbal score	NA

No Child Left Behind, 2003-04
Attendence rate (target = 90%)	96.0%
Drop rate	NA
Highly-qualified teachers	98.5%
District needs improvement?(AYP)	No

Municipal Finance

Fiscal Year 2005
Total tax levy	$39,796,955
County levy	9,931,674
County taxes	8,675,213
County library	769,204
County health	0
County open space	487,257
School levy	24,163,248
Local muni. budget	5,702,033
Misc. revenues	5,697,342
Total aid	$1,793,060
CMPTRA	188,568
Muni. block grant	40,289
Energy tax receipts	1,494,203
Homeland security	70,000

Fiscal Year 2006
Total aid	$1,793,060
CMPTRA	136,271
Muni. block grant	40,289
Energy tax receipts	1,546,500
Homeland security	70,000

Taxes
	2003	2004	2005
General tax rate per $100	3.63	3.910	4.250
Net valuation taxable	$853,789,317	$884,756,502	$936,560,490
State equalized value	$1,287,960,955	$1,532,084,914	$1,795,553,087
County equalization ratio	73.58	66.29	57.69

Demographics & Socio-Economic Characteristics
(2000 U.S. Census, except as noted)

Population
1980*	11,402
1990*	15,592
2000	17,592
Male	8,593
Female	8,999
2004 (estimate)*	18,485
Persons per sq. mi. of land	412

Race & Hispanic Origin, 2000
Race
White	16,917
Black/African American	146
Amer. Indian/Alaska Natv.	15
Asian	329
Natv. Hawaiian/Pac. Islander	9
Other Race	62
Two or more races	114
Hispanic origin, total	389
Mexican	47
Puerto Rican	127
Cuban	62
Other Hispanic	153

Age & Nativity, 2000
Under 5 years	1,213
18 years and over	12,281
21 years and over	11,797
65 years and over	1,449
85 years and over	337
Median Age	38.3
Native born	16,537
Foreign born	1,055

Educational Attainment, 2000
Population 25 years and over	11,313
0-8 yrs of school	1.8%
High School grad or higher	96.3%
Bachelor's degree or higher	53.2%
Graduate degree	20.0%

Income & Poverty, 1999
Per capita income	$37,489
Median household income	$97,763
Median family income	$104,926
Persons in poverty	397
H'holds receiving public assistance	30
H'holds receiving social security	999

Households, 2000
Total households	5,755
With persons under 18	2,780
With persons over 65	960
Family households	4,874
One-person households	701
Persons per household	3.02
Persons per family	3.31

Labor & Employment
Total civilian labor force, 2004**	8,939
Unemployment rate	3.0%
Total civilian labor force, 2000	9,048
Unemployment rate	2.7%

Employed persons 16 years and over by occupation, 2000
Managers & professionals	4,827
Service occupations	849
Sales & office occupations	2,178
Farming, fishing & forestry	18
Construction & maintenance	523
Production & transportation	406
Self-employed persons	634

*US Census Bureau
**New Jersey Department of Labor

General Information
Washington Township
43 Schooley's Mtn Rd
Long Valley, NJ 07853
908-876-3315
Web site	www.wtmorris.org
Land area (sq. miles)	44.86
Water area (sq. miles)	0
Type of government	Township
Form of government	TC

Government

Legislative Districts
US Congressional	11
State Legislative	24

Local Officials, 2006
Mayor	Tracy Tobin
Admin/Manager	Dianne S. Gallets
Clerk	Dianne S. Gallets
Finance Dir/Treas	Kevin Lifer
Engineer	Leon C. Hall
Attorney	John Jansen
Tax assessor	Dolores Pecorari
Tax collector	Amy Monahan
Building officer	Frederick Jordan
Zoning officer	Frederick Jordan
Public Works	NA

Housing & Construction

Housing Units, 2000*
Total	5,890
Median rent	$1,052
Median SF home value	$279,300

New Privately Owned Housing Units Authorized by Building Permit
	Units	Value
Total, 2004	58	$11,083,476
Single family	58	$11,083,476
Total, 2005	45	$11,609,601
Single family	45	$11,609,601

Real Property Valuation - parcels, 2005
	Number	Valuation
Total		$1,663,181,300
Vacant	532	33,965,000
Residential	5,511	1,459,046,400
Commercial	165	54,665,900
Industrial	22	24,463,800
Apartments	5	21,625,100
Farm land	218	65,127,600
Farm homestead	462	4,287,500

Average Property Value & Tax, 2005
Residential value	$244,991
Property tax	$7,941
FAIR rebate	$460

Public Library
Washington Twp Public Library
37 E Springtown Rd
Long Valley, NJ 07853
908-876-3596
Director	Virginia Scarlatelli

Library statistics, 2004
	Total	per capita
Volumes	62,643	3.56
Expenditure	$808,531	$45.96

Public Safety

Police
Chief	NA
Number of officers, 2004	34

Crime, 2004	Number	Rate
Total	144	7.9
Violent	14	0.8
Non-violent	130	7.1
Domestic Viol.	107	NA

Emergency/Fire
Director	NA

Public School District
(for school year 2004-2005 except as noted)

Washington Township School District
53 W Mill Rd
Long Valley, NJ 07853
908-876-4172
Superintendent	Gerald Vernotica
Grade plan	K-8
Enrollment	2,940.0
Students per teacher	12.9
Per pupil expenditure	$10,922
Median faculty salary	$55,400
Median administrator salary	$110,890
Grade 12 enrollment	NA
High school graduation rate	NA

Assessment test results
(percent scoring at proficient or advanced level)
	Language	Math
Grade 3	93.7%	88.9%
Grade 8	91.7%	85.4%
High school	NA	NA

SAT
Percent tested	NA
Average SAT math score	NA
Average SAT verbal score	NA

No Child Left Behind, 2003-04
Attendence rate (target = 90%)	95.8%
Drop rate	NA
Highly-qualified teachers	97.9%
District needs improvement?(AYP)	No

Municipal Finance

Fiscal Year 2005
Total tax levy	$54,007,123
County levy	6,976,848
County taxes	5,715,036
County library	0
County health	0
County open space	1,261,812
School levy	38,068,438
Local muni. budget	8,961,838
Misc. revenues	6,292,909
Total aid	$1,969,822
CMPTRA	714,541
Muni. block grant	68,979
Energy tax receipts	1,115,503
Homeland security	70,000

Fiscal Year 2006
Total aid	$1,969,821
CMPTRA	675,498
Muni. block grant	60,979
Energy tax receipts	1,154,545
Homeland security	70,000

Taxes
	2003	2004	2005
General tax rate per $100	2.89	3.060	3.250
Net valuation taxable	$1,608,623,633	$1,633,315,657	$1,666,244,077
State equalized value	$2,301,321,363	$2,565,319,392	$2,856,581,651
County equalization ratio	77.06	69.90	63.62

Demographics & Socio-Economic Characteristics
(2000 U.S. Census, except as noted)

Population
1980*	4,243
1990*	5,367
2000	6,248
Male	3,053
Female	3,195
2004 (estimate)*	6,809
Persons per sq. mi. of land	387

Race & Hispanic Origin, 2000
Race
White	5,997
Black/African American	107
Amer. Indian/Alaska Natv.	4
Asian	59
Natv. Hawaiian/Pac. Islander	0
Other Race	31
Two or more races	50
Hispanic origin, total	135
Mexican	7
Puerto Rican	44
Cuban	21
Other Hispanic	63

Age & Nativity, 2000
Under 5 years	435
18 years and over	4,373
21 years and over	4,177
65 years and over	609
85 years and over	57
Median Age	37.6
Native born	5,994
Foreign born	254

Educational Attainment, 2000
Population 25 years and over	4,049
0-8 yrs of school	2.7%
High School grad or higher	90.8%
Bachelor's degree or higher	32.0%
Graduate degree	8.8%

Income & Poverty, 1999
Per capita income	$29,141
Median household income	$77,458
Median family income	$84,348
Persons in poverty	189
H'holds receiving public assistance	36
H'holds receiving social security	497

Households, 2000
Total households	2,099
With persons under 18	955
With persons over 65	442
Family households	1,740
One-person households	297
Persons per household	2.95
Persons per family	3.26

Labor & Employment
Total civilian labor force, 2004**	3,488
Unemployment rate	2.9%
Total civilian labor force, 2000	3,271
Unemployment rate	4.5%

Employed persons 16 years and over by occupation, 2000
Managers & professionals	1,168
Service occupations	396
Sales & office occupations	949
Farming, fishing & forestry	15
Construction & maintenance	375
Production & transportation	220
Self-employed persons	142

*US Census Bureau
**New Jersey Department of Labor

General Information
Township of Washington
350 Route 57 West
Washington, NJ 07882
908-689-7200
Web site	www.washington-twp-warren.org
Land area (sq. miles)	17.58
Water area (sq. miles)	0.02
Type of government	Township
Form of government	TC

Government
Legislative Districts
US Congressional	5
State Legislative	23

Local Officials, 2006
Mayor	David Dempski
Admin/Manager	NA
Clerk	Mary Ann O'Neil
Finance Dir/Treas	Jo Ann Fascenelli (Actg)
Engineer	Robert Miller
Attorney	Edward J. Glynn
Tax assessor	Michael Schmidt
Tax collector	Evan Howell
Building officer	Michael McCartney
Zoning officer	Thomas Bocko
Public Works	Peter de Boer

Housing & Construction
Housing Units, 2000*
Total	2,174
Median rent	$822
Median SF home value	$185,400

New Privately Owned Housing Units Authorized by Building Permit
	Units	Value
Total, 2004	73	$9,548,093
Single family	73	$9,548,093
Total, 2005	28	$3,694,257
Single family	28	$3,694,257

Real Property Valuation - parcels, 2005
	Number	Valuation
Total		$625,885,749
Vacant	395	19,982,500
Residential	2,147	508,931,299
Commercial	93	66,999,100
Industrial	6	3,807,200
Apartments	3	1,880,300
Farm land	94	21,757,600
Farm homestead	200	2,527,750

Average Property Value & Tax, 2005
Residential value	$217,920
Property tax	$5,695
FAIR rebate	$523

Public Library
No public municipal library.

Library statistics, 2004
	Total	per capita
Volumes	NA	NA
Expenditure	NA	NA

Public Safety
Police
Chief	James McDonald
Number of officers, 2004	13

Crime, 2004	Number	Rate
Total	108	16.3
Violent	4	0.6
Non-violent	104	15.7
Domestic Viol.	54	NA

Emergency/Fire
Director	John Kappus

Public School District
(for school year 2004-2005 except as noted)

Washington Township School District
16 Castle St
Washington, NJ 07882
908-689-1119
Superintendent	Janet Razze
Grade plan	K-6
Enrollment	671.0
Students per teacher	12.8
Per pupil expenditure	$10,885
Median faculty salary	$58,025
Median administrator salary	$82,612
Grade 12 enrollment	NA
High school graduation rate	NA

Assessment test results
(percent scoring at proficient or advanced level)
	Language	Math
Grade 3	87.1%	81.2%
Grade 8	NA	NA
High school	NA	NA

SAT
Percent tested	NA
Average SAT math score	NA
Average SAT verbal score	NA

No Child Left Behind, 2003-04
Attendence rate (target = 90%)	95.5%
Drop rate	NA
Highly-qualified teachers	100%
District needs improvement?(AYP)	No

Municipal Finance
Fiscal Year 2005
Total tax levy	$16,401,610
County levy	4,391,026
County taxes	3,631,170
County library	349,774
County health	0
County open space	410,081
School levy	9,633,356
Local muni. budget	2,377,228
Misc. revenues	2,706,967
Total aid	$817,215
CMPTRA	280,359
Muni. block grant	24,499
Energy tax receipts	462,357
Homeland security	50,000

Fiscal Year 2006
Total aid	$817,215
CMPTRA	264,177
Muni. block grant	24,499
Energy tax receipts	478,539
Homeland security	50,000

Taxes
	2003	2004	2005
General tax rate per $100	2.62	2.550	2.620
Net valuation taxable	$578,162,224	$602,677,368	$627,661,363
State equalized value	$586,847,568	$653,938,794	$748,195,688
County equalization ratio	108.51	98.52	92.13

Demographics & Socio-Economic Characteristics

(2000 U.S. Census, except as noted)

Population

1980*	5,290
1990*	5,110
2000	5,613
Male	2,741
Female	2,872
2004 (estimate)*	5,789
Persons per sq. mi. of land	962

Race & Hispanic Origin, 2000

Race
White	4,732
Black/African American	189
Amer. Indian/Alaska Natv.	5
Asian	553
Natv. Hawaiian/Pac. Islander	5
Other Race	40
Two or more races	89
Hispanic origin, total	168
Mexican	10
Puerto Rican	31
Cuban	27
Other Hispanic	100

Age & Nativity, 2000

Under 5 years	334
18 years and over	4,386
21 years and over	4,276
65 years and over	914
85 years and over	87
Median Age	43
Native born	4,754
Foreign born	859

Educational Attainment, 2000

Population 25 years and over	4,144
0-8 yrs of school	2.1%
High School grad or higher	93.9%
Bachelor's degree or higher	57.0%
Graduate degree	31.5%

Income & Poverty, 1999

Per capita income	$58,653
Median household income	$101,944
Median family income	$120,764
Persons in poverty	121
H'holds receiving public assistance	0
H'holds receiving social security	645

Households, 2000

Total households	2,098
With persons under 18	676
With persons over 65	558
Family households	1,618
One-person households	399
Persons per household	2.62
Persons per family	3

Labor & Employment

Total civilian labor force, 2004**	3,392
Unemployment rate	2.4%
Total civilian labor force, 2000	2,699
Unemployment rate	3.7%

Employed persons 16 years and over by occupation, 2000
Managers & professionals	1,318
Service occupations	192
Sales & office occupations	570
Farming, fishing & forestry	0
Construction & maintenance	152
Production & transportation	157
Self-employed persons	288

*US Census Bureau
**New Jersey Department of Labor

General Information

Borough of Watchung
15 Mountain Blvd
Watchung, NJ 07069
908-756-0080

Web site	NA
Land area (sq. miles)	6.02
Water area (sq. miles)	0.02
Type of government	Borough
Form of government	B

Government

Legislative Districts

US Congressional	7
State Legislative	21

Local Officials, 2006

Mayor	Albert Ellis
Admin/Manager	Laureen Fellin
Clerk	Laureen Fellin
Finance Dir/Treas	W. Hance
Engineer	Maser Consulting
Attorney	Albert E. Cruz
Tax assessor	David Gill
Tax collector	Catherine Park
Building officer	Edward Bennett
Zoning officer	Edward Bennett
Public Works	C. Gunther

Housing & Construction

Housing Units, 2000*

Total	2,155
Median rent	$854
Median SF home value	$429,400

New Privately Owned Housing Units Authorized by Building Permit

	Units	Value
Total, 2004	26	$9,023,900
Single family	26	$9,023,900
Total, 2005	43	$10,339,700
Single family	35	$9,539,700

Real Property Valuation - parcels, 2005

	Number	Valuation
Total		$1,764,712,900
Vacant	229	49,840,700
Residential	1,872	1,353,040,400
Commercial	85	314,230,900
Industrial	7	6,705,800
Apartments	1	40,000,000
Farm land	1	888,300
Farm homestead	1	6,800

Average Property Value & Tax, 2005

Residential value	$722,396
Property tax	$11,180
FAIR rebate	$605

Public Library

Watchung Branch Library†
12 Stirling Rd
Watchung, NJ 07060
908-561-0117
Branch Librarian ... Douglas Poswencyk

Library statistics, 2004

	Total	per capita
Volumes	NA	NA
Expenditure	NA	NA

†Branch of County Library

Public Safety

Police

Chief	John Frosoni
Number of officers, 2004	28

Crime, 2004	Number	Rate
Total	363	63.3
Violent	4	0.7
Non-violent	359	62.6
Domestic Viol.	34	NA

Emergency/Fire

Director ... Stephen Peterson

Public School District

(for school year 2004-2005 except as noted)

Watchung Borough School District
One Parenty Way
Watchung, NJ 07069
908-755-8121

Superintendent	M. L. Malyska
Grade plan	K-8
Enrollment	657.0
Students per teacher	11.3
Per pupil expenditure	$11,917
Median faculty salary	$49,148
Median administrator salary	$106,393
Grade 12 enrollment	NA
High school graduation rate	NA

Assessment test results

(percent scoring at proficient or advanced level)
	Language	Math
Grade 3	96.1%	92.3%
Grade 8	81.9%	86.5%
High school	NA	NA

SAT

Percent tested	NA
Average SAT math score	NA
Average SAT verbal score	NA

No Child Left Behind, 2003-04

Attendence rate (target = 90%)	95.9%
Drop rate	NA
Highly-qualified teachers	95.1%
District needs improvement?(AYP)	No

Municipal Finance

Fiscal Year 2005

Total tax levy	$27,335,762
County levy	6,455,126
County taxes	5,348,017
County library	592,826
County health	0
County open space	514,283
School levy	14,072,214
Local muni. budget	6,808,422
Misc. revenues	4,845,113
Total aid	$1,077,058
CMPTRA	343,806
Muni. block grant	22,359
Energy tax receipts	660,893
Homeland security	50,000

Fiscal Year 2006

Total aid	$1,077,057
CMPTRA	320,674
Muni. block grant	22,359
Energy tax receipts	684,024
Homeland security	50,000

Taxes

	2003	2004	2005
General tax rate per $100	1.54	1.550	1.550
Net valuation taxable	$1,490,344,799	$1,605,968,053	$1,766,331,608
State equalized value	$1,527,931,924	$1,667,434,752	$1,854,611,096
County equalization ratio	110.37	103.42	103.65

Demographics & Socio-Economic Characteristics
(2000 U.S. Census, except as noted)

Population
1980*	8,126
1990*	10,940
2000	10,494
Male	5,255
Female	5,239
2004 (estimate)*	10,679
Persons per sq. mi. of land	295

Race & Hispanic Origin, 2000
Race
White	9,733
Black/African American	439
Amer. Indian/Alaska Natv.	22
Asian	94
Natv. Hawaiian/Pac. Islander	1
Other Race	70
Two or more races	135
Hispanic origin, total	217
Mexican	24
Puerto Rican	127
Cuban	6
Other Hispanic	60

Age & Nativity, 2000
Under 5 years	635
18 years and over	7,793
21 years and over	7,407
65 years and over	854
85 years and over	72
Median Age	36.1
Native born	10,161
Foreign born	324

Educational Attainment, 2000
Population 25 years and over	6,979
0-8 yrs of school	4.3%
High School grad or higher	82.9%
Bachelor's degree or higher	12.8%
Graduate degree	3.5%

Income & Poverty, 1999
Per capita income	$21,676
Median household income	$59,075
Median family income	$63,693
Persons in poverty	590
H'holds receiving public assistance	44
H'holds receiving social security	779

Households, 2000
Total households	3,542
With persons under 18	1,491
With persons over 65	610
Family households	2,790
One-person households	591
Persons per household	2.9
Persons per family	3.27

Labor & Employment
Total civilian labor force, 2004**	6,077
Unemployment rate	3.1%
Total civilian labor force, 2000	6,043
Unemployment rate	7.5%

Employed persons 16 years and over by occupation, 2000
Managers & professionals	1,585
Service occupations	822
Sales & office occupations	1,560
Farming, fishing & forestry	6
Construction & maintenance	894
Production & transportation	725
Self-employed persons	337

*US Census Bureau
**New Jersey Department of Labor

General Information
Township of Waterford
2131 Auburn Ave
Atco, NJ 08004
856-768-2300
Web site	www.waterfordtwp.org
Land area (sq. miles)	36.19
Water area (sq. miles)	0.07
Type of government	Township
Form of government	TC

Government

Legislative Districts
US Congressional	3
State Legislative	6

Local Officials, 2006
Mayor	Anthony L. Clark
Admin/Manager	Donna E. Heaton
Clerk	Virginia Chandler
Finance Dir/Treas	Gabriella Pilla
Engineer	Chris Rehmann
Attorney	Marie-Louise Procacci
Tax assessor	Deborah Hample
Tax collector	NA
Building officer	Michael Borek
Zoning officer	David Heath
Public Works	Ronald Miller

Housing & Construction

Housing Units, 2000*
Total	3,671
Median rent	$725
Median SF home value	$116,500

New Privately Owned Housing Units
Authorized by Building Permit
	Units	Value
Total, 2004	23	$2,453,424
Single family	23	$2,453,424
Total, 2005	31	$3,374,536
Single family	31	$3,374,536

Real Property Valuation - parcels, 2005
	Number	Valuation
Total		$456,414,800
Vacant	447	10,522,900
Residential	3,500	395,510,400
Commercial	125	35,951,200
Industrial	5	1,225,400
Apartments	4	2,144,900
Farm land	71	9,491,700
Farm homestead	205	1,568,300

Average Property Value & Tax, 2005
Residential value	$107,174
Property tax	$4,479
FAIR rebate	$495

Public Library
Waterford Twp Public Library
2204 Atco Ave
Atco, NJ 08004
856-767-7727
Director	Eva Lynch

Library statistics, 2004
	Total	per capita
Volumes	25,979	2.48
Expenditure	$243,227	$23.18

Public Safety

Police
Chief	John Bekisz
Number of officers, 2004	20

Crime, 2004	Number	Rate
Total	227	21.3
Violent	19	1.8
Non-violent	208	19.5
Domestic Viol.	30	NA

Emergency/Fire
Director	James Jankowski

Public School District
(for school year 2004-2005 except as noted)

Waterford Township School District
1106 Old White Horse Pike
Waterford, NJ 08089
856-767-0331
Superintendent	Gary Dentino
Grade plan	K-12
Enrollment	959.0
Students per teacher	11.0
Per pupil expenditure	$11,672
Median faculty salary	$62,068
Median administrator salary	$91,960
Grade 12 enrollment	NA
High school graduation rate	NA

Assessment test results
(percent scoring at proficient or advanced level)
	Language	Math
Grade 3	83.4%	79.2%
Grade 8	NA	NA
High school	NA	NA

SAT
Percent tested	NA
Average SAT math score	NA
Average SAT verbal score	NA

No Child Left Behind, 2003-04
Attendence rate (target = 90%)	94.9%
Drop rate	NA
Highly-qualified teachers	100%
District needs improvement?(AYP)	No

Municipal Finance

Fiscal Year 2005
Total tax levy	$19,130,929
County levy	4,690,706
County taxes	4,629,946
County library	0
County health	0
County open space	60,760
School levy	9,769,956
Local muni. budget	4,670,267
Misc. revenues	3,686,586
Total aid	$1,576,789
CMPTRA	562,845
Muni. block grant	47,870
Energy tax receipts	886,380
Homeland security	70,000

Fiscal Year 2006
Total aid	$1,576,790
CMPTRA	531,822
Muni. block grant	47,870
Energy tax receipts	917,404
Homeland security	70,000

Taxes
	2003	2004	2005
General tax rate per $100	4.04	4.018	4.180
Net valuation taxable	$451,357,223	$453,875,714	$457,779,934
State equalized value	$532,952,206	$600,393,800	$685,196,728
County equalization ratio	92.05	84.69	75.53

Demographics & Socio-Economic Characteristics
(2000 U.S. Census, except as noted)

Population

1980*	46,474
1990*	47,025
2000	54,069
Male	25,699
Female	28,370
2004 (estimate)*	55,402
Persons per sq. mi. of land	2,326

Race & Hispanic Origin, 2000

Race

White	48,687
Black/African American	895
Amer. Indian/Alaska Natv.	54
Asian	3,066
Natv. Hawaiian/Pac. Islander	11
Other Race	631
Two or more races	725
Hispanic origin, total	2,754
Mexican	164
Puerto Rican	726
Cuban	320
Other Hispanic	1,544

Age & Nativity, 2000

Under 5 years	3,313
18 years and over	41,543
21 years and over	39,201
65 years and over	8,765
85 years and over	1,236
Median Age	40
Native born	45,291
Foreign born	8,824

Educational Attainment, 2000

Population 25 years and over	37,298
0-8 yrs of school	4.4%
High School grad or higher	89.2%
Bachelor's degree or higher	41.5%
Graduate degree	15.4%

Income & Poverty, 1999

Per capita income	$35,349
Median household income	$83,651
Median family income	$95,114
Persons in poverty	1,443
H'holds receiving public assistance	155
H'holds receiving social security	5,528

Households, 2000

Total households	18,755
With persons under 18	6,801
With persons over 65	5,650
Family households	14,370
One-person households	3,797
Persons per household	2.74
Persons per family	3.19

Labor & Employment

Total civilian labor force, 2004**	26,714
Unemployment rate	3.2%
Total civilian labor force, 2000	28,103
Unemployment rate	3.9%

Employed persons 16 years and over by occupation, 2000

Managers & professionals	13,791
Service occupations	2,614
Sales & office occupations	7,897
Farming, fishing & forestry	21
Construction & maintenance	1,627
Production & transportation	2,070
Self-employed persons	1,629

*US Census Bureau
**New Jersey Department of Labor

General Information
Township of Wayne
475 Valley Rd
Wayne, NJ 07470
973-694-1800

Web site	www.waynetownship.com
Land area (sq. miles)	23.82
Water area (sq. miles)	1.37
Type of government	Township
Form of government	Mayor-Council

Government

Legislative Districts

US Congressional	8
State Legislative	40

Local Officials, 2006

Mayor	Scott Rumana
Admin/Manager	Neal Bellet
Clerk	Katherine Pusterla
Finance Dir/Treas	Robert Miller
Engineer	Fernando Zapato
Attorney	Mark Semeraro
Tax assessor	Dorothy Kreitz
Tax collector	Carl Smith
Building officer	Len Talerico
Zoning officer	John Ellicott
Public Works	George Holzapfel

Housing & Construction

Housing Units, 2000*

Total	19,218
Median rent	$943
Median SF home value	$284,800

New Privately Owned Housing Units Authorized by Building Permit

	Units	Value
Total, 2004	29	$7,031,100
Single family	29	$7,031,100
Total, 2005	22	$5,304,055
Single family	22	$5,304,055

Real Property Valuation - parcels, 2005

	Number	Valuation
Total		$5,374,545,400
Vacant	502	68,935,400
Residential	16,701	3,776,507,400
Commercial	556	1,192,393,900
Industrial	86	214,759,100
Apartments	9	120,181,300
Farm land	7	1,677,100
Farm homestead	11	91,200

Average Property Value & Tax, 2005

Residential value	$225,981
Property tax	$7,961
FAIR rebate	$585

Public Library
Wayne Public Library
475 Valley Rd
Wayne, NJ 07470
973-694-4272

Director . . . . Jody Treadway

Library statistics, 2004

	Total	per capita
Volumes	202,474	3.74
Expenditure	$2,838,660	$52.50

Public Safety

Police

Chief	Donald Stouthamer
Number of officers, 2004	118

Crime, 2004	Number	Rate
Total	1,325	24
Violent	32	0.6
Non-violent	1,293	23.4
Domestic Viol.	276	NA

Emergency/Fire

Director . . . . Dennis Ferray

Public School District
(for school year 2004-2005 except as noted)

Wayne Township School District
50 Nellis Drive
Wayne, NJ 07470
973-633-3032

Administrator	Maria Nuccetelli
Grade plan	K-12
Enrollment	8,769.0
Students per teacher	11.9
Per pupil expenditure	$11,543
Median faculty salary	$55,395
Median administrator salary	$109,550
Grade 12 enrollment	650.0
High school graduation rate	NA

Assessment test results
(percent scoring at proficient or advanced level)

	Language	Math
Grade 3	93.7%	92.3%
Grade 8	91.4%	83.3%
High school	94.2%	93.3%

SAT

Percent tested	NA
Average SAT math score	NA
Average SAT verbal score	NA

No Child Left Behind, 2003-04

Attendance rate (target = 90%)	95.6%
Drop rate	0.9%
Highly-qualified teachers	98.7%
District needs improvement?(AYP)	No

Municipal Finance

Fiscal Year 2005

Total tax levy	$189,681,774
County levy	47,370,672
County taxes	46,469,090
County library	0
County health	0
County open space	901,582
School levy	102,383,427
Local muni. budget	39,927,674
Misc. revenues	22,084,131
Total aid	$5,975,332
CMPTRA	1,990,239
Muni. block grant	212,006
Energy tax receipts	3,610,292
Homeland security	140,000

Fiscal Year 2006

Total aid	$5,975,333
CMPTRA	1,863,879
Muni. block grant	212,006
Energy tax receipts	3,736,653
Homeland security	140,000

Taxes

	2003	2004	2005
General tax rate per $100	3.10	3.300	3.530
Net valuation taxable	$5,315,338,931	$5,365,364,575	$5,384,588,548
State equalized value	$7,976,198,876	$8,943,653,098	$9,779,492,459
County equalization ratio	71.92	66.64	59.94

Demographics & Socio-Economic Characteristics
(2000 U.S. Census, except as noted)

Population
1980*	13,168
1990*	12,385
2000	13,501
Male	6,582
Female	6,919
2004 (estimate)*	13,195
Persons per sq. mi. of land	15,531

Race & Hispanic Origin, 2000
Race
White	9,862
Black/African American	483
Amer. Indian/Alaska Natv.	27
Asian	630
Natv. Hawaiian/Pac. Islander	14
Other Race	1,882
Two or more races	603
Hispanic origin, total	5,487
Mexican	177
Puerto Rican	822
Cuban	1,182
Other Hispanic	3,306

Age & Nativity, 2000
Under 5 years	643
18 years and over	11,265
21 years and over	10,900
65 years and over	1,650
85 years and over	192
Median Age	35
Native born	8,272
Foreign born	5,229

Educational Attainment, 2000
Population 25 years and over	10,010
0-8 yrs of school	12.7%
High School grad or higher	76.0%
Bachelor's degree or higher	37.5%
Graduate degree	13.0%

Income & Poverty, 1999
Per capita income	$29,269
Median household income	$50,196
Median family income	$52,613
Persons in poverty	1,535
H'holds receiving public assistance	161
H'holds receiving social security	1,336

Households, 2000
Total households	5,975
With persons under 18	1,323
With persons over 65	1,250
Family households	3,061
One-person households	2,126
Persons per household	2.26
Persons per family	3.02

Labor & Employment
Total civilian labor force, 2004**	7,559
Unemployment rate	5.5%
Total civilian labor force, 2000	7,854
Unemployment rate	5.8%

Employed persons 16 years and over by occupation, 2000
Managers & professionals	3,121
Service occupations	983
Sales & office occupations	2,152
Farming, fishing & forestry	5
Construction & maintenance	319
Production & transportation	818
Self-employed persons	458

*US Census Bureau
**New Jersey Department of Labor

General Information
Township of Weehawken
400 Park Ave
Weehawken, NJ 07086
201-319-6022
Web site	www.weehawken-nj.us
Land area (sq. miles)	0.85
Water area (sq. miles)	0.66
Type of government	Township
Form of government	OMCL

Government
Legislative Districts
US Congressional	13
State Legislative	33

Local Officials, 2006
Mayor	Richard Turner
Admin/Manager	James Marchetti
Clerk	Rola Dahboul (Actg.)
Finance Dir/Treas	Dominick Facchini
Engineer	Mayo Lynch
Attorney	Richard Venino
Tax assessor	Paul Sadlon
Tax collector	NA
Building officer	Frank Tattoli
Zoning officer	NA
Public Works	NA

Housing & Construction
Housing Units, 2000*
Total	6,159
Median rent	$781
Median SF home value	$231,200

New Privately Owned Housing Units Authorized by Building Permit
	Units	Value
Total, 2004	3	$585,000
Single family	3	$585,000
Total, 2005	2	$390,000
Single family	2	$390,000

Real Property Valuation - parcels, 2005
	Number	Valuation
Total		$1,008,434,623
Vacant	200	90,327,130
Residential	2,442	478,123,840
Commercial	69	322,007,403
Industrial	28	60,185,900
Apartments	121	57,790,350
Farm land	0	0
Farm homestead	0	0

Average Property Value & Tax, 2005
Residential value	$195,792
Property tax	$5,675
FAIR rebate	$647

Public Library
Weehawken Public Library
49 Hauxhurst Ave
Weehawken, NJ 07086
201-863-7823
Director	Philip Greco

Library statistics, 2004
	Total	per capita
Volumes	41,169	3.05
Expenditure	$700,154	$51.86

Public Safety
Police
Chief	W. McCullen/J. Fulcher
Number of officers, 2004	60

Crime, 2004	Number	Rate
Total	418	31.3
Violent	26	1.9
Non-violent	392	29.4
Domestic Viol.	55	NA

Emergency/Fire
Director	Jeffrey Welz (PS Dir)

Public School District
(for school year 2004-2005 except as noted)

Weehawken Township School District
53 Liberty Place
Weehawken, NJ 07086
201-867-2243
Superintendent	Kevin McLellan
Grade plan	K-12
Enrollment	1,189.5
Students per teacher	10.1
Per pupil expenditure	$12,036
Median faculty salary	$52,570
Median administrator salary	$104,305
Grade 12 enrollment	54.5
High school graduation rate	94.7%

Assessment test results
(percent scoring at proficient or advanced level)
	Language	Math
Grade 3	81.0%	83.6%
Grade 8	89.6%	80.5%
High school	77.2%	70.0%

SAT
Percent tested	81%
Average SAT math score	473
Average SAT verbal score	467

No Child Left Behind, 2003-04
Attendence rate (target = 90%)	95.3%
Drop rate	0.6%
Highly-qualified teachers	100%
District needs improvement?(AYP)	No

Municipal Finance
Fiscal Year 2005
Total tax levy	$31,338,730
County levy	8,673,857
County taxes	8,509,918
County library	0
County health	0
County open space	163,940
School levy	11,929,088
Local muni. budget	10,735,785
Misc. revenues	13,720,621
Total aid	$3,108,047
CMPTRA	2,394,060
Muni. block grant	54,193
Energy tax receipts	589,089
Homeland security	70,000

Fiscal Year 2006
Total aid	$3,108,047
CMPTRA	2,373,442
Muni. block grant	54,193
Energy tax receipts	609,707
Homeland security	70,000

Taxes
	2003	2004	2005
General tax rate per $100	2.98	3.030	3.105
Net valuation taxable	$967,464,912	$974,249,403	$1,009,544,129
State equalized value	$1,351,396,720	$1,559,529,320	$1,876,476,076
County equalization ratio	76.11	71.59	62.44

Demographics & Socio-Economic Characteristics

(2000 U.S. Census, except as noted)

Population

1980*	2,303
1990*	2,331
2000	2,317
Male	1,128
Female	1,189
2004 (estimate)*	2,321
Persons per sq. mi. of land	2,384

Race & Hispanic Origin, 2000

Race

White	2,260
Black/African American	25
Amer. Indian/Alaska Natv.	2
Asian	15
Natv. Hawaiian/Pac. Islander	0
Other Race	0
Two or more races	15
Hispanic origin, total	17
Mexican	8
Puerto Rican	4
Cuban	1
Other Hispanic	4

Age & Nativity, 2000

Under 5 years	148
18 years and over	1,716
21 years and over	1,657
65 years and over	320
85 years and over	33
Median Age	41.2
Native born	2,281
Foreign born	36

Educational Attainment, 2000

Population 25 years and over	1,584
0-8 yrs of school	0.3%
High School grad or higher	97.2%
Bachelor's degree or higher	42.2%
Graduate degree	15.8%

Income & Poverty, 1999

Per capita income	$34,116
Median household income	$71,625
Median family income	$82,505
Persons in poverty	57
H'holds receiving public assistance	2
H'holds receiving social security	233

Households, 2000

Total households	844
With persons under 18	316
With persons over 65	211
Family households	652
One-person households	166
Persons per household	2.7
Persons per family	3.13

Labor & Employment

Total civilian labor force, 2004**	1,495
Unemployment rate	5.1%
Total civilian labor force, 2000	1,233
Unemployment rate	7.4%

Employed persons 16 years and over by occupation, 2000

Managers & professionals	818
Service occupations	91
Sales & office occupations	266
Farming, fishing & forestry	4
Construction & maintenance	86
Production & transportation	77
Self-employed persons	82

*US Census Bureau
**New Jersey Department of Labor

General Information

Borough of Wenonah
PO Box 66
1 South West Ave
Wenonah, NJ 08090
856-468-5228

Web site	www.wenonahnj.us
Land area (sq. miles)	0.97
Water area (sq. miles)	0
Type of government	Borough
Form of government	B

Government

Legislative Districts

US Congressional	1
State Legislative	3

Local Officials, 2006

Mayor	Thomas Capaldi
Admin/Manager	Dawn Marie Human
Clerk	Dawn Marie Human
Finance Dir/Treas	Karen Sweeney
Engineer	KLE Consultants
Attorney	Brian Duffield
Tax assessor	Roy Duffield
Tax collector	NA
Building officer	Bob Kunkle
Zoning officer	NA
Public Works	NA

Housing & Construction

Housing Units, 2000*

Total	860
Median rent	$665
Median SF home value	$161,600

New Privately Owned Housing Units Authorized by Building Permit

	Units	Value
Total, 2004	6	$799,452
Single family	6	$799,452
Total, 2005	5	$690,744
Single family	5	$690,744

Real Property Valuation - parcels, 2005

	Number	Valuation
Total		$135,885,500
Vacant	37	1,113,300
Residential	818	132,566,400
Commercial	12	2,205,800
Industrial	0	0
Apartments	0	0
Farm land	0	0
Farm homestead	0	0

Average Property Value & Tax, 2005

Residential value	$162,062
Property tax	$6,971
FAIR rebate	$562

Public Library

Wenonah Public Library
101 E Mantua Ave
Wenonah, NJ 08090
856-468-6323

Director	Ann Zuber

Library statistics, 2004

	Total	per capita
Volumes	12,736	5.50
Expenditure	$56,564	$24.41

Public Safety

Police

Chief	Glenn Scheetz
Number of officers, 2004	6

Crime, 2004	Number	Rate
Total	16	6.9
Violent	0	0
Non-violent	16	6.9
Domestic Viol.	2	NA

Emergency/Fire

Director	Andrew Sole III

Public School District

(for school year 2004-2005 except as noted)

Wenonah School District
200 N Clinton Ave
Wenonah, NJ 08090
856-468-6000

Administrator	Christine Smith
Grade plan	K-6
Enrollment	234.0
Students per teacher	10.9
Per pupil expenditure	$10,457
Median faculty salary	$44,415
Median administrator salary	$97,461
Grade 12 enrollment	NA
High school graduation rate	NA

Assessment test results

(percent scoring at proficient or advanced level)

	Language	Math
Grade 3	97.2%	97.2%
Grade 8	NA	NA
High school	NA	NA

SAT

Percent tested	NA
Average SAT math score	NA
Average SAT verbal score	NA

No Child Left Behind, 2003-04

Attendance rate (target = 90%)	96.6%
Drop rate	NA
Highly-qualified teachers	88.9%
District needs improvement?(AYP)	No

Municipal Finance

Fiscal Year 2005

Total tax levy	$5,852,996
County levy	1,221,280
County taxes	1,145,099
County library	0
County health	0
County open space	76,181
School levy	3,510,494
Local muni. budget	1,121,223
Misc. revenues	802,814
Total aid	$264,488
CMPTRA	116,651
Muni. block grant	10,200
Energy tax receipts	112,637
Homeland security	0

Fiscal Year 2006

Total aid	$264,488
CMPTRA	112,709
Muni. block grant	10,200
Energy tax receipts	116,579
Homeland security	25,000

Taxes

	2003	2004	2005
General tax rate per $100	3.65	3.957	4.302
Net valuation taxable	$134,644,015	$135,424,808	$136,070,523
State equalized value	$166,165,636	$189,554,154	$219,716,653
County equalization ratio	88.04	81.03	71.41

Demographics & Socio-Economic Characteristics
(2000 U.S. Census, except as noted)

Population
1980*	2,299
1990*	2,251
2000	2,383
Male	1,193
Female	1,190
2004 (estimate)*	2,847
Persons per sq. mi. of land	131

Race & Hispanic Origin, 2000
Race
White	2,337
Black/African American	15
Amer. Indian/Alaska Natv.	2
Asian	17
Natv. Hawaiian/Pac. Islander	0
Other Race	1
Two or more races	11
Hispanic origin, total	17
Mexican	1
Puerto Rican	3
Cuban	1
Other Hispanic	12

Age & Nativity, 2000
Under 5 years	116
18 years and over	1,879
21 years and over	1,826
65 years and over	330
85 years and over	37
Median Age	42.9
Native born	2,274
Foreign born	109

Educational Attainment, 2000
Population 25 years and over	1,782
0-8 yrs of school	3.8%
High School grad or higher	89.6%
Bachelor's degree or higher	37.0%
Graduate degree	12.6%

Income & Poverty, 1999
Per capita income	$33,877
Median household income	$73,380
Median family income	$79,605
Persons in poverty	39
H'holds receiving public assistance	8
H'holds receiving social security	280

Households, 2000
Total households	949
With persons under 18	288
With persons over 65	245
Family households	697
One-person households	202
Persons per household	2.51
Persons per family	2.93

Labor & Employment
Total civilian labor force, 2004**	1,552
Unemployment rate	2.6%
Total civilian labor force, 2000	1,411
Unemployment rate	2.2%

Employed persons 16 years and over by occupation, 2000
Managers & professionals	581
Service occupations	145
Sales & office occupations	353
Farming, fishing & forestry	19
Construction & maintenance	147
Production & transportation	135
Self-employed persons	154

*US Census Bureau
**New Jersey Department of Labor

General Information
Township of West Amwell
150 Rocktown-Lambertville
Lambertville, NJ 08530
609-397-2054
Web site	www.westamwelltwp.org
Land area (sq. miles)	21.72
Water area (sq. miles)	0.18
Type of government	Township
Form of government	TC

Government

Legislative Districts
US Congressional	12
State Legislative	23

Local Officials, 2006
Mayor	Thomas J. Molnar
Admin/Manager	NA
Clerk	Lora L. Olsen
Finance Dir/Treas	Jane Luhrs
Engineer	Robert Clerico
Attorney	Phillip Faherty III
Tax assessor	David Gill
Tax collector	Catherine L. Park
Building officer	Ed Novel
Zoning officer	Eugene Venettone
Public Works	Randy Hoagland

Housing & Construction

Housing Units, 2000*
Total	984
Median rent	$865
Median SF home value	$198,800

New Privately Owned Housing Units Authorized by Building Permit
	Units	Value
Total, 2004	45	$8,856,320
Single family	45	$8,856,320
Total, 2005	35	$7,679,247
Single family	35	$7,679,247

Real Property Valuation - parcels, 2005
	Number	Valuation
Total		$507,571,199
Vacant	198	14,428,400
Residential	895	368,686,300
Commercial	41	25,112,399
Industrial	7	11,864,400
Apartments	3	1,476,900
Farm land	144	83,411,400
Farm homestead	281	2,591,400

Average Property Value & Tax, 2005
Residential value	$315,712
Property tax	$4,919
FAIR rebate	$568

Public Library

No public municipal library.

Library statistics, 2004
	Total	per capita
Volumes	NA	NA
Expenditure	NA	NA

Public Safety

Police
Chief	Stephen Bartzak
Number of officers, 2004	5

Crime, 2004	Number	Rate
Total	35	12.6
Violent	0	0
Non-violent	35	12.6
Domestic Viol.	22	NA

Emergency/Fire
Director	Jeff Ent

Public School District
(for school year 2004-2005 except as noted)

West Amwell Township School District
1417 Route 179
Lambertville, NJ 08530
609-397-0819
Superintendent	Todd Fay
Grade plan	K-6
Enrollment	226.0
Students per teacher	9.0
Per pupil expenditure	$13,357
Median faculty salary	$45,605
Median administrator salary	$93,993
Grade 12 enrollment	NA
High school graduation rate	NA

Assessment test results
(percent scoring at proficient or advanced level)
	Language	Math
Grade 3	92.0%	96.0%
Grade 8	NA	NA
High school	NA	NA

SAT
Percent tested	NA
Average SAT math score	NA
Average SAT verbal score	NA

No Child Left Behind, 2003-04
Attendence rate (target = 90%)	96.2%
Drop rate	NA
Highly-qualified teachers	87%
District needs improvement?(AYP)	No

Municipal Finance

Fiscal Year 2005
Total tax levy	$7,922,250
County levy	1,861,550
County taxes	1,580,532
County library	132,265
County health	0
County open space	148,754
School levy	5,546,789
Local muni. budget	513,911
Misc. revenues	2,621,026
Total aid	$1,409,001
CMPTRA	1,143,162
Muni. block grant	9,849
Energy tax receipts	209,370
Homeland security	25,000

Fiscal Year 2006
Total aid	$1,409,001
CMPTRA	1,135,834
Muni. block grant	9,849
Energy tax receipts	216,698
Homeland security	25,000

Taxes
	2003	2004	2005
General tax rate per $100	1.78	1.580	1.560
Net valuation taxable	$392,419,657	$459,706,044	$508,423,351
State equalized value	$366,884,496	$429,688,428	$515,172,106
County equalization ratio	98.75	102.35	102.72

Demographics & Socio-Economic Characteristics
(2000 U.S. Census, except as noted)

Population
1980*	11,407
1990*	10,422
2000	11,233
Male	5,330
Female	5,903
2004 (estimate)*	11,096
Persons per sq. mi. of land	2,197

Race & Hispanic Origin, 2000
Race
White	10,541
Black/African American	100
Amer. Indian/Alaska Natv.	4
Asian	432
Natv. Hawaiian/Pac. Islander	4
Other Race	68
Two or more races	84
Hispanic origin, total	314
Mexican	23
Puerto Rican	85
Cuban	68
Other Hispanic	138

Age & Nativity, 2000
Under 5 years	813
18 years and over	8,463
21 years and over	8,241
65 years and over	2,142
85 years and over	376
Median Age	41
Native born	10,262
Foreign born	971

Educational Attainment, 2000
Population 25 years and over	7,982
0-8 yrs of school	1.7%
High School grad or higher	93.4%
Bachelor's degree or higher	48.1%
Graduate degree	18.2%

Income & Poverty, 1999
Per capita income	$38,345
Median household income	$83,396
Median family income	$94,379
Persons in poverty	227
H'holds receiving public assistance	48
H'holds receiving social security	1,353

Households, 2000
Total households	3,990
With persons under 18	1,469
With persons over 65	1,351
Family households	3,114
One-person households	767
Persons per household	2.75
Persons per family	3.17

Labor & Employment
Total civilian labor force, 2004**	5,583
Unemployment rate	1.3%
Total civilian labor force, 2000	5,819
Unemployment rate	2.7%

Employed persons 16 years and over by occupation, 2000
Managers & professionals	3,819
Service occupations	596
Sales & office occupations	1,699
Farming, fishing & forestry	0
Construction & maintenance	325
Production & transportation	221
Self-employed persons	356

*US Census Bureau
**New Jersey Department of Labor

General Information
Township of West Caldwell
30 Clinton Rd
West Caldwell, NJ 07006
973-226-2300
Web site	www.westcaldwell.com
Land area (sq. miles)	5.05
Water area (sq. miles)	0
Type of government	Township
Form of government	B

Government
Legislative Districts
US Congressional	11
State Legislative	27

Local Officials, 2006
Mayor	Joseph Tempesta Jr.
Admin/Manager	Benedict Martorana
Clerk	Benedict Martorana
Finance Dir/Treas	Russell Jarger
Engineer	Benedict Martorana
Attorney	Joseph Maddaloni
Tax assessor	Richard Hamilton Jr.
Tax collector	Kathleen Bruchac
Building officer	Jock Watkins
Zoning officer	John Bock
Public Works	William Frint

Housing & Construction
Housing Units, 2000*
Total	4,044
Median rent	$1,193
Median SF home value	$265,900

New Privately Owned Housing Units
Authorized by Building Permit
	Units	Value
Total, 2004	5	$1,095,996
Single family	5	$1,095,996
Total, 2005	4	$864,846
Single family	4	$864,846

Real Property Valuation - parcels, 2005
	Number	Valuation
Total		$1,115,007,200
Vacant	96	9,805,300
Residential	3,479	754,399,800
Commercial	154	160,039,800
Industrial	65	182,640,200
Apartments	6	8,040,700
Farm land	0	0
Farm homestead	6	81,400

Average Property Value & Tax, 2005
Residential value	$216,494
Property tax	$7,403
FAIR rebate	$623

Public Library
West Caldwell Public Library
30 Clinton Rd
West Caldwell, NJ 07006
973-226-5441
Director	April Judge

Library statistics, 2004
	Total	per capita
Volumes	58,599	5.22
Expenditure	$948,083	$84.40

Public Safety
Police
Chief	Charles Tubbs
Number of officers, 2004	28

Crime, 2004	Number	Rate
Total	110	9.9
Violent	6	0.5
Non-violent	104	9.3
Domestic Viol.	28	NA

Emergency/Fire
Director	Charles Holden

Public School District
(for school year 2004-2005 except as noted)

Caldwell-West Caldwell School District
Harrison Bldg Gray St
West Caldwell, NJ 07006
973-228-6979
Superintendent	Daniel Gerardi
Grade plan	K-12
Enrollment	2,617.0
Students per teacher	12.0
Per pupil expenditure	$11,912
Median faculty salary	$51,875
Median administrator salary	$103,339
Grade 12 enrollment	207.0
High school graduation rate	97.6%

Assessment test results
(percent scoring at proficient or advanced level)
	Language	Math
Grade 3	95.8%	88.5%
Grade 8	85.0%	78.1%
High school	95.4%	91.6%

SAT
Percent tested	96%
Average SAT math score	551
Average SAT verbal score	542

No Child Left Behind, 2003-04
Attendence rate (target = 90%)	96.7%
Drop rate	0.6%
Highly-qualified teachers	95.7%
District needs improvement?(AYP)	No

Municipal Finance
Fiscal Year 2005
Total tax levy	$38,155,371
County levy	8,666,063
County taxes	8,484,588
County library	0
County health	0
County open space	181,475
School levy	20,447,492
Local muni. budget	9,041,817
Misc. revenues	6,371,330
Total aid	$1,859,565
CMPTRA	586,004
Muni. block grant	45,773
Energy tax receipts	1,157,788
Homeland security	70,000

Fiscal Year 2006
Total aid	$1,859,565
CMPTRA	545,482
Muni. block grant	45,773
Energy tax receipts	1,198,310
Homeland security	70,000

Taxes
	2003	2004	2005
General tax rate per $100	3.25	3.320	3.420
Net valuation taxable	$1,108,743,400	$1,113,542,500	$1,115,842,700
State equalized value	$1,617,422,903	$1,792,555,238	$1,964,857,721
County equalization ratio	74.86	74.86	62.10

Demographics & Socio-Economic Characteristics

(2000 U.S. Census, except as noted)

Population

1980*	1,091
1990*	1,026
2000	1,095
Male	527
Female	568
2004 (estimate)*	1,067
Persons per sq. mi. of land	900

Race & Hispanic Origin, 2000

Race

White	921
Black/African American	159
Amer. Indian/Alaska Natv.	4
Asian	0
Natv. Hawaiian/Pac. Islander	0
Other Race	6
Two or more races	5
Hispanic origin, total	20
Mexican	7
Puerto Rican	7
Cuban	0
Other Hispanic	6

Age & Nativity, 2000

Under 5 years	37
18 years and over	880
21 years and over	862
65 years and over	267
85 years and over	33
Median Age	46.3
Native born	1,043
Foreign born	52

Educational Attainment, 2000

Population 25 years and over	870
0-8 yrs of school	4.7%
High School grad or higher	83.1%
Bachelor's degree or higher	31.8%
Graduate degree	9.9%

Income & Poverty, 1999

Per capita income	$25,663
Median household income	$37,500
Median family income	$47,031
Persons in poverty	81
H'holds receiving public assistance	12
H'holds receiving social security	213

Households, 2000

Total households	507
With persons under 18	121
With persons over 65	202
Family households	302
One-person households	178
Persons per household	2.16
Persons per family	2.8

Labor & Employment

Total civilian labor force, 2004**	650
Unemployment rate	3.5%
Total civilian labor force, 2000	536
Unemployment rate	9.0%

Employed persons 16 years and over by occupation, 2000

Managers & professionals	197
Service occupations	81
Sales & office occupations	127
Farming, fishing & forestry	8
Construction & maintenance	56
Production & transportation	19
Self-employed persons	61

*US Census Bureau
**New Jersey Department of Labor

General Information

Borough of West Cape May
732 Broadway
West Cape May, NJ 08204
609-884-1005

Web site	westcapemay.us
Land area (sq. miles)	1.19
Water area (sq. miles)	0
Type of government	Borough
Form of government	Comm.

Government

Legislative Districts

US Congressional	2
State Legislative	1

Local Officials, 2006

Mayor	Pamela Kaithern
Admin/Manager	NA
Clerk	Lisa Stefankiewicz
Finance Dir/Treas	John Hansen
Engineer	Andrew Simkins
Attorney	Frank Corrado
Tax assessor	Arthur Amonette
Tax collector	Bruce Macleod
Building officer	Bill Callahan
Zoning officer	Norman Roach
Public Works	Rob Flynn

Housing & Construction

Housing Units, 2000*

Total	1,004
Median rent	$703
Median SF home value	$174,100

New Privately Owned Housing Units
Authorized by Building Permit

	Units	Value
Total, 2004	7	$1,204,954
Single family	7	$1,204,954
Total, 2005	7	$2,935,563
Single family	7	$2,935,563

Real Property Valuation - parcels, 2005

	Number	Valuation
Total		$307,019,100
Vacant	138	19,493,000
Residential	849	256,750,500
Commercial	34	28,934,400
Industrial	0	0
Apartments	2	746,700
Farm land	4	936,100
Farm homestead	13	158,400

Average Property Value & Tax, 2005

Residential value	$298,038
Property tax	$3,503
FAIR rebate	$721

Public Library

No public municipal library.

Library statistics, 2004

	Total	per capita
Volumes	NA	NA
Expenditure	NA	NA

Public Safety

Police

Chief	Diane Sorantino
Number of officers, 2004	0

Crime, 2004	Number	Rate
Total	44	40.2
Violent	2	1.8
Non-violent	42	38.4
Domestic Viol.	7	NA

Emergency/Fire

Director	Charles McPherson

Public School District

(for school year 2004-2005 except as noted)

West Cape May School District
301 Moore St
West Cape May, NJ 08204
609-884-4614

Administrator	David G. Lamborne
Grade plan	K-6
Enrollment	71.0
Students per teacher	8.6
Per pupil expenditure	$12,582
Median faculty salary	$40,670
Median administrator salary	$60,447
Grade 12 enrollment	NA
High school graduation rate	NA

Assessment test results

(percent scoring at proficient or advanced level)

	Language	Math
Grade 3	90.9%	100%
Grade 8	NA	NA
High school	NA	NA

SAT

Percent tested	NA
Average SAT math score	NA
Average SAT verbal score	NA

No Child Left Behind, 2003-04

Attendence rate (target = 90%)	95.7%
Drop rate	NA
Highly-qualified teachers	100%
District needs improvement?(AYP)	No

Municipal Finance

Fiscal Year 2005

Total tax levy	$3,611,307
County levy	809,873
County taxes	680,890
County library	95,919
County health	0
County open space	33,064
School levy	2,023,847
Local muni. budget	777,586
Misc. revenues	696,728
Total aid	$150,572
CMPTRA	29,656
Muni. block grant	4,490
Energy tax receipts	91,426
Homeland security	25,000

Fiscal Year 2006

Total aid	$150,572
CMPTRA	26,456
Muni. block grant	4,490
Energy tax receipts	94,626
Homeland security	25,000

Taxes

	2003	2004	2005
General tax rate per $100	1.85	1.080	1.180
Net valuation taxable	$170,883,100	$305,108,652	$307,279,703
State equalized value	$259,779,720	$327,910,365	$394,606,014
County equalization ratio	75.75	116.28	93.04

Demographics & Socio-Economic Characteristics
(2000 U.S. Census, except as noted)

Population
1980*	18,002
1990*	19,380
2000	19,368
Male	9,354
Female	10,014
2004 (estimate)*	20,464
Persons per sq. mi. of land	1,287

Race & Hispanic Origin, 2000
Race
White	17,875
Black/African American	984
Amer. Indian/Alaska Natv.	45
Asian	219
Natv. Hawaiian/Pac. Islander	4
Other Race	82
Two or more races	159
Hispanic origin, total	341
Mexican	29
Puerto Rican	172
Cuban	9
Other Hispanic	131

Age & Nativity, 2000
Under 5 years	1,137
18 years and over	14,807
21 years and over	14,147
65 years and over	2,357
85 years and over	168
Median Age	37.5
Native born	18,995
Foreign born	373

Educational Attainment, 2000
Population 25 years and over	13,226
0-8 yrs of school	2.7%
High School grad or higher	85.7%
Bachelor's degree or higher	21.7%
Graduate degree	6.8%

Income & Poverty, 1999
Per capita income	$24,219
Median household income	$50,583
Median family income	$64,477
Persons in poverty	1,015
H'holds receiving public assistance	74
H'holds receiving social security	1,954

Households, 2000
Total households	7,719
With persons under 18	2,583
With persons over 65	1,700
Family households	5,129
One-person households	2,115
Persons per household	2.49
Persons per family	3.07

Labor & Employment
Total civilian labor force, 2004**	13,220
Unemployment rate	3.8%
Total civilian labor force, 2000	10,862
Unemployment rate	4.2%

Employed persons 16 years and over by occupation, 2000
Managers & professionals	3,524
Service occupations	1,173
Sales & office occupations	3,158
Farming, fishing & forestry	25
Construction & maintenance	941
Production & transportation	1,789
Self-employed persons	331

*US Census Bureau
**New Jersey Department of Labor

General Information
Township of West Deptford
400 Crown Point Rd
Thorofare, NJ 08086
856-845-4004
Web site	www.westdeptford.com
Land area (sq. miles)	15.90
Water area (sq. miles)	1.86
Type of government	Township
Form of government	TC

Government

Legislative Districts
US Congressional	1
State Legislative	3

Local Officials, 2006
Mayor	Anna Docimo
Admin/Manager	Gerald White
Clerk	Raymond Sherman
Finance Dir/Treas	Richard Giuliani
Engineer	T & M Associates
Attorney	Michael Angelini
Tax assessor	Alicia Melson
Tax collector	George Damminger
Building officer	Robert DeAngelo
Zoning officer	Norman W. Hill Jr.
Public Works	Edward J. Phelps

Housing & Construction

Housing Units, 2000*
Total	7,999
Median rent	$687
Median SF home value	$120,100

New Privately Owned Housing Units Authorized by Building Permit
	Units	Value
Total, 2004	227	$20,967,875
Single family	196	$18,600,225
Total, 2005	426	$26,888,289
Single family	228	$16,813,362

Real Property Valuation - parcels, 2005
	Number	Valuation
Total		$1,356,135,000
Vacant	1,058	58,320,900
Residential	6,091	683,071,400
Commercial	278	302,143,600
Industrial	14	265,264,300
Apartments	11	45,290,400
Farm land	12	1,674,100
Farm homestead	43	370,300

Average Property Value & Tax, 2005
Residential value	$111,419
Property tax	$3,856
FAIR rebate	$572

Public Library
West Deptford Public Library
420 Crown Point Rd
Thorofare, NJ 08086
856-845-5593
Director ... Marie Downes

Library statistics, 2004
	Total	per capita
Volumes	76,177	3.93
Expenditure	$912,113	$47.09

Public Safety

Police
Chief	James Mehaffey
Number of officers, 2004	40

Crime, 2004	Number	Rate
Total	470	23.5
Violent	31	1.5
Non-violent	439	21.9
Domestic Viol.	285	NA

Emergency/Fire
Director ... J. Gill/J. Trautner

Public School District
(for school year 2004-2005 except as noted)

West Deptford Township School District
675 Grove Road
West Deptford, NJ 08066
856-848-4300
Superintendent	Edward Wasilewski Jr.
Grade plan	K-12
Enrollment	3,256.0
Students per teacher	13.7
Per pupil expenditure	$10,682
Median faculty salary	$63,130
Median administrator salary	$85,800
Grade 12 enrollment	225.0
High school graduation rate	94.4%

Assessment test results
(percent scoring at proficient or advanced level)
	Language	Math
Grade 3	88.2%	88.3%
Grade 8	80.3%	76.5%
High school	86.8%	81.8%

SAT
Percent tested	74%
Average SAT math score	507
Average SAT verbal score	496

No Child Left Behind, 2003-04
Attendence rate (target = 90%)	94.5%
Drop rate	1.9%
Highly-qualified teachers	98.9%
District needs improvement?(AYP)	No

Municipal Finance

Fiscal Year 2005
Total tax levy	$48,525,324
County levy	11,528,518
County taxes	10,809,134
County library	0
County health	0
County open space	719,385
School levy	24,689,942
Local muni. budget	12,306,863
Misc. revenues	12,943,055
Total aid	$2,766,248
CMPTRA	1,170,903
Muni. block grant	84,800
Energy tax receipts	1,440,545
Homeland security	70,000

Fiscal Year 2006
Total aid	$2,786,248
CMPTRA	1,120,484
Muni. block grant	84,000
Energy tax receipts	1,490,964
Homeland security	90,000

Taxes
	2003	2004	2005
General tax rate per $100	3.11	3.299	3.462
Net valuation taxable	$1,372,055,423	$1,409,564,433	$1,402,042,348
State equalized value	$1,701,246,650	$1,788,223,685	$2,138,889,928
County equalization ratio	91.05	80.65	77.97

Demographics & Socio-Economic Characteristics
(2000 U.S. Census, except as noted)

Population
1980*	7,380
1990*	7,690
2000	8,258
Male	3,857
Female	4,401
2004 (estimate)*	8,241
Persons per sq. mi. of land	2,854

Race & Hispanic Origin, 2000
Race
White	7,781
Black/African American	184
Amer. Indian/Alaska Natv.	6
Asian	100
Natv. Hawaiian/Pac. Islander	3
Other Race	41
Two or more races	143
Hispanic origin, total	241
Mexican	29
Puerto Rican	63
Cuban	20
Other Hispanic	129

Age & Nativity, 2000
Under 5 years	409
18 years and over	6,458
21 years and over	5,165
65 years and over	1,206
85 years and over	129
Median Age	33.8
Native born	7,676
Foreign born	582

Educational Attainment, 2000
Population 25 years and over	4,722
0-8 yrs of school	4.7%
High School grad or higher	87.1%
Bachelor's degree or higher	34.9%
Graduate degree	14.3%

Income & Poverty, 1999
Per capita income	$27,651
Median household income	$71,852
Median family income	$80,127
Persons in poverty	303
H'holds receiving public assistance	26
H'holds receiving social security	838

Households, 2000
Total households	2,448
With persons under 18	915
With persons over 65	889
Family households	1,860
One-person households	522
Persons per household	2.77
Persons per family	3.25

Labor & Employment
Total civilian labor force, 2004**	4,460
Unemployment rate	2.6%
Total civilian labor force, 2000	4,169
Unemployment rate	14.7%

Employed persons 16 years and over by occupation, 2000
Managers & professionals	1,391
Service occupations	532
Sales & office occupations	1,120
Farming, fishing & forestry	0
Construction & maintenance	357
Production & transportation	156
Self-employed persons	244

*US Census Bureau
**New Jersey Department of Labor

General Information
Borough of West Long Branch
PO Box 639
West Long Branch, NJ 07764
732-229-1756
Web site	www.westlongbranch.org
Land area (sq. miles)	2.89
Water area (sq. miles)	0.02
Type of government	Borough
Form of government	B

Government
Legislative Districts
US Congressional	12
State Legislative	11

Local Officials, 2006
Mayor	Janet W. Tucci
Admin/Manager	NA
Clerk	Lori Cole
Finance Dir/Treas	Gail Watkins
Engineer	T & M Associates
Attorney	Greg Baxter
Tax assessor	Charles Heck
Tax collector	Charlotte C. Rolly
Building officer	Michael Jahn
Zoning officer	NA
Public Works	Earl S. Reed Jr.

Housing & Construction
Housing Units, 2000*
Total	2,535
Median rent	$639
Median SF home value	$203,300

New Privately Owned Housing Units Authorized by Building Permit
	Units	Value
Total, 2004	9	$2,002,335
Single family	9	$2,002,335
Total, 2005	6	$1,202,694
Single family	6	$1,202,694

Real Property Valuation - parcels, 2005
	Number	Valuation
Total		$669,480,500
Vacant	85	7,072,100
Residential	2,261	523,224,400
Commercial	157	135,726,000
Industrial	2	1,506,000
Apartments	2	966,000
Farm land	3	973,200
Farm homestead	4	12,800

Average Property Value & Tax, 2005
Residential value	$231,010
Property tax	$7,091
FAIR rebate	$626

Public Library
West Long Branch Public Library
95 Poplar Ave
West Long Branch, NJ 07764
732-222-5993
Director	David Lisa

Library statistics, 2004
	Total	per capita
Volumes	35,831	4.34
Expenditure	$283,500	$34.33

Public Safety
Police
Chief	Arthur N. Cosentino
Number of officers, 2004	20

Crime, 2004	Number	Rate
Total	332	40.4
Violent	21	2.6
Non-violent	311	37.9
Domestic Viol.	26	NA

Emergency/Fire
Director	Jonathan Tucci

Public School District
(for school year 2004-2005 except as noted)

West Long Branch School District
135 Locust Ave
West Long Branch, NJ 07764
732-222-5900
Superintendent	Joan Kelly
Grade plan	K-8
Enrollment	746.0
Students per teacher	12.5
Per pupil expenditure	$10,453
Median faculty salary	$43,900
Median administrator salary	$101,846
Grade 12 enrollment	NA
High school graduation rate	NA

Assessment test results
(percent scoring at proficient or advanced level)
	Language	Math
Grade 3	94.4%	97.2%
Grade 8	90.7%	78.7%
High school	NA	NA

SAT
Percent tested	NA
Average SAT math score	NA
Average SAT verbal score	NA

No Child Left Behind, 2003-04
Attendence rate (target = 90%)	95.9%
Drop rate	NA
Highly-qualified teachers	100%
District needs improvement?(AYP)	No

Municipal Finance
Fiscal Year 2005
Total tax levy	$20,573,978
County levy	3,527,689
County taxes	3,165,485
County library	174,372
County health	0
County open space	187,832
School levy	12,461,022
Local muni. budget	4,585,266
Misc. revenues	2,867,583
Total aid	$1,182,794
CMPTRA	429,777
Muni. block grant	33,649
Energy tax receipts	669,368
Homeland security	50,000

Fiscal Year 2006
Total aid	$1,182,793
CMPTRA	406,349
Muni. block grant	33,649
Energy tax receipts	692,795
Homeland security	50,000

Taxes
	2003	2004	2005
General tax rate per $100	2.66	2.829	3.070
Net valuation taxable	$677,208,428	$678,983,905	$670,250,333
State equalized value	$922,250,345	$1,065,546,755	$1,210,275,069
County equalization ratio	80.71	73.43	63.69

Demographics & Socio-Economic Characteristics

(2000 U.S. Census, except as noted)

Population

1980*	22,750
1990*	25,430
2000	26,410
Male	13,224
Female	13,186
2004 (estimate)*	28,217
Persons per sq. mi. of land	374

Race & Hispanic Origin, 2000

Race
White	25,110
Black/African American	326
Amer. Indian/Alaska Natv.	159
Asian	269
Natv. Hawaiian/Pac. Islander	4
Other Race	160
Two or more races	382
Hispanic origin, total	893
Mexican	97
Puerto Rican	305
Cuban	97
Other Hispanic	394

Age & Nativity, 2000

Under 5 years	1,863
18 years and over	19,222
21 years and over	18,480
65 years and over	2,212
85 years and over	251
Median Age	37
Native born	24,882
Foreign born	1,528

Educational Attainment, 2000

Population 25 years and over	17,657
0-8 yrs of school	2.6%
High School grad or higher	89.3%
Bachelor's degree or higher	27.2%
Graduate degree	8.0%

Income & Poverty, 1999

Per capita income	$28,612
Median household income	$74,124
Median family income	$80,264
Persons in poverty	1,085
H'holds receiving public assistance	132
H'holds receiving social security	1,702

Households, 2000

Total households	9,190
With persons under 18	3,863
With persons over 65	1,592
Family households	7,186
One-person households	1,536
Persons per household	2.84
Persons per family	3.23

Labor & Employment

Total civilian labor force, 2004**	14,553
Unemployment rate	3.7%
Total civilian labor force, 2000	14,817
Unemployment rate	4.3%

Employed persons 16 years and over by occupation, 2000
Managers & professionals	5,003
Service occupations	1,533
Sales & office occupations	4,182
Farming, fishing & forestry	19
Construction & maintenance	1,868
Production & transportation	1,575
Self-employed persons	913

*US Census Bureau
**New Jersey Department of Labor

General Information

Township of West Milford
1480 Union Valley Rd
West Milford, NJ 07480
973-728-7000

Web site	www.westmilford.org
Land area (sq. miles)	75.44
Water area (sq. miles)	4.97
Type of government	Township
Form of government	CM '50

Government

Legislative Districts

US Congressional	5
State Legislative	26

Local Officials, 2006

Mayor	Joseph A. Di Donato
Admin/Manager	Richard Kunze
Clerk	Antoinette Battaglia
Finance Dir/Treas	Arthur Magnotti
Engineer	Richard Mc Fadden
Attorney	Fred Semrau
Tax assessor	Brian Townsend
Tax collector	Rita DeNivo
Building officer	Kurt Wagner
Zoning officer	James Lupo
Public Works	Gerald Storms

Housing & Construction

Housing Units, 2000*

Total	9,909
Median rent	$835
Median SF home value	$171,200

New Privately Owned Housing Units
Authorized by Building Permit

	Units	Value
Total, 2004	55	$9,459,707
Single family	50	$9,030,118
Total, 2005	62	$10,155,682
Single family	47	$8,866,915

Real Property Valuation - parcels, 2005

	Number	Valuation
Total		$1,493,375,000
Vacant	1,366	54,309,100
Residential	9,831	1,313,342,600
Commercial	277	88,664,800
Industrial	29	10,267,800
Apartments	1	550,000
Farm land	114	25,550,300
Farm homestead	257	690,400

Average Property Value & Tax, 2005

Residential value	$130,257
Property tax	$6,348
FAIR rebate	$522

Public Library

West Milford Township Library
1490 Union Valley Rd
West Milford, NJ 07480
973-728-2820

Director .... Patricia Hannon

Library statistics, 2004

	Total	per capita
Volumes	34,276	1.30
Expenditure	$733,398	$27.77

Public Safety

Police

Chief	Paul Costello
Number of officers, 2004	45

Crime, 2004	Number	Rate
Total	454	16.3
Violent	23	0.8
Non-violent	431	15.4
Domestic Viol.	192	NA

Emergency/Fire

Director .... Ed Steines (Comm)

Public School District

(for school year 2004-2005 except as noted)

West Milford Township School District
46 Highlander Drive
West Milford, NJ 07480
973-697-1700

Administrator	Glenn Kamp
Grade plan	K-12
Enrollment	4,654.0
Students per teacher	12.1
Per pupil expenditure	$11,438
Median faculty salary	$65,700
Median administrator salary	$107,749
Grade 12 enrollment	364.0
High school graduation rate	94.3%

Assessment test results

(percent scoring at proficient or advanced level)
	Language	Math
Grade 3	92.0%	90.1%
Grade 8	79.7%	72.7%
High school	86.1%	84.4%

SAT

Percent tested	71%
Average SAT math score	524
Average SAT verbal score	511

No Child Left Behind, 2003-04

Attendence rate (target = 90%)	94.5%
Drop rate	1.4%
Highly-qualified teachers	98.5%
District needs improvement?(AYP)	No

Municipal Finance

Fiscal Year 2005

Total tax levy	$73,052,590
County levy	15,118,582
County taxes	14,830,929
County library	0
County health	0
County open space	287,653
School levy	41,213,666
Local muni. budget	16,720,342
Misc. revenues	11,886,507
Total aid	$3,970,290
CMPTRA	1,075,659
Muni. block grant	111,273
Energy tax receipts	1,935,671
Homeland security	90,000

Fiscal Year 2006

Total aid	$3,970,290
CMPTRA	1,007,911
Muni. block grant	111,273
Energy tax receipts	2,003,419
Homeland security	90,000

Taxes

	2003	2004	2005
General tax rate per $100	4.47	4.650	4.880
Net valuation taxable	$1,471,456,429	$1,487,606,432	$1,498,956,607
State equalized value	$2,487,669,364	$2,849,449,769	$3,218,026,207
County equalization ratio	66.59	59.15	52.10

Demographics & Socio-Economic Characteristics
(2000 U.S. Census, except as noted)

Population
1980*	39,194
1990*	38,125
2000	45,768
Male	22,470
Female	23,298
2004 (estimate)*	46,231
Persons per sq. mi. of land	45,450

Race & Hispanic Origin, 2000
Race
White	27,503
Black/African American	1,626
Amer. Indian/Alaska Natv.	305
Asian	1,339
Natv. Hawaiian/Pac. Islander	15
Other Race	11,515
Two or more races	3,465
Hispanic origin, total	36,038
Mexican	2,982
Puerto Rican	2,791
Cuban	8,991
Other Hispanic	21,274

Age & Nativity, 2000
Under 5 years	3,049
18 years and over	35,562
21 years and over	33,621
65 years and over	5,828
85 years and over	614
Median Age	34
Native born	15,937
Foreign born	29,831

Educational Attainment, 2000
Population 25 years and over	30,669
0-8 yrs of school	25.7%
High School grad or higher	54.4%
Bachelor's degree or higher	16.4%
Graduate degree	7.3%

Income & Poverty, 1999
Per capita income	$16,719
Median household income	$31,980
Median family income	$34,083
Persons in poverty	8,635
H'holds receiving public assistance	759
H'holds receiving social security	4,149

Households, 2000
Total households	16,719
With persons under 18	5,867
With persons over 65	4,613
Family households	11,042
One-person households	4,593
Persons per household	2.74
Persons per family	3.3

Labor & Employment
Total civilian labor force, 2004**	20,842
Unemployment rate	5.8%
Total civilian labor force, 2000	20,406
Unemployment rate	10.0%

Employed persons 16 years and over by occupation, 2000
Managers & professionals	3,626
Service occupations	3,686
Sales & office occupations	4,828
Farming, fishing & forestry	34
Construction & maintenance	1,316
Production & transportation	4,868
Self-employed persons	858

*US Census Bureau
**New Jersey Department of Labor

General Information
Town of West New York
428 60th St
West New York, NJ 07093
201-295-5200

Web site	NA
Land area (sq. miles)	1.02
Water area (sq. miles)	0.31
Type of government	Town
Form of government	Comm.

Government
Legislative Districts
US Congressional	13
State Legislative	33

Local Officials, 2006
Mayor	Albio Sires
Admin/Manager	Richard Turner
Clerk	Carmela Riccie
Finance Dir/Treas	Darren Maloney
Engineer	Schoor DePalma-R Tango
Attorney	George Campen
Tax assessor	Salvatore Bonaccorsi
Tax collector	NA
Building officer	Franco Zanardelli
Zoning officer	Franco Zanardelli
Public Works	NA

Housing & Construction
Housing Units, 2000*
Total	17,360
Median rent	$681
Median SF home value	$218,400

New Privately Owned Housing Units
Authorized by Building Permit
	Units	Value
Total, 2004	537	$73,554,894
Single family	1	$163,579
Total, 2005	296	$45,054,949
Single family	2	$170,000

Real Property Valuation - parcels, 2005
	Number	Valuation
Total		$928,340,150
Vacant	428	39,135,600
Residential	3,965	422,757,950
Commercial	736	233,711,900
Industrial	173	48,669,900
Apartments	405	184,064,800
Farm land	0	0
Farm homestead	0	0

Average Property Value & Tax, 2005
Residential value	$106,622
Property tax	$4,462
FAIR rebate	$685

Public Library
West New York Public Library
425 60th St
West New York, NJ 07093
201-295-5135

Director	Wei Liang Lai

Library statistics, 2004
	Total	per capita
Volumes	67,840	1.48
Expenditure	$688,705	$15.05

Public Safety
Police
Chief	Timothy Griffin
Number of officers, 2004	126

Crime, 2004	Number	Rate
Total	1,057	22.8
Violent	133	2.9
Non-violent	924	19.9
Domestic Viol.	522	NA

Emergency/Fire
Director	Brion McEldowney

Public School District
(for school year 2004-2005 except as noted)

West New york School District
6028 Broadway
West New York, NJ 07093
201-553-4000

Superintendent	Anthony Yankovich
Grade plan	K-12
Enrollment	6,602.0
Students per teacher	10.8
Per pupil expenditure	$13,335
Median faculty salary	$54,207
Median administrator salary	$108,000
Grade 12 enrollment	311.0
High school graduation rate	97.7%

Assessment test results
(percent scoring at proficient or advanced level)
	Language	Math
Grade 3	78.1%	80.8%
Grade 8	68.8%	62.5%
High school	67.6%	64.8%

SAT
Percent tested	73%
Average SAT math score	428
Average SAT verbal score	416

No Child Left Behind, 2003-04
Attendence rate (target = 90%)	94.9%
Drop rate	0.7%
Highly-qualified teachers	87.6%
District needs improvement?(AYP)	No

Municipal Finance
Fiscal Year 2005
Total tax levy	$43,559,841
County levy	8,814,236
County taxes	8,647,092
County library	0
County health	0
County open space	167,145
School levy	13,055,557
Local muni. budget	21,690,048
Misc. revenues	26,336,757
Total aid	$8,620,711
CMPTRA	6,944,834
Muni. block grant	179,457
Energy tax receipts	1,356,420
Homeland security	140,000

Fiscal Year 2006
Total aid	$8,620,710
CMPTRA	6,897,359
Muni. block grant	179,457
Energy tax receipts	1,403,894
Homeland security	140,000

Taxes
	2003	2004	2005
General tax rate per $100	4.47	4.596	4.689
Net valuation taxable	$913,649,842	$925,443,050	$929,118,780
State equalized value	$1,405,182,778	$1,632,619,673	$1,973,489,337
County equalization ratio	71.6	65.02	56.66

Demographics & Socio-Economic Characteristics

(2000 U.S. Census, except as noted)

Population

1980*	39,510
1990*	39,103
2000	44,943
Male	21,110
Female	23,833
2000 (revised)	45,012
2004 (estimate)*	44,832
Persons per sq. mi. of land	3,700

Race & Hispanic Origin, 2000

Race

White	30,359
Black/African American	7,848
Amer. Indian/Alaska Natv.	63
Asian	3,635
Natv. Hawaiian/Pac. Islander	17
Other Race	1,584
Two or more races	1,437
Hispanic origin, total	4,514
Mexican	277
Puerto Rican	672
Cuban	214
Other Hispanic	3,351

Age & Nativity, 2000

Under 5 years	2,988
18 years and over	34,477
21 years and over	33,258
65 years and over	7,818
85 years and over	1,523
Median Age	39.4
Native born	33,369
Foreign born	11,483

Educational Attainment, 2000

Population 25 years and over	31,694
0-8 yrs of school	4.7%
High School grad or higher	86.3%
Bachelor's degree or higher	43.1%
Graduate degree	19.0%

Income & Poverty, 1999

Per capita income	$34,412
Median household income	$69,254
Median family income	$83,375
Persons in poverty	2,461
H'holds receiving public assistance	228
H'holds receiving social security	4,630

Households, 2000

Total households	16,480
With persons under 18	5,699
With persons over 65	5,053
Family households	11,682
One-person households	4,050
Persons per household	2.66
Persons per family	3.19

Labor & Employment

Total civilian labor force, 2004**	19,876
Unemployment rate	2.7%
Total civilian labor force, 2000	22,909
Unemployment rate	4.4%

Employed persons 16 years and over by occupation, 2000

Managers & professionals	10,344
Service occupations	2,417
Sales & office occupations	6,116
Farming, fishing & forestry	22
Construction & maintenance	1,263
Production & transportation	1,738
Self-employed persons	1,514

*US Census Bureau
**New Jersey Department of Labor

General Information

Township of West Orange
66 Main St
West Orange, NJ 07052
973-325-4155

Web site	www.westorange.org
Land area (sq. miles)	12.12
Water area (sq. miles)	0.11
Type of government	Township
Form of government	MC '50

Government

Legislative Districts

US Congressional	8, 10
State Legislative	27

Local Officials, 2006

Mayor	John McKeon
Admin/Manager	John Sayers
Clerk	Nancy O'Hara
Finance Dir/Treas	Edward Coleman
Engineer	Leonard Lepore
Attorney	Richard Trenk
Tax assessor	Kevin Dillon
Tax collector	Joseph Antonucci
Building officer	Russell DeSaneis
Zoning officer	Geniece Gary-Adams
Public Works	NA

Housing & Construction

Housing Units, 2000*

Total	16,901
Median rent	$857
Median SF home value	$209,200

New Privately Owned Housing Units Authorized by Building Permit

	Units	Value
Total, 2004	15	$2,757,781
Single family	15	$2,757,781
Total, 2005	7	$1,394,318
Single family	7	$1,394,318

Real Property Valuation - parcels, 2005

	Number	Valuation
Total		$1,529,837,500
Vacant	334	16,135,600
Residential	12,873	1,222,444,700
Commercial	427	239,621,000
Industrial	44	10,072,000
Apartments	43	41,394,500
Farm land	1	150,800
Farm homestead	1	18,900

Average Property Value & Tax, 2005

Residential value	$94,956
Property tax	$9,352
FAIR rebate	$580

Public Library

West Orange Public Library
46 Mt Pleasant Ave
West Orange, NJ 07052
973-736-0198

Director............. Cynthia Chamberlin

Library statistics, 2004

	Total	per capita
Volumes	150,887	3.36
Expenditure	$2,147,434	$47.78

Public Safety

Police

Chief	James Abbott
Number of officers, 2004	112

Crime, 2004	Number	Rate
Total	1,228	27.2
Violent	78	1.7
Non-violent	1,150	25.5
Domestic Viol.	216	NA

Emergency/Fire

Director................... Dennis Boyle

Public School District

(for school year 2004-2005 except as noted)

West Orange School District
179 Eagle Rock Ave
West Orange, NJ 07052
973-669-5430

Superintendent	Jerry Tarnoff
Grade plan	K-12
Enrollment	6,345.0
Students per teacher	10.4
Per pupil expenditure	$12,993
Median faculty salary	$53,410
Median administrator salary	$106,129
Grade 12 enrollment	404.0
High school graduation rate	90.4%

Assessment test results

(percent scoring at proficient or advanced level)

	Language	Math
Grade 3	85.6%	83.7%
Grade 8	70.5%	58.3%
High school	85.6%	72.3%

SAT

Percent tested	90%
Average SAT math score	498
Average SAT verbal score	475

No Child Left Behind, 2003-04

Attendence rate (target = 90%)	95.3%
Drop rate	2.4%
Highly-qualified teachers	97.5%
District needs improvement?(AYP)	No

Municipal Finance

Fiscal Year 2005

Total tax levy	$151,010,758
County levy	25,021,866
County taxes	24,497,880
County library	0
County health	0
County open space	523,986
School levy	89,644,683
Local muni. budget	36,344,208
Misc. revenues	21,212,557
Total aid	$6,119,424
CMPTRA	1,966,060
Muni. block grant	176,223
Energy tax receipts	3,831,924
Homeland security	140,000

Fiscal Year 2006

Total aid	$6,119,425
CMPTRA	1,831,943
Muni. block grant	176,223
Energy tax receipts	3,966,042
Homeland security	140,000

Taxes

	2003	2004	2005
General tax rate per $100	8.80	9.350	9.850
Net valuation taxable	$1,533,153,833	$1,538,633,007	$1,533,221,711
State equalized value	$4,629,087,660	$5,211,645,620	$5,840,844,613
County equalization ratio	36.43	36.43	29.47

Demographics & Socio-Economic Characteristics
(2000 U.S. Census, except as noted)

Population
1980*	11,293
1990*	10,982
2000	10,987
Male	5,288
Female	5,699
2004 (estimate)*	11,298
Persons per sq. mi. of land	3,821

Race & Hispanic Origin, 2000
Race
White	9,507
Black/African American	347
Amer. Indian/Alaska Natv.	9
Asian	421
Natv. Hawaiian/Pac. Islander	4
Other Race	348
Two or more races	351
Hispanic origin, total	1,105
Mexican	38
Puerto Rican	355
Cuban	60
Other Hispanic	652

Age & Nativity, 2000
Under 5 years	669
18 years and over	8,834
21 years and over	8,527
65 years and over	1,680
85 years and over	144
Median Age	38.1
Native born	8,675
Foreign born	2,312

Educational Attainment, 2000
Population 25 years and over	8,001
0-8 yrs of school	9.3%
High School grad or higher	81.8%
Bachelor's degree or higher	25.2%
Graduate degree	8.2%

Income & Poverty, 1999
Per capita income	$29,758
Median household income	$60,273
Median family income	$67,292
Persons in poverty	368
H'holds receiving public assistance	79
H'holds receiving social security	1,289

Households, 2000
Total households	4,397
With persons under 18	1,286
With persons over 65	1,219
Family households	3,025
One-person households	1,121
Persons per household	2.49
Persons per family	3.01

Labor & Employment
Total civilian labor force, 2004**	6,652
Unemployment rate	3.5%
Total civilian labor force, 2000	6,036
Unemployment rate	3.4%

Employed persons 16 years and over by occupation, 2000
Managers & professionals	2,305
Service occupations	705
Sales & office occupations	1,668
Farming, fishing & forestry	0
Construction & maintenance	423
Production & transportation	730
Self-employed persons	334

*US Census Bureau
**New Jersey Department of Labor

General Information
Borough of West Paterson
5 Brophy Lane
West Paterson, NJ 07424
973-345-8100
Web site	www.westpaterson.com
Land area (sq. miles)	2.96
Water area (sq. miles)	0.14
Type of government	Borough
Form of government	SM '50

Government
Legislative Districts
US Congressional	8
State Legislative	34

Local Officials, 2006
Mayor	Pat Lepore
Admin/Manager	John Pavlik
Clerk	John Pavlik
Finance Dir/Treas	John McCluskey
Engineer	Thomas Solfaro
Attorney	Albert Buglione
Tax assessor	Tim Henderson
Tax collector	John McCluskey
Building officer	Felix Esposito
Zoning officer	NA
Public Works	George Galbraith

Housing & Construction
Housing Units, 2000*
Total	4,497
Median rent	$854
Median SF home value	$195,100

New Privately Owned Housing Units Authorized by Building Permit
	Units	Value
Total, 2004	9	$1,125,362
Single family	7	$650,362
Total, 2005	29	$1,086,217
Single family	13	$928,579

Real Property Valuation - parcels, 2005
	Number	Valuation
Total		$796,988,562
Vacant	93	18,200,798
Residential	2,957	551,968,824
Commercial	198	152,609,260
Industrial	27	37,815,200
Apartments	6	36,392,800
Farm land	0	0
Farm homestead	1	1,680

Average Property Value & Tax, 2005
Residential value	$186,603
Property tax	$6,679
FAIR rebate	$672

Public Library
Alfred H. Baumann Library
7 Brophy Lane
West Paterson, NJ 07424
973-345-8120
Director	Robert E. Lindsley

Library statistics, 2004
	Total	per capita
Volumes	41,944	3.82
Expenditure	$390,487	$35.54

Public Safety
Police
Chief	Robert Reda
Number of officers, 2004	25

Crime, 2004	Number	Rate
Total	262	23.3
Violent	26	2.3
Non-violent	236	21
Domestic Viol.	113	NA

Emergency/Fire
Director	Joseph Macones

Public School District
(for school year 2004-2005 except as noted)

West Paterson School District
853 McBride Ave
West Paterson, NJ 07424
973-278-5535
Administrator	Frederick Lijoi
Grade plan	K-8
Enrollment	918.0
Students per teacher	10.8
Per pupil expenditure	$11,404
Median faculty salary	$49,535
Median administrator salary	$92,822
Grade 12 enrollment	NA
High school graduation rate	NA

Assessment test results
(percent scoring at proficient or advanced level)
	Language	Math
Grade 3	85.7%	87.9%
Grade 8	74.6%	66.4%
High school	NA	NA

SAT
Percent tested	NA
Average SAT math score	NA
Average SAT verbal score	NA

No Child Left Behind, 2003-04
Attendence rate (target = 90%)	96.4%
Drop rate	NA
Highly-qualified teachers	100%
District needs improvement?(AYP)	No

Municipal Finance
Fiscal Year 2005
Total tax levy	$28,551,487
County levy	6,872,237
County taxes	6,741,365
County library	0
County health	0
County open space	130,872
School levy	14,651,406
Local muni. budget	7,027,843
Misc. revenues	3,023,883
Total aid	$1,192,734
CMPTRA	535,482
Muni. block grant	48,054
Energy tax receipts	532,524
Homeland security	70,000

Fiscal Year 2006
Total aid	$1,192,733
CMPTRA	516,843
Muni. block grant	48,054
Energy tax receipts	551,162
Homeland security	70,000

Taxes
	2003	2004	2005
General tax rate per $100	3.15	3.420	3.580
Net valuation taxable	$796,095,265	$800,333,022	$797,734,270
State equalized value	$1,193,546,124	$1,303,348,997	$1,475,919,093
County equalization ratio	75.98	66.70	61.38

Demographics & Socio-Economic Characteristics

(2000 U.S. Census, except as noted)

Population

1980*	360
1990*	453
2000	448
Male	217
Female	231
2004 (estimate)*	420
Persons per sq. mi. of land	1,592

Race & Hispanic Origin, 2000

Race

White	429
Black/African American	0
Amer. Indian/Alaska Natv.	0
Asian	1
Natv. Hawaiian/Pac. Islander	0
Other Race	10
Two or more races	8
Hispanic origin, total	17
Mexican	1
Puerto Rican	15
Cuban	0
Other Hispanic	1

Age & Nativity, 2000

Under 5 years	22
18 years and over	364
21 years and over	352
65 years and over	87
85 years and over	6
Median Age	47.3
Native born	449
Foreign born	0

Educational Attainment, 2000

Population 25 years and over	348
0-8 yrs of school	4.0%
High School grad or higher	69.0%
Bachelor's degree or higher	5.2%
Graduate degree	1.4%

Income & Poverty, 1999

Per capita income	$17,839
Median household income	$33,393
Median family income	$50,625
Persons in poverty	29
H'holds receiving public assistance	9
H'holds receiving social security	95

Households, 2000

Total households	202
With persons under 18	45
With persons over 65	70
Family households	118
One-person households	74
Persons per household	2.22
Persons per family	2.92

Labor & Employment

Total civilian labor force, 2004**	278
Unemployment rate	9.9%
Total civilian labor force, 2000	234
Unemployment rate	12.0%

Employed persons 16 years and over by occupation, 2000

Managers & professionals	94
Service occupations	47
Sales & office occupations	73
Farming, fishing & forestry	0
Construction & maintenance	31
Production & transportation	21
Self-employed persons	2

*US Census Bureau
**New Jersey Department of Labor

General Information

Borough of West Wildwood
701 West Glenwood Ave
West Wildwood, NJ 08260
609-522-4845

Web site	www.westwildwoodnj.com
Land area (sq. miles)	0.26
Water area (sq. miles)	0.09
Type of government	Borough
Form of government	Comm.

Government

Legislative Districts

US Congressional	2
State Legislative	1

Local Officials, 2006

Mayor	Christopher Fox
Admin/Manager	NA
Clerk	Dorothy Tomlin
Finance Dir/Treas	Judson Moore
Engineer	John Faeirheller
Attorney	Ronald Stagliano
Tax assessor	Joseph Gallagher
Tax collector	NA
Building officer	Michael Preston
Zoning officer	NA
Public Works	James Fox

Housing & Construction

Housing Units, 2000*

Total	775
Median rent	$765
Median SF home value	$87,600

New Privately Owned Housing Units Authorized by Building Permit

	Units	Value
Total, 2004	15	$1,406,650
Single family	15	$1,406,650
Total, 2005	20	$3,293,600
Single family	16	$2,683,600

Real Property Valuation - parcels, 2005

	Number	Valuation
Total		$201,494,800
Vacant	185	30,690,600
Residential	732	162,260,600
Commercial	11	6,567,500
Industrial	0	0
Apartments	5	1,976,100
Farm land	0	0
Farm homestead	0	0

Average Property Value & Tax, 2005

Residential value	$221,667
Property tax	$3,071
FAIR rebate	$748

Public Library

No public municipal library.

Library statistics, 2004

	Total	per capita
Volumes	NA	NA
Expenditure	NA	NA

Public Safety

Police

Chief	Alan Fox
Number of officers, 2004	5

Crime, 2004	Number	Rate
Total	23	53.5
Violent	3	7
Non-violent	20	46.5
Domestic Viol.	8	NA

Emergency/Fire

Director	Daniel Spiegel

Public School District

(for school year 2004-2005 except as noted)

West Wildwood School District†
701 W Glenwood Ave
West Wildwood, NJ 08260

†No schools in district - sends children to North Wildwood schools.

Grade plan	NA
Enrollment	NA
Students per teacher	NA
Per pupil expenditure	NA
Median faculty salary	NA

Assessment test results

(percent scoring at proficient or advanced level)

	Language	Math
Grade 3	NA	NA
Grade 8	NA	NA
High school	NA	NA

SAT

Percent tested	NA
Average SAT math score	NA
Average SAT verbal score	NA

No Child Left Behind, 2003-04

Attendence rate (target = 90%)	NA
Drop rate	NA
Highly-qualified teachers	NA
District needs improvement?(AYP)	NA

Municipal Finance

Fiscal Year 2005

Total tax levy	$2,792,420
County levy	428,948
County taxes	360,564
County library	50,857
County health	0
County open space	17,527
School levy	1,010,281
Local muni. budget	1,353,191
Misc. revenues	378,246
Total aid	$81,944
CMPTRA	13,486
Muni. block grant	1,982
Energy tax receipts	41,476
Homeland security	25,000

Fiscal Year 2006

Total aid	$81,943
CMPTRA	12,034
Muni. block grant	1,982
Energy tax receipts	42,927
Homeland security	25,000

Taxes

	2003	2004	2005
General tax rate per $100	2.87	1.100	1.390
Net valuation taxable	$61,352,203	$205,753,260	$201,571,529
State equalized value	$108,626,422	$180,732,888	$226,408,547
County equalization ratio	67.93	186.18	113.85

Demographics & Socio-Economic Characteristics

(2000 U.S. Census, except as noted)

Population

1980*	8,542
1990*	16,021
2000	21,907
Male	10,858
Female	11,049
2004 (estimate)*	24,458
Persons per sq. mi. of land	940

Race & Hispanic Origin, 2000

Race

White	15,670
Black/African American	605
Amer. Indian/Alaska Natv.	17
Asian	4,986
Natv. Hawaiian/Pac. Islander	2
Other Race	236
Two or more races	391
Hispanic origin, total	892
Mexican	177
Puerto Rican	152
Cuban	63
Other Hispanic	500

Age & Nativity, 2000

Under 5 years	1,541
18 years and over	14,939
21 years and over	14,470
65 years and over	1,349
85 years and over	110
Median Age	37
Native born	17,001
Foreign born	4,906

Educational Attainment, 2000

Population 25 years and over	14,026
0-8 yrs of school	1.5%
High School grad or higher	96.9%
Bachelor's degree or higher	73.9%
Graduate degree	39.0%

Income & Poverty, 1999

Per capita income	$48,511
Median household income	$116,335
Median family income	$127,877
Persons in poverty	548
H'holds receiving public assistance	63
H'holds receiving social security	961

Households, 2000

Total households	7,282
With persons under 18	3,730
With persons over 65	993
Family households	5,986
One-person households	1,061
Persons per household	3.01
Persons per family	3.36

Labor & Employment

Total civilian labor force, 2004**	9,254
Unemployment rate	2.3%
Total civilian labor force, 2000	11,228
Unemployment rate	3.0%

Employed persons 16 years and over by occupation, 2000

Managers & professionals	7,731
Service occupations	487
Sales & office occupations	2,230
Farming, fishing & forestry	0
Construction & maintenance	175
Production & transportation	264
Self-employed persons	526

*US Census Bureau
**New Jersey Department of Labor

General Information

Township of West Windsor
PO Box 38
271 Clarksville Rd
West Windsor, NJ 08550
609-799-2400

Web site	www.westwindsornj.org
Land area (sq. miles)	26.01
Water area (sq. miles)	0.32
Type of government	Township
Form of government	Mayor-Council

Government

Legislative Districts

US Congressional	12
State Legislative	14

Local Officials, 2006

Mayor	Shing-Fu Hsueh
Admin/Manager	Christopher R. Marion
Clerk	Sharon Young
Finance Dir/Treas	Joanne R. Louth
Engineer	Jim Parvesse
Attorney	Michael Herbert
Tax assessor	Steven Benner
Tax collector	Rita Carr
Building officer	Joseph Valeri
Zoning officer	Sam Surtees
Public Works	George Spille

Housing & Construction

Housing Units, 2000*

Total	7,450
Median rent	$1,198
Median SF home value	$333,800

New Privately Owned Housing Units Authorized by Building Permit

	Units	Value
Total, 2004	605	$23,595,345
Single family	112	$7,434,731
Total, 2005	159	$15,336,428
Single family	159	$15,336,428

Real Property Valuation - parcels, 2005

	Number	Valuation
Total		$2,646,422,850
Vacant	809	68,207,100
Residential	7,352	1,760,419,100
Commercial	243	717,208,350
Industrial	15	65,523,400
Apartments	4	25,344,200
Farm land	32	8,607,400
Farm homestead	105	1,113,300

Average Property Value & Tax, 2005

Residential value	$236,225
Property tax	$10,041
FAIR rebate	$508

Public Library

West Windsor Branch Library†
333 N Post Rd
Princeton Jnc, NJ 08550
609-799-0462

Branch Librarian	Kaija Greenberg

Library statistics, 2004

	Total	per capita
Volumes	NA	NA
Expenditure	NA	NA

†Branch of County Library

Public Safety

Police

Chief	Joseph Pica
Number of officers, 2004	46

Crime, 2004	Number	Rate
Total	546	22.7
Violent	16	0.7
Non-violent	530	22
Domestic Viol.	58	NA

Emergency/Fire

Director	Jim Yates

Public School District

(for school year 2004-2005 except as noted)

West Windsor-Plainsboro Reg. School Dist.
PO Box 505
Princeton Junction, NJ 08550
609-716-5000

Administrator	Robert Loretan
Grade plan	K-12
Enrollment	9,097.0
Students per teacher	11.1
Per pupil expenditure	$12,653
Median faculty salary	$56,100
Median administrator salary	$104,475
Grade 12 enrollment	644.0
High school graduation rate	NA

Assessment test results

(percent scoring at proficient or advanced level)

	Language	Math
Grade 3	96.2%	96.0%
Grade 8	91.6%	88.8%
High school	95.7%	94.4%

SAT

Percent tested	NA
Average SAT math score	NA
Average SAT verbal score	NA

No Child Left Behind, 2003-04

Attendence rate (target = 90%)	96.5%
Drop rate	0.3%
Highly-qualified teachers	98.6%
District needs improvement?(AYP)	No

Municipal Finance

Fiscal Year 2005

Total tax levy	$112,907,847
County levy	27,211,358
County taxes	23,768,852
County library	2,107,525
County health	0
County open space	1,334,980
School levy	68,191,307
Local muni. budget	17,505,182
Misc. revenues	13,403,144
Total aid	$3,102,983
CMPTRA	595,848
Muni. block grant	85,898
Energy tax receipts	2,331,237
Homeland security	90,000

Fiscal Year 2006

Total aid	$3,102,983
CMPTRA	514,255
Muni. block grant	85,898
Energy tax receipts	2,412,830
Homeland security	90,000

Taxes

	2003	2004	2005
General tax rate per $100	4.11	4.130	4.260
Net valuation taxable	$2,580,293,449	$2,639,912,126	$2,656,180,318
State equalized value	$3,985,009,188	$4,412,163,611	$5,038,278,297
County equalization ratio	68.8	64.75	59.73

Demographics & Socio-Economic Characteristics

(2000 U.S. Census, except as noted)

Population

1980*	3,383
1990*	6,004
2000	7,217
Male	3,418
Female	3,799
2004 (estimate)*	8,429
Persons per sq. mi. of land	763

Race & Hispanic Origin, 2000

Race

White	5,110
Black/African American	1,535
Amer. Indian/Alaska Natv.	20
Asian	219
Natv. Hawaiian/Pac. Islander	3
Other Race	132
Two or more races	198
Hispanic origin, total	448
Mexican	24
Puerto Rican	296
Cuban	8
Other Hispanic	120

Age & Nativity, 2000

Under 5 years	525
18 years and over	5,104
21 years and over	4,888
65 years and over	659
85 years and over	39
Median Age	35.8
Native born	6,730
Foreign born	470

Educational Attainment, 2000

Population 25 years and over	4,729
0-8 yrs of school	2.0%
High School grad or higher	90.9%
Bachelor's degree or higher	26.2%
Graduate degree	6.9%

Income & Poverty, 1999

Per capita income	$26,594
Median household income	$63,973
Median family income	$69,656
Persons in poverty	180
H'holds receiving public assistance	12
H'holds receiving social security	518

Households, 2000

Total households	2,525
With persons under 18	1,158
With persons over 65	467
Family households	1,966
One-person households	456
Persons per household	2.83
Persons per family	3.24

Labor & Employment

Total civilian labor force, 2004**	3,884
Unemployment rate	3.5%
Total civilian labor force, 2000	3,724
Unemployment rate	3.2%

Employed persons 16 years and over by occupation, 2000

Managers & professionals	1,301
Service occupations	521
Sales & office occupations	1,208
Farming, fishing & forestry	0
Construction & maintenance	170
Production & transportation	404
Self-employed persons	108

*US Census Bureau
**New Jersey Department of Labor

General Information

Township of Westampton
710 Rancocas Rd
Westampton, NJ 08060
609-267-1891

Web site	www.westampton.com
Land area (sq. miles)	11.04
Water area (sq. miles)	0.12
Type of government	Township
Form of government	TC

Government

Legislative Districts

US Congressional	4
State Legislative	7

Local Officials, 2006

Mayor	Dan Miller
Admin/Manager	Donna Ryan
Clerk	Donna Ryan
Finance Dir/Treas	Robert Hudnell
Engineer	David Denton
Attorney	Michael Mouber
Tax assessor	Marie Procacci
Tax collector	Marge O'Dell
Building officer	Gene Blair
Zoning officer	Gene Blair
Public Works	NA

Housing & Construction

Housing Units, 2000*

Total	2,581
Median rent	$1,112
Median SF home value	$127,300

New Privately Owned Housing Units
Authorized by Building Permit

	Units	Value
Total, 2004	102	$10,881,825
Single family	84	$9,460,025
Total, 2005	66	$14,512,790
Single family	66	$14,512,790

Real Property Valuation - parcels, 2005

	Number	Valuation
Total		$620,631,050
Vacant	232	13,891,500
Residential	2,945	417,541,700
Commercial	103	172,621,100
Industrial	2	11,261,400
Apartments	0	0
Farm land	23	4,220,700
Farm homestead	68	1,094,650

Average Property Value & Tax, 2005

Residential value	$138,943
Property tax	$3,960
FAIR rebate	$500

Public Library

No public municipal library.

Library statistics, 2004

	Total	per capita
Volumes	NA	NA
Expenditure	NA	NA

Public Safety

Police

Chief	Steven VanSciver
Number of officers, 2004	23

Crime, 2004	Number	Rate
Total	221	27.7
Violent	22	2.8
Non-violent	199	25
Domestic Viol.	65	NA

Emergency/Fire

Director	Wylie Johnson

Public School District

(for school year 2004-2005 except as noted)

Westampton Township School District
710 Rancocas Rd
Westampton, NJ 08060
609-267-2053

Superintendent	Richard Ballard
Grade plan	K-8
Enrollment	980.0
Students per teacher	12.0
Per pupil expenditure	$9,780
Median faculty salary	$44,421
Median administrator salary	$91,999
Grade 12 enrollment	NA
High school graduation rate	NA

Assessment test results
(percent scoring at proficient or advanced level)

	Language	Math
Grade 3	94.8%	87.4%
Grade 8	85.2%	67.7%
High school	NA	NA

SAT

Percent tested	NA
Average SAT math score	NA
Average SAT verbal score	NA

No Child Left Behind, 2003-04

Attendence rate (target = 90%)	95.4%
Drop rate	NA
Highly-qualified teachers	96.6%
District needs improvement?(AYP)	No

Municipal Finance

Fiscal Year 2005

Total tax levy	$17,738,488
County levy	3,948,291
County taxes	3,312,632
County library	289,817
County health	0
County open space	345,841
School levy	10,653,370
Local muni. budget	3,136,827
Misc. revenues	3,842,493
Total aid	$958,856
CMPTRA	275,842
Muni. block grant	28,298
Energy tax receipts	604,716
Homeland security	50,000

Fiscal Year 2006

Total aid	$958,856
CMPTRA	254,677
Muni. block grant	28,298
Energy tax receipts	625,881
Homeland security	50,000

Taxes

	2003	2004	2005
General tax rate per $100	2.65	2.779	2.852
Net valuation taxable	$548,650,157	$587,828,709	$622,307,010
State equalized value	$672,777,630	$814,427,688	$943,175,220
County equalization ratio	90.95	81.55	72.11

Demographics & Socio-Economic Characteristics

(2000 U.S. Census, except as noted)

Population

1980*	30,447
1990*	28,870
2000	29,644
Male	14,209
Female	15,435
2004 (estimate)*	30,062
Persons per sq. mi. of land	4,465

Race & Hispanic Origin, 2000

Race

White	26,675
Black/African American	1,151
Amer. Indian/Alaska Natv.	27
Asian	1,208
Natv. Hawaiian/Pac. Islander	3
Other Race	185
Two or more races	395
Hispanic origin, total	836
Mexican	104
Puerto Rican	176
Cuban	103
Other Hispanic	453

Age & Nativity, 2000

Under 5 years	2,369
18 years and over	21,235
21 years and over	20,704
65 years and over	4,015
85 years and over	528
Median Age	38.6
Native born	26,940
Foreign born	2,704

Educational Attainment, 2000

Population 25 years and over	20,052
0-8 yrs of school	1.8%
High School grad or higher	95.4%
Bachelor's degree or higher	62.5%
Graduate degree	29.8%

Income & Poverty, 1999

Per capita income	$47,187
Median household income	$98,390
Median family income	$112,145
Persons in poverty	791
H'holds receiving public assistance	93
H'holds receiving social security	2,626

Households, 2000

Total households	10,622
With persons under 18	4,454
With persons over 65	2,716
Family households	8,181
One-person households	2,052
Persons per household	2.77
Persons per family	3.2

Labor & Employment

Total civilian labor force, 2004**	15,709
Unemployment rate	2.5%
Total civilian labor force, 2000	14,907
Unemployment rate	2.2%

Employed persons 16 years and over by occupation, 2000

Managers & professionals	8,811
Service occupations	1,102
Sales & office occupations	3,510
Farming, fishing & forestry	8
Construction & maintenance	484
Production & transportation	660
Self-employed persons	942

*US Census Bureau
**New Jersey Department of Labor

General Information

Town of Westfield
425 E Broad St
Westfield, NJ 07090
908-789-4033

Web site	NA
Land area (sq. miles)	6.73
Water area (sq. miles)	0.02
Type of government	Town
Form of government	SC

Government

Legislative Districts

US Congressional	7
State Legislative	21

Local Officials, 2006

Mayor	Andrew Skibitsky
Admin/Manager	James Gildea
Clerk	Claire Gray
Finance Dir/Treas	Liy-Huei Tsai
Engineer	Kenneth Marsh
Attorney	Robert Cockren
Tax assessor	Ann Switzer
Tax collector	Susan Noon
Building officer	Steve Freedman
Zoning officer	Kathleen Neville
Public Works	Claude Shafter

Housing & Construction

Housing Units, 2000*

Total	10,819
Median rent	$1,048
Median SF home value	$346,000

New Privately Owned Housing Units Authorized by Building Permit

	Units	Value
Total, 2004	38	$8,919,150
Single family	38	$8,919,150
Total, 2005	77	$19,550,466
Single family	77	$19,550,466

Real Property Valuation - parcels, 2005

	Number	Valuation
Total		$1,843,799,300
Vacant	204	8,171,300
Residential	9,131	1,631,230,100
Commercial	427	179,952,300
Industrial	4	1,988,100
Apartments	12	22,453,300
Farm land	0	0
Farm homestead	1	4,200

Average Property Value & Tax, 2005

Residential value	$178,628
Property tax	$10,431
FAIR rebate	$580

Public Library

Westfield Memorial Library
550 East Broad St
Westfield, NJ 07090
908-789-4090

Director.....................Phillip Israel

Library statistics, 2004

	Total	per capita
Volumes	150,851	5.09
Expenditure	$1,739,797	$58.69

Public Safety

Police

Chief	John Parizeau
Number of officers, 2004	60

Crime, 2004	Number	Rate
Total	350	11.7
Violent	4	0.1
Non-violent	346	11.6
Domestic Viol.	111	NA

Emergency/Fire

Director.....................Daniel Kelly

Public School District

(for school year 2004-2005 except as noted)

Westfield School District
302 Elm St
Westfield, NJ 07090
908-789-4420

Superintendent	William Foley
Grade plan	K-12
Enrollment	5,889.0
Students per teacher	11.5
Per pupil expenditure	$11,887
Median faculty salary	$58,588
Median administrator salary	$108,648
Grade 12 enrollment	367.0
High school graduation rate	98.9%

Assessment test results

(percent scoring at proficient or advanced level)

	Language	Math
Grade 3	94.8%	94.2%
Grade 8	90.8%	85.0%
High school	95.5%	93.1%

SAT

Percent tested	99%
Average SAT math score	589
Average SAT verbal score	574

No Child Left Behind, 2003-04

Attendence rate (target = 90%)	95.8%
Drop rate	0.2%
Highly-qualified teachers	98.2%
District needs improvement?(AYP)	No

Municipal Finance

Fiscal Year 2005

Total tax levy	$107,806,714
County levy	22,805,731
County taxes	21,905,092
County library	0
County health	0
County open space	900,639
School levy	67,415,638
Local muni. budget	17,585,346
Misc. revenues	14,784,159
Total aid	$4,484,903
CMPTRA	1,986,685
Muni. block grant	126,326
Energy tax receipts	2,231,892
Homeland security	140,000

Fiscal Year 2006

Total aid	$4,484,904
CMPTRA	1,908,569
Muni. block grant	126,326
Energy tax receipts	2,310,009
Homeland security	140,000

Taxes

	2003	2004	2005
General tax rate per $100	5.26	5.580	5.840
Net valuation taxable	$1,828,115,010	$1,835,542,535	$1,846,085,079
State equalized value	$5,064,030,499	$5,623,362,292	$6,245,213,393
County equalization ratio	38.86	34.58	30.81

Demographics & Socio-Economic Characteristics
(2000 U.S. Census, except as noted)

Population
1980*	4,786
1990*	4,573
2000	4,500
Male	2,183
Female	2,317
2004 (estimate)*	4,471
Persons per sq. mi. of land	4,636

Race & Hispanic Origin, 2000
Race
White	4,206
Black/African American	122
Amer. Indian/Alaska Natv.	6
Asian	45
Natv. Hawaiian/Pac. Islander	1
Other Race	58
Two or more races	62
Hispanic origin, total	133
Mexican	21
Puerto Rican	59
Cuban	2
Other Hispanic	51

Age & Nativity, 2000
Under 5 years	253
18 years and over	3,396
21 years and over	3,236
65 years and over	633
85 years and over	63
Median Age	36.6
Native born	4,398
Foreign born	102

Educational Attainment, 2000
Population 25 years and over	3,033
0-8 yrs of school	4.5%
High School grad or higher	75.5%
Bachelor's degree or higher	8.9%
Graduate degree	1.2%

Income & Poverty, 1999
Per capita income	$18,747
Median household income	$39,570
Median family income	$49,005
Persons in poverty	389
H'holds receiving public assistance	41
H'holds receiving social security	535

Households, 2000
Total households	1,812
With persons under 18	590
With persons over 65	471
Family households	1,126
One-person households	577
Persons per household	2.48
Persons per family	3.15

Labor & Employment
Total civilian labor force, 2004**	2,769
Unemployment rate	6.8%
Total civilian labor force, 2000	2,388
Unemployment rate	5.0%

Employed persons 16 years and over by occupation, 2000
Managers & professionals	406
Service occupations	350
Sales & office occupations	707
Farming, fishing & forestry	0
Construction & maintenance	339
Production & transportation	406
Self-employed persons	108

*US Census Bureau
**New Jersey Department of Labor

General Information
Borough of Westville
1035 Broadway
Westville, NJ 08093
856-456-0030

Web site	www.westvillenj.com
Land area (sq. miles)	0.96
Water area (sq. miles)	0.39
Type of government	Borough
Form of government	B

Government

Legislative Districts
US Congressional	1
State Legislative	5

Local Officials, 2006
Mayor	William Packer III
Admin/Manager	William Bittner Jr.
Clerk	Richard Burr
Finance Dir/Treas	Richard Burr
Engineer	Norman Rogers III
Attorney	Robert Becker Jr.
Tax assessor	Roy Duffield
Tax collector	Christine Helder
Building officer	Robert Kunkle
Zoning officer	NA
Public Works	Donna Domico

Housing & Construction

Housing Units, 2000*
Total	1,938
Median rent	$569
Median SF home value	$91,500

New Privately Owned Housing Units
Authorized by Building Permit
	Units	Value
Total, 2004	2	$202,561
Single family	2	$202,561
Total, 2005	6	$553,821
Single family	6	$553,821

Real Property Valuation - parcels, 2005
	Number	Valuation
Total		$160,726,800
Vacant	70	1,378,200
Residential	1,396	120,978,000
Commercial	99	23,266,800
Industrial	16	8,786,100
Apartments	10	6,317,700
Farm land	0	0
Farm homestead	0	0

Average Property Value & Tax, 2005
Residential value	$86,660
Property tax	$3,545
FAIR rebate	$598

Public Library
Westville Public Library
1035 Broadway
Westville, NJ 08093
856-456-0357

Director	Gwen Carotenuto

Library statistics, 2004
	Total	per capita
Volumes	22,837	5.07
Expenditure	$105,907	$23.53

Public Safety

Police
Chief	Frederick Lederer
Number of officers, 2004	10

Crime, 2004	Number	Rate
Total	136	30.4
Violent	7	1.6
Non-violent	129	28.8
Domestic Viol.	57	NA

Emergency/Fire
Director	Chuck Murtaugh

Public School District
(for school year 2004-2005 except as noted)

Westville School District
101 Birch St
Westville, NJ 08093
856-456-0235

Superintendent	Shannon Whalen
Grade plan	K-6
Enrollment	362.0
Students per teacher	9.9
Per pupil expenditure	$10,287
Median faculty salary	$50,705
Median administrator salary	$73,335
Grade 12 enrollment	NA
High school graduation rate	NA

Assessment test results
(percent scoring at proficient or advanced level)
	Language	Math
Grade 3	63.8%	78.8%
Grade 8	NA	NA
High school	NA	NA

SAT
Percent tested	NA
Average SAT math score	NA
Average SAT verbal score	NA

No Child Left Behind, 2003-04
Attendence rate (target = 90%)	95.9%
Drop rate	NA
Highly-qualified teachers	100%
District needs improvement?(AYP)	No

Municipal Finance

Fiscal Year 2005
Total tax levy	$6,589,465
County levy	1,253,884
County taxes	1,175,675
County library	0
County health	0
County open space	78,209
School levy	3,591,581
Local muni. budget	1,744,000
Misc. revenues	3,035,000
Total aid	$575,660
CMPTRA	256,708
Muni. block grant	20,010
Energy tax receipts	273,942
Homeland security	25,000

Fiscal Year 2006
Total aid	$575,660
CMPTRA	247,120
Muni. block grant	20,010
Energy tax receipts	283,530
Homeland security	25,000

Taxes
	2003	2004	2005
General tax rate per $100	3.47	3.707	4.091
Net valuation taxable	$161,008,476	$161,085,863	$161,075,099
State equalized value	$179,216,915	$194,297,020	$220,529,982
County equalization ratio	92.97	89.84	82.87

Demographics & Socio-Economic Characteristics
(2000 U.S. Census, except as noted)

Population

1980*	10,714
1990*	10,446
2000	10,999
Male	5,218
Female	5,781
2004 (estimate)*	11,051
Persons per sq. mi. of land	4,768

Race & Hispanic Origin, 2000
Race

White	9,525
Black/African American	629
Amer. Indian/Alaska Natv.	15
Asian	483
Natv. Hawaiian/Pac. Islander	1
Other Race	184
Two or more races	162
Hispanic origin, total	660
Mexican	135
Puerto Rican	113
Cuban	60
Other Hispanic	352

Age & Nativity, 2000

Under 5 years	762
18 years and over	8,631
21 years and over	8,392
65 years and over	1,752
85 years and over	320
Median Age	38.6
Native born	9,317
Foreign born	1,682

Educational Attainment, 2000

Population 25 years and over	8,052
0-8 yrs of school	4.8%
High School grad or higher	88.1%
Bachelor's degree or higher	37.4%
Graduate degree	11.7%

Income & Poverty, 1999

Per capita income	$32,083
Median household income	$59,868
Median family income	$77,105
Persons in poverty	474
H'holds receiving public assistance	58
H'holds receiving social security	1,315

Households, 2000

Total households	4,485
With persons under 18	1,348
With persons over 65	1,279
Family households	2,878
One-person households	1,395
Persons per household	2.42
Persons per family	3.08

Labor & Employment

Total civilian labor force, 2004**	6,247
Unemployment rate	3.3%
Total civilian labor force, 2000	5,874
Unemployment rate	2.1%

Employed persons 16 years and over by occupation, 2000

Managers & professionals	2,444
Service occupations	839
Sales & office occupations	1,678
Farming, fishing & forestry	0
Construction & maintenance	372
Production & transportation	417
Self-employed persons	311

*US Census Bureau
**New Jersey Department of Labor

General Information
Borough of Westwood
101 Washington Ave
Westwood, NJ 07675
201-664-7100

Web site	www.westwoodnj.gov
Land area (sq. miles)	2.32
Water area (sq. miles)	0
Type of government	Borough
Form of government	B

Government

Legislative Districts

US Congressional	5
State Legislative	39

Local Officials, 2006

Mayor	Thomas D. Wanner
Admin/Manager	Kenneth Gabbert
Clerk	Eileen Sarubbi
Finance Dir/Treas	Raymond Herr
Engineer	Stephen Boswell
Attorney	Russell Huntington
Tax assessor	Barbara Potash
Tax collector	NA
Building officer	Leroy Humes
Zoning officer	NA
Public Works	NA

Housing & Construction

Housing Units, 2000*

Total	4,610
Median rent	$996
Median SF home value	$239,300

New Privately Owned Housing Units
Authorized by Building Permit

	Units	Value
Total, 2004	6	$1,002,800
Single family	6	$1,002,800
Total, 2005	7	$1,246,900
Single family	7	$1,246,900

Real Property Valuation - parcels, 2005

	Number	Valuation
Total		$1,586,967,300
Vacant	103	10,789,100
Residential	3,051	1,192,944,600
Commercial	237	234,973,500
Industrial	34	37,146,400
Apartments	29	111,113,700
Farm land	0	0
Farm homestead	0	0

Average Property Value & Tax, 2005

Residential value	$391,001
Property tax	$7,382
FAIR rebate	$585

Public Library
Westwood Public Library
49 Park Ave
Westwood, NJ 07675
201-664-0583

Director	Phyllis Palley

Library statistics, 2004

	Total	per capita
Volumes	45,810	4.16
Expenditure	$625,057	$56.83

Public Safety

Police

Chief	Frank Regino
Number of officers, 2004	28

Crime, 2004	Number	Rate
Total	130	11.8
Violent	10	0.9
Non-violent	120	10.9
Domestic Viol.	41	NA

Emergency/Fire

Director	John Domville

Public School District
(for school year 2004-2005 except as noted)

Westwood Regional School District
701 Ridgewood Rd
Township of Washington, NJ 07676
201-664-2765

Superintendent	Roy Montesano
Grade plan	K-12
Enrollment	2,641.0
Students per teacher	10.9
Per pupil expenditure	$13,071
Median faculty salary	$48,659
Median administrator salary	$113,303
Grade 12 enrollment	160.0
High school graduation rate	98.1%

Assessment test results
(percent scoring at proficient or advanced level)

	Language	Math
Grade 3	97.0%	92.0%
Grade 8	84.0%	77.7%
High school	95.1%	88.7%

SAT

Percent tested	81%
Average SAT math score	538
Average SAT verbal score	503

No Child Left Behind, 2003-04

Attendance rate (target = 90%)	96.2%
Drop rate	1.2%
Highly-qualified teachers	97.8%
District needs improvement?(AYP)	No

Municipal Finance

Fiscal Year 2005

Total tax levy	$30,013,529
County levy	3,177,059
County taxes	3,017,654
County library	0
County health	0
County open space	159,405
School levy	17,176,494
Local muni. budget	9,659,975
Misc. revenues	3,858,674
Total aid	$1,436,482
CMPTRA	447,374
Muni. block grant	45,708
Energy tax receipts	872,695
Homeland security	70,000

Fiscal Year 2006

Total aid	$1,436,483
CMPTRA	416,830
Muni. block grant	45,708
Energy tax receipts	903,240
Homeland security	70,000

Taxes

	2003	2004	2005
General tax rate per $100	3.12	1.750	1.890
Net valuation taxable	$805,346,886	$1,590,222,103	$1,589,647,810
State equalized value	$1,340,011,458	$1,586,738,077	$1,707,096,016
County equalization ratio	68.47	117.75	100.22

Demographics & Socio-Economic Characteristics
(2000 U.S. Census, except as noted)

Population
1980*	1,260
1990*	1,957
2000	2,257
Male	1,085
Female	1,172
2004 (estimate)*	2,325
Persons per sq. mi. of land	191

Race & Hispanic Origin, 2000
Race
White	2,076
Black/African American	108
Amer. Indian/Alaska Natv.	9
Asian	18
Natv. Hawaiian/Pac. Islander	0
Other Race	23
Two or more races	23
Hispanic origin, total	86
Mexican	24
Puerto Rican	42
Cuban	2
Other Hispanic	18

Age & Nativity, 2000
Under 5 years	141
18 years and over	1,694
21 years and over	1,628
65 years and over	387
85 years and over	29
Median Age	39.4
Native born	2,191
Foreign born	59

Educational Attainment, 2000
Population 25 years and over	1,530
0-8 yrs of school	5.6%
High School grad or higher	79.5%
Bachelor's degree or higher	14.2%
Graduate degree	4.4%

Income & Poverty, 1999
Per capita income	$18,987
Median household income	$45,882
Median family income	$49,800
Persons in poverty	115
H'holds receiving public assistance	29
H'holds receiving social security	297

Households, 2000
Total households	851
With persons under 18	283
With persons over 65	276
Family households	624
One-person households	183
Persons per household	2.65
Persons per family	3.06

Labor & Employment
Total civilian labor force, 2004**	1,033
Unemployment rate	5.3%
Total civilian labor force, 2000	1,098
Unemployment rate	3.8%

Employed persons 16 years and over by occupation, 2000
Managers & professionals	355
Service occupations	228
Sales & office occupations	310
Farming, fishing & forestry	0
Construction & maintenance	139
Production & transportation	124
Self-employed persons	46

*US Census Bureau
**New Jersey Department of Labor

General Information
Township of Weymouth
45 S Jersey Ave
Dorothy, NJ 08317
609-476-2633
Web site	www.weymouthnj.org
Land area (sq. miles)	12.20
Water area (sq. miles)	0.37
Type of government	Township
Form of government	TC

Government

Legislative Districts
US Congressional	2
State Legislative	2

Local Officials, 2006
Mayor	Amelia A. Messina
Admin/Manager	Bonnie Yearsley
Clerk	Bonnie Yearsley
Finance Dir/Treas	Ronald Trebing
Engineer	Fralinger Engineering
Attorney	James J. Carroll
Tax assessor	Bernadette Leonardi
Tax collector	Debra D'Amore
Building officer	(State)
Zoning officer	Jay Laubenger
Public Works	Ronald Carroll

Housing & Construction

Housing Units, 2000*
Total	909
Median rent	$725
Median SF home value	$119,000

New Privately Owned Housing Units Authorized by Building Permit
	Units	Value
Total, 2004	8	$445,188
Single family	8	$445,188
Total, 2005	2	$23,050
Single family	2	$23,050

Real Property Valuation - parcels, 2005
	Number	Valuation
Total		$90,894,500
Vacant	326	5,653,400
Residential	644	74,847,200
Commercial	32	8,431,900
Industrial	1	206,700
Apartments	2	1,439,900
Farm land	3	287,400
Farm homestead	5	28,000

Average Property Value & Tax, 2005
Residential value	$115,370
Property tax	$2,809
FAIR rebate	$483

Public Library

No public municipal library.

Library statistics, 2004
	Total	per capita
Volumes	NA	NA
Expenditure	NA	NA

Public Safety

Police
Chief	(State)
Number of officers, 2004	0

Crime, 2004	Number	Rate
Total	25	10.8
Violent	2	0.9
Non-violent	23	9.9
Domestic Viol.	8	NA

Emergency/Fire
Director	Robert Gibney

Public School District
(for school year 2004-2005 except as noted)

Weymouth Township School District
1202 Eleventh Ave
Dorothy, NJ 08317
609-476-2412
Administrator	Donna Van Horn
Grade plan	K-12
Enrollment	245.0
Students per teacher	9.4
Per pupil expenditure	$9,792
Median faculty salary	$41,299
Median administrator salary	$77,279
Grade 12 enrollment	NA
High school graduation rate	NA

Assessment test results
(percent scoring at proficient or advanced level)
	Language	Math
Grade 3	92.0%	92.0%
Grade 8	72.4%	65.5%
High school	NA	NA

SAT
Percent tested	NA
Average SAT math score	NA
Average SAT verbal score	NA

No Child Left Behind, 2003-04
Attendance rate (target = 90%)	95.5%
Drop rate	NA
Highly-qualified teachers	100%
District needs improvement?(AYP)	No

Municipal Finance

Fiscal Year 2005
Total tax levy	$2,225,032
County levy	507,566
County taxes	414,286
County library	45,955
County health	22,615
County open space	24,710
School levy	1,451,713
Local muni. budget	265,753
Misc. revenues	789,148
Total aid	$400,588
CMPTRA	90,148
Muni. block grant	8,850
Energy tax receipts	276,590
Homeland security	25,000

Fiscal Year 2006
Total aid	$375,588
CMPTRA	80,467
Muni. block grant	8,850
Energy tax receipts	286,271
Homeland security	NA

Taxes
	2003	2004	2005
General tax rate per $100	2.18	2.073	2.435
Net valuation taxable	$86,916,598	$88,406,333	$91,389,523
State equalized value	$106,947,949	$118,990,314	$115,013,243
County equalization ratio	84.4	81.27	74.17

Demographics & Socio-Economic Characteristics

(2000 U.S. Census, except as noted)

Population

1980*	5,485
1990*	5,405
2000	6,298
Male	3,043
Female	3,255
2004 (estimate)*	6,239
Persons per sq. mi. of land	2,855

Race & Hispanic Origin, 2000

Race
White	5,170
Black/African American	277
Amer. Indian/Alaska Natv.	28
Asian	198
Natv. Hawaiian/Pac. Islander	0
Other Race	454
Two or more races	171
Hispanic origin, total	1,462
Mexican	147
Puerto Rican	391
Cuban	18
Other Hispanic	906

Age & Nativity, 2000

Under 5 years	464
18 years and over	4,660
21 years and over	4,479
65 years and over	711
85 years and over	91
Median Age	35.7
Native born	5,430
Foreign born	868

Educational Attainment, 2000

Population 25 years and over	4,218
0-8 yrs of school	5.1%
High School grad or higher	80.9%
Bachelor's degree or higher	22.7%
Graduate degree	7.9%

Income & Poverty, 1999

Per capita income	$25,168
Median household income	$56,580
Median family income	$64,957
Persons in poverty	517
H'holds receiving public assistance	45
H'holds receiving social security	607

Households, 2000

Total households	2,328
With persons under 18	871
With persons over 65	558
Family households	1,599
One-person households	616
Persons per household	2.7
Persons per family	3.28

Labor & Employment

Total civilian labor force, 2004**	3,462
Unemployment rate	2.2%
Total civilian labor force, 2000	3,369
Unemployment rate	6.7%

Employed persons 16 years and over by occupation, 2000
Managers & professionals	1,079
Service occupations	379
Sales & office occupations	990
Farming, fishing & forestry	9
Construction & maintenance	267
Production & transportation	420
Self-employed persons	94

*US Census Bureau
**New Jersey Department of Labor

General Information

Borough of Wharton
10 Robert St
Wharton, NJ 07885
973-361-8444

Web site	www.whartonnj.com
Land area (sq. miles)	2.19
Water area (sq. miles)	0.03
Type of government	Borough
Form of government	B

Government

Legislative Districts

US Congressional	11
State Legislative	25

Local Officials, 2006

Mayor	William Chegwidden
Admin/Manager	Jon Rheinhardt
Clerk	Susan Best
Finance Dir/Treas	Jon Rheinhardt
Engineer	Schoor Depalma
Attorney	George Johnson
Tax assessor	Donald Sherman
Tax collector	NA
Building officer	Joseph Monetmarano
Zoning officer	Pedro Moreno
Public Works	Walter Van Kirk

Housing & Construction

Housing Units, 2000*

Total	2,394
Median rent	$867
Median SF home value	$165,300

New Privately Owned Housing Units Authorized by Building Permit

	Units	Value
Total, 2004	1	$60,000
Single family	1	$60,000
Total, 2005	1	$60,000
Single family	1	$60,000

Real Property Valuation - parcels, 2005

	Number	Valuation
Total		$347,232,900
Vacant	56	3,882,000
Residential	1,685	235,364,400
Commercial	78	57,911,700
Industrial	10	28,603,100
Apartments	15	21,322,300
Farm land	1	146,900
Farm homestead	2	2,500

Average Property Value & Tax, 2005

Residential value	$139,518
Property tax	$5,448
FAIR rebate	$560

Public Library

Wharton Public Library
15 South Main St
Wharton, NJ 07885
973-361-1333
Director.............Nancy Kaminetsky

Library statistics, 2004

	Total	per capita
Volumes	34,664	5.50
Expenditure	$258,830	$41.10

Public Safety

Police

Chief	Anthony Fernandez
Number of officers, 2004	21

Crime, 2004	Number	Rate
Total	157	25.2
Violent	11	1.8
Non-violent	146	23.5
Domestic Viol.	80	NA

Emergency/Fire

Director....................Doug Ploth

Public School District

(for school year 2004-2005 except as noted)

Wharton Borough School District
137 E Central Ave
Wharton, NJ 07885
973-361-2592

Superintendent	Richard Bitondo
Grade plan	K-8
Enrollment	796.0
Students per teacher	10.0
Per pupil expenditure	$11,399
Median faculty salary	$43,735
Median administrator salary	$94,750
Grade 12 enrollment	NA
High school graduation rate	NA

Assessment test results

(percent scoring at proficient or advanced level)

	Language	Math
Grade 3	83.1%	84.5%
Grade 8	69.3%	60.6%
High school	NA	NA

SAT

Percent tested	NA
Average SAT math score	NA
Average SAT verbal score	NA

No Child Left Behind, 2003-04

Attendence rate (target = 90%)	95.4%
Drop rate	NA
Highly-qualified teachers	91.9%
District needs improvement?(AYP)	No

Municipal Finance

Fiscal Year 2005

Total tax levy	$13,577,635
County levy	1,639,414
County taxes	1,342,912
County library	0
County health	0
County open space	296,502
School levy	9,789,469
Local muni. budget	2,148,751
Misc. revenues	3,776,282
Total aid	$843,411
CMPTRA	331,885
Muni. block grant	24,695
Energy tax receipts	436,831
Homeland security	50,000

Fiscal Year 2006

Total aid	$843,411
CMPTRA	316,596
Muni. block grant	24,695
Energy tax receipts	452,120
Homeland security	50,000

Taxes

	2003	2004	2005
General tax rate per $100	3.25	3.570	3.910
Net valuation taxable	$345,035,652	$346,223,906	$347,730,762
State equalized value	$541,402,247	$608,464,576	$695,044,497
County equalization ratio	73.1	63.73	56.86

Demographics & Socio-Economic Characteristics
(2000 U.S. Census, except as noted)

Population
1980*	2,748
1990*	3,603
2000	4,245
Male	2,124
Female	2,121
2004 (estimate)*	5,395
Persons per sq. mi. of land	197

Race & Hispanic Origin, 2000
Race
White	4,090
Black/African American	51
Amer. Indian/Alaska Natv.	8
Asian	26
Natv. Hawaiian/Pac. Islander	2
Other Race	14
Two or more races	54
Hispanic origin, total	90
Mexican	6
Puerto Rican	29
Cuban	11
Other Hispanic	44

Age & Nativity, 2000
Under 5 years	236
18 years and over	3,299
21 years and over	3,160
65 years and over	772
85 years and over	55
Median Age	41.5
Native born	4,029
Foreign born	216

Educational Attainment, 2000
Population 25 years and over	3,086
0-8 yrs of school	4.3%
High School grad or higher	81.4%
Bachelor's degree or higher	22.4%
Graduate degree	5.4%

Income & Poverty, 1999
Per capita income	$24,783
Median household income	$54,732
Median family income	$66,127
Persons in poverty	201
H'holds receiving public assistance	47
H'holds receiving social security	610

Households, 2000
Total households	1,668
With persons under 18	502
With persons over 65	562
Family households	1,179
One-person households	420
Persons per household	2.47
Persons per family	2.98

Labor & Employment
Total civilian labor force, 2004**	2,204
Unemployment rate	5.0%
Total civilian labor force, 2000	2,006
Unemployment rate	2.8%

Employed persons 16 years and over by occupation, 2000
Managers & professionals	640
Service occupations	282
Sales & office occupations	514
Farming, fishing & forestry	7
Construction & maintenance	233
Production & transportation	272
Self-employed persons	151

*US Census Bureau
**New Jersey Department of Labor

General Information
Township of White
555 CR 519
Belvidere, NJ 07823
908-475-2093
Email	clerk@whitetwp-nj.com
Land area (sq. miles)	27.37
Water area (sq. miles)	0.38
Type of government	Township
Form of government	TC

Government

Legislative Districts
US Congressional	5
State Legislative	23

Local Officials, 2006
Mayor	James Ashe
Admin/Manager	NA
Clerk	Kathleen Reinalda
Finance Dir/Treas	Kathleen Reinalda
Engineer	Paul Sterbenz
Attorney	Brian Smith
Tax assessor	Bernard Murdoch
Tax collector	Susan Luthringer
Building officer	Ralph Price
Zoning officer	(Vacant)
Public Works	NA

Housing & Construction

Housing Units, 2000*
Total	1,770
Median rent	$531
Median SF home value	$163,700

New Privately Owned Housing Units
Authorized by Building Permit
	Units	Value
Total, 2004	125	$7,939,623
Single family	125	$7,939,623
Total, 2005	99	$6,759,251
Single family	76	$5,559,465

Real Property Valuation - parcels, 2005
	Number	Valuation
Total		$624,903,840
Vacant	229	15,406,300
Residential	1,468	380,920,450
Commercial	86	42,349,200
Industrial	10	139,562,250
Apartments	6	6,912,100
Farm land	135	36,274,000
Farm homestead	322	3,479,540

Average Property Value & Tax, 2005
Residential value	$214,749
Property tax	$3,282
FAIR rebate	$658

Public Library
No public municipal library.

Library statistics, 2004
	Total	per capita
Volumes	NA	NA
Expenditure	NA	NA

Public Safety

Police
Chief	NA
Number of officers, 2004	0

Crime, 2004	Number	Rate
Total	40	7.8
Violent	1	0.2
Non-violent	39	7.6
Domestic Viol.	15	NA

Emergency/Fire
Director	NA

Public School District
(for school year 2004-2005 except as noted)

White Township School District
565 County Route 519
Belvidere, NJ 07823
908-475-4773
Administrator	Linda Heilman
Grade plan	K-12
Enrollment	462.0
Students per teacher	11.3
Per pupil expenditure	$11,798
Median faculty salary	$53,828
Median administrator salary	$114,250
Grade 12 enrollment	NA
High school graduation rate	NA

Assessment test results
(percent scoring at proficient or advanced level)
	Language	Math
Grade 3	93.2%	91.0%
Grade 8	83.3%	78.6%
High school	NA	NA

SAT
Percent tested	NA
Average SAT math score	NA
Average SAT verbal score	NA

No Child Left Behind, 2003-04
Attendence rate (target = 90%)	96.0%
Drop rate	NA
Highly-qualified teachers	100%
District needs improvement?(AYP)	No

Municipal Finance

Fiscal Year 2005
Total tax levy	$9,576,980
County levy	3,803,132
County taxes	3,143,117
County library	303,816
County health	0
County open space	356,199
School levy	5,649,011
Local muni. budget	124,837
Misc. revenues	2,553,042
Total aid	$448,366
CMPTRA	181,132
Muni. block grant	16,645
Energy tax receipts	237,147
Homeland security	0

Fiscal Year 2006
Total aid	$448,366
CMPTRA	172,832
Muni. block grant	16,645
Energy tax receipts	245,447
Homeland security	NA

Taxes
	2003	2004	2005
General tax rate per $100	2.33	1.470	1.530
Net valuation taxable	$369,621,888	$620,695,880	$626,559,297
State equalized value	$522,359,932	$584,500,197	$660,648,774
County equalization ratio	74.26	118.21	106.21

Demographics & Socio-Economic Characteristics

(2000 U.S. Census, except as noted)

Population

1980*	4,913
1990*	4,484
2000	5,436
Male	2,657
Female	2,779
2004 (estimate)*	5,211
Persons per sq. mi. of land	4,038

Race & Hispanic Origin, 2000

Race
White	3,835
Black/African American	905
Amer. Indian/Alaska Natv.	21
Asian	26
Natv. Hawaiian/Pac. Islander	8
Other Race	481
Two or more races	160
Hispanic origin, total	958
Mexican	163
Puerto Rican	668
Cuban	9
Other Hispanic	118

Age & Nativity, 2000

Under 5 years	412
18 years and over	4,038
21 years and over	3,802
65 years and over	770
85 years and over	83
Median Age	35.5
Native born	5,294
Foreign born	251

Educational Attainment, 2000

Population 25 years and over	3,531
0-8 yrs of school	8.2%
High School grad or higher	66.3%
Bachelor's degree or higher	6.8%
Graduate degree	1.8%

Income & Poverty, 1999

Per capita income	$13,682
Median household income	$23,981
Median family income	$28,288
Persons in poverty	1,448
H'holds receiving public assistance	201
H'holds receiving social security	821

Households, 2000

Total households	2,333
With persons under 18	694
With persons over 65	625
Family households	1,273
One-person households	891
Persons per household	2.3
Persons per family	3.06

Labor & Employment

Total civilian labor force, 2004**	2,459
Unemployment rate	17.0%
Total civilian labor force, 2000	2,644
Unemployment rate	21.4%

Employed persons 16 years and over by occupation, 2000
Managers & professionals	383
Service occupations	533
Sales & office occupations	599
Farming, fishing & forestry	33
Construction & maintenance	209
Production & transportation	322
Self-employed persons	169

*US Census Bureau
**New Jersey Department of Labor

General Information

City of Wildwood
4400 New Jersey Ave
Wildwood, NJ 08260
609-522-2444

Web site	www.wildwoodnj.org
Land area (sq. miles)	1.29
Water area (sq. miles)	0.09
Type of government	City
Form of government	MC '50

Government

Legislative Districts

US Congressional	2
State Legislative	1

Local Officials, 2006

Mayor	Ernest Troiano Jr.
Admin/Manager	NA
Clerk	Christopher Wood
Finance Dir/Treas	Jeanette Powers
Engineer	Mark DeBlasio
Attorney	Marcus Karavan
Tax assessor	Joseph Gallagher
Tax collector	Faith Wilson
Building officer	Michael Preston
Zoning officer	NA
Public Works	Matthew Christopher

Housing & Construction

Housing Units, 2000*

Total	6,488
Median rent	$526
Median SF home value	$84,000

New Privately Owned Housing Units Authorized by Building Permit

	Units	Value
Total, 2004	349	$38,193,250
Single family	48	$4,991,650
Total, 2005	300	$33,139,428
Single family	46	$3,347,199

Real Property Valuation - parcels, 2005

	Number	Valuation
Total		$1,724,490,300
Vacant	358	89,726,800
Residential	3,456	886,886,000
Commercial	615	533,997,600
Industrial	6	5,766,900
Apartments	292	208,113,000
Farm land	0	0
Farm homestead	0	0

Average Property Value & Tax, 2005

Residential value	$256,622
Property tax	$3,631
FAIR rebate	$705

Public Library

No public municipal library.

Library statistics, 2004

	Total	per capita
Volumes	NA	NA
Expenditure	NA	NA

Public Safety

Police

Chief	Joseph Fisher
Number of officers, 2004	45

Crime, 2004	Number	Rate
Total	713	135.6
Violent	80	15.2
Non-violent	633	120.3
Domestic Viol.	139	NA

Emergency/Fire

Director	Conrad Johnson

Public School District

(for school year 2004-2005 except as noted)

Wildwood City School District
4300 Pacific Ave
Wildwood, NJ 08260
609-522-4157

Superintendent	Dennis Anderson
Grade plan	K-12
Enrollment	861.5
Students per teacher	7.5
Per pupil expenditure	$16,648
Median faculty salary	$56,241
Median administrator salary	$79,300
Grade 12 enrollment	60.0
High school graduation rate	67.8%

Assessment test results

(percent scoring at proficient or advanced level)
	Language	Math
Grade 3	63.3%	66.1%
Grade 8	31.9%	20.9%
High school	55.1%	56.2%

SAT

Percent tested	37%
Average SAT math score	459
Average SAT verbal score	447

No Child Left Behind, 2003-04

Attendence rate (target = 90%)	90.8%
Drop rate	11.9%
Highly-qualified teachers	78.1%
District needs improvement?(AYP)	No

Municipal Finance

Fiscal Year 2005

Total tax levy	$24,443,621
County levy	3,167,549
County taxes	2,662,870
County library	375,307
County health	0
County open space	129,372
School levy	7,523,218
Local muni. budget	13,752,855
Misc. revenues	8,803,824
Total aid	$1,345,156
CMPTRA	337,493
Muni. block grant	21,315
Energy tax receipts	936,348
Homeland security	50,000

Fiscal Year 2006

Total aid	$1,345,156
CMPTRA	304,721
Muni. block grant	21,315
Energy tax receipts	969,120
Homeland security	50,000

Taxes

	2003	2004	2005
General tax rate per $100	3.38	3.430	1.420
Net valuation taxable	$509,537,929	$544,676,623	$1,727,550,881
State equalized value	$827,709,436	$1,164,564,343	$1,677,559,605
County equalization ratio	82.57	61.56	134.57

Demographics & Socio-Economic Characteristics
(2000 U.S. Census, except as noted)

Population
1980*	4,149
1990*	3,631
2000	3,980
Male	1,854
Female	2,126
2004 (estimate)*	3,862
Persons per sq. mi. of land	3,352

Race & Hispanic Origin, 2000
Race
White	3,776
Black/African American	49
Amer. Indian/Alaska Natv.	4
Asian	19
Natv. Hawaiian/Pac. Islander	0
Other Race	88
Two or more races	44
Hispanic origin, total	168
Mexican	44
Puerto Rican	89
Cuban	1
Other Hispanic	34

Age & Nativity, 2000
Under 5 years	171
18 years and over	3,255
21 years and over	3,167
65 years and over	1,013
85 years and over	132
Median Age	46.7
Native born	3,746
Foreign born	124

Educational Attainment, 2000
Population 25 years and over	2,955
0-8 yrs of school	3.5%
High School grad or higher	79.5%
Bachelor's degree or higher	26.4%
Graduate degree	8.9%

Income & Poverty, 1999
Per capita income	$23,741
Median household income	$36,579
Median family income	$47,462
Persons in poverty	231
H'holds receiving public assistance	51
H'holds receiving social security	783

Households, 2000
Total households	1,833
With persons under 18	417
With persons over 65	755
Family households	1,114
One-person households	634
Persons per household	2.17
Persons per family	2.76

Labor & Employment
Total civilian labor force, 2004**	2,261
Unemployment rate	8.9%
Total civilian labor force, 2000	1,908
Unemployment rate	15.4%

Employed persons 16 years and over by occupation, 2000
Managers & professionals	604
Service occupations	295
Sales & office occupations	475
Farming, fishing & forestry	5
Construction & maintenance	114
Production & transportation	91
Self-employed persons	160

*US Census Bureau
**New Jersey Department of Labor

General Information
Borough of Wildwood Crest
6101 Pacific Ave
Wildwood Crest, NJ 08260
609-522-3843
Web site	www.wildwoodcrest.org
Land area (sq. miles)	1.15
Water area (sq. miles)	0.15
Type of government	Borough
Form of government	Comm.

Government
Legislative Districts
US Congressional	2
State Legislative	1

Local Officials, 2006
Mayor	Carl H. Groon
Admin/Manager	Kevin Yecco
Clerk	Kevin Yecco
Finance Dir/Treas	Stephen Ritchie
Engineer	Ralph Petrella
Attorney	Doreen Corino
Tax assessor	Jason Hesley
Tax collector	NA
Building officer	JCOW
Zoning officer	Elizabeth Terenik
Public Works	Donald Twist

Housing & Construction
Housing Units, 2000*
Total	4,862
Median rent	$610
Median SF home value	$147,600

New Privately Owned Housing Units
Authorized by Building Permit
	Units	Value
Total, 2004	194	$18,583,181
Single family	96	$8,057,198
Total, 2005	357	$46,333,160
Single family	96	$14,635,480

Real Property Valuation - parcels, 2005
	Number	Valuation
Total		$1,310,880,800
Vacant	234	53,411,500
Residential	4,022	996,076,500
Commercial	178	248,122,200
Industrial	0	0
Apartments	40	13,270,600
Farm land	0	0
Farm homestead	0	0

Average Property Value & Tax, 2005
Residential value	$247,657
Property tax	$3,074
FAIR rebate	$797

Public Library
Wildwood Crest Library†
6301 Ocean Ave
Wildwood Crest, NJ 08260
609-522-0564
Director	William Smith

Library statistics, 2004
	Total	per capita
Volumes	NA	NA
Expenditure	NA	NA

†Privately owned

Public Safety
Police
Chief	Thomas DePaul
Number of officers, 2004	22

Crime, 2004	Number	Rate
Total	167	43
Violent	13	3.3
Non-violent	154	39.6
Domestic Viol.	65	NA

Emergency/Fire
Director	Albert Beers

Public School District
(for school year 2004-2005 except as noted)

Wildwood Crest School District
9100 Pacific Ave
Wildwood Crest, NJ 08260
609-729-3760
Superintendent	Dennis Anderson
Grade plan	K-12
Enrollment	316.0
Students per teacher	8.2
Per pupil expenditure	$13,942
Median faculty salary	$69,300
Median administrator salary	$95,000
Grade 12 enrollment	NA
High school graduation rate	NA

Assessment test results
(percent scoring at proficient or advanced level)
	Language	Math
Grade 3	91.5%	91.4%
Grade 8	71.1%	76.3%
High school	NA	NA

SAT
Percent tested	NA
Average SAT math score	NA
Average SAT verbal score	NA

No Child Left Behind, 2003-04
Attendence rate (target = 90%)	95.9%
Drop rate	NA
Highly-qualified teachers	100%
District needs improvement?(AYP)	No

Municipal Finance
Fiscal Year 2005
Total tax levy	$16,276,170
County levy	3,839,464
County taxes	3,227,990
County library	454,729
County health	0
County open space	156,745
School levy	4,831,458
Local muni. budget	7,605,248
Misc. revenues	6,810,556
Total aid	$566,218
CMPTRA	157,619
Muni. block grant	15,889
Energy tax receipts	367,710
Homeland security	25,000

Fiscal Year 2006
Total aid	$566,217
CMPTRA	144,749
Muni. block grant	15,889
Energy tax receipts	380,579
Homeland security	25,000

Taxes
	2003	2004	2005
General tax rate per $100	1.22	1.230	1.250
Net valuation taxable	$1,237,721,798	$1,259,386,493	$1,311,305,112
State equalized value	$1,237,350,593	$1,495,593,341	$1,848,731,301
County equalization ratio	127.82	100.03	84.20

Demographics & Socio-Economic Characteristics
(2000 U.S. Census, except as noted)

Population
1980*	39,912
1990*	36,291
2000	33,008
Male	15,633
Female	17,375
2004 (estimate)*	33,114
Persons per sq. mi. of land	4,306

Race & Hispanic Origin, 2000
Race
White	8,144
Black/African American	22,021
Amer. Indian/Alaska Natv.	99
Asian	562
Natv. Hawaiian/Pac. Islander	12
Other Race	866
Two or more races	1,304
Hispanic origin, total	1,998
Mexican	103
Puerto Rican	1,273
Cuban	46
Other Hispanic	576

Age & Nativity, 2000
Under 5 years	2,024
18 years and over	23,939
21 years and over	22,672
65 years and over	4,246
85 years and over	239
Median Age	37.9
Native born	30,299
Foreign born	2,709

Educational Attainment, 2000
Population 25 years and over	21,431
0-8 yrs of school	2.7%
High School grad or higher	87.2%
Bachelor's degree or higher	18.9%
Graduate degree	5.9%

Income & Poverty, 1999
Per capita income	$21,799
Median household income	$60,869
Median family income	$64,338
Persons in poverty	1,934
H'holds receiving public assistance	342
H'holds receiving social security	3,260

Households, 2000
Total households	10,713
With persons under 18	4,617
With persons over 65	3,086
Family households	8,780
One-person households	1,607
Persons per household	3.07
Persons per family	3.36

Labor & Employment
Total civilian labor force, 2004**	23,506
Unemployment rate	5.5%
Total civilian labor force, 2000	16,077
Unemployment rate	7.0%

Employed persons 16 years and over by occupation, 2000
Managers & professionals	4,869
Service occupations	2,348
Sales & office occupations	4,574
Farming, fishing & forestry	31
Construction & maintenance	929
Production & transportation	2,207
Self-employed persons	505

*US Census Bureau
**New Jersey Department of Labor

General Information
Township of Willingboro
1 Salem Rd
Willingboro, NJ 08046
609-877-2200

Web site	NA
Land area (sq. miles)	7.69
Water area (sq. miles)	0.33
Type of government	Township
Form of government	CM '50

Government

Legislative Districts
US Congressional	3
State Legislative	7

Local Officials, 2006
Mayor	Jeffrey E. Ramsey
Admin/Manager	Denise Rose
Clerk	Marie Annese
Finance Dir/Treas	Joann Diggs
Engineer	Remington & Vernick
Attorney	Michael Armstrong
Tax assessor	William Tantum
Tax collector	NA
Building officer	Duane Wallace
Zoning officer	NA
Public Works	NA

Housing & Construction

Housing Units, 2000*
Total	11,124
Median rent	$1,100
Median SF home value	$96,700

New Privately Owned Housing Units Authorized by Building Permit
	Units	Value
Total, 2004	74	$1,940,428
Single family	26	$932,428
Total, 2005	71	$1,862,600
Single family	42	$1,253,600

Real Property Valuation - parcels, 2005
	Number	Valuation
Total		$1,083,883,300
Vacant	115	5,405,400
Residential	10,968	1,013,319,400
Commercial	152	58,196,200
Industrial	10	6,813,000
Apartments	0	0
Farm land	1	146,000
Farm homestead	1	3,300

Average Property Value & Tax, 2005
Residential value	$92,381
Property tax	$4,037
FAIR rebate	$626

Public Library
Willingboro Public Library
220 Willingboro Pkwy
Willingboro, NJ 08046
609-877-6668

Director . . . . Chris King

Library statistics, 2004
	Total	per capita
Volumes	77,384	2.34
Expenditure	$1,258,802	$38.14

Public Safety

Police
Chief	NA
Number of officers, 2004	71

Crime, 2004	Number	Rate
Total	838	25.3
Violent	117	3.5
Non-violent	721	21.8
Domestic Viol.	230	NA

Emergency/Fire
Director . . . . Tony Burnett

Public School District
(for school year 2004-2005 except as noted)

Willingboro Township School District
440 Beverly-Rancocas Rd
Willingboro, NJ 08046
609-835-8600

Superintendent	Melindo Persi (Int)
Grade plan	K-12
Enrollment	5,661.0
Students per teacher	11.1
Per pupil expenditure	$10,173
Median faculty salary	$45,511
Median administrator salary	$83,045
Grade 12 enrollment	265.0
High school graduation rate	93.1%

Assessment test results
(percent scoring at proficient or advanced level)
	Language	Math
Grade 3	83.3%	76.6%
Grade 8	55.0%	28.5%
High school	73.2%	47.5%

SAT
Percent tested	65%
Average SAT math score	417
Average SAT verbal score	430

No Child Left Behind, 2003-04
Attendance rate (target = 90%)	93.4%
Drop rate	1.3%
Highly-qualified teachers	95.4%
District needs improvement?(AYP)	No

Municipal Finance

Fiscal Year 2005
Total tax levy	$47,547,413
County levy	6,311,673
County taxes	5,714,584
County library	0
County health	0
County open space	597,089
School levy	22,638,940
Local muni. budget	18,596,800
Misc. revenues	12,083,328
Total aid	$4,757,152
CMPTRA	2,605,427
Muni. block grant	158,797
Energy tax receipts	1,852,928
Homeland security	140,000

Fiscal Year 2006
Total aid	$4,757,152
CMPTRA	2,540,575
Muni. block grant	158,797
Energy tax receipts	1,917,780
Homeland security	140,000

Taxes
	2003	2004	2005
General tax rate per $100	3.95	4.153	4.370
Net valuation taxable	$1,080,802,186	$1,084,991,092	$1,088,105,440
State equalized value	$1,358,645,111	$1,482,666,328	$1,750,209,812
County equalization ratio	88.74	79.55	73.09

Demographics & Socio-Economic Characteristics
(2000 U.S. Census, except as noted)

Population
1980*	1,785
1990*	1,576
2000	1,514
Male	691
Female	823
2004 (estimate)*	1,511
Persons per sq. mi. of land	8,561

Race & Hispanic Origin, 2000
Race
White	1,468
Black/African American	5
Amer. Indian/Alaska Natv.	3
Asian	2
Natv. Hawaiian/Pac. Islander	1
Other Race	10
Two or more races	25
Hispanic origin, total	37
Mexican	3
Puerto Rican	16
Cuban	8
Other Hispanic	10

Age & Nativity, 2000
Under 5 years	76
18 years and over	1,198
21 years and over	1,156
65 years and over	241
85 years and over	35
Median Age	38.9
Native born	1,472
Foreign born	42

Educational Attainment, 2000
Population 25 years and over	1,112
0-8 yrs of school	3.7%
High School grad or higher	79.2%
Bachelor's degree or higher	8.0%
Graduate degree	1.9%

Income & Poverty, 1999
Per capita income	$21,565
Median household income	$37,000
Median family income	$47,167
Persons in poverty	113
H'holds receiving public assistance	12
H'holds receiving social security	233

Households, 2000
Total households	694
With persons under 18	191
With persons over 65	199
Family households	395
One-person households	266
Persons per household	2.18
Persons per family	2.92

Labor & Employment
Total civilian labor force, 2004**	835
Unemployment rate	5.1%
Total civilian labor force, 2000	807
Unemployment rate	7.4%

Employed persons 16 years and over by occupation, 2000
Managers & professionals	140
Service occupations	142
Sales & office occupations	241
Farming, fishing & forestry	4
Construction & maintenance	90
Production & transportation	130
Self-employed persons	19

*US Census Bureau
**New Jersey Department of Labor

General Information
Township of Winfield
12 Gulfstream Ave
Winfield, NJ 07036
908-925-3850
Web site	www.winfield-nj.org
Land area (sq. miles)	0.18
Water area (sq. miles)	0
Type of government	Township
Form of government	TC

Government
Legislative Districts
US Congressional	7
State Legislative	22

Local Officials, 2006
Mayor	David P. Wright Sr.
Admin/Manager	NA
Clerk	Laura Reinertsen
Finance Dir/Treas	Sue Wright
Engineer	John Ziemian
Attorney	Frank Capece
Tax assessor	Thomas Boyle
Tax collector	Kimberley Allorto
Building officer	Matthew Valvano
Zoning officer	NA
Public Works	NA

Housing & Construction
Housing Units, 2000*
Total	697
Median rent	$463
Median SF home value	$74,000

New Privately Owned Housing Units Authorized by Building Permit
	Units	Value
Total, 2004	0	$0
Single family	0	$0
Total, 2005	0	$0
Single family	0	$0

Real Property Valuation - parcels, 2005
	Number	Valuation
Total		$1,382,200
Vacant	1	220,200
Residential	689	1,072,000
Commercial	1	90,000
Industrial	0	0
Apartments	0	0
Farm land	0	0
Farm homestead	0	0

Average Property Value & Tax, 2005
Residential value	$1,556
Property tax	$2,472
FAIR rebate	$641

Public Library
No public municipal library.

Library statistics, 2004
	Total	per capita
Volumes	NA	NA
Expenditure	NA	NA

Public Safety
Police
Chief	Walter L. Berg
Number of officers, 2004	9

Crime, 2004	Number	Rate
Total	24	15.8
Violent	0	0
Non-violent	24	15.8
Domestic Viol.	15	NA

Emergency/Fire
Director	Debra Daly

Public School District
(for school year 2004-2005 except as noted)

Winfield Township School District
Gulfstream Ave
Winfield, NJ 07036
908-486-7410
Superintendent	Alice D'Ambola
Grade plan	K-12
Enrollment	119.0
Students per teacher	7.3
Per pupil expenditure	$13,137
Median faculty salary	$45,686
Median administrator salary	$80,889
Grade 12 enrollment	NA
High school graduation rate	NA

Assessment test results
(percent scoring at proficient or advanced level)
	Language	Math
Grade 3	NA	NA
Grade 8	73.3%	53.4%
High school	NA	NA

SAT
Percent tested	NA
Average SAT math score	NA
Average SAT verbal score	NA

No Child Left Behind, 2003-04
Attendance rate (target = 90%)	95.7%
Drop rate	NA
Highly-qualified teachers	100%
District needs improvement?(AYP)	No

Municipal Finance
Fiscal Year 2005
Total tax levy	$2,203,187
County levy	63,815
County taxes	61,296
County library	0
County health	0
County open space	2,519
School levy	1,292,278
Local muni. budget	847,095
Misc. revenues	550,373
Total aid	$317,449
CMPTRA	240,412
Muni. block grant	6,896
Energy tax receipts	45,141
Homeland security	25,000

Fiscal Year 2006
Total aid	$317,449
CMPTRA	238,832
Muni. block grant	6,896
Energy tax receipts	46,721
Homeland security	25,000

Taxes
	2003	2004	2005
General tax rate per $100	134.27	143.888	158.877
Net valuation taxable	$1,386,492	$1,386,257	$1,386,732
State equalized value	$13,306,065	$13,729,976	$15,289,217
County equalization ratio	9.25	8.75	8.25

Demographics & Socio-Economic Characteristics

(2000 U.S. Census, except as noted)

Population

1980*	20,034
1990*	30,087
2000	34,611
Male	17,039
Female	17,572
2004 (estimate)*	36,061
Persons per sq. mi. of land	625

Race & Hispanic Origin, 2000

Race

White	22,670
Black/African American	10,154
Amer. Indian/Alaska Natv.	104
Asian	449
Natv. Hawaiian/Pac. Islander	10
Other Race	547
Two or more races	677
Hispanic origin, total	1,492
Mexican	217
Puerto Rican	958
Cuban	38
Other Hispanic	279

Age & Nativity, 2000

Under 5 years	2,838
18 years and over	24,646
21 years and over	23,558
65 years and over	2,939
85 years and over	401
Median Age	34.4
Native born	33,353
Foreign born	1,306

Educational Attainment, 2000

Population 25 years and over	22,366
0-8 yrs of school	6.3%
High School grad or higher	82.2%
Bachelor's degree or higher	18.6%
Graduate degree	4.3%

Income & Poverty, 1999

Per capita income	$21,254
Median household income	$55,990
Median family income	$62,045
Persons in poverty	2,007
H'holds receiving public assistance	239
H'holds receiving social security	2,544

Households, 2000

Total households	11,661
With persons under 18	5,354
With persons over 65	2,193
Family households	9,002
One-person households	2,187
Persons per household	2.87
Persons per family	3.28

Labor & Employment

Total civilian labor force, 2004**	15,711
Unemployment rate	5.0%
Total civilian labor force, 2000	17,665
Unemployment rate	6.1%

Employed persons 16 years and over by occupation, 2000

Managers & professionals	5,187
Service occupations	2,484
Sales & office occupations	4,699
Farming, fishing & forestry	78
Construction & maintenance	2,003
Production & transportation	2,138
Self-employed persons	811

*US Census Bureau
**New Jersey Department of Labor

General Information

Township of Winslow
125 S Route 73
Braddock, NJ 08037
609-567-0700

Web site	www.winslowtownship.com
Land area (sq. miles)	57.70
Water area (sq. miles)	0.40
Type of government	Township
Form of government	TC

Government

Legislative Districts

US Congressional	1
State Legislative	6

Local Officials, 2006

Mayor	Sue Ann Metzner
Admin/Manager	David P. Fanslau
Clerk	Deborah Puchakjian
Finance Dir/Treas	Steven Dringus
Engineer	Adams, Rehmann & Heggan
Attorney	Raymond J. Zane
Tax assessor	Stephen Kessler
Tax collector	Constance Hegyi
Building officer	Herb Leary
Zoning officer	Churchill & Assoc.
Public Works	Edward McGlinchey

Housing & Construction

Housing Units, 2000*

Total	12,413
Median rent	$738
Median SF home value	$112,800

New Privately Owned Housing Units Authorized by Building Permit

	Units	Value
Total, 2004	580	$49,914,642
Single family	580	$49,914,642
Total, 2005	552	$75,488,231
Single family	552	$75,488,231

Real Property Valuation - parcels, 2005

	Number	Valuation
Total		$1,329,838,070
Vacant	2,549	50,204,400
Residential	11,336	1,113,457,400
Commercial	296	88,084,250
Industrial	16	20,908,000
Apartments	27	31,709,300
Farm land	210	21,114,120
Farm homestead	521	4,360,600

Average Property Value & Tax, 2005

Residential value	$94,275
Property tax	$3,982
FAIR rebate	$503

Public Library

South County Regional Library†
35 Coopers Folly Rd
Atco, NJ 08004
856-753-2537

Branch Librarian ... Nancy Bennett

Library statistics, 2004

	Total	per capita
Volumes	NA	NA
Expenditure	NA	NA

†Branch of County Library

Public Safety

Police

Chief	Anthony Bello
Number of officers, 2004	78

Crime, 2004	Number	Rate
Total	838	23.8
Violent	153	4.4
Non-violent	685	19.5
Domestic Viol.	540	NA

Emergency/Fire

Director ... Michael Scardino

Public School District

(for school year 2004-2005 except as noted)

Winslow Township School District
30 Cooper Folly Rd
Atco, NJ 08004
856-767-2850

Superintendent	Michael Schreiner (Int)
Grade plan	K-12
Enrollment	6,243.0
Students per teacher	10.9
Per pupil expenditure	$11,363
Median faculty salary	$66,173
Median administrator salary	$92,345
Grade 12 enrollment	337.0
High school graduation rate	85.7%

Assessment test results

(percent scoring at proficient or advanced level)

	Language	Math
Grade 3	84.1%	77.8%
Grade 8	54.3%	37.3%
High school	80.1%	58.5%

SAT

Percent tested	60%
Average SAT math score	460
Average SAT verbal score	460

No Child Left Behind, 2003-04

Attendence rate (target = 90%)	93.7%
Drop rate	3.2%
Highly-qualified teachers	100%
District needs improvement?(AYP)	Yes

Municipal Finance

Fiscal Year 2005

Total tax levy	$56,373,949
County levy	15,049,739
County taxes	13,870,248
County library	997,580
County health	0
County open space	181,911
School levy	33,559,710
Local muni. budget	7,764,500
Misc. revenues	16,987,300
Total aid	$8,061,832
CMPTRA	1,630,886
Muni. block grant	135,711
Energy tax receipts	6,125,451
Homeland security	140,000

Fiscal Year 2006

Total aid	$8,061,832
CMPTRA	1,416,495
Muni. block grant	135,711
Energy tax receipts	6,339,842
Homeland security	140,000

Taxes

	2003	2004	2005
General tax rate per $100	3.81	3.911	4.224
Net valuation taxable	$1,234,166,024	$1,273,579,767	$1,334,696,902
State equalized value	$1,519,721,739	$1,725,269,443	$2,048,023,480
County equalization ratio	87.37	81.21	73.73

Demographics & Socio-Economic Characteristics
(2000 U.S. Census, except as noted)

Population
1980*	2,809
1990*	2,678
2000	2,716
Male	1,596
Female	1,120
2004 (estimate)*	2,616
Persons per sq. mi. of land	327

Race & Hispanic Origin, 2000
Race
White	1,450
Black/African American	880
Amer. Indian/Alaska Natv.	6
Asian	3
Natv. Hawaiian/Pac. Islander	0
Other Race	299
Two or more races	78
Hispanic origin, total	577
Mexican	19
Puerto Rican	478
Cuban	5
Other Hispanic	75

Age & Nativity, 2000
Under 5 years	249
18 years and over	1,993
21 years and over	1,895
65 years and over	283
85 years and over	26
Median Age	36.4
Native born	2,680
Foreign born	36

Educational Attainment, 2000
Population 25 years and over	1,765
0-8 yrs of school	24.2%
High School grad or higher	58.1%
Bachelor's degree or higher	4.5%
Graduate degree	1.1%

Income & Poverty, 1999
Per capita income	$13,335
Median household income	$30,298
Median family income	$31,786
Persons in poverty	383
H'holds receiving public assistance	82
H'holds receiving social security	209

Households, 2000
Total households	773
With persons under 18	370
With persons over 65	181
Family households	558
One-person households	178
Persons per household	2.77
Persons per family	3.21

Labor & Employment
Total civilian labor force, 2004**	1,126
Unemployment rate	7.4%
Total civilian labor force, 2000	954
Unemployment rate	9.0%

Employed persons 16 years and over by occupation, 2000
Managers & professionals	182
Service occupations	290
Sales & office occupations	176
Farming, fishing & forestry	10
Construction & maintenance	82
Production & transportation	128
Self-employed persons	56

*US Census Bureau
**New Jersey Department of Labor

General Information
Borough of Woodbine
501 Washington
Woodbine, NJ 08270
609-861-2153
Web site	www.boroughofwoodbine.net
Land area (sq. miles)	8.00
Water area (sq. miles)	0
Type of government	Borough
Form of government	B

Government

Legislative Districts
US Congressional	2
State Legislative	1

Local Officials, 2006
Mayor	William Pikolycky
Admin/Manager	NA
Clerk	Lisa Garrison
Finance Dir/Treas	John Miller
Engineer	Bruce Graham
Attorney	Michael Benson
Tax assessor	John Miller
Tax collector	Lisa Garrison
Building officer	DCA
Zoning officer	Milt Truxton
Public Works	Claude Wise

Housing & Construction

Housing Units, 2000*
Total	1,080
Median rent	$463
Median SF home value	$80,600

New Privately Owned Housing Units Authorized by Building Permit
	Units	Value
Total, 2004	11	$307,504
Single family	11	$307,504
Total, 2005	6	$304,952
Single family	6	$304,952

Real Property Valuation - parcels, 2005
	Number	Valuation
Total		$57,966,200
Vacant	492	5,863,500
Residential	510	33,192,800
Commercial	62	12,183,500
Industrial	7	1,854,900
Apartments	2	1,931,800
Farm land	35	2,828,800
Farm homestead	30	110,900

Average Property Value & Tax, 2005
Residential value	$61,674
Property tax	$1,475
FAIR rebate	$618

Public Library
Upper Cape Branch†
801 Webster
Woodbine, NJ 08270
609-463-6350
Librarian	Andrew Martin

Library statistics, 2004
	Total	per capita
Volumes	NA	NA
Expenditure	NA	NA

†Branch of County Library

Public Safety

Police
Chief	(State)
Number of officers, 2004	2

Crime, 2004	Number	Rate
Total	98	36.6
Violent	18	6.7
Non-violent	80	29.9
Domestic Viol.	61	NA

Emergency/Fire
Director	Manuel Gonzalez

Public School District
(for school year 2004-2005 except as noted)

Woodbine School District
801 Webster Ave
Woodbine, NJ 08270
609-861-5174
Superintendent	Robert Manning
Grade plan	K-12
Enrollment	237.0
Students per teacher	10.2
Per pupil expenditure	$12,856
Median faculty salary	$61,123
Median administrator salary	$87,000
Grade 12 enrollment	NA
High school graduation rate	NA

Assessment test results
(percent scoring at proficient or advanced level)
	Language	Math
Grade 3	52.0%	54.2%
Grade 8	41.4%	10.0%
High school	NA	NA

SAT
Percent tested	NA
Average SAT math score	NA
Average SAT verbal score	NA

No Child Left Behind, 2003-04
Attendence rate (target = 90%)	94.7%
Drop rate	NA
Highly-qualified teachers	73%
District needs improvement?(AYP)	No

Municipal Finance

Fiscal Year 2005
Total tax levy	$1,405,291
County levy	239,483
County taxes	201,346
County library	28,359
County health	0
County open space	9,778
School levy	923,250
Local muni. budget	242,558
Misc. revenues	2,788,455
Total aid	$466,174
CMPTRA	338,737
Muni. block grant	11,718
Energy tax receipts	115,104
Homeland security	0

Fiscal Year 2006
Total aid	$466,174
CMPTRA	334,709
Muni. block grant	11,718
Energy tax receipts	119,132
Homeland security	NA

Taxes
	2003	2004	2005
General tax rate per $100	2.26	2.350	2.400
Net valuation taxable	$56,152,190	$57,114,372	$58,772,528
State equalized value	$84,375,943	$93,370,374	$115,967,893
County equalization ratio	79.55	66.55	60.81

Demographics & Socio-Economic Characteristics
(2000 U.S. Census, except as noted)

Population
1980*	90,074
1990*	93,086
2000	97,203
Male	48,640
Female	48,563
2004 (estimate)*	100,775
Persons per sq. mi. of land	4,380

Race & Hispanic Origin, 2000
Race
White	68,848
Black/African American	8,507
Amer. Indian/Alaska Natv.	167
Asian	14,054
Natv. Hawaiian/Pac. Islander	24
Other Race	3,212
Two or more races	2,391
Hispanic origin, total	8,956
Mexican	390
Puerto Rican	3,838
Cuban	680
Other Hispanic	4,048

Age & Nativity, 2000
Under 5 years	6,161
18 years and over	75,460
21 years and over	72,777
65 years and over	13,005
85 years and over	1,042
Median Age	37.1
Native born	76,332
Foreign born	20,871

Educational Attainment, 2000
Population 25 years and over	68,845
0-8 yrs of school	5.2%
High School grad or higher	84.0%
Bachelor's degree or higher	26.8%
Graduate degree	8.9%

Income & Poverty, 1999
Per capita income	$25,087
Median household income	$60,683
Median family income	$68,492
Persons in poverty	4,565
H'holds receiving public assistance	643
H'holds receiving social security	9,953

Households, 2000
Total households	34,562
With persons under 18	12,405
With persons over 65	9,529
Family households	25,423
One-person households	7,484
Persons per household	2.71
Persons per family	3.19

Labor & Employment
Total civilian labor force, 2004**	56,628
Unemployment rate	4.3%
Total civilian labor force, 2000	49,753
Unemployment rate	4.8%

Employed persons 16 years and over by occupation, 2000
Managers & professionals	17,681
Service occupations	4,982
Sales & office occupations	14,186
Farming, fishing & forestry	85
Construction & maintenance	4,000
Production & transportation	6,429
Self-employed persons	1,604

*US Census Bureau
**New Jersey Department of Labor

General Information
Township of Woodbridge
1 Main St
Woodbridge, NJ 07095
732-634-4500

Web site	NA
Land area (sq. miles)	23.01
Water area (sq. miles)	1.21
Type of government	Township
Form of government	MC '50

Government

Legislative Districts
US Congressional	7, 13
State Legislative	19

Local Officials, 2006
Mayor	Frank Pelzman
Admin/Manager	Robert M. Landolfi
Clerk	John Mitch
Finance Dir/Treas	Margaret Gorman
Engineer	Scott Thomson
Attorney	James Nolan Jr.
Tax assessor	Richard Duda
Tax collector	Richard Lorentzen
Building officer	Lawrence Esoldo
Zoning officer	Lawrence Clement
Public Works	Jerry Macintyre

Housing & Construction

Housing Units, 2000*
Total	35,298
Median rent	$879
Median SF home value	$158,100

New Privately Owned Housing Units Authorized by Building Permit
	Units	Value
Total, 2004	34	$2,263,177
Single family	17	$2,020,865
Total, 2005	1	$100,500
Single family	1	$100,500

Real Property Valuation - parcels, 2005
	Number	Valuation
Total		$3,203,945,452
Vacant	945	53,599,852
Residential	26,389	1,958,918,000
Commercial	1,066	702,161,900
Industrial	171	301,040,800
Apartments	75	188,224,900
Farm land	0	0
Farm homestead	0	0

Average Property Value & Tax, 2005
Residential value	$74,232
Property tax	$4,742
FAIR rebate	$606

Public Library
Woodbridge Public Library
George Frederick Plaza
Woodbridge, NJ 07095
732-634-4450

Director	John Hurley

Library statistics, 2004
	Total	per capita
Volumes	392,614	4.04
Expenditure	$5,648,442	$58.11

Public Safety
Police
Chief	William Trenery
Number of officers, 2004	192

Crime, 2004	Number	Rate
Total	3,223	32
Violent	324	3.2
Non-violent	2,899	28.7
Domestic Viol.	810	NA

Emergency/Fire
Director	NA

Public School District
(for school year 2004-2005 except as noted)

Woodbridge Township School District
School Street
Woodbridge, NJ 07095
732-602-8549

Superintendent	Vincent Smith
Grade plan	K-12
Enrollment	13,401.0
Students per teacher	11.8
Per pupil expenditure	$10,790
Median faculty salary	$58,000
Median administrator salary	$100,143
Grade 12 enrollment	934.0
High school graduation rate	NA

Assessment test results
(percent scoring at proficient or advanced level)
	Language	Math
Grade 3	85.9%	88.2%
Grade 8	79.1%	71.3%
High school	84.3%	79.2%

SAT
Percent tested	NA
Average SAT math score	NA
Average SAT verbal score	NA

No Child Left Behind, 2003-04
Attendence rate (target = 90%)	94.8%
Drop rate	1%
Highly-qualified teachers	94.2%
District needs improvement?(AYP)	No

Municipal Finance

Fiscal Year 2005
Total tax levy	$205,171,400
County levy	28,964,843
County taxes	26,237,720
County library	0
County health	0
County open space	2,727,123
School levy	135,031,557
Local muni. budget	41,175,000
Misc. revenues	48,520,790
Total aid	$30,677,440
CMPTRA	11,139,510
Muni. block grant	407,339
Energy tax receipts	18,990,591
Homeland security	140,000

Fiscal Year 2006
Total aid	$30,677,440
CMPTRA	10,474,839
Muni. block grant	407,339
Energy tax receipts	19,655,262
Homeland security	140,000

Taxes
	2003	2004	2005
General tax rate per $100	5.85	6.090	6.390
Net valuation taxable	$3,172,026,415	$3,190,263,565	$3,211,856,485
State equalized value	$7,654,503,897	$9,023,574,575	$10,593,194,212
County equalization ratio	44.43	41.44	35.28

Demographics & Socio-Economic Characteristics

(2000 U.S. Census, except as noted)

Population

1980*	10,353
1990*	10,904
2000	10,307
Male	4,815
Female	5,492
2004 (estimate)*	10,437
Persons per sq. mi. of land	5,024

Race & Hispanic Origin, 2000

Race

White	7,467
Black/African American	2,353
Amer. Indian/Alaska Natv.	23
Asian	102
Natv. Hawaiian/Pac. Islander	14
Other Race	132
Two or more races	216
Hispanic origin, total	406
Mexican	28
Puerto Rican	235
Cuban	17
Other Hispanic	126

Age & Nativity, 2000

Under 5 years	669
18 years and over	7,754
21 years and over	7,385
65 years and over	1,702
85 years and over	264
Median Age	37
Native born	10,030
Foreign born	277

Educational Attainment, 2000

Population 25 years and over	6,842
0-8 yrs of school	6.4%
High School grad or higher	80.3%
Bachelor's degree or higher	21.9%
Graduate degree	6.9%

Income & Poverty, 1999

Per capita income	$21,592
Median household income	$41,827
Median family income	$53,630
Persons in poverty	1,324
H'holds receiving public assistance	138
H'holds receiving social security	1,305

Households, 2000

Total households	4,051
With persons under 18	1,428
With persons over 65	1,199
Family households	2,588
One-person households	1,283
Persons per household	2.43
Persons per family	3.08

Labor & Employment

Total civilian labor force, 2004**	6,087
Unemployment rate	8.0%
Total civilian labor force, 2000	4,670
Unemployment rate	5.4%

Employed persons 16 years and over by occupation, 2000

Managers & professionals	1,592
Service occupations	713
Sales & office occupations	1,134
Farming, fishing & forestry	12
Construction & maintenance	335
Production & transportation	634
Self-employed persons	209

*US Census Bureau
**New Jersey Department of Labor

General Information

City of Woodbury
33 Delaware St
Woodbury, NJ 08096
856-845-1300

Web site	www.woodbury.nj.us
Land area (sq. miles)	2.08
Water area (sq. miles)	0.04
Type of government	City
Form of government	SC

Government

Legislative Districts

US Congressional	1
State Legislative	5

Local Officials, 2006

Mayor	Leslie Clark
Admin/Manager	Thomas Bowe
Clerk	Thomas Bowe
Finance Dir/Treas	Robert Law
Engineer	Joseph Schiavo
Attorney	Michael Aimino
Tax assessor	Roy Duffield
Tax collector	Lorraine Roberts
Building officer	Robert Kunkle
Zoning officer	John Leech
Public Works	Michael Walsh

Housing & Construction

Housing Units, 2000*

Total	4,310
Median rent	$523
Median SF home value	$97,100

New Privately Owned Housing Units Authorized by Building Permit

	Units	Value
Total, 2004	8	$1,076,388
Single family	8	$1,076,388
Total, 2005	10	$937,030
Single family	10	$937,030

Real Property Valuation - parcels, 2005

	Number	Valuation
Total		$371,752,800
Vacant	172	4,825,500
Residential	2,909	265,175,300
Commercial	290	87,743,100
Industrial	3	2,017,800
Apartments	21	11,991,100
Farm land	0	0
Farm homestead	0	0

Average Property Value & Tax, 2005

Residential value	$91,157
Property tax	$4,867
FAIR rebate	$601

Public Library

Woodbury Public Library
33 Delaware St
Woodbury, NJ 08096
856-845-2611

Director ... Jean Wipf

Library statistics, 2004

	Total	per capita
Volumes	56,750	5.51
Expenditure	$280,458	$27.21

Public Safety

Police

Chief	Reed Merinuk
Number of officers, 2004	27

Crime, 2004	Number	Rate
Total	538	51.5
Violent	52	5
Non-violent	486	46.6
Domestic Viol.	188	NA

Emergency/Fire

Director ... Drew Bain

Public School District

(for school year 2004-2005 except as noted)

Woodbury School District
25 N Broad St
Woodbury, NJ 08096
856-853-0123

Superintendent	Joseph Jones
Grade plan	K-12
Enrollment	1,497.5
Students per teacher	9.4
Per pupil expenditure	$12,766
Median faculty salary	$48,268
Median administrator salary	$90,250
Grade 12 enrollment	89.5
High school graduation rate	88.3%

Assessment test results

(percent scoring at proficient or advanced level)

	Language	Math
Grade 3	74.5%	74.5%
Grade 8	51.6%	54.5%
High school	76.7%	71.1%

SAT

Percent tested	75%
Average SAT math score	511
Average SAT verbal score	517

No Child Left Behind, 2003-04

Attendence rate (target = 90%)	94.1%
Drop rate	1.3%
Highly-qualified teachers	91.1%
District needs improvement?(AYP)	No

Municipal Finance

Fiscal Year 2005

Total tax levy	$20,064,827
County levy	3,180,819
County taxes	2,982,780
County library	0
County health	0
County open space	198,040
School levy	11,022,638
Local muni. budget	5,861,370
Misc. revenues	4,904,806
Total aid	$1,848,341
CMPTRA	924,715
Muni. block grant	47,713
Energy tax receipts	805,913
Homeland security	70,000

Fiscal Year 2006

Total aid	$1,848,340
CMPTRA	896,508
Muni. block grant	47,713
Energy tax receipts	834,119
Homeland security	70,000

Taxes

	2003	2004	2005
General tax rate per $100	4.78	5.023	5.339
Net valuation taxable	$375,490,624	$375,290,791	$375,825,278
State equalized value	$446,481,122	$489,853,624	$556,695,716
County equalization ratio	90.65	84.10	76.40

Demographics & Socio-Economic Characteristics

(2000 U.S. Census, except as noted)

Population

1980*	3,460
1990*	3,392
2000	2,988
Male	1,437
Female	1,551
2004 (estimate)*	3,010
Persons per sq. mi. of land	2,455

Race & Hispanic Origin, 2000

Race

White	2,879
Black/African American	46
Amer. Indian/Alaska Natv.	8
Asian	30
Natv. Hawaiian/Pac. Islander	0
Other Race	14
Two or more races	11
Hispanic origin, total	37
Mexican	2
Puerto Rican	23
Cuban	1
Other Hispanic	11

Age & Nativity, 2000

Under 5 years	179
18 years and over	2,207
21 years and over	2,113
65 years and over	396
85 years and over	29
Median Age	38.3
Native born	2,896
Foreign born	92

Educational Attainment, 2000

Population 25 years and over	2,012
0-8 yrs of school	4.1%
High School grad or higher	86.5%
Bachelor's degree or higher	22.9%
Graduate degree	7.8%

Income & Poverty, 1999

Per capita income	$24,001
Median household income	$63,266
Median family income	$70,167
Persons in poverty	121
H'holds receiving public assistance	14
H'holds receiving social security	284

Households, 2000

Total households	1,027
With persons under 18	421
With persons over 65	286
Family households	826
One-person households	171
Persons per household	2.89
Persons per family	3.24

Labor & Employment

Total civilian labor force, 2004**	2,048
Unemployment rate	2.1%
Total civilian labor force, 2000	1,537
Unemployment rate	4.0%

Employed persons 16 years and over by occupation, 2000

Managers & professionals	439
Service occupations	162
Sales & office occupations	473
Farming, fishing & forestry	6
Construction & maintenance	175
Production & transportation	221
Self-employed persons	69

*US Census Bureau
**New Jersey Department of Labor

General Information

Borough of Woodbury Heights
500 Elm Ave
Woodbury Heights, NJ 08097
856-848-2832

Email	janetpz@bwhnj.com
Land area (sq. miles)	1.23
Water area (sq. miles)	0
Type of government	Borough
Form of government	B

Government

Legislative Districts

US Congressional	1
State Legislative	5

Local Officials, 2006

Mayor	Harry Elton Jr.
Admin/Manager	NA
Clerk	Janet Pizzi
Finance Dir/Treas	Sandra Kraus
Engineer	Mark Brunermer
Attorney	Barry Lozuke
Tax assessor	Brian Schneider
Tax collector	Sandra Kraus
Building officer	Robert Kunkle
Zoning officer	NA
Public Works	David Baresich

Housing & Construction

Housing Units, 2000*

Total	1,045
Median rent	$742
Median SF home value	$124,300

New Privately Owned Housing Units Authorized by Building Permit

	Units	Value
Total, 2004	6	$529,600
Single family	6	$529,600
Total, 2005	8	$852,917
Single family	8	$852,917

Real Property Valuation - parcels, 2005

	Number	Valuation
Total		$191,978,300
Vacant	128	3,346,800
Residential	1,062	149,578,300
Commercial	84	29,634,200
Industrial	12	8,911,800
Apartments	3	507,200
Farm land	0	0
Farm homestead	0	0

Average Property Value & Tax, 2005

Residential value	$140,846
Property tax	$5,071
FAIR rebate	$600

Public Library

No public municipal library.

Library statistics, 2004

	Total	per capita
Volumes	NA	NA
Expenditure	NA	NA

Public Safety

Police

Chief	Leo Selb
Number of officers, 2004	7

Crime, 2004	Number	Rate
Total	123	41
Violent	8	2.7
Non-violent	115	38.3
Domestic Viol.	24	NA

Emergency/Fire

Director	Robbie Conley

Public School District

(for school year 2004-2005 except as noted)

Woodbury Heights School District
100 Academy Ave
Woodbury Heights, NJ 08097
856-848-7001

Administrator	Janie Haines
Grade plan	K-6
Enrollment	255.0
Students per teacher	10.5
Per pupil expenditure	$10,977
Median faculty salary	$41,700
Median administrator salary	$95,000
Grade 12 enrollment	NA
High school graduation rate	NA

Assessment test results

(percent scoring at proficient or advanced level)

	Language	Math
Grade 3	80.8%	88.4%
Grade 8	NA	NA
High school	NA	NA

SAT

Percent tested	NA
Average SAT math score	NA
Average SAT verbal score	NA

No Child Left Behind, 2003-04

Attendance rate (target = 90%)	96.4%
Drop rate	NA
Highly-qualified teachers	100%
District needs improvement?(AYP)	No

Municipal Finance

Fiscal Year 2005

Total tax levy	$6,927,515
County levy	1,438,742
County taxes	1,261,539
County library	93,231
County health	0
County open space	83,972
School levy	3,889,675
Local muni. budget	1,599,098
Misc. revenues	1,553,167
Total aid	$447,607
CMPTRA	186,655
Muni. block grant	14,842
Energy tax receipts	221,110
Homeland security	25,000

Fiscal Year 2006

Total aid	$447,608
CMPTRA	178,917
Muni. block grant	14,842
Energy tax receipts	228,849
Homeland security	25,000

Taxes

	2003	2004	2005
General tax rate per $100	3.20	3.343	3.601
Net valuation taxable	$190,804,792	$192,375,616	$192,398,519
State equalized value	$193,259,184	$208,903,727	$230,031,706
County equalization ratio	106.55	98.73	92.07

Demographics & Socio-Economic Characteristics
(2000 U.S. Census, except as noted)

Population

1980*	5,644
1990*	5,303
2000	5,745
Male	2,757
Female	2,988
2004 (estimate)*	5,886
Persons per sq. mi. of land	1,768

Race & Hispanic Origin, 2000

Race

White	5,391
Black/African American	50
Amer. Indian/Alaska Natv.	2
Asian	257
Natv. Hawaiian/Pac. Islander	0
Other Race	11
Two or more races	34
Hispanic origin, total	134
Mexican	16
Puerto Rican	30
Cuban	28
Other Hispanic	60

Age & Nativity, 2000

Under 5 years	406
18 years and over	4,027
21 years and over	3,901
65 years and over	768
85 years and over	133
Median Age	40.7
Native born	5,162
Foreign born	583

Educational Attainment, 2000

Population 25 years and over	3,791
0 8 yrs of school	1.0%
High School grad or higher	96.1%
Bachelor's degree or higher	58.3%
Graduate degree	27.0%

Income & Poverty, 1999

Per capita income	$53,461
Median household income	$123,022
Median family income	$133,925
Persons in poverty	86
H'holds receiving public assistance	7
H'holds receiving social security	454

Households, 2000

Total households	1,824
With persons under 18	892
With persons over 65	451
Family households	1,605
One-person households	193
Persons per household	3.08
Persons per family	3.31

Labor & Employment

Total civilian labor force, 2004**	2,836
Unemployment rate	1.3%
Total civilian labor force, 2000	2,692
Unemployment rate	1.4%

Employed persons 16 years and over by occupation, 2000

Managers & professionals	1,528
Service occupations	138
Sales & office occupations	810
Farming, fishing & forestry	0
Construction & maintenance	96
Production & transportation	83
Self-employed persons	271

*US Census Bureau
**New Jersey Department of Labor

General Information

Borough of Woodcliff Lake
188 Pascack Rd
Woodcliff Lake, NJ 07677
201-391-4977

Web site	www.wclnj.com
Land area (sq. miles)	3.33
Water area (sq. miles)	0.21
Type of government	Borough
Form of government	B

Government

Legislative Districts

US Congressional	5
State Legislative	39

Local Officials, 2006

Mayor	Joseph T. La Paglia
Admin/Manager	Edward Sandve
Clerk	Lorinda Sciara
Finance Dir/Treas	Kathleen Rizza (Dep Treas)
Engineer	NA
Attorney	Mark Madaio
Tax assessor	Barbara Potash
Tax collector	Lois Frezza
Building officer	Nick Saluzzi
Zoning officer	NA
Public Works	Ed Barboni

Housing & Construction

Housing Units, 2000*

Total	1,842
Median rent	$1,258
Median SF home value	$450,700

New Privately Owned Housing Units Authorized by Building Permit

	Units	Value
Total, 2004	12	$4,409,604
Single family	12	$4,409,604
Total, 2005	35	$11,445,800
Single family	35	$11,445,800

Real Property Valuation - parcels, 2005

	Number	Valuation
Total		$1,550,723,900
Vacant	69	13,457,100
Residential	1,842	1,157,148,000
Commercial	51	378,733,100
Industrial	0	0
Apartments	0	0
Farm land	4	1,367,100
Farm homestead	4	18,600

Average Property Value & Tax, 2005

Residential value	$626,851
Property tax	$10,926
FAIR rebate	$583

Public Library

No public municipal library.

Library statistics, 2004

	Total	per capita
Volumes	NA	NA
Expenditure	NA	NA

Public Safety

Police

Chief	Anthony Jannicelli
Number of officers, 2004	18

Crime, 2004	Number	Rate
Total	47	8
Violent	3	0.5
Non-violent	44	7.5
Domestic Viol.	14	NA

Emergency/Fire

Director	George Fusco

Public School District

(for school year 2004-2005 except as noted)

Woodcliff Lake School District
100 Dorchester Rd
Woodcliff Lake, NJ 07675
201-391-6570

Superintendent	Edward Michaelson
Grade plan	K-8
Enrollment	895.0
Students per teacher	10.8
Per pupil expenditure	$11,813
Median faculty salary	$45,119
Median administrator salary	$105,682
Grade 12 enrollment	NA
High school graduation rate	NA

Assessment test results

(percent scoring at proficient or advanced level)

	Language	Math
Grade 3	99.0%	96.0%
Grade 8	96.0%	89.0%
High school	NA	NA

SAT

Percent tested	NA
Average SAT math score	NA
Average SAT verbal score	NA

No Child Left Behind, 2003-04

Attendence rate (target = 90%)	96.1%
Drop rate	NA
Highly-qualified teachers	100%
District needs improvement?(AYP)	No

Municipal Finance

Fiscal Year 2005

Total tax levy	$27,060,202
County levy	3,276,967
County taxes	3,113,051
County library	0
County health	0
County open space	163,916
School levy	17,502,277
Local muni. budget	6,280,958
Misc. revenues	2,874,584
Total aid	$779,211
CMPTRA	150,188
Muni. block grant	23,204
Energy tax receipts	544,633
Homeland security	50,000

Fiscal Year 2006

Total aid	$779,211
CMPTRA	131,126
Muni. block grant	23,204
Energy tax receipts	563,695
Homeland security	50,000

Taxes

	2003	2004	2005
General tax rate per $100	1.48	1.610	1.750
Net valuation taxable	$1,542,688,774	$1,544,731,387	$1,552,518,524
State equalized value	$1,483,782,605	$1,628,842,233	$1,780,819,596
County equalization ratio	117.26	103.97	94.83

Demographics & Socio-Economic Characteristics

(2000 U.S. Census, except as noted)

Population

1980*	2,285
1990*	2,063
2000	1,170
Male	582
Female	588
2000 (revised)	1,292
2004 (estimate)*	1,364
Persons per sq. mi. of land	14

Race & Hispanic Origin, 2000

Race

White	1,147
Black/African American	7
Amer. Indian/Alaska Natv.	1
Asian	4
Natv. Hawaiian/Pac. Islander	0
Other Race	2
Two or more races	9
Hispanic origin, total	14
Mexican	2
Puerto Rican	6
Cuban	0
Other Hispanic	6

Age & Nativity, 2000

Under 5 years	57
18 years and over	868
21 years and over	824
65 years and over	90
85 years and over	7
Median Age	38.4
Native born	1,125
Foreign born	35

Educational Attainment, 2000

Population 25 years and over	781
0-8 yrs of school	4.5%
High School grad or higher	83.0%
Bachelor's degree or higher	18.4%
Graduate degree	6.1%

Income & Poverty, 1999

Per capita income	$26,126
Median household income	$59,271
Median family income	$65,972
Persons in poverty	33
H'holds receiving public assistance	8
H'holds receiving social security	76

Households, 2000

Total households	425
With persons under 18	164
With persons over 65	69
Family households	323
One-person households	81
Persons per household	2.75
Persons per family	3.15

Labor & Employment

Total civilian labor force, 2004**	730
Unemployment rate	5.0%
Total civilian labor force, 2000	662
Unemployment rate	3.6%

Employed persons 16 years and over by occupation, 2000

Managers & professionals	181
Service occupations	91
Sales & office occupations	147
Farming, fishing & forestry	8
Construction & maintenance	118
Production & transportation	93
Self-employed persons	41

*US Census Bureau
**New Jersey Department of Labor

General Information

Township of Woodland
PO Box 388
Chatsworth, NJ 08019
609-726-1700

Web site	NA
Land area (sq. miles)	95.94
Water area (sq. miles)	0.45
Type of government	Township
Form of government	TC

Government

Legislative Districts

US Congressional	3
State Legislative	8

Local Officials, 2006

Mayor	Robert DePetris
Admin/Manager	Maryalice Brown
Clerk	Maryalice Brown
Finance Dir/Treas	John Cicalese
Engineer	Robert Callaway
Attorney	Anthony Drollas
Tax assessor	Harry Renwick
Tax collector	Stephanie Ettinger
Building officer	Dan McGonigle
Zoning officer	NA
Public Works	NA

Housing & Construction

Housing Units, 2000*

Total	448
Median rent	$579
Median SF home value	$129,300

New Privately Owned Housing Units Authorized by Building Permit

	Units	Value
Total, 2004	5	$326,600
Single family	5	$326,600
Total, 2005	7	$1,103,400
Single family	7	$1,103,400

Real Property Valuation - parcels, 2005

	Number	Valuation
Total		$95,998,542
Vacant	3,066	6,172,033
Residential	456	64,739,950
Commercial	22	4,373,200
Industrial	13	6,145,400
Apartments	0	0
Farm land	45	13,236,887
Farm homestead	122	1,331,072

Average Property Value & Tax, 2005

Residential value	$114,310
Property tax	$3,233
FAIR rebate	$524

Public Library

No public municipal library.

Library statistics, 2004

	Total	per capita
Volumes	NA	NA
Expenditure	NA	NA

Public Safety

Police

Chief	NA
Number of officers, 2004	0

Crime, 2004	Number	Rate
Total	44	32.5
Violent	2	1.5
Non-violent	42	31
Domestic Viol.	10	NA

Emergency/Fire

Director .... Walter Leap

Public School District

(for school year 2004-2005 except as noted)

Woodland Township School District
2 Giles Avenue
Chatsworth, NJ 08019
609-726-1230

Superintendent	William Randazzo
Grade plan	K-8
Enrollment	151.0
Students per teacher	10.1
Per pupil expenditure	$15,652
Median faculty salary	$51,150
Median administrator salary	$68,691
Grade 12 enrollment	NA
High school graduation rate	NA

Assessment test results

(percent scoring at proficient or advanced level)

	Language	Math
Grade 3	84.6%	92.3%
Grade 8	70.6%	64.7%
High school	NA	NA

SAT

Percent tested	NA
Average SAT math score	NA
Average SAT verbal score	NA

No Child Left Behind, 2003-04

Attendence rate (target = 90%)	95.3%
Drop rate	NA
Highly-qualified teachers	100%
District needs improvement?(AYP)	No

Municipal Finance

Fiscal Year 2005

Total tax levy	$2,729,291
County levy	578,580
County taxes	485,362
County library	42,500
County health	0
County open space	50,718
School levy	2,150,711
Local muni. budget	0
Misc. revenues	1,925,970
Total aid	$694,822
CMPTRA	105,937
Muni. block grant	9,027
Energy tax receipts	107,498
Homeland security	0

Fiscal Year 2006

Total aid	$694,822
CMPTRA	102,175
Muni. block grant	9,027
Energy tax receipts	111,260
Homeland security	NA

Taxes

	2003	2004	2005
General tax rate per $100	2.43	2.660	2.829
Net valuation taxable	$93,995,156	$95,602,905	$96,509,652
State equalized value	$110,245,316	$125,544,055	$151,316,482
County equalization ratio	96.86	85.26	76.01

Demographics & Socio-Economic Characteristics
(2000 U.S. Census, except as noted)

Population
1980*	2,578
1990*	2,547
2000	2,796
Male	1,362
Female	1,434
2004 (estimate)*	2,757
Persons per sq. mi. of land	12,759

Race & Hispanic Origin, 2000
Race
White	1,354
Black/African American	635
Amer. Indian/Alaska Natv.	16
Asian	343
Natv. Hawaiian/Pac. Islander	0
Other Race	324
Two or more races	124
Hispanic origin, total	576
Mexican	29
Puerto Rican	456
Cuban	5
Other Hispanic	86

Age & Nativity, 2000
Under 5 years	219
18 years and over	1,889
21 years and over	1,773
65 years and over	244
85 years and over	27
Median Age	30.8
Native born	2,401
Foreign born	395

Educational Attainment, 2000
Population 25 years and over	1,679
0-8 yrs of school	11.0%
High School grad or higher	69.3%
Bachelor's degree or higher	8.0%
Graduate degree	1.7%

Income & Poverty, 1999
Per capita income	$14,757
Median household income	$39,138
Median family income	$39,669
Persons in poverty	388
H'holds receiving public assistance	83
H'holds receiving social security	228

Households, 2000
Total households	912
With persons under 18	445
With persons over 65	197
Family households	684
One-person households	189
Persons per household	3.07
Persons per family	3.52

Labor & Employment
Total civilian labor force, 2004**	1,280
Unemployment rate	3.4%
Total civilian labor force, 2000	1,321
Unemployment rate	5.4%

Employed persons 16 years and over by occupation, 2000
Managers & professionals	260
Service occupations	226
Sales & office occupations	353
Farming, fishing & forestry	0
Construction & maintenance	71
Production & transportation	332
Self-employed persons	29

*US Census Bureau
**New Jersey Department of Labor

General Information
Borough of Woodlynne
200 Cooper Ave
Woodlynne, NJ 08107
856-962-8300

Web site	NA
Land area (sq. miles)	0.22
Water area (sq. miles)	0.02
Type of government	Borough
Form of government	B

Government

Legislative Districts
US Congressional	1
State Legislative	5

Local Officials, 2006
Mayor	Jeraldo Fuentes
Admin/Manager	NA
Clerk	Veronica Gitto
Finance Dir/Treas	Veronica Gitto
Engineer	Edward Vernick
Attorney	Michael McKenna
Tax assessor	Bruce Coyle
Tax collector	NA
Building officer	William Joseph
Zoning officer	NA
Public Works	NA

Housing & Construction

Housing Units, 2000*
Total	1,012
Median rent	$635
Median SF home value	$56,800

New Privately Owned Housing Units Authorized by Building Permit
	Units	Value
Total, 2004	0	$0
Single family	0	$0
Total, 2005	0	$0
Single family	0	$0

Real Property Valuation - parcels, 2005
	Number	Valuation
Total		$50,304,250
Vacant	18	298,800
Residential	876	45,579,500
Commercial	27	3,695,050
Industrial	0	0
Apartments	7	730,900
Farm land	0	0
Farm homestead	0	0

Average Property Value & Tax, 2005
Residential value	$52,031
Property tax	$3,417
FAIR rebate	$595

Public Library
Woodlynne Public Library
200 Cooper Ave
Woodlynne, NJ 08107
856-962-7172

Director....................Ann Vennell

Library statistics, 2004
	Total	per capita
Volumes	NA	NA
Expenditure	NA	NA

Public Safety

Police
Chief	NA
Number of officers, 2004	8

Crime, 2004	Number	Rate
Total	102	36.7
Violent	19	6.8
Non-violent	83	29.9
Domestic Viol.	50	NA

Emergency/Fire
Director................ Patrick Hallahan

Public School District
(for school year 2004-2005 except as noted)

Woodlynne Borough School District
131 Elm Ave
Woodlynne, NJ 08107
856-962-8822

Superintendent	Patricia T. Doloughty
Grade plan	K-12
Enrollment	481.0
Students per teacher	13.5
Per pupil expenditure	$9,909
Median faculty salary	$40,494
Median administrator salary	$71,789
Grade 12 enrollment	NA
High school graduation rate	NA

Assessment test results
(percent scoring at proficient or advanced level)
	Language	Math
Grade 3	55.8%	40.4%
Grade 8	41.1%	41.0%
High school	NA	NA

SAT
Percent tested	NA
Average SAT math score	NA
Average SAT verbal score	NA

No Child Left Behind, 2003-04
Attendence rate (target = 90%)	93.0%
Drop rate	NA
Highly-qualified teachers	100%
District needs improvement?(AYP)	No

Municipal Finance

Fiscal Year 2005
Total tax levy	$3,307,016
County levy	525,381
County taxes	484,222
County library	34,812
County health	0
County open space	6,347
School levy	1,584,173
Local muni. budget	1,197,463
Misc. revenues	1,128,725
Total aid	$288,632
CMPTRA	153,662
Muni. block grant	11,145
Energy tax receipts	98,825
Homeland security	25,000

Fiscal Year 2006
Total aid	$288,632
CMPTRA	150,203
Muni. block grant	11,145
Energy tax receipts	102,284
Homeland security	25,000

Taxes
	2003	2004	2005
General tax rate per $100	5.46	5.983	6.568
Net valuation taxable	$50,461,690	$50,424,228	$50,350,552
State equalized value	$59,338,770	$63,270,367	$73,279,802
County equalization ratio	91.98	85.04	79.68

Demographics & Socio-Economic Characteristics
(2000 U.S. Census, except as noted)

Population
1980*	7,929
1990*	7,506
2000	7,644
Male	3,632
Female	4,012
2004 (estimate)*	7,657
Persons per sq. mi. of land	6,970

Race & Hispanic Origin, 2000
Race
White	6,957
Black/African American	64
Amer. Indian/Alaska Natv.	6
Asian	384
Natv. Hawaiian/Pac. Islander	1
Other Race	135
Two or more races	97
Hispanic origin, total	556
Mexican	11
Puerto Rican	138
Cuban	87
Other Hispanic	320

Age & Nativity, 2000
Under 5 years	467
18 years and over	6,021
21 years and over	5,876
65 years and over	1,297
85 years and over	153
Median Age	40.3
Native born	6,481
Foreign born	1,162

Educational Attainment, 2000
Population 25 years and over	5,590
0-8 yrs of school	5.6%
High School grad or higher	84.4%
Bachelor's degree or higher	27.7%
Graduate degree	6.2%

Income & Poverty, 1999
Per capita income	$29,865
Median household income	$60,949
Median family income	$72,500
Persons in poverty	119
H'holds receiving public assistance	37
H'holds receiving social security	979

Households, 2000
Total households	3,024
With persons under 18	926
With persons over 65	952
Family households	2,138
One-person households	781
Persons per household	2.53
Persons per family	3.07

Labor & Employment
Total civilian labor force, 2004**	4,393
Unemployment rate	3.2%
Total civilian labor force, 2000	4,086
Unemployment rate	3.3%

Employed persons 16 years and over by occupation, 2000
Managers & professionals	1,563
Service occupations	376
Sales & office occupations	1,227
Farming, fishing & forestry	0
Construction & maintenance	334
Production & transportation	452
Self-employed persons	219

*US Census Bureau
**New Jersey Department of Labor

General Information
Borough of Wood-Ridge
85 Humboldt St
Wood-Ridge, NJ 07075
201-939-0202
Web site	njwoodridge.org
Land area (sq. miles)	1.10
Water area (sq. miles)	0
Type of government	Borough
Form of government	B

Government

Legislative Districts
US Congressional	9
State Legislative	36

Local Officials, 2006
Mayor	Paul Sarlo
Admin/Manager	Nicholas Fargo
Clerk	Diane Thornley
Finance Dir/Treas	Nicholas Fargo
Engineer	Michael Neglia
Attorney	Paul Barbire
Tax assessor	Stuart Stolarz
Tax collector	Sharon Curran
Building officer	Paul Clemente
Zoning officer	NA
Public Works	Richard Gennarelli

Housing & Construction

Housing Units, 2000*
Total	3,087
Median rent	$966
Median SF home value	$196,800

New Privately Owned Housing Units Authorized by Building Permit
	Units	Value
Total, 2004	12	$1,729,301
Single family	10	$1,503,001
Total, 2005	7	$983,651
Single family	5	$956,651

Real Property Valuation - parcels, 2005
	Number	Valuation
Total		$734,311,500
Vacant	35	3,207,700
Residential	2,484	577,705,800
Commercial	70	47,161,300
Industrial	23	87,080,400
Apartments	13	19,156,300
Farm land	0	0
Farm homestead	0	0

Average Property Value & Tax, 2005
Residential value	$232,571
Property tax	$5,668
FAIR rebate	$620

Public Library
Wood Ridge Memorial Library
231 Hackensack St
Wood Ridge, NJ 07075
201-438-2455
Director	John Trause

Library statistics, 2004
	Total	per capita
Volumes	37,785	4.94
Expenditure	$327,878	$42.89

Public Safety

Police
Chief	Joseph Rutigliano
Number of officers, 2004	21

Crime, 2004	Number	Rate
Total	64	8.4
Violent	5	0.7
Non-violent	59	7.7
Domestic Viol.	22	NA

Emergency/Fire
Director	Thomas Sarracino

Public School District
(for school year 2004-2005 except as noted)

Wood-Ridge School District
89 Hackensack St
Wood-Ridge, NJ 07075
201-933-6778
Superintendent	Elaine Giugliano
Grade plan	K-12
Enrollment	1,076.0
Students per teacher	12.6
Per pupil expenditure	$11,196
Median faculty salary	$48,400
Median administrator salary	$99,197
Grade 12 enrollment	71.5
High school graduation rate	93.7%

Assessment test results
(percent scoring at proficient or advanced level)
	Language	Math
Grade 3	85.9%	85.9%
Grade 8	85.4%	76.4%
High school	85.6%	81.8%

SAT
Percent tested	84%
Average SAT math score	495
Average SAT verbal score	496

No Child Left Behind, 2003-04
Attendence rate (target = 90%)	94.6%
Drop rate	1.9%
Highly-qualified teachers	93%
District needs improvement?(AYP)	No

Municipal Finance

Fiscal Year 2005
Total tax levy	$17,914,845
County levy	1,924,783
County taxes	1,828,516
County library	0
County health	0
County open space	96,268
School levy	9,872,977
Local muni. budget	6,117,085
Misc. revenues	3,141,016
Total aid	$1,231,252
CMPTRA	656,523
Muni. block grant	32,844
Energy tax receipts	491,885
Homeland security	50,000

Fiscal Year 2006
Total aid	$1,231,252
CMPTRA	639,307
Muni. block grant	32,844
Energy tax receipts	509,101
Homeland security	50,000

Taxes
	2003	2004	2005
General tax rate per $100	2.08	2.120	2.440
Net valuation taxable	$733,995,795	$732,042,797	$735,037,403
State equalized value	$833,328,559	$938,515,566	$1,034,972,406
County equalization ratio	100.08	88.08	77.98

Demographics & Socio-Economic Characteristics
(2000 U.S. Census, except as noted)

Population
1980*	3,250
1990*	3,154
2000	3,136
Male	1,459
Female	1,677
2004 (estimate)*	3,273
Persons per sq. mi. of land	2,062

Race & Hispanic Origin, 2000
Race
White	2,667
Black/African American	405
Amer. Indian/Alaska Natv.	6
Asian	23
Natv. Hawaiian/Pac. Islander	0
Other Race	8
Two or more races	27
Hispanic origin, total	49
Mexican	12
Puerto Rican	14
Cuban	2
Other Hispanic	21

Age & Nativity, 2000
Under 5 years	183
18 years and over	2,360
21 years and over	2,270
65 years and over	517
85 years and over	66
Median Age	37.9
Native born	3,031
Foreign born	105

Educational Attainment, 2000
Population 25 years and over	2,129
0-8 yrs of school	2.8%
High School grad or higher	92.8%
Bachelor's degree or higher	31.6%
Graduate degree	9.8%

Income & Poverty, 1999
Per capita income	$24,182
Median household income	$44,533
Median family income	$56,328
Persons in poverty	171
H'holds receiving public assistance	10
H'holds receiving social security	434

Households, 2000
Total households	1,304
With persons under 18	435
With persons over 65	380
Family households	840
One-person households	401
Persons per household	2.38
Persons per family	3

Labor & Employment
Total civilian labor force, 2004**	1,509
Unemployment rate	4.0%
Total civilian labor force, 2000	1,617
Unemployment rate	3.1%

Employed persons 16 years and over by occupation, 2000
Managers & professionals	604
Service occupations	227
Sales & office occupations	345
Farming, fishing & forestry	4
Construction & maintenance	87
Production & transportation	270
Self-employed persons	83

*US Census Bureau
**New Jersey Department of Labor

General Information
Borough of Woodstown
PO Box 286
Woodstown, NJ 08098
856-769-2200
Web site	www.historicwoodstown.org
Land area (sq. miles)	1.59
Water area (sq. miles)	0.04
Type of government	Borough
Form of government	B

Government
Legislative Districts
US Congressional	2
State Legislative	3

Local Officials, 2006
Mayor	Richard S. Pfeffer
Admin/Manager	NA
Clerk	Jeanette M. Gerlack
Finance Dir/Treas	James Hackett
Engineer	Remington & Vernick
Attorney	George G. Rosenberger
Tax assessor	Edwin Kay
Tax collector	Elaine Urion
Building officer	Joe Willie
Zoning officer	Andrew Hoglen
Public Works	Frank Mitchell

Housing & Construction
Housing Units, 2000*
Total	1,389
Median rent	$644
Median SF home value	$118,800

New Privately Owned Housing Units Authorized by Building Permit
	Units	Value
Total, 2004	14	$1,327,850
Single family	14	$1,327,850
Total, 2005	21	$1,629,025
Single family	21	$1,629,025

Real Property Valuation - parcels, 2005
	Number	Valuation
Total		$145,376,100
Vacant	181	3,415,200
Residential	1,025	116,105,300
Commercial	74	17,424,700
Industrial	0	0
Apartments	11	8,298,200
Farm land	1	63,900
Farm homestead	13	68,800

Average Property Value & Tax, 2005
Residential value	$111,921
Property tax	$4,315
FAIR rebate	$583

Public Library
Woodstown-Pilesgrove Library
14 School Ln
Woodstown, NJ 08098
856-769-0098
Director	Ruth Fritz

Library statistics, 2004
	Total	per capita
Volumes	NA	NA
Expenditure	NA	NA

Public Safety
Police
Chief	George Lacy
Number of officers, 2004	7

Crime, 2004	Number	Rate
Total	41	12.6
Violent	9	2.8
Non-violent	32	9.8
Domestic Viol.	58	NA

Emergency/Fire
Director	Carl Castiglio

Public School District
(for school year 2004-2005 except as noted)

Woodstown-Pilesgrove Reg. School District
135 E Ave
Woodstown, NJ 08098
856-769-1664
Superintendent	Robert Bumpus
Grade plan	K-12
Enrollment	1,581.0
Students per teacher	11.6
Per pupil expenditure	$10,541
Median faculty salary	$61,252
Median administrator salary	$89,683
Grade 12 enrollment	131.0
High school graduation rate	95.1%

Assessment test results
(percent scoring at proficient or advanced level)
	Language	Math
Grade 3	84.8%	82.6%
Grade 8	80.8%	70.0%
High school	89.6%	82.6%

SAT
Percent tested	66%
Average SAT math score	518
Average SAT verbal score	510

No Child Left Behind, 2003-04
Attendence rate (target = 90%)	94.3%
Drop rate	0.6%
Highly-qualified teachers	98.4%
District needs improvement?(AYP)	No

Municipal Finance
Fiscal Year 2005
Total tax levy	$5,659,777
County levy	1,929,965
County taxes	1,891,695
County library	0
County health	0
County open space	38,270
School levy	2,689,252
Local muni. budget	1,040,560
Misc. revenues	1,667,286
Total aid	$407,389
CMPTRA	223,038
Muni. block grant	13,801
Energy tax receipts	145,550
Homeland security	25,000

Fiscal Year 2006
Total aid	$407,390
CMPTRA	217,944
Muni. block grant	13,801
Energy tax receipts	150,645
Homeland security	25,000

Taxes
	2003	2004	2005
General tax rate per $100	3.49	3.832	3.856
Net valuation taxable	$144,702,311	$145,511,258	$146,799,686
State equalized value	$180,900,501	$188,938,195	$214,556,688
County equalization ratio	89.14	79.99	76.83

Demographics & Socio-Economic Characteristics
(2000 U.S. Census, except as noted)

Population
1980*	1,129
1990*	1,459
2000	3,032
Male	1,505
Female	1,527
2004 (estimate)*	6,115
Persons per sq. mi. of land	292

Race & Hispanic Origin, 2000
Race
White	2,763
Black/African American	138
Amer. Indian/Alaska Natv.	0
Asian	34
Natv. Hawaiian/Pac. Islander	0
Other Race	59
Two or more races	38
Hispanic origin, total	118
Mexican	26
Puerto Rican	65
Cuban	0
Other Hispanic	27

Age & Nativity, 2000
Under 5 years	309
18 years and over	2,081
21 years and over	2,001
65 years and over	206
85 years and over	21
Median Age	33.8
Native born	2,959
Foreign born	73

Educational Attainment, 2000
Population 25 years and over	1,918
0-8 yrs of school	4.0%
High School grad or higher	88.1%
Bachelor's degree or higher	29.2%
Graduate degree	11.6%

Income & Poverty, 1999
Per capita income	$29,503
Median household income	$83,790
Median family income	$87,111
Persons in poverty	88
H'holds receiving public assistance	8
H'holds receiving social security	151

Households, 2000
Total households	959
With persons under 18	496
With persons over 65	152
Family households	838
One-person households	82
Persons per household	3.13
Persons per family	3.35

Labor & Employment
Total civilian labor force, 2004**	955
Unemployment rate	6.8%
Total civilian labor force, 2000	1,531
Unemployment rate	2.8%

Employed persons 16 years and over by occupation, 2000
Managers & professionals	664
Service occupations	123
Sales & office occupations	395
Farming, fishing & forestry	36
Construction & maintenance	127
Production & transportation	143
Self-employed persons	92

*US Census Bureau
**New Jersey Department of Labor

General Information
Township of Woolwich
121 Woodstown Rd
Woolwich, NJ 08085
856-467-2666
Web site	www.woolwichtwp.org
Land area (sq. miles)	20.94
Water area (sq. miles)	0.24
Type of government	Township
Form of government	TC

Government

Legislative Districts
US Congressional	2
State Legislative	3

Local Officials, 2006
Mayor	Giuseppe Chila
Admin/Manager	NA
Clerk	Jane DiBella
Finance Dir/Treas	John Schock
Engineer	Frank S. Morris
Attorney	Timothy Scaffidi
Tax assessor	Bruce Komito
Tax collector	Mary Folker
Building officer	James Sabetta
Zoning officer	Mark Fruits
Public Works	Anthony Bertino

Housing & Construction

Housing Units, 2000*
Total	1,026
Median rent	$763
Median SF home value	$194,800

New Privately Owned Housing Units Authorized by Building Permit
	Units	Value
Total, 2004	514	$52,853,894
Single family	285	$34,066,494
Total, 2005	387	$50,288,773
Single family	387	$50,288,773

Real Property Valuation - parcels, 2005
	Number	Valuation
Total		$434,893,100
Vacant	701	22,023,200
Residential	1,957	347,136,500
Commercial	64	43,606,200
Industrial	1	633,900
Apartments	0	0
Farm land	119	15,848,000
Farm homestead	275	5,645,300

Average Property Value & Tax, 2005
Residential value	$158,056
Property tax	$5,962
FAIR rebate	$397

Public Library
Swedesboro Public Library†
1442 Kings Highway
Swedesboro, NJ 08085
856-467-0111
Director	Marge Dombrosky

Library statistics, 2004
	Total	per capita
Volumes	NA	NA
Expenditure	NA	NA

†Joint library with Swedesboro Boro

Public Safety
Police
Chief	Russell Marino
Number of officers, 2004	18

Crime, 2004	Number	Rate
Total	139	25.2
Violent	5	0.9
Non-violent	134	24.3
Domestic Viol.	7	NA

Emergency/Fire
Director	Edward Barber

Public School District
(for school year 2004-2005 except as noted)

Swedesboro-Woolwich School District
15 Fredrick Blvd
Woolwich Township, NJ 08085
856-241-1136
Superintendent	Richard Fisher
Grade plan	K-6
Enrollment	1,058.0
Students per teacher	10.3
Per pupil expenditure	$10,104
Median faculty salary	$36,720
Median administrator salary	$83,637
Grade 12 enrollment	NA
High school graduation rate	NA

Assessment test results
(percent scoring at proficient or advanced level)
	Language	Math
Grade 3	88.6%	85.9%
Grade 8	NA	NA
High school	NA	NA

SAT
Percent tested	NA
Average SAT math score	NA
Average SAT verbal score	NA

No Child Left Behind, 2003-04
Attendence rate (target = 90%)	95.0%
Drop rate	NA
Highly-qualified teachers	100%
District needs improvement?(AYP)	No

Municipal Finance

Fiscal Year 2005
Total tax levy	$16,461,123
County levy	4,543,935
County taxes	3,984,529
County library	294,471
County health	0
County open space	264,935
School levy	9,857,885
Local muni. budget	2,059,303
Misc. revenues	3,366,900
Total aid	$603,720
CMPTRA	113,555
Muni. block grant	11,889
Energy tax receipts	428,276
Homeland security	25,000

Fiscal Year 2006
Total aid	$603,720
CMPTRA	98,565
Muni. block grant	11,889
Energy tax receipts	443,266
Homeland security	50,000

Taxes
	2003	2004	2005
General tax rate per $100	3.59	3.671	3.773
Net valuation taxable	$341,176,142	$399,709,411	$436,394,102
State equalized value	$471,237,765	$604,577,106	$727,808,709
County equalization ratio	77.98	72.40	66.02

Demographics & Socio-Economic Characteristics
(2000 U.S. Census, except as noted)

Population

1980*	3,031
1990*	3,843
2000	748
Male	364
Female	384
2004 (estimate)*	749
Persons per sq. mi. of land	426

Race & Hispanic Origin, 2000

Race
White	373
Black/African American	226
Amer. Indian/Alaska Natv.	4
Asian	54
Natv. Hawaiian/Pac. Islander	0
Other Race	54
Two or more races	37
Hispanic origin, total	84
Mexican	27
Puerto Rican	27
Cuban	1
Other Hispanic	29

Age & Nativity, 2000

Under 5 years	58
18 years and over	526
21 years and over	496
65 years and over	64
85 years and over	5
Median Age	31.2
Native born	632
Foreign born	115

Educational Attainment, 2000

Population 25 years and over	434
0-8 yrs of school	4.1%
High School grad or higher	80.4%
Bachelor's degree or higher	7.8%
Graduate degree	1.4%

Income & Poverty, 1999

Per capita income	$14,489
Median household income	$27,500
Median family income	$29,375
Persons in poverty	179
H'holds receiving public assistance	11
H'holds receiving social security	46

Households, 2000

Total households	312
With persons under 18	118
With persons over 65	51
Family households	182
One-person households	108
Persons per household	2.37
Persons per family	3.09

Labor & Employment

Total civilian labor force, 2004**	1,274
Unemployment rate	10.1%
Total civilian labor force, 2000	364
Unemployment rate	6.9%

Employed persons 16 years and over by occupation, 2000
Managers & professionals	46
Service occupations	117
Sales & office occupations	94
Farming, fishing & forestry	0
Construction & maintenance	21
Production & transportation	61
Self-employed persons	7

*US Census Bureau
**New Jersey Department of Labor

General Information
Borough of Wrightstown
21 Saylors Pond Rd
Wrightstown, NJ 08562
609-723-4450

Web site	NA
Land area (sq. miles)	1.76
Water area (sq. miles)	0
Type of government	Borough
Form of government	B

Government

Legislative Districts

US Congressional	3, 4
State Legislative	8

Local Officials, 2006

Mayor	Thomas Harper
Admin/Manager	NA
Clerk	Ellen Thorne
Finance Dir/Treas	Frank Van Gelder
Engineer	Remington Vernick
Attorney	Nicholas Costa
Tax assessor	Douglas Kolton
Tax collector	NA
Building officer	Larry Nixon
Zoning officer	Laru Nikon
Public Works	NA

Housing & Construction

Housing Units, 2000*

Total	339
Median rent	$623
Median SF home value	$98,900

New Privately Owned Housing Units Authorized by Building Permit

	Units	Value
Total, 2004	1	$150,000
Single family	1	$150,000
Total, 2005	1	$137,250
Single family	1	$137,250

Real Property Valuation - parcels, 2005

	Number	Valuation
Total		$24,705,150
Vacant	26	791,800
Residential	110	10,088,050
Commercial	48	10,059,200
Industrial	2	302,500
Apartments	8	3,451,150
Farm land	0	0
Farm homestead	2	12,450

Average Property Value & Tax, 2005

Residential value	$90,183
Property tax	$1,638
FAIR rebate	$602

Public Library

No public municipal library.

Library statistics, 2004

	Total	per capita
Volumes	NA	NA
Expenditure	NA	NA

Public Safety

Police

Chief	NA
Number of officers, 2004	0

Crime, 2004	Number	Rate
Total	36	48.1
Violent	8	10.7
Non-violent	28	37.4
Domestic Viol.	8	NA

Emergency/Fire

Director	Joseph McFarland

Public School District
(for school year 2004-2005 except as noted)

New Hanover Township School District
122 Fort Dix St
Wrightstown, NJ 08562
609-723-2139

Superintendent	George Pratt
Grade plan	K-12
Enrollment	150.0
Students per teacher	7.7
Per pupil expenditure	$16,987
Median faculty salary	$44,418
Median administrator salary	$72,500
Grade 12 enrollment	NA
High school graduation rate	NA

Assessment test results
(percent scoring at proficient or advanced level)

	Language	Math
Grade 3	80.0%	73.3%
Grade 8	75.0%	75.0%
High school	NA	NA

SAT

Percent tested	NA
Average SAT math score	NA
Average SAT verbal score	NA

No Child Left Behind, 2003-04

Attendence rate (target = 90%)	94.9%
Drop rate	NA
Highly-qualified teachers	88.9%
District needs improvement?(AYP)	No

Municipal Finance

Fiscal Year 2005

Total tax levy	$563,732
County levy	123,154
County taxes	103,312
County library	9,046
County health	0
County open space	10,795
School levy	440,578
Local muni. budget	0
Misc. revenues	1,023,810
Total aid	$533,084
CMPTRA	435,681
Muni. block grant	16,816
Energy tax receipts	80,587
Homeland security	0

Fiscal Year 2006

Total aid	$533,085
CMPTRA	432,861
Muni. block grant	16,816
Energy tax receipts	83,408
Homeland security	NA

Taxes

	2003	2004	2005
General tax rate per $100	2.33	2.204	2.150
Net valuation taxable	$25,709,553	$25,812,925	$26,247,785
State equalized value	$26,764,057	$25,686,596	$26,104,212
County equalization ratio	104.64	96.06	100.52

Demographics & Socio-Economic Characteristics
(2000 U.S. Census, except as noted)

Population
1980*	15,500
1990*	15,372
2000	16,508
Male	7,880
Female	8,628
2004 (estimate)*	17,206
Persons per sq. mi. of land	2,628

Race & Hispanic Origin, 2000
Race
White	15,607
Black/African American	77
Amer. Indian/Alaska Natv.	25
Asian	611
Natv. Hawaiian/Pac. Islander	2
Other Race	74
Two or more races	112
Hispanic origin, total	376
Mexican	19
Puerto Rican	94
Cuban	62
Other Hispanic	201

Age & Nativity, 2000
Under 5 years	1,185
18 years and over	11,837
21 years and over	11,512
65 years and over	2,603
85 years and over	481
Median Age	40.9
Native born	14,978
Foreign born	1,530

Educational Attainment, 2000
Population 25 years and over	11,122
0-8 yrs of school	2.5%
High School grad or higher	93.8%
Bachelor's degree or higher	56.6%
Graduate degree	23.0%

Income & Poverty, 1999
Per capita income	$49,375
Median household income	$103,614
Median family income	$117,864
Persons in poverty	290
H'holds receiving public assistance	39
H'holds receiving social security	1,607

Households, 2000
Total households	5,541
With persons under 18	2,410
With persons over 65	1,573
Family households	4,634
One-person households	819
Persons per household	2.89
Persons per family	3.22

Labor & Employment
Total civilian labor force, 2004**	8,320
Unemployment rate	2.0%
Total civilian labor force, 2000	7,574
Unemployment rate	2.8%

Employed persons 16 years and over by occupation, 2000
Managers & professionals	4,139
Service occupations	453
Sales & office occupations	2,109
Farming, fishing & forestry	5
Construction & maintenance	289
Production & transportation	364
Self-employed persons	691

*US Census Bureau
**New Jersey Department of Labor

General Information
Township of Wyckoff
Scott Plaza
340 Franklin Ave
Wyckoff, NJ 07481
201-891-7000

Web site	www.wycoff-nj.com
Land area (sq. miles)	6.55
Water area (sq. miles)	0.02
Type of government	Township
Form of government	TC

Government

Legislative Districts
US Congressional	5
State Legislative	40

Local Officials, 2006
Mayor	Joseph Fiorenzo
Admin/Manager	Robert Shannon Jr.
Clerk	Joyce Santimauro
Finance Dir/Treas	Diana McLeod
Engineer	Lawrence Edler
Attorney	Robert Landel
Tax assessor	Pamela Steele
Tax collector	NA
Building officer	Thomas Gensheimer
Zoning officer	Fred Depken
Public Works	Scott Fisher

Housing & Construction

Housing Units, 2000*
Total	5,638
Median rent	$1,114
Median SF home value	$417,500

New Privately Owned Housing Units Authorized by Building Permit
	Units	Value
Total, 2004	37	$9,763,731
Single family	35	$9,363,731
Total, 2005	25	$10,439,497
Single family	25	$10,439,497

Real Property Valuation - parcels, 2005
	Number	Valuation
Total		$2,143,975,971
Vacant	107	16,799,400
Residential	5,521	1,985,041,571
Commercial	134	115,331,800
Industrial	18	24,163,300
Apartments	2	886,000
Farm land	3	1,732,700
Farm homestead	2	21,200

Average Property Value & Tax, 2005
Residential value	$359,417
Property tax	$9,241
FAIR rebate	$605

Public Library
Wyckoff Public Library
200 Woodland Ave
Wyckoff, NJ 07481
201-891-4866

Director | Judy Schmitt

Library statistics, 2004
	Total	per capita
Volumes	56,517	3.42
Expenditure	$821,980	$49.79

Public Safety

Police
Chief	John Ydo
Number of officers, 2004	25

Crime, 2004	Number	Rate
Total	130	7.7
Violent	7	0.4
Non-violent	123	7.2
Domestic Viol.	62	NA

Emergency/Fire
Director | Edward Pettit

Public School District
(for school year 2004-2005 except as noted)

Wyckoff Township School District
241 Morse Ave
Wyckoff, NJ 07481
201-848-5701

Superintendent	James Bender
Grade plan	K-8
Enrollment	2,572.0
Students per teacher	12.7
Per pupil expenditure	$10,824
Median faculty salary	$55,335
Median administrator salary	$130,554
Grade 12 enrollment	NA
High school graduation rate	NA

Assessment test results
(percent scoring at proficient or advanced level)
	Language	Math
Grade 3	95.5%	94.0%
Grade 8	96.6%	85.5%
High school	NA	NA

SAT
Percent tested	NA
Average SAT math score	NA
Average SAT verbal score	NA

No Child Left Behind, 2003-04
Attendence rate (target = 90%)	96.6%
Drop rate	NA
Highly-qualified teachers	96.7%
District needs improvement?(AYP)	No

Municipal Finance

Fiscal Year 2005
Total tax levy	$55,207,473
County levy	7,284,373
County taxes	6,919,819
County library	0
County health	0
County open space	364,555
School levy	40,124,458
Local muni. budget	7,798,641
Misc. revenues	6,234,202
Total aid	$1,688,182
CMPTRA	506,963
Muni. block grant	67,263
Energy tax receipts	1,043,956
Homeland security	70,000

Fiscal Year 2006
Total aid	$1,688,182
CMPTRA	470,425
Muni. block grant	67,263
Energy tax receipts	1,080,494
Homeland security	70,000

Taxes
	2003	2004	2005
General tax rate per $100	2.31	2.430	2.580
Net valuation taxable	$2,079,470,889	$2,110,797,277	$2,147,223,666
State equalized value	$3,252,730,939	$3,579,601,091	$3,972,661,732
County equalization ratio	71.9	63.93	58.93

The New Jersey Municipal Data Book

2006

State & Municipal Profiles Series™

County Profiles

**State &
Municipal
Profiles
Series**

Demographics & Socio-Economic Characteristics

(2000 U.S. Census, except as noted)

Population

1990*	224,327
2000	252,552
2004 (estimate)*	268,693
Male	130,464
Female	138,229
Persons per sq. mi. of land	478.9

Race & Hispanic Origin, 2004**

White	198,881
Black/African American	48,403
Amer. Indian/Alaska Natv.	892
Asian	16,491
Natv Hawaiian/Pac Islander	186
Two or more races	3,840
Hispanic origin, total	36,701

Age & Nativity, 2004**

Under 5 years	17,891
18 years and over	201,232
15 to 44 years	111,938
45 to 64 years	64,977
65 years and over	35,775
85 years and over	4,833
Median Age	37.5
Native born, 2000	222,757
Foreign born, 2000	29,795

Educational Attainment, 2000

Population 25 years and over	168,546
0-8 yrs of school	6.5%
High School grad or higher	78.2%
Bachelor's degree or higher	18.7%
Graduate degree	5.8%

Income & Poverty, 1999

Per capita income	$21,034
Median household income	$43,933
Median family income	$51,710
Persons in poverty	25,906
H'holds receiving public assistance	2,828
H'holds receiving social security	26,955

Households, 2000

Total households	95,024
With persons under 18	33,919
With persons over 65	24,974
Family households	63,151
One-person households	25,661
Persons per household	2.59
Persons per family	3.16

Labor & Employment

Total civilian labor force, 2005**	136,300
Unemployment rate	5.0%

*Labor Employment for Major Industries, 2012 Projection***

Total non-farm payroll empl	165,100
Construction	5.0%
Manufacturing	2.3%
Wholesale trade	2.0%
Retail trade	11.0%
Transp & warehousing	1.5%
Information	0.8%
Finance & insurance	1.5%
Real estate	1.1%
Professional & technical	3.5%
Management	0.4%
Administration	3.8%
Education	1.2%
Health & social svcs	5.0%
Accommodations	34.9%
Government	13.7%

*US Census Bureau; **NJ Dept of Labor
***NJ Labor Planning Analysis

General Information

Atlantic County
1333 Atlantic Ave
Atlantic City, NJ 08401
609-345-6700

Website	www.aclink.org
Land Area (sq. miles)	561.1
Water Area (sq. miles)	110.4
Class	Fifth
Government form	CEP (OCCL-1972)
Number of Freeholders	9
Number of municipalities	23

Government & Voters

Legislative Districts

US Congressional	2
State Legislative	1, 2, 9

Registered Voters, November 2005

Total	157,202
Democrat	33,538
Republican	37,428
Unaffiliated	85,675

County Officials, 2006

County Executive	Dennis Levinson
Manager/Admin	Helen Walsh
Clerk	Michael Garvin
Finance Dir/Treas	George Boileau
Tax Administrator	Lois Finifter
Surrogate	James Carney
Prosecutor	Jeffrey Blitz
Planning/Develop	NA

County School District

6260 Old Harding Hwy
Mays Landing, NJ 08330
609-625-0004

Superintendent	Daniel Loggi
Number of districts	26

Housing & Construction

Total Housing Units, 2000-2004

2000*	114,090
Median rent	$677
Median SF home value	$122,000
2001	115,913
2002	117,445
2003	119,297
2004 (estimate)	121,192

New Privately Owned Housing Units
Authorized by Building Permit

	Units	Value
Total, 2004	2,075	$254,456,099
Single family	1,970	$244,035,152
Total, 2005	1,993	$233,889,239
Single family	1,830	224,513,401

Real Property Valuation - parcels, 2005

(sum of all municipalities in county)

	Number	Valuation
Total		$25,186,386,700
Vacant	29,507	1,110,023,925
Residential	96,352	15,040,036,650
Non-residential	6,169	8,939,379,375
Commercial	5,602	8,319,314,920
Industrial	188	131,041,555
Apartments	379	288,822,900
Farm land	661	78,491,800
Farm homestead	1,669	18,454,950

Public Safety

Police

Sheriff	James McGettigan
Officers, 2004	
Sheriff's department	92
County officers	164
Municipal police	961
Prosecutors, 2004	72

Crime, 2004	Number	Rate
Total	12,184	46.3
Violent	1,408	5.3
Non-violent	10,776	40.9
Arson	52	NA
Domestic Viol.	5,608	NA

Emergency/Fire

Fire Marshal	Harold Swartz

Public Library

Atlantic County Library
40 Farragut Ave
Mays Landing, NJ 08330
609-625-2776

Director	William Paullin

Library statistics, 2004

	Total	per capita
Volumes	466,660	2.57
Expenditure	$6,186,700	$34.12
Library weekly hours		64
Full-time equivalent staff		78

Income Tax, 2002

Number of returns	108,928
Total taxable income	$4,114,374,000
Net charged tax	$105,637,000
Average gross income	$42,661
Average income tax	$970

County Finance

(sum of all municipalities in county)

Fiscal Year 2004

Total tax levy	$688,327,031
County taxes	104,857,219
County library	5,848,907
County health	3,988,097
County open space	5,565,170
Muni. budget	256,667,747
Misc. revenues	121,189,037

Fiscal Year 2005

Total tax levy	$733,369,659
County levy	128,141,732
County taxes	110,840,470
County library	6,548,972
County health	4,111,871
County open space	6,640,419
School levy	341,714,317
Muni. budget	263,513,612
Misc. revenues	154,852,477
Total aid	$38,640,318
CMPTRA	9,126,204
Muni. block grant	1,032,540
Energy tax receipts	26,999,215
Homeland security	1,210,000

Fiscal Year 2006

Total aid	$38,619,893
CMPTRA	8,185,806
Muni. block grant	1,032,540
Energy tax receipts	27,944,188
Homeland security	1,185,000

Taxes†

	2003	2004	2005
Net valuation taxable	$21,315,081,924	$22,107,060,573	$25,152,364,169
State equalized value	$27,118,819,658	$32,408,380,703	$38,719,302,252

† sum of all municipalities in county

Bergen County

Demographics & Socio-Economic Characteristics
(2000 U.S. Census, except as noted)

Population
1990*	825,380
2000	884,118
2004 (estimate)*	902,998
Male	436,449
Female	466,549
Persons per sq. mi. of land	3,856.1

Race & Hispanic Origin, 2004**
White	719,557
Black/African American	52,452
Amer. Indian/Alaska Natv.	1,949
Asian	118,537
Natv Hawaiian/Pac Islander	222
Two or more races	10,281
Hispanic origin, total	114,354

Age & Nativity, 2004**
Under 5 years	53,002
18 years and over	695,130
15 to 44 years	354,166
45 to 64 years	242,059
65 years and over	133,875
85 years and over	20,188
Median Age	40.2
Native born, 2000	661,817
Foreign born, 2000	222,301

Educational Attainment, 2000
Population 25 years and over	623,469
0-8 yrs of school	5.5%
High School grad or higher	86.6%
Bachelor's degree or higher	38.2%
Graduate degree	14.2%

Income & Poverty, 1999
Per capita income	$33,638
Median household income	$65,241
Median family income	$78,079
Persons in poverty	43,417
H'holds receiving public assistance	4,829
H'holds receiving social security	93,396

Households, 2000
Total households	330,817
With persons under 18	113,056
With persons over 65	95,469
Family households	235,070
One-person households	81,573
Persons per household	2.64
Persons per family	3.17

Labor & Employment
Total civilian labor force, 2005**	468,600
Unemployment rate	3.5%

*Labor Employment for Major Industries, 2012 Projection***
Total non-farm payroll empl	519,350
Construction	3.6%
Manufacturing	8.1%
Wholesale trade	9.3%
Retail trade	12.1%
Transp & warehousing	3.1%
Information	3.4%
Finance & insurance	4.2%
Real estate	1.4%
Professional & technical	7.0%
Management	3.0%
Administration	8.0%
Education	1.7%
Health & social svcs	3.6%
Accommodations	5.7%
Government	9.9%

*US Census Bureau; **NJ Dept of Labor
***NJ Labor Planning Analysis

General Information
Bergen County
One Bergen County Plaza
Hackensack, NJ 07601
201-336-6000

Website	www.co.bergen.nj.us
Land Area (sq. miles)	234.2
Water Area (sq. miles)	12.6
Class	First
Government form	CEP (OCCL 1972)
Number of Freeholders	7
Number of municipalities	70

Government & Voters

Legislative Districts
US Congressional	5, 9
State Legislative	32, 35, 36, 37, 38, 39, 40

Registered Voters, November 2005
Total	506,070
Democrat	106,296
Republican	98,410
Unaffiliated	298,793

County Officials, 2006
County Executive	Dennis McNerney
Manager/Admin	Timothy Dacey
Clerk	Kathleen Donovan
Finance Dir/Treas	Alfred Dispoto
Tax Administrator	Robert Layton
Surrogate	Michael Dressler
Prosecutor	John Molinelli
Planning/Develop	NA

County School District
327 E Ridgewood Ave
Paramus, NJ 07652
201-646-6804
Superintendent	Aaron Graham
Number of districts	77

Housing & Construction

Total Housing Units, 2000-2004
2000*	339,820
Median rent	$872
Median SF home value	$250,300
2001	342,776
2002	344,102
2003	345,413
2004 (estimate)	344,721

New Privately Owned Housing Units
Authorized by Building Permit
	Units	Value
Total, 2004	2,142	$394,147,014
Single family	914	$293,455,950
Total, 2005	2,984	$532,255,463
Single family	1,218	367,178,534

Real Property Valuation - parcels, 2005
(sum of all municipalities in county)
	Number	Valuation
Total		$109,013,572,251
Vacant	6,642	1,631,715,190
Residential	244,511	82,498,543,736
Non-residential	15,809	24,845,896,225
Commercial	11,318	15,297,368,771
Industrial	2,812	5,166,664,434
Apartments	1,679	4,381,863,020
Farm land	56	36,535,700
Farm homestead	86	881,400

Public Safety

Police
Sheriff	Leo McGuire

Officers, 2004
Sheriff's department	430
County officers	693
Municipal police	2,177
Prosecutors, 2004	171

Crime, 2004	Number	Rate
Total	15,285	17
Violent	1,116	1.2
Non-violent	14,169	15.8
Arson	62	NA
Domestic Viol.	4,902	NA

Emergency/Fire
Fire Marshal	Bryan Hennig

Public Library
No County Library
(Library statistics are the sum of all municipal libraries in the county)

Library statistics, 2004
	Total	per capita
Volumes	3,845,272	4.46
Expenditure	$45,822,116	$53.14
Library weekly hours	56.9	
Full-time equivalent staff	650	

Income Tax, 2002
Number of returns	378,936
Total taxable income	$27,567,279,000
Net charged tax	$738,971,000
Average gross income	$79,423
Average income tax	$1,950

County Finance
(sum of all municipalities in county)

Fiscal Year 2004
Total tax levy	$709,606,707
County taxes	241,956,754
County library	0
County health	0
County open space	3,626,154
Muni. budget	189,963,221
Misc. revenues	101,959,812

Fiscal Year 2005
Total tax levy	$2,538,517,374
County levy	272,091,713
County taxes	258,445,112
County library	0
County health	0
County open space	13,646,602
School levy	1,507,451,853
Muni. budget	758,973,823
Misc. revenues	384,211,606
Total aid	$127,685,676
CMPTRA	40,539,882
Muni. block grant	3,656,392
Energy tax receipts	78,949,703
Homeland security	4,365,000

Fiscal Year 2006
Total aid	$127,718,890
CMPTRA	37,809,857
Muni. block grant	3,656,392
Energy tax receipts	81,712,942
Homeland security	4,365,000

Taxes†

	2003	2004	2005
Net valuation taxable	$86,830,101,555	$98,456,094,134	$109,204,537,237
State equalized value	$119,997,204,154	$134,755,914,959	$152,020,919,861

† sum of all municipalities in county

Demographics & Socio-Economic Characteristics

(2000 U.S. Census, except as noted)

Population

1990*	395,066
2000	423,394
2000 (revised)	423,391
2004 (estimate)*	449,685
Male	222,455
Female	227,230
Persons per sq. mi. of land	558.9

Race & Hispanic Origin, 2004**

White	351,028
Black/African American	73,956
Amer. Indian/Alaska Natv.	1,008
Asian	15,703
Natv Hawaiian/Pac Islander	180
Two or more races	7,810
Hispanic origin, total	21,507

Age & Nativity, 2004**

Under 5 years	27,318
18 years and over	340,673
15 to 44 years	190,244
45 to 64 years	112,801
65 years and over	57,238
85 years and over	6,698
Median Age	38.0
Native born, 2000	396,713
Foreign born, 2000	26,681

Educational Attainment, 2000

Population 25 years and over	285,553
0-8 yrs of school	3.3%
High School grad or higher	87.2%
Bachelor's degree or higher	28.4%
Graduate degree	9.2%

Income & Poverty, 1999

Per capita income	$26,339
Median household income	$58,608
Median family income	$67,481
Persons in poverty	19,280
H'holds receiving public assistance	2,715
H'holds receiving social security	39,555

Households, 2000

Total households	154,371
With persons under 18	57,893
With persons over 65	37,115
Family households	111,581
One-person households	35,419
Persons per household	2.65
Persons per family	3.14

Labor & Employment

Total civilian labor force, 2005**	243,100
Unemployment rate	3.6%

*Labor Employment for Major Industries, 2012 Projection****

Total non-farm payroll empl	227,950
Construction	3.9%
Manufacturing	8.3%
Wholesale trade	6.3%
Retail trade	13.5%
Transp & warehousing	4.3%
Information	1.5%
Finance & insurance	7.9%
Real estate	1.8%
Professional & technical	5.3%
Management	0.9%
Administration	6.6%
Education	1.4%
Health & social svcs	3.9%
Accommodations	6.0%
Government	13.7%

*US Census Bureau; **NJ Dept of Labor
***NJ Labor Planning Analysis

General Information

Burlington County
County Office Bldg
49 Rancocas Rd
Mt. Holly, NJ 08060
609-265-5000

Website	www.co.burlington.nj.us
Land Area (sq. miles)	804.6
Water Area (sq. miles)	14.9
Class	Second
Government form	BCF
Number of Freeholders	5
Number of municipalities	40

Government & Voters

Legislative Districts

US Congressional	1, 2, 3, 4
State Legislative	7, 8, 9, 30

Registered Voters, November 2005

Total	245,992
Democrat	51,837
Republican	52,930
Unaffiliated	139,657

County Officials, 2006

County Executive	None
Manager/Admin	Fred Galdo
Clerk	Phillip Haines
Finance Dir/Treas	Christine J. Nociti
Tax Administrator	Linda Stewart
Surrogate	Elton A. Conda
Prosecutor	Robert Bernardi
Planning/Develop	NA

County School District

3 Union St
Mt Holly, NJ 08060
609-265-5060

Superintendent	Walter Keiss
Number of districts	42

Housing & Construction

Total Housing Units, 2000-2004

2000*	161,311
Median rent	$758
Median SF home value	$137,400
2001	164,592
2002	166,648
2003	168,869
2004 (estimate)	169,905

New Privately Owned Housing Units Authorized by Building Permit

	Units	Value
Total, 2004	1,516	$174,653,615
Single family	1,302	$161,432,129
Total, 2005	1,460	$194,616,311
Single family	1,275	185,755,566

Real Property Valuation - parcels, 2005

(sum of all municipalities in county)

	Number	Valuation
Total		$26,442,597,352
Vacant	16,246	536,504,072
Residential	139,385	20,385,870,877
Non-residential	6,001	5,163,438,747
Commercial	5,057	3,639,729,267
Industrial	594	843,584,830
Apartments	350	680,124,650
Farm land	1,472	309,168,307
Farm homestead	3,129	47,615,339

Public Safety

Police

Sheriff	Jean Stanfield

Officers, 2004

Sheriff's department	72
County officers	120
Municipal police	786
Prosecutors, 2004	48

Crime, 2004

	Number	Rate
Total	9,137	20.6
Violent	849	1.9
Non-violent	8,288	18.7
Arson	77	NA
Domestic Viol.	3,570	NA

Emergency/Fire

Fire Marshal	Robert Rose

Public Library

Burlington County Library
5 Pioneer Blvd
Mount Holly, NJ 08060
609-267-9660

Director	Gail Sweet

Library statistics, 2004

	Total	per capita
Volumes	966,596	2.92
Expenditure	$8,189,049	$24.73
Library weekly hours		68
Full-time equivalent staff		101

Income Tax, 2002

Number of returns	176,169
Total taxable income	$9,407,203,000
Net charged tax	$252,863,000
Average gross income	$59,223
Average income tax	$1,435

County Finance

(sum of all municipalities in county)

Fiscal Year 2004

Total tax levy	$828,147,099
County taxes	126,432,000
County library	7,859,889
County health	0
County open space	12,819,656
Muni. budget	134,109,537
Misc. revenues	183,195,038

Fiscal Year 2005

Total tax levy	$890,649,034
County levy	162,072,479
County taxes	138,630,002
County library	8,957,239
County health	0
County open space	14,485,235
School levy	575,550,479
Muni. budget	153,026,078
Misc. revenues	192,852,131
Total aid	$65,209,049
CMPTRA	21,721,800
Muni. block grant	1,819,774
Energy tax receipts	38,956,381
Homeland security	1,855,000

Fiscal Year 2006

Total aid	$65,209,050
CMPTRA	20,358,331
Muni. block grant	1,819,774
Energy tax receipts	40,319,851
Homeland security	1,855,000

Taxes†

	2003	2004	2005
Net valuation taxable	$23,468,676,090	$24,071,970,740	$26,531,761,430
State equalized value	$31,124,384,343	$35,348,897,217	$40,667,753,763

† sum of all municipalities in county

Camden County

Demographics & Socio-Economic Characteristics
(2000 U.S. Census, except as noted)

Population
1990*	502,824
2000	508,932
2004 (estimate)*	516,282
Male	249,752
Female	266,530
Persons per sq. mi. of land	2,322.5

Race & Hispanic Origin, 2004**
White	381,205
Black/African American	103,667
Amer. Indian/Alaska Natv.	1,572
Asian	22,372
Natv Hawaiian/Pac Islander	457
Two or more races	7,009
Hispanic origin, total	56,811

Age & Nativity, 2004**
Under 5 years	34,888
18 years and over	381,074
15 to 44 years	215,781
45 to 64 years	127,002
65 years and over	62,718
85 years and over	8,719
Median Age	36.7
Native born, 2000	473,582
Foreign born, 2000	35,350

Educational Attainment, 2000
Population 25 years and over	331,765
0-8 yrs of school	5.9%
High School grad or higher	80.3%
Bachelor's degree or higher	24.0%
Graduate degree	8.4%

Income & Poverty, 1999
Per capita income	$22,354
Median household income	$48,097
Median family income	$57,429
Persons in poverty	52,121
H'holds receiving public assistance	7,165
H'holds receiving social security	50,015

Households, 2000
Total households	185,744
With persons under 18	71,459
With persons over 65	46,059
Family households	129,844
One-person households	46,556
Persons per household	2.68
Persons per family	3.23

Labor & Employment
Total civilian labor force, 2005**	270,000
Unemployment rate	4.5%

*Labor Employment for Major Industries, 2012 Projection****

Total non-farm payroll empl	231,850
Construction	4.6%
Manufacturing	6.8%
Wholesale trade	5.0%
Retail trade	12.1%
Transp & warehousing	3.2%
Information	1.6%
Finance & insurance	3.5%
Real estate	1.2%
Professional & technical	7.8%
Management	0.6%
Administration	6.8%
Education	1.8%
Health & social svcs	4.6%
Accommodations	5.7%
Government	15.2%

*US Census Bureau; **NJ Dept of Labor
***NJ Labor Planning Analysis

General Information
Camden County
520 Market St
Camden, NJ 08102
856-225-5431

Website	www.co.camden.nj.us
Land Area (sq. miles)	222.3
Water Area (sq. miles)	5.3
Class	Second
Government form	BCF
Number of Freeholders	7
Number of municipalities	37

Government & Voters

Legislative Districts
US Congressional	1, 3
State Legislative	4, 5, 6, 7

Registered Voters, November 2005
Total	304,874
Democrat	89,529
Republican	34,834
Unaffiliated	179,134

County Officials, 2006
County Executive	None
Manager/Admin	Ross Angilella
Clerk	James Beach
Finance Dir/Treas	Mark Lonetto
Tax Administrator	Sheri Garton
Surrogate	Patricia Jones
Prosecutor	James Lynch (Actg)
Planning/Develop	NA

County School District
509 Forrest Hall
Blackwood, NJ 08012
856-401-2400

Superintendent	Daniel Mastrobuono
Number of districts	40

Housing & Construction

Total Housing Units, 2000-2004
2000*	199,679
Median rent	$635
Median SF home value	$111,200
2001	200,394
2002	200,934
2003	201,867
2004 (estimate)	202,772

New Privately Owned Housing Units Authorized by Building Permit
	Units	Value
Total, 2004	1,413	$134,328,000
Single family	1,222	$122,202,504
Total, 2005	1,666	$181,923,291
Single family	1,163	146,984,532

Real Property Valuation - parcels, 2005
(sum of all municipalities in county)

	Number	Valuation
Total		$20,372,779,997
Vacant	14,236	326,745,202
Residential	153,650	15,464,923,554
Non-residential	9,157	4,533,460,645
Commercial	7,835	3,331,913,451
Industrial	690	526,262,340
Apartments	632	675,284,854
Farm land	340	40,720,720
Farm homestead	858	6,929,876

Public Safety

Police
Sheriff	Michael McLaughlin

Officers, 2004
Sheriff's department	182
County officers	320
Municipal police	1,360
Prosecutors, 2004	112

Crime, 2004	Number	Rate
Total	20,415	39.7
Violent	3,153	6.1
Non-violent	17,262	33.6
Arson	253	NA
Domestic Viol.	6,773	NA

Emergency/Fire
Fire Marshal	Paul Hartstein

Public Library
Camden County Library
203 Laurel Rd
Voorhees, NJ 08043
856-772-1636

Director	Claudia Sumler

Library statistics, 2004
	Total	per capita
Volumes	469,983	1.94
Expenditure	$7,704,771	$31.73
Library weekly hours		67
Full-time equivalent staff		90

Income Tax, 2002
Number of returns	196,166
Total taxable income	$8,809,857,000
Net charged tax	$209,969,000
Average gross income	$50,182
Average income tax	$1,070

County Finance
(sum of all municipalities in county)

Fiscal Year 2004
Total tax levy	$850,762,240
County taxes	208,571,733
County library	7,270,724
County health	0
County open space	2,567,238
Muni. budget	164,791,288
Misc. revenues	290,972,108

Fiscal Year 2005
Total tax levy	$914,067,319
County levy	228,831,150
County taxes	218,471,732
County library	7,489,127
County health	0
County open space	2,870,295
School levy	500,011,261
Muni. budget	185,224,912
Misc. revenues	312,683,690
Total aid	$124,281,544
CMPTRA	77,603,162
Muni. block grant	2,225,365
Energy tax receipts	42,388,036
Homeland security	2,025,000

Fiscal Year 2006
Total aid	$124,281,539
CMPTRA	76,119,578
Muni. block grant	2,225,365
Energy tax receipts	43,871,615
Homeland security	2,025,000

Taxes†

	2003	2004	2005
Net valuation taxable	$20,226,389,476	$20,307,603,928	$20,476,422,500
State equalized value	$25,376,120,018	$28,175,208,294	$33,115,842,531

† sum of all municipalities in county

Demographics & Socio-Economic Characteristics
(2000 U.S. Census, except as noted)

Population
1990*	95,089
2000	102,326
2004 (estimate)*	100,758
Male	48,500
Female	52,258
Persons per sq. mi. of land	394.8

Race & Hispanic Origin, 2004**
White	94,079
Black/African American	5,024
Amer. Indian/Alaska Natv.	164
Asian	727
Natv Hawaiian/Pac Islander	35
Two or more races	729
Hispanic origin, total	3,805

Age & Nativity, 2004**
Under 5 years	5,027
18 years and over	79,097
15 to 44 years	35,839
45 to 64 years	26,881
65 years and over	20,681
85 years and over	3,182
Median Age	43.3
Native born, 2000	99,038
Foreign born, 2000	3,288

Educational Attainment, 2000
Population 25 years and over	72,878
0-8 yrs of school	4.6%
High School grad or higher	81.9%
Bachelor's degree or higher	22.0%
Graduate degree	6.5%

Income & Poverty, 1999
Per capita income	$24,172
Median household income	$41,591
Median family income	$51,402
Persons in poverty	8,549
H'holds receiving public assistance	1,029
H'holds receiving social security	15,857

Households, 2000
Total households	42,148
With persons under 18	12,049
With persons over 65	14,480
Family households	27,372
One-person households	12,732
Persons per household	2.36
Persons per family	2.94

Labor & Employment
Total civilian labor force, 2005**	60,000
Unemployment rate	6.0%

*Labor Employment for Major Industries, 2012 Projection***
Total non-farm payroll empl	46,850
Construction	5.8%
Manufacturing	1.7%
Wholesale trade	1.2%
Retail trade	17.2%
Transp & warehousing	1.1%
Information	1.0%
Finance & insurance	2.6%
Real estate	2.2%
Professional & technical	3.0%
Management	0.3%
Administration	2.8%
Education	1.0%
Health & social svcs	5.8%
Accommodations	20.1%
Government	19.6%

*US Census Bureau; **NJ Dept of Labor
***NJ Labor Planning Analysis

General Information
Cape May County
4 Moore Rd
Cape May Court House, NJ 08210
609-465-1000

Website	www.capemaycountygov.net
Land Area (sq. miles)	255.2
Water Area (sq. miles)	365.1
Class	Sixth
Government form	BCF
Number of Freeholders	5
Number of municipalities	16

Government & Voters

Legislative Districts
US Congressional	2
State Legislative	1

Registered Voters, November 2005
Total	66,683
Democrat	9,332
Republican	26,256
Unaffiliated	30,698

County Officials, 2006
County Executive	None
Manager/Admin	Stephen O'Connor
Clerk	Rita Marie Fulginiti
Finance Dir/Treas	Edmund J. Grant Jr.
Tax Administrator	George R. Brown III
Surrogate	W. Robert Hentges
Prosecutor	Robert L. Taylor
Planning/Develop	NA

County School District
4 Moore Rd
Cape May Court House, NJ 08210
609-465-1283

Superintendent	Albert Monillas
Number of districts	19

Housing & Construction

Total Housing Units, 2000-2004
2000*	91,047
Median rent	$650
Median SF home value	$137,600
2001	92,289
2002	93,451
2003	94,624
2004 (estimate)	96,405

New Privately Owned Housing Units Authorized by Building Permit
	Units	Value
Total, 2004	2,149	$310,694,974
Single family	1,101	$184,173,613
Total, 2005	2,432	$416,876,803
Single family	1,124	239,337,063

Real Property Valuation - parcels, 2005
(sum of all municipalities in county)
	Number	Valuation
Total		$30,930,815,600
Vacant	12,309	1,104,991,300
Residential	77,197	26,782,351,100
Non-residential	4,396	3,014,632,500
Commercial	3,735	2,565,657,900
Industrial	25	22,809,300
Apartments	636	426,165,300
Farm land	208	24,584,800
Farm homestead	512	4,255,900

Public Safety

Police
Sheriff	John Callinan
Officers, 2004	
Sheriff's department	115
County officers	134
Municipal police	343
Prosecutors, 2004	19

Crime, 2004	Number	Rate
Total	4,925	48.4
Violent	368	3.6
Non-violent	4,557	44.7
Arson	36	NA
Domestic Viol.	1,294	NA

Emergency/Fire
Director	Frank McCall

Public Library
Cape May County Library
30 W Mechanic St
Cape May Court House, NJ 08210
609-463-6350

Director	Andrew Martin

Library statistics, 2004
	Total	per capita
Volumes	304,262	3.5
Expenditure	$4,770,753	$54.87
Library weekly hours		74
Full-time equivalent staff		50

Income Tax, 2002
Number of returns	39,648
Total taxable income	$1,608,407,000
Net charged tax	$45,319,000
Average gross income	$45,682
Average income tax	$1,143

County Finance
(sum of all municipalities in county)

Fiscal Year 2004
Total tax levy	$302,439,410
County taxes	70,971,990
County library	6,029,689
County health	0
County open space	2,854,461
Muni. budget	105,943,539
Misc. revenues	102,249,145

Fiscal Year 2005
Total tax levy	$324,428,177
County levy	82,623,375
County taxes	73,072,666
County library	6,002,216
County health	0
County open space	3,548,494
School levy	123,418,444
Muni. budget	118,386,356
Misc. revenues	101,553,783
Total aid	$22,037,154
CMPTRA	2,631,833
Muni. block grant	420,092
Energy tax receipts	18,597,382
Homeland security	480,000

Fiscal Year 2006
Total aid	$22,241,578
CMPTRA	2,185,350
Muni. block grant	420,092
Energy tax receipts	19,136,214
Homeland security	480,000

Taxes†

	2003	2004	2005
Net valuation taxable	$20,506,918,312	$27,407,693,230	$30,959,289,578
State equalized value	$27,910,886,683	$34,423,715,017	$43,138,710,236

† sum of all municipalities in county

Demographics & Socio-Economic Characteristics
(2000 U.S. Census, except as noted)

Population
1990*	138,053
2000	146,438
2004 (estimate)*	151,183
Male	77,259
Female	73,924
Persons per sq. mi. of land	309.0

Race & Hispanic Origin, 2004**
White	112,583
Black/African American	32,685
Amer. Indian/Alaska Natv.	1,547
Asian	1,674
Natv Hawaiian/Pac Islander	426
Two or more races	2,268
Hispanic origin, total	32,536

Age & Nativity, 2004**
Under 5 years	10,518
18 years and over	113,074
15 to 44 years	65,936
45 to 64 years	34,845
65 years and over	18,976
85 years and over	2,593
Median Age	35.6
Native born, 2000	137,431
Foreign born, 2000	9,007

Educational Attainment, 2000
Population 25 years and over	96,899
0-8 yrs of school	11.3%
High School grad or higher	68.5%
Bachelor's degree or higher	11.7%
Graduate degree	3.7%

Income & Poverty, 1999
Per capita income	$17,376
Median household income	$39,150
Median family income	$45,403
Persons in poverty	20,367
H'holds receiving public assistance	2,605
H'holds receiving social security	14,694

Households, 2000
Total households	49,143
With persons under 18	19,296
With persons over 65	13,463
Family households	35,185
One-person households	11,604
Persons per household	2.73
Persons per family	3.19

Labor & Employment
Total civilian labor force, 2005**	69,900
Unemployment rate	6.0%

*Labor Employment for Major Industries, 2012 Projection****

Total non-farm payroll empl	64,900
Construction	4.1%
Manufacturing	13.1%
Wholesale trade	3.8%
Retail trade	14.5%
Transp & warehousing	3.8%
Information	1.5%
Finance & insurance	3.1%
Real estate	0.8%
Professional & technical	2.2%
Management	0.6%
Administration	2.7%
Education	1.6%
Health & social svcs	4.1%
Accommodations	4.7%
Government	23.3%

*US Census Bureau; **NJ Dept of Labor
***NJ Labor Planning Analysis

General Information
Cumberland County
Administration Bldg
790 E Commerce St
Bridgeton, NJ 08302
856-453-2138
Website	www.co.cumberland.nj.us
Land Area (sq. miles)	489.3
Water Area (sq. miles)	187.3
Class	Third
Government form	BCF
Number of Freeholders	7
Number of municipalities	14

Government & Voters

Legislative Districts
US Congressional	2
State Legislative	1, 3

Registered Voters, November 2005
Total	81,783
Democrat	16,135
Republican	13,401
Unaffiliated	51,985

County Officials, 2006
County Executive	None
Manager/Admin	David W. Gray
Clerk	Gloria Noto
Finance Dir/Treas	Gary Simmerman
Tax Administrator	Patricia A. Belmont
Surrogate	Arthur J. Marchand
Prosecutor	Ronald Casella
Planning/Develop	NA

County School District
19 Landis Ave
Bridgeton, NJ 08302
856-451-0211
Superintendent	D. Mastrobuono (Actg)
Number of districts	16

Housing & Construction

Total Housing Units, 2000-2004
2000*	52,863
Median rent	$616
Median SF home value	$91,200
2001	53,150
2002	53,398
2003	53,692
2004 (estimate)	53,736

New Privately Owned Housing Units Authorized by Building Permit
	Units	Value
Total, 2004	566	$54,640,550
Single family	564	$54,632,949
Total, 2005	591	$64,432,382
Single family	575	62,596,781

Real Property Valuation - parcels, 2005
(sum of all municipalities in county)
	Number	Valuation
Total		$5,106,215,405
Vacant	11,988	160,880,175
Residential	39,302	3,591,384,100
Non-residential	3,092	1,136,354,930
Commercial	2,655	748,367,430
Industrial	263	262,207,000
Apartments	174	125,780,500
Farm land	1,542	181,429,700
Farm homestead	3,059	36,166,500

Public Safety

Police
Sheriff	Michael Barruzza

Officers, 2004
Sheriff's department	51
County officers	70
Municipal police	291
Prosecutors, 2004	19

Crime, 2004	Number	Rate
Total	7,519	50.4
Violent	1,167	7.8
Non-violent	6,352	42.5
Arson	49	NA
Domestic Viol.	3,464	NA

Emergency/Fire
Fire Marshal	Robert Hoffman Jr.

Public Library
Cumberland County Library
800 E Commerce St
Bridgeton, NJ 08302
856-453-2210
Director	Nancy Forester

Library statistics, 2004
	Total	per capita
Volumes	117,406	1.74
Expenditure	$1,136,523	$16.86
Library weekly hours		60
Full-time equivalent staff		11

Income Tax, 2002
Number of returns	52,676
Total taxable income	$1,774,594,000
Net charged tax	$41,330,000
Average gross income	$37,951
Average income tax	$785

County Finance
(sum of all municipalities in county)

Fiscal Year 2004
Total tax levy	$143,545,979
County taxes	50,045,000
County library	0
County health	1,285,000
County open space	547,544
Muni. budget	36,064,168
Misc. revenues	66,795,144

Fiscal Year 2005
Total tax levy	$162,477,947
County levy	60,927,533
County taxes	58,950,001
County library	0
County health	1,378,000
County open space	599,534
School levy	58,862,886
Muni. budget	42,687,528
Misc. revenues	71,829,499
Total aid	$24,946,881
CMPTRA	13,108,296
Muni. block grant	610,809
Energy tax receipts	10,902,783
Homeland security	320,000

Fiscal Year 2006
Total aid	$24,946,884
CMPTRA	12,726,700
Muni. block grant	610,809
Energy tax receipts	11,284,382
Homeland security	320,000

Taxes†

	2003	2004	2005
Net valuation taxable	$4,234,599,515	$4,398,496,715	$5,137,949,473
State equalized value	$5,261,748,424	$5,753,815,196	$6,673,320,616

† sum of all municipalities in county

Demographics & Socio-Economic Characteristics
(2000 U.S. Census, except as noted)

Population
1990*	778,206
2000	793,633
2000 (revised)	792,305
2004 (estimate)*	796,684
Male	380,794
Female	415,890
Persons per sq. mi. of land	6,309.5

Race & Hispanic Origin, 2004**
White	408,160
Black/African American	341,004
Amer. Indian/Alaska Natv.	2,515
Asian	33,683
Natv Hawaiian/Pac Islander	1,038
Two or more races	10,284
Hispanic origin, total	136,445

Age & Nativity, 2004**
Under 5 years	61,215
18 years and over	584,006
15 to 44 years	338,711
45 to 64 years	187,437
65 years and over	91,954
85 years and over	13,604
Median Age	35.5
Native born, 2000	625,468
Foreign born, 2000	168,165

Educational Attainment, 2000
Population 25 years and over	513,570
0-8 yrs of school	9.3%
High School grad or higher	75.6%
Bachelor's degree or higher	27.5%
Graduate degree	10.9%

Income & Poverty, 1999
Per capita income	$24,943
Median household income	$44,944
Median family income	$54,818
Persons in poverty	120,006
H'holds receiving public assistance	18,478
H'holds receiving social security	71,485

Households, 2000
Total households	283,736
With persons under 18	110,244
With persons over 65	68,588
Family households	193,498
One-person households	75,839
Persons per household	2.72
Persons per family	3.3

Labor & Employment
Total civilian labor force, 2005**	367,400
Unemployment rate	5.4%

*Labor Employment for Major Industries, 2012 Projection****

Total non-farm payroll empl	414,250
Construction	3.1%
Manufacturing	5.7%
Wholesale trade	4.3%
Retail trade	7.7%
Transp & warehousing	8.3%
Information	2.4%
Finance & insurance	6.7%
Real estate	1.7%
Professional & technical	6.1%
Management	1.5%
Administration	6.9%
Education	2.9%
Health & social svcs	3.1%
Accommodations	4.3%
Government	17.9%

*US Census Bureau; **NJ Dept of Labor
***NJ Labor Planning Analysis

General Information
Essex County
Hall of Records
PO Box 690
Newark, NJ 07101
973-621-4921

Website	www.co.essex.nj.us
Land Area (sq. miles)	126.3
Water Area (sq. miles)	3.3
Class	First
Government form	CEP (OCCL 1972)
Number of Freeholders	9
Number of municipalities	22

Government & Voters

Legislative Districts
US Congressional	8, 10, 11, 13
State Legislative	21, 27, 28, 29, 34, 36, 40

Registered Voters, November 2005
Total	403,279
Democrat	148,486
Republican	41,830
Unaffiliated	212,658

County Officials, 2006
County Executive	J. DeVincenzo Jr.
Manager/Admin	Joyce Wilson Harley
Clerk	Christopher Durkin
Finance Dir/Treas	Paul Hopkins II
Tax Administrator	Joan Codey Durkin
Surrogate	Joseph Brennan
Prosecutor	Paula Dow
Planning/Develop	NA

County School District
155 Fairview Ave
Cedar Grove, NJ 07009
973-857-5700

Superintendent	Anthony Marino
Number of districts	22

Housing & Construction

Total Housing Units, 2000-2004
2000*	301,011
Median rent	$675
Median SF home value	$208,400
2001	302,151
2002	303,119
2003	304,123
2004 (estimate)	304,878

New Privately Owned Housing Units Authorized by Building Permit
	Units	Value
Total, 2004	2,343	$206,455,512
Single family	436	$82,257,090
Total, 2005	3,117	$333,598,761
Single family	713	169,029,239

Real Property Valuation - parcels, 2005
(sum of all municipalities in county)

	Number	Valuation
Total		$34,929,744,031
Vacant	8,726	623,494,200
Residential	148,920	23,569,209,631
Non-residential	16,914	10,735,746,400
Commercial	12,195	7,235,264,500
Industrial	2,035	2,088,980,500
Apartments	2,684	1,411,501,400
Farm land	7	1,106,600
Farm homestead	23	187,200

Public Safety

Police
Sheriff	Armando Fontoura
Officers, 2004	
Sheriff's department	520
County officers	800
Municipal police	2,833
Prosecutors, 2004	255

Crime, 2004	Number	Rate
Total	39,067	49.1
Violent	6,779	8.5
Non-violent	32,288	40.5
Arson	270	NA
Domestic Viol.	4,367	NA

Emergency/Fire
Director	NA

Public Library
No County Library
(Library statistics are the sum of all municipal libraries in the county)

Library statistics, 2004
	Total	per capita
Volumes	3,938,581	5.02
Expenditure	$43,485,241	$55.46
Library weekly hours		58.8
Full-time equivalent staff		581

Income Tax, 2002
Number of returns	299,712
Total taxable income	$16,315,514,000
Net charged tax	$429,700,000
Average gross income	$60,010
Average income tax	$1,434

County Finance
(sum of all municipalities in county)

Fiscal Year 2004
Total tax levy	$1,550,144,336
County taxes	311,643,294
County library	0
County health	0
County open space	6,086,808
Muni. budget	499,585,780
Misc. revenues	764,339,920

Fiscal Year 2005
Total tax levy	$1,621,658,734
County levy	326,192,215
County taxes	319,343,292
County library	0
County health	0
County open space	6,848,921
School levy	770,517,775
Muni. budget	524,948,747
Misc. revenues	708,827,896
Total aid	$216,293,374
CMPTRA	150,934,411
Muni. block grant	3,409,218
Energy tax receipts	59,885,395
Homeland security	2,015,000

Fiscal Year 2006
Total aid	$216,293,375
CMPTRA	148,888,121
Muni. block grant	3,409,218
Energy tax receipts	61,981,383
Homeland security	2,015,000

Taxes†

	2003	2004	2005
Net valuation taxable	$33,130,098,983	$33,977,666,249	$35,083,477,855
State equalized value	$59,713,593,631	$67,054,964,079	$76,819,824,317

† sum of all municipalities in county

Demographics & Socio-Economic Characteristics

(2000 U.S. Census, except as noted)

Population

1990*	230,082
2000	254,673
2004 (estimate)*	271,806
Male	131,844
Female	139,962
Persons per sq. mi. of land	837.1

Race & Hispanic Origin, 2004**

White	236,647
Black/African American	26,715
Amer. Indian/Alaska Natv.	507
Asian	5,092
Natv Hawaiian/Pac Islander	75
Two or more races	2,770
Hispanic origin, total	8,077

Age & Nativity, 2004**

Under 5 years	15,950
18 years and over	204,722
15 to 44 years	117,277
45 to 64 years	68,600
65 years and over	31,307
85 years and over	3,660
Median Age	37.1
Native born, 2000	246,107
Foreign born, 2000	8,566

Educational Attainment, 2000

Population 25 years and over	164,801
0-8 yrs of school	3.9%
High School grad or higher	84.3%
Bachelor's degree or higher	22.0%
Graduate degree	6.4%

Income & Poverty, 1999

Per capita income	$22,708
Median household income	$54,273
Median family income	$62,482
Persons in poverty	15,395
H'holds receiving public assistance	1,340
H'holds receiving social security	23,822

Households, 2000

Total households	90,717
With persons under 18	36,196
With persons over 65	21,150
Family households	67,197
One-person households	19,242
Persons per household	2.75
Persons per family	3.22

Labor & Employment

Total civilian labor force, 2005**	148,000
Unemployment rate	4.1%

*Labor Employment for Major Industries, 2012 Projection****

Total non-farm payroll empl	113,600
Construction	6.6%
Manufacturing	8.5%
Wholesale trade	9.6%
Retail trade	16.1%
Transp & warehousing	2.0%
Information	1.1%
Finance & insurance	2.2%
Real estate	1.0%
Professional & technical	4.4%
Management	0.1%
Administration	6.8%
Education	0.9%
Health & social svcs	6.6%
Accommodations	7.0%
Government	16.4%

*US Census Bureau; **NJ Dept of Labor
***NJ Labor Planning Analysis

General Information

Gloucester County
PO Box 337
Woodbury, NJ 08096
856-853-3237

Website	www.co.gloucester.nj.us
Land Area (sq. miles)	324.7
Water Area (sq. miles)	12.2
Class	Third
Government form	BCF
Number of Freeholders	7
Number of municipalities	24

Government & Voters

Legislative Districts

US Congressional	1, 2
State Legislative	3, 4, 5

Registered Voters, November 2005

Total	170,790
Democrat	47,704
Republican	28,232
Unaffiliated	93,500

County Officials, 2006

County Executive	None
Manager/Admin	John Fisher III
Clerk	James Hogan
Finance Dir/Treas	Jean DuBois
Tax Administrator	Edward J. Burek
Surrogate	Stephen Salvatore
Prosecutor	Sean Dalton
Planning/Develop	NA

County School District

1492 Tanyard Rd
Sewell, NJ 08080
856-468-6500

Superintendent	H. Mark Stanwood
Number of districts	29

Housing & Construction

Total Housing Units, 2000-2004

2000*	95,054
Median rent	$645
Median SF home value	$120,100
2001	96,631
2002	98,198
2003	99,922
2004 (estimate)	101,285

New Privately Owned Housing Units Authorized by Building Permit

	Units	Value
Total, 2004	2,050	$205,150,706
Single family	1,638	$183,575,400
Total, 2005	2,100	$236,941,123
Single family	1,883	226,814,009

Real Property Valuation - parcels, 2005

(sum of all municipalities in county)

	Number	Valuation
Total		$13,823,547,338
Vacant	12,288	367,018,302
Residential	84,935	9,963,845,400
Non-residential	4,260	3,282,492,936
Commercial	3,886	2,259,998,820
Industrial	182	792,593,716
Apartments	192	229,900,400
Farm land	1,338	175,798,700
Farm homestead	3,170	34,392,000

Public Safety

Police

Sheriff	Gilbert Miller III

Officers, 2004

Sheriff's department	66
County officers	122
Municipal police	583
Prosecutors, 2004	56

Crime, 2004	Number	Rate
Total	8,132	30.5
Violent	649	2.4
Non-violent	7,483	28
Arson	53	NA
Domestic Viol.	3,227	NA

Emergency/Fire

Fire Marshal	William Reiger

Public Library

Gloucester County Library
389 Wolfert Station Rd
Mullica Hill, NJ 08062
856-223-6000

Director	Robert Wetherall

Library statistics, 2004

	Total	per capita
Volumes	182,400	2.16
Expenditure	$3,148,212	$37.31
Library weekly hours		66
Full-time equivalent staff		29

Income Tax, 2002

Number of returns	104,041
Total taxable income	$4,805,060,000
Net charged tax	$105,126,000
Average gross income	$51,554
Average income tax	$1,010

County Finance

(sum of all municipalities in county)

Fiscal Year 2004

Total tax levy	$486,709,538
County taxes	100,700,000
County library	2,664,023
County health	0
County open space	3,356,358
Muni. budget	102,967,773
Misc. revenues	111,345,702

Fiscal Year 2005

Total tax levy	$530,962,199
County levy	123,431,530
County taxes	112,900,000
County library	3,017,415
County health	0
County open space	7,514,118
School levy	293,443,256
Muni. budget	114,087,413
Misc. revenues	123,938,554
Total aid	$36,166,008
CMPTRA	13,710,971
Muni. block grant	1,048,607
Energy tax receipts	20,015,138
Homeland security	1,145,000

Fiscal Year 2006

Total aid	$36,281,003
CMPTRA	13,010,439
Muni. block grant	1,048,607
Energy tax receipts	20,715,665
Homeland security	1,310,000

Taxes†

	2003	2004	2005
Net valuation taxable	$13,271,095,721	$13,641,295,755	$13,964,405,380
State equalized value	$16,262,089,515	$18,242,255,166	$21,382,135,336

† sum of all municipalities in county

Demographics & Socio-Economic Characteristics
(2000 U.S. Census, except as noted)

Population
1990*	553,099
2000	608,975
2004 (estimate)*	606,240
Male	298,789
Female	307,451
Persons per sq. mi. of land	12,985.0

Race & Hispanic Origin, 2004**
White	432,682
Black/African American	91,935
Amer. Indian/Alaska Natv.	3,770
Asian	65,006
Natv Hawaiian/Pac Islander	776
Two or more races	12,071
Hispanic origin, total	249,844

Age & Nativity, 2004**
Under 5 years	42,938
18 years and over	465,476
15 to 44 years	287,904
45 to 64 years	132,575
65 years and over	67,100
85 years and over	9,689
Median Age	35.0
Native born, 2000	374,378
Foreign born, 2000	234,597

Educational Attainment, 2000
Population 25 years and over	408,799
0-8 yrs of school	13.5%
High School grad or higher	70.5%
Bachelor's degree or higher	25.3%
Graduate degree	8.9%

Income & Poverty, 1999
Per capita income	$21,154
Median household income	$40,293
Median family income	$44,053
Persons in poverty	93,149
H'holds receiving public assistance	11,179
H'holds receiving social security	53,146

Households, 2000
Total households	230,546
With persons under 18	76,670
With persons over 65	52,809
Family households	143,532
One-person households	68,078
Persons per household	2.6
Persons per family	3.27

Labor & Employment
Total civilian labor force, 2005**	292,400
Unemployment rate	5.2%

*Labor Employment for Major Industries, 2012 Projection****

Total non-farm payroll empl.	281,100
Construction	2.7%
Manufacturing	4.7%
Wholesale trade	5.8%
Retail trade	9.5%
Transp & warehousing	10.3%
Information	3.1%
Finance & insurance	14.2%
Real estate	1.5%
Professional & technical	4.8%
Management	1.0%
Administration	8.1%
Education	2.3%
Health & social svcs	2.7%
Accommodations	4.3%
Government	13.8%

*US Census Bureau; **NJ Dept of Labor
***NJ Labor Planning Analysis

General Information
Hudson County
Administration Annex
567 Pavonia Ave
Jersey City, NJ 07306
201-795-6000

Website	www.hudsoncountynj.org
Land Area (sq. miles)	46.7
Water Area (sq. miles)	15.7
Class	First
Government form	CEP (OCCL-1972)
Number of Freeholders	9
Number of municipalities	12

Government & Voters

Legislative Districts
US Congressional	9, 10, 13
State Legislative	31, 32, 33

Registered Voters, November 2005
Total	309,738
Democrat	134,486
Republican	24,660
Unaffiliated	149,549

County Officials, 2006
County Executive	Thomas DeGise
Manager/Admin	Abraham Antun
Clerk	Javier E. Inclan
Finance Dir/Treas	Wade Frazee
Tax Administrator	Donald Kenny
Surrogate	Donald DeLeo
Prosecutor	Edward DeFazio
Planning/Develop	Stephen Marks

County School District
595 County Ave
Secaucus, NJ 07094
201-319-3850

Superintendent	Robert Osak
Number of districts	13

Housing & Construction

Total Housing Units, 2000-2004
2000*	240,618
Median rent	$703
Median SF home value	$150,300
2001	241,539
2002	242,058
2003	242,985
2004 (estimate)	244,332

New Privately Owned Housing Units Authorized by Building Permit
	Units	Value
Total, 2004	3,808	$266,557,070
Single family	386	$32,691,173
Total, 2005	4,699	$472,203,197
Single family	367	35,741,530

Real Property Valuation - parcels, 2005
(sum of all municipalities in county)
	Number	Valuation
Total		$20,636,516,611
Vacant	7,648	799,550,820
Residential	90,298	10,794,542,730
Non-residential	15,722	9,042,423,061
Commercial	9,558	4,627,914,731
Industrial	1,990	2,679,972,630
Apartments	4,174	1,734,535,700
Farm land	0	0
Farm homestead	0	0

Public Safety

Police
Sheriff	Joseph Cassidy
Officers, 2004	
Sheriff's department	196
County officers	296
Municipal police	1,940
Prosecutors, 2004	100

Crime, 2004	Number	Rate
Total	21,357	35.2
Violent	4,095	6.7
Non-violent	17,262	28.4
Arson	71	NA
Domestic Viol.	5,298	NA

Emergency/Fire
Emerg Mgmt	Frank Pizzuta

Public Library
No County Library
(Library statistics are the sum of all municipal libraries in the county)

Library statistics, 2004	Total	per capita
Volumes	1,314,351	2.21
Expenditure	$15,954,254	$26.78
Library weekly hours	60	
Full-time equivalent staff	216	

Income Tax, 2002
Number of returns	245,912
Total taxable income	$9,045,047,000
Net charged tax	$153,294,000
Average gross income	$40,491
Average income tax	$623

County Finance
(sum of all municipalities in county)

Fiscal Year 2004
Total tax levy	$852,623,966
County taxes	206,850,478
County library	0
County health	0
County open space	3,496,943
Muni. budget	333,532,740
Misc. revenues	529,031,504

Fiscal Year 2005
Total tax levy	$892,368,169
County levy	217,180,282
County taxes	213,055,993
County library	0
County health	0
County open space	4,124,292
School levy	323,670,126
Muni. budget	351,517,763
Misc. revenues	551,414,615
Total aid	$184,906,614
CMPTRA	112,419,974
Muni. block grant	2,476,481
Energy tax receipts	68,724,454
Homeland security	1,285,000

Fiscal Year 2006
Total aid	$184,906,613
CMPTRA	110,014,618
Muni. block grant	2,476,481
Energy tax receipts	71,129,809
Homeland security	1,285,000

Taxes†
	2003	2004	2005
Net valuation taxable	$19,953,608,073	$20,284,583,440	$20,699,232,068
State equalized value	$33,716,604,663	$39,560,229,241	$48,159,722,307

† sum of all municipalities in county

Demographics & Socio-Economic Characteristics
(2000 U.S. Census, except as noted)

Population
1990*	107,776
2000	121,989
2004 (estimate)*	129,746
Male	64,202
Female	65,544
Persons per sq. mi. of land	301.8

Race & Hispanic Origin, 2004**
White	121,758
Black/African American	3,569
Amer. Indian/Alaska Natv.	213
Asian	3,457
Natv Hawaiian/Pac Islander	6
Two or more races	743
Hispanic origin, total	4,348

Age & Nativity, 2004**
Under 5 years	7,639
18 years and over	97,896
15 to 44 years	50,269
45 to 64 years	39,241
65 years and over	14,183
85 years and over	1,698
Median Age	40.4
Native born, 2000	114,281
Foreign born, 2000	7,708

Educational Attainment, 2000
Population 25 years and over	83,548
0-8 yrs of school	2.8%
High School grad or higher	91.5%
Bachelor's degree or higher	41.8%
Graduate degree	16.3%

Income & Poverty, 1999
Per capita income	$36,370
Median household income	$79,888
Median family income	$91,050
Persons in poverty	3,027
H'holds receiving public assistance	518
H'holds receiving social security	9,101

Households, 2000
Total households	43,678
With persons under 18	16,819
With persons over 65	8,535
Family households	32,837
One-person households	8,722
Persons per household	2.69
Persons per family	3.14

Labor & Employment
Total civilian labor force, 2005**	70,800
Unemployment rate	2.9%

*Labor Employment for Major Industries, 2012 Projection****

Total non-farm payroll empl	59,200
Construction	7.9%
Manufacturing	5.4%
Wholesale trade	3.6%
Retail trade	13.3%
Transp & warehousing	1.4%
Information	1.7%
Finance & insurance	3.8%
Real estate	0.8%
Professional & technical	11.7%
Management	NA
Administration	4.7%
Education	NA
Health & social svcs	7.9%
Accommodations	4.9%
Government	17.1%

*US Census Bureau; **NJ Dept of Labor
***NJ Labor Planning Analysis

General Information
Hunterdon County
PO Box 2900
71 Main St
Flemington, NJ 08822
908-788-1102

Website	www.co.hunterdon.nj.us
Land Area (sq. miles)	429.9
Water Area (sq. miles)	7.8
Class	Third
Government form	BCF
Number of Freeholders	3
Number of municipalities	26

Government & Voters

Legislative Districts
US Congressional	7, 12
State Legislative	23, 24

Registered Voters, November 2005
Total	77,956
Democrat	9,462
Republican	27,434
Unaffiliated	40,628

County Officials, 2006
County Executive	None
Manager/Admin	Cynthia Yard
Clerk	Dorothy Tirpok
Finance Dir/Treas	Charles Balogh
Tax Administrator	Athan Efstathiou
Surrogate	Susan Hoffman
Prosecutor	J. Patrick Barnes
Planning/Develop	NA

County School District
10 Court St
Flemington, NJ 08822
908-788-1414
Superintendent	Frank Dragotta (Int)
Number of districts	30

Housing & Construction

Total Housing Units, 2000-2004
2000*	45,032
Median rent	$867
Median SF home value	$245,000
2001	45,717
2002	46,333
2003	46,866
2004 (estimate)	47,527

New Privately Owned Housing Units Authorized by Building Permit
	Units	Value
Total, 2004	648	$116,222,318
Single family	627	$114,444,618
Total, 2005	513	$99,679,719
Single family	443	96,195,719

Real Property Valuation - parcels, 2005
(sum of all municipalities in county)
	Number	Valuation
Total		$17,248,543,610
Vacant	4,203	359,202,152
Residential	40,542	13,087,698,900
Non-residential	2,306	2,359,846,133
Commercial	2,031	1,873,126,823
Industrial	155	370,149,710
Apartments	120	116,569,600
Farm land	3,190	1,388,040,250
Farm homestead	5,333	53,756,175

Public Safety

Police
Sheriff	William Doyle

Officers, 2004
Sheriff's department	25
County officers	46
Municipal police	182
Prosecutors, 2004	21

Crime, 2004	Number	Rate
Total	1,293	10.1
Violent	64	0.5
Non-violent	1,229	9.6
Arson	4	NA
Domestic Viol.	531	NA

Emergency/Fire
Fire Marshal	Allen Layton

Public Library
Hunterdon County Library
314 State Route 12
Flemington, NJ 08822
908-788-1444
Director	Janet Friend

Library statistics, 2004
	Total	per capita
Volumes	413,058	3.66
Expenditure	$5,028,268	$44.61
Library weekly hours		75
Full-time equivalent staff		33

Income Tax, 2002
Number of returns	50,067
Total taxable income	$4,095,142,000
Net charged tax	$143,701,000
Average gross income	$89,868
Average income tax	$2,870

County Finance
(sum of all municipalities in county)

Fiscal Year 2004
Total tax levy	$375,846,551
County taxes	65,037,000
County library	4,738,268
County health	0
County open space	5,599,000
Muni. budget	37,993,040
Misc. revenues	62,146,740

Fiscal Year 2005
Total tax levy	$401,392,965
County levy	78,691,766
County taxes	67,086,001
County library	5,290,766
County health	0
County open space	6,315,000
School levy	276,426,175
Muni. budget	46,275,022
Misc. revenues	62,951,097
Total aid	$21,188,918
CMPTRA	6,271,930
Muni. block grant	496,260
Energy tax receipts	13,944,108
Homeland security	555,000

Fiscal Year 2006
Total aid	$21,201,342
CMPTRA	5,796,311
Muni. block grant	496,260
Energy tax receipts	14,432,151
Homeland security	455,000

Taxes†
	2003	2004	2005
Net valuation taxable	$15,037,748,905	$15,981,607,720	$17,298,026,128
State equalized value	$16,952,327,609	$18,808,542,834	$21,163,094,853

† sum of all municipalities in county

Demographics & Socio-Economic Characteristics
(2000 U.S. Census, except as noted)

Population
1990*	325,824
2000	350,761
2004 (estimate)*	365,271
Male	178,565
Female	186,706
Persons per sq. mi. of land	1,616.8

Race & Hispanic Origin, 2004**
White	258,000
Black/African American	75,246
Amer. Indian/Alaska Natv.	920
Asian	25,905
Natv Hawaiian/Pac Islander	622
Two or more races	4,578
Hispanic origin, total	41,501

Age & Nativity, 2004**
Under 5 years	23,462
18 years and over	277,561
15 to 44 years	158,977
45 to 64 years	89,411
65 years and over	44,231
85 years and over	6,585
Median Age	36.5
Native born, 2000	302,102
Foreign born, 2000	48,659

Educational Attainment, 2000
Population 25 years and over	231,139
0-8 yrs of school	5.9%
High School grad or higher	81.8%
Bachelor's degree or higher	34.0%
Graduate degree	15.5%

Income & Poverty, 1999
Per capita income	$27,914
Median household income	$56,613
Median family income	$68,494
Persons in poverty	28,570
H'holds receiving public assistance	3,453
H'holds receiving social security	32,324

Households, 2000
Total households	125,807
With persons under 18	45,528
With persons over 65	31,729
Family households	86,288
One-person households	32,246
Persons per household	2.62
Persons per family	3.16

Labor & Employment
Total civilian labor force, 2005**	194,200
Unemployment rate	3.7%

Labor Employment for Major Industries, 2012 Projection***
Total non-farm payroll empl	255,650
Construction	2.4%
Manufacturing	3.1%
Wholesale trade	2.9%
Retail trade	9.2%
Transp & warehousing	1.9%
Information	3.0%
Finance & insurance	5.9%
Real estate	1.1%
Professional & technical	8.2%
Management	1.1%
Administration	5.3%
Education	9.8%
Health & social svcs	2.4%
Accommodations	4.9%
Government	26.5%

*US Census Bureau; **NJ Dept of Labor
***NJ Labor Planning Analysis

General Information
Mercer County
PO Box 8068
640 S Broad St
Trenton, NJ 08650
609-989-6518

Website	www.mercercounty.org
Land Area (sq. miles)	225.9
Water Area (sq. miles)	2.9
Class	Second
Government form	CEP (OCCL-1972)
Number of Freeholders	7
Number of municipalities	13

Government & Voters

Legislative Districts
US Congressional	4, 12
State Legislative	12, 14, 15, 30

Registered Voters, November 2005
Total	200,615
Democrat	51,579
Republican	26,644
Unaffiliated	120,958

County Officials, 2006
County Executive	Brian Hughes
Manager/Admin	Andrew A. Mair
Clerk	Paula Sollamie-Covello
Finance Dir/Treas	David Miller
Tax Administrator	Martin Guhl
Surrogate	Diane Gerofsky
Prosecutor	Joseph Bacchini
Planning/Develop	NA

County School District
1075 Old Trenton Rd
Trenton, NJ 08960
609-588-5877
Superintendent	Carol Perry
Number of districts	11

Housing & Construction

Total Housing Units, 2000-2004
2000*	133,280
Median rent	$727
Median SF home value	$147,400
2001	134,624
2002	135,770
2003	136,986
2004 (estimate)	137,573

New Privately Owned Housing Units
Authorized by Building Permit
	Units	Value
Total, 2004	1,641	$148,611,147
Single family	938	$108,191,532
Total, 2005	1,321	$143,746,985
Single family	1,220	130,745,600

Real Property Valuation - parcels, 2005
(sum of all municipalities in county)
	Number	Valuation
Total		$22,550,116,549
Vacant	7,664	445,825,609
Residential	103,436	16,063,620,160
Non-residential	6,475	5,818,406,532
Commercial	5,821	4,512,900,298
Industrial	297	673,464,800
Apartments	357	632,041,434
Farm land	603	207,591,800
Farm homestead	1,243	14,672,448

Public Safety

Police
Sheriff	Kevin Larkin
Officers, 2004	
Sheriff's department	95
County officers	195
Municipal police	929
Prosecutors, 2004	100

Crime, 2004	Number	Rate
Total	11,501	31.8
Violent	1,785	4.9
Non-violent	9,716	26.8
Arson	50	NA
Domestic Viol.	3,551	NA

Emergency/Fire
Fire Marshal	George Lenhardt

Public Library
Mercer County Library
2751 Brunswick Pke
Lawrenceville, NJ 08648
609-989-6807
Director	Ellen Brown

Library statistics, 2004
	Total	per capita
Volumes	679,441	4.74
Expenditure	$9,843,105	$68.69
Library weekly hours	66	
Full-time equivalent staff	108	

Income Tax, 2002
Number of returns	137,217
Total taxable income	$8,556,801,000
Net charged tax	$261,565,000
Average gross income	$68,352
Average income tax	$1,906

County Finance
(sum of all municipalities in county)

Fiscal Year 2004
Total tax levy	$783,567,290
County taxes	169,622,003
County library	9,167,350
County health	0
County open space	6,212,463
Muni. budget	164,504,556
Misc. revenues	271,726,650

Fiscal Year 2005
Total tax levy	$840,053,076
County levy	204,705,923
County taxes	185,297,504
County library	8,995,386
County health	0
County open space	10,413,033
School levy	457,242,382
Muni. budget	178,104,773
Misc. revenues	277,078,988
Total aid	$113,961,546
CMPTRA	71,967,452
Muni. block grant	1,478,472
Energy tax receipts	39,394,917
Homeland security	1,120,000

Fiscal Year 2006
Total aid	$113,961,546
CMPTRA	70,588,628
Muni. block grant	1,478,472
Energy tax receipts	40,773,741
Homeland security	1,120,000

Taxes†

	2003	2004	2005
Net valuation taxable	$21,984,112,989	$22,361,669,631	$22,632,242,082
State equalized value	$30,344,187,402	$34,068,413,088	$38,497,371,705

† sum of all municipalities in county

Demographics & Socio-Economic Characteristics
(2000 U.S. Census, except as noted)

Population
1990*	671,780
2000	750,162
2004 (estimate)*	785,095
Male	386,901
Female	398,194
Persons per sq. mi. of land	2,534.9

Race & Hispanic Origin, 2004**
White	552,669
Black/African American	81,195
Amer. Indian/Alaska Natv.	2,506
Asian	137,066
Natv Hawaiian/Pac Islander	373
Two or more races	11,286
Hispanic origin, total	124,126

Age & Nativity, 2004**
Under 5 years	53,430
18 years and over	596,820
15 to 44 years	348,018
45 to 64 years	185,836
65 years and over	93,552
85 years and over	12,453
Median Age	36.4
Native born, 2000	568,401
Foreign born, 2000	181,761

Educational Attainment, 2000
Population 25 years and over	501,552
0-8 yrs of school	6.2%
High School grad or higher	84.4%
Bachelor's degree or higher	33.0%
Graduate degree	12.5%

Income & Poverty, 1999
Per capita income	$26,535
Median household income	$61,446
Median family income	$70,749
Persons in poverty	48,205
H'holds receiving public assistance	5,047
H'holds receiving social security	67,122

Households, 2000
Total households	265,815
With persons under 18	98,362
With persons over 65	66,229
Family households	190,930
One-person households	59,544
Persons per household	2.74
Persons per family	3.23

Labor & Employment
Total civilian labor force, 2005**	421,300
Unemployment rate	3.9%

*Labor Employment for Major Industries, 2012 Projection*** *
Total non-farm payroll empl	477,100
Construction	3.4%
Manufacturing	9.8%
Wholesale trade	8.0%
Retail trade	10.2%
Transp & warehousing	4.9%
Information	3.1%
Finance & insurance	5.3%
Real estate	1.0%
Professional & technical	10.0%
Management	1.4%
Administration	12.1%
Education	1.0%
Health & social svcs	3.4%
Accommodations	4.1%
Government	12.3%

*US Census Bureau; **NJ Dept of Labor
***NJ Labor Planning Analysis

General Information
Middlesex County
75 Bayard St
New Brunswick, NJ 08901
732-745-3000

Website	www.co.middlesex.nj.us
Land Area (sq. miles)	309.7
Water Area (sq. miles)	12.8
Class	Second
Government form	BCF
Number of Freeholders	7
Number of municipalities	25

Government & Voters

Legislative Districts
US Congressional	6, 7, 12, 13
State Legislative	13, 14, 17, 18, 19, 22

Registered Voters, November 2005
Total	393,101
Democrat	111,884
Republican	43,683
Unaffiliated	235,707

County Officials, 2006
County Executive	None
Manager/Admin	Walter DeAngelo
Clerk	Elaine Flynn
Finance Dir/Treas	James Phillips
Tax Administrator	Irving Verosloff
Surrogate	Kevin J. Hoagland
Prosecutor	Bruce Kaplan
Planning/Develop	NA

County School District
1501 Livingston Ave
N Brunswick, NJ 08902
732-249-2900
Superintendent	Patrick Piegari
Number of districts	25

Housing & Construction

Total Housing Units, 2000-2004
2000*	273,637
Median rent	$845
Median SF home value	$168,500
2001	276,436
2002	278,121
2003	279,914
2004 (estimate)	280,757

New Privately Owned Housing Units
Authorized by Building Permit

	Units	Value
Total, 2004	2,622	$316,330,730
Single family	1,899	$249,445,689
Total, 2005	3,215	$343,131,087
Single family	1,747	246,624,593

Real Property Valuation - parcels, 2005
(sum of all municipalities in county)

	Number	Valuation
Total		$43,721,453,142
Vacant	15,339	1,147,502,967
Residential	202,058	28,406,768,400
Non-residential	10,994	14,057,187,375
Commercial	8,013	6,394,492,800
Industrial	2,128	5,493,593,975
Apartments	853	2,169,100,600
Farm land	430	92,001,100
Farm homestead	1,080	17,993,300

Public Safety

Police
Sheriff	Joseph C. Spicuzzo
Officers, 2004	
Sheriff's department	194
County officers	328
Municipal police	1,602
Prosecutors, 2004	134

Crime, 2004	Number	Rate
Total	17,620	22.6
Violent	1,655	2.1
Non-violent	15,965	20.4
Arson	127	NA
Domestic Viol.	5,000	NA

Emergency/Fire
Fire Marshal	Michael Gallagher

Public Library
No County Library
(Library statistics are the sum of all municipal libraries in the county)

Library statistics, 2004
	Total	per capita
Volumes	2,559,838	3.42
Expenditure	$34,711,317	$46.38
Library weekly hours		59.5
Full-time equivalent staff		460

Income Tax, 2002
Number of returns	310,076
Total taxable income	$15,748,523,000
Net charged tax	$383,156,000
Average gross income	$56,479
Average income tax	$1,236

County Finance
(sum of all municipalities in county)

Fiscal Year 2004
Total tax levy	$1,593,808,393
County taxes	224,822,000
County library	0
County health	0
County open space	20,638,298
Muni. budget	348,972,866
Misc. revenues	371,800,410

Fiscal Year 2005
Total tax levy	$1,683,812,610
County levy	248,014,422
County taxes	224,664,999
County library	0
County health	0
County open space	23,349,422
School levy	1,058,252,043
Muni. budget	377,546,149
Misc. revenues	410,127,828
Total aid	$155,110,902
CMPTRA	63,542,127
Muni. block grant	3,028,709
Energy tax receipts	86,136,859
Homeland security	2,250,000

Fiscal Year 2006
Total aid	$155,110,903
CMPTRA	60,527,336
Muni. block grant	3,028,709
Energy tax receipts	89,151,651
Homeland security	2,390,000

Taxes†

	2003	2004	2005
Net valuation taxable	$40,319,659,553	$40,745,446,402	$43,857,896,282
State equalized value	$67,673,758,246	$77,008,954,372	$88,317,049,132

† sum of all municipalities in county

Demographics & Socio-Economic Characteristics
(2000 U.S. Census, except as noted)

Population
1990*	553,124
2000	615,301
2004 (estimate)*	636,298
Male	310,210
Female	326,088
Persons per sq. mi. of land	1,348.3

Race & Hispanic Origin, 2004**
White	545,972
Black/African American	52,005
Amer. Indian/Alaska Natv.	1,087
Asian	30,258
Natv Hawaiian/Pac Islander	199
Two or more races	6,777
Hispanic origin, total	46,703

Age & Nativity, 2004**
Under 5 years	40,192
18 years and over	474,339
15 to 44 years	251,786
45 to 64 years	171,694
65 years and over	79,410
85 years and over	11,394
Median Age	39.1
Native born, 2000	551,494
Foreign born, 2000	63,807

Educational Attainment, 2000
Population 25 years and over	413,058
0-8 yrs of school	3.7%
High School grad or higher	87.9%
Bachelor's degree or higher	34.6%
Graduate degree	12.8%

Income & Poverty, 1999
Per capita income	$31,149
Median household income	$64,271
Median family income	$76,823
Persons in poverty	38,242
H'holds receiving public assistance	4,003
H'holds receiving social security	57,896

Households, 2000
Total households	224,236
With persons under 18	85,287
With persons over 65	55,114
Family households	160,233
One-person households	53,456
Persons per household	2.7
Persons per family	3.24

Labor & Employment
Total civilian labor force, 2005**	329,900
Unemployment rate	3.8%

*Labor Employment for Major Industries, 2012 Projection****

Total non-farm payroll empl	296,050
Construction	5.8%
Manufacturing	3.1%
Wholesale trade	3.6%
Retail trade	14.5%
Transp & warehousing	2.1%
Information	3.2%
Finance & insurance	4.3%
Real estate	1.5%
Professional & technical	9.5%
Management	0.5%
Administration	5.4%
Education	2.9%
Health & social svcs	5.8%
Accommodations	7.6%
Government	13.4%

*US Census Bureau; **NJ Dept of Labor
***NJ Labor Planning Analysis

General Information
Monmouth County
Hall of Records
One E Main St
Freehold, NJ 07728
732-431-7310

Website	www.visitmonmouth.com
Land Area (sq. miles)	471.9
Water Area (sq. miles)	193.2
Class	Fifth
Government form	BCF
Number of Freeholders	5
Number of municipalities	53

Government & Voters

Legislative Districts
US Congressional	4, 6, 12
State Legislative	10, 11, 12, 13, 30

Registered Voters, November 2005
Total	398,044
Democrat	66,348
Republican	77,547
Unaffiliated	252,706

County Officials, 2006
County Executive	None
Manager/Admin	Louis Paparozzi
Clerk	M. Claire French
Finance Dir/Treas	Benjamin Danskin
Tax Administrator	Matthew Clark
Surrogate	Marie Muhler
Prosecutor	Luis Valentin
Planning/Develop	NA

County School District
3680 Hwy 9
Freehold, NJ 07728
732-431-7810

Superintendent	Eugenia Lawson
Number of districts	55

Housing & Construction

Total Housing Units, 2000-2004
2000*	240,884
Median rent	$759
Median SF home value	$203,100
2001	245,243
2002	247,294
2003	249,553
2004 (estimate)	249,852

New Privately Owned Housing Units Authorized by Building Permit
	Units	Value
Total, 2004	2,628	$410,856,945
Single family	2,179	$390,165,734
Total, 2005	2,548	$405,532,948
Single family	1,893	392,832,904

Real Property Valuation - parcels, 2005
(sum of all municipalities in county)

	Number	Valuation
Total		$65,356,564,458
Vacant	17,966	1,299,927,319
Residential	199,898	53,934,369,834
Non-residential	10,560	9,656,855,390
Commercial	9,010	7,588,884,440
Industrial	520	872,367,350
Apartments	1,030	1,195,603,600
Farm land	1,509	437,114,900
Farm homestead	2,550	28,297,015

Public Safety

Police
Sheriff	Joseph Oxley
Officers, 2004	
Sheriff's department	464
County officers	546
Municipal police	1,499
Prosecutors, 2004	82

Crime, 2004	Number	Rate
Total	14,065	22.2
Violent	1,366	2.2
Non-violent	12,699	20.1
Arson	45	NA
Domestic Viol.	5,328	NA

Emergency/Fire
Fire Marshal	Tim Smith

Public Library
Monmouth County Library
125 Symmes Dr
Manalapan, NJ 07726
732-431-7235

Director	Kenneth Sheinbaum

Library statistics, 2004
	Total	per capita
Volumes	1,341,708	3.36
Expenditure	$10,901,062	$27.28
Library weekly hours		68
Full-time equivalent staff		105

Income Tax, 2002
Number of returns	249,640
Total taxable income	$17,760,553,000
Net charged tax	$513,685,000
Average gross income	$78,010
Average income tax	$2,058

County Finance
(sum of all municipalities in county)

Fiscal Year 2004
Total tax levy	$1,530,657,446
County taxes	260,752,374
County library	9,936,071
County health	1,442,602
County open space	16,000,000
Muni. budget	307,343,903
Misc. revenues	310,513,965

Fiscal Year 2005
Total tax levy	$1,618,315,191
County levy	297,685,044
County taxes	269,650,000
County library	10,478,307
County health	1,556,731
County open space	15,999,998
School levy	979,394,815
Muni. budget	341,235,337
Misc. revenues	320,665,064
Total aid	$107,899,400
CMPTRA	39,303,565
Muni. block grant	2,548,565
Energy tax receipts	63,154,647
Homeland security	2,855,000

Fiscal Year 2006
Total aid	$107,923,226
CMPTRA	37,116,977
Muni. block grant	2,548,565
Energy tax receipts	65,352,676
Homeland security	2,855,000

Taxes†
	2003	2004	2005
Net valuation taxable	$51,152,695,353	$57,090,882,529	$65,515,271,859
State equalized value	$76,889,245,190	$88,455,723,375	$103,449,533,181

† sum of all municipalities in county

Demographics & Socio-Economic Characteristics
(2000 U.S. Census, except as noted)

Population
1990*	421,353
2000	470,212
2004 (estimate)*	488,173
Male	239,591
Female	248,582
Persons per sq. mi. of land	1,040.9

Race & Hispanic Origin, 2004**
White	430,195
Black/African American	14,724
Amer. Indian/Alaska Natv.	782
Asian	37,747
Natv Hawaiian/Pac Islander	164
Two or more races	4,561
Hispanic origin, total	45,263

Age & Nativity, 2004**
Under 5 years	31,904
18 years and over	367,016
15 to 44 years	193,392
45 to 64 years	134,321
65 years and over	59,237
85 years and over	7,350
Median Age	39.3
Native born, 2000	397,574
Foreign born, 2000	72,638

Educational Attainment, 2000
Population 25 years and over	323,881
0-8 yrs of school	3.5%
High School grad or higher	90.6%
Bachelor's degree or higher	44.1%
Graduate degree	17.0%

Income & Poverty, 1999
Per capita income	$36,964
Median household income	$77,340
Median family income	$89,773
Persons in poverty	17,872
H'holds receiving public assistance	1,699
H'holds receiving social security	38,460

Households, 2000
Total households	169,711
With persons under 18	63,242
With persons over 65	37,765
Family households	124,907
One-person households	36,555
Persons per household	2.72
Persons per family	3.18

Labor & Employment
Total civilian labor force, 2005**	266,400
Unemployment rate	3.1%

*Labor Employment for Major Industries, 2012 Projection***
Total non-farm payroll empl	357,450
Construction	4.0%
Manufacturing	6.4%
Wholesale trade	7.4%
Retail trade	9.8%
Transp & warehousing	3.1%
Information	3.6%
Finance & insurance	7.5%
Real estate	1.8%
Professional & technical	10.7%
Management	3.2%
Administration	8.6%
Education	2.4%
Health & social svcs	4.0%
Accommodations	4.6%
Government	12.0%

*US Census Bureau; **NJ Dept of Labor
***NJ Labor Planning Analysis

General Information
Morris County
PO Box 900
Morristown, NJ 07963
973-285-6000
Website	www.co.morris.nj.us
Land Area (sq. miles)	469.0
Water Area (sq. miles)	12.3
Class	Second
Government form	BCF
Number of Freeholders	7
Number of municipalities	39

Government & Voters

Legislative Districts
US Congressional	11
State Legislative	16, 21, 24, 25, 26

Registered Voters, November 2005
Total	296,992
Democrat	41,229
Republican	97,336
Unaffiliated	157,035

County Officials, 2006
County Executive	None
Manager/Admin	John Bonanni
Clerk	Joan Bramhall
Finance Dir/Treas	Glenn Roe
Tax Administrator	Ralph Meloro
Surrogate	John Pecoraro
Prosecutor	Michael Rubbinaccio
Planning/Develop	Walter Krich

County School District
PO Box 900
Morristown, NJ 07963
973-285-8332
Superintendent	Thomas Kane
Number of districts	40

Housing & Construction

Total Housing Units, 2000-2004
2000*	174,379
Median rent	$883
Median SF home value	$257,400
2001	177,476
2002	178,869
2003	180,590
2004 (estimate)	181,257

New Privately Owned Housing Units Authorized by Building Permit
	Units	Value
Total, 2004	1,427	$220,790,527
Single family	888	$185,095,564
Total, 2005	2,521	$282,098,311
Single family	903	214,593,575

Real Property Valuation - parcels, 2005
(sum of all municipalities in county)
	Number	Valuation
Total		$62,027,632,792
Vacant	9,893	1,229,486,204
Residential	146,236	45,689,330,230
Non-residential	8,107	14,642,662,012
Commercial	6,726	10,455,808,911
Industrial	996	2,564,928,201
Apartments	385	1,621,924,900
Farm land	722	452,337,200
Farm homestead	1,394	13,817,146

Public Safety

Police
Sheriff	Edward Rochford

Officers, 2004
Sheriff's department	247
County officers	353
Municipal police	1,080
Prosecutors, 2004	73

Crime, 2004	Number	Rate
Total	7,178	14.9
Violent	514	1.1
Non-violent	6,664	13.8
Arson	33	NA
Domestic Viol.	2,644	NA

Emergency/Fire
Fire Marshal	Philip Wilk

Public Library
Morris County Free Library
30 East Hanover Ave
Whippany, NJ 07981
973-285-6934
Director	Joanne Kares

Library statistics, 2004
	Total	per capita
Volumes	222,028	0.45
Expenditure	$7,352,062	$15.64
Library weekly hours	69	
Full-time equivalent staff	66	

Income Tax, 2002
Number of returns	201,360
Total taxable income	$16,836,627,000
Net charged tax	$559,926,000
Average gross income	$90,954
Average income tax	$2,781

County Finance
(sum of all municipalities in county)

Fiscal Year 2004
Total tax levy	$1,359,123,374
County taxes	166,093,003
County library	0
County health	0
County open space	34,434,862
Muni. budget	298,140,304
Misc. revenues	226,766,048

Fiscal Year 2005
Total tax levy	$1,442,508,274
County levy	209,577,044
County taxes	171,660,446
County library	0
County health	0
County open space	37,916,596
School levy	900,373,918
Muni. budget	332,557,318
Misc. revenues	240,939,933
Total aid	$66,920,423
CMPTRA	23,534,162
Muni. block grant	1,898,216
Energy tax receipts	38,685,300
Homeland security	2,270,000

Fiscal Year 2006
Total aid	$66,965,428
CMPTRA	22,180,178
Muni. block grant	1,898,216
Energy tax receipts	40,039,289
Homeland security	2,315,000

Taxes†

	2003	2004	2005
Net valuation taxable	$55,913,590,879	$57,903,087,324	$62,177,814,928
State equalized value	$70,806,891,990	$78,454,629,822	$88,095,915,466

† sum of all municipalities in county

Demographics & Socio-Economic Characteristics
(2000 U.S. Census, except as noted)

Population
1990*	433,203
2000	510,916
2004 (estimate)*	553,251
Male	263,441
Female	289,810
Persons per sq. mi. of land	869.5

Race & Hispanic Origin, 2004**
White	520,862
Black/African American	18,295
Amer. Indian/Alaska Natv.	936
Asian	8,694
Natv Hawaiian/Pac Islander	186
Two or more races	4,278
Hispanic origin, total	33,794

Age & Nativity, 2004**
Under 5 years	34,644
18 years and over	424,854
15 to 44 years	205,090
45 to 64 years	124,859
65 years and over	116,654
85 years and over	20,759
Median Age	40.8
Native born, 2000	477,764
Foreign born, 2000	33,152

Educational Attainment, 2000
Population 25 years and over	358,354
0-8 yrs of school	4.5%
High School grad or higher	83.0%
Bachelor's degree or higher	19.5%
Graduate degree	6.1%

Income & Poverty, 1999
Per capita income	$23,054
Median household income	$46,443
Median family income	$56,420
Persons in poverty	34,945
H'holds receiving public assistance	3,848
H'holds receiving social security	83,067

Households, 2000
Total households	200,402
With persons under 18	60,798
With persons over 65	78,100
Family households	137,803
One-person households	54,186
Persons per household	2.51
Persons per family	3.06

Labor & Employment
Total civilian labor force, 2005**	249,900
Unemployment rate	4.3%

*Labor Employment for Major Industries, 2012 Projection****

Total non-farm payroll empl	171,300
Construction	6.3%
Manufacturing	3.5%
Wholesale trade	2.3%
Retail trade	18.1%
Transp & warehousing	1.8%
Information	0.8%
Finance & insurance	2.6%
Real estate	1.6%
Professional & technical	4.8%
Management	0.2%
Administration	3.5%
Education	2.2%
Health & social svcs	6.3%
Accommodations	7.9%
Government	14.9%

*US Census Bureau; **NJ Dept of Labor
***NJ Labor Planning Analysis

General Information
Ocean County
PO Box 2191
Toms River, NJ 08754
732-244-2121

Website	www.co.ocean.nj.us
Land Area (sq. miles)	636.3
Water Area (sq. miles)	279.6
Class	Fifth
Government form	BCF
Number of Freeholders	5
Number of municipalities	33

Government & Voters

Legislative Districts
US Congressional	3, 4
State Legislative	9, 10, 30

Registered Voters, November 2005
Total	347,950
Democrat	48,987
Republican	82,485
Unaffiliated	214,998

County Officials, 2006
County Executive	None
Manager/Admin	Alan W. Avery Jr.
Clerk	Carl W. Block
Finance Dir/Treas	Julie N. Tarrant
Tax Administrator	Barbara Raney
Surrogate	Jeffrey W. Moran
Prosecutor	Thomas F. Kelaher
Planning/Develop	D. J. McKeon (Asst Dir)

County School District
212 Washington St
Toms River, NJ 08753
732-929-2079

Superintendent	Bruce Greenfield
Number of districts	30

Housing & Construction

Total Housing Units, 2000-2004
2000*	248,711
Median rent	$819
Median SF home value	$131,300
2001	255,366
2002	258,946
2003	262,222
2004 (estimate)	265,447

New Privately Owned Housing Units
Authorized by Building Permit

	Units	Value
Total, 2004	3,818	$452,045,328
Single family	3,300	$436,745,321
Total, 2005	2,866	$423,250,058
Single family	2,706	402,591,145

Real Property Valuation - parcels, 2005
(sum of all municipalities in county)

	Number	Valuation
Total		$51,955,407,023
Vacant	36,109	1,656,531,870
Residential	227,137	45,017,389,185
Non-residential	7,130	5,228,294,752
Commercial	6,355	4,007,679,552
Industrial	399	480,962,300
Apartments	376	739,652,900
Farm land	265	48,182,300
Farm homestead	493	5,008,916

Public Safety

Police
Sheriff	William Polher
Officers, 2004	
Sheriff's department	106
County officers	177
Municipal police	1,064
Prosecutors, 2004	71

Crime, 2004	Number	Rate
Total	11,302	20.7
Violent	895	1.6
Non-violent	10,407	19.1
Arson	78	NA
Domestic Viol.	5,553	NA

Emergency/Fire
Fire Marshal	Daniel Mulligan

Public Library
Ocean County Library
101 Washington St
Toms River, NJ 08753
732-349-6200

Director	Elaine H. McConnell

Library statistics, 2004
	Total	per capita
Volumes	994,824	1.95
Expenditure	$24,397,437	$47.87
Library weekly hours	68	
Full-time equivalent staff	234	

Income Tax, 2002
Number of returns	216,502
Total taxable income	$8,856,646,000
Net charged tax	$226,735,000
Average gross income	$46,682
Average income tax	$1,047

County Finance
(sum of all municipalities in county)

Fiscal Year 2004
Total tax levy	$1,039,754,632
County taxes	224,198,148
County library	23,636,901
County health	8,450,000
County open space	7,452,000
Muni. budget	228,916,344
Misc. revenues	230,634,519

Fiscal Year 2005
Total tax levy	$1,124,543,618
County levy	281,719,876
County taxes	239,224,898
County library	24,615,778
County health	8,950,004
County open space	8,929,201
School levy	577,140,223
Muni. budget	265,683,522
Misc. revenues	237,417,050
Total aid	$69,945,035
CMPTRA	17,945,416
Muni. block grant	2,033,841
Energy tax receipts	47,685,711
Homeland security	1,875,000

Fiscal Year 2006
Total aid	$70,259,621
CMPTRA	16,590,998
Muni. block grant	2,033,841
Energy tax receipts	49,324,596
Homeland security	1,875,000

Taxes†

	2003	2004	2005
Net valuation taxable	$37,685,422,733	$41,809,703,330	$52,045,082,824
State equalized value	$60,841,488,476	$72,738,192,367	$87,967,181,739

† sum of all municipalities in county

Demographics & Socio-Economic Characteristics
(2000 U.S. Census, except as noted)

Population
1990*	453,060
2000	489,049
2000 (revised)	490,377
2004 (estimate)*	500,427
Male	243,100
Female	257,327
Persons per sq. mi. of land	2,700.8

Race & Hispanic Origin, 2004**
White	390,791
Black/African American	76,833
Amer. Indian/Alaska Natv.	3,360
Asian	21,422
Natv Hawaiian/Pac Islander	1,169
Two or more races	6,852
Hispanic origin, total	166,300

Age & Nativity, 2004**
Under 5 years	40,631
18 years and over	365,429
15 to 44 years	211,364
45 to 64 years	116,209
65 years and over	58,512
85 years and over	8,462
Median Age	35.4
Native born, 2000	358,758
Foreign born, 2000	130,291

Educational Attainment, 2000
Population 25 years and over	316,401
0-8 yrs of school	11.8%
High School grad or higher	73.3%
Bachelor's degree or higher	21.2%
Graduate degree	7.0%

Income & Poverty, 1999
Per capita income	$21,370
Median household income	$49,210
Median family income	$56,054
Persons in poverty	59,072
H'holds receiving public assistance	6,487
H'holds receiving social security	43,664

Households, 2000
Total households	163,856
With persons under 18	65,753
With persons over 65	42,848
Family households	119,689
One-person households	36,301
Persons per household	2.92
Persons per family	3.42

Labor & Employment
Total civilian labor force, 2005**	237,000
Unemployment rate	5.2%

*Labor Employment for Major Industries, 2012 Projection*** *
Total non-farm payroll empl	194,500
Construction	5.4%
Manufacturing	10.9%
Wholesale trade	6.0%
Retail trade	13.3%
Transp & warehousing	2.5%
Information	1.5%
Finance & insurance	3.5%
Real estate	1.2%
Professional & technical	4.1%
Management	2.4%
Administration	7.8%
Education	1.6%
Health & social svcs	5.4%
Accommodations	4.9%
Government	15.7%

*US Census Bureau; **NJ Dept of Labor
***NJ Labor Planning Analysis

General Information
Passaic County
Administration Bldg
401 Grand St
Paterson, NJ 07505
973-881-3632
Website	www.passaiccountynj.org
Land Area (sq. miles)	185.3
Water Area (sq. miles)	11.8
Class	Second
Government form	BCF
Number of Freeholders	7
Number of municipalities	16

Government & Voters

Legislative Districts
US Congressional	5, 8, 9, 11
State Legislative	26, 34, 35, 36, 40

Registered Voters, November 2005
Total	245,594
Democrat	51,070
Republican	43,705
Unaffiliated	149,725

County Officials, 2006
County Executive	None
Manager/Admin	Anthony DeNova
Clerk	Karen Brown
Finance Dir/Treas	M. Cherone (Actg)
Tax Administrator	James Murner
Surrogate	Willam Bate
Prosecutor	James Avigliano
Planning/Develop	NA

County School District
501 River St
Paterson, NJ 07524
973-569-0241
Superintendent	Robert Gilmartin (Int)
Number of districts	20

Housing & Construction

Total Housing Units, 2000-2004
2000*	170,048
Median rent	$747
Median SF home value	$190,600
2001	170,286
2002	170,648
2003	171,065
2004 (estimate)	170,978

New Privately Owned Housing Units
Authorized by Building Permit
	Units	Value
Total, 2004	763	$87,414,927
Single family	437	$65,759,546
Total, 2005	677	$76,239,653
Single family	229	43,177,165

Real Property Valuation - parcels, 2005
(sum of all municipalities in county)
	Number	Valuation
Total		$21,288,317,981
Vacant	6,683	355,480,878
Residential	105,522	15,485,021,573
Non-residential	9,525	5,414,577,021
Commercial	7,023	3,384,685,240
Industrial	1,415	1,448,039,753
Apartments	1,087	581,852,028
Farm land	143	32,203,500
Farm homestead	338	1,035,009

Public Safety

Police
Sheriff	Jerry Speziale
Officers, 2004	
Sheriff's department	667
County officers	758
Municipal police	1,126
Prosecutors, 2004	91

Crime, 2004	Number	Rate
Total	14,803	29.7
Violent	2,319	4.7
Non-violent	12,484	25.1
Arson	24	NA
Domestic Viol.	4,719	NA

Emergency/Fire
Coordinator	Joseph Forbes

Public Library
No County Library
(Library statistics are the sum of all municipal libraries in the county)

Library statistics, 2004
	Total	per capita
Volumes	1,142,012	2.36
Expenditure	$14,366,693	$29.73
Library weekly hours		56
Full-time equivalent staff		195

Income Tax, 2002
Number of returns	199,912
Total taxable income	$8,027,110,000
Net charged tax	$197,112,000
Average gross income	$45,577
Average income tax	$986

County Finance
(sum of all municipalities in county)

Fiscal Year 2004
Total tax levy	$904,418,302
County taxes	193,502,857
County library	0
County health	0
County open space	3,575,641
Muni. budget	273,448,273
Misc. revenues	225,778,023

Fiscal Year 2005
Total tax levy	$963,272,286
County levy	213,393,844
County taxes	209,321,069
County library	0
County health	0
County open space	4,072,777
School levy	455,846,532
Muni. budget	294,031,908
Misc. revenues	230,644,928
Total aid	$94,135,729
CMPTRA	62,171,672
Muni. block grant	2,004,344
Energy tax receipts	27,829,643
Homeland security	1,340,000

Fiscal Year 2006
Total aid	$94,135,728
CMPTRA	61,197,634
Muni. block grant	2,004,344
Energy tax receipts	28,803,680
Homeland security	1,340,000

Taxes†
	2003	2004	2005
Net valuation taxable	$20,972,139,025	$21,208,000,480	$21,335,720,331
State equalized value	$35,071,347,133	$40,106,449,757	$45,466,073,584

† sum of all municipalities in county

Demographics & Socio-Economic Characteristics

(2000 U.S. Census, except as noted)

Population

1990*	65,294
2000	64,285
2004 (estimate)*	65,346
Male	31,630
Female	33,716
Persons per sq. mi. of land	193.4

Race & Hispanic Origin, 2004**

White	54,084
Black/African American	9,923
Amer. Indian/Alaska Natv.	235
Asian	449
Natv Hawaiian/Pac Islander	31
Two or more races	624
Hispanic origin, total	3,040

Age & Nativity, 2004**

Under 5 years	3,777
18 years and over	49,539
15 to 44 years	26,050
45 to 64 years	17,326
65 years and over	9,205
85 years and over	1,351
Median Age	39.0
Native born, 2000	62,665
Foreign born, 2000	1,620

Educational Attainment, 2000

Population 25 years and over	42,789
0-8 yrs of school	7.1%
High School grad or higher	79.4%
Bachelor's degree or higher	15.2%
Graduate degree	4.0%

Income & Poverty, 1999

Per capita income	$20,874
Median household income	$45,573
Median family income	$54,890
Persons in poverty	5,980
H'holds receiving public assistance	723
H'holds receiving social security	7,398

Households, 2000

Total households	24,295
With persons under 18	8,788
With persons over 65	6,508
Family households	17,371
One-person households	5,907
Persons per household	2.6
Persons per family	3.08

Labor & Employment

Total civilian labor force, 2005**	31,700
Unemployment rate	4.6%

*Labor Employment for Major Industries, 2012 Projection****

Total non-farm payroll empl	23,500
Construction	5.5%
Manufacturing	13.0%
Wholesale trade	1.3%
Retail trade	10.9%
Transp & warehousing	3.0%
Information	NA
Finance & insurance	2.6%
Real estate	0.9%
Professional & technical	2.1%
Management	NA
Administration	NA
Education	NA
Health & social svcs	5.5%
Accommodations	6.4%
Government	19.1%

*US Census Bureau; **NJ Dept of Labor
***NJ Labor Planning Analysis

General Information

Salem County
Court House
92 Market St
Salem, NJ 08079
856-935-7510

Website	www.salemco.org
Land Area (sq. miles)	337.9
Water Area (sq. miles)	34.7
Class	Third
Government form	BCF
Number of Freeholders	7
Number of municipalities	15

Government & Voters

Legislative Districts

US Congressional	2
State Legislative	3

Registered Voters, November 2005

Total	40,941
Democrat	9,179
Republican	7,373
Unaffiliated	24,145

County Officials, 2006

County Executive	None
Manager/Admin	Deborah Turner-Fox
Clerk	Gilda Gill
Finance Dir/Treas	Joanne Bell
Tax Administrator	Linda Stewart
Surrogate	Nicki Burke
Prosecutor	John Lenahan
Planning/Develop	NA

County School District

94 Market St
Salem, NJ 08079
856-935-7510

Superintendent	Michael Elwell
Number of districts	15

Housing & Construction

Total Housing Units, 2000-2004

2000*	26,158
Median rent	$602
Median SF home value	$105,200
2001	26,330
2002	26,493
2003	26,643
2004 (estimate)	26,790

New Privately Owned Housing Units Authorized by Building Permit

	Units	Value
Total, 2004	334	$32,629,550
Single family	289	$31,318,944
Total, 2005	294	$32,209,660
Single family	282	31,722,512

Real Property Valuation - parcels, 2005

(sum of all municipalities in county)

	Number	Valuation
Total		$3,249,518,160
Vacant	4,710	91,683,450
Residential	19,514	2,050,342,550
Non-residential	1,229	801,698,805
Commercial	1,118	368,031,185
Industrial	53	381,358,170
Apartments	58	52,309,450
Farm land	1,860	260,597,750
Farm homestead	4,122	45,195,605

Public Safety

Police

Sheriff	John Cooksey
Officers, 2004	
Sheriff's department	118
County officers	135
Municipal police	125
Prosecutors, 2004	17

Crime, 2004	Number	Rate
Total	1,662	25.6
Violent	184	2.8
Non-violent	1,478	22.8
Arson	15	NA
Domestic Viol.	973	NA

Emergency/Fire

Fire Marshal	John Turner Jr.

Public Library

No County Library
(Library statistics are the sum of all municipal libraries in the county)

Library statistics, 2004

	Total	per capita
Volumes	93,763	2.34
Expenditure	$365,963	$9.13
Library weekly hours		38.3
Full-time equivalent staff		10

Income Tax, 2002

Number of returns	24,645
Total taxable income	$988,772,000
Net charged tax	$21,224,000
Average gross income	$44,918
Average income tax	$861

County Finance

(sum of all municipalities in county)

Fiscal Year 2004

Total tax levy	$100,966,995
County taxes	36,320,365
County library	0
County health	0
County open space	0
Muni. budget	10,187,839
Misc. revenues	51,432,843

Fiscal Year 2005

Total tax levy	$109,522,421
County levy	40,562,972
County taxes	39,755,570
County library	0
County health	0
County open space	807,403
School levy	57,124,245
Muni. budget	11,835,202
Misc. revenues	51,467,412
Total aid	$24,033,761
CMPTRA	7,772,882
Muni. block grant	286,868
Energy tax receipts	15,764,764
Homeland security	245,000

Fiscal Year 2006

Total aid	$24,294,691
CMPTRA	7,482,043
Muni. block grant	286,868
Energy tax receipts	16,302,725
Homeland security	220,000

Taxes†

	2003	2004	2005
Net valuation taxable	$2,868,412,508	$3,236,055,644	$3,266,149,495
State equalized value	$3,534,422,584	$3,902,539,838	$4,246,589,649

† sum of all municipalities in county

Demographics & Socio-Economic Characteristics
(2000 U.S. Census, except as noted)

Population
1990*	240,279
2000	297,490
2004 (estimate)*	316,750
Male	155,366
Female	161,384
Persons per sq. mi. of land	1,039.6

Race & Hispanic Origin, 2004**
White	250,450
Black/African American	27,402
Amer. Indian/Alaska Natv.	522
Asian	34,964
Natv Hawaiian/Pac Islander	117
Two or more races	3,295
Hispanic origin, total	33,586

Age & Nativity, 2004**
Under 5 years	22,787
18 years and over	234,308
15 to 44 years	128,909
45 to 64 years	83,461
65 years and over	34,714
85 years and over	4,548
Median Age	38.4
Native born, 2000	243,553
Foreign born, 2000	53,937

Educational Attainment, 2000
Population 25 years and over	204,343
0-8 yrs of school	4.2%
High School grad or higher	89.6%
Bachelor's degree or higher	46.5%
Graduate degree	19.1%

Income & Poverty, 1999
Per capita income	$37,970
Median household income	$76,933
Median family income	$90,605
Persons in poverty	11,061
H'holds receiving public assistance	1,298
H'holds receiving social security	23,221

Households, 2000
Total households	108,984
With persons under 18	41,460
With persons over 65	22,612
Family households	78,409
One-person households	24,864
Persons per household	2.69
Persons per family	3.19

Labor & Employment
Total civilian labor force, 2005**	174,700
Unemployment rate	3.2%

*Labor Employment for Major Industries, 2012 Projection***
Total non-farm payroll empl	211,800
Construction	3.6%
Manufacturing	8.7%
Wholesale trade	7.9%
Retail trade	11.1%
Transp & warehousing	2.4%
Information	6.3%
Finance & insurance	5.8%
Real estate	0.9%
Professional & technical	9.7%
Management	3.5%
Administration	11.3%
Education	1.2%
Health & social svcs	3.6%
Accommodations	5.1%
Government	7.4%

*US Census Bureau; **NJ Dept of Labor
***NJ Labor Planning Analysis

General Information
Somerset County
PO Box 3000
Somerville, NJ 08876
908-231-7000
Website	www.co.somerset.nj.us
Land Area (sq. miles)	304.7
Water Area (sq. miles)	0.4
Class	Second
Government form	BCF
Number of Freeholders	5
Number of municipalities	21

Government & Voters

Legislative Districts
US Congressional	7, 11, 12
State Legislative	16, 27, 21, 22

Registered Voters, November 2005
Total	166,648
Democrat	23,429
Republican	39,746
Unaffiliated	102,677

County Officials, 2006
County Executive	None
Manager/Admin	Richard E. Williams
Clerk	Brett A. Radi
Finance Dir/Treas	Brian Newman
Tax Administrator	William Linville
Surrogate	Frank G. Bruno
Prosecutor	Wayne J. Forrest
Planning/Develop	Robert P. Bzik

County School District
92 E Main St
Somerville, NJ 08876
908-231-7171
Superintendent	David Livingston
Number of districts	20

Housing & Construction

Total Housing Units, 2000-2004
2000*	112,023
Median rent	$898
Median SF home value	$235,000
2001	114,696
2002	116,012
2003	117,122
2004 (estimate)	117,972

New Privately Owned Housing Units Authorized by Building Permit
	Units	Value
Total, 2004	1,362	$222,745,845
Single family	797	$146,550,602
Total, 2005	1,105	$183,278,302
Single family	709	149,243,489

Real Property Valuation - parcels, 2005
(sum of all municipalities in county)
	Number	Valuation
Total		$48,943,543,927
Vacant	5,669	733,164,150
Residential	98,190	38,089,673,249
Non-residential	4,546	9,205,649,515
Commercial	3,714	6,629,695,680
Industrial	609	1,974,721,215
Apartments	223	601,232,620
Farm land	891	897,480,090
Farm homestead	1,677	17,576,923

Public Safety

Police
Sheriff	Frank J. Provenzano

Officers, 2004
Sheriff's department	180
County officers	224
Municipal police	603
Prosecutors, 2004	44

Crime, 2004	Number	Rate
Total	4,706	15.1
Violent	311	1
Non-violent	4,395	14.1
Arson	21	NA
Domestic Viol.	2,303	NA

Emergency/Fire
Director	LeRoy Gunzelman III

Public Library
Somerset County Library
1 Vogt Dr
Bridgewater, NJ 08807
908-526-4016
Director	Jim Hecht

Library statistics, 2004
	Total	per capita
Volumes	791,138	4.89
Expenditure	$10,188,890	$61.95
Library weekly hours	69	
Full-time equivalent staff	108	

Income Tax, 2002
Number of returns	128,099
Total taxable income	$11,716,988,000
Net charged tax	$390,214,000
Average gross income	$98,722
Average income tax	$3,046

County Finance
(sum of all municipalities in county)

Fiscal Year 2004
Total tax levy	$874,548,639
County taxes	150,228,574
County library	9,255,153
County health	0
County open space	13,513,077
Muni. budget	140,311,475
Misc. revenues	139,244,846

Fiscal Year 2005
Total tax levy	$945,317,079
County levy	182,799,005
County taxes	157,589,774
County library	10,054,593
County health	0
County open space	15,154,638
School levy	588,483,194
Muni. budget	174,034,884
Misc. revenues	150,839,279
Total aid	$43,535,816
CMPTRA	13,942,148
Muni. block grant	1,178,461
Energy tax receipts	27,070,207
Homeland security	1,345,000

Fiscal Year 2006
Total aid	$43,555,815
CMPTRA	12,994,688
Muni. block grant	1,178,461
Energy tax receipts	28,017,666
Homeland security	1,365,000

Taxes†

	2003	2004	2005
Net valuation taxable	$39,570,002,155	$40,595,111,147	$49,036,713,110
State equalized value	$44,442,841,658	$49,547,368,719	$55,171,930,705

† sum of all municipalities in county

Demographics & Socio-Economic Characteristics
(2000 U.S. Census, except as noted)

Population
1990* 130,943
2000 144,166
2000 (revised).................... 144,170
2004 (estimate)*................. 152,218
   Male 75,512
   Female 76,706
   Persons per sq. mi. of land 292.0

Race & Hispanic Origin, 2004**
White......................... 145,982
Black/African American 2,279
Amer. Indian/Alaska Natv......... 176
Asian 2,537
Natv Hawaiian/Pac Islander 13
Two or more races 1,231
Hispanic origin, total 7,149

Age & Nativity, 2004**
Under 5 years 8,824
18 years and over 112,606
15 to 44 years 62,390
45 to 64 years 43,421
65 years and over................ 14,397
85 years and over................. 1,887
Median Age....................... 38.5
Native born, 2000 135,995
Foreign born, 2000 8,171

Educational Attainment, 2000
Population 25 years and over....... 95,094
0-8 yrs of school................... 2.9%
High School grad or higher 89.8%
Bachelor's degree or higher 27.2%
Graduate degree.................... 8.7%

Income & Poverty, 1999
Per capita income................ $26,992
Median household income........ $65,266
Median family income $73,335
Persons in poverty 5,693
H'holds receiving public assistance 839
H'holds receiving social security 10,734

Households, 2000
Total households 50,831
   With persons under 18 21,353
   With persons over 65........... 9,281
   Family households.............. 38,805
   One-person households 9,614
Persons per household 2.8
Persons per family.................. 3.24

Labor & Employment
Total civilian labor force, 2005** 82,900
   Unemployment rate............... 3.7%
*Labor Employment for Major Industries, 2012 Projection***
Total non-farm payroll empl........ 45,150
   Construction...................... 6.6%
   Manufacturing.................... 3.9%
   Wholesale trade 3.1%
   Retail trade 13.6%
   Transp & warehousing 2.3%
   Information..................... 1.2%
   Finance & insurance.............. 2.4%
   Real estate 0.8%
   Professional & technical........... 7.0%
   Management...................... 3.0%
   Administration.................... 4.8%
   Education....................... 1.2%
   Health & social svcs.............. 6.6%
   Accommodations................. 7.9%
   Government 16.3%

*US Census Bureau; **NJ Dept of Labor
***NJ Labor Planning Analysis

General Information
Sussex County
Administration Center
One Spring St
Newton, NJ 07860
973-579-0210
Website .... www.sussex.nj.us
Land Area (sq. miles) 521.3
Water Area (sq. miles)............... 14.7
Class........................... Third
Government form .... BCF
Number of Freeholders................. 5
Number of municipalities 24

Government & Voters

Legislative Districts
US Congressional 5, 11
State Legislative 24

Registered Voters, November 2005
Total........................... 88,004
   Democrat...................... 9,070
   Republican.................... 30,900
   Unaffiliated 47,653

County Officials, 2006
County Executive .... None
Manager/Admin .... John H. Eskilson
Clerk................... Erma Gormley
Finance Dir/Treas .... Bernard A. Re
Tax Administrator.......... Carol Dennis
Surrogate............. Nancy Fitzgibbons
Prosecutor................ David Weaver
Planning/Develop...................... NA

County School District
262 White Lake Rd
Sparta, NJ 07871
973-579-6996
Superintendent........... Barry Worman
Number of districts.................... 26

Housing & Construction

Total Housing Units, 2000-2004
2000* 56,528
   Median rent..................... $790
   Median SF home value $157,700
2001 57,335
2002 58,070
2003 58,678
2004 (estimate)................. 59,045

New Privately Owned Housing Units Authorized by Building Permit

	Units	Value
Total, 2004	612	$92,450,915
Single family	558	$89,517,662
Total, 2005	668	$108,831,316
Single family	661	108,452,499

Real Property Valuation - parcels, 2005
(sum of all municipalities in county)

	Number	Valuation
Total		$10,631,902,129
Vacant	10,815	329,856,482
Residential	53,050	8,748,339,330
Non-residential	2,459	1,176,117,512
Commercial	2,173	981,004,712
Industrial	194	133,172,300
Apartments	92	61,940,500
Farm land	1,671	347,304,245
Farm homestead	3,481	30,284,560

Public Safety

Police
Sheriff..................... Robert Untig
Officers, 2004
   Sheriff's department 116
   County officers 148
   Municipal police 201
Prosecutors, 2004 32

Crime, 2004	Number	Rate
Total	1,774	11.7
Violent	116	0.8
Non-violent	1,658	11
Arson	4	NA
Domestic Viol.	1,274	NA

Emergency/Fire
Fire Marshal .... Thomas Davis

Public Library
Sussex County Library
125 Morris Turnpike
Newton, NJ 07860
973-948-3660
Director................ Stanley Polokoff

Library statistics, 2004

	Total	per capita
Volumes	288,069	2.28
Expenditure	$4,157,738	$32.98
Library weekly hours		.65
Full-time equivalent staff		.55

Income Tax, 2002
Number of returns................. 57,463
Total taxable income....... $3,301,878,000
Net charged tax $92,155,000
Average gross income............. $64,342
Average income tax............... $1,604

County Finance
(sum of all municipalities in county)

Fiscal Year 2004
Total tax levy $334,107,580
   County taxes.............. 56,625,654
   County library 4,025,268
   County health............. 1,112,530
   County open space......... 2,509,221
   Muni. budget............. 60,063,769
   Misc. revenues 58,919,265

Fiscal Year 2005
Total tax levy $350,850,361
   County levy................ 67,781,102
   County taxes.............. 59,427,893
   County library 4,181,023
   County health............. 1,112,529
   County open space......... 3,059,659
   School levy 216,729,861
   Muni. budget............. 66,339,393
   Misc. revenues 62,065,774
Total aid..................... $17,756,199
   CMPTRA.................... 7,305,419
   Muni. block grant 586,294
   Energy tax receipts......... 8,744,268
   Homeland security 580,000

Fiscal Year 2006
Total aid..................... $17,756,201
   CMPTRA.................... 6,999,369
   Muni. block grant 586,294
   Energy tax receipts.......... 9,050,320
   Homeland security 580,000

Taxes†

	2003	2004	2005
Net valuation taxable	$10,053,675,654	$10,223,380,295	$10,669,612,715
State equalized value	$13,057,609,951	$14,973,612,169	$17,141,051,415

† sum of all municipalities in county

Demographics & Socio-Economic Characteristics
(2000 U.S. Census, except as noted)

Population
1990*	493,819
2000	522,541
2004 (estimate)*	531,957
Male	257,320
Female	274,637
Persons per sq. mi. of land	5,150.2

Race & Hispanic Origin, 2004**
White	380,931
Black/African American	119,506
Amer. Indian/Alaska Natv.	1,853
Asian	23,067
Natv Hawaiian/Pac Islander	456
Two or more races	6,144
Hispanic origin, total	122,788

Age & Nativity, 2004**
Under 5 years	38,528
18 years and over	395,712
15 to 44 years	218,615
45 to 64 years	130,162
65 years and over	68,742
85 years and over	11,062
Median Age	37.5
Native born, 2000	391,625
Foreign born, 2000	130,916

Educational Attainment, 2000
Population 25 years and over	351,903
0-8 yrs of school	8.8%
High School grad or higher	79.3%
Bachelor's degree or higher	28.5%
Graduate degree	10.9%

Income & Poverty, 1999
Per capita income	$26,992
Median household income	$55,339
Median family income	$65,234
Persons in poverty	43,319
H'holds receiving public assistance	5,764
H'holds receiving social security	51,634

Households, 2000
Total households	186,124
With persons under 18	70,298
With persons over 65	51,537
Family households	133,352
One-person households	43,918
Persons per household	2.77
Persons per family	3.28

Labor & Employment
Total civilian labor force, 2005**	267,100
Unemployment rate	4.6%

*Labor Employment for Major Industries, 2012 Projection****

Total non-farm payroll empl	265,900
Construction	4.9%
Manufacturing	13.2%
Wholesale trade	5.7%
Retail trade	12.0%
Transp & warehousing	5.4%
Information	1.6%
Finance & insurance	3.3%
Real estate	1.4%
Professional & technical	7.6%
Management	0.9%
Administration	7.2%
Education	1.5%
Health & social svcs	4.9%
Accommodations	4.9%
Government	12.2%

*US Census Bureau; **NJ Dept of Labor
***NJ Labor Planning Analysis

General Information
Union County
10 Elizabethtown Plaza
Elizabeth, NJ 07207
908-527-4000

Website	www.unioncountynj.org
Land Area (sq. miles)	103.3
Water Area (sq. miles)	2.2
Class	Second
Government form	CMP (OCCL-1972)
Number of Freeholders	9
Number of municipalities	21

Government & Voters

Legislative Districts
US Congressional	7, 10, 13
State Legislative	20, 21, 22, 29

Registered Voters, November 2005
Total	268,810
Democrat	87,829
Republican	39,405
Unaffiliated	140,660

County Officials, 2006
County Executive	None
Manager/Admin	George Devanney
Clerk	Joanne Rajoppi
Finance Dir/Treas	Lawrence Caroselli
Tax Administrator	Christopher Duryee
Surrogate	James LaCorte
Prosecutor	Thomas Romankow
Planning/Develop	NA

County School District
300 North Ave E
Westfield, NJ 07090
908-654-9860

Superintendent	Glenn Tillou
Number of districts	21

Housing & Construction

Total Housing Units, 2000-2004
2000*	192,945
Median rent	$752
Median SF home value	$188,800
2001	193,541
2002	193,797
2003	194,180
2004 (estimate)	194,227

New Privately Owned Housing Units Authorized by Building Permit
	Units	Value
Total, 2004	1,399	$116,828,671
Single family	411	$50,653,912
Total, 2005	1,155	$131,267,530
Single family	514	85,196,166

Real Property Valuation - parcels, 2005
(sum of all municipalities in county)
	Number	Valuation
Total		$23,897,916,928
Vacant	4,000	229,228,500
Residential	127,331	17,110,073,175
Non-residential	10,497	6,557,147,533
Commercial	7,788	3,111,459,900
Industrial	1,558	2,822,005,233
Apartments	1,151	623,682,400
Farm land	5	1,302,600
Farm homestead	12	165,120

Public Safety

Police
Sheriff	Ralph Froehlich
Officers, 2004	
Sheriff's department	160
County officers	548
Municipal police	1,438
Prosecutors, 2004	75

Crime, 2004	Number	Rate
Total	16,962	32
Violent	2,005	3.8
Non-violent	14,957	28.3
Arson	42	NA
Domestic Viol.	4,416	NA

Emergency/Fire
Director	LeRoy Gunzelman III

Public Library
No County Library
(Library statistics are the sum of all municipal libraries in the county)

Library statistics, 2004
	Total	per capita
Volumes	1,982,860	3.81
Expenditure	$22,136,979	$42.49
Library weekly hours		55.8
Full-time equivalent staff		338

Income Tax, 2002
Number of returns	216,117
Total taxable income	$12,026,332,000
Net charged tax	$313,458,000
Average gross income	$61,615
Average income tax	$1,450

County Finance
(sum of all municipalities in county)

Fiscal Year 2004
Total tax levy	$1,183,908,011
County taxes	203,832,767
County library	0
County health	0
County open space	7,880,101
Muni. budget	385,264,648
Misc. revenues	280,993,143

Fiscal Year 2005
Total tax levy	$1,249,092,865
County levy	225,244,960
County taxes	216,332,767
County library	0
County health	0
County open space	8,912,191
School levy	620,003,705
Muni. budget	403,844,206
Misc. revenues	300,422,838
Total aid	$121,629,791
CMPTRA	55,348,221
Muni. block grant	2,160,938
Energy tax receipts	62,330,632
Homeland security	1,790,000

Fiscal Year 2006
Total aid	$121,629,792
CMPTRA	53,166,650
Muni. block grant	2,160,938
Energy tax receipts	64,512,204
Homeland security	1,790,000

Taxes†

	2003	2004	2005
Net valuation taxable	$23,804,111,241	$23,934,764,600	$23,947,228,345
State equalized value	$48,914,191,723	$54,710,432,326	$61,959,181,493

† sum of all municipalities in county

Demographics & Socio-Economic Characteristics
(2000 U.S. Census, except as noted)

Population
1990*	91,607
2000	102,437
2000 (revised)	102,433
2004 (estimate)*	110,018
Male	53,709
Female	56,309
Persons per sq. mi. of land	307.4

Race & Hispanic Origin, 2004**
White	103,774
Black/African American	3,021
Amer. Indian/Alaska Natv.	111
Asian	2,257
Natv Hawaiian/Pac Islander	3
Two or more races	852
Hispanic origin, total	5,744

Age & Nativity, 2004**
Under 5 years	6,902
18 years and over	82,256
15 to 44 years	45,141
45 to 64 years	28,326
65 years and over	13,680
85 years and over	2,093
Median Age	38.6
Native born, 2000	96,520
Foreign born, 2000	5,917

Educational Attainment, 2000
Population 25 years and over	69,457
0-8 yrs of school	4.4%
High School grad or higher	84.9%
Bachelor's degree or higher	24.4%
Graduate degree	7.6%

Income & Poverty, 1999
Per capita income	$25,728
Median household income	$56,100
Median family income	$66,223
Persons in poverty	5,492
H'holds receiving public assistance	857
H'holds receiving social security	10,250

Households, 2000
Total households	38,660
With persons under 18	14,258
With persons over 65	9,416
Family households	27,485
One-person households	9,270
Persons per household	2.61
Persons per family	3.12

Labor & Employment
Total civilian labor force, 2005**	59,600
Unemployment rate	3.6%

*Labor Employment for Major Industries, 2012 Projection****

Total non-farm payroll empl	42,600
Construction	4.3%
Manufacturing	14.4%
Wholesale trade	2.0%
Retail trade	18.7%
Transp & warehousing	NA
Information	0.8%
Finance & insurance	2.0%
Real estate	0.7%
Professional & technical	3.1%
Management	0.6%
Administration	4.9%
Education	2.6%
Health & social svcs	4.3%
Accommodations	6.5%
Government	14.2%

*US Census Bureau; **NJ Dept of Labor
***NJ Labor Planning Analysis

General Information
Warren County
165 County Rte 519 S
Belvidere, NJ 07823
908-475-6200

Website	www.co.warren.nj.us
Land Area (sq. miles)	357.9
Water Area (sq. miles)	4.9
Class	Third
Government form	BCF
Number of Freeholders	3
Number of municipalities	23

Government & Voters

Legislative Districts
US Congressional	5
State Legislative	23

Registered Voters, November 2005
Total	61,759
Democrat	9,768
Republican	19,615
Unaffiliated	32,017

County Officials, 2006
County Executive	None
Manager/Admin	Steve Marvin
Clerk	Terrance D. Lee
Finance Dir/Treas	Charles Houck
Tax Administrator	Melissa Pritchett
Surrogate	Susan Dickey
Prosecutor	Thomas S. Ferguson
Planning/Develop	David Dech

County School District
537 Oxford St
Belvidere, NJ 07823
908-475-6327

Superintendent	William King
Number of districts	25

Housing & Construction

Total Housing Units, 2000-2004
2000*	41,157
Median rent	$689
Median SF home value	$155,500
2001	42,177
2002	42,866
2003	43,661
2004 (estimate)	44,088

New Privately Owned Housing Units
Authorized by Building Permit

	Units	Value
Total, 2004	620	$76,174,005
Single family	573	$75,429,774
Total, 2005	556	$71,477,466
Single family	437	62,706,799

Real Property Valuation - parcels, 2005
(sum of all municipalities in county)

	Number	Valuation
Total		$8,904,515,175
Vacant	4,200	198,332,890
Residential	32,909	6,420,991,477
Non-residential	2,172	1,756,952,953
Commercial	1,835	919,463,503
Industrial	197	664,085,450
Apartments	140	173,404,000
Farm land	1,851	488,899,000
Farm homestead	3,998	39,338,855

Public Safety

Police
Sheriff	Sal Simonetti
Officers, 2004	
Sheriff's department	18
County officers	54
Municipal police	153
Prosecutors, 2004	36

Crime, 2004	Number	Rate
Total	1,557	14.3
Violent	119	1.1
Non-violent	1,438	13.2
Arson	12	NA
Domestic Viol.	1,314	NA

Emergency/Fire
Fire Marshal	Joseph Lake

Public Library
Warren County Library
199 Hardwick St
Belvidere, NJ 07823
908-475-6322

Director	Thomas Carney

Library statistics, 2004
	Total	per capita
Volumes	235,634	3.63
Expenditure	$4,020,792	$61.95
Library weekly hours		61
Full-time equivalent staff		7.0

Income Tax, 2002
Number of returns	41,672
Total taxable income	$2,063,239,000
Net charged tax	$53,965,000
Average gross income	$55,693
Average income tax	$1,295

County Finance
(sum of all municipalities in county)

Fiscal Year 2004
Total tax levy	$214,821,930
County taxes	50,702,940
County library	3,690,294
County health	0
County open space	5,518,885
Muni. budget	29,609,307
Misc. revenues	47,132,686

Fiscal Year 2005
Total tax levy	$230,597,957
County levy	64,889,259
County taxes	54,618,571
County library	4,072,742
County health	0
County open space	6,197,939
School levy	130,663,273
Muni. budget	35,069,424
Misc. revenues	49,899,018
Total aid	$17,169,789
CMPTRA	5,737,391
Muni. block grant	424,754
Energy tax receipts	10,454,202
Homeland security	590,000

Fiscal Year 2006
Total aid	$17,169,788
CMPTRA	5,371,493
Muni. block grant	424,754
Energy tax receipts	10,820,099
Homeland security	540,000

Taxes†

	2003	2004	2005
Net valuation taxable	$7,795,252,331	$8,483,068,417	$8,937,084,483
State equalized value	$8,981,871,535	$10,121,603,065	$11,573,645,964

† sum of all municipalities in county

The New Jersey Municipal Data Book

2006

State & Municipal Profiles Series™

[ip]

**State &
Municipal
Profiles
Series**

Atlantic County

Absecon City
Atlantic City
Brigantine City
Buena Borough
Buena Vista Township
Corbin City
Egg Harbor City
Egg Harbor Township
Estell Manor City
Folsom Borough
Galloway Township
Hamilton Township
Hammonton Town
Linwood City
Longport Borough
Margate City
Mullica Township
Northfield City
Pleasantville City
Port Republic City
Somers Point City
Ventnor City
Weymouth Township

Bergen County

Allendale Borough
Alpine Borough
Bergenfield Borough
Bogota Borough
Carlstadt Borough
Cliffside Park Borough
Closter Borough
Cresskill Borough
Demarest Borough
Dumont Borough
East Rutherford Borough
Edgewater Borough
Elmwood Park Borough
Emerson Borough
Englewood City
Englewood Cliffs
  Borough
Fair Lawn Borough
Fairview Borough
Fort Lee Borough
Franklin Lakes Borough
Garfield City
Glen Rock Borough
Hackensack City
Harrington Park Borough

Bergen County, continued

Hasbrouck Heights
  Borough
Haworth Borough
Hillsdale Borough
Ho-Ho-Kus Borough
Leonia Borough
Little Ferry Borough
Lodi Borough
Lyndhurst Township
Mahwah Township
Maywood Borough
Midland Park Borough
Montvale Borough
Moonachie Borough
New Milford Borough
North Arlington Borough
Northvale Borough
Norwood Borough
Oakland Borough
Old Tappan Borough
Oradell Borough
Palisades Park Borough
Paramus Borough
Park Ridge Borough
Ramsey Borough
Ridgefield Borough
Ridgefield Park Village
Ridgewood Village
River Edge Borough
River Vale Township
Rochelle Park Township
Rockleigh Borough
Rutherford Borough
Saddle Brook Township
Saddle River Borough
South Hackensack
  Township
Teaneck Township
Tenafly Borough
Teterboro Borough
Upper Saddle River
  Borough
Waldwick Borough
Wallington Borough
Washington Township
Westwood Borough
Woodcliff Lake Borough
Wood-Ridge Borough
Wyckoff Township

Burlington County

Bass River Township
Beverly City
Bordentown City
Bordentown Township
Burlington City
Burlington Township
Chesterfield Township
Cinnaminson Township
Delanco Township
Delran Township
Eastampton Township
Edgewater Park
  Township
Evesham Township
Fieldsboro Borough
Florence Township
Hainesport Township
Lumberton Township
Mansfield Township
Maple Shade Township
Medford Township
Medford Lakes Borough
Moorestown Township
Mount Holly Township
Mount Laurel Township
New Hanover Township
North Hanover Township
Palmyra Borough
Pemberton Borough
Pemberton Township
Riverside Township
Riverton Borough
Shamong Township
Southampton Township
Springfield Township
Tabernacle Township
Washington Township
Westampton Township
Willingboro Township
Woodland Township
Wrightstown Borough

Camden County

Audubon Borough
Audubon Park Borough
Barrington Borough
Bellmawr Borough
Berlin Borough
Berlin Township
Brooklawn Borough
Camden City

Camden County, continued

Cherry Hill Township
Chesilhurst Borough
Clementon Borough
Collingswood Borough
Gibbsboro Borough
Gloucester City
Gloucester Township
Haddon Township
Haddon Heights Borough
Haddonfield Borough
Hi-Nella Borough
Laurel Springs Borough
Lawnside Borough
Lindenwold Borough
Magnolia Borough
Merchantville Borough
Mount Ephraim Borough
Oaklyn Borough
Pennsauken Township
Pine Hill Borough
Pine Valley Borough
Runnemede Borough
Somerdale Borough
Stratford Borough
Tavistock Borough
Voorhees Township
Waterford Township
Winslow Township
Woodlynne Borough

Cape May County

Avalon Borough
Cape May City
Cape May Point Borough
Dennis Township
Lower Township
Middle Township
North Wildwood City
Ocean City
Sea Isle City
Stone Harbor Borough
Upper Township
West Cape May Borough
West Wildwood Borough
Wildwood City
Wildwood Crest Borough
Woodbine Borough
Cumberland County
Bridgeton City
Commercial Township

*Cape May County
continued on next page*

Cape May County
continued

Deerfield Township
Downe Township
Fairfield Township
Greenwich Township
Hopewell Township
Lawrence Township
Maurice River Township
Millville City
Shiloh Borough
Stow Creek Township
Upper Deerfield
    Township
Vineland City

Essex County

Belleville Township
Bloomfield Township
Caldwell Borough
Cedar Grove Township
East Orange City
Essex Fells Borough
Fairfield Township
Glen Ridge Borough
Irvington Township
Livingston Township
Maplewood Township
Millburn Township
Montclair Township
Newark City
North Caldwell Borough
Nutley Township
Orange City Township
Roseland Borough
South Orange Village
    Township
Verona Township
West Caldwell Township
West Orange Township

Gloucester County

Clayton Borough
Deptford Township
East Greenwich
    Township
Elk Township
Franklin Township
Glassboro Borough
Greenwich Township
Harrison Township
Logan Township

Gloucester County, continued

Mantua Township
Monroe Township
National Park Borough
Newfield Borough
Paulsboro Borough
Pitman Borough
South Harrison Township
Swedesboro Borough
Washington Township
Wenonah Borough
West Deptford Township
Westville Borough
Woodbury City
Woodbury Heights
    Borough
Woolwich Township

Hudson County

Bayonne City
East Newark Borough
Guttenberg Town
Harrison Town
Hoboken City
Jersey City
Kearny Town
North Bergen Township
Secaucus Town
Union City
Weehawken Township
West New York Town
Hunterdon County
Alexandria Township
Bethlehem Township
Bloomsbury Borough
Califon Borough
Clinton Town
Clinton Township
Delaware Township
East Amwell Township
Flemington Borough
Franklin Township
Frenchtown Borough
Glen Gardner Borough
Hampton Borough
High Bridge Borough
Holland Township
Kingwood Township
Lambertville City
Lebanon Borough
Lebanon Township
Milford Borough

Hudson County, continued

Raritan Township
Readington Township
Stockton Borough
Tewksbury Township
Union Township
West Amwell Township

Mercer County

East Windsor Township
Ewing Township
Hamilton Township
Hightstown Borough
Hopewell Borough
Hopewell Township
Lawrence Township
Pennington Borough
Princeton Borough
Princeton Township
Trenton City
Washington Township
West Windsor Township
Middlesex County
Carteret Borough
Cranbury Township
Dunellen Borough
East Brunswick Township
Edison Township
Helmetta Borough
Highland Park Borough
Jamesburg Borough
Metuchen Borough
Middlesex Borough
Milltown Borough
Monroe Township
New Brunswick City
North Brunswick
    Township
Old Bridge Township
Perth Amboy City
Piscataway Township
Plainsboro Township
Sayreville Borough
South Amboy City
South Brunswick
    Township
South Plainfield Borough
South River Borough
Spotswood Borough
Woodbridge Township

Monmouth County

Aberdeen Township
Allenhurst Borough
Allentown Borough
Asbury Park City
Atlantic Highlands
    Borough
Avon-by-the-Sea
    Borough
Belmar Borough
Bradley Beach Borough
Brielle Borough
Colts Neck Township
Deal Borough
Eatontown Borough
Englishtown Borough
Fair Haven Borough
Farmingdale Borough
Freehold Borough
Freehold Township
Hazlet Township
Highlands Borough
Holmdel Township
Howell Township
Interlaken Borough
Keansburg Borough
Keyport Borough
Lake Como Borough*
Little Silver Borough
Loch Arbour Village
Long Branch City
Manalapan Township
Manasquan Borough
Marlboro Township
Matawan Borough
Middletown Township
Millstone Township
Monmouth Beach
    Borough
Neptune Township
Neptune City Borough
Ocean Township
Oceanport Borough
Red Bank Borough
Roosevelt Borough
Rumson Borough
Sea Bright Borough
Sea Girt Borough
Shrewsbury Borough
Shrewsbury Township
Spring Lake Borough

formerly South Belmar

Monmouth County, continued

Spring Lake Heights
  Borough
Tinton Falls Borough
Union Beach Borough
Upper Freehold
  Township
Wall Township
West Long Branch
  Borough

Morris County

Boonton Town
Boonton Township
Butler Borough
Chatham Borough
Chatham Township
Chester Borough
Chester Township
Denville Township
Dover Town
East Hanover Township
Florham Park Borough
Hanover Township
Harding Township
Jefferson Township
Kinnelon Borough
Lincoln Park Borough
Long Hill Township
Madison Borough
Mendham Borough
Mendham Township
Mine Hill Township
Montville Township
Morris Township
Morris Plains Borough
Morristown Town
Mount Arlington
  Borough
Mount Olive Township
Mountain Lakes Borough
Netcong Borough
Parsippany-Troy Hills
  Township
Pequannock Township
Randolph Township
Riverdale Borough
Rockaway Borough
Rockaway Township
Roxbury Township
Victory Gardens Borough

Morris County, continued

Washington Township
Wharton Borough

Ocean County

Barnegat Township
Barnegat Light Borough
Bay Head Borough
Beach Haven Borough
Beachwood Borough
Berkeley Township
Brick Township
Dover Township
Eagleswood Township
Harvey Cedars Borough
Island Heights Borough
Jackson Township
Lacey Township
Lakehurst Borough
Lakewood Township
Lavallette Borough
Little Egg Harbor
  Township
Long Beach Township
Manchester Township
Mantoloking Borough
Ocean Township
Ocean Gate Borough
Pine Beach Borough
Plumsted Township
Point Pleasant Borough
Point Pleasant Beach
  Borough
Seaside Heights Borough
Seaside Park Borough
Ship Bottom Borough
South Toms River
  Borough
Stafford Township
Surf City Borough
Tuckerton Borough

Passaic County

Bloomingdale Borough
Clifton City
Haledon Borough
Hawthorne Borough
Little Falls Township
North Haledon Borough
Passaic City
Paterson City

Passaic County, continued

Pompton Lakes Borough
Prospect Park Borough
Ringwood Borough
Totowa Borough
Wanaque Borough
Wayne Township
West Milford Township
West Paterson Borough

Salem County

Alloway Township
Carneys Point Township
Elmer Borough
Elsinboro Township
Lower Alloways Creek
  Township
Mannington Township
Oldmans Township
Penns Grove Borough
Pennsville Township
Pilesgrove Township
Pittsgrove Township
Quinton Township
Salem City
Upper Pittsgrove
  Township
Woodstown Borough

Somerset County

Bedminster Township
Bernards Township
Bernardsville Borough
Bound Brook Borough
Branchburg Township
Bridgewater Township
Far Hills Borough
Franklin Township
Green Brook Township
Hillsborough Township
Manville Borough
Millstone Borough
Montgomery Township
North Plainfield Borough
Peapack & Gladstone
  Borough
Raritan Borough
Rocky Hill Borough
Somerville Borough
South Bound Brook
  Borough
Warren Township
Watchung Borough

Sussex County

Andover Borough
Andover Township
Branchville Borough
Byram Township
Frankford Township
Franklin Borough
Fredon Township
Green Township
Hamburg Borough
Hampton Township
Hardyston Township
Hopatcong Borough
Lafayette Township
Montague Township
Newton Town
Ogdensburg Borough
Sandyston Township
Sparta Township
Stanhope Borough
Stillwater Township

Sussex County, cont.

Sussex Borough
Vernon Township
Walpack Township
Wantage Township

Union County

Berkeley Heights
  Township
Clark Township
Cranford Township
Elizabeth City
Fanwood Borough
Garwood Borough
Hillside Township
Kenilworth Borough
Linden City
Mountainside Borough
New Providence Borough
Plainfield City
Rahway City
Roselle Borough
Roselle Park Borough
Scotch Plains Township
Springfield Township
Summit City
Union Township
Westfield Town
Winfield Township

continued on next page

Warren County

Allamuchy Township
Alpha Borough
Belvidere Town
Blairstown Township
Franklin Township
Frelinghuysen Township
Greenwich Township
Hackettstown Town
Hardwick Township
Harmony Township
Hope Township
Independence Township
Knowlton Township
Liberty Township
Lopatcong Township
Mansfield Township
Oxford Township
Phillipsburg Town
Pohatcong Township
Washington Borough
Washington Township
White Township

Public School District Data

(for school year 2004-2005 except as noted)

Hopewell Valley Regional School District

425 South Main St
Pennington, NJ 8534
Mercer County
609-737-4000
www.hvrsd.k12.nj.us

Chief Administrator . . . . . . Judith Ferguson
Grade plan. K-12
Number of schools. 6
Number of schools. 6
Enrollment 3,895
Students per teacher 10.2
Per pupil expenditure $13,335
Median faculty salary $55,827
Median administrator salary. $99,418
Grade 12 enrollment 251
High school graduation rate 98.40%

Assessment test results
(percent scoring at proficient or advanced level)

	Language	Math
Grade 3	94.50%	93.50%
Grade 8	89.20%	85.40%
High school	95.20%	93.30%

SAT
Percent tested 97%
Average SAT math score. 580
Average SAT verbal score. 543

No Child Left Behind (NCLB), 2003-04
Attendence rate (target = 90%) 96.30%
Drop rate. 0.10%
Highly-qualified teachers. 97.70%
District needs improvement?(AYP) . . . . . No

Long Beach Island School District

200 Barnegat Ave
Surf City, NJ 8008
Ocean County
609-494-2341
www.lbischools.org

Superintendent (Int) . . . . Dennis Fyffe
Grade plan. K-6
Number of schools. 2
Number of schools. 2
Enrollment 286
Students per teacher 8.5
Per pupil expenditure $21,397
Median faculty salary $68,223
Median administrator salary. $92,000
Grade 12 enrollment . . . . .NA
High school graduation rate . . . . .NA

Assessment test results
(percent scoring at proficient or advanced level)

	Language	Math
Grade 3	97.40%	92.10%
Grade 8	NA	NA
High school	NA	NA

SAT
Percent tested . . . . .NA
Average SAT math score. . . . . .NA
Average SAT verbal score. . . . . .NA

No Child Left Behind (NCLB), 2003-04
Attendence rate (target = 90%) 94.20%
Drop rate. . . . . .NA
Highly-qualified teachers. 100%
District needs improvement?(AYP) . . . . . No

Northern Valley Regional School District

162 Knickerbocker Rd
Demarest, NJ 7627
Bergen County
201-768-2200
www.nvnet.org

Superintendent. . . . . Jan Furman
Grade plan. .12-Sep
Number of schools. 2
Number of schools. 2
Enrollment 2,376
Students per teacher 9
Per pupil expenditure $12,887
Median faculty salary $70,305
Median administrator salary. $128,057
Grade 12 enrollment 556
High school graduation rate . . . . .NA

Assessment test results
(percent scoring at proficient or advanced level)

	Language	Math
Grade 3	NA	NA
Grade 8	NA	NA
High school	97%	92.60%

SAT
Percent tested . . . . .NA
Average SAT math score. . . . . .NA
Average SAT verbal score. . . . . .NA

No Child Left Behind (NCLB), 2003-04
Attendence rate (target = 90%) 96.60%
Drop rate. 0.20%
Highly-qualified teachers. 99.30%
District needs improvement?(AYP) . . . . . No

Shore Regional High School District

Monmouth Park Hwy
West Long Branch, NJ 7764
Monmouth County
732-222-9300
shoreregional.org

Superintendent. . . . . .Leonard G. Schnappauf
Grade plan. .12-Sep
Number of schools. 1
Number of schools. 1
Enrollment 722.5
Students per teacher 11.9
Per pupil expenditure $15,332
Median faculty salary $60,050
Median administrator salary. $95,008
Grade 12 enrollment 154
High school graduation rate 100%

Assessment test results
(percent scoring at proficient or advanced level)

	Language	Math
Grade 3	NA	NA
Grade 8	NA	NA
High school	97.20%	87.90%

SAT
Percent tested 100%
Average SAT math score. 519
Average SAT verbal score. 509

No Child Left Behind (NCLB), 2003-04
Attendence rate (target = 90%) 95.30%
Drop rate. 0%
Highly-qualified teachers. 100%
District needs improvement?(AYP) . . . . . No

ORDER FORM

Title	Qty	Edition	Price	Extended Price	Standing Order YES	Standing Order NO
State & Municipal Profiles Series™						
Almanac of the 50 States 2006		Hardcover	$80		☐	☐
Almanac of the 50 States 2006		Paper	$70		☐	☐
California Cities, Towns & Counties 2006		CD	$105		☐	☐
California Cities, Towns & Counties 2006		Paper	$105		☐	☐
Connecticut Municipal Profiles 2006		CD	$74		☐	☐
Connecticut Municipal Profiles 2006		Paper	$74		☐	☐
Florida Municipal Profiles 2006		CD	$95		☐	☐
Florida Municipal Profiles 2006		Paper	$95		☐	☐
Massachusetts Municipal Profiles 2006		CD	$97		☐	☐
Massachusetts Municipal Profiles 2006		Paper	$97		☐	☐
The New Jersey Municipal Data Book 2006		CD	$105		☐	☐
The New Jersey Municipal Data Book 2006		Paper	$105		☐	☐
North Carolina Municipal Profiles 2006		CD	$95		☐	☐
North Carolina Municipal Profiles 2006		Paper	$95		☐	☐
American Profiles Series™						
Black Americans: A Statistical Sourcebook 2006		Hardcover	$75		☐	☐
Hispanic Americans: A Statistical Sourcebook 2006		Hardcover	$70		☐	☐
Asian Americans: A Statistical Sourcebook 2006		Hardcover	$70		☐	☐

Offer and prices valid until 12/31/06

Purchase orders accepted from libraries, government agencies, and educational institutions.

Prepayment required from all other organizations.

Order Subtotal	_____
(Required ONLY for shipments to California) CA Sales Tax	_____
Shipping & Handling	_____
Total	_____

Please complete the following shipping and billing information. If paying by credit card or PO please call **(877)544-4636** or fax your completed order form to **(877)544-4635**. To pay by check, please mail this form and your payment to the address below.

Information Publications, Inc.
2995 Woodside Rd., Suite 400-182
Woodside, CA 94062

U.S. Ground Shipping Rates

Order Subtotal	Shipping & Handling
$0-$80	$6
$81-$105	$8
$106-$200	$12
$201-$300	$16
$301-$400	$20
>$400	Call

Call for Int'l or Express Shipping Rates

Shipping Information (UPS/FedEx tracking number sent via email)

Organization Name		
Shipping Contact		
Address (No PO Boxes, please)		
City	State	Zip
Email Address (req'd if want tracking #)	Phone #	

Payment Information (mark choice)

☐ **Check**	☐ **Credit Card** ☐ Visa ☐ MC ☐ AMEX	☐ **Purchase Order** (attach PO to this form)
Check #	CC#	PO #
	Exp Date	

Credit Card Billing Information   ☐ Check if same as Shipping Address

Name on Credit Card		
Billing Address of Credit Card		
City	State	Zip
Signature		

2995 WOODSIDE RD., SUITE 400-182
WOODSIDE, CA 94062

WWW.INFORMATIONPUBLICATIONS.COM

TOLL FREE PHONE 877-544-INFO (4636)
TOLL FREE FAX 877-544-4635

• Since 1980, A Trusted Ready Reference Resource for Easy-To-Use Federal, State and Local Information •

Title	Qty	Edition	Price	Extended Price	Standing Order YES	Standing Order NO
State & Municipal Profiles Series™						
Almanac of the 50 States 2006		Hardcover	$80		☐	☐
Almanac of the 50 States 2006		Paper	$70		☐	☐
California Cities, Towns & Counties 2006		CD	$105		☐	☐
		Paper	$105		☐	☐
Connecticut Municipal Profiles 2006		CD	$74		☐	☐
		Paper	$74		☐	☐
Florida Municipal Profiles 2006		CD	$95		☐	☐
		Paper	$95		☐	☐
Massachusetts Municipal Profiles 2006		CD	$97		☐	☐
		Paper	$97		☐	☐
The New Jersey Municipal Data Book 2006		CD	$105		☐	☐
		Paper	$105		☐	☐
North Carolina Municipal Profiles 2006		CD	$95		☐	☐
		Paper	$95		☐	☐
American Profiles Series™						
Black Americans: A Statistical Sourcebook 2006		Hardcover	$75		☐	☐
Hispanic Americans: A Statistical Sourcebook 2006		Hardcover	$70		☐	☐
Asian Americans: A Statistical Sourcebook 2006		Hardcover	$70		☐	☐

Offer and prices valid until 12/31/06

Purchase orders accepted from libraries, government agencies, and educational institutions.

Prepayment required from all other organizations.

Order Subtotal _____

(Required ONLY for shipments to California) CA Sales Tax _____

Shipping & Handling _____

Total _____

Please complete the following shipping and billing information. If paying by credit card or PO please call **(877)544-4636** or fax your completed order form to **(877)544-4635**. To pay by check, please mail this form and your payment to the address below.

Information Publications, Inc.
2995 Woodside Rd., Suite 400-182
Woodside, CA 94062

U.S. Ground Shipping Rates	
Order Subtotal	Shipping & Handling
$0-$80	$6
$81-$105	$8
$106-$200	$12
$201-$300	$16
$301-$400	$20
>$400	Call

Call for Int'l or Express Shipping Rates

Shipping Information (UPS/FedEx tracking number sent via email)

Organization Name		
Shipping Contact		
Address (No PO Boxes, please)		
City	State	Zip
Email Address (req'd if want tracking #)	Phone #	

Payment Information (mark choice)

	☐ **Check**	☐ **Credit Card** ☐ Visa ☐ MC ☐ AMEX	☐ **Purchase Order** (attach PO to this form)
	Check #	CC#	PO #
		Exp Date	

Credit Card Billing Information   ☐ Check if same as Shipping Address

Name on Credit Card		
Billing Address of Credit Card		
City	State	Zip
Signature		

2995 WOODSIDE RD., SUITE 400-182
WOODSIDE, CA 94062   **WWW.INFORMATIONPUBLICATIONS.COM**   TOLL FREE PHONE 877-544-INFO (4636)
TOLL FREE FAX 877-544-4635

• **Since 1980, A Trusted Ready Reference Resource for Easy-To-Use Federal, State and Local Information** •

Title	Qty	Edition	Price	Extended Price	Standing Order	
					YES	NO
State & Municipal Profiles Series™						
Almanac of the 50 States 2006		Hardcover	$80		☐	☐
Almanac of the 50 States 2006		Paper	$70		☐	☐
California Cities, Towns & Counties 2006		CD	$105		☐	☐
		Paper	$105		☐	☐
Connecticut Municipal Profiles 2006		CD	$74		☐	☐
		Paper	$74		☐	☐
Florida Municipal Profiles 2006		CD	$95		☐	☐
		Paper	$95		☐	☐
Massachusetts Municipal Profiles 2006		CD	$97		☐	☐
		Paper	$97		☐	☐
The New Jersey Municipal Data Book 2006		CD	$105		☐	☐
		Paper	$105		☐	☐
North Carolina Municipal Profiles 2006		CD	$95		☐	☐
		Paper	$95		☐	☐
American Profiles Series™						
Black Americans: A Statistical Sourcebook 2006		Hardcover	$75		☐	☐
Hispanic Americans: A Statistical Sourcebook 2006		Hardcover	$70		☐	☐
Asian Americans: A Statistical Sourcebook 2006		Hardcover	$70		☐	☐

Offer and prices valid until 12/31/06

Order Subtotal _____

(Required ONLY for shipments to California) CA Sales Tax _____

Purchase orders accepted from libraries, government agencies, and educational institutions.

Shipping & Handling _____

Prepayment required from all other organizations.

Total _____

Please complete the following shipping and billing information. If paying by credit card or PO please call **(877)544-4636** or fax your completed order form to **(877)544-4635**. To pay by check, please mail this form and your payment to the address below.

Information Publications, Inc.
2995 Woodside Rd., Suite 400-182
Woodside, CA 94062

U.S. Ground Shipping Rates	
Order Subtotal	Shipping & Handling
$0-$80	$6
$81-$105	$8
$106-$200	$12
$201-$300	$16
$301-$400	$20
>$400	Call

Call for Int'l or Express Shipping Rates

Shipping Information (UPS/FedEx tracking number sent via email)

Organization Name		
Shipping Contact		
Address (No PO Boxes, please)		
City	State	Zip
Email Address (req'd if want tracking #)	Phone #	

Payment Information (mark choice)	☐ **Check**	☐ **Credit Card** ☐ Visa ☐ MC ☐ AMEX	☐ **Purchase Order** (attach PO to this form)
	Check #	CC#	PO #
		Exp Date	

Credit Card Billing Information   ☐ Check if same as Shipping Address

Name on Credit Card		
Billing Address of Credit Card		
City	State	Zip
Signature		

• Since 1980, A Trusted Ready Reference Resource for Easy-To-Use Federal, State and Local Information •